TIME CHARTERS
FOURTH EDITION

定期傭船契約

第四版

郷原 資亮 監訳

石井 達夫
小川　優　訳
白水　隆

信山社

TIME CHARTERS

FOURTH EDITION

By

MICHAEL WILFORD
London, Solicitor
Clyde & Co.

TERENCE COGHLIN
Chairman, Thomas Miller & Co.

JOHN D. KIMBALL
New York, Attorney
Healy & Baillie

the original English edition published by Lloyd's of London Press Ltd.
Copyright © 1995, Michael Wilford, Terence Coghlin, John D. Kimball
All rights reserved.

Japanese Translation Rights granted by
Informa Professional Publishing to Shinzansha
Japanese Translation © 2001, Motosuke Gohara

推薦の辞

　平成11 (1999) 年におけるわが国の海上貿易量は8億5,000万トン（金額にして約55兆6,000億円）に達する。このうち輸入貨物4億1,100万トン（全輸入貨物量の70.6％）輸出貨物3,500万トン（全輸出貨物量の36.2％）がわが国商船隊によって輸送された。

　今日これだけの貨物量がわが国商船隊によって輸送されているが，しかし，その商船隊の国籍（船籍）別構成に注目する時，日本の国籍（船籍）を有する船舶は，わずかに154雙（1,667万重量トン）にすぎない。残りの1,842雙（8,409万重量トン）は，全て，外国傭船（1,083雙4,138万重量トン）か，仕組船（759雙4,271万重量トン）（便宜置籍船）である。

　外国傭船であれ仕組船であれ，わが国海運企業が，外国籍の船舶を利用するには，何らかの契約を必要とする。その大部分が海事法分野に特有の定期傭船契約という契約方式に拠っている。しかも，この契約方式に関する法律的研究は，英国において，判例あるいは，仲裁判断の蓄積により，もっとも進んでいるといわれる。海事紛争の解決を基本的には依然として英国の法制に依拠している世界の海運市場において，わが国海運企業の法益を，そして結局，わが国の国益を擁護するために定期傭船契約に関する英国法，あるいはそれに準ずる米国法の研究は，不可欠であるといえよう。

　このような観点から，MR. MICHAEL WILFORD, MR. TERENCE COGHLIN および MR. JOHN D. KIMBALL 三氏による "TIME CHARTERS" を邦訳した本書は，海運関係者はもちろんのこと，海運に関係する貿易，保険等の関連業界，研究機関・学界の関係各位には必読の文献であると確信する。

　原著は，英国および米国の一流の海事法専門の弁護士による執筆であり，初版刊行以来，世界の海運関係者の間で，評価の高い著書である。

　訳者は，日本を代表する海運企業の法務あるいは営業を経験した実務家である。海運取引の特にこの分野は，実務経験がなければ理解が難しいといわれる。原著者と翻訳者のよき組合せが，このような秀れた文献を生んだものと，心からの敬意を表したい。

　なお，最後に，特に一言付言したい。

　翻訳の作業は，当然のことながら，多忙な本務以外の貴重な時間を充当して行われたものと考える。この厖大な内容量と非英語圏の関係者が難渋しがちな

英米の判決文の読解を主体とした作業の困難に想いを致す時，訳者の情熱とエネルギーにはただ感服のほかはない。

本書を広く関係各位に推薦する次第である。

国土交通副大臣
泉　信也

第四版 訳者はしがき

　本書は，MR. TERENCE COGHLIN, MR. MICHAEL WILFORD, MR. JOHN D. KIMBALL 三氏による共著 "TIME CHARTERS" 第四版(1995)の邦語訳である。

　海運取引における定期傭船契約の占める役割については，多くの言葉を費す要はあるまい。就中，定期傭船契約に関する紛争の解決例を，海運先進国たる英国を中心とする英米法圏における多くの判例，仲裁判断の分析・体系化を通じて理解しておくことは，海運に関係する者にとって，必須の要諦であろう。

　原著書初版（1978年）の翻訳に筆者を含む実務家4名（田中淳夫，中家章，森荘太郎）が挑戦したのは，上述のような本書の重要性を認識したが故でありその成果を刊行しえた（1981年）のは，監修者窪田宏教授および校閲者小川洋一弁護士のご指導の賜物であった。

　しかしながら，原著者たちのこの主題に賭ける情熱は衰えを知らず，1995年には遂に第四版が誕生した。

　そこで，初版のメンバーとは異なる実務家3名を迎え，初版に比し2倍以上に増量された第四版の翻訳を行った。

　筆者のほか，石井達夫（㈱エム・オー・エル・アジャストメントクレイムグループ）が中心となって，小川優（㈱商船三井総務部法規・保険チーム），白水隆（国際エネルギー輸送㈱海技安全グループ）の協力の下，共同作業による訳述を纏めたのが本書である。

　MR. TERENCE COGHLIN 他の原著者は，私たちによる翻訳出版を再び快諾しただけではなく，初版の場合と同様，私たちの質問に親切かつ丁寧に答えてくれた。心からの謝意を表したい。

　最後の校正作業を行っている最中に，TERENCE COGHLIN 氏が U. K. P. & I CLUB の管理会社 THOMAS MILLER 社会長を本年（2001年）7月に退任するとの報に接した。翻訳書刊行という形で，本書を最初にわが国に紹介できたのは，同氏と筆者とのご縁に負うものであった。

　ここに，同氏との長年に亘る友情に感謝し，本書の刊行に同氏退任祝賀の意をも含めたい。

　また，わが国運輸行政の最高責任者である 泉信也国土交通副大臣より，「推薦の辞」を頂いたことは，私たちにとって大きな喜びであり，光栄でもある。

最後に，この種の地味な実務書の出版をお引き受け頂いた信山社の袖山貴氏および刊行に至るまで大変なご協力を賜った編集工房INABAの稲葉文子氏に満腔の謝意を表したい。

　平成13年6月

郷 原 資 亮

凡　例

(1) 各種契約書式の訳文は，日本海運集会所編纂『新訂定期傭船契約書式集』（平成8年）を参照した。
(2) 原書・訳書双方の利用価値を高め，かつ読者の便宜を増進する観点から，原書の頁数を訳文の左側に□で表示した。
(3) 判例索引，法索引，事項索引は，原書の頁数（本書□内頁数）で表記している。
(4) 実務において，半ば日常用語として定着している英語についても，出来る限り日本語に翻訳したが，用語の性質上，またはその慣用語となっているもの等については，英語のままとしたもの（例：リーエン）がある。

感謝のことば

　私たちは，オックスフォード大学の Worcester College の王室弁護士である Francis Reynolds 教授に特別の謝意を表したい。今回も彼は，貴重な助言を与えてくれ，心から感謝する。
　私たちは，Stan Bonnick にもタンカーの定期傭船の問題についての助力に深謝する。
　最後に，蚯蚓(みみず)の走ったような手書きの原稿を首尾よく処理してくれた秘書の Helen Godel と Mavis Taylor に感謝したい。

M. T. W.
T. G. C.

　私は，忍耐強く不断に助けてくれた秘書の Annette O'Reilly に感謝の意を記したい。この版を執筆するについては Marianna Rubino と Morgan Kennedy が助けてくれた。つらい仕事をやり遂げた彼らに謝意を表したい。

J. D. K.

第四版の序文

　本書の第三版が1989年に出版されて以降，定期傭船契約の領域で多くの重大な判決が下された。その中には，定期傭船契約法の重要な発展をもたらしたものがある。新版が必要となった所以である。

　その他の点に関しては，従来の傾向が続いた。Mustill 卿（私たちは，1978年の初版本で当時王室弁護士であった卿の励ましに謝意を表明した）は，1995年の *The Gregos* 事件の弁論で，私たちが，第二版の序文でひとつの傾向として把握した傭船契約の解釈の方法を補強して次のように述べた。「実用性ということでは，私は Saville 判事と見解を同じくする。即ち，この種の問題のよりよい解決は，二つの解決法のうち一方を選択した場合の実際の結果について推測するよりも，契約内容を考察することにより生れる。当然のことながら，判事の誰しもが，契約文言の故にやむなく無理な解釈を強いられることのない限り，明らかに不合理な結果を生む解釈に賛同することはない。何故なら，それは，契約当事者の意図ではあり得ないからである。しかし，明白な不条理がなく，その解釈が，より道理に適った結果を生むという一方の側の単なる主張だけでは，誤審のおそれがある。……私は，むしろ傭船契約それ自身に集中する方を選ぶ。……」

　この第四版の乾貨物の章の枠組みとして，今一度1946年10月3日改訂版のニューヨーク・プロデュース書式を使用する。この年季の入った書式は最近現代化された。新版が，1981年に合衆国船舶仲立業・代理店協会（ASBA）によって発行された。これは，ASBATIME と呼ばれている。それは，本書第三版の末尾に収録されている。再草案を行うに際しては ASBA の配慮により，ボルティック国際海運集会所（BIMCO）や英国海運集会所（General Council of British Shipping，現在の The Chamber of Shipping）等の関係者との協議が広く行われたが，その新書式は，実務では殆んど利用されなかった。たいていの契約は，1946年版に基いて，引き続き締結された。しかし，それは契約当事者により大規模な削除や修正や追加がなされてきた。契約当事者の多くは，長年にわたって当事者自身による複合的な改定を行ってきており，特定の必要に対応し，また，選択を行ったのである。

　別の改訂版が昨年 ASBA と BIMCO および FONASBA（the Federation of National Associations of Ship Brokers and Agents）からなる合同作業グループにより発行された。これが NYPE 93 として知られているものである。ASBATIME に導入された修正，追加を参考として，さらに発展させたものである。1946年版の用語法の実質や細目の変更に加えて，NYPE 93 は傭船開始時およびオフハイヤー検査，危険品，戦争，徴用，荷役業者による船体損傷，船艙清掃，係船返戻，書類，密輸，密航を扱う新条項を導入した。

NYPE 93 を生み出した人々の仕事が広く称賛されている一方で，業界が AS-BATIME 版以上に広く，それを使用するかどうかを予言するには，時期尚早である。ニューヨーク・プロデュース書式の主要な使用者たちは，1946年版を基にそれぞれに手を入れた修正版に不自由を感じていないので，新しい使用したことのない印刷書式の長所を認めず今一度これを利用しないことは，ありうることである。

　したがって，この版では，1946年版をそのまま利用することにした。ASBATIME の代わりに NYPE 93 年版を本書に入れ，本文中では同版による1946年版の変更を参照するに止めた。NYPE 93 の変更の功罪あるいは有効性を模索することが必要であるとか，望ましいとは考えていない。やがて新書式が，広く使用されるようになれば，本書の続版でそれをもっと取り扱わねばならないことになろう——1946年版を外して，NYPE 93 を続版の章の枠組として，使用するとしても——しかし，それは，第四版では，時期尚早と考える。

　よく使用される英国のタンカー書式である Shelltime に適用される英国法に関し，新しい章を追加した。この章の枠組として Shelltime 4 書式を使用することを認めてくれたシェル社に感謝する。これは，STB 書式に関する米国法の章の対編である。さらに，それはこの本の主力がニューヨーク・プロデュース書式であるということから生じる乾貨物重点との均衡を当面保つものである。最近，英国法廷でタンカー定期傭船についての訴訟の判決がいくつか出た。そのことは，新しくこの章を設けることを十分に有意義なものとした。以前，私たちはそれらの判決例は，第二版の序文に記したように不十分であると判断していた。本書の乾貨物の部分と比較してまだ範囲が狭いが，判例の増加とともに，これを拡張したい。

　私たちは，この本の本来の目的は変わっていないことを再確認したい。初版の序文に次のように述べた。

　「本書は，定期傭船契約に関する判例法を纏め，傭船や運航の実務者（そして，またおそらく，その助言者）が，その疑問点につき，指導的判例を簡便に参照する一助となることを目的としている」。

　本版を含め続版による修正や追加は，この目的を念頭において行われた。読者が，今後共本書を簡便に使用し，日々の傭船契約問題の法律的側面に関する有用な手引書として使用することを希望する。

　最後に英国の共著者は，私たちが不可能と考えていたことを成就したことについて出版社と John Kimball を含む尊敬すべき著者たちに祝賀の言葉を述べたい。すなわち，定期傭船契約の分野をニューヨーク・プロデュース書式が支配してきたような形では何らの傭船契約書式が存しない航海傭船契約に本書の構成を応用することは不可能と考えてきたのである。私たちは，ロイズ海事法図書の姉妹編である『航海傭船』の関係者皆さんのご多幸を祈る。

　本書の中では，米国法は各米国契約法の章毎に縁線を引き，各論題毎に英国法と区分している。

　私たちは，1995年8月1日現在の法令を述べることを意図した。

初版訳書序文

　M. Wilford, T. Coghlin, N. Healy, Jr. 三氏共著による "Time Charters" を，郷原資亮氏外三氏が翻訳して纏め上げたのが，本『定期傭船契約―基本書式とその実務指針―』である。

　原著 "Time Charters" は，この三氏により，定期傭船契約締結当事者や当該船を運航する当事者が，通常持つと思われる疑問点及び紛争の解決に指導的な英法廷判決やニューヨークの仲裁判断を，主として The New York Produce Exchange Form (1946) の条項に従って整理収録したものであり，従来の傭船契約に関する著作とは可成り趣を異にしているものである。

　原著者の一人，T. Coghlin 氏は，Thomas Millers & Son 社の中堅有望な Partner の一人だが，同社は The United Kingdom Mutual Steam Ship Assurance Association Ltd. (所謂 U. K. P. & I. Club) その他四つの類似 Club の Manager 会社として，それ等 Club の運営を全面的に受託している会社であり，この関係から，わが国海運界にも Coghlin 氏を知る人が多い。同社には，海運業務に於ける極めて広範且つ多岐に渉る紛争事例が殺到していよう事は，想像に難くないので，法律家としてそれ等一つ一つの実務的解決に多忙な同氏にとって，かかる型式の著作の発想があってもおかしく無いと思う。

　前述のように，本書は定期傭船契約書式として日々使用されているものに即して論述されているものであるから，日頃多忙な契約締結担当者，運航担当者にとって，本書は問題解決のためのレーダー・ジャイロコンパスの如きもので，これ程有難く心強く思われるものは，あるまい。実務担当者の座右の書として御薦め致し度い。

　本書は郷原氏外三氏の翻訳により，初めて日本人にとって有効な価値ある本となったと言っても過言ではあるまい。

　訳者はそのはしがきに，外国語による実務的に価値の高い著作であろうとも，日本人にとってその文献の実用性は半減すると言っている。これは実務者であるが故に理解される事であり，この厖大な原著を翻訳せんと決意した情熱の源泉も実務者精神であろう。同氏外二氏は海運会社の中堅管理職として，日頃多忙な海運実務に従事して居り，日常業務遂行に支障を与えずに，かかる大仕事を為しとげた事には多大の労苦があった事と推察すると共に，翻訳も極めてスムースで訳文とは思わせぬのも，これ等業務に高度の知識と豊富な経験を持っているためと存じ心より敬意を表し度い。

　昭和56年8月

大阪商船三井船舶株式会社
代表取締役会長
U. K. P. & I. CLUB 理事
元・日本船主協会会長

永井典彦

目　　次

推薦の辞 …………………………………………………… 泉　信也 …… *3*

第四版 訳者はしがき ……………………………………… 郷原資亮 …… *5*
感謝のことば ……………………………………………………………… *7*
第四版の序文 ……………………………………………………………… *9*
初版訳書序文 ……………………………………………… 永井典彦 …… *11*
判 例 索 引（Table of Cases）…………………………………………… *31*
法 令 索 引（Table of Legislation）…………………………………… *123*

定期傭船契約書［英語原文］

the Text of the New York Produce Exchange Form （ニューヨーク・
　プロデュース書式全文）……………………………………………… *4*
the Text of NYPE 93（NYPE 93 書式全文）………………………… *8*
the Text of Baltime Form（ボルタイム書式全文）………………… *20*
the Text of Shelltime Form（シェルタイム書式全文）…………… *24*
the Text of STB Form of Tanker Time Charter（タンカー定期傭船
　STB 書式全文）……………………………………………………… *35*

定期傭船契約書［和訳］

ニューヨーク・プロデュース書式 …………………………………… *48*
NYPE 93 書式 …………………………………………………………… *53*
ボルタイム書式 ………………………………………………………… *63*
シェルタイム書式 ……………………………………………………… *67*
タンカー定期傭船 STB 書式 ………………………………………… *81*

ニューヨーク・プロデュース書式

契約の成立 ……………………………………………………………… *97*
　特別な形式は不要 …………………………………………………… *97*
　基本的条項すべてについて明確な合意の必要性 ………………… *97*
　傭船契約書署名前の成約 …………………………………………… *100*
　「契約締結を条件として　subject to contract」……………………… *100*
　「検査結果，許可または承諾を条件に　subject to survey, permission or
　　approval」…………………………………………………………… *101*
　「細目を条件として　subject details」……………………………… *102*

「～を条件として subject to」の他の用法 ……………………………………103
　　どの法律により決定されるか …………………………………………………104
　米　国　法 ……………………………………………………………………………105
　　適　用　法 ………………………………………………………………………105
　　解釈の規則 ………………………………………………………………………106
　　契約の成立 ………………………………………………………………………106
　　基本的条項 ………………………………………………………………………107
　　「細目を条件として sub details」 ……………………………………………108
　　「主要条件 main terms」 ………………………………………………………108
　　傭船契約書署名前の成約 ………………………………………………………109

契約の当事者 ……………………………………………………………………………111
　一　般　原　則 ……………………………………………………………………111
　　権限のある代理人が本人のために契約を締結する場合であって，かつ，本人の契
　　　約との関係を契約の相手方が知っている場合(顕名された本人の代理人 dis-
　　　closed principal) ……………………………………………………………111
　　代理人の権限 ……………………………………………………………………111
　　自己を代理人と表示しているにもかかわらず，実は本人である場合 …………115
　　権限のある代理人が自己の名において本人のために契約を締結したが，相手方が
　　　本人の存在を知らないか，あるいは本人と契約との関係を知らない場合（隠
　　　された本人 undisclosed principal) …………………………………………116
　　代理人として行為している者が，本人と称する者から授権されていなかった場合 …118
　　法　の　抵　触 …………………………………………………………………121
　米　国　法 ……………………………………………………………………………122
　　船主あるいは傭船者の同一性 …………………………………………………122
　　代　理　人 ………………………………………………………………………122
　　実際の権限 ………………………………………………………………………123
　　表　見　代　理 …………………………………………………………………124
　　追　　　認 ………………………………………………………………………125
　　隠された本人 ……………………………………………………………………125
　　代理人の本人に対する責任 ……………………………………………………126
　　「法人格の否認」 ………………………………………………………………126
　　保　証　人 ………………………………………………………………………129
　　仲　裁　協　定 …………………………………………………………………130

船舶の表示 ………………………………………………………………………………131
　序 ……………………………………………………………………………………131
　交渉の過程でなされる表示 ………………………………………………………132
　　(1) 責任を生じない表示 …………………………………………………………132
　　(2) 不　実　表　示 ………………………………………………………………132
　　不実表示による契約の解除 ……………………………………………………132
　　不実表示に基づく損害賠償 ……………………………………………………134
　　不実表示の責任を排除する条項 ………………………………………………135
　　契約の一部となる不実表示 ……………………………………………………136

契約の条項 ………………………………………………………136
"De minimis"の原則（「些細なことを問わない」という原則）……136
契約違反の救済方法 ……………………………………………137
損　害　賠　償 …………………………………………………137
特定履行命令と差止命令 ………………………………………137
契約を消滅したものとして扱う権利 …………………………138
契約条件（contractual terms）の分類 ………………………138
権利放棄と確約 …………………………………………………142
個々の記載事項 …………………………………………………144
本船が表示を遵守すべき時期 …………………………………144
表示に合致しない本船の引渡 …………………………………144
船　　　　名 ……………………………………………………145
代　　　　船 ……………………………………………………145
売　　　　船 ……………………………………………………146
国　籍（flag）……………………………………………………147
船体，機関および装備を完全な稼働状態に保持すること …147
船級に関する表示 ………………………………………………152
ベール容積と載貨重量 …………………………………………152
速力と燃料消費 …………………………………………………155
ＮＹＰＥ 93 ………………………………………………………158
本船の動静 ………………………………………………………158
米　国　法 …………………………………………………………159
船　　　　名 ……………………………………………………160
国　籍（flag）……………………………………………………160
船体，機関および装備を完全な稼働状態に保持すること …161
堪航性担保義務違反の結果 ……………………………………161
海上物品運送法とハーター法 …………………………………163
船級に関する表示 ………………………………………………164
ベール容積と載貨重量 …………………………………………164
総／純トン数 ……………………………………………………165
「約 about」………………………………………………………165
速力と燃料消費 …………………………………………………166
燃　料　消　費 …………………………………………………170
本船の動静 ………………………………………………………171
傭船期間 ……………………………………………………………173
「賃貸」と「賃借」………………………………………………173
引　　　　渡 ……………………………………………………173
傭船期間（期間超過・期間不足）………………………………173
最　終　航　海 …………………………………………………173
最終航海の指図 …………………………………………………175
無効な最終航海指図 ……………………………………………177
傭船期間の真の範囲 ……………………………………………178

目　次

「最終航海」条項の効果 …………………………………………………181
期間満了前返船 ……………………………………………………………182
特定航海の継続期間をもって定める傭船期間 ………………………183
　米　国　法 ………………………………………………………………185
期間超過／期間不足：黙示の許容期間 ………………………………185
最短／最長 …………………………………………………………………186
明示の許容期間 ……………………………………………………………187
「約 about」 …………………………………………………………………188
妥当な許容期間の範囲 ……………………………………………………189
傭船期間満了後の返船 ……………………………………………………190
最終航海は適法な航海か …………………………………………………191
期間満了前返船 ……………………………………………………………191
返 船 場 所 ……………………………………………………………………192
返 船 通 知 ……………………………………………………………………192

航 路 定 限 ……………………………………………………………………193
航路定限の目的 ……………………………………………………………193
定限外航海の指図 …………………………………………………………193
航路定限より狭められた航海を対象とする定期傭船契約 …………193
傭船者の指図に従うことの効果 …………………………………………194
定限外航海に対する損害賠償の程度 ……………………………………194
航路定限外航行に関する協定 ……………………………………………195
　米　国　法 ………………………………………………………………196
航 路 定 限 ……………………………………………………………………196

再 傭 船 自 由 …………………………………………………………………199
再傭船の効果 ………………………………………………………………199
船長に代わって再傭船者が船荷証券に署名する権限 ………………199
再傭船契約に基づく運賃の支払 …………………………………………200
　米　国　法 ………………………………………………………………201
再傭船の自由 ………………………………………………………………201
船長に代わって船荷証券に再傭船者が署名する権限 ………………202
期間の計算開始の時 ………………………………………………………202

引　渡　地 ……………………………………………………………………203
常に浮揚状態で安全に碇泊 ………………………………………………203
期間の計算開始の時 ………………………………………………………203

引渡時の本船の状態 …………………………………………………………205
一 般 原 則 ……………………………………………………………………205
あらゆる点において運送業務に適合し船体堅牢強固 ………………206
解約条項を適用しようとする場合の準備 ………………………………206
清掃した船艙での貨物受取準備完了 ……………………………………207
貨物荷役機器と装置 ………………………………………………………207
商業的に判断される準備完了 ……………………………………………208

| 特別な装置 ……………………………………………………………210
| あらゆる点で適合した；本船の物理的状態を超えて ……………211
| 推定的（*prima facie*）事実問題 …………………………………213
| 本船の受取 ………………………………………………………213
| 損害賠償の算定 …………………………………………………214
| 米　国　法………………………………………………………………215
| 積荷準備完了 ……………………………………………………215
| 船艙を清掃して …………………………………………………216
| 船体の堅牢強固 …………………………………………………216

適法な貨物 ……………………………………………………………219
| 違法な貨物 ………………………………………………………219
| 傭船契約上除外された貨物の船積 ……………………………219
| 除外貨物引受の効果 ……………………………………………220
| 危　険　貨　物 …………………………………………………221
| 傭船者の黙示の義務 ……………………………………………221
| 米国海上物品運送法 ……………………………………………222
| ニューヨーク・プロデュース書式第8条に基づく船主に対する補償 …224
| 警告の欠如 ………………………………………………………224
| ボルタイム書式 …………………………………………………224
| 特　別　報　酬 …………………………………………………225
| 適法な航路において ……………………………………………225
| 米　国　法………………………………………………………………226
| 適法な貨物 ………………………………………………………226
| 麻　　　　薬 ……………………………………………………227
| 危　険　貨　物 …………………………………………………227
| 米国の他の法規制 ………………………………………………230

安全港と安全バース …………………………………………………231
| 一　般　原　則 …………………………………………………231
| 安全性の要素 ……………………………………………………231
| 当　該　期　間 …………………………………………………232
| 特　定　の　船　舶 ……………………………………………234
| 接近時の安全性 …………………………………………………234
| 使用上の安全性 …………………………………………………236
| 出港時の安全性 …………………………………………………238
| 異　常　事　態 …………………………………………………239
| 危険と政治的非安全性 …………………………………………240
| 適切な航海操船技術により回避可能な危険 …………………241
| 事実と法律 ………………………………………………………242
| 傭船者の第一義的義務は，本船に配船を指図するときに生じる …242
| 指定した後に港が非安全となる。傭船者の第二義的義務 ……243
| 傭船者の知らない非安全性 ……………………………………244
| 「相当の注意」条項 ……………………………………………244

非安全と予見される港への配船指図の結果 ································245
　　　船長または乗組員の過失の効果 ···247
　　　安全に関する黙示の条項 ···249
　　　明示された港 ···250
　　　バースの安全性 ···251
　　　常に浮揚状態で安全に碇泊 ··252
　　　航海傭船契約と定期傭船契約 ···253
　　　使用条項による選択的請求 ··253
　　　戦争条項との相互作用 ··254
　　米　国　法···255
　　　非安全港またはバースの指定 ···255
　　　常に浮揚状態で安全に碇泊 ··255
　　　安　全　港　間 ···255
　　　特定の船舶 ···257
　　　接近および出港時の安全性 ··257
　　　氷 ··259
　　　使用上の安全性 ··259
　　　危　　　険 ··261
　　　適切な航海操船技術による回避可能性 ··································262
　　　指定港またはバースの受入れ ···262
　　　過失の介在 ···264
　　　寄　与　過　失 ···265

保守条項 ··267
　　　給　　　料 ··267
　　　船舶の保険 ···267
　　　保　守　条　項 ···267
　　　保守条項のその他の類型 ···268
　　米　国　法···270
　　　船艙清掃費用の責任 ··271
　　　変化する法的要件 ···271

傭船者の手配および費用負担 ···275
　　　傭船者の手配義務の一般的性質 ···275
　　　燃　　　料 ··276
　　　港　　　費 ··278
　　　水　先　料 ··278
　　　代　理　人 ··279
　　　その他一切の通常費用 ··280
　　　オフハイヤー期間 ···280
　　米　国　法···281
　　　傭船者が手配し，支払う ···281
　　　燃　　　料 ··281
　　　水　先　料 ··283

船艙清掃費用 …………………………………………284
燃　　料 …………………………………………………285
　　引渡時および返船時の量 ……………………………285
　　燃料の所有権 …………………………………………286
　　価　　格 ………………………………………………286
　　質 ………………………………………………………287
　米　国　法 ………………………………………………288
　　量 ………………………………………………………288
　　価　　格 ………………………………………………288
　　質 ………………………………………………………288

期間の計算 ………………………………………………289
　　地方標準時または経過時間 …………………………289
　米　国　法 ………………………………………………291

返　　船 …………………………………………………293
　　傭船期間終了時の返船 ………………………………293
　　傭船料の支払は返船まで継続する …………………293
　　同様に良好な状態での返船 …………………………293
　　損傷を受けた本船の返船 ……………………………294
　　通常の損耗 ……………………………………………295
　　期限前早期返船 ………………………………………295
　　約定以外の場所での返船 ……………………………296
　米　国　法 ………………………………………………297
　　同様に良好な状態での返船 …………………………297
　　通常の損耗を除く ……………………………………298
　　約定以外の場所での返船 ……………………………299
　　荷　　敷 ………………………………………………299

傭船料の支払と本船の引揚 ……………………………301
　　一　般　原　則 ………………………………………301
　　現　　金 ………………………………………………302
　　船主が合意した支払方法の変更 ……………………304
　　支払傭船料の不足 ……………………………………304
　　本船の使用が妨げられた場合の傭船料の支払 ……305
　　支払期日に本船がオフハイヤーとなっているときの傭船料の支払 …………305
　　傭船契約の条項により許容される傭船料からの控除 ……306
　　損害賠償請求金額の控除：衡平法上の相殺 ………307
　　傭船者が控除できる金額 ……………………………310
　　控除する権利を誠実に信じることでは十分ではない ……311
　　半　月　毎　に ………………………………………311
　　前　払　に　て ………………………………………311
　　支払期日が銀行休日にあたる場合 …………………312
　　絶対的義務 ……………………………………………312

目　次

　　最後の半月分の傭船料 …………………………………………………313
　　履　行　拒　絶 ……………………………………………………………313
　　本船引揚の権利 ……………………………………………………………314
　　従前承認された支払方法に起因する支払の遅滞 ………………………314
　　支払遅滞の事前の承認 ……………………………………………………315
　　本船引揚は最終的なものでなければならない …………………………315
　　遅滞した傭船料の支払：引揚権の効果 …………………………………316
　　本船引揚の通知 ……………………………………………………………316
　　権利消滅（forfeiture）に対する衡平法上の救済 ………………………317
　　反厳格解釈条項（NYPE 93 の第11条(b)項を含む）……………………317
　　本船引揚権の放棄 …………………………………………………………319
　　本船引揚の効果 ……………………………………………………………322
　　「あるいは，本傭船契約の違反により」………………………………324
　　本船引揚と損害賠償請求権 ………………………………………………327
　　差　止　命　令 ……………………………………………………………329
　米　国　法 ……………………………………………………………………330
　　現　　　金 …………………………………………………………………330
　　傭船料満額以下の支払／控除 ……………………………………………330
　　傭船料の支払不履行 ………………………………………………………332
　　「前払にて」………………………………………………………………332
　　船主の態度による変更 ……………………………………………………333
　　警告が必要なのか …………………………………………………………334
　　本船引揚の通知 ……………………………………………………………335
　　遅滞した傭船料支払の受領 ………………………………………………335
　　期限遅れの支払提示 ………………………………………………………335
　　船上に貨物がある場合の引揚 ……………………………………………335
　　銀行の過誤 …………………………………………………………………336
　　「あるいは，本傭船契約の違反により」………………………………337
　　本船引揚の効果 ……………………………………………………………337
　　不法な引揚または解約の際の損害賠償 …………………………………338
　　傭船者が本船を使用するのを船主が拒否する権利 ……………………340

期間の計算を開始する時 …………………………………………………………341
　　傭船期間の開始 ……………………………………………………………342
　　前渡立替金 …………………………………………………………………343
　　常に浮揚状態で安全に碇泊 ………………………………………………343
　　傭船者が貨物積載可能な船艙 ……………………………………………343
　米　国　法 ……………………………………………………………………344
　　期間の計算を開始する時 …………………………………………………344

極 力 迅 速 …………………………………………………………………………345
　　航海の遂行 …………………………………………………………………345
　　機　関　士 …………………………………………………………………345
　　免責条項に従って …………………………………………………………345

|　　　慣習上の助力 …………………………………………………………346
|　米　国　法 ………………………………………………………………348
|　　　極　力　迅　速 ……………………………………………………348
|　　　慣習上の助力 …………………………………………………………349
本船使用条項 ……………………………………………………………………351
　　傭船者の指図に服従 ……………………………………………………351
　　黙示の補償 ………………………………………………………………353
　　他の条項との関係 ………………………………………………………355
　　明示の補償 ………………………………………………………………355
　　船荷証券の署名から生じる補償 ………………………………………355
　　傭船者の過失によらない補償 …………………………………………356
　　使　用（Employment）……………………………………………356
　　因　果　関　係 …………………………………………………………358
　　通常費用と航海危険 ……………………………………………………359
　　代　　　理 ………………………………………………………………360
　米　国　法 ………………………………………………………………361
　　使　用　条　項 …………………………………………………………361
　　船主と傭船者との間の補償の権利 ……………………………………362
貨物の積込，積付，荷均および揚荷 ………………………………………363
　　傭船者への責任の転嫁 …………………………………………………363
　　揚　　　荷 ………………………………………………………………363
　　海上物品運送法の効果 …………………………………………………364
　　ボルタイム書式 …………………………………………………………365
　　船長の監督の下に ………………………………………………………366
　　「および船長の責任」 …………………………………………………367
　　甲板積貨物 ………………………………………………………………368
　　1945年法改革（寄与過失）に関する法 ………………………………369
　　ニューヨーク・プロデュース書式に関するP&Iクラブ間の協定 …370
　　海損バース基準条項 ……………………………………………………375
　　傭船者は船主のP&I補償の利益を受ける ……………………………375
　米　国　法 ………………………………………………………………376
　　船長の監督の下に ………………………………………………………377
　　クラブ間協定 ……………………………………………………………382
　　訴訟告知（Vouching-in）………………………………………………383
船荷証券（B/L）の署名 ………………………………………………………385
　　呈示された（As presented）…………………………………………385
　　傭船契約以上の責任を船主に課する船荷証券 ………………………386
　　補償請求が生じるとき …………………………………………………388
　　異常な性質の条件または傭船契約と「明らかに矛盾している」条件 …389
　　仕向港が傭船契約の航路定限外にある船荷証券 ……………………389
　　傭船契約により要求される条項を摂取していない船荷証券 ………390

貨物の状態につき不実記載のある船荷証券	390
不正確な日付の船荷証券	391
船積貨物の数量または性質を誤表示している船荷証券	391
艙内積と誤って表示する船荷証券	392
デマイズ条項（demise clause）を含む船荷証券	392
「運賃前払」船荷証券	392
外国の裁判管轄条項を含む船荷証券	393
傭船契約上の権利を侵害することなく	393
署名の効果；船主のあるいは傭船者の船荷証券	394
米　国　法	401
メーツ・レシート（Mate's receipts）	401
船荷証券（Bill of lading）	401
船荷証券の署名	401
船長自身が署名した船荷証券	402
傭船者またはその代理人が署名した船荷証券	402
中間の定期傭船者	404
船荷証券の追認	405
不堪航または不法行為について貨物所有者に対する船主の直接責任	405
呈示された	406
傭船契約以上の責任を船主に課する船荷証券	406
傭船契約上の「権利を侵害することなく」署名された船荷証券	407
船荷証券発行の際の明示の制限	408
船荷証券を請求する荷送人の権利	408
貨物の引渡前に船荷証券の呈示を請求する船長の権利	408
運送人の同一性または「デマイズ」条項	409
ボルタイム書式	409
航　海　日　誌	411
米　国　法	412
傭船者の航海指図	412
航　海　日　誌	413
傭船契約の継続	415
傭船契約を継続する選択権の行使	415
14行の傭船者任意の許容期間についての効果	415
米　国　法	416
傭船契約の継続	416
解　約　条　項	419
原　　　則	419
傭船者による約定日以前の使用	419
準備完了の要件	420
準備完了の通知	420
解約期日までに本船を引き渡すことは船主の絶対的義務ではない	422

目　次

　　解約期日前に解約する権利（義務）はない …………423
　　解約権の行使 …………424
　　解約選択権とその他の権利 …………424
米　国　法 …………425
　　解約期日 …………425
　　引渡時の状態 …………426

オフハイヤー条項 …………427
　　一般原則 …………427
　　債務不履行はオフハイヤーの要件ではない …………428
　　時間の喪失 …………428
　　「正味喪失時間」オフハイヤー条項と「期間」オフハイヤー条項 …………429
　　傭船料全額の支払義務が再開する時期 …………430
　　部分的業務不能 …………432
　　傭船開始前に発生した事由 …………433
　　人員の不足 …………433
　　故　障 …………434
　　本船もしくは貨物の海損事故による滞船 …………434
　　もしくは本船の完全な稼働を妨げるその他一切の事由によって …………435
　　傭船者の義務違反により生じた事由 …………442
　　傭船料支払の停止 …………443
　　オフハイヤー期間中の燃料およびその他の義務 …………443
　　船主または傭船者のその他の救済手段についての効果 …………444
　　ニューヨーク・プロデュース書式99行から101行に規定されている本船速力の低下について …………445
米　国　法 …………447
　　一般原則 …………447
　　時間の喪失 …………447
　　傭船料の再開 …………448
　　人員の不足 …………448
　　本船または貨物の海損事故による滞船 …………451
　　入　渠 …………452
　　火　災 …………452
　　船体，機関または装備の故障または損傷 …………452
　　その他の一切の事由 …………453
　　本船の差押え（アレスト） …………455
　　航海中の速力の減少 …………457
　　傭船者のその他の義務 …………457
　　船主と傭船者のその他の救済についての効果 …………457
　　傭船者に解約の選択権を付与する条項 …………459

傭船契約の履行不能 …………461
　　本船の滅失 …………461
　　履行不能の法理 …………461

目 次

　　事実問題と法律問題 …………………………………………462
　　傭船船舶の喪失による履行不能 ……………………………464
　　遅延による履行不能 …………………………………………464
　　傭船始期の遅延 ………………………………………………465
　　航海のための傭船期間の延長 ………………………………466
　　傭船期間内に業務を中断させるもの ………………………467
　　当事者が考慮した事態もしくは契約に規定された事態 …469
　　中断の程度の評価 ……………………………………………470
　　経済的損失 ……………………………………………………473
　　過失の効果 ……………………………………………………474
　　履行不能に伴う義務 …………………………………………477
　米 国 法 ……………………………………………………………480
　　反対給付が得られなかった前払金 …………………………480
　　傭船契約の履行不能 …………………………………………480
　　事態は予見不可能であることを要する ……………………481
　　危険の分担 ……………………………………………………482
　　商業的に実行不可能な履行 …………………………………483
　　契約の履行を妨げる第三者の債務不履行 …………………484
　　法律の変更 ……………………………………………………485
　　輸出禁止令 ……………………………………………………487
　　全損の効果――代船条項 ……………………………………487
　　推 定 全 損 ……………………………………………………488

一般免責条項 …………………………………………………………489
　　一 般 原 則 ……………………………………………………489
　　本船滅失に限らない …………………………………………489
　　米国海上物品運送法 …………………………………………489
　　天　　　災 ……………………………………………………490
　　公　　　敵 ……………………………………………………490
　　火　　　災 ……………………………………………………490
　　君主，統治者および人民による抑留 ………………………491
　　海洋，河川の危険および事故 ………………………………492
　　機関，汽罐，蒸気航海 ………………………………………492
　　航海上の過誤 …………………………………………………492
　　常に相互に免責される ………………………………………493
　　米国海上物品運送法における免責条項 ……………………493
　　免責条項および102行と103行の第1文 ……………………494
　　免責条項の解釈に関する一般的解説 ………………………494
　　これらの原則に対する最近の修正 …………………………495
　　根本的な契約違反 ……………………………………………495
　米 国 法 ……………………………………………………………497
　　相互免責条項 …………………………………………………497
　　天　　　災 ……………………………………………………498

         火　　　　災 ……………………………………………………498
         君主，統治者および人民による抑留 …………………………500
         海洋，河川の危険および事故 …………………………………501
         機　　　　関 ……………………………………………………502
         航海上の過誤 ……………………………………………………503
         米国海上物品運送法における免責条項 ………………………503
         解釈の規範 ………………………………………………………504

   自 由 条 項 …………………………………………………………505
         離　　　　路 ……………………………………………………505

   仲　　　　裁 ………………………………………………………507
         この章の範囲 ……………………………………………………507
         仲裁の場所 ………………………………………………………507
         仲裁人によって適用される法律の選択 ………………………507
         1991年4月1日以前に締結された傭船契約 …………………508
         1991年4月1日以降に締結された傭船契約 …………………509
         仲裁合意，管轄および仲裁手続を規制する法律 ……………509
         米国海上物品運送法第3条6項の出訴期限の摂取 …………509
         仲裁人の選任 ……………………………………………………511
         仲裁の開始 ………………………………………………………511
         仲　裁　法 ………………………………………………………511
         「3人の（仲裁人）」に関して …………………………………511
         仲裁人の数が特定されていない場合 …………………………512
         実務家（Commercial men）……………………………………512
         仲裁付託の場合の訴訟手続の停止 ……………………………512
         当事者が仲裁人を起用しない場合 ……………………………512
         仲裁を行う際の仲裁人の権限 …………………………………513
         裁判所の権限 ……………………………………………………514
         1979年法の下での裁判所への上訴 ……………………………515
         控訴院への上訴 …………………………………………………516
         利子についての仲裁人の権限 …………………………………517
         暫定仲裁判断 ……………………………………………………517
   米　国　法 …………………………………………………………518
         仲裁の合意 ………………………………………………………518
         法　の　選　択 …………………………………………………518
         仲裁に関する制定法 ……………………………………………518
         書面による仲裁合意 ……………………………………………518
         仲裁判断を待って，訴訟手続を停止 …………………………520
         仲裁の強制 ………………………………………………………521
         仲裁の併合 ………………………………………………………523
         仲裁人，審判人の選任 …………………………………………525
         「実　務　家」 …………………………………………………526
         仲裁開始前の証拠開示手続 ……………………………………527

仲裁付託を条件とした係争 …………………………………527
仲裁の放棄 …………………………………………………529
利子，報酬，費用に関して仲裁判断を下す権限 …………529
懲罰的損害賠償 ……………………………………………530
仲裁判断実現を目的とする担保 ……………………………532
担保の提供を裁定する仲裁人の権限 ………………………533
仲裁判断の確認 ……………………………………………534
仲裁判断の破棄 ……………………………………………536
明らかな法の無視 …………………………………………547
公序良俗違反 ………………………………………………549
外国仲裁判断の承認および執行に関する条約 ……………549
仲裁判断の第三者拘束力 …………………………………552
手続を開始する時期 ………………………………………553

リ ー エ ン …………………………………………………555
英国法と米国法の重要な違い ………………………………555
積荷に対する船主のリーエンの性質 ………………………555
リーエンはどの貨物に対して行使しうるか ………………556
リーエンを行使する場所 …………………………………557
再運送賃に対する船主のリーエンの性質 …………………558
「再運送賃」の意味 …………………………………………558
船主に支払われるべき再運送賃 …………………………559
傭船者に支払われるべき再運送賃 ………………………561
再傭船者に支払われるべき運賃 …………………………561
請求の優先 …………………………………………………562
船主のリーエンが担保権として登記されるとき …………562
運賃前払の船荷証券（B/L）………………………………563
本傭船契約において支払われるべきすべての金額 ………563
本船に対する傭船者のリーエン …………………………564
一切のリーエンもしくは財産上の負担 …………………565

米 国 法 …………………………………………………567
海事リーエン ………………………………………………567
未履行の契約 ………………………………………………567
船主のリーエン ……………………………………………568
船主のリーエンを行使できる時期 ………………………570
「運賃前払」の船荷証券 ……………………………………574
自 助 ………………………………………………………575
傭船者のリーエン …………………………………………576
傭船者のリーエンの優先権 ………………………………577
傭船者発注による物品供給者のリーエン ………………578
納入業者のリーエンの優先度 ……………………………583
再傭船者のリーエン ………………………………………583
アレストから本船を解放する義務 ………………………584

海事リーエンがついている傭船者の財物 ……………………………………585
海難救助 ………………………………………………………………………587
　　　得られた純救助料の分配 ………………………………………………587
船主負担の燃料 ………………………………………………………………589
　　　船主が支払うべき燃料費 ………………………………………………589
　　　米　国　法 ………………………………………………………………590
入渠と設備 ……………………………………………………………………591
米国海上物品運送法 …………………………………………………………593
　　　ハーター法および米国海上物品運送法（1936年）の摂取 …………594
　　　ハーター法 ………………………………………………………………594
　　　米国海上物品運送法 ……………………………………………………594
　　　米国海上物品運送法の摂取の方法 ……………………………………596
　　　ニューヨーク・プロデュース書式においては，すべての航海に米国法が適用される ………………………………………………………………………597
　　　各航海における堪航性担保義務 ………………………………………597
　　　米国法のその他の効果 …………………………………………………598
　　　船主と傭船者間の業務の分担 …………………………………………601
　　　双方過失衝突条項 ………………………………………………………601
　　　米　国　法 ………………………………………………………………603
　　　ハーター法と海上物品運送法 …………………………………………603
　　　運送人としての船主と傭船者 …………………………………………603
　　　手続の開始時期 …………………………………………………………604
　　　双方過失衝突条項 ………………………………………………………607
　　　裁判管轄条項 ……………………………………………………………608
傭船契約の性質 ………………………………………………………………611
　　　氷　条　項 ………………………………………………………………611
　　　船舶の賃貸借ではない …………………………………………………611
　　　賃貸借（demise）契約 …………………………………………………611
　　　定期傭船契約 ……………………………………………………………612
　　　航海傭船契約 ……………………………………………………………613
　　　航　　海 …………………………………………………………………613
　　　保険塡補の範囲 …………………………………………………………614
　　　本船の損傷に関する船主の傭船者に対するクレームの効果 ………614
　　　傭船者による保険料払戻条項 …………………………………………615
　　　米　国　法 ………………………………………………………………619
　　　氷　条　項 ………………………………………………………………619
　　　定期傭船者の本船に対する利害 ………………………………………619
　　　「船主は……につき責任がある」 ………………………………………620
　　　保　　険 …………………………………………………………………621
手　数　料 ……………………………………………………………………623

〜からの電信による授権 ………………………………………………624
　米　国　法………………………………………………………………625
　　　手　数　料 ………………………………………………………625

ボルタイム書式

ボルタイム書式 ……………………………………………………………629
　第1条 ― 期間／引渡港／引渡時 …………………………………630
　第2条 ― 航　　　路 …………………………………………………631
　第3条 ― 船主の支給 …………………………………………………632
　第4条 ― 傭船者の支給 ………………………………………………632
　第5条および第6条 ― 燃料／傭船料 ………………………………634
　第7条 ― 返　　　船 …………………………………………………635
　第8条 ― 貨物スペース ………………………………………………637
　第9条 ― 船　　　長 …………………………………………………637
　第9条 続 ― 船長（使用と補償）……………………………………639
　米　国　法 ……………………………………………………………641
　　船荷証券を発行する傭船者の権利 ………………………………641
　第10, 11条および12条 ― 指図と航海日誌／傭船料の支払停止等／汽罐の掃除 …642
　第13条 ― 責任と免責 …………………………………………………644
　第13条 続 ― ストライキ等 …………………………………………650
　第13条 続 ― 傭船者の責任 …………………………………………652
　第14条および第15条 ― 前渡金／除外港 …………………………653
　第16, 17条および第18条 ― 本船の滅失／時間外／リーエン ……656
　第19条および第20条 ― 海難救助／再傭船 ………………………656
　第21条 ― 戦　　　争 …………………………………………………658
　米　国　法 ……………………………………………………………662
　　戦争危険条項 ………………………………………………………662
　第22条 ― 解　　　約 …………………………………………………663
　第23, 24条および第25条 ― 仲裁／共同海損／手数料 ……………664

シェルタイム書式

シェルタイム書式 …………………………………………………………667
　第1条 ― 本船の表示および状態 ……………………………………668
　第2条 ― 乗組員およびその義務 ……………………………………671
　第3条 ― 保船義務 ……………………………………………………672
　第4条 ― 期間および航路定限 ………………………………………676
　第5条 ― 傭船開始・傭船解約 ………………………………………679
　第6条 ― 船主負担費目 ………………………………………………681
　第7条 ― 傭船者負担費目 ……………………………………………681

| 目　次 |

| 第 8 条 ― 傭 船 料 率 …………………………………………………682
| 第 9 条 ― 傭船料の支払 ………………………………………………683
| 第10条 ― 貨物積載場所 ………………………………………………684
| 第11条 ― 時間外手当 …………………………………………………685
| 第12条 ― 指図および航海日誌 ………………………………………685
| 第13条 ― 船 荷 証 券 …………………………………………………687
| 第14条 ― 乗組員の行為 ………………………………………………689
| 第15条 ― 引渡時および返船時の燃料 ………………………………690
| 第16条 ― 荷役業者，水先人，曳船 …………………………………692
| 第17条 ― 定員外の乗船 ………………………………………………693
| 第18条 ― 再　傭　船 …………………………………………………693
| 第19条 ― 最 終 航 海 …………………………………………………694
| 第20条 ― 本船の滅失 …………………………………………………695
| 第21条 ― オフハイヤー ………………………………………………698
| 第22条 ― 定 期 入 渠 …………………………………………………704
| 第23条 ― 検　　　船 …………………………………………………705
| 第24条 ― 本船の細目および性能 ……………………………………708
| 第25条 ― 海 難 救 助 …………………………………………………712
| 第26条 ― リ ー エ ン …………………………………………………712
| 第27条 ― 免　　　責 …………………………………………………714
| 第28条 ― 有 害 貨 物 …………………………………………………718
| 第29条 ― 燃料油の品質 ………………………………………………719
| 第30条 ― 諸　　　掛 …………………………………………………720
| 第31条 ― 繋　　　船 …………………………………………………720
| 第32条 ― 徴　　　用 …………………………………………………721
| 第33条 ― 戦争の勃発 …………………………………………………722
| 第34条 ― 戦争による追加費用 ………………………………………723
| 第35条 ― 戦 争 危 険 …………………………………………………725
| 第36条 ― 双方過失衝突条項 …………………………………………729
| 第37条 ― ニュー・ジェイソン条項 …………………………………731
| 第38条 ― 至 上 条 項 …………………………………………………732
| 第39条 ― TOVALOP（油濁責任に関するタンカー船主間自主協定）……734
| 第40条 ― 輸 出 制 限 …………………………………………………736
| 第41条 ― 法および訴訟 ………………………………………………737
| 第42条 ― 解　　　釈 …………………………………………………738

タンカー定期傭船STB書式

STB書式によるタンカー定期傭船契約に関する米国法上の解説 ……………741

付録A（略）
　ハーター法1893
　米国海上物品運送法1936
付録B（略）
　ヘーグ・ヴィスビー・ルール
付録C（略）
　1950年仲裁法
　1975年仲裁法
　1979年仲裁法
付録D（略）
　米国仲裁法
　外国仲裁判断の承認と執行に関する条約

事項索引……………………………………………………………………793

判例索引 (Table of Cases)

該当判例は原書の頁で掲記（原書頁数は訳文の左肩□内に表記）
（判例の事実関係を記載している頁数は，太字で示した）。

A/B Helsingfors S. S. Co. Ltd. v. Rederi A/B Rex—The White Rose [1969] 2 Lloyd's
　Rep. 52; [1969] 1 W. L. R. 1098; [1969] 3 All E. R. 374 (Q. B.) ········297, **298**, 299, 563
A. B. Marintrans v. Comet Shipping—The Shinjitsu Maru No. 5 [1985] 1 Lloyd's Rep.
　568; [1985] 1 W. L. R. 1270; [1985] 3 All E. R. 442, (Q. B.) ····················**307**, 308, 309
A&D Properties Inc. v. The Volta River, 1984 AMC 464 (E. D. La. 1983) ··········**175-176**
AES Express, The (1990) 20 N. S. W. L. R. 57 ···264, **265**
A. P. J. Priti, The—Atkins International H. A. v. Islamic Republic of Iran Shipping
　Lines [1987] 2 Lloyd's Rep. 37, (C. A.) ·······································**194**, 195, 196, 197
A/S Acadia v. Curtis Bay Towing Co. (1967) 304 F. Supp. 1050 (E. D. Pa.) ············226
A/S Awilco v. Fulvia S. p. A. di Navigazione—The Chikuma [1981] 1 Lloyd's Rep.
　371; [1981] 1 W. L. R. 314; [1981] 1 All E. R. 652, (H. L.); rev'g [1980] 2 Lloyd's
　Rep. 409. (C. A.); restoring [1979] 1 Lloyd's Rep. 367, (Q. B.) ·······················**244**, 584
A/S Brovanor v. Central Gulf S. S. Corp. (1970) 323 F. Supp. 1029 (S. D. N. Y.) ········318
A/S Custodia v. Lessin Int'l Inc. (1974) 503 F. 2d 318 (2d Cir.) ·····················**447**, 450
A/S Hansen Tangens Rederi III v. Total Transport Corp.—The Sagona [1984] 1
　Lloyd's Rep. 194, (Q. B.) ···221, 292, 293, **294**, 583
A/S Iverans Rederei v. KG M. S. Holstencruiser Seeschiffahrtsgesellschaft m. b. H—
　The Holstencruiser [1992] 2 Lloyd's Rep. 378, (Q. B.) ·······························**313-314**
A/S J. Ludwig Mowinckels Rederi v. Dow Chemical Co. (1970) 25 N. Y. 2d 576;
　307 N. Y. S. 2d 660 ···56
Aaby v. States Marine Corp.—The Tendo (1948) 80 F. Supp. 328 (S. D. N. Y.); aff'd
　(1950) 181 F. 2d 383; 1950 AMC 947 (2d Cir.); cert. denied (1950) 340 U. S. 829
　··108, 110, **389**
Aaby v. States Marine Corp. (1951) 107 F. Supp. 484 (S. D. N. Y.) ·····················278, 279
Abu Dhabi National Tanker Co. v. Product Star Shipping Ltd.—The Product Star
　(No. 2) [1993] 1 Lloyd's Rep. 397, (C. A.); rev'g [1991] 2 Lloyd's Rep. 468, (Q. B.)
　···569, **612**
Actis Co. Ltd. v. The Sanko Steamship Co. Ltd.—The Aquacharm [1982] 1 Lloyd's
　Rep. 7; [1982] 1 W. L. R. 119 [1982] 1 All E. R. 390, (C. A.); aff'g [1980] 2 Lloyd's
　Rep. 237, (Q. B.) ·····························**293**, 297, 298, **304**, 370, **371**, 372, 374, 515, 517, **518**
Active Glass Corp. v. Architectural and Ornamental Iron Workers Local Union
　(1995) U. S. Dist. Lexis 1500 (S. D. N. Y.) ··453
Ada, The (1918) 250 F. 194 (2d. Cir.) ···56
Adamastos Shipping Co. Ltd. v. Anglo-Saxon Petroleum Co.—The Saxon Star [1958]
　1 Lloyd's Rep. 73; [1959] A. C. 133; [1958] 2 W. L. R. 688; [1958] 1 All E. R.
　725, (H. L.); rev'g [1957] 1 Lloyd's Rep. 272; [1957] 2 Q. B. 233; [1957] 2 W. L.
　R. 908; [1957] 2 All E. R. 311, (C. A.); restoring [1957] 1 Lloyd's Rep. 79; [1957]

2 Q. B. 233; [1957] 2 W. L. R. 509; [1957] 1 All E. R. 673, (Q. B.)
··212, 286, **514-515**, 516, 517, 519, 531, 561, 603
Adelaide Steamship Co. Ltd. v. The Crown (No. 2) (1925) 23 Ll. L. Rep. 49, 259; *sub nom.* Adelaide S. S. Co. Ltd. v. A. -G. [1926] A. C. 172; 31 Com. Cas. 145; 42 T. L. R. 180; 95 L. J. K. B. 213; *sub nom.* Adelaide S. S. Co. Ltd. v. The King, 134 L. T. 258; 16 Asp. M. L. C. 579, (H. L.); (1924) 18 Ll. L. Rep. 453; *sub nom.* Adelaide S. S. Co. Ltd. v. The King, 30 Com. Cas. 1; 40 T. L. R. 595; 131 L. T. 548; 16 Asp. M. L. C. 366, (C. A.); (1923) 17 Ll. L. Rep. 324; *sub nom.* Adelaide S. S. Co. Ltd. v. The King, 29 Com. Cas. 165; 40 T. L. R. 194; 131 L. T. 548; 16 Asp. M. L. C. 366, (K. B.) ········373
Adelfoi, The, 1972 AMC 1742 (Arb. at N. Y.) ··117, 135
Aden Refinery Co. Ltd. v. Ugland Management Co. Ltd. [1986] 2 Lloyd's Rep. 336; [1987] Q. B. 650; [1986] 3 W. L. R. 949; [1986] 3 All E. R. 737, (C. A.) ···············446
Aditya Vaibhav, The—Century Textiles and Industry Ltd v. Tomoe Shipping Co. (Singapore) Pte. Ltd. [1991] 1 Lloyd's Rep. 573, (Q. B.); [1993] 1 Lloyd's Rep. 63, (Q. B.) ···**249**, 251, 252, 594
Admiralty Flyer, The SMA 349 (Arb. at N. Y. 1967) ···································272, 274
Adventure, The, SMA 3161 (Arb. at N. Y 1995) ··301, 499
Advest Inc. v. McCarthy (1990) 914 F. 2d 6 (1st Cir.) ···473
Aegean Dolphin, The—Dolphin Hellas Shipping S. A. v. Itemslot Ltd. [1992] 2 Lloyd's Rep. 178, (Q. B.) ···92, 104
Aegnoussiotis Shipping Corp. v. A/S Kristian Jebsen's Rederi—The Aegnoussiotis [1977] 1 Lloyd's Rep. 268, (Q. B.) ···257, 258, 480, 481
Aegnoussiotis, The—Aegnoussiotis Shipping Corp. v. A/S Kristian Jebsen's Rederi [1977] 1 Lloyd's Rep. 268, (Q. B.) ···257, 258, 480, 481
Aello, The—Sociedad Financiera de Bienes Raices v. Agrimpex [1960] 1 Lloyd's Rep. 623; [1961] A. C. 135; [1960] 3 W. L. R. 145; [1960] 2 All E. R. 578, (H. L.) ······**159**
Aetolia, The, SMA 1993 (Arb. at N. Y. 1984); SMA 2157 (Arb. at N. Y. 1985)
···270, 300, 318
Afovos Shipping Co. S. A. v. R. Pagnan & F. Lli—The Afovos [1983] 1 Lloyd's Rep. 335; [1983] 1 W. L. R. 195; [1983] 1 All E. R. 449, (H. L.); [1982] 1 Lloyd's Rep. 562; [1982] 1 W. L. R. 848; [1982] 3 All E. R. 18, (C. A.); [1980] 2 Lloyd's Rep. 469, (Q. B.) ···245, 253, **259-260**, 268, 269, 584
Afovos, The—Afovos Shipping Co. S. A. v. R. Pagnan & F. Lli [1983] 1 Lloyd's Rep. 335; [1983] 1 W. L. R. 195; [1983] 1 All E. R. 449, (H. L.); [1982] 1 Lloyd's Rep. 562; [1982] 1 W. L. R. 848; [1982] 3 All E. R. 18, (C. A.); [1980] 2 Lloyd's Rep. 469, (Q. B.) ···245, 253, **259-260**, 268, 269, 584
African Glen, The, 1969 AMC 1465 (A. S. B. C. A. 1969) ··427
Agathon, The (No. 2)—Empresa Cubana de Fletes v. Kissavos Shipping Co. S. A. [1984] 1 Lloyd's Rep. 183, Q. B. ···534, **535**, 567
Aghia Marina, The, SMA 1236 (Arb. at N. Y. 1978) ···113, 114, 116
Agia Erini II, The, SMA 1602 (Arb. at N. Y. 1981) ···633
Agia Skepti, The, SMA 2891 (Arb. at N. Y. 1992) ···350
Agios Giorgis, The—Steelwood Carriers Inc. v. Evimeria Cia. Nav. S. A. [1976] 2

判例索引　　33

Lloyd's Rep. 192, (Q. B.) ···246, **256-257**, 279, 285, 480
Agios Lazaros, The—Nea Agrex S. A. v. Baltic Shipping Co. Ltd. [1976] 2 Lloyd's
　Rep. 47; [1976] Q. B. 933; [1976] 2 W. L. R. 925; [1976] 2 All E. R. 842, (C. A.)
　··313, 439, 440, 515, 517, 518, 520, **561**
Agios Nikolaos III, The, SMA 2540 (Arb. at N. Y. 1988) ·······························457
Agios Panteleimon, The, SMA 1477 (Arb. at N. Y. 1980) ·······························317
Aira Force S. S. Co. v. Christie (1892) 9 T. L. R. 104. (C. A.) ···························532
Akra Aktion, The—Antria Shipping Co. Ltd. v. Triton Int'l Carriers Ltd., 1980 AMC
　678 (S. D. N. Y. 1976) ···491
Akt. Adalands v. Michael Whitaker Ltd. (1913) 18 Com. Cas. 229, (Q. B.) ···············563
Akt. Brunsgaard v. Standard Oil of N. J. (1922) 283 F. 106 (2d Cir.) ·····················346
Akt. Dampsk. Thorbjorn v. Harrison & Co. (1918) 260 F. 287 (S. D. N. Y.) ·········493, 494
Akt. Fido v. Lloyd Brasileiro (1919) 267 F. 733 (S. D. N. Y.); aff'd (1922) 283 F. 62
　(2d Cir.); cert. denied (1922) 260 U. S. 737 ··173
Aktieselskabet Nord-Osterso Rederiet v. Casper, Edgar & Co. (1923) 14 Ll. L. Rep.
　203, (H. L.); (1922) 11 Ll. L. Rep. 146. (C. A.); (1922) 10 Ll. L. Rep. 362, (K. B.) ······403
Al Bida, The—Arab Maritime Petroleum Transport Co. v. Luxor Trading Corp.
　[1987] 1 Lloyd's Rep. 124. (C. A.); [1986] 1 Lloyd's Rep. 142, (Q. B.) ···102, **105-106**, 600
Al Wahab, The—Amin Rasheed Shipping Corp. v. Kuwait Insurance Co. [1984] A. C.
　50; [1983] 2 Lloyd's Rep. 365; [1983] 3 W. L. R. 241; [1983] 2 All E. R. 884, (H.
　L.); [1983] 1 Lloyd's Rep. 235; [1983] 1 W. L. R. 228; [1983] 1 All E. R. 873, (C.
　A.); [1982] 1 Lloyd's Rep. 638; [1982] 1 W. L. R. 961, (Q. B.) ·······························437
Alamo Chemical Transportation Co. v. The Overseas Valdes (1979) 469 F. Supp.
　203; 1979 AMC 2033 (E. D. La.)···72, 526
Alaskan Trader, The (No. 2) —Clea Shipping Corp. v. Bulk Oil International Ltd.
　[1983] 2 Lloyd's Rep. 645; [1984] 1 All E. R. 129 (Q. B.) ·······················**130**, 236
Albion Sugar Co. Ltd. v. William Tankers Ltd.—The John S. Darbyshire [1977] 2
　Lloyd's Rep. 457, (Q. B.) ··53, 586
Albis Co. v. Munson (1905) 139 F. 234 (2d Cir.) ···384
Alcazar, The, SMA 1512 (Arb. at N. Y. 1981) ···382
Alecos M. The—Sealace Shipping Co. Ltd. v. Oceanvoice Ltd. [1991] 1 Lloyd's Rep.
　120, (C. A.); rev'g [1990] 1 Lloyd's Rep. 82, (Q. B.) ·······································237
Alexandros Koryzis, The, SMA 271 (Arb. at N. Y. 1968) ···································284
Alexandros P, The—Alexandros Shipping Co. of Piraeus v. MSC Mediterranean
　Shipping Co. of Geneva [1986] 1 Lloyd's Rep. 421, (Q. B.) ·······························308
Alexandros Shipping Co. of Piraeus v. MSC Mediterranean Shipping Co. of Geneva—
　The Alexandros P [1986] 1 Lloyd's Rep. 421, (Q. B.) ·······································308
Alfred C. Toepfer Schiffahrtsgesellschaft G. m. b. H. v. Tossa Marine Co. Ltd., Tossa
　Marine Co. Ltd. v. Alfred C. Toepfer Schiffahrtsgesellschaft G. m. b. H.—The Derby
　[1985] 2 Lloyd's Rep. 325, (C. A.); [1984] 1 Lloyd's Rep. 635, (Q. B.)
　···154, 156, 158, 159, **160**, 574
Alhambra, The (1881) 6 P. D. 68; 44 L. T. 637; 50 L. J. P. 36; 4 Asp. M. L. C. 410, (C.
　A.) ··180

Aliakmon Maritime Corp. v. Trans Ocean Shipping Ltd.—The Aliakmon Progress
  [1978] 2 Lloyd's Rep. 499, (C. A.) ···251, 515, **518**, 519
Aliakmon Progress, The—Aliakmon Maritime Corp. v. Trans Ocean Shipping Ltd.
  [1978] 2 Lloyd's Rep. 499, (C. A.) ···251, 515, **518**, 519
Aljassim v. The South Star (1971) 323 F. Supp. 918; 1971 AMC 1703 (S. D. N. Y.) ······**340**
Allen v. The Contessa (1961) 196 F. Supp. 649; 1961 AMC 2190 (S. D. Tex.) ··········500
Allied Marine Transport Ltd. v. Vale do Rio Doce Navegacao S. A.—The Leonidas D
  [1985] 2 Lloyd's Rep. 18; [1985] 1 W. L. R. 925; [1985] 2 All E. R. 796, (C. A.) ···443
Allseas Maritime v. The Mimosa (1983) 574 F. Supp. 844 (S. D. Tex.) ·······················527
Alma Shipping Corp. v. Mantovani—The Dione [1975] 1 Lloyd's Rep. 115, (C. A.);
  rev'g [1974] 1 Lloyd's Rep. 86, (Q. B.) ·····················122, 123, 125, 126, **127**, 128, 590, 619
Alma, The, SMA 261 (Arb. at N. Y. 1964) ···117, 119
Almacenes Fernandez S. A. v. Golodetz (1945) 148 F. 2d 625 (2d Cir.); 1961 AMC
  1974··79
Almak, The—Rudolf A. Oetker v. IFA Internationale Frachtagentur A. G. [1985] 1
  Lloyd's Rep. 557, (Q. B.) ···330, 331
Alonzo, The (1869) F. Cas. No. 257 (D. Me.) ···344, 346
Alpha Trading Ltd. v. DunnShaw-Patten Ltd. [1981] 1 Lloyd's Rep. 122; [1981] Q.
  B. 290; [1981] 2 W. L. R. 169; [1981] 1 All E. R. 482, (C. A.) ·····························541
Alucentro Div. Dell 'Alusuisse Italia S. p. A. v. The Hafnia, 1992 AMC 267 (Fla.
  1991) ··448
Alumina Transp. Corp. v. Occidental Chemical Co., SMA 2136 (Arb. at N. Y. 1985) ···278
American Asiatic Co. v. Robert Dollar Co. (1922) 282 F. 743 (9th Cir.); cert. denied
  (1922) 261 U. S. 615···385
American Casualty Co. v. L-J Inc. (1994) 35 F. 3d 133 (4th Cir.) ·····························451
American Centennial Ins. Co. v. National Casualty Co. (1991) 951 F. 2d 107 (6th
  Cir.) ··452
American President Lines Ltd. v. United States (1961) 208 F. Supp. 573; 1968 AMC
  830 (N. D. Cal.) ··207, 300
American Steel Barge Co. v. Chesapeake & Ohio Coal Agency Co. (1902) 115 F.
  669 (1st Cir.) ···**491**, 492, 493, 494, 496
American Tobacco Co. v. Goulandris (1959) 173 F. Supp. 140 (S. D. N. Y.); aff'd
  (1960) 281 F. 2d 179; 1962 AMC 2655 (2d Cir.); modified on other grounds, Lekas
  & Drivas Inc. v. Goulandris (1962) 306 F. 2d 426 (2d Cir.) ·································428
American Tobacco Co. v. The Katingo Hadjipatera (1948) 81 F. Supp. 438, 446 (S. D.
  N. Y.); mod. on other grounds (1951) 194 F. 2d 449 (2d Cir.) ·····························429
American Trading & Production Corp. v. Shell International Marine Ltd. (1972) 453
  F. 2d 939 (2d Cir.) ··413
American Union Transport Inc. v. United States, 1976 AMC 1480 (N. D. Cal) ······**526**, 637
Americas Ins. Co. v. Seagull Compania Naviera S. A. (1985) 774 F. 2d 64, 67 (2d
  Cir.) ··472
Amerocean, The, 1952 AMC 1559 (Arb. at N. Y.) ···215
Amin Rasheed Shipping Corp. v. Kuwait Insurance Co.—The Al Wahab [1984] A. C.

50; [1983] 2 Lloyd's Rep. 365; [1983] 2 W. L. R. 241; [1983] 2 All E. R. 884, (H.
  L.); [1983] 1 Lloyd's Rep. 235; [1983] 1 W. L. R. 228; [1983] 1 All E. R. 873, (C.
  A.); [1982] 1 Lloyd's Rep. 638; [1982] 1 W. L. R. 961, (Q. B.) ·····················437
Amoco Cadiz, The 1984 AMC 2124 (N. D. Ill.) ··78
Amoco Overseas Co. v. The Avenger (1975) 387 F. Supp. 589; 1975 AMC 782 (S. D.
  N. Y.) ··448
Amoco Texas City, The, 1979 AMC 690 (Arb. at N. Y. 1977) ··························204
Anaconda, The v. American Sugar Refining Co. (1944) 322 U. S. 42 ·············460
Anastasia (Owners) v. Ugleexport Charkow (1934) 49 Ll. L. Rep. 1; 39 Com. Cas.
  238; 50 T. L. R. 361; 151 L. T. 261; 18 Asp. M. L. C. 482, (H. L.) ·····················217
Anders Utkilens Rederi A/S v. Compagnie Tunisienne de Navigation—The
  Golfstraum [1976] 2 Lloyd's Rep. 97, (Q. B.) ···**546**
Anderson v. Anderson [1895] 1 Q. B. 749; 11 T. L. R. 253, (C. A.) ·····················373
Anderson v. Munson (1900) 104 F. 913 (S. D. N. Y.) ··132
Andre et Compagnie S. A. v. Marine Transocean Ltd.—The Splendid Sun [1981] 2
  Lloyd's Rep. 29; [1981] Q. B. 694; [1981] 3 W. L. R. 43; [1981] 2 All E. R. 993,
  (C. A.); aff'g [1980] 1 Lloyd's Rep. 333, (Q. B.) ···443
Andrews & Co. v. United States (1954) 124 F. Supp. 362; 1954 AMC 2221 (Ct. Cl.);
  aff'd (1954) 292 F. 2d 280 (Ct. Cl.) ···543
Andros City, The, SMA 1156 (Arb. at N. Y. 1977) ···**288-289**
Andros Compania Maritima v. Andre & Cie. S. A. (1977) 430 F. Supp. 88; 1977
  AMC 668 (S. D. N. Y.) ···460
Andros Compania Maritima S. A. v. Marc Rich & Co. A. G. (1978) 579 F. 2d 691;
  1978 AMC 2108 (2d Cir.) ···**469**, 472, 473
Andros Island, The, SMA 1548 (Arb. at N. Y. 1980) ································386, 430
Andros Mentor, The, SMA 2125 (Arb. at N. Y. 1985) ······················144, 300, 349, **350**
Andros Oceania, The, SMA 2012 (Arb. at N. Y. 1984) ································384, 386
Angantyr, The, 1971 AMC 2503 (Arb. at N. Y.) ···**216**
Angelakis (G. & N.) Shipping Co. S. A. v. Compagnie National Algerienne de
  Navigation—The Attika Hope [1988] 1 Lloyd's Rep. 439, (Q. B.) ·············484, **485**
Angelia, The—Trade and Transport Inc. v. Iino Kaiun Kaisha Ltd. [1972] 2 Lloyd's
  Rep. 154; [1973] 1 W. L. R. 210; [1973] 2 All E. R. 144, (Q. B.) ·············394, 395
Angelic Grace, The—Japan Line Ltd. v. Aggeliki Charis Compania Maritima S. A.
  and Davies and Potter [1980] 1 Lloyd's Rep. 288, (C. A.) ···························446
Angelica, The, SMA 504 (Arb. at N. Y. 1970) ··111
Angelina Cas. v. Exxon Corp. (1989) 876 F. 2d 40; 1989 AMC 2677 (5th Cir.) ··········56
Anglo-Northern Trading Co. Ltd. v. Emlyn Jones & Williams [1918] 1 K. B. 372; 23
  Com. Cas. 231; 34 T. L. R. 27; 118 L. T. 196; 87 L. J. K. B. 309; [1917] W. N. 320; 14
  Asp. M. L. C. 242, (C. A.); aff'g [1917] 2 K. B. 78; 22 Com. Cas. 194; 33 T. L. R. 302;
  116 L. T. 414; 14 Asp. M. L. C. 18, (K. B.) ···401
Anglo-Saxon Petroleum Co. v. Adamastos Shipping Co. Ltd.—The Saxon Star [1958]
  1 Lloyd's Rep. 73; [1959] A. C. 133; [1958] 2 W. L. R. 688; [1958] 1 All E. R.
  725, (H. L.); rev'g [1957] 1 Lloyd's Rep. 271; [1957] 2 Q. B. 233; [1957] 2 W. L. R.

908; [1957] 2 All E.R. 311, (C.A.); *restoring* [1957] 1 Lloyd's Rep. 79; [1957] 2
Q.B. 233; [1957] 2 W.L.R. 509; [1957] 1 All E.R. 673, (Q.B.)
··212, 286, **514-515**, 516, 517, 519, 531, 561, 603
Anita, The—Panamanian Oriental S.S. Corp. *v.* Wright [1971] 1 Lloyd's Rep. 487;
[1971] 1 W.L.R. 882; [1971] 2 All E.R. 1028, (C.A.); *rev'g* [1970] 2 Lloyd's Rep.
365, (Q.B.) ··421
Ann Stathatos, The—Royal Greek Government *v.* Minister of Transport (1949) 83 Ll.
L. Rep. 228; 66 T.L.R. (Pt. 1) 504, (K.B.) ·····························295, **297**, 299, 552, 553, **555**
Annangel Glory, The—Annangel Glory Compania Naviera *v.* M. Golodetz Ltd. [1988]
1 Lloyd's Rep. 45, (Q.B.); 1988 P.C.C. 37 ··486
Anoula A, The, SMA 307 (Arb. at N.Y. 1967) ···385
Antaios Compania Naviera S.A. *v.* Salen Rederierna A.B.—The Antaios (No. 2)
[1984] 2 Lloyd's Rep. 235; [1985] A.C. 191; [1984] 3 W.L.R. 592; [1984] 3 All
E.R. 229, (H.L.); [1983] 2 Lloyd's Rep. 473; [1983] 1 W.L.R. 1362; [1983] 3 All
E.R. 777, (C.A.) ···262, 263, 265, 267, 445, 446
Antaios, The—Maritime Transport Overseas G.m.b.H. *v.* Unitramp [1981] 2 Lloyd's
Rep. 284, (Q.B.) ··532, **534**
Antaios, The (No. 2)—Antaios Compania Naviera S.A. *v.* Salen Rederierna A.B.
[1984] 2 Lloyd's Rep. 235; [1985] A.C. 191; [1984] 3 W.L.R. 592; [1984] 3 All
E.R. 229, (H.L.); [1983] 2 Lloyd's Rep. 473; [1983] 1 W.L.R. 1362; [1983] 3 All
E.R. 777, (C.A.) ···262, 263, 265, 267, 445, 446
Antclizo, The—Food Corp. of India *v.* Antclizo Shipping Corp. [1988] 2 Lloyd's Rep.
93; [1988] 1 W.L.R. 603; [1988] 2 All E.R. 513. (H.L.); [1987] 2 Lloyd's Rep.
130, (C.A.) ···443
Antco Shipping Co. Ltd. *v.* Sidemar S.p.A. (1976) 417 F. Supp. 207 (S.D.N.Y.) ···········79
Anthony Shipping Co. Ltd. *v.* Hugo Neu Corp. (1980) 482 F. Supp. 965; 1980 AMC
1477 (S.D.N.Y) ···474
Antilles Shipping Co. Ltd. *v.* Texaco Inc. (1970) 321 F. Supp. 166; 1971 AMC 1291
(S.D.N.Y.) ··225
Antonis, The, SMA 273 (Arb. at N.Y. 1959) ··284
Antria Shipping Co. Ltd. *v.* Triton Int'l Carriers Ltd., 1980 AMC 681 (E.D. Pa.
1978); *aff'd without opinion* (1979) 609 F. 2d 500 (3d Cir.) ·······························275, 494
Antria Shipping Co. Ltd. *v.* Triton Int'l Carriers Ltd.—The Akra Aktion, 1980 AMC
678 (S.D.N.Y. 1976) ···491
Anwar Al Sabar, The—Gulf Steel Co. Ltd. *v.* Al Khalifa Shipping Co. Ltd. [1980] 2
Lloyd's Rep. 261, (Q.B.) ···325
Apex, The—Phoenix Shipping Corp. *v.* Apex Shipping Corp. [1982] 2 Lloyd's Rep.
407, (Q.B.) ···**534**
Apiliotis, The—Reinante Transoceanic Navegacion S.A. *v.* President of India [1985]
1 Lloyd's Rep. 255, (Q.B.) ··186, 187
Apollo, The—Sidermar S.p.A. *v.* Apollo Corp. [1978] 1 Lloyd's Rep. 200, (Q.B.)
··**371-372**, 373, 374
Apollonius, The-Cosmos Bulk Transport Inc. *v.* China National Foreign Trade

判例索引

Transportation Corp. [1978] 1 Lloyd's Rep. 53; [1978] 1 All E. R. 322, (Q. B.)
···101, **104**, 285, 368, 375, 379, **551**, 554, 556, **559-560**
Appeal of U. S. Lines Inc., 1977 AMC 318 (A. S. B. C. A. 1976) ·····························203, 209
Aquacharm, The—Actis Co. Ltd. *v.* The Sanko Steamship Co. Ltd. [1982] 1 Lloyd's
  Rep. 7; [1982] 1 W. L. R. 119; [1982] 1 All E. R. 390, (C. A.); *aff'g* [1980] 2
  Lloyd's Rep. 237, (Q. B.) ·······················**293**, 297, 298, **304**, 370, **371**, 372, 374, 515, 517, **518**
Arab Maritime Petroleum Transport Co. *v.* Luxor Trading Corp.—The Al Bida
  [1987] 1 Lloyd's Rep. 124, (C.A.); [1986] 1 Lloyd's Rep. 142, (Q. B.) ···102, **105-106**, 600
Aragon, The—Segovia Compania Naviera S. A. *v.* R. Pagnan & F. Lli [1977] 1
  Lloyd's Rep. 343, (C. A.); *aff'g* [1975] 2 Lloyd's Rep. 216; [1975] 1 Lloyd's Rep.
  628, (Q. B.) ···131
Aramco Servs. Co. *v.* EAC Bulk Transp. Inc., 1993 AMC 1885 (Fla.) ················454-455
Arbitration between East Asiatic Co. and Transamerican Steamship Corp. (The
  Camara and Cinchoma), 1988 AMC 1086 (S. D. N. Y. 1987) ·····························461
Arbitration between Guinomar and Martin Marietta Aluminium Inc., SMA 2534
  (Arb. at N. Y. 1988) ··278
Arbitration between Herlofson Mgmt A/S and Ministry of Supply, Kingdom of
  Jordan (*Re*) (1991) 765 F. Supp. 78; 1991 AMC 2959 ···72
Arbitration between Horizon Development Corp. Ltd. and Mantua Oil Co., SMA
  2734 (Arb. at N. Y. 1990) ···58
Arbitration between National Shipping Co. of Saudi Arabia and Transamerican
  Steamship Corp., 1993 AMC 684 (S. D. N. Y. 1992) ·······································467-468
Arbitration between Sun Refining & Marketing Co. and Statheros Shipping Corp.
  (1991) 761 F. Supp. 293; 1991 AMC 1874 (S. D. N. Y.); *aff'd without opinion* (1991)
  948 F. 2d 1277; 1992 AMC 1216 (2d Cir.) ··467
Archangelos III, The, SMA 2541 (Arb. at N. Y. 1988) ·····································457
Arctic Confidence, The, SMA 2987 (Arb. at N. Y. 1992) ·································133
Arctic Skou, The—Ove Skou *v.* Rudolf A. Oetker [1985] 2 Lloyd's Rep. 478, (Q. B.)
  ··231, 583
Ardennes (Owners of Cargo) *v.* Ardennes (Owners)—The Ardennes (1950) 84 Ll.
  L. Rep. 340; [1951] 1 K. B. 55; 66 T. L. R. (Pt. 2) 312; [1950] 2 All E. R. 517, (K.
  B.) ···86
Ardennes, The (1950) 84 Ll. L. Rep. 340; [1951] 1 K. B. 55; 66 T. L. R. (Pt. 2) 312;
  [1950] 2 All E. R. 517, (K. B.) ···86
Areti S., The, 1965 AMC 2116 (Arb. at N. Y.) ···119
Aretusa, The, SMA 835 (Arb. at N. Y. 1973) ···136
Argentine Transport, The, 1956 AMC 1772 (Arb. at N. Y.) ·······························223
Argo Leader, The, SMA 2065 (Arb. at N. Y. 1985) ·····································213, 391
Argo Master, The, SMA 1489 (Arb. at N. Y. 1980) ···116
Argo Merchant, The, SMA 2101 (Arb. at N. Y. 1985) ·······································636
Argo Sky, The, SMA 627 (Arb. at N. Y. 1971) ···································117, 233, 241
Argonaut, The—MSC Mediterranean Shipping Co. S. A. *v.* Alianca Bay Shipping Co.
  Ltd. [1985] 2 Lloyd's Rep. 216, (Q. B.) ···**307**, 308

Arianna, The—Athenian Tankers Management S. A. v. Pyrena Shipping Inc. [1987]
　2 Lloyd's Rep. 376, (Q. B.) ···154, **156-157**, 160, 356, 357, **575**, 581
Ariel Maritime v. Zust Bachmeier (1991) 762 F. Supp. 55; 1991 AMC 2048 (S. D. N.
　Y.) ··74
Aries Tanker Corp. v. Total Transport Ltd.—The Aries [1977] 1 Lloyd's Rep. 334;
　[1977] 1 W. L. R. 185; [1977] 1 All E. R. 398, (H. L.) ·······································249
Aries, The—Aries Tanker Corp. v. Total Transport Ltd. [1977] 1 Lloyd's Rep. 334;
　[1977] 1 W. L. R. 185; [1977] 1 All E. R. 398, (H. L.) ·······································249
Arietta Venizelos, The, 1973 AMC 1012 (Arb. at N. Y. 1972) ·················144, **204**, 276
Arild (S. S.) v. S. A. de Navigation Hovrani (1923) 15 Ll. L. Rep. 50; [1923] 2 K. B.
　141; 28 Com. Cas. 328; 92 L. J. K. B. 616; [1923] W. N. 132, (Q. B.) ···········**222**, 377, 548
Arizona, The, SMA 1259 (Arb. at N. Y. 1978) ··223, 239
Armagas Ltd. v. Mundogas S. A.—The Ocean Frost [1986] 2 Lloyd's Rep. 109
　[1986] A. C. 717; [1986] 2 W. L. R. 1063; [1986] 2 All E. R. 385, (H. L.); [1985] 1
　Lloyd's Rep. 1; [1985] 3 W. L. R. 640; [1985] 3 All E. R. 795, (Q. B. and C. A.) ···**68**, 69
Armement Adolf Deppe v. John Robinson & Co. Ltd. [1917] 2 K. B. 204; 22 Com.
　Cas. 300; 116 L. T. 664; 86 L. J. K. B. 1103; 14 Asp. M. L. C. 84, (Q. B.) ···············155, **157**
Arochem Corp. v. Wilomi Inc. (1992) 962 F. 2d 496; 1992 AMC 2342 (5th Cir.) ······**493**
Arta Shipping Co. Ltd. v. Thai Europe Tapioca Service Ltd.—The Johnny [1977] 2
　Lloyd's Rep. 1, (C. A.); aff'g [1997] 1 Lloyd's Rep. 257, (Q. B.) ················127, 549, **550**
Asbestos Corp. Ltd. v. Compagnie de Navigation Fraissinet—The Marquette (1973)
　480 F. 2d 669; 1973 AMC 1683 (2d Cir.) ···428, 429
Ashburner v. Balchen (1852) 7 N. Y. 262 ··114
Ask, The (1907) 156 F. 678 (S. D. N. Y.) ···**389**, 390
Aspa Maria, The—Gulf Shipping Lines Ltd. v. Cia. Nav. Alanje S. A. [1976] 2
　Lloyd's Rep. 643, (C. A.) ···**353**
Aspen Trader, The—Libra Shipping and Trading Corp. Ltd. v. Northern Sales Ltd.
　[1981] 1 Lloyd's Rep. 273, (C. A.) ···440
Asphalt Int'l v. Enterprise (1981) 514 F. Supp. 1111 (S. D. N. Y.); aff'd (1982) 667 F.
　2d 261 (2d Cir.) ···417
Associated Metals & Minerals Corp. v. The Arktis Sky (1992) 978 F. 2d 47; 1993
　AMC 509 (2d Cir.) ···317
Associated Metals & Minerals Corp. v. The Jasmine (1993) 983 F. 2d 410; 1993
　AMC 957 (2d Cir.) ···522
Associated Portland Cement Manufacturers Ltd. v. Teigland Shipping A/S— The
　Oakworth [1975] 1 Lloyd's Rep. 581, (C. A.) ··87, 531
Astra Trust Ltd. v. Adams [1969] 1 Lloyd's Rep. 81, (Q. B.) ························52, 586
Astraea, The (1903) 124 F. 83 (E. D. N. Y.) ···115, 116
Astro Amo Compania Naviera S. A. v. Elf Union S. A.—The Zographia M [1976] 2
　Lloyd's Rep. 382, (Q. B.) ·· 245, 253, 254
Astro Energy, The, SMA 2771 (Arb. at N. Y. 1991) ·································116, 117, 119
Asty Maritime Co. Ltd. and Panagiotis Stravelakis v. Rocco Giuseppe & Figli S. n. c.
　and Others—The Astyanax [1985] 2 Lloyd's Rep. 109, (C. A.); [1984] 2 Lloyd's

Rep. 459, (Q. B.) ··**67**
Astyanax, The—Asty Maritime Co. Ltd. and Panagiotis Stravelakis *v.* Rocco
　Giuseppe & Figli S. n. c. and Others [1985] 2 Lloyd's Rep. 109, (C. A.); [1984] 2
　Lloyd's Rep. 459, (Q. B.) ··**67**
Athanassia, The, SMA 2752 (Arb. at N. Y. 1991) ···301
Athanasia Comninos and Georges Chr. Lemos, The [1990] 1 Lloyd's Rep. 277, (Q. B.)
　···167, 168, 169, 295, **297**, 424, 520
Athenian Horizon, The, SMA 1197 (Arb. at N. Y. 1977) ···················223, **274**, 275, 388
Athenian Tankers Management S. A. *v.* Pyrena Shipping Inc.—The Arianna [1987]
　2 Lloyd's Rep. 376, (Q. B.) ·······················154, **156-157**, 160, 356, 357, **575**, 581
Athenoula, The, SMA 1410 (Arb. at N. Y. 1980) ···625, 627
Athos, The-Telfair Shipping Corp. *v.* Athos Shipping Co. S. A., Solidor Shipping Co.
　Ltd., Horizon Finance Corp. and A. N. Cominos [1983] 1 Lloyd's Rep. 127, (C. A.);
　[1981] 2 Lloyd's Rep. 74, (Q. B.) ·····························265, **266-267**, 531, **533-534**
Atkins *v.* Fibre Disintegrating Co. (1868) 2 Fed. Cas. 78 (E. D. N. Y.) (No. 601); *aff'd*
　(1873) 85 U. S. (18 Wall.) 272 ··**200**, 205, **206**
Atkins International H. A. *v.* Islamic Republic of Iran Shipping Lines—The A. P. J.
　Priti [1987] 2 Lloyd's Rep. 37, (C. A.) ··**194**, 195, 196, 197
Atlanta, The (1948) 82 F. Supp. 218; 1948 AMC 1769 (S. D. Ga.) ···························118
Atlantic & Great Lakes S. S. Corp. *v.* Steelmet Inc., 74 Civ. 5048 (S. D. N. Y. 22
　February 1977) (not officially reported); *aff'd* 565 F. 2d 848; 1978 AMC 107 (2d
　Cir. 1977) ···59
Atlantic & Gulf Stevedores Inc. *v.* The Rosa Roth (1984) 587 F. Supp. 103; 1985
　AMC 718 (S. D. N. Y.) ···500
Atlantic Duchess, The—Atlantic Oil Carriers Ltd. *v.* British Petroleum Co. Ltd.
　[1957] 2 Lloyd's Rep. 55, (Q. B.) ···168
Atlantic Emperor, The—Marc Rich & Co. A. G. *v.* Societa Italiana Impianti P. A.
　[1992] 1 Lloyd's Rep. 342, (E. C. J.); [1989] 1 Lloyd's Rep. 548, (C. A.) ·············55
Atlantic Glory, The, SMA 76 (Arb. at N. Y 1962) ·······································113, 233
Atlantic Lines and Navigation Co. Inc. *v.* Didymi Corp. and Leon Corp.—The
　Didymi and The Leon [1984] 1 Lloyd's Rep. 583, (C. A.) ································128
Atlantic Lines and Navigation Co. Inc. *v.* Hallam Ltd.—The Lucy [1983] 1 Lloyd's
　Rep. 188, (Q. B.) ··**82-83**, 143
Atlantic Master, The, SMA 510 (Arb. at N. Y.) ···119
Atlantic Oil Carriers Ltd. *v.* British Petroleum Co. Ltd.—The Atlantic Duchess
　[1957] 2 Lloyd's Rep. 55, (Q. B.) ···168
Atlantic Richfield Co. *v.* Interstate Oil Transp. Co. (1986) 784 F. 2d 106 (2d Cir.);
　cert. denied (1986) 479 U. S. 817 ···323
Atlantic Shipping Co. S. A. *v.* Tradax Internacional S. A.—The Bratislava [1977] 2
　Lloyd's Rep. 269, (Q. B.) ··440
Atlas Chartering Services Inc. *v.* World Trade Group Inc. (1978) 453 F. Supp. 861;
　1978 AMC 2033 (S. D. N. Y.) ··460
Atlas, The (1876) 93 U. S. 302 ··526

Attika Hope, The—Angelakis (G. & N.) Shipping Co. S. A. v. Compagnie National
 Algerienne de Navigation [1988] 1 Lloyd's Rep. 439, (Q. B.) ·····························484, **485**
Attica Sea Carriers Corp. v. Ferrostaal Poseidon Bulk Reederei G. m. b. H. —The
 Puerto Buitrago [1976] 1 Lloyd's Rep. 250, (C. A.)   ································130, **236**, 237
August Leonhardt, The—Lokumal (K.) & Sons London Ltd. v. Lotte Shipping Co.
 Pte. Ltd. [1985] 1 Lloyd's Rep. 28, (C. A.); [1984] 1 Lloyd's Rep. 322; (1984) 134
 New L. J. 125, (Q. B.)   ···69
Augvald, The, 1965 AMC 1614 (Arb. at N. Y.) ··108, **163**
Aurora, The (1816) 14 U. S. (1 Wheat.) 96 ··339
Austin Friars, The (1894) 71 L. T. 27; 10 T. L. R. 633; 7 Asp. M. L. C. 503, (P. D. A.) ···159
Australian Oil Refining Pty. Ltd. v. R. W. Miller & Co. Pty. Ltd. [1968] 1 Lloyd's
 Rep. 448; (1967) 41 A. L. J. R. 280, (H. C. Aust.)   ·····································519, 603

B. H. Inc. v. Anthony M. Meyerskin Inc. (1957) 149 F. Supp. 219 (E. D. N. Y) ············241
B. P. Exploration v. Hunt (No. 2) [1982] 2 W. L. R. 253; [1982] 1 All E. R. 925, (H.
 L.); [1979] 1 W. L. R. 783; [1981] 1 W. L. R. 232, (C. A.)   ·····························394, 408
B. V. Oliehandel Jungkind v. Coastal International [1983] 2 Lloyd's Rep. 463 ············586
B. V. S. and the Khuzestan Water and Power Authority v. Kerman Shipping Co. S.
 A.—The Kerman [1982] 1 Lloyd's Rep. 62; [1982] 1 W. L. R. 166; [1982] 1 All
 E. R. 616, (Q. B.)   ···445
Badagry, The—Terkol Rederierne v. Petroleo Brasileiro S. A. [1985] 1 Lloyd's Rep.
 395, (C. A.)   ···**95**, 396, 591
Baesler v. Continental Grain Co. (1990) 900 F. 2d 1193 (8th Cir.)   ·····························452
Baker Castor Oil Co. v. Insurance Co. of North America (1944) 60 F. Supp. 32; 1945
 AMC 168 (S. D. N. Y.); aff'd (1946) 157 F. 2d 3; 1946 AMC 1115 (2d Cir.); cert.
 denied (1947) 329 U. S. 800   ···429
Balder London, The—Gatoil Anstalt v. Omennial Ltd. [1980] 2 Lloyd's Rep. 489, (Q.
 B.)   ···**262**
Balder London, The (No. 2) —Gatoil Anstalt v. Omennial Ltd. [1983] 1 Lloyd's Rep.
 492, (Q. B.)   ···87
Baleares, The—Geogas SA v. Trammo Gas [1991] 2 Lloyd's Rep. 318; [1991] 1 W.
 L. R. 776; [1991] 3 All E. R. 554; (1991) 135 S. J. (LB) 101; (1991) 141 New L.
 J. 1037, (H. L.); aff'g [1991] 1 Lloyd's Rep. 349; [1991] 2 Q. B. 139; [1991] 2 W. L.
 R. 794; [1991] 2 All E. R. 710, (C. A.); rev'g [1990] 2 Lloyd's Rep. 130, (Q. B.) ······446
Ballard Shipping Co. (Re) (1991) 752 F. Supp. 546; 1991 AMC 721 (D. R. I.); later
 proceedings (1991) 772 F. Supp. 721; 1992 AMC 402 (D. R. I.); modified on other
 grounds (1994) 32 F. 3d 623; 1994 AMC 2705 (1st Cir.)   ·····································449
Balli Trading Ltd. v. Afalona Shipping Co. Ltd.-The Coral [1993] 1 Lloyd's Rep. 1;
 (1992) 136 S. J. (LB) 259, (C. A.); rev'g [1992] 2 Lloyd's Rep. 158, (Q. B.) ············305
Bamburi, The [1982] 1 Lloyd's Rep. 312 ···421
Banes, The (1915) 221 F. 416 (2d Cir.)   ···**149**
Banja Luka, The, SMA 1293 (Arb. at N. Y. 1979)   ···203
Bank Line v. Capel (Arthur) & Co. [1919] A. C. 435; 88 L. J. K. B. 211; 35 T. L. R.

150; 120 L. T. 129; 14 Asp. M. L. C. 370; [1919] W. N. 20; 63 S. J. 177, (H. L.)
···359, 394, **396**, 399, 400, 404

Bank of Boston Connecticut (formerly Colonial Bank) *v.* European Grain & Shipping Ltd.—The Dominique [1989] A. C. 1056; [1989] 2 W. L. R. 440; [1989] 1 All E. R. 545; (1989) 133 S. J. 219, (H. L.); *rev'g* [1988] 1 Lloyd's Rep. 215, [1988] 3 W. L. R. 60; [1988] 3 All E. R. 233; [1988] 1 F. T. L. R. 327; (1988) 132 S. J. 896, (C. A.); *rev'g* [1987] 1 Lloyd's Rep. 239, (Q. B.) ···249

Bankers Trust International Ltd. *v.* Todd Shipyards Corp.—The Halcyon Isle [1980] 2 Lloyd's Rep. 325; [1981] A. C. 221; [1980] 3 W. L. R. 400; [1980] 3 All E. R. 197, (P. C.) ··488

Baravati *v.* Josephthal, Lyon & Ross Inc. (1994) 28 F. 3d 704 (7th Cir.) ················458

Barbier *v.* Shearson Lehman Hutton Inc. (1991) 948 F. 2d 117 (2d Cir.) ················459

Bardons & Oliver Inc. *v.* Amtorg Trading Corp. (1948) 123 N. Y. S. 2d 633 (Sup. Ct.); *aff'd without opinion* (1949) 275 App. Div. 748; (1949) 88 N. Y. S. 2d 272 (1st Dept.); *aff'd* (1950) 301 N. Y. 622; (1950) 93 N. E. 2d 915 ·······································**414**

Barker *v.* Moore & McCormack Co. (1930) 40 F. 2d 410; 1930 AMC 779 (2d Cir.)
··**383-384**

Baron Venture, The, SMA 2138 (Arb. at N. Y. 1985) ···78

Barton *v.* Armstrong [1976] A. C. 104; [1975] 2 W. L. R. 1050; [1975] 2 All E. R. 465, (P. C.) ··82

Barwick Mills (E. T.) Inc. *v.* Hellenic Lines Ltd. (1971) 331 F. Supp. 161 (S. D. Ga.); *aff'd* (1973) 472 F. 2d 1406 (5th Cir.) ···339

Basma *v.* Weekes [1950] A. C. 441; 66 T. L. R. (Pt. 1) 1047; [1950] 2 All E. R. 146, (P. C.) ··62

Batis, The—Batis Maritime Corporation *v.* Petroleos del Mediterraneo S. A. [1990] 1 Lloyd's Rep. 345, (Q. B.) ···125, 190, 191, 197

Batis Maritime Corporation *v.* Petroleos del Mediterraneo S. A.—The Batis [1990] 1 Lloyd's Rep. 345, (Q. B.) ···125, 190, 191, 197

Baumwoll Manufactur Von Carl Scheibler *v.* Furness [1893] A. C. 8; 62 L. J. Q. B. 201; 68 L. T. 1; 9 T. L. R. 71; 7 Asp. M. L. C. 263, (H. L.); *aff'g* [1892] 1 Q. B. 253, (C. A.) ···529

Bay Master, The, 1969 AMC 359 (E. D. N. Y.) ···536

Bay State Yacht Sales Inc. *v.* Squantum Engine & Service Co. Inc. (1990) 117 B. R. 16; 1991 AMC 94 (Bank. D. Mass) ···504

Bede, The—Rahcassi Shipping Co. S. A. *v.* Blue Star Line Ltd. [1967] 2 Lloyd's Rep. 261; [1969] 1 Q. B. 173; [1967] 3 W. L. R. 1382; [1967] 3 All E. R. 301, (Q. B.) ···441

Bedeburn, The, 1931 AMC 1678 (Arb. 1931) ···115

Begbie *v.* Phosphate Sewage Co. (1876) 1 Q. B. D. 679; *aff'g* (1875) L. R. 10 Q. B. 491
··82

Behn *v.* Burness (1863) 3 B. & S. 751; 32 L. J. Q. B. 204; 8 L. T. 207; 1 Mar. L. C. (O. S.) 329; 122 E. R. 281, (Ex. Ch.) ···106

Bela Krajina, The—Splosna Plovba of Piran *v.* Agrelak S. S. Corp. [1975] 1 Lloyd's Rep. 139, (Q. B.) ···**286**

Belize, The (1938) 25 F. Supp. 663 (S. D. N. Y.); *appeal dismissed* (1939) 101 F. 2d 1005 (2d Cir.) ···**460**
Bell Aerospace Co. Division of Textron Inc. *v*. Local 516 (1974) 500 F. 2d. 921 (2d Cir.) ···464
Bellcore Maritime Corp. *v*. F. Lli Moretti Cereali S. p. A.—The Mastro Giorgis [1983] 2 Lloyd's Rep. 66, (Q. B.) ···372, 373, 374
Belvedere *v*. Compania Ploman de Vapores S. A. (1951) 189 F. 2d 148 ; 1951 AMC 1217 (5th Cir.) ··491
Ben Line Steamers *v*. Pacific Steam Navigation Co.—The Benlawyers [1989] 2 Lloyd's Rep. 51, (Q. B.) ···313
Benlawyers, The—Ben Line Steamers *v*. Pacific Steam Navigation Co. [1989] 2 Lloyd's Rep. 51. (Q. B.) ··313
Ben Shipping Co. (Pte.) Ltd. *v*. An-Board Bainne—The C. Joyce [1986] 2 Lloyd's Rep. 285, (Q. B.) ··326, 327
Bengal Pride, The—Ministry of Food, Government of Bangladesh *v*. Bengal Liner Ltd. [1986] 1 Lloyd's Rep. 167, (Q. B.) ···442
Bennington, The, SMA 940 (Arb. at N. Y. 1975) ···203
Benship International *v*. Demand Shipping—The Lendoudis Evangelos II (1988) (L. M. L. N. 408, 24 June 1995) ···131
Bentsen *v*. Taylor [1893] 2 Q. B. 274 ; 63 L. J. Q. B. 15 ; 69 L. T. 487 ; 9 T. L. R. 552 ; 7 Asp. M. L. C. 385 ··106
Berdex Int'l Inc. *v*. The Kapitan Grishin, 1992 AMC 1559 (N. C. Cal.) ·········495, 496
Bergan *v*. Int'l Freighting Corp. (1958) 254 F. 2d 231 ; 1958 AMC 1303 (2d Cir.) ······537
Berge Sund, The—Sig Bergesen D. Y. A/S *v*. Mobil Shipping and Transportation Co. [1993] 2 Lloyd's Rep. 453, (C. A.) ; [1992] 1 Lloyd's Rep. 460, (Q. B.) ···295, 297, 298, 364, 371, 375, 378, 586, **595**
Berge Tasta, The—Skibs. A/S Snefonn *v*. Kawasaki Kisen Kaisha [1975] 1 Lloyd's Rep. 422, (Q. B.) ···121, 128, 531
Bergen Bay, The, SMA 3060 (Arb. at N. Y. 1993) ···388
Bergesen *v*. Joseph Muller Corp. (1983) 710 F. 2d 928 ; 1983 AMC 1960 (2d Cir.) ··463, 476
Bergesen D. Y. A/S *v*. Lindholm, 1991 AMC 2839 ; 760 F. Supp. 976 (D. Conn.) ············77
Berkshire, The [1974] 1 Lloyd's Rep. 185, (Q. B.) ····································329, 331, 335, 336
Bermuda, The, SMA 3097 (Arb. at N. Y. 1994) ···461
Bermuda Express N. V. *v*. The Lista (1989) 872 F. 2d 554 ; 1989 AMC 1537 (3d Cir.) ; *cert. denied* (1989) 493 U. S. 819 ···500
Bertina, The, SMA 3144 (Arb. at N. Y. 1995) ···350
Beverly Hills Nat. Bank & Trust Co. *v*. Compania de Navegacion Almirante S. A., Panama—The Searaven (1971) 437 F. 2d 301 (9th Cir.) ; *cert. denied* (1971) 402 U. S. 966 ··493, 496
Binship, The, SMA 1416 (Arb. at N. Y. 1980) ···386, 432
Bird of Paradise, The (1867) 72 U. S. 545 ···491
Birmingham and District Land Co. *v*. L. N. W. R. (1888) 40 Ch. D. 268 ; 60 L. T. 527,

(C. A.) ···92
Bjorn Ragne, The, SMA 1298 (Arb. at N. Y. 1979) ···································214
Bjorneford, The (1921) 271 F. 682 (2d Cir.) ··213
Black Falcon, The—Shipping Corporation of India Ltd. v. NSB Niederelbe
　Schiffahrtsgesellschaft m. b. H. & Co. [1991] 1 Lloyd's Rep. 77, (Q. B.) ······125, 128, 129
Blanchard Lumber Co. v. S. S. Anthony II (1967) 259 F. Supp. 857, 865-66; 1967
　AMC 103, 120-21 (S. D. N. Y.) ···346
Blandon, The (1922) 287 F. 722 (S. D. N. Y.) ··343
Blane Steamships Ltd. v. Minister of Transport [1951] 2 Lloyd's Rep. 155; [1951] 2
　K. B. 965; [1951] 2 T. L. R. 763, (C. A.) ···396
Blankenstein, The—Damon Compania Naviera S. A. v. Hapag Lloyd International S. A.
　[1985] 1 Lloyd's Rep. 93; [1985] 1 W. L. R. 435; [1985] 1 All E. R. 475, (C. A.);
　[1983] 2 Lloyd's Rep. 522; [1983] 3 All E. R. 510, (Q. B.) ····························52
Bless River, The, SMA 1889 (Arb. at N. Y. 1983) ···································346
Blue Sympathy Shipping Co. v. Serviocean International S. A., 1994 AMC 2522 (S. D.
　N. Y.) ··461
Board of Commissioners of the Port of New Orleans v. The Space King, 1978 AMC
　856 (E. D. La.) ···209, 318
Board of Trade v. Temperley Steam Shipping Co. Ltd. (1927) 27 Ll. L. Rep. 230, (C.
　A.) ··376
Bold Venture, The (1986) 638 F. Supp. 87; 1987 AMC 182 (W. D. Wash.) ···············499
Bolton (H. L.) (Engineering) Co. Ltd. v. T. J. Graham & Sons Ltd. [1957] 1 Q. B.
　159; [1956] 3 W. L. R. 804; [1956] 3 All E. R. 624, (C. A.) ····························558
Bombay & Persia Steam Navigation v. Shipping Controller (1921) 7 Ll. L. Rep. 226,
　(C. A.); 4 Ll. L. Rep. 290 ···607
Bonar v. Dean Whitter Reynolds Inc. (1988) 835 F. 2d 1378 (11th Cir.) ···········458, **465**
Boni, The, SMA 3053 (Arb. at N. Y. 1994) ···278, 429
Booker (George) & Co. v. The Pocklington S. S. Co. Ltd. [1899] 2 Q. B. 690; 5 Com.
　Cas. 15; 69 L. J. Q. B. 10; 81 L. T. 524; 16 T. L. R. 19; 9 Asp. M. L. C. 22, (Q. B.) ········**507**
Bordatxoa, The, SMA 891 (Arb. at N. Y. 1974) ···································233
Bosma v. Larsen [1966] 1 Lloyd's Rep. 22, (Q. B.) ···································552, 553
Boucraa, The—L'Office Cherifien des Phosphates and Unitramp S. A. v. Yamashita-
　Shinnihon Steamship Co. Ltd. [1994] 1 Lloyd's Rep. 251; [1994] 1 A. C. 486;
　[1994] 2 W. L. R. 39; [1994] 1 All E. R. 20; (1994) 138 S. J. (LB) 19, (H. L.);
　rev'g [1993] 2 Lloyd's Rep. 149; [1993] 3 W. L. R. 266; [1993] 3 All E. R. 686;
　[1993] N. P. C. 64, (C. A.) ···443
Boukadoura Maritime Corp. v. Société Anonyme Marocaine de l'Industrie et du
　Raffinage—The Boukadoura [1989] 1 Lloyd's Rep. 393, (Q. B.) ·················**331**, 586
Boukadoura, The—Boukadoura Maritime Corp. v. Société Anonyme Marocaine de
　l'Industrie et du Raffinage [1989] 1 Lloyd's Rep. 393, (Q. B.) ·················**331**, 586
Bourgeois v. Bergen Juno, 1979 AMC 1396 (E. D. La 1978) ···························321
Boyd v. Moses (1869) 74 U. S. 192 ···175
Boyd, Weir & Sewell Inc. v. Fritzen-Halcyon Lijn Inc., 1989 AMC 1159 (S. D. N. Y.

1989) ···543
Boyle v. Rederij Shipmair VI, 1979 AMC 2844 (E. D. Pa.) ························**456**
Boyle v. Walker. See Walker v. Boyle.
Brabant, The—Gesellschaft Bürgerlichen Rechts and Others v. Stockholms
　Rederiaktiebolag Svea [1965] 2 Lloyd's Rep. 546; [1967] 1 Q. B. 588; [1966] 2 W.
　L. R. 909; [1966] 1 All E. R. 961, (Q. B.) ··556,**557**,560
Bradley (F. C.) & Sons v. Federal Steam Navigation Co. (1927) 27 Ll. L. Rep. 221,
　395; 137 L. T. 266; 17 Asp. M. L. C. 265, (H. L.); (1926) 24 Ll. L. Rep. 59, 446, (C.
　A.); (1925) 22 Ll. L. Rep. 336, 424, (Q. B.) ··97
Brandeis Intsel Ltd. v. Calabrian Chemicals Corp. (1987) 656 F. Supp. 160 (S. D. N.
　Y.) ···476
Brandt (H. O.) & Co. v. H. N. Morris & Co. Ltd. [1917] 2 K. B. 784; 87 L. J. K. B.
　101; 117 L. T. 196, (C. A.) ··62, 63
Brass v. Maitland (1856) 6 E. & B. 470; 26 L. J. Q. B. 49; 2 Jur. (N. S.) 710 ··············167
Bratislava, The—Atlantic Shipping Co. S. A. v. Tradax Internacional S. A. [1977] 2
　Lloyd's Rep. 269, (Q. B.) ··440
Brauer & Co. (G. B.) Ltd. v. James Clark (Brush Materials) Ltd. [1952] 2 Lloyd's
　Rep. 147; [1952] 2 All E. R. 497; [1952] 2 T. L. R. 349, (C. A.) ························52
Brede, The—Henriksens Rederi A/S v. T. H. Z. Rolimpex [1973] 2 Lloyd's Rep. 333;
　[1974] Q. B. 233; [1973] 3 W. L. R. 556; [1973] 3 All E. R. 589, (C. A.) ················249
Bremer Handelsgesellschaft m. b. H. v. Westzucker G. m. b. H. (No. 2) [1981] 2
　Lloyd's Rep. 130, (C. A.); [1981] 1 Lloyd's Rep. 214, (Q. B.) ························444
Bremer Vulkan Schiffbau und Maschinenfabrik v. South India Shipping Corp. [1981]
　1 Lloyd's Rep. 253; [1981] A. C. 909; [1981] 2 W. L. R. 141; [1981] 1 All E. R.
　289, (H. L.) ··442, 443
Breynton, The, 1934 AMC 1473 (Arb. at N. Y. 1933) ··207
Bridgestone Maru No. 3, The—Navigas International Ltd. v. Trans-Offshore Inc.
　[1985] 2 Lloyd's Rep. 62, (Q. B.) ························365, 372, 377, 574, **577**, 583, 592, **593**
Brier v. Northstar Marine Inc., 1993 AMC 1194 (D. N. J. 1992) ························475
Bright Evelyn, The, SMA 2914 (Arb. at N. Y. 1992) ··430
Brimnes, The—Tenax S. S. Co. v. The Brimnes (Owners) [1974] 2 Lloyd's Rep. 241;
　[1975] Q. B. 929; [1974] 3 W. L. R. 613; [1974] 3 All E. R. 88, (C. A.); aff'g
　[1972] 2 Lloyd's Rep. 465; [1973] 1 W. L. R. 386; [1973] 1 All E. R. 769, (Q. B.)
　··244, 245, 255, 260, 261, 268
Britain S. S. Co. v. Munson S. S. Line (1929) 31 F. 2d 530 (2d Cir.) ······**132**, **135**, 136, 138
Britain Steamship Co. v. The King—The Petersham, 3 Ll. L. Rep. 163, 205; 4 Ll. L.
　Rep. 245; [1921] 1 A. C. 99; 89 L. J. K. B. 881; 25 Com. Cas 301; [1920] W. N. 271;
　123 L. T. 721; 64 S. J. 737; 15 Asp. 58, (H. L.) ··609
British Bank of the Middle East v. Sun Life Assurance Co. of Canada [1983] 2
　Lloyd's Rep. 9 ··68
British West Indies Produce Inc. v. The Atlantic Clipper (1973) 353 F. Supp. 548;
　1973 AMC 163 (S. D. N. Y.) ··**341**
Brogden v. Metropolitan Railway Company (1877) 2 App. Cas. 666, (H. L.) ············52

判例索引　　　　　　　　　　　　　　45

Brookhurst, The, SMA 87 (Arb. at N. Y. 1960) ···270
Brostrom & Son v. Dreyfus & Co. (1932) 44 Ll. L. Rep. 136 ; 38 Com. Cas. 79, (K. B.)
　···179-180, 191
Brotherhood of Railroad Trainmen v. Central of Georgia Co. (1969) 415 F. 2d 403
　(5th Cir.) ···**472**
Brown, Jenkinson & Co. Ltd. v. Percy Dalton (London) Ltd. [1957] 2 Lloyd's Rep.
　1 ; [1957] 2 Q. B. 621 ; [1957] 2 All E. R. 844, (C. A.) ; rev'g [1957] 1 Lloyd's Rep.
　31 ··**330-331**
Brys & Gylsen Ltd. v. J. J. Drysdale & Co. (1920) 4 Ll. L. Rep. 24, (K. B.) ···220, 221, 303
Buckeye State, The (1941) 39 F. Supp. 344 (W. D. N. Y.) ·······································**428**
Budd & Co. Ltd. v. Johnson, Englehart & Co. Ltd. (1920) 2 Ll. L. Rep. 27, (K. B.) ······253
Bulk Charters (Pty) Ltd. v. Korea Shipping Corp., 1981 AMC 2877 (S. D. N. Y.) ·········58
Bulkley v. Naumkeag Steam Cotton Co. (1860) 65 U. S. 386 ···································339
Bunga Kenanga, The—Malaysian International Shipping Corp. v. Empresa Cubana de
　Fletes [1981] 1 Lloyd's Rep. 518, (Q. B.) ···238, 550
Bunge Corp. v. Republic of Brazil (1972) 353 F. Supp. 64 ; 1973 AMC 1219 (E. D. La.)
　···111
Bunge Corp. v. The Furness Bridge (1977) 588 F. 2d 790 ; 1977 AMC 2109 (5th
　Cir.) ; cert. denied (1978) 435 U. S. 924 ···206
Bunge Corp. v. Tradax Export S. A. [1981] 2 Lloyd's Rep. 1 ; [1981] 1 W. L. R. 711 ;
　[1981] 2 All E. R. 513, (H. L.) ; aff'g [1980] 1 Lloyd's Rep. 294, (C. A.) ; rev'g [1979]
　2 Lloyd's Rep. 477, (Q. B.) ···88, 89, 90, 91, 269
Bunge Edible Oil Corp. v. The Torm Rask (1991) 756 F. Supp. 261 ; 1991 AMC 1102
　(E. D. La.) ; aff'd (1992) 949 F. 2d 786 ; 1992 AMC 2227 (5th Cir.) ; cert. denied
　(1992) —U. S. —; 120 L. Ed. 2d 875 ; 112 S. Ct. 2998 ···344
Bunn v. Global Marine Inc. (1970) 428 F. 2d 40 ; 1970 AMC 1539 (5th Cir.) ············490
Burrell & Sons v. F. Green & Co. [1915] 1 K. B. 391 ; 20 Com. Cas. 84 ; 84 L. J. K. B.
　192 ; 112 L. T. 105 ; 12 Asp. M. L. C. 589, (C. A.) ; aff'g [1914] 1 K. B. 293 ; 19 Com.
　Cas. 81 ; 83 L. J. K. B. 499 ; 109 L. T. 970 ; 12 Asp. M. L. C. 411, (K. B.) ·····················555
Byzantine Maritime Corp. v. Matthew Shipping Co. Ltd., SMA 972 (Arb. at N. Y.
　1975) ···116

C. A. Venezolana de Navegacion v. Bank Line—The Roachbank [1988] 2 Lloyd's Rep.
　337, (C. A.) ; [1987] 2 Lloyd's Rep. 498, (Q. B.) ·····························370, 371, **372**, 374, 375, 446
C. H. Z. Rolimpex v. Eftavrysses Compania Naviera S. A.—The Panaghia Tinnou
　[1986] 2 Lloyd's Rep. 586, (Q. B.) ···305
CN Marine Inc. v. Stena Line A/B and Regie Voor Maritiem Transport—The Stena
　Nautica (No. 2) [1982] 2 Lloyd's Rep. 336 ; [1982] Com. L. R. 203, (C. A.) ·············87
CPC Gallia, The [1994] 1 Lloyd's Rep. 68 ··54
CSX Transp. Inc. v. United Transp. Union (1991) 950 F. 2d 872 ·······················451-452
C. T. Shipping Ltd. v. DMI Ltd. (1991) 774 F. Supp. 146 (S. D. N. Y.) ················**458**
C. Joyce, The—Ben Shipping Co. (Pte.) Ltd. v. An-Board Bainne [1986] 2 Lloyd's
　Rep. 285 ; [1986] 2 All E. R. 177, (Q. B.) ··326, 327

Cactus Pipe & Supply Co. *v.* The Montmartre (1985) 756 F. 2d 1103 ; 1985 AMC
   2150 (5th Cir.) ··342
Caldas (*Re*) (1972) 350 F. Supp. 566 ; 1973 AMC 1243 (E. D. Pa.) ; *aff'd without opinion
   sub nom.* Re Anderson, Clayton & Co. (1973) 485 F. 2d 678 (3d Cir.) ···············429
Caldwell Co. *v.* Connecticut Mills (1929) 225 App. Div. 270 ; (1929) 232 N. Y. S. 625 ;
   aff'd (1929) 251 N. Y. 565 ; (1929) 168 N. E. 429 ···543
Caledonia, The (1895) 157 U. S. 124 ··**110**, 427
California *v.* The Norfolk (1977) 435 F. Supp. 1039 ; 1978 AMC 144 (N. D. Cal.) ···225, 226
California, The, SMA 2736 (Arb. at N. Y. 1990) ···74
Caliopi Carras, The, SMA 1111 (Arb. at N. Y. 1977) ···416
Camara and Cinchoma, The, 1988 AMC 1086 (S. D. N. Y. 1987) ································461
Cameron-Hawn Realty Co. *v.* City of Albany (1913) 207 N. Y. 377 ; 101 N. E. 162 ·····**412**
Canada Rice Mills *v.* Union Marine & General Ins. Co. (1940) 67 Ll. L. Rep. 549 ;
   [1941] A. C. 55 ; 57 T. L. R. 41 ; 110 L. J. P. C. 1 ; 164 L. T. 367 ; [1940] 4 All E. R.
   169, (P. C.) ··422
Canadia, The (1917) 241 F. 233 (3d Cir.) ···381, 384
Canadian Gulf Line (*Re*) (1938) 98 F. 2d 711 ; 1938 AMC 1123 (2d Cir.) ···············456
Canadian Pacific (Bermuda) *v.* Canadian Transport Co.—The H. R. Macmillan [1974]
   1 Lloyd's Rep. 311, (C. A.) ; *aff'g* [1973] 1 Lloyd's Rep. 27, (Q. B.) ···········365, 368, 378
Canadian Pacific Railway Co. *v.* Board of Trade (1925) 22 Ll. L. Rep. 1, (H. L.) ········**237**
Cape Palmas, The, SMA 440 (Arb. at N. Y. 1964) ···115
Capel *v.* Soulidi [1916] 2 K. B. 365 ; 85 L. J. K. B. 1169 ; 114 L. T. 921 ; 32 T. L. R. 508 ;
   1916 W. N. 204 ; 13 Asp. M. L. C. 361, (C. A.) ···401
Capetan Costis I, The, SMA 1622 (Arb. at N. Y. 1981) ···538
Capozziello *v.* Lloyd Brasileiro (1971) 443 F. 2d 1155 ; 1971 AMC 1477 (2d Cir.) ········57
Captain Demosthenes, The, SMA 1569 (Arb. at N. Y. 1981) ··································278
Captain Diamantis, The—Mammoth Bulk Carriers Ltd. *v.* Holland Bulk Transport B.
   V. [1978] 1 Lloyd's Rep. 346, (C. A.) ; *aff'g* [1977] 1 Lloyd's Rep. 362, (Q. B.) ···218, **227**
Captain George K., The—Palmco Shipping Inc. *v.* Continental Ore Corp. [1970] 2
   Lloyd's Rep. 21, (Q. B.) ··**398**
Captain John, The, 1973 AMC 2005 (Arb. at N. Y.) ·······························**163**, 213, 389
Car & Universal Finance Co. Ltd. *v.* Caldwell [1965] 1 Q. B. 525 ; [1964] 2 W. L. R.
   600 ; [1964] 1 All E. R. 290, (C. A.) ···83
Carbon Slate Co. *v.* Ennis (1902) 114 F. 260 (3d Cir.) ·································**201-202**
Carcich *v.* Rederi A/B Nordie (1968) 389 F. 2d 692 ; 1968 AMC 299 (2d Cir.) ··········449
Cardinal Shipping Corp. *v.* The Seisho Maru, 1985 AMC 2630 ; (1984) 744 F. 2d 461
   (5th Cir.) ···277, 499, 504
Care Shipping Corp. *v.* Latin American Shipping Corp.—The Cebu [1983] 1 Lloyd's
   Rep. 302 ; [1983] Q. B. 1005 ; [1983] 2 W. L. R. 829 ; [1983] 1 All E. R. 1121, (Q.
   B.) ··481, 482, **485**, 602
Cargill *v.* Empresa Nicaraguense Dealimentos (1994) 25 F. 3d 223 (4th Cir.) ············454
Cargill International S. A. *v.* CPN Tankers (Bermuda) Ltd.—The Ot Sonja [1993] 2
   Lloyd's Rep. 435, (C. A.) ··439, 520

Cargill Int'l S. A. v. The Pavel Dybenko (1993) 991 F. 2d 1012;1994 AMC 2258 (2d Cir.) ··57
Cargo Carriers v. Brown S. S. Co. (1950) 95 F. Supp. 288 (W. D. N. Y.) ·······················428
Cargo Ships El-Yam Ltd. v. Invotra N. V. [1958] 1 Lloyd's Rep. 39, (Q. B.) ···94, 101, **103**
Cargo Ships EI-Yam Ltd. v. Stearns & Foster Co. (1955) 149 F. Supp. 754 ; 1957 AMC 668 (S. D. N. Y.) ···115, 116
Carib Prince, The (1898) 170 U. S. 655 ···110
Caribbean Nostalgia, The, SMA 1788 (Arb. at N. Y. 1983) ···208
Caribbean Sky, The, SMA 2827 (Arb. at N. Y. 1992) ··317
Caribbean Steamship Co. S. A. v. Sonmez Denizcilik ve Ticaret A. S. (1979) 598 F. 2d 1264 ; 1979 AMC 1270 (2d Cir.) ···**456**, 457
Caribbean Trader, The, SMA 41 (Arb. at N. Y. 1964) ···543
Caribbean Wave, The, SMA 278 (Arb. at N. Y. 1961) ···361
Carib Eve, The, SMA 2749 (Arb. at N. Y. 1991) ···110, 318
Carnival, The—Prekookeanska Plovidba v. Felstar Shipping Corporation and Sotromar Srl. and STC Scantrade A. B. (Third Party) [1994] 2 Lloyd's Rep. 14, (C. A.); [1992] 1 Lloyd's Rep. 449, (Q. B.) ··182, 187, 195
Caroline Horn, The, SMA 649 (Arb. at N. Y. 1971) ···202
Caroline P, The—Telfair Shipping Corp. v. Inersea Carriers S. A. [1983] 2 Lloyd's Rep. 351 ; [1984] 2 Lloyd's Rep. 466 ; [1985] 1 W. L. R. 553 ; [1985] 1 All E. R. 243, (Q. B.) ··295, 327, **328**, 553
Caterpillar Overseas S. A. v. The Expeditor (1963) 318 F. 2d 720 ; 1963 AMC 1662 (2d Cir.);*cert. denied* (1963) 375 U. S. 942 ···522
Catlin v. United States (1945) 324 U. S. 229 ···451
Catz American Co. v. Pearl Grange Fruit Exchange Inc. (1968) 292 F. Supp. 549 (S. D. N. Y.) ···465
Cavcar Company v. The Suzdal (1983) 723 F. 2d 1096 ; 1984 AMC 609 (3d Cir.) ·······343
Cebu, The—Care Shipping Corp. v. Latin American Shipping Corp. [1983] 1 Lloyd's Rep. 302 ; [1983] Q. B. 1005 ; [1983] 2 W. L. R. 829 ; [1983] 1 All E. R. 1121, (Q. B.) ···481, 482, **485**, 602
Cebu, The (No. 2)—Itex Italgrani Export S. A. v. Care Shipping Corporation [1990] 2 Lloyd's Rep. 316 ; [1993] Q. B. 1 ; [1991] 3 W. L. R. 609 ; [1992] 1 All E. R. 91, (Q. B.) ···482, 602
Cehave N. V. v. Bremer Handelsgesellschaft m. b. H.—The Hansa Nord [1975] 2 Lloyd's Rep. 445 ; [1976] Q. B. 44 ; [1975] 3 W. L. R. 447 ; [1975] 3 All E. R. 739, (C. A.) ··89, 90
Centennial Insurance Co. v. Constellation Enterprise, 1987 AMC 1155 (S. D. N. Y. 1986) ···341
Central Hanover Bank & Trust Co. v. Siemens & Halske Akt. (1936) 15 F. Supp. 927 (S. D. N. Y.); *aff'd on opinion below* (1936) 84 F. 2d 993 (2d Cir.);*cert. denied* (1936) 299 U. S. 585···415
Central Marine Service Inc. v. Ocean Marine Contractors Inc., 1984 AMC 1730 (5th Cir. 1982) (*per curiam*) ···58

Central Trust, The, 1971 AMC 200 (Can. Exch. 1970) ···144
Century Textiles and Industry Ltd. v. Tomoe Shipping Co. (Singapore) Pte. Ltd.—
　The Aditya Vaibhav [1991] 1 Lloyd's Rep. 573, (Q. B.); [1993] 1 Lloyd's Rep. 63,
　(Q. B.) ···249, 251, 252, 594
Cephalonian Shipping Co. S. A. (The matter of), 1979 AMC 1451 (S. D. N. Y.) ······**470, 471**
Cepheus, The, 1990 AMC 1058 (Arb. at N. Y. 1990) ··205
Ceres, The (1896) 72 F. 936 (2d Cir.); *cert. denied* (1896) 163 U. S. 706 ···················115
Challenger, The, 1978 AMC 2037 (Arb. at N. Y. 1978) ···207
Chandris v. Isbrandtsen-Moller Co. (1950) 84 Ll. L. Rep. 347; [1951] 1 K. B. 240; 66
　T. L. R. (Pt. 2) 358; [1950] 2 All E. R. 618, (C. A.) ·························**165-166**, 169, 373
Channel Island Ferries Ltd. v. Cenargo Navigation Ltd.—The Rozel [1994] 2 Lloyd's
　Rep. 161 ···237
Charalambos N. Pateras, The—Nippon Yusen Kaisha v. Acme Shipping Corp. [1972]
　1 Lloyd's Rep. 1; [1972] 1 W. L. R. 74; [1972] 1 All E. R. 35, (C. A.); *aff'g* [1971]
　2 Lloyd's Rep. 42, (Q. B.) ··247, 249, 285, 553, 556
Chartwell Shipping v. Q. N. S. Paper Co. (1989) 62 D. L. R. (4th) 36 ·························64
Chattahoochee, The (1898) 173 U. S. 540 ··526
Cheik Boutros v. Ceylon Shipping Lines Ltd.—The Madeleine [1967] 2 Lloyd's Rep.
　224, (Q. B.) ···97, **100**, 121, 154, **159**, 355, **356**, 359, 530
Chellew Navigation Co. Ltd. v. A. R. Appelquist Kolimport A. G. (1933) 45 Ll. L. Rep.
　190; 38 Com. Cas. 218; 49 T. L. R. 295, (K. B.) ···**159, 236**
Chemical Venture, The—Pearl Carriers Inc. v. Japan Line Ltd. [1993] 1 Lloyd's Rep.
　508, (Q. B.) ···186, 188, **189-190**, 191, 579, **580-581**, 605, 612
Cheshire, The, SMA 3129 (Arb. at N. Y. 1994) ··461
Chevron Transport Corp. v. Astro Venecedor Compania Naviera S. A. (1969) 300 F.
　Supp. 179; 1969 AMC 1582 (S. D. N. Y.) ···468
Chi Sun Hua Steel Co. Ltd. v. Crest Tankers Inc. (1989) 708 F. Supp. 18; 1989 AMC
　2551 (D. N. H.); 1990 AMC 2816 (N. D. Cal.) ··57, 501
Chikuma, The—A/S Awilco v. Fulvia S. p. A. di Navigazione [1981] 1 Lloyd's Rep.
　371; [1981] 1 W. L. R. 314; [1981] 1 All E. R. 652, (H. L.); *rev'g* [1980] 2 Lloyd's
　Rep. 409, (C. A.); *restoring* [1979] 1 Lloyd's Rep. 367, (Q. B.) ····································**244**, 584
Chilean Nitrate Sales Corp. v. Marine Transportation Co. Ltd.—The Hermosa [1982]
　1 Lloyd's Rep. 570, (C. A.); *aff'g* [1980] 1 Lloyd's Rep. 638, (Q. B.)
　···**99**, 100, 161, 212, 364, 517
China National Foreign Trade Transportation Corp. v. Evlogia Shipping Co. Ltd.—
　The Mihalios Xilas [1979] 2 Lloyd's Rep. 303; [1979] 1 W. L. R. 1018; [1979] 2
　All E. R. 1044, (H. L.); *rev'g* [1978] 2 Lloyd's Rep. 397; [1978] 1 W. L. R. 1257;
　[1979] 1 All E. R. 657, (C. A.); *restoring* [1976] 2 Lloyd's Rep. 697; [1976] 3 All E.
　R. 865, (Q. B.) ··93, **246**, 254, 255, 260, 261, 262, **263**, 264
China Ocean Shipping Co. v. The Owners Of the Vessel Andros—The Xingcheng
　[1987] 2 Lloyd's Rep. 210; [1987] 1 W. L. R. 1213; (1987) 131 S. J. 972, (P. C.) ······604
China Trade & Devel. Corp. v. The Choong Yong (1987) 837 F. 2d 33; 1988 AMC
　880 (2d Cir.) ··76

China Trident, The, SMA 2756 (Arb. at N. Y. 1991) ···109, 458
Chiswell Shipping and Liberian Jaguat Transports Inc. *v.* National Iranian Tankers
  Co.—The World Symphony and The World Renown [1992] 2 Lloyd's Rep. 115.
  (C. A.); *aff'g* [1991] I Lloyd's Rep. 251, (Q. B.) ································**129, 446, 590-591**
Chris, The, SMA 199 (Arb. at N. Y. 1958) ···117, 239, 381
Christensen *v.* Hindustan Steel Ltd. [1971] 1 Lloyd's Rep. 395; [1971] 1 W. L. R.
  1369; [1971] 2 All E. R. 811, (Q. B.) ···358
Christie & Vesey Ltd. *v.* Maatschappij Tot Exploitatie Van Schepen en Andere
  Zaken Helvetia N. V.—The Helvetia-S. [1960] 1 Lloyd's Rep. 540, (Q. B.) ···**557**, 570, 571
Christin T, The, SMA 2527 (Arb. at N. Y. 1988) ··241
Christina Pezas, The (1957) 149 F. Supp. 678; 1958 AMC 240 (S. D. N. Y.) ················109
Christman *v.* Maristella Compania Naviera (1971) 349 F. Supp. 845 (S. D. N. Y.); *aff'd*
  on opinion below (1972) 468 F. 2d 620 (2d Cir.) ···57
Chrysalis, The—Vinava Shipping Co. Ltd. *v.* Finelvet A. G. [1983] 1 Lloyd's Rep. 503;
  [1983] 1 W. L. R. 1469; [1983] 2 All E. R. 658, (Q. B.) ·································403, 404
Chrysanthi G. L., The, SMA 1417 (Arb. at N. Y. 1980) ···381
Chrysovalandou Dyo, The—Santiren Shipping Ltd. *v.* Unimarine S. A. [1981] 1
  Lloyd's Rep. 159; [1981] 1 All E. R. 340, (Q. B.) ·····················87, 249, 250, 252, 254, 481
Cia Estrella Blanca Ltda *v.* The Nictric (1965) 247 F. Supp. 161 (D. Ore); *aff'd per*
  curiam (1966) 368 F. 2d 575 (9th Cir.) ···390
Cia Platamon de Navegacion S. A. *v.* Empresa Colombiana de Petroleos (1979) 478
  F. Supp. 66; 1980 AMC 538 (S. D. N. Y.) ···448
Ciampa *v.* British India Steam Navigation Co. [1915] 2 K. B. 774; 20 Com. Cas. 247;
  84 L. J. K. B. 1653, (K. B.) ···156, 159, 421
Ciechocinek, The—Ismail *v.* Polish Ocean Lines [1976] 1 Lloyd's Rep. 489; [1976] Q.
  B. 893; [1976] 3 W. L. R. 477; [1976] 1 All E. R. 902, (C. A.); [1975] 2 Lloyd's
  Rep. 170, (Q. B.) ··308
Cielo Rosso, The, 1980 AMC 2088 (Arb. at N. Y.) ···57, 354
Citibank N. A. *v.* Hobbs Savill & Co. Ltd.—The Panglobal Friendship [1978] 1
  Lloyd's Rep. 368. (C. A.) ···488
Cities Service Transp. Co. *v.* Gulf Refining Co. (1935) 79 F. 2d 521; 1935 AMC 1513
  (2d Cir.) ··199, 208
City and Westminster Properties (1934) Ltd. *v.* Mudd [1959] Ch. 129; [1958] 3 W.
  L. R. 312; [1958] 2 All E. R. 733, (Q. B.) ···86
Clan Line Steamers Ltd. *v.* Ove Skou Rederi A/S [1969] 2 Lloyd's Rep. 155, (Q. B.)
  ···315
Clea Shipping Corp. *v.* Bulk Oil International Ltd.—The Alaskan Trader (No. 2)
  [1983] 2 Lloyd's Rep. 645; [1984] 1 All E. R. 129, (Q. B.) ·································**130**
Cleobolus Shipping Co. Ltd *v.* Intertanker Ltd.—The Cleon [1983] 1 Lloyd's Rep.
  586, (Q. B. and C. A.) ··442
Cleon, The—Cleobolus Shipping Co. Ltd *v.* Intertanker Ltd. [1983] 1 Lloyd's Rep.
  586, (Q. B. and C. A.) ··442
Clough *v.* London & North Western Railway Co. (1871) L. R. 7 Exch. 26; 41 L. J. Ex.

17;25 L. T. 708, (Ex. Ch.) ··83
Clyde Commercial S. S. Co. v. West India S. S. Co. (1909) 169 F. 275 (2d Cir.); *cert. denied* (1909) 214 U. S. 523 ····································272, **380**, 381, 410, **427**, 429, 639
Coastal Corpus Christi, The, SMA 2828 (Arb. at N. Y. 1992) ···································113
Coastal States Gas Corp. v. Atlantic Tankers Ltd. (1976) 546 F. 2d 15; 1976 AMC 2337 (2d Cir.) ··**79**
Cobec Brazilian Trading and Warehousing v. H. & J. Isbrandtsen (1979) 79 Civ. 3833 (S. D. N. Y.) (unreported) ···60
Coca-Cola Co. v. The Norholt (1971) 333 F. Supp. 946; 1972 AMC 388 (S. D. N. Y.) ···10, **164**, 318-319
Cochin Refineries v. Triton Shipping, 1978 AMC 444 (Arb. at N. Y.) ·······················273
Cofinco Inc. v. Bakrie & Bros., N. V. (1975) 395 F. Supp. 613 (S. D. N. Y.) ········**468**, **472**
Collen v. Wright (1857) 8 E. & B. 647; 27 L. J. Q. B. 215; 30 L. T. O. S. 209; 4 Jur. N. S. 357; 6 W. R. 123; 120 E. R. 241, (Ex. Ch.) ··69
Colonial Bank v. European Grain and Shipping Ltd.—The Dominique [1989] 1 Lloyd's Rep. 431; [1989] A. C. 1056; [1989] 2 W. L. R. 440, (H. L.); [1989] 1 All E. R. 545; (1989) 133 S. J. 219. (H. L.); *rev'g* [1988] 1 Lloyd's Rep. 215; [1988] 3 W. L. R. 60; [1988] 3 All E. R. 233; [1988] 1 F. T. L. R. 327; (1988) 132 S. J. 896. (C. A.); *rev'g* [1987] 1 Lloyd's Rep. 239, (Q. B.) ··249
Colonial Penn Insur. Co. v. Omaha Indemnity Co. (1991) 943 F. 2d 327 (3d Cir.) ······463
Columbia Liberty, The, SMA 2220 (Arb. at N. Y. 1986) ·······································629
Commercial Metals v. The Luckyman, 1994 AMC 673 (E. D. Pa.) ·······························340
Commercial Union Ins. v. Gilbane Building Co. (1993) 992 F. 2d 386 (1st Cir.) ············449
Commonwealth Coatings Corp. v. Continental Casualty Co. (1968) 393 U. S. 145 ···466, 467
Commonwealth Oil Refining Co. Inc. v. The Grand Commonwealth, 1978 AMC 975 (M. D. Fla.) ···**464**
Compagnie Algerienne de Meaunerie v. Katana Societa di Navigazione Maritime S. p. A.—The Nizeti [1960] 1 Lloyd's Rep. 132; [1960] 2 Q. B. 115; [1960] 2 W. L. R. 719; [1960] 2 All E. R. 55, (C. A.); [1958] 2 Lloyd's Rep. 502; [1959] 1 Q. B. 527; [1959] 2 W. L. R. 366; [1959] 1 All E. R. 272, (Q. B.) ·····································156
Compagnie Generale Maritime v. Diakan Spirit S. A.—The Ymnos [1981] 1 Lloyd's Rep. 550; [1982] 2 Lloyd's Rep. 574, (Q. B.) ···89, 91
Compagnie Tunisienne de Navigation S. A. v. Compagnie d'Armement Maritime S. A. [1970] 2 Lloyd's Rep. 99; *sub nom.* Compagnie d'Armement Maritime S. A. v. Compagnie Tunisienne de Navigation S. A. [1971] A. C. 572; [1970] 3 W. L. R. 389; [1970] 3 All E. R. 71, (H. L.) ···**438**
Compania Chilena de Navigation Interociania v. Norton, Lilly & Co. (1987) 652 F. Supp. 1512; 1987 AMC 1565 (S. D. N. Y.) ··461
Compania de Naviera Nedelka S. A. v. Tradax Internacional S. A.—The Tres Flores [1973] 2 Lloyd's Rep. 247; [1974] Q. B. 264; [1973] 3 W. L. R. 545; [1973] 3 All E. R. 967, (C. A.); *aff'g* [1972] 2 Lloyd's Rep. 384, (Q. B.) ················155, 157, **357**, 358
Compania de Navegacion la Flecha v. Brauer (1897) 168 U. S. 104 ····························427
Compania de Vapores Insco S. A. v. Missouri Pacific R. Co. (1956) 232 F. 2d 657

(5th Cir.); *cert. denied* (1956) 352 U. S. 800 ···428
Compania Espanola de Petroleos S. A. *v.* Nereus Shipping S. A. (1975) 527 F. 2d
　966 ; 1975 AMC 2421 (2d Cir.); *cert. denied* (1976) 426 U. S. 936 ··················**79**, 452, 453
Compania Naviera Aisgiannis S. A. *v.* Holt, 1984 AMC 2228 (E. D. Pa. 1983) ···············60
Compania Naviera Asiastic *v.* Burmah Oil, 1977 AMC 1538 (S. D. N. Y.) ··················109
Compania Naviera Bachi *v.* Henry Hosegood & Son Ltd. (1938) 60 Ll. L. Rep 236 ;
　158 L. T. 356 ; [1938] 2 All E. R. 189 ; 19 Asp. M. L. C. 186, (K. B.) ························562
Compania Naviera Maropan S. A. *v.* Bowater's Lloyd Pulp & Paper Mills Ltd. —The
　Stork [1955] 1 Lloyd's Rep. 349 ; [1955] 2 Q. B. 68 ; [1955] 2 W. L. R. 998 ; [1955]
　2 All E. R. 241, (C. A.); *aff'g* [1954] 2 Lloyd's Rep. 397 ; [1955] 2 Q. B. 68 ; [1954]
　3 W. L. R. 894 ; [1954] 3 All E. R. 563, (Q. B.) ··················178, 190, 192, **193**, 195, 197, 293
Compania Naviera Micro S. A. *v.* Shipley International Inc.—The Parouth [1982] 2
　Lloyd's Rep. 351, (C. A.) ···55, 438
Compania Panemena Maritima San Gerassimo S. A. *v.* J. E. Hurley Lumber Co.
　(1957) 244 F. 2d 286 ; 1957 AMC 1759 (2d Cir.) ···464
Compania Sud Americana de Vapores *v.* Shipmair B. V. —The Teno [1977] 2
　Lloyd's Rep. 289, (Q. B.) ··249, 250
Compania Venetico de Navegacion S. A. *v.* Presthus Chartering A/S, SMA 1110
　(Arb. at N. Y. 1977) ···116
Complaint of Koala Shipping & Trading Inc. (1984) 587 F. Supp. 140 (S. D. N. Y.) ······464
Comptoir Commercial Anversois and Power (*Re*) [1920] 1 K. B. 868 ; 122 L. T. 567 ;
　30 T. L. R. 101, (C. A.) ···394
Concordia Fjord, The—D/S A/S Idaho *v.* Colossus Maritime S. A. [1984] 1 Lloyd's
　Rep. 385, (Q. B.) ···143, 188, 613
Cone (Moses H.) Memorial Hosp. *v.* Mercury Constr. Corp. (1983) 460 U. S. 1 ·········453
Congress Coal and Transp. Co. Inc. *v.* International S. S. Co., 1925 AMC 701 (Penn.)
　··543
Consolidated Investment & Contracting Co. *v.* Saponaria Shipping Ltd. —The Virgo
　[1978] 2 Lloyd's Rep. 167, (C. A.) ··440
Constantine (Joseph) S. S. Line Ltd. *v.* Imperial Smelting Corp. (1941) 70 Ll. L. Rep.
　1 ; [1942] A. C. 154 ; 110 L. J. K. B. 433 ; 165 L. T. 27 ; 57 T. L. R. 485 ; 46 Com. Cas.
　258 ; [1941] 2 All E. R. 165, (H. L.) ···405, 406, **407**
Constantine & Pickering S. S. Co. *v.* West India S. S. Co. (1914) 231 F. 472 (S. D. N.
　Y.) ···136
Constellation, The, SMA 3012 (Arb. at N. Y. 1993) ···233
Consumers Import Co. *v.* Kabushiki-Kaisha Kawasaki Zosenjo (1943) 320 U. S. 249 ;
　1943 AMC 1209···429
Conti-Lines *v.* The Baroness V, 1992 AMC 681 (N. D. Fla.) ··501
Conticommodity Services Inc. *v.* Philipp & Lion (1980) 613 F. 2d 1222 (2d Cir.)
　··**450**, 451, 523, 524
Continental Chartering and Brokerage Inc. *v.* T. J. Stevenson & Co. (1987) 678 F.
　Supp. 58 ; 1988 AMC 617 (S. D. N. Y.) ··460-461
Continental Grain Co. *v.* American Commercial Barge Line Co. (1964) 332 F. 2d 26

(7th Cir.) ···339
Continental Trader, The, SMA 1503 (Arb. at N. Y. 1980) ·······································**288**
Cook Inlet v. Amer. T. & P., 1976 AMC 160 (S. D. N. Y.) ····································208
Cooper v. Offshore Express (1989) 171 F. Supp. 1180; 1990 AMC 666 (W. D. La.);
　aff'd without opinion (1990) 915 F. 2d 1569 (5th Cir.) ·································321-322
Coral, The—Balli Trading Ltd. v. Afalona Shipping Co. Ltd. [1993] 1 Lloyd's Rep. 1
　(C. A.); (1992) 136 S. J. (LB) 259, (C. A.); rev'g [1992] 2 Lloyd's Rep. 158, (Q. B.)
　··305
Cordoba Shipping Co. Ltd. v. Maro Shipping Ltd. (1980) 494 F. Supp. 1183 ; 1980
　AMC 1945 (D. Conn.) ···78
Corfu Island, The—Naxos Shipping Co. v. Thegra Shipping Co. (1973) unreported
　(Ackner, J.) ···249
Cornish Shipping v. Ferromet, 1995 AMC 235 (S. D. N. Y. 1995) ·······················496
Corona, The, SMA 961 (Arb. at N. Y. 1975) ··416
Cory v. Burr (1883) 8 App. Cas. 393 ···606
Cosmar Compania Naviera S. A. v. Total Transport Corp.—The Isabelle [1984] 1
　Lloyd's Rep. 366, (C. A.); [1982] 2 Lloyd's Rep. 81, (Q. B.) ·························196, 296
Cosmos Bulk Transport Inc. v. China National Foreign Trade Transportation Corp.
　—The Apollonius [1978] 1 Lloyd's Rep. 53; [1978] 1 All E. R. 322, (Q. B.)
　··101, **104**, 285, 368, 375, 379, **551**, 554, 556, **559-560**
Costa Rican Trader, The, SMA 203 (Arb. at N. Y. 1967) ···································117
Cotton v. Sloan [1993] 4 F. 3d 176 (2d Cir.) ···449
County & District Properties Ltd. v. C. Jenner & Son Ltd. [1976] 2 Lloyd's Rep. 728;
　280 E. G. 1589, (Q. B.) ···552
Court Line Ltd. v. Canadian Transport Co. Ltd. (1940) 67 Ll. L. Rep. 161; [1940] A.
　C. 934 ; 56 T. L. R. 802 ; 163 L. T. 317 ; 45 Com. Cas. 276 ; 110 L. J. K. B. 14 ; [1940] 3
　All E. R. 112 ; 19 Asp. M. L. C. 374, (H. L.) ·······································221, 303, **306**, 315
Court Line Ltd. v. Dant & Russell Inc. (1939) 64 Ll. L. Rep. 212 ; 44 Com. Cas. 345 ;
　161 L. T. 35 ; [1939] 3 All E. R. 314 ; 19 Asp. M. L. C. 307, (K. B.)
　···**370**, 371, 374, 375, **399-400**, 402
Court Line Ltd. v. Finelvet A. G.—The Jevington Court [1966] 1 Lloyd's Rep. 683,
　(Q. B.) ···554, **555**
Court Line v. The King (1945) 78 Ll. L. Rep. 390 ; [1945] W. N. 147 ; 61 T. L. R. 418 ;
　173 L. T. 162 ; [1945] 2 All E. R. 357, (C. A.); (1943-44) 77 Ll. L. Rep. 529 ···········591
Courtney & Fairbairn Ltd. v. Tolaini Brothers (Hotels) Ltd. [1975] 1 W. L. R. 297 ;
　[1975] 1 All E. R. 716, (C. A.) ··50
Craig v. Lake Asbestos of Quebec Ltd. (1988) 843 F. 2d 145 (3d Cir.) ······················78
Crane Nest, The, 1939 AMC 1186 (Arb. at N. Y.) ··538
Crawford v. A. E. A Prowting Ltd. [1973] Q. B. 1 ; [1972] 2 W. L. R. 749 ; [1972] 1
　All E. R. 1199, (Q. B.) ··443
Cremdean Properties v. Nash (1977) 244 E. G. 547, (C. A.) ·······························82, 85
Crisp v. United States & Australasia S. S. Co. (1903) 124 F. 748 (S. D. N. Y.) ·········**201**
Crossman v. Burrill (1900) 179 U. S. 100 ···**345**

Crow v. Myers (1890) 41 F. 806 (E. D. Va.) ···162
Czarnikow Ltd. v. Koufos-The Heron II [1967] 2 Lloyd's Rep. 457; [1967] 3 W. L. R.
　1491; [1967] 3 All E. R. 686; [1969] 1 A. C. 350, (H. L.); [1966] 1 Lloyd's Rep.
　595; [1966] 2 Q. B. 695; [1966] 2 W. L. R. 1397; [1966] 2 All E. R. 593, (C. A.);
　[1966] 1 Lloyd's Rep. 259, (Q. B.) ···92, 358
Czarnikow-Rionda Co. v. Federal Sugar Refining (1930) 255 N. Y. 33; 173 N. E. 913 ···278

Dr. Beck & Co. v. General Electric Co. (1962) 210 F. Supp. 86 (S. D. N. Y.) ················**73**
D/S A/S Idaho v. Colossus Maritime S. A.—The Concordia Fjord [1984] 1 Lloyd's
　Rep. 385, (Q. B.) ···143, 188, 613
D/S A/S Idaho v. The Peninsular and Oriental Steam Navigation Company—The
　Strathnewton [1983] 1 Lloyd's Rep. 219, (C. A.); [1982] 2 Lloyd's Rep. 296, (Q. B.)
　··311, 313
D/S Ove Skou v. Herbert (1966) 365 F. 2d 341; 1966 AMC 2223 (5th Cir.); cert.
　denied (1970) 400 U. S. 902 ···**321**
Daffodil B, The—Danae Shipping Corp. v. T. P. A. O. and Guven Turkish Insurance Co.
　Ltd. [1983] 1 Lloyd's Rep. 498, (Q. B.) ··435
Dagmar, The—Tage Berglund v. Montoro Shipping Corp. [1968] 2 Lloyd's Rep. 563,
　(Q. B.) ··**182**, 192
Dagny Skou, The, SMA 2416 (Arb. at N. Y. 1987) ···271
Daihatsu Motor Co. v. Terrain Vehicles Inc. (1993) 13 F. 3d 196 (7th Cir.) ············462
Daisy Manufacturing v. NCR Corp. (1994) 29 F. 3d 389 (8th Cir.) ·······················448
Dalny, The—Tarmarea S. R. L. v. Rederiaktiebolaget Sally [1979] 2 Lloyd's Rep. 439;
　[1979] 1 W. L. R. 1320; [1979] 2 All E. R. 989, (Q. B.) ··································443
Damon Compania Naviera S. A. v. Hapag Lloyd International S. A.—The Blankenstein
　[1985] 1 Lloyd's Rep. 93; [1985] 1 W. L. R. 435; [1985] 1 All E. R. 475, (C. A.);
　[1983] 2 Lloyd's Rep. 522; [1983] 3 All E. R. 510, (Q. B.) ···································52
Damps. Dannebrog v. Signal Oil & Gas Co. (1940) 310 U. S. 268 ·······················499
Damps. Norden v. Isbrandtsen-Moller Co.—The Katonia (1930) 43 F. 2d 560; 1930
　AMC 1441 (S. D. N. Y.) ··**117**
Dampskibs Akt. Thor v. Tropical Fruit Co. (1922) 281 F. 740 (2d Cir.) ···················149
Dampskibs, etc. v. Munson Line S. S. Co. (1927) 20 F. 2d 345 (2d. Cir); cert. denied
　275 U. S. 561 ··239
Danae Shipping Corp. v. T. P. A. O. and Guven Turkish Insurance Co. Ltd.—The
　Daffodil B [1983] 1 Lloyd's Rep. 498, (Q. B.) ··435
Danita, The, SMA 2514 (Arb. at N. Y. 1988) ··113
Dannah, The [1993] 1 Lloyd's Rep. 351···308
Davis v. Dittman (1925) 6 F. 2d 141 (2d Cir.) ···343
Davis Contractors Ltd. v. Fareham U. D. C. [1956] A. C. 696; [1956] 3 W. L. R. 37;
　[1956] 2 All E. R. 145, (H. L.) ···393, 394, 395, **397**, 404
Davison v. Von Lingen (1885) 113 U. S. 40 ···108, **119**, 361
Davison Chemical Co. v. Eastern Transp. Co. (1929) 30 F. 2d 862; 1929 AMC 161
　(4th Cir.) ··**431**

Dawson Line Ltd. *v.* A. G. "Adler" fuer Chemische Industrie (1931) 41 Ll. L. Rep. 75;
  [1932] 1 K. B. 433; 101 L. J. K. B. 57; 146 L. T. 187; 37 Com. Cas. 28; 18 Asp. M. L.
  C. 273, (C. A.) ··326
Dean Witter Reynolds Inc. *v.* Byrd (1985) 470 U. S. 213 ··453
Dearle *v.* Hall (1828) 3 Russ. 1; 2 L. J. Ch. 62 ···485
Debenham's Ltd. *v.* Perkins (1925) 133 L. T. 252; [1925] All E. R. 234 ·····················62
Decro-Wall International S. A. *v.* Practitioners in Marketing [1971] 1 W. L. R. 361;
  [1971] 2 All E. R. 216, (C. A.) ··99, 268
Deiulemar di Navigazione S. p. A. (In the matter of), 1994 AMC 2250 (E. D. La.) ······455
Del E. Webb Const. *v.* Richardson Hospital Auth. (1987) 823 F. 2d 145 (5th Cir.) ···452
Delaware, The (1872) 81 U. S. 579 ···346
Delian Spirit, The—Shipping Developments Corp. *v.* V/O Sojuzneftexport [1971] 1
  Lloyd's Rep. 506; [1972] 1 Q. B. 103; [1971] 2 W. L. R. 1434; [1971] 2 All E. R.
  1067, (C. A.) ··**159**
Deloitte Noraudit *v.* Deloitte Haskins & Sell ls (1993) 9 F. 3d 1060 (2d Cir.) ············448
Delta Commodities Inc. *v.* The Jo Oak, 1990 AMC 820 (E. D. La. 1989) ···············206
De Mattos *v.* Gibson (1858) 4 De G. & J. 276; 28 L. J. Ch. 498, (C. A.) ············87, **95-96**
De Meza and Stuart *v.* Apple, Van Straten, Shena and Stone [1975] 1 Lloyd's Rep.
  498, (C. A.); *aff'g* [1974] 1 Lloyd's Rep. 508, (Q. B.) ··309
Democritos, The—Marbienes Cia. Nav. *v.* Ferrostaal A. G. [1976] 2 Lloyd's Rep. 149,
  (C. A.); *aff'g* [1975] 1 Lloyd's Rep. 386, (Q. B.)
  ··124, **126**, 128, 131, 153, 161, 355, **358**, 359, 360, 377, 408
Demosthenes V, The (No. 1) —Gerani Compania Naviera S. A. *v.* General Organisation
  for Supply Goods and Alfred C. Toepfer [1982] 1 Lloyd's Rep. 275, (Q. B.) ······158, 358
Demsey & Assoc. *v.* The Sea Star (1972) 461 F. 2d 1009; 1972 AMC 1440 (2d Cir.)
  ··164, 317, 340, 342, 449
Denholm Shipping Co. *v.* W. E. Hedger Co. (1931) 47 F. 2d 213; 1931 AMC 297 (2d
  Cir.) ··113, **114-115**
Denny, Mott & Dickson Ltd. *v.* James B. Fraser & Co. Ltd. [1944] A. C. 265; [1944]
  1 All E. R. 678; 113 L. J. P. C. 37; 171 L. T. 345; 60 T. L. R. 419, (H. L.) ············402, **403**
Derby, The—Alfred C. Toepfer Schiffahrtsgesellschaft G. m. b. H. *v.* Tossa Marine Co.
  Ltd., Tossa Marine Co. Ltd. *v.* Alfred C. Toepfer Schiffahrtsgesellschaft G. m. b. H.
  [1985] 2 Lloyd's Rep. 325, (C. A.); [1984] 1 Lloyd's Rep. 635, (Q. B.)
  ··154, 156, 158, 159, **160**, 574
Derry *v.* Peek (1889) 14 App. Cas. 337; 58 L. J. Ch. 864; 61 L. T. 265; 5 T. L. R. 625,
  (H. L.) ···84
Derrynane, The, 1954 AMC 1015 (Arb. at N. Y.) ···136, 225
Desormeaux *v.* Oceans Int'l Corp., 1979 AMC 1962 (W. D. La.) ································321
Diamond, The, [1906] P. 282; 95 L. T. 550; 75 L. J. P. 90; 10 Asp. M. L. C. 286, (P. D.
  A.) ··421
Diana Compania Maritima S. A. of Panama *v.* Sub-freights of the Admiralty Flyer
  (1968) 280 F. Supp. 607; 1968 AMC 2093 (S. D. N. Y.) ·······················275, 491, 496
Diana Prosperity, The—Reardon Smith Line Ltd. *v.* Yngvar Hansen-Tangen and

Sanko Steamship Co. Ltd. [1976] 2 Lloyd's Rep. 621; [1976] 1 W. L. R. 989;
 [1976] 3 All E. R. 570. (H. L.); *aff'g* [1976] 2 Lloyd's Rep. 60. (C. A.) ···90, 93, **94**, 106, 573
Didymi Corp. *v.* Atlantic Lines and Navigation Co. Inc.—The Didymi [1987] 2
 Lloyd's Rep. 166; [1988] 2 Lloyd's Rep. 108, (C. A.) ································51, **106**, 598
Didymi, The—Didymi Corp. *v.* Atlantic Lines and Navigation Co. Inc. [1987] 2
 Lloyd's Rep. 166; [1988] 2 Lloyd's Rep. 108, (C. A.) ································51, **106**, 598
Didymi, The, and The Leon—Atlantic Lines and Navigation Co. Inc. *v.* Didymi Corp.
 and Leon Corp. [1984] 1 Lloyd's Rep. 583, (C. A.) ·····································128
Dione, The—Alma Shipping Corp. *v.* Mantovani [1975] 1 Lloyd's Rep. 115, (C. A.);
 rev'g [1974] 1 Lloyd's Rep. 86, (Q. B.) ····················122, 123, 125, 126, **127**, 128, 590, 619
Director, The (1886) 26 F. 708 (D. Ore.) ··491
Dirphys, The, SMA 283 (Arb. at N. Y.) ···536
Discaria, The—Islamic Republic of Iran Shipping Lines *v.* P. & O. Bulk Shipping Ltd.
 [1985] 2 Lloyd's Rep. 489, (Q. B.) ···**535**
Disney *v.* Furness (1897) 79 F. 810 (D. Md.) ···162
Dodds *v.* Walker [1981] 1 W. L. R. 1027, (H. L.); *aff'g* [1980] 1 W. L. R. 1061, (C. A.)
 ··253
Dolphin Hellas Shipping S. A. *v.* Itemslot Ltd.—The Aegean Dolphin [1992] 2
 Lloyd's Rep. 178, (Q. B.) ··92, 104
Dominica Mining Co. *v.* Port Everglades Towing Co. (1969) 318 F. Supp. 500; 1970
 AMC 123 (S. D. Fla.) ···113
Dominion Coal Co. Ltd. *v.* Roberts (1920) 4 Ll. L. Rep. 434, (K. B.) ·······················395
Dominique, The, SMA 2535 (Arb. at N. Y. 1989) ·······································279
Dominique, The—Bank of Boston Connecticut (formerly Colonial Bank) *v.* European
 Grain & Shipping Ltd. [1989] 1 Lloyd's Rep. 431; [1989] A. C. 1056; [1989] 2 W.
 L. R. 440; [1989] 1 All E. R. 545; (1989) 133 S. J. 219, (H. L.); *rev'g* [1988] 1
 Lloyd's Rep. 215; [1988] 3 W. L. R. 60; [1988] 3 All E. R. 233; [1988] 1 F. T. L.
 R. 327; (1988) 132 S. J. 896, (C. A.); *rev'g* [1987] 1 Lloyd's Rep. 239, (Q. B.) ·········249
Domino Group *v.* Charlie Parker Mem. Foundation (1993) 985 F. 2d 417 (8th Cir.)
 ···463, 464
Doros, The, SMA 616 (Arb. at N. Y. 1971) ··233
Dorothea Boulton, The, SMA 1211 (Arb. at N. Y. 1978.) ·································318
Dow Chemical Pacific Ltd. *v.* Rascator Maritime S. A. (1986) 782 F. 2d 329 (2d Cir.)
 ··77
Doyle *v.* Olby [1969] 2 Q. B. 158; [1969] 2 W. L. R. 673; [1969] 2 All E. R. 119, (C.
 A.) ···85
Drayer *v.* Krasner (1978) 572 F. 2d 348; *cert. denied* 436 U. S. 948 ···················465
Dreyfus (Louis) & Cie *v.* Parnaso Compania Naviera S. A. [1960] 1 Lloyd's Rep.
 117; [1960] 2 Q. B. 49; [1960] 2 W. L. R. 637; [1960] 1 All E. R. 759, (C. A.);
 rev'g [1959] 1 Lloyd's Rep. 125; [1959] 1 Q. B. 498; [1959] 2 W. L. R. 405;
 [1959] 1 All E. R. 502, (Q. B.) ···**102-103**, 128
Drosia, The, SMA 1303 (Arb. at N. Y. 1979) ···115, 138
Drughorn *v.* Red. A/B Transatlantic [1919] A. C. 203; 24 Com. Cas. 45; 88 L. J. K. B.

233;120 L.T. 70;35 T.L.R. 73;14 Asp. M.L.C. 400, (H.L.) ·····················67
Drummond Coal Co. v. Interocean Shipping Co., 1985 AMC 1152 (S.D. Ala. 1985) ···176
Duche v. Thomas and John Brocklebank (1930) 40 F. 2d 418;1930 AMC 717 (2d Cir.) ·····················431
Dugdale v. Lovering (1875) L.R. 10 C.P. 196;44 L.J.C.P. 197;32 L.T. 155, (C.P.) ·····················294
Duncan v. Koster—The Teutonia [1872] L.R. 4 P.C. 171;8 Moo. P.C.C.N.S. 411;41 L.J. Adm. 57;26 L.T. 48;20 W.R. 421;17 E.R. 366;1 Asp. M.L.C. 214, (P.C.) ·····················181, 186, 291
Dunlop v. Selfridge [1915] A.C. 847;84 L.J.K.B. 1680;113 L.T. 386;31 T.L.R. 399, (H.L.) ·····················147
Dunlop S.S. Co. v. Tweedie Trading Co. (1908) 162 F. 490 (S.D.N.Y.);aff'd (1910) 178 F. 673 (2d Cir.) ·····················381

E.A.S.T. Inc. v. The Alaia, 1988 AMC 1396 (E.D. La. 1987); (1989) 876 F. 2d 1168;1989 AMC 2024 (5th Cir.) ·····················460, 491, 498
E.B. Michaels v. Mariforum Shipping S.A. (1980) 624 F. 2d 411;1980 AMC 1901 (2d Cir.) ·····················462, **463**, 464
E.T. Barwick Mills Inc. v. Hellenic Lines Ltd. (1971) 331 F. Supp. 161 (S.D. Ga.); aff'd (1973) 472 F. 2d 1406 (5th Cir.) ·····················339
Eagle Transport Ltd. v. O'Connor (1978) 449 F. Supp. 58 (S.D.N.Y.) ·····················79
Earle & Stoddart Inc. v. Ellerman's Wilson Line (1932) 287 U.S. 420;1933 AMC 1 ···429
East Asiatic Co. and Transamerican Steamship Corp. (The Camara and Cinchona) (Arbitration between) 1988 AMC 1086 (S.D.N.Y. 1987) ·····················461
East Asiatic Trading Co. v. Navibec Shipping Ltd., 1979 AMC 1043 (S.D.N.Y. 1978) ·····················495
Easte Eagle, The, 1971 AMC 236 (Arb. at N.Y. 1970) ·····················202
Eastern City, The—Leeds Shipping Co. v. Société Francaise Bunge [1958] 2 Lloyd's Rep. 127, (C.A.);aff'g [1957] 2 Lloyd's Rep. 153, (Q.B.) ·····················177, **178, 181**, 182, 183, 186, 199, 579
Eastern Mediterranean Maritime (Liechtenstein) Ltd. v. Unimarine S.A.—The Marika M [1981] 2 Lloyd's Rep. 622, (Q.B.) ·····················365, **366**
Eastern Saga, The—Oxford Shipping Co. v. Nippon Yusen Kaisha [1984] 2 Lloyd's Rep. 373; [1984] 3 All E.R. 835, (Q.B.) ·····················443
Eastern Street, The, SMA 1352 (Arb. at N.Y. 1979) ·····················108
Ecay v. Godfrey (1947) 80 Ll.L.Rep. 286, (K.B.) ·····················81-82
Econolines Inc. and Mohammed Al-Haddad, et al, 1980 AMC 424 (Arb. at N.Y. 1979) ·····················414
Eddie S.S. Co. Ltd. v. Eastern Development Inc., SMA 1051 (Arb. at N.Y. 1979) ······278
Edison S.S. Corp. v. Eastern Minerals (1958) 167 F. Supp. 601 (D. Mass.) ···383, **385-386**
Edward R. Smith, The—Hildebrand v. Geneva Mill Co. (1929) 32 F. 2d 343;1929 AMC 962 (M.D. Ala.) ·····················111
Edwin I. Morrison, The (1893) 153 U.S. 199 ·····················110

判例索引   57

Effy, The—Zim Israel Navigation Co. Ltd. v. Effy Shipping Corp. [1972] 1 Lloyd's
Rep. 18, (Q. B.) ··**246**, 256
Efphlia, The, SMA 1359 (Arb. at N. Y. 1979) ·······································229, 627
Efploia Shipping Corp. Ltd. v. Canadian Transport Co. Ltd.—The Pantanassa [1958]
  2 Lloyd's Rep. 449, (Q. B.) ···102, **227**
Egle, The, SMA 815 (Arb. at N. Y. 1973) ··272, 274
El Champion, The—Pacific Navigators Corp. v. Islamic Republic of Iran Shipping
  Lines [1985] 2 Lloyd's Rep. 275, (Q. B.) ···**535**
Elbe Ore, The, SMA 2561 (Arb. at N. Y. 1989); confirmed 1989 AMC 2874 (S. D. N.
  Y.) ···278
Elder, Dempster & Co. v. Dunn & Co. (1909) 15 Com. Cas. 49; 101 L. T. 578; 11
  Asp. M. L. C. 337, (H. L.) ···326
Elder, Dempster & Co. Ltd. v. Paterson, Zochonis & Co. Ltd. (1924) 18 Ll. L. Rep.
  319; [1924] A. C. 522; 93 L. J. K. B. 625; 131 L. T. 449; 40 T. L. R. 464; 29 Com. Cas.
  340; 16 Asp. M. L. C. 351, (H. L.); rev'g sub nom. Paterson, Zochonis & Co. v. Elder,
  Dempster & Co. [1923] 1 K. B. 420, (C. A.); aff'g (1922) 2 Ll. L. Rep. 69, (Q. B.) ······**334**
Electronic Switching Industries Inc. v. Faradyne Electric Corp. (1987) 833 F. 2d 418
  (2d Cir.) ··77
Elite Inc. v. Texaco Panama (1991) 777 F. Supp. 189; 1992 AMC 698 (S. D. N. Y.) ······473
Elizabeth Entz, The, SMA 588 (Arb. at N. Y. 1971) ························133, 138, 619
Ellen Klautschke, The, SMA 361 (Arb. at N. Y. 1965) ·······························239
Ellerman Lines Ltd. v. Lancaster Maritime Co. Ltd.—The Lancaster [1980] 2
  Lloyd's Rep. 497, (Q. B.) ···484, 487, 488
Ellerman Lines Ltd. v. The President Harding (1960) 187 F. Supp. 948 (S. D. N. Y.);
  aff'd (1961) 288 F. 2d 288 (2d Cir.) ···279
Ellis Pontos, The, SMA 2116 (Arb. at N. Y. 1985) ·······································459
Elna, II, The, SMA 576 (Arb. at N. Y. 1957) ··241
Elpis Maritime Co. Ltd. v. Marti Chartering Co. Inc.—The Maria D [1991] 2 Lloyd's
  Rep. 311; [1992] 1 A. C. 21; [1991] 3 W. L. R. 330; [1991] 3 All E. R. 758; (1991)
  135 S. J. (LB) 100; (1991) 141 New L. J. 1109, (H. L.); rev'g [1991] 1 Lloyd's Rep.
  521, (C. A.) ···64
Ely, The (1901) 110 F. 563 (S. D. N. Y.); aff'd (1903) 122 F. 447 (2d Cir.); cert.
  denied (1903) 189 U. S. 514 ··149
Emily S. Malcolm, The (1922) 278 F. 943 (3d Cir.) ······································114
Emmanuel C, The, SMA 1575 (Arb. at N. Y. 1981) ·····································162
Emmanuel C, The—Industrie Chimiche Italia Centrale S. p. A. v. Nea Ninemia
  Shipping Co. S. A. [1983] 1 Lloyd's Rep. 310, (Q. B.) ·····················422, 605
Employers Ins. v. National Union Fire Ins. (1991) 933 F. 2d 1481 (9th Cir.) ············468
Empresa Cubana de Fletes v. Kissavos Shipping Co. S. A.—The Agathon (No. 2)
  [1984] 1 Lloyd's Rep. 183, (Q. B.) ·······································534, **535**, 567
Empresa Cubana de Fletes v. Lagonisi Shipping Co. Ltd.—The Georgios C. [1971] 1
  Lloyd's Rep. 7; [1971] 1 Q. B. 488; [1971] 2 W. L. R. 221; [1971] 1 All E. R. 193,
  (Q. B. and C. A.) ·······································87, 244, 257, 258, 268, 548

Endeavor, The, 1978 AMC 1742 (Arb. at N. Y. 1977) ··162,**215**
Enerchem Avance, The, SMA 2907 (Arb. at N. Y. 1992) ··461
Energy Explorer, The, SMA 3033 (Arb. at N. Y. 1993) ··416
Epps v. Rothnie [1945] K. B. 562;114 L. J. K. B. 511;173 L. T. 353;61 T. L. R. 533;
　　[1946] 1 All E. R. 146, (C. A.) ··66
Epstein v. United States (1949) 86 F. Supp. 740 (S. D. N. Y.) ··346
Equilease Corp. v. The Sampson (1986) 793 F. 2d 598;1986 AMC 1826 (5th Cir.)
　　(en banc);cert. denied (1986) 479 U. S. 984 ··500
Erechthion, The—New Line v. Erechthion Shipping Co. S. A. [1987] 2 Lloyd's Rep.
　　180, (Q. B.); [1987] 1 F. T. L. R 525 ··196,198,219,**296**,297
Erie, The, SMA 497 (Arb. at N. Y. 1970) ··276
Erisort, The, SMA 1022 (Arb. at N. Y. 1976) ··414
Ert Stefanie, The—Société Anonyme des Minerais v. Grant Trading Inc. [1987] 2
　　Lloyd's Rep. 371; [1989] 1 Lloyd's Rep. 349, (C. A.) ··557,558
Essex Envoy, The (1929) 34 Ll. L. Rep. 191; 35 Com. Cas. 61; 141 L. T. 432; 18 Asp.
　　M. L. C. 54, (P. D. A.) ··368
Essi Gina, The, SMA 534 (Arb. at N. Y. 1970) ··**273**,275,276
Esso Petroleum Co. Ltd. v. Mardon [1976] 2 Lloyd's Rep. 305; [1976] Q. B. 801;
　　[1976] 2 W. L. R. 583; [1976] 2 All E. R. 5, (C. A.) ··84
Esso Standard Oil S. A. v. The Sabrina (1957) 154 F. Supp. 720; 1957 AMC 691 (D.
　　C. Z.) ···**203**
Etablissement Biret & Cie. S. A. v. Yukiteru Kauin KK and Nissui Shipping Corp.
　　—The Sun Happiness [1984] 1 Lloyd's Rep. 381, (Q. B.) ··64
Eugenia, The—Ocean Tramp Tankers Corp. v. V/O Sovfracht [1963] 2 Lloyd's Rep.
　　381; [1964] 2 Q. B. 226; [1964] 2 W. L. R. 114; [1964] 1 All E. R. 161, (C. A.);
　　rev'g [1963] 2 Lloyd's Rep. 155, (Q. B.) ········296,**397-398**,400,404,405,**408**,409,531,**567**
Eurogas, The, SMA 3005 (Arb. at N. Y. 1993) ··461
Eurolines Shipping Co. S. A. v. Metal Transp. Corp. (1980) 491 F. Supp. 590; 1980
　　AMC 2445 (S. D. N. Y.) ··462
European-American Banking Corp. v. The Rosaria (1978) 486 F. Supp. 245 (S. D.
　　Miss.) ···490,498,543
Eurotrader, The—Irish Agricultural Wholesale Society Ltd. v. Partenreederei M. S.
　　Eurotrader [1987] 1 Lloyd's Rep. 418, (C. A.) ··440
Eurymedon, The—New Zealand Shipping Co. Ltd. v. A. M. Satterthwaite & Co. Ltd.
　　[1974] 1 Lloyd's Rep. 534; [1975] A. C. 154; [1974] 2 W. L. R. 865; [1974] 1 All
　　E. R. 1015, (P. C.) ···334
Euryplus, The (1982) 677 F. 2d 225 (2d Cir.) ··428,429
Eurytan, The, SMA 289 (Arb. at N. Y. 1968) ··119
Eva Borden, The, SMA 219 (Arb. at N. Y.) ··207
Evaggelos Th, The—Vardinoyannis v. Egyptian General Petroleum Corp. [1971] 2
　　Lloyd's Rep. 200, (Q. B.) ··186,**194**,197,198
Evans (J.) & Sons (Portsmouth) Ltd. v. Andrea Merzario Ltd. [1976] 2 Lloyd's
　　Rep. 165; [1976] 1 W. L. R. 1078; [1976] 2 All E. R. 930, (C. A.) ··86

判 例 索 引

Evanthia M. The—Petroleo Brasileiro S. A.—Petrobas Fronto National de Petroleiros
—Fronape v. Elounda Shipping Co. [1985] 2 Lloyd's Rep. 154, (Q. B.) ············106,601
Evia, The (No. 2) —Kodros Shipping Corp. v. Empresa Cubana de Fletes [1982] 2
Lloyd's Rep. 307; [1983] 1 A. C. 736; [1982] 3 W. L. R. 637; [1982] 3 All E. R.
350, (H. L.); aff'g [1982] 1 Lloyd's Rep. 334, (C. A.); rev'g [1981] 2 Lloyd's Rep. 613,
(Q. B.) ···143, 178, 183, 184, 185, 186, **187-188**, 189, 190, 193, 194,
197, 400, 403, **404**, 407, 532, 564, 565, 567, **568**, 579, 581, 607, 609
Evra Corp. v. Swiss Bank Corp. (1981) 522 F. Supp. 820 (N. D. Ill.); rev'd (1982)
673 F. 2d 951 (7th Cir.) ···275
Evra Corp. v. Swiss Bank Corp. (1982) 673 F. 2d 951 (7th Cir); cert. denied (1982)
459 U. S. 1017··278
Evryalos, The, 1980 AMC 296 (S. D. N. Y. 1979) ···471
Excel Shipping Corp. v. Seatrain Int'l (1984) 584 F. Supp. 734; 1986 AMC 1587 (E.
D. N. Y.) ···340
Exercise Shipping Co. Ltd. v. Bay Maritime Lines Ltd.—The Fantasy [1992] 1
Lloyd's Rep. 235, (C. A.); aff'g [1991] 2 Lloyd's Rep. 391, (Q. B.) ···················308
Exi, The, SMA 2709 (Arb. at N. Y. 1990) ···345
Exmar N. V. v. BP Shipping Ltd.—The Gas Enterprise [1993] 2 Lloyd's Rep. 352, (C.
A.) ···106, 599
Exportkhleb v. Maistros Corp. (1992) 790 F. Supp. 70; 1992 AMC 1804 (S. D. N. Y.);
aff'd without opinion (1992) 979, F. 2d 845; 1993 AMC 608 (2d Cir.) ············452
Exxon Corp. v. Central Gulf Lines Inc. (1991) 780 F. Supp. 191; 1992 AMC 1660 (S.
D. N. Y.); (1991) 500 U. S. 603; 1991 AMC 1817 ···································500, 501

F. C. Bradley & Sons v. Federal Steam Navigation Co. (1927) 27 Ll. L. Rep. 221, 395;
137 L. T. 266; 17 Asp. M. L. C. 265, (H. L.); (1926) 24 Ll. L. Rep. 59, 446, (C. A.);
(1925) 22 Ll. L. Rep. 336, 424, (Q. B.) ···97
FFM Matarengi, The, SMA 2592 (Arb. at N. Y. 1988)························117, 118, 119
Fagan v. Green and Edwards Ltd. [1926] 1 K. B. 102; 134 L. T. 191; 95 L. J. K. B. 363,
(K. B.) ··423
Fahnestock & Co. v. Waltman (1991) 935 F. 2d 512 (2d Cir.); cert. denied (1991) 502
U. S. 942 and cert. denied (1992) 502 U. S. 1120; later proceedings (1992) 792 F.
Supp. 31 (E. D. Pa.); aff'd without opinion (1993) 989 F. 2d 490 (3d Cir.) ···········459
Fairlie v. Fenton (1870) L. R. 5 Ex. 169; 39 L. J. (Ex.) 107; 22 L. T. 373, (Exch.) ·········61
Falls of Keltie S. S. Co. v. United States & Australasia. S. S. Co. (1901) 108 F. 416
(S. D. N. Y.) ···118, 384
Family Anthony, The, SMA 1820 (Arb. at N. Y. 1983) ·····································382
Famosa Shipping Co. Ltd. v. Armada Bulk Carriers Ltd.-The Fanis [1994] 1 Lloyd's
Rep. 633, (Q. B.) ··161
Fanis, The—Famosa Shipping Co. Ltd. v. Armada Bulk Carriers Ltd. [1994] 1
Lloyd's Rep. 633, (Q. B.) ···161
Fantasy, The—Exercise Shipping Co. Ltd. v. Bay Maritime Lines Ltd. [1992] 1
Lloyd's Rep. 235, (C. A.); aff'g [1991] 2 Lloyd's Rep. 391, (Q. B.) ···················308

Farland, The—Nichimen Company v. The Farland (1972) 462 F. 2d 319 (2d Cir.)
....**316, 317,** 320, 431
Farrell Lines v. Nalfleet Bull & Roberts Inc. (1995) U. S. Dist. Lexis 1091 (S. D. N. Y.) 323
Father Thames, The [1979] 2 Lloyd's Rep. 364, (Q. B.) 529
Federal Calumet, The, SMA 1667 (Arb. at N. Y. 1982) 203
Federal Commerce & Navigation Co. Ltd. v. Associated Metals & Minerals Corp. 1979 AMC 1733 (S. D. N. Y. 1978) 457
Federal Commerce & Navigation Co. v. Kanematsu-Gosho Ltd. (1972) 457 F. 2d 387; 1972 AMC 946 (2d Cir.) 470
Federal Commerce & Navigation Co. v. The Marathonian (1975) 392 F. Supp. 908 (S. D. N. Y.); *aff'd per curiam* (1975) 528 F. 3d 907 (2d Cir.); *cert. denied* (1976) 425 U. S. 975 536
Federal Commerce & Navigation Co. Ltd. v. Molena Alpha Inc.—The Nanfri [1979] 1 Lloyd's Rep. 201; [1979] A. C. 757; [1978] 3 W. L. R. 991; [1979] 1 All E. R. 307, (H. L.); *aff'g* [1978] 2 Lloyd's Rep. 132; [1978] Q. B. 927; [1978] 3 W. L. R. 309; [1978] 3 All E. R. 1066, (C. A.); *rev'g* [1978] 1 Lloyd's Rep. 581, (Q. B.) 88, 99, **248,** 249-252, **325-326,** 327-329, **332,** 333, 482, 484, 486, 548
Federal Fraser, The, SMA 1804 (Arb. at N. Y. 1983) 361
Federal Insurance Co. v. Sabine Towing & Transp. Co. (1986) 783 F. 2d 347 (2d Cir.) 278
Federal Voyager, The, 1955 AMC 880 (Arb. at N. Y. 1953) 136, 138
Fenton v. Dublin S. S. (1838) 8 A. & E. 835 529
Fernandez v. Chios Shipping (1976) 71 Civ. 2786 (S. D. N. Y.) (unreported); *aff'd* (1976) 542 F. 2d 145 (2d Cir.) **320,** 321
Fernglen, The, 1971 AMC 213 (Arb. at N. Y. 1970) 172, 233, 288
Fertilizer Corp. of India v. IDI Management Inc. (1981) 517 F. Supp. 948 (S. D. Ohio); *reconsideration denied* (1982) 530 F. Supp. 542 (S. D. Ohio) 476, 477
Fibrosa Spolka Akcyina v. Fairbairn Lawson Combe Barbour [1943] A. C. 32; 111 L. J. K. B. 433; 167 L. T. 101; 58 T. L. R. 308; [1942] 2 All E. R. 122, (H. L.) **401,** 407
Ficus, The, SMA 2473 (Arb. at N. Y. 1988) 109
Field Line (Cardiff) Ltd. v. South Atlantic S. S. Line (1912) 201 F. 301 (5th Cir.) 344, **345**
Filikos Shipping Corp. v. Shipmair B. V.—The Filikos [1983] 1 Lloyd's Rep. 9, (C. A.); [1981] 2 Lloyd's Rep. 555, (Q. B.) 303, 305, 315, 547
Filikos, The—*See* Filikos Shipping Corp. v. Shipmair B. V.
Fina Samco, The—International Fina Services AG v. Katrina Shipping Ltd. and Tonen Tanker Kabushiki Kaisha [1995] 2 Lloyd's Rep. 344 (C. A.); [1994] 1 Lloyd's Rep. 153, (Q. B.) 574, **577-578,** 584, 594
Finagrain Compagnie Commerciale Agricole et Financiere S. A. v. Federal Commerce and Navigation (1974) Ltd. (1980) 80 Civ. 0839 (S. D. N. Y.) 457, 464, **473-474**
Finlay v. Liverpool and Great Western S. S. Co. Ltd. (1870) 23 L. T. 251; 3 Asp. M. L. C. (O. S.) 487, (Exch.) 421

Finnfalcon, The, SMA 2873 (Arb. at N. Y. 1992) ···322
Finora Co. v. Amitie Shipping Ltd. (1995) 54 F. 3d 209; 1995 U. S. App. Lexis 12110
　(4th Cir.); aff'g (1994) 852 F. Supp. 1298; 1995 AMC 607 (D. S. C. 1994) ············275, 495
Fiona, The—Mediterranean Freight Services Ltd. v. BP Oil International Ltd. [1994]
　2 Lloyd's Rep. 506, (C. A.); [1993] 1 Lloyd's Rep. 257, (Q. B.) ············168, 169, 604, **606**
First Energy (U. K.) v. Hungarian International Bank [1993] 2 Lloyd's Rep. 194;
　[1993] B. C. C. 533; [1993] B. C. L. C. 1409; [1993] N. P. C. 34, (C. A.) ·················69
First Options of Chicago Inc. v. Kaplan (1995) 514 U. S.—; 115 S. Ct.—; 131 L. Ed.
　1995 U. S. Lexis 2d. 985; aff'g (1994) 19 F. 3d 1503 (3d Cir.) ·····························455
Fisser v. International Bank (1960) 282 F. 2d 231 (2d Cir.) ··································**75**
Flagship Group v. Peninsula Cruise (1991) 771 F. Supp. 756; 1992 AMC 815 (E. D.
　Va.) ···500
Flash, The (1847) F. Cas. No. 4, 857 (S. D. N. Y.) ···339
Flat-Top Fuel Co. Inc. v. Martin (1936) 85 F. 2d 39; 1936 AMC 1296 (2d Cir.) ·········149
Flender Corp. v. Techna-Quip Co. (1992) 953 F. 2d 273 (7th Cir.) ·················470, 472
Fletcher (W. & R.) (New Zealand) Ltd. v. Sigurd Haavik Aksjeselskap—The
　Vikfrost [1980] 1 Lloyd's Rep. 560, (C. A.) ··147
Florosynth Inc. v. Pickholz (1984) 750 F. 2d 171 (2d Cir.) ···································464
Folkways Music Publishers Inc. v. Weiss (1993) 989 F. 2d 108 (2d Cir.) ···················473
Food Corp. of India v. Antclizo Shipping Corp.—The Antclizo [1988] 2 Lloyd's Rep.
　93; [1988] 1 W. L. R. 603; [1988] 2 All E. R. 513, (H. L.); [1987] 2 LIoyd's Rep.
　130, (C. A.) ··443
Forestships International Ltd. v. Armonia Shipping and Finance Corporation—The
　Ira [1995] 1 Lloyd's Rep. 103 ··365
Forsikringsaktieselskapet Vesta v. Butcher [1989] 1 Lloyd's Rep. 331; [1989] A. C.
　852; [1989] 2 W. L. R. 290; [1989] 1 All E. R. 402; 1989 Fin. L. R. 223; (1989)
　133 S. J. 184, (H. L.); aff'g [1988] 1 Lloyd's Rep. 19; [1988] 3 W. L. R. 565; [1988]
　2 All E. R. 43, (C. A.); [1988] 1 F. T. L. R. 78; [1988] F. L. R. 67, (C. A.); aff'g;
　[1986] 2 Lloyd's Rep. 179; [1986] 2 All E. R. 488, (Q. B.) ·····················307, 309, 310
Forsythe International (U. K.) Ltd. v. Silver Shipping Co. Ltd. and Petroglobe
　International Ltd.—The Saetta [1993] 2 Lloyd's Rep. 268; [1994] 1 W. L. R. 1334;
　[1994] 1 All E. R. 851, (Q. B.) ···228, **588-589**
Fort Gaines, The (1927) 21 F. 2d 865; 1927 AMC 1778 (D. Md.) ···························213
Fort Morgan S. S. Co. v. Baltimore & Jamaica Trad. Co. (1922) 284 F. 1 (4th Cir.) ···390
Foss Launch & Tug Co. v. Char Ching Shipping USA Ltd. (1987) 808 F. 2d 697;
　1987 AMC 913 (9th Cir.); certi. denied (1987) 484 U. S. 828 ······························500
Foster v. C. F. Turley Jr. (1986) 808 F. 2d 38 (10th Cir.) ······························464, 465
Fotochrome Inc. v. Copal Co. (1975) 517 F. 2d 512 (2d Cir.) ·······························476
Fowler (L. C.) & Sons Ltd. v. St. Stephen's College Board of Governors [1991] 3 N.
　Z. L. R. 304··62
France Fenwick v. The Crown [1927] 1 K. B. 458; (1926) 26 Ll. L. Rep. 52;
　[1926] W. N. 288; 43 T. L. R. 18; 96 L. J. K. B. 144; 32 Com. Cas. 116; 136 L. T. 358 ···608
Francosteel Corp. v. Tien Cheung (1973) 375 F. Supp. 794; 1973 AMC 2370 (S. D. N.

Y.) ··················524, **525**
Fraser v. Equitorial Shipping Co. Ltd.—The Ijaola [1979] 1 Lloyd's Rep. 103, (Q. B.) ···**64**
Fraser & White v. Bee (1900) 17 T. L. R. 101; 49 W. R. 336; 45 S. J. 102, (Q. B.)
 ··················**220**, 221, 376, 531
Freedom General Shipping S. A. v. Tokai Shipping Co. Ltd.-The Khian Zephyr
 [1982] 1 Lloyd's Rep. 73, (Q. B.) ··················**304**, 439
Freeman v. Reed (1863) 4 B. & S. 174; 32 L. J. M. C. 226; 10 Jur. (N. S.) 149; 122 E.
 R. 425 ··················**253**
Freeman & Lockyer v. Buckhurst Park Properties [1964] 2 Q. B. 480; [1964] 2 W.
 L. R. 618; [1964] 1 All E. R. 630, (C. A.) ··················**68**
Freights of the Kate, The (1894) 63 F. 707 (S. D. N. Y.) ··················**492**
French v. Newgass (1878) 3 C. P. D. 163; 47 L. J. C. P. 361; 38 L. T. 164; 3 Asp. M. L.
 C. 574, (C. A.) ··················**101**
French (L.) & Co. v. Leeston Shipping Co. (1922) 10 Ll. L. Rep. 448; [1922] 1 A. C.
 451; 27 Com. Cas. 257; 38 T. L. R. 459; 127 L. T. 169; 91 L. J. K. B. 655; 15 Asp. M. L.
 C. 544, (H. L.) ··················**541**
French Marine v. Compagnie Napolitaine d'Eclairage et de Chauffage par le Gas
 [1921] 2 A. C. 494; 27 Com. Cas. 69; 90 L. J. K. B. 1068; 125 L. T. 833; 37 T. L. R.
 923; 15 Asp. M. L. C. 358, (H. L.) ··················**487**
Fri, The (1907) 154 F. 333 (2d Cir.) ··················**339**
Fried, Krupp GmbH v. Solidarity Carriers Inc. (1987) 674 F. Supp. 1022; 1988 AMC
 1383 (S. D. N. Y.); aff'd without opinion (1987) 838 F. 2d 1202 (2d Cir.) ··················**78**
Fu Chiao, The, SMA 1089 (Arb. at N. Y. 1977) ··················**108**
Furness, Withy & Co. v. Rederi A/B Banco [1917] 2 K. B. 873; 23 Com. Cas. 99; 87
 L. J. K. B. 11; 117 L. T. 313; 14 Asp. M. L. C. 137, (K. B.) ··················**421**
Furness Withy (Australia) Pty. Ltd. v. Black Sea Shipping Co.—The Roman Karmen
 [1994] 1 Lloyd's Rep. 644, (Q. B.) ··················**282**

G. A. Tomlinson, The (1923) 293 F. 51 (W. D. N. Y.) ··················**342**, 343
G. G. Post, The (1945) 64 F. Supp. 191, (W. D. N. Y.) ··················**241**
Gabrielle Wesch, The, 1981 AMC 1324 (Arb. at N. Y. 1981) ··················**430**, 505
Gadd v. Houghton (1876) 1 Ex. D. 357; 46 L. J. (Ex.) 71; 35 L. T. 222, (C. A.) ··········**63**
Galahad, The, SMA 3057 (Arb. at N. Y. 1994) ··················**354**
Gans S. S. Line v. Wilhelmsen—The Themis (1921) 275 F. 254 (2d Cir.); cert. denied
 sub nom. Barber & Co. v. Wilhelmsen (1921) 257 U. S. 655 ··················**339**, 340, 427, 428
Garbis Maritime Corp. v. Philippine National Oil Co.—The Garbis [1982] 2 Lloyd's
 Rep. 283, (Q. B.) ··················**325**, 329
Garbis, The—Garbis Maritime Corp. v. Philippine National Oil Co. [1982] 2 Lloyd's
 Rep. 283, (Q. B.) ··················**325**, 329
Garden City, The [1982] 2 Lloyd's Rep. 382, (Adm.) ··················**559**
Gardner v. The Calvert (1958) 253 F. 2d 395 (3d Cir.); cert. denied (1958) 356 U. S.
 960 ··················**72**, 278
Garrett v. Moore-McCormack Co. (1942) 317 U. S. 239 ··················**56**

判 例 索 引

Garrity v. Lyle Stuart Inc. (1976) 40 N. Y 2d 354; (1976) 386 N. Y. S. 2d 831; 353
N. E. 2d 793 ···459
Gas Enterprise, The—Exmar N. V. v. BP Shipping Ltd. [1993] 2 Lloyd's Rep. 352, (C.
A.) ···106, 599
Gatoil Anstalt v. Omennial Ltd. —The Balder London [1980] 2 Lloyd's Rep. 489, (Q.
B.) ···**262**
Gatoil Anstalt v. Omennial Ltd. —The Balder London (No. 2) [1983] 1 Lloyd's Rep.
492, (Q. B.) ···87
Gator Shipping Corp. v. Trans-Asiatic Oil Ltd.—The Odenfeld [1978] 2 Lloyd's Rep.
357, (Q. B.) ···130, 236
Gazelle, The (1888) 128 U. S. 474 ··**201**
Geipel v. Smith (1872) L. R. 7 Q. B. 404; 41 L. J. Q. B. 153; 26 L. T. 361; 1 Asp. M. L.
C. 268, (Q. B.) ···403
Gemini Shipping v. Seas Shipping, SMA 1253 (Arb. at N. Y. 1978) ···············414
Geogas SA v. Trammo Gas—The Baleares [1991] 2 Lloyd's Rep. 318; [1991] 1 W. L.
R. 776; [1991] 3 All E. R. 554; (1991) 135 S. J. (LB) 101; (1991) 141 New L. J.
1037, (H. L.); aff'g [1991] 1 Lloyd's Rep. 349; [1991] 2 Q. B. 139; [1991] 2 W. L.
R. 794; [1991] 2 All E. R. 710, (C. A.); rev'g [1990] 2 Lloyd's Rep. 130, (Q. B.) ······446
George J. Goulandris, The (1941) 36 F. Supp. 827; 1941 AMC 1804 (D. Me.) ······429, 570
George Mitchell (Chesterhall) Ltd. v. Finney Lock Seeds Ltd. [1983] 2 Lloyd's Rep.
272; [1983] A. C. 803; [1983] 3 W. L. R. 163; [1983] 2 All E. R. 737, (H. L.);
[1983] 1 Lloyd's Rep. 168; [1983] Q. B. 284, (C. A.); [1981] 1 Lloyd's Rep. 476,
(Q. B.) ··426
George Vergottis, The, SMA 1214 (Arb. at N. Y. 1978) ······························503
Georges Christos Lemos, The, (third party proceedings) [1991] 2 Lloyd's Rep. 107
··293, 295, 299
Georgios, The, SMA 2005 (Arb. at N. Y. 1984) ··116
Georgios C., The—Empresa Cubana de Fletes v. Lagonisi Shipping Co. Ltd. [1971] 1
Lloyd's Rep. 7; [1971] 1 Q. B. 488; [1971] 2 W. L. R. 221; [1971] 1 All E. R. 193,
(Q. B. and C. A.) ···87, 244, 257, 258, 268, 548
Gerani Compania Naviera S. A. v. General Organisation for Supply Goods and Alfred
C. Toepfer—The Demonsthenes V (No. 1) [1982] 1 Lloyd's Rep. 275, (Q. B.) ···158, 358
Gerber & Co. v. The Sabine Howaldt (1970) 437 F. 2d 580 (2d Cir.) ···············431
Gerdt Oldendorff, The, SMA 1981 (Arb. at N. Y. 1984) ······························241
Gesellschaft Bürgerlichen Rechts and Others v. Stockholms Rederiaktiebolag Svea—
The Brabant [1965] 2 Lloyd's Rep. 546; [1967] 1 Q. B. 588; [1966] 2 W. L. R.
909; [1966] 1 All E. R. 961, (Q. B.) ···556, **557**, 560
Getty Oil Co. v. Norse Management Co. (Pte.) Ltd. (1989) 711 F. Supp. 175 (S. D. N.
Y.) ···71
Gewa Chartering B. V. v. Remco Shipping Lines Ltd.—The Remco [1984] 2 Lloyd's
Rep. 205, (Q. B.) ··**65**
Ghikas, The, SMA 686 (Arb. at N. Y. 1972) ··116
Giannis N. K., The [1994] 2 Lloyd's Rep. 171, (Q. B.) ·······························168, 169

Giertsen v. George Turnbull & Co., 1908 S. C. 1101 ; 45 Sc. L. R. 916 ; 16 S. L. T. 250,
(Ct. of Sess.) ···97, 154, 211, 369
Gilbert-Ash (Northern) Ltd. v. Modern Engineering (Bristol) Ltd. [1974] A. C. 689 ;
[1973] 3 W. L. R. 421 ; [1973] 3 All E. R. 195 ; 72 L. G. R. 1, (H. L.) ·······················250
Gilla, The, 1972 AMC 1738 (Arb. at N. Y. 1972) ··361
Gill & Duffus v. Société pour l'Exportation des Sucres S. A. [1986] 1 Lloyd's Rep.
322, (C. A.); [1985] 1 Lloyd's Rep. 621, (Q. B.) ···91
Giovanna Lolli-ghetti, The, 1974 AMC 2161 (Arb. at N. Y.) ·································417
Giulia, The (1914) 218 F. 744 (2d Cir.) ···431
Glasgow Shipowner's Co. v. Bacon (1905) 139 F. 541 (2d Cir.) ·····························117
Glidden Co. v. Hellenic Lines Ltd. (1960) 275 F. 2d 253 (2d Cir.) ··························412
Glynn v. Margetson & Co. [1893] A. C. 351 ; 62 L. J. Q. B. 466 ; 69 L. T. 1 ; 9 T. L. R.
437 ; 7 Asp. M. L. C. 366, (H. L.) ···424, 425
Glynn v. United Steel Works Corp. (1935) 160 Misc. 405 ; 289 N. Y. S. 1037 (Sup.
Ct.) ···415
Glynwed Steels Limited v. Great Lakes and European Lines Inc., 1979 AMC 1290
(N. D. Ill. 1978) ···340, 342
Golar Kansai, The, SMA 1263 (Arb. at N. Y. 1978) ·······································627, 628, 629
Golden Chase Steamship Inc. v. Valmar de Navegacion S. A. (1984) 724 F. 2d 129 ;
1984 AMC 2040 (5th Cir.) (per curiam) ··73
Golden Dolphin, The, SMA 2797 (Arb. at N. Y. 1987) ··164
Golden Eagle Liberia Ltd. v. Amoco Transport Co. (1979) 422 N. Y. 2d 270 ; 1979
AMC 698 (N. Y. County, Special Term, Part 1, 1979) ·····································464
Golden Gate, The, SMA 2188 (Arb. at N. Y. 1986) ··417
Golden Shimizu, The, SMA 2991 (Arb. at N. Y. 1993) ··351
Goldsmith v. Rodger [1962] 2 Lloyd's Rep. 249, (C. A.) ··82
Golfstraum, The—Anders Utkilens Rederi A/S v. Compagnie Tunisienne de
Navigation [1976] 2 Lloyd's Rep. 97, (Q. B.) ··546
Gonzalez v. Industrial Bank (1962) 12 N. Y. 2d 33 ; 234 N. Y. S. 2d 210 ·················415
Good Helmsman, The—Harmony Shipping Co. S. A. v. Saudi-Europe Line Ltd. [1981] 1
Lloyd's Rep. 377, (C. A.) ···228, 368, 372, 542
Goodbody & Co. v. Balfour, Williamson & Co. (Re) (1899) 5 Com. Cas. 59 ; 82 L. T.
484 ; 9 Asp. M. L. C. 69, (C. A.) ···180
Goodpasture Inc. v. The Pollux (1979) 602 F. 2d 84 ; 1979 AMC 2515 reh. denied ;
(1979) 606 F. 2d 321 (5th Cir.) ···492
Gota River, The, SMA 1241 (Arb. at N. Y. 1978) ··416
Goulandris v. Goldman [1957] 2 Lloyd's Rep. 207 ; [1958] 1 Q. B. 74 ; [1957] 3 W. L.
R. 596 ; [1957] 3 All E. R. 100 ; 101 S. J. 762, (Q. B.) ·······································604
Government of Ceylon v. Société Franco-Tunisienne d'Armement-Tunis—The Massalia
(No. 2) [1960] 2 Lloyd's Rep. 352 ; [1962] 2 Q. B. 416 ; [1961] 2 W. L. R. 161 ;
[1960] 3 All E. R. 797, (Q. B.) ···358
Government of India v. Cargill (1989) 867 F. 2d 130 (2d Cir.) ·······················450, 471, 473
Government of the Republic of Spain v. North of England S. S. Co. (1938) 61 Ll. L.

Rep. 44 ; 54 T. L. R. 852, (K. B.) ··**569**
Government of the United Kingdom of Great Britain v. Boeing Co. (1993) 998 F. 2d
  68 ; 1993 AMC 2913 (2d Cir.) ···**79**, 452, 453
Gow v. Gans S. S. Line (1909) 174 F. 215 (2d Cir.) ·····································381
Grace (G. W.) & Co. Ltd. v. General Steam Navigation Co.—The Sussex Oak (1950)
  83 Ll. L. Rep. 297 ; [1950] 2 K. B. 383 ; 66 T. L. R. (Pt. 1) 147 ; [1950] 1 All E. R.
  201, (K. B.) ··141, 165, 179, **180, 183**, 190, 292, 564, **565**
Grace Lines Inc. v. Central Gulf S. S. Corp. (1969) 416 F. 2d 977 (5th Cir.); *cert.*
  denied (1970) 398 U. S. 939 ···525
Grace V, The, SMA 1760 (Arb. at N. Y. 1982) ··**116**, 381
Grampian Steamship Co. v. Carver & Co. (1893), 9 T. L. R. 210 ·······················155
Grand, The, SMA 2548 (Arb. at N. Y. 1989) ···118
Grand Champion Tankers Ltd. v. Norpipe A/S—The Marion [1984] 2 Lloyd's Rep. 1 ;
  [1984] A. C. 563 ; [1984] 2 W. L. R. 942 ; [1984] 2 All E. R. 243, (H. L.) ; [1983] 2
  Lloyd's Rep. 156, (C. A.) ; [1982] 2 Lloyd's Rep. 52, (Q. B.) ·······························557, 559
Grand Explorer, The, SMA 551 (Arb. at N. Y. 1963) ···108, 163
Grand Integrity, The, SMA 671 (Arb. at N. Y. 1971) ···116
Grand Zenith, The, 1979 AMC 2179 (Arb. at N. Y.) ; SMA 2186 (Arb. at N. Y. 1986)
  ···417
Granit v. Benship International [1994] 1 Lloyd's Rep. 526, (Q. B.) ·························54
Granite State Insur. Co. v. The Caraibe (1993) 825 F. Supp. 1113 ; 1994 AMC 680 (D.
  P. R.) ···522
Gray & Co. v. Christie & Co. (1889) 5 T. L. R. 577, (Q. B.) ··································**126**
Gray (P. N.) & Co. v. Cavalliotis (1921) 276 F. 565 (E. D. N. Y.) ; *aff'd without opinion*
  (1923) 293 F. 1018 (2d Cir.) ···415
Great Circle Lines Ltd. v. Matheson & Co. Ltd., 1982 AMC 567 (S. D. N. Y. 1981),
  aff'd (1982) 681 F. 2d 121 ; 1982 AMC 2321 (2d Cir.) ···························55, 59, 60
Green and Silley Weir v. British Railways Board (1980) *The Times*, 8 October 1980 ;
  [1980] 17 B. L. R. 94 ··553
Greenwell v. Ross (1888) 34 F. 656 (Ed. D. La.) ···162
Greenwich Marine Inc. v. Federal Commerce & Navigation Co. Ltd.—The Mavro
  Vetranic [1985] 1 Lloyd's Rep. 580, (Q. B.) ···91
Gregos, The—Torvald Klaverness v. Arni Maritime [1995] 1 Lloyd's Rep. 1 ; [1994]
  1 W. L. R. 1465 ; [1994] 4 All E. R. 998 ; (1994) 144 New L. J. 1550, (H. L.) ; *rev'g*
  [1994] 1 Lloyd's Rep. 335, (C. A.) ; *rev'g* [1992] 2 Lloyd's Rep. 40, (Q. B.)
  ···122, **123-124, 125**, 127, 190, 192, 549
Griparion, The [1994] 1 Lloyd's Rep. 533, (Q. B.) ·······································130, 237
Groves, Maclean & Co. v. Volkart Bros. (1884) C. & E. 309 ; (1885) 1 T. L. R. 454,
  (C. A.) ; *aff'g* (1884) 1 T. L. R. 92, (Q. B.) ···155
Grow v. Steel Gas Screw Loraine K (1962) 310 F. 2d 547 ; 1963 AMC 2044 (6th
  Cir.) ···501
Guldborg, The, 1932 AMC 1206 (S. D. N. Y.) ···215
Gulf Oil Trading Co. v. The Caribe Mar (1985) 757 F. 2d 743 ; 1985 AMC 2726

(5th Cir.) ··502
Gulf Oil Trading Co. v. The Freedom, 1988 AMC 2738 (D. Or. 1985) ···············502
Gulf Pacific, The, SMA 3036 (Arb. at N. Y. 1993) ··································72, 73, 354
Gulf Sea, The, SMA 3095 (Arb. at N. Y. 1994) ···413
Gulf Shipping Lines Ltd. v. Compania Naviera Alanje S. A.-The Aspa Maria [1976]
　2 Lloyd's Rep. 643, (C. A.) ···**353**
Gulf Steel Co. Ltd. v. Al Khalifa Shipping Co. Ltd.—The Anwar Al Sabar [1980] 2
　Lloyd's Rep. 261, (Q. B.) ···325
Gulf Trading v. The Tento, 1979 AMC 753 (N. D. Cal.) ·····································502
Gulf Trading & Transp. Co. v. The Hoegh Shield (1981) 658 F. 2d 363; 1982 AMC
　1138 (5th Cir.) ··500, 503
Gyda, The (1969) 406 F. 2d 1039; 1971 AMC 2070 (6th Cir.) ····························175

H. Schuldt v. Standard Fruit & Steamship Co., 1979 AMC 2470 (S. D. N. Y. 1978)
　··202, 225, 537
H. L. Bolton (Engineering) Co. Ltd. v. T. J. Graham & Sons Ltd. [1975] 1 Q. B. 159;
　[1956] 3 W. L. R. 804; [1956] 3 All E. R. 624, (C. A.) ······································558
H. R. Macmillan, The—Canadian Pacific (Bermuda) Ltd. v. Canadian Transport Co.
　Ltd. [1974] 1 Lloyd's Rep. 311, (C. A.); aff'g [1973] 1 Lloyd's Rep. 27, (Q. B.)
　··365, 368, 378
Hadley v. Baxendale (1854) 9 Ex. 341; 156 E. R. 145 ···························275, 277, 446
Halcoussis Shipping Ltd. v. Golden Eagle Liberia Ltd. (1989) U. S. Dist. Lexis 11401
　(S. D. N. Y.) ···476
Halcyon Isle, The—Bankers Trust International Ltd. v. Todd Shipyards Corp. [1980]
　2 Lloyd's Rep. 325; [1981] A. C. 221; [1980] 3 W. L. R. 400; [1980] 3 All E. R.
　197, (P. C.) ···488
Halcyon S. S. Co. Ltd. v. Continental Grain Co. (1943) 75 Ll. L. Rep. 80; [1943] K. B.
　355; 112 L. J. K. B. 382; 168 L. T. 349; 59 T. L. R. 278; [1943] 1 All E. R. 558, (C.
　A.) ···141, 247, 249, 329
Hale v. Co-Mar Offshore Corp. 1986 AMC 1620 (W. D. La.) ·······························56
Halekulani, The, SMA 1633 (Arb. at N. Y. 1981) ···626
Halifax, The and The White Sea, SMA 2984 (Arb. at N. Y. 1993) ······················384
Hall Bros. S. S. Co. Ltd. v. R. & W. Paul Ltd. (1914) 19 Com. Cas. 384; 111 L. T. 811;
　30 T. L. R. 598; 12 Asp. M. L. C. 543, (K. B.) ··**180**, 191
Hall Corp. v. Cargo ex steamer Mont Louis (1933) 62 F. 2d 603 (2d Cir.) ············493
Hallborg, The, SMA 2639 (Arb. at N. Y. 1990) ···461
Haluapo v. Akashi Kaiun, K. K. S. A. M. Inc. (1984) 748 F. 2d 1363; 1985 AMC 1107
　(9th Cir.) ···320
Hamilton & Co. v. Mackie & Sons (1889) 5 T. L. R. 677, (C. A.) ························516
Hamilton, Fraser & Co. v. Pandorf & Co. (1887) 12 App. Cas. 518; 57 L. J. Q. B. 24;
　57 L. T. 726; 3 T. L. R. 768; 6 Asp. M. L. C. 212, (H. L.) ·····································422
Hamlet, The, SMA 2780 (Arb. at N. Y. 1991) ···272
Hammonds v. Barclay (1802) 2 East 227; 102 E. R. 356 ······································480

Hanak v. Green [1958] 2 Q.B. 9; [1958] 2 W.L.R. 755; [1958] 2 All E.R. 141, (C.
 A.) ···250
Handy Leader, The, SMA—(Arb. at N.Y. 1995) ···133
Hannah Blumenthal, The—Paal Wilson & Co. A/S v. Partenreederei Hannah
 Blumenthal [1983] 1 Lloyd's Rep. 103; [1983] 1 A.C. 854; [1982] 3 W.L.R. 1149,
 (H.L.); [1982] 1 Lloyd's Rep. 582; [1982] 3 W.L.R. 49, (C.A.); [1981] 2 Lloyd's
 Rep. 438; [1981] 3 W.L.R. 823; [1982] 1 All E.R. 197, (Q.B.) ·······························443
Hans Leonhardt, The, SMA 2820 (Arb. at N.Y. 1991) ···345
Hans Sachs, The, SMA 1493 (Arb. at N.Y. 1980) ···137
Hansa Nord, The—Cehave N.V. v. Bremer Handelsgesellschaft m.b.H. [1975] 2
 Lloyd's Rep. 445; [1976] Q.B. 44; [1975] 2 W.L.R. 447; [1975] 3 All E.R. 739,
 (C.A.) ···89, 90
Hansen v. Harrold Bros. [1894] 1 Q.B. 612; 63 L.J.Q.B. 744; 70 L.T. 475; 10 T.L.R.
 327; 7 Asp. M.L.C. 464, (C.A.) ··325, 333
Hanskar Shipping Co. v. Iron Ore Co. of Canada, 1980 AMC 1249 (S.D.N.Y.) ··········450
Happy Empress, The, SMA 2599 (Arb. at N.Y. 1989) ···118
Har Rai, The, SMA 1868 (Arb. at N.Y. 1983) ···134
Harbutt's Plasticine Ltd. v. Wayne Tank & Pump Co. Ltd. [1970] 1 Lloyd's Rep. 15;
 [1970] 1 Q.B. 447; [1970] 2 W.L.R. 198; [1970] 1 All E.R. 225, (C.A.) ·······425, 426
Harding, The, SMA 959 (Arb. at N.Y. 1975) ···203
Hargreaves Transport Ltd. v. Lynch [1969] 1 W.L.R. 215; [1969] 1 All E.R. 455;
 20 P. & C.R. 143, (C.A.) ···52
Harmony Shipping Co. S.A. v. Saudi-Europe Line Ltd.—The Good Helmsman [1981]
 1 Lloyd's Rep. 377, (C.A.) ···228, 368, 372, 542
Harpagus, The, SMA 323 (Arb. at N.Y. 1868) ···58
Harper & Co. v. Vigers Brothers [1909] 2 K.B. 549; 100 L.T. 887; 25 T.L.R. 627;
 14 Com. Cas. 213; 78 L.J.K.B. 867; 11 Asp. M.L.C. 275, (K.B.) ·······················61, **66**
Harris v. S.P. Shipping (1993) 818 F. Supp. 149; 1993 AMC 1558 (E.D. Va.) ············321
Harrison v. Huddersfield Steamship (1903) 19 T.L.R. 386 ···334
Hart Enterprises Int'l Inc. v. Anhui Provincial Import & Export Corp. (1995) U.S.
 Dist. Lexis 7432 (S.D.N.Y.) ···447
Hartbridge, The (1932) 57 F. 2d 672 (2d Cir.); cert. denied sub nom. Munson S.S.
 Line v. North England S.S. Co. (1933) 288 U.S. 601 ··464
Hartford Fire Insurance Co. v. Calmar S.S. Corp. (1975) 404 F Supp. 442; 1976
 AMC 2636 (W.D. Wash.); aff'd (1977) 554 F. 2d 1068 (9th Cir.) ······················111, 522
Hasbro Industries Inc. v. The St. Constantine, 1980 AMC 1425 (D. Hawaii) ············523
Haverton, The, SMA 743 (Arb. at N.Y. 1973) ···233
Hayes v. Wilh.Wilhelmsen Enterprises Ltd. (1987) 818 F. 2d 1557; 1988 AMC 259
 (11th Cir.) ···321
Hayn v. Culliford (1879) 4 C.P.D. 182 (C.A.); (1878) 3 C.P.D. 410 ···························264
Hayn Roman & Co. S.A. v. Cominter (U.K.) Ltd. [1982] 1 Lloyd's Rep. 295, (Q.B.)
 ···444
Hector Steamship v. V/O Sovfracht (1945) 78 Ll.L. Rep. 275; [1945] K.B. 343; 172

L. T. 268; 61 T. L. R. 264, (K. B.) ···122, 549
Hedley Byrne & Co. Ltd. v. Heller & Partners Ltd. [1963] 1 Lloyd's Rep. 485;
 [1964] A. C. 465; [1963] 3 W. L. R. 101; [1963] 2 All E. R. 575, (H. L.) ·········84, 310
Heidberg, The—Partenreederei M/S Heidberg v. Grosvenor Grain and Feed Co. Ltd.
 [1994] 2 Lloyd's Rep. 287; [1993] 2 Lloyd's Rep. 324, (Q. B.) ·······························439
Heilgers & Co. v. Cambrian Steam Navigation Co. Ltd. (1917) 34 T. L. R. 72, (C. A.)
 ···400
Heinz Horn, The (1968) 404 F. 2d 412; 1968 AMC 2548 (5th Cir.); cert. denied
 (1969) 394 U. S. 943···112
Helen Miller, The—St. Vincent Shipping Co. Ltd. v. Bock, Godeffroy & Co. [1980] 2
 Lloyd's Rep. 95, (Q. B.) ···143, 195, 532
Helindas, The, SMA 1589 (Arb. at N. Y. 1981) ···279
Hellas in Eternity, The, LMLN 221—23 April 1988 ···304
Helle Skou, The—Sofial S. A. v. Ove Skou Rederi [1976] 2 Lloyd's Rep. 205, (Q. B.)
 ···282, 358
Hellenic Bulk Transport S. A. v. Burmah Oil Tankers Ltd., SMA 1086 (Arb. at N. Y.
 1976) ···116
Helvetia-S, The—Christie & Vesey Ltd. v. Maatschappij Tot Exploitatie Van Schepen
 en Andere Zaken Helvetia N. V. [1960] 1 Lloyd's Rep. 540, (Q. B.) ········557, 570, 571
Henderson v. Merrett Syndicates Ltd. [1994] 3 W. L. R. 761 (H. L.); [1994] 2
 Lloyd's Rep. 193; [1994] 3 All E. R. 506, (H. L.) ···86, 310
Henrik Sif, The [1982] 1 Lloyd's Rep. 456, (Q. B.) ··69
Henriksens Rederi A/S v. T. H. Z. Rolimpex—The Brede [1973] 2 Lloyd's Rep. 333;
 [1974] Q. B. 233; [1973] 3 W. L. R. 556; [1973] 3 All E. R. 589, (C. A.) ···············249
Hercules Inc. v. Stevens Shipping Co. Inc. (1983) 698 F. 2d 726; 1983 AMC 1786
 (5th Cir.) (en banc) ···525
Hermine, The—Unitramp v. Garnac Grain Co. Inc. [1979] 1 Lloyd's Rep. 212. (C. A.);
 rev'g [1978] 2 Lloyd's Rep. 37, (Q. B.) ···177, 179, 183
Hermosa, The—Chilean Nitrate Sales Corp. v. Marine Transportation Co. Ltd. [1982]
 1 Lloyd's Rep. 570, (C. A.); aff'g [1980] 1 Lloyd's Rep. 638, (Q. B.)
 ···99, 100, 161, 212, 364, 517
Heron II, The—Czarnikow Ltd. v. Koufos [1967] 2 Lloyd's Rep. 457; [1967] 2 W. L.
 R. 1491; [1967] 3 All E. R. 686; [1969] 1 A. C. 350, (H. L.); [1966] 1 Lloyd's
 Rep. 595; [1966] 2 Q. B. 695; [1966] 2 W. L. R. 1397; [1966] 2 All E. R. 593, (C.
 A.); [1966] 1 Lloyd's Rep. 259, (Q. B.) ···92, 358
Hidrocarburos y Derivados C. A. v. Lemos (1978) 453 F. Supp. 160 (S. D. N. Y.) ······71, 74
Hildebrand v. Geneva Mill Co.—The Edward R. Smith (1929) 32 F. 3d 343; 1929
 AMC 962 (M. D. Ala.) ···111
Hill Steam Shipping Co. v. Hugo Stinnes Ltd., 1941 S. C. 324 ···65
Hillas & Co. Ltd. v. Arcos Ltd. (1932) 43 Ll. L. Rep. 359; 38 Com. Cas. 23; 147 L. T.
 503, (H. L.) ··49-50
Himoff Indus. v. Seven Seas Shipping Corp., 1976 AMC 1030 (N. Y. Sup. 1976) ···58, 119
Hines v. British Steel Corp. (1990) 907 F. 2d 726; 1990 AMC 2986 (7th Cir.) ·········321

Hira II, The, SMA 2246 (Arb. at N.Y. 1986) ··386
Hirji Mulji and Others v. Cheong Yue S.S. Co. [1926] A.C. 497; 24 Ll. L. Rep. 210; 42
　　T. L. R. 359; 31 Com. Cas. 199; 17 Asp. M. L. C. 8, (H. L.) ·························**394**
Hispanica de Petroleos S. A. and Compania Iberica Refinadera S. A. v. Vencedora
　　Oceanica Navegacion S. A.; Same v. Same and West of England Ship Owners
　　Mutual Protection and Indemnity Association (Luxembourg) —The Kapetan
　　Markos N. L. (No. 2) [1987] 2 Lloyd's Rep. 321, (C. A.) ····························334
Hoegh Mallard, The, SMA 2679 (Arb. at N.Y. 1990) ·······························225, 386
Hofflinghouse & Co. Ltd. v. C-Trade S. A.—The Intra Transporter [1986] 2 Lloyd's
　　Rep. 132, (C. A.); [1985] 2 Lloyd's Rep. 158, (Q. B.) ································54
Hogarth v. Alexander Miller, Brothers & Co. [1891] A.C. 48; 60 L. J. P. C. 1; 64 L. T.
　　205; 7 T. L. R. 120; 7 Asp. M. L. C. 1, (H. L.) ·································**364**, 367, 371
Holborn Oil Trading Ltd. v. Interpetrol Bermuda Ltd. (1991) 774 F. Supp. 840; 1992
　　AMC 819 (S. D. N. Y.) ···**76-77**
Holland, The, SMA 2114 (Arb. at N.Y. 1985) ···319
Holstencruiser, The—A/S Iverans Rederei v. KG M. S. Holstencruiser
　　Seeschiffahrtsgesellschaft m. b. H. & Co. [1992] 2 Lloyd's Rep. 378 ···················313
Hongkong Fir Shipping Co. Ltd. v. Kawasaki Kisen Kaisha—The Hongkong Fir
　　[1961] 2 Lloyd's Rep. 478; [1962] 2 Q. B. 26; [1962] 2 W. L. R. 474; [1962] 1 All
　　E. R. 474, (C. A.); aff'g [1961] 1 Lloyd's Rep. 159; [1961] 2 W. L. R. 716; [1961] 2
　　All E. R. 257, (Q. B.) ·····················88, 89, 90, 91, 92, **97-98**, 99, 100, 154, 160, 161, 212, 559
Hongkong Fir, The—Hongkong Fir Shipping Co. Ltd. v. Kawasaki K.K. [1961] 2
　　Lloyd's Rep. 478; [1962] 2 Q. B. 26; [1962] 2 W. L. R. 474; [1962] 1 All E. R.
　　474, (C. A.); aff'g [1961] 1 Lloyd's Rep. 159; [1961] 2 W. L. R. 716; [1961] 2 All
　　E. R. 257, (Q. B.) ······················88, 89, 90, 91, 92, **97-98**, 99, 100, 154, 160, 161, 212, 559
Hopeville, The, 1968 AMC 2650 (Arb. at N.Y.) ··284
Horlock v. Beal [1916] 1 A.C. 486; 85 L. J. K. B. 602; 114 L. T. 193; 32 T. L. R. 251; 21
　　Com. Cas. 201; 13 Asp. M. L. C. 250, (H. L.) ···403
Horn v. Cia. de Navegacion Fruco S. A.—The Heinz Horn (1968) 404 F. 2d 412;
　　1968 AMC 2548 (5th Cir.); cert. denied (1969) 394 U. S. 943 ·························112
Houda, The—Kuwait Petroleum Corporation v. I & D Oil Carriers Ltd. [1994] 2
　　Lloyd's Rep. 541. (C. A.); rev'g [1993] 1 Lloyd's Rep. 333, (Q. B.) ···291, **292**, 585, **587**, 595
Houston City, The—Reardon Smith Line v. Australian Wheat Board [1956] 1 Lloyd's
　　Rep. 1; [1956] A.C. 266; [1956] 2 W. L. R. 403; [1956] 1 All E. R. 456, (P. C.);
　　rev'g [1954] 2 Lloyd's Rep. 148 (High Ct. Aust.); restoring [1953] 1 Lloyd's Rep.
　　131 ··**182**, 184, 190, 192, 195, 197
Howard Marine & Dredging Co. Ltd. v. A. Ogden (Excavations) Ltd. [1978] 1
　　Lloyd's Rep. 334; [1978] Q. B. 574; [1978] 2 W. L. R. 515; [1978] 2 All E. R.
　　1134, (C. A.) ···52, 84, 85
Hsing May, The, SMA 3019 (Arb. at N.Y. 1993) ···428
Hudson Trading Co. v. Hasler & Co. Inc. (1926) 11 F. 2d 666 (S. D. N. Y.) ················71
Hudson Valley Light Weight Aggregate Corp. v. Windsor Bldg. & Supply Co. (1971)
　　446 F. 2d 750 (2d Cir.) ··240

Hughes v. Metropolitan Railway (1877) 2 App. Cas. 439; 46 L. J. C. P. 583; 36 L. T.
932, (H. L.) ···92
Humble v. Hunter (1848) 12 Q. B. 310; 17 L. J. Q. B. 350; 11 L. T. O. S. 265; 12 Jur.
1021; 116 E. R. 885 ··66
Humble Oil & Refining Co. v. Philadelphia Ship Maintenance Co. (1971) 444 F. 2d
727 (3rd Cir.) ···323
Hurley (J. E.) Lumber Co. v. Compania Panamena Maritima San Gerassimo S. A.,
1958 AMC 2502 (Arb. at N. Y.) ···114
Hurst v. Usborne (1856) 18 C. B. 144; 25 L. J. C. P. 209; 27 L. T. O. S. 80; 139 E. R.
1321, (C. P.) ···101
Hygrade Operators Inc. and Leevac Marine Inc. (In the matter of), SMA 2851 (Arb.
at N. Y. 1992)··240
Hyundai Corp. USA v. Hull Ins. Proceeds of The Vulca (1992) 800 F. Supp. 124;
1993 AMC 434 (D. N. J.); aff'd 54 F. 3d 768; (1995) U. S. App. Lexis 11714 (3d
Cir.) ··149, 342, 522
Hyundai Merchant Marine v. Gesuri Chartering—The Peonia [1991] 1 Lloyd's Rep.
100, (C. A. & Q. B.) ··121, **122-123**, 128, 129, 549, 590

I/S Stavborg v. National Metal Converters Inc. (1974) 500 F. 2d 424 (2d Cir.) ···462, **473**
Ijaola, The—Fraser v. Equitorial Shipping Co. Ltd. [1979] 1 Lloyd's Rep. 103, (Q. B.) ···64
Iligan International Corp. v. The John Weyerhaeuser (1974) 372 F. Supp. 859; 1974
AMC 1719 (S. D. N. Y.); aff'd (1974) 507 F. 2d 68 (2d Cir.); cert. denied (1974) 421
U. S. 956 ··112, 163
Ilissos, The—Royal Greek Government v. Minister of Transport (1948) 82 Ll. L. Rep.
196; [1949] 1 K. B. 525; [1949] L. J. R. 670; 65 T. L. R. 32; [1949] 1 All E. R. 171,
(C. A.); aff'g (1948) 81 Ll. L. Rep. 355; [1949] 1 K. B. 7; 64 T. L. R. 283; [1948] 1
All E. R. 904, (K. B.) ···363, **368**, 554
Imperial Ethiopian Gov't v. Baruch-Foster Corp. (1976) 535 F. 2d 334, 335 n. 2 (5th
Cir.) ··475
Independence, The, SMA 3049 (Arb. at N. Y. 1994) ················58, 60, 72, 73, 78, 278, 279
Induna (Steamship) Co. Ltd. v. British Phosphate Commissioners (1949) 82 Ll. L.
Rep. 430; [1949] 2 K. B. 430; [1949] L. J. R. 1058; 65 T. L. R. 149; [1949] 1 All E.
R. 522, (K. B.) ···421
Indussa Corp. v. The Ranborg (1967) 377 F. 2d 200; 1967 AMC 589 (2d Cir.) ···448, **527**
Industrial y Frutera Colombiana S. A. v. The Brisk (1952) 195 F. 2d 1015; 1952
AMC 738 (5th Cir.) ···460
Industrie Chimiche Italia Centrale S. p. A. v. Nea Ninemia Shipping Co. S. A.—The
Emmanuel C [1983] 1 Lloyd's Rep. 310, (Q. B.) ···422, 605
Inman S. S. Co. Ltd. v. James Bischoff (1882) 7 App. Cas. 670; 47 L. T. 581; 52 L. J.
Q. B. 169; 5 Asp. M. L. C. 6, (H. L.) ···**482**
Instituto Cubano de Estab. v. The Theotokos (1957) 153 F. Supp. 85 (S. D. N. Y.)
(before trial); 155 F. Supp. 945 (S. D. N. Y.) (after trial) ·······································71
Instituto Cubano de Est. del Azucar v. The Golden West (1957) 246 F. 2d 802; 1957

判例索引   71

AMC 1481 (2d Cir.); *certi. denied* (1957) 355 U. S. 884 ·······················339
Insurance Company of North America *v.* The American Argosy (1984) 732 F. 2d
　299 ; 1984 AMC 1547 (2d Cir.) ···342, 343
Inter-American Shipping Enterprises Ltd. *v.* The T. T. Tula, 1982 AMC 951 (E. D.
　Va. 1981) ···498
Interbras Cayman Co. *v.* Orient Victory Shipping Co. S. A. (1981) 663 F. 2d 4 ; 1982
　AMC 737 (2d Cir.) ··450
Interbulk Ltd. *v.* Pontei dei Sospiri Shipping Co.—The Standard Ardour [1988] 2
　Lloyd's Rep. 159, (Q. B.) ···439, 520
Intermar Progress, The, SMA 2468 (Arb. at N. Y. 1988) ·················390, 413
International Bulk Carriers *v.* Evlogia Shipping—The Mihalios Xilas [1978] 2 Lloyd's
　Rep. 186, (Q. B.) ···256, 257, 480, 481, 551, 566
International Fina Services AG *v.* Katrina Shipping Ltd. and Tonen Tanker
　Kabushiki Kaisha—The Fina Samco [1995] 2 Lloyd's Rep. 344, (C. A.); [1994] 1
　Lloyd's Rep. 153, (Q. B.) ··574, **577-578**, 584, 594
International Mercantile Marine Co. *v.* Fels (1909) 170 F. 275 (2d Cir.) ··········173, 175
International Produce Inc. *v.* A/S Rosshavet (1981) 638 F. 2d 548 ; 1981 AMC 472
　(2d Cir.); *cert. denied* (1981) 451 U. S. 1017 ····································466
International Sea Tankers Inc. *v.* Hemisphere Shipping Co. Ltd.—The Wenjiang
　[1982] 1 Lloyd's Rep. 128; [1982] 2 All E. R. 437. (C. A.); *rev'g in part* [1981] 2
　Lloyd's Rep. 308, (Q. B.) ···370
International Sea Tankers Inc. *v.* Hemisphere Shipping Co. Ltd.—The Wenjiang (No.
　2) [1983] 1 Lloyd's Rep. 400, (Q. B.) ·······································399, 404
Interocean Shipping Co. *v.* The Lygaria, 1981 AMC 2244 (D. Md.) ·················491, 498
Interocean Shipping Co. *v.* National Shipping & Trading Corp. (1972) 462 F. 2d 673
　(2d Cir.) ··79, 450
Interocean Shipping Co. *v.* National Shipping & Trading Corp. (1975) 523 F. 2d 527
　(2d Cir.); *cert. denied* (1976) 423 U. S. 1054 ······················57, 58, 59, 60, 71, 72, 78, 450
Interstate Steel Corp. *v.* The Crystal Gem (1970) 317 F. Supp. 112 (S. D. N. Y.) ······318
In the matter of the Arbitration between Sun Oil Co. *v.* Western Sea Transport
　Ltd., 1978 AMC 1372 (S. D. N. Y.) ··474
In the matter of the complaint of Ta Chi Navigation (Panama) Corp. (The
　Eurypylus) (1982) 677 F. 2d 225 (2d Cir.) ···································428, 429
Int'l Produce Inc. *v.* The Frances Salman, 1975 AMC 1521 (S. D. N. Y.) ············318
Intra Transporter, The—Hofflinghouse & Co. Ltd. *v.* C-Trade S. A. [1986] 2 Lloyd's
　Rep. 132, (C. A.); [1985] 2 Lloyd's Rep. 158, (Q. B.) ·································54
Ioanna, The—Ocean Glory Compania Naviera S. A. *v.* A/S P. V. Christensen [1985] 2
　Lloyd's Rep. 164, (Q. B.) ··105, 363, 368, 376, **379**
Ion, The—Nippon Yusen Kaisha *v.* Pacifica Navegacion S. A. [1980] 2 Lloyd's Rep.
　245, (Q. B.) ···311
Ionian S. S. Co. *v.* United Distillers of America Inc. (1956) 236 F. 2d 78 (5th Cir.) ···214
Ionic, The, SMA 2519 (Arb. at N. Y. 1988) ······································115, 627
Ira, The—Forestships International Ltd. *v.* Armonia Shipping and Finance

Corporation [1995] 1 Lloyd's Rep. 103 ···365
Iran Aircraft Industries v. Avco Corp. (1992) 980 F. 2d 141 (2d Cir.) ·······················476
Irby v. Tokai Lines, 1990 AMC 1042 (E. D. Pa.) ···321
Irene's Grace, The, SMA 1213 (Arb. at N. Y. 1978) ···503
Irish Agricultural Wholesale Society Ltd. v. Partenreederei M. S. Eurotrader—The
　　Eurotrader [1987] 1 Lloyd's Rep. 418, (C. A.) ···440
Irrawaddy, The (1897) 171 U. S. 187 ···614
Irwin Schroder, The [1970] Ex. C. R. 426··168
Isaacs & Sons Ltd. v. William McAllum & Co. Ltd. (1921) 6 Ll. L. Rep. 289; [1921]
　　3 K. B. 377; 90 L. J. K. B. 1105; 125 L. T. 794; 37 T. L. R. 408; 15 Asp. M. L. C. 411,
　　(K. B.) ··93, 95, **96**, 101, 104
Isabelle, The—Cosmar Compania Naviera S. A. v. Total Transport Corp. [1984] 1
　　Lloyd's Rep. 366, (C. A.); [1982] 2 Lloyd's Rep. 81, (Q. B.) ·······························196, 296
Isbrandtsen Co. v. George S. Boutwell, 1958 AMC 351 (S. D. N. Y. 1957) ·····················318
Islamic Republic of Iran Shipping Lines v. P. & O. Bulk Shipping Ltd.—The Discaria
　　[1985] 2 Lloyd's Rep. 489, (Q. B.) ···535
Island Archon, The—Triad Shipping Co. v. Stellar Chartering & Brokerage Inc. [1995]
　　1 All E. R. 595, (C. A.); aff'g [1993] 2 Lloyd's Rep. 388, (Q. B.); [1994] 2 Lloyd's
　　Rep. 227 (C. A.) ···293, **294**, 295, 297, 298, 326-328
Islander Shipping Enterprises S. A. v. Empresa Maritima del Estado S. A.—The
　　Khian Sea [1979] 1 Lloyd's Rep. 545, (C. A.); aff'g [1977] 2 Lloyd's Rep. 439, (Q.
　　B.) ···181, **182**, 183
Ismail v. Polish Ocean Lines—The Ciechocinek [1976] 1 Lloyd's Rep. 489; [1976] Q.
　　B. 893; [1976] 3 W. L. R. 477; [1976] 1 All E. R. 902, (C. A.); [1975] 2 Lloyd's
　　Rep. 170, (Q. B.) ··308
Istros (Owners) v. F. W. Dahlstrom & Co. (1930) 38 Ll. L. Rep. 84; [1931] 1 K. B.
　　247; 100 L. J. K. B. 141; 144 L. T. 124; 36 Com. Cas. 65; 18 Asp. M. L. C. 177, (K. B.)
　　··285, 286, 551, 557
Italmare Shipping Co. v. Ocean Tanker Co. Inc.—The Rio Sun [1981] 2 Lloyd's Rep.
　　489; [1982] 1 W. L. R. 158; [1982] 1 All E. R. 517, (C. A.); [1982] 1 Lloyd's Rep.
　　404, (Q. B.) ···259, 260, 445
Itel Containers Int'l Corp. v. Atlanttrafik Express Service Ltd. (1992) 982 F. 2d 765;
　　1993 AMC 608 (2d Cir.); rev'g (1991) 1992 AMC 622 (S. D. N. Y.); (1990) 909 F.
　　2d 698 (2d Cir.) ··77, 500
Itel Taurus, The, SMA 1220 (Arb. at N. Y. 1977) ···**138**, 208
Itex Italgrani Export S. A. v. Care Shipping Corporation—The Cebu (No. 2) [1990] 2
　　Lloyd's Rep. 316; [1993] Q. B. 1; [1991] 3 W. L. R. 609; [1992] 1 All E. R. 91,
　　(Q. B.) ··482, 602

J. Lauritzen A/S v. Korea Shipping Corp., 1986 AMC 2450 (S. D. N. Y.) ·····················60
J. Lauritzen A/S v. Wijsmuller B. V.—The Super Servant Two [1990] 1 Lloyd's Rep.
　　1, (C. A.); aff'g [1989] 1 Lloyd's Rep. 148, (Q. B.) ···394, 405, **406**, 407
J. Vermaas' Scheepvaartbedrijf N. V. v. Association Technique de l'Importation

Charbonnière—The Laga [1966] 1 Lloyd's Rep. 582, (Q. B.) ·················**562**
J. Zeevi & Sons Ltd. v. Grindlays Bank (Uganda) Ltd. (1975) 37 N. Y. 2d 220 ; 371
   N. Y. S. 2d 892 ; *cert. denied* 423 U. S. 806 ··················415
J. E. Hurley Lumber Co. v. Compania Panamena Maritima San Gerassimo S. A., 1958
   AMC 2502 (Arb. at N. Y.) ··················114
Jackson v. Union Marine Insurance Co. (1874) L. R. 10 C. P. 125 ; 44 L. J. C. P. 27 ; 31
   L. T. 789 ; 2 Asp. M. L. C. 435, (Ex. Ch.) ··················397, 405
Jadranska Slobodna Plovidba v. Gulf Shipping Lines Ltd.—The Matija Gubec [1983]
   1 Lloyd's Rep. 24, (Q. B.) ··················127
Jagat Padmini, The, SMA 1097 (Arb. at N. Y. 1977) ··················137, 354
Jalamohan, The—Ngo Chew Hong Edible Oil Pte. Ltd. v. Scindia Steam Navigation
   Co. Ltd. [1988] 1 Lloyd's Rep. 443 ; [1988] 1 F. T. L. R. 340, (Q. B.) ··················332
Jamaica Commodity Trading v. Connell Rice & Sugar (1991) 766 F. Supp. 138 (S. D.
   N. Y.) ; (1991) U. S. Dist. Lexis 8976 (S. D. N. Y.) ··················323, 477
Japan Line Ltd. v. Aggeliki Charis Compania Maritima S. A. and Davies and Potter—
   The Angelic Grace [1980] 1 Lloyd's Rep. 288, (C. A.) ··················446
Japy Frères & Co. v. Sutherland & Co. (1921) 6 Ll. L. Rep. 381 ; (1921) 91 L. J. K. B.
   19 ; 125 L. T. 211 ; 37 T. L. R. 446 ; 26 Com. Cas. 227 ; 15 Asp. M. L. C. 198, (K. B.)
   ··················131, 550
Jaramar, The, 1969 AMC 354 (Arb. at N. Y.) ··················239
Jason, The (1912) 225 U. S. 32··················636
Jebsen v. A Cargo of Hemp (1915) 228 F. 143 (D. Mass.) ··················491, 494, **495**
Jerom, The, SMA 2790 (Arb. at N. Y. 1991) ··················144, 388
Jevington Court, The—Court Line Ltd. v. Finelvet A. G. [1966] 1 Lloyd's Rep. 683, (Q.
   B.) ··················554, **555**
Jhansi Ki Rani, The—Sanko Steamship Co. Ltd. v. The Shipping Corp. of India [1980]
   2 Lloyd's Rep. 569, (Q. B.) ··················442
John S. Darbyshire, The—Albion Sugar Co. Ltd. v. William Tankers Ltd. [1977] 2
   Lloyd's Rep. 457, (Q. B.) ··················53, 586
John Wiley & Sons Inc. v. Livingston (1964) 376 U. S. 543 ··················451
Johnny, The—Arta Shipping Co. Ltd. v. Thai Europe Tapioca Service Ltd. [1977] 2
   Lloyd's Rep. 1, (C. A.) ; *aff'g* [1977] 1 Lloyd's Rep. 257, (Q. B.) ··················127, 549, **550**
Johnston Bros. v. Saxon Queen S. S. Co. (1913) 108 L. T. 564 ; 12 Asp. M. L. C. 305,
   (K. B.) ··················**181**
Jones v. Hough (1879) 5 Ex. D. 115 ; 49 L. J. Q. B. 211 ; 42 L. T. 108 ; 4 Asp. M. L. C.
   248, (C. A.) ··················**325**
Jones v. Sea Tow Services, 1994 AMC 1107 ; 828 F. Supp. 1002 (E. D. N. Y. 1993) ;
   rev'd and remanded 1994 AMC 2661 ; 30 F. 3d 360 (2d Cir.) ··················475
Jones Tug & Barge Co. v. The Liberty Manufacturer, 1978 AMC 1183 (C. D. Cal.
   1976) ··················503
Joo Seng Hong Kong Co. v. The Unibulkfir (1979) 483 F. Supp. 43 (S. D. N. Y.) ········342
Joseph Grant, The (1857) Fed. Cas. No. 7538 (D. Wis.) ··················344
Joseph Travers v. Cooper [1915] 1 K. B. 73, (C. A.) ··················308

Jugoslavenska Linijska Plovidba v. Hulsman—The Primorje [1980] 2 Lloyd's Rep. 74
··**62, 64**
Jugotanker-Turisthotel v. Mt. Ve Balik Kurumu, SMA 1133 (Arb. at N.Y. 1977) ······543
Julia, The, SMA 552 (Arb. at N.Y.) ···137
Junior K, The—Star Steamship Society v. Beogradska Plovidba [1988] 2 Lloyd's Rep.
583, (Q.B.) ···**53-54**

K. H. Enterprise, The—K. H. Enterprise (Cargo Owners) v. Pioneer Container
(Owners) [1994] 1 Lloyd's Rep. 593; [1994] 2 A.C. 324; [1994] 3 W.L.R. 1;
[1994] 2 All E.R. 250; (1994) 138 S.J. (LB) 85, (P.C.) ···································335
K. H. Enterprise (Cargo Owners) v. Pioneer Container (Owners) —The K. H.
Enterprise [1994] 1 Lloyd's Rep. 593; [1994] 2 A.C. 324; [1994] 3 W.L.R. 1;
[1994] 2 All E.R. 250; (1994) 138 S.J. (LB) 85, (P.C.) ···································335
K/S Penta Shipping A/S v. Ethiopian Shipping Lines Corporation—The Saga Cob
[1992] 2 Lloyd's Rep. 545, (C.A.); rev'g [1992] 2 Lloyd's Rep. 398, (Q.B.)
··**181**, 183, 184-186, 188-190, **579-580**
Kaleej International v. Gulf Shipping Lines (1986) 6 N.S.W.L.R. 569, (C.A.) ············337
Kanchenjunga, The—Motor Oil Hellas (Corinth) Refineries S.A. v. Shipping Corp. of
India [1990] 1 Lloyd's Rep. 391, (H.L.); aff'g [1989] 1 Lloyd's Rep. 354; (1989)
132 S.J. 19, (C.A.); aff'g [1987] 2 Lloyd's Rep. 509, (Q.B.)
··92, 93, 125, 142, 161, 190, **191**, 260, 261, 293, 360, **611**
Kanuth v. Prescott, Ball & Turben Inc. (1991) 949 F. 2d 1175 (D.C. Cir.); motion to
enforce judgment granted (1992) U.S. Dist. Lexis 3943 ·······································471
Kapetan Antonis, The, 1989 AMC 551 (Arb. at N.Y. 1988) ·······························175, 459
Kapetan Markos N. L., The (No. 2) —Hispanica de Petroleos S.A. and Compania
Iberica Refinadera S.A. v. Vencedora Oceanica Navegacion S.A.; Same v. Same
and West of England Ship Owners Mutual Protection and Indemnity Association
(Luxembourg) [1987] 2 Lloyd's Rep. 321, (C.A.) ···334
Karavos Compania Naviera S.A. v. Atlantica Export Corp. (1978) 588 F. 2d 1; 1978
AMC 2634 (2d Cir.) ···**73**
Karen C, The, SMA 3042 (Arb. at N.Y. 1994) ··380
Karin M, The, SMA 2869 (Arb. at N.Y. 1992) ···271, 279, 287
Karpinnen v. Karl Kiefer Machine Co. (1951) 187 F. 2d 32 (2d Cir.) ·······························465
Karran v. Peabody (1906) 145 F. 166 (2d Cir.) ··361
Karsales (Harrow) v. Wallis [1956] 1 W.L.R. 936; [1956] 2 All E.R. 866, (C.A.) ···104
Kartini, The, SMA 1958 and 2196 (Arb. at N.Y. 1984 and 1985) ···························176
Katina, The, SMA 1310 (Arb. at N.Y. 1979) ···270
Katonia, The—Damps. Norden v. Isbrandtsen-Moller Co. (1930) 43 F. 2d 560; 1930
AMC 1441 (S.D.N.Y.) ···**117**
Katz v. Uvegi, 18 Misc. 2d 576; 187 N.Y.S. 2d 511 (Sup. Ct. 1959); aff'd 11 A.D. 2d
773; 205 N.Y.S. 2d 972 (App. Div. 1960) ···**469**
Kawasaki Kisen Kabushiki Kaisha v. Bantham Steamship Co. Ltd. (hire) (1938) 61
Ll. L. Rep. 331; [1938] 2 K.B. 790; 43 Com. Cas. 355; 107 L.J.K.B. 604; 159 L.T.

判例索引

432;54 T. L. R. 1095; [1938] 3 All E. R. 690, 19 Asp. M. L. C. 233, (C. A.); *aff'g*
 (1938) 60 Ll. L. Rep. 70; [1938] 1 K. B. 805;43 Com. Cas. 355; 158 L. T. 349;54 T.
 L. R. 436; Asp. M. L. C. 180, (K. B.) ················253, 282, **608**
Kawasaki Kisen Kabushiki Kaisha *v.* Bantham Steamship Co. Ltd. (No. 2) (war)
 (1939) 63 Ll. L. Rep. 155; [1939] 2 K. B. 544; 44 Com. Cas. 170; 55 T. L. R. 503;
 108 L. J. K. B. 709; 161 L. T. 25; [1939] 1 All E. R. 819; 19 Asp. M. L. C. 274, (C.
 A.) ················569, 611
Kawasaki K. K. K. *v.* Belships Co. Ltd., Skibs A/S (1939) 63 Ll. L. Rep. 175; 160 L. T.
 359; [1939] 2 All E. R. 108; 19 Asp. M. L. C. 278, (K. B.) ················**569**
Keighley, Maxsted & Co. *v.* Durant [1901] A. C. 240; 70 L. J. K. B. 662; 84 L. T. 777; 17
 T. L. R. 527, (H. L.) ················68
Kennedy *v.* Weston & Co. (1905) 136 F. 166 (5th Cir.) ················344
Keokuk, The (1870) 76 U. S. (9 Wall.) 517 ················491
Kerman, The—B. V. S. and the Khuzestan Water and Power Authority *v.* Kerman
 Shipping Co. S. A. [1982] 1 Lloyd's Rep. 62; [1982] 1 W. L. R. 166; [1982] 1 All
 E. R. 616, (Q. B.) ················445
Kerr-McGee Refining Corp. *v.* The Triumph (1991) 924 F. 2d 467; 1991 AMC 1051
 (2d Cir.); *cert. denied* (1991) 502 U. S. 821 ················463, 464, 471
Keystone Shipping *v.* Cie Marocaine, 1990 AMC 2971 (S. D. N. Y.) ················73
Khian Sea, The—Islander Shipping Enterprises S. A. *v.* Empresa Maritima del Estado
 S. A. [1979] 1 Lloyd's Rep. 545, (C. A.); *aff'g* [1977] 2 Lloyd's Rep. 439, (Q. B.)
 ················181, **182**, 183
Khian Zephyr, The—Freedom General Shipping S. A. *v.* Tokai Shipping Co. Ltd.
 [1982] 1 Lloyd's Rep. 73, (Q. B.) ················304, 439
Kimball, The (1835) 70 U. S. 37 ················492
Kinoshita & Co. (*Re*) (1961) 287 F. 2d 951; 1961 AMC 1974 (2d Cir.) ················79
Kirno Hill Corp. *v.* Holt (1980) 618 F. 2d 982; 1980 AMC 254 (2d Cir.) ······56, 71, 74, 78
Kirkawa Corporation *v.* Gatoil Overseas Inc.—The Peter Kirk [1990] 1 Lloyd's Rep.
 154, (Q. B.) ················443
Kitsa, The, SMA 3119 (Arb. at N. Y. 1994) ················386
Knud II, The—Steamship Co. Gorm *v.* United States Shipping Bd. Emergency Fleet
 Corp. (1922) 285 F. 142 (2d Cir.) ················**233-234**
Knutsford (S. S.) Ltd. *v.* Tillmanns & Co. [1908] A. C. 406; 99 L. T. 399; 24 T. L. R.
 786; 77 L. J. K. B. 977; 13 Com. Cas. 334; 11 Asp. M. L. C. 105, (H. L.); *aff'g* [1908] 2
 K. B. 385; 99 L. T. 399, 24 T. L. R. 454; 13 Com. Cas. 244; 11 Asp. M. L. C. 105, (C.
 A.) ················179
Koala Shipping & Trading Inc. (Complaint of) (1984) 587 F. Supp. 140 (S. D. N. Y.) ···464
Koch Fuel *v.* South Star, 1988 AMC 1226 (E. D. N. Y. 1987) ················455
Kodros Shipping Corp. *v.* Empresa Cubana de Fletes—The Evia (No. 2) [1982] 2
 Lloyd's Rep. 307; [1983] 1 A. C. 736; [1982] 3 W. L. R. 637; [1982] 3 All E. R.
 350, (H. L.); *aff'g* [1982] 1 Lloyd's Rep. 334, (C. A.); *rev'g* [1981] 2 Lloyd's Rep. 613,
 (Q. B.) ················143, 178, 183,
  184, 185, 186, **187-188**, 189, 190, 193, 194, 197, 400,

403, **404**, 407, 532, 564, 565, 567, **568**, 579, 581, 607, 609
Komninos S. The [1991] 1 Lloyd's Rep. 370 ··438
Konkar Kinos, The, SMA 2631 (Arb. at N. Y. 1990) ································351
Konkar Maritime Enterprises S. A. v. Compagnie Belge d'Affretement (The Konkar
　Pioneer) (1987) 668 F. Supp. 267; 1989 AMC 182 (S. D. N. Y.) ·····················461
Konkar Pioneer, The (1987) 668 F. Supp. 267; 1989 AMC 182 (S. D. N. Y.) ···461, 469, 471
Konkar Victory, The, SMA 1798 (Arb. at N. Y. 1983) ···································206
Kopac Int'l Inc. v. The Bold Venture (1986) 638 F. Supp. 87 (W. D. Wash.) ············499
Kossick v. United Fruit Co. (1961) 365 U. S. 731; 6 L. Ed. 2d 56 ····················56, 57
Kostas Melas, The, 1988 AMC 68 (S. D. N. Y. 1983) ···································453
Kostas Melas, The—S. L. Sethia Liners Ltd. v. Naviagro Maritime Corp. [1981] 1
　Lloyd's Rep. 18, (Q. B.) ···248, 250, 252, 446
Koycegiz, The, SMA 2700 (Arb. at N. Y. 1990) ···279
Krauss Brothers Lumber Co. v. Dimon Steamship Corp. (1933) 290 U. S. 117 ············491
Kristiandsands Tankrederi A/S v. Standard Tankers (Bahamas) Ltd.—The Polyglory
　[1977] 2 Lloyd's Rep. 353, (Q. B.) ···**186**, 187, 192
Kroft Entertainment Inc. v. CBS Songs (1987) 653 F. Supp. 1530 (S. D. N. Y.) ············57
Kronprinzessin Cecilie, The (1917) 244 U. S. 12 ·····································411, 569
Kruger & Co. Ltd. v. Moel Tryvan Ship Co. Ltd. [1907] A. C. 272; 97 L. T. 143; 23
　T. L. R. 677; 76 L. J. K. B. 985; 13 Com. Cas. 1; 10 Asp. M. L. C. 465, (H. L.); aff'g
　[1907] 1 K. B. 809, (C. A.) ···**326**, 327, 328
Krulewitch v. National Importing & Trading Co. Inc. (1921) 195 A. D. 544; 186 N. Y.
　S. 838 ··**414**, 415
Kuwait Petroleum Corporation v. I & D Oil Carriers Ltd.—The Houda [1994] 2
　Lloyd's Rep. 541, (C. A.); rev'g [1993] 1 Lloyd's Rep. 333, (Q. B.) ···291, **292**, 585, **587**, 595

L. C. Fowler & Sons Ltd. v. St. Stephen's College Board of Governors [1991] 3 N. Z.
　L. R. 304···62
LEP International v. Atlanttrafic Express Service (1987) 10 N. S. W. L. R. 614 ······336, 553
Labrador Rex, The, SMA 2472 (Arb. at N. Y. 1988) ····································318
Laconia, The—Mardorf Peach & Co. Ltd. v. Attica Sea Carriers Corp. [1977] 1
　Lloyd's Rep. 315; [1977] A. C. 850; [1977] 2 W. L. R. 286; [1977] 1 All E. R. 545,
　(H. L.); rev'g [1976] 1 Lloyd's Rep. 395; [1976] Q. B. 835; [1976] 2 W. L. R. 668;
　[1976] 2 All E. R. 249, (C. A.) ·····················244, 245, 254, 257, 258, **260-261**, 262, 266, 548
Lady Gwendolen, The [1965] 1 Lloyd's Rep. 335; [1965] P. 294; [1965] 3 W. L. R.
　91; [1965] 2 All E. R. 283, (C. A.); aff'g [1964] 2 Lloyd's Rep. 99; [1964] 3 W. L.
　R. 1062; [1964] 3 All E. R. 447, (Adm.) ···557, 558
Laga, The—J. Vermaas' Scheepvaartbedrijf N. V. v. Association Technique de
　l'Importation Charbonnière [1966] 1 Lloyd's Rep. 582, (Q. B.) ···························**562**
Lakatoi Express, The (1990) 19 N. S. W. L. R. 285 ····································264, 487
Lake Steam Shipping Co. v. Bacon (1904) 129 F. 819 (S. D. N. Y.); aff'd on opinion
　below (1906) 145 F. 1022 (2d Cir.) ··385
Lake Union Drydock Co. v. The Polar Viking (1978) 446 F. Supp. 1286; 1978 AMC

1477 (W. D. Wash.) ···502
Lamyrefs, The, 1970 AMC 1966 (Arb. at N. Y.) ·····································138
Lancaster, The—Ellerman Lines Ltd. v. Lancaster Maritime Co. Ltd. [1980] 2 Lloyd's
　Rep. 497, (Q. B.) ···484, 487, 488
Landy Michaels Realty v. Local 32B-32J (1992) 954 F. 2d 794 (2d Cir.) ··················451
La Pintada Compania Navegacion S. A. v. President of India—The La Pintada [1984]
　2 Lloyd's Rep. 9; [1984] 3 W. L. R. 10, (H. L.); [1984] 1 Lloyd's Rep. 305; [1983]
　1 Lloyd's Rep. 37, (Q. B.) ···446
La Pintada, The—La Pintada Compania Navegacion S. A. v. President of India [1984]
　2 Lloyd's Rep. 9; [1984] 3 W. L. R. 10, (H. L.); [1984] 1 Lloyd's Rep. 305; [1983]
　1 Lloyd's Rep. 37, (Q. B.) ···446
Largo, The, SMA 1230 (Arb. at N. Y. 1978) ·······································**350**, 390
Larissa, The—Showa Oil Tanker Co. Ltd. v. Maravan S. A. [1983] 2 Lloyd's Rep. 325.
　(Q. B.) ···106, **601**
Larrinaga & Co. Ltd. v. The Société Franco-Américaine des Phosphates de Medulla
　(1923) 14 Ll. L. Rep. 457; 92 L. J. K. B. 455; 129 L. T. 65; 39 T. L. R. 316; 29 Com.
　Cas. 1; 16 Asp. M. L. C. 133, (H. L.) ···395, 404
Larrinaga S. S. Co. Ltd. v. The Crown (1944) 78 Ll. L. Rep. 167; [1945] A. C. 246;
　114 L. J. K. B. 129; 61 T. L. R. 241; 172 L. T. 177; [1945] 1 All E. R. 329, (H. L.)
　··**296**, 298, 299, 552
Larsen v. 150 Bales of Sisal Grass (1906) 147 F. 783 (S. D. Ala.) ············492, 493, 494
Lauritzen (J.) A/S v. Korea Shipping Corp., 1986 AMC 2450 (S. D. N. Y.) ···············60
Lauritzen (J.) A/S v. Wijsmuller B. V.—The Super Servant Two [1990] 1 Lloyd's
　Rep. 1, (C. A.); aff'g [1989] 1 Lloyd's Rep. 148, (Q. B.) ····················394, 405, **406**, 407
Leaf v. International Galleries [1950] 2 K. B. 86; 66 T. L. R. (Pt. 1) 1031; [1950] 1
　All E. R. 693, (C. A.) ···83
Ledee v. Ceramiche Ragno (1982) 684 F. 2d 184, 185-86 (1st Cir.) ······················475
Lee Cooper Ltd. v. Jeakins & Sons Ltd. [1964] 1 Lloyd's Rep. 300; [1967] 2 Q. B.
　1; [1965] 3 W. L. R. 753; [1965] 1 All E. R. 280 ···147
Leeds Shipping Co. v. Société Francaise Bunge—The Eastern City [1958] 2 Lloyd's
　Rep. 127, (C. A.); [1957] 2 Lloyd's Rep. 153, (Q. B.) ···177, **178, 181**, 182, 183, 186, 199, 579
Lelaps, The, SMA 2840 (Arb. at N. Y. 1992) ···288
Lendoudis Evangelos II, The—Benship International v. Demand Shipping (1988) (L.
　M. L. N. 408, 24 June 1995) ···131
Lenoudis Kiki, The, SMA 2323 (Arb. at N. Y. 1986) ································385, 497
Lensen Shipping Ltd. v. Anglo-Soviet Shipping Co. (1935) 52 Ll. L. Rep. 141; 40 Com.
　Cas. 320, (C. A.) ···**189**, 190, 195, 376, 378, 563
Leolga Compania de Navigacion v. John Glynn & Sons Ltd. [1953] 2 Lloyd's Rep.
　47; [1953] 2 Q. B. 374; [1953] 1 W. L. R. 846; [1953] 2 All E. R. 327, (Q. B.) ···**165**, 378
Leon Corporation v. Atlantic Lines Navigation Co. Inc.—The Leon [1985] 2 Lloyd's
　Rep. 470, (Q. B.) ···250, 251
Leon, The—Leon Corp. v. Atlantic Lines Navigation Co. Inc. [1985] 2 Lloyd's Rep.
　470, (Q. B.) ···250, 251

Leon, The, and The Didymi—Atlantic Lines & Navigation Co. Inc. *v.* Didymi Corp.
　and Leon Corp. [1984] 1 Lloyd's Rep. 583, (C. A.) ……………………………………128
Leonidas D. The—Allied Marine Transport Ltd. *v.* Vale do Rio Doce Navegacao S. A.
　[1985] 2 Lloyd's Rep. 18; [1985] 1 W. L. R. 925; [1985] 2 All E. R. 796, (C. A.) …443
Leonidas Glory, The, SMA 2753 (Arb. at N. Y. 1991) ……………………………………117
Leprechaun Spirit, The, SMA 1056 (Arb. at N. Y. 1976) …………………………………536
Les Affreteurs Reunis S. A. *v.* Leopold Walford (London) Ltd. [1919] A. C. 801 ; 24
　Com. Cas. 268 ; 88 L. J. K. B. 861 ; 121 L. T. 393 ; 35 T. L. R. 542 ; 14 Asp. M. L. C. 451,
　(H. L.) ………………………………………………………………………………61, 541
Leslie Shipping *v.* Welstead (1921) 7 Ll. L. Rep. 251 ; [1921] 3 K. B. 420 ; 125 L. T.
　858 ; 91 L. J. K. B. 12 ; 15 Asp. M. L. C. 413, (K. B.) ………………………………268, 378
Leslie, The, SMA 1341 (Arb. at N. Y. 1979) ……………………………………108, 224
Levy *v.* Costerton (1816) 4 Camp. 389 ; 1 Stark. 212……………………………………159
Liberian Shipping Corp. *v.* A. King & Sons Ltd.—The Pegasus [1967] 1 Lloyd's Rep.
　302 ; [1967] 2 Q. B. 86 ; [1967] 2 W. L. R. 856 ; [1967] 1 All E. R. 934, (C. A.) ……440
Liberian Statesman, The, SMA 2092 (Arb. at N. Y. 1985) …………………………………458
Liberian Vertex Transports Inc. *v.* Associated Bulk Carriers Ltd. (1984) 738 F. 2d
　85 ; 1984 AMC 2841 (2d Cir.) ………………………………………………………463
Liberty Bell Venture, The, SMA 3147 (Arb. at N. Y. 1992) ………………………………461
Liberty Navigation and T. Co. *v.* Kinoshita & Co. Ltd. (1960) 285 F. 2d 343 (2d Cir.) ;
　cert. denied (1961) 366 U. S. 949 ……………………………………………………277
Libra Shipping and Trading Corp. Ltd. *v.* Northern Sales Ltd.—The Aspen Trader
　[1981] 1 Lloyd's Rep. 273, (C. A.) ……………………………………………………440
Lidgett *v.* Williams (1845) 4 Hare 456 ; 14 L. J. Ch. 459 ; 10 Jur. 42 ; 67 E. R. 727 ;
　aff'd 5 L. T. O. S. 169 …………………………………………………………………49
Lilliana Dimitrova, The, SMA 3075 (Arb. at N. Y. 1994) …………………………………461
Lilly, Wilson & Co. *v.* Smales, Eeles & Co. [1892] 1 Q. B. 456 ; 8 T. L. R. 410 ……………**69**
Limerick S. S. Co. v. Stott & Co. (1920) 5 Ll. L. Rep. 190, 226, 446, (K. B.) ; (1921) 7
　Ll. L. Rep. 5, 69 ; [1921] 2 K. B. 613 ; 37 T. L. R. 674 ; 90 L. J. K. B. 865 ; 125 L. T.
　516, (C. A.) ………………………………………………………180, **183**, 235, **564**, 565
Lips, The—President of India *v.* Lips Maritime Corp. [1987] 2 Lloyd's Rep. 311 ;
　[1988] A. C. 395 ; [1987] 3 W. L. R. 572 ; [1987] 3 All E. R. 110 ; [1987] 2 F. T. L.
　R. 477 ; [1987] F. L. R. 313, (H. L.) ; *rev'g* [1987] 1 Lloyd's Rep. 131 ; [1987] 2 W.
　L. R. 906 ; [1987] 1 All E. R. 957 ; [1987] 1 F. T. L. R. 50 ; [1987] F. L. R. 91 ;
　(1987) 131 S. J. 422, (C. A.) ; *rev'g* (1894) 134 New L. J. 969 ……………………446
Lloyd Royal Belge S. A. *v.* Stathatos (1917) 34 T. L. R. 70, (C. A.) ………………………407
Loch Rannoch, The (1911) 192 F. 219 (D. Me.) ; *aff'd* (1913) 208 F. 884 (1st Cir.) …344
L'Office Cherifien des Phosphates and Unitramp S. A. *v.* Yamashita-Shinnihon
　Steamship Co. Ltd.—The Boucraa [1994] 1 Lloyd's Rep. 251 ; [1994] A. C. 486 ;
　[1994] 2 W. L. R. 39 ; [1994] 1 All E. R. 20 ; (1994) 138 S. J. (LB) 19, (H. L.) ; *rev'g*
　[1993] 2 Lloyd's Rep. 149 ; [1993] 3 W. L. R. 266 ; [1993] 3 All E. R. 686 ; [1993]
　N. P. C. 64, (C. A.) ……………………………………………………………………443
Lok Manya, The (1980) *unreported* (C. A.) ; (1979) *unreported* (Q. B.) ………………251

判例索引　　　79

Lokumal (K.) & Sons London Ltd. *v.* Lotte Shipping Co. Pte. Ltd.—The August
　Leonhardt [1985] 2 Lloyd's Rep. 28, (C. A.); [1984] 1 Lloyd's Rep. 322; (1984)
　134 New L. J. 125, (Q. B.) ···69
Lombard North Central *v.* Butterworth [1987] Q. B. 527; [1987] 2 W. R. L. 7; [1987]
　1 All E. R. 267, (C. A.) ···269
London Confidence, The, SMA 1257 (Arb. at N. Y. 1978) ·······················386, 622
London Explorer, The—London & Overseas Freighters *v.* Timber Shipping [1971] 1
　Lloyd's Rep. 523; [1972] A. C. 1; [1971] 2 W. L. R. 1360; [1971] 2 All E. R. 599,
　(H. L.) ··122, 123, 125, 127, 523
London Glory, The, S. M. A. 1771 (Arb. at N. Y. 1982) ·······························225
London & Overseas Freighters *v.* Timber Shipping—The London Explorer [1971] 1
　Lloyd's Rep. 523; [1972] A. C. 1; [1971] 2 W. L. R. 1360; [1971] 2 All E. R. 599,
　(H. L.) ··122, 123, 125, 127, 523
Long *v.* Lloyd [1958] 1 W. L. R. 753; [1958] 2 All E. R. 402, (C. A.) ·····················83
Long Hope, The, SMA 2664 (Arb. at N. Y. 1990) ···214
Lord Strathcona S. S. Co. Ltd. *v.* Dominion Coal Co. Ltd. (1925) 23 Ll. L. Rep. 145;
　[1926] A. C. 108; 95 L. J. P. C. 71; 134 L. T. 227; 42 T. L. R. 86; 31 Com. Cas. 80; 16
　Asp. M. L. C. 585, (P. C.) ···95, 96
Lorentzen *v.* White Shipping Co. Ltd.(1943) 74 Ll. L. Rep. 161, (K. B.) ·················**104**
Lougheed & Co. Ltd. *v.* Suzuki (1926) 216 App. Div. 487; (1926) 215 N. Y. S. 505;
　aff'd (1926) 243 N. Y. 648; (1926) 154 N. E. 642 ···543
Love & Stewart Ltd. *v.* S. Instone & Co. Ltd. (1917) 33 T. L. R. 475, (H. L.) ···············54
Lovell *v.* Davis, 101 U. S. 541 (1879) ···119, 120
Loveland (S. C.) Co. *v.* Eastern States Farmer's Exch. (1937) 92 F. 2d 180 (3d Cir.);
　cert. denied (1937) 302 U. S. 762 ···343
Lovelock *v.* Exportles [1968] 1 Lloyd's Rep. 163, (C. A.) ·································**50**
Lowber *v.* Bangs (1865) 69 U. S. 728 ···287
Lowry & Co. *v.* The Le Moyne d'Iberville (1966) 253 F. Supp. 396; 1966 AMC 2195
　(S. D. N. Y.) ··448
Lucerna, The, SMA 2579 (Arb. at N. Y. 1988) ···361
Lucille, The—Uni-Ocean Lines Ltd. *v.* C-Trade S. A. [1984] 1 Lloyd's Rep. 244, (C.
　A.); [1983] 1 Lloyd's Rep. 387, (Q. B.) ·······································185, 186, 188, 197
Luckenbach *v.* McCahan Sugar Co. (1918) 248 U. S. 139 ·································**213**
Luckenbach *v.* Pierson (1915) 229 F. 130 (2d Cir.) ·································274, 275
Luckenbach Overseas Corp. *v.* Sub-freights of the Audrey J. Luckenbach (1963) 232
　F. Supp. 572; 1965 AMC 692 (S. D. N. Y. 1963) ·······························**491-492**, 496
Luckenbach S. S. Co. *v.* Coast Mfg. & Sup. Co. (1960) 185 F. Supp. 910; 1960 AMC
　2076 (E. D. N. Y.) ···173
Luckenbach S. S. Co. *v.* W. R. Grace & Co. (1920) 267 F. 676 (4th Cir.) ·················570
Lucy, The—Atlantic Lines & Navigation Co. Inc. *v.* Hallam Ltd. [1983] 1 Lloyd's
　Rep. 188, (Q. B.) ···**82-83**, 143
Luigi Monta *v.* Cechofracht Co. Ltd. [1956] 2 Lloyd's Rep. 97; [1956] 2 Q. B. 552;
　[1956] 3 W. L. R. 480; [1956] 2 All E. R. 769, (Q. B.) ·······························**568**, 608

Lumber Carrier, The, SMA 252 (Arb. at N. Y. 1955) ···225
Lutetian, The—Tradax Export S. A. v. Dorada Compania Naviera S. A. [1982] 2
 Lloyd's Rep. 140, (Q. B.) ···246, 247, 248, 252, 259, 377, 584
Lyeth v. Chrysler Corp. (1991) 929 F. 2d 891 (2d Cir.) ···469
Lyons-Magnus Inc. v. American Hawaiian S. S. Co. (1941) 41 F. Supp. 575 ; 1941
 AMC 1550 (S. D. N. Y.) ···524
Lysland, The, SMA 419 (Arb. at N. Y. 1969) ···239

MCT Shipping Corp. v. Sabet (1980) 497 F. Supp. 1078 (S. D. N. Y.) ·················494
MMI Int'l v. Skyros 1991 AMC 1264 (N. D. Cal. 1990) ···504
MSC Mediterranean Shipping Co. S. A. v. Alianca Bay Shipping Co. Ltd.—The
 Argonaut [1985] 2 Lloyd's Rep. 216, (Q. B.) ···**307**, 308
Maaslot, The, SMA 3074 (Arb. at N. Y. 1994) ···461
Machitis, The, 1978 AMC 1120 (S. D. N. Y.) ···471, **473**
McAllister Bros. Inc. v. A & S Transp. Co., SMA 1989 (Arb. at N. Y. 1984) ·········278
McCreary Tire & Rubber Co. v. CEAT S. p. A. (1974) 501 F. 2d 1032 (3d Cir.) ······460
McDermott Int'l Inc. v. Underwriters at Lloyd's (1993) 981 F. 2d 744 (5th Cir.);
 cert. denied (1993) —U. S.—; 113 S. Ct. 2442 ; 124 L. Ed. 2d 660 ···451
McIllroy v. Paine Webber Inc. (1993) 989 F. 2d 817 (5th Cir.) ···465
MacIver & Co. v. Tate Steamers Ltd. [1903] 1 K. B. 362 ; 72 L. J. K. B. 253 ; 88 L. T.
 182 ; 19 T. L. R. 217 ; 8 Com. Cas. 124 ; 9 Asp. M. L. C. 362, (C. A); aff'g (1902) 18
 T. L. R. 379, (K. B.) ···**218**
Mackenzie McAllister v. United States, 1942 AMC 1215 (E. D. N. Y.) ·················300
McNear v. Leblond (1903) 123 F. 384 (9th Cir.) ···277
McNeil Higgins Co. v. Old Dominion S. S. Co. (1916) 235 F. 854 (7th Cir.) ·············428
Madeirense do Brasil S/A v. Stulman—Emrick Lumber Co. (1945) 147 F. 2d 399 (2d
 Cir.); cert. denied (1945) 325 U. S. 861 ···**411-412**
Madeleine, The—Cheik Boutros v. Ceylon Shipping Lines Ltd. [1967] 2 Lloyd's Rep.
 224, (Q. B.) ···97, **100**, 121, 154, **159**, 355, **356**, 359, 530
Magdalene, The, SMA 579 (Arb. at N. Y. 1957) ···202
Mages Foundation v. Thrifty Corp. (1990) 916 F. 2d 402 (7th Cir.) ···449
Magnhild (Owners) v. McIntyre Brothers & Co. (1921) 6 Ll. L. Rep. 190 ; [1921] 2
 K. B. 97 ; 37 T. L. R. 413 ; 124 L. T. 771 ; 26 Com. Cas. 185 ; 90 L. J. K. B. 527 ; 15 Asp.
 M. L. C. 230, (C. A.); (1920) 4 Ll. L. Rep. 130 ; [1920] 3 K. B. 321 ; 25 Com. Cas.
 347 ; 124 L. T. 160 ; 15 Asp. M. L. C. 107 ; 36 T. L. R. 744, (K. B.) ···554, **555**
Mahroos v. The Tatiana L, 1988 AMC 757 (S. D. N. Y. 1986) ···341
Majestic, The (1897) 166 U. S. 375 ···431
Malaysian International Shipping Corp. v. Empresa Cubana de Fletes—The Bunga
 Kenanga [1981] 1 Lloyd's Rep. 518, (Q. B.) ···238, 550
Mallozzi v. Caparelli S. p. A. [1976] 1 Lloyd's Rep. 407, (C. A.) ···50, 51
Mammoth Bulk Carriers Ltd. v. Holland Bulk Transport B. V.—The Captain
 Diamantis [1978] 1 Lloyd's Rep. 346. (C. A.); aff'g [1977] 1 Lloyd's Rep. 362, (Q.
 B.) ···218, **227**

Mana, The, SMA 2669 (Arb. at N. Y. 1990) ···144
Managua, The, SMA 352 (Arb. at N. Y. 1966) ···240
Manchester Trust, The v. Furness, Withy & Co. Ltd. [1895] 2 Q. B. 539; 1 Com.
　Cas. 39; 73 L. T. 110; 8 Asp. M. L. C. 57; sub nom. The Manchester Trust Ltd. v.
　Furness, Withy & Co. Ltd., 11 T. L. R. 530; 64 L. J. Q. B. 766, (C. A.) ·················333
Mandolyna, The, SMA 2115 (Arb. at N. Y. 1985); SMA 1967 (Arb. at N. Y. 1984)
　··224, 385
Mangalia, The, SMA 2839 (Arb. at N. Y. 1991) ···116, 351
Manhattan Prince, The—Sanko Steamship Co. Ltd. v. Fearnley & Eger A/S [1985] 1
　Lloyd's Rep. 140, (Q. B.) ···211, **372-373**, 374, **593**
Manila Enterprise, The, SMA 2060 (Arb. at N. Y. 1983) ·····························116, 458
Marabueno Compania Naviera S. A. v. Cayman Caribbean Carriers, 1984 AMC 1849
　(S. D. N. Y.) ··463
Marathon, The, SMA 2425 (Arb. at N. Y. 1987) ···457
Marathon Int'l Petroleum Supply Co. v. I. T. I. Shipping S. A. (1990) 740 F. Supp. 984
　(S. D. N. Y.) ··323
Marbienes Compania Naviera v. Ferrostaal A. G.—The Democritos [1976] 2 Lloyd's
　Rep. 149, (C. A.); aff'g [1975] 1 Lloyd's Rep. 386, (Q. B.)
　···124, **126**, 128, 131, 153, 161, 355, **358**, 359, 360, 377, 408
Marchessini & Co. (New York) v. Pacific Marine Co. (1964) 2227 F. Supp. 17; 1964
　AMC 1538 (S. D. N. Y.) ···543
Marchessini (P. D.) & Co. (New York) Inc. v. H. W. Robinson & Co. (1967) 287 F.
　Supp. 728; 1968 AMC 2084 (S. D. N. Y.) ···73
Mardorf, Peach & Co. Ltd. v. Attica Sea Carriers Corp. of Liberia—The Laconia
　[1977] 1 Lloyd's Rep. 315; [1977] A. C. 850; [1977] 2 W. L. R. 286; [1977] 1 All
　E. R. 545, (H. L.); rev'g [1976] 1 Lloyd's Rep. 395; [1976] Q. B. 835; [1976] 2 W.
　L. R. 668; [1976] 2 All E. R. 249, (C. A.) ·······244, 245, 254, 257, 258, **260-261**, 262, 266, 548
Mare Felice, The, SMA 1954 (Arb. at N. Y. 1984) ···240
Mare Felice, The, 1974 AMC 2150 (Arb. at N. Y. 1971) ·······································271
Maredelanto Compania Naviera S. A. v. Bergbauhandel G. m. b. H.—The Mihalis
　Angelos [1970] 2 Lloyd's Rep. 43; [1971] 1 Q. B. 164; [1970] 3 W. L. R. 601;
　[1970] 3 All E. R. 125, (C. A.); rev'g [1970] 1 Lloyd's Rep. 118, (Q. B.)
　··86, 90, 92, **107**, 359
Mareva A. S., The—Mareva Navigation Co. Ltd. v. Canaria Armadora S. A. [1977] 1
　Lloyd's Rep. 368, (Q. B.) ·······································124, 125, **127**, 363, 368, **369**, 370, 371
Mareva Navigation Co. Ltd. v. Canaria Armadora S. A.—The Mareva A. S. [1977] 1
　Lloyd's Rep. 368, (Q. B.) ·······································124, 125, **127**, 363, 368, **369**, 370, 371
Margaronis Navigation Agency Ltd. v. Henry W. Peabody & Co. of London Ltd.
　[1964] 2 Lloyd's Rep. 153; [1965] 2 Q. B. 430; [1964] 3 W. L. R. 873; [1964] 3
　All E. R. 333, (C. A.) ···86
Maria D, The—Elpis Maritime Co. Ltd. v. Marti Chartering Co. Inc. [1991] 2 Lloyd's
　Rep. 311; [1992] 1 A. C. 21; [1991] 3 W. L. R. 330; [1991] 3 All E. R. 758; (1991)
　135 S. J. (LB) 100; (1991) 141 New L. J. 1109, (H. L.); rev'g [1991] 1 Lloyd's Rep.

521, (C. A.) ··64
Maria G. Culucundis, The, 1954 AMC 325 (Arb. at N. Y. 1952) ················272
Maria G. L., The, SMA 2506 (1988) ··204
Maria Glyptis, The, SMA 2223 (Arb. at N. Y. 1986) ·······························385
Maria K, The, SMA 1324 (Arb. at N. Y. 1979) ···172
Maria Lemos, The, SMA 74 (Arb. at N. Y. 1963) ··108
Maria Sitinas, The, 1985 AMC 1790 (S. D. N. Y.) ··457
Marifortuna Naviera S. A. v. Government of Ceylon [1970] 1 Lloyd's Rep. 247, (Q. B.) ··515, 561
Marika M, The—Eastern Mediterranean Maritime (Liechtenstein) Ltd. v. Unimarine S. A.[1981] 2 Lloyd's Rep. 622, (Q. B.) ···365, **366**
Marine Fuel Supply & Towing Inc. v. The Ken Lucky (1988) 859 F. 2d 1405 ; 1989 AMC 390 (9th Cir.) ··502
Marine Products Export Corporation v. The Globe Galaxy, 1987 AMC 2310 (S. D. N. Y.); later proceedings 1992 AMC 1336 (S. D. N. Y.); aff'd (1992) 977 F. 2d 66 ; 1993 AMC 190 (2d Cir.) ···453, **454**
Marine Sulphur Queen, The (1972) 460 F. 2d 89 ; 1972 AMC 1122 (2d Cir.) ; cert. denied (1972) 409 U. S. 982 ··427, 522
Marine Traders Inc. v. Seasons Navigation Corp. (1970) 422 F. 2d 804 ; 1970 AMC 346 (2d Cir.) ···493
Marion, The—Grand Champion Tankers Ltd. v. Norpipe A/S [1984] 2 Lloyd's Rep. 1 ; [1984] A. C. 563 ; [1984] 2 W. L. R. 942 ; [1984] 2 All E. R. 243, (H. L.) ; [1983] 2 Lloyd's Rep. 156, (C. A.) ; [1982] 2 Lloyd's Rep. 52, (Q. B.) ·······················557, 559
Maritime National Fish Ltd. v. Ocean Trawlers Ltd. (1935) 51 Ll. L. Rep. 299 ; [1935] A. C. 524 ; 104 L. J. P. C. 88 ; 153 L. T. 425 ; 18 Asp. M. L. C. 551, (P. C.) ·············**405-406**
Maritime Transport Overseas G. m. b. H. v. Unitramp—The Antaios [1981] 2 Lloyd's Rep. 284, (Q. B.) ···532, **534**
Maritime Ventures Int'l Inc. v. Caribbean Trading & Fidelity Ltd. (1988) 689 F. Supp. 1341 (S. D. N. Y.) ···**77**
Maro, The SMA 2533 (Arb. at N. Y. 1988) ···119, **224**
Marquette, The (1973) 480 F. 2d 669 ; 1973 AMC 1683 (2d Cir.) ·······················428, 429
Marseille Fret S. A. v. D. Oltmann Schiffahrts G. m. b. H. & Co. K. G. —The Trado [1982] 1 Lloyd's Rep. 157, (Q. B.) ··353
Marta Z, The, SMA 2602 (Arb. at N. Y. 1989) ··362
Martin v. The Southwark (1903) 191 U. S. 1 ··162, **163**
Marubeni America Corp. v. The Unity (1992) 802 F. Supp. 1353 ; 1993 AMC 141 (D. Md.) ··460
Marubeni-Iida (A) Inc. v. Toko Kaiun Kabushiki Kaisha (1971) 327 F. Supp. 519 (S. D. Tex.) ···525
Maruka, The, SMA 2609 (Arb. at N. Y. 1989) ···73
Mary Ellen Conway, The, 1973 AMC 772 (Arb. at N. Y.) ··417
Mary L, The (1990) *unreported* (Evans, J.) ··313
Mary Lou, The—Transoceanic Petroleum Carriers v. Cook Industries Inc. [1981] 2

Lloyd's Rep. 272, (Q. B.) ·····························177, 178, 179, **183-184**, 185, 186, 192, 193, 195
Maryland Trader, The, SMA 849 (Arb. at N. Y. 1974) ···205
Massalia, The—Government of Ceylon v. Société Franco-Tunisienne d'Armement-
  Tunis (demurrage) [1960] 2 Lloyd's Rep. 352; [1962] 2 Q. B. 416; [1961] 2 W. L.
  R. 161; [1960] 3 All E. R. 797, (Q. B.) ···358
Massalia, The—Société Franco-Tunisienne d'Armement-Tunis v. Sidermar S. p. A.
  (frustration) [1960] 1 Lloyd's Rep. 594; [1961] 2 Q. B. 278; [1960] 3 W. L. R.
  701; [1960] 2 All E. R. 529, (Q. B.) ··398
Massari v. Forest Lumber Co. (1923) 290 F. 470; 1923 AMC 1111 (S. D. Fla.) ········108
Mastro Giorgis, The—Bellcore Maritime Corp. v. F. Lli. Moretti Cereali S. p. A. [1983]
  2 Lloyd's Rep. 66, (Q. B.) ···372, 373, 374
Mastrobuono v. Shearson Lehman Hutton Inc. (1995) —U. S.—; 115 S. Ct. 1212; 131
  L. Ed. 2d 76 ···459
Matija Gubec, The—Jadranska Slobodna Plovidba v. Gulf Shipping Lines Ltd. [1983]
  1 Lloyd's Rep. 24 (Q. B.) ···127
Mavro Vetranic, The—Greenwich Marine Inc. v. Federal Commerce & Navigation Co.
  Ltd. [1985] 1 Lloyd's Rep. 580, (Q. B.) ···91
Maxine Footwear Co. Ltd. v. Canadian Government Merchant Marine Ltd. [1959] 2
  Lloyd's Rep. 105; [1959] A. C. 589; [1959] 3 W. L. R. 232; 103 S. J. 561; [1959] 2
  All E. R. 740, (P. C.) ···420
Meade-King, Robinson & Co. v. Jacobs & Co. [1915] 2 K. B. 640; 84 L. J. K. B. 1133;
  20 Com. Cas. 288; 113 L. T. 298; 13 Asp. M. L. C. 105; 31 T. L. R. 316, (C. A.) ········554
Medina v. Marvirazon Compania Naviera S. A. (1983) 709 F. 2d 124; 1983 AMC
  2113 (1st Cir.) ···501
Mediolanum Shipping Co. v. Japan Lines Ltd.—The Mediolanum [1984] 1 Lloyd's
  Rep. 136, (C. A.); [1982] 1 Lloyd's Rep. 47, (Q. B.) ······························**196**, 219, 296
Mediolanum, The—Mediolanum Shipping Co. v. Japan Lines Ltd. [1984] 1 Lloyd's
  Rep. 136, (C. A.); [1982] 1 Lloyd's Rep. 47, (Q. B.) ······························**196**, 219, 296
Medita, The, SMA 1150 (Arb. at N. Y. 1977) ·······················115, 119, **134**, 287, 300
Medita, The, SMA 2347 (Arb. at N. Y. 1986) ···206
Mediterranean Freight Services Ltd. v. BP Oil International Ltd.—The Fiona [1994]
  2 Lloyd's Rep. 506, (C. A.); [1993] 1 Lloyd's Rep. 257, (Q. B.) ···········168, 169, 604, **606**
Meling v. Minos Shipping Co. Ltd.—The Oliva [1972] 1 Lloyd's Rep. 458, (Q. B.) ······419
Meltemi, The, SMA 491 (Arb. at N. Y. 1970) ···276
Mencke v. A Cargo of Java Sugar (1902) 187 U. S. 248 ···································202
Menke v. Monchecourt (1994) 17 F. 3d 1007 (7th Cir.) ···································457
Mente & Co. v. Isthmian S. S. Co. (The Quarrington Court) (1940) 36 F. Supp. 278;
  1940 AMC 1546 (S. D. N. Y.); aff'd (1941) 122 F. 2d 266; 1941 AMC 1234 (2d Cir.)
  ···340, 522
Merak, The [1964] 2 Lloyd's Rep. 527; [1965] P. 223; [1965] 2 W. L. R. 250;
  [1965] 1 All E. R. 230, (C. A.) ···439
Merak, The—Varverakis v. Compagnia de Navegacion Artico S. A. [1976] 2 Lloyd's
  Rep. 250, (Q. B. and C. A.) ···53

Mercandian Queen, The, SMA 2713 (Arb. at N. Y. 1990) ··200
Mercandian Supplier II, The, SMA 2509 (Arb. at N. Y. 1988) ····························172, 388
Mercantile S. S. Co. Ltd. *v.* Tyser (1881) 7 Q. B. D. 73 ··422
Merit Ins. Co. *v.* Leatherby Ins. Co. (1983) 714 F. 2d 673 (7th Cir.); *cert. denied* 464
    U. S. 1009; (1984) 737 F. 2d 580 (7th Cir.); *cert. denied* (1984) 469 U. S. 918 ········466
Mermaid I, The, SMA 1836 (Arb. at N. Y. 1983) ···278, 413
Merrill Lynch Commodities Inc. *v.* Richal Shipping Corp. (1984) 581 F. Supp. 933 (S.
    D. N. Y.) ··79
Merrill Lynch Pierce Fenner & Smith Inc. *v.* Bobker (1986) 808 F. 2d 930 (2d Cir.)
    ···**472-473**
Messis, The, SMA 2167 (Arb. at N. Y. 1985) ···387
Mesologi, The, 1971 AMC 2498 (Arb. at N. Y.) ···318
Messiniaki Floga, The (1985) 606 F. Supp. 692; 1985 AMC 2190 (S. D. N. Y.) ············461
Metropolitan Coal Co. *v.* Howard (1946) 155 F. 2d 780 (2d Cir.) ······························113
Metropolitan Water Board *v.* Dick, Kerr & Co. [1918] A. C. 119; 87 L. J. K. B. 370;
    117 L. T. 766; 34 T. L. R. 113; 82 J. P. 61; 161 L. G. R. 1, (H. L.) ····························399
Metropolitan World Tankers Corp. *v.* P. N. Pertambangan Minjakdangas Dumi
    National, 1976 AMC 421 (S. D. N. Y.) ··460
Meyer *v.* R. F. Sanderson & Co. (1916) 32 T. L. R. 428 ··128
Miami, The, SMA 240 (Arb. at N. Y. 1967) ···117
Micada Compania Naviera S. A. *v.* Texim [1968] 2 Lloyd's Rep. 57, (Q. B.) ··············**170**
Michael C. Lemos, The, SMA 1906 (Arb. at N. Y. 1983) ···205
Michael L, The, SMA 1301 (Arb. at N. Y. 1979) ··361
Michaels (E. B.) *v.* Mariforum Shipping S. A. (1980) 624 F. 2d 411; 1980 AMC 1901
    (2d Cir.) ··462, **463**, 464
Middlesex Mut. Ins. Co. *v.* Levine (1982) 675 F. 2d 1197 (11th Cir.) ·························467
Midland Bank Trust Co. Ltd. *v.* Hett, Stubbs & Kemp [1979] Ch. 384; [1978] 3 W.
    L. R. 167; [1978] 3 All E. R. 571, (Q. B.) ··86
Midland Silicones Ltd. *v.* Scruttons Ltd. [1961] 2 Lloyd's Rep. 365; [1962] A. C. 446;
    [1962] 2 W. L. R. 186; [1962] 1 All E. R. 1, (H. L.); *aff'g* [1960] 1 Lloyd's Rep.
    571; [1961] 1 Q. B. 106, (C. A.) ··334
Midland Tar Distillers Inc. *v.* The Lotos (1973) 362 F. Supp. 1311; 1973 AMC 1924
    (S. D. N. Y.) ··448
Midwest Shipping Co. Inc. *v.* D. I. Henry (Jute) Ltd. [1971] 1 Lloyd's Rep. 375, (Q.
    B.) ···**291**
Miguel de Larrinaga S. S. Co. *v.* D. L. Flack & Son (1925) 21 Ll. L. Rep. 284, (C. A.);
    aff'g (1924) 20 Ll. L. Rep. 268, (K. B.) ···**562-563**
Mihalis Angelos, The—Maredelanto Cia. Nav. *v.* Bergbauhandel G. m. b. H. [1970] 2
    Lloyd's Rep. 43; [1971] 1 Q. B. 164; [1970] 3 W. L. R. 601; [1970] 3 All E. R. 125,
    (C. A.); *rev'g* [1970] 1 Lloyd's Rep. 118, (Q. B.) ···86, 90, 92, **107**, 359
Mihalios Xilas, The—China National Foreign Trade Transportation Corp. *v.* Evlogia
    Shipping Co. Ltd. [1979] 2 Lloyd's Rep. 303; [1979] 1 W. L. R. 1018; [1979] 2 All
    E. R. 1044, (H. L.); *rev'g* [1978] 2 Lloyd's Rep. 397; [1978] 1 W. L. R. 1257; [1979]

1 All E. R. 657, (C. A.); *restoring* [1976] 2 Lloyd's Rep. 697; [1976] 3 All E. R. 865, (Q. B.) ··93, **246**, 254, 255, 260, 261, 262, **263**, 264
Mihalios Xilas, The—International Bulk Carriers v. Evlogia Shipping [1978] 2 Lloyd's Rep. 186, (Q. B.) ··256, 257, 480, 481, 551, 566
Milanovich v. Costa Crociere (1992) 954 F. 2d 763; 1993 AMC 1034 (D. C. Cir. 1992) ···56
Milburn & Co. v. Jamaica Fruit Importing and Trading Co. of London [1900] 2 Q. B. 540; 83 L. T. 321; 69 L. J. Q. B. 860; 16 T. L. R. 515; 5 Com. Cas. 346; 9 Asp. M. L. C. 122, (C. A.) ··**327-328**
Millar (W.) & Co. Ltd. v. Freden (Owners) [1918] 1 K. B. 611; 87 L. J. K. B. 524; 118 L. T. 522; 34 T. L. R. 234; 14 Asp. M. L. C. 247, (C. A.) ··**101**
Miller v. Law Accident Insurance Co. [1903] 1 K. B. 712; 88 L. T. 370; 72 L. J. K. B. 428; 19 T. L. R. 331; 8 Com. Cas. 161; 9 Asp. M. L. C. 386, (C. A.) ······················421
Miller (James) & Partners v. Whitworth Street Estates (Manchester) Ltd. [1970] 1 Lloyd's Rep. 269; [1970] A. C. 583; [1970] 2 W. L. R. 728; [1970] 1 All E. R. 796, (H. L.) ···439
Milly Gregos, The, SMA 2190 (Arb. at N. Y. 1986) ··118, 241
Ming Autumn, The, SMA 2189 (Arb. at N. Y. 1986) ···510
Ming Belle, The, SMA 2043 (Arb. at N. Y. 1984) ···505
Ming Summer, The, SMA 2490 (Arb. at N. Y. 1988) ···536
Mini Lap, The, SMA 1077 (Arb. at N. Y. 1976) ···115
Ministry of Food, Government of Bangladesh v. Bengal Liner Ltd.—The Bengal Pride [1986] 1 Lloyd's Rep. 167, (Q. B.) ···442
Minturn v. Maynard (1855) 17 How. 477 ···501
Miseroachi & Co. S. p. A. v. Peavey Int'l Inc. (15 September 1978) 78 Civ. 1571 (S. D. N. Y.) (*unreported*) ··**467**
Misphah, The (1878) F. Cas. No. 9678 (D. Del.) ···344
Mistral, The, SMA 2724 (Arb. at N. Y. 1990) ···497
Mitchell v. Steel [1916] 2 K. B. 610 ··169
Mitchell (George) (Chesterhall) Ltd. v. Finney Lock Seeds Ltd. [1983] 2 Lloyd's Rep. 272; [1983] A. C. 803; [1983] 3 W. L. R. 163; [1983] 2 All E. R. 737, (H. L.); [1983] 1 Lloyd's Rep. 168; [1983] Q. B. 284, (C. A.); [1981] 1 Lloyd's Rep. 476, (Q. B.) ···426
Mitsubishi Corp. v. The Oinoussian Strength (1994) U. S. Dist. Lexis 2625 (S. D. N. Y.) ··450, 460
Mmecen S. A. v. Inter Ro-Ro S. A.—The Samah [1981] 1 Lloyd's Rep. 40, (Q. B.) ···54, 69
Mobil Oil Indonesia Inc. v. Asamera Oil (Indonesia) Ltd. (1977) 43 N. Y. 2d 275; (1977) 401 N. Y. S. 2d 186; (1977) 372 N. E. 2d 21; (1980) 487 F. Supp. 63 (S. D. N. Y.) ···464, 465
Moel Tryvan Ship Co. v. Andrew Weir & Co. [1910] 2 K. B. 844; 79 L. J. K. B. 898; 103 L. T. 161; 15 Com. Cas. 307; 11 Asp. M. L. C. 469, (C. A.) ··································359
Mohammad Bin Abdul Rahman Orri v. Seawind Navigation Co. S. A.—The Winner [1986] 1 Lloyd's Rep. 36, (Q. B.) ···54
Molthes Rederi A/S v. Ellerman's Wilson Line Ltd. (1926) 26 Ll. L. Rep. 259; [1927]

1 K. B. 710; 32 Com. Cas. 106; 96 L. J. K. B. 414; 136 L. T. 767; 17 Asp. M. L. C. 219,
 (K. B.) ··483, **484**
Monarch S. S. Co. Ltd. v. A/B Karlshamns Oljefabriker (1948) 82 Ll. L. Rep. 137;
 [1949] A. C. 196; [1949] L. J. R. 772; 65 T. L. R. 217; [1949] 1 All E. R. 1, (H. L.) ···405
Mondella v. The Elie V. (1963) 223 F. Supp. 390; 1965 AMC 2672 (S. D. N. Y.)
 ···213, 536, 537
Mondial Trading Co. G. m. b. H. v. Gill & Duffus Zuckerhandelsgesellschaft m. b. H.
 [1980] 2 Lloyd's Rep. 376, (Q. B.) ···445
Monica S, The [1967] 2 Lloyd's Rep. 113; [1968] P. 741; [1968] 2 W. L. R. 431;
 [1967] 3 All E. R. 740, (Adm.) ···488
Montauk Oil Transp. Corp. v. Sonat Marine Inc. (1989) 871 F. 2d 1169; 1989 AMC
 1147 (2d Cir.) ···383
Montecristo, The, SMA 2941 (Arb. at N. Y. 1993) ···278
Monterosso Shipping Co. v. International Transport Workers' Federation—The Rosso
 [1982] 2 Lloyd's Rep. 120; [1982] 3 All E. R. 841; [1982] Com. L. R. 152; (1982)
 126 S. J. 591. (C. A.) ···55
MoPrusman Ltd. v. Ariel Maritime, 1992 AMC 1059 (S. D. N. Y. 1991) ······················78
Moran Towing Co. v. Gammino Constr. Co. (1966) 363 F. 2d 108; 1966 AMC 2263
 (1st Cir.) ···**240**
Morelite Const. Corp. v. New York City District Council Carpenters Benefit Funds
 (1984) 748 F. 2d 79 (2d Cir.) ··**466**
Morewitz v. Imbros Shipping Co. Ltd., 1979 AMC 1622 (E. D. Va. 1978) ················537
Morris v. Levison (1876) 1 C. P. D. 155; 34 L. T. 576; 3 ASP M. L. C. 171 ···········102, 103
Morris v. Martin (C. W.) [1965] 2 Lloyd's Rep. 63; [1966] 1 Q. B. 716; [1965] 3 W.
 L. R. 276; [1965] 2 All E. R. 725, (C. A.) ···334
Morris v. New York State Dep't of Taxation and Finance (1993) 82 N. Y. 2d 135;
 603 N. Y. S. 2d 807; 623 N. E. 2d 1157 ···76
Moses H. Cone Memorial Hosp. v. Mercury Constr. Corp. (1983) 460 U. S. 1 ··········453
Moshill, The, SMA 2069 (Arb. at N. Y. 1985) ···277
Motor Oil Hellas (Corinth) Refineries S. A. v. Shipping Corp. of India—The
 Kanchenjunga [1990] 1 Lloyd's Rep. 391, (H. L.); aff'g [1989] 1 Lloyd's Rep. 354;
 (1989) 132 S. J. 19, (C. A.); aff'g [1987] 2 Lloyd's Rep. 509, (Q. B.)
 ··92, 93, 125, 142, 161, 190, **191**, 260, 261, 293, 360, **611**
Mount Athos, The, SMA 1570 (Arb. at N. Y. 1981) ······································115, 118, 321
Mozart Festival, The, SMA 2393 (Arb. at N. Y. 1987) ···200
Muggenburg, The, SMA 898 (Arb. at N. Y. 1974) ···239
Muncaster Castle, The—Riverstone Meat Co. Pty. Ltd. v. Lancashire Shipping Co.
 Ltd. [1961] 1 Lloyd's Rep. 57; [1961] A. C. 807; [1961] 2 W. L. R. 269; [1961] 1
 All E. R. 495, (H. L.) ···557
Munson S. S. Line v. Elswick Steam Shipping Co. (1913) 207 F. 984 (S. D. N. Y.); aff'd
 per curiam (1914) 214 F. 84 (2d Cir.) ···136, 138
Munson S. S. Line v. Miramar S. S. Co. (1908) 166 F. 722 (2d Cir.); mod. on other
 grounds (1909) 167 F. 960 (2d Cir.); cert. denied (1909) 214 U. S. 526

··117-118, 163, 384, 385
Muratore v. The Scotia Prince (1987) 663 F. Supp. 484 ; 1988 AMC 859 (D. Me.
　1987) ··458
Murray Oil Products Co. v. Mitsui & Co. (1944) 146 F. 2d 381 (2d Cir.) ·············460
Muskegon, The (1924) 10 F. 2d 817 (S. D. N. Y.) ································343
Mykali II, The, SMA 2240 (Arb. at N. Y. 1986) ·····························118, 510
Myriam, The, 1992 AMC 1625 (Arb. at N. Y.) ···································270

N. H. Shipping Corp. v. Freights of the Jackie Hause (1960) 181 F. Supp. 165 (S. D.
　N. Y.) ···492, 493
N. V. Stoom. Maats. "De Maas" v. Nippon Yusen Kaisha—The Pendrecht [1980] 2
　Lloyd's Rep. 56, (Q. B.) ···440
Naess Shipping Agencies Inc. v. SSI Navigation Inc., 1985 AMC 346 (N. D. Cal. 1984)
　···543
Naiad, The, SMA 1177 ; 1978 AMC 2049 (Arb. at N. Y. 1977) ···············202, 207
Nanfri, The—Federal Commerce & Navigation Co. Ltd. v. Molena Alpha Inc. [1979]
　1 Lloyd's Rep. 201 ; [1979] A. C. 757 ; [1978] 3 W. L. R. 991, [1979] 1 All E. R. 307,
　(H. L.); aff'g [1978] 2 Lloyd's Rep. 132 ; [1978] Q. B. 927 ; [1978] 3 W. L. R. 309 ;
　[1978] 3 All E. R. 1066, (C. A.); rev'g [1978] 1 Lloyd's Rep. 581, (Q. B.)
　·····························88, 99, **248**, 249-252, **325-326**, 327-329, **332**, 333, 482, 484, 486, 548
Napier, The, SMA 525 (Arb. at N. Y. 1970) ·····································239
Narnian Sea, The, 1991 AMC 274 (Arb. at N. Y. 1990) ···············129, 135, 354, 591
Nassau Sand & Gravel Co. v. Red Star Towing and Transp. Co. (1932) 62 F. 2d
　356 (2d Cir.) ··207
National Bulk Carriers Inc. v. Princess Management Co. Ltd. (1979) 597 F. 2d 819
　(2d Cir.) ···465
National Carriers Ltd. v. Panalpina (Northern) Ltd. [1981] A. C. 675 ; [1981] 1 All E.
　R. 161, (H. L.) ···394, 395, 399, 402
National Iranian Oil Co. v. Mapco International Inc. (1992) 983 F. 2d 485 (3d Cir.) ···524
National Shipping Co. of Saudi Arabia and Transamerican Steamship Corp.
　(Arbitration between) 1993 AMC 684 (S. D. N. Y. 1992) ···············467-468
National Transp. Corp. v. Texaco, 1976 AMC 1549 (Arb. at N. Y.) ···············381
Naviera Amazonica Peruana S. A. v. Compania Internacional de Seguros del Peru
　[1988] 1 Lloyd's Rep. 116, (C. A.) ······································439
Naviera Mogor S. A. v. Société Metallurgique de Normandie—The Nogar Marin
　[1988] 1 Lloyd's Rep. 412 ; [1988] 1 F. T. L. R. 349. (C. A.); aff'g [1987] 1 Lloyd's
　Rep. 456 ; [1987] 1 F. T. L. R. 243, (Q. B.) ···············294, 326, 327, **330**, 331, 585
Navieros Oceanikos S. A. v. The Mobil Trader (1977) 554 F. 2d 43, (2d Cir.) ······56, 57
Navigas International Ltd. v. Trans-Offshore Inc.—The Bridgestone Maru No.3
　[1985] 2 Lloyd's Rep. 62, (Q. B.) ·················365, 372, 377, 574, **577**, 583, 592, **593**
Navigator, The, SMA 287 (Arb. at N. Y. 1968) ; 1977 AMC 739 ·······················111
Navigazione Alta Italia S. p. A. v. Concordia Maritime Chartering A. B.—The Stena
　Pacifica [1990] 2 Lloyd's Rep. 234, (Q. B.) ·····················439, 603, **604**

Naxos Shipping Co. v. Thegra Shipping Co.—The Corfu Island (1973) *unreported*
(Ackner, J.) ···249
Nea Agrex S. A. v. Baltic Shipping Co. Ltd.—The Agios Lazaros [1976] 2 Lloyd's
Rep. 47; [1976] Q. B. 933; [1976] 2 W. L. R. 925; [1976] 2 All E. R. 842, (C. A.)
··313, 439, 440, 515, 517, 518, 520, **561**
Nea Tyhi, The [1982] 1 Lloyd's Rep. 606, (Q. B.) ·······································**69**, **338**
Nea Tyhi, The, SMA 2571 (Arb. at N. Y. 1989)···204
Nelson (Thomas) & Sons v. Dundee East Coast Shipping Co., 1907 S. C. 927; 44 Sc.
L. R. 661; 15 S. L. T. 38 ··153, 360, 361
Nema, The—Pioneer Shipping Ltd. v. B. T. P. Tioxide Ltd. [1981] 2 Lloyd's Rep. 239;
[1982] A. C. 724; [1981] 3 W. L. R. 292; [1981] 2 All E. R. 1030, (H. L.); *aff'g*
[1980] 2 Lloyd's Rep. 339; [1980] Q. B. 547; [1980] 3 W. L. R. 326; [1980] 3 All
E. R. 117, (C. A.); *rev'g* [1980] 2 Lloyd's Rep. 83, (Q. B.) ···**395**, 396, 399, 401-403, 444, 445
Neptune Kiku, The, SMA 2102 (Arb. at N. Y. 1985)···································113
Nesbitt v. Lushington (1792) 4 T. R. 783; 100 E. R. 1300 ··························421
Neubros Corp. v. Northwestern Nat. Ins. Co. (1972) 359 F. Supp. 310 (E. D. N. Y.) ······240
New England Energy Inc. v. Keystone Shipping Co. (1988) 855 F. 2d 1; 1989 AMC
537 (1st Cir.); *cert. denied* (1989) 489 U. S. 1077 ·····························452
New Horizon,The—Tramp Shipping Corp. v. Greenwich Marine Inc. [1975] 2 Lloyd's
Rep. 314; [1975] 1 W. L. R. 1042; [1975] 2 All E. R. 989; [1975] I. C. R. 261, (C.
A.)···**562**
New Rotterdam Insurance Co. v. The Loppersum (1963) 215 F. Supp. 563 (S. D. N.
Y.) ···428
New Way, The, 1977 AMC 88 (Arb. at N. Y. 1976) ···································144
New York and Cuba Mail Steamship Co. v. Eriksen & Christensen (1922) 10 Ll. L.
Rep. 772; 27 Com. Cas. 330, (K. B.) ···**157**, 356-357
New York Cent. R. R. v. New York, N. H. & H. R. R. (1960) 275 F. 2d 865 (2d Cir.) ···343
New York Getty, The, SMA 2200 (Arb. at N. Y. 1986) ·······························**241**
New Zealand Insur. v. The Greenland Rex, 1991 OR 1992 AMC 21 (S. D. N. Y.) ········450
New Zealand Shipping Co. Ltd. v. A. M. Satterthwaite & Co. Ltd.—The Eurymedon
[1974] 1 Lloyd's Rep. 534; [1975] A. C. 154; [1974] 2 W. L. R. 865; [1974] 1 All
E. R. 1015, (P. C.) ···334
Newa Line v. Erechthion Shipping Co. S. A.—The Erechthion [1987] 2 Lloyd's Rep.
180; [1987] 1 F. T. L. R. 525, (Q. B.) ···196, 198, 219, **296**, 297
Newman & Dale v. Lamport & Holt [1896] 1 Q. B. 20; 73 L. T. 475; 65 L. J. Q. B.
102; 12 T. L. R. 18; 1 Com. Cas. 161; 8 Asp. M. L. C. 76 ·······················**219**
Newspaper Guild of New York v. New York Post Corp. (1983) No. 32 Civ. 7226
(DNE) (S. D. N. Y. 14 July) ···465
Ngo Chew Hong Edible Oil Pte. Ltd. v. Scindia Steam Navigation Co. Ltd.—The
Jalamohan [1988] 1 Lloyd's Rep. 443; [1998] 1 F. T. L. R. 340, (Q. B.) ···········332
Niarchos (London) Ltd. v. Shell Tankers Ltd. [1961] 2 Lloyd's Rep. 496, (Q. B.)
··95, **396**, 417, 575, 591
Nichimen Company v. The Farland (1972) 462 F. 2d 319 (2d Cir.) ······**316**, **317**, 320, 431

Nicolaou v. Minister of War Transport (1944) 77 Ll. L. Rep. 495 ; 60 T. L. R. 524 ; 171
L. T. 159 ; [1944] 2 All E. R. 322···608
Nicolene v. Simmonds [1953] 1 Q. B. 543 ; [1953] 1 Lloyd's Rep. 189 ; [1953] 2 W.
L. R. 717 ; [1953] 1 All E. R. 882, (C. A.) ; *aff'g* [1952] 2 Lloyd's Rep. 419, (Q. B.) ······50
Nidarholm, The (1931) 282 U. S. 681 ··316
Nilam, The, SMA 2705 (Arb. at N. Y. 1990) ··116
Nippon Yusen Kaisha v. Acme Shipping Corp.—The Charalambos N. Pateras [1972]
1 Lloyd's Rep. 1 ; [1972] 1 W. L. R. 74 ; [1972] 1 All E. R. 35, (C. A.) ; *aff'g* [1971]
2 Lloyd's Rep. 42, (Q. B.) ···247, 249, 285, 553, 556
Nippon Yusen Kaisha v. Pacifica Navegacion S. A.—The Ion [1980] 2 Lloyd's Rep.
245, (Q. B.) ···311
Nissho-Iwai Co. Ltd. v. The Stolt Lion (1980) 617 F. 2d 907 ; 1980 AMC 867 (2d Cir.) ;
rev'g 1979 AMC 2415 (S. D. N. Y.) ··301, 316, 522
Nissos Samos, The—Samos Shipping Enterprises v. Eckhardt & Co. K. G. [1985] 1
Lloyd's Rep. 378, (Q. B.) ···54
Nitram Inc. v. The Cretan Life (1979) 599 F. 2d 1359 (5th Cir.) ···317
Nizeti, The—Compagnie Algerienne de Meunerie v. Katana Societa di Navigazione
Marittima S. p. A. [1960] 1 Lloyd's Rep. 132 ; [1960] 2 Q. B. 115 ; [1960] 2 W. L. R.
719 ; [1960] 2 All E. R. 55, (C. A.) ; [1958] 2 Lloyd's Rep. 502 ; [1959] 1 Q. B.
527 ; [1959] 2 W. L. R. 366 ; [1959] 1 All E. R. 272, (Q. B.) ···156
Nobel's Explosive Co. Ltd. v. Jenkins & Co. [1896] 2 Q. B. 326 ; 1 Com. Cas. 436 ; 65
L. J. Q. B. 638 ; 75 L. T. 163 ; 12 T. L. R. 522 ; 8 Asp. M. L. C. 181 ··421
Noemijulia Steamship Co. Ltd. v. Minister of Food (1950) 84 Ll. L. Rep. 354 ; [1951]
1 K. B. 223 ; 66 T. L. R. (Pt. 2) 342 ; [1950] 2 All E. R. 699, (C. A.) ; *aff'g* (1950) 83
Ll. L. Rep. 500 ; 66 T. L. R. (Pt. 1) 819, (K. B.) ···**155**, 156, 158, 356, 357, 550
Nogar Marin, The—Naviera Mogor S. A. v. Société Metallurgique de Normadie [1988]
1 Lloyd's Rep. 412 ; [1988] 1 F. T. L. R. 349, (C. A.) ; *aff'g* [1987] 1 Lloyd's Rep.
456 ; [1987] 1 F. T. L. R. 243, (Q. B.) ···294, 326, 327, **330**, 331, 585
North Atlantic and Gulf S. S. Co. (*Re*) (1962) 204 F. Supp. 899 ; 1963 AMC 871 (S. D.
N. Y.) ; *aff'd* (1963) 320 F. 2d 628 (2d Cir.) ···492, **495**
North Emperor, The, SMA 1284 (Arb. at N. Y. 1978) ···318
North Hills, The, 1973 AMC 2318 (Arb. at N. Y. 1972) ···114, **233**
North Marchioness, The, SMA 77 (Arb. at N. Y. 1962) ···241
North River Ins. Co. v. Philadelphia Reinsurance Corp. (1994) 856 F. Supp. 850 (S. D.
N. Y.) ···453
Northern Clipper, The, 1967 AMC 1557 (Arb. at N. Y.) ···116, 117, 118
Northern Light, The, SMA 2645 (Arb. at N. Y. 1990) ···224
Northern Pacific R. Co. v. American Trading Co. (1904) 195 U. S. 439 ···430
Northern S. S. Co. v. Earn Line S. S. Co. (1910) 175 F. 529 (2d Cir.) ···382, 389
Northern Star, The, SMA 1494 (Arb. at N. Y. 1980) ···**628**
Northern Tankers (Cyprus) Ltd. v. Lexmar Corp. (1992) 781 F. Supp. 289 ; 1992
AMC 1021 (S. D. N. Y.) ···57
Norwegian Shipping & Trade Mission v. Nitrate Corp. of Chile Ltd., 1942 AMC 1523

(Arb. at N. Y.) ··389
Noto, The, 1979 AMC 116 (Arb. at N. Y. 1976) ·································271, 274, 275, 361
Nourse (James) Ltd. v. Elder Dempster & Co. Ltd. (1922) 13 Ll. L. Rep. 197, (K. B.)
 ··219, 376
Nova (Jersey) Knit Ltd. v. Kammgarn Spinnerei G. m. b. H. [1977] 1 Lloyd's Rep.
 463; [1977] 1 W. L. R. 713; [1977] 2 All E. R. 463, (H. L.); rev'g [1976] 2 Lloyd's
 Rep. 155, (C. A.) ··442
Nova Scotia Steel Co. v. Sutherland S. S. Co. (1889) 5 Com. Cas. 106 ······················263
Noyes v. Munson S. S. Line (1909) 173 F. 814 (S. D. N. Y.) ························118, 381, 384
N'tchengue, The, SMA 2665 (Arb. at N. Y. 1990) ···430
Nugent v. Smith (1876) 1 C. P. D. 423; 34 L. T. 827; 3 Asp. M. L. C. 198, (C. A.) ········420
Nyquist v. Randall (1987) 819 F. 2d 1014 (11th Cir.) ··278

O/Y Wasa S. S. Co. Ltd. v. Newspaper Pulp & Wood Export (1949) 82 Ll. L. Rep.
 936, (K. B.) ··67
Oak Pearl, The, SMA 2427 (Arb. at N. Y. 1986) ··278
Oakes v. Turquand & Harding (1867) L. R. 2 H. L. 325; 36 L. J. (Ch.) 949; 16 L. T.
 808, (H. L.) ··82
Oakworth, The—Associated Portland Cement Manufacturers Ltd. v. Teigland
 Shipping A/S [1975] 1 Lloyd's Rep. 581, (C. A.) ···87, 531
Occidental World Wide Investment Corp. v. Skibs A/S Avanti [1976] 1 Lloyd's Rep.
 293, (Q. B.) ··404
Ocean Advance, The, SMA 1677 (Arb. at N. Y. 1982) ··272
Ocean Commander, The, SMA 2930 (Arb. at N. Y. 1992) ·································412, 414
Ocean Dove, The, SMA 2750 (Arb. at N. Y. 1991) ··344
Ocean Frost, The—Armagas Ltd. v. Mundogas S. A. [1986] 2 Lloyd's Rep. 109;
 [1986] A. C. 717; [1986] 2 W. L. R. 1063; [1986] 2 All E. R. 385, (H. L.); [1985] 1
 Lloyd's Rep. 1; [1985] 3 W. L. R. 640; [1985] 3 All E. R. 795, (Q. B. and C. A.) ···68, 69
Ocean Glory Compania Naviera S. A. v. A/S P. V. Christensen—The Ioanna [1985] 2
 Lloyd's Rep. 164, (Q. B.) ··105, 363, 368, 376, 379
Ocean Industries Inc. v. Soros Assoc. Int'l Inc. (1971) 328 F. Supp. 944 (S. D. N. Y.) ···447
Ocean Prince, The, SMA 2517 (Arb. at N. Y. 1988) ··318
Ocean Star Tankers S. A. v. Total Transport Corp.—The Taygetos [1982] 2 Lloyd's
 Rep. 272, (Q. B.) ··535, 610
Ocean Tramp Tankers Corp. v. V/O Sovfracht—The Eugenia [1963] 2 Lloyd's Rep.
 381; [1964] 2 Q. B. 226; [1964] 2 W. L. R. 114; [1964] 1 All E. R. 161, (C. A.);
 rev'g [1963] 2 Lloyd's Rep. 155, (Q. B.) ···········296, 397-398, 400, 404, 405, 408, 409, 531, 567
Oceania Shipping Corp. v. Thos. P. Gonzalez Corp. (1977) 442 F. Supp. 997 (S. D. N.
 Y.) ···457
Oceanic Amity, The and The Satya Kailash—Seven Seas Transportation Ltd. v.
 Pacifico Union Marina Corp. [1984] 1 Lloyd's Rep. 588; [1984] 2 All E. R. 140;
 [1983] 1 All E. R. 672, (C. A.); [1982] 2 Lloyd's Rep. 465, (Q. B.) ····················422
Oceanic First, The, SMA 1054 (Arb. at N. Y. 1976); SMA 1158 (Arb. at N. Y. 1977)

··**199, 203, 208, 209**
Oceanic Trading Corp. v. The Freights of the Diana (1970) 423 F. 2d 1 (2d Cir.) ···493
Oceanis, The, SMA 2772 (Arb. at N. Y. 1991) ··58, 60
Oceano, The (1906) 148 F. 131 (S. D. N. Y.) ···**490, 497-498**
Octonia Sun, The, 1988 AMC 832 (Arb. at N. Y.) ··458
Odenfeld, The—Gator Shipping Corp. v. Trans-Asiatic Oil Ltd. [1978] 2 Lloyd's Rep.
  357, (Q. B.) ··130, 236
Office of Supply, Government of the Republic of Korea v. N. Y. Navigation Co. Inc.
  (1972) 469 F. 2d 377;1973 AMC 1238 (2d Cir.) ···523
Offshore Logistics Inc. v. Tallentire (1986) 477 U. S. 207 ······································56
Ogden v. Graham (1861) 1 B. & S. 773;31 L. J. Q. B. 26;5 L. T. 396;8 Jur. N. S.
  613;10 W. R. 77;121 E. R. 901 ···**185-186**
Oinoussian Virtue, The (No. 2) —Schiffahrtsagentur Hamburg Middle East Line G. m.
  b. H. v. Virtue Shipping Corp. [1981] 2 Lloyd's Rep. 300, (Q. B.) ·······················**534**
Okehampton, The [1913] P. 173;83 L. J. P. 5;110 L. T. 130;29 T. L. R. 731;18 Com.
  Cas. 320;12 Asp. M. L. C. 428 ··**338**
Okura & Co. v. Navara Shipping Corp. S. A. [1982] 2 Lloyd's Rep. 537, (C. A.);
  [1981] 1 Lloyd's Rep. 561, (Q. B.) ··52
Oliva, The—Meling v. Minos Shipping Co. Ltd. [1972] 1 Lloyd's Rep. 458, (Q. B.)
  ··419, 424
Olivera v. Union Insurance Co. (1818) 16 U. S. 183;4 L. Ed. 365 ··························429
Olympia & York Florida Equity Corp. v. Gould (1985) 776 F. 2d 42 (2d Cir.) ········472
Olympic Armour, The, SMA 1840 (Arb. at N. Y. 1983) ·······································538
Olympic Garland, The, SMA 1209 (Arb. at N. Y. 1978) ······································115, 118
OMI Charger, The, SMA 2769 (Arb. at N. Y. 1991) ··624
Omina, The, SMA 3116 (Arb. at N. Y. 1994) ···205, 388
Oneida Nav. Co. v. L. Richardson & Co. (1922) 282 F. 241 (2d Cir.) ·····················163
Ontario Paper Co. v. Neff (1919) 261 F. 353 (7th Cir.) ··114
Orduna, The, SMA 2967 (Arb. at N. Y. 1993) ···416
Orduna S. A. v. Zen-Noh Grain Corp. (1990) 913 F. 2d 1149;1991 AMC 346 (5th
  Cir.) ···**200**, 201
Ore & Chemical Corp. v. Stinnes Interoil Inc. (1985) 606 F. Supp. 1510;611 F. Supp.
  237 (S. D. N. Y.) ··453
Ore Carriers of Liberia Inc. v. Navigen Corp. (1969) 332 F. Supp. 72;1971 AMC 505
  (S. D. N. Y.);aff'd (1970) 435 F. 2d 549;1971 AMC 513 (2d Cir.) ·······················209
Orient Horizon, The, SMA 1709 (Arb. at N. Y. 1982) ··**388**
Orient Lakes, The, SMA 181 (Arb. at N. Y. 1964) ···273
Orient Mid-East Great Lakes Service v. Int'l Export Lines Ltd. (1963) 315 F. 2d
  519;1964 AMC 1810 (4th Cir.) ··58
Orient Point, The, SMA 246 (Arb. at N. Y. 1961) ···361
Oriental Commercial & Shipping v. Rosseel N. V. (1989) 125 F. R. D. 398 (S. D. N. Y.) ···455
Orion Shipping & Trading v. Eastern States Petroleum Corp. (1963) 312 F. 2d 299;
  cert. denied (1963) 373 U. S. 949;SMA 573 (Arb. at N. Y. 1962) (2nd Cir.) ······227, 278

Orri (Mohammad Bin Abdul Rahman) v. Seawind Navigation Co. S. A.—The Winner
[1986] 1 Lloyd's Rep. 36, (Q. B.) ···54
Osaka Shosen Kaisha v. Pacific Export Lbr. Co. (1923) 260 U. S. 490·······················491
Osrok, The, SMA 654 (Arb. at N. Y. 1971) ··524
Ot Sonja, The—Cargill International S. A. v. CPN Tankers (Bermuda) Ltd. [1993] 2
  Lloyd's Rep. 435, (C. A.) ··439, 520
Otelia, The, 1980 AMC 424 (Arb. at N. Y. 1979) ··430
Ottley v. Schwartzberg (1987) 819 F. 2d 373 (2d Cir.) ·······························463, 472
Otto Candies Inc. v. McDermott International Inc. (1985) 600 F. Supp. 1334 (E. D.
  La.); aff'd (1986) 785 F. 2d 1033 (5th Cir.) ··240
Otto Wolff Handelsgesellschaft mbH v. Sheridan Transportation Co., 1992 AMC 2646
  (E. D. Va.); dismissed on other grounds (1992) 800 F. Supp. 1359; 1993 AMC 406 (E.
  D. Va.) ··448
Ove Skou v. Rudolf A. Oetker—The Arctic Skou [1985] 2 Lloyd's Rep. 478, (Q. B.)
  ··231, 583
Overbrooke Estates v. Glencombe Properties [1974] 1 W. L. R. 1335; [1974] 3 All E.
  R. 511, (Q. B.) ···85
Overseas Oil v. The Phibro Energy, 1989 AMC 847 (S. D. N. Y.) ························74
Overseas Transportation Co. v. Mineralimportexport-The Sinoe [1972] 1 Lloyd's Rep.
  201, (C. A.); aff'g [1971] 1 Lloyd's Rep. 514, (Q. B.) ·······································220
Oxford Shipping Co. v. Nippon Yusen Kaisha—The Eastern Saga [1984] 2 Lloyd's
  Rep. 373; [1984] 3 All E. R. 835, (Q. B.) ··443

P. D. Marchessini & Co. (New York) Inc. v. H. W. Robinson & Co. (1967) 287 F.
  Supp. 728; 1968 AMC 2084 (S. D. N. Y.) ··73
P. N. Gray & Co. v. Cavalliotis (1921) 276 F. 565 (E. D. N. Y.); aff'd without opinion
  (1923) 293 F. 1018 (2d Cir.) ···415
Paal Wilson & Co. A/S v. Partenreederei Hannah Blumenthal—The Hannah
  Blumenthal [1983] 1 Lloyd's Rep. 103; [1983] 1 A. C. 854; [1982] 3 W. L. R. 1149,
  (H. L.); [1982] 1 Lloyd's Rep. 582; [1982] 3 W. L. R. 49, (C. A.); [1981] 2 Lloyd's
  Rep. 438; [1981] 3 W. L. R. 823; [1982] 1 All E. R. 197, (Q. B.) ···················443
Pacbaron, The, SMA 2660 (Arb. at N. Y. 1990) ··344
Pacduke, The, SMA 2586 (Arb. at N. Y. 1989) ···172, 503
Pacglory, The, SMA 2737 (Arb. at N. Y. 1990) ···233
Pacific Caribbean (U. S. A.) Inc. (Re), 1985 AMC 2045 (Bankr. N. D. Cal. 1984) ········493
Pacific Employers Ins. Co. v. The Gloria (1985) 767 F. 2d 229 (5th Cir.) ···············340
Pacific Lumber & Shipping Co. Inc. v. Star Shipping A/S (1979) 464 F. Supp. 1314;
  1979 AMC 2137 (W. D. Wash.) ··448-449
Pacific Navigators Corp. v. Islamic Republic of Iran Shipping Lines—The El
  Champion [1985] 2 Lloyd's Rep. 275, (Q. B.) ··535
Pacific Phosphate Co. Ltd. v. Empire Transport Co. Ltd. (1920) 36 T. L. R. 750 ···400, **401**
Pacific Sun, The, SMA 1789 (Arb. at N. Y. 1983); 1983 AMC 830 ·········129, 135, 591
Packing, The, SMA 2858 (Arb. at N. Y. 1992) ··224, 233

Pacsea and Pacsun, The, SMA 746 (Arb. at N.Y. 1972) ·····························**110-111**,214
Padro v. Vessel Charters Inc. (1990) 731 F. Supp. 145 ; 1990 AMC 1664 (S. D. N. Y.) ···322
Palace Shipping Co. v. Gans S.S. Line [1916] 1 K. B. 138 ; 21 Com. Cas. 270 ; 85 L. J. K.
  B. 415 ; 115 L. T. 414 ; 32 T. L. R. 207 ; 13 Asp. M. L. C. 494, (K. B.) ···············**180-181**,186
Palmco Shipping Inc. v. Continental Ore Corp.—The Captain George K [1970] 2
  Lloyd's Rep. 21, (Q. B.) ···**398**
Pamela, The—Schelde Delta Shipping B. V. v. Astarte Shipping Ltd. [1995] 2 Lloyd's
  Rep. 249 ···259
Pan Cargo Shipping Corp. v. United States (1964) 234 F. Supp. 623 ; 1965 AMC 2649
  (S. D. N. Y.) ; aff'd (1967) 323 F. 2d 525 ; 1967 AMC 850 (2d Cir.) ; cert. denied
  (1967) 386 U. S. 836 ···**204-205**, 207, 300
Pan Ocean Shipping Co. Ltd. v. Creditcorp Ltd.—The Trident Beauty [1994] 1
  Lloyd's Rep. 365 ; [1994] 1 W. L. R. 161 ; [1994] 1 All E. R. 470 ; (1994) 144 New
  L. J. 1203, (H. L.) ; aff'g [1993] 1 Lloyd's Rep. 443 ; (1993) 137 S. J. (LB) 53, (C. A.)
  ··253, **264**
Panaghia P, The [1983] 2 Lloyd's Rep. 653 ··541
Panaghia Tinnou, The—C. H. Z. Rolimpex v. Eftavrysses Compania Naviera S. A.
  [1986] 2 Lloyd's Rep. 586, (Q. B.) ···305
Panagiotis Xilas, The, SMA 1035 (Arb. at N. Y. 1976) ································116, 118, 119
Panagos D. Pateras, SMA 1566 (Arb. at N. Y. 1981) ···**538**
Panamanian Oriental S. S. Corp. v. Wright—The Anita [1971] 1 Lloyd's Rep. 487 ;
  [1971] 1 W. L. R. 882 ; [1971] 2 All E. R. 1028, (C. A.) ; rev'g [1970] 2 Lloyd's Rep.
  365, (Q. B.) ···421
Panamax Venus, The, SMA 1979 (see SMA 2040) (Arb. at N. Y. 1984) ···················119
Panchaud Frères S. A. v. Etablissements General Grain Co. [1970] 1 Lloyd's Rep. 53,
  (C. A.) ; rev'g [1969] 2 Lloyd's Rep. 109, (Q. B.) ···93
Pando Compania Naviera S. A. v. Filmo S. A. S. [1975] 1 Lloyd Rep. 560 ; [1975] Q.
  B. 742 ; [1975] 2 W. L. R. 636 ; [1975] 2 All E. R. 515, (Q. B.) ···························**441**, 455
Pandora, The, 1973 AMC 1561 (Arb. at N. Y. 1972) ··273
Pandora, The (No. 2), SMA 755-A (Arb. at N. Y. 1973) ·····································275, 276
Pandora, The, SMA 1466 (Arb. at N. Y. 1980) ··492, 504
Panglobal Friendship, The—Citibank N. A. v. Hobbs, Savill & Co. Ltd. [1978] 1
  Lloyd's Rep. 368, (C. A.) ···488
Pantanassa, The—Efploia Shipping Corp. Ltd. v. Canadian Transport Co. Ltd. [1958]
  2 Lloyd's Rep. 449, (Q. B.) ··102, **227**
Paragon Oil Co. v. Republic Tankers S. A. (1962) 310 F. 2d 169 ; 1963 AMC 158 (2d
  Cir.) ··208
Paramount Carriers Corp. v. Cook Industries Inc. (1979) 465 F. Supp. 599 ; 1979
  AMC 875 (S. D. N. Y.) ···460, 477
Park S. S. Co. v. Cities Service Oil Co. (1951) 188 F. 2d 804 ; 1951 AMC 851 (2d Cir.) ;
  cert. denied (1951) 342 U. S. 802 ··**199**
Paros Shipping Corp. v. Nafta (G. B.) Ltd.—The Paros [1987] 2 Lloyd's Rep. 269, (Q.
  B.) ··327, 333

Paros, The—Paros Shipping Corp. *v*. Nafta (G. B.) Ltd. [1987] 2 Lloyd's Rep. 269. (Q.
 B.) ···327, 333
Paros, The, SMA 1025 (Arb. at N. Y. 1976) ···**413**
Parouth, The—Compania Naviera Micro S. A. *v*. Shipley International Inc. [1982] 2
 Lloyd's Rep. 351, (C. A.) ···55, 438
Parsons & Whittemore Overseas Co. Inc. *v*. Société Generale de L'Industrie du
 Papier (1974) 508 F. 2d 969 (2d Cir.) ···476
Partenreederei M/S Heidberg *v*. Grosvenor Grain and Feed Co. Ltd.—The Heidberg
 [1994] 2 Lloyd's Rep. 287; [1993] 2 Lloyd's Rep. 324, (Q. B.) ···························439
Passalacqua (Wm.) Builders *v*. Resnick Developers South Inc. (1991) 933 F. 2d 131
 (2d Cir.) ···**75, 76,** 77
Paul *v*. Birch (1743) 2 Akt. 621 ··481
Payne *v*. The Tropic Breeze (1969) 412 F. 2d 707; 1970 AMC 1850 (1st Cir.) ·········634
Pearl Carriers Inc. *v*. Japan Line Ltd.—The Chemical Venture [1993] 1 Lloyd's Rep.
 508, (Q. B.) ···186, 188, **189-190**, 191, 579, **580-581**, 605, 612
Peerless, The (1923) 2 F. 2d 395; 1923 AMC 236 (S. D. N. Y.) ·······························503
Pegasus, The—Liberian Shipping Corp. *v*. A. King & Sons Ltd. [1967] 1 Lloyd's Rep.
 302; [1967] 2 Q. B. 86; [1967] 2 W. L. R. 856; [1967] 1 All E. R. 934. (C. A.) ······440
Pendleton *v*. Benner Line (1918) 246 U. S. 353 ···637
Pendrecht, The—N. V. Stoom. Maats. "De Maas" *v*. Nippon Yusen Kaisha [1980] 2
 Lloyd's Rep. 56, (Q. B.) ··440
Penelope, The [1928] P. 180; 44 T. L. R. 597; 139 L. T. 355; 97 L. J. P 127; 17 Asp. M.
 L. C. 486 ···401, **402**
Pennsylvania Shipping Co. *v*. Compagnie Nationale de Navigation (1936) 55 Ll. L.
 Rep. 271; 42 Com. Cas. 45; 155 L. T. 294; [1936] 2 All E. R. 1167, (K. B.) ·········**91**, 576
Penta, The, 1981 AMC 532 (Arb. at N. Y. 1980) ···109
Penta, The, SMA 1603 (Arb. at N. Y. 1981) ···115, **270**, 272, 553
Peonia, The—Hyundai Merchant Marine Co. Ltd. *v*. Gesuri Chartering Co. Ltd. [1991]
 1 Lloyd's Rep. 100, (C. A. & Q. B.) ···121, **122-123**, 128, 129, 549, 590
Peoples' Security Life Insur. *v*. Monumental Life Insur. (1993) 991 F. 2d 141 (4th
 Cir.) ··457, 466, 469
Perez *v*. Cia Tropical Exportadora (1950) 182 F. 2d 874; 1950 AMC 1264 (5th Cir.) ···149
Pergamos, The, SMA 3090 (Arb. at N. Y. 1994) ···273
Pesquerias y Secaderos de Bacalao de Espana *v*. Beer (1949) 82 Ll. L. Rep. 501;
 [1949] W. N. 189; [1949] 1 All E. R. 845, (H. L.); *aff'g* (1947) 80 Ll. L. Rep. 318,
 (C. A.); *rev'g* 79 Ll. L. Rep. 417; (1946) 175 L. T. 495 ·······································610
Peter Cremer G. m. b. H. *v*. Sugat Food Industries Ltd.—The Rimon [1981] 2 Lloyd's
 Rep. 640, (Q. B.) ···440
Peter Kirk, The—Kirkawa Corporation *v*. Gatoil Overseas Inc. [1990] 1 Lloyd's Rep.
 154, (Q. B.) ···443
Petersham, The—Britain S. S. Co. *v*. The King, 3 Ll. L. Rep. 163, 205; 4 Ll. L. Rep. 245;
 [1921] 1 A. C. 99; 89 L. J. K. B. 881; 25 Com. Cas. 301; [1920] W. N. 271; 123 L. T.
 721; 64 S. J. 737; 15 Asp. 58, (H. L.) ···609

Petition of Southern Transp. Co. (1963) 211 F. Supp. 940 (E. D. Va.) ························214
Petroleo Brasileiro S. A.—Petrobas Fronto National de Petroleiros—Fronape v.
　Elounda Shipping Co.—The Evanthia M [1985] 2 Lloyd's Rep. 154, (Q. B.) ······106, 601
Petroleum Export Corp. v. Kerr S. S. Co. (1929) 32 F. 2d 969; 1929 AMC 905 (9th
　Cir.) ··108
Peyman v. Lanjani [1985] Ch. 457; [1985] 2 W. L. R. 154; [1984] 3 All E. R. 703,
　(C. A.) ··93
Phassa, The, SMA 2650 (Arb. at N. Y. 1990) ···345
Philippine Bear, The, 1960 AMC 670 (A. S. B. C. A. 1959) ···431
Philippine Bulk Shipping Inc. v. Int'l Minerals & Chemical Corp. (1973) 376 F. Supp.
　654 (S. D. N. Y.) ··74
Phoenix Shipping Corp. v. Apex Shipping Corp.—The Apex [1982] 2 Lloyd's Rep.
　407, (Q. B.) ···**534**
Phosphate Mining Co. v. Rankin (1915) 21 Com. Cas. 248; 115 L. T. 211 ; 86 L. J. K. B.
　358; 13 Asp. M. L. C. 418, (K. B.) ···421
Photo Production Ltd. v. Securicor Transport Ltd. [1980] 1 Lloyd's Rep. 545; [1980]
　A. C. 827; [1980] 2 W. L. R. 283; [1980] 1 All E. R. 556, (H. L.) ···········88, 89, 98, 425, 426
Piedmont & Georges Creek Coal Co. v. Seaboard Fisheries Co. (1920) 254 U. S. 1······500
Pierce v. Winsor (1861) F. Cas. Nos. 11, 150 and 11, 151 (D. C. D. Mass. and C. C. D.
　Mass.) ··173
Pioneer Container, The—K. H. Enterprise (Cargo Owners) v. Pioneer Container
　(Owners) [1994] 1 Lloyd's Rep. 593; [1994] 2 A. C. 324; [1994] 3 W. L. R. 1;
　[1994] 2 All E. R. 250; (1994) 138 S. J. (LB) 85, (P. C.); *sub nom.* The K. H.
　Enterprise [1994] 1 Lloyd's Rep. 593 ···335
Pioneer Shipping Ltd. v. B. T. P. Tioxide Ltd.—The Nema [1981] 2 Lloyd's Rep. 239;
　[1982] A. C. 724; [1981] 3 W. L. R. 292; [1981] 2 All E. R. 1030, (H. L.); *aff'g*
　[1980] 2 Lloyd's Rep. 339; [1980] Q. B. 547; [1980] 3 W. L. R. 326; [1980] 3 All
　E. R. 117, (C. A.); *rev'g* [1980] 2 Lloyd's Rep. 83, (Q. B.) ······**395**, 396, 399, 401-403, 444, 445
Pitria Star Navigation Co. v. Monsanto Co., 1986 AMC 2966 (E. D. La. 1984) ······173,**174**
Plod, The and The Voce, SMA 2719 (Arb. at N. Y. 1990) ···241, 381
Polar Shipping Ltd. v. Oriental Shipping Corp. (1982) 680 F. 2d 627; 1982 AMC
　2330 (9th Cir.) ··451, 477
Polar Steamship Corp. v. Overseas S. Corp. (1943) 136 F. 2d 835 (4th Cir.); *cert.*
　denied (1943) 320 U. S. 774 ···278
Pole v. Cetcovitch (1860) 9 C. B. (N. S.) 430 ···291
Polemis v. Furness, Withy & Co. (1921) 8 Ll. L. Rep. 263, 351; [1921] 3 K. B. 560;
　27 Com. Cas. 25; 90 L. J. K. B. 1353; 37 T. L. R. 940; 126 L. T. 154; 15 Asp. M. L. C.
　398, (C. A.) ···**420**, 423, 561
Poliskie Line Oceanic v. Hooker Chemical Corp., 499 F. Supp. 94; 1980 AMC 1748
　(S. D. N. Y.) ···175
Pollux I, The, SMA 3004 (Arb. at N. Y. 1993) ···233
Pollux Marine Agencies Inc. v. Louis Dreyfus Corp. (1978) 455 F. Supp. 211 (S. D. N.
　Y.); *aff'd* (1979) 595 F. 2d 1209 (2d Cir.) ···56, 57, 59

Polyglory, The—Kristiandsands Tankrederi v. Standard Tankers (Bahamas) [1977] 2
 Lloyd's Rep. 353, (Q. B.) ···**186**, 187, 192
Polyxeni, The, SMA 1961 (Arb. at N. Y. 1984) ···389
Pomona, The, SMA 118 (Arb. at N. Y. 1966) ··118
Pope v. Nickerson (1844) F. Cas. No. 11,273 (C. C. D. Mass.) ································339
Port Line Ltd. v. Ben Line Steamers Ltd. [1958] 1 Lloyd's Rep. 290; [1958] 2 Q. B.
 146; [1958] 2 W. L. R. 551; [1958] 1 All E. R. 787, (Q. B.) ············95, 96, **400**, 530, 608
Portsmouth S. S. Co. Ltd. v. Liverpool & Glasgow Salvage Association (1929) 34 Ll.
 L. Rep. 459, (K. B.) ··291, 295, **298**, 299
Post Chaser, The—Société Italo-Belge v. Palm and Vegetable Oils (Malaysia) [1981]
 2 Lloyd's Rep. 695; [1982] 1 All E. R. 19, (Q. B.) ···92
Poznan, The (1921) 276 F. 418 (S. D. N. Y.) ···343, **411**
Prairie Grove, The, 1976 AMC 2589 (Arb. at N. Y.) ···**524**
Praxiteles, The, SMA 104 and 600 (Arb. at N. Y. 1964) ··117
Prebensens Damps. A/S v. Munson S. S. Line (1919) 258 F. 227 (2d Cir.) ···············135
Prekookeanska Plovidba v. Felstar Shipping Corporation and Sotromar Srl. and STC
 Scantrade A. B. (Third Party) —The Carnival [1994] 2 Lloyd's Rep. 14, (C. A.);
 [1992] 1 Lloyd's Rep. 449, (Q. B.) ···182, 187, 195
President of India v. Hariana Overseas Corporation—The Takafa [1990] 1 Lloyd's
 Rep. 536, (Q. B.) ··286
President of India v. La Pintada Compania Navegacion S. A.—The La Pintada [1984]
 2 Lloyd's Rep. 9; [1984] 3 W. L. R. 10, (H. L.); [1984] 1 Lloyd's Rep. 305; [1983]
 1 Lloyd's Rep. 37, (Q. B.) ···446
President of India v. Lips Maritime Corp.—The Lips [1987] 2 Lloyd's Rep. 311;
 [1988] A. C. 395; [1987] 3 W. L. R. 572; [1987] 3 All E. R. 110; [1987] 2 F. T. L.
 R. 477; [1987] F. L. R. 313, (H. L.); rev'g [1987] 1 Lloyd's Rep. 131; [1987] 2 W. L.
 R. 906; [1987] 1 All E. R. 957; [1987] 1 F. T. L. R. 50; [1987] F. L. R. 91; (1987)
 131 S. J. 422, (C. A.); rev'g (1984) 134 New L. J. 969 ···446
Primorje, The—Jugoslavenska Linijska Plovidba v. Hulsman [1980] 2 Lloyd's Rep. 74,
 (Q. B.) ··**62**, 64
Probulk Carriers Ltd. & Pacific Commerce Line, SMA 2817 (Arb. at N. Y. 1991) ······233
Procter and Gamble Ltd. v. The Fraser, 1992 AMC 1575 (E. D. La.) ················341, 343
Procter and Gamble Ltd. v. The Stolt Llandaff, 1981 AMC 1880 (E. D. La.); aff'd
 (1982) 664 F. 2d 1285; 1982 AMC 2517 (5th Cir.) ··522
Procyon, The, SMA 2674 (Arb. at N. Y. 1990) ··139
Product Star, The (No. 2) —Abu Dhabi National Tanker Co. v. Product Star
 Shipping Ltd. [1993] 1 Lloyd's Rep. 397, (C. A.); rev'g [1991] 2 Lloyd's Rep. 468,
 (Q. B.) ···569, **612**
Progreso, The (1892) 50 F. 835 (3d Cir.) ···361
Prometheus, The, SMA 1154 (Arb. at N. Y. 1977) ···239
Proodos Marine Carriers Co. v. Overseas Shipping & Logistics (1984) 578 F. Supp.
 207 (S. D. N. Y.) ···463
Protective Life Ins. v. Lincoln Nat'l Life Ins. (1989) 873 F. 2d 281 (11th Cir.) ·········452

Protectus Alpha Navigation Co. Ltd. v. North Pacific Grain Growers Inc. (1985) 767
F. 2d 1379; 1986 AMC 56 (9th Cir. 1985) ···458
Proton, The, SMA 160 (Arb. at N. Y. 1966) ··273
Pteroti Compania Naviera S. A. v. National Coal Board [1958] 1 Lloyd's Rep. 245;
  [1958] 1 Q. B. 469; [1958] 2 W. L. R. 505; [1958] 1 All E. R. 603, (Q. B.) ············355
Puerto Buitrago, The—Attica Sea Carriers Corp. v. Ferrrostaal Poseidon Bulk
  Reederei G. m. b. H. [1976] 1 Lloyd's Rep. 250, (C. A.) ·····························130, **236**, 237
Puerto Rico Maritime Shipping Authority v. Star Lines Ltd. (1978) 454 F. Supp. 368
  (S. D. N. Y.) ··**462**
Punjab Bank v. De Boinville [1992] 1 Lloyd's Rep. 7; [1992] 1 W. L. R. 1138; [1992]
  3 All E. R. 104; (1991) 141 New L. J. 85, (C. A.) ···128
Pyrene Co. Ltd. v. Scindia Steam Navigation Co. Ltd. [1954] 1 Lloyd's Rep. 321;
  [1954] 2 Q. B. 402; [1954] 2 W. L. R. 1005; [1954] 2 All E. R. 158, (Q. B.) ···304-305, 521
Pyrgos, The, SMA 896 (Arb. at N. Y. 1974) ··201, **208**
Pythia, The—Western Sealanes Corp. v. Unimarine S. A. [1982] 2 Lloyd's Rep. 160,
  (Q. B.) ···**304**, 365, 366
Pyxis Special Shipping Co. v. Dritsas & Kaglis Bros.—The Scaplake [1978] 2
  Lloyd's Rep. 380, (Q. B.) ···**64**, 67

Quarrington Court, The (1940) 36 F. Supp. 278 (S. D. N. Y.); aff'd (1941) 122 F. 2d
  266 (2d Cir.) ···340
Queen Ltd. (Re) (1973) 361 F. Supp. 1009; 1973 AMC 646 (E. D. Pa.) ·················500
Quigley & Co. v. The Safir (1989) 750 F. Supp. 790; 1990 AMC 2104 (S. D. Tex.) ······432
Quinn v. Burch Bros. (Builders) [1966] 2 Q. B. 370; [1966] 2 W. L. R. 1017; [1966]
  2 All E. R. 283. (C. A.) ···309

Radcliffe & Co. v. Compagnie Général Transatlantique (1918) 24 Com. Cas. 40; 35 T.
  L. R. 65, (C. A.) ···369
Rahcassi Shipping Co. S. A. v. Blue Star Line Ltd.—The Bede [1967] 2 Lloyd's Rep.
  261; [1969] 1 Q. B. 173; [1967] 3 W. L. R. 1382; [1967] 3 All E. R. 301, (Q. B.) ···441
Rainbow Line Inc. v. The Tequila, 341 F. Supp. 459; 1972 AMC 1540 (S. D. N. Y);
  aff'd (1973) 480 F. 2d 1024; 1973 AMC 1431 (2d Cir.) ············**490**, 491, 496, **498**, 499
Rainwater v. National Home Ins. Co. (1991) 944 F. 2d 190 (4th Cir.); amended, slip
  opinion (1991) 22 October, 4th Cir.···462
Ramsay Scarlett & Co. Inc. v. The Koh Eun (1978) 462 F. Supp. 277; 1979 AMC
  970 (E. D. Va.) ···344, **502**, 503
Rayner v. Grote (1846) 15 M. & W. 359; 16 L. J. Ex. 79; 8 L. T. (O. S.) 474 ·············65
Raynes v. Ballantyne (1898) 14 T. L. R. 399, (H. L.) ··293
Raytheon Co. v. Automated Business Systems Inc. (1989) 882 F. 2d 6 (1st Cir.) ······458
Reardon Smith Line Ltd. v. Australian Wheat Board—The Houston City [1956] 1
  Lloyd's Rep. 1; [1956] 1 A. C. 266; [1956] 2 W. L. R. 403; [1956] 1 All E. R. 456,
  (P. C.); rev'g [1954] 2 Lloyd's Rep. 148, (High Ct. Aust.); restoring [1953] 1 Lloyd's
  Rep. 131 ···**182**, 184, 190, 192, 195, 197

Reardon Smith Line Ltd. v. Ministry of Agriculture [1963] 1 Lloyd's Rep. 12; [1963] A. C. 691; [1963] 2 W. L. R. 439; [1963] 1 All E. R. 545, (H. L.); *rev'g in part* [1961] 1 Lloyd's Rep. 385; [1962] 1 Q. B. 42; [1961] 3 W. L. R. 110; [1961] 2 All E. R. 577, (C. A.); *aff'g* [1959] 2 Lloyd's Rep. 229; [1960] 1 Q. B. 439; [1959] 3 W. L. R. 665; [1959] 3 All E. R. 434, (Q. B.) ···402, 422

Reardon Smith Line Ltd. v. Yngvar Hansen-Tangen and Sanko Steamship Co. Ltd. —The Diana Prosperity [1976] 2 Lloyd's Rep. 621; [1976] 1 W. L. R. 989; [1976] 3 All E. R. 570, (H. L.); *aff'g* [1976] 2 Lloyd's Rep. 60, (C. A.) ············90, 93, **94**, 106, 573

Reconstruction Finance Corp. v. Harrisons & Crosfield Ltd. (1953) 204 F. 2d 366; 1953 AMC 1012 (2d Cir.); *cert. denied* (1953) 346 U. S. 854 ·······························524

Recovery Services International v. The Tatiana L, 1988 AMC 788 (S. D. N. Y. 1986) ···346

Rederi A/B Soya v. Evergreen Marine, 1972 AMC 1555 (E. D. Va. 1971) ···············536

Rederi A/B "Unda" v. Burdon & Co. (1937) 57 Ll. L. Rep. 95; 42 Com. Cas. 239, (C. A.) ···158

Rederi Sverre Hansen A/S v. Phs. Van Ommeren (1921) 6 Ll. L. Rep. 193 ··············142

Rederiaktiebolaget Urania v. Zachariades (1931) 41 Ll. L. Rep. 145 ·····················102

Redwood Empire Production Credit Assoc. v. Fishing Vessel Owners Marine Ways Inc. (1981) 530 F. Supp. 75 (W. D. Wash.) ···499

Regent Ranger, The, SMA 1564 (Arb. at N. Y. 1981) ···205

Reinante Transoceanic Navegacion S. A. v. President of India—The Apiolitis [1985] 1 Lloyd's Rep. 255, (Q. B.) ···186, 187

Reindeer Steamship Co. Ltd. v. Forslind & Son (1908) 13 Com. Cas. 214; 24 T. L. R. 529, (C. A.) ···130

Reliant, The, SMA 3077 (Arb. at N. Y. 1994) ···322

Remco, The—Gewa Chartering B. V. v. Remco Shipping Lines Ltd. [1984] 2 Lloyd's Rep. 205, (Q. B.) ··**65**

Rena K, The [1978] 1 Lloyd's Rep. 545; [1979] Q. B. 377; [1978] 3 W. L. R. 431; [1979] 1 All E. R. 397, (Q. B.) ···442

Renton (G. H.) & Co. v. Palmyra Trading Corp. [1956] 2 Lloyd's Rep. 379; [1957] A. C. 149; [1957] 2 W. L. R. 45; [1956] 3 All E. R. 957, (H. L.) ···················305, 604

Repetto v. Millar's Karri & Jarrah Forrests Ltd. [1901] 2 K. B. 306, 310; 70 L. J. K. B. 561; 84 L. T. 836; 17 T. L. R. 421; 9 Asp. M. L. C. 215; 6 Com. Cas. 129 ···············64

Resolute Maritime Inc. and Another v. Nippon Kaiji Kyokai and Others—The Skopas [1983] 1 Lloyd's Rep. 431; [1983] 1 W. R. L. 857; [1983] 2 All E. R. 1, (Q. B.) ······84

Resolven, The (1892) 9 T. L. R. 75, (P. D. A.) ··102, 103

Retla Steamship v. Canpotex, 1977 AMC 1594 (Arb. at N. Y.) ······························416

Rewia, The [1991] 2 Lloyd's Rep. 325. (C. A.); *rev'g* [1990] 1 Lloyd's Rep. 69, (Q. B.) ···333, 334, **337**, 338

Rhodian River Shipping Co. S. A. and Rhodian Sailor Shipping Co. S. A. v. Halla Maritime Corp.—The Rhodian River [1984] 1 Lloyd's Rep. 373, (Q. B.) ·············69

Rhodian River, The—Rhodian River Shipping Co. S. A. and Rhodian Sailor Shipping Co. S. A. v. Halla Maritime Corp. [1984] 1 Lloyd's Rep. 373, (Q. B.) ·················69

Rhone Mediterranee Compagnia v. Lauro, 1984 AMC 1575; 712 F. 2d 50 (3d Cir.

1983) ···475
Rich (Marc) & Co. A. G. v. Societa Italiana Impianti P. A.—The Atlantic Emperor
[1992] 1 Lloyd's Rep. 342, (E. C. J.); [1989] 1 Lloyd's Rep. 548, (C. A.) ················55
Richards & Co. v. Wreschner (1915) 156 N. Y. S. 1054 (Sup. Ct.); aff'd (1916) 174 A.
D. 484 ; 158 N. Y. S. 1129 ···415
Richmond Shipping Ltd. v. Agro Co. of Canada Ltd.—The Simonburn (No. 2) [1973]
2 Lloyd's Rep. 145, (Q. B.) ···440
Richmond Shipping Ltd. v. D/S and A/S Vestland—The Vestland [1980] 2 Lloyd's
Rep. 171, (Q. B.) ···484, **488**
Rickards v. Forestal Land, Timber & Railways Co. Ltd. [1942] A. C. 50 ; 46 Com.
Cas. 335 ; 57 T. L. R. 672 ; 110 L. J. K. B. 593 ; 165 L. T. 257 ; [1941] 3 All E. R. 62 ;
sub nom. Forestal Land, Timber & Railways Co. Ltd. v. Rickards (1941) 70 Ll. L.
Rep. 173, (H. L.) ···421
Riffe Petroleum Co. v. Cibro Sales Corp. (1979) 601 F. 2d 1385 ; 1979 AMC 1611
(10th Cir.) ···537
Rijn, The—Santa Martha Baay Scheepvaart & Handelsmaatschappij N. V. v. Scanbulk
A/S [1981] 2 Lloyd's Rep. 267, (Q. B.) ···238, **375**, 379, 554
Riley v. Kingsley Underwriting Agencies Ltd. (1992) 969 F. 2d 953 (10th Cir.); cert
denied (1992) —U. S.—; 113 S. Ct. 658 ; 121 L. Ed. 2d 584 ·······························475
Rimon, The—Peter Cremer G. m. b. H. v. Sugat Food Industries Ltd. [1981] 2 Lloyd's
Rep. 640, (Q. B.) ··440
Rio Sun, The—Italmare Shipping Co. v. Ocean Tanker Co. Inc. [1981] 2 Lloyd's Rep.
489 ; [1982] 1 W. L. R. 158 ; [1982] 1 All E. R. 517, (C. A.); [1982] 1 Lloyd's Rep.
404, (Q. B.) ···259, 260, 445
Riverstone Meat Co. Pty. Ltd. v. Lancashire Shipping Co. Ltd.—The Muncaster
Castle [1961] 1 Lloyd's Rep. 57 ; [1961] A. C. 807 ; [1961] 2 W. L. R. 269 ; [1961]
1 All E. R. 495, (H. L.) ··557
Roachbank, The—C. A. Venezolana de Navegacion v. Bank Line [1988] 2 Lloyd's
Rep. 337, (C. A.); [1987] 2 Lloyd's Rep. 498, (Q. B.) ·············370, 371, **372**, 374, 375, 446
Robbins v. Day (1992) 954 F. 2d 679 (11th Cir.); cert. denied —U. S.—; 113 S. Ct.
201 ; 121 L. Ed. 143 ···472
Roberta, The (1938) 60 Ll. L. Rep. 84, (C. A.) ···559
Robertina, The, SMA 1151 (Arb. at N. Y. 1977) ·······················113, 273, 287, 318, 381
Robertson v. Amazon Tug & Lighterage Co. Ltd. (1881) 7 Q. B. D. 598 ; 51 L. J. Q. B.
68 ; 46 L. T. 146 ; 4 Asp. M. L. C. 496, (C. A.) ··104
Robins Dry Dock & Repair Co. v. Flint (1927) 275 U. S. 303························536, 537
Roby v. Hyundai Merchant Marine (1988) 700 F. Supp. 316 ; 1989 AMC 1726 (E. D.
La.) ···321
Roman Bernard, The, SMA 1202 (Arb. at N. Y. 1978) ·····································**207-208**
Roman Karmen, The—Furness Withy (Australia) Pty. Ltd. v. Black Sea Shipping Co.
[1994] 1 Lloyd's Rep. 644, (Q. B.) ··282
Romandie, The, SMA 1092 (Arb. at N. Y. 1977) ································**133**, 137, 138, 619
Romano v. West India Fruit and Steamship Co. (1945) 151 F. 2d 727 ; 1946 AMC 90

(5th Cir.) ···108, **112-113**, 116
Ropner *v.* Inter-American S. S. Co. (1917) 243 F. 549 (2d Cir.) ·······························133
Rosalia, The (1920) 264 F. 285 (2d Cir.) ···431
Ross Industries *v.* The Gretke Oldendorff (1980) 483 F. Supp. 195; 1980 AMC 1397
 (E. D. Tex.) ···340
Ross Isle, The, SMA 1340 (Arb. at N. Y. 1979) ·······································202, 466
Rossiter *v.* Miller (1878) 3 App. Cas. 1124; 39 L. T. 173; 48 L. J. (Ch.) 10, (H. L.) ·······49
Rosso, The—Monterosso Shipping Co. *v.* International Transport Workers' Federation
 [1982] 2 Lloyd's Rep. 120; [1982] 3 All E. R. 841; [1982] Com. L. R. 152; (1982)
 126 S. J. 591, (C. A.) ···55
Rountree Co. *v.* Dampskibs Aktieselskabet Oy II, 1934 AMC 26 (Cty. Ct. N. Y. 1933)
 ···544
Routh *v.* MacMillan (1863) 9 L. T. 541; 2 H. & C. 750; 33 L. J. (Ex.) 38; 1 Asp. M. L.
 C. (O. S.) 402 ···101
Rowe *v.* Turner Hopkins & Partners [1980] 2 N. Z. L. R. 550 ·······························309
Royal Greek Government *v.* Minister of Transport—The Ann Stathatos (1949) 83 Ll.
 L. Rep. 228; 66 T. L. R. (Pt. 1) 504, (K. B.) ·······························295, **297**, 299, 552, 553, **555**
Royal Greek Government *v.* Minister of Transport—The Ilissos (1948) 82 Ll. L. Rep.
 196; [1949] 1 K. B. 525; [1949] L. J. R. 670; 65 T. L. R. 32; [1949] 1 All E. R.
 171, (C. A.); *aff'g* (1948) 81 Ll. L. Rep. 355; [1949] 1 K. B. 7; 64 T. L. R. 283;
 [1948] 1 All E. R. 904, (K. B.) ···363, **368**, 554
Royal Insurance Co. *v.* The Maracaibo (1980) 488 F. Supp. 521 (S. D. N. Y.) ·······431-432
Royal Prince, The, 1927 AMC 62 (S. D. N. Y. 1926) ···224
Royscot Trust Ltd. *v.* Rogerson [1991] 2 Q. B. 297; [1991] 3 W. L. R. 57; [1991] 3
 All E. R. 294; [1992] R. T. R. 99; (1992) 11 Tr. L. R. 23; [1991] C. C. L. R. 45;
 (1991) 135 S. J. 444; (1991) 141 New L. J. 493, (C. A.) ·······································85
Rozel, The—Channel Island Ferries Ltd. *v.* Cenargo Navigation Ltd. [1994] 2 Lloyd's
 Rep. 161, (Q. B.) ···237
Rudolf A. Oetker *v.* IFA Internationale Frachtagentur A. G.—The Almak [1985] 1
 Lloyd's Rep. 557, (Q. B.) ···330, 331
Rudolf A. Oetker *v.* Koninklijke Nederlandsche Stoomboot-Maatschappij N. V., SMA
 508 (Arb. at N. Y. 1970) ···162
Russell *v.* Niemann (1864) 34 L. J. C. P. 10; 17 C. B. N. S. 163; 5 New Rep. 190; 10 L.
 T. 786; 2 Asp. M. L. C. 72; 144 E. R. 66, (C. P.) ·······························420
Ruth, The, SMA 2462 (Arb. at N. Y. 1987) ···525
Ruxley Electronics *v.* Forsyth [1995] 3 W. L. R. 118 (H. L.) ·······································237
Rygja, The (1908) 161 F. 106 (2d Cir.) ···**135, 137**

S. A. Cockerill *v.* The Kyung Ju, 1983 AMC 1517 (M. D. Fla. 1982) ·······························341
S. C. Loveland Co. *v.* Eastern States Farmer's Exch. (1937) 92 F. 2d 180 (3d Cir.);
 cert. denied (1937) 302 U. S. 762 ···343
SCAC Transport (USA) Inc. *v.* The Danaos (1988) 845 F. 2d 1157; 1988 AMC 1827
 (2d Cir.) ···323, 477

判例索引　　　　　　　　　　　101

S. L. Sethia Liners Ltd. v. Naviagro Maritime Corp.—The Kostas Melas [1981] 1
　Lloyd's Rep. 18, (Q. B.) ···248, 250, 252, 446
S. O. Stray and Co. v. Trottier Ide and Co. (1922) 280 F. 249 (D. Mass.) ···················114
Sabine Towing & Transp. Co. v. Merit Ventures Inc. (1983) 575 F. Spp. 1442 (E. D.
　Tex.) ···77
Sabrina, The (1957) 154 F. Supp. 720 ; 1957 AMC 691 (D. C. Z.) ·································207
Saetta, The—Forsythe International (U. K.) Ltd. v. Silver Shipping Co. Ltd. and
　Petroglobe International Ltd. [1993] 2 Lloyd's Rep. 268 ; [1994] 1 W. L. R. 1334 ;
　[1994] 1 All E. R. 851, (Q. B.) ···228, **588-589**
Saga Cob, The—K/S Penta Shipping A/S v. Ethiopian Shipping Lines Corporation
　[1992] 2 Lloyd's Rep. 545, (C. A.); rev'g [1992] 2 Lloyd's Rep. 398, (Q. B.)
　··181, 183, 184-186, 188-190, **579-580**
Sagona, The—A/S Hansen Tangens Rederi III v. Total Transport Corp. [1984] 1
　Lloyd's Rep. 194, (Q. B.) ···221, 292, 293, **294**, 583
Sail America v. The Prosperity (1991) 778 F. Supp. 1282 ; 1992 AMC 1617 (S. D. N.
　Y.) ···341
Saint Anna, The [1980] 1 Lloyd's Rep. 180, (Adm.) ···219, 588
Saint John Marine Co. v. United States, 1994 AMC 2526 ; 1994 U. S. Dist. Lexis 8334
　(S. D. N. Y.) ···496
St. Paul Fire and Marine Ins. Co. v. United States Lines (1958) 258 F. 2d 374 ; 1958
　AMC 2385 (2d Cir.); cert. denied (1959) 359 U. S. 910 ···525
St. Vincent Shipping Co. Ltd. v. Bock, Godeffroy & Co.—The Helen Miller [1980] 2
　Lloyd's Rep. 95, (Q. B.) ···**143**, 195, **532**
Sally Stove, The, SMA 2320 (Arb. at N. Y. 1986) ···497
Samah, The—Mmecen S. A. v. Inter Ro-Ro S. A. [1981] 1 Lloyd's Rep. 40, (Q. B.) ···54, 69
Sammi Line Co. Ltd. v. Altamar Navegacion S. A., 1985 AMC 1790 (S. D. N. Y.) ·········457
Samos Shipping Enterprises v. Eckhardt & Co. K. G.—The Nissos Samos [1985] 1
　Lloyd's Rep. 378, (Q. B.) ···54
Samuel, Samuel & Co. v. West Hartlepool Steam Navigation Co. (1906) 11 Com.
　Cas. 115 ; (1907) 12 Com. Cas. 203, (K. B.) ···**334**, **486-487**
Samuel W. Hall, The (1892) 49 F. 281 (S. D. N. Y.) ···361
San Juan Venturer, The, 1974 AMC 1053 (Arb. at N. Y.) ···274
San Martine Compania de Nav. S. A. v. Saguenay Term. Ltd. (1961) 293 F. 2d 796
　(9th Cir.) ···472
Sanday v. United States Shipping Board Emergency Fleet Corp. (1925) 6 F. 2d 384
　(2d Cir.); cert. denied (1925) 269 U. S. 556 ···**361**
Sanko Steamship Co. v. Cook Indus. Inc. (1973) 495 F. 2d 1260 ·································467
Sanko Steamship Co. Ltd. v. Fearnley & Eger A/S—The Manhattan Prince [1985] 1
　Lloyd's Rep. 140, (Q. B.) ···211, **372-373**, 374, **593**
Sanko Steamship Co. Ltd. v. Kano Trading Ltd. [1978] 1 Lloyd's Rep. 156, (C. A.) ······94
Sanko Steamship Co. Ltd. v. Newfoundland Refining Co. Ltd., 1976 AMC 417 (S. D.
　N. Y.); aff'd on opinion below, 1976 AMC 417 (2d Cir.) ···460
Sanko Steamship Co. Ltd. v. The Shipping Corp. of India—The Jhansi Ki Rani

[1980] 2 Lloyd's Rep. 569, (Q. B.) ···442
Santa Carina, The—Vlassopulos (N. & J.) Ltd. v. Ney Shipping Ltd. [1977] 1 Lloyd's
　Rep. 478, (C. A.) ···62
Santa Clara, The (1922) 281 F. 725 (2d Cir.) ···173
Santa Katerina, The, 1974 AMC 1383 (Arb. at N. Y.) ·····································354
Santa Martha Baay Scheepvaart & Handelsmaatschhappij N. V. v. Scanbulk A/S—
　The Rijn [1981] 2 Lloyd's Rep. 267, (Q. B.) ·······························238, 375, 379, 554
Santiren Shipping Ltd. v. Unimarine S. A.—The Chrysovalandou Dyo [1981] 1
　Lloyd's Rep. 159; [1981] 1 All E. R. 340, (Q. B.) ···············87, 249, 250, 252, 254, 481
Santona, The (1907) 152 Fed. 516 (S. D. N. Y.) ···316
Sarah, The, SMA 2671 (Arb. at N. Y. 1990) ··172
Sargasso, The—Stargas S. p. A. v. Petredec Ltd. [1994] 1 Lloyd's Rep. 412
　···251, 441, 520, 594
Sarma Navigation S. A. v. Navibec Shipping Ltd., 1979 AMC 1040 (S. D. N. Y. 1978) ···496
Sarpen, The [1916] P. 306···608
Saturnus, The (1918) 250 F. 407 (2d Cir.); *cert. denied* (1918) 247 U. S. 521··············490
Satya Kailash, The and The Oceanic Amity—Seven Seas Transportation Ltd. v.
　Pacifico Union Marina Corp. [1984] 1 Lloyd's Rep. 588; [1984] 2 All E. R. 140;
　[1983] 1 All E. R. 672. (C. A.); [1982] 2 Lloyd's Rep. 465, (Q. B.)
　···422, 514, **515-516**, 518, 519, 603, 605
Saudi Crown, The [1986] 1 Lloyd's Rep. 261··69
Savage v. Blakney (1970) 119 C. L. R. 435, (Aus.) ···85
Saxis S. S. Co. v. Multifacs International Traders Inc. (1967) 375 F. 2d 577; 1967
　AMC 1178 (2d Cir.) ··149
Saxon Star; The—Adamastos Shipping Co. Ltd. v. Anglo-Saxon Petroleum Co. [1958]
　1 Lloyd's Rep. 73; [1959] A. C. 133; [1958] 2 W. L. R. 688; [1958] 1 All E. R.
　725, (H. L.); *rev'g* [1957] 1 Lloyd's Rep. 271; [1957] 2 Q. B. 233; [1957] 2 W. L. R.
　908; [1957] 2 All E. R. 311, (C. A.); *restoring* [1957] 1 Lloyd's Rep. 79; [1957] 2
　Q. B. 233; [1957] 2 W. L. R. 509; [1957] 1 All E. R. 673, (Q. B.)
　···212, 286, **514-515**, 516, 517, 519. 531, 561, 603
Scaldia, The, SMA 905 (Arb. at N. Y. 1975) ·······································133, 137, 138, 619
Scales (Pacific) Ltd. v. Temperley S. S. Co. (1925) 23 Ll. L. Rep. 312, (K. B.) ······220, 547
Scammell (G.) & Nephew Ltd. v. H. C. and J. G. Ouston [1941] A. C. 251; 46 Com.
　Cas. 190; 110 L. J. K. B. 197; 164 L. T. 379; 57 T. L. R. 280; [1941] 1 All E. R. 14,
　(H. L.) ··49, **50**
Scan Venture, The, SMA 1627 (Arb. at N. Y. 1982) ·······································**345**
Scandinavian Trading Tanker Co. A. B. v. Flota Petrolera Ecuatoriana—The
　Scaptrade [1983] 2 Lloyd's Rep. 253; [1983] 2 A. C. 694; [1983] 3 W. L. R. 203;
　[1983] 2 All E. R. 763, (H. L.); [1983] 1 Lloyd's Rep. 146; [1983] Q. B. 529;
　[1983] 2 W. L. R. 248; [1983] 1 All E. R. 301, (C. A.); [1981] 2 Lloyd's Rep 425,
　(Q. B.) ··87, 256, 258, **262**, 263
Scaplake, The—Pyxis Special Shipping Co. v. Dritsas & Kaglis Bros. [1978] 2 Lloyd's
　Rep. 380, (Q. B.) ··**64**, 67

Scaptrade, The—Scandinavian Trading Tanker Co. A. B. v. Flota Petrolera
Ecuatoriana [1983] 2 Lloyd's Rep. 253; [1983] 2 A. C. 694; [1983] 3 W. L. R. 203;
[1983] 2 All E. R. 763, (H. L.); [1983] 1 Lloyd's Rep. 146; [1983] Q. B. 529;
[1983] 2 W. L. R. 248; [1983] 1 All E. R. 301, (C. A.); [1981] 2 Lloyd's Rep. 425;
(Q. B.) ··87, 256, 258, **262**, 263
Schelde Delta Shipping B. V. v. Astarte Shipping Ltd.—The Pamela [1995] 2 Lloyd's
Rep. 249 ··259
Schiffahrtsagentur Hamburg Middle East Line G. m. b. H. v. Virtue Shipping Corp.
Monrovia—The Oinoussian Virtue (No. 2) [1981] 2 Lloyd's Rep. 300, (Q. B.) ········**534**
Schiffbek, The, 1934 AMC 713 (Arb. at N. Y.) ··203
Schilling v. A/S D/S Dannebrog (1963) 320 F. 2d 628; 1964 AMC 678 (2d Cir.)
··496, 498, 499
Schmaltz v. Avery (1851) 16 Q. B. 655; 20 L. J. Q. B. 228; 17 L. T. O. S. 27; 15 Jur.
291; 117 E. R. 1031 ···**65**, 66
Schmitz v. Zilveti (1994) 20 F. 3d 1043 (9th Cir.) ··467
Schoenamsgruber v. Hamburg American Line (1935) 294 U. S. 454 ···························460
Scholl v. Chuang Hui Marine Co. Ltd. (1986) 646 F. Supp. 137; 1987 AMC 1162 (D.
Conn.) ··633
Schoonmaker-Connors Co. Inc. v. Lambert Transp. Co. (1920) 269 F. 583 (2d Cir.) ···133
Schooner Freeman, The v. Buckingham (1856) 59 U. S. 182 ······················**339**, 490, 498
Schuldt (H.) v. Standard Fruit & S. S. Co., 1979 AMC 2470 (S. D. N. Y. 1978)
··202, 225, 537
Scotiacliffe Hall, The, SMA 1364 (Arb. at N. Y. 1980) ······································503, 505
Scottish Navigation Co. Ltd. v. W. A. Souter & Co. [1917] 1 K. B. 222; 86 L. J. K. B.
336; 115 L. T. 812; 33 T. L. R. 70; 22 Com. Cas. 154; 13 Asp. M. L. C. 539, (C. A.) ······**398**
Scruttons Ltd. v. Midland Silicones Ltd. See Midland Silicones Ltd. v. Scruttons Ltd.
Sea & Land Securities Ltd. v. William Dickinson & Co. Ltd. (1942) 72 Ll. L. Rep.
159; [1942] 2 K. B. 65; 111 L. J. K. B. 698; 167 L. T. 173; 58 T. L. R. 210; [1942] 1
All E. R. 503, (C. A.); rev'g (1941) 71 Ll. L. Rep. 166, (K. B.) ····················249, 378, 530
Sea Calm Shipping Co. S. A. v. Chantiers Navals de L'Esterel S. A.—The Uhenbels
[1986] 2 Lloyd's Rep. 294, (Q. B.) ··93
Sea Dragon Inc. (Re) (1983) 574 F. Supp. 367; 1984 AMC 699 (S. D. N. Y.) ···············474
Seafaith, The, 1955 AMC 2062 (Arb. at N. Y. 1954) ··389
Seaford, The, 1975 AMC 1553 (Arb. at N. Y.) ··214
Sealace Shipping Co. Ltd. v. Oceanvoice Ltd.—The Alecos M [1991] 1 Lloyd's Rep.
120, (C. A.); rev'g [1990] 1 Lloyd's Rep. 82, (Q. B.) ··237
Seamaid, The, 1967 AMC 1362 (Arb. at N. Y. 1966) ···**115**, 116
Sea Ranger, The, SMA 1240 (Arb. at N. Y 1978) ···386, **387**
Searaven, The (1971) 437 F. 2d 301 (5th Cir.); cert. denied (1971) 402 U. S. 966 ···493, 496
Seas Shipping Co. Inc. v. United States, 1951 AMC 503 (S. D. N. Y.) ························538
Sedco v. Petroleos Mexicanos (1985) 767 F. 2d 1140; 1986 AMC 706 (5th Cir.) ········475
Segovia Compania Naviera S. A. v. R. Pagnan & F. Lli—The Aragon [1977] 1
Lloyd's Rep. 343, (C. A.); aff'g [1975] 2 Lloyd's Rep. 216; [1975] 1 Lloyd's Rep.

628, (Q. B.) ··131
Seguros Banvenez S. A. v. The Oliver Drescher (1985) 761 F. 2d 855; 1985 AMC
 2168 (2d Cir.) ··317, 449, **505**
Sen Mar. Inc. v. Tiger Petroleum Corp. (1991) 774 F. Supp. 879 (S. D. N. Y.) ······474-475
Senicoll Sierra, The, SMA 2966 (Arb. at N. Y. 1993) ···340
Serena, The, SMA 1159 (Arb. at N. Y. 1997) ··**111**
Serrano v. U. S. Lines Co. (1965) 238 F. Supp. 383; 1965 AMC 1038 (S. D. N. Y.) ········**174**
Sethia Liners (S. L.) Ltd. v. Naviagro Maritime Corp.—The Kostas Melas [1981] 1
 Lloyd's Rep. 18, (Q. B.) ···248, 250, 252, 446
Seven Seas Transportation Ltd. v. Atlantic Shipping Co. S. A. [1975] 2 Lloyd's Rep.
 188, (Q. B.) ··247, 248, 249, 482
Seven Seas Transportation Ltd. v. Pacifico Union Marina Corp.—The Satya Kailash
 [1984] 1 Lloyd's Rep. 588; [1984] 2 All E. R. 140; [1983] 1 All E. R. 672, (C. A.);
 [1982] 2 Lloyd's Rep. 465, (Q. B.) ·····························422, 514, **515-516**, 518, 519, 603, 605
Severoles, The, 1935 AMC 1135 (Arb. at N. Y.) ··241
Sevin v. Deslands (1860) 30 L. J. (Ch.) 457 ··87
Shackleford, The—Surrey Shipping Co. Ltd. v. Compagnie Continentale (France) S. A.
 [1978] 2 Lloyd's Rep. 154; [1978] 1 W. L. R. 1080, (C. A.); aff'g [1978] 1 Lloyd's
 Rep. 191, (Q. B.) ···358
Shamrock v. Storey (1899) 81 L. T. 413; 16 T. L. R. 6; 8 Asp. M. L. C. 590; 5 Com.
 Cas. 21 ···50
Shaw v. South African Marine Corp., 1983 AMC 1578 (E. D. Va. 1982) ··············321
Shearson Lehman Hutton Inc. v. Wagoner (1991) 944 F. 2d 114 (2d Cir.) ··············450
Sheet Metal Workers Int'l Assn., Local 420 v. Kinney Air Cond. Co. (1985) 756 F.
 2d 742 (9th Cir.) ··467
Sheffield Corporation v. Barclay [1905] A. C. 392 ··328
Shell Oil Co. v. The Gilda (1986) 790 F. 2d 1209 (5th Cir.) ······························522
Shena, The and The Ave, SMA 2893 (Arb. at N. Y. 1992) ······················277, 380, 390
Shillito, The (1897) 3 Com. Cas. 44, (P. D. A.) ···486
Shimone, The, SMA 3092 (Arb. at N. Y. 1994) ···274
Shinjitsu Maru No. 5, The—A. B. Marintrans v. Comet Shipping Co. Ltd. [1985] 1
 Lloyd's Rep. 568; [1985] 1 W. L. R. 1270; [1985] 3 All E. R. 442, (Q. B.) ···**307**, 308, 309
Shipping Corporation of India Ltd. v. NSB Niederelbe Schiffahrtsgesellschaft m. b. H.
 & Co.—The Black Falcon [1991] 1 Lloyd's Rep. 77, (Q. B.) ···············125, 128, 129
Shipping Developments Corp. v. V/O Sojuzneftexport—The Delian Spirit [1971] 1
 Lloyd's Rep. 506; [1972] 1 Q. B. 103; [1971] 2 W. L. R. 1434; [1971] 2 All E. R.
 1067, (C. A.) ··**159**
Shipping Transportation Enterprises v. Transatlantic Petroleum, 1992 AMC 663 (S.
 D. N. Y. 1991) ···457
Showa Oil Tanker Co. Ltd. v. Maravan S. A.—The Larissa [1983] 2 Lloyd's Rep. 325,
 (Q. B.) ··106, **601**
Siderbulk Ltd. v. Nagos Maritime Inc., 1993 AMC 2566 (S. D. N. Y. 1992) ···········460
Siderius Inc. v. The Amilla (1989) 880 F. 2d 662; 1989 AMC 2533 (2d Cir.) ······322, 343

Sidermar S. p. A. v. Apollo Corp.—The Apollo [1978] 1 Lloyd's Rep. 200, (Q. B.)
....**371-372**, 373, 374
Sidney Blumenthal & Co. v. Atlantic Coast Line R. Co. (1943) 139 F. 2d 288 (2d
 Cir.); *cert. denied* (1944) 321 U. S. 795 428
Siegleman v. Cunard White Star (1955) 221 F. 2d 189 (2d Cir.) 56
Sig Bergesen D. Y A/S/ v. Mobil Shipping and Transportation Co.—The Berge
 Sund [1993] 2 Lloyd's Rep. 453, (C. A.); [1992] 1 Lloyd's Rep. 460, (Q. B.)
....295, 297, 298, 364, 371, 375, 378, 586, **595**
Silvercove, The, SMA 813A (Arb. at N. Y. 1976) 202
Silver Hawk, The, SMA 1857 (Arb. at N. Y. 1983) 223
Silverhawk, The, SMA 1041 (Arb. at N. Y. 1976) 524
Simonburn, The (No. 2) —Richmond Shipping Ltd. v. Agro Co. of Canada Ltd.
 [1973] 2 Lloyd's Rep. 145, (Q. B.) 440
Sindall (William) v. Cambridgeshire C. C. [1994] 3 All E. R. 932; 92 L. G. R. 121;
 [1993] E. G. C. S. 105; [1993] N. P. C. 82, (C. A.); [1994] 1 W. L. R. 1016 85
Sinoe, The—Overseas Transportation Co. v. Mineralimportexport [1972] 1 Lloyd's
 Rep. 201, (C. A.); *aff'g* [1971] 1 Lloyd's Rep. 514, (Q. B.) 220
Siordet v. Hall (1828) 4 Bing. 607; 1 Moo. & P. 561; 6 L. J. O. S. C. P. 137; 130 E. R.
 902 420
Siu Yin Kwan v. Eastern Insurance Ltd. [1994] 1 Lloyd's Rep. 616; [1994] 2 A. C.
 199; [1994] 2 W. L. R. 370; [1994] 1 All E. R. 213; (1994) 138 S. J. (LB) 26;
 (1994) 144 New L. J. 87, (P. C.) 67
Skadi, The, SMA 789 (Arb. at N. Y. 1973) 116
Skagerak (A/S) v. Saremine S. A. (1939) 64 Ll. L. Rep. 153, 55 T. L. R. 821, (K. B.) ...158
Skibs. A/S Snefonn v. Kawasaki Kisen Kaisha—The Berge Tasta [1975] 1 Lloyd's
 Rep. 422, (Q. B.) 121, 128, 531
Skopas, The—Resolute Maritime Inc. and Another v. Nippon Kaiji Kyokai and
 Others [1983] 1 Lloyd's Rep. 431; [1983] 1 W. L. R. 857; [1983] 2 All E. R. 1, (Q.
 B.) 84
Smailes (Thomas) & Sons v. Evans & Reid [1917] 2 K. B. 54; 86 L. J. K. B. 1072; 22
 Com. Cas. 225; 116 L. T. 595, 33 T. L. R. 233; 14 Asp. M. L. C. 59 ....**365**
Smith v. Dart & Son (1884) 14 Q. B. D. 105; 1 T. L. R. 99; 5 Asp. M. L. C. 360; 52 L.
 T. 218; 54 L. J. Q. B. 121, (C. A.) **178**, 181, 355, 358
Smith v. Eric S. Bush [1990] 1 A. C. 831; [1989] 2 W. L. R. 790; [1989] 2 All E. R.
 514; (1990) 9 Tr. L. R. 1; 87 L. G. R. 685; (1989) 21 H. L. R. 424; [1989] 17 E. G.
 68 and [1989] 18 E. G. 99; (1989) 133 S. J. 597; (1989) 139 New L. J. 576; (1989)
 153 L. G. Rev. 984, (H. L.); *aff'g* [1988] Q. B. 743; [1987] 3 All E. R. 179; (1987)
 19 H. L. R. 287; [1987] 1 E. G. L. R. 157; [1988] T. L. R. 77; (1987) 131 S. J. 1423;
 (1987) 137 New L. J. 362, (C. A.) 85
Smith Barney, Harris, Upham & Co. v. Luckie, Merrill Lynch, Pierce Fenner &
 Smith Inc. v. Manhard (1995) 85 N. Y. 2d 193; 623 N. Y. S. 2d 800 450
Snia Società di Navigazione v. Suzuki & Co. (1924) 18 Ll. L. Rep. 333; 29 Com. Cas.
 284, (C. A.); (1924) 17 Ll. L. Rep. 78, (K. B.) **100**, 161, 212

Soares Financial Group Inc. v. Nat'l Assoc. of Securities Dealers (1994) U. S. Dist.
Lexis 8245 (N. D. Cal.) ···450
Sobel v. Hertz, Warner & Co. (1972) 469 F. 2d 1211 (2d Cir.) ·······················472,473
Sociedad Financiera de Bienes Raices S. A. v. Agrimpex—The Aello [1960] 1 Lloyd's
Rep. 623; [1961] A. C. 135; [1960] 3 W. L. R. 145; [1960] 2 All E. R. 578, (H. L.) ···**159**
Sociedade Portuguesa de Navios Tanques v. Polaris A/S [1952] 1 Lloyd's Rep. 407,
(C. A.); aff'g [1952] 1 Lloyd's Rep. 71, (K. B.) ···**52**
Société Anonyme des Minerais v. Grant Trading Inc.—The Ert Stefanie [1987] 2
Lloyd's Rep. 371; [1989] 1 Lloyd's Rep. 349, (C. A.) ·····································557,558
Société Anonyme Maritime et Commerciale v. Anglo-Iranian Oil Co. Ltd. [1954] 1
Lloyd's Rep. 1; [1954] 1 All E. R. 529; [1954] 1 W. L. R. 492, (C. A.); [1953] 2
Lloyd's Rep. 466; [1953] 1 W. L. R. 1379, (Q. B.); [1953] 2 All E. R. 1325 ········**95**,575
Société Franco-Tunisienne d'Armement v. Sidermar S. p. A.—The Massalia [1960] 1
Lloyd's Rep. 594; [1961] 2 Q. B. 278; [1960] 3 W. L. R. 701; [1960] 2 All E. R.
529, (Q. B.) ···398
Société Italo-Belge v. Palm and Vegetable Oils (Malaysia)—The Post Chaser [1981]
2 Lloyd's Rep. 695; [1982] 1 All E. R. 19, (Q. B.) ···92
Société Navale de L'Ouest v. Sutherland & Co. (1920) 4 Ll. L. Rep. 58, 185; (1920)
3 Ll. L. Rep. 262; 36 T. L. R. 682 ···95
Socomet v. Sliedrecht, 1975 AMC 314 (S. D. N. Y.) ··318
Sofia Shipping Co. v. Amoco Transp. Co. (1986) 628 F. Supp. 116; 1986 AMC 2163
(S. D. N. Y.) ···277
Sofial S. A. v. Ove Skou Rederi-The Helle Skou [1976] 2 Lloyd's Rep. 205, (Q. B.)
···282,358
Sokoloff v. National City Bank (1924) 239 N. Y. 158; 145 N. E. 917 ··············415
Solar, The, SMA 2666 (Arb. at N. Y. 1990) ···272
Solhaug, The (1931) 2 F. Supp. 294 (S. D. N. Y.) ·····································493,495
Solholt, The—Sotiros Shipping Inc. and Aeco Maritime S. A. v. Sameiet Solholt [1983]
1 Lloyd's Rep. 605, (C. A.); [1981] 2 Lloyd's Rep. 574, (Q. B.) ······························54
Solomon, The, SMA 3107 (Arb. at N. Y. 1990) ···208
Son Shipping Co. v. DeFosse & Tanghe (1952) 199 F. 2d 687; 1952 AMC 1931 (2d
Cir.) ···448,450,**523**
Sorrentino v. Buerger [1915] 3 K. B. 367; 84 L. J. K. B. 1937; 21 Com. Cas. 33. (C. A.);
aff'g [1915] 1 K. B. 307 ···95
Sotiros Shipping Inc. and Aeco Maritime S. A. v. Sameiet Solholt—The Solholt [1983]
1 Lloyd's Rep. 605, (C. A.); [1981] 2 Lloyd's Rep. 574, (Q. B.) ······························54
Sounion, The—Summit Investment Inc. v. British Steel Corp. [1987] 1 Lloyd's Rep.
230; [1987] 1 F. T. L. R. 169, (C. A.); rev'g [1986] 2 Lloyd's Rep. 593, (Q. B.) ········509
Southern Pacific Co. v. Jensen (1917) 244 U. S. 205; 37 S. Ct. 524 ···············56
Southern Seas Navigation Ltd. v. Petroleos Mexicanos (1985) 606 F. Supp. 692; 1985
AMC 2190 (S. D. N. Y.) ···461,463
Southwestern Sugar & Molasses Corp. v. The Eliza Jane Nicholson (1954) 126 F.
Supp. 666; 1955 AMC 746 (S. D. N. Y. 1954) ···448

Span Terza, The [1982] 2 Lloyd's Rep. 72, (Adm.); [1983] 1 Lloyd's Rep. 441, (C.
 A.); [1984] 1 Lloyd's Rep. 119; [1984] 1 W. L. R. 27, (H. L.) ············219, 228, 588, 589
Spanish Amer. Skin Co. v. Buanno Transp. Co., 1975 AMC 910 (N. Y. Civ.)·············524
Spence v. Crawford [1939] 3 All E. R. 271, (H. L.) ··83
Spence v. Mariehamns R/S (1985) 766 F. 2d 1504; 1986 AMC 685 (11th Cir.) ·········318
Sperry International Trade Inc. v. Government of Israel (1982) 689 F. 2d 301 (2d
 Cir.) ··461
Sphere Drake Ins. v. Marine Towing Inc. (1994) 16 F. 3d 666; 1994 AMC 1581 (5th
 Cir.); cert. denied (1994) —U. S.—; 115 S. Ct. 195; 130 L. Ed. 2d 127; Lexis 6329451,
 474
Spier v. Calzaturificio Tecnica S. p. A. (1987) 663 F. Supp. 871 (S. D. N. Y.) ·············477
Spinney's v. Royal Insurance [1980] 1 Lloyd's Rep. 406, (Q. B.) ·····················609, 610
Spiro v. Lintern [1973] 1 W. L. R. 1002; [1975] 3 All E. R. 319; 117 S. J. 584, (C. A.) ···69
Splendid Sun, The—Andre et Compagnie S. A. v. Marine Transocean Ltd. [1981] 2
 Lloyd's Rep. 29; [1981] Q. B. 694; [1981] 3 W. L. R. 43; [1981] 2 All E. R. 993,
 (C. A.); aff'g [1980] 1 Lloyd's Rep. 333, (Q. B.) ···443
Splosna Plovba of Piran v. Agrelak S. S. Corp. (1974) 381 F. Supp. 1368 (S. D. N. Y.) ···462
Splosna Plovba of Piran v. Agrelak S. S. Corp.—The Bela Krajina [1975] 1 Lloyd's
 Rep. 139, (Q. B.) ··286
Spray Cap, The, SMA 1706 (Arb. at N. Y. 1982) ··116
Spring v. Guardian Assurance [1994] 3 W. L. R. 354; [1994] 3 All E. R. 129; [1994]
 I. C. R. 596; [1994] I. R. L. R. 460; (1994) 138 S. J. (LB) 183; (1994) 144 New L.
 J. 971, (H. L.); rev'g [1993] 2 All E. R. 273; [1993] I. C. R. 412; [1993] I. R. L. R.
 122; (1993) 12 Tr. L. R. 33; (1993) 137 S. J. (LB) 47; (1993) 143 New L. J. 365,
 (C. A.); rev'g [1992] I. R. L. R. 173; (1992) 11 Tr. L. R. 100 ···································84
Spyros Lemos, The, 1967 AMC 2357 (Arb. at N. Y.) ···273
Stadt Schleswig, The, 1971 AMC 362 (Arb. at N. Y. 1970)···204
Stag Line v. Ellerman & Papayanni Lines (1949) 82 Ll. L. Rep. 826, (K. B.) ···195, 197, 296
Stag Line Ltd. v. Foscolo, Mango & Co. Ltd. (1931) 41 Ll. L. Rep. 165; [1932] A. C.
 328; 101 L. J. K. B. 165; 146 L. T. 305; 37 Com. Cas. 54; 48 T. L. R. 127; 18 Asp. M. L.
 C. 266, (H. L.) ···435
Standard Ardour, The—Interbulk Ltd. v. Pontei dei Sospiri Shipping Co. [1988] 2
 Lloyd's Rep. 159, (Q. B.) ···439, 520
Standard Navigazione S. p. A. v. The K. Z. Michalos, 1981 AMC 748 (S. D. Tex.) ······537
Standard Tankers (Bahamas) Co. Ltd. v. The Akti (1977) 438 F. Supp. 153; 1978
 AMC 181 (E. D. N. C.) ··466, 468, 469
Stanton v. Richardson (1875) 45 L. J. Q. B. 78; 33 L. T. 193; 3 Asp. M. L. C. 23, (H.
 L.); aff'g (1874) L. R. 9 C. P. 390, (Ex. Ch.) ···98, 100
Stargas S. p. A. v. Petredec Ltd.—The Sargasso [1994] 1 Lloyd's Rep. 412
 ··251, 441, 520, 594
Star Steamship Society v. Beogradska Plovidba—The Junjor K [1988] 2 Lloyd's Rep.
 583, (Q. B.) ···**53-54**
Stavros Commantaros, The, 1961 AMC 370 (Arb. at N. Y.) ···241

Steamship Co. Gorm v. United States Shipping Bd. Emergency Fleet Corp.—The
Knud II (1922) 285 F. 142 (2d Cir.) ···233-234
Steamship Knutsford Co. v. Barber & Co. (1919) 261 F. 866 (2d Cir.); cert. denied
(1920) 252 U. S. 586 ··384-385, 389
Stedor Enterprises Ltd. v. Armtex Inc. (1991) 947 F. 2d 727 (4th Cir.) ················451
Steelwood Carriers Inc. v. Evimeria Cia. Nav. S. A.—The Agios Giorgis [1976] 2
Lloyd's Rep. 192, (Q. B.) ···246, 256-257, 279, 285, 480
Stena Nautica, The, (No. 2) —CN Marine Inc. v. Stena Line A/B and Regie Voor
Maritiem Transport [1982] 2 Lloyd's Rep. 336; [1982] Com. L. R. 203, (C. A.) ········87
Stena Pacifica, The—Navigazione Alta Italia S. p. A. v. Concordia Maritime Chartering
A. B. [1990] 2 Lloyd's Rep. 234, (Q. B.) ··439, 603, **604**
Stephens v. Harris & Co. (1887) 57 L. T. 618; 3 T. L. R. 720; 57 L. J. Q. B. 203; 6 Asp.
M. L. C. 192, (C. A.) ···562
Sterling Navigation Co. Ltd. (Re) (1983) 31 B. R. 619; 1983 AMC 2240 (S. D. N. Y.) ···493
Sterns Ltd. v. Salterns Ltd. (1922) 12 Ll. L. Rep. 385, (K. B.) ·······························103
Steven v. Bromley & Son [1919] 2 K. B. 722; 24 Com. Cas. 252; 121 L. T. 354; 35 T.
L. R. 594; 88 L. J. K. B. 1147; 14 Asp. M. L. C. 455, (C. A.) ·····················**166**, 170
Stewart v. P. Van Ommeren [1918] 2 K. B. 560; 88 L. J. K. B. 32; 119 L. T. 637; 14
Asp. M. L. C. 359; 62 S. S. 739 ···254
Stinnes Interoil G. m. b. H. v. A. Halcoussis & Co.—The Yanxilas [1982] 2 Lloyd's
Rep. 445, (Q. B.) ···64, 67
Stolt Capricorn, The, SMA 2359 (Arb. at N. Y. 1987) ·································390, 627
Stolt Lion, The, SMA 1188 (Arb. at N. Y. 1977) ·····································162, **215**
Stolt Loyalty, The [1993] 2 Lloyd's Rep. 281, (Q. B.) ······································69
Stolt Pam, The, SMA 1026 (Arb. at N. Y. 1976) ···109
Stoot v. Fluor Drilling Services (1988) 851 F. 2d 1514; 1989 AMC 20 (5th Cir.) ········56
Stork, The—Compania Naviera Maropan S. A. v. Bowater's Lloyd Pulp & Paper Mills
Ltd. [1955] 1 Lloyd's Rep. 349; [1955] 2 Q. B. 68; [1955] 2 W. L. R. 998; [1955]
2 All E. R. 241, (C. A.); aff'g [1954] 2 Lloyd's Rep. 397; [1955] 2 Q. B. 68; [1954]
3 W. L. R. 894; [1954] 3 All E. R. 563, (Q. B.) ···············178, 190, 192, **193**, 195, 197, 293
Stove Vulkan, The, SMA 292 (Arb. at N. Y. 1968) ···························**115**, 116, 117, 118
Straits of Dover Steamship Co. v. Munson (1899) 99 F. 690 (S. D. N. Y.); aff'd (1900)
100 F. 1055 (2d Cir.) ···132
Strathlorne S. S. Co. v. Andrew Weir & Co. (1934) 50 Ll. L. Rep. 185; 40 Com. Cas.
168, (C. A.); aff'g (1934) 49 Ll. L. Rep. 306, (K. B.) ···············221, **293-294**, 295, 328, 481
Strathnewton, The—D/S A/S Idaho v. The Peninsular and Oriental Steam Navigation
Company [1983] 1 Lloyd's Rep. 219, (C. A.); [1982] 2 Lloyd's Rep. 296, (Q. B.)
···311, 313
Stray (S. O.) & Co. v. Trottier, Ide & Co. (1922) 280 F. 249 (D. Mass.) ···············114
Strong v. United States (1878) 154 U. S. 632 ···213
Stuyvesant, The, SMA 1722 (Arb. at N. Y. 1982) ···538
Stylianos Restis, The, 1974 AMC 2343 (S. D. N. Y. 1972) ·······························174, 175
Styria, The (1900) 101 F. 728 (2d Cir.); mod. on other grounds (1902) 186 U. S. 1

判例索引 109

··287, 429, 570
Suart v. Haigh (1893) 9 T. L. R. 488, (H. L.) ··**70**
Sucrest Corp. v. Jennifer (1978) 455 F. Supp. 371; 1978 AMC 2520 (D. Me.) ············173
Sudbrook Trading Estate Ltd. v. Eggleton [1983] 1 A. C. 444; [1982] 3 W. L. R. 315;
　[1982] 3 All E. R. 1, (H. L.) ··50
Suisse Atlantique Société d'Armement Maritime v. N. V. Rotterdamsche Kolen
　Centrale [1966] 1 Lloyd's Rep. 529; [1967] 1 A. C. 361; [1966] 2 W. L. R. 944;
　[1966] 2 All E. R. 61, (H. L.) ··425, 426
Summit Investment Inc. v. British Steel Corp.—The Sounion [1987] 1 Lloyd's Rep.
　230; [1987] 1 F. T. L. R. 169, (C. A.), rev'g [1986] 2 Lloyd's Rep. 593, (Q. B.) ·········509
Sun Happiness, The—Etablessement Biret & Cie. S. A. v. Yukiteru Kauin KK and
　Nissui Shipping Corp. [1984] 1 Lloyd's Rep. 381, (Q. B.) ·····································64
Sun Oil Co. v. Dalzell Towing Co. Inc. (1932) 55 F. 2d 63 (2d Cir.); aff'd (1932) 287
　U. S. 291 ··57-58
Sun Oil Co. v. Western Sea Transport Ltd. (in the matter of the Arbitration
　between) 1978 AMC 1372 (S. D. N. Y.) ···474
Sun Refining & Marketing Co. v. Statheros Shipping Corp. (Arbitration between)
　(1991) 761 F. Supp. 293; 1991 AMC 1874 (S. D. N. Y.); aff'd without opinion (1991)
　948 F. 2d 1277; 1992 AMC 1216 (2d Cir.) ···467
Sun Ship Inc. v. Matson Navigation Co. (1986) 785 F. 2d 59 (3d Cir.) ···············471
Suncorp Insurance and Finance v. Milano Assecurazioni [1993] 2 Lloyd's Rep. 225,
　(Q. B.) ···68
Sunil Industries v. The Ogden Fraser, 1981 AMC 2670 (S. D. N. Y.) ················343, 344
Sunkist Growers Inc. v. Adelaide Shipping Lines Ltd. (1979) 603 F. 2d 1327 (9th
　Cir.); cert. denied (1980) 449 U. S. 1012 ···429
Sunkist Soft Drinks Inc. v. Sunkist Growers Inc. (1993) 10 F. 3d 753 (11th Cir.) ···448, 467
Super Servant Two, The—Lauritzen (J.) A/S v. Wijsmuller B. V. [1990] 1 Lloyd's
　Rep. 1, (C. A.); aff'g [1989] 1 Lloyd's Rep. 148, (Q. B.) ·······················394, 405, **406**, 407
Superhulls Cover Case No. 2, The—Youell v. Bland Welch & Co. Ltd. [1990] 2
　Lloyd's Rep. 431, (Q. B.) ···309
Surrey Shipping Co. Ltd. v. Compagnie Continentale (France) S. A.—The
　Shackleford [1978] 2 Lloyd's Rep. 154; [1978] 1 W. L. R. 1080, (C. A.); aff'g [1978]
　1 Lloyd's Rep. 191, (Q. B.) ···358
Sussex Oak, The—G. W. Grace & Co. v. General Steam Navigation Co. (1950) 83 Ll.
　L. Rep. 297; [1950] 2 K. B. 383; 66 T. L. R. (Pt. 1) 147; [1950] 1 All E. R. 201, (K.
　B.) ···141, 165, 179, **180, 183**, 190, 292, 564, **565**
Sutherland v. Compagnie Napolitaine D'Eclairage (1920) 36 T. L. R. 724; (1920) 2
　Ll. L. Rep. 294; 4 Ll. L. Rep. 74, (C. A.) ···608
Suzuki & Co. Ltd. v. T. Beynon & Co. Ltd. (1926) 24 Ll. L. Rep. 49; 42 T. L. R. 269;
　95 L. J. K. B. 397; 134 L. T. 449; 31 Com. Cas. 183; 17 Asp. M. L. C. 1, (H. L.); aff'g
　(1924) 20 Ll. L. Rep. 179, (C. A.); aff'g (1924) 18 Ll. L. Rep. 415, (K. B.) ······**285-286**, 551
Svenska Lloyd Rederi A/B v. Niagassas (1921) 8 Ll. L. Rep. 500, (K. B.) ···············**55**
Sverdrup Corp. v. WHC Constructors (1993) 989 F. 2d 148 (4th Cir.) ·····················463

Swan, The [1968] 1 Lloyd's Rep. 5 (Adm.) ·· **63**
Swift & Company Packers v. Compania Colombiana Del Caribe S. A. (1950) 339 U. S.
  684 ·· 75
Swiss Bank Corp. v. Lloyds Bank Ltd. [1982] A. C. 584 (C. A. and H. L.); [1981] 2
  W. L. R. 893; [1981] 2 All E. R. 449; (1981) 125 S. J. 495, (H. L.); *aff'g* [1980] 3
  W. L. R. 457; [1980] 2 All E. R. 419; (1980) 124 S. J. 741, (C. A.); *rev'g* [1979] Ch.
  548; [1979] 3 W. L. R. 201; [1979] 2 All E. R. 853; (1978) 123 S. J. 536, (Q. B.)
  ··· 95, 96
Sykes (F. & G.) (Wessex) Ltd. v. Fine Fare Ltd. [1967] 1 Lloyd's Rep. 53, (C. A.) ···51
Syra, The, SMA 297 (Arb. at N. Y. 1968) ···109
Sze Hai Tong Bank v. Rambler Cycle Co. [1959] 2 Lloyd's Rep. 114; [1959] A. C.
  576; [1959] 3 W. L. R. 214; [1959] 3 All E. R. 182, (P. C.) ···························292, 424

TFL Prosperity, The—Tor Line A. B. v. Alltrans Group of Canada Ltd. [1984] 1
  Lloyd's Rep. 123; [1984] 1 W. L. R. 48; [1984] 1 All E. R. 103, (H. L.); [1983] 2
  Lloyd's Rep. 18, (C. A.); [1982] 1 Lloyd's Rep. 617, (Q. B.)
  ··103, 551, 553, **556**, 557, 560, 561, 563
TTT Stevedores of Texas Inc. v. The Jagat Vijeta (1983) 696 F. 2d 1135; 1983
  AMC 1980 (5th Cir.) ···500
Ta Chi Navigation (Panama) Corp. (The Eurypylus) (in the matter of the
  complaint of) (1982) 677 F. 2d 225 (2d Cir.) ···428, 429
Tagart, Beaton & Co. v. James Fisher & Sons [1903] 1 K. B. 391; 88 L. T. 451; 8
  Com. Cas. 133; 9 Asp. M. L. C. 381; 72 L. J. K. B. 202, (C. A.) ·······················484, **485**
Tage Berglund v. Montoro Shipping Corp.—The Dagmar [1968] 2 Lloyd's Rep. 563,
  (Q. B.) ···**182**, 192
Tai Hing v. Liu Chong Hing Bank [1985] 2 Lloyd's Rep. 313; [1986] A. C. 80;
  [1985] 3 W. L. R. 317; [1985] 2 All E. R. 947; [1986] F. L. R. 14; (1985) 129 S.
  J. 503; (1985) 135 New L. J. 680, (P. C.) ···309
Taisho Marine & Fire v. The Sea-Land Endurance (1987) 815 F. 2d 1270; 1987
  AMC 1730 (9th Cir.) ···431
Taiwan Navigation Co. Ltd. v. Seven Seas Merchants Corp. (1959) 172 F. Supp. 721
  (S. D. N. Y.) ···78
Takafa, The—President of India v. Hariana Overseas Corporation [1990] 1 Lloyd's
  Rep. 536, (Q. B.) ···286
Tamplin (F. A.) S. S. Co. v. Anglo-Mexican Petroleum Products Co. [1916] 2 A. C.
  397; 85 L. J. K. B. 1389; 21 Com. Cas. 299; 115 L. T. 315; 32 T. L. R. 677; 13 Asp. M.
  L. C. 467, (H. L.) ···**399**, 401
Tankexpress A/S v. Compagnie Financière Belge des Pétroles S. A. (1948) 82 Ll. L.
  Rep. 43; [1949] A. C. 76; [1949] L. J. R. 170; [1948] 2 All E. R. 939, (H. L.);
  (1947) 80 Ll. L. Rep. 365, (C. A.); (1946) 79 Ll. L. Rep. 451, (K. B.)
  ···243, 247, 253, 254, **255**
Tankers Int'l Navigation Corp. v. National Shipping & Trading Corp., 499 N. Y. S. 2d
  697; 1987 AMC 478 (A. D. 1 1986) ···543, **544**

Tarmarea S. R. L. v. Rederiaktiebolaget Sally—The Dalny [1979] 2 Lloyd's Rep. 439;
[1979] 1 W. L. R. 1320; [1979] 2 All E. R. 989, (Q. B.) ·································443
Tarstar Shipping Co. v. Century Shipping Ltd. (1978) 451 F. Supp. 317; 1979 AMC
1101 (S. D. N. Y.); aff'd on opinion below 1979 AMC 1096; (1979) 597 F. 2d 837;
1979 AMC 1096 (2d Cir.) ··494
Tatem v. Gamboa (1938) 61 Ll. L. Rep. 149; [1939] 1 K. B. 132; 108 L. J. K. B. 34; 43
Com. Cas. 343; 160 L. T. 159; [1938] 3 All E. R. 135; 19 Asp. M. L. C. 216, (K. B.)
···396, **400**
Taygetos, The—Ocean Star Tankers S. A. v. Total Transport Corp. [1982] 2 Lloyd's
Rep. 272, (Q. B.) ··**535**, 610
Taylor v. Weir (1901) 110 F. 1005 (D. Or.) ···543
Tecomar S. A. (Re Complaint of) (1991) 765 F. Supp. 1150; 1991 AMC 2432 (S. D. N.
Y.) ···432
Teheran-Europe Co. Ltd. v. S. T. Belton (Tractors) Ltd. [1968] 2 Lloyd's Rep. 37;
[1968] 2 Q. B. 545; [1968] 3 W. L. R. 205; [1968] 2 All E. R. 886, (C. A.) ········64, 66
Tehno-Impex v. Gebr. Van Weelde Scheepvaartkantoor B. V. [1981] 1 Lloyd's Rep.
587; [1981] 1 Q. B. 648; [1981] 2 W. L. R. 821; [1981] 2 All E. R. 669, (C. A.);
rev'g [1980] 1 Lloyd's Rep. 484, (Q. B.) ···446
Telfair Shipping Co. v. Institute Rio (Re), 1978 AMC 1120 (S. D. N. Y.) ···············457
Telfair Shipping Corp. v. Athos Shipping Co. S. A., Solidor Shipping Co. Ltd., Horizon
Finance Corp. and A. N. Cominos—The Athos [1983] 1 Lloyd's Rep. 127, (C. A.);
[1981] 2 Lloyd's Rep. 74, (Q. B.) ··························265, **266-267**, 531, **533-534**
Telfair Shipping Corp. v. Inersea Carriers S. A.—The Caroline P [1984] 2 Lloyd's
Rep. 466; [1985] 1 W. L. R. 533; [1985] 1 All E. R. 243, (Q. B.) ·········295, 327, **328**, 553
Temple Moat, The—Temple Steamship Co. Ltd. v. V/O Sovfracht (1945) 79 Ll. L.
Rep. 1; 62 T. L. R. 43; 173 L. T. 373, (H. L.); aff'g (1944) 77 Ll. L. Rep. 257; 60 T. L. R.
257; 170 L. T. 378, (C. A.) ···**131**, **141-142**, 296, 408, 531
Temple Steamship Co. v. Mercator Marine Corp., 1959 AMC 641 (Arb. at N. Y 1958)
···385
Temple Steamship Co. Ltd. v. V/O Sovfracht—The Temple Moat (1945) 79 Ll. L.
Rep. 1; 62 T. L. R. 43; 173 L. T. 373, (H. L.); aff'g (1944) 77 Ll. L. Rep. 257; 60 T. L. R.
257; 170 L. T. 378, (C. A.) ···**131**, **141-142**, 296, 408, 531
Tempus Shipping Co. Ltd. v. Louis Dreyfus & Co. Ltd. (1930) 40 Ll. L. Rep. 217;
[1931] A. C. 726; 100 L. J. K. B. 673; 145 L. T. 490; 36 Com. Cas. 318; 47 T. L. R. 542;
18 Asp. M. L. C. 243, (H. L.); aff'g [1931] 1 K. B. 195; 37 Ll. L. Rep. 273, (C. A.); rev'g
in part [1930] 1 K. B. 699; 36 Ll. L. Rep. 159, (K. B.) ································421
Tenax Steamship Co. Ltd. v. The Brimnes (Owners)-The Brimnes [1974] 2 Lloyd's
Rep. 241; [1975] Q. B. 929; [1974] 3 W. L. R. 613; [1974] 3 All E. R. 88, (C. A.);
aff'g [1972] 2 Lloyd's Rep. 465; [1973] 1 W. L. R. 386; [1973] 1 All E. R. 769, (Q.
B.) ···244, 245, 255, 260, 261, 268
Tendo, The (1948) 80 F. Supp. 328 (S. D. N. Y.); aff'd (1950) 181 F. 2d 383; 1950
AMC 947 (2d Cir.); cert. denied (1950) 340 U. S. 829 ·····················108, 110, **389**
Teno, The—Compania Sud Americana de Vapores v. Shipmair B. V. [1977] 2 Lloyd's

Rep. 289, (Q. B.) ···249, 250
Tequila, The, 341 F. Supp. 459 ; 1972 AMC 1540 (S. D. N. Y.) ; *aff'd* (1973) 480 F. 2d
　1024 ; 1973 AMC 1431 (2d Cir.) ··**490**, 491, 496, **498**, 499
Terkol Rederierne *v*. Petroleo Brasileiro S. A.―The Badagry [1985] 1 Lloyd's Rep.
　395, (C. A.) ···**95**, 396, 591
Termagant, The (1914) 19 Com. Cas. 239 ; 30 T. L. R. 377, (K. B.) ······························147
Tesco Supermarkets Ltd. *v*. Nattrass [1972] A. C. 153 ; [1971] 2 W. L. R. 1166 ;
　[1971] 2 All E. R. 127, (H. L.) ··558
Teutonia, The―Duncan *v*. Koster (1872) L. R. 4 P. C. 171 ; 8 Moo. P. C. N. S. 411 ; 41 L.
　J. Adm. 57 ; 26 L. T. 48 ; 20 W. R. 421 ; 17 E. R. 366 ; 1 Asp. M. L. C. 214, (P. C.)
　··181, 186, 291
Texas Co. *v*. Hogarth Shipping Co. (1921) 256 U. S. 619 ·······································**416**
Thames, The (1881) 10 F. 848 (S. D. N. Y.) ··543
Thekos, The, SMA 2253 (Arb. at N. Y. 1986) ···271
Themis, The (1917) 244 F. 545 (S. D. N,. Y.) ···133, **134**
Themis, The―Gans S. S. Line *v*. Wilhelmsen (1921) 275 F. 254 (2d Cir.) ; *cert. denied*
　(1921) 257 U. S. 655 ··339, 340, 427, 428
Theodora, The, SMA 2333 (Arb. at N. Y. 1985) ···391
Theofilos J. Vatis, The, SMA 1994 (Arb. at N. Y. 1984) ··239
Theokeetor, The, SMA 604 (Arb. at N. Y.) ···241
Thomas A. & Thomas Q., The, 1979 AMC 202 (Arb. at N. Y. 1978) ·······················**416**
Thomas Jordan Inc. *v*. Mayronne Drilling Mud Chem. & Eng'r Serv. (1954) 214 F.
　2d 410 (5th Cir.) ···110
Thomas Neison & Sons *v*. Dundee East Coast Shipping Co., 1907 S. C. 927 ; 44 Sc. L.
　R. 661 ; 15 S. L. T. 38 ··153, 360, 361
Thomas Witter *v*. TBP Industries (1994) (unreported) ···83
Thomson & Co. *v*. T & J. Brocklebank Ltd. [1918] 1 K. B. 655 ; 87 L. J. K. B. 616 ; 118
　L. T. 573 ; 34 T. L. R. 284 ; 14 Asp. M. L. C. 253, (K. B.) ···**102**
Thorgerd, The, 1926 AMC 160 (Arb. at N. Y. 1925) ···137
Three Sisters, The, SMA 345 (Arb. at N. Y. 1969) ···503
Thunderbird, The, SMA 54 (Arb. at N. Y. 1964) ··383
Thunderhead, The, SMA 617 (Arb. at N. Y. 1971) ···233
Thyssen Inc. *v*. The Eurounity (1994) 21 F. 2d 533 ; 1994 AMC 1638 (2d Cir.) ········431
Thyssen Inc. *v*. The Fortune Star (1985) 777 F. 2d 57 ; 1986 AMC 1318 (2d Cir.)
　···317, 458
Thyssen Steel Corp. *v*. The Adonis (1973) 364 F. Supp. 1332 ; 1974 AMC 389 (S. D.
　N. Y. 1973) ···**342**
Tibermede *v*. Graham & Co. (1921) 7 Ll. L. Rep. 250, (K. B.) ·····································**103**
Tillmanns & Co. *v*. S. S. Knutsford Ltd. [1908] A. C. 406 ; 77 L. J. K. B. 977 ; 99 L. T.
　399 ; 24 T. L. R. 786 ; 13 Com. Cas. 334 ; 11 Asp. M. L. C. 105, (H. L.) ; *aff'g* [1908] 2
　K. B. 385 ; 99 L. T. 399 ; 24 T. L. R. 454 ; 13 Com. Cas. 244 ; 11 Asp. M. L. C. 105, (C.
　A.) ···329, 333, **335-336**, 337
Todd Shipyards Corp. *v*. Cunard Lines Ltd. (1991) 943 F. 2d 1056 ; 1992 AMC 328

(9th Cir.) ···457-458
Topgallant Lines Inc. (Re) (1992) 125 B. R. 682; 1992 AMC 2511 (Bankr. S. D. Ga.);
 modified on other grounds (1993) 154 B. R. 368; 1993 AMC 2775 (S. D. Ga.); aff'd
 without opinion (1994) 20 F. 3d 1175 (11th Cir.) ·······································493, 499
Toepfer v. Lenersan-Poortman N. V. [1980] 1 Lloyd's Rep. 143, (C. A.); aff'g [1978] 2
 Lloyd's Rep. 555, (Q. B.) ··92
Toho Bussan Kaisha Ltd. v. American President Lines (1959) 265 F. 2d 418; 1959
 AMC 1114 (2d Cir.) ··343
Toledo, The (1939) 30 F. Supp. 93 (E. D. N. Y.); aff'd (1941) 122 F. 2d 255 (2d Cir.);
 cert. denied (1941) 314 U. S. 689 ···110, 427, 432, 433
Tonnelier & Bolckow, Vaughan & Co. v. Smith & Weatherill & Co. (1897) 2 Com.
 Cas. 258; 77 L. T. 277; 13 T. L. R. 560; 8 Asp. M. L. C. 327, (C. A.) ········254, 481, 487, 548
Tonnevold v. Finn Friis [1916] 2 K. B. 551 ···606
Toplis, v. Grane (1839) 5 Bing. N. C. 636; 2 Arn. 110; 7 Scott 620; 9 L. J. P. C. 180;
 132 E. R. 1245···294
Tor Line A. B. v. Alltrans Group of Canada Ltd.—The TFL Prosperity [1984] 1
 Lloyd's Rep. 123; [1984] 1 W. L. R. 48; [1984] 1 All E. R. 103, (H. L.); [1983] 2
 Lloyd's Rep. 18, (C. A.); [1982] 1 Lloyd's Rep. 617, (Q. B.)
 ···103, 551, 553, **556**, 557, 560, 561, 563
Tordenskjold, The, SMA 1091 (Arb. at N. Y. 1977) ··108, **109**, 390
Tore Knudsen, The, SMA 1108 (Arb. at N. Y. 1977) ··416
Torres v. Cool Carriers (1994) 26 Cal. App. 4th 900; 31 Cal. Rptr. 2d 790; 1994
 AMC 2690 ··321
Torvald Klaverness v. Arni Maritime—The Gregos [1995] 1 Lloyd's Rep. 1; [1994]
 1 W. L. R. 1465; [1994] 4 All E. R. 998; (1994) 144 New L. J. 1550, (H. L.); rev'g
 [1994] 1 Lloyd's Rep. 335, (C. A.); rev'g [1992] 2 Lloyd's Rep. 40, (Q. B.)
 ···122, **123-124**, **125**, 127, 190, 549
Totem Marine Tug & Barge Inc. v. North American Towing Inc. (1979) 607 F. 2d
 649; 1980 AMC 1961 (5th Cir.) ···468, 470
Toxon, The, SMA 913 (Arb. at N. Y. 1974) ···58
Toxotis, The, SMA 855 (Arb. at N. Y. 1974) ··233
Toyota of Berkeley v. Automobile Salesmen's Union, Local 1095 (1987) 834 F. 2d
 751 (9th Cir.); cert. denied (1988) 486 U. S. 1043; amended 856 F. 2d 1572 (9th
 Cir.) ··467
Tradax Export S. A. v. Dorada Compania Naviera S. A.—The Lutetian [1982] 2
 Lloyd's Rep. 140, (Q. B.) ···246, 247, 248, 252, 259, 377, 584
Tradax Export S. A. v. Volkswagenwerk A. G. [1970] 1 Lloyd's Rep. 62; [1970] 1
 Q. B. 537; [1970] 2 W. L. R. 339; [1970] 1 All E. R. 420, (C. A.) ·······································440
Tradax International S. A. v. Government of Pakistan, 1973 AMC 1609 (Arb. at N. Y.
 1973)··414
Trade and Transport Inc. v. Caribbean S. S. Co. (1974) 384 F. Supp. 782; 1975 AMC
 1065 (S. D. Tex.) ···207
Trade and Transport Inc. v. Iino Kaiun Kaisha Ltd.—The Angelia [1972] 2 Lloyd's

Rep. 154; [1973] 1 W. L. R. 210; [1973] 2 All E. R. 144, (Q. B.) ··················394, 395
Trade and Transport Inc. v. Natural Petroleum Charters Inc. (1991) 931 F. 2d 191
  (2d Cir.) ··454
Trade Arbed Inc. v. The Ellispontos (1980) 482 F. Supp. 991 (S. D. Tex.) ·············522
Trade Banner Line Inc. v. Caribbean S. S. Co. S. A. (1975) 521 F. 2d 229; 1975
  AMC 2515 (5th Cir.) ··202
Trade Endeavor, The, SMA 1916 (Arb. at N. Y. 1983) ··116
Trade Fortitude, The, 1974 AMC 2195 (Arb. at N. Y.) ··**570**
Trade Greece, The, SMA 1643 (Arb. at N. Y. 1982) ···78
Trade Yonder, The, SMA 2435 (Arb. at N. Y. 1987) ··136, 322
Trado, The—Marseille Fret S. A. v. D. Oltmann Schiffahrts G. m. b. H. & Co. K. G.
  [1982] 1 Lloyd's Rep. 157, (Q. B.) ···353
Trafalgar Shipping Co. v. Int'l Milling Co. (1968) 401 F. 2d 568; 1969 AMC 1006
  (2d Cir.) ··450
Trafalgar, The, 1938 AMC 463 (Arb. at N. Y.) ··241
Tramp Oil and Marine Ltd. v. The Mermaid I (1986) 630 F. Supp. 630; 1987 AMC
  129 (D. P. R.); aff'd (1986) 805 F. 2d 42; 1987 AMC 866 (1st Cir.) ····················501
Tramp Shipping Corp. v. Greenwich Marine Inc.—The New Horizon [1975] 2
  Lloyd's Rep. 314; [1975] 1 W. L. R. 1042; [1975] 2 All E. R. 989; [1975] I. C. R.
  261, (C. A.) ··**562**
Transatlantic Bulk Shipping Ltd. v. Saudi Chartering S. A., 1985 AMC 2432 (S. D. N.
  Y.) ···475-476
Transatlantic Financing Corp. v. United States (1966) 363 F. 2d 312; 1966 AMC
  1717 (D. C. Cir.) ···**410**, 413
Transmarine Seaways Corp. v. Marc Rich & Co. A. G. (1978) 480 F. Supp. 352; 1979
  AMC 1496 (S. D. N. Y.), aff'd without opinion (1980) 614 F. 2d 1291; 1979 AMC
  2906 (2d Cir.); cert. denied (1980) 445 U. S. 930 ··467
Transoceanic Petroleum Carriers v. Cook Industries Inc.—The Mary Lou [1981] 2
  Lloyd's Rep. 272, (Q. B.) ····················177, 178, 179, **183-184**, 185, 186, 192, 193, 195
Transportacion Maritima Mexicana S. A. (Re) (1983) 636 F. Supp. 474 (S. D. N. Y.) ···**452**
Transvenezuelian Shipping Co. S. A. v. Czarnikow-Rionda Co. Inc., 1982 AMC 1458
  (S. D. N. Y.) ··457, 641
Travers (Joseph) v. Cooper [1915] 1 K. B. 73 (C. A.) ··308
Treana, The, SMA 2929 (Aarb. At N. Y. 1992) ··271
Treasure Island, The, SMA 1898 (Arb. at N. Y. 1983) ··113
Trechman S. S. Co. v. Munson S. S. Line (1913) 203 F. 692 (2d Cir.) ····················132
Tres Flores, The—Compania de Nav. Nedelka S. A. v. Tradax Internacional S. A.
  [1973] 2 Lloyd's Rep. 247; [1974] Q. B. 264; [1975] 3 W. L. R. 545; [1975] 3 All
  E. R. 967, (C. A.); aff'g [1972] 2 Lloyd's Rep. 384, (Q. B.) ·················155, 157, **357**, 358
Triad Shipping Co. v. Stellar Chartering & Brokerage Inc.—The Island Archon
  [1994] 2 Lloyd's Rep. 227; [1995] 1 All E. R. 595, (C. A.); aff'g [1993] 2 Lloyd's
  Rep. 388, (Q. B.) ···293, **294**, 295, 297, 298, 326-328
Trident Beauty, The—Pan Ocean Shipping Co. Ltd. v. Creditcorp Ltd. [1994] 1

判例索引   115

Lloyd's Rep. 365 ; [1994] 1 W. L. R. 161 ; [1994] 1 All E. R. 470 ; (1994) 144 New
L. J. 1203, (H. L.); aff'g [1993] 1 Lloyd's Rep. 443 ; (1993) 137 S. J. (LB) 53, (C. A.)
···253, **264**
Trinity Navigator, The, SMA 2609 (Arb. at N. Y. 1989) ·······························74
Triton Container Int'l v. Itapage (1990) 774 F. Supp. 1349 ; 1991 AMC 2319 (M. D.
Fla.) ···500
Tropez Comfort, The, SMA 2616 (Arb. at N. Y. 1989)································361
Tropic Breeze, The (1972) 456 F. 2d 137, 1972 AMC 1622 (1st Cir.) ···············505
Tropical Gas Co. v. The Mundogas Caribe (1974) 388 F. Supp. 647 ; 1975 AMC 987
(D. P. R.) ···448
Tropical Veneer, The, SMA 1172 (Arb. at N. Y. 1977) ························**202**, 203
Tropigas Far East, The, SMA 1594 (Arb. at N. Y. 1981) ···························354
Tropwind, The (No. 1) —Tropwood A. G. v. Jade Enterprises Ltd. [1977] 1 Lloyd's
Rep. 397, (Q. B.) ···192, **266**, 267
Tropwind, The (No. 2) —Tropwood A. G. of Zug v. Jade Enterprises Ltd. [1982] 1
Lloyd's Rep. 232, (C. A.); [1981] 1 Lloyd's Rep. 45, (Q. B.) ···············258, 263, 264, 268
Tropwood A. G. v. Jade Enterprises Ltd. —The Tropwind (No. 1) [1977] 1 Lloyd's
Rep. 397, (Q. B.) ···192, **266**, 267
Tropwood A. G. of Zug v. Jade Enterprises Ltd. —The Tropwind (No. 2) [1982] 1
Lloyd's Rep. 232, (C. A.); [1981] 1 Lloyd's Rep. 45, (Q. B.) ···············258, 263, 264, 268
Trust 38, The, SMA 2911 (Arb. at N. Y. 1992) ·······································319
Tsakiroglou & Co. v. Noblee Thorl G. m. b. H. [1961] 1 Lloyd's Rep. 329 ; [1962] A. C.
93 ; [1961] 2 W. L. R. 633 ; [1961] 2 All E. R. 179, (H. L.) ·······················394, 395
Tube Products of India v. The Rio Grande (1971) 334 F. Supp. 1039 ; 1971 AMC
1629 (S. D. N. Y.) ···340, 343
Tubos de Acero de Mexico v. Dynamic Shipping Inc. (1966) 249 F. Supp. 583 ; 1966
AMC 1903 (S. D. N. Y.) ···71
Tudor Marine Ltd. v. Tradax Export S. A. —The Virgo [1976] 2 Lloyd's Rep. 135,
(C. A.) ···**63-64**
Tug Diane, The, SMA 819 (Arb. at N. Y. 1973) ·······································111
Tully v. Howling (1877) 2 Q. B. D. 182 ; 46 L. J. Q. B. 388 ; 36 L. T. 163 ; 3 Asp. M. L. C.
368 ···98
Tulsa, The SMA 2794 (Arb. at N. Y. 1991) ·······································317, 341
Turmoil, The, SMA 2842 (Arb. at N. Y. 1992) ·······································413
Turner v. Green [1895] 2 Ch. 205 ; 64 L. J. (Ch.) 539 ; 72 L. T. 763 ·······················82
Turner v. Haji Goolam Mahomed Azam [1904] A. C. 826 ; 74 L. J. P. C. 17 ; 91 L. T.
216 ; 20 T. L. R. 599 ; 9 Asp. M. L. C. 588, (P. C.) ·························**147**, 333, **479**
Turner v. Japan Lines Ltd. (1981) 651 F. 2d 1300 ; 1981 AMC 2223 (9th Cir.); cert.
denied (1982) 459 U. S. 967 and amended (1983) 702 F. 2d 752 ; 1984 AMC 2703
(9th Cir.) ···320, 321
Tuscaloosa Steel Corp. v. The Naimo 1993 AMC 622 (S. D. N. Y. 1992) ···············341
Tweedie Trading Co. v. George D. Emery Co. (1907) 154 F. 472 (2d Cir.) ···············**381**
Tweedie Trading Co. v. James P. McDonald Co. (1902) 114 F. 985 (S. D. N. Y.) ·······**415**

Tweedie Trading Co. v. New York & Boston Dyewood Co. (1903) 127 F. 2d 278
  (2d Cir); cert. denied (1903) 193 U. S. 669···206, 300
Tweedie Trading Co. v. Sangstand (1910) 180 F. 691 (2d Cir.) ·····················133, 134
Tynedale Steam Shipping Co. Ltd. v. Anglo-Soviet Shipping Co. Ltd. (1936) 54 Ll. L.
  Rep. 341 ; 41 Com. Cas. 206 ; 154 L. T. 414 ; 52 T. L. R. 304 ; [1936] 1 All E. R. 389 ;
  19 Asp. M. L. C. 16, (C. A.) ···211, 364, 366, 367
Tyrer v. Hessler (1902) 7 Com. Cas. 166 ; (1902) 18 T. L. R. 589 ; 86 L. T. 697 ; 9
  Asp. M. L. C. 292, (C. A.) ··142, 263

U. G. S. Finance v. National Mortgage Bank of Greece [1964] 1 Lloyd's Rep. 446, (C.
  A.) ···425
U. S. Offshore v. Seabulk Offshore, 1991 AMC 616 (S. D. N. Y.) ························473
Ugland Trailer, The—Re Welsh Irish Ferries Ltd. [1985] 2 Lloyd's Rep. 372 ; [1986]
  Ch. 471 ; [1985] 3 W. L. R. 610, (Ch. D.) ··486
Uhenbels, The—Sea Calm Shipping Co. S. A. v. Chantiers Navals de L'Esterel S. A.
  [1986] 2 Lloyd's Rep. 294, (Q. B.) ···93
Ultimo Cabinet Corp. v. The Mason Lykes, 1991 AMC 1343 (S. D. N. Y.) ············343
Ultramar, The, 1981 AMC 1831 (Arb. at N. Y.) ···216
Unibulk Fir, The, SMA 1505 (Arb. at N. Y. 1980) ··318
Unimarine S. A. v. Interessentslskapet Wind Endeavor, 1984 AMC 405 (S. D. N. Y.
  1981) ··463
Uninav v. Molena Trust, 1973 AMC 1386 (S. D. N. Y.); aff'd (1974) 490 F. 2d 1406
  (2d Cir.) ··58
Uni-Ocean Lines Ltd. v. C-Trade S. A.—The Lucille [1984] 1 Lloyd's Rep. 244, (C.
  A.); [1983] 1 Lloyd's Rep. 387, (Q. B.) ·······································185, 186, 188, 197
Union Fish Co. v. Erickson (1919) 248 U. S. 308 ; (1919) 63 L. Ed. 261 ···············56
Union Harvest, The, SMA 2626 (Arb. at N. Y. 1989) ·······································301
Union Industrielle et Maritime v. Nimpex International Inc. (1972) 459 F. 2d 926 ;
  1972 AMC 1494 (7th Cir.) ···493, 494
Union Mariner, The, SMA 89 (Arb. at N. Y. 1960) ···117
Unione Stearinerie Lanza and Wiener (Re) [1917] 2 K. B. 558 ; 86 L. J. K. B. 1236 ;
  117 L. T. 337, (D. C.) ···442
United Bounty, The, SMA 2040 (Arb. at N. Y. 1984) ·······························116, 119, 351
United Faith, The, SMA 1409 (Arb. at N. Y. 1980) ···382
United Nations Children's Fund v. The Nordstern (1965) 251 F. Supp. 833 (S. D. N.
  Y.) ···340, 343
United Scientific Holdings v. Burnley Borough Council [1978] A. C. 904 ; [1977] 2 W.
  L. R. 806, (H. L.) ··268
United States v. Atlantic Mutual Ins. Co. (1952) 343 U. S. 236 ; 1952 AMC 659 ········526
United States v. Buffalo Coal Mining Co. (1965) 345 F. 2d 517 (9th Cir.)··············**411**
United States v. Carver (1923) 260 U. S. 482 ···499
United States v. The Freights of the Mt. Shasta (1927) 274 U. S. 466 ; 1927 AMC
  943···493, 494

判例索引   117

United States v. Gen. Douglas MacArthur Sr. Vil. Inc. (1974) 508 F. 2d 377 (2d Cir.)
···411
United States v. Ira S. Bushey & Sons Inc. (1973) 363 F. Supp. 110 (D. Vt.); aff'd
without opinion (1973) 487 F. 2d 1393 (2d Cir.); cert. denied (1974) 417 U. S. 976 ······78
United States v. Jon. T. Chemicals Inc. (1985) 768 F. 2d 686 (5th Cir.); cert. denied,
475 U. S. 10 ···78
United States v. Reliable Transfer Co. Inc. (1975) 421 U. S. 397 ·······························208
United States v. The Lucie Schulte (1965) 343 F. 2d 897; 1965 AMC 1516 (2d Cir.)
··499, 504
United States v. The Marilena P (1969) 433 F. 2d 164; 1969 AMC 1155 (4th Cir.)
···108, 382, 383, 522
United States v. The South Star (1954) 210 F. 2d 44 (2d Cir.) ·······························524
United States Barite Corp. v. The Haris, 1982 AMC 925 (S. D. N. Y) ························448
United Steelworkers of America v. Enterprise Wheel & Car Corp. (1960) 363 U. S.
593···474
United Transp. Co. v. Berwind-White Coal Mining Co. (1926) 13 F. 2d 282 (2d Cir.) ···277
Unitramp v. Garnac Grain Co. Inc.—The Hermine [1979] 1 Lloyd's Rep. 212, (C. A.);
rev'g [1978] 2 Lloyd's Rep. 37, (Q. B.) ···177, **179**, 183
Unitramp Ltd. v. Mediterranean Brokerage, 1994 AMC 476 (E. D. La. 1993) ············460
Universal American Barge Corp. v. J-Chem Inc. (1991) 946 F. 2d 1131; 1993 AMC
1888 (5th Cir.) ··323
Universal Cargo Carriers Corp. v. Pedro Citati [1957] 2 Lloyd's Rep. 191; [1957] 1
W. L. R. 979; [1957] 3 All E. R. 234, (C. A.); aff'g [1957] 1 Lloyd's Rep. 174;
[1957] 2 Q. B. 401; [1957] 2 W. L. R. 703; [1957] 2 All E. R. 70, (Q. B.) ··············394
Universal Shipping Inc. v. Panamanian Flag Barge (1976) 563 F. 2d 483; 1978 AMC
1458 (1st Cir.) ··500
Universal Steam Navigation Co. Ltd. v. James McKelvie & Co. (1923) 15 Ll. L. Rep.
99; [1923] A. C. 492; 92 L. J. K. B. 647; 129 L. T. 395; 28 Com. Cas. 353; 39 T. L. R.
480; 16 Asp. M. L. C. 184, (H. L.) ···**62-63**
Universe Explorer, The, 1985 AMC 1014 (Arb. at N. Y. 1984) ············144, 205, 391, 430
Uranus, The, 1977 AMC 586 (Arb. at N. Y.) ···**270**, 524
U. S. 219 (No. 11), The (1937) 21 F. Supp. 466 (E. D. Pa.) ·······································274

V/O Rasnoimport v. Guthrie & Co. Ltd. [1966] 1 Lloyd's Rep. 1, (Q. B.) ···················69
Valmar, The (1941) 38 F. Supp. 618; 1941 AMC 872 (E. D. Pa.) ································490
Van Hawk, The, 1975 AMC 254 (Arb. at N. Y.) ···163
Vanderspar & Co. v. Duncan & Co. (1891) 8 T. L. R. 30··165
Vardinoyannis v. Egyptian General Petroleum Corp.—The Evaggelos Th [1971] 2
Lloyd's Rep. 200, (Q. B.) ···186, **194**, 197, 198
Varley v. Tarrytown Associates Inc. (1973) 477 F. 2d 208 (2d Cir.) ···························462
Varverakis v. Compagnia de Navigacion Artico S. A.—The Merak [1976] 2 Lloyd's
Rep. 250, (C. A.) ···53
Vaughan and Others v. Campbell, Heatley & Co. (1885) 2 T. L. R. 33, (C. A.) ······155, **158**

Vellore S. S. Co. Ltd. *v.* Steengrafe (1915) 229 F. 394 (2d Cir.) ································544
Velma, The, SMA 958 (Arb. at N. Y. 1975) ································78
Vendelso, The, SMA 663 (Arb. at N. Y. 1971) ································118
Venetia, The, SMA 1351 (Arb. at N. Y. 1979) ································223
Venezolana (C. A.) de Navegacion *v.* Bank Line—The Roachbank [1988] 2 Lloyd's
　Rep. 337, (C. A.); [1987] 2 Lloyd's Rep. 498, (Q. B.) ··············370, 371, **372**, 374, 375, 446
Venezuela, The [1980] 1 Lloyd's Rep. 393, (Q. B.) ································334, **337-338**
Venore Transportation Co. *v.* The Struma (1978) 583 F. 2d 708 ; 1978 AMC 2146
　(4th Cir.) ································536
Venore Transportation Co. *v.* Oswego Shipping Corp. (1974) 498 F. 2d 469 ; 1974
　AMC 827 (2d Cir.); *cert. denied* (1974) 419 U. S. 998 ································199, 207
Vermaas' J. Scheepvaartbedrijf N. V. *v.* Association Technique de l'Importation
　Charbonnière—The Laga [1966] 1 Lloyd's Rep. 582, (Q. B.) ································**562**
Vermont I, The, SMA 747 (Arb. at N. Y. 1970) ································272, 273
Vestland, The—Richmond Shipping Ltd. *v.* D/S and A/S Vestland [1980] 2 Lloyd's
　Rep. 171, (Q. B.) ································484, **488**
Vikfrost, The—W. & R. Fletcher (New Zealand) Ltd. *v.* Sigurd Haavik Aksjeselskap
　[1980] 1 Lloyd's Rep. 560, (C. A.) ································147, 329, **332-333**, 336, **337**
Vimar Seguros y Reaseguros S. A. *v.* The Sky Reefer (1995) 515 U. S.—; 115 S. Ct.
　—1995 U. S. Lexis 4067 ; 132 L. Ed. 2d. 462 ; 1995 AMC 1817 ································448, 527
Vinava Shipping Co. Ltd. *v.* Finelvet A. G.—The Chrysalis [1983] 1 Lloyd's Rep. 503 ;
　[1983] 1 W. L. R. 1469 ; [1983] 2 All E. R. 658, (Q. B.) ································403, 404
Virgo, The—Consolidated Investment & Contracting Co. *v.* Saponaria Shipping Ltd :
　[1978] 2 Lloyd's Rep. 167, (C. A.) ································440
Virgo, The—Tudor Marine Ltd. *v.* Tradax Export S. A. [1976] 2 Lloyd's Rep. 135, (C.
　A.) ································**63-64**
Vitol Trading S. A. *v.* SCS Control Services (1989) 874 F. 2d 76 (2d Cir.) ··············278
Vlassopulos (N. & J.) Ltd. *v.* Ney Shipping Ltd.—The Santa Carina [1977] 1 Lloyd's
　Rep. 478, (C. A.) ································62
Vogemann *v.* Zanzibar S. S. Co. Ltd. (1902) 7 Com. Cas. 254, (C. A.); *aff'g* (1901) 6
　Com. Cas. 253, (K. B.) ································**365-366**, 369
Volere, The, SMA 1885 (Arb. at N. Y. 1983) ································78
Volt Information Sciences *v.* Board of Trustees of the Leland Stanford Jr. University
　(1989) 489 U. S. 468 ································**450**, 453
Von Hatzfeldt-Wildenburg *v.* Alexander [1912] 1 Ch. 284 ; 81 L. J. Ch. 184 ; 105 L. T.
　434, (Ch. D.) ································51

W. Millar & Co. Ltd. *v.* Freden (Owners) [1918] 1 K. B. 611 ; 87 L. J. K. B. 524 ; 118
　L. T. 522 ; 34 T. L. R. 234 ; 14 Asp. M. L. C. 247, (C. A.) ································**101**
W. K. Webster & Co. *v.* American President Lines Ltd. (1994) 32 F. 3d. 665 ; 1995
　AMC 134 (2d Cir.) ································454, 473
W. & R. Fletcher (New Zealand) Ltd. *v.* Sigurd Haavik Aksjeselskap—The Vikfrost
　[1980] 1 Lloyd's Rep. 560, (C. A.) ································147, 329, **332-333**, 336, **337**

Wm. Passalacqua Builders v. Resnick Developers South Inc. (1991) 933 F. 2d 131
(2d Cir.) ···75, 76, 77
Walker v. Boyle; Boyle v. Walker [1982] 1 W. L. R. 495; [1982] 1 All E. R. 634;
(1982) 44 P. & C. R. 20; (1982) 261 E. G. 1090; (1981) 125 S. J. 724, (Q. B.) ·········85
Walker v. Transp. Co. (1866) 70 U. S. 150 ···429
Wallis, Son & Wells v. Pratt & Haynes [1911] A. C. 394; 80 L. J. K. B. 1058, 105 L. T.
146; 27 T. L. R. 431, (H. L.) ···424
Warm Springs, The, SMA 134 (Arb. at N. Y. 1966) ···111
Warnock v. Daiichi Chuo Kisen Kaisha, 1983 AMC 1463 (E. D. Ore. 1981) ···············321
Warren Adams, The (1896) 74 F. 413 (2d Cir); cert. denied (1896) 163 U. S. 679 ······431
Warth Line v. Merinda Marine 1992 AMC 1406 (S. D. N. Y. 1991) ·······························470
Waterside Ocean Navigation v. Int'l Nav. Ltd. (1984) 737 F. 2d 150; 1985 AMC 349
(2d Cir.) ··476, 477
Watson S. S. Co. v. Merryweather & Co. (1913) 18 Com. Cas. 294; 108 L. T. 1031; 12
Asp. M. L. C. 353, (K. B.) ···**126**
Watt v. Cargo of Lumber (1908) 161 F. 104 (2d Cir.) ···346
Watts v. Camors (1885) 115 U. S. 353 ···113, 114
Watts, Watts & Co. v. Mitsui & Co. [1917] A. C. 227; 22 Com. Cas. 242; 86 L. J. K. B.
873; 116 L. T. 353; 33 T. L. R. 262; 13 Asp. M. L. C. 580, (H. L.) ·························421
Wave, The—Woodstock Shipping Co. v. Kyma Compania Naviera S. A. [1981] 1
Lloyd's Rep. 521, (Q. B.) ···69
Waverly v. Carnoud Metalbox Engineering [1994] 1 Lloyd's Rep. 38, (Q. B.) ············444
Webster (W. K.) & Co. v. American President Lines Ltd. (1994) 32 F. 3d 665; 1995
AMC 134 (2d Cir.) ···454, 473
Wehner v. Dene Steam Shipping Co. Ltd. [1905] 2 K. B. 92; 10 Com. Cas. 139; 74 L.
J. K. B. 550; 21 T. L. R. 339, (K. B.) ···264, 333, **483**
Weir and Others v. Union Steamship Co. Ltd. [1900] A. C. 525; 69 L. J. K. B. 809; 82
L. T. 91; 5 Com. Cas. 363; 9 Asp. M. L. C. 111 ···296, 298, 550
Welsh Irish Ferries Ltd. (Re) —The Ugland Trailer [1985] 2 Lloyd's Rep. 372;
[1985] 3 W. L. R. 610, (Ch. D.) ···486
Wenjiang, The—International Sea Tankers Inc. v. Hemisphere Shipping Co. Ltd.
[1982] 1 Lloyd's Rep. 128; [1982] 2 All E. R. 437, (C. A.); rev'g in part [1981] 2
Lloyd's Rep. 308, (Q. B.) ···370, 399
Wenjiang, The (No. 2) —International Sea Tankers Inc. v. Hemisphere Shipping Co.
Ltd. [1983] 1 Lloyd's Rep. 400, (Q. B.) ···399, 404
West of Eng. v. McAllister (1993) 829 F. Supp. 122; 1993 AMC 2559 (E. D. Pa.);
motion to vacate denied (1993) 829 F. Supp. 125; 1993 AMC 2563 (E. D. Pa.) ·········460
Westchester Fire Insurance Co. v. Buffalo Housewrecking & Salvage Co. (1941) 40
F. Supp. 378; 1941 AMC 1601 (W. D. N. Y.); aff'd (1942) 129 F. 2d 319; 1942 AMC
1052 (2d Cir.) ··173, 175
Western Bulk Carriers (Australia) Pty. Ltd. v. P. S. Int'l Inc. (1994) 164 B. R. 616;
1994 AMC 1981 (S. D. Ind.) ···494
Western Electric Co. Inc. v. Communication Workers of America, AFL-CIO (1978)

450 F. Supp. 876 (S. D. N. Y); *aff'd without opinion* (1978) 591 F. 2d 1333 (2d Cir.)
....**469-470**
Western Sealanes Corp. *v.* Unimarine S. A.—The Pythia [1982] 2 Lloyd's Rep. 160,
(Q. B.) **304**, 365, 366
Western Woolen Mill Co. *v.* Northern Assurance Co. of London (1905) 139 F. 637
(8th Cir.); *cert. denied* (1905) 199 U. S. 608 428
Westfal-Larsen & Co. A/S *v.* Colonial Sugar Refining Co. Ltd. [1960] 2 Lloyd's Rep.
206, (Sup. Ct. (N. S. W.)) 556, 557
Westmoreland, The (1936) 86 F. 2d 96; 1936 AMC 1680 (2d Cir.) 111, 433
Weyerhaeuser Company *v.* Western Seas Shipping Co. (1984) 743 F. 2d 635; 1985
AMC 30 (9th Cir.); *cert. denied* (1984) 469 U. S. 1061 452
White *v.* Turnbull, Martin & Co. (1898) 3 Com. Cas. 183; 78 L. T. 726; 14 T. L. R.
401; 8 Asp. M. L. C. 406, (C. A.) 541
White & Carter (Councils) Ltd. *v.* McGregor [1962] A. C. 413; [1962] 2 W. L. R. 17;
[1961] 3 All E. R. 1178; 1962 S. C. (H. L.) 1; 1962 S. L. T. 9, (H. L.) 130
White Rose, The—A/B Helsingfors S. S. Co. Ltd. *v.* Rederi A/B Rex [1969] 2
Lloyd's Rep. 52; [1969] 1 W. L. R. 1098; [1969] 3 All E. R. 374, (Q. B.)
....297, **298**, 299, 563
Whitwood Chemical Co. *v.* Hardman [1891] 2 Ch. 416; 60 L. J. Ch. 428; 64 L. T. 716,
(C. A.) 87
Wickman Machine Tool Sales Ltd. *v.* Schuler A. G. [1973] 2 Lloyd's Rep. 53; [1974]
A. C. 235; [1973] 2 W. L. R. 683; [1973] 2 All E. R. 39, (H. L.); *aff'g* [1972] 1 W.
L. R. 840; [1972] 2 All E. R. 1173, (C. A.) 90
Wildwood, The (1943) 133 F. 2d 765; 1943 AMC 320 (9th Cir.) 570
Wilko *v.* Swan (1935) 346 U. S. 427 472
William J. Quillan (1910) 180 F. 681 (2d Cir.); *cert. denied* (1910) 218 U. S. 682 173
William Sindall *v.* Cambridgeshire C. C. [1994] 3 All E. R. 932; [1994] 1 W. L. R.
1016..85
Williams *v.* East India Co. (1802) 3 East 192 167
Williams Bros. (Hull) Ltd. *v.* Naamlooze Venootschap W. H. Berghuys Kolenhandel
(1915) 21 Com. Cas. 253; 86 L. J. K. B. 334, (K. B.) 562
Williamson *v.* Compania Anonima Venezolana de Navegacion (1971) 446 F. 2d 1339;
1971 AMC 2083 (2d Cir.) 174
Willoughby Roofing & Supply Co. Inc. *v.* Kajjma Int'l Inc. (1984) 598 F. Supp. 353
(N. D. Ala.); *aff'd per curiam* (1985) 776 F. 2d 269 (11th Cir.) 458
Wilson *v.* Job Inc. (1992) 958 F. 2d 653 (5th Cir.) 57
Wilson *v.* Rankin (1865) L. R. 1 Q. B. 162; 35 L. J. Q. B. 87; 13 L. T. 564; 2 Asp; M. L.
C. (O. S.) 161, 287..159
Wilson Shipping Corp. Ltd. *v.* Tamarack Corp., SMA 645 (Arb. at N. Y. 1971) 241
Wilston S. S. Co. Ltd. *v.* Andrew Weir & Co. (1925) 22 Ll. L. Rep. 521; 31 Com. Cas.
111, (K. B.) 333, **337**
Winner, The—Mohammad Bin Abdul Rahman Orri *v.* Seawind Navigation Co. S. A.
[1986] 1 Lloyd's Rep. 36, (Q. B.) 54

Wismar, The, SMA 1454 (Arb. at N. Y. 1980) ··················172, 175, 387, 503, 504
Witfuel, The, SMA 1381 (Arb. at N. Y. 1979) ···172, 619
With v. O'Flanagan [1936] Ch. 575; [1936] 1 All E. R. 727; 105 L. J. (Ch.) 247; 154
  L. T. 634 ···82
Witter (Thomas) v. TBP Industries ··83
Woodar Investment Development Ltd. v. Wimpey Construction U. K. Ltd. [1980] 1
  W. L. R. 277; [1980] 1 All E. R. 571, (H. L.) ···88, 89
Woodstock Shipping Co. v. Kyma Compania Naviera S. A.—The Wave [1981] 1
  Lloyd's Rep. 521, (Q. B.) ···69
Work v. Leathers (1878) 97 U. S. 379 ···110, 163
World Aegeus, The, SMA 2488 (Arb. at N. Y. 1988) ···272
World Brilliance Corp. v. Bethlehem Steel Co. (1965) 342 F. 2d 362; 1965 AMC 881
  (2d Cir.) ···450
World Magnate Shipping v. Rederi A/B Soya [1975] 2 Lloyd's Rep. 498, (Q. B.) ······531
World Symphony and The World Renown, The—Chiswell Shipping and Liberian
  Jaguar Transports Inc. v. National Iranian Tankers Co. [1992] 2 Lloyd's Rep. 115,
  (C. A.); aff'g [1991] 2 Lloyd's Rep. 251, (Q. B) ···································129, 446, 590-591
Wulfsberg v. Weardale (1916) 115 L. T. 146 (C. A.) ···265
Wye Shipping Co. Ltd. v. Compagnie du Chemin de Fer Paris-Orleans (1922) 10 Ll.
  L. Rep. 85; [1922] 1 K. B. 617; 91 L. J. K. B. 553; 38 T. L. R. 274, (K. B.) ···················236

Xantho, The (1887) 12 App. Cas. 503; 56 L. J. P. 116; 57 L. T. 701; 3 T. L. R. 766; 6
  Asp. M. L. C. 207, (H. L.) ··422
Xingcheng, The—China Ocean Shipping Co. v. The Owners of The Vessel Andros
  [1987] 2 Lloyd's Rep. 210; [1987] 1 W. L. R. 1213; (1987) 131 S. J. 972, (P. C.) ······604

Yanxilas, The—Stinnes Interoil G. m. b. H. v. A. Halcoussis & Co. [1982] 2 Lloyd's
  Rep. 445, (Q. B.) ···64, 67
Yasuda Fire & Marine Ins. v. Continental Cas. Co. (1994) 37 F. 3d 345 (7th Cir.) ······470
Yasuda Fire & Marine Ins. Co. Ltd. v. The Indian City, 1981 AMC 1451 (M. D. Fla.
  1980) ··342
Yaye Maru, The (1921) 274 F. 195 (4th Cir.); cert. denied (1921) 257 U. S. 638 ········380
Yeramex Int'l v. The Tendo (1979) 595 F. 2d 943; 1979 AMC 1282 (4th Cir.); rev'g
  1977 AMC 1807 (E. D. Va.) ···318, 340
Ymnos, The—Compagnie Generale Maritime v. Diakan Spirit S. A. [1982] 2 Lloyd's
  Rep. 574, (Q. B.) ···89, 91
Youell v. Bland Welch & Co. Ltd. (No. 2) (The Superhulls Cover Case) [1990] 2
  Lloyd's Rep. 431, (Q. B.) ···309
Young Mechanic, The (1855) 30 F. Cas. 873 (No. 18, 180) (C. C. D. Me.) ··············490
Ypapadi, The, SMA 2814 (Arb. at N. Y. 1991) ···117

Zacharia T, The, SMA 2224 (Arb. at N. Y. 1986) ··632
Zakynthos, The, SMA 2097 (Arb. at N. Y. 1985) ··58

Zaneta, The, 1970 AMC 807 (Arb. at N.Y. 1968) ···201, 208
Zannis, The, SMA 2074 (Arb. at N.Y. 1985) ···224
Zarati S.S. Co. Ltd. *v.* Frames Tours Ltd. [1955] 2 Lloyd's Rep. 278, (Q.B.) ···············52
Zeevi (J.) & Sons Ltd. *v.* Grindlays Bank (Uganda) Ltd. (1975) 37 N.Y. 2d 220;
    (1975) 371 N.Y.S. 2d 892; *cert. denied* (1975) 423 U.S. 806 ·······························415
Zidell Inc. *v.* Pacific Northern Marine Corp., 1990 AMC 922 (D. Or. 1990) ···············239
Zim Israel Navigation Co. Ltd. *v.* Effy Shipping Corp. —The Effy [1972] 1 Lloyd's
    Rep. 18, (Q.B.) ···**246**, 256
Zoe Christina, The, SMA 2777 (Arb. at N.Y. 1991) ··206
Zographia M, The—Astro Amo Cia. Nav. *v.* Elf Union S.A. [1976] 2 Lloyd's Rep.
    382, (Q.B.) ···245, 253, 254

法令索引 (Table of Legislation)

ここに記載する頁数は，原書のそれを示す。

Administration of Justice Act 1956……1956年司法の運営に関する法律……488
Administration of Justice Act 1981……1981年司法の運営に関する法律……441
Administration of Justice Act 1982……1982年司法の運営に関する法律……441
Administration of Justice Act 1985……1985年司法の運営に関する法律……442
Arbitration Act 1950 (as amended by the Arbitration Acts 1975 and 1979, by the Administration of Justice Acts 1982 and 1985 and the Courts and Legal Services Act 1990)……1950年仲裁法 ……657 et seq.
    s. 4(1) ……442
    6 ……441
    7 ……442
    8 ……443
    (1)(amended by s. 6(1) of the Arbitration Act 1979) ……443
    9 ……441
    10(1)(a)(c)(d) ……443
        (2) ……443
        (3)(added by the Administration of Justice Act 1985) ……443
        (A)-(D)(added by the Courts and Legal Services Act 1990) ……442,443
    12(1) ……442,443
        (6) ……444
    13A(added by the Courts and Legal Services Act 1990) ……443
    14 ……446
    19A(added by the Administration of Justice Act 1982) ……446
    ss. 27, 29(2), 33, 44(3) ……440
Arbitration Act 1975 (as amended by the Administration of Justice Acts 1981, 1982 and 1985 and the Courts and Legal Services Act 1990)……1975年仲裁法……441, 667 et seq.
    s. 1 ……442
Arbitration Act 1979 (as amended by s. 148 of the Supreme Court Act 1981, the Administration of Justice Acts 1981, 1982 and 1985 and the Courts and Legal Services Act 1990)……1979年仲裁法 ……441, 668 et seq.
    s. 1 ……444
    (2), (3)(a), (4) ……445
    (6A), (7) ……446
    3(1), (6) ……445
    4(1)(c)(i), (ii) ……445
    5(1), (2) ……444
    6(1)(amending s. 8(1) of the Arbitration Act 1950) ……443
    (2) ……441
Bankruptcy Act (U.S.)……破産法 ……492

COGSA — *See* U. S. Carriage of Goods by Sea Act 1936
CPLR (New York)
　s. 3002(b) ……74
Carriage of Explosives or Dangerous Substances Act 1970, 46 U. S. C., s. 170
　(repealed in 1983 by Pub. L. 98-89, s. 4(6), 97 Stat. 600-605)
　……1970年爆発物または危険物質の運送法 ……176
Carriage of Goods by Sea Act 1924……1924年海上物品運送法
　Sched., art. 111, r. 2 ……304
Carriage of Goods by Sea Act 1971……1971年海上物品運送法 ……561
Civil Liability (Contribution) Act 1978……1978年民事責任（寄与）法 ……187
Companies Act 1985……1985年会社法
　s. 395 (formerly s. 95 of the Companies Act 1948) ……486
　ss. 409, 410 ……486
Compensation (Defence) Act 1939……1939年賠償（抗弁）法
　s. 17(1) ……607
Constitution of the United States……米国憲法 ……56
Contracts (Applicable Law) Act 1990……1990年契約（適用）法 ……55, 437
Convention on the Law Applicable to Contractual Obligations (The "Rome Convention")
　……契約責任に適用される法律に関する国際条約（ローマ条約）……55, 437
　art. 3. 1 ……438
　arts. 3. 1, 8. 1, 8. 2 ……55
　art. 4. 1 ……438
Convention on the Recognition and Enforcement of Foreign Arbitral Awards (UN)
(The "New York Convention")……外国仲裁判断の承認と執行に関する国連条約
（ニューヨーク条約）……460, 474-476, 677 *et seq.*
　art. V……476
　　(1)(b)(c) ……476
　　(2) ……476
　　(b) ……477
　　Ⅵ ……476, 477
Courts and Legal Services Act 1990……1990年裁判所及び法的サービス法
　s. 101 ……442
Federal Arbitration Act, 9 U. S. C. (U.S.)……連邦仲裁法
　ss. 1-14 ……447
　s. 2 ……475
　　3 ……79, 449
　　4 ……79, 450, 524
　　5 ……450, 453, 454
　　8 ……459, 460, 477
　　9 ……461-463
　　10 ……463-465
　　(a) ……465, 472
　　(a)(4) ……459

(b)	466, 472
(c)	468, 472
(d)	469, 472, 476
11	463
12	464
16(a)(1)(D), (E)	451
201 *et seq.*	463
ss. 201-208	447, 474
s. 207	463, 475
208	475

Federal Maritime Lien Act 1910, 46 U.S.C., ss. 971-975 (amended on 23 November 1988 by Public Law 100-710) (U.S.)……1910年連邦海事リーエン法……500
 ss. 971-975 …… 500
 s. 971 (as amended in 1971) …… 500, 502
 ss. 972, 973 …… 501
 s. 974 …… 502
  1304(4) …… 300
Fire Statute (U.S.)……火災法 …… 428, 429
H.R. Rep. No. 100-918, 100th Cong., 2d Sess. 14, 15, 36 (1988) (U.S.) …… 500
Hague Rules (as amended by the Brussels Protocol 1968)……ヘーグ・ルール…651, *et seq.*
Hague/Hague-Visby Rules………ヘーグ・ヴィスビー・ルール…………154, 651, *et seq.*
 art. III, r. 1 …… 169, 606
   6 …… 439, 440, 561, 603-605
    (bis) …… 440, 603-605
  IV …… 561
   r. 1 …… 574
    2 …… 602
    3 …… 295, 297, 520
    4 …… 603
    6 …… 168, 169, 606
Hamburg Rules 1978……ハンブルグ・ルール …… 615
Harter Act 1893, 46 U.S.C.A. (U.S.)……ハーター法
…………………………111, 433, 513, 514, 522, 526, 642, 643 *et seq.*
 ss. 1-3 …… 643
 s. 3 …… 517, 519, 614
  4 …… 346, 643-644
 ss. 5-7 …… 644
International Convention for the Prevention of Pollution from Ships (MARPOL 73/78)
 ……1973年の船舶による汚染防止のための国際条約（及び同条約に関する1978年議定書）
……………………………………………………………………413
International Convention on Civil Liability for Oil Pollution Damage 1969 ("CLC")
 ……1969年の油による汚染損害についての民事責任に関する国際条約
 art. 111 …… 640

Judiciary Act 1789 (U.S.)……1789年裁判所法 …………………………………………56
Law Reform (Contributory Negligence) Act 1945
　……1945年法改革（寄与・過失）に関する法 ……………………193, 307, 309, 310
Law Reform (Frustrated Contracts) Act 1943
　……1943年法改革（履行不能により消滅する契約）に関する法 ………………531
　s. 1(2), (3) …………………………………………………………………………408
　　2(3) …………………………………………………………………408, 409, 591
　　(4) …………………………………………………………………………409
Limitation Act 1939……1939年出訴期限法
　s. 27(3) ………………………………………………………………………………440
Limitation Act 1980……1980年出訴期限法 …………………………………………604
　s. 34(3)(a) …………………………………………………………………………440
Limitation of Liability Act (U.S.)……責任制限法 ……………………………344, 428
Marine Insurance Act 1906……1906年海上保険法
　ss. 61, 62 ……………………………………………………………………………591
Maritime Drug Law Enforcement Act 1986 (U.S.)……1986年米国海事麻薬法施行法
　ss. 1901-1904 ………………………………………………………………………173
Merchant Shipping Act 1894……1894年商船法
　s. 502 (as amended by the Merchant Shipping (Liability of Shipowners and Others)
　　Act 1958) …………………………………………………………………………420
　　502(i) ………………………………………………………………………………421
　　503 …………………………………………………………………………………558
Merchant Shipping Code of the USSR……ソ連商船法典 ………………………344
Misrepresentation Act 1967……1967年不実表示法
　s. 1 ……………………………………………………………………………………86
　　2(1) ………………………………………………………………………………83-85
　　(2) …………………………………………………………………82, 83, 85, 86
　　(3) …………………………………………………………………………………85
　　3 (as amended by s. 8(1) of the Unfair Contract Terms Act 1977) …………85, 560
New York Civil Practice Law and Rules……ニューヨーク民事実務法と規則
　s. 7501 ………………………………………………………………………………447
New York General Construction Law (McKinney Supps. 1974)……ニューヨーク解釈一般法
　s. 25 …………………………………………………………………………………272
North Carolina Unfair Trade Practices Act……ノースカロライナ不公正取引慣行法 ……469
Pomerene Act (U.S.)……ポメリン法 ……………………………………………346
Port and Tanker Safety Act 1973 (U.S.)……1973年港とタンカーの安全に関する法…216, 413
Public Law 100-710 (amending on 23 November 1988 the Ship Mortgage Act, 46
　U.S.C., s. 953. and the Federal Maritime Lien Act 1910, 46 U.S.C., ss. 971-975)(U.S.)
　……公法 ……………………………………………………………………499, 500
Restatement (Second) of Agency (U.S.)……代理に関するリステイトメント（第2版）
　s. 8(B) …………………………………………………………………………………73
　ss. 26, 33-34…………………………………………………………………………71-72
　　82-104 ………………………………………………………………………………74

法　令　索　引　　　127

```
    s. 379 ································································································74
    399 ··································································································75
Restatement (Second) of Contracts (U.S.)······契約に関するリステイトメント (第2版)
    ss. 201-208 ······················································································57
    s. 261 et seq. ···············································································410
    347 ································································································277
Restatement (Second) of Torts (U.S.)······不法行為に関するリステイトメント (第2版)
    s. 388 ····························································································174
Sale of Goods Act 1893······1893年動産売買法····················································89
Sale of Goods Act 1979······1979年動産売買法····················································89
    ss. 13-15 ·························································································90
Ship Mortgage Act, 46 U.S.C., s. 953 (amended on 23 November 1988 by Public Law
    100-710) (U.S.)······船舶モーゲージ法 ·····················································499
Statute of Frauds (U.S.)······詐欺防止法 ····························································56
Supreme Court Act 1981······1981年最高法院法 ·················································488
Unfair Contract Terms Act 1977······1977年不公正契約条項法·························425, 426
    s. 8(1) (amending s. 3 of the Misrepresentation Act 1967)·························85, 560
    27 ···································································································85
    Sched. 2 ···························································································85
Uniform Commercial Code (UCC) (U.S.)······統一商事法典 ·······························56
U.S./USSR Maritime Agreement······米国・ソ連海運協定 ································382
U.S. Arbitration Act······米国仲裁法 ·····················································673 et seq.
U.S. Carriage of Goods by Sea Act 1936 (COGSA)······1936年米国海上物品運送法
    ··············································111 et seq., 513 et seq., 522 et seq., 636 et seq., 642, 644 et seq.
    s. 1(a) ····························································································439
    2·····························································································286, 519
    3(1) ···················································································514, 517, 518
        (2) ·············································································304, 305
        (3) ··························································································346
        (6) ·············································································439, 440, 520
        (8) ·············································································448, 518, 527
    4·········································································································519
        (1) ·············································································154, 515, 518, 519
        (2) ······································································419, 423, 432-433, 518, 519, 561
            (a) ·································································286, 419, 422, 515, 516, 518
            (b) ·····················································································420, 429, 523
            (c) ·····························································································422
    s. 4(2)(d)(f) ············································································420
        (g) ·····························································································421, 422
        (3) ·······························································································169, 174, 423, 433, 520
        (4) ·······························································································300, 435, 520
        (6) ·······························································································168-170, 174, 175, 520
    1004(2)(c) ·······························································································431
```

  1303(6) ··523
  1304(3) ··174
U. S. Coast Guard Regulations, 46 C. F. R.······米国コーストガード規則・連邦危険物規則集
 ss. 30-40, 98, 146-154, 171-176 ··176
U. S. Code (U. S. C.)······合衆国法典
 9 U. S. C. (*See* Federal Arbitration Act (U. S.))
 28 U. S. C.
  s. 1333 ··56
 45 U. S. C.
  ss. 2101, 3701-3718··176
 46 U. S. C.
  s. 182 ··428
  183 ··637
  183 *et seq.* ··344
  186 ··637
  971 (as amended in 1971) ··500, 502
  ss. 972, 973 ··501
  s. 1304(4) ··300
  ss. 1901-1904 ··173
   11301-11303 ··351
  ss. 31301(4) ··500
  ss. 31301(5), (6), 31321-31330 ··499
  s. 31326(b)(2) ··504
 49 U. S. C.
  ss. 381-124 ··346
York-Antwerp Rules 1950······1950年ヨーク・アントワープ・ルール ··636
York-Antwerp Rules 1974······1974年ヨーク・アントワープ・ルール ··614
 1990 Amendment ··614
York-Antwerp Rules 1994······1994年ヨーク・アントワープ・ルール ··614, 636

TIME CHARTERS
定期傭船契約

定期傭船契約書

［英語原文］

the Text of the New York Produce Exchange Form
the Text of the NYPE 93
the Text of the Baltime Form
the Text of the Shelltime Form
the Text of the STB Form of Tanker Time Charter

Time Charter

GOVERNMENT FORM

Approved by the New York Produce Exchange

November 6th, 1913—Amended October 20th, 1921; August 6th, 1931; October 3rd, 1946

....day of.................................19.........

This Charter Party, made and concluded in ....

1
2 Between ....of..................................
3 Owners of the good..
4 of.......................................tons gross register, and..indicated horse power
5 and with hull, machinery and equipment in a thoroughly efficient state, and classed
6 .... { Steamship / Motorship } ....tons net register, having engines of ....tons of 2240 lbs.
7 at.........................of about...cubic feet bale capacity, and about...........................tons of 2240 lbs.
8 deadweight capacity (cargo and bunkers, including fresh water and stores not exceeding one and one-half percent of ship's deadweight capacity,
9 allowing a minimum of fifty tons) on a draft of..................feet..................inches on....................Summer freeboard, inclusive of permanent bunkers,
10 which are of the capacity of about...........................knots on a consumption of about....................tons of fuel, and capable of steaming, fully laden, under good weather
11 conditions about..tons of best Welsh coal—best grade fuel oil—best grade Diesel oil,
12 now.............................and...Charterers of the City of..
13 **Witnesseth**, That the said Owners agree to let, and the said Charterers agree to hire the said vessel, from the time of delivery, for
14 about ....within below mentioned trading limits.
15 Charterers to have liberty to sublet the vessel for all or any part of the time covered by this Charter, but Charterers remaining responsible for
16 the fulfillment of this Charter Party.
17 Vessel to be placed at the disposal of the Charterers, at...
18
19 in such dock or at such wharf or place (where she may safely lie, always afloat, at all times of tide, except as otherwise provided in clause No. 6), as
20 the Charterers may direct. If such dock, wharf or place be not available time to count as provided for in clause No. 5. Vessel on her delivery to be
21 ready to receive cargo with clean-swept holds and tight, staunch, strong and in every way fitted for the service, having water ballast, winches and
22 donkey boiler with sufficient steam power, or if not equipped with donkey boiler, then other power sufficient to run all the winches at one and the same
23 time (and with full complement of officers, seamen, engineers and firemen for a vessel of her tonnage), to be employed, in carrying lawful merchan-
24 dise, including petroleum or its products, in proper containers, excluding
25 (vessel is not to be employed in the carriage of Live Stock, but Charterers are to have the privilege of shipping a small number on deck at their risk,
26 all necessary fittings and other requirements to be for account of Charterers), in such lawful trades, between safe port and/or ports in British North
27 America, and/or United States of America, and/or West Indies, and/or Central America, and/or Caribbean Sea, and/or Gulf of Mexico, and/or
28 Mexico, and/or South America............................and/or Asia, and/or Australia, and/or Tasmania, and/or New Zealand, but excluding Magdalena River, River St. Lawrence between
29 and/or Africa, and/or Asia, and/or Australia, and/or Tasmania, and/or New Zealand, but excluding Magdalena River, River St. Lawrence between
30 October 31st and May 15th, Hudson Bay and all unsafe ports; also excluding, when out of season, White Sea, Black Sea and the Baltic,
31
32
33
34

NEW YORK PRODUCE EXCHANGE FORM

as the Charterers or their Agents shall direct, on the following conditions:

1. That the Owners shall provide and pay for all provisions, wages and consular shipping and discharging fees of the Crew; shall pay for the insurance of the vessel, also for all the cabin, deck, engine-room and other necessary stores, including boiler water and maintain her class and keep the vessel in a thoroughly efficient state in hull, machinery and equipment for and during the service.

2. That the Charterers shall provide and pay for all the fuel except as otherwise agreed, Port Charges, Pilotages, Agencies, Commissions, Consular Charges (except those pertaining to the Crew) and all other usual expenses except those before stated, but when the vessel puts into a port for causes for which vessel is responsible, then all such charges incurred shall be paid by the Owners. Fumigations ordered because of illness of the crew to be for Owners account. Fumigations ordered because of cargoes carried or ports visited while vessel is employed under this charter to be for Charterers account. All other fumigations to be for Charterers account after vessel has been on charter for a continuous period of six months or more.

    Charterers are to provide necessary dunnage and shifting boards, also any extra fittings requisite for a special trade or unusual cargo, but Owners to allow them the use of any dunnage and shifting boards already aboard vessel. Charterers to have the privilege of using shifting boards for dunnage, they making good any damage thereto.

3. That the Charterers, at the port of delivery, and the Owners, at the port of re-delivery, shall take over and pay for all fuel remaining on board the vessel at the current prices in the respective ports, the vessel to be delivered with not less than .... tons and not more than .... tons and to be re-delivered with not less than .... tons and not more than............tons.

4. That the Charterers shall pay for the use and hire of the said Vessel at the rate of .... United States Currency per ton on vessel's total deadweight carrying capacity, including bunkers and stores, on............summer freeboard, per Calendar Month, commencing on and from the day of her delivery, as aforesaid, and at and after the same rate for any part of a month; hire to continue until the hour of the day of her re-delivery in like good order and condition, ordinary wear and tear excepted, to the Owners (unless lost) at .... unless otherwise mutually agreed. Charterers are to give Owners not less than............days notice of vessel's expected date of re-delivery, and probable port.

5. Payment of said hire to be made in New York in cash in United States Currency, semi-monthly in advance, and for the last half month or part of same the approximate amount of hire, and should same not cover the actual time, hire is to be paid for the balance day by day, as it becomes due, if so required by Owners, unless bank guarantee or deposit is made by the Charterers, otherwise failing the punctual and regular payment of the hire, or bank guarantee, or on any breach of this Charter Party, the Owners shall be at liberty to withdraw the vessel from the service of the Charterers, without prejudice to any claim they (the Owners) may otherwise have on the Charterers. Time to count from 7 a.m. on the working day following that on which written notice of readiness has been given to Charterers or their Agents before 4 p.m., but if required by Charterers, they to have the privilege of using vessel at once, such time used to count as hire.

    Cash for vessel's ordinary disbursements at any port may be advanced as required by the Captain, by the Charterers or their Agents, subject to 2½% commission and such advances shall be deducted from the hire. The Charterers, however, shall in no way be responsible for the application of such advances.

6. That the cargo or cargoes be laden and/or discharged in any dock or at any wharf or place that Charterers or their Agents may direct, provided the vessel can safely lie always afloat at any time of tide, except at such places where it is customary for similar size vessels to safely lie aground.

7. That the whole reach of the Vessel's Hold, Decks, and usual places of loading (not more than she can reasonably stow and carry), also accommodations for Supercargo, if carried, shall be at the Charterers' disposal, reserving only proper and sufficient space for Ship's officers, crew, tackle, apparel, furniture, provisions, stores and fuel. Charterers have the privilege of passengers as far as accommodations allow, Charterers paying Owners .... per day per passenger for accommodations and meals. However, it is agreed that in case any fines or extra expenses are incurred in the consequence of the carriage of passengers, Charterers are to bear such risk and expense.

8. That the Captain shall prosecute his voyages with the utmost despatch, and shall render all customary assistance with ship's crew and boats. The Captain (although appointed by the Owners), shall be under the orders and directions of the Charterers as regards employment and agency; and Charterers are to load, stow, and trim the cargo at their expense under the supervision of the Captain, who is to sign Bills of Lading for cargo as presented, in conformity with Mate's or Tally Clerk's receipts.

9. That if the Charterers shall have reason to be dissatisfied with the conduct of the Captain, Officers, or Engineers, the Owners shall on receiving particulars of the complaint, investigate the same, and, if necessary, make a change in the appointments.

10. That the Charterers shall have permission to appoint a Supercargo, who shall accompany the vessel and see that voyages are prosecuted

with the utmost despatch. He is to be furnished with free accommodation, and same fare as provided for Captain's table, Charterers paying at the rate of $1.00 per day. Owners to victual Pilots and Customs Officers, and also, when authorized by Charterers or their Agents, to victual Tally Clerks, Stevedore's Foreman, etc., Charterers paying at the current rate per meal, for all such victualling.

11. That the Charterers shall furnish the Captain from time to time with all requisite instructions and sailing directions, in writing, and the Captain shall keep a full and correct Log of the voyage or voyages, which are to be patent to the Charterers or their Agents, and furnish the Charterers, their Agents or Supercargo, when required, with a true copy of daily Logs, showing the course of the vessel and distance run and the consumption of fuel.

12. That the Captain shall use diligence in caring for the ventilation of the cargo.

13. That the Charterers shall have the option of continuing this charter for a further period of ....days previous to the expiration of the first-named term, or any declared option.

14. That if required by Charterers, time not to commence before ....and should vessel not have given written notice of readiness on or before .... but not later than 4 p.m. Charterers or their Agents to have the option of cancelling this Charter at any time not later than the day of vessel's readiness.

15. That in the event of the loss of time from deficiency of men or stores, fire, breakdown or damages to hull, machinery or equipment, grounding, detention by average accidents to ship or cargo, drydocking for the purpose of examination or painting bottom, or by any other cause preventing the full working of the vessel, the payment of hire shall cease for the time thereby lost; and if upon the voyage the speed be reduced by defect in or breakdown of any part of her hull, machinery or equipment, the time so lost, and the cost of any extra fuel consumed in consequence thereof, and all extra expenses shall be deducted from the hire.

16. That should the Vessel be lost, money paid in advance and not earned (reckoning from the date of loss or of being last heard of) shall be returned to the Charterers at once. The act of God, enemies, fire, restraint of Princes, Rulers and People, and all dangers and accidents of the Seas, Rivers, Machinery, Boilers and Steam Navigation, and errors of Navigation throughout this Charter Party, always mutually excepted.

The vessel shall have the liberty to sail with or without pilots, to tow and to be towed, to assist vessels in distress, and to deviate for the purpose of saving life and property.

17. That should any dispute arise between Owners and the Charterers, the matter in dispute shall be referred to three persons at New York, one to be appointed by each of the parties hereto, and the third by the two so chosen; their decision or that of any two of them, shall be final, and for the purpose of enforcing any award, this agreement may be made a rule of the Court. The Arbitrators shall be commercial men.

18. That the Owners shall have a lien upon all cargoes, and all sub-freights for any amounts due under this Charter, including General Average contributions, and the Charterers to have a lien on the Ship for all monies paid in advance and not earned, and any overpaid hire or excess deposit to be returned at once. Charterers will not suffer, nor permit to be continued, any lien or encumbrance incurred by them or their agents, which might have priority over the title and interest of the owners in the vessel.

19. That all derelicts and salvage shall be for Owners' and Charterers' equal benefit after deducting Owners' and Charterers' expenses and Crew's proportion. General Average shall be adjusted, stated and settled, according to Rules 1 to 15, inclusive, 17 to 22, inclusive, and Rule F of York-Antwerp Rules 1924, at such port or place in the United States as may be selected by the carrier, and as to matters not provided for by these Rules, according to the laws and usages at the port of New York. In such adjustment disbursements in foreign currencies shall be exchanged into United States money at the rate prevailing on the dates made and allowances for damage to cargo claimed in foreign currency shall be converted at the rate prevailing on the last day of discharge at the port or place of final discharge of such damaged cargo from the ship. Average agreement or bond and such additional security, as may be required by the carrier, must be furnished before delivery of the goods. Such cash deposit as the carrier or his agents may deem sufficient as additional security for the contribution of the goods and for any salvage and special charges thereon, shall, if required, be made by the goods, shippers, consignees or owners of the goods to the carrier before delivery. Such deposit shall, at the option of the carrier, be payable in United States money and be remitted to the adjuster. When so remitted the deposit shall be held in a special account at the place of adjustment in the name of the adjuster pending settlement of the General Average and refunds or credit balances, if any, shall be paid in United States money.

In the event of accident, danger, damage, or disaster, before or after commencement of the voyage resulting from any cause whatsoever, whether due to negligence or not, for which, or for the consequence of which, the carrier is not responsible, by statute, contract, or otherwise, the goods, the shipper and the consignee, jointly and severally, shall contribute with the carrier in general average to the payment of any sacrifices, losses, or expenses of a general average nature that may be made or incurred, and shall pay salvage and special charges incurred in respect of the goods. If a salving ship is owned or operated by the carrier, salvage shall be paid for as fully and in the same manner as if such salving ship or ships belonged to strangers.

NEW YORK PRODUCE EXCHANGE FORM

132   Provisions as to General Average in accordance with the above are to be included in all bills of lading issued hereunder.
133   20. Fuel used by the vessel while off hire, also for cooking, condensing water, or for grates and stoves to be agreed to as to quantity, and the
134 cost of replacing same, to be allowed by Owners.
135   21. That as the vessel may be from time to time employed in tropical waters during the term of this Charter, Vessel is to be docked at a
136 convenient place, bottom cleaned and painted whenever Charterers and Captain think necessary, at least once in every six months, reckoning from
137 time of last painting, and payment of the hire to be suspended until she is again in proper state for the service.
138
139
140   22. Owners shall maintain the gear of the ship as fitted, providing gear (for all derricks) capable of handling lifts up to three tons, also
141 providing ropes, falls, slings and blocks. If vessel is fitted with derricks capable of handling heavier lifts, Owners are to provide necessary gear for
142 same, otherwise equipment and gear for heavier lifts shall be for Charterers' account. Owners also to provide on the vessel lanterns and oil for
143 night work, and vessel to give use of electric light when so fitted, but any additional lights over those on board to be at Charterers' expense. The
144 Charterers to have the use of any gear on board the vessel.
145   23. Vessel to work night and day, if required by Charterers, and all winches to be at Charterers' disposal during loading and discharging;
146 steamer to provide one winchman per hatch to work winches day and night, as required, Charterers agreeing to pay officers, engineers, winchmen,
147 deck hands and donkeymen for overtime work done in accordance with the working hours and rates stated in the ship's articles. If the winches,
148 port or labor unions, prevent crew from driving winches, shore Winchmen to be paid by Charterers. In the event of a disabled winch or winches, or
149 insufficient power to operate winches, Owners to pay for shore engine, or engines, in lieu thereof, if required, and pay any loss of time occasioned
150 thereby.
151   24. It is also mutually agreed that this Charter is subject to all the terms and provisions of and all the exemptions from liability contained
152 in the Act of Congress of the United States approved on the 13th day of February, 1893, and entitled "An Act relating to Navigation of Vessels,
153 etc.", in respect of all cargo shipped under this charter to or from the United States of America. It is further subject to the following clauses, both
154 of which are to be included in all bills of lading issued hereunder:
155   U.S.A. Clause Paramount
156   This bill of lading shall have effect subject to the provisions of the Carriage of Goods by Sea Act of the United States, approved April
157 16, 1936, which shall be deemed to be incorporated herein, and nothing herein contained shall be deemed a surrender by the carrier of
158 any of its rights or immunities or an increase of any of its responsibilities or liabilities under said Act. If any term of this bill of lading
159 be repugnant to said Act to any extent, such term shall be void to that extent, but no further.
160   Both-to-Blame Collision Clause
161   If the ship comes into collision with another ship as a result of the negligence of the other ship and any act, neglect or default of the
162 Master, mariner, pilot or the servants of the Carrier in the navigation or in the management of the other ship, the owners of the goods carried
163 hereunder will indemnify the Carrier against all loss or liability to the other or non-carrying ship or her owners in so far as such loss
164 or liability represents loss of, or damage to, or any claim whatsoever of the owners of said goods, paid or payable by the other or non-
165 carrying ship or her owners to the owners of said goods and set off, recouped or recovered by the other or non-carrying ship or her
166 owners as part of their claim against the carrying ship or carrier.
167   25 The vessel shall not be required to enter any ice-bound port, or any port where lights or light-ships have been or are about to be with-
168 drawn by reason of ice, or where there is risk that in the ordinary course of things the vessel will not be able on account of ice to safely enter the
169 port or to get out after having completed loading or discharging.
170   26. Nothing herein stated is to be construed as a demise of the vessel to the Time Charterers. The owners to remain responsible for the
171 navigation of the vessel, insurance, crew, and all other matters, same as when trading for their own account.
172   27. A commission of $2\frac{1}{2}$ per cent is payable by the Vessel and Owners to
173
174 on hire earned and paid under this Charter, and also upon any continuation or extension of this Charter.
175   28. An address commission of $2\frac{1}{2}$ per cent payable to .... on the hire earned and paid under this Charter.

The original Charter Party in our possession.   As .... For Owners
                                        By cable authority from
                                           BROKERS.

Code Name: "NYPE 93"
Recommended by:
The Baltic and International Maritime Council (BIMCO)
The Federation of National Associations of
Ship Brokers and Agents (FONASBA)

TIME CHARTER©

New York Produce Exchange Form

Issued by the Association of Ship Brokers and Agents (U.S.A.), Inc.

November 6th, 1913—Amended October 20th, 1921; August 6th, 1931; October 3rd, 1946; Revised June 12th, 1981; September 14th, 1993.

THIS CHARTER PARTY, made and concluded in 1
this .... day of .... 19.................................. 2

Between.. 3
.... 4
Owners of the Vessel described below, and 5
.... 6
.... 7
Charterers. 8

Description of Vessel 9

Name .... Flag .... Built ....(year). 10
Port and number of Registry 11
Classed .... in 12
Deadweight ....long*/metric* tons (cargo and bunkers, including freshwater and 13
stores not exceeding .... long*/metric* tons) on a salt water draft of 14
on summer freeboard. 15
Capacity .... cubic feet grain .... cubic feet bale space. 16
Tonnage.. GT/GRT. 17
Speed about .... knots, fully laden, in good weather conditions up to and including maximum 18
Force .... on the Beaufort wind scale, on a consumption of about .... long*/metric* 19
tons of 20

* *Delete as appropriate.* 21
For further description see Appendix "A" (if applicable) 22

1. **Duration** 23

The Owners agree to let and the Charterers agree to hire the Vessel from the time of delivery for a period 24
of 25
.... 26
.... 27
....within below mentioned trading limits. 28

2. **Delivery** 29

The Vessel shall be placed at the disposal of the Charterers at 30
.... 31
.... 32
.... The Vessel on her delivery 33
shall be ready to receive cargo with clean-swept holds and tight, staunch, strong and in every way fitted 34
for ordinary cargo service, having water ballast and with sufficient power to operate all cargo-handling gear 35
simultaneously. 36

The Owners shall give the Charterers not less than .... days notice of expected date of delivery.

3. On-Off Hire Survey

Prior to delivery and redelivery the parties shall, unless otherwise agreed, each appoint surveyors, for their respective accounts, who shall not later than at first loading port/last discharging port respectively, conduct joint on-hire/off-hire surveys, for the purpose of ascertaining quantity of bunkers on board and the condition of the Vessel. A single report shall be prepared on each occasion and signed by each surveyor, without prejudice to his right to file a separate report setting forth items upon which the surveyors cannot agree. If either party fails to have a representative attend the survey and sign the joint survey report, such party shall nevertheless be bound for all purposes by the findings in any report prepared by the other party. On-hire survey shall be on Charterers' time and off-hire survey on Owners' time.

4. Dangerous Cargo/Cargo Exclusions

(a) The Vessel shall be employed in carrying lawful merchandise excluding any goods of a dangerous, injurious, flammable or corrosive nature unless carried in accordance with the requirements or recommendations of the competent authorities of the country of the Vessel's registry and of ports of shipment and discharge and of any intermediate countries or ports through whose waters the Vessel must pass. Without prejudice to the generality of the foregoing, in addition the following are specifically excluded: livestock of any description, arms, ammunition, explosives, nuclear and radioactive materials, ...
....
....
....
....
....
....
....
....

(b) If IMO-classified cargo is agreed to be carried, the amount of such cargo shall be limited to .... tons and the Charterers shall provide the Master with any evidence he may reasonably require to show that the cargo is packaged, labelled, loaded and stowed in accordance with IMO regulations, failing which the Master is entitled to refuse such cargo or, if already loaded, to unload it at the Charterers' risk and expense.

5. Trading Limits

The Vessel shall be employed in such lawful trades between safe ports and safe places within ....
....excluding
....
....
....as the Charterers shall direct.

6. Owners to Provide

The Owners shall provide and pay for the insurance of the Vessel, except as otherwise provided, and for all provisions, cabin, deck, engine-room and other necessary stores, including boiler water; shall pay for wages, consular shipping and discharging fees of the crew and charges for port services pertaining to the crew; shall maintain the Vessel's class and keep her in a thoroughly efficient state in hull, machinery and equipment for and during the service, and have a full complement of officers and crew.

7. Charterers to Provide

The Charterers, while the Vessel is on hire, shall provide and pay for all the bunkers except as otherwise agreed; shall pay for port charges (including compulsory watchmen and cargo watchmen and compulsory garbage disposal), all communication expenses pertaining to the Charterers' business at cost, pilotages, towages, agencies, commissions, consular charges (except those pertaining to individual crew members or flag of the Vessel), and all other usual expenses except those stated in Clause 6, but when the Vessel puts into a port for causes for which the Vessel is responsible (other than by stress of weather), then all such charges incurred shall be paid by the Owners. Fumigations ordered because of illness of the crew shall be for the Owners' account. Fumigations ordered because of cargoes carried or ports visited while the Vessel is employed under this Charter Party shall be for the Charterers' account. All other fumigations shall be for the Charterers' account after the Vessel has been on charter for a continuous period of six months or more.

The Charterers shall provide and pay for necessary dunnage and also any extra fittings requisite for a special trade or unusual cargo, but the Owners shall allow them the use of any dunnage already aboard the Vessel. Prior to redelivery the Charterers shall remove their dunnage and fittings at their cost and in their time.

8. Performance of Voyages

(a) The Master shall perform the voyages with due despatch, and shall render all customary assistance with the Vessel's crew. The Master shall be conversant with the English language and (although appointed by the Owners) shall be under the orders and directions of the Charterers as regards employment and agency; and the Charterers shall perform all cargo handling, including but not limited to loading, stowing, trimming, lashing, securing, dunnaging, unlashing, discharging, and tallying, at their risk and expense, under the supervision of the Master.

(b) If the Charterers shall have reasonable cause to be dissatisfied with the conduct of the Master or officers, the Owners shall, on receiving particulars of the complaint, investigate the same, and, if necessary, make a change in the appointments.

9. Bunkers

(a) The Charterers on delivery, and the Owners on redelivery, shall take over and pay for all fuel and diesel oil remaining on board the Vessel as hereunder. The Vessel shall be delivered with: .... long*/metric* tons of fuel oil at the price of .... per ton; .... tons of diesel oil at the price of .... per ton. The vessel shall be redelivered with: .... tons of fuel oil at the price of .... per ton; .... tons of diesel oil at the price of .... per ton.

* Same tons apply throughout this clause.

(b) The Charterers shall supply bunkers of a quality suitable for burning in the Vessel's engines and auxiliaries and which conform to the specification(s) as set out in Appendix A.

The Owners reserve their right to make a claim against the Charterers for any damage to the main engines or the auxiliaries caused by the use of unsuitable fuels or fuels not complying with the agreed specification(s). Additionally, if bunker fuels supplied do not conform with the mutually agreed specification(s) or otherwise prove unsuitable for burning in the Vessel's engines or auxiliaries, the Owners shall not be held responsible for any reduction in the Vessel's speed performance and/or increased bunker consumption, nor for any time lost and any other consequences.

10. Rate of Hire/Redelivery Areas and Notices

The Charterers shall pay for the use and hire of the said Vessel at the rate of $.................................. U.S. currency, daily, or $.. U.S. currency per ton on the Vessel's deadweight carrying capacity, including bunkers and stores, on .... summer freeboard, per 30 days, commencing on and from the day of her delivery, as aforesaid, and at and after the same rate for any part of a month; hire shall continue until the hour of the day of her redelivery in like good order and condition, ordinary wear and tear excepted, to the Owners (unless Vessel lost) at..
....
....
.... unless otherwise mutually agreed.

The Charterers shall give the Owners not less than .... days notice of the Vessel's expected date and probable port of redelivery.

For the purpose of hire calculations, the times of delivery, redelivery or termination of charter shall be adjusted to GMT.

NYPE 93

11. **Hire Payment**

(a) *Payment*

Payment of Hire shall be made so as to be received by the Owners or their designated payee in ...., viz .... in .... currency, or in United States Currency, in funds available to the Owners on the due date, 15 days in advance, and for the last month or part of same the approximate amount of hire, and should same not cover the actual time, hire shall be paid for the balance day by day as it becomes due, if so required by the Owners. Failing the punctual and regular payment of the hire, or on any fundamental breach whatsoever of this Charter Party, the Owners shall be at liberty to withdraw the Vessel from the service of the Charterers without prejudice to any claims they (the Owners) may otherwise have on the Charterers.

At any time after the expiry of the grace period provided in Sub-clause 11 (b) hereunder and while the hire is outstanding, the Owners shall, without prejudice to the liberty to withdraw, be entitled to withhold the performance of any and all of their obligations hereunder and shall have no responsibility whatsoever for any consequences thereof, in respect of which the Charterers hereby indemnify the Owners, and hire shall continue to accrue and any extra expenses resulting from such withholding shall be for the Charterers' account.

(b) *Grace Period*

Where there is failure to make punctual and regular payment of hire due to oversight, negligence, errors or omissions on the part of the Charterers or their bankers, the Charterers shall be given by the Owners .... clear banking days (as recognized at the agreed place of payment) written notice to rectify the failure, and when so rectified within those ....days following the Owners' notice, the payment shall stand as regular and punctual.

Failure by the Charterers to pay the hire within .... days of their receiving the Owners' notice as provided herein, shall entitle the Owners to withdraw as set forth in Sub-clause 11 (a) above.

(c) *Last Hire Payment*

Should the Vessel be on her voyage towards port of redelivery at the time the last and/or the penultimate payment of hire is/are due, said payment(s) is/are to be made for such length of time as the Owners and the Charterers may agree upon as being the estimated time necessary to complete the voyage, and taking into account bunkers actually on board, to be taken over by the Owners and estimated disbursements for the Owners' account before redelivery. Should same not cover the actual time, hire is to be paid for the balance, day by day, as it becomes due. When the Vessel has been redelivered, any difference is to be refunded by the Owners or paid by the Charterers, as the case may be.

(d) *Cash Advances*

Cash for the Vessel's ordinary disbursements at any port may be advanced by the Charterers, as required by the Owners, subject to 2½ percent commission and such advances shall be deducted from the hire. The Charterers, however, shall in no way be responsible for the application of such advances.

12. **Berths**

The Vessel shall be loaded and discharged in any safe dock or at any safe berth or safe place that Charterers or their agents may direct, provided the Vessel can safely enter, lie and depart always afloat at any time of tide.

13. **Spaces Available**

(a) The whole reach of the Vessel's holds, decks, and other cargo spaces (not more than she can reasonably and safely stow and carry), also accommodations for supercargo, if carried, shall be at the Charterers' disposal, reserving only proper and sufficient space for the Vessel's officers, crew, tackle, apparel, furniture, provisions, stores and fuel.

(b) In the event of deck cargo being carried, the Owners are to be and are hereby indemnified by the Charterers for any loss and/or damage and/or liability of whatsoever nature caused to the Vessel as a result of the carriage of deck cargo and which would not have arisen had deck cargo not been loaded.

14. Supercargo and Meals

The Charterers are entitled to appoint a supercargo, who shall accompany the Vessel at the Charterers' risk and see that voyages are performed with due despatch. He is to be furnished with free accommodation and same fare as provided for the Master's table, the Charterers paying at the rate of .... per day. The Owners shall victual pilots and customs officers, and also, when authorized by the Charterers or their agents, shall victual tally clerks, stevedore's foreman, etc. Charterers paying at the rate of .... per meal for all such victualling.

15. Sailing Orders and Logs

The Charterers shall furnish the Master from time to time with all requisite instructions and sailing directions, in writing, in the English language, and the Master shall keep full and correct deck and engine logs of the voyage or voyages, which are to be patent to the Charterers or their agents, and furnish the Charterers, their agents or supercargo, when required, with a true copy of such deck and engine logs, showing the course of the Vessel, distance run and the consumption of bunkers. Any log extracts required by the Charterers shall be in the English language.

16. Delivery/Cancelling

If required by the Charterers, time shall not commence before .... and should the Vessel not be ready for delivery on or before.................................. but not later than.................................. hours, the Charterers shall have the option of cancelling this Charter Party.

Extension of Cancelling

If the Owners warrant that, despite the exercise of due diligence by them, the Vessel will not be ready for delivery by the cancelling date, and provided the Owners are able to state with reasonable certainty the date on which the Vessel will be ready, they may, at the earliest seven days before the Vessel is expected to sail for the port or place of delivery, require the Charterers to declare whether or not they will cancel the Charter Party. Should the Charterers elect not to cancel, or should they fail to reply within two days or by the cancelling date, whichever shall first occur, then the seventh day after the expected date of readiness for delivery as notified by the Owners shall replace the original cancelling date. Should the Vessel be further delayed, the Owners shall be entitled to require further declarations of the Charterers in accordance wtih this Clause.

17. Off Hire

In the event of loss of time from deficiency and/or default and/or strike of officers or crew, or deficiency of stores, fire, breakdown of, or damages to hull, machinery or equipment, grounding, detention by the arrest of the Vessel, (unless such arrest is caused by events for which the Charterers, their servants, agents or subcontractors are responsible), or detention by average accidents to the Vessel or cargo unless resulting from inherent vice, quality or defect of the cargo, drydocking for the purpose of examination or painting bottom, or by any other similar cause preventing the full working of the Vessel, the payment of hire and overtime, if any, shall cease for the time thereby lost. Should the Vessel deviate or put back during a voyage, contrary to the orders or directions of the Charterers, for any reason other than accident to the cargo or where permitted in lines 257 to 258 hereunder, the hire is to be suspended from the time of her deviating or putting back until she is again in the same or equidistant position from the destination and the voyage resumed therefrom. All bunkers used by the Vessel while off hire shall be for the Owners' account. In the event of the Vessel being driven into port or to anchorage through stress of weather, trading to shallow harbors or to rivers or ports with bars, any detention of the Vessel and/or expenses resulting from such detention shall be for the Charterers' account. If upon the voyage the speed be reduced by defect in, or breakdown of, any part of her hull, machinery or equipment, the time so lost, and the cost of any extra bunkers consumed in consequence thereof, and all extra proven expenses may be deducted from the hire

18. Sublet

Unless otherwise agreed, the Charterers shall have the liberty to sublet the Vessel for all or any part of the time covered by this Charter Party, but the Charterers remain responsible for the fulfillment of this Charter Party.

19. Drydocking

The Vessel was last drydocked ....

* (a) The Owners shall have the option to place the Vessel in drydock during the currency of this Charter at a convenient time and place, to be mutually agreed upon between the Owners and the Charterers, for bottom cleaning and painting and/or repair as required by class or dictated by circumstances.

* (b) Except in case of emergency no drydocking shall take place during the currency of this Charter Party.

* *Delete as appropriate*

20. Total Loss

Should the Vessel be lost, money paid in advance and not earned (reckoning from the date of loss or being last heard of) shall be returned to the Charterers at once.

21. Exceptions

The act of God, enemies, fire, restraint of princes, rulers and people, and all dangers and accidents of the seas, rivers, machinery, boilers, and navigation, and errors of navigation throughout this Charter, always mutually excepted.

22. Liberties

The Vessel shall have the liberty to sail with or without pilots, to tow and to be towed, to assist vessels in distress, and to deviate for the purpose of saving life and property.

23. Liens

The Owners shall have a lien upon all cargoes and all sub-freights and/or sub-hire for any amounts due under this Charter Party, including general average contributions, and the Charterers shall have a lien on the Vessel for all monies paid in advance and not earned, and any overpaid hire or excess deposit to be returned at once.

The Charterers will not directly or indirectly suffer, nor permit to be continued, any lien or encumbrance, which might have priority over the title and interest of the Owners in the Vessel. The Charterers undertake that during the period of this Charter Party, they will not procure any supplies or necessaries or services, including any port expenses and bunkers, on the credit of the Owners or in the Owners' time.

24. Salvage

All derelicts and salvage shall be for the Owners' and the Charterers' equal benefit after deducting Owners' and Charterers' expenses and crew's proportion

25. General Average

General average shall be adjusted according to York-Antwerp Rules 1974, as amended 1990, or any subsequent modification thereof, in .... and settled in .... currency.

The Charterers shall procure that all bills of lading issued during the currency of the Charter Party will contain a provision to the effect that general average shall be adjusted according to York-Antwerp Rules 1974, as amended 1990, or any subsequent modification thereof and will include the "New Jason Clause" as per Clause 31.

Time charter hire shall not contribute to general average.

26. Navigation

Nothing herein stated is to be construed as a demise of the Vessel to the Time Charterers. The Owners shall remain responsible for the navigation of the Vessel, acts of pilots and tug boats, insurance, crew, and all other matters, same as when trading for their own account.

27. Cargo Claims

Cargo claims as between the Owners and the Charterers shall be settled in accordance with the Inter-Club New York Produce Exchange Agreement of February 1970, as amended May, 1984, or any subsequent modification or replacement thereof.

28. Cargo Gear and Lights

The Owners shall maintain the cargo handling gear of the Vessel which is as follows:...

....

....

....

providing gear (for all derricks or cranes) capable of lifting capacity as described. The Owners shall also provide on the Vessel for night work lights as on board, but all additional lights over those on board shall be at the Charterers' expense. The Charterers shall have the use of any gear on board the Vessel. If required by the Charterers, the Vessel shall work night and day and all cargo handling gear shall be at the Charterers' disposal during loading and discharging. In the event of disabled cargo handling gear, or insufficient power to operate the same, the Vessel is to be considered to be off hire to the extent that time is actually lost to the Charterers and the Owners to pay stevedore stand-by charges occasioned thereby, unless such disablement or insufficiency of power is caused by the Charterers' stevedores. If required by the Charterers, the Owners shall bear the cost of hiring shore gear in lieu thereof, in which case the Vessel shall remain on hire.

29. Crew Overtime

In lieu of any overtime payments to officers and crew for work ordered by the Charterers or their agents, the Charterers shall pay the Owners, concurrently with the hire .... per month or pro rata.

30. Bills of Lading

(a) The Master shall sign the bills of lading or waybills for cargo as presented in conformity with mates or tally clerk's receipts. However, the Charterers may sign bills of lading or waybills on behalf of the Master, with the Owner's prior written authority, always in conformity with mates or tally clerk's receipts.

(b) All bills of lading or waybills shall be without prejudice to this Charter Party and the Charterers shall indemnify the Owners against all consequences or liabilities which may arise from any inconsistency between this Charter Party and any bills of lading or waybills signed by the Charterers or by the Master at their request.

(c) Bills of lading covering deck cargo shall be claused: "Shipped on deck at Charterers', Shippers' and Receivers' risk, expense and responsibility, without liability on the part of the Vessel, or her Owners for any loss, damage, expense or delay howsoever caused."

31. Protective Clauses

This Charter Party is subject to the following clauses all of which are also to be included in all bills of lading or waybills issued hereunder:

(a) CLAUSE PARAMOUNT

"This bill of lading shall have effect subject to the provisions of the Carriage of Goods by Sea Act of the United States, the Hague Rules, or the Hague-Visby Rules, as applicable, or such other similar national legislation as may mandatorily apply by virtue of origin or destination of the bills of lading, which shall be deemed to be incorporated herein and nothing herein contained shall be deemed a surrender by the carrier of any of its rights or immunities or an increase of any of its responsibilities or liabilities under said applicable Act. If any term of this bill of lading be repugnant to said applicable Act to any extent, such term shall be void to that extent, but no further."

and

(b) BOTH-TO-BLAME COLLISION CLAUSE

"If the ship comes into collision with another ship as a result of the negligence of the other ship and any act, neglect or default of the master, mariner, pilot or the servants of the carrier in the navigation or in the management of the ship, the owners of the goods carried hereunder will indemnify the carrier against all loss or liability to the other or non-carrying ship or her owners insofar as such loss or liability represents loss of, or damage to, or any claim whatsoever of the owners of said goods, paid or payable by the other or non-carrying ship or her owners to the owners of said goods and set off, recouped or recovered by the other or non-carrying ship or her owners as part of their claim against the carrying ship or carrier.

The foregoing provisions shall also apply where the owners, operators or those in charge of any ships or objects other than, or in addition to, the colliding ships or objects are at fault in respect to a collision or contact."

and

(c) NEW JASON CLAUSE

"In the event of accident, danger, damage or disaster before or after the commencement of the voyage resulting from any cause whatsoever, whether due to negligence or not, for which, or for the consequences of which, the carrier is not responsible, by statute, contract, or otherwise the goods, shippers, consignees, or owners of the goods shall contribute wth the carrier in general average to the payment of any sacrifices, losses, or expenses of a general average nature that may be made or incurred, and shall pay salvage and special charges incurred in respect of the goods.

If a salving ship is owned or operated by the carrier, salvage shall be paid for as fully as if salving ship or ships belonged to strangers. Such deposit as the carrier or his agents may deem sufficient to cover the estimated contribution of the goods and any salvage and special charges thereon shall, if required, be made by the goods, shippers, consignees or owners of the goods to the carrier before delivery."

and

(d) U.S. TRADE—DRUG CLAUSE

"In pursuance of the provisions of the U.S. Anti Drug Abuse Act 1986 or any re-enactment thereof, the Charterers warrant to exercise the highest degree of care and dilligence in preventing unmanifested narcotic drugs and marijuana to be loaded or concealed on board the Vessel.

Non-compliance with the provisions of this clause shall amount to breach of warranty for consequences of which the Charterers shall be liable and shall hold the Owners, the Master and the crew of the Vessel harmless and shall keep them indemnified against all claims whatsoever which may arise and be made against them individually or jointly. Furthermore, all time lost and all expenses incurred, including fines, as a result of the Charterers' breach of the provisions of this clause shall be for the Charterers' account and the Vessel shall remain on hire.

Should the Vessel be arrested as a result of the Charterers' non-compliance with the provisions of this clause, the Charterers shall at their expense take all reasonable steps to secure that within a reasonable time the Vessel is released and at their expense put up the bails to secure release of the Vessel.

The Owners shall remain responsible for all time lost and all expenses incurred, including fines, in the event that unmanifested narcotic drugs and marijuana are found in the possession or effects of the Vessel's personnel."

and

(e) WAR CLAUSES

"(i) No contraband of war shall be shipped. The Vessel shall not be required, without the consent of the Owners, which shall not be unreasonably withheld, to enter any port or zone which is involved in a state of war, warlike operations, or hostilities, civil strife, insurrection or piracy whether there be a declaration of war or not, where the Vessel, cargo or crew might reasonably be expected to be subject to capture, seizure or arrest, or to a hostile act by a belligerent power (the term "power" meaning any de jure or de facto authority or any purported governmental organization maintaining naval, military or air forces).

(ii) If such consent is given by the Owners, the Charterers will pay the provable additional cost of insuring the Vessel against hull risks in an amount equal to the value under her ordinary hull policy but not exceeding a valuation of .... In addition, the Owners may purchase and the Charterers will pay for war risk insurance on ancillary risks such as loss of hire, freight disbursements, total loss, blocking and trapping, etc. If such insurance is not obtainable commercially or through a government program, the Vessel shall not be required to enter or remain at any such port or zone.

(iii) In the event of the existence of the conditions described in (i) subsequent to the date of this Charter, or while the Vessel is on hire under this Charter, the Charterers shall, in respect of voyages to any such port or zone assume the provable additional cost of wages and insurance properly incurred in connection with master, officers and crew as a consequence of such war, warlike operations or hostilities.

(iv) Any war bonus to officers and crew due to the Vessels's trading or cargo carried shall be for the Charterers' account."

32. War Cancellation

In the event of the outbreak of war (whether there be a declaration of war or not) between any two or more of the following countries: ....
....
....
....
either the Owners or the Charterers may cancel this Charter Party. Whereupon, the Charterers shall redeliver the Vessel to the Owners in accordance with Clause 10; if she has cargo on board, after discharge thereof at destination, or, if debarred under this Clause from reaching or entering it, at a near open and safe port as directed by the Owners; or, if she has no cargo on board, at the port at which she then is; or, if at sea, at a near open and safe port as directed by the Owners. In all cases hire shall continue to be paid in accordance with Clause 11 and except as aforesaid all other provisions of this Charter Party shall apply until redelivery.

33. Ice

The Vessel shall not be required to enter or remain in any icebound port or area, nor any port or area where lights or lightships have been or are about to be withdrawn by reason of ice, nor where there is risk that in the ordinary course of things the Vessel will not be able on account of ice to safely enter and remain in the port or area or to get out after having completed loading or discharging. Subject to the Owners' prior approval the Vessel is to follow ice-breakers when reasonably required with regard to her size, construction and ice class.

34. Requisition

Should the Vessel be requisitioned by the government of the Vessel's flag during the period of this Charter Party, the Vessel shall be considered to be off hire during the period of such requisition, and any hire paid by the said government in respect of such requisition period shall be retained by the Owners. The period during which the Vessel is on requisition to the said government shall count as part of the period provided for in this Charter Party.

If the period of requisition exceeds .... months, either party shall have the option of cancelling this Charter Party and no consequential claim may be made by either party.

35. Stevedore Damage

Notwithstanding anything contained herein to the contrary, the Charterers shall pay for any and all damage to the Vessel caused by stevedores provided the Master has notified the Charterers and/or their agents in writing as soon as practical but not later than 48 hours after any damage is discovered. Such notice to specify the damage in detail and to invite Charterers to appoint a surveyor to assess the extent of such damage.

(a) In case of any and all damage(s) affecting the Vessel's seaworthiness and/or the safety of the crew and/or affecting the trading capabilities of the Vessel, the Charterers shall immediately arrange for repairs of such damage(s) at their expense and the Vessel is to remain on hire until such repairs are completed and if required passed by the Vessel's classification society.

(b) Any and all damage(s) not described under point (a) above shall be repaired at the Charterers' option, before or after redelivery concurrently with the Owners' work. In such case no hire and/or expenses will be paid to the Owners except and insofar as the time and/or the expenses required for the repairs for which the Charterers are responsible, exceed the time and/or expenses necessary to carry out the Owners' work.

36. Cleaning of Holds

The Charterers shall provide and pay extra for sweeping and/or washing and/or cleaning of holds between voyages and/or between cargoes provided such work can be undertaken by the crew and is permitted by local regulations, at the rate of .... per hold.

In connection with any such operation, the Owners shall not be responsible if the Vessel's holds are not accepted or passed by the port or any other authority. The Charterers shall have the option to redeliver the Vessel with unclean/unswept holds against a lumpsum payment of..................................in lieu of cleaning.

37. Taxes

Charterers to pay all local, State, National taxes and/or dues assessed on the Vessel or the Owners resulting from the Charterers' orders herein, whether assessed during or after the currency of this Charter Party including any taxes and/or dues on cargo and/or freights and/or sub-freights and/or hire (excluding taxes levied by the country of the flag of the Vessel or the Owners).

38. Charterers' Colors

The Charterers shall have the privilege of flying their own house flag and painting the Vessel with their own markings. The Vessel shall be repainted in the Owners' colors before termination of the Charter Party. Cost and time of painting, maintaining and repainting those changes effected by the Charterers shall be for the Charterers' account.

39. Laid Up Returns

The Charterers shall have the benefit of any return insurance premium receivable by the Owners from their underwriters as and when received from underwriters by reason of the Vessel being in port for a minimum period of 30 days if on full hire for this period or pro rata for the time actually on hire.

40. Documentation

The Owners shall provide any documentation relating to the Vessel that may be required to permit the Vessel to trade within the agreed trade limits, including, but not limited to certificates of financial responsibility for oil pollution, provided such oil pollution certificates are obtainable from the Owners' P & I club, valid international tonnage certificate, Suez and Panama tonnage certificates, valid certificate of registry and certificates relating to the strengh and/or serviceability of the Vessel's gear.

41. Stowaways

(a) (i) The Charterers warrant to exercise due care and diligence in preventing stowaways in gaining access to the Vessel by means of secreting away in the goods and/or containers shipped by the Charterers.

(ii) If, despite the exercise of due care and diligence by the Charterers, stowaways have gained access to the Vessel by means of secreting away in the goods and/or containers shipped by the Charterers, this shall amount to breach of charter for the consequences of which the Charterers shall be liable and shall hold the Owners harmless and shall keep them indemnified against all claims whatsoever which may arise and be made against them. Furthermore, all time lost and all expenses whatsoever and howsoever incurred, including fines, shall be for the Charterers' account and the Vessel shall remain on hire.

(iii) Should the Vessel be arrested as a result of the Charterers' breach of charter according to sub-clause (a)(ii) above, the Charterers shall take all reasonable steps to secure that, within a reasonable time, the Vessel is released and at their expense put up bail to secure release of the Vessel.

(b) (i) If, despite the exercise of due care and diligence by the Owners, stowaways have gained access to the Vessel by means other than secreting away in the goods and/or containers shipped by the Charterers, all time lost and all expenses whatsoever and howsoever incurred, including fines, shall be for the Owners' account and the Vessel shall be off hire.

(ii) Should the Vessel be arrested as a result of stowaways having gained access to the Vessel by means other than secreting away in the goods and/or containers shipped by the Charterers, the Owners shall take all reasonable steps to secure that, within a reasonable time, the Vessel is released and at their expense put up bail to secure release of the Vessel.

42. Smuggling

In the event of smuggling by the Master, Officers and/or crew, the Owners shall bear the cost of any fines, taxes, or imposts levied and the Vessel shall be off hire for any time lost as a result thereof.

43. Commissions

A commission of .... percent is payable by the Vessel and the Owners to ....
....
....
....
on hire earned and paid under this Charter, and also upon any continuation or extension of this Charter.

44. Address Commission

An address commission of .... percent is payable to ....
....
....
.... on hire earned and paid under this Charter.

45. Arbitration*

(a)   NEW YORK
All disputes arising out of this contract shall be arbitrated at New York in the following manner, and subject to U.S. Law:

One Arbitrator is to be appointed by each of the parties hereto and a third by the two so chosen. Their decision or that of any two of them shall be final, and for the purpose of enforcing any award, this agreement may be made a rule of the court. The Arbitrators shall be commercial men, conversant with shipping matters. Such Arbitration is to be conducted in accordance with the rules of the Society of Maritime Arbitrators Inc.

For disputes where the total amount claimed by either party does not exceed US $ ....** the arbitration shall be conducted in accordance with the Shortened Arbitration Procedure of the Society of Maritime Arbitrators Inc.

(b)   LONDON
All disputes arising out of this contract shall be arbitrated at London and, unless the parties agree forthwith on a single Arbitrator, be referred to the final arbitrament of two Arbitrators carrying on business in London who shall be members of the Baltic Mercantile & Shipping Exchange and engaged in Shipping, one to be appointed by each of the parties, with power to such Arbitrators to appoint an Umpire. No award shall be questioned or invalidated on the ground that any of the Arbitrators is not qualified as above, unless objection to his action be taken before the award is made. Any dispute arising hereunder shall be governed by English Law.

For disputes where the total amount claimed by either party does not exceed US $ ....** the arbitration shall be conducted in accordance with the Small Claims Procedure of the London Maritime Arbitrators Association.

* Delete para (a) or (b) as appropriate

** Where no figure is supplied in the blank space this provision only shall be void but the other provisions of this clause shall have full force and remain in effect.

If mutually agreed, clauses .... to ...., both inclusive, as attached hereto are fully incorporated in this Charter Party.

APPENDIX "A" 525

To Charter Party dated 526
Between.. Owners 527
and .... Charterers 528

Further details of the Vessel: 529
530

THE BALTIC AND INTERNATIONAL MARITIME CONFERENCE
(Formerly The Baltic and White Sea Conference)

UNIFORM TIME-CHARTER

.... 19 ....

IT IS THIS DAY MUTUALLY AGREED between .... Owners	1
of the Vessel called ....of........................ tons gross Register, tons net	2
classed .... of ....indicated horse power,	3
carrying about ....tons deadweight on Board of Trade summer freeboard inclusive	4
of bunkers, stores, provisions and boiler water, having as per builder's plan ....cubic-feet	5
grain capacity, exclusive of permanent bunkers, which contain about .... tons, and fully loaded capable bale	6
of steaming about .... knots in good weather and smooth water on a consumption of about	7
................................tons best Welsh coal, or about................................. tons oil-fuel, now................................	8
and	9
of .... Charterers, as follows:	10
1. The Owners let, and the Charterers hire the Vessel for a period of	11
calendar months from the time (not a Sunday or a legal Holiday unless taken over) the Vessel is delivered	12
and placed at the disposal of the Charterers between 9 a.m. and 6 p.m., or between 9 a.m. and 2 p.m.	13
if on Saturday, at	14
.... in such available berth where she can safely lie always afloat, as the Charterers	15
may direct, she being in every way fitted for ordinary cargo service.	16
The Vessel to be delivered	17
2. The Vessel to be employed in lawful trades for the carriage of lawful merchandise only	18
between good and safe ports or places where she can safely lie always afloat within the following	19
limits:	20

    No live stock nor injurious, inflammable or dangerous goods (such as acids, explosives, calcium   21
carbide, ferro silicon, naphtha, motor spirit, tar, or any of their products) to be shipped.   22
    3. The Owners to provide and pay for all provisions and wages, for insurance of the Vessel, for all   23
deck and engine-room stores and maintain her in a thoroughly efficient state in hull and machinery   24
during service.   25
    The Owners to provide one winchman per hatch. If further winchmen are required, or if the   26
stevedores refuse or are not permitted to work with the Crew, the Charterers to provide and pay   27
qualified shore-winchmen.   28
    4. The Charterers to provide and pay for all coals, including galley coal, oil-fuel, water for boilers,   29
port charges, pilotages (whether compulsory or not), canal steersmen, boatage, lights, tug-assistance,   30
consular charges (except those pertaining to the Master, Officers and Crew), canal, dock and other dues   31
and charges, including any foreign general municipality or state taxes, also all dock, harbour and   32
tonnage dues at the ports of delivery and re-delivery (unless incurred through cargo carried before delivery   33
or after re-delivery), agencies, commissions, also to arrange and pay for loading, trimming, stowing   34
(including dunnage and shifting boards, except any already on board), unloading, weighing, tallying and   35
delivery of cargoes, surveys on hatches, meals supplied to officials and men in their service and all   36
other charges and expenses whatsoever including detention and expenses through quarantine (including   37
cost of fumigation and disinfection).   38

All ropes, slings and special runners actually used for loading and discharging and any special gear, including special ropes, hawsers and chains required by the custom of the port for mooring to be for the Charterers' account. The Vessel to be fitted with winches, derricks, wheels and ordinary runners capable of handling lifts up to 2 tons.

5. The Charterers at port of delivery and the Owners at port of re-delivery to take over and pay for all coal or oil-fuel remaining in the Vessel's bunkers at current price at the respective ports. The Vessel to be re-delivered with not less than .... tons and not exceeding ....tons of coal or oil-fuel in the Vessel's bunkers.

6. The Charterers to pay as hire: ....
per 30 days, commencing in accordance with clause 1 until her re-delivery to the Owners.
Payment of hire to be made in cash, in .... without discount, every 30 days, in advance.

In default of payment the Owners to have the right of withdrawing the Vessel from the service of the Charterers, without noting any protest and without interference by any court or any other formality whatsoever and without prejudice to any claim the Owners may otherwise have on the Charterers under the Charter.

7. The Vessel to be re-delivered on the expiration of the Charter in the same good order as when delivered to the Charterers (fair wear and tear excepted) at an ice-free port in the Charterers' option in

....
....

between 9 a.m. and 6 p.m., and 9 a.m. and 2 p.m. on Saturday, but the day of re-delivery shall not be a Sunday or legal Holiday.

The Charterers to give the Owners not less than ten day's notice at which port and on about which day the Vessel will be re-delivered

Should the Vessel be ordered on a voyage by which the Charter period will be exceeded the Charterers to have the use of the Vessel to enable them to complete the voyage, provided it could be reasonably calculated that the voyage would allow re-delivery about the time fixed for the termination of the Charter, but for any time exceeding the termination date the Charterers to pay the market rate if higher than the rate stipulated herein.

8. The whole reach and burthen of the Vessel, including lawful deck-capacity to be at the Charterer's disposal, reserving proper and sufficient space for the Vessel's Master, Officers, Crew, tackle, apparel, furniture, provisions and stores.

9. The Master to prosecute all voyages with the utmost despatch and to render customary assistance with the Vessel's Crew. The Master to be under the orders of the Charterers as regards employment agency, or other arrangements. The Charterers to indemnify the Owners against all consequences or liabilities arising from the Master, Officers or Agents signing Bills of Lading or other documents or otherwise complying with such orders, as well as from any irregularity in the Vessel's papers or for overcarrying goods. The Owners not to be responsible for shortage, mixture, marks, nor for number of pieces or packages, nor for damage to nor claims on cargo caused by bad stowage or otherwise

If the Charterers have reason to be dissatisfied with the conduct of the Master, Officers, or Engineers, the Owners, on receiving particulars of the complaint, promptly to investigate the matter, and, if necessary and practicable, to make a change in the appointments.

10. The Charterers to furnish the Master with all instructions and sailing directions and the Master and Engineer to keep full and correct logs accessible to the Charterers or their Agents.

11. (A) In the event of drydocking or other necessary measures to maintain the efficiency of the Vessel, deficiency of men or Owners' stores, breakdown of machinery, damage to hull or other accident, either hindering or preventing the working of the vessel and continuing for more than twentyfour consecutive hours, no hire to be paid in respect of any time lost thereby during the period in which the Vessel is unable to perform the service immediately required. Any hire paid in advance to be adjusted accordingly.

(B) In the event of the Vessel being driven into port or to anchorage through stress of weather, trading to shallow harbours or to rivers or ports with bars or suffering an accident to her cargo, any detention of the Vessel and/or expenses resulting from such detention to be for the Charterers' account even if such detention and/or expenses, or the cause by reason of which either is incurred, be due to, or be contributed to by, the negligence of the Owners' servants.

12. Cleaning of boilers whenever possible to be done during service, but if impossible the Charterers to give the Owners necessary time for cleaning. Should the Vessel be detained beyond 48 hours hire to cease until again ready.

13. The Owners only to be responsible for delay in delivery of the Vessel or for delay during the currency of the Charter and for loss or damage to goods onboard, if such delay or loss has been caused by want of due diligence on the part of the Owners or their Manager in making the Vessel seaworthy and fitted for the voyage or any other personal act or omission or default of the Owners or their Manager. The Owners not to be responsible in any other case nor for damage or delay whatsoever and howsoever caused even if caused by the neglect or default of their servants. The Owners not to be liable for loss or damage arising or resulting from strikes, lock-outs or stoppage or restraint of labour (including the Master, Officers or Crew) whether partial or general.

The Charterers to be responsible for loss or damage caused to the Vessel or to the Owners by goods being loaded contrary to the terms of the Charter or by improper or careless bunkering or loading, stowing or discharging of goods or any other improper or negligent act on their part or that of their servants.

14. The Charterers or their Agents to advance to the Master, if required, necessary funds for

ordinary disbursements for the Vessel's account at any port charging only interest at 6 per cent p.a., such advances to be deducted from hire.

15. The Vessel not to be ordered to nor bound to enter: a) any place where fever or epidemics are prevalent or to which the Master, Officers and Crew by law are not bound to follow the Vessel b) any ice-bound place or any place where lights, lightships, marks and buoys are or are likely to be withdrawn by reason of ice on the Vessel's arrival or where there is risk that ordinarily the Vessel will not be able on account of ice to reach the place or to get out after having completed loading or discharging. The Vessel not to be obliged to force ice. If on account of ice the Master considers it dangerous to remain at the loading or discharging place for fear of the Vessel being frozen in and/or damaged, he has liberty to sail to a convenient open place and await the Charterers' fresh instructions. Unforeseen detention through any of above causes to be for the Charterers' account.

16. Should the Vessel be lost or missing, hire to cease from the date when she was lost. If the date of loss cannot be ascertained half hire to be paid from the date the Vessel was last reported until the calculated date of arrival at the destination. Any hire paid in advance to be adjusted accordingly.

17. The Vessel to work day and night if required. The Charterers to refund the Owners their outlays for all overtime paid to Officers and Crew according to the hours and rates stated in the Vessel's articles.

18. The Owners to have a lien upon all cargoes and sub-freights belonging to the Time-Charterers and any Bill of Lading freight for all claims under this Charter, and the Charterers to have a lien on the Vessel for all moneys paid in advance and not earned.

19. All salvage and assistance to other vessels to be for the Owners' and the Charterers' equal benefit after deducting the Master's and Crew's proportion and all legal and other expenses including hire paid under the charter for time lost in the salvage, also repairs of damage and coal or oil-fuel consumed. The Charterers to be bound by all measures taken by the Owners in order to secure payment of salvage and to fix its amount.

20. The Charterers to have the option of subletting the Vessel, giving due notice to the Owners, but the original Charterers always to remain responsible to the Owners for due performance of the Charter.

21. (A) The Vessel unless the consent of the Owners be first obtained not to be ordered nor continue to any place or on any voyage nor be used on any service which will bring her within a zone which is dangerous as the result of any actual or threatened act of war, war hostilities, warlike operations, acts of piracy or of hostility or malicious damage against this or any other vessel or its cargo by any person, body or State whatsoever, revolution, civil war, civil commotion or the operation of international law, nor be exposed in any way to any risks or penalties whatsoever consequent upon the imposition of Sanctions, nor carry any goods that may in any way expose her to any risks of seizure, capture, penalties or any other interference of any kind whatsoever by the belligerent or fighting powers or parties or by any Government or Ruler.

(B) Should the Vessel approach or be brought or ordered within such zone, or be exposed in any way to the said risks, (1) the Owners to be entitled from time to time to insure their interests in the Vessel and/or hire against any of the risks likely to be involved thereby on such terms as they shall think fit, the Charterers to make a refund to the Owners of the premium on demand; and (2) notwithstanding the terms of clause 11 hire to be paid for all time lost including any lost owing to loss of or injury to the Master, Officers, or Crew or to the action of the Crew in refusing to proceed to such zone or to be exposed to such risks.

(C) In the event of the wages of the Master, Officers and/or Crew or the cost of provisions and/or stores for deck and/or engine room and/or insurance premiums being increased by reason of or during the existence of any of the matters mentioned in section (A) the amount of any increase to be added to the hire and paid by the Charterers on production of the Owners' account therefor, such account being rendered monthly.

(D) The Vessel to have liberty to comply with any orders or directions as to departure, arrival, routes, ports of call, stoppages, destination, delivery or in any otherwise whatsoever given by the Government of the nation under whose flag the Vessel sails or any other Government or any person (or body) acting or purporting to act with the authority of such Government or by any committee or person having under the terms of the war risks insurance on the Vessel the right to give any such orders or directions.

(E) In the event of the nation under whose flag the Vessel sails becoming involved in war, hostilities, warlike operations, revolution, or civil commotion, both the Owners and the Charterers may cancel the Charter and, unless otherwise agreed, the Vessel to be redelivered to the Owners at the port of destination or, if prevented through the provisions of section (A) from reaching or entering it, then at a near open and safe port at the Owners' option, after discharge of any cargo on board.

(F) If in compliance with the provisions of this clause anything is done or is not done, such not to be deemed a deviation.

22. Should the Vessel not be delivered by the .... day of .... 19........................, the Charterers to have the option of cancelling.

If the Vessel cannot be delivered by the cancelling date, the Charterers, if required, to declare within 48 hours after receiving notice thereof whether they cancel or will take delivery of the Vessel.

23. Any dispute arising under the Charter to be referrred to arbitration in London (or such other place as may be agreed) one Arbitrator to be nominated by the Owners and the other by the Charterers, and in case the Arbitrators shall not agree then to the decision of an Umpire to be appointed by them, the award of the Arbitrators or the Umpire to be final and binding upon both parties.

BALTIME FORM

24. General Average to be settled according to York/Antwerp Rules, 1974. Hire not to contribute to General Average.
25. The Owners to pay a commission of.. to .... on any hire paid under the Charter, but in no case less than is necessary to cover the actual expenses of the Brokers and a reasonable fee for their work, If the full hire is not paid owing to breach of Charter by either of the parties the party liable therefor to indemnify the Brokers against their loss of commission.
    Should the parties agree to cancel the Charter, the Owners to indemnify the Brokers against any loss of commission but in such case the commission not to exceed the brokerage on one year's hire.

**Code word for this Charter Party
"SHELLTIME 4"**

Issued December 1984

Time Charter Party

LONDON, 19

IT IS THIS DAY AGREED between 1

of (hereinafter referred to as "Owners"), being owners of the 2

good vessel called 3

(hereinafter referred to as "the vessel") described as per Clause 1 hereof and 4

of (hereinafter referred to as "Charterers"): 5

Description and Condition of Vessel

1. At the date of delivery of the vessel under this charter 6
    (a) she shall be classed; 7
    (b) she shall be in every way fit to carry crude petroleum and/or its products; 8

    (c) she shall be tight, staunch, strong, in good order and condition, and in every way fit for the 9
service, with her machinery, boilers, hull and other equipment (including but not limited to hull stress calculator 10
and radar) in a good and efficient state; 11
    (d) her tanks, valves and pipelines shall be oil-tight; 12
    (e) she shall be in every way fitted for burning 13

        at sea – fueloil with a maximum viscosity of Centistokes at 50 degrees Centigrade/any 14
            commercial grade of fueloil ("ACGFO") for main propulsion, marine diesel oil/ACGFO 15
            for auxiliaries 16
        in port – marine diesel oil/ACGFO for auxiliaries; 17

    (f) she shall comply with the regulations in force so as to enable her to pass through the Suez and 18
Panama Canals by day and night without delay; 19
    (g) she shall have on board all certificates, documents and equipment required from time to time by 20
any applicable law to enable her to perform the charter service without delay; 21
    (h) she shall comply with the description in Form B appended hereto, provided however that if there 22
is any conflict between the provisions of Form B and any other provision, including this Clause 1, of this charter 23
such other provision shall govern. 24

Shipboard Personnel and their Duties

2. (a) At the date of delivery of the vessel under this charter 25
        (i) she shall have a full and efficient complement of master, officers and crew for a vessel of her 26
tonnage, who shall in any event be not less than the number required by the laws of the flag state and who shall be 27
trained to operate the vessel and her equipment competently and safely; 28
        (ii) all shipboard personnel shall hold valid certificates of competence in accordance with the 29
requirements of the law of the flag state; 30
        (iii) all shipboard personnel shall be trained in accordance with the relevant provisions of the 31
International Convention on Standards of Training, Certification and Watchkeeping for Seafarers, 1978; 32
        (iv) there shall be on board sufficient personnel with a good working knowledge of the English 33
language to enable cargo operations at loading and discharging places to be carried out efficiently and safely 34
and to enable communications between the vessel and those loading the vessel or accepting discharge therefrom to be 35
carried out quickly and efficiently. 36
    (b) Owners guarantee that throughout the charter service the master shall with the vessel's officers 37
and crew, unless otherwise ordered by Charterers, 38
        (i) prosecute all voyages with the utmost despatch; 39
        (ii) render all customary assistance; and 40
        (iii) load and discharge cargo as rapidly as possible when required by Charterers or their agents 41
to do so, by night or by day, but always in accordance with the laws of the place of loading or discharging (as the 42
case may be) and in each case in accordance with any applicable laws of the flag state. 43

Duty to Maintain

3. (i) Throughout the charter service Owners shall, whenever the passage of time, wear and tear or any 44
event (whether or not coming within Clause 27 hereof) requires steps to be taken to maintain or restore the 45
conditions stipulated in Clauses 1 and 2(a), exercise due diligence so as to maintain or restore the vessel. 46
    (ii) If at any time whilst the vessel is on hire under this charter the vessel fails to comply with the 47

SHELLTIME FORM

requirements of Clauses 1, 2(a) or 10 then hire shall be reduced to the extent necessary to indemnify Charterers for such failure. If and to the extent that such failure affects the time taken by the vessel to perform any services under this charter, hire shall be reduced by an amount equal to the value, calculated at the rate of hire, of the time so lost.

Any reduction of hire under this sub-Clause (ii) shall be without prejudice to any other remedy available to Charterers, but where such reduction of hire is in respect of time lost, such time shall be excluded from any calculation under Clause 24.

(iii) If Owners are in breach of their obligation under Clause 3(i) Charterers may so notify Owners in writing; and if, after the expiry of 30 days following the receipt by Owners of any such notice, Owners have failed to demonstrate to Charterers' reasonable satisfaction the exercise of due diligence as required in Clause 3(i), the vessel shall be off-hire, and no further hire payments shall be due, until Owners have so demonstrated that they are exercising such due diligence.

Furthermore, at any time while the vessel is off-hire under this Clause 3 Charterers have the option to terminate this charter by giving notice in writing with effect from the date on which such notice of termination is received by Owners or from any later date stated in such notice. This sub-Clause (iii) is without prejudice to any rights of Charterers or obligations of Owners under this charter or otherwise (including without limitation Charterers' rights under Clause 21 hereof).

Period Trading Limits

4. Owners agree to let and Charterers agree to hire the vessel for a period of commencing from the time and date of delivery of the vessel, for the purpose of carrying all lawful merchandise (subject always to Clause 28) including in particular

in any part of the world, as Charterers shall direct, subject to the limits of the current British Institute Warranties and any subsequent amendments thereof. Notwithstanding the foregoing, but subject to Clause 35, Charterers may order the vessel to ice-bound waters or to any part of the world outside such limits provided that Owners consent thereto (such consent not to be unreasonably withheld) and that Charterers pay for any insurance premium required by the vessel's underwriters as a consequence of such order.

Charterers shall use due diligence to ensure that the vessel is only employed between and at safe places (which expression when used in this charter shall include ports, berths, wharves, docks, anchorages, submarine lines, alongside vessels or lighters, and other locations including locations at sea) where she can safely lie always afloat. Notwithstanding anything contained in this or any other clause of this charter, Charterers do not warrant the safety of any place to which they order the vessel and shall be under no liability in respect thereof except for loss or damage caused by their failure to exercise due diligence as aforesaid. Subject as above, the vessel shall be loaded and discharged at any places as Charterers may direct, provided that Charterers shall exercise due diligence to ensure that any ship-to-ship transfer operations shall conform to standards not less than those set out in the latest published edition of the ICS/OCIMF Ship-to-Ship Transfer Guide.

The vessel shall be delivered by Owners at a port in

at Owners' option and redelivered to Owners at a port in

at Charterers' option.

Laydays/ Cancelling

5. The vessel shall not be delivered to Charterers before   and Charterers shall have the option of cancelling this charter if the vessel is not ready and at their disposal on or before

Owners to Provide

6. Owners undertake to provide and to pay for all provisions, wages, and shipping and discharging fees and all other expenses of the master, officers and crew; also, except as provided in Clauses 4 and 34 hereof, for all insurance on the vessel, for all deck, cabin and engine-room stores, and for water; for all drydocking, overhaul, maintenance and repairs to the vessel; and for all fumigation expenses and de-rat certificates. Owners' obligations under this Clause 6 extend to all liabilities for customs or import duties arising at any time during the performance of this charter in relation to the personal effects of the master, officers and crew, and in relation to the stores, provisions and other matters aforesaid which Owners are to provide and pay for and Owners shall refund to Charterers any sums Charterers or their agents may have paid or been compelled to pay in respect of any such liability. Any amounts allowable in general average for wages and provisions and stores shall be credited to Charterers insofar as such amounts are in respect of a period when the vessel is on-hire.

Charterers to Provide

7. Charterers shall provide and pay for all fuel (except fuel used for domestic services), towage and pilotage and shall pay agency fees, port charges, commissions, expenses of loading and unloading cargoes, canal dues and all charges other than those payable by Owners in accordance with Clause 6 hereof, provided that all charges for the said items shall be for Owners' account when such items are consumed, employed or incurred for Owners' purposes or while the vessel is off-hire (unless such items reasonably relate to any service given or

distance made good and taken into account under Clause 21 or 22); and provided further that any fuel used in connection with a general average sacrifice or expenditure shall be paid for by Owners.

Rate of Hire

8. Subject as herein provided, Charterers shall pay for the use and hire of the vessel at the rate of　　　　　per day, and pro rata for any part of a day, from the time and date of her delivery (local time) until the time and date of her redelivery (local time) to Owners.

Payment of Hire

9. Subject to Clause 3 (iii), payment of hire shall be made in immediately available funds to:

　　　　　Account
in　　　　　per calendar month in advance, less:
　　　　　(i) any hire paid which Charterers reasonably estimate to relate to off-hire periods, and
　　　　　(ii) any amounts disbursed on Owners' behalf, any advances and commission thereon, and charges which are for Owners' account pursuant to any provision hereof, and
　　　　　(iii) any amounts due or reasonably estimated to become due to Charterers under Clause 3(ii) or 24 hereof,

any such adjustments to be made at the due date for the next monthly payment after the facts have been ascertained. Charterers shall not be responsible for any delay or error by Owners' bank in crediting Owners' account provided that Charterers have made proper and timely payment.

In default of such proper and timely payment,
　　　　　(a) Owners shall notify Charterers of such default and Charterers shall within seven days of receipt of such notice pay to Owners the amount due including interest, failing which Owners may withdraw the vessel from the service of Charterers without prejudice to any other rights Owners may have under this charter or otherwise; and
　　　　　(b) Interest on any amount due but not paid on the due date shall accrue from the day after that date up to and including the day when payment is made, at a rate per annum which shall be 1% above the U.S. Prime Interest Rate as published by the Chase Manhattan Bank in New York at 12.00 New York time on the due date, or, if no such interest rate is published on that day, the interest rate published on the next preceding day on which such a rate was so published, computed on the basis of a 360 day year of twelve 30-day months, compounded semi-annually.

Space Available to Charterers

10. The whole reach, burthen and decks of the vessel and any passenger accommodation (including Owners' suite) shall be at Charterers' disposal, reserving only proper and sufficient space for the vessel's master, officers, crew, tackle, apparel, furniture, provisions and stores, provided that the weight of stores on board shall not, unless specially agreed, exceed 　　　　　tonnes at any time during the charter period.

Overtime

11. Overtime pay of the master, officers and crew in accordance with ship's articles shall be for Charterers' account when incurred, as a result of complying with the request of Charterers or their agents, for loading, discharging, heating of cargo, bunkering or tank cleaning.

Instructions and Logs

12. Charterers shall from time to time give the master all requisite instructions and sailing directions, and he shall keep a full and correct log of the voyage or voyages, which Charterers or their agents may inspect as required. The master shall when required furnish Charterers or their agents with a true copy of such log and with properly completed loading and discharging port sheets and voyage reports for each voyage and other returns as Charterers may require. Charterers shall be entitled to take copies at Owners' expense of any such documents which are not provided by the master.

Bills of Lading

13. (a) The master (although appointed by Owners) shall be under the orders and direction of Charterers as regards employment of the vessel, agency and other arrangements, and shall sign bills of lading as Charterers or their agents may direct (subject always to Clauses 35(a) and 40) without prejudice to this charter. Charterers hereby indemnify Owners against all consequences or liabilities that may arise
　　　　　(i) from signing bills of lading in accordance with the directions of Charterers or their agents, to the extent that the terms of such bills of lading fail to conform to the requirements of this charter, or (except as provided in Clause 13(b)) from the master otherwise complying with Charterers' or their agents' orders;
　　　　　(ii) from any irregularities in papers supplied by Charterers or their agents.
　　　(b) Notwithstanding the foregoing, Owners shall not be obliged to comply with any orders from

SHELLTIME FORM 27

Charterers to discharge all or part of the cargo
(i) at any place other than that shown on the bill of lading and/or
(ii) without presentation of an original bill of lading
unless they have received from Charterers both written confirmation of such orders and an indemnity in a form acceptable to Owners.

Conduct of Vessel's Personnel

14. If Charterers complain of the conduct of the master or any of the officers or crew, Owners shall immediately investigate the complaint. If the complaint proves to be well founded, Owners shall, without delay, make a change in the appointments and Owners shall in any event communicate the result of their investigations to Charterers as soon as possible.

Bunkers at Delivery and Redelivery

15. Charterers shall accept and pay for all bunkers on board at the time of delivery, and Owners shall on redelivery (whether it occurs at the end of the charter period or on the earlier termination of this charter) accept and pay for all bunkers remaining on board, at the then-current market prices at the port of delivery or redelivery, as the case may be, or if such prices are not available payment shall be at the then-current market prices at the nearest port at which such prices are available; provided that if delivery or redelivery does not take place in a port payment shall be at the price paid at the vessel's last port of bunkering before delivery or redelivery, as the case may be. Owners shall give Charterers the use and benefit of any fuel contracts they may have in force from time to time, if so required by Charterers, provided suppliers agree.

Stevedores, Pilots, Tugs

16. Stevedores when required shall be employed and paid by Charterers, but this shall not relieve Owners from responsibility at all times for proper stowage, which must be controlled by the master who shall keep a strict account of all cargo loaded and discharged. Owners hereby indemnify Charterers, their servants and agents against all losses, claims, responsibilities and liabilities arising in any way whatsoever from the employment of pilots, tugboats or stevedores, who although employed by Charterers shall be deemed to be the servants of and in the service of Owners and under their instructions (even if such pilots, tugboat personnel or stevedores are in fact the servants of Charterers their agents or any affiliated company); provided, however, that
(i) the foregoing indemnity shall not exceed the amount to which Owners would have been entitled to limit their liability if they had themselves employed such pilots, tugboats or stevedores, and
(ii) Charterers shall be liable for any damage to the vessel caused by or arising out of the use of stevedores, fair wear and tear excepted, to the extent that Owners are unable by the exercise of due diligence to obtain redress therefor from stevedores.

Supernumeraries

17. Charterers may send representatives in the vessel's available accommodation upon any voyage made under this charter, Owners finding provisions and all requisites as supplied to officers, except liquors, Charterers paying at the rate of   per day for each representative while on board the vessel.

Sub-letting

18. Charterers may sub-let the vessel, but shall always remain responsible to Owners for due fulfilment of this charter.

Final Voyage

19. If when a payment of hire is due hereunder Charterers reasonably expect to redeliver the vessel before the next payment of hire would fall due, the hire to be paid shall be assessed on Charterers' reasonable estimate of the time necessary to complete Charterers' programme up to redelivery, and from which estimate Charterers may deduct amounts due or reasonably expected to become due for
(i) disbursements on Owners' behalf or charges for Owners' account pursuant to any provision hereof, and
(ii) bunkers on board at redelivery pursuant to Clause 15.
Promptly after redelivery any overpayment shall be refunded by Owners or any underpayment made good by Charterers.
If at the time this charter would otherwise terminate in accordance with Clause 4 the vessel is on a ballast voyage to a port of redelivery or is upon a laden voyage, Charterers shall continue to have the use of the vessel at the same rate and conditions as stand herein for as long as necessary to complete such ballast voyage, or to complete such laden voyage and return to a port of redelivery as provided by this charter, as the case may be.

Loss of Vessel

20. Should the vessel be lost, this charter shall terminate and hire shall cease at noon on the day of her loss; should the vessel be a constructive total loss, this charter shall terminate and hire shall cease at noon on the day on which the vessel's underwriters agree that the vessel is a constructive total loss; should the vessel be missing, this charter shall terminate and hire shall cease at noon on the day on which she was last heard of. Any hire paid in advance and not earned shall be returned to Charterers and Owners shall reimburse Charterers for the value of the estimated quantity of bunkers on board at the time of termination, at the price paid by Charterers at the last bunkering port.

Off-hire

21. (a) On each and every occasion that there is loss of time (whether by way of interruption in the vessel's service or, from reduction in the vessel's performance, or in any other manner)
   (i) due to deficiency of personnel or stores; repairs; gas-freeing for repairs; time in and waiting to enter drydock for repairs; breakdown (whether partial or total) of machinery, boilers or other parts of the vessel or her equipment (including without limitation tank coatings); overhaul, maintenance or survey; collision, stranding, accident or damage to the vessel; or any other similar cause preventing the efficient working of the vessel; and such loss continues for more than three consecutive hours (if resulting from interruption in the vessel's service) or cumulates to more than three hours (if resulting from partial loss of service); or
   (ii) due to industrial action, refusal to sail, breach of orders or neglect of duty on the part of the master, officers or crew; or
   (iii) for the purpose of obtaining medical advice or treatment for or landing any sick or injured person (other than a Charterers' representative carried under Clause 17 hereof) or for the purpose of landing the body of any person (other than a Charterers' representative), and such loss continues for more than three consecutive hours; or
   (iv) due to any delay in quarantine arising from the master, officers or crew having had communication with the shore at any infected area without the written consent or instructions of Charterers or their agents, or to any detention by customs or other authorities caused by smuggling or other infraction of local law on the part of the master, officers, or crew; or
   (v) due to detention of the vessel by authorities at home or abroad attributable to legal action against or breach of regulations by the vessel, the vessel's owners, or Owners (unless brought about by the act or neglect of Charterers); then
   without prejudice to Charterers' rights under Clause 3 or to any other rights of Charterers hereunder or otherwise the vessel shall be off-hire from the commencement of such loss of time until she is again ready and in an efficient state to resume her service from a position not less favourable to Charterers than that at which such loss of time commenced; provided, however, that any service given or distance made good by the vessel whilst off-hire shall be taken into account in assessing the amount to be deducted from hire.
   (b) If the vessel fails to proceed at any guaranteed speed pursuant to Clause 24, and such failure arises wholly or partly from any of the causes set out in Clause 21(a) above, then the period for which the vessel shall be off-hire under this Clause 21 shall be the difference between
   (i) the time the vessel would have required to perform the relevant service at such guaranteed speed, and
   (ii) the time actually taken to perform such service (including any loss of time arising from interruption in the performance of such service).
   For the avoidance of doubt, all time included under (ii) above shall be excluded from any computation under Clause 24.
   (c) Further and without prejudice to the foregoing, in the event of the vessel deviating (which expression includes without limitation putting back, or putting into any port other than that to which she is bound under the instructions of Charterers) for any cause or purpose mentioned in Clause 21(a), the vessel shall be off-hire from the commencement of such deviation until the time when she is again ready and in an efficient state to resume her service from a position not less favourable to Charterers than that at which the deviation commenced, provided, however, that any service given or distance made good by the vessel whilst so off-hire shall be taken into account in assessing the amount to be deducted from hire. If the vessel, for any cause or purpose mentioned in Clause 21(a), puts into any port other than the port to which she is bound on the instructions of Charterers, the port charges, pilotage and other expenses at such port shall be borne by Owners. Should the vessel be driven into any port or anchorage by stress of weather hire shall continue to be due and payable during any time lost thereby.
   (d) If the vessel's flag state becomes engaged in hostilities, and Charterers in consequence of such hostilities find it commercially impracticable to employ the vessel and have given Owners written notice thereof then from the date of receipt by Owners of such notice until the termination of such commercial impracticability the vessel shall be off-hire and Owners shall have the right to employ the vessel on their own account.
   (e) Time during which the vessel is off-hire under this charter shall count as part of the charter period.

Periodical Drydocking

22. (a) Owners have the right and obligation to drydock the vessel at regular intervals of drydock the vessel, not less than
   On each occasion Owners shall propose to Charterers a date on which they wish to before such date, and Charterers shall offer a port for

such periodical drydocking and shall take all reasonable steps to make the vessel available as near to such date as practicable.

Owners shall put the vessel in drydock at their expense as soon as practicable after Charterers place the vessel at Owners' disposal clear of cargo other than tank washings and residues. Owners shall be responsible for and pay for the disposal into reception facilities of such tank washings and residues and shall have the right to retain any monies received therefor, without prejudice to any claim for loss of cargo under any bill of lading or this charter.

(b) If a periodical drydocking is carried out in the port offered by Charterers (which must have suitable accommodation for the purpose and reception facilities for tank washings and residues), the vessel shall be off-hire from the time she arrives at such port until drydocking is completed and she is in every way ready to resume Charterers' service and is at the position at which she went off-hire or a position no less favourable to Charterers, whichever she first attains. However,

(i) provided that Owners exercise due diligence in gas-freeing, any time lost in gas-freeing to the standard required for entry into drydock for cleaning and painting the hull shall not count as off-hire, whether lost on passage to the drydocking port or after arrival there (notwithstanding Clause 21), and

(ii) any additional time lost in further gas-freeing to meet the standard required for hot work or entry to cargo tanks shall count as off-hire, whether lost on passage to the drydocking port or after arrival there.

Any time which, but for sub-Clause (i) above, would be off-hire, shall not be included in any calculation under Clause 24.

The expenses of gas-freeing, including without limitation the cost of bunkers, shall be for Owners account.

(c) If Owners require the vessel, instead of proceeding to the offered port, to carry out periodical drydocking at a special port selected by them, the vessel shall be off-hire from the time when she is released to proceed to the special port until she next presents for loading in accordance with Charterers' instructions, provided, however, that Charterers shall credit Owners with the time which would have been taken on passage at the service speed had the vessel not proceeded to drydock. All fuel consumed shall be paid for by Owners but Charterers shall credit Owners with the value of the fuel which would have been used on such notional passage calculated at the guaranteed daily consumption for the service speed, and shall further credit Owners with any benefit they may gain in purchasing bunkers at the special port.

(d) Charterers shall, insofar as cleaning for periodical drydocking may have reduced the amount of tank-cleaning necessary to meet Charterers' requirements, credit Owners with the value of any bunkers which Charterers calculate to have been saved thereby, whether the vessel drydocks at an offered or a special port.

Ship Inspection

23. Charterers shall have the right at any time during the charter period to make such inspection of the vessel as they may consider necessary. This right may be exercised as often and at such intervals as Charterers in their absolute discretion may determine and whether the vessel is in port or on passage. Owners affording all necessary co-operation and accommodation on board provided, however,

(i) that neither the exercise nor the non-exercise, nor anything done or not done in the exercise or non-exercise, by Charterers of such right shall in any way reduce the master's or Owners' authority over, or responsibility to Charterers or third parties for, the vessel and every aspect of her operation, nor increase Charterers' responsibilities to Owners or third parties for the same; and

(ii) that Charterers shall not be liable for any act, neglect or default by themselves, their servants or agents in the exercise or non-exercise of the aforesaid right.

Detailed Description and Performance

24. (a) Owners guarantee that the speed and consumption of the vessel shall be as follows: -

Average speed in knots	Maximum average bunker consumption	
	main propulsion – fuel oil/diesel oil tonnes	auxiliaries fuel oil/diesel oil tonnes
Laden		

The foregoing bunker consumptions are for all purposes except cargo heating and tank cleaning and shall be pro-rated between the speeds shown.

The service speed of the vessel is   knots laden and   knots in ballast and in the absence of Charterers' orders to the contrary the vessel shall proceed at the service speed. However if more than one laden and one ballast speed are shown in the table above Charterers shall have the right to order the vessel to steam at any speed within the range set out in the table (the "ordered speed").

If the vessel is ordered to proceed at any speed other than the highest speed shown in the table, and the average speed actually attained by the vessel during the currency of such order exceeds such ordered speed plus 0.5 knots (the "maximum recognised speed"), then for the purpose of calculating any increase or decrease of hire under this Clause 24 the maximum recognised speed shall be used in place of the average speed actually attained.

For the purposes of this charter the "guaranteed speed" at any time shall be the then-current ordered speed or the service speed, as the case may be

The average speeds and bunker consumptions shall for the purposes of this Clause 24 be calculated by reference to the observed distance from pilot station to pilot station on all sea passages during each period stipulated in Clause 24(c), but excluding any time during which the vessel is (or but for Clause 22(b) (i) would be) off-hire and also excluding "Adverse Weather Periods", being (i) any periods during which reduction of speed is necessary for safety in congested waters or in poor visibility (ii) any days, noon to noon, when winds exceed force 8 on the Beaufort Scale for more than 12 hours.

(b) If during any year from the date on which the vessel enters service (anniversary to anniversary) the vessel falls below or exceeds the performance guaranteed in Clause 24(a) then if any shortfall or excess results

(i) from a reduction or an increase in the average speed of the vessel, compared to the speed guaranteed in Clause 24(a), then an amount equal to the value at the hire rate of the time so lost or gained, as the case may be, shall be deducted from or added to the hire paid;

(ii) from an increase or a decrease in the total bunkers consumed, compared to the total bunkers which would have been consumed had the vessel performed as guaranteed in Clause 24(a), an amount equivalent to the value of the additional bunkers consumed or the bunkers saved, as the case may be, based on the average price paid by Charterers for the vessel's bunkers in such period, shall be deducted from or added to the hire paid.

The addition to or deduction from hire so calculated for laden and ballast mileage respectively shall be adjusted to take into account the mileage steamed in each such condition during Adverse Weather Periods, by dividing such addition or deduction by the number of miles over which the performance has been calculated and multiplying by the same number of miles plus the miles steamed during the Adverse Weather Periods, in order to establish the total addition to or deduction from hire to be made for such period.

Reduction of hire under the foregoing sub-Clause (b) shall be without prejudice to any other remedy available to Charterers.

(c) Calculations under this Clause 24 shall be made for the yearly periods terminating on each successive anniversary of the date on which the vessel enters service, and for the period between the last such anniversary and the date of termination of this charter if less than a year. Claims in respect of reduction of hire arising under this Clause during the final year or part year of the charter period shall in the first instance be settled in accordance with Charterers' estimate made two months before the end of the charter period. Any necessary adjustment after this charter terminates shall be made by payment by Owners to Charterers or by Charterers to Owners as the case may require.

Payments in respect of increase of hire arising under this Clause shall be made promptly after receipt by Charterers of all the information necessary to calculate such increase.

Salvage

25. Subject to the provisions of Clause 21 hereof, all loss of time and all expenses (excluding any damage to or loss of the vessel or tortious liabilities to third parties) incurred in saving or attempting to save life or in successful or unsuccessful attempts at salvage shall be borne equally by Owners and Charterers provided that Charterers shall not be liable to contribute towards any salvage payable by Owners arising in any way out of services rendered under this Clause 25.

All salvage and all proceeds from derelicts shall be divided equally between Owners and Charterers after deducting the master's, officers' and crew's share.

Lien

26. Owners shall have a lien upon all cargoes and all freights, sub-freights and demurrage for any amounts due under this charter: and Charterers shall have a lien on the vessel for all monies paid in advance and not earned, and for all claims for damages arising from any breach by Owners of this charter.

Exceptions

27. (a) The vessel, her master and Owners shall not, unless otherwise in this charter expressly provided, be liable for any loss or damage or delay or failure arising or resulting from any act, neglect or default of the master, pilots, mariners or other servants of Owners in the navigation or management of the vessel; fire, unless caused by the actual fault or privity of Owners; collision or stranding; dangers and accidents of the sea; explosion, bursting of boilers, breakage of shafts or any latent defect in hull, equipment or machinery; provided, however, that Clauses 1, 2, 3 and 24 hereof shall be unaffected by the foregoing. Further, neither the vessel, her master or Owners, nor Charterers shall, unless otherwise in this charter expressly provided, be liable for any loss or damage

SHELLTIME FORM 31

or delay or failure in performance hereunder arising or resulting from act of God, act of war, seizure under legal process, quarantine restrictions, strikes, lock-outs, riots, restraints of labour, civil commotions or arrest or restraint of princes, rulers or people.

    (b) The vessel shall have liberty to sail with or without pilots, to tow or go to the assistance of vessels in distress and to deviate for the purpose of saving life or property.

    (c) Clause 27(a) shall not apply to or affect any liability of Owners or the vessel or any other relevant person in respect of

        (i) loss or damage caused to any berth, jetty, dock, dolphin, buoy, mooring line, pipe or crane or other works or equipment whatsoever at or near any place to which the vessel may proceed under this charter, whether or not such works or equipment belong to Charterers, or

        (ii) any claim (whether brought by Charterers or any other person) arising out of any loss of or damage to or in connection with cargo. All such claims shall be subject to the Hague-Visby Rules or the Hague Rules, as the case may be, which ought pursuant to Clause 38 hereof to have been incorporated in the relevant bill of lading (whether or not such Rules were so incorporated) or, if no such bill of lading is issued, to the Hague-Visby Rules.

    (d) In particular and without limitation, the foregoing subsections (a) and (b) of this Clause shall not apply to or in any way affect any provision in this charter relating to off-hire or to reduction of hire.

Injurious Cargoes

    28. No acids, explosives or cargoes injurious to the vessel shall be shipped and without prejudice to the foregoing any damage to the vessel caused by the shipment of any such cargo, and the time taken to repair such damage, shall be for Charterers' account. No voyage shall be undertaken, nor any goods or cargoes loaded, that would expose the vessel to capture or seizure by rulers or governments.

Grade of Bunkers

    29. Charterers shall supply marine diesel oil/fuel oil with a maximum viscosity of   Centistokes at 50 degrees Centigrade/ACGFO for main propulsion and diesel oil/ACGFO for the auxiliaries. If Owners require the vessel to be supplied with more essential bunkers they shall be liable for the extra cost thereof.

    Charterers warrant that all bunkers provided by them in accordance herewith shall be of a quality complying with the International Marine Bunker Supply Terms and Conditions of Shell International Trading Company and with its specification for marine fuels as amended from time to time.

Disbursements

    30. Should the master require advances for ordinary disbursements at any port, Charterers or their agents shall make such advances to him, in consideration of which Owners shall pay a commission of two and a half per cent. and all such advances and commission shall be deducted from hire.

Laying up

    31. Charterers shall have the option, after consultation with Owners, of requiring Owners to lay up the vessel at a safe place nominated by Charterers, in which case the hire provided for under this charter shall be adjusted to reflect any net increases in expenditure reasonably incurred or any net saving which should reasonably be made by Owners as a result of such lay-up. Charterers may exercise the said option any number of times during the charter period.

Requisition

    32. Should the vessel be requisitioned by any government, de facto or de jure, during the period of this charter, the vessel shall be off-hire during the period of such requisition, and any hire paid by such government in respect of such requisition period shall be for Owners' account. Any such requisition period shall count as part of the charter period.

Outbreak of War

    33. If war or hostilities break out between any two or more of the following countries: U.S.A., U.S.S.R., P.R.C., U.K., Netherlands – both Owners and Charterers shall have the right to cancel this charter.

Additional War Expenses

    34. If the vessel is ordered to trade in areas where there is war (de facto or de jure) or threat of war, Charterers shall reimburse Owners for any additional insurance premia, crew bonuses and other expenses which are reasonably incurred by Owners as a consequence of such orders, provided that Charterers are given notice of such expenses as soon as practicable and in any event before such expenses are incurred, and provided further that Owners obtain from their insurers a waiver of any subrogated rights against Charterers in respect of any claims by Owners under their war risk insurance arising out of compliance with such orders.

War Risks

35. (a) The master shall not be required or bound to sign bills of lading for any place which in his or Owners' reasonable opinion is dangerous or impossible for the vessel to enter or reach owing to any blockade, war, hostilities, warlike operations, civil war, civil commotions or revolutions.

(b) If in the reasonable opinion of the master or Owners it becomes, for any of the reasons set out in Clause 35(a) or by the operation of international law, dangerous, impossible or prohibited for the vessel to reach or enter, or to load or discharge cargo at, any place to which the vessel has been ordered pursuant to this charter (a "place of peril"), then Charterers or their agents shall be immediately notified by telex or radio messages, and Charterers shall thereupon have the right to order the cargo, or such part of it as may be affected, to be loaded or discharged, as the case may be, at any other place within the trading limits of this charter (provided such other place is not itself a place of peril). If any place of discharge is or becomes a place of peril, and no orders have been received from Charterers or their agents within 48 hours after dispatch of such messages, then Owners shall be at liberty to discharge the cargo or such part of it as may be affected at any place which they or the master may in their or his discretion select within the trading limits of this charter and such discharge shall be deemed to be due fulfilment of Owners' obligations under this charter so far as cargo so discharged is concerned.

(c) The vessel shall have liberty to comply with any directions or recommendations as to departure, arrival, routes, ports of call, stoppages, destinations, zones, waters, delivery or in any other wise whatsoever given by the government of the state under whose flag the vessel sails or any other government or local authority or by any person or body acting or purporting to act as or with the authority of any such government or local authority including any de facto government or local authority or by any person or body acting or purporting to act as or with the authority of any such government or local authority or by any committee or person having under the terms of the war risks insurance on the vessel the right to give any such directions or recommendations. If by reason of or in compliance with any such directions or recommendations anything is done or is not done, such shall not be deemed a deviation.

If by reason of or in compliance with any such direction or recommendation the vessel does not proceed to any place of discharge to which she has been ordered pursuant to this charter, the vessel may proceed to any place which the master or Owners in his or their discretion select and there discharge the cargo or such part of it as may be affected. Such discharge shall be deemed to be due fulfilment of Owners' obligations under this charter so far as cargo so discharged is concerned.

Charterers shall procure that all bills of lading issued under this charter shall contain the Chamber of Shipping War Risks Clause 1952.

Both to Blame Collision Clause

36. If the liability for any collision in which the vessel is involved while performing this charter falls to be determined in accordance with the laws of the United States of America, the following provision shall apply:

"If the ship comes into collision with another ship as a result of the negligence of the other ship and any act, neglect or default of the master, mariner, pilot or the servants of the carrier in the navigation or in the management of the ship, the owners of the cargo carried hereunder will indemnify the carrier against all loss, or liability to the other or non-carrying ship or her owners in so far as such loss or liability represents loss of, or damage to, or any claim whatsoever of the owners of the said cargo, paid or payable by the other or non-carrying ship or her owners as part of their claim against the carrying ship or carrier."

"The foregoing provisions shall also apply where the owners, operators or those in charge of any ship or ships or objects other than, or in addition to, the colliding ships or objects are at fault in respect of a collision or contact."

Charterers shall procure that all bills of lading issued under this charter shall contain a provision in the foregoing terms to be applicable where the liability for any collision in which the vessel is involved falls to be determined in accordance with the laws of the United States of America.

New Jason Clause

37. General average contributions shall be payable according to the York/Antwerp Rules, 1974, and shall be adjusted in London in accordance with English law and practice but should adjustment be made in accordance with the law and practice of the United States of America, the following provision shall apply:

"In the event of accident, danger, damage or disaster before or after the commencement of the voyage, resulting from any cause whatsoever, whether due to negligence or not, for which, or for the consequence of which, the carrier is not responsible by statute, contract or otherwise, the cargo, shippers, consignees or owners of the cargo shall contribute with the carrier in general average to the payment of any sacrifices, losses or expenses of a general average nature that may be made or incurred and shall pay salvage and special charges incurred in respect of the cargo."

"If a salving ship is owned or operated by the carrier, salvage shall be paid for as fully as if the said salving ship or ships belonged to strangers. Such deposit as the carrier or his agents may deem sufficient to cover the estimated contribution of the cargo and any salvage and special charges thereon shall, if required, be made by the cargo, shippers, consignees or owners of the cargo to the carrier before delivery."

Charterers shall procure that all bills of lading issued under this charter shall contain a provision in the foregoing terms, to be applicable where adjustment of general average is made in accordance with the laws and practice of the United States of America.

SHELLTIME FORM 33

Clause Paramount

38. Charterers shall procure that all bills of lading issued pursuant to this charter shall contain the following clause:

"(1) Subject to sub-clause (2) hereof, this bill of lading shall be governed by, and have effect subject to, the rules contained in the International Convention for the Unification of Certain Rules relating to Bills of Lading signed at Brussels on 25th August 1924 (hereafter the "Hague Rules") as amended by the Protocol signed at Brussels on 23rd February 1968 (hereafter the "Hague-Visby Rules"). Nothing contained herein shall be deemed to be either a surrender by the carrier of any of his rights or immunities or any increase of any of his responsibilities or liabilities under the Hague-Visby Rules."

"(2) If there is governing legislation which applies the Hague Rules compulsorily to this bill of lading, to the exclusion of the Hague-Visby Rules, then this bill of lading shall have effect subject to the Hague Rules. Nothing herein contained shall be deemed to be either a surrender by the carrier of any of his rights or immunities or an increase of any of his responsibilities under the Hague Rules."

"(3) If any term of this bill of lading is repugnant to the Hague-Visby Rules, or Hague Rules if applicable, such term shall be void to that extent but no further."

"(4) Nothing in this bill of lading shall be construed as in any way restricting, excluding or waiving the right of any relevant party or person to limit his liability under any available legislation and/or law."

TOVALOP

39. Owners warrant that the vessel is:
(i) a tanker in TOVALOP and
(ii) properly entered in   P & I Club

and will so remain during the currency of this charter.

When an escape or discharge of Oil occurs from the vessel and causes or threatens to cause Pollution Damage, or when there is the threat of an escape or discharge of Oil (i.e. a grave and imminent danger of the escape or discharge of Oil which, if it occurred, would create a serious danger of Pollution Damage, whether or not an escape or discharge in fact subsequently occurs), then Charterers may, at their option, upon notice to Owners or master, undertake such measures as are reasonably necessary to prevent or minimise such Pollution Damage or to remove the Threat, unless Owners promptly undertake the same. Charterers shall keep Owners advised of the nature and result of any such measures taken by them and, if time permits, the nature of the measures intended to be taken by them. Any of the aforementioned measures taken by Charterers shall be deemed taken on Owners' authority as Owners' agent, and shall be at Owners' expense except to the extent that:

(1) any such escape or discharge or Threat was caused or contributed to by Charterers, or

(2) by reason of the exceptions set out in Article III, paragraph 2, of the 1969 International Convention on Civil Liability for Oil Pollution Damage, Owners are or, had the said Convention applied to such escape or discharge or to the Threat, would have been exempt from liability for the same, or

(3) the cost of such measures together with all other liabilities, costs and expenses of Owners arising out of or in connection with such escape or discharge or Threat exceeds one hundred and sixty United States Dollars (US $160) per ton of the vessel's Tonnage or sixteen million eight hundred thousand United States Dollars (US $16,800,000), whichever is the lesser, save and insofar as Owners shall be entitled to recover such excess under either the 1971 International Convention on the Establishment of an International Fund for Compensation for Oil Pollution Damage or under CRISTAL;

PROVIDED ALWAYS that if Owners in their absolute discretion consider said measures should be discontinued, Owners shall so notify Charterers and thereafter Charterers shall have no right to continue said measures under the provisions of this Clause 39 and all further liability to Charterers under this Clause 39 shall thereupon cease.

The above provisions are not in derogation of such other rights as Charterers or Owners may have under this charter or may otherwise have or acquire by law or any International Convention or TOVALOP.

The term "TOVALOP" means the Tanker Owners' Voluntary Agreement Concerning Liability for Oil Pollution dated 7th January 1969, as amended from time to time, and the term "CRISTAL" means the Contract Regarding an Interim Supplement to Tanker Liability for Oil Pollution dated 14th January 1971, as amended from time to time. The terms "Oil", "Pollution Damage", and "Tonnage" shall for the purposes of this Clause 39 have the meanings ascribed to them in TOVALOP.

Export Restrictions

40. The master shall not be required or bound to sign bills of lading for the carriage of cargo to any place to which export of such cargo is prohibited under the laws, rules or regulations of the country in which the cargo was produced and/or shipped.

Charterers shall procure that all bills of lading issued under this charter shall contain the following clause:

"If any laws rules or regulations applied by the government of the country in which the cargo was produced and/or shipped, or any relevant agency thereof, impose a prohibition on export of the cargo to the place of discharge designated in or ordered under this bill of lading, carriers shall be entitled to require cargo owners forthwith to nominate an alternative discharge place for the discharge of the cargo, or such part of it as may be affected, which alternative place shall not be subject to the prohibition, and carriers shall be entitled to accept orders from cargo owners to proceed to and discharge at such alternative place. If cargo owners fail to nominate an alternative, place within 72 hours after they or their agents have received from carriers notice of such prohibition, carriers shall be at liberty to discharge the cargo or such part of it as may be affected by the prohibition at any safe place on which they or the master may in their or his absolute discretion decide and which is not subject to the prohibition, and such discharge shall constitute due performance of the contract contained in this bill of lading so far as the cargo so discharged is concerned".

The foregoing provision shall apply mutatis mutandis to this charter, the references to a bill of lading being deemed to be references to this charter.

Law and Litigation

41. (a) This charter shall be construed and the relations between the parties determined in accordance with the laws of England.

(b) Any dispute arising under this charter shall be decided by the English Courts to whose jurisdiction the parties hereby agree.

(c) Notwithstanding the foregoing, but without prejudice to any party's right to arrest or maintain the arrest of any maritime property, either party may, by giving written notice of election to the other party, elect to have any such dispute referred to the arbitration of a single arbitrator in London in accordance with the provisions of the Arbitration Act 1950, or any statutory modification or re-enactment thereof for the time being in force.

   (i) A party shall lose its right to make such an election only if:
       (a) it receives from the other party a written notice of dispute which –
           (1) states expressly that a dispute has arisen out of this charter;
           (2) specifies the nature of the dispute; and
           (3) refers expressly to this clause 41(c)
       and
       (b) it fails to give notice of election to have the dispute referred to arbitration not later than 30 days from the date of receipt of such notice of dispute.
   (ii) The parties hereby agree that either party may –
       (a) appeal to the High Court on any question of law arising out of an award;
       (b) apply to the High Court for an order that the arbitrator state the reasons for his award;
       (c) give notice to the arbitrator that a reasoned award is required; and
       (d) apply to the High Court to determine any question of law arising in the course of the reference.

(d) It shall be a condition precedent to the right of any party to a stay of any legal proceedings in which maritime property has been, or may be, arrested in connection with a dispute under this charter, that that party furnishes to the other party security to which that other party would have been entitled in such legal proceedings in the absence of a stay.

Construction

42. The side headings have been included in this charter for convenience of reference and shall in no way affect the construction hereof.

STB FORM 35

CODE WORD FOR THIS CHARTER PARTY
STB TIME

....
Vessel Name

TANKER TIME CHARTER PARTY

....
Place   Date

IT IS THIS DAY MUTUALLY AGREED between ....
....
as Owner/Chartered Owner (herein called "Owner") of the ....
.... (herein called "Vessel") and
....
(herein called "Charterer") that the Owner lets and the Charterer hires the use and services of the Vessel for the carriage of .... , in bulk, and such other lawful merchandise as may be suitable for a vessel of her description, for the period and on the terms and conditions hereinafter set forth.

TERM

1. (a) The term of this Charter shall be for a period of about .... (hereinafter "Original Period") plus any extensions thereof as provided in (b) below. The Original Period shall commence at the time when the Vessel is placed at the Charterer's disposal as provided in Clause 5. The word "about" as used above shall mean "14 days more or less" and shall apply to the term of this Charter consisting of the Original Period plus any extensions as hereinafter provided.

EXTENSIONS

(b) Charterer shall have the option of extending the term of this Charter for a period of .... (hereinafter "Extended Period") by written notice to Owner at least 30 days previous to the expiration of the Original Period. The term of this Charter may be extended by Charterer also for periods (hereinafter "Off/Hire Extensions") of all or any part of the time the Vessel is off hire during the Original Period and/or Extended Period, if any, by giving written notice to Owner at least 30 days before the expiration of the Original Period or Extended Period, as the case may be, and, if Charterer so elects and gives a further written notice to Owner at least 30 days before the expiration of any such Off-Hire Extension, all or any part of the time the Vessel is off hire following the previous notice shall be added to the term of this Charter.

VESSEL PARTICULARS

2. The following are particulars and capacities of the Vessel and her equipment:
A. **Cargo Carrying Capacity**
   I. Total cargo tank capacity when 100% full .... US Barrels
   II. Weight of stores, etc., permanently
       deducted from cargo carrying capacity .... L.T.
   III. a. Fresh water consumption per day .... L.T.
        b. Capacity of evaporators per day .... L.T.
        c. Quantity of fresh water deductible
           from cargo carrying capacity on a
           daily basis .... L.T.
   IV. Estimated loss of cargo carrying capacity due
       to "sag" when fully loaded with light, medium,
       heavy cargo
                            Light   .... L.T.
                            Medium   .... L.T.
                            Heavy   .... L.T.

V. The Vessel can carry .... tons (of 2,240 lbs.) total deadweight (as   42
   certified by Classification Society) of cargo, bunkers, water, and stores on an assigned   43
   summer mean draft of ....ft......................in. and an assigned freeboard of   44
   .... ft............................ in.   45
B. **Other Tank Capacities**   46
   I. Total capacity of fuel tanks for propulsion   .... US Barrels   47
   II. Total capacity of fresh water tanks   .... L.T.   48
   III. Total capacity of segregated ballast tanks   .... L.T.   49
C. **Capacity of Pumps**   50
   I. Cargo Pumps   51
      a. Number   52
      b. Make   53
      c. Type   54
      d. Design rated capacity of each pump in   55
         U.S. Barrels per hour and corresponding   .... US Bbls/Hr.   56
         head in feet   .... Feet/Head   57
   II. Stripping Pumps   58
      a. Number   59
      b. Design capacity of each pump in U.S.   60
         Barrels per hour for the guaranteed   .... US Bbls/Hr.   61
         discharge head of   .... Feet/Head   62
   III. Segregated Ballast Pumps   63
      a. Number   64
      b. Design capacity each pump   .... US Bbls/Hr.   65
D. **Cargo Loading/Discharge Manifold**   66
   The whole manifold is made of steel or comparable material and is strengthened and supported   67
   to avoid damage from loading and discharge equipment and to withstand a maximum load from   68
   any direction equivalent to the safe working load of the cargo hose lifting equipment.   69
   I. a. Number of manifold connections   70
      b. Diameter of manifold connections   71
      c. Distance from centers of manifold connections   72
      d. Distance from manifold connections to ship's side   73
      e. Distance center of manifold connection to deck   74
      f. Distance bow/center of manifold   75
      g. Safe working load of cargo hose lifting equipment .... tons.   76
   II. Cargo Manifold Reducing Pieces   77
      Vessels from 16 to 60 MDWT are equipped with a sufficient number of cargo manifold   78
      reducing pieces of steel or a comparable material to permit presenting of flanges of 8", 10"   79
      and 12" (ASA) cargo hoses/arms at all manifold connections on one side of the vessel.   80
      Vessels over 60 MDWT are equipped with a sufficient number of cargo manifold reducing   81
      pieces of steel or a comparable material to premit presenting of flanges of 10", 12" and 16"   82
      (ASA) cargo hose/arms at all manifold connections on one side of the vessel.   83
E. **Heating Coils**   84
   I. Type of coils and material of which manufactured   85
   II. Ratio heating surface/volume   86
      a. Center Tanks   Ft.^{2}/40 Ft.^{3} 87
      b. Wing Tanks   Ft.^{2}/40 Ft.^{3} 88
F. **Cargo Loading/Performance**   89
   Vessel can load homogeneous cargo at maximum rate of .... B/H.   90
G. **Vessel Particulars**   91
   I. Length overall .... ft .... In.   92
   II. Fully loaded summer draft in salt water of a density of 1.025   93
      ....ft........................inches on an assigned freeboard of   94
   III. Fresh Water allowance.............................. In.   95
   IV. Light ship draft   Forward .... Ft .... In.   96
                           Aft .... Ft .... In.   97
                           Mean .... Ft .... In.   98
   V. Moulded Depth   99
   VI. Light ship freeboard............................Ft........................ In.   100
   VII. TPI on light ship draft   101
   VIII. TPI on summer draft   102
   IX. Extreme beam   103
   X. Gross Reg. Tons   104
   XI. Net Reg. Tons   105
   XII. Suez Canal Tonnage   106
   XIII. Panama Canal Tonnage   107
   XIV. Flag of Registry   108
   XV. Call letters   109
   XVI. Classification Society   110
   XVII. Maximum bunkers aboard when vessel is placed at Charterer's disposal to be   111
        112

XVIII. Owner shall provide Charterer with copies of the Vessel's plans upon Charterer's request therefor, provided, in the case of a newbuilding, that Owner need not provide same until such plans are available to him from the building yard.

XIX. Vessel is equipped with a fresh water evaporator which will be maintained in good operating condition. Owners warrant that this evaporator is capable of making sufficient fresh water to supply the vessel's needs.

XX. Owner warrants vessel is capable of heating cargo to 135°F. and of maintaining same throughout entire discharge. Should vessel fail to heat cargo in accordance with Charterer's instructions, Charterer shall have the option to:
 a) Delay discharge of the cargo
 b) Delay berthing of the Vessel
 c) Discontinue discharge and remove vessel from berth until cargo is heated in accordance with Charterer's instructions.
All time lost to be considered as off-hire and for Owner's account. In addition any expenses incurred in moving vessel from berth will be for Owner's account.

HIRE

3. (a) The Charterer shall pay hire for the use of the Vessel at the rate of .... in .... currency per ton (of 2,240 lbs.) on Vessel's deadweight as shown in Clause 2. A. per calendar month, payment to be made in advance monthly at .... by check without discount commencing with the date and hour the Vessel is placed at Charterer's disposal hereunder and continuing to the date and hour when the Vessel is released to Owner at the expiration of this Charter except as otherwise expressed in this Charter. Any hire paid in advance and not earned shall be returned to the Charterer at once. In no event will initial payment of hire be made until Charter Party is signed and Vessel placed at Charterer's disposal as herein provided.

DEDUCTIONS

(b) The Charterer shall be entitled to deduct from hire payments: (1) any disbursements for Owner's account and any advances to the Master or Owner's agents, including commissions thereon, (2) layup savings calculated in accordance with Clause 17, (3) any previous overpayments of hire including offhire and including any overpayments of hire concerning which a bona fide dispute may exist but in the latter event the Charterer shall furnish an adequate bank guarantee or other good and sufficient security on request of the Owner, (4) any Clause 8 and 9 claims, and (5) any other sums to which Charterer is entitled under this charter. The Charterer shall be entitled to $2\frac{1}{2}\%$ commission on any sums advanced or disbursements made for the Owner's account. However, the Owner shall have the option of making advances to the Charterer or its designated agent for disbursements (provided such advances are deemed adequate and reasonable by the Charterer), and, in such event, no commissions shall be paid.

FINAL VOYAGE

(c) Should the Vessel be on her final voyage at the time a payment of hire becomes due, said payment shall be made for the time estimated by Charterer to be necessary to complete the voyage and effect release of the Vessel to Owner, less all deductions provided for in sub-paragraph (b) of this Clause which shall be estimated by Charterer if the actual amounts have not been received and also less the amount estimated by Charterer to become payable by the Owner for fuel and water on release as provided in Clause 19. (b). Upon redelivery any difference between the estimated and actual amounts shall be refunded to or paid by the Charterer as the case may require.

LOSS OF VESSEL

(d) Should the Vessel be lost or be missing and presumed lost, hire shall cease at the time of her loss or, if such time is unknown, at the time when the Vessel was last heard of. If the Vessel should become a constructive total loss, hire shall cease at the time of the casualty resulting in such loss. In either case, any hire paid in advance and not earned shall be returned to the Charterer. If the Vessel should be off hire or missing when a payment of hire would otherwise be due, such payment shall be postponed until the off-hire period ceases or the safety of the Vessel is ascertained, as the case may be.

REDUCTION IN HIRE

(e) If the Vessel shall not fulfill the Owner's Warranty or any other part of her description as warranted in Clause 4, Charterer shall be entitled without prejudice to a reduction in the hire to correct for the deficiency and to any other rights the Charterer may have.

DEFAULT

(f) In default of punctual and regular payment as herein specified, the Owner will notify .... at .... whereupon the Charterer shall make payment of the amount due within ten (10) days of receipt of notification from the Owner, failing which the Owner

will have the right to withdraw the Vessel from the service of the Charterer without prejudice to any 169
claim the Owner may otherwise have against the Charterer under this Charter. 170

INCREMENT

(g) The rate of hire set forth in sub-paragraph (a) of this Clause includes an increment of 171
$ .... to cover in full any expenses for Charterer's account for extra victualling 172
by the Master, telephone calls, radio messages, telegrams and cables and all overtime worked by the 173
Vessel's officers and crew at Charterer's request. 174
(h) The rate of charter hire set forth in this Clause 3 is equivalent to $ 175
per hour. 176

WARRANTIES

4. Owner warrants that at the time the Vessel is placed at Charterer's disposal, the Vessel shall 177
fulfill the descriptions, particulars and capabilities set forth in Clause 2 above, and shall be tight, 178
staunch, and strong, in thoroughly efficient order and condition and in every way fit, manned, 179
equipped, and supplied for the service contemplated, with holds, cargo tanks, pipelines, and valves 180
clear, clean, and tight and with pumps, heating coils, and all other equipment in good working order. 181
Such description, particulars, and capabilities of the Vessel shall be maintained by Owner throughout 182
the period of the Vessel's service hereunder so far as possible by the exercise of due diligence. 183

HIRE

5. (a) The use and services of the Vessel shall be placed at the disposal of the Charterer at 184
.... (hereinafter "Port of Delivery") at such readily 185
accessible dock, wharf, or other place as the Charterer may direct. Charter hire shall commence when 186
the Vessel is at such dock, wharf, or place and in all respects ready to perform this Charter and ready 187
for sea and written notice thereof has been given by the Master to the Charterer or its Agents at the 188
Port of Delivery. 189

LAYDAYS

(b) Hire shall not commence before 190
.... , except 191
with Charterer's consent, and the Vessel shall be placed at Charterer's disposal in accordance with 192
the provisions hereof no later than .... in default of which Charterer shall 193
have the option to cancel this Charter declarable not later than the day of the Vessel's readiness. 194
Cancellation by Charterer or acceptance of the use of the Vessel's services shall be without prejudice 195
to any claims for damages Charterer may have for late tender of the Vessel's services. 196

USE OF VESSEL

(c) The whole reach and burthen of the Vessel (but not more than she can reasonably stow 197
and safely carry) shall be at the Charterer's disposal, reserving proper and sufficient space for Vessel's 198
Officers, Crew, Master's cabin, tackle, apparel, furniture, fuel, provisions, and stores. 199

TRADING LIMITS

6. (a) The Vessel may be employed in any part of the World trading between and at ports, 200
places, berths, docks, anchorages, and submarine pipe-lines in such lawful trades as the Charterer or 201
its agents may direct, subject to Institute Warranties and Clauses attached hereto but may be sent to 202
ports and places on the North American Lakes, the St. Lawrence River and tributaries between May 203
15 and November 15 and through the Straits of Magellan and around Cape Horn and The Cape of 204
Good Hope at any time of the year without payment of any extra premium. Notwithstanding the 205
foregoing restrictions, the Vessel may be sent to Baltic Sea ports not North of Stockholm, and to 206
Helsingfors and Abo, Finland, and other ports and places as set forth in the Institute Warranties and 207
Clauses, provided, however, that Charterer shall reimburse Owner for any additional premia properly 208
assessed by Vessel's underwriters and payable by Owner for breach of such trade warranties. 209

BERTHS

(b) The Vessel shall be loaded, discharged, or lightened, at any port, place, berth, dock, 210
anchorage, or submarine line or alongside lighters or lightening vessels as Charterer may direct. 211
Notwithstanding anything contained in this Clause or any other provisions of this Charter, Charterer 212
shall not be deemed to warrant the safety of any port, berth, dock, anchorage, and/or submarine line 213
and shall not be liable for any loss, damage, injury, or delay resulting from conditions at such ports, 214
berths, docks, anchorages, and submarine lines not caused by Charterer's fault or neglect or which 215
could have been avoided by the exercise of reasonable care on the part of the Master or Owner. 216

FUEL

(c) The Charterer shall accept and pay for all fuel in the Vessel's bunkers at the time the 217
vessel is placed at Charterer's disposal not exceeding the maximum quantity in Clause 2 above. 218
Any excess quantity shall be removed by the Owner at its expense before such time unless the 219

Charterer elects to accept such excess at the price determined as hereinafter provided or at such other price as may be mutually agreed. Payment for such fuel shall be in accordance with The Exxon International Contract Price List current for the date when and the port or place where the vessel is placed at Charterer's disposal under the Charter or the nearest port to which such list applies.

CARGO

7. The Charterer shall have the option of shipping any lawful dry cargo in bulk for which the Vessel and her tanks are suitable and any lawful merchandise in cases and/or cans and/or other packages in the Vessel's forehold, 'tween decks, and/or other suitable space available, subject, however, to the Master's approval as to kind and character, amount and stowage. All charges for dunnage, loading, stowing, and discharging so incurred shall be paid by the Charterer.

SPEED, FUEL AND PUMPING WARRANTIES

8. The Owner warrants that the Vessel is capable of maintaining and shall maintain throughout the period of this Charter Party on all sea passages from Seabuoy to Seabuoy a guaranteed average speed under all weather conditions of .... knots in a laden condition and .... knots in ballast (speed will be determined by taking the total miles at sea divided by the total hours at sea as shown in the log books excluding stops at sea and any sea passage covered by an off-hire calculation) on a guaranteed daily consumption of .... tons (of 2,240 lbs.) of Diesel/Bunker C/High Viscosity Fuel Oil maximum .... seconds Redwood No.1 at 100 degrees F. for main engine, and .... tons (of 2,240 lbs.) of Diesel for auxiliaries for propulsion.
For each day that heat is applied to cargo the guaranteed daily consumption is ....bbls. of Diesel/Bunker C/High Viscosity Fuel Oil maximum............................ seconds Redwood No. 1 at 100 degrees F. per tank day. For each hour that tank cleaning is required, the guaranteed consumption is .... bbls. of Diesel/Bunker C/High Viscosity Fuel Oil maximum .... seconds Redwood No.1 at 100 degrees F. per machine hour.
The Charterer is entitled to the full capabilities of the Vessel and the Owner warrants that the Vessel is capable of discharging a cargo of petroleum at the following minimum rates:
Light petroleum (viscosity less than 320 SSU at 100°F.) .... bbls/hr
Medium petroleum (viscosity of 320 to 3200 SSU at 100°F.) .... bbls/hr
Heavy petroleum (viscosity above 3200 SSU at 100°F.) .... bbls/hr
or of maintaining a pressure of 100 PSI at ship's rail should the foregoing minimum rates not be met. Charterer is to be compensated at $ .... per hour or pro rata for each part of an hour that Vessel takes in excess of the pumping rates as stipulated above. The owner understands and agrees that he will receive no credit or compensation if the Vessel is able to discharge at a rate greater than those specified above. Any delay to Vessel's discharge caused by shore conditions shall be taken into account in the assessment of pumping performance. Pumping performance shall be reviewed in accordance with Clause 9.

ADJUSTMENT OF HIRE

9. (a) The speed and consumption guaranteed by the Owner in Clause 8 will be reviewed by the Charterer after three calendar months counting from the time of delivery of the Vessel to the Charterer in accordance with this Charter Party and thereafter at the end of each three (3) calendar month period. If at the end of each twelve (12) calendar month period (or at any time during the term of this charter) it is found that the Vessel has failed to maintain as an average during the preceding twelve (12) calendar month period (or for any other twelve month period during the term of this Charter) the speed and/or consumption warranted, the Charterer shall be retroactively compensated in respect of such failings as follows:
(b) Speed—Payment to Charterer of $ .... per hour or pro rata for each part of an hour that Vessel steams in excess of the equivalent time Vessel would have taken at the guaranteed speed warranted in Clause 8 as calculated in accordance with Attachment 1—"Performance Calculations".
(c) Consumption—the Owner to reimburse the Charterer for each ton of 2,240 lbs. or pro rata for part of a ton in excess of the guaranteed daily consumption for main engine and/or auxilliaries and/or heating and/or tank cleaning including any excess not borne by the Owner in accordance with the off hire clause of this Charter Party at the average price for the particular grade of oil as set forth in the then current Exxon International Contract Price List at..for the total period under review provided that Vessel's actual speed is in accordance with Clause 8. To the extent the Vessel's speed is less than that warranted, fuel consumption allowed will be determined in accordance with Attachment 1—"Performance Calculations".
(d) The basis for determining the Vessel's performance (a) and (b) above shall be the statistical data supplied by the Master in accordance with Clause 14. (5).
(e) Owner to have similar privileges under this Clause for receiving compensation as Charterers do should Vessel performance as concerns speed be in excess or consumption for propulsion be below the descriptions outlined herein.
(f) The Charterer shall provide Owner with an opportunity to review any cliam submitted by Charterer under this Clause, and the Owner shall complete such review, and provide Charterer with the results thereof within 30 days from the date such claim was mailed by Charterer to Owner.

Charterer may deduct from hire any amount to which it is entitled under this Clause after the expiration of 40 days from the date of Charterer's mailing of a claim relating thereto to Owner.
 In the event of Charterer having a claim in respect of Vessel's performance during the final year or part of the Charter period and any extension thereof, the amount of such claim shall be withheld from hire in accordance with Charterer's estimate made about two months before the end of the Charter period and any necessary adjustment after the end of the Charter shall be made by the Owner to the Charterer or the Charterer to the Owner as the case may require.

LIENS

10. The Owner shall have a lien on all cargoes for all amounts due under this Charter, and the Charterer shall have a lien on the Vessel for all moneys paid in advance and not earned, all disbursements and advances for the Owner's account, for the value of any of Charterer's fuel used or accepted for Owner's account, for all amounts due to Charterer under Clause 9, and other provisions of this Charter and for any damages sustained by the Charterer as a result of breach of this Charter by the Owner.

OFF HIRE

11. (a) In the event of loss of time from breakdown of machinery, interference by authorities, collision, stranding, fire, or other accident or damage to the Vessel, not caused by the fault of the Charterer, preventing the working of the Vessel for more than twelve consecutive hours, or in the event of loss of time from deficiency of men or stores, breach of orders or neglect of duty by the Master, Officers, or Crew, or from deviation for the purpose of landing any injured or ill person on board other than any person who may be carried at Charterer's request, payment of hire shall cease for all time lost until the Vessel is again in an efficient state to resume her service and has regained a point of progress equivalent to that when the hire ceased hereunder; cost of fuel consumed while the Vessel is off hire hereunder, as well as all port charges, pilotages, and other expenses incurred during such period and consequent upon the putting in to any port or place other than to which the Vessel is bound, shall be borne by the Owner; but should the Vessel be driven into port or to anchorage by stress of weather or on account of accident to her cargo, such loss of time, shall be for Charterer's account. If upon the voyage the speed of the Vessel be reduced on her next port or an excess fuel consumption increased by breakdown, casualty, or inefficiency of Master, Officers, or Crew, so as to cause a delay of more than twenty-four hours in arriving at the Vessel's next port or an excess consumption of more than one day's fuel, hire for the time lost and cost of extra fuel consumed, if any, shall be borne by the Owner. Any delay by ice or time spent in quarantine shall be for Charterer's account, except delay in quarantine resulting from the Master, Officers, or Crew having communications with the shore at an infected port, where the Charterer has given the Master adequate written notice of infection, which shall be for Owner's account, as shall also be any loss of time through detention by authorities as a result of charges of smuggling or of other infraction of law by the Master, Officers, or Crew.

(b) If the periods of time lost for which hire does not cease to be payable under the foregoing provisions of this Clause because each such period or delay is not of more than twelve (12) hours duration exceed in the aggregate one hundred and forty-four (144) hours in any charter party year (and pro rata for part of a year), hire shall not be payable for the excess and any hire overpaid by the Charterer shall be repaid by the Owner.

(c) In the event of loss of time by detention of the Vessel by authorities at any place in consequence of legal proceeding against the Vessel or the Owner, payment of charter hire shall cease for all time so lost. Cost of fuel and water consumed as well as all additional port charges, pilotages, and other expenses incurred during the time so lost shall be borne by the Owner. If any such loss of time shall exceed thirty consecutive days, the Charterer shall have the option to cancel this Charter by written notice given to the Owner while the vessel remains so detained without prejudice to any other right Charterer may have in the premises.

DRYDOCKING

12. (a) Owner, at its expense, shall drydock, clean, and paint Vessel's bottom and make all overhaul and other necessary repairs at reasonable intervals not to exceed twenty-four (24) months for which purpose Charterer shall allow Vessel to proceed to an appropriate port. Owner shall be solely responsible therefor, and also for gasfreeing the Vessel, upon each occasion. All towing, pilotage, fuel, water and other expenses incurred while proceeding to and from and while in drydock, shall also be for Owner's account. Fuel used during such drydocking or repair as provided in this Clause or Clause 15 or in proceeding to or from the port of drydocking or repair, will be charged to Owner by Charterer at the price charged to Charterer by its bunker supplier at such port if bunkers are obtained there or at the next replenishment port.

(b) In case of drydocking pursuant to this Clause at a port where Vessel is to load, discharge or bunker, under Charterer's orders, hire shall be suspended from the time the Vessel received free pratique on arrival, if in ballast, or upon completion of discharge of cargo, if loaded, until Vessel is again ready for service. In case of drydocking at a port other than where Vessel loads, discharges, or bunkers, under Charterer's orders, the following time and bunkers shall be deducted from hire: total time and bunkers including repair port call for the actual voyage from last port of call under Charterer's orders to next port of call under Charterer's orders, less theoretical voyage time and bunkers for the direct voyage from said last port of call to said next port of call. Theoretical voyage will be calculated on the basis of the seabuoy to seabuoy distance at the warranted speed and consumption per Clause 8.

OWNER PROVIDES

13. The Owner shall provide and pay for all provisions, deck and engine room stores, galley and cabin stores, galley and crew fuel, insurance on the Vessel, wages of the Master, Officers, and Crew, all certificates and other requirements necessary to enable the Vessel to be employed throughout the trading limits herein provided, consular fees pertaining to the Master, Officers, and Crew, all fresh water used by the Vessel and all other expenses connected with the operation, maintenance, and navigation of the Vessel.

MASTER'S DUTIES

14. (a) The Master, although appointed by and in the employ of the Owner and subject to Owner's direction and control, shall observe the orders of Charterer in connection with Charterer's agencies, arrangements, and employment of the Vessel's services hereunder. Nothing in this Clause or elsewhere in this Charter shall be construed as creating a demise of the Vessel to Charterer nor as vesting Charterer with any control over the physical operation or navigation of the Vessel.

(b) The Master and the Engineers shall keep full and correct logs of the voyages, which are to be patent to the Charterer and its agents, and abstracts of which are to be mailed directly to the Charterer from each port of call.

(c) If the Charterer shall have reason to be dissatisfied with the conduct of the Master or Officers, the Owner shall, on receiving particulars of the complaint, investigate it and if necessary, make a change in the appointments.

FUEL, PORT CHARGES, ETC.

15. (a) The Charterer (except during any period when the Vessel is off hire) shall provide and pay for all fuel except for galley and Crew as provided in Clause 13. The Charterer shall also pay for all port charges, light dues, dock dues, Panama and other Canal dues, pilotage, consular fees, (except those pertaining to Master, Officers, and Crew), tugs necessary for assisting the Vessel in, about, and out of port for the purpose of carrying out this Charter, Charterer's agencies and commissions incurred for Charterer's account and crew expense incurred for connecting and disconnecting cargo hoses and arms. The Owner shall, however, reimburse the Charterer for any fuel used or any expenses incurred in making a general sacrifice or expenditure, and for any fuel consumed during drydocking or repair of the Vessel.

TUGS AND PILOTS

(b) In engaging pilotage and tug assistance, Charterer is authorized by Owner to engage them on behalf of Owner on the usual terms and conditions for such services then prevailing at the ports or places where such services are engaged, including provisions there prevailing, if any, making pilots, tug captains, or other personnel of any tug the borrowed servants of the Owner.

(c) Neither the Charterer nor its agents nor any of its associated or affiliated companies, nor any of their agents or employees, shall be under any responsibility for any loss, damage, or liability arising from any negligence, incompetence, or incapacity of any pilot, tug captain, or other personnel of any tug, or arising from the terms of the contract of employment thereof or for any unseaworthiness or insufficiency of any tug or tugs, the services of which are arranged by Charterer on behalf of Owner, and Owner agrees to indemnify and hold Charterer, its agents, associated and affiliated companies and their employees harmless from and against any and all such consequences.

(d) Charterer shall have the option of using its own tugs and pilots, or tugs or pilots made available or employed by any associated or affiliated companies, to render towage or pilotage services to the Vessel. In this event, the terms and conditions relating to such services prevailing at the port where such services are rendered and applied by independent tugboat owners or pilots, shall be applicable, and Charterer, its associated or affiliated companies and their pilots shall be entitled to all exemptions from and limitations of liability, applicable to said independent tugboat owners or pilots and their published tariff terms and conditions.

ADDITIONAL EQUIPMENT

16. The Charterer, subject to the Owner's approval not to be unreasonably withheld, shall be at liberty to fit any additional pumps and/or gear for loading or discharging cargo it may require beyond that which is on board at the commencement of the Charter, and to make the necessary connections with steam or water pipes, such work to be done at its expense and time, and such pumps and/or gear so fitted to be considered its property, and the Charterer shall be at liberty to remove it at its expense and time during or at the expiry of this Charter; the Vessel to be left in her original condition to the Owner's satisfaction.

LAY-UP

17. The Charterer shall have the option of laying up the Vessel for all or any portion of the term of this Charter, in which case hire hereunder shall continue to be paid, but there shall be credited against such hire the whole amount which the Owner shall save (or reasonably should save) during

such period of layup through reduction in expenses, less any extra expenses to which the Owner is put as a result of such layup.
Should the Charterer, having exercised the option granted hereunder, desire the Vessel again to be put into service, the Owner will, upon receipt of written notice from the Charterer to such effect, immediately take steps to restore the Vessel to service as promptly as possible. The option granted to the Charterer hereunder may be exercised one or more times during the currency of this Charter or any extension thereof.

18. (a) In the event that title to the Vessel shall be requisitioned or seized by any government authority (or the Vessel shall be seized by any person or government under circumstances which are equivalent to requisition of title), this Charter shall terminate automatically as of the effective date of such requisition or seizure.

REQUISITION

(b) In the event that the Vessel should be requisitioned for use or seized by any government authority on any basis not involving, or not equivalent to, requisition of title, she shall be off hire hereunder during the period of such requisition, and any hire or any other compensation paid in respect of such requisition shall be for Owner's account, provided, however, that if such requisition continues for a period in excess of 90 days, the Charterer shall have the option to terminate this Charter upon written notice to the Owner. Any periods of off-hire under this Clause shall be subject to the Charterer's option for off-hire extension set forth in Clause 1 (b) hereof.

REDELIVERY

19. (a) Unless the employment of the Vessel under this Charter shall previously have been terminated by loss of the Vessel or otherwise, the Charterer shall release the Vessel to the Owner's use, free of cargo, at the expiration of the term of this Charter stated in Clause 1 (including any extension thereof provided in said Clause or elsewhere in this Charter), at .... (herein called "Port of Redelivery") and shall give written notice of the date and hour of such release. At the Charterer's option, the vessel may be released to the Owner with tanks in a clean or dirty condition.

(b) The Owner shall accept and pay for all fuel in the Vessel's bunkers when this Charter terminates. Payment for such fuel shall be made in accordance with the Exxon International Company Contract Price List current for the date when and the port or place where the Vessel is redelivered by Charterer to Owners under this Charter, or the nearest port to which such list applies.

BILLS OF LADING

20. (a) Bills of Lading shall be signed by the Master as presented, the master attending daily, if required, at the offices of the Charterer or its Agents. However, at Charterer's option, the Charterer or its Agents may sign Bills of Lading on behalf of the Master. All Bills of Lading shall be without prejudice to this Charter and the Charterer shall indemnify the Owner against all consequences or liabilities which may arise from any inconsistency between this Charter and any bills of lading or other documents signed by the Charterer or its Agents or by the Master at their request or which may arise from an irregularity in papers supplied by the Charterer or its Agents.

(b) The carriage of cargo under this Charter Party and under all Bills of Lading issued for the cargo shall be subject to the statutory provisions and other terms set forth or specified in subparagraphs (i) to (vi) of this Clause and such terms shall be incorporated verbatim or be deemed incorporated by the reference in any such Bill of Lading. In such subparagraphs and in any Act referred to therein, the word "carrier" shall include the Owner and the Chartered Owner of the Vessel.

(i) *Clause Paramount*. This bill of lading shall have effect subject to the provisions of the Carriage of Goods by Sea Act of the United States, approved April 16, 1936, except that if this Bill of Lading is issued at a place where any other Act, ordinance, or legislation gives statutory effect to the International Convention for the Unification of Certain Rules relating to Bills of Lading at Brussels, August 1924, then this Bill of Lading shall have effect subject to the provisions of such Act, ordinance, or legislation. The applicable Act, ordinance, or legislation (hereinafter called "Act") shall be deemed to be incorporated herein and nothing herein contained shall be deemed a surrender by the Owner or Carrier of any of its rights or immunities or an increase of any of its responsibilities or liabilities under the Act. If any term of this Bill of Lading be repugnant to the Act to any extent, such term shall be void to that extent but no further.

(ii) *New Jason Clause*. In the event of accident, danger, damage, or disaster before or after the commencement of the voyage, resulting from any cause whatsoever, whether due to negligence or not, for which, or for the consequences of which, the Carrier is not responsible, by statute, contract or otherwise, the cargo, shippers, consignees, or owners of the cargo shall contribute with the Carrier in General Average to the payment of any sacrifices, losses, or expenses of a General Average nature that may be made or incurred and shall pay salvage and special charges incurred in respect of the cargo. If a salving ship is owned or operated by the Carrier, salvage shall be paid for as fully as if the said salving ship or ships belonged to strangers. Such deposit as the Carrier or its Agents may deem sufficient to cover the estimated contribution of the cargo and any salvage and special charges thereon shall, if required, be made by the cargo, shippers, consignees or owners of the cargo to the Carrier before delivery.

(iii) *General Average*. General Average shall be adjusted, stated, and settled according to

York/Antwerp Rules 1950, as amended, and, as to matters not provided for by those rules, according to the laws and usages at the Port of New York. If a General Average statement is required, it shall be prepared at such port by an Adjuster from the Port of New York appointed by the Carrier and approved by the Charterer of the Vessel. Such Adjuster shall attend to the settlement and the collection of the General Average, subject to customary charges. General Average Agreements and/or security shall be furnished by Carrier and/or Charterer of the Vessel, and/or Carrier and/or Consignee of cargo, if requested. Any cash deposit being made as security to pay General Average and/or salvage shall be remitted to the Average Adjuster and shall be held by him at his risk in a special account in a duly authorized and licensed bank at the place where the General Average statement is prepared.

(iv) *Both to Blame.* If the Vessel comes into collision with another ship as a result of the negligence of the other ship and any act, neglect or default of the Master, mariner, pilot, or the servants of the Carrier in the navigation or in the management of the Vessel, the owners of the cargo carried hereunder shall indemnify the Carrier against all loss or liability to the other or noncarrying ship or her owners in so far as such loss or liability represents loss of, or damage to, or any claim whatsoever of the owners of said cargo, paid or payable by the other or recovered by the other or noncarrying ship or her owners as part of their claim against the carrying ship or Carrier. The foregoing provisions shall also apply where the owners, operators, or those in charge of any ships or objects other than, or in addition to, the colliding ships or object are at fault in respect of a collision or contract.

(v) *Limitation of Liability.* Any provision of this Charter to the contrary notwithstanding, the Carrier shall have the benefit of all limitations of, and exemptions from, liability accorded to the Owner or Chartered Owner of vessels by any statute or rule of law for the time being.

(vi) *Deviation Clause.* The Vessel shall have liberty to sail with or without pilots, to tow or be towed, to go to the assistance of vessels in distress, to deviate for the purpose of saving life or property or of landing any ill or injured person on board, and to call for fuel at any port or ports in or out of the regular course of the voyage.

21. *War Risks.* (a) No contraband of war shall be shipped, but petroleum and/or its products shall not be deemed contraband of war for the purposes of this Clause. Vessel shall not, however, be required, without the consent of Owner, which shall not be unreasonably withheld, to enter any port or zone which is involved in a state of war, warlike operations, or hostilities, civil strife, insurrection or piracy whether there be a declaration of war or not, where it might reasonably be expected to be subject to capture, seizure or arrest, or to a hostile act by a belligerent power (the term "power" meaning any de jure or de facto authority or any other purported governmental organization maintaining naval, military, or air forces).

(b) For the purposes of this Clause it shall be unreasonable for Owner to withhold consent to any voyage, route, or port of loading or discharge if insurance against all risks defined in Article 21 (a) is then available commercially or under a Government program in respect of such voyage, route or port of loading or discharge. If such consent is given by Owner, Charterer will pay the provable additional cost of insuring Vessel against Hull war risks in an amount equal to the value under her ordinary hull policy but not exceeding.. In addition, Owner may purchase war risk insurance on ancillary risks such as loss of hire, freight disbursements, total loss, etc., if he carries such insurance for ordinary marine hazards. If such insurance is not obtainable commercially or through a Government program, Vessel shall not be required to enter or remain at any such port or zone.

(c) In the event of the existence of the conditions described in Article 21 (a) subsequent to the date of this Charter, or while vessel is on hire under this Charter, Charterer shall, in respect of voyages to any such port or zone assume the provable additional cost of wages and insurance properly incurred in connection with Master, Officers and Crew as a consequence of such war, warlike operations or hostilities.

EXCEPTIONS

22. (a) The Vessel, her Master and Owner shall not, unless otherwise in this Charter expressly provided, be responsible for any loss or damage to cargo arising or resulting from: any act, neglect, default or barratry of the Master, Pilots, mariners or other servants of the Owner in the navigation or management of the Vessel; fire, unless caused by the personal design or neglect of the Owner; collision, stranding, or peril, danger or accident of the sea or other navigable waters; or from explosion, bursting of boilers, breakage of shafts, or any latent defect in hull, equipment or machinery. And neither the Vessel, her Master or Owner, nor the Charterer, shall, unless otherwise in this Charter expressly provided, be responsible for any loss or damage or delay or failure in performing hereunder arising or resulting from: act of God; act of war; perils of the seas; act of public enemies, pirates or assailing thieves; arrest or restraint of princes, rulers or people, or seizure under legal process provided bond is promptly furnished to release the Vessel or cargo; strike or lockout or stoppage or restraint of labor from whatever cause, either partial or general; or riot or civil commotion.

NUMBER OF GRADES

(b) The Owner warrants the Vessel is constructed and equipped to carry .... grades of oil. If for any reason the Vessel, upon arrival at a loading port, is unable to load the required number of grades, the Charterer will do its utmost to provide a suitable cargo consistent with Vessel's capabilities. However, if this is not possible the Vessel is to proceed to the nearest repair port in ballast and will there repair all bulkhead leaks necessary, any time and expense being for Owner's account.

(c) The exceptions stated in subparagraph (a) of this Clause shall not affect the Owner's undertakings with respect to the condition, particulars and capabilities of the Vessel, or the provisions for payment and cessation of hire or the obligations of the Owner under Clause 20 in respect of the loading, handling, stowage, carriage, custody, care and discharge of cargo.

23. All salvage moneys carried by the Vessel shall be divided equally between the Owner and the Charterer after deducting Master's, Officers' and Crew's share, legal expenses, hire of Vessel during time lost, value of fuel consumed, repairs of damage, if any, and any other extraordinary loss or expense sustained as a result of the service, which shall always be a first charge on such money.

24. Owner warrants that the Vessel is entered in TOVALOP and will remain so entered during the currency of this Charter, provided, however, that if Owner acquires the right to withdraw from TOVALOP under Clause VIII thereof, nothing herein shall prevent it from exercising that right.

OIL POLLUTION

Where an escape or discharge of oil occurs from the Vessel and threatens to cause pollution damage to coastlines, Charterer may, at its option, and upon notice to Owner or Master, undertake such measures as are reasonably necessary to prevent or mitigate such damage, unless Owner promptly undertakes same. Charterer shall keep Owner advised of the nature of the measures intended to be taken by it. Any of the aforementioned measures actually taken by Charterer shall be at Owner's expense (except to the extent that such escape or discharge was caused or contributed to by Charterer), provided that if Owner considers said measure should be discontinued, Owner may so notify Charterer and thereafter Charterer shall have no right to continue said measures under the provisions of this Clause and all further liability to Charterer thereunder shall thereupon cease.

If any dispute shall arise between Owner and Charterer as to the reasonableness of the measures undertaken and/or the expenditure incurred by Charterer hereunder, such dispute shall be referred to arbitration as herein provided.

The provisions of this Clause are not in derogation of such other rights as Charterer or Owner may have under this Charter, or may otherwise have or acquire by law or any International Convention.

CLEAN SEAS

25. The Owner agrees to participate in the Charterer's program covering oil pollution avoidance. Such program aims to prevent the discharge into the sea anywhere in the world of all oil, oil water or ballast, chemicals or oily waste material in any form if the said material is of a persistent nature, except under extreme circumstances whereby the safety of the Vessel, cargo or life would be imperiled.

The Owner agrees to adhere to the oil pollution avoidance instructions provided by the Charterer in the Charterer's Vessel Instruction Manual together with any amendments which may be issued in writing or by radio to cover special cases or changes in International and National Regulations or Laws. The Master will contain on board the Vessel all oily residues from consolidated tank washings, dirty ballast, etc. Such residues shall be contained in one compartment after the separation of all possible water has taken place by safe methods employing the use of settlement and decanting or mechanic separation to approved and recognized standards.

The oily residue will be pumped ashore at the loading or discharge terminal either as segregated oily, dirty ballast, commingling with cargo or as is possible for Charterer to arrange with each cargo.

If the Charterer requires that demulsifiers be used for the separation of oil and water, the cost of such demulsifiers will be at the Charterer's expense.

Owner will also arrange for the Vessel to adhere to Charterer's oil pollution program during off-hire periods within the term of this Charter including the preparing of cargo tanks for drydocking and repairs. In the latter case, the Charterer agrees to bear costs for the disposal of oil residues.

Vessel will take all necessary precautions while loading and discharging cargo or bunkers as well as ballast to ensure that no oil will escape overboard.

Nothing in the Charterer's instructions shall be construed as permission to pollute the sea by the discharge of oil or oily water etc. The Owner agrees to instruct the Master to furnish Charterer with a report covering oil pollution avoidance together with details of the quantity of oil residue on board on arrival at the loading port.

PRODUCTS

26. Owner hereby agrees to receive sales representatives of affiliates of Charterer which market marine products. However, Owner is under no obligation to purchase from said affiliates, and said affiliates are under no obligation to sell to Owner any of such products. Owner designates the following as the appropriate persons or organizations with whom said affiliates should deal:
    Name ....
    Address ....

CHANGE OF OWNERSHIP

27. Owner's rights and obligations under this Charter are not transferable by Sale or Assignment without Charterer's consent. In the event of the Vessel being sold without its consent in addition to its other rights, Charterer may, at its absolute discretion, terminate the Charter, whereupon the Owner shall reimburse Charterer for any hire paid in advance and not earned, the cost of bunkers, for any sums to which Charterer is entitled under the Charter, and for any damages which Charterer may sustain.

ARBITRATION

28. Any and all differences and disputes of whatsoever nature arising out of this Charter shall be put to arbitration in the City of New York pursuant to the laws relating to arbitration there in force, before a board of three persons, consisting of one arbitrator to be appointed by the Owner, one by the Charterer, and one by the two so chosen. The decision of any two of the three on any point or points shall be final. Until such time as the arbitrators finally close the hearings either party shall have the right by written notice served on the arbitrators and on an officer of the other party to specify further disputes or differences under this Charter for hearing and determination. The arbitrators may grant any relief which they, or a majority of them, deem just and equitable and within the scope of the agreement of the parties, including, but not limited to, specific performance. Awards pursuant to this Clause may inlude costs, including a reasonable allowance for attorney's fees, and judgments may be entered upon any award made hereunder in any Court having jurisdiction in the premises.

ASSIGNMENT

29. (a) Charterer, upon notice to Owner, may assign this Charter Party to any of its affiliates.

SUBLET

(b) Charterer shall also have the right to sublet the Vessel, but in the event of a sublet, Charterer shall always remain responsible for the fulfillment of this Charter in all its terms and conditions.

LAWS

30. The interpretation of the Charter and of the rights and obligations of the parties shall be governed by the laws applicable to Charter Parties made in the City of New York. The headings of Clauses are for convenience of reference only and shall not affect the interpretation of this Charter. No modification, waiver or discharge of any term of this Charter shall be valid unless in writing and signed by the party to be charged therewith.

IN WITNESS, WHEREOF, THE PARTIES HAVE CAUSED THIS CHARTER TO BE EXECUTED IN DUPLICATE THE DAY AND YEAR HEREIN FIRST ABOVE WRITTEN.

....
WITNESS TO SIGNATURE OF

....
WITNESS TO SIGNATURE OF

定期傭船契約書

［和訳］

ニューヨーク・プロデュース書式
NYPE 93 書式
ボルタイム書式
シェルタイム書式
タンカー定期傭船 STB 書式

ニューヨーク・プロデュース書式

定期傭船契約書
ガヴァメント・フォーム

ニューヨーク・プロデュース・エクスチェンジ承認
1913年11月6日発行—1921年10月20日改訂—1931年8月6日改訂，1946年10月3日改訂

　本傭船契約書は，19………年………月………日に，………………において，………………国｜汽船・機船｜………………の総トン数………………トン，純トン数………………トン，機関………………指示馬力，完全な稼働状態にある船体・機関・装備を有し，………………船級協会船級………………艙内載貨容積ベールにて約………………立方フィート，燃料約………トンの容積の常備用燃料庫を含めた………………夏期乾舷による………………フィート………インチの喫水を基準とする載貨重量トン（2,240ポンドを1トンとする）約………………トン（貨物・燃料，本船載貨重量トンの1.5パーセント以下で最低50トンの清水・船用品を含む），平穏な天候状態における満載航海速力約………………ノット，燃料消費最高最良ウェルズ炭—極上燃料油—極上ディーゼル油にて約………………トン，現在………………中の良好な………号の船主………………と………………市の傭船者………………との間に，締結したものであって，上記船主が，上記船舶をその引渡のときから向こう，約………………の期間，下記航路限定内で上記傭船者に貸し渡し，上記傭船者がこれを借り受けることに合意した旨の証となるものである。傭船者は，本契約期間の全部または一部につき，本船を再傭船に出すことができる。ただし，その場合でも，傭船者は，本傭船契約の履行義務を免れない。

　本船は，………………所在の（別に第6条に定める場合を除き，本船が，潮時に関係なく，常時浮揚状態で安全に碇泊しうる）傭船者が指図するドック，埠頭，またはその他の場所において，傭船者の使用に供されるものとする。かかるドック，埠頭，またはその他の場所が使用できないときは，第5条の規定により期間の計算を行う。本船は，引渡時において，船艙を清掃して貨物積取の準備を整え，船体堅牢強固で，水バラスト，ウインチ，十分なる蒸気力ある補汽罐，補汽罐のないときは，すべてのウインチを同時に運転するに足りる他の動力（および，本船のトン数相応の航海士，甲板員，機関士，機関員の全定員）を備え，あらゆる点において，運送業務に適していなければならない。本船は適切な容器に入れた石油または石油製品を含み，………………を除外する適法な貨物の運送に（家畜の運送は除外する。ただし，傭船者は，自己の危険において少数の家畜を甲板積とする権利を有するが，これに要する造作その他の必要整備は，傭船者の負担とする）適法な航路において使用されるものとし，英領北アメリカ，アメリカ合衆国，西インド諸島，中央アメリカ，カリブ海，メキシコ湾，メキシコ，南アメリカ，………………欧州，アフリカ，アジア，オーストラリア，タスマニアおよび／またはニュージーランド（ただし，Magdalena河，10月31日から5月15日までのSt. Lawrence河，Hudson湾および一切の非安全港，および季節外の白海，黒海，バルチック海，………………を除外する）の，傭船者またはその代理人が指示する，安全な一または数港間に配船されるものとし，その他以下の条項によるものとする。

1. 船主は，乗組員の一切の食料品・給料・乗船地および下船地における領事館費を準備して，その費用を支払い，船舶保険料，ならびに船室・甲板・機関室その他に必要なすべて

の船用品（罐水を含む）の費用を支払うほか，本船の船級を維持し，傭船期間中，船体・機関および装備を完全な稼働状態に置くものとする。

2．傭船者は，すべての燃料費（別段の定めがある場合を除く）・港費・水先料・代理店料・仲介手数料・領事館料（乗組員に関するものを除く），その他通常費用を生じる一切の事項（前記のものを除く）の手配を行い，支払うものとする。ただし，本船の責任に帰すべき事由で入港した場合は，上記費用は，船主の負担とする。乗組員の発病のため，命じられた燻蒸消毒は，船主の負担とする。運送品，またはこの契約により本船を使用中の本船の寄港地のゆえに命じられた，燻蒸費用消毒の費用は，傭船者の負担とする。その他一切の燻蒸消毒費は，本船を連続6ヶ月以上の期間傭船した場合において，爾後，傭船者の負担となる。

　荷敷・仕切板，および特殊な航海または特殊な貨物のために必要な装備品は傭船者が供給するものとする。ただし，船主は既に本船にある一切の荷敷・仕切板の使用を認めなければならない。この場合，傭船者は仕切板を荷敷に代用する権利を有するが，これによって生ずる一切の損害を賠償しなければならない。

3．傭船者は，引渡港において，または船主は，返船港において，本船内の一切の残留燃料を引き取り，それぞれの港における時価で，その代金を支払う。ただし，引渡の際，最低……………トン以上，最高……………トン以下，返船の際，最低……………トン以上，最高……………トン以下を，本船が保有していなければならない。

4．傭船者は，本船の使用ならびに用役に対し，夏期乾舷……………における本船の総載貨重量トン（燃料・船用品を含む）につき，1暦月毎トン当たり……………米国ドルの割合で，上記引渡の日から支払をなすものとする。1ヶ月未満の期間についても，同一の料率による。

　傭船料の支払は，通常の損耗を除き，本船を同様に良好な状態で……………において船主に返船する日の返船時間までとする（滅失の場合を除く）。ただし，別段の合意があるときは，この限りでない。傭船者は，船主に対して，返船の予定日および予定港を少なくとも，その……………日以前に通知しなければならない。

5．前条の傭船料の支払は，New York において現金（米国通貨）により，毎半月分を前払するものとする。最終の半月，またはこれに満たない期間に対する傭船料は，概算額によるものとし，その概算額が，実際の期間に及ばない場合においては，傭船料の不足額につき，その弁済期の到来する毎に，船主の要求により，連日これを支払わなければならない。ただし，傭船者が銀行の保証を受け，または供託をしていた場合は，この限りではない。傭船料を遅滞なく定期に支払わない場合，銀行保証がない場合，もしくは本契約に違反した場合，船主は自由に傭船者の運航から本船を引き揚げることができる。この場合，船主が傭船者に対して有すべき他の一切の請求は妨げられない。

　期間の計算は，傭船者またはその代理人が，午後4時前に書面による準備完了の通知を受け取った日に続く作業日の午前7時から開始する。ただし，傭船者は，要求すれば，本船を即時に使用する権利を有し，その使用時間を傭船期間に算入するものとする。

　傭船者またはその代理人は，船長の求めにより，2.5パーセントの手数料を徴して，いずれの港における通常の諸掛に必要な現金を，立て替えるものとする。立替金は傭船料から控除する。ただし，上記立替金の使用について，傭船者は一切責任を負わないものとする。

6．貨物の船積または揚荷は，傭船者またはその代理人が指示するドック・埠頭またはその他の場所で行う。ただし，本船が潮時の如何を問わず，常時浮揚状態で安全に碇泊できる

ことを要するが、同じ寸法の船舶が慣習上座洲状態で安全に碇泊できる場所を含む。

7. 本船の区画は、本船の職員・部員、揚貨機、装具、備品、食料品、船用品および燃料のための相当かつ十分な船腹を除き、本船の船艙・甲板、その他通常の積付場所の全容積（本船が相当な積付および運送をなしうる限度を超えない）、および上乗人が同乗する場合、その居住区を含めて、すべて傭船者の使用に委ねなければならない。傭船者は乗客設備の収容限度まで、乗客を乗せる権利を有する。傭船者は船主に対し、乗客設備の費用ならびに食費として、乗客1人当たり1日……………を支払う。ただし、旅客運送の結果、負担金または特別の費用を生ずるときは、傭船者がその危険と費用を負担するものとする。

8. 船長はその航海を極力迅速に遂行し、本船の乗組員および端艇をもって、慣習上なすべき一切の助力を提供するものとする。

　船長は（船主により任命されたことにかかわりなく）本船の使用および代理業務に関しては、傭船者の命令・指示に従わなければならない。

　傭船者は、自らの費用により、船長の監督の下に、積込・積付および荷均を行う。

　船長は、船荷証券の呈示がなされた場合、メーツ・レシートまたはタリー・シートの記載に基づいて、これに署名しなければならない。

9. 傭船者に、船長・航海士、または機関士の行為を不満足とする相当な理由がある場合、船主は、その苦情の詳細を受け取りしだい、その事実を取り調べ、要すれば、配乗を変更するものとする。

10. 傭船者は、随意に1名の上乗人を任命することができる。上乗人は本船と同航し、航海の極力迅速な遂行を確認するものとする。上乗人に対しては、居住設備を無償で提供し、サロン待遇を与えるものとする。この場合、傭船者は1日につき1ドルの割合で、その食費を支弁しなければならない。船主は、水先人・税関吏の食事を供するほか、傭船者またはその代理人の承諾がある限り、検数人・船内荷役フォアマンその他の者の食事を供するものとする。これら一切の食費は、傭船者が、毎食、時価で支払う。

11. 傭船者は随時、船長に対し書面により、一切の必要な指図、および航海上の指示を与えるものとする。船長は、傭船者またはその代理人の用に供すべき、または航海に関する完全かつ正確な航海日誌を作成し、傭船者、その代理人または上乗人の要求がある場合には、本船の針路・航海距離・燃料消費高を記した航海日誌の正本を提出しなければならない。

12. 船長は貨物の換気の実施に注意するものとする。

13. 傭船者は傭船期間をさらに……………………………………………間、継続する権利を有する。その場合、当初定めた傭船期間もしくは明示の選択期間の満了する…………日前に、船主もしくはその代理人に書面でその旨を通知しなければならない。

14. 傭船者の要求があるときは、傭船期間は……………より前には開始しない。本船が……………の午後4時までに書面による準備完了の通知をしないときは、傭船者またはその代理人は、本船の準備完了前ならば、いつでも本契約を任意に解約することができる。

15. 人員または船用品の不足、火災、船体・機関もしくは装備の故障または損傷、座礁、本船または積荷の海損事故による滞船、船底の検査または塗装のための入渠、その他本船の完全な稼働を妨げる一切の事由により時間を喪失したときは、傭船料の支払は、それによって喪失した時間について中断する。船体、機関または装備の欠陥または故障により、航海中速力が低下したときは、それによって喪失した時間、その結果余分に消費した燃料

費，その他一切の費用が，傭船料より控除される。
16. 本船が滅失したときは，反対給付が得られなかった前払金（滅失また最後の消息があった日から起算する）を，直ちに傭船者に返還しなければならない。

　本傭船期間中，天災，公敵，火災，君主・統治者および人民による抑留，海上，河川，機器，汽罐および汽船航海の一切の危険および事故，ならびに航海上の過誤について，当事者は相互に免責されるものとする。

　水先人を同乗させまたは同乗させずに航行すること，曳航しまたは曳航されること，遭難船舶を救援すること，人命・財産を救助する目的で離路することは，本船の自由とする。
17. 船主と傭船者との間に争いを生じたときには，係争事項を New York において，3名の仲裁人に付託するものとする。この場合，双方の当事者が各々1名を選定し，選定を受けたこれらの2名の者が共同してさらに第三の者を選定する。これら仲裁人全員，もしくはいずれか2名の裁定を終局のものとして，これに従う。仲裁判断の執行については，前記の合意をもって裁判所の命令とみなす。仲裁人は実務家に限る。
18. 船主は本契約上当然受け取るべき一切の金額（共同海損分担金を含む）につき，すべての積荷，再運送賃の上にリーエンを有し，傭船者は反対給付が得られなかった一切の前払金につき，本船の上にリーエンを有するものとする。既払傭船料または供託金の超過分は，直ちに返還されなければならない。傭船者またはその代理人は，船主の船舶に対する権利，利益を害することあるべきリーエンその他の負担の発生，存続を認めないものとする。
19. 一切の漂流物および救助料については，船主および傭船者の費用と乗組員の分配額を控除した後，船主と傭船者は均等に利益を受けるものとする。

——原書115行—132行訳省略——

20. 本船がオフハイヤー中に使用する燃料および炊事，造水または暖炉やストーブ用の燃料についても，その使用量を協議するものとし，船主はその補給費用を負担する。
21. 本傭船期間中，本船を熱帯水域に使用したときは，適当な場所において入渠させるものとする。船底の掃除および塗装は，傭船者ならびに船長が必要と認めたときに行うほか，前回の塗装のときから，少なくとも6ヶ月を経過する毎に行う。傭船料の支払は，本船が再び適切な稼働状態に戻るまで中止される。
22. 船主は本船装備の設備を維持し，3トン以下の積揚貨物の荷役に堪える（すべてのデリック用の）索具のほか，綱・吊索・スリングおよび滑車を準備しなければならない。本船が前記のトン数以上の重量を有する貨物の荷役に堪えるデリックを装備するときは，船主において，これに要する索具を準備するものとする。ただし，その装備がないときは，上記の重量を有する貨物のための属具および索具は，傭船者の負担とする。船主はまた，本船に夜間作業用のカンテラおよび灯油を準備し，かつ，本船に電灯設備があるときは，これを使用に供するものとする。ただし，船内の灯火以外に増設した一切の灯火の費用は傭船者の負担とする。傭船者は本船上のあらゆる器具を使用することができる。
23. 本船は，傭船者の要求がある場合，昼夜ともに作業に従事するものとし，積荷および揚荷中，全ウィンチを傭船者の使用に委ねるものとする。本船は，艙口毎に1人のウィンチマンを配置し，要求がある場合には，昼夜にわたりウィンチを運転しなければならない。傭船者は，本船の諸規定に定められた作業時間ならびに賃率に従い，航海士・機関士・ウィンチマン・甲板員および補汽罐手の時間外労働に対し支払を行う。港則または労働組合の規約が，乗組員によるウィンチの運転を禁止している場合には，陸上ウィンチマンの

費用を傭船者が支払う。ウィンチの運転の不能，もしくはこれに要する動力の不足を生じたときは，船主は陸上の荷役機械，または要求があればこれに代わるその他の機械の費用を支払い，かつ，それによって時間を喪失したときは，その支払を行うものとする。

24. この傭船契約の下で，米国を仕向地または積地とするすべての貨物については，本契約は1893年2月13日米国連邦議会の承認を経た「船舶の航海等に関する法律」に定める一切の条項・規定および免責条項に従うものであることも，またここに合意する。上記のほか，傭船契約は，本契約の下で発行する一切の船荷証券に挿入されるべき下記二条項にも従うものとする。

米国至上条項

本船荷証券は，1936年4月16日に承認された米国海上物品運送法の規定により，その効力を有し，かつ，それらの規定が本証券に挿入されているものとみなすほか，本証券に定めるいかなる事項も，同法に基づく運送人の権利もしくは免責の特権を放棄し，またはその責任もしくは義務を加重しないものとみなす。本証券の文言が，上記の法律と抵触するときは，その文言はその抵触を限度として無効となるものとする。

双方過失衝突条項

相手船の過失と，本船の船長・乗組員・水先人その他運送人の被用者の航海もしくは船舶の取扱に関する行為・怠慢または懈怠の結果，本船と相手船が衝突し，相手船たる非積載船またはその船主が，本証券記載物品の滅失，損傷，その他貨物所有者の請求一切につき，これを貨物所有者に対して賠償したかまたは賠償義務を負い，かかる損害を衝突損害の一部として，積載船または運送人に求償し，相殺または回収した場合，貨物所有者は，運送人が被った上記損害を補償するものとする。

25. 本船は結氷港，もしくは結氷を理由として灯標または灯船が撤去されているか撤去のおそれのある港，もしくは結氷のため通常の方法では本船が安全に入港し，もしくは積荷・揚荷後出港できないような危険がある港には，配船されないものとする。
26. 本契約書記載のいかなる事項も，定期傭船者に対する船舶賃貸借とは，解釈しないものとする。船主は，常に本船の航海，船舶保険，乗組員，その他一切の事項につき，自己の計算において航海する場合と同一の責任を負う。
27. 本船および船主は，本契約およびその継続または延長により受け取り，支払われる傭船料の2.5パーセントを仲介料として………に支払うものとする。
28. 本契約により受け取る傭船料のうち，2.5パーセントをアドレス・コミッションとして……………………………………………に支払うものとする。

からの電信による授権によって

原傭船契約書を所持。

船主の代わりに………………として

仲立人

NYPE93書式

コードネーム：NYPE93
ボルティック国際海運集会所（BIMCO）および海運仲立業協会（FONASBA）推薦：

定期傭船契約書

ニューヨーク・プロデュース・エクスチェンジ書式
アメリカ合衆国海運仲立業代理店協会発行

1913年11月6日発行―1921年10月20日；1931年8月6日；1946年10月3日修正
1981年6月12日；1993年9月14日改訂

本傭船契約は，本日19.........年........月........日に，......................において下記明細の本船の<u>船主</u>........................<u>と傭船者</u>............................との間で締結された。

船舶の明細
船名.....................国籍......................建造（年）.....................
船籍港および登録番号.............................
船級..................
夏期乾舷による..................の海水喫水における重量トン数.................ロングトン＊／メトリックトン＊（................ロングトン＊／メトリックトン＊を超えない清水および船用品を含む貨物および燃料）
容積..............立方フィート（グレーン）...............立方フィート（ベール） 総トン数...............トン
ビューフォート風力階級.................以下の平穏な天候状態において，................の約.............ロングトン＊／メトリックトン＊の燃料消費量の下における満載航海速力約............ノット

＊適宜抹消のこと
　その他の明細があるときは，追加規定"A"参照

1．期　　　間
船主は，本船引渡のときから向こう................................の期間，下記航路定限において，本船を貸し渡し，傭船者はこれを借り受けることに合意する。

2．引　　　渡
本船は，..............................において傭船者の使用に供される。本船は，引渡時において，船艙を清掃して貨物積取の準備を整え，船体堅牢強固で，水バラストを有し，かつすべての荷役装置を同時に運転するに足りる動力を備え，あらゆる点において通常の貨物運送業務に適していなければならない。
船主は，引渡予定日の通知をその予定日の...............前に傭船者に発しなければならない。

3．傭船開始時・返船時検査
他に別段の定めがない限り，本船の引渡および返船の前に，各当事者は各自の費用負担でそれぞれ検査人を指名し，それらの検査人は，本船上の燃料の量および本船の状態を確認するため最初の船積港・最後の揚荷港以前に共同の傭船開始・返船検査を行う。両検査人は，検査ごとに1通の報告書を作成し，署名する。ただし，検査人間で合意できない項目を記載した別個の報告書を提出することを

妨げない。一方の当事者が検査に代表者を立ち会わせず、共同の検査報告書に署名させない場合においても、その当事者は他の当事者の作成した報告書の調査結果について、すべての点で拘束される。傭船開始検査は傭船者負担の時間として、返船検査は船主負担の時間としてそれぞれ計算する。

4．危険品・除外貨物

(a) 本船は、一切の危険性、有害性、可燃性または腐食性を有する物品を除外する適法な貨物の運送に使用される。ただし、本船の船籍国、積揚を行う国もしくは港および本船がその海域を通過せざるをえない途中の国もしくは港の関係当局の要求または勧告に従って運送する場合を除く。上記の一般規定を害することなく、さらに以下の貨物を特に除外する。すなわち、あらゆる種類の家畜、武器、弾薬、爆発物、核物質および放射性物質、……………。

(b) IMO で指定された貨物の運送が合意されたときは、その貨物の量は……………トンに限定されるものとし、傭船者は船長に対して、IMO 規則に従って梱包、表示、船積および積付が行われていることを示すために船長が要求する証拠を提出しなければならない。それがないときは、船長はその貨物の船積を拒否することができ、また既に船積されたときは、傭船者の危険と費用で揚荷することができる。

5．就航区域

本船は、傭船者の指示により、……………を除く、……………内の安全な港および場所の間の適法な航路に使用される。

6．船主負担

船主は、他に別段の定めがある場合を除き、船舶保険、一切の食料品、船室、甲板、機関室その他必要なすべての船用品（罐水を含む）を手配し、かつその費用を支払い、乗組員の給料、乗組員の乗船地および下船地における領事館費、乗組員にかかる港費を支払うほか、本船の船級を維持し、傭船期間中、船体、機関および装備を完全な稼働状態に置き、職員および部員の定員を確保する。

7．傭船者負担

傭船者は、本船の傭船期間中、別段の定めがある場合を除き、すべての燃料を手配し、かつその支払をなし、（強制見張、貨物見張および強制廃棄物処分を含む）港費、傭船者の業務に関するすべての通信費（実費）、水先料、曳航料、代理店料、手数料、領事館費（各乗組員および本船の国籍に関するものを除く）その他第6条に記載されたものを除く一切の通常の費用を支払う。ただし、（天候上の理由を除き）本船の責任に帰すべき事由で入港したときは、それによって生ずる一切の費用は、船主の負担とする。乗組員の発病のため命じられた燻蒸消毒は、船主の負担とする。本傭船契約に基づく本船の使用中の運送品または寄港地のゆえに命じられた燻蒸消毒は、傭船者の負担とする。その他一切の燻蒸消毒費用は、本船を連続6ヶ月以上傭船した場合において、爾後、傭船者の負担とする。

傭船者は、必要な荷敷および特別の航海または貨物に必要な追加装備品を備え、その支払をなすが、船主は、既に本船にある一切の荷敷の使用を傭船者に認めなければならない。傭船者は、返船前に自己の費用と時間を負担して追加の荷敷および装備品を本船から撤去しなければならない。

8．航海遂行

(a) 船長は、相当な迅速さをもって航海を遂行し、本船の乗組員をもって慣習上なすべき一切の助力を提供する。船長は、英語に精通し、（船主により任命されたことにかかわりなく）本船の使用および代理業務に関しては、傭船者の命令・指示に従わなければならない。傭船者は、自己の危険と費用により、船長の監督の下で、船積、積付、荷均、ラッシング、固縛、荷敷、アンラッシング、揚荷および検数を含む貨物のすべての取扱を行うものとする。

(b) 傭船者に船長または職員の行為を不満足とする相当な理由がある場合、船主は、その苦情の詳細を受け取り次第、その事実を取り調べ、要すれば、配乗を変更するものとする。

9．燃　　　料

(a) 傭船者は引渡の際、船主は返船の際、本船内の一切の残留燃料油およびディーゼル油を以下の条件で引き取り、その代金を支払う。本船は、トン当たり……………の価格の燃料油……………ロングトン*／メトリックトン*と、トン当たり……………の価格のディーゼル油……………トンと共

に，引き渡される。本船は，トン当たり……………の価格の燃料油……………トンと，トン当たり……………の価格のディーゼル油……………トンと共に，返船される。
  ＊本条項では同一トンを適用する。
 (b) 傭船者は，本船の主機関および補機関の使用に適し，かつ，追加規定Aに表示された明細に適合する質の燃料油を提供しなければならない。
    船主は，不適当な燃料油または合意された明細に適合しない燃料油の使用によって生ずる主機関または補機関のすべての損害について，傭船者に対して賠償請求する権利を留保する。さらに，提供された燃料油が相互に合意した明細に適合せず，またはその他の理由で本船の主機関もしくは補機関に使用するのに不適当であると証明されたときは，船主は，本船の航海速力の低下および／または燃料消費量の増加および時間の喪失その他の結果について責任を負わない。

10．傭船料率・返船場所と返船通知

　傭船者は，本船の使用および用役に対し，1日当たり米貨……………米ドルの割合または燃料および船用品を含む……………夏期乾舷における本船の総重量トン数について，米国通貨により30日当たり1トン米貨……………米ドルの割合による金額を，上記引渡の日から支払をなすものとする。1ヶ月未満の期間についても，同一の割合による。

　傭船料の支払は，通常の損耗を除き，本船を傭船開始時と同様に良好な状態で……………において船主に返船する日の返船時間までとする（滅失の場合を除く）。ただし，別段の合意があるときは，この限りではない。

　傭船者は，返船の予定日および予定港を少なくともその………日以前に船主に通知しなければならない。

　傭船料の計算にあたっては，引渡または返船，傭船終了の各時間を，GMT（グリニッジ標準時）によって調整する。

11．傭船料支払

 (a) 支　　払

　傭船料は，船主または船主の指定する……………における受取人，すなわち……………に対し，……………通貨または米国通貨により，支払期日に船主が使用可能なように，15日分ずつ前払されなければならない。最終の月またはそれに満たない期間に対する傭船料は，概算額によるものとし，その概算額が実際の期間に及ばないときは，傭船料の不足額につき船主の要求により，その弁済期が到来するごとに，連日支払われなければならない。傭船料を遅滞なく，定期に支払わない場合，または本傭船契約の根本的な違反があったときは，船主は，自由に傭船者の運航から本船を引き揚げることができる。この場合船主が傭船者に対して有すべき他の一切の請求は妨げられない。

　第11条(b)に規定された猶予期間の満了後は，傭船料が未払であるときはいつでも，船主は引揚権を妨げられることなく，本傭船契約上のいかなる義務の履行も中断することができる。その結果について，船主は一切責任を負わず，傭船者は船主に補償する。この場合，傭船料は引き続き発生し，そのような中断によって生ずる一切の追加費用は傭船者の勘定とする。

 (b) 猶　予　期　間

　傭船者またはその銀行の側の見落とし，不注意，誤りまたは怠慢により傭船料が遅滞なく，かつ定期に支払われないときは，船主は，正味………日の（約定された支払地で認められている）銀行営業日前に，書面による不払の補正通知を傭船者に発する。その通知に従って，上記………日以内に支払われたときは，支払は定期に，かつ遅滞なく支払われたものとする。

　ここに規定された船主の通知を傭船者が受けた後………日以内に傭船料が支払われないときは，船主は，上記第11条(a)に規定したとおり本船を引き揚げることができる。

 (c) 傭船料の最終支払

　最終および・またはその直前の傭船料支払時に，本船が返船港向けの航海を行っているときは，その支払は，本船上に残留する燃料油および返船前に船主が引き取るべき燃料油と船主のための概算諸掛を考慮し，その航海を完了するのに要する見込について船主と傭船者が合意した期間について行われる。その支払額が実際の期間に満たないときは，傭船料は日々支払われるものとする。本船の返船

後，差額が生じたときは，それぞれに応じて，差額を船主が返還し，または傭船者が支払う。

(d) 立 替 前 払

傭船者は，船主の要求によりいずれの港における本船の通常の諸掛として必要な現金を2.5パーセントの手数料を徴して立て替える。立替金は傭船料から控除する。ただし，傭船者はかかる立替金の使用について一切責任を負わないものとする。

12. バ ー ス

本船は，傭船者またはその代理人が指示するいかなる安全なドック，安全なバースまたは安全な場所においても船積および揚荷を行う。ただし，それらは，潮時の如何を問わず本船が常時浮揚して，安全に到着し，碇泊し，発航できるところでなければならない。

13. 提 供 容 積

(a) 本船の職員，部員，揚貨機，装具，備品，食料品，船用品および燃料のための相当かつ十分な船腹を除き，本船の区画は，(本船が相当かつ安全な積付および運送をなしうる限度を超えない) 本船の船艙，甲板その他貨物用の場所ならびに上乗人が同乗する場合，その居住区を含めてすべて，傭船者の使用に委ねなければならない。

(b) 甲板積貨物が運送されたときは，傭船者は，甲板積貨物の運送の結果本船に生じたいかなる種類の滅失および・または損傷および・または責任および甲板積貨物を積まなかったならば生じなかったはずのいかなる種類の滅失および・または損傷および・または責任についても，船主に対して補償する。

14. 上乗人と食事

傭船者は，自己の危険で本船に乗船して航海が相当の迅速さで遂行されることを確認する上乗人を任命することができる。上乗人は，無償で居住設備の提供とサロン待遇を受ける。この場合，傭船者は1日当たり……………の割合の金額を支払う。船主は，水先人および税関吏の食料を提供し，傭船者またはその代理人の承諾する限り，検数人，船内荷役フォアマンその他の者に食事を供するものとする。傭船者は，これら一切の食費として1食当たり……………の割合の金額を支払う。

15. 航海上の指図と航海日誌

傭船者は，随時，船長に対し，英語の書面により一切の必要な指図および航海上の指示を与えるものとする。船長は，傭船者またはその代理人の使用に供する，完全かつ正確な甲板部および機関部の航海日誌を作成し，傭船者，その代理人または上乗人の要求がある場合には，本船の針路，航走距離および燃料消費量を記載した甲板部および機関部の概要日誌の正本を提出しなければならない。傭船者から要求される日誌は，すべて英語で書かれなければならない。

16. 引渡・解約

傭船者から要求があるときは，傭船期間は……………より前には開始しない。本船が……………の…………時以前に引渡準備を整えないときは，傭船者は本傭船契約を任意に解約することができる。

解約期日の延長

船主が，相当の注意を尽くしたにもかかわらず，解約期日までに本船の引渡準備が整わないと判断し，かつ，本船の新たな準備整頓予定日を合理的に推定して定めることができるときは，船主は本船の引渡港または引渡地への発航予定日の早くとも7日前に，傭船者に本傭船契約を解約するか否かを宜言することを要求できる。傭船者が解約しないとき，または2日以内もしくは解約期日のいずれか早い時期までに回答しないときは，船主が通知する新たな引渡準備整頓予定日の7日後が当初の解約期日に代わる。本船がさらに遅延したときは，船主は本条項に従って傭船者の (解約権行使の) 宣告を再度求めることができる。

17. オフハイヤー

職員もしくは部員の不足および・または怠慢および・またはストライキ，船用品の不足，火災，船体，機関もしくは装備の故障または損傷，座礁，本船のアレストによる拘留 (そのアレストが傭船者，その代理人または下請業者が責任を負うべき事由によって生じた場合を除く)，貨物の固有の瑕疵，性質または欠陥によらない本船または貨物の海損事故による滞船，船底の検査または塗装のため

の入渠その他，本船の完全な稼働を阻害する，一切の事由によって時間を喪失したときは，傭船料および時間外手当の支払は，それによって喪失した期間について中断する。本船が航海中，傭船者の指図または指示に反し，または貨物の事故もしくは本傭船契約の257行から258行目で容認されている場合以外の事由により離路し，または引き返したときは，本船が離路を開始し，または引き返し始めた時点から，本船が再びその開始地点または目的地から等距離の地点において航海を再開するまで，傭船料の支払は中断する。オフハイヤー中に本船が使用したすべての燃料は，船主の負担とする。悪天候のため港または錨地への避難を余儀なくされたとき，または水深の浅い港，浅瀬のある河川もしくは港へ航行したときは，本船の滞船および・またはよって生ずる費用は傭船者の負担とする。船体，機関または装備の欠陥または故障により，航海中速力が低下したときは，それによって喪失した時間，その結果余分に消費した燃料の代金その他一切の証明された費用は，傭船料から控除する。

18．再 傭 船

別段の定めがない限り，傭船者は，本契約期間の全部または一部につき，本船を再傭船に出すことができる。ただし，傭船者は，本契約履行の義務を負う。

19．入 渠

本船の前回の入渠は，……………実施した。

*(a) 船主は，本傭船期間中，船級の要求または事情により船底の掃除および塗装および・または修理のため，船主と傭船者が合意した都合のよい時期と場所で，本船を入渠させることができる。

*(b) 緊急の場合を除き，本傭船期間中，本船の入渠は行わない。

＊適宜抹消のこと

20．全 損

本船が滅失したときは，前払金のうち反対給付が得られなかった分（滅失または最後に消息のあった日から起算する）は，直ちに傭船者に返還しなければならない。

21．免 責

本傭船期間中，天災，公敵，火災，君主・統治者・人民による抑留，海上・河川，機器・汽罐および航海の一切の危険および事故，ならびに航海上の過誤について，両当事者は相互に免責されるものとする。

22．自 由

水先人を同乗させ，または同乗させずに航行すること，曳航しまたは曳航されること，遭難船舶を救援すること，人命・財産を救助する目的で離路することは本船の自由とする。

23．リーエン

船主は，本傭船契約上当然，然るべき一切の金額（共同海損分担金を含む）につき，すべての積荷，再運送賃および・または再傭船料の上にリーエンを有し，傭船者は，反対給付が得られなかった一切の前払金につき，本船の上にリーエンを有するものとする。一切の既払傭船料または供託金の超過分は，直ちに返還されなければならない。

傭船者は，直接または間接を問わず，船主の船舶に対する権利，利益を害することあるべきリーエンその他の負担の発生を認めないものとする。傭船者は本傭船期間中，港費および燃料を含め，船用品またはサービスを船主の信用貸しでまたは船主の時間で調達しないことを保証する。

24．救 助

一切の漂流物および救助料については，船主および傭船者の費用および乗組員の分配額を控除した後，船主と傭船者は均等に利益を受けるものとする。

25．共同海損

共同海損は，1990年改正の1974年ヨーク・アントワープ・ルールまたは以後の改正規則に従って……………において，……………通貨によって精算する。

傭船者は，本傭船期間中に発行されるすべての船荷証券に，共同海損は1990年改正の1974年ヨーク・アントワープ・ルールまたは以後の改正規則に従って精算する旨の規定および第31条の「ニュー・ジェイソン条項」を挿入することを保証する。

定期傭船料は共同海損を分担しない。
26. 航　　海
本傭船契約書に記載のいかなる事項も，定期傭船者に対する船舶の賃貸借としては，解釈しないものとする。船主は，常に本船の航海，水先人および曳船の行為，船舶保険，乗組員その他の一切の事項につき，自己の計算において航海する場合と同一の責任を負う。
27. 貨物クレーム
船主と傭船者の間における貨物クレームは，1984年5月改正の1970年2月ニューヨーク・プロデュース書式に関するPIクラブ間協定または以後の改正のものに従って精算する。
28. 荷役用機器と灯火
船主は，本船に..........................荷役用機器を装備し，記載された揚貨能力を有する（すべてのデリックまたはクレーン用）機器を提供する。船主はまた，本船の夜間作業用の照明を備える。ただし，船内の灯火以外に増設した一切の灯火の費用は，傭船者の負担とする。本船のいずれの機器も傭船者の使用に委ねられる。傭船者が要求したときは，本船は昼夜作業を行い，積揚中，すべての荷役用機器は，傭船者の使用に委ねられる。荷役用機器の運転不能または動力不足を生じたときは，傭船者の荷役作業員が引き起こしたものでない限り，傭船者が実際に喪失した時間は，オフハイヤーとみなされ，それによって生じた荷役作業員の待機料は，船主が支払う。傭船者が要求したときは，船主は，これに代わる陸上の装置の賃借料を負担する。その場合，本船はオンハイヤーとする。
29. 乗組員時間外
傭船者は，傭船者またはその代理人が命じた職員および部員の時間外労働の対価として，1ヶ月当たり..............1ヶ月未満は按分して，傭船料と共に船主に支払う。
30. 船荷証券
(a) 船長は，メーツ・レシートまたは検数人のタリー・シートの記載に従って呈示された船荷証券または海上貨物運送状に署名しなければならない。ただし，傭船者は，事前に船主から書面による権限を受け，常にメーツ・レシートまたは検数人のタリー・シートに従って発行される船荷証券または海上貨物運送状に，船長に代わって署名することができる。
(b) いかなる船荷証券または海上貨物運送状も，本傭船契約を侵害してはならず，傭船者は，本傭船契約と自己またはその要請により船長が署名した一切の船荷証券または海上貨物運送状との間の不一致から生ずるすべての結果または責任について，船主に補償する。
(c) 甲板積貨物に対する船荷証券には，「傭船者，荷送人および荷受人の危険，費用および責任で甲板上に積載した。それによって生ずる一切の減失，損傷または遅延につき，本船または船主の側に責任を課さない」旨の条項が挿入されなければならない。
31. 保護条項
本傭船契約は，以下の条項に従うものとし，それら一切の条項は，本傭船契約に基づき発行されるすべての船荷証券または海上貨物運送状に挿入される。
(a) 至上条項
「本船荷証券は，米国海上物品運送法，ヘーグ・ルール，ヘーグ・ヴィスビー・ルールその他船荷証券の発行地または仕向地において強行法として適用されるべき同種の国内法の規定によりその効力を有し，かつ，それらの規定が本証券に挿入されているものとみなすほか，本証券に定めるいかなる事項も，上記の法に基づく運送人の権利もしくは免責の特権を放棄し，またはその責任もしくは義務を加重させないものとみなす。本証券の文言が，同法と抵触するときは，その文言はその抵触を限度として無効となるものとする。」

および
(b) 双方過失衝突条項
「相手船の過失と本船の船長，乗組員，水先人またはその他運送人の被用者の航海もしくは船舶の取扱に関する行為・怠慢または懈怠の結果，本船と相手船が衝突し，相手船たる非積載船またはその船主が，本証券記載物品の減失・損傷その他貨物所有者の請求一切につき，これを貨物所有者に対し

て賠償したかまたは賠償義務を負い，かかる損害を衝突損害の一部として，積載船または運送人に求償し，相殺または回収した場合，貨物所有者は，運送人が被った上記損害を補償するものとする。

上記の規定は，衝突船舶または衝突物体以外のいずれかの船舶または物体の所有者，運航者もしくは管理者に衝突または接触について過失がある場合にも適用する。」

および

(c) ニュー・ジェイソン条項

「航海の開始前または開始後に，過失によると否とを問わず，かつ原因の如何を問わず，事故，危険，損害または災害が発生し，その原因またはその原因の結果について，運送人が法律，契約その他によって責任を負わないときは，貨物，荷送人，荷受人または貨物の所有者は，それによって生じた共同海損の性質を有する犠牲，損失または費用を船主と分担し，かつ貨物について生じた救助料および特別の費用を支払わなければならない。

救助船が運送人によって所有され，または運航されている場合においても，その救助船が第三者の所有に属する場合と同様に，救助料は全額支払わなければならない。貨物，荷送人，荷受人または貨物の所有者は，要求があれば，運送人またはその代理人が貨物の見積分担金，一切の救助料および特別の費用を補償するに十分と認める金額を，貨物の引渡前に運送人に預託しなければならない。」

および

(d) 合衆国向け航海 ― 麻薬条項

「1986年合衆国薬物乱用禁止法またはその改正法の規定に従って，傭船者は，積荷目録に記載されていない麻薬およびマリファナが本船上に積み込まれ，または隠されるのを防止するため最大限の注意を尽くすことを担保する。

本規定に傭船者が従わないときは，傭船者は，担保違反として船主に対して責任を負い，船主，本船の船長および乗組員に害が加わらないようにし，彼らに対して個々にまたは連帯でなされ，生じるいかなるクレームについても補償しなければならない。さらに，傭船者による本規定違反の結果生ずるすべての喪失時間，罰金を含むすべての支出は，傭船者の勘定とし，本船はオンハイヤーとする。

傭船者の本規定違反の結果，本船がアレストされたときは，傭船者は，自己の費用で相当の期間内に本船の解放を確実にするためあらゆる相当な手段を尽くし，自己の費用で本船解放を確実にするための保釈金を提供しなければならない。

麻薬およびマリファナが本船の乗組員等の所持品から見つかったときは，船主は，すべての喪失時間および罰金を含む支出について責任を負わなければならない。」

および

(e) 戦争条項

「(i) 戦時禁制品は，一切船積してはならない。本船は，船主の承諾（その承諾は不当に差し控えてはならない）なしに，宣戦布告の有無を問わず，戦争状態，軍事的行為，敵対行為，内戦，暴動または海賊行為に巻き込まれ，船舶，貨物または乗組員が交戦国の権力による捕獲，アレスト，抑留または敵対行為を受けやすいと合理的に予想される一切の港または場所に入ることを要求されない（「権力」という語は，海軍，陸軍もしくは空軍を持つ法律上または事実上の官憲または一切の政府機関を名乗る者を意味する）。

(ii) 船主が承諾を与えたときは，傭船者は，通常の船体保険証券上の価額に等しい保険価額（評価額……………を超えない）で，本船に船体戦争保険を付すための証明可能な割増保険料を支払う。さらに，船主は不稼働損失，運賃滞費，全損，封鎖等の付随的危険に対する戦争危険保険を付すことができ，傭船者は，その保険料を支払う。そのような保険が民間保険または国家保険を利用できないときは，本船はそのような港または区域に入り，または碇泊することを要求されない。

(iii) 本傭船契約日の後，または本船が本傭船契約に基づく傭船期間中に，(i)項に記載された状況がある場合，そのような港または地域への航海に関し，傭船者は，そのような戦争，軍事的行為または敵対行為の結果，船舶，職員および部員に関して生じた証明可能な割増賃金および割増保険料を負担する。

(iv) 本船の航海または運送される貨物に起因して職員および部員に支給される特別手当は，すべて傭船者の勘定とする。」

32. 戦争による解約

....のいずれか二国または二国以上の国家間で戦争(宣戦布告の有無を問わない)が勃発した場合,船主または傭船者のいずれも本傭船契約を解約することができる。その場合,傭船者は,第10条に従って,本船が貨物を積載している場合は,仕向地において,または本条に基づき仕向地への到着もしくは入港が妨げられるときは,船主の指示する付近の安全な開港において揚荷した後,本船が貨物を積載していない場合は,その時碇泊している港において,または航海中のときは船主の指示する付近の安全な開港において,返船する。いずれの場合においても,傭船料は,第11条に従って継続して支払われる。本条に規定したものを除き,本傭船契約の他の規定は,すべて返船時まで適用される。

33. 結　　　氷

本船は,結氷港もしくは結氷地域,結氷を理由として灯標もしくは灯船が撤去されているか,撤去のおそれのある港もしくは地域,または結氷のため通常の方法では本船が安全に入港碇泊できない危険のあるような港もしくは地域,船積・揚荷完了後出港できないおそれのある港もしくは地域のいずれに向けても,入港または碇泊を命じられない。本船の寸法,構造および氷の程度に関して要求されるのが相当であるときは,船主の事前の承諾を得て,本船は,砕氷船の後について行くことができる。

34. 徴　　　用

本傭船契約期間中,本船が旗国政府により徴用されたときは,本船は,その徴用期間,オフハイヤーとみなされ,政府がその徴用期間に関して支払う傭船料は,船主が取得する。本船が政府に徴用されている期間は,本傭船契約に定められた期間の一部として計算する。

徴用期間が................ヶ月を超えるときは,いずれの当事者も本傭船契約を解約することができ,それによって生ずる損害については,いずれの当事者も賠償を請求できない。

35. 荷役作業員による損傷

本傭船契約中の反対の規定如何にかかわらず,荷役作業員が本船にもたらした一切の損傷について,船長が実務上できるだけ速やかに,かつ発見後48時間以内に書面で傭船者および・またはその代理人に通知したときは,傭船者は,補償しなければならない。その通知は,損傷を詳細に示し,傭船者に対して損傷の程度を見積るため検査人を指名するよう要求するものとする。

(a) 一切の損傷が,本船の堪航能力および・または乗組員の安全および,または本船の取引上の能力に影響を及ぼす場合,傭船者は直ちに自己の費用でそのような損傷を修理するよう手配しなければならず,本船はその修理が完了するまで傭船が継続し,要求があれば本船の船級協会の検査に合格しなければならない。

(b) 上記(a)に記載されていない一切の損傷は,傭船者の選択により返船の前または後に船主の作業と同時に修理される。その場合,傭船料および・または費用は,傭船者が責任を負う修理のために要した時間および・または費用が,船主の作業を行うのに必要な時間および・または費用を超える場合を除き,支払われない。

36. 船艙清掃

航海ごとにおよび・または貨物ごとに船艙を掃き,および・または水洗いし,および・または清掃する作業が乗組員によって行われ,かつそれが現地の規則で認められているときは,傭船者は,そのための手配をし,かつ1船艙につき....................の割合で追加費用を支払わなければならない。

そのような一切の作業に関し,本船の船艙が港湾当局その他の検査に合格しなくても,船主は,責任を負わない。傭船者は,その選択により船艙を清掃せずに,代わりに一括合計....................を支払って返船することができる。

37. 税　　　金

傭船者の指図の結果,本船または船主に課された一切の地方税,州税および国税は,本傭船契約の期間中,期間後いずれであるかを問わず,(本船の置籍国または船主所属国によって課されたものを除き)貨物および・または運賃および・または再運送賃および・または傭船料に対する税金を含め,傭船者が支払わなければならない。

38. 傭船者マーク

傭船者は，本船に自社の旗を掲げ，自社の社色を塗装する権利を有する。本船は，傭船終了前に船主の社色に塗装し直されなければならない。傭船者の行うこれらの塗装，保守および再塗装に要する時間と費用は，傭船者の負担とする。

39. 繋船返戻金

傭船者は，本船が最短30日間港内に停泊したことにより，船主が保険者から受け取ることができ，かつ実際に受け取った一切の割増保険料の払戻額について，その碇泊した期間がすべて傭船期間中であるときは全額，一部が傭船期間中であるときは按分して利益を得る。

40. 書　　類

船主は，油濁に対する賠償資力証明書が船主のPIクラブから取得できるときは，その証明書，国際トン数証明書，スエズ運河およびパナマ運河トン数証明書，国籍証書，本船の索具の強度および・または能力に関する証明書を含め，合意された航路定限内の航海を可能にするために要求される，本船に関する一切の書類を備えなければならない。

41. 密　航　者

(a)(i)　傭船者は，自己が船積する貨物および・またはコンテナの中に隠れて密航者が本船に入り込むのを防ぐため，相当の注意を尽くすことを担保する。

(ii)　傭船者が相当の注意を尽くしても，傭船者が船積した貨物および・またはコンテナの中に隠れて密航者が本船に入り込んだときは，傭船契約違反となり，傭船者は，その結果について責任を負い，船主に害が及ばないようにし，かつ船主に対してなされる一切のクレームを補償しなければならない，さらに，それによって生じた一切の喪失時間および罰金を含む費用は，傭船者の勘定とし，本船は傭船を継続する。

(iii)　上記(a)(ii)による傭船者の契約違反の結果，本船がアレストされたときは，傭船者は，相当の期間内に本船が解放されることを確実にするため，あらゆる適当な手段を尽くし，自己の費用で本船の解放を確実にするため保釈金を提供しなければならない。

(b)(i)　船主が相当の注意を尽くしても，傭船者が船積した貨物および・またはコンテナの中に隠れる以外の方法で密航者が本船に入り込んだときは，それによって生じた一切の喪失時間および罰金を含む費用は，船主の勘定とし，本船はオフハイヤーとなる。

(ii)　傭船者が船積した貨物および・またはコンテナの中に隠れる以外の方法で密航者が本船に入り込んだ結果，本船がアレストされたときは，船主は，相当の期間内に本船が解放されることを確実にするため，あらゆる相当な手段を尽くし，自己の費用で本船の解放を確実にするため保釈金を提供しなければならない。

42. 密　　輸

船長，職員および・または部員が密輸を行ったときは，船主は，一切の罰金，税金または賦課金を負担しなければならず，本船はその結果生じた喪失時間についてオフハイヤーとなる。

43. 手　数　料

本船および船主は，本傭船契約およびその継続または延長により受け取る傭船料について，..........パーセントの手数料を...........................に支払う。

44. アドレスコミッション

本傭船契約により受け取り，支払われる傭船料につき，..........パーセントのアドレスコミッションを...........................に支払うものとする。

45. 仲　　裁*

(a)　NEW YORK

本契約から生じるすべての紛争は，New Yorkにおいて，以下の方法で合衆国法に従って仲裁により解決する。

本契約の各当事者が仲裁人を1名ずつ指名し，その2名の仲裁人が第三仲裁人を指名する。仲裁人全員または2名（多数決）の判断は，最終のものとして，仲裁判断執行のためにこの合意を裁判所の

命令とすることができる。仲裁人は，海運事情に通じた実務家でなければならない。この仲裁は，海事仲裁人協会の規則に従って行われる。

　各当事者の請求金額の総額が米貨……………ドル＊＊を超えない紛争に関する仲裁は，海事仲裁人協会の短縮仲裁手続に従って行われる。

(b) **LONDON**

　本契約から生ずるすべての紛争は，Londonにおいて仲裁により解決する。両当事者が直ちに単独仲裁人によることを合意しない限り，ボルティック商業および海運取引所の会員で，Londonにおいて事業を営む2名の仲裁人による最終の仲裁に付託される。仲裁人は，各当事者が1名ずつ指名し，それらの仲裁人は審判人を指名する権限を有する。いずれかの仲裁人が上記の資格を有しないことを埋由に，仲裁判断に異議を唱え，または無効を申し立ててはならない。ただし，仲裁判断が下される前にその仲裁人の行為について不服が申し立てられたときは，この限りではない。本契約に基づき発生するすべての紛争には英国法が適用される。

　各当事者の請求金額の総額が米貨……………ドル＊＊を超えない紛争に関する仲裁は，London海事仲裁人協会の少額仲裁手続に従って行われる。

　＊　(a)または(b)を適宜抹消のこと
　＊＊　この空欄に数字が記載されない場合，この規定のみが無効となり，本条の他の規定は完全に効力を有する。

　……………………条から……………………条まで（両条を含む）の追加規定が本傭船契約に完全に挿入されたことを，相互に合意する。

追加規定 "A"

　船主……………………と傭船者……………………との間の……………………日付傭船契約書に添付

本船の追加明細：

ボルタイム書式

ボルティック アンド インターナショナル
マリタイム コンファレンス
（前 ボルティック アンド ホワイト シー コンファレンス）

統一定期傭船契約書

................19................

　本日ここに，船主....................と，その所有に係る....................号，総トン数／純トン数................トン，船級....................指示馬力，商務省夏期乾舷における載貨重量トン約....................トン（燃料，船用品，食料品および罐水を含む），造船所図面上，艙内載貨容積グレーン／ベールにて................立方フィート（約....................トンをいれる常備用燃料庫を除く），燃料消費高最良ウェールズ炭にて約....................トン，もしくは燃料油にて約....................トンの消費量で，天候良好，海上平穏の状態における満載航海速力約................ノット，現在....................中の船舶に関し，....................の傭船者....................との間で，下記のとおり合意した。

1．船主は本船を貸し渡し，傭船者は借り受けることとし，その期間は....................暦月間とする。傭船開始時は（受渡のない限り日曜日または公休日を除く），午前9時から午後6時まで，土曜日ならば午前9時から午後2時までの間に....................における，傭船者の指示する本船が常時浮揚状態で安全に碇泊し，利用できるバースにおいて，あらゆる点において通常の貨物運送業務に適する状態をもって本船が引き渡され，傭船者の使用に委ねられたときとする。
　　本船は，....................引き渡されるものとする。

2．本船は，適法な貨物の運送のための適法な航路に使用するものとし，その航路は，本船が常時浮揚して安全に碇泊できる下記の区域内の良好かつ安全な港，その他の場所の間に限る：................
....
....家畜または（酸類・爆発物・カーバイド・珪素鉄・ナフサ・ガソリン・タールおよびその製品のような）有毒性・発火性もしくは危険性を有する貨物を船積してはならない。

3．船主は一切の食料および給料，船舶保険料，甲板および機関室用のすべての船用品を準備して，その費用を支払い，傭船期間中，船体ならびに機関を完全な稼働状態に維持しなければならない。
　　船主は，艙口毎に，1人のウィンチマンを配置しなければならない。ただし，その増員を要する場合，または船内荷役作業員が乗組員との共同荷役を拒否するか，その共同荷役を認められていない場合，傭船者は資格のある陸上ウィンチマンを配置し，かつその費用を支払うものとする。

4．傭船者は賄用石炭を含むすべての石炭・燃料油・罐水の費用，港費，水先料（強制水先料であると否とを問わない），運河操舵手賃，通船料，灯台料，曳船料・領事館費（船長・職員および部員に関するものを除く），運河通航料，桟橋料，その他の税金ならびに料金（外国の一般地方税または国税を含む）のほか，引渡港・返船港における桟橋料，港税およびトン税（ただし本船の引渡前または返船後の運送品について生じたものを除く），代理店料，仲介料をも手配して，これを支払わねばならない。積込・荷均・積浮（荷敷・仕切板を含む。ただし，既に本船に在るものを除く）・揚荷・検量・検数・積荷の引渡・艙口検査，就業中の役人，または被用者に支給した食事，検疫（燻蒸消毒・殺菌消毒を含む）による抑留およびその費用も含むその他の諸費用の手配とその支払とは，すべて傭船者の負担とする。
　　積込および揚荷に実際に使用する一切の綱・スリング・特別の動索および一切の特別の索具（港

の慣習により必要とする**繋船用の特別の綱・大索・鎖を含む**）は，傭船者の負担である。ただし，本船は2トン以下の積揚貨物の荷役に堪えるウィンチ・デリック・滑車および普通の動索を装備するものとする。

5. 傭船者は引渡港において，また船主は返船港において，本船燃料庫内の一切の石炭または燃料油の残高を引き取り，それぞれの港における時価で，その代金を支払う。ただし，最低..............トン以上，最高..............トン以下の石炭または燃料油を，本船燃料庫内に残置して，返船しなければならない。

6. 傭船者は傭船料として，30日につき..............を，第1条による傭船開始のときから，船主に返船するときまで支払うものとする。傭船料の支払は現金により，..............において，毎30日分を前払するものとし，減額を認めない。

　この支払がないときは，船主は催告，裁判所の介入その他の手続によることなく，傭船者の業務から本船を引き揚げる権利を有する。この場合，船主が傭船者に対して本契約上有する他の一切の請求は妨げられない。

7. 返船は傭船期間の満了と同時に，傭船者が本船の引渡を受けたときと同様の良好な状態で，（正当な自然損耗を除き）結氷していない傭船者任意の港..............において，午前9時から午後6時（土曜日は午後2時）までの間に行うものとする。ただし，返船日は，日曜日または公休日であってはならない。

　傭船者が船主に対して行う返船の予定港および予定日の通知は，その少なくとも10日以前でなければならない。

　本船の指示された航海が傭船期間を超過する場合には，傭船者は，本船を使用してその航海を完了することができる。この場合，右の航海については，所定の傭船終了時頃に返船しうる相当の見込があったことを要する。ただし，傭船終了日以後の期間については傭船者は，市場料率が本契約に定めた傭船料率を超える場合，その市場料率を支払わねばならない。

8. 傭船者が使用できる船腹は，本船の船長・職員・部員，揚荷機，装具，備品，食料および船用品のための相当かつ十分な船腹を除き，本船の区画および全積載力（適法な甲板積載力を含む）に及ぶものとする。

9. 船長はすべての航海を極力迅速に遂行し，本船の乗組員により，慣習上なすべき助力を提供するものとする。船長は本船の使用，代理店業務，またはその他の手配に関しては，傭船者の指図に従わなければならない。傭船者は船長・職員または代理人が船荷証券その他の証書に署名するか，もしくはかかる指図に従ったため，および本船の書類の不正確または持越貨物によって生ずる一切の結果または責任につき，船主に補償するものとする。船主は荷不足・混合・荷印・貨物の個数，もしくは積付不良その他によって生じる積荷の損害または請求に対しては，その責めに任じない。

　傭船者において船長・航海士，または機関士の行為を不満足とする相当な理由があるときは，船主は苦情の詳細を受け取りしだい，直ちにその事実を取り調べ，必要かつ可能な場合，これを交代させるものとする。

10. 傭船者は一切の指図，および航海上の指示を，船長に与えるものとする。船長および機関士は，完全かつ正確な航海日誌を作成し，傭船者またはその代理人の閲覧に供しなければならない。

11. (A)　入渠その他本船の稼働状態を維持するに必要な処置，人員または船用品の不足，機関の故障，船体の損傷その他の事故により，連続24時間を超えて本船の業務が阻害された場合，本船が即時に提供すべき業務を履行しえないために喪失した一切の時間に対しては，傭船料の支払を要しない。傭船料の前払があったときは，これをその時間に応じて精算しなければならない。

　(B)　本船が荒天のため港湾または錨地に避難したとき，水深の浅い湾または沙洲のある河川・港湾に寄港したとき，もしくは本船の積荷に事故を生じた場合，滞船および／またはこれによって生じた費用は，傭船者の負担とする。この場合，滞船および／またはその費用，もしくはその原因が，船主の被用者の単独の過失によるか寄与過失によるかを問わない。

12. 汽罐の掃除は，できる限り業務期間中に行うものとする。これが不可能な場合には，傭船者は掃除に必要な時間を船主に供与しなければならない。本船が48時間を超えて滞船するときは，傭船料の支払は，本船が再び準備完了となるまで中止する。

13. 本船引渡の遅延, 傭船期間中の遅延, 積荷の減失, 損傷については, 本船を堪航状態におくにつき船主または船舶管理人に相当の注意が欠けていたために生じた場合, もしくはそれが船主または船舶管理人自身の作為・不作為または懈怠から生じた場合に限り, 船主はその責任を負担する。これ以外の場合については, 船主はたとえ自己の被用者の怠慢または懈怠に起因するいかなる損害または遅延を生じても責任を負わない。船主は局地的・全般的の別なく, ストライキ・ロックアウトもしくは労働の停止または制限 (船長・職員または部員を含む) から生じる減失または損傷を負担しない。

本契約に違反して船積した貨物により, または燃料積取・貨物の積込・積付・揚荷の不適当あるいは不注意により, または傭船者もしくはその被用者の怠慢な行為または過失によって, 本船もしくは船主に減失または損傷を生じたときは, 傭船者はその責めに任じなければならない。

14. 傭船者またはその代理人は, 船長の求めにより, いずれの港においても, 通常の船用金として必要な金員を立て替えるものとする。この場合, 船主は右の立替金について年6分の利子以外負担しない。立替金は傭船料から控除する。

15. 本船は(a)熱病または流行病の蔓延している場所, もしくは船長・職員および部員が法律の規定により本船と同航する義務のない場所, (b)結氷地, または本船の到着時に結氷を理由として灯火・灯船・標識・浮標が撤去されているか, または撤去のおそれのある場所, もしくは結氷のため通常の方法では到底本船が到着しまたは積取・揚荷の完了後において出港できない危険が現存する場所のいずれに向けても, 配船を命ぜられ, もしくは入港の義務を負うことがない。本船には, 結氷を強行突破する義務はないものとする。結氷のため船長が積地または揚地に碇泊するときは, 凍結およびまたは損害を被るおそれがあると認めた場合, 船長は随意に最寄りの開放地に回航して, 新たに傭船者の指図を待つことができる。

前項の事由による予見しえない滞留は, 傭船者の負担である。

16. 本船が滅失するか, または行方不明となったときは, その滅失の日から傭船料の支払を中止する。減失の日が確定しないときは, 本船につき最後の通信があった日から起算して, 仕向地到着を予定された日まで, 傭船料の半額を支払う。前払傭船料は, すべてこれに応じて精算するものとする。

17. 本船は要求がある場合, 昼夜, 作業するものとする。この場合, 傭船者は本船の船員雇用契約に定められた時間ならびに料率に従って船主が職員および部員に支払った一切の時間外労働の費用を償還しなければならない。

18. 船主は本契約に基づく一切の請求権につき, 定期傭船者のすべての積荷, 再運送賃, および船荷証券運賃の上に, リーエンを有し, 傭船者は反対給付が得られなかった一切の前払金につき, 本船の上にリーエンを有するものとする。

19. 他船に対してなした, あらゆる救助・救援については, 船長および乗組員への分配額, 一切の法定その他の費用 (救助のため喪失した時間に対し本契約により支払う傭船料, ならびに損傷の修理, 消費した石炭または燃料油を含む) を控除した後, 船主と傭船者とにおいて均等の利益を受けるものとする。傭船者は, 船主が救助料の支払を確保し, かつその金額を定めるためになした一切の処置に従わねばならない。

20. 傭船者は, 船主に対し, 相当の通知をなして, 任意に本船を他に再傭船させることができる。ただし, 原傭船者は常に船主に対し, 本契約履行の責任を免れない。

21. (A) 本船は, 現実のまたは切迫せる交戦行為, 戦争, 敵対行為, 軍事的行為, 私人・団体・国家のいずれによるかを問わず, 本船その他の船舶または その積荷に対する海賊行為または敵対・悪意の加害行為, 革命, 内乱, 暴動または国際法上の行為のため危険となっている区域内航行を必要とする一切の場所または航海につき, 配船の指示を受けまたはこれを続行しもしくはかかる業務に使用されることも, 制裁権の発動に基づく一切の危険または刑罰に曝されることも, 交戦国または交戦団体もしくは官憲によるあらゆる種類の没収・捕獲・刑罰その他の処分を受けるおそれのある貨物の運送も要求されないものとする。ただし, 予め船主の承諾を得た場合は, この限りでない。

(B) 本船が, かかる危険区域に近づき, 立ち入り, またはその水域へ配船を命ぜられたとき, も

しくは前項記載の危険に曝されたときは，(1)これに関連するおそれのある一切の危険に対し，船主自ら適当とする条件により，本船および／または，傭船料に関する自己の利益を，随時，保険に付することができる。傭船者は船主の請求があるときは，その保険料を償還すべきものとする。また(2)船長・職員または部員の死傷，もしくは乗組員がその危険水域への航行，またはその危険に曝されることを拒否したために喪失した時間その他，全喪失時間に対しては，第11条の規定にかかわらず，傭船料を支払わねばならない。

(C) (A)項記載のいずれかの事実が存在するため，またはその存在期間中に，船長・職員および／または部員の給料もしくは食料品および／または甲板および／または機関室用の船用品の費用および／または保険料が増加するに至った場合，船主からこれに関する計算書の提出を受けたときは，傭船者はその増加額を傭船料に付加して支払うものとする。右の計算書は毎月これを提出する。

(D) 本船は，本船の旗国政府その他の政府，もしくはかかる政府の権限を行使するかまたは行使しているとみられる個人（団体），もしくはかかる本船に関する戦争保険条項により権限を賦与された委員会または個人から受ける発航・到着・航路・寄港地・停船・仕向地・引渡その他一切の事項についての命令または指示に従うことができる。

(E) 本船の旗国に戦争，敵対行為，軍事的行為，革命，または暴動が波及するに至った場合，船主ならびに傭船者は本契約を解約することができる。ただし，特約がないときは，仕向港において返船するものとし，仕向港に到達または入港することが(A)項の規定上許されないときは，本船の一切の荷物を揚荷した後，船主が選定した最寄りの安全な開港において返船するものとする。

(F) 本条項の規定に従ってなした作為もしくは不作為は，離路とみなされない。

22. 19......年......月......日までに本船の引渡がないときは，傭船者は本契約を解約することができる。

解約期日までに本船の引渡ができない場合，傭船者は，船主の要求があれば，その旨の通知受領後48時間以内に，解約もしくは本船引取の意思を表示しなければならない。

23. 本契約に関して生じる一切の紛争は，ロンドン（または合意により定めたその他の地）において，これを船主・傭船者双方が各々1名宛選任した仲裁人の仲裁判断に付託するものとする。仲裁人の判断が一致しないときは，双方の仲裁人は共同して審判人を選任し，その裁定を求める。両当事者は，仲裁人もしくは審判人の仲裁判断を終局のものとして，これに従う。

24. 共同海損は1950年ヨーク・アントワープ・ルールに準拠して決済するものとする。傭船料は共同海損を分担しない。

25. 船主は本契約により受け取る一切の傭船料につき，.........................の手数料を........................に対して支払うものとする。ただし，いかなる場合においても，仲立人の実際に要した費用，およびその業務に相当する報酬を下回らないものとする。当事者の一方の契約違反により，傭船料全額について支払がない場合には，その当事者が仲立人に対し，手数料の損失を塡補する責任を負うものとする。

両当事者の合意により本契約を解約したときは，船主が仲立人に対して手数料の一切の損失を補償する。ただし，その場合でも，手数料の額は1年分の傭船料に対する仲立料を超えないものとする。

シェルタイム書式

本傭船契約書の略称
"SHELLTIME 4"
1984年12月発行

定期傭船契約
ロンドン, 19

　本契約は，本日，本契約第1条に表示された..............................と称する良好な船（以下「本船」という）の船主である..............................所在の..............................（以下「船主」という）と..............................所在の..............................（以下「傭船者」という）との間で合意したものである。

本船の表示および状態

1. 本契約に基づき，本船の引渡日において，
   (a) 本船は................の船級を保持すること，
   (b) 本船は原油ならびに・もしくは精製油の運送にあらゆる面で適すること，
   (c) 本船は船体堅牢，水密で良好な状態にあり，その機関，汽罐，船体その他装備（少なくとも船体応力計算機，レーダーを含む）も良好，能率的な状態にして，あらゆる面で航海に適すること，
   (d) 本船のタンク，バルブおよびパイプラインは油密であること，
   (e) 本船は，
      航海中：主機に，摂氏50度において最大粘度......CSの燃料油・市販のいずれの等級の燃料油（ACGFO）を，補機に舶用ディーゼル油（ACGFO）を，
      碇泊中：補機に舶用ディーゼル油・ACGFOを，焚くのにあらゆる面で適合していること，
   (f) 本船は，昼夜を問わず遅滞なくスエズ運河およびパナマ運河を通航できるよう施行中の規則に準拠していること，
   (g) 本船には，本契約を遅滞なく履行するために，いずれの適用法によるにせよ随時必要とされるすべての証書類と備品を具備していること，
   (h) 本船は，本契約に添付された書式Bの要目に適合すること，ただし，書式Bの条項と本条を含む本契約の他の条項との間に抵触あるときは，本契約の条項が優先すること。

乗組員およびその義務

2. (a) 本契約に基づき，本船の引渡日において，
   (i) 本船には，本船のトン数に見合う適正かつ必要な定員数の船長，職員および部員が乗り組むものとし，それらの員数は，いかなる場合においても，旗国法により要求される数を下回ってはならず，また，それらは本船およびその装備を十分かつ安全に操作するよう訓練されていること，
   (ii) すべての乗組員は，旗国法の要求に従い，正当な資格証明書を保持すること，
   (iii) すべての乗組員は，1978年の船員の訓練，資格証明および当直の基準に関する国際条約（STCW条約）の関係条項に従って訓練されていること，
   (iv) 本船には，積揚地において荷役が効率的かつ安全に遂行されるよう，また本船と荷送人または荷受人との間の意思疎通が迅速かつ能率よく行われるよう，英語の適切な実用的知識をもった十分な数の船員が乗り組むものとする。
   (b) 船主は，傭船者より別途の指図がない限り，本契約を通じて，船長が本船職員および部員と共に，
   (i) 極力迅速に全航海を遂行すること，

(ii) 一切の慣習上の助力を提供すること，および

(iii) 傭船者またはその代理人より要求あったときは，昼夜を問わず，可能な限り迅速に船積および揚荷を行うこと，ただし，積地または揚地の法（その場合による）に常に従い，またそれぞれの場合に旗国のいかなる適用法にも従って船積および揚荷を行うことを保証する。

保船義務

3．(i) 傭船業務を通じて，船主は，時の経過，自然損耗，その他の事由（本契約第27条に該当すると否とを問わない）により，第1条および第2条(a)に記載された状態を維持しまたは修復する措置をとる必要が生じたときは，相当の注意を尽くして本船の維持または修復を行うものとする。

(ii) 本契約に基づき本船のオンハイヤー中，本船が第1条，第2条(a)または第10条の要件に適合しなくなったときは，傭船料はそのような不適合に対して傭船者に補償するのに十分な金額を差し引くものとする。このような不適合によって，本船の本契約の履行に要する時間が影響されるときは，傭船料は，その喪失時間を傭船料率に基づいて計算された額と等しい額を差し引き減額するものとする。

本項(ii)による傭船料の控除は，傭船者の取りうるその他の賠償請求の権利を損なわない。ただし，その傭船料の控除が喪失時間に関するものである場合には，その喪失時間は第24条に基づく計算から除外されるものとする。

(iii) 船主が第3条(i)項に基づく義務に違反している場合には，傭船者はその旨を船主に書面で通知することができる。船主がその通知を受け取った後30日を経過しても，船主が第3条(i)項で要求される相当の注意を尽くしていることを，傭船者の相応の満足を得るまで行わなかったときは，本船はオフハイヤーとなり，以後の傭船料の支払は，船主がそうした相当の注意を尽くしていることを示すまで中断するものとする。

さらに，本船が第3条に基づきオフハイヤーとなっているときにはいつでも，傭船者は書面による解約通知を発し本契約を終了する選択権を有する。その場合の解約は，そうした通知が船主に受け取られる日またはその通知に記載された日以降より効力を生じる。本第3条(iii)項は，本契約あるいは，その他に基づく，傭船者の一切の権利（本契約第21条に基づく傭船者の権利を無条件に含む）または船主の義務を損なうものではない。

期間および航路定限

4．船主は本船を提供することに合意し，傭船者は，本船の引渡日時から開始する．．．．．．．．．．．．．．．．．．．．．．の期間に，特に．．．．．．．．．．．．．．．．．．．を含め，あらゆる適法な貨物（第28条には常に従う）を運送する目的で，英国の現行協会担保航路定限およびその後に改正された航路定限に準拠した，傭船者の指図する世界全域で，傭船することに合意する。前記にかかわらず，ただし，第35条に従い，傭船者は，船主の承諾を得て（この承諾は不当に保留されてはならない），かつ傭船者の指図の結果本船の保険者により請求される割増保険料を傭船者が支払うことを条件として，結氷海域または上述の定限外の世界全域に本船を仕向けることができる。

傭船者は，本船を常時浮揚して安全に碇泊できる安全な場所間および安全な場所（この表現が本契約で使用される場合は，港，バース，埠頭，ドック，錨地，海底油管，他船または艀の舷側，および海上の指定地を含むその他の指定地を含む）においてのみ使用するよう，相当の注意を尽くすものとする。本条または本契約の他の条項の記述にかかわらず，傭船者は，自己が本船を仕向けるいかなる場所の安全性も保証するものではなく，上述の相当の注意を尽くさなかったことにより生じた滅失または損傷を除いては，それに関し何ら責任を負わないものとする。上記を条件として，本船は，傭船者の指示するいかなる場所においても船積し，揚荷するものとする。ただし，傭船者は，船舶間積み替え荷役が少なくともICS・OCIMFのShip-to-Ship Transfer Guideの最新版に記載されている基準に従うよう，相当の注意を尽くすものとする。

本船は，船主任意の．．．．．．．．．．．．．．．．．．．．．．．にある港において船主より引き渡され，傭船者任意の．．．．．．．．．．．．．．．．．．．．．．．．．にある港において船主に返船されるものとする。

傭船開始・傭船解約

5．本船は，..........日以前には傭船者に引き渡されないものとし，本船が，..........日またはそれ以前に使用準備が整わず，傭船者の使用に委ねられないときは，傭船者は本契約を解約する選択権を有するものとする。

船主負担費目

6．船主は，船長，職員および部員の一切の食料，賃金，乗船および下船費用，その他一切を支給し，その費用を支払う義務を負い，さらに本契約第4条および第34条に規定されたものを除き，本船に係わる一切の保険，すべての甲板，船室および機関室の備品，水，本船の一切の入渠，分解検査，保守および修理，また一切の燻蒸費用および鼠族駆除証明書につき，その費用を支払うことを保証する。本第6条に基づく船主の義務は，船長，職員および部員の手回品に関し，また，船主が支給し支払うべき船用品，食料および上述のその他の物に関し，本契約履行中に生じる関税または輸入税についてのあらゆる債務を含むものとし，船主は，傭船者またはその代理人がこのような債務を支払いまたは支払うことを余儀なくされた金額については，傭船者に補償するものとする。賃金，食料および船用品につき共同海損に容認される金額は，その金額が本船のオンハイヤー期間についてのものである限り，傭船者に返還される。

傭船者負担費目

7．傭船者は，一切の燃料（船内用燃料を除く）曳船および水先人を手配し，その費用を支払うものとし，また代理店料，港費，手数料，貨物の船積および揚荷費用，運河通航料，および第6条により船主が支払うべき諸掛以外の一切の費用を支払うものとする。ただし，これらの費用が船主のために消費され，使用され，または生ずるとき，または本船がオフハイヤーにあるとき（そのような費目が第21条または第22条に基づき，提供した業務または短縮された距離が，傭船料からの控除額の算定に際し考慮されることに相当な関係がある場合を除く），そのような費目の全費用は船主の負担とし，さらに共同海損犠牲または費用に関連して使用された一切の燃料は船主が支払うものとする。

傭 船 料 率

8．本条の規定に従い，傭船者は，本船の使用ならびに傭船につき，1日当たり，また1日に満たない部分は按分で，..........の料率で，本船引渡日時（引渡地時）から船主への本船返船日時（返船地時）まで支払うものとする。

傭船料の支払

9．第3条(iii)項を条件として，傭船料の支払は，直ちに使用可能な資金として，.....................の.......................にある口座に毎暦月次の費用を控除して前払するものとする。

　(i) 既に支払われた傭船料に対して，傭船者がオフハイヤー期間に関連して正当に見積る一切の金額，

　(ii) 船主のための立替金，前払金およびそれに関する手数料，また本契約の各条項に従って船主負担となる費用，および

　(iii) 本契約第3条(ii)項または第24条に基づき傭船者に支払われるべき，または傭船者に支払われることになる正当に見積られた一切の金額。

　その精算については，その事実が確定した後の次回の月例支払期日に行うものとする。傭船者は，期限までに正当に支払を行ったものに限り，船主の取引銀行が船主の口座への入金に際し惹き起した遅延または過失には一切責任を負わない。

　期限までに適正に支払がなされなかったときは，

(a) 船主はその不履行を傭船者に通知し，傭船者はその通知を受け取ってから7日以内に利息を付した相当額を船主に支払うものとする。これを怠ったときは，船主は，本契約またはその他において，船主に存する他の一切の権利を損なうことなく，本船を傭船者の運航から引き揚げることができる，また

(b) 支払期日に支払われなかった金額に対する利息は，支払期日の翌日から支払のなされる日を含む日までについて発生し，年利は，支払期日の New York 時間正午現在において New York の

チェイス・マンハッタン銀行が発表する米国プライムレートに1パーセント上乗せしたものとする。その日にレートが発表されない場合には、次に発表された日のレートによるものとし、30日を1ヶ月とする12ヶ月、つまり1年を360日として半年複利で計算する。

貨物積載場所

10. 本船の全部、積載場所、甲板およびいかなる旅客用船室（船主の室を含む）も、本船の船長、職員、部員、索具、装具、備品、食料および船用品のための適切かつ十分な場所を除き、すべて傭船者の使用に委ねられる。ただし、船内の船用品の重量は、特に合意のない限り、傭船期間中いかなる時も………トンを超えてはならない。

時間外手当

11. 本船の就業規則に基づく船長、職員および部員の時間外手当は、それが傭船者またはその代理人の要請に応じて船積、揚荷、貨物の加熱、補油またはタンク清掃を行った結果生じたときは、傭船者の負担とする。

指図および航海日誌

12. 傭船者は、随時一切の必要な指図および航海指図を船長に与えるものとし、船長は完全で正確な航海日誌を作成し、傭船者またはその代理人が必要に応じ閲覧できるようにするものとする。船長は、要求があるときは、傭船者またはその代理人に同航海日誌の正本および完全な船積港および揚荷港の手仕舞書類、各航海毎の航海報告書その他報告書を提出するものとする。傭船者は、船長が提出しない書類については、船主費用で複写する権利を有するものとする。

船荷証券

13. (a) 船長は（船主により任命されるとはいえ）、本船の使用、代理行為その他の手配に関し、傭船者の命令および指図に従うものとし、本契約上の権利を損なうことなく、傭船者またはその代理人の指図のとおり船荷証券に署名しなければならない（ただし、常に第35条(a)および第40条を条件とする）。

    傭船者は、

    (i) 傭船者またはその代理人の指図に従って船荷証券に署名したことにより生ずる一切の結果または責任のうち、その船荷証券の条項が本契約の条件に反する部分に対し、または（第13条(b)の場合を除き）船長が別途傭船者またはその代理人の指図に従ったことにより生ずる一切の結果または責任に対し、また

    (ii) 傭船者またはその代理人が提供した書類の不備により生ずる一切の結果または責任に対し、船主に補償するものとする。

    (b) 前項の規定にかかわらず、船主は、

    (i) 船荷証券に記載されていない場所において、かつ・または

    (ii) 船荷証券の正本の提出を受けることなく、

    傭船者からの貨物の全部または一部の揚荷指図に従う義務はないものとする。ただし、船主が傭船者からその指図の確認書と船主が受入可能な補償状の双方を受け取った場合は、この限りではない。

乗組員の行為

14. 傭船者が、船長またはいかなる職員もしくは部員であろうとも、その行為に不満を表明した場合、船主は直ちにその不満を調査するものとする。その不満が十分根拠あると認められるときは、船主は遅滞なく任命を変更するものとする。また、船主はいかなる時にも、調査の結果を可及的速やかに傭船者に通知するものとする。

引渡および返船時の燃料

15. 傭船者は、引渡時、本船にある一切の燃料油を受け取り、代価を支払うものとし、船主は返船時（本契約の契約期間の満了時であると中途での終了時であるとを問わず）、本船に残存する一切の燃料油を受け取り、代価を支払うものとする。その代価は、引渡港または返船港それぞれにおけるその時の市場価格によるものとし、その市場価格が利用できないときは、それが利用可能な最寄りの

港におけるその時の市場価格で支払うものとする。ただし，引渡また返船が港で行われないときは，それぞれ引渡または返船の直前の補油港で支払われた価格で支払うものとする。船主は，傭船者の要求により，供給者の同意を得て，船主が随時有する一切の有効な補油契約を傭船者に利用できるようにし，その便宜を与えるものとする。

荷役業者，水先人，曳船

16. 荷役業者を必要とするときは，傭船者により雇傭され，支払がなされるものとする。ただし，これをもって，船長をしてすべての積揚貨物を常に厳密に計算させ監督をさせるべき船主の適切な積付義務を免除するものではない。船主はこれにより，傭船者により雇傭された者とはいえ，船主の被用者となりその業務に従事し，その指揮下にあるとみなすべき水先人，曳船乗務員または荷役業者（たとえその水先人，曳船乗務員または荷役業者が実際に傭船者，その代理人，またはその関係会社の被用者であっても）の雇傭により生ずる一切の損害，請求，責任および義務に対し，傭船者，その被用者および代理人に補償するものとする。

ただし，
(i) 上記の補償は，船主が自らそのような水先人，曳船および荷役業者を雇傭した場合にその責任を制限する権利を有することになる額を超えないものとする。また
(ii) 傭船者は，自然損耗を除き，荷役業者の使用により本船に生じたあらゆる損害につき，船主が相当の努力をしたにもかかわらず荷役業者からその賠償を得ることができない場合に限って，責任を負うものとする。

定員外の乗船

17. 傭船者は，本契約に基づくいかなる航海においても，本船の船室が利用できるときは代表者を乗船させることができる。船主は，酒類を除き，職員と同じ食事および一切の必需品を支給し，傭船者は，本船乗船期間中，代表者1人につき1日当たり……………の……………料金を支払う。

再 傭 船

18. 傭船者は本船を再傭船に出すことができる。ただし，本契約の正当な履行について常に船主に対し責任を負うものとする。

最 終 航 海

19. 本契約に基づく傭船料支払期日が到来したときに，傭船者が次回の傭船料支払期日の到来前に本船の返船を正当に予測する場合，その支払傭船料は，返船に至るまでの傭船者の計画を遂行するのに必要であると，傭船者が合理的に予測する時間に基づき算出するものとし，傭船者はその算出額から，
(i) 船主のための立替金または本契約の条項により船主負担となる費用，および
(ii) 第15条により，返船時本船にある燃料
に対して支払義務のある，または支払義務が生ずると合理的に予想される金額を控除することができる。

返船後，直ちに，支払超過額は船主から返戻され，支払不足額は傭船者から支払われるものとする。

本契約が第4条により終了するときに，本船が返船港へ空船航海をしているか，または積荷航海中である場合には，傭船者は，その空船航海を終了するのに必要とされる期間，または当該積荷航海を終了して本契約に定められた返船港へ回航するのに必要とされる期間につき，本契約に定めるものと同一の傭船料率と条件で本船を引き続き使用するものとする。

本船の滅失

20. 本船が滅失したときは，本契約は終了し，傭船料は本船滅失の日の正午に停止するものとする。本船が推定全損となったときは，本契約は終了し，傭船料は，本船の保険者が本船の推定全損に同意した日の正午に停止するものとする。本船が行方不明になったときは，本契約は終了し，傭船料は最後に本船の消息があった日の正午に停止するものとする。前払傭船料のうち反対給付が得られなかった分は傭船者に返戻するものとし，船主は，本契約終了時の本船の推定燃料油量につき，傭船者が最終補油港で支払った価格で傭船者に返戻するものとする。

オフハイヤー

21. (a) 時間の喪失（本船業務の中断によるものであろうと，業務の能率の低下によるものであろうと，またその他いかなる原因によるものであろうと）が，
    (i) 乗組員の欠員または船用品の不足，修繕，修繕のためのガス・フリー，修繕のため入渠した期間およびその待ち時間，機関，汽罐または本船の他の箇所もしくは本船の属具（無条件にタンク・コーティング部を含む）の故障（部分的であると全体的であるとを問わない），分解検査，保守または検査，衝突，座礁，本船の事故もしくは損傷その他これに類する本船の効率的稼働を妨げる原因により生じ，かつ，そのような喪失時間が3連続時間を超えるとき（本船業務の中断による場合）または合計3時間を超えるとき（業務の一部の損失による場合），または
    (ii) 船長，職員または部員の側の罷業，就航拒否，指図違反または業務怠慢のため生ずるとき，または
    (iii) 病人または負傷者（本契約第17条に基づき乗船している傭船者の代表者を除く）の診察，治療を得るため，もしくは下船させるために，または（傭船者の代表者を除く）遺体を下船させるために生じ，かつ，そのような時間の喪失が3連続時間を超えるとき，または
    (iv) 船長，職員または部員が，傭船者またはその代理人の書面による同意または指図なしに，伝染病流行地域に上陸したことにより検疫停船期間が延長することによって生ずるとき，または船長，職員もしくは部員の側の密輸その他現地法違反により，税関その他当局に抑留されるために生ずるとき，または
    (v) 本船もしくは本船船主に対する訴訟，または本船もしくは本船船主の規則違反（ただし，傭船者の行為または怠慢により生じたものでないこと）に起因して，国内または外国当局に本船が抑留されたことで生ずるときは，

    いかなる場合にも，第3条に基づく傭船者の権利または本契約に基づき，もしくは本契約外での傭船者のその他の権利を損なうことなく，本船はそのような時間の喪失の開始時から，本船が再び使用準備を整え，稼働状態で，そのような時間の喪失が始まった地点より傭船者に不利益とならない地点から本船業務を再開するまで，オフハイヤーとなるものとする。ただし，オフハイヤー期間に本船が提供した業務または短縮した距離は，傭船料の控除額の算定にあたり考慮するものとする。

    (b) 本船が第24条に基づく保証速力で航行できず，しかもそれが全面的であろうと部分的であろうと，上記第21条(a)に規定する原因のいずれかによるときは，本第21条に基づき本船がオフハイヤーとなる期間は，
    (i) 本船がその担保速力で当該業務を遂行するのに要したであろう時間と
    (ii) その業務を遂行するのに実際に要した時間（同業務の遂行中断による時間の喪失を含む）との差とする。

    疑義を避けるため，上記(ii)に該当するすべての時間は，第24条に基づく一切の計算から除外するものとする。

    (c) さらに，また前記権利を損なうことなく，本船が第21条(a)に記載されたいずれかの原因または目的のために，本船が離路（離路という語には本船が傭船者の指図によらずに港に引き返し，または指図以外の港に入港することを無条件に含む）する場合には，そのような離路の開始時から，本船が再び準備を整え，稼働状態で，その離路が始まった地点より傭船者によって不利益とならない地点から本船業務を再開するまで，本船はオフハイヤーとする。ただし，同オフハイヤー期間に本船が提供した業務または短縮された距離は，傭船料の控除額の算定にあたり考慮するものとする。本船が，第21条(a)に記載されたいずれかの原因または目的のために，傭船者の指図によらない港に入るときには，そのような港での港費，水先料その他の費用は船主負担とする。悪天候により，本船がどの港またはどの錨地であれ避難を余儀なくされるときは，傭船料は，それによって生ずる時間の損失についても中断することなく支払われるものとする。

    (d) 本船の旗国が参戦し，その戦争行為のため傭船者が本船を商業的に使用不可能と判断し，船主にその旨を書面で通知したときは，本船は，船主がその通知を受け取った日からその商業的に使用不可能の事態が終了するまで，オフハイヤーとし，船主は自己の費用で本船を使用する権利を

(e) 本船が本契約に基づきオフハイヤーとなる期間は，備船期間の一部に含めるものとする。

定 期 入 渠

22. (a) 船主は，..................毎に本船を入渠させる権利および義務を有する。その都度船主は本船の入渠を希望する日を少なくとも.........前までに備船者に申し出るものとし，一方，備船者は定期入渠を行うための港を申し出，その期日に実務上可能な限り近い日に本船を利用できるよう合理的なあらゆる手続を取るものとする。

　　　備船者がタンクの洗浄液と残滓以外の貨物を揚げ切って，本船を船主の使用に委ねた後，船主は，実務的に可及的速やかに自己の費用で本船を入渠させるものとする。船主は，タンクの洗浄液および残滓を受入施設で処理する義務を負い，その費用を支払うものとし，またそれによって得られる金銭を収得する権利を有する。ただし，これにより船荷証券または本契約に基づく積荷損害賠償請求権は損なわれない。

(b) 定期入渠が，備船者の申し出た港（入渠を行うための適切な設備およびタンクの洗浄液と残滓の受入施設を有さなければならない）において行われるときは，本船がその港に到着したときより，入渠が終了して，あらゆる点で備船者の業務を再開する準備が整い本船がオフハイヤーとなった地点または備船者にとってそれより不利益とならない地点のいずれかに最初に到達するまで，本船はオフハイヤーとする。ただし，

(i) 船主がガス・フリーを行うのに相当の注意を尽くすことを条件として，船体の清掃と塗装の目的で入渠するために要求される基準までガス・フリーを行う際に生じた喪失時間は，（第21条にかかわらず）入渠する港に向かう途中で生じたものであろうと，その港に到着後に生じたものであろうと，オフハイヤーとして計算されないものとする。また

(ii) 火気工事をするため，または貨物タンクへ入るために要求される基準に合致するために，さらにガス・フリーの実施により喪失した追加時間は，それが入渠港への途上で生じたものであろうと，その港に到着後に生じたものであろうと，オフハイヤーとして計算する。

　　　上記(i)による場合を除き，オフハイヤーとなる期間は，第24条に基づくいかなる計算にも含まれないものとする。

　　　ガス・フリーの費用は，無条件に燃料費を含め，船主負担とする。

(c) 船主が，申出のあった港へ行く代わりに，自ら選んだ専用港で定期入渠を行うことを要求する場合には，本船がその専用港へ向かうために解放されたときから，次に備船者の指図に従って船積のために提供されるまでの間は，本船はオフハイヤーになるものとする。ただし，本船がその船渠へ向かわなかったと仮定して，常用速力で航海するのに要したであろう時間については備船者が船主に対し負担するものとする。消費した燃料は一切船主が支払うものとする。ただし，前記の仮定の航海で消費されたとみられる燃料を常用速力に対する1日当たりの保証消費量で算出し，その代価を備船者は船主に対し負担するものとする。さらに備船者は船主に対し，その専用港での燃料購入に際し得られる便益を供与するものとする。

(d) 本船の入渠が申出のあった港で行われるか，専用港で行われるかに関係なく，定期入渠を行うための清掃が備船者の要求を満たすのに必要なタンク清掃の総量を減少する場合に限り，備船者はそれによって節約されたと算定される燃料代を船主に支払うものとする。

検　　船

23. 備船者は，本備船期間中いかなる時でも，本船に対し自ら必要と考える検査を行う権利を有するものとする。この権利は，備船者がまったく自らの任意で決定する都度または間隔毎に，かつ，本船が碇泊中であると航海中であるとを問わず，行使できるものとする。他方，船主は一切の必要な協力と船内便宜を提供するものとする。ただし，

(i) 備船者がその権利を行使すると否とにかかわらず，またはその権利の行使，不行使によって何らかのことが行われると否とにかかわらず，本船および本船運航のあらゆる状況に対する船長または船主の権限ないしはそれらに関する備船者または第三者に対する船長または船主の責任は，決して軽減しないものとし，かつ，同じくそれらに関する船主または第三者に対する備船者の責任も増加しないものとする。また

(ii) 傭船者は，上記権利の行使・不行使による自己，その被用者または代理人によるいかなる作為，過失もしくは懈怠に対し責任を負わないものとする。

本船の細目および性能

24. (a) 船主は本船の速力および燃料消費量が次のとおりであることを保証する。

	平均速力（ノット）	最大平均燃料消費量	
		主機	補機
		燃料油・ディーゼル油	燃料油・ディーゼル油
貨物積載時		トン	トン
		燃料油・ディーゼル油	燃料油・ディーゼル油
空船時		トン	トン

　上記燃料消費量は，貨物の加熱とタンク清掃を除くすべての用途を含み，記載の両速力の間で比例按分するものとする。

　本船の常用速力は，貨物積載時………ノット，空船時………ノットで，傭船者の別段の指図がない限り，本船は常用速力で航行するものとする。ただし，上掲の表に貨物積載時速力と空船時速力がそれぞれ二つ以上記載されているときは，傭船者は，その表に示された範囲内のいかなる速力（「指図速力」）でも本船に航行指図を出す権利を有するものとする。

　本船が，同表に記載された最高速力以外の速力で航行するよう指図され，その指図の期間中に本船の実際に達成した平均速力が，指図速力プラス0.5ノット（「最大認知速力」）を上回るときは，本第24条に基づき傭船料の増減を計算する際，実際に達成した平均速力に置きかえて最大認知速力を用いるものとする。

　本契約に基づく「担保速力」とは，いずれの時点にせよ，その時点での指図速力または常用速力を指すものとする。

　本第24条に基づく平均速力および平均燃料消費量は，第24条(c)に規定された各期間における全航行水域上のパイロット・ステーションからパイロット・ステーションまでの測定距離を参照して計算するものとする。ただし，上記期間からは，本船がオフハイヤーとなった（または第22条(b)(i)がなければオフハイヤーとなっていたであろう）期間を除外し，また(i)輻輳水域や視界不良水域で安全のため減速が必要だった期間，(ii)ビューフォート風力階級で8を上回る強風が12時間以上にわたり吹いた日（正午から正午を基準）など，「荒天期間」も除くものとする。

(b) 本船が，業務を開始した日を基準とする年間（開始日から開始日までの年単位）を通じ，第24条(a)で担保された性能を上回った場合，または下回った場合には，そのような性能の過不足が，

(i) 第24条(a)の保証速力に比較して，本船の平均速力が増加または減少したときは，節約または喪失された時間につき傭船料率によって算出した額に見合う金額を，それぞれ支払傭船料に上乗せするか，または傭船料から控除するものとする。

(ii) 本船が第24条担保どおりの性能を出していた場合に消費したであろう総燃料油量に比較して，実際に消費した総燃料油量が増加，または減少するときは，余分に消費され，または節約された燃料油につき，当該期間に傭船者が本船の燃料油代に支払った平均価格に基づき算出した価額に見合う額を，それぞれ支払傭船料に上乗せするか，または傭船料から控除するものとする。

　積載航行距離および空船航行距離につき各々以上のように計算された傭船料の増額または減額は，荒天期間の各状況の中で航海した距離を考慮して調整するものとする。すなわち，当該期間に対して支払うべき傭船料の増額ないし減額の総計を確定するために，当該の増額ないし減額を，当該の性能で航行した距離で除し，それに「同距離に荒天期間中に航海した距離を加算した数」を乗ずるものとする。

　前記本条(b)に基づく傭船料の減額は，傭船者の取りうるその他のいかなる救済方法に拠る権利をも損なわないものとする。

(c) 本第24条に基づく計算は，毎年本船が業務を開始した日に応当する日を終了日とする1年間毎に，そして1年に満たないときは前回の応当日から本契約の終了日までの期間につき行うものとする。本傭船期間の最終年または最終の1年に満たない期間において本条に基づき生ずる傭船料

の減額に関する請求は，まず最初に本傭船期間の終了２ヶ月前になされる傭船者の見積に従って精算するものとする。本契約終了後精算の必要があれば，場合に応じ船主が傭船者に，または傭船者が船主にそれぞれ支払うものとする。

本条に基づき生ずる傭船料の増額についての支払は，傭船者がその増額を計算するのに必要なすべての資料を入手しだい速やかに行うものとする。

海難救助

25. 本契約第21条の規定を条件として，人命の救助またはその試みもしくは成功または不成功に終わった海難救助の試みから生じた一切の喪失時間および費用（本船の滅失もしくは損傷または第三者に対する不法行為責任を除く）は，船主と傭船者が等分して負担するものとする。ただし，傭船者は，本第25条に基づき提供される救助作業により何らかの点で生じた，船主が負担すべき救助料を分担する責任を負わないものとする。

すべての救助料ならびに遺棄物の売上金は，船長，職員および部員の受取分を控除した後，船主と傭船者の間で等分するものとする。

リーエン

26. 船主は，本契約に基づき支払われる一切の金額に対して，すべての貨物，すべての運賃，再運送賃および滞船料の上にリーエンを有するものとし，傭船者は，反対給付が得られなかった一切の前払金および船主の本契約違反により生じるすべての損害賠償請求につき，本船上にリーエンを有するものとする。

免　責

27. (a) 本契約書に別段の明示の規定がない限り，本船，本船船長ならびに船主は，船長，水先人，船員その他船主の被用者の航行または本船の取扱に関する行為，過失または不履行，船主の故意または重過失に基づかない火災，衝突または座礁，海上の危険および事故，汽罐の爆発，破裂，シャフトの破損，船体または装備もしくは機関の隠れた欠陥により生じる，またはその結果によるいかなる滅失，損傷，遅延または不履行に対しても，責任を負わない。ただし，本契約第１条，第２条，第３条および第24条は上記によって影響を受けないものとする。さらに，本船，本船船長，船主または傭船者は本契約書に別段の明示の規定のない限り，不可抗力，戦争行為，裁判上の差押え，検疫上の制限，ストライキ，ロックアウト，暴動，労働制限，内乱，君主または統治者または人民による拘留または拘束から生じるまたはその結果によるいかなる滅失，損傷，遅延または本契約の不履行に対しても，責任を負わない。

    (b) 本船は，水先人をつけてまたは水先人なしで航行し，遭難中の船舶を曳航し，またはその救助に向かい，また人命もしくは財産を救助するために離路する自由を有するものとする。

    (c) 第27条(a)は，次のものについては船主，本船その他一切の関係者のいかなる責任に対しても適用されず，または影響を与えないものとする。

    (i) 傭船者の所有物であると否とを問わず，本契約に基づく本船の仕向地またはその近くにあるすべてのバース，桟橋，ドック，繋留柱，ブイ，繋船索，パイプ，クレーンその他一切の構造物または設備に与えた損害または損傷，または

    (ii) 貨物に対する，または貨物に関する一切の滅失もしくは損傷から生じるあらゆる賠償請求（傭船者またはその他の者によって提起されたかどうかを問わない）。かかるすべての損害賠償請求は，本契約第38条に従って当該船荷証券に摂取されることになるヘーグ・ヴィスビー・ルールまたはヘーグ・ルールにそれぞれ従うものとし（各ルールがその趣旨で摂取されているか否かを問わない），かかる船荷証券が発行されていないときは，ヘーグ・ヴィスビー・ルールによるものとする。

    (d) 特に，かつ無条件に，上記本条(a)および(b)は，オフハイヤーまたは傭船料の減額に関する本契約のいかなる規定にも適用されず，またはいかなる点でも影響を与えないものとする。

有害貨物

28. いかなる酸類，爆発物または本船に有害な貨物を船積してはならず，前述の規定に拠る権利を損なうことなく，かかる貨物の船積に起因する本船への一切の損害，また同損害の修繕に要した時間

は，傭船者の負担とする。統治者または政府によって本船が拿捕または差押えられる危険のある航海は引き受けないものとし，またそのような危険のあるいかなる物品または貨物も船積しないものとする。

燃料油の品質

29. 傭船者は，主機用として，摂氏50度において最大粘度………cs/ACGFO の舶用ディーゼル油・燃料油を，また補機用として，ディーゼル油・ACGFO を供給するものとする。船主が本船に，より高価な燃料油を供給するよう要求するときは，船主はその割増費用を負担するものとする。

傭船者は，本条に基づいて供給する一切の燃料油が International Marine Bunker Supply Terms and Conditions of Shell International Trading Company および随時改正される舶用燃料油に関するその細則に合致する品質であることを保証する。

諸　　掛

30. 船長が，港において通常の諸掛のために立替金を要求するときは，船主がそれに対して2.5パーセントの手数料を支払うことを条件に傭船者またはその代理人は船長に立替払をなすものとし，かかる一切の立替金および手数料は傭船料から控除するものとする。

繋　　船

31. 傭船者は，船主と協議の後，傭船者によって指定された安全港において本船を繋船するよう船主に要求する選択権を有するものとする。その場合は，本契約で定めた傭船料は，相当な理由によって生じた費用の純増分，またかかる繋船の結果船主によって合理的になされた純節約分を反映するように調整するものとする。傭船者は，傭船期間中，同上権利を何回でも行使することができる。

徴　　用

32. 本傭船期間中，本船がいずれの政府により，その政府が事実上または法律的に確立された政府であるか否かを問わず，徴用された場合は，本船はその徴用期間中オフハイヤーとする。その徴用期間に対してかかる政府により支払われた傭船料は，船主の収得とする。かかる徴用期間はすべて傭船期間の一部として算入するものとする。

戦争の勃発

33. 戦争または敵対行為が次の国家のうちの二国またはそれ以上の国々の間で勃発した場合は，船主および傭船者は共に本契約を解約する権利を有する：米国，ソビエト，中華人民共和国，連合王国，オランダ。

戦争による追加費用

34. 本船が，（事実上であれ，宣戦布告がなされている場合であれ）戦争状態にあるまたはそのおそれのある区域へ就航するように指図された場合は，傭船者は，かかる指図に従う結果として，船主に当然に生じる保険料の割増金，船員の特別手当ならびにその他の費用を船主に補償するものとする。ただし，傭船者はかかる費用につき，実務上できる限り速やかに，かついずれの場合にも，その費用が発生する前に，通知を受けるものとする。さらに船主は，かかる指図に従った結果生じる戦争危険保険に基づく船主の請求に関して，保険者が傭船者に対して有する代位請求権を，保険者より放棄せしめるものとする。

戦争危険

35. (a) 船長は，封鎖，戦争，敵対行為，軍事的行為，内乱，暴動または革命が原因で，本船の入港または到着が危険または不可能であると，自らまたは船主が合理的に判断した場合は，いかなる場所であれ，そのような場所向けの船荷証券に署名を要求されることはなく，または署名を義務付けられることもない。

(b) 船長または船主の合理的な判断において，第35条(a)に規定されたいずれかの事由によりまたは国際法の適用により，本傭船契約上指図された場所への本船の到着，入港もしくは積揚が危険または不可能となり，または禁止された場合は（かかる場所を「危険地」という），傭船者またはその代理人はテレックスまたは無線機により連絡を受けしだい，その貨物をまたは影響をうけるその一部を本傭船契約上の就航区域内にある他の場所での，船積または揚荷を指図する権利を有

するものとする（ただし，その場所自体が危険地でないものとする）。揚荷場所が危険地であるか，または危険地となり，かつ，その旨の連絡が発せられてから48時間以内に，傭船者またはその代理人が何らの指図も行わなかった場合は，船主はその貨物をまたは影響をうけるその一部を，船主または船長の裁量により，本備船契約中の就航区域内で選択するいかなる場所においても，揚荷することができる。かかる揚荷は，そのように揚荷された貨物に関する限り，本備船契約上の船主の義務の正当な履行とみなすものとする。

(c) 本船は出航，到着，航路，寄港地，停ము，仕向地，海域，水域，引渡その他一切の事項に関し，本船の旗国政府，事実上の政府もしくは地方官憲を含むその他の政府もしくは地方官憲またはそのような政府もしくは地方官憲の権限をもって行為しまたは行為すると称する者もしくは団体によって，または本船に関する戦争危険保険の条項に基づき指図または勧告をする権限を有する委員会もしくは者によってなされた一切の指図または勧告に従う権利を有する。そのような指図または勧告によりまたはそれに従った何らかの作為または不作為があっても，それは離路とはみなされない。

本船がそのような指図もしくは勧告によりまたはそれに従うことによって，本契約に基づいて指定された揚荷地へ航行しない場合は，本船は船長または船主がその裁量により選択する場所へ航行し，そこでその貨物をまたは影響を被るその一部を揚荷することができる。かかる揚荷は，そのように揚荷された貨物に関する限り，本備船契約上の船主の義務の正当な履行とみなすものとする。

傭船者は，本契約に基づき発行されるすべての船荷証券に，1952年海運会議所「戦争危険」約款を含むことを保証する。

双方過失衝突条項

36. 本船の本契約履行中に生じた衝突に関する責任が，米国の法律に基づき裁定されることになる場合には，次の条項を適用する。

「本船が相手船の過失と，本船の航行または本船の取扱に関する船長，乗組員，水先人または船主の被用者の行為，過失または不履行の結果，相手船と衝突した場合には，本契約に基づき運送される貨物の所有者は，相手船，すなわち非搭載船またはその所有者に対して運送人が負う損失または債務につき次の限度において運送人に補償するものとする。すなわち，このような損失または債務が当該貨物の滅失，損傷または貨物所有者の有する一切の請求額に相当するものとして，相手船，すなわち非搭載船またはその所有者により相殺，控除もしくは回収されたものに限る。」

「前記の規定は，衝突船舶または衝突物体以外のいずれの船舶または物体の所有者，運航者もしくは管理者が，衝突または接触につき過失ある場合にも適用する。」

傭船者は，本契約に基づき発行されるすべての船荷証券に，本船が関係する衝突に関する責任が米国の法律によって裁定される場合には，上記条項が適用される旨の規定を含むことを保証する。

ニュー・ジェイソン条項

37. 共同海損分担金は1974年のヨーク・アントワープ・ルールに従って支払うものとし，かつLondonで英国の法律と慣習に従って精算するものとする。ただし，その精算が米国の法律と慣習に従ってなされる場合には，次の条項を適用するものとする。

「航海の開始前または開始後，事由の如何を問わず，過失によると否とを問わず，法律，契約その他により運送人が責任を負わない，またはその結果について責任を負わない事故，危険，損害または災害が発生したときは，貨物，荷送人，荷受人または貨物の所有者は，支払われるまたは支払うことになる共同海損の性質を有する犠牲，損害または費用を共同海損において運送人と分担し，貨物について生じた救助料および特別の費用を支払わなければならない。」

「救助船が運送人の所有または運航するものである場合も，救助船が第三者の所有下にある場合と同一の救助料全額を支払わなければならない。もし要求があれば，貨物，荷送人，荷受人または貨物所有者は，運送人またはその代理人が貨物の概算分担金ならびに貨物に関する救助料および特別の費用を塡補するのに足りるとみなす金員を貨物の引渡前に運送人に予託しなければならない。」

傭船者は，本契約に基づき発行されるすべての船荷証券に，前記条項の規定を取り入れて，共同海損の精算が米国の法律と慣習によって行われる場合に，上記条項の規定が適用されるようにする

ことを保証する。

至上条項

38. 傭船者は,本契約に基づき発行されるすべての船荷証券が,次の条項を含むことを保証する。

「(1)本条第(2)項を条件として,本船荷証券は1968年2月23日Brusselsで署名された議定書(以下「ヘーグ・ヴィスビー・ルール」という)により修正された,1924年8月25日Brusselsで署名された船荷証券に関するある規則の統一のための国際条約(以下「ヘーグ・ルール」という)の規則に準拠し,かつ同規則による効力を有するものとする。本証券中に,ヘーグ・ヴィスビー・ルールに基づく運送人の権利もしくは免責を放棄し,または運送人の責任もしくは義務を加重させるものは一切含まれていないものとみなす。」

「(2)ヘーグ・ヴィスビー・ルールを排除して,ヘーグ・ルールを強制的に本船荷証券に適用する準拠法がある場合は,本船荷証券はヘーグ・ルールにより効力を有する。本証券に,ヘーグ・ルールに基づく運送人の権利もしくは免責を放棄し,または運送人の責任もしくは義務を加重させるものは一切含まれていないものとみなす。」

「(3)本船荷証券の条項が,ヘーグ・ヴィスビー・ルールまたは準拠法がヘーグ・ルールの場合これに反するときは,その条件に反する範囲のみを無効とする。」

「(4)本船荷証券の条項は,いかなる場合においても,適用可能な制定法および・または法律に基づき当事者の責任を制限する当事者の権利を制限,排除または放棄するように解釈してはならない。」

TOVALOP (油濁責任に関するタンカー船主間自主協定)

39. 船主は本船が,
    (i) TOVALOP加入船であり,かつ,
    (ii) 正式に......P&Iクラブに加入していること,
そして本契約期間中本船がこれを維持することを担保する。

本船からの油の流出もしくは排出が油濁損害を発生させ,または発生させるおそれがあるときは,または油の流出もしくは排出のおそれがあるとき(すなわち,もし発生すれば,油濁損害の重大な危険を招来するであろう,油の流出もしくは排出の重大かつ切迫した危険であって,その後実際に流出もしくは排出が生じたと否とを問わない)は,傭船者は自らの選択により船主または船長に通知して,その油濁損害を防止または軽減するために,またはその危険を除去するために合理的に必要とされる措置を講ずることができる。ただし,船主が直ちに同様の措置を講ずるときはこの限りでない。傭船者は,自己のとった措置の種類と結果につき,また時間の許すときは自ら予定している措置の種類につき,船主に絶えず連絡するものとする。傭船者がとった上記のいかなる措置も,船主の代理人として船主の権限に基づきなされたものとみなし,かつその費用は,以下の場合を除き,船主の負担とする。

(1) そのような流出もしくは排出またはそのおそれが,傭船者に原因があるか,または傭船者が寄与している場合,

(2) 1969年の油による汚染損害についての民事責任に関する国際条約第3条第2項に規定された免責事項によって,船主がその流出もしくは排出またはそのおそれに関する責任を免除される場合,または同条約の適用により免除されたであろう場合,

(3) そのような措置の費用とその流出もしくは排出またはそのおそれから生じ,またはそれらに関連して生じる船主のその他一切の責任および諸費用が,本船の1総トン当たり米貨160ドルまたは米貨1,680万ドルのいずれか低い金額を超える場合,ただし,船主が1971年油による汚染損害の補償のための国際基金の設立に関する国際条約またはCRISTALのいずれかにより,その超えた金額を回収する権利を有する場合を除く。

ただし,船主は,まったく自らの任意で,上記の措置を続行すべきではない,と判断したときは,常に傭船者にその旨を通知する。その後は,傭船者は本条第39条の規定に基づく上記の措置を続行する権利を有せず,本条第39条に基づく傭船者に対するそれ以上の一切の責任は,そのときをもって終了する。

上記の規定は,傭船者または船主が本契約に基づき有する,または法律もしくは国際条約もしく

はTOVALOPによって有するまたは取得する，その他の権利を損なうものではない。
　「TOVALOP」とは，1969年1月7日付け油濁責任に関するタンカー船主間自主協定であって，随時改正されたものをいう。また「CRISTAL」とは，1971年1月14日付けタンカーの油濁責任に対する臨時追加補償制度に関する契約であって，随時改正されたものをいう。「油」，「油濁損害」および「総トン」とは，本条第39条においてはTOVALOPにてそれぞれの語に付した意味を有するものとする。

輸出制限

40. 船長は，仕向地向けの貨物の輸出がその貨物の産出国および・または船積国の法律，規則または条例によって禁止されている場合は，その地向けの貨物運送に対する船荷証券への署名を要求されず，またその義務もない。
　傭船者は本契約に基づき発行されるすべての船荷証券に次の条項が含まれることを担保する。
　「貨物産出国および・または船積国の，またはその関係機関によって適用される法律，規則または条例が，本船荷証券に指定された，またはそれに基づき指図される揚地向けの貨物の輸出を禁止している場合は，運送人は直ちに荷主に対して，その貨物または影響を被るその一部を揚荷するために，代替揚地を指定するよう要求する権利を有する。その代替揚地は上記の禁止を受けない場所とし，かつ運送人は荷主よりかかる代替揚地へ航行し揚荷を行う指図を受ける権利を有するものとする。荷主またはその代理人が運送人からそのような禁止についての通知を受けてより72時間以内に代替地を指定しなかった場合は，運送人はその貨物または影響を被るその一部を，運送人または船長の絶対的裁量において決定した，上記の禁止を受けない安全な場所で揚荷することができる。かかる揚荷は，そのように揚荷された貨物に関する限り，本船荷証券が表象する契約の正当な履行を構成するものとする。」
　上記の規定は本契約にも準用し，船荷証券の箇所は本契約と読み替えるものとみなす。

法および訴訟

41. (a) 本傭船契約は英国法により解釈され，当事者間の関係は英国法により決定される。
　(b) 本傭船契約に基づき生じるいかなる紛争も，英国裁判所により解決されるものとし，当事者はここにその管轄権を合意する。
　(c) 上記の規定にかかわらず，海上財産をアレストし，またはアレストを維持するいかなる者の権利も損なうことなく，いずれの当事者も，他の当事者に対し書面による選択の通知を交付することにより，1950年仲裁法またはその時に施行されているその修正法または改正法の規定に従ってLondonの単独仲裁人にその紛争の仲裁を付託することを選択することができる。
　　(i) 当事者は次の場合にのみその選択の権利を失う。
　　　(a) 当事者が，
　　　　(1) 紛争が本傭船契約から生じたことを明記し，
　　　　(2) 紛争の性質を記載し，かつ
　　　　(3) 本条第41条(c)に明確に言及する
　　　　　紛争についての通知書を相手方から受け取り
　　　　そして
　　　(b) 当事者が紛争についての通知書の受領の日から30日以内に，その紛争を仲裁に付託する旨の選択通知を交付しなかった場合
　　(ii) 両当事者は，ここにいずれの当事者も次のことを行いうることに合意する。
　　　(a) 仲裁判断から生じる法律問題に関し，高等法院に上訴すること
　　　(b) 高等法院に対して，仲裁人がその仲裁判断に理由を付記する命令を申請すること，
　　　(c) 仲裁人に，理由を付した仲裁判断が要求されることを通知すること，かつ
　　　(d) 高等法院に対し，仲裁手続の過程で生じる法律問題の判断を申請すること。
　(d) いずれかの当事者が本傭船契約に基づく紛争に関連して，海上財産がアレストされたか，またはアレストされる法的手続を停止する権利を行使するためには，その当事者が，停止がない場合にそのような法的手続において相手方が提供を受ける権利を有することになるとみられる担保を相手方に提供することが停止条件となる。

解　釈

42. 条項の見出しは，参照の便宜のため本傭船契約に挿入したものであって，本傭船契約の解釈にいかなる影響も及ぼすものではない。

タンカー定期傭船STB書式

本傭船契約の略号
STB

....
船舶名

タンカー定期傭船契約書

....
場所　　　日付

　本日，...................．（以下，単に「本船」と称する）の船主／傭船船主...................．（以下，単に「船主」と称する）と...................．（以下，単に「傭船者」と称する）との間で，...................．．．．．．．の撒積運送，およびその他本契約に表示する船舶に積載しうる適法な貨物の運送のために，以下の傭船期間，約定条件で本船を使用運航する権利を，船主は賃貸し傭船者は賃借りすることを合意する。

期　　間

1．(a)．本契約の期間は，約...................．（以下，「原期間」と称する）であり，これに下記(b)に規定する幾ばくかの延長期間が付加される。原期間は，第5条の規定に基づいて，本船が傭船者の使用に委ねられた時点より開始する。上記に使用した「約」という語は，「プラスマイナス14日」を意味し，原期間と，後に規定する幾ばくかの延長期間より成る本契約の期間に適用される。

延　　長

　(b)．傭船者は，原期間満了の少なくとも30日前に，船主に書面により通知することによって，...................．間（以下単に「延長期間」と称する），本契約の期間を延長する権利を有する。本契約の期間は，本船が原期間および／もしくは延長期間中にオフハイヤーとなった場合，原期間もしくは延長期間の満了の少なくとも30日前に船主に対して書面により通知することにより傭船者はそのオフハイヤー期間の全部または一部につき，本契約の期間を延長する（以下，単に「オフハイヤー延長期間」と称する）ことができる。さらに傭船者はオフハイヤー期間満了の少なくとも30日前に，船主に対しさらに書面により通知することにより，先の通知の後に本船がオフハイヤーになった場合，その期間の全部または一部を本契約の期間に付加することができる。

本船要目

2．本船の要目，容量，装備は次のとおりである。

A．貨物積載容量
- Ⅰ．100パーセント積載時の全積荷タンク容量　　　　　　…………USバレル
- Ⅱ．積荷積載容量から常時控除される船用品等重量　　　…………ロング・トン
- Ⅲ．a．1日当たり清水消費量　　　　　　　　　　　　　…………ロング・トン
  　b．1日当たり造水量　　　　　　　　　　　　　　　…………ロング・トン
  　c．積荷積載容量より控除される清水1日当たりの量　…………ロング・トン
- Ⅳ．軽質油，中質油，重質油各満載時の「サグ」のための積荷積載容量の見積損失
  　　　　　　　　　　　　軽質油　　…………ロング・トン
  　　　　　　　　　　　　中質油　　…………ロング・トン
  　　　　　　　　　　　　重質油　　…………ロング・トン

Ⅴ．本船は，夏期満載喫水………フィート………インチ，乾舷………フィート………インチで，積荷，燃料，水，船用品を，総載貨重量屯………トン（2,240ポンド）（船級協会証明），運送できる。

B．その他のタンク容量
　Ⅰ．推進用燃料タンク全容量　　　　　　　　………USバレル
　Ⅱ．清水タンク全容量　　　　　　　　　　　　………ロング・トン
　Ⅲ．バラスト専用タンク全容量　　　　　　　　………ロング・トン

C．ポンプ性能
　Ⅰ．貨物ポンプ
　　a．数　　　量　　　　　　　　　　　　　………
　　b．製　　　造　　　　　　　　　　　　　………
　　c．型　　　式　　　　　　　　　　　　　………
　　d．時間当たりUSバレルでの各ポンプの定格容量　………USバレル／時間
　　　　および対応する揚程　　　　　　　　　………フィート／揚程
　Ⅱ．ストリッピング・ポンプ
　　a．数　　　量　　　　　　　　　　　　　………
　　b．各ポンプの定格容量　　　　　　　　　………USバレル／時間
　　　　およびこれに対応する保証吐出揚程　　………フィート／揚程
　Ⅲ．専用バラストポンプ
　　a．数　　　量　　　　　　　　　　　　　………
　　b．各ポンプの定格容量　　　　　　　　　………USバレル／時間

D．積荷／揚荷マニホールド
マニホールドは，すべて鋼製またはそれに準ずる材質製で，荷役設備による損害防止の補強がなされており，かつ荷役ホース昇降装置安全荷重と同等の，どの方向からの最大荷重にも耐えるだけの，強度を保持するものとする。
　Ⅰ．a．マニホールド連結口の数量　　　　　………
　　　b．マニホールド連結口の径　　　　　　………
　　　c．マニホールド連結口の中心間距離　　………
　　　d．マニホールド連結口と舷側間の距離　………
　　　e．マニホールド連結口中心の甲板からの高さ　………
　　　f．マニホールド中心・船首間距離　　　………
　　　g．荷役ホース昇降装置安全荷重　　　　………トン
　Ⅱ．貨物マニホールド・レデューサー
　　16ないし60MDWTの船舶は，鋼製またはそれに準ずる材質製の十分な数の荷油マニホールド・レデューサーを装備しており，これによって船舶の片舷のマニホールド連結口全部に，8"，10"，12"（ASA）のフランジの荷役ホース／アームを連結できる。
　　60MDWTを超える船舶は，鋼製またこれに準ずる材質製の十分な数の荷油マニホールド・レデューサーを装備しており，これによって船舶の片舷のマニホールド連結口全部に，10"，12"，16"（ASA）のフランジの荷役ホース／アームを連結できる。

E．加　熱　管
　Ⅰ．加熱管の型式および材質
　Ⅱ．加熱面積／容積比
　　a．中央タンク　　　………平方フィート／40立方フィート
　　b．両翼タンク　　　………平方フィート／40立方フィート

F．荷油積込性能
本船は，同質荷油を最高レート………バレル／時間で積み込むことができる。

G．本　船　要　目

タンカー定期傭船STB書式

Ⅰ. 全　　　長　　　　　　　　…………フィート…………インチ
Ⅱ. 比重1.025塩水での夏期満載喫水　　…………フィート…………インチ
　　そのときの指定乾舷
Ⅲ. 淡水における喫水沈下量　　　　　　　……………インチ
Ⅳ. 空船喫水　舳　　　　　　…………フィート…………インチ
　　　　　　艫　　　　　　…………フィート…………インチ
　　　　　　平均　　　　　…………フィート…………インチ
Ⅴ. 型　　　深　　　　　……………
Ⅵ. 空船時乾舷　　　　　…………フィート…………インチ
Ⅶ. 空船時のトン・パー・インチ　　……………
Ⅷ. 夏期満載喫水でのトン・パー・インチ　……………
Ⅸ. 全　　　幅　　　　　……………
Ⅹ. 総トン数　　　　　　……………
Ⅺ. 純トン数　　　　　　……………
Ⅻ. スエズ運河トン数　　……………
ⅩⅢ. パナマ運河トン数　　……………
ⅩⅣ. 船　籍　国
ⅩⅤ. 信　号　符　字
ⅩⅥ. 船　級　協　会
ⅩⅦ. 本船の傭船者引渡時の最大積載燃料　……………
ⅩⅧ. 船主は，傭船者の要求に応じて本船の図面の写を提供する。新造船の場合には船主は，造船所より図面を受け取った後，写を提供すれば足りる。
ⅩⅨ. 本船は造水器を装備しており，それは良好に作動するように調整されるものとし，船主は，この造水器が本船に必要な量の造水能力を有することを保証する。
ⅩⅩ. 船主は，本船が荷油を華氏135度に加熱し，揚荷中継続してその状態を維持する性能を有することを保証する。もし本船が傭船者の指図どおりに，荷油を加熱できない場合には，傭船者は次のいずれかを選択する権利を有する。
　　a）揚荷を遅らせる。
　　b）本船の着桟を遅らせる。
　　c）揚荷を中止し，荷油が傭船者の指図どおりに加熱されるまで本船を離桟させる。
　　これらの喪失時間すべては，オフハイヤーとみなされ，船主負担となる。さらに，離桟費用一切も船主負担となる。

傭　船　料

3.（a）. 傭船者は，本船の使用に対して，第２条Ａに表示する載貨重量トン１トン（2,240ポンド），１ヶ月当たり，……………の通貨……………の率で，傭船料を支払う。本契約に別段の定めなき限り，支払は暦月毎に前払で，割引なし小切手にて，……………において，本船が傭船者の使用に委ねられた日時に始まり，傭船契約が満了し本船が船主に返船される日時まで，継続して支払われる。反対給付が得られなかった前払傭船料一切は，直ちに傭船者に返還される。本契約書に署名がなされ，本船がここに規定するように傭船者の使用に委ねられるまでは，いかなる場合にも，傭船料の第１期の支払はなされない。

控　　　除

（b）. 傭船者は，傭船料支払額から次に挙げるものを控除することができる。(1)船主負担となる立替金，船長または船主代理人への前払金一切。これには対応する手数料を含む。(2)第17条に基づき算出される係船割戻金。(3)傭船料の事前超過支払額一切。これにはオフハイヤー分，および善意の争いある傭船料超過支払額が含まれる。ただし，後者において傭船料は，船主の要求があれば，十分な銀行保証，または他の信用ある十分な担保を提供しなければならない。(4)第

8条，第9条の請求。および(5)本契約上傭船者に控除権を与えたその他一切の金額。傭船者は，船主負担となる前払金，または立替金の2.5パーセントを手数料として取得する権利を有する。ただし，船主は立替金について，傭船者もしくはその指定する代理人に前払をなす権利を有する（ただし，かかる前払金を，傭船者が十分かつ妥当とみなすことを条件に）。この場合には手数料の支払を要しない。

最 終 航 海

(c). 本船が，傭船料支払期日に最終航海中である場合，当該支払は，当該航海を完遂し，本船を船主に返船するに必要であると傭船者が予定した期間についてなされ，そこから，本条(b)に規定する全控除額，もし実際の額が不明であれば傭船者見積額，および第19条(b)に規定する船主に支払義務のある返船時の燃料，清水代の傭船者見積額を控除する。返船時において，見積額と実際額の差額を，傭船者に返還するか，あるいは傭船者が追加支払しなければならない。

本船の滅失

(d). 本船が滅失するか，もしくは行方不明で滅失と推定される場合，傭船料は滅失時，それが不明なら本船の最後の消息の時点で中止される。本船が推定全損となった場合には，傭船料は当該全損の原因たる事故の時点で中止となる。いずれの場合にも，反対給付が得られなかった前払傭船料は傭船者に返還される。もし本船が，傭船料支払時期にオフハイヤー中であるか，または行方不明である場合，傭船料支払は，場合によりオフハイヤー期間が終了するか，または本船の安全が確認されるまで延期される。

傭船料の減額

(e). 本船が，第4条の船主担保，その他の担保された船舶表示を満たさない場合，傭船者は，欠陥の是正その他傭船者が有すべき一切の権利を取得する。ただし，傭船者の傭船料減額の権利は，損なわれない。

遅 滞

(f). ここに規定する期限どおりの定期の支払が遅滞した場合，船主は，.....................所在の.....................に通知をなす。この場合傭船者は船主からの通知受領後10日以内に支払をなさなければならず，これを怠った場合，船主は同人が傭船者に対して有する本契約上の他の請求権を害さずに，本船を傭船者の業務から引き揚げる権利を有する。

増 額

(g). 本条(a)に規定する傭船料は，傭船者負担の，船長による臨時食事提供，電話，無線，電報，電信，および傭船者の要求でなした本船の職員，部員の時間外労働の費用を全額まかなう...............ドルの増額分を含むものである。

(h). 本条第3条に規定する傭船料率は，時間当たり...............ドルに相当する。

担 保

4．船主は，本船が傭船者の使用に委ねられたときに，上記第2条に表示した表示，要目，性能を満たすこと，堅牢，強固であること，完全に性能を発揮しうる状態でかつすべての点で適応性をもつこと，乗組員が配乗されていること，艤装されていること，さらには予定される運航のために積荷タンク，荷油管，弁を清浄かつ堅牢な状態で，またポンプ・加熱管，その他すべての装備を良好な状態で提供することを担保する。船主は，本契約上本船が使用される全期間，相当の注意を尽くすことにより本船は上記表示，要目，性能をできる限り維持しなければならない。

傭 船

5．(a). 本船は傭船者の指示する.....................（以下，「引渡港」という）の，直に接岸しうる

ドック，埠頭その他の場所で，傭船者の使用に委ねられなければならない。傭船料は，本船がかかるドック，埠頭または場所において，すべての点で本契約の遂行および航海の準備が完了し，船長が引渡港で傭船者またはその代理人に，その旨の書面による通知をなしたときより開始する。

碇 泊 期 間

(b). 傭船は，傭船者が同意する場合を除いては……………………以前には開始しない。本船は，ここに規定するところに従い……………………より以前に傭船者の使用に提供されなければならず，これを怠った場合，傭船者は本船が準備完了となる日以前に宣言することにより，本契約を解約する権利を有する。傭船者による解約，または本船の運航業務の受領は，本船の運航業務の提供の遅延に対し傭船者が有する損害賠償請求権を害するものではない。

本 船 の 使 用

(c). 本船の全載貨容積（ただし，本船が適切に積載し，安全に運送できる量を最大限として）は，本船の船長，職員，部員の船室，器具，装備，艤装具，燃料，食料，船用品のための十分かつ適当なスペースを保留して，傭船者の使用に供されなければならない。

航 路 定 限

6．(a). 本船は，ここに添付する協会担保航路定限条款に従い，世界中のいかなる港，場所，埠頭，ドック，錨地，海中パイプラインおよびそれらの間の傭船者，またはその代理人が指図する適法な航海に使用される。ただし，5月15日から11月15日までの間の北アメリカの湖水，St. Lawrence河およびその支流，年間を通じてのMagellan海峡通過，Horn岬，喜望峰周辺への配船は，保険料割増金の支払なしにできる。上記の制限にかかわらず，本船をStockholm以南のバルト海諸港，フィンランドのHelsingfors，Abo，その他協会担保航路定限条款に規定する港，場所に配船することができる。ただし，傭船者は，当該航路定限違反に対して船主が支払うべき本船の保険者により適切に査定された追加保険料を船主に支払うものとする。

碇 泊 場 所

(b). 本船は，傭船者が指図する港，場所，バース，ドック，錨地，海底ラインにおいて，艀あるいは瀬取船に横付けして積荷，揚荷，瀬取をしなければならない。本条，その他本契約書の他の規定にかかわらず，傭船者が港，バース，ドック，錨地および／または海中パイプラインの安全を担保したものとはみなされない。また傭船者は，港，バース，ドック，錨地，海中パイプラインの状態を原因とするいかなる滅失，損傷，負傷または遅延について，それが傭船者の過失，怠慢に起因しない場合，あるいは船長または船主が相当の注意を尽せば回避しえた場合，一切の責任を負わない。

燃 料

(c). 傭船者は，本船が傭船者の使用に委ねられたときに積載している燃料を，上記第2条に表示した最大量を限度として，受け取り，その代金を支払わなければならない。超過量については，傭船者がその選択で，後に規定するところに従い決定される価格，または相互の合意に基づく価格で，これを受け取ることができるが，傭船者が超過分を受け取らない場合には，本船が傭船者の使用に委ねられる前に，船主は自らの費用で当該超過量を本船から移出しなければならない。燃料代金の支払は，本船が本契約により傭船者の使用に委ねられた日，およびその港，場所におけるエッソ国際契約価格表の値，または同表に掲載される最寄りの港における表値に従い行われる。

貨 物

7．傭船者は，本船およびそのタンクに適合する適法な撒，乾貨物の船積，および箱，罐，その他梱

包された適法な商品を船首船艙，中甲板，その他適切な利用可能スペースへ船積する権利を有する。ただし，種類，特性，数量，載貨方法に関する船長の同意を条件とする。荷敷，積込，保管，揚荷についての費用一切は，傭船者が負担する。

速力，燃料，ポンプ能力の担保

8．本船は本契約期間中，シーブイとシーブイとの間の海上航行において，主機については最大粘度が華氏100度において..............秒レッドウッドNo.1のディーゼル油／Ｃ重油／高粘度燃料，..............トン（2,240ポンド），補機についてはディーゼル油..............トン（2,240ポンド）の1日当たり保証燃料消費量で，満載状態では..............ノット，空荷状態では..............ノット（速力は，オフハイヤーとして計算される航海時間および海上での停船を除き，航海日誌記載の全航走距離を全航海時間で除することにより算出される）を，あらゆる気象条件の下で維持することを船主は担保する。

積荷が加熱されている間の1日当たり保証燃料消費量は，1タンク，1日当たり，最大粘度が華氏100度において..............秒レッドウッドNo.1のディーゼル油／Ｃ重油／高粘度燃料，..............バレルである。タンク清掃中の保証消費量は，1機1時間当たり，最大粘度が華氏100度において..............秒レッドウッドNo.1のディーゼル油／Ｃ重油／高粘度燃料，..............バレルである。

傭船者は，本船の全性能を使用する権利を有し，船主は本船が最低でも以下のレートで荷油を揚荷する性能を有することを担保する。

軽質油（華氏100度で粘度320セーボルト・ユニバーサル未満）..............バレル／時間

中質油（華氏100度で粘度320セーボルト・ユニバーサル以上，3,200セーボルト・ユニバーサル以下）..............バレル／時間

重質油（華氏100度で粘度3,200セーボルト・ユニバーサルを超える）..............バレル／時間

上記の値を満足しない場合には，舷側で100ポンド／平方インチの圧力を維持することができるもの。

傭船者は，上記揚荷レートを下回った所要時間につき1時間当たり..............ドル，1時間未満については，これに按分比例して補償を受ける。船主は，本船が上記レートを超えて揚荷できる場合にも，支払ないし補償を受けないことを了承し，これに同意する。陸側の状態に起因する本船の揚荷の遅延は，すべて揚荷実績の査定において考慮されるべきものとする。揚荷実績は，第9条に従い精査される。

傭船料の調整

9．(a)．第8条で船主が保証した速力および燃料消費量は，本傭船契約に従い傭船者に本船が引き渡されたときより3暦月後，以後3暦月毎に傭船者により精査される。各12暦月の期間の最終日に（または傭船期間中いつでも），本船がそれに先行する12暦月間（または傭船期間中の他のいずれかの12暦月間）の保証速力および／または保証燃料消費量を平均して維持できなかったことが判明した場合，傭船者は当該違反に関して，以下に従って遡及して補償を受ける。

(b)．速力―傭船者に対し，第8条で担保した本船の保証速力での推定所要時間の超過分につき，1時間当たり..............ドル，1時間未満は按分比例により支払う。超過時間は添付書1――「性能計算書」――により算定される。

(c)．燃料消費量―船主は傭船者に，本船の実際の速力が第8条に適合していることを前提として精査した上で，主機，補機，加熱および／またはタンク洗浄についての1日当たり保証消費量を超えるトン数（2,240ポンド）について，1トン未満は按分比例で当該全検査対象期間について..............でのエッソ国際契約価格表の既述特定油種の平均価格に従い，償還する。超過分は，本傭船契約のオフハイヤー条項に従って，船主負担にならないものをも含む。本船の速力が保証速力を下回る場合，その程度に応じて消費量は添付書1――「性能計算書」――により算定される。

(d)．上記(a)および(b)における本船実績の判断基準は，第14条(b)に従って船長の提出する統計資料を基礎とする。

(e). 船主は，本船の実績上，速力が保証を超えるか，または，燃料消費量がそれ以下である場合には，本条において傭船者が有すると同様の補償を受領する権利を有する。

(f). 傭船者は，本条により提起する請求について，船主に検討の機会を与え，船主は検討後，傭船者が船主に当該請求書を郵送した日より30日以内に，その結果を傭船者に提出しなければならない。傭船者は，船主に対する請求書の郵送の日より40日経過後，本条により権利を認められる金額を，傭船料より控除できる。

　傭船者が，傭船期間および延長期間の最終年または最終部分の間の本船実績に関し，請求権を有する場合，当該請求額は傭船期間終了約2ヶ月前になされた傭船者の見積に従い，傭船料より控除される。そして，傭船期間終了後，必要な調整は船主が傭船者に対し，場合により傭船者が船主に対しなすこととする。

リーエン

10. 船主は，本契約により支払われるべき全金額について，すべての積荷にリーエンを有する。傭船者は，反対給付が得られなかった前払全金額，船主負担の立替金，前渡金，船主負担となる使用された，または受け取られた傭船者の燃料一切の代金，第9条およびその他本契約の規定により傭船者に対して支払うべき全金額，および船主の本契約不履行の結果，傭船者が被った全損害金額について本船の上にリーエンを有する。

オフハイヤー

11. (a). 傭船者の過失を原因としない機関の故障，官憲の介入，衝突，座礁，火災その他本船の事故もしくは損害により時間の喪失が生じ，それが本船の稼働を連続12時間を超えて妨げる場合，もしくは人員，船用品の不足，船長，職員，部員による指揮命令違反または義務不履行，または傭船者の要請で運送される者以外の船内傷病者を上陸させる目的での離路により時間の喪失が生じる場合，傭船料の支払は，本船がその運航業務を再開するに十分な状態となり，オフハイヤー開始時の原点に復帰するまでの全喪失時間中停止される。本契約に基づく本船のオフハイヤー期間中および仕向地以外の港，場所に向かったため生じた消費燃料代，港費一切，水先料，その他の費用は船主負担とする。ただし本船が気象状態により，もしくは積荷の事故のために港または錨地に入る場合，その喪失時間は傭船者負担とする。機関故障，災害，あるいは船長，職員，部員の非能率により，航海中本船の速力が低下し，または燃料消費量が増加した場合，それによって本船の次港到達が24時間以上遅延し，または消費量が1日分の消費量を超えた場合，その喪失時間または超過燃料消費量は船主負担とする。結氷による遅延，または検疫のための時間は，傭船者負担とする。ただし，傭船者が船長に伝染病流行についての十分な書面による通知をなしたにもかかわらず，その伝染病流行港で船長，職員，部員が，陸上と交通することにより生じた検疫による遅延は，船主負担とする。船長，職員，部員がなした密輸その他の法律違反の追及の結果としての，官憲の抑留による喪失時間についても同様とする。

(b). 本条前段により喪失時間または遅延が12時間以下であることを理由に傭船料支払が停止されなかった喪失時間が，各傭船契約年において（1年に満たない部分はその割合で）合計144時間を超えた場合，その超過分につき傭船料は支払われず，船主は過払傭船料を傭船者に返還する。

(c). 本船または船主に対する法的手段の結果たる官憲による抑留によって喪失時間が生じた場合，それがいかなる地においてであっても，その全喪失時間について傭船料支払は停止される。当該喪失時間中生じた消費燃料および水の代金，さらには追加港費，水先料，その他の費用一切は船主負担となる。この喪失時間が30日を超えて継続する場合，傭船者は，本船の抑留中に船主に，書面で通知することによって，本契約を解約することができる。この場合，傭船者の有する前述の他のいかなる権利も害されない。

入　渠

12. (a). 船主は，自らの負担において24ヶ月を超えない適当な間隔をおき，入渠，清掃，船底塗装，

すべての分解検査その他必要な修繕を行い，傭船者は，この目的のため本船が適当な港に向かうことを許容する。船主は，上記および本船のガス・フリーについてすべての責任をもつ。ドックへのおよびドックからの回航中および入渠中に生じる曳航費用，水先料，燃料費，清水代その他の費用もまた船主負担とする。本条または第15条に規定するドック中または修繕中，もしくはドックまたは修繕港への，またはそこからの航行中に消費された燃料は，それが当該地または次の補給港で得られたものである場合には，この燃料供給者が傭船者に請求した価格で，傭船者は船主負担として請求する。

(b). 本船が傭船者の指図に従い積荷，揚荷，燃料補給をする港で本条に基づき入渠する場合，傭船料は，本船が空船のときは，到着時点で検疫済証を得たときから，積荷あるときは揚荷終了のときから，再び運航業務の準備ができるまで，支払われない。傭船者の指図に従い，本船が積荷，揚荷，燃料補給をなす港以外の港で入渠する場合，以下の時間および燃料費用は，傭船料より控除される。すなわち，傭船者が指図した最終寄港地より次の寄港地までの修繕のための寄港を含む実際の航海所要時間および燃料費用より，当該最終寄港地より次の寄港地まで直航したと仮定した場合の航海所要時間および燃料費用を減じた時間および費用である。この仮定の航海は，シーブイからシーブイまでの距離を基準に，第8条の保証速力および保証燃料消費量で算定される。

船主負担費目

13. 船主は，食料費，甲板部，機関部の船用品，厨房・船室の船用品の費用，厨房・船室の燃料費，本船保険料，船長・職員・部員の賃金，本船を本契約に規定する航行区域に運航させるために必要な証明書その他の書類一切の費用，船長・職員・部員に関する費用一切を負担しかつ支払う。

船長の義務

14. (a). 船長は，船主によって任命され，その被用者たる立場にあり，その指揮命令に従うが，傭船者の代理，運航手配，本契約による本船の運航業務利用に関しては傭船者の指図を遵守する。本条および本契約のいずれの条項も，傭船者に対する本船の賃貸借を構成するもの，あるいは傭船者が本船の物理的管理または航海を支配する権限を傭船者に与えるものと解釈されてはならない。

(b). 船長および機関士は，航海日誌を脱落なくかつ正確に記載する。それは，傭船者およびその代理人の閲覧に供され，かつその抄録は各寄港地で傭船者に直接送付される。

(c). 傭船者が，船長または職員の行為を不満足とする理由がある場合，船主はその苦情内容聴取後，直ちにそれを調査し，かつ必要あれば交代させるものとする。

燃料費，港費等

15. (a). 傭船者は，（本船のオフハイヤー期間を除き），第13条で規定する厨房および乗組員のための燃料費以外のすべての燃料を手配し，その費用を支払う。傭船者はまた，すべての港費，艀費，埠頭料，パナマその他の運河通行料，水先料，領事証明手数料（船長・職員・部員に関するものを除く），本契約を実行するための出入港および港内碇泊のための必要な曳船使用料，傭船者負担分として生じる代理店費および手数料，荷役ホースおよびアームの連結，取りはずしより生じる乗組員の費用を支払う。しかし船主は，共同海損犠牲損害または費用として使用した燃料費ないし生じた費用，および入渠中または修繕中消費した燃料費を，傭船者に償還する。

曳船および水先人

(b). 水先案内および曳船を使用する場合，船主は，当該業務を必要とする港または場所において，慣行となっている当該業務についての通常の条件で，もしあれば水先人，曳船の船長その他乗組員を船主派遣被用者とする条件で，船主に代わってこれらを雇い入れる権限を傭船者に与える。

(c). 傭船者，その代理人，関連会社，子会社，それらの代理人または被用者は，水先人，曳船の船長その他乗組員の過失，無能力，不適任に起因する，あるいはこれらの者の雇用契約条件から発生する，さらには傭船者が船主に代わって手配した曳船の不堪航ないし性能不足に起因する責任，減失，損傷につき何らの責任を負うものではない。そして船主は，かかる結果の一切について傭船者，その代理人，関連会社，子会社，その被用者に責任を負わせないこと，また損害を負担させないことに同意する。

(d). 本船に曳船ないし水先案内の業務を提供するについては，傭船者は，自己の曳船，水先人，あるいは関連会社ないし子会社が利用しているか，ないし雇用している曳船，水先人を使用する権利を有する。この場合，当該労務が提供される港に普及している，独立の曳船所有者ないし水先人が用いる当該労務に関する諸条件が適用され，そして傭船者，関連会社，子会社，その水先人には，上記独立曳船所有者ないし水先人に適用されるすべての免責，責任制限，およびその公表されたタリフ条件が認められる。

追加装備

16. 傭船者は，傭船開始時に本船にある積荷ないし揚荷のためのポンプおよび／または，設備の他に，必要なポンプおよび／または設備を追加設置する自由を有し，さらに必要な蒸気管または水道管と連結することができる。ただし，船主の同意を必要とするが，船主は理由なくこれを拒否できない。この設置は，傭船者の費用と時間でなされ，かつ設置されたポンプおよび／または設備は傭船者の財産とみなされ，さらに傭船者は，その費用と時間で本契約期間中，または満了時にこれを撤去する自由を有する。本船は船主の満足するよう，その原状に回復されなければならない。

繋　　　船

17. 傭船者は，本傭船期間の全部または一部にわたり本船を**繋**船する権利を有し，この場合，傭船料は継続して支払われる。しかし，この傭船料に対しては，船主は，**繋**船中の費用削減により節約する（ないし合理的にみて節約すべき）額から，**繋**船により船主が負担すべき増加費用を控除した額を，減額する。

傭船者が本条により付与された権利を行使した後に，本船を再び運航させることを希望するならば，船主は，傭船者からその旨の書面による通知を受領した後直ちに，本船をできるだけ，速やかに運航業務に復帰させる措置を講ずる。本条により付与された傭船者の権利は，本傭船期間またはその延長期間中，一度ないし数度行使することができる。

徴　　　用

18. (a). 本船の権原が，いかなる政府当局により徴用，または奪取された場合には（もしくは，本船が，いかなる人または政府当局によって権原の徴用と同じ状況の下で奪取を受けた場合にも），本契約は，当該徴用ないし奪取の実際の開始日を以て自動的に終了する。

(b). 本船がいかなる政府当局により使用のため徴用，または奪取された場合にも，それが権原徴用または，それと同等のものでない限り，本船はその徴用期間中オフハイヤーとなる。そして，当該徴用に関して支払われる傭船料その他補償金一切は，船主勘定となる。しかしながら，当該徴用が90日を超えて継続するならば，傭船者は，船主に対し書面による通知をなし，本契約を終了させる権利を有する。本条によるオフハイヤー期間中については，本契約第1条(b)に規定するオフハイヤー延長期間についての傭船者の権利が適用される。

返　　　船

19. (a). 本契約による本船の業務が，本船の滅失その他により事前に終了したものでない場合，傭船者は，第1条に定める契約期間（同条または本契約の他の規定による延長期間を含む）の満了時に……………（以下，「返船港」という）において，本船を空船状態で船主の使用に供すべく返還し，その返船日時を書面により通知する。本船のタンクを洗浄して，船主に返船するかどうかは傭船者の任意とする。

(b). 船主は，本契約終了時に本船に積載されている燃料タンク内の燃料一切を受け取り，かつその代金を支払う。当該燃料代金支払は，エクソン国際会社契約価格表により，本船が傭船者から船主に返船された日付，および港または場所，もしくはその表が適用になる最寄り港の表値に従ってなされる。

船荷証券

20. (a). 船荷証券は，呈示どおりに船長により署名されるものとし，要求あれば，船長が，傭船者またはその代理人の事務所に毎日出頭する。しかし，傭船者の選択により，傭船者またはその代理人が，船長にかわって船荷証券に署名することもできる。いかなる船荷証券も本契約上の権利を害するものではない。また本契約と，船荷証券，その他傭船者その代理人，またはその要求によって船長が署名した書類との間の不一致，または傭船者またはその代理人の提供した書類の不備により生じるすべての結果ないし責任について，傭船者は船主に補償する。

(b). 本傭船契約および積荷につき発行された船荷証券に基づく積荷運送は，制定法規およびその他本条(i)ないし(vi)に規定する条項に従う。また，これら条項は，すべての船荷証券に逐語的に摂取され，あるいは船荷証券上に引用されることにより摂取されたものとみなされる。上記当該条項および法律にいう「運送人」とは，本船船主および傭船船主を含む。

(i). 至上条項。本船船荷証券は，1936年4月16日承認された米国海上物品運送法に準拠し効力を有する。ただし，他の一定の法律，命令，規則が1924年8月Brusselsにおける船荷証券に関する若干の規則の統一のための国際条約を国内法化している地で発行される場合には，本船荷証券は，当該法律，命令，規則に準拠し効力を有する。適用される法律，命令，規則（以下，「法律」という）は，ここに摂取しているものとみなされる。そして，ここに規定するいかなる条項も，船主または運送人による当該法律上の権利ないし免責の放棄，もしくは責任の加重とみなされるものではない。本船荷証券中の条項が法律と矛盾する場合，その条項はその抵触する範囲およびその限度で無効となる。

(ii). ニュー・ジェイソン条項。航海開始の前後を問わず，また原因の如何，過失の有無を問わず，事故，危険，損害，災害が生じ，かかる事態およびその結果に対して運送人が法律，契約その他により責任を負わない場合，貨物，荷送人，貨物所有者は，支払われるまたは支払われることになる共同海損の性質を有する犠牲，損害または費用を共同海損において運送人と分担し，かつ積荷に関して生じた救助料および特別費用を支払う。救助船が運送人により所有ないし管理されている場合，救助料は，当該救助船が第三者に属する場合と同等に控除なく支払われる。荷送人，荷受人，貨物所有者は要求があれば，貨物引渡前に運送人に対して，運送人またはその代理人が積荷分担金，救助料，特別費用を回収するために十分とみなす額を供託しなければならない。

(iii). 共同海損。共同海損は，1950年改正ヨーク・アントワープ・ルールおよびこれに規定なき事項については，New York港の法律および慣習に準拠し，精算され，書類が作成され，決済される。共同海損精算書が要求される場合には，それは，運送人が選任し，本船傭船者が同意したNew York港の精算人によって同港で作成される。当該精算人は慣行的報酬を得て共同海損の決済，徴収をなすものとする。本船の運送人，傭船者，積荷の運送人および／または荷受人は，要求があれば共同海損同意書または保証状を提出する。共同海損および／または救助料の支払保証としてなされる現金供託は，海損精算人に送金され，当該精算人により，またその責任において，共同海損精算書作成地の正当に認可され，免許を有する銀行の特別口座に保管される。

(iv). 双方過失。本船が，他船の過失および本船船長，船員，水先人その他運送人の被用者の航海もしくは船舶取扱上の行為，過失または怠慢の結果，他船と衝突した場合，本契約に基づき運送された積荷の所有者は，運送人に対して，相手船たる非積載船ないしその船主に対するすべての損失ないし債務を，次の限度において補償する。すなわちそれが積載船または運送人に対する求償の一部として相手船により支払われたかまたは支払われるべき，あるいは相手船，非積載船ないしその船主により回収された上記積荷所有者の全滅失，損傷ないし求

償分に限る。以上の規定は，衝突船または衝突物体以外の，船舶または物体の所有者，運航者または管理者に，衝突，接触につき過失ある場合にもまた適用する。
- (v). 責任制限。本契約中の反対の規定にもかかわらず，運送人は，現行の制定法ないし法の原則による船主または傭船者の責任制限ないし免責の利益を有する。
- (vi). 離路条項。本船は，水先人の有無にかかわらず航行し，曳航し，または曳航され，遭難船の救助に向かい，人命，財産の救助または船上の傷病者を上陸させる目的で離路し，あるいは航海の通常航路上および航路外の港に燃料補給のため寄港する自由を有する。

21. 戦争危険条項。(a). いかなる戦時禁制品も船積してはならない。ただし，石油および／または石油製品は，本条における戦時禁制品とはみなされない。しかしながら，本船は，船主の同意──それは理由なく拒否されるべきではないが──なくして，宣戦布告の有無にかかわらず戦争，軍事的行為，または敵対行為，内乱，暴動，海賊行為下にあり，拿捕，没収，アレスト，または交戦国（「国（power）」とは，陸海空軍を保有する法律上または事実上の政府その他政府機関一切を意味する）による敵対行為を受けることが合理的に予期される港，地帯に入港，入域することを要求されない。
    - (b). 本条の趣旨に照らして，第21条(a)に規定する一切の危険についての保険を，その航海，航路，積揚港に関して商業上または政府の施策上，付保しうる場合には，船主の当該航海，航路，積揚港に関する同意拒否は不当なものとなる。船主が同意した場合，傭船者は，本船の普通船体保険証券上の保険価額につき本船を船体戦争保険に付保するについて相当の割増保険料を，...............を超えない限度で支払う。さらに船主が，不稼働損失，運賃積費，全損等の付帯危険について普通の海上危険に付保している場合，船主は，かかる危険につき戦争危険保険を付すことができる。もし当該保険が，商業上ないし政府の施策上得られない場合には，本船はそのような港または地域に入りまたは滞まることを要しない。
    - (c). 本契約締結日以降または本船の本契約に基づく傭船中，第21条(a)に規定する状況が存在している場合，傭船者は，そのような港または地域への航海に関して当該戦争，軍事的行為，敵対行為の結果，船長，職員および部員に支払うべき正当な割増賃金および割増保険料を負担する。

免　　責

22. (a). 本船，その船長および船主は，本契約書に別段の規定ない限り，以下に起因する積荷の滅失，損傷に対しては責任を負わない。すなわち，船長，水先人，船員その他船主の被用者の本船航海あるいは船舶取扱上の行為，過失，怠慢または不履行，火災（ただし，船主自身の故意，過失を原因とするものを除く），衝突，座礁，海上その他可航水域における危険または事故，爆発，汽罐の破裂，シャフトの折損，その他船体，艤装，機器の隠れたる瑕疵。さらに，本船，その船長および船主あるいは傭船者は，本契約書に別段の規定がない限り，以下に起因する契約上の滅失，損傷，遅延または契約不履行について責任を負わない。すなわち，天災；戦争行為；海の危険；公敵，海賊，強盗の行為；君主，統治者，人民によるアレスト，抑留もしくは法的手続による差押え（ただし，本船または積荷を解放するために直ちに保証金が提供されることを条件とする）；原因の如何を問わず部分的または全般的たるとを問わず，ストライキ，ロックアウト，労働の停止，制限；暴動または内乱。

複 数 等 級

- (b). 船主は，本船が...............等級の油を運送するために建造かつ艤装されたものであることを担保する。何らかの理由で，本船が積荷港へ到着したときに，要求された数の等級の異なる油を積載できない場合，傭船者は本船の能力に合致する適当な貨物を提供するため，最善を尽くすものとする。ただし，これが不可能であれば，本船は，空船状態で最寄りの修繕港へ向かい，そこで必要なすべての隔壁の漏れを修理する。当該時間および費用は船主負担とする。
- (c). 本条(a)に述べた免責事由は，本船の状態，要目，性能，傭船料の支払および停止の規定，もしくは貨物の積込，取扱，保管，運送，管理，注意，揚荷についての，第20条に基づく船主の

義務に何ら影響するものではない。
23. 本船が収得した救助料一切は，救助料に対して最優先権を有する船長，職員，部員の取得分，法的手続費用，喪失時間中の本船傭船料，消費燃料費用，もしあれば損害修理費，その他救助の結果として生じた特別損失および費用一切を控除した上で，船主，傭船者間で均等に分配される。
24. 船主は，本船がTOVALOPに加盟し，かつ本契約有効期間中，継続して加盟することを担保する。しかしながら，その規約第Ⅷ条により，船主がTOVALOPを脱退する権利を得る場合，本契約のいかなる条項も当該権利の行使を妨げるものではない。

油　濁

　本船から油の流出，排出を生じ，海岸への油濁損害を生じるおそれがある場合，船主が速やかに措置を講じないときは，傭船者はその裁量で船主ないし船長に通知して，損害を防止し，または最小限に止めるために必要な合理的措置をとることができる。傭船者は，その講じようとする措置の内容を，常に船主に通知するものとする。傭船者が現実にとった上記措置の費用は，船主負担とする（油の流出，排出原因が傭船者にある場合，あるいは傭船者が流出，排出に寄与している場合は，その限りにおいて例外とする）。ただし，船主が当該措置を中止すべきだと考えるならば，船主は傭船者にその旨通知でき，その後傭船者は，本条項により当該措置を続行する権利を有せず，以後の行為に対する傭船者の責任は消滅することを条件とする。

　ここに規定した，傭船者によりとられた措置および/または生じた費用の妥当性に関して，船主・傭船者間に意見の不一致が生じた場合，当該紛争は本契約書に規定する仲裁に付託される。

　本条の規定は，傭船者または船主が本契約に基づき，あるいは別途法律または国際条約により有するか，もしくは取得する他の権利を害するものではない。

汚染防止

25. 船主は，油濁防止に関する傭船者の計画に参画する。その計画は，本船，積荷または人命が危険に曝される極端な状況を除き，世界中どこであろうと，油，油濁水，バラスト，化学製品，その他いかなる形態であろうと，持続性残滓油の海洋投棄を防止する目的を持つ。

　船主は，傭船者の提供した，傭船者本船指図便覧中の油濁防止要領を，遵守することに同意する。当該指図書便覧は，国際あるいは国内法規制上の特別の事態または変更を網羅するための書面または電信により発行される改定をも含む。船長は，本船船上に集合タンク洗浄の油濁残水，汚濁バラスト等を保持する。かかる残水は，沈殿分離または機械的分離法を用いた安全な方法で，公認された水準にまで，可能な限り水分を分離した後に，1区画に保持する。

　油濁残水は，分離油，汚濁バラスト，積荷との混合物として，傭船者が各積荷を調整するのに可能な限り，積荷または揚荷ターミナルで陸揚される。

　傭船者が，抗乳化剤を油水分離のため使用することを要求するならば，当該抗乳化剤の費用は傭船者負担である。

　船主は，入渠または修理のための積荷タンク準備を含む，本契約期間内のオフハイヤー期間中に，傭船者の油濁防止計画を遵守すべく，本船を整備する。この場合には，傭船者は，油濁残水投棄の費用を負担する。

　本船は，積揚荷役，燃料補給，バラスティングの際に，油を船外に排出しないことを確実にするために，必要なあらゆる予防策を講ずる。

　いかなる傭船者の指図も，油または油濁水の排出等による海洋汚染の容認と解されるべきではない。船主は，船長に対し，傭船者へ積荷港到達時の船上油濁残水量の詳細も併記した油濁防止に関する報告書の提出を，指図することに同意する。

製　品

26. 船主は，ここに船用製品を商う傭船者の子会社の販売部と接することに同意する。しかしながら，船主はこの子会社から当該生産物を購買する義務はなく，この子会社が船主に販売する義務もない。船主は，当該子会社と交渉する適当な人物ないし組織として次の者を指定する。

名称 ....
住所 ....

所有者の変更

27. 本契約上の船主の権利および義務は，傭船者の同意なくして売却または譲渡により移転するものではない。本船がその同意なく他の権利と共に売却された場合，傭船者は，そのまったくの自由裁量で傭船契約を終了させることができる。その場合，船主は傭船者に対し，反対給付が得られなかった前払傭船料，燃料費用，本契約上傭船者に支払われるべき金額一切，および傭船者が被る損害一切を償還する。

仲　　裁

28. いかなる性質のものであれ，本契約から生ずる一切の紛議，紛争は，New York 市で効力を有する仲裁に関する法律に従って，New York 市において3名で構成する仲裁委員会に付託される。同委員会は，船主により任命された仲裁人，傭船者により任命された仲裁人，およびこの2人が選任した仲裁人により構成される。3名のうち，いずれか2名の，いかなる争点についての判断も最終のものとする。各当事者は，仲裁人が聴聞を終結するときまで，仲裁人または相手方に書面で通知することによって，本契約上の他の紛争または紛議を審問，裁決の目的として指定する権利を有する。仲裁人は，全員一致または多数決をもって，当事者の合意の範囲内で正当かつ衡平とみなされる救済を与えることができる。かかる救済は，特定の履行行為を含むがそれに限られない。本条による裁定額は諸費用を含み，そこには，妥当な弁護士費用も含まれる。本条による裁定に基づき当該事項につき管轄を有する裁判所において，判決を取得することができる。

譲　　渡

29. (a). 傭船者は，船主に対して通知の上，本傭船契約をその関連会社に譲渡できる。

転　　貸

(b). 傭船者は，また本船を再傭船に出す権利を有する。しかし，この場合にも，傭船者は常に本契約全条項，全条件に基づく本契約の履行につき責任を負う。

法　　律

30. 本傭船契約およびその当事者の権利，義務の解釈は，New York 市で締結された傭船契約に適用される法律に準拠する。各条項の見出しは引用，参考の便宜のためのものにすぎず，本契約の解釈に影響を与えるものではない。本契約書のいかなる条項の変更，権利放棄または取消も，書面によりなされ，かつ，その責任を負う当事者により署名されない限り無効とする。

以上の証拠として本契約書は当事者により本契約書冒頭記載の年月日に2通作成された。

....　　　　　..............................
..............の証拠としての署名
....　　　　　..............................
..............の証拠としての署名

ニューヨーク・プロデュース書式

契約の成立

THE NEW YORK PRODUCE EXCHANGE
TIME CHARTER (1946)

"1. This Charter Party, made and concluded in .... day of .... 19......"

定期傭船契約書〔ニューヨーク・プロデュース書式〕(1946)

「本傭船契約書は，19......年......月......日に，......において，締結したものであって，」

特別な形式は不要

　傭船契約に特別な形式は必要ではない。当事者が拘束力ある傭船契約を締結したかどうかは，契約法の一般原則が決めることである。したがって，傭船契約は当事者の署名がなくても，また合意事項を印刷書式に基づいて作成していなくても，拘束力を持ちうる。ある船舶を傭船するという口頭の合意でさえも，証明されれば，拘束力がある（この点については，*Lidgett* v. *Williams* (1845) 14 L. J. Ch. 459 事件における Wigram 副大法官の見解参照）。船主および傭船者（またはそれぞれを代理した仲立人）が文書またはテレックスもしくはファクスにより，傭船契約の基本事項すべてにつき合意済みであれば，裁判所は合意が成立したものとみなす。ただし，このような交渉過程で，後日傭船契約書を作成し署名するまでは，合意に拘束されない旨の意思を示すものがある場合は，この限りではない。傭船実務の用語では，その時点で，成約 (fixture) があったことになる。

基本的条項すべてについて明確な合意の必要性

　当事者がすべての基本的条項について明確な合意に達するまでは，契約は存在しえないというのが基本原則である。Blackburn 卿は，*Rossiter* v. *Miller* (1878) 3 App. Cas. 1124 事件で，次のように判示した（同判例集1151頁）。「合意の基本的明細が，後刻決着をつけるべく残されている場合，契約は存在しない」。当事者が例えば，支払傭船料率というような，ある重要な事項について合意できないか，合意することを怠っている場合に契約が存在しえないことは明らかである。当事者が重要事項について合意してはいるが，曖昧なまたは漠然とした用語が用いられているため，調査してもその当事者の合意に確かな意味を持たせることができない事例では，事態は，より困難を極める。

　このような事例について，裁判所は，当事者が使用した文言に確実な意味を発見するよう，一般に懸命の努力をする。例えば，裁判所は特に当事者自身が全面的合意に達していたと信じている場合に，外観上の契約を維持するよう，当事者間の従前の取引や，あるいは，特定の売買に関係ある用語の通常の意味を参照する。Maugham 子爵は，*Scammell* v. *Ouston* [1941] A. C. 251 事件において，次のように述べている（同判例集255頁）。「当事者が拘束力ある契約を締結したと思い込んでいると裁判所が確信を持った場合には，当事者が精通している取引に

関係する商業上の書類の中に，他の契約ではとても考えられないような一定の条項（それも特に履行手段に関わる条項）が当然含まれていると解することに，裁判所は積極的である。*Hillas & Co. v. Arcos, Ltd.* 事件参照」。Maugham子爵が参照した判例の事実関係は次のとおりである。

材木商人が，ロシア産の「平均的規格の針葉樹22,000本分」を1930年中に購入する契約を締結した。契約では，1931年度には，同年度についての売主の公式価格表からの表示値引価格で「100,000本分」を購入する選択権が与えられてはいたが，木材の種類，寸法，品質，船積の方法について細目の定めはなかった。1930年の購入分については，問題が起きなかったが，売主は，拘束力ある契約とするには，文言が不確実に過ぎることを理由として，1931年度についての選択権による責任を免れようとした。貴族院は，1931年度についての選択権は，拘束力があると判示した。すなわち，先の文言上の空白は，1930年度の契約の文言を参照して埋めることができるし，また，その文言自体曖昧な場合には，(例えば，針葉樹を単に「平均的規格の」と記載したように)，その意味は，条理に適い公平であることとを当然の前提とすることによって確定しうる，というのである。
Hillas v. *Arcos* (1932) 43 Ll. L. Rep. 359.
(*Shamrock* v. *Storey* (1899) 81 L.T. 413 事件も参照)

ただし，裁判所が重要事項にそうしたはっきりした意味を確定することができないときは，裁判所は契約はまったく存在しないと宣言すると思われる。

有蓋貨物自動車の売買契約書に「この注文は売買代金残額を，2年間に亘る買取権付物品貸借契約条項に基づき，支払うことができるという了解の下になされるものである」と規定していた。貴族院は契約が存在しないと判断した。買取権付物品貸借契約条項には，多くの異なる形態がある以上，この約定は意味がきわめて不明確で，そのため，この契約は，肝心な点の合意が欠けている。Maugham子爵は，「有効な契約を成立させるためには，当事者は意図する所をかなり確実に決定できるようにその意思を表明しなければならない。これができなければ，契約の当事者が同一の意図を有したと認め難いことは言うまでもない。換言すれば，意思の合致も，単なる憶測に過ぎなくなるであろう」と述べた。Wright卿は，「契約は，裁判所がその契約に実際的な意味を付与できる程度に明確でなければならないということが必要な要件である。その文言は，当事者がそれ以上の合意をしなくても各当事者による約束や履行が十分確実になされ得るように明確であるか，または，明確にできるものでなくてはならない」と述べた。
Scammell v. *Ouston* [1941] A. C. 251.

一方，意味のない文言は，完璧な契約に何の意味も付加しえないのであれば，無視できる (*Nicolene* v. *Simmonds* [1953] 1 Q. B. 543 事件参照)。自己矛盾のある条項は，当事者の重要な権利と義務に影響を与えることなしにその条項を契約から切り離しができる場合，契約を無効にするものではない。

木材販売契約書の仲裁条項は，あらゆる紛争 (any dispute) は Londonの仲裁に付し，かつ他のあらゆる紛争 (any other dispute) は Moscowで仲裁に付すと規定していた。
控訴院は，当該仲裁条項はすべて意味がなく，すべて無視すべきであると判示した。その条項は契約の他の部分から切り離し可能であり，貨物の引渡不能と欠陥品質に関する当事者間の紛争は，裁判所の審理による，とした。
Lovelock v. *Exportles* [1968] 1 Lloyd's Rep. 163.

一般原則として，基本的な事項を当事者間の後日の交渉に委ねているような合意は，強行可

能な契約ではない。*Courtney & Fairbairn* v. *Tolaini Bros.* [1975] 1 W. L. R. 297 事件と *Mallozzi* v. *Carapelli* [1976] 1 Lloyd's Rep. 407 事件参照。だからといって，当事者が指名する者に決定を委ねる合意が，必ずしも無効というわけではない。ただし，その決定が明示あるいは黙示の客観的基準に合致しているものである限りにおいてである。*Sudbrook Trading Estate Ltd* v. *Eggleton* [1983] 1 A.C. 444 事件において貴族院は，自由保有権の復帰購入の選択権を賃借人に与える賃貸借契約の1条項を支持して，次のように判示した。「価格は賃借人と賃貸人がそれぞれ指名した評定者の協議による。ただし，合意が成立しない場合には，両評定者により指名された審判人による」。賃借人が，この選択権を行使しようとするも，賃貸人が，価格評定者を指名せず，価格についての合意は成立しなかった。貴族院は，次のように判示した。契約上価格評定者を規定することで当事者は客観的基準を取り入れた。すなわち，その価格は（契約に指名された個人の主観的決定に比べて）公正でかつ合理的でなければならない。例えば，当事者は公正・合理的な価格で売買に合意したし，正確な価格に到達するために設定された仕組それ自身は契約の基本的な部分ではないが，その主要な目的に従属するものであった。したがって，その仕組が壊れたときに，裁判所が介入し，契約に設定した客観的基準に沿って価格を査定することは許されることであった。控訴院は，この判決を，客観的な基準を設定する一方で，当事者自身に査定が委ねられている契約に適用した。*Didymi Corporation* v. *Atlantic Lines and Navigation* (*The Didymi*) [1988] 2 Lloyd's Rep. 108 事件で，ニューヨーク・プロデュース書式の追加条項に，本船が規定の速力および燃料消費より良好な平均成績を達成した場合，「船主・傭船者間で相互に合意できる金額分だけ……公平に」計算される傭船料を増額することにより船主は，補塡されるとの規定があった。控訴院は，補塡契約は有効であるとの Hobhouse 判事の判決（[1987] 2 Lloyd's Rep. 166.）を支持した。基本的合意はその状況では，船主は補塡されるべきで，正確な金額を計算する手続は単に仕組の問題に過ぎないというものであった。しかし，「公平（equitably）に」という語を用いた客観的基準の条項は，裁判所の決定には必須の要素であった。Nourse 卿判事は，次のように述べた。「したがって，当事者が客観的基準に合意していたのであるから，契約が規定する人々——彼らが当事者であるけれども——の同一性は，まったく問題ではないように思える。本事案についての私の見解は，契約に……言及して定めるべき基準を当事者が規定していたということに全面的に依拠していることを強調したい。当事者の間で『後日合意されるべき』価格，賃貸料，賃借料または他の金額による販売，賃貸，傭船，または他のいかなる契約であれ，法律上，有効な契約であると私は考えているわけではない。*Mallozzi* v. *Carapelli S. p. A.* 事件が……分類されるのはまさしくこの範疇の事件である」。

控訴院は，また，重要事項を，当事者自身の後日の合意に委ねることを明示した契約で，合意不成立の場合の解決方法が仲裁条項により定まっていれば，当該契約を進んで支持しようとしてきた。*Sykes* v. *Fine Fare* [1967] 1 Lloyd's Rep. 53 事件において，記録長官 Denning 卿は次のように述べた。「『[初年度以降に] 当事者間で合意されるべき数字』という文言は，契約を契約ではなくするような不確実さをもたらすものではないと私は確信する。合意が成立しない場合には，数字は……仲裁条項に基づき，仲裁人が確定する妥当な数字であると記載することにより，この契約は有効となる」。

前出 *Didymi Corporation* v. *Atlantic Lines and Navigation* 事件で控訴院は，*Sykes* v. *Fine Fare* 事件を支持した上でこれを引用し，次のように言った。*Sykes* v. *Fine Fare* 事件で，必要とあれば，判決のために別の根拠を示すことができた。すなわち，この事件の実体法上の権利関係は，争われた契約が当事者の相当の出費によって既に一部履行されていたため，異常に強力であった。この事件は，注意して扱うべきであるが，しかし，契約が部分的に履行されてい

るなら，裁判所はこの種の条項を有効とする十分な用意があるように見えることをこの事件は例証している。

傭船契約書署名前の成約

　当事者がその最終の合意を傭船契約書に記載しようと考えている場合，この傭船契約書は，単に，既に合意されている契約の条項を記録するだけのものなのか，あるいは，契約書が作成されて承認（または署名）されるまではまったく拘束力を持たないものなのかという問題を生じることがある。これは，契約が成立した，と主張する当事者がその根拠としている交信内容を解釈して決定する他はない問題である。Parker 判事は，*Von Hatzfeldt-Wildenburg* v. *Alexander* [1912] 1 Ch. 284 事件で次のように述べた（同判例集288頁）。「契約の成立を示すとされた文書や書状中に，当事者がさらに契約書を作成することを予定している場合，契約書作成が，当該取引の条件をなすのか，あるいは，それが，既に合意された取引の事実上の履行方法に関する当事者の希望の単なる表明に過ぎないかは，解釈の問題である。この点は，判例によって十分に確立しているように思われる。前者の場合には，条件が成就していないため，また法が契約を締結するという合意に拘束力を認めないがため，拘束力ある契約は存在しない。52後者の場合には，拘束力ある契約が存在しており，それ以上の形式的な文書は無視してよい」。この点につき最近の判決を参照：*Okura* v. *Navara* [1981] 1 Lloyd's Rep. 561, [1982] 2 Lloyd's Rep. 537（C. A.）事件と *The Blankenstein* [1983] 2 Lloyd's Rep. 522, [1985] 1 Lloyd's Rep. 93（C. A.）事件。

　傭船契約書の作成，署名以前に，拘束力ある契約が成立するのが通常である。しかし，時々，重要な条項が傭船契約書の作成が済むまで，最終的に合意をみなかったり，あるいは，一方の当事者が，傭船契約書の署名まで，契約には拘束されないという留保をしたりすることがある。次の事件は，その一例である。

　　Polarsol 号の長期定期傭船のための交渉は，傭船者に新規傭船契約の成約を禁止するポルトガル政府の指示により打ち切られた。船主は，拘束ある合意が既に成立していたと主張した。McNair 判事は，傭船契約が日々略式で成約されることを認めたが，他方，特に本件では，当事者が往復文書中で，傭船契約書署名前は拘束を受けないという意思を明白にしていたこと，さらに，銀行保証に関するある重要事項が，政府の指示が通知された日までには合意に達していなかったことも認めた。その上で McNair 判事は，当事者を拘束する契約は存在しないと判示し，控訴院もこれを支持した。
　　Sociedade Portuguesa de Navios Tanques v. *Polaris* [1952] 1 Lloyd's Rep. 71 と 407（C. A.）。
　　（*Zarati Steamship* v. *Frames Tours* [1955] 2 Lloyd's Rep. 278 事件も参照）

「契約締結を条件として　subject to contract」

　傭船以外の事件においては，交渉過程において「契約締結を条件として」という文言その他これと類似の文言を用いた場合，後日正式に契約が締結されるまでは，拘束されないものとする趣旨を示すものであると繰り返し判示されてきた。このような文言を用いることは，傭船契約の交渉過程でも，同様の効果を持つものと考えられる。この点，前出 *Sociedade Portuguesa de Navios Tanques* v. *Polaris* 事件における Somervell 卿判事の意見参照。（同判例集417頁）

　ただし，*Howard Marine* v. *Ogden* [1978] 1 Lloyd's Rep. 334 事件参照。本件では，艀傭船の申込が「艀利用の可能性と傭船契約書締結を条件」としてなされた。その後，諸条項が合意されたけれども，傭船契約書は遂に署名されなかった。しかし，艀が傭船者に引き渡されて使

用されたときに，契約は合意済条項どおりに成立したと判示された。これは，*Brogden* v. *Metropolitan Railway*（1877）2 App. Cas. 666 事件の先例に従ったものである。

「検査結果，許可または承諾を条件に subject to survey, permission or approval」

　当事者が交渉の過程で，「検査結果を条件に」「政府の許可を得た上で」または「荷送人の承諾を得た上で」という文言を使用した場合には，(a)拘束力のある契約はまったく存在しないのか，(b)即時に拘束力を有するが，検査が遂行されたか，許可または承諾が与えられた場合のみ，その主たる義務が，実施される契約なのか，(c)即時に拘束力を有する契約であるが，要件が満たされない場合，拘束力を失うものなのか，を決めるのは，その文脈に関連する交信すべての解釈の問題である。(b)に解釈される場合には，検査が遂行されるか，許可または承諾が与えられるまで，契約の主たる義務は，作動しない。しかし，一方または双方の当事者には要件を満たすことを妨害しない義務，それどころか要件を満たすために妥当なことをする義務がある。この点 *Brauer* v. *Clark* [1952] 2 Lloyd's Rep. 147 事件および *Hargreaves Transport* v. *Lynch* [1969] 1 W. L. R. 215 事件参照。

　Astra Trust v. *Adams* [1969] 1 Lloyd's Rep. 81 事件で，解釈(a)が採用された。「満足できる検査結果を条件として」の文言は，拘束力ある売買船契約の成立を当分の間は妨げると判示された。同事件で，Megaw 判事は，買主が満足するような検査報告書を受け取るまでは，いずれの当事者も，暫定的に合意した条項によって拘束されないと判示した。その時点までなら，[53]いずれの当事者も自由に取り消すことができる。その文言が単に「検査の上で subject to survey」であっても，判決は同じものになるであろう。この判決の趣旨は，上記の「契約締結を条件として」についてと同じ効果を「（満足できる）検査結果を条件に」という文言に与えようとするものである。

　記録長官 Denning 卿は，その後の売買契約事件，*The Merak* [1976] 2 Lloyd's Rep. 250 事件において，Megaw 判事の判決の正当性について疑問を表明し，そのような文言があっても，場合によっては，直ちに拘束力ある契約が成立することがありうるとの見解を述べた。つまり，買主には検査義務が，売主には検査を許容する義務が，それぞれ発生し，おそらく，客観的見地から検査結果が不満足なものであると認められる場合に限り，契約が消滅することになるというのである。

　上記 *The Merak* 事件で控訴院は，全面的にノルウェー売買書式に拠る売買契約のテレックス交渉において，「外見上の検査の上で subject to superficial inspection」という文言を用いた場合につき，即時に拘束力ある契約（ただし，検査後に買主が受領拒絶できるノルウェー売買書式の通常の印刷条項を含む）の成立を妨げないと判示した。

　しかし，後出の事件では，「2 度の試験航海が満足に完了した上で，subject to satisfactory completion of two trial voyages」という文言は，これらの試験航海が満足裡に完了して，当事者が契約締結に同意しない限り，かつ同意するときまで，傭船契約は何ら拘束力を持たないとする趣旨であると判示された。

　ある澱粉製造業者が，自己の工場に澱粉を運ぶ目的で，*John S. Darbyshire* 号について，「2 度の試験航海が満足に完了した上で」という限定を付けて定期傭船に同意した。この限定は，傭船者が，自己の負担で同船に取り付けた圧搾空気管設備により，運送中澱粉を十分活性化し，泥炭状態に維持することを確認したいがため，設定されたものであった。第 2 回目の試験航海後，当該業者は，定期傭

船契約をするつもりはないと言った。商事裁判所において，当該業者は定期傭船契約として拘束力を持つような合意は何らなされていない旨，主張した。Mocatta 判事はこれを承認した。同判事は，当該文言があるために，定期傭船契約各条項は「当事者が，さらにその文書によって拘束さるべきことを合意した場合に使用するために，いわば条件付き捺印証書として，作成され，合意されたもの」として扱われる，と述べている。

The John S. Darbyshire [1977] 2 Lloyd's Rep. 457.

「〜を条件として subject to」で始まる条項が使用された多くの不動産売買契約の判例があるが，その中の幾つかでは，契約の場所についての複雑な検討が行なわれている。傭船契約紛争にこういう判例を適用する際には注意を払わねばならない。なぜなら，多くの判例はその当事者の出身諸国における特別な不動産売買の実務により影響を受けているからである。特に，どちらの当事者も通常滞在しないので，拘束を受けることのない合意から契約の取り交わしまでの期間英国にいるかも知れないということで影響を受けている。Coote 著，*Agreements subject to finance*, 40 Conv. (N. S.) 37 (1976) 参照。

「細目を条件として　subject details」

傭船契約書交渉でよく使用される表現「細目を条件として subject to details あるいは単に sub details」は，主要な契約条件全てについての合意にもかかわらず，少なくとも詳細が合意されない場合，および少なくとも合意されるまでは，通常英国法に基づく拘束力ある契約の成立を妨げる。米国の判例では反対の効果があることを留意するべきである（後出108頁を参照）。しかし次の事件は，合衆国の法廷はこの点について海運取引が機能している方法と歩調があっていないことを Steyn 判事が示唆したものである（しかし，Davies [1992] LMCLQ 351 (358頁) を参照）。

　Junior K 号の航海傭船契約の交渉の後で，船主の仲立人は傭船者の仲立人にテレックスを送り，「細目を条件としてここに電話会話による成約を確認 Confirm telcons here recap fixture sub details」で始まり，「Gencon 傭船契約書式の細目を条件として sub dets Gencon CP」で終わる合意条件を述べた。このテレックスは，傭船契約のすべての基本的条件を含んでいた。未解決の事項は，交渉の中で，特段取り上げられなかった。船主は，拘束力ある契約が存在したと主張した。Steyn 判事は中間申立に基いて，船主の主張は勝訴の現実的見込がないと判示した。同判事は，次のように述べた。「当事者同士が Gencon 書式の契約を心に描いたことは，明白であるが，その細部について熟慮してはいなかった。『Gencon 傭船契約書の細目を条件として』という表現によって，船主は，傭船契約の詳細について交渉が行われるまで，契約としての拘束を受けたくないということを明確にした。そういう議論が一連の条項について行われたかも知れない。だからといって，船主が標準書式の詳細な条項のすべてを喜んでそのまま受け入れるということにはならない。つまり，Gencon 書式のいくつかの条項が，交渉の過程で修正されるのが普通なのである。いずれにしても Gencon 標準書式自身が明確な選択条項を複数含んでいる……こういう選択について何ら議論は行われていない……この背景で，『Gencon 傭船契約書式の細目を条件として』の条項は，未だ議論されなかった Gencon 傭船契約書式の細目につき合意がなされることを条件とする取決めであることを意味することは明白であると思う」。

The Juior K [1988] 2 Lloyd's Rep. 583.

（*The Solholt* [1981] 2 Lloyd's Rep. 574 事件（同判例集576頁）で Staughton 判事が表明した見解および *The Intra Transporter* [1985] 2 Lloyd's Rep. 158 事件（同判例集163頁）で Leggatt 判事が表明した見解も参照）

The Nissos Samos［1985］1 Lloyd's Rep. 378 の売買船契約事件で，Leggatt 判事は385頁に所見を述べている。「『細目を条件として』は仲立業においてよく知られた表現であり，両当事者間で議論される細目のどこかで，誠意を尽くしてもいずれかが満足しないならば，契約から手をひく権利があることを意味する」。しかし，Steyn 判事は，前出 *The Junior K* 事件で，Leggatt 判事が誠意を尽くすとの条件に言及する限りにおいて，同判事は厳密な法的立場ではなく仲立業の見解を単に記録し述べたに過ぎないと考えた。拘束力ある契約が成立していない場合，交渉から当事者が撤収する理由は通常，関係がない。

　さらに，仲立業の通常の実務において「細目」のように思われる，またはみなされているような事柄は，基本的な契約上の重要事項である。*The Winner*［1986］1 Lloyd's Rep. 36 事件（同判例集38頁）において，傭船契約上の傭船者の明細あるいは指名が意味する傭船者の「名称 the style」は，最終的に成約される以前に確認を要する細目とみなされる事項の一つであるとの証拠が仲立人によって出された。

　一方，Parker 判事は，*The Samah*［1981］1 Lloyd's Rep. 40 事件で，次のように述べた（同判例集42頁）。「多くのことが未定として残っているときに契約し，予想していなかったようなある条件の受諾を約束することは疑うべくもなくありうることである」。しかし，現代英国判例の趨勢は，「細目を条件として subject to details」という条件の設定は，当事者が未だ拘束されることを意図していないとの見解を明確に支持している。*The Samah* 事件で，2隻の船舶の傭船の交渉が行われた。傭船者と後日議論される予定の「充分な仕様変更を条件として subject to satisfactory modifications」船舶が取決められたと述べたテレックスがある段階で，送られた。テレックスは，「定期傭船ニューヨーク・プロデュース書式　傭船者の仮細目を条件として NYPE TC sub charts proforma details……」で終わっていた。拘束力ある傭船契約は，次の段階で効力を生じるが，この段階では拘束力ある契約は存在しないと判示された。*The CPC Gallia*［1994］1 Lloyd's Rep. 68（「Conline booking note-subject to details/logical amendments」）事件と *Granit* v. *Benship International*［1994］1 Lloyd's Rep. 526 事件を参照。そこでは，傭船契約交渉が「細目を条件として subject to details」行われた場合，拘束力ある契約ではないということが，共通の根拠である。Ball［1984］LMCLQ 250 および Debattista［1985］LMCLQ 241 と［1988］LMCLQ 439 および Davies［1992］LMCLQ 351（357頁）を広く参照。

「～を条件として　subject to」の他の用法

　「～を条件として」という文言は，当事者が，例えば「戦争危険条項の定めるところによる subject to war risks clause」の場合のように，ある特別の文言または条項を単に交渉の場に乗せるためにだけ用いることがある。このような文言を使用した申出でも，相手方がそれに応ずれば，拘束力ある合意が成立することとなる。しかし文言全体から，その意図する特別条項の同一性が明確でなければならない。さもなければ，そのような文言は「双方が然るべき戦争危険条項につき合意できたならば」との意味に解され，拘束力ある契約の成立を妨げるおそれがあるからである。例えば，*Love & Stewart* v. *Instone*（1917）33 T. L. R. 475 事件では，一定数量の石炭の売買条件が「ストライキおよびロックアウト条項の定めるところによって」という限定を付して合意された。貴族院は次のとおり判示した。当事者は契約中にそのような条項を入れるべきことに合意してはいたけれども，その条項の内容について合意していなかったのであるから契約は存在しない。次の事案もまた，この点を明らかにしている。

汽船 Ring 号の買受希望者の代理人が「乾ドック条項の定めるところにより，英貨22,000ポンドから1パーセント引きのファームオッファー」を行った。船舶所有者の代理人はこれに答えて，「……売主がお申込を承諾したことをここにお知らせ致します。そこで，当方は，契約書を月曜日にお送り致します」と言った。Bailhache 判事は，契約は締結されていないとして，次のように述べた。「一定の内容の通常の乾ドック条項というものは，私の知る限りでは存在しないというだけで十分である。本件の申込と承諾とは対応してはいるが，内容の定まっていない乾ドック条項を条件にしているから，本件では，そのことが当事者間の契約の成立を妨げている。当事者は，契約を締結したと話し合っていたし，事実，両当事者は契約締結を意図していた。しかし，契約締結を意図していたという事実だけでは不十分である」。

Svenska Lloyd v. *Niagassas*（1921）8 Ll.L. Rep. 500.

どの法律により決定されるか

拘束力ある契約が締結されたかを決定する際に，英国裁判所と外国の裁判所は，その国の法の抵触規定を適用する。英国の裁判所に関する限り，英国の裁判所は1991年4月1日以降締結された（あるいは締結される予定の）契約に契約義務に適用される法律に関するローマ条約を発効させる1990年契約（適用）法を適用する。この法律は後出507頁で扱われる。基本的原則は，条約の3.1条に「契約は当事者が選択する法律に準拠する」と述べられている。したがって，契約が締結されたかどうかについて紛争がある場合には，非常に難しい問題が生じる。なぜならそのときには当事者が法について合意していたかどうかの問題自身が争点であるがゆえである。例えば，「細目を条件として sub details」の合意の効果についてのある国の理解は，後出109頁の *Great Circle Lines* v. *Matheson* 事件のように，他の国では異なるものになるかも知れない。交渉の場に乗せるある特定の条項が契約の部分か否かということに関しても問題は生じる。条項が法の選択，訴訟あるいは仲裁の場所に言及している場合，その条項は契約の準拠法の決定に関係する。この状況のために，条約は8.1条で次のように規定している。「契約あるいは契約の条件の存在と有効期限は，契約あるいは条件の効力をこの条約に基づき管轄する法により決定される」。この概念は通常「推定上のプロパー・ロー putative proper law」の概念として言及される。その概念は，紛争を巡る事実関係を調べることで，そしてそれが合意されているか否かの問題が争点であろうとも，交渉で重要な役割を果たす条項，すなわち法，裁判管轄，または仲裁の条項の選択を特に考慮して確認されると思われる。少なくとも，そういう条項の一つだけが申し立てられた場合，他方の当事者が契約に同意していないので，当条項にも同意していないと言い立てたとしても，その条項は，決定的効果をもたらす。*The Parouth* [1982] 2 Lloyd's Rep. 351 事件と *The Atlantic Emperor* [1989] 1 Lloyd's Rep. 548 事件参照。そういう条項のない場合には，*The Rosso* [1982] 2 Lloyd's Rep. 120 事件におけるように，事は客観的に評価されなければならない。

契約上の申込への黙示的同意が簡単には推察されない，そして単に通知に対して回答または異議を申し立てることができないことからその黙示的同意が特にしばしば推察されない裁判管轄地で営業を遂行する者を主として保護するために，8.2条は次の条件を含んでいる。

「それにもかかわらず，先行する条項に特定される法に従って自らの行為の効果を決定することは状況から合理的ではないと思えることに同意しなかったことを確認するために，当事者は自らの常居所のある国の法に依拠する」。

本件について，広く Dicey & Morris 著『法の抵触』（*The Conflict of Laws*）（12版）の1248頁から1252頁を参照。

56 米 国 法

適 用 法

　米国において傭船契約紛争は州裁判所あるいは連邦裁判所，仲裁で決せられる。どの裁判地が選択されようとも準拠法は合衆国一般海事法である。一般海事法は海運に影響を及ぼす連邦法と共に最高裁判所と下級裁判所の判例法からなる。傭船契約事件では仲裁裁定が，先例としての拘束力がなくとも，時々，指針として引用される。

　海事事件は連邦裁判管轄の適正な主題として合衆国憲法上特別の承認を得ている。米国の裁判所は海事事件を管轄する法の統一性を推進する重要性を長らく認めてきた。結果として海事法は州法に優先する。*Southern Pacific Co.* v. *Jensen*, 244 U.S. 205 (1917)。1789年裁判所法（現在では 28 U.S.C. §1333 に法典化されている）の「訴人救済 Savings to Suiters」条項により，船籍相違管轄権を行使して，大概の海事事件の請求者が海事を管轄する連邦裁判所で訴えるか，あるいは州裁判所・連邦裁判所でのコモン・ローの救済を求めるかの選択肢を持っているとしても，海事法の優先は真実である。*A/S J. Ludwig Mowinckels Rederi* v. *Dow Chemical Co.*, 25 N.Y. 2d 576, 307 N.Y.S. 2d 660 (1970)。請求原因が海事である場合には，事件が州裁判所に持ち込まれたとしてもいつでも連邦実体法が最高権威である。例として *Kossick* v. *United Fruit Co.*, 365 U.S. 731 (1961); *Offshore Logistics* v. *Tallentire*, 477 U.S. 207, 222-223 (1986); *Garrett* v. *Moore-McCormack Co.*, 317 U.S. 239 (1942) の各事件を参照。

　傭船契約は長らく海事契約であると考えられてきた。*The Ada*, 250 F. 194 (2d Cir. 1918)。傭船契約を管轄する一般海事法は通常契約と代理法の原則を包含する。*Kirno Hill Corp.* v. *Holt*, 618 F. 2d 982, 985 (2d Cir. 1980); *Navieros Oceanikos S. A.* v. *The Mobil Trader*, 554 F. 2d 43, 47 (2d Cir. 1977)。傭船契約は詐欺防止法あるいは米国統一商事法典のような州法に支配されない。*Union Fish Co.* v. *Erickson*, 248 U.S. 308 (1919)。

　州法あるいは外国法の適用を特別に定める法の選択条項を含むことは傭船契約の当事者の自由である。例えば傭船契約は，当事者間の紛争は New York 州の法律に準拠すると定めうる。この種の法の選択条項は有効であり，通常裁判所は効力を認める。*Milanovich* v. *Costa Crociere*, 954 F. 2d 763, 1993 AMC 1034, 1040 (D. C. Cir. 1992) 事件参照。選択された特定の州が当事者，あるいはその取引と実質的な関係があるのであれば，あるいは州法が海事法，または公序に抵触しないのであれば，この種の条項は，有効である。*Stoot* v. *Fluor Drilling Services*, 851 F. 2d 1514, 1989 AMC 20, 24 (5th Cir. 1988); *Hale* v. *Co-Mar Offshore Corp.*, 1986 AMC 1620, 1624-1625 (W. D. La. 1984)。一般的には *Angelina Cas.* v. *Exxon Corp.*, 876 F. 2d 40, 1989 AMC 2677 (5th Cir. 1989) 事件を参照。この事件では，傭船契約は Louisiana 法と連邦海事法の両方を摂取しており，裁判所は連邦法が管轄すると判示した。外国法の適用を定める法の選択条項も，法の選択が誠実であり，選択された法が契約に何らかの関係をもっている限りにおいて，有効である。*Siegleman* v. *Cunard White Star*, 221 F. 2d 189, 195 (2d Cir. 1955)。

　米国の大多数の傭船契約紛争は，New York で仲裁により解決されている。しかし，契約の締結が争点であれば，その問題は通常最初に連邦裁判所において審理されなければならない。例として，*Pollux Marine Agencies Inc.* v. *Louis Dreyfus Corp.*, 455 F. Supp. 211 (S. D. N. Y. 1978)，原審維持 595 F. 2d 1209 (2d Cir. 1979) 事件を参照。例えば，海事法で開廷する

57 New York の連邦裁判所は，一旦 New York における仲裁を定める海事契約が存在すると申

し立てられる場合には，管轄権を持つと考えられる。契約の存在と仲裁条項の存在が認められれば，傭船契約違反と損害賠償の問題は通常仲裁人に付託される。

仲裁人が，拘束力のある契約が存在するか否かを決定することを合意することは当事者に委ねられる。いくぶん異常な事件で，裁判所は傭船契約が成立したか否かを仲裁人が決定すると判示した。*Northern Tankers (Cyprus) Ltd.* v. *Lexmar Corp.*, 781 F. Supp. 289, 1992 AMC 1021 (S.D.N.Y. 1992). この事件では，船主は傭船者の傭船契約の拒否から生じた損害賠償請求の仲裁を請求した。傭船者は仲裁に付する請求を受諾したが，抗弁として傭船契約は合意されていないとの主張をした。こういう状況で，裁判所は，仲裁協定が存するとし，仲裁が傭船者の抗弁により生じた問題を裁定すべしと判断した。本件のより完全な解説については後出518頁参照。

解釈の規則

傭船契約書は普通の契約法により規制される。「……［A］傭船契約書は，他の拘束力ある協定と同様の解釈の規則に支配される一種の契約である」。*Cargill Int'l S. A.* v. *The Pavel Dybenko*, 991 F. 2d 1012, 1019, 1994 AMC 2258 (2d Cir. 1993).

一般海事法で適用される普通の契約原則の下で，傭船契約の語法は，使用用語の明白な意味に十分な効力を与えると解釈される。傭船契約は全体として読まなければならない。傭船契約の曖昧な条項には明白な意味が与えられるべきであり，裁判所は当事者がその意思を決定するために選択した用語を越えることを考えない。一般に *Wilson* v. *Job Inc.*, 958 F. 2d 653, 657 (5th Cir. 1992) 事件を参照。当事者の使用する言葉が複数の解釈になりやすい場合には，曖昧であるとみなされ，裁判所はその意味に関して事実関係を究明するために外部の証拠にたよる。例として *Kroft Entertainment Inc.* v. *CBS Songs*, 653 F. Supp. 1530, 1533 (S.D.N.Y. 1987)；*Chi Sun Hua Steel Co. Ltd.* v. *Crest Tankers*, 1990 AMC 2816, 2817-2818 (N.D. Cal. 1990). 裁判所は次のような要因を検討する。特定の解釈が余分なことを新たに生み出すか，または引き起こさないようにするか，当該傭船契約に限定的な定義の存在，紛争となる条項の言葉の幅，契約全体を取り巻く条項。*Capozziello* v. *Lloyd Brasileiro*, 443 F. 2d 1155, 1159, 1971 AMC 1477 (2d Cir. 1971). 傭船契約に含まれている言葉が曖昧である場合に，紛争となる条項はその傭船契約を起草した当事者に不利であるとの観点から解釈され，他方の当事者がそうであろうと確信した意味を与えられる。前出 *Navieros Oceanikos S. A.* v. *The Mobil Trader*. この解釈の規則は *Restatement (Second) of Contracts*. §§ 201-208 で詳細に解説されている。

契約の成立

傭船契約は，当事者がその基本的条項について合意したときに成立する。*Christman* v. *Maristella Compania Naviera*, 349 F. Supp. 845 (S.D.N.Y. 1971), 下記の理由で原審判断維持 468 F. 2d 620 (2d Cir. 1972)；*Interocean Shipping Co.* v. *National Shipping and Trading Corp.*, 523 F. 2d 527, 534 (2d Cir. 1975), 裁量上告拒絶 423 U. S. 1054 (1976)；前出 *Pollux Marine Agencies Inc.* v. *Louis Dreyfus Corp.*；*The Cielo Rosso*, 1980 AMC 2088 (Arb. at N. Y. 1980). 拘束力ある傭船契約とするためには，書類に両当事者が署名することは必要ではない。口頭の傭船契約も有効であり，拘束力がある。*Kossick* v. *United Fruit Co.*, 365 U.S. 731 (1961)；前出 *Interocean Shipping Co.* v. *National Shipping and Trading Corp.* 同時に，口頭による海事契約は，書面にある条項に言及して，これを契約中に取り入れてもよい。*Sun Oil*

58 *Co.* v. *Dalzell Towing Co.* Inc., 55 F. 2d 63 (2d Cir. 1932), 原審維持 287 U.S. 291 (1932); *The Independence,* SMA 3049 (Arb. at N.Y. 1994). 当事者は, 署名された書面の協定がなくとも契約の条件を反映する一連の交渉を行動によって確認できる。*Arbitration between Horizon Development Corp. Ltd. and Mantua Oil Co.,* SMA 2734 (Arb. at N.Y. 1990) 事件を参照。成約の要点 (a fixture recap) は船主と傭船者の間の契約条件の証拠ともなる。例として *The Oceanis,* SMA 2772 (Arb. at N.Y. 1991) 事件参照。*Central Marine Service Inc.* v. *Ocean Marine Contractors Inc.,* 1984 AMC 1730 (5th Cir. 1982) (全員一致) 事件において裁判所は, 海事法証言規則は書面による協定が後刻口頭で変更されたという証明を禁止していないと述べた。

もちろん, 当事者は, 傭船契約が特別の条件 (conditions) を条件とすることに同意するかも知れない。その条件 (conditions) が同意されるなら, 傭船契約が成立する前に条件 (conditions) は満たされるか, 放棄されねばならない。当事者は条件 (conditions) の遂行につき誠実に行動する義務がある。*The Zakynthos,* SMA 2097 (Arb. at N.Y. 1985) 事件で成約のテレックスは傭船者に有利な次の条件を含んでいた。「今航 Curaçao での検船後の好評価報告を条件として」。検船後傭船者は本船を拒否し, 傭船契約は破棄されたものと考えられた。しかし, 仲裁審は, 合理的な基準は条項に黙示されており, したがってそれは「合理的原因なくして本船を拒否する白紙委任状を付与するものではない」と裁定した。傭船者が本船を拒否するのは気まぐれな行動であると仲裁審は判断し, したがって本件は傭船契約違反であり, 船主は損害の回収を認められると裁定した。

「細目を条件として sub details」に関し, 米国で遵守される規則については後で検討する。

基本的条項

ある条項が本来「基本的」なものであるかどうかは, 当事者の意思による事実問題である。*Uninav* v. *Molena Trust,* 1973 AMC 1386 (S.D.N.Y. 1973), 原審維持 490 F. 2d 1406 (2d Cir. 1974) 事件では, 船員の時間外労働手当を巡って傭船契約当事者が一度も合意していない場合には, 拘束力ある契約は存在しないと判示された。船員の時間外労働手当は, その傭船契約の基本的要素と考えられたのである。前出 *Interocean Shipping Co.* v. *National Shipping and Trading Corp.* 事件では, 引渡区域, 保険条項および乾ドック条項についての合意が傭船契約には不可欠であると考えられた。同様に, *Orient Mid-East Great Lakes Service* v. *Int'l Export Lines Ltd.,* 315 F. 2d 519, 1964 AMC 1810 (4th Cir. 1963) 事件では, 船主が保持を許される船用品および燃料の数量について当事者が合意に達していなかった以上, 傭船契約は存在しない, と裁判所は判示した。*Himoff Indus* v. *Seven Seas Shipping Corp.,* 1976 AMC 1030 (N.Y. Sup., 1976) 事件で, 裁判所は, 解約期日および返船通知期間ならびに成約の他の重要な条項について意思の合致がない場合には, 傭船契約は存在しないと判示した。*Bulk Charters (Pty) Limited* v. *Korea Shipping Corporation,* 1981 AMC 2877 (S.D.N.Y. 1981) 事件で, 船艙の清掃の代わりに一括支払を定める条項の提案に不同意のために「主要条件 main term」についての両者の合意はなく, したがって傭船契約は成立していないと判示された。仲裁人が多くの傭船契約で「主要条件 main terms」と考える多くの条項に関する合意の欠如は, 問題の傭船契約の成立には不可欠なものではないと裁定した *The Independence,* SMA 3049 (Arb. at N.Y. 1994) 事件参照。

原則として当事者は, 他の場合なら重要ではないような特定の傭船契約条項についての合意が, やがて成立する「成約」の前提条件であると約定することもできる。例えば, *The Toxon,*

SMA 913 (Arb. at N.Y. 1974) 事件では, 船主も, その仲立人も見たことがない新しいモービル定期傭船契約書式に基づく傭船契約を, 傭船者が提案した。船主は成約前に新書式を閲読する権利を留保することを明示し, 書式を閲読した上で, 数多くの変更を求めた。傭船者はこの要求に応じなかった。結局, 傭船契約は存在しないと判断された。The Harpagus, SMA 323 (Arb. at. N.Y. 1968) 事件参照。同事件において, 傭船者側の申込を承諾する船主のテレックスの内容が「双方で合意すべき細目を除き承諾, 引渡区域は10月5日までに明示すべき[59]ものとする」というものであった場合について, 成約は存在しないと判断された。仲裁審によれば, これは事実上新たな申込ということである。すなわち,「申込内容の変更は, それがいかなる文言を使用して為されても, 新たな申込となる」というのである。

「細目を条件として　sub details」

「主要条件　main terms」

「細目を条件として sub details」成約するという, 既に普及している慣行があるが, それは, 拘束力ある契約が成立する以前に, いちいち全部の傭船契約条項について合意する必要があることを意味するものとは, 通常解されていない。1度基本的条項について同意があった場合に, 契約は存在していると思われるし, 残っている細目の交渉は補助的な仕事である。前出 *Interocean Shipping Co.* v. *National Shipping and Trading Corp.*, 523 F. 2d 527, 535 (2d Cir. 1975), 裁量上告拒絶 423 U.S. 1054 (1976) 事件で, 裁判所が述べているように,「……『細目を条件として sub details』というのは, 空白欄を充たすことを意味するのであって, 全交渉過程を再検討することを意味しない」。*Atlantic & Great Lakes S. S. Corp.* v. *Steelmet. Inc.*, 74 Civ. 5048 (S. D. N. Y., Feb. 22, 1977), 原審維持 565 F. 2d 848, 1978 AMC 107 (2d Cir. 1977) 事件で, 同じような結果が得られたが, 裁判所は,「Genjascrap sub details」という文言は, 意思の合致および契約書作成のための停止条件を構成するものではないと判示した。

この原則は, 前出 *Pollux Marine Agencies Inc.* v. *Louis Dreyfus Corp.* 事件で説明されている。そこでは仲立人が撒積船の3年間の傭船契約の交渉を始めた。明確に交渉された初期の問題点の一つが「国際運輸労連 ITF 条項」であった。当事者はその条項に同意できないので, その1点で交渉は決裂した。しかし, 数日後妥協点が示唆され, 標準的 ITF 条項の代わりの条項が受諾できることが判った。それから他の条項についてのやりとりが精力的に再開され, 金曜日の遅くにすべての基本的条項が合意された。そこで仲立人は慣例の成約テレックスを打った。そこには全合意条件を述べて,「細目を条件として sub details」といういつもの限定条件を付した。翌月曜日に当事者は細目の作成を合意に基づき傭船者の仮の定期傭船契約書式を使って作業を開始した。この交渉が進展するうちに, 傭船者は前に合意された代替 ITF 条項を修正しようとした。船主は異を唱えた。しかし, 成約があったとの立場を「損なうことなく without prejudice」, 船主は文言の再検討に同意しようとした。一方, 交渉は「細目 details」について継続された。月曜日の営業終了までにすべての細目につき合意された。残るは代替 ITF 条項のみであった。妥協に到達しようと苦心したが, 交渉は終了し傭船者は成約は合意されていないと主張した。

しかし, 結局船主は傭船者の拒否に対して損害賠償の請求を行い仲裁を求めた。傭船者は, 傭船契約が, 合意されていたことを否定したので, 傭船者は仲裁を拒否し, そうして問題は New York の裁判所に付託された。公判の後で, 裁判所は, 当事者は金曜日にすべての基本的条件につき事実上, 合意に達した, そして「細目を条件として sub details」という条件は

拘束力ある成約の停止条件ではない，月曜日に代替ITF条項についての再交渉を行うことに傭船者が固執するのは拒絶することであると判断した。その決定は第2巡回区控訴裁判所で支持された。

Great Circle Lines Ltd. v. *Matheson & Co. Ltd.,* 1982 AMC 567 (S.D.N.Y. 1981)，原審維持 681 F. 2d 121, 1982 AMC 2321 (2d Cir. 1982) 事件で同じような結果となった。再び，主要条件の交渉は金曜日に決着して，「成約の要点 fixture recap」が「細目を条件として subject details」仲立人により送られた。続いて両当事者は先に合意された「主要条件 main terms」のいくつかを含む各種の条項の変更を提案した。しかし被告船主は原告傭船者が Londonの仲裁に合意したと執拗に主張した。合意された傭船契約ニューヨーク・プロデュース書式により，仲裁地は New York であった。裁判所は仲裁地は特別にやりとりしなかった細目であると判断した。裁判所は，次に，拘束力ある契約は既に存在しているので船主は条件の変更を当然には要求できないと判示した。傭船者は修正を提案したが，修正は示唆に過ぎなかった。契約は既に締結されていたし，どちらの当事者も変更を一方的に強要することはできなかった。*Cobec Brazilian Trading and Warehousing* v. *H. & J. Isbrandtsen,* 79 Civ. 3833 (S.D.N.Y. 1979) 事件も参照。

前出 *Great Circle Lines* 事件で，第2巡回区裁判所は主要条件には「傭船者の名前と船主の名前，本船とその特質，引渡の時と場所，傭船期間，返船の場所，傭船料，傭船契約の印刷書式，一方の当事者が重要と考える他のどんな条件をも含む」と述べた (1982 AMC at 2326)。さらに裁判所は重要でない条件には，「使用燃料，本船速力，傭船者への本船の引渡の正確な時間，口銭，故障，傭船契約延長の選択権，貨物積載容量，滞船料，両当事者が重要でないと考える他の事」を含むことに着目した (1982 AMC at 2327)。しかし，第2巡回区裁判所が「重要でない minor」と分類した多くの項目がしばしば大抵の定期傭船契約では非常に重大な「主要 main」条件であることは明らかである。それらの項目を裁判所が「重要でない minor」とした事実にもかかわらず，一方あるいは双方の当事者がその条件は重要であると表示すれば，その項目が主要条件とみなされることはあり得る。

J. Lauritzen A/S v. *Korea Shipping Corporation,* 1986 AMC 2450 (S.D.N.Y 1986) 事件で，米国から日本向け4回の穀物船積の運送契約の成約につき紛争が生じた。「成約・細目条件 fixture sub-details」とはり札されたテレックスによる要点が，船主から傭船者に送られたが，その後成約テレックスに参照された仮傭船契約書式に含まれる運賃支払条項に関し不同意が生じた。裁判所は，運賃支払条項は主要条件か重要でない細目かという問題は，公判で解決されるべき実質的事実についての真の問題を提示したと判示した。

傭船契約書署名前の成約

通常，船舶を傭船する旨の口頭の合意は，後日，成約書またはテレックスによって確認される。そして合意された細目は，最終的にタイプで打たれるか，または印刷された傭船契約書に記載され，両当事者がこれに署名する。そこでの最終の傭船契約書は，契約の証拠となり，それ以前のすべての口頭または文書による細目についての合意は，その傭船契約書の中に書き込まれているものとみなされる。前出 *Interocean Shipping Co.* v. *National Shipping and Trading Corp.* この原則は，成約テレックスと最終の傭船契約書との間に相違がある場合には，特に重要である。例えば *Interocean* 事件では，成約テレックスと最終文書との間に，航路定限，速力，性能，違約金および支払方法といった細目に関して，多数の相違があった。裁判所は，この不一致は契約を無効にしないと判示して，次のように述べた。すなわち，テレックスの文言

は,「どちらの当事者に有利であるかどうかを問わず,その後の契約書の中に書き込まれたものとみなされるべきである。脱漏したり,変更した規定の適用を必要とした当事者は,最終の書面にその規定を挿入することを要求できたはずである」(523 F. 2d at 535)。

　The Oceanis, SMA 2772 (Arb. at N.Y. 1991) 事件で,成約の要点 (a fixture recap) は船主が正式の傭船契約書に署名することを拒否した場合に,傭船契約条項の証拠となると考えられた。前出 *The Independence* 事件で,船主が署名した書面の契約書は傭船者の署名拒否にかかわらず合意された条件を確認するものと考えられた。

　しかし *Compania Naviera Aisgiannis S. A.* v. *Holt,* 1984 AMC 2228 (E.D.Pa. 1983) 事件で,最終の書面による傭船契約書は傭船者として存在しない会社を指定した。そこで裁判所は,代わりに成約テレックスで使用された名前を挿入した。

契約の当事者

"2. Between..
3. Owners of the good............................ |Steamship/Motorship| ....
12. .... and .... Charterers of the City of
...."

「船主......................が，その所有にかかわる良好な..............国 |汽船／機船| ....
の..............号を..............市の傭船者..............との間に」

一 般 原 則

定期傭船契約書の前文に，船主および傭船者として記載された者は，傭船契約上の請求権を有するか，あるいは逆に請求を受ける当事者であるのが普通であるが，必ずしもそうであるとは限らない。仲立人が介在している場合，誰が訴え，または訴えられるのかを確定するためには，代理に関する法の一般原則を適用しなければならないことが多い。Pickford 判事が *Harper* v. *Vigers* [1909] 2 K.B. 549 事件で指摘したとおり，「仲立人に限らず誰でも傭船契約締結のための代理人となれるのと同じで，仲立人は傭船契約締結のための代理人に過ぎない」（仲立人の手数料を請求する傭船者の権利については，*Les Afréteurs Réunis* v. *Walford* [1919] A.C. 801 事件と後出623頁参照）。代理の効果は，これを4項目に分けて検討する。

権限のある代理人が本人のために契約を締結する場合であって，かつ，本人の契約との関係を契約の相手方が知っている場合（顕名された本人の代理人 disclosed principal）

基 本 原 則

正当な権限を有する代理人が，本人の名前を示し，本人のために契約を締結する場合，代理人が，本人の代理人としてのみ行為していることを示して署名すれば，代理人ではなくて，本人がその契約の当事者となる。これを「代理人が抜ける the agent drops out」という。このような事情の下で，仲立人が提起した訴訟が効を奏さずに終った事件につき *Fairlie* v. *Fenton* (1870) L.R. 5 Ex. 169 事件参照。

代理人の権限

仲立人のような代理人は，本人の代わりに傭船契約を締結することを明示的に授権される。あるいは，四囲の状況の中で，本人の発言と行為により，代理人は，然るべく授権されていると代理人自身に納得させ，黙示の権限を与えられる。明示であれ，黙示であれ，「何かを行うことを授権された代理人は，主たる行為に付随することを行う権限を（通常）暗黙裡に有している」。したがって，傭船契約を締結する権限を有する代理人は，傭船契約に署名する権限を通常黙示的に有する。

62 責めを負うべきかつ権限のある代理人

しかし，代理人が自ら契約上の責めに任じたり，契約上の権利を主張することがあるが，それは，このような意思が，契約によりまたは契約書の署名方法によって示されている場合である。代理人が自己の署名に，それ相応の資格制限を付けずに署名すれば，このような意思を示すに十分と思われる。現に，Scrutton 卿判事は，*Brandt* v. *Morris*［1917］2 K.B. 784 事件（同判例集797頁）において，このことを「強力な一応の推定（*prima facie*）」と呼んだほどである。その代理人が，代理人として行為していることを，相手方が知っている場合でも，同じことになると判示されてきた。*Basma* v. *Weekes*［1950］A.C. 441. 口頭契約に関しては，そのような厳格な原則はない。*Vlassopulos* v. *Ney Shipping*［1977］1 Lloyd's Rep. 478 事件で，控訴院は次のように判示した。すなわち，ボルチック取引所の仲立人は，他人のために代理人として行為することが一般に知られているので，このような仲立人が，他のボルチックの仲立人と電話により締結した補油契約については，自己が代理人に過ぎない旨をその際には明示的に述べていなかったとしても，代理人自身責任を負うものではないというのがそれである。

代理人が責任と権限を持つ場合，古い判例は，それは，本人の代わりであるということを当然のことと考えた。しかし，代理人は，本人と**同様**に，契約の当事者でありうるということでもある。特に，本人の氏名が表示されていない場合，この代理人が当事者であることは，徐々に認められるところとなっている。後出参照。しかし，隠れた本人の場合と同じように，ここでも本人または代理人のどちらか一方に対する判決を得ることにより，あるいはたぶん一方を提訴する「選定」をしただけでもう一方の責任は消滅するという（確立していないが）判例がある。*Debenham's* v. *Perkins*（1925）133 L.T. 252（同判例集254頁）事件参照。法律のこの危険な領域についての価値ある最近の議論については，ニュージーランドの判例 *L.C. Fowler & Sons* v. *St. Stephen's College Board of Governors*［1991］3 N.Z.L.R. 304 事件を参照。

名前の表示された本人の代理人であると自らを表示して，交渉に臨んだが，最終的に，代理権に触れずに，かつ正式傭船契約書に署名することもせずに契約を結んだ場合に，代理人が個人的に契約上責任を負うか否かという問題は，傭船契約にまで至った交渉の中でなされた陳述および四囲の状況を検討することにより認定されるであろう。

> 船主の本船 *Rab* 号の部分傭船のための交渉は，仲立人を通して「インドネシア政府のために on account of」B.&S. と記載された傭船者候補と行われた。結果として，*Rab* 号の商売は成立しなかった。船主は新たに条件を交渉するという条件で，他の所有船 *Primorje* 号を同じ貨物に提案した。成約が実現し，傭船者として B.&S. と明記して傭船契約書が作成された。新規交渉において，あるいは傭船契約書中にも，本人に代わって代理人として行為する B.&S. についてまったくふれていなかった。その傭船契約書に船主は署名したが，B.&S. は署名していなかった。B.&S. が単に仲介者として行為したと主張したのは，傭船契約が履行され，クレームが提起された後のことであった。「インドネシア政府のために」傭船すると原契約交渉で言及したにもかかわらず B.&S. は本人として契約したと判示された。
>
> *The Primorje*［1980］2 Lloyd's Rep. 74.

「代理人として」署名

しかし，「本人に代って for and on behalf of」または「本人のために on account of」あるいは「代理人として as agent」契約に署名することは，契約上本人に帰属する権利義務を自らが有することを避けようとする代理人の明白な意思を示すものである。したがって，契約書中に，それと反対の特に明白な文言がない限り，代理人自身の責任の推定は排除されていることになる。

Ariadne Irene 号の船主代理人，T. H. S. & Co. と「傭船者 J. Mck. & Co.」とが傭船契約を締結した。傭船契約は「(代理人としての) J. Mck. & Co. に代わって J. A. Mck —— For and on behalf of J. Mck. & Co. (as Agents), J. A. Mck.」と署名された。船主は，傭船契約書が署名されたとき，J. Mck. & Co. が他人のために行為していることを知っていた。

　船主は，傭船契約に基づき，J. Mck. & Co. を相手取って，訴えを提起したが，J. Mck. & Co. は，自分は本人ではないと抗弁した。貴族院は，「代理人として (as agents)」と署名することによって，J. Mck. & Co. は，傭船契約に基づく自己の責任を免れていると判示した。Shaw 卿は，次のように述べた。「……商事契約の当事者の署名に『代理人』という言葉を付記することは，本人か代理人かという問題の解決上，常に決め手となる。まったく起こりそうもない憶測上の事例（そこでなら，この決め手が，契約の他の部分により潰されることがあるかもしれないが）を想像力に訴えて描くことはできよう。しかし，それを除けば，署名に，『代理人』という用語を付記することは，代理関係存在の決定的な主張であり……本人の責任を代理人に負わせることは決してないということである」。

63

　Universal Steam Navigation v. *McKelvie* [1923] A. C. 492.

　本件では，傭船契約書本文中には，代理人が「傭船者 Charterers」として記載されているにもかかわらず，署名の後に「代理人として as Agents」の文言があったので，代理人自身の一切の責任を排除する効果が認められた。

署名に続く他の文言

　署名の後に他の文言を追加しても，それは，代理人が契約の当事者となるとか，契約に基づいて訴えられることとかを防止するのに，それほどの効果はない。次に挙げる事案は，そのことを物語っている。それとともに，裁判所が，当事者の意思を発見するために契約書に使用された特定の文言だけを考察するのではなく，これを取り巻く状況をも斟酌することを示している。

　モーターボート Swan 号の所有者が，自ら取締役である会社へ，そのボートを賃貸した。船主は，ボートの修理を注文したが，その注文は，賃貸先会社の用箋に記載されていて，所有者がその氏名の後に「取締役」という文言を付して署名したものであった。修理業者は，署名した者が，そのボートの所有者であることを知っていた。Brandon 判事は，次のように判示した。所有者は結果的に会社の代理人として契約を締結したことになった。しかし，所有者はまた，この契約（一部口頭で一部は書面による）に基づき所有者自身訴求を受ける。なぜなら，所有者は，ボートの所有者として修理代金を支払うだろう，という修理業者のもっともな推定を否定しなかったからである。

　Brandon 判事は，「Aが本人Cの存在を明らかにして，そのCのためにBと契約を締結する場合，A，C両者が契約上の責任を負うのか，Cのみが責任を負うのかは，当事者の意思如何によって決まる。この意思は，1）契約の性質，2）契約の条項，3）周囲の状況……から認定される……」と述べた。

　The Swan [1968] 1 Lloyd's Rep. 5.

契約書本文に示された代理関係

　代理人は，自己の署名を適当に限定する方法により契約に基づく自らの責任を排除することができるだけでなく，代わりに自己の法律上の地位が単に代理人のそれに止まるものであることを，契約書本文で明らかにすることができる。Archibald 判事は，*Gadd* v. *Houghton* (1876) 1 Ex. D. 357 事件（同判例集361頁）で次のように指摘した。「代理人が自ら責任を負わない形で契約する通常の方法は，代理人として署名することである。しかし，それが唯一の方法ではない。代理人が，ただ代理人として契約したということが，契約書本文から明らかであれば，

通常，代理人は自己の責を免れうる」。

本人のみ，代理人のみあるいは，本人および代理人の双方が責任あるのかという問題は，したがって，契約を巡る状況をも斟酌して，全体として契約を解釈する問題である。前出 Brandt v. Morris［1917］2 K. B. 784 事件および The Swan［1968］1 Lloyd's Rep. 5 事件参照。この二つの判例は，このことを説明しているし，裁判所はそのような問題を判断するにあたって，契約の一部分を不当に重視することを避けることを示している。

Virgo 号の傭船契約で，その7行目に，傭船者は，「Tradax Export S. A.」であると記載されており，傭船契約は，「Tradax Export S. A. の代理人としての Greenwich Marine Incorporated」が署名していた。ところが，傭船契約書の「追加条項」第31条は，「本船は，在カイロ General Organization for Supply Goods に代わりかつそのために傭船されたものである」と規定していた。Tradax Export S. A. 社は，第31条の文言に依拠して，同社自身は，代理人に過ぎず，傭船者ではないことを立証しようと努めた。

控訴院は，傭船契約の全趣旨から見ると，Tradax Export S. A. が本人であって，傭船者としての義務を有すると解され，31条の文言は，同社の立場を変更しようという反対の意思を明白に示したものではないと判示した。

Megaw 卿判事は，以下のように述べた。すなわち，「傭船契約でも他の契約でも，契約上その氏名を示された者が，その契約の当事者本人であるのか，一代理人に過ぎないのか，また，代理人であるとして，この者もまた，その契約に基づき法律上の義務を負うのかどうか，の問題が生じた場合には，法は契約書面に記載されている限り，およそ関連のあるすべての規定を調査し，斟酌すべきことを要求している。例えば署名というような契約の一部分だけを見てはならない。契約条項や契約書の，どの部分にしろ，関連する事項すべてを考慮する必要がある」。

Tudor Marine v. Tradax Export (The Virgo)［1976］2 Lloyd's Rep. 135.
(The Sun Happiness［1984］1 Lloyd's Rep. 381 事件も参照)

Scaplake 号は「傭船者として」C. D. M. に傭船された。傭船契約の第29条は次のように規定していた。「運賃と滞船料は実際の傭船者 D. & K. により……あるいはその役員個人により保証される。」傭船契約書は，C. D. M. と D. & K. により2ヶ所に署名された。傭船契約書の補遺の一つには，C. D. M. と D. & K. の両者が，他の一つには，C. D. M. のみが署名した。

D. & K. は C. D. M. の本人として傭船契約上責任があると船主は主張した。Mocatta 判事は，次のように判示した。「D. & K. は傭船契約書とその重要な補遺に署名をし，実際の傭船者と記載されているので，ただ単に運賃および滞船料の支払保証人であるとみなされることはない」。この特色と四囲の商売環境は，C. D. M. と D. & K. は，傭船契約の当事者であり，責任があることを示している。

The Scaplake［1978］2 Lloyd's Rep. 380.

(前出 The Primorje［1980］2 Lloyd's Rep. 74 事件，および (運航船主として as operating Owners) The Yanxilas［1982］2 Lloyd's Rep. 445 事件，(管理運航者として as managing operators，本人の代わりに on behalf of our principals) カナダの判例 Chartwell Shipping v. Q. N. S. Paper (1989) 62 D. L. R. (4th) 36事件参照)

本人の氏名が表示されない場合

正当に授権された代理人が，その名前が表示されていない本人のために契約を公然と締結する場合，その本人の立場は，原則として前述したところと同じである。しかし，このような場合，裁判所としては，本人が名指しされている場合に比べて，その代理人が契約に基づく責任を本人と共に負うと判断しやすいと思われる。Teheran-Europe v. Belton (Tractors)［1968］2 Lloyd's Rep. 37 事件 (後出117頁) の Diplock 卿判事の判旨参照。

外国人が本人

外国人である本人に代わり英国人が代理人として契約した場合，代理人は契約上個人的に責任を負うとの推定がかつてはあった。今日ではそういう推定はありえない。*Teheran-Europe* v. *Belton*（*Tractors*）[1968] 2 Lloyd's Rep. 37 事件参照。しかし，ある特別な状況の下では代理人が本人と共に個人的に責任ありという正しい推定がありうる。*Fraser* v. *Equitorial Shipping*（*The Ijaola*）[1979] 1 Lloyd's Rep. 103（同判例集111頁）事件参照。

代理人の権利

一般に，契約の相手方に対して責任を負うような代理人には，逆に，その相手方を訴える権利がある。「一方の側の責任の存在は，他方の側の相互に関係のある権利の存在を伴う」。*Repetto* v. *Millar's Karri & Jarrah Forests* [1901] 2 K.B. 306, 310. しかし，これは，必ずしもそうであるとは限らない。考えてみるに，契約を適切に解釈した場合には，代理人が責任を引き受けてもこれに見合った権利がないとか，あるいは稀な状況では，見合った責任なく権利のみがあるという場合がありうるからである。

保　証　人

代理人は傭船契約上の当事者の義務を保証することがある。これは別個の契約である。そういう場合の例としては，*The Maria D* [1992] 1 A.C. 21 事件参照。

65 自己を代理人と表示しているにもかかわらず，実は本人である場合

そのような者は，少なくとも権限の担保の違反のため，原則としてその契約に基づく責任を負う（後出参照）。その者が契約上権利を持つかどうかは，想定された本人が表示されているかどうかによる。

本人の氏名が表示されている場合

契約を締結する者が，本人となる意思がありながら，契約書には，他人の氏名を挙げてこれを本人として，自己をその代理人と表示した場合，相手方が本人として氏名を表示された者の地位や名声を信頼して，契約を締結したという事情があれば，自己を代理人と表示した者は，その契約に基づいて本人として訴えることはできない。実際のところ，本人の氏名が表示されている場合に，自己を代理人として表示した者が訴えを提起できるかさえ疑わしい。ただし，相手方が，事の真相に気付いているにもかかわらず，その契約を認めている場合は別である。*Rayner* v. *Grote*（1846）15 M. & W. 359 事件参照。

Librekcem の子会社である Afrab は，指定本船あるいは，代船を基に，瀝青の船積のため Gewa と傭船契約を結んだ。指定の本船は，必要な時期に利用できず，したがって Gewa は，Afrab に約束したことを履行するため Remco 号の傭船を交渉した。実は，Gewa は，自分のために傭船したのであったが，Gewa は船主側仲立人に対して，Gewa は Afrab あるいは Librekcem の他の子会社の代理人として傭船すると言明したことが事実として確認された。Gewa は，次の理由で Remco 号の船主に傭船契約を強制できないと判示された。

(a) Remco 号の船主は，本人であると彼らが信じた当事者の身元が，重要であることを示した。つまり，船主は，Librekcem グループは喜んで傭船契約を結べる大きなグループであることを知っていた。一方で，船主は，Gewa が傭船者であることを知っていたなら，ある種の運賃保証を要求した

(b) *Remco* 号の船主は，事の真相を承知していたならば，契約に至らなかったであろう。
   The Remco [1984] 2 Lloyd's Rep. 205.

本人の氏名が表示されない場合

一方，本人になるはずの者が，その氏名を表示されていなければ，相手方が，このような本人の身元を重要視するはずはないから，代理人として契約を締結した者が，本人として契約に基づいて訴える権利を有すると判示されてきた。しかし，これらの判決は批判されてきており（*Hill Steam Shipping* v. *Stinnes*, 1941 S. C. 324 事件および *Bowstead on Agency*（第15版），478～479頁参照），注意して扱われるべきである。

> G. Schmaltz & Co. は「傭船者の代理人 agents of the freighter」として船舶を傭船し，次のように約定した。すなわち，「本傭船契約は他の当事者に代わって締結されたものであって，G. Schmaltz & Co. のすべての責任は，貨物が船積されたときに直ちに消滅することを約諾する」というのがそれである。G. Schmaltz & Co. の船主に対する訴訟において，G. Schmaltz & Co. は，自己が本来の権利を有する傭船者であるという立証を認められ，したがって，この契約に基づいて，本人として提訴する権利があると判断された。Patterson 判事は，*Rayner* v. *Grote*（1846）15 M. & W. 359（同判例集365頁）事件にある Alderson 判事が言い渡した判決の一部を肯定的に引用しているが，その一節は，次のとおりである。「例えば，本人として氏名を表示された者の技能や支払能力が契約の重要な構成要素であると考えるのが適切である事例が多いが，そのような場合，代理人が自己を真正の本人であると主張し，自己の名において訴えを提起できないことは明白である。まったく履行されていないか，真実の本人不明のまま一部履行されたような履行未済の契約の場合は，このことが一般原則である，という議論は正しいと思われる」。Patterson 判事は，さらに続けて次のように述べている。「この一節にはまったく同感である。とは言っても，これは，本人と考えられる者の氏名が契約上表示されている場合に限って適用されうるものであることは，明らかである。本人の氏名が表示されていなければ，どう考えてみても，契約の相手方が，かかる本人と契約を締結する気になるはずがない」。
> *Schmaltz* v. *Avery*（1851）16 Q. B. 655.

66 Harper & Co. は，後日船名を指定することになっていた船舶の「船主代理人として as agents for owners」傭船契約を締結し，傭船契約書に「船主の授権により，かつ，その代理人として By authority of and as agents for owners」署名した。実際には Harper & Co. は本人に代わって行為したのではなく，まさに自己の計算において投機的に傭船契約を締結したのであった。傭船者は，もし，そのときにこの事実を知っていたならば傭船契約を締結しなかったであろうという証拠を提出した。それにもかかわらず，Pickford 判事は，*Schmaltz* v. *Avery* 事件に従って，Harper & Co. 以外に本人という者はいないのであるから，Harper & Co. は傭船契約に基づいて傭船者を訴えることができると判示した。
Harper v. *Vigers* [1909] 2 K. B. 549.

権限のある代理人が自己の名において本人のために契約を締結したが，相手方が本人の存在を知らないか，あるいは本人と契約との関係を知らない場合（隠された本人 undisclosed principal）

この本人は，「隠された undisclosed」本人と言われている。この場合の一般原則は，本人か代理人（少なくとも，本人が名乗り出るまでは）のどちらかが，契約に基づいて提訴できるということである。同様に，本人か代理人のどちらかが契約に基づいて提訴される。もっとも，相手方が，その一方に対する判決を得ることにより，あるいは相手方が，その一方のみを目当

てとして「選定した」と判断されればおそらく，その一方を提訴する権利を失うものと思われる。

Diplock 卿判事は，*Teheran-Europe* v. *Belton*（*Tractors*）[1968] 2 Lloyd's Rep. 37 事件（同判例集41頁）において次のように述べた。「契約上誰が請求する権利を有し，誰が請求を受ける義務を負うかを確定するにあたって一つの有益な出発点は，契約が書面による場合，その契約書をよく精読することである。その場合に，若干の基本的原則に留意する必要がある。第1に，人は，自分に代わって契約を締結する権限を実際に与えた代理人か，またはそのような権限を与えたと相手方に信じさせた代理人を通じて，契約を締結することができるということである。しかし，ここでは，実際に代理権限がある場合のみが問題となる。権限を有する代理人が本人に代わって契約を締結する際，その相手方が，代理人に授権した本人が誰であろうともその本人を契約当事者として扱う意思を実際持っているか，その意思があると代理人に信ぜしめた場合には，代理人が本人を明らかにすること，さらに，代理人が本人のために契約するのだということすら，まったく重要ではない。通常の商事契約の場合，代理人は，相手方が本人と契約する意思を持つと推測して差し支えない。ただし，相手方がそれと反対の意思を明白にしている場合，あるいは，相手方の反対の意思を代理人が推認するに足るだけの事情がある場合はこの限りでない」。

代理人が自らを「船主」と表示する場合

しかし，契約条件，あるいは四囲の状況によっては，隠された（undisclosed）本人の介入を排除する場合がある。後出 *Humble* v. *Hunter* 事件で，代理人が傭船契約書に，自らを「船主」と表示している場合には，そのような表示は，代理関係存在の可能性を否定し，したがってまた，隠された（undisclosed）本人が，自己を真実の船主であると立証する可能性をも否定する意味を持つから，その隠された（undisclosed）本人は訴えを提起しえないと判示された。しかしこの判例は，その有効性に疑問のあるものとみるべきであると言われている（例えば，*Epps* v. *Rothnie* [1945] K. B. 562 事件における Scott 卿判事の判決参照）。それは，書面による契約の条項に抵触したり，これを変更したりするような口頭の証拠を排除する原則の適用に基づくものであって，もし，広くこの原則による場合には，書面による契約は，隠された（undisclosed）本人の介入を大きく制限することになるであろう。

> 「*Ann* 号の船主である C. J. Humble」と，傭船者である Hunter との間で傭船契約が締結された。C. J. Humble は，実際には，真の所有者の息子であった。本件につき裁判所は，自らを船主として表示した者が，実は単なる代理人であったことを立証することは許されないと判示した。その理由として，裁判所は，そのような証拠は傭船契約上の明文の記載，すなわち，C. J. Humble は船主であるという記載に抵触するからであるとした。「船主」という表示が，言外に代理の意味を持つことはありえないと判断されたのである。
> *Humble* v. *Hunter* (1848) 12 Q. B. 310.

67 自己を「傭船者」または「管理船主 disponent」と表示した代理人

例えば上記判決が正当で「船主」という表示が代理の可能性を真っ向から排除しても，「傭船者」および「管理船主 disponents」という表示では，代理関係を排除したことにはならない。

> 定期傭船契約が「スクリュー汽船，*England* 号の船主，Messrs. Fred. Drughorn, Ltd.」と「傭船者，Gothenburg の Wilh. R. Lundgren」との間で締結された。傭船契約書には「Swedish South African Line，支配人 Wilh. R. Lundgren」と頭書され，「Wilh. R. Lundgren の電信の授権により，かつ

その代理人として」代理人による署名があった。Lundgren は，実際には，Red. Transatlantic の代理人として傭船をしていた。貴族院は，この契約書は一方の当事者を「傭船者」として記載し，他人の代理人として傭船しようとしている可能性を排除していないから，代理関係の存在を容認しうると判示した。

Drughorn v. *Red. A/B Transatlantic* 〔1919〕A. C. 203.

「良好な汽船 *Elle* 号の管理船主（disponent owners)」である N. V. Stoomschip「Hannah」により傭船契約が締結され，「管理船主（disponents)」からの電話による授権の下で，かつその代理人として」仲立人が，これに署名した。傭船契約書は多くの条項中に「船主」という記載があった。Morris 判事は，本傭船契約を全体として解釈すれば，「管理船主（disponent owners)」という文言は，船舶の所有者以外の何者かを表示していると判示した。つまり O/Y Wasa Steamship Co. が船舶の所有者であり，真実の本人でもあるという証拠は，傭船契約の条項と矛盾しないから，容認しうるというのである。

O/Y Wasa Steamship v. *Newspaper Pulp & Wood Export* (1949) 82 Ll.L. Rep. 936.

しかし，次の判例では，「管理船主（disponent owner)」と記載される人物が，船主の管理会社の被用者であったとしても，船主は，隠された本人として，傭船契約を実行できないと判示された。係争となった傭船契約に関して，船主と「管理船主（disponent owner)」の関係は，代理関係に矛盾するとの証拠が示された。

Astyanax 号の航海傭船契約の交渉は，船主の代理人として授権された仲立人と傭船者の間で行われた。しかし，運賃に課されるアルゼンチンの税金を避けるため，船主は，「管理船主（disponent owner）として」ピレウスの P. S. として傭船契約に記載されることに合意した。P. S. は，船主の管理会社の被用者で，ギリシャ人であり，アルゼンチンとの二重課税協定の特典を享受できた。仲立人との交信の中で，管理船主（disponent owner）P. S. と船主であるキプロスの会社の間の定期傭船契約が先行することが認められた。しかしながら，船主は，P. S. が，単なる被指名者であるとの理由で，隠された本人として航海傭船契約を実行しようとした。Leggatt 判事の判決を取り消し，控訴院は，次のように判示した。提起された先行する定期傭船契約は単なる見せかけと，意図されてはいないので，たとえ，P. S. が，最終的に個人的な損害関係にはない立場にあるといえども，傭船者であり，再傭船契約の管理船主（disponent owner）である P. S. の立場は，本人としての船主の代理人たる単なる代理行為と矛盾する。彼自身が本人である。

The Astyanax 〔1985〕2 Lloyd's Rep. 109.

（「本当の傭船者 actual charterers」について，〔1978〕2 Lloyd's Rep. 380 と前出114頁の *The Scaplake* 事件と，「運航船主として as operating Owners」について，*The Yanxilas* 〔1982〕2 Lloyd's Rep. 445 事件も参照）

現在では，契約条件が，隠された本人の介入を明示的にあるいは黙示的に排除しているかということが，問われている。*Siu Yin Kwan* v. *Eastern Insurance* 〔1994〕1 Lloyd's Rep. 616 事件と前出117頁の Diplock 卿判事の引用を参照。とはいえ，本人が介入していないことを確認するのは容易なことではない。

代理人として行為している者が，本人と称する者から授権されていなかった場合

ここまでは，本人の代わりに署名する代理人は，そのように署名することを授権されているとの前提であった。しかし，代理人が授権されていないことがある。そこで，本人が契約を追

認しているか，あるいは，代理人は外見上あるいは表面上の権限を持っているかどうかの問題が生じる。そのような権限がなければ，代理人は権限の担保の違反の責めを負うこととなる。

68 追　　認

権限のない代理人により本人として表示された者なら，その代理人のなした行為を後に追認することで，例えば，代理人が権限なしに締結した傭船契約を採用することで，代理権の欠陥を治癒することができる。このような追認権能は，前出の「隠された undisclosed」本人にはない。*Keighley, Maxsted* v. *Durant* [1901] A. C. 240 事件参照。この権能は不当に行使されないよう一定の制限の下にある。代理人が権限なしに締結した契約に，本人が追認すれば，同様に本人がその責めに任ずることになろう。だからといって本人の指示を越えたことにつき本人に対する代理人の責任を必ずしも免除することにはならない。*Suncorp Insurance and Finance* v. *Milano Assecurazioni* [1993] 2 Lloyd's Rep. 225 事件（同判例集234と235頁）参照。

表見あるいは外観代理

表見あるいは外観代理の法理に基づき本人は，また責任を負うことがありうるし，しばしば現に責任を負っている。実際に権限を有しないが，本人により権限を有する者としての外観を創出された代理人の行為が存する場合，表見あるいは外観代理の法理により，本人は拘束される。

表見代理は代理人1人の宣言あるいは行為により確定されるものではない。本人は，自らの宣言あるいは行為により，あるいは，然るべく授権された代理人の宣言あるいは行為により，代理人は本人に代わり代理人として行為することを授権されていると相手側当事者に合理的に理解させなければならなかった（*British Bank of The Middle East* v. *Sun Life Assurance Co. of Canada* [1983] 2 Lloyd's Rep. 9 事件参照）。例えば，通常適当な権限を持つ代理人に本人が事柄を委ねるときにこの関係が生じる。

The Ocean Frost 事件で，Keith 卿は以下のように述べた。「表見代理は，本人が言葉と行為で代理人が必要な実際の権限を持つことを示し，代理人と交渉する相手側当事者がその表示を信頼して代理人と契約を締結したときに，生じる。この場合に，本人は実際の権限が存在したことを否定することを許されない。よく出会う事例では，本人が代理人を，問題となる種類の取引を行う権限を持っていると外部世界で一般にみなされる立場に置いたときに生じるが，表見代理は，性質上一般的である。表見一般代理は，代理人が個別の契約相手と交渉するある方法をもって，本人がこの交渉の方法を黙認し，その結果の取引を引き受けるときにも生じる」（表見代理の存在の確証するため充足されねばならない個別条件について，*Freeman & Lockyer* v. *Buckhurst Park Properties* [1964] 2 Q. B. 480（同判例集505頁）の Diplock 卿判事の判決も参照）。

　Ocean Frost 号は，売買契約で Mundogas から Armagas に売却された。Armagas は，買船後 Mundogas へ3年間の傭船（貸船）に基づいてのみ取引に入る用意があった。Mundogas は，1年間のみの傭船に同意する用意があった。仲立人と Mundogas の傭船課長でもあった，運輸担当の副社長は，詐欺的手配を行い，3年間の見かけ上の「厳秘」定期傭船契約に Mundogas の代理人として署名した。別の1年間の定期傭船契約も署名された。1年の定期傭船契約の期限終了時に詐欺的手配が明らかになった。Mundogas は3年間の契約の有効性を否定した。Armagas は否認による損害の賠償を求めた。

　控訴院に至るまでの間に，運輸担当の副社長兼 Mundogas の傭船課長は，この事件の具体的状況の下で，3年間の定期傭船契約を締結する実際の権限あるいは，表見一般代理権を持っていなかった

ということは，共通の認識となった。しかし，Mundogasは，彼を二つの地位に指名することで，彼がArmagasに傭船契約の承認を通知する権限を持つと表示したため，彼がMundogasを拘束する表見上の特定代理権を持つのかが，紛議となった。控訴院と貴族院で次のように判示された。Armagasは3年間の傭船契約はMundogasの承認を要することを承知していたのであり，彼は3年間の傭船契約を結ぶ表見代理権を明らかに持っていなかったのだから，二つの地位への指名によりMundogas（傭船者）は，彼が3年間の傭船契約の承認を通知する権限を持つことを示したことにはならない。

Armagas v. *Mundogas*（*The Ocean Frost*）［1985］1 Lloyd's Rep. 1（Q. B. and C. A.）および［1986］2 Lloyd's Rep. 109（H. L.）．

69 *The Rhodian River*［1984］1 Lloyd's Rep. 373 事件において，同一株主と同一取締役がいる2個の別々の1社1隻所有会社の傭船課長は，一方の会社から他方の会社に傭船に出す実際の権限も表見代理権もないと判示された。間違いで，Rhodian River Companyは，他方の会社の本船 *Rhodian Sailor* 号の傭船契約の船主と記名された。彼が，各々の会社の傭船課長として各会社の本船を貸船する実際の権限は，他方の会社の本船を貸船する付随的権限を含むものとはみなされなかった。この傭船課長が，通常そういう権限を持つとの結論を正当化する証拠は何もなかった（傭船仲立人が本人を拘束する表見代理権を持っていたと判示された判決については，*The Samah*［1981］1 Lloyd's Rep. 40 と *The Wave*［1981］1 Lloyd's Rep. 521 の各事件を参照。*The Nea Tyhi*［1982］1 Lloyd's Rep. 606（後出399頁）と *The Saudi Crown*［1986］1 Lloyd's Rep. 261 各事件も参照）。

代理人には契約に同意する権限はなかったが，上司が同意したか否かを報告する権限を持っていたとの意見の一致を見ることは時々ある。前出 *The Ocean Frost* 事件と調和させるのが困難であるが，*First Energy*（*U. K.*）v. *Hungarian International Bank*［1993］2 Lloyd's Rep. 194 事件判決を参照。

たとえ契約時点で存在する表見代理を確認できないとしても，本人は，自らのその後の行為によって取引は授権されていなかったと表明することは，禁反言の法則により禁じられる。*Spiro* v. *Lintern*［1973］1 W. L. R. 1002 事件参照。本人は，代理人の行為についても同様禁反言の法則に従う。*The Henrik Sif*［1982］1 Lloyd's Rep. 456 と *The Stolt Loyalty*［1993］2 Lloyd's Rep. 281 の各事件参照。*The August Leonhardt*［1985］1 Lloyd's Rep. 28 事件参照。

権限担保違反

しかし，本人がその責めに任じない場合，代理人は，代理人が自ら主張する権限を正当に有しているという，黙示の担保（後出139頁）に違反したことによる損害賠償の請求を契約の相手方からつきつけられることもある。*Collen* v. *Wright*（1857）8 E. & B. 647 事件および *V/O Rasnoimport* v. *Guthrie*［1966］1 Lloyd's Rep. 1（貨物ブローカーの船荷証券署名の責任）事件参照。この担保は本来絶対的なものであり，代理人が自分は確かに権限を持っていると誠実に信じていても，代理人はそれをもって，相手方の請求に対する抗弁とはなしえない。

「電報の授権により」

しかし，代理人は，自分は権限を担保しないということを明確にすることができる。代理人が，本人からの「電報の授権により」署名した場合，代理人が担保するのは，当該傭船契約書に署名する権限を外見上与える電報を自分が持っているということ以外の何物でもないと判示された。

仲立人は Pocklington 号の傭船契約書に，傭船者の「電報授権により」という文言を自己の署名の前に附して，傭船者の代理人として署名した。傭船契約書における運賃率は傭船者からの電報で授権されたのだが，それは電報会社によって誤って伝達されたもので，傭船者が実際に申し込んでいたものより高く定められていた。仲立人が，自分が持っていなかった権限を持っていることを担保したという理由で，船主は，仲立人に対し損害賠償の訴えを起こした。これに対し，仲立人は，次のような反証をあげ，それは，Denman 判事により受理された。すなわち，「電報授権により」という文言は，「傭船者の代理人が，その署名しようとする傭船契約を認める電報――その電報が正しいものとして――を持っていることを約束するというだけで，それ以上の広範囲の担保約束ではないことを意味するものであって，このことは，業界でよく理解されている」というものであった。以上の結果，代理権の存在に関する絶対的担保は，このような文言の使用により有効に排除された，と判示された。
Lilly, Wilson v. Smales, Eeles ［1892］1 Q. B. 456.

しかしながら，この判決は，以下に述べる翌1893年の貴族院判決と一致するとは言い難い。

70 ロンドンの仲立人は，ボンベイの会社から電報を受け取った。その電報は，この仲立人に，Eastbourne 号の傭船契約書にコロンボの傭船者の代理人として署名する権限を明白に与える電報であった。仲立人は，これに基づき傭船契約書を作成し，コロンボの傭船者の代理人であるボンベイの会社を傭船者として表示し，ボンベイの会社からの「電報授権による」代理人として署名した。実際には，コロンボの傭船者はボンベイの会社にかかる権限を与えていなかった。船主は，担保約束違反を理由として，仲立人に対して訴えを提起した。これに対し，仲立人は，そこで使用された文言は，コロンボの傭船者が実際に権限を与えていない限り，契約が成立しないことを明示していると主張した。貴族院はこの主張を退け，仲立人は責めを負うと判示した。Watson 卿は次のとおり述べている。「控訴人の依拠する文言は，船主，傭船者間の契約の有効性が未確認の条件に左右されるというようなことを示すには十分ではない。文言を素直に読めば，その文言は，控訴人が傭船者を代理する権限を引き出した根拠を記述しているに過ぎないように思える」。
Suart v. Haigh（1893）9 T. L. R. 488.

通信手段が改善された今日，第三者が，代理人が立場を説明するための適当な手段を講じて，本人が遠く離れた所にいる事実に何らかの方法で言及するとしても，代理人の権限を担保していると考えることには十分な理由がある。

法 の 抵 触

上述の命題は英国法の命題である。本人が或る国に居住し，代理人が本人とは別の他国に居住している場合のように代理が国境を越えて機能する場合，困難な問題が生じる。契約により本人を拘束し，権利を与える代理人の権能の問題は，問題の契約の準拠法が支配するが，本人と代理人の間の問題は，両者の間の契約（存在するなら）に適用される法が支配するというのが，一般的見解である。しかしながら，事は，大変難しい。特に代理人が行為する場所の法律が，関連する（Dicey & Morris 著『法の抵触』（The Conflict of Laws）（12版）1452頁およびその次の頁以降参照）。

71 米 国 法

定期傭船契約の当事者は船主と傭船者である。しかしながら，傭船契約書に「船主」と記載された者が，本船の登録船主以外の者であることは，異常なことではない。裸傭船者，定期傭船者あるいは航海傭船者でも再傭船契約することを選択できる。そうなれば，再傭船者との関係は，本船の「管理船主 (disponent owner)」となる。再傭船契約上，管理船主 (disponent owner) を単に「船主 owner」と記載するのは，海運界では，普通のことである。したがって，同一船の別の傭船契約上，ある者が，「船主」であったり「傭船者」であるのは，珍しいことではない。

一般的海事法で適用される通常の契約原則が傭船契約の当事者が誰であるかを決定すると判示している。一般海事法は，代理原則を含む。*Interocean Shipping Co.* v. *National Shipping and Trading Corp.*, 523 F. 2d 527, 539 (2d Cir. 1975), 裁量上告拒絶 423 U. S. 1054 (1976). *Kirno Hill Corp.* v. *Holt*, 618 F. 2d 982, 985 (2d Cir. 1980).

船主あるいは傭船者の同一性

単に「良好な船舶 [Victory 号] の船主の代理人として」と記述し，それ以上船主の名前を詳しく述べることなく，傭船契約に署名するのが，仲立人その他の者にとって一般的な慣行になっている。これで本人の同一性を確認するのに十分であると判示されている。*Getty Oil Co.* v. *Norse Management Co. (Pte.) Ltd.*, 711 F. Supp. 175, 177 (S. D. N. Y. 1989)；*Instituto Cubano de Estab.* v. *The Theotokos*, 153 F. Supp. 85 (S. D. N. Y. 1957) (公判前), 155 F. Supp. 945 (S. D. N. Y.) (公判後)；*Tubos de Acero de Mexico* v. *Dynamic Shipping Inc.*, 249 F. Supp. 583, 1966 AMC 1903 (S. D. N. Y. 1966)；*Hudson Trading Co.* v. *Hasler & Co. Inc.*, 11 F. 2d 666, 667 (S. D. N. Y. 1926). しかし，この文脈において，本船名が明確に記載されることが，基本的な事項である。例えば，仲立人が「後で船名が指定される本船の船主の代理人として」署名した場合，本人の同一性の識別は十分とは言えないし，仲立人は隠された本人の代理人として傭船契約の当事者とみなされるであろう (*Hidrocarburos y Derivados C. A.* v. *Lemos*, 453 F. Supp. 160, 171 (S. D. N. Y. 1978) 事件を参照)。Haight 判事が，この事件で言及したように，「潜在的な本人 potential principal」の代理に関する法は認められない。もちろん，引用例において，一度本船が指定されて同一性が認識される以上，本人は十分に表示されたことになろう。

代 理 人

明示された本人の代理人として行為する者自身は傭船契約の当事者ではない。上記 *Interocean Shipping Co.* v. *National Shipping and Trading Corp.* 事件。代理人が，傭船契約に拘束されるかを決定する重要な基準は，本人の氏名が表示されているかではなく，本人の同一性が認識されているかである。事実上ある者が授権された代理人であるか否かという問題は，単純ではない。代理は，実際の権限あるいは表見代理により生じる。ある状況では，本人は代理関係の存在を否定することを禁じられるであろう。

実際の権限

　実際の権限は，代理人が本人に代わって行為できることを本人から代理人に対して意思表示し，かつ代理人が本人を代理することについて同意した場合のみ存在する。代理関係は，文書72契約である必要はない。しかし，常に諾成契約である（*Restatement（Second）of Agency* §§ 26, 33-34）。したがって，本人は，明示的に自分の代わりに行為する権限を代理人に委託するか，または本人の書面，あるいは口頭，あるいは他の行為が，本人に代わって行為する権限を代理人に与えるものと代理人が納得するか，いずれかの要件を満たす方法による。

　傭船契約の交渉および成約の権限を，船主や傭船者から与えられている仲立人は，当事者の代理人とみなされるのが普通である。前出 *Interocean Shipping Co.* v. *National Shipping and Trading Corp.* 事件で，第2巡回区控訴裁判所は，1人の仲立人を通じて双方当事者が傭船条件の交渉を行い，その仲立人がその成約確認のテレックスを双方当事者へ送った場合には，仲立人自身，自己を単なる仲立人と考え，傭船者も仲立人を代理人とする意図がなかったとしても，その仲立人は，船主および傭船者の代理人であると判示した。「代理は，当事者の表示行為から判断される法律上の概念であり，当事者が行為するにあたっての内心の意図や信念によって定まるものではない」（523 F. 2d at 537）。

　代理関係を生じるためには，特別な形式の文言は必要ない。本人に代わって行為する権限は，「合理的に解釈して，代理人に本人のために行為することを希望していると代理人に確信させる本人の書面，あるいは口頭，あるいは他の行為によって生じる」。*Re Arbitration between Herlofson Mgmt A/S and Ministry of Supply, Kingdom of Jordan*, 765 F. Supp. 78, 1991 AMC 2959, 2968 (S. D. N. Y. 1991).

　会社の役員は，通常会社を拘束する一定の権限を持っているが，それは，会社の内規による。したがって，会社と取引する際に第三者は，契約書に真に権限ある役員が署名しているかを常に注意して確認すべきである。

　Gardner v. *The Calvert*, 253 F. 2d 395, 398 (3d Cir. 1958) 事件で，社長と締結した口頭による傭船契約の違反として傭船者は船主，社長を訴え，さらに対物訴訟で本船を訴えた。契約違反で会社の責任を認め，社長個人への訴えを退けて，裁判所は次のように述べた。

　　「なお，その上に，会社の社長が会社の最高執行責任者および代理人として行為するのは，普通のことであり，会社の法律上の目的の範囲内で，会社の権限ある代理人の為した契約は，会社を拘束する」。

　同時に，会社の定款あるいは内規によりある種の取引に取締役会の承認を必要とするのは，普通である。社長あるいは，最高執行責任者でさえ，取締役会の承認なくして，会社を拘束する権限はない。

　The Independence, SMA 3049 (Arb. at N. Y. 1994) 事件で，仲裁人は会社の社長には5年間の定期傭船契約を約束する実際の権限があったと裁定した。同じように *The Gulf Pacific*, SMA 3036 (Arb. at N. Y. 1993) 事件で，代理人は4年間だけ裸傭船契約期間を延長する選択を行使する実際の権限を持つと裁定された。代理人は傭船について決定をする総括的権限を授与されていた。選択権が行使されたのは会社立て直しの後であるにもかかわらず，その権限はそっくりそのまま有効であると仲裁審は裁定した。この事件が例証するように，本人は代理人の行動を取り締まることのできない危険を覚悟して授権しているのである。

　明示の限定的指示が代理人に与えられない限り，付与された実際の権限は，代理人が義務を

遂行するのに合理的に必要であると判断する行為をする権能を代理人にもたらす。これは元来委託された業務に付随する契約を本人に代わり交渉する権能を含む。したがって，貨物所有者の代理人が艀による貨物の引渡の手配を授権された場合に，委託された業務の代理人の遂行に必要な付随事項である艀傭船契約を交渉する権限も，代理関係の特質に鑑み代理人は付与されていると推断された。*Alamo Chemical Transportation Co.* v. *The Overseas Valdes* 469 F. Supp. 203, 1979 AMC 2033（E. D. La. 1979）.

73 表見代理

表見代理は実際の権限とは異なる基礎に拠り，本人の行為が第三者に代理人は本人を拘束する権限を持つことを示すと合理的に認知される場合に存在すると考えられる。*Dr. Beck & Co.* v. *General Electric Co.,* 210 F. Supp. 86, 90（S. D. N. Y. 1962）事件で，表見代理は，簡潔に次のように定義された。

　表見代理は，別の者は自分の代理人であるという本人の表明——その表明は，実際の権限が生じる場合のように代理人に対してではなく第三者に対してなされる——から生じる。……表見代理が存する場合，第三者は代理人が実際に授権された場合と同様に本人に関する権利を持つ。……権限の外観は本人によって作り出されなければならない。代理人が自らの行為と表明により権限の外観を成功裏に作り出すことがあるが，そういう外観は表見代理を作り出すことにはならない。……
　第三者が代理人の権限のない不実表示により惑わされる危険を負い，本人が責任を負うのは，本人が表示の権限を与えた場合か，または合理的な者が代理人には権限があると推断するような何事かを本人がなした場合のみであるという代理に関する法の基本的命題は，不変である（210. F. Supp. at 90）.

代理人の権限の把握は，あらゆる状況に照らして合理的でなければならない。この問題をよく説明しているのは，*Karavos Compania Naviera S. A.* v. *Atlantica Export Corp.,* 588 F. 2d 1, 1978 AMC 2634（2d Cir. 1978）事件である。船主は，表示された傭船者 Atlantica が，本船の受取を拒否したときに，傭船者は傭船契約に違反したと訴えた。船主は，Atlantica の代わりに傭船契約の交渉を行い，これを締結したという代理人 Alfred Repetti の事実上の取決めに Atlantica は拘束されると主張した。Repetti は Atlantica の事務所から傭船契約の交渉を行ったし，その事務所にいる間に提案された傭船契約に関する電話やテレックスを受領した。しかし，Repetti は Atlantica を拘束する実際の権限を持っていなかった。裁判所は，Repetti は Atlantica の代わりに傭船契約を締結する権限を持つと船主が信ずるに足る理由は，船主の立場から見て Atlantica の側には何ら存しないと判断した。裁判所によると，Atlantica が，Repetti が事務所で働き，通信手段を使うのを許可していたからといって，船主が Repetti の立場について当然に照会する義務から解放され Atlantica を傭船契約に拘束する権限を Repetti が持っていると信じる正当な事由はない。裁判所は，さらに「船主が，Repetti は Atlantica の被用者であると信じる正当な事由があろうとも，Repetti の権限は何かということを船主は問わねばならない」と述べた。裁判所が言及したように，「商業会社の被用者の誰もが，連続傭船契約はもちろんのこと，1回の定期傭船契約を締結する権限を持つわけではない」（588 F. 2d. at 10）.

P. D. Marchessini & Co.（New York）Inc. v. *H. W. Robinson & Co.,* 287 F. Supp. 728, 1968 AMC 2084（S. D. N. Y. 1967）事件参照。同事件で船主には貨物船積契約に署名するという船会社の被用者の表見代理権に拠る正当事由はないと裁判所は判示した（*Keystone Shipping* v.

Cie Marocaine, 1990 AMC 2971, 2974-2976 (S.D.N.Y. 1990) 事件も参照）。しかし，代理人が傭船者を拘束する表見代理権を持つと判示した前出 *The Independence* および *The Gulf Pacific* 事件を参照。*The Maruka,* SMA 2609（Arb. at N.Y. 1989）事件で，長年に亘って傭船者のために仕事をして来た仲立人は，傭船契約の付属協定を交渉する表見代理権を持つと推定された。

　本人が意図してあるいは不注意で代理関係があると信じさせた場合，あるいは本人は第三者に真実を通知する適当な手続をとらなかった場合，第三者が代理関係があったと信じて，第三者が自分の立場を変更したとしても，当事者が代理人の権限を否定することは許されない。それはたとえ第三者が彼をその取引の本人であると信じており，それゆえに，立場を変えるかも知れないということを本人が知っていたとしてもそうである（*Restatement（Second）of Agency* § 8(B)。一般的には，前出 *Karavos Compania Naviera S. A.* v. *Atlantica Export Corp.,* 588 F. 2d at 11 事件参照）。

　しかし，*Golden Chase Steamship Inc.* v. *Valmar de Navegacion S. A.,* 724 F. 2d 129, 1984 AMC 2040（5th Cir. 1984）（全員一致）事件で，代理人と交渉する者はその業界の慣習を熟知していると推定され，したがってその業界で代理人に慣習上許されていない権限のない行為について本人に責任ありとすることはできないと述べられた。裁判所は次のように理由を述べた。「New York 海運仲立人の間の慣習により，最終条件提示が本人の代わりになされ，あるいは確認される毎に，各仲立人は毎回本人から個別かつ明示の権限を付与されなければならない。……傭船契約を締結する権限の非常に限定された性質は表見代理の成立にはなじまない」(1984 AMC at 2042)。

追　　認

　人は，事前の承認なく自分のために行われたかまたは行われるということになっていた行為や取引の当事者となることを選択できる。このように，代理人によりなされた授権されていない行為を本人が追認すると，行為が遂行されたときにその行為は授権されたとみなされることとなる（*Restatement（Second）of Agency* §§ 82-104 参照）。*The Trinity Navigator,* SMA 2609（Arb. at N.Y. 1989）事件で，仲立人が結んだ傭船契約は，傭船者により追認されたと判示された。

隠された本人

　隠された本人は傭船契約上その権利を行使できるし，また傭船契約の他方の当事者が，その権利を行使する行為に従うこととなる（*Kirno Hill Corp.* v. *Holt,* 618 F. 2d 982, 984 (2d Cir. 1980)；*Philippine Bulk Shipping Inc.* v. *International Minerals & Chemical Corp.,* 376 F. Supp. 654 (S.D.N.Y. 1973)）。同時に，隠された本人のために行為する代理人は傭船契約の当事者であり，したがってその本人のあらゆる権利と義務を有することとなる（*Hidrocarburos y Derivados C. A.* v. *Lemos,* 453 F. Supp. 160, 168 (S.D.N.Y. 1978)；*Overseas Oil* v. *The Phibro Energy,* 1989 AMC 847, 849 (S.D.N.Y. 1989)；*Ariel Maritime* v. *Zust Bachmeier,* 762 F. Supp. 55, 1991 AMC 2048 (S.D.N.Y. 1991)；*The California,* SMA 2736（Arb. at N.Y. 1990））。

　代理人あるいは隠された本人のどちらか一方に対して提訴することは，当然その判決が満足すべきものでない限り残る一方当事者に対する提訴を妨げる救済策を選んだことにはならな

い。New York 州法上，この原則は，CPLR §3002(b)に収められている。

代理人の本人に対する責任

　代理人は有能に注意深く行動する義務があり，代理人の地位にある者に要求される標準的な知識がないか，あるいは標準的な注意を尽くせないことから生じる誤謬あるいは懈怠につき本人に対し責任がある (*Restatement (Second) of Agency* §379)。例えば，本人が承認した文言を変更した傭船契約を仲立人が準備し署名した場合，結果として生じる損害につき仲立人は本人に対し責任を負う。代理人は完全な基準で履行することを決して期待されておらず，小さな誤謬や不注意により，通常，代理人が本人に対する責任を問われることはない。しかし，代理人は一般に人が傭船仲立人に合理的に期待する程度の注意を払って行動しなければならない。

　代理人は，また本人が付与した権限の範囲内で行動することを要求される。代理人が，権限を越えた行動をとっても本人を拘束するので，本人に対して責任を負う。前述のように，代理人は遂行しようとするすべての行為を個別具体的に正確にはっきりさせる必要はない。実際，反対の特段の指示がなされない限り，代理人は義務を果たす際に自らの判断を下すことを期待され，業務を遂行するに適当と思う手段をとることができる。

75　その代理人が義務に違反し，あるいは違反するおそれがある場合に，本人が取りうる広い範囲の救済がある。最も重要な救済は契約義務を遂行できないことについて契約上の訴訟や代理義務の遂行の過失についての不法行為訴訟，原状回復訴訟，金銭収支報告を求める訴訟，差止命令訴訟を含む (*Restatement (Second) of Agency* §399 参照)。

「法人格の否認」

　通常，法人は法人の営業活動から生じる負債あるいは請求に対する人的責任から株主を隔離する。しかし，事件によっては，当事者の「法人格」は否認され，傭船契約の当事者は単に署名のための分身 (*alter ego*) と判断される (*Fisser v. International Bank*, 282 F. 2d 231, 233-234 (2d Cir.1960) 事件参照)。石炭輸入業者は訴訟を提起し，International Bank が，原告と第三者 Allied Transportation の間の運送契約違反の請求を仲裁に付託することを求めた。裁判所は法律判断として，裁判所が銀行は Allied の分身 (*alter ego*) であると判断するなら International Bank は契約に署名していなくてもその契約の仲裁条項に拘束されると述べた。

> 　分身 (*alter ego*) 学説の適用の結果として，法人の別個の存在と関係なく法人を管理する者とその法人は，一つの実在として扱われる。そして少なくとも，契約の分野で一個人の行為は全員の行為である。……手先の契約違反による損害に応える親の義務と，その損害の程度を仲裁に付す義務の間を区別する妥当な根拠はない。……われわれはこれまで，損害賠償に応える義務は，「人形使い」が署名を「人形に指示」したように，分身理論がその親に義務を負わせる契約から生じると判断した。……われわれは今，親がその人形と同様に契約に拘束されるなら，親は仲裁に付されるべきであると判断する (282 F. 2d at 234-235)。

　しかし，法廷に出された事実に基づき，原告は Allied が International の単なる手先であることを証明できないと裁判所は判断し，International を仲裁に付す要はないと判示した (282 F. 2d at 235-241)。

　海事管轄の裁判所は法人格を否認する権能を有するとするのが，長い間，米国の規則であっ

た。*Swift & Company Packers* v. *Compania Colombiana Del Caribe S. A.*, 339 U.S. 684, 689 n. 4（1950）事件で，最高裁は，「分身問題に判決を下す海事法廷の管轄権に疑問の余地はない」と述べた。

　法人格否認の学説の起源は，*Wm. Passalacqua Builders* v. *Resnick Developers South Inc.*, 933 F. 2d 131 (2nd Cir.1991) 事件で詳しく吟味された。この事件は，New York 州法下で裁定された非海事事件であるが，そこで研究された原則は一般海事法下の海事事件に適用されるべきである。*Passalacqua Builders* 事件は不動産開発に関連して提供された未払労働と役務についての判決を強制する訴訟が関連していた。判決を受けた開発業者は支払えず，あるいは支払おうとしなかったので，原告は訴訟を提起し，開発業者は「見せかけ（shell）」会社であり，一族所有の会社と個人株主グループの単なる分身（alter ego）であることの証明を試みた。地方裁判所は被告有利の判決を出したが，第２巡回区控訴裁判所は判決を覆して，法人格否認の要件について広範囲にわたる法則を策定した。

　この学説の歴史的起源を再検討して，裁判所はそこに衡平法上とコモン・ロー上の構成要素があると考えた。海事事件の管轄権を有する地方裁判所側は，単に衡平法上の救済を与えるのに伝統的に消極的なので，海事事件に関係する者にとり，このことは意義深い（例として *China Trade & Devel. Corp.* v. *The Choong Yong*, 837 F. 2d 33, 1988 AMC 880 (2d Cir. 1987) 事件参照）。*Passalacqua Builders* 事件で裁判所は，法人格否認は衡平法上の訴訟手続におけるとまったく同様に，コモン・ロー上の訴訟の適当な救済形式であると力説した。通常陪審裁判の権利がない海事事件では大抵問題ないが，陪審員により法人格否認問題が判定されるべきか否かに関する限り，*Passalacqua Builders* 事件のこの区別は意義深い。

　同裁判所は法人格否認の二重の基準を設定しにかかった。まず第１に，親会社あるいは個人株主が，「(1)子会社が，本当の行為者である親会社の『単なる手先となる』管理を行った，(2)その管理は詐欺または他の悪行を為すために使用された，(3)詐欺または悪行の結果，原告の不当な損失または傷害となる」場合には，法人組織は，無視される。933 F. 2d at 138. また一方，法人が個人あるいは親会社により管理され，法人自らの事業よりも個人あるいは親会社の目的の遂行のために使用される場合，法人格は無視される（同上）。

　裁判所が述べたように「したがって，責任は，詐欺を示すこと，あるいは第三者に対する悪行となる支配会社による完全管理に基づき，断定される」（同上 at 135）。

　この要素に対する第１審裁判所の事実審理の範囲は，限定されず，裁判所は，10項目を取り上げた。それは，法人格否認は救済の適当な形式であることを示そうとしていると指摘した。

　　(1)法人存在の重要部分である形式と付属品の不存在，つまり株式の発行，取締役の選任，法人記録の保存などの不存在，(2)不適当な資本化，(3)資金が法人の目的よりむしろ個人の目的のために法人に投入され，使用されるか，(4)所有権，役員，取締役と従業員の重複，(5)法人組織の共通事務所空間，住所，電話番号，(6)支配会社といわれるものにより示される業務判断の程度，(7)関連法人が支配会社と離れて取引するかどうか，(8)法人は独立の収益センターとして扱われるか，(9)グループの他の会社による支配会社の負債の支払あるいは保証，(10)自らのものであるかのように他の法人によって使われた資産を問題の法人が，所有していたか（同上 at 139）。

　しかし，*Passalacqua* 事件の判決の２年後，New York 控訴裁判所は，*Morris* v. *New York State Dep't of Taxation and Finance*, 82 N. Y. 2d 135, 603 N. Y. S. 2d 807, 623 N. E. 2d 1157 (1993) 事件においてもっと限定的な基準を採用した。*Morris* 事件で裁判所は，New York 州法の下で法人格は，詐欺あるいは悪行が認定されない限り，否認されないと判示した。New York 州法についての決定的説明として，*Morris* 事件は *Passalacqua* 事件を覆し，第２巡回区

裁判所は、法人が株主の「手先（instrumentality）」、あるいは「分身（alter ego）」であることを単に示すことで法人格否認に十分であると判示した。

本稿執筆の時点では、海事法を適用する裁判所が Passalacqua 事件で要約された二股の基準に従うか、あるいは Morris 事件で採用されたもっと限定的な基準に還るかどうかは不透明である。

Holborn Oil Trading Ltd. v. Interpetrol Bermuda Ltd., 774 F. Supp. 840, 1992 AMC 819 (S. D. N. Y. 1991) 事件は、この原則の適用を解説している。船主は訴訟を提起し、傭船者から支払期限がきている未払の滞船料の回収を試み、被告の法人格を否認しようとした。被告は、次の理由で、略式裁判を申請した。つまり、被告は傭船者とは完全に別個の存在である、傭船契約に関与していない、特に船主は、滞船料につき貨物にリーエンを有するので、船主は傭船契約締結に際し、被告をまったく当てにしていなかった。裁判所は、その裁定申請を否認し、原告は、具体的事実についての真の問題が存在し公判を必要とすることを十分に示したと判示した。裁判所は、そう判示して、法人格否認に関する判例法を再検討した。裁判所は、準拠法は一般海事法であるが、New York 州法下の前出 Passalacqua Builders 事件で控訴院により説明された基準は違わず、適用されると判示した。裁判所が述べたように「New York 州法と連邦コモン・ローの下での、法人格否認の基準を比較することにより、詐欺あるいは支配を証明することを要求する二つの基準が一点に向かうことが明らかとなった」。

それから裁判所は、法人格否認に関する重要な事実と密接な関係のある問題が、公判を正当化するために示されたかどうかを決定すべく、Passalacqua Builders 事件で挙げられた要素を検討して、本件はそれに該当する事案であるとの結論を出した。

Maritime Ventures Int'l Inc. v. Caribbean Trading & Fidelity Ltd., 689 F. Supp. 1341 (S. D. N. Y. 1988) 事件も、この原則を説明している。同事件は、Senhorita 号の航海傭船の不履行についての損害賠償であった。傭船者は資産のない単なる見せかけ法人であったので、傭船者の分身であると船主が主張する数人の個人に対して船主は損害賠償を強制しようとした。裁判所は、船主は法人格否認のための一応の証拠のある事案としての証明をし、さらに傭船者の自称役員が、個人の財産として会社を利用し、会社の手続を無視し会社の資本をひどく削減したことを示す証明責任を果たしたと、考えた（しかし、本事件は、示談解決されて、法人格否認の申立の本案審理は行われなかった）。

Bergesen d. y. A/S v. Lindholm, 1991 AMC 2839, 760 F. Supp. 976 (D. Conn. 1991) 事件は、3年間の定期傭船を傭船者が拒否したことから生じた損害賠償であった。船主は、傭船者と他の海運会社を管理している同じ個人により所有されていると申し立て、1群の会社の不動産の仮差押えを求めた。仮差押えは、Connecticut 州法の下で、求められた。同州法の下で、原告の基礎となる損害賠償請求の妥当性を支える十分な原因があるかどうかについての裁判所の決定が求められた。審理の後で裁判所は、海運と不動産グループ各種会社の法人格を否認すべきであるとの原告の主張とともに、原告の損害賠償請求を妥当であると考えるに足る原因がある、と判断した。Sabine Towing & Transp. Co. v. Merit Ventures Inc., 575 F. Supp. 1442 (E. D. Tex. 1983) 事件に倣って、裁判所は、単独あるいは組み合わせで法人格否認の基礎となる15の要素を挙げた。「(1)親と子会社の間で、共通あるいは重複する株式の所有、(2)共通あるいは重複する取締役および役員、(3)同じ会社事務所の使用、(4)子会社の不適当な資本化、(5)親会社による子会社への資金提供、(6)親会社が子会社の持株会社としてのみ存在、(7)親会社が、子会社の財産や資産を自己のものとして使用、(8)非公式な会社間貸金取引、(9)親会社による子会社の設立、(10)親会社と子会社の連結所得税申告、(11)親会社と本人による子会社の意思決定、(12)子会社の取締役は子会社の利益のために独立して行動せず、親会社の利益によって行動

する。, ⒀親会社に有利な親会社と子会社間の契約, ⒁正式な法的要件の非遵守, ⒂第三者への詐欺, 悪行あるいは不正の存在」。

　これらの基準は提出された事実に基づいて満たされ, Connecticut 州法の下で確立された同じような基準もまた満たされたと考えた裁判所は, 原告の損害賠償の妥当性を支持する原因が示されたと判示し, 仮差押えは, 許可された。

　以下の例にとどまらない, 本件に関する重要な多くの他の判決がある。Dow Chemical Pacific Ltd. v. Rascator Maritime S. A., 782 F. 2d 329 (2d Cir. 1986); Itel Containers International Corp. v. Atlanttrafik Express Service Ltd., 909 F. 2d 698 (2d Cir. 1990); Electronic Switching Industries Inc. v. Faradyne Electric Corp., 833 F. 2d 418 (2d Cir. 1987); Kirno Hill Corp. v. Holt, 618 F. 2d 982 (2d Cir. 1980); MoPrusman Ltd. v. Ariel Maritime, 1992 AMC 1059 (S. D. N. Y. 1991).

　契約紛争におけるよりも不法行為事件で法人格を否認する方が, 一般的により容易である。しかし, 法人形式を無視させるために会社支配と損害との間の因果関係を請求者が証明しなければならないかどうかについての, 明白な法則は存しない。Craig v. Lake Asbestos of Quebec Ltd., 843 F. 2d 145 (3rd Cir. 1988) 事件では, それを証明することを要求した。United States v. Jon. T. Chemicals Inc., 768 F. 2d 686 (5th Cir. 1985), 裁量上告拒絶 475 U. S. 10 事件, あるいは, United States v. Ira S. Bushey & Sons Inc., 363 F. Supp. 110, 115 (D. Vt. 1973), 理由を付さず原審判断維持 487 F. 2d 1393 (2d Cir. 1973), 裁量上告拒絶 417 U. S. 976 (1974) 事件では, そのような証明は, 要求されなかった。同様に The Amoco Cadiz, 1984 AMC 2124 (N. D. Ⅲ. 1984) 事件で, 裁判所は Standard Oil Company (Indiana) とその Delaware 州とリベリアの子会社の「法人格を否認し」, Amoco Cadiz 号の座礁事故とその結果原油流出から生じた損害につき親会社は責任ありとした。裁判所は, 子会社に対して Standard が行使する管理は子会社の実在が Standard の「単なる手先」に過ぎない程度と判断した。

　完全に確立した法に反した仲裁裁定が多くある。すなわち, 商業仲裁人は子会社に帰属する損害賠償請求を主張するために, 法人格を否認することをその会社に許している。The Baron Venture, SMA 2138 (Arb. at N. Y. 1985) 事件では, 仲裁審は, 本船を傭船した親会社が子会社に帰属する貨物滅失損害賠償請求を行うことを許した。子会社は, 傭船契約または仲裁協定の当事者ではなかった。The Volere, SMA 1885 (Arb. at N. Y. 1983) と The Trade Greece, SMA 1643 (Arb. at N. Y. 1982), The Velma, SMA 958 (Arb. at N. Y. 1975) 事件で, 同じような裁定が出された。ある仲裁人は, そういう「近道」を許すことで商業的公正を考えているようだが, こういう裁定は法律問題としては明確に誤りであると考えられている。

　The Baron Venture 事件で裁定を無効にする申立が貨物滅失に責任ありとされた傭船者から行われた。地方裁判所は, 傭船者に同意したが, 裁定は法律上誤りであるが, 「仲裁人は, 結論は確立した先例と慣行に基づくと明白に理解している」ので, 法を明白に無視してはいないと結論づけた (Fried, Krupp GmbH v. Solidarity Carriers Inc., 674 F. Supp. 1022, 1027, 1988 AMC 1383 (S. D. N. Y. 1987), 理由を付さず原審判断維持 838 F. 2d 1202 (2d Cir. 1987). 後出547頁の解説参照)。

保　証　人

　一方の当事者の傭船契約に基づく義務の単なる保証人は, 契約の当事者ではない。上記 Interocean Shipping Co. v. National Shipping and Trading Corp. 事件。傭船契約が, 別段の取決

めがなければ、保証人は保証を引き受けた義務の不履行があった後はじめて、あてにされる。

通常、保証人は傭船契約の仲裁条項に拘束されるとみなされない。その保証契約は紛争の解決方法について何ら規定しておらず、傭船契約は「船主と傭船者」間の紛争の仲裁を定めていたが、保証人は仲裁条項に拘束されないと判示された例、*Cordoba Shipping Co. Ltd.* v. *Maro Shipping Ltd.*, 494 F. Supp. 1183, 1980 AMC 1945 (D. Conn. 1980) 事件を参照。*Taiwan Navigation Co. Ltd.* v. *Seven Seas Merchants Corp.*, 172 F. Supp. 721 (S.D.N.Y. 1959) 事件で、同様の結果となった。仲裁人は、その条件はあまりに不明確で強制できないので、保証人は拘束されないと判断した *The Independence*, SMA 3049 (Arb. at N.Y. 1994) 事件も参照。

79 しかし、保証人は仲裁条項に拘束されると判示した例がある。*Compania Espanola de Petroleos S. A.* v. *Nereus Shipping S. A.*, 527 F 2d 966, 973 (2d Cir. 1975), 裁量上告拒絶426 U.S. 936 (1976) 事件（これは *Gov't of the United Kingdom* v. *Boeing Co.*, 998 F. 2d 68 (2d Cir. 1993) 事件で、他の理由に基づき破棄されたが）で、裁判所は次のように述べた。

> ……仲裁条項がその条件により、船主と傭船者の間に生じた紛争に限らず、あらゆる紛争に適用される場合に、仲裁協定は原当事者のみならず、後に拘束されることに同意する者すべてを拘束する。……

Coastal States Gas Corp. v. *Atlantic Tankers Ltd.*, 546 F. 2d 15, 1976 AMC 2337 (2d Cir. 1976) 事件で、傭船者の保証人は、仲裁条項に拘束されると判示された。その傭船契約は、「性質の如何を問わず、本契約に起因するあらゆる紛議、紛争は仲裁に付託されるものとする」と規定していた。裁判所によれば、保証人は、「……仲裁を原船主と〔傭船者〕間の紛争に限定するという仲裁条項を……，自己の保証にからませることにより自衛しえたのに、かかる自衛のための約定をしなかったのであるから、もはや本裁判所において、そのような保護を受けることはできない」としている (1976 AMC at 2340)。*Merrill Lynch Commodities Inc.* v. *Richal Shipping Corp.*, 581 F. Supp. 933, 940 (S.D.N.Y. 1984); *Antco Shipping Co. Ltd.* v. *Sidemar S. p. A.*, 417 F. Supp. 207 (S.D.N.Y. 1976) 事件も参照。

保証人が仲裁に拘束されるという事実は、船主に実質的な手続上の利点をもたらした。この理由は、傭船契約上の義務の保証として行為する合意は、通常海事契約ではなく、例えば、詐欺に関する州法に従うというようなことである。*Interocean Shipping Co.* v. *National Shipping and Trading Corp.*, 462 F. 2d 673, 678 (2d Cir. 1972) 事件参照。しかし、海事契約であると判示された保証の例として *Eagle Transport Ltd.* v. *O'Connor*, 449 F. Supp. 58 (S.D.N.Y. 1978) 事件参照。さらに、保証人に対する裁定が付与されることにより、船主はその責任の確定のため別途訴訟を提起する必要がなくなる。

仲 裁 協 定

ある者が傭船契約の仲裁条項の当事者であるかどうかの問題は、仲裁を強制するあるいは仲裁期間訴訟を中断させる訴えにより連邦仲裁法に従って裁判所により決定される問題である。9 U.S.C. §§3 または4。*Interocean Shipping Co.* v. *National Shipping and Trading Corp.*, 462 F. 2d 673, 676-677 (2d Cir. 1972); *Re Kinoshita & Co.*, 287 F. 2d 951, 953 (2d Cir. 1961); *Almacenes Fernandez S. A.* v. *Golodetz*, 148 F. 2d 625, 1961 AMC 1974 (2d Cir. 1945) 各事件参照。後出518-524頁の解説参照。

船舶の表示

[81]

"4. of .... tons gross register, and .... tons net register, having engines of .... indicated horse power
5. and with hull, machinery and equipment in a thoroughly efficient state, and classed ....
6. at .... of about .... cubic feet bale capacity, and about .... tons of 2,240lbs.
7. deadweight capacity (cargo and bunkers, including fresh water and stores not exceeding one and one-half percent of ship's deadweight capacity,
8. allowing a minimum of fifty tons) on a draft of .... feet .... inches on .... Summer freeboard, inclusive of permanent bunkers,
9. which are of the capacity of about .... tons of fuel, and capable of steaming, fully laden, under good weather
10. conditions about .... knots on a consumption of about .... tons of best Welsh coal-best grade fuel oil-best grade Diesel oil,
11. now ...."

「総トン数......トン、純トン数......トン、機関......指示馬力、完全な稼働状態にある船体・機関・装備を有し、......船級協会船級......艙内載貨容積ベールにて約......立方フィート、燃料約......トンの容積の常備用燃料庫を含めた......夏期乾舷による......フィート......インチの喫水を基準とする載貨重量トン(2,240ポンドを1トンとする)約......トン(貨物・燃料、本船載貨重量トンの1.5パーセント以下で最低50トンの清水・船用品を含む)、平穏な天候状態における満載航海速力約......ノット、燃料消費高最良ウェルズ炭―極上燃料油―極上ディーゼル油にて約......トン、現在......中の船舶に関して......」

序

ニューヨーク・プロデュース書式の4行から11行の備船の明細または他の定期傭船契約書式の同等の文言の効力を評価するためには、表示と約束の効力に関する英国法の一般原則を考慮する必要がある。したがって、ここでこの原則についての説明を行い、本書を通して参照する。4行から11行へのこの原則の適用は、この章の後で次の見出しで検討する。

本船が表示を遵守すべき時期：144頁
表示と合致しない本船の引渡：144頁
船名：145頁
代船と売船：145/146頁
国籍：147頁
船体、機関および装備を完全に稼働状態に保持すること：147頁
船級に関する表示：152頁
ベール容積と載貨重量：152頁
速力と燃料消費：155頁
本船の動静：158頁

交渉の過程でなされる表示

(1) 責任を生じない表示

　曖昧なまたは過分な賞賛（単なる「ほめそやし」）や，単なる意見の開陳，「約因」を欠いて
[82]いるとして相手方から対価を得る見込のない意思の表示は，法的効力をまったく有しない（例
として *Ecay* v. *Godfrey*（1947）80 Ll.L. Rep. 286 事件を参照）。しかし商業関係では裁判所は，
なかなか表示をこの範疇で扱おうとはしないであろう。表示が書面による署名契約の一部であ
るように見える場合には，事実上裁判所は別の行動をとるだろう。

(2) 不 実 表 示

　不実表示は事実の虚偽の表示である。意見や意思の単なる開陳は不実表示にはならない。し
かし，交渉の過程で行われた意見の開陳は，その意見を裏付ける事実が存在することや意見は
正当な考えであるという暗黙の表示を意味するかもしれない。次にそういう事実がなかった
り，意見が正当な考えでないのであれば，その表示は不実表示となる。したがって，*Crem-
dean Properties* v. *Nash*（1977）244 E.G. 547（同判例集551頁）事件で Bridge 卿判事は次の
ように述べた。「情報を伝えたり，意見や信念を述べるときに，人は表示をしていないという
理由を私は理解できない」。

　契約の交渉過程における沈黙は，それが重要な事実に関する場合でも，表示とはならない
（*Turner* v. *Green* [1895] 2 Ch. 205）。しかし，半分だけ真実を述べることは，部分的には真
実を明らかにしていても，他の部分を隠しているという意味で，不実表示となることがある
（*Oakes* v. *Turquand*（1867）L.R. 2 H.L. 325）。表示がなされた時点で真実であっても，その
後，表示をなした当事者が知りえたことに照らして，真実でなくなれば，契約締結前にその表
示を修正しないことは不実表示である（*With* v. *O'Flanagan* [1936] Ch. 575）。

　不実表示は，それが相手方に契約を締結させる動機となった場合にのみ，相手方に救済の道
をも与える。例として後出の *The Lucy* 事件を参照。不実表示となるには，それが動機のすべ
てである必要はないが，少なくとも，一つの動機であることが必要である（*Barton* v. *Armstrong* [1976] A.C. 104 事件（同判例集118頁）参照）。しかしながら，不実表示された相手方
が，その表示が真実でないことを知っているとき，あるいは不実表示に拠る前にそのことに気
づくとき，その相手方は，表示が真実でないことを熟知している場合に限り，不実表示に対す
る救済を与えられない。*Begbie* v. *Phosphate Sewage*（1875）L.R. 10 Q.B. 491。

不実表示による契約の解除

　不実表示が，詐欺的に，不注意に，または善意でなされようと，いずれにせよ不実表示によ
り契約を締結することになった当事者は，通常，契約を解除する権利を有する。契約の解除と
は，履行すること（またはさらに継続して履行すること）を拒否し，支払った金員または譲っ
た財産を回収すべく訴訟を起こせることを意味する。例として *Goldsmith* v. *Rodger* [1962] 2
Lloyd's Rep. 249 事件参照。しかし，この権利は，1967年不実表示法第2条第2項の適用に
よって排除されることがあり，さらにまた，以下に要約するその他の場合にはこれを喪失する
こともある。

Lucy 号は，ある一定の免責条項付の再定期傭船の条件が既存の原定期傭船契約に正確に一致していることに基づいて再定期傭船された。その原傭船契約の写は交渉中に再傭船者に送付された。実際は，航路定限外の航海に関して，原傭船契約は船主と傭船者間の実際の合意を反映していなかった。再傭船が約9ヶ月間継続した後で，再傭船者がこのことに気づいたとき，再傭船者は契約の解除を目論んだ。Mustill 判事は，実際の合意を（善意で）開陳せずに再傭船者に原傭船契約書の写を送付することは契約解除を正当化できる黙示の不実表示となるが，証拠に基づくと再傭船者は傭船契約の締結に際して航路定限外の航海に関する条件に拠っていないと判示した。したがって，再傭船者は契約を解除できなかった。

　Mustill 判事は，202頁で傍論として，仮に証拠に基づき別の結論に至ったならば，次のように判示しようという気持になったであろうと述べた。「善意の不実表示が役務履行の契約の動機となる事件では，当事者の衡平法上の権利を完全に調整するために，契約解除の命令に付加物として金員を支払う命令が課せられることが（あるいは先行する解除が有効であるとの判断が）しばしば必要であるが，契約が部分的に履行されたことは契約解除の阻却事由とはならない」。したがって，契約解除を命令することは，裁判所の自由であったろうし，その場合には判事は，契約解除に代わる別の道として損害賠償（これについては，下記を参照）を命令するため1967年不実表示法第2条第2項に基づく裁量権を行使したであろう。

　The Lucy [1983] 1 Lloyd's Rep. 188.

1967年不実表示法第2条第2項

　この条項により，裁判所または仲裁人が「契約解除によって相手方に及ぼす損失を考慮するだけでなく，不実表示の性質，契約を存続させた場合に生ずる損失をも考慮にいれて，衡平の原則に適うと考えた場合」には，契約解除に代えて損害賠償の裁定を下すこともできる。事実，本項は，裁判所または仲裁人に対し，公正と思われる場合に，契約解除権に代えて，損害賠償を命ずる裁量権を与えている。しかし，不実表示が詐欺的である場合には，適用されない（下記参照）。

　前出 *The Lucy* 事件で，Mustill 判事は，自身の見解では同法第2条第2項により裁判所は過去に生じた契約解除を遡及して無効にできるが，この状況下での裁量権の行使は恐るべき困難を引き起こすと所見を述べた。再傭船者が目論んだ契約解除は履行の拒絶として受け入れられず，権利関係を毀損することはないとの合意に基づき，本船が返船されるまで傭船が継続したので，*The Lucy* 事件では，困難の度合いは減少した。崩壊しつつあった現物市場で仮に再傭船者が本船を返船すれば生じる原傭船者の損害は巨大なものであったであろうから，同判事は，契約解除の代わりに損害賠償の裁定の裁量を下したのであろう。船主と原傭船者間の特別協定が別のものであるからといって再傭船料率になんらかの実質的な差異があったとの証拠はなかった。そしてたとえ不実表示が傭船契約を結ぶ気にさせる動機であったとしても，それはまったく些細なことであった。

その他の場合における解除権の喪失

　次の場合においても，解除権を喪失する。(a)もともと解除権を有する当事者が，問題の事実を知りながら，契約の継続を明示または黙示をもって表明する場合（*Car and Universal Finance* v. *Caldwell* [1965] 1 Q.B. 525 事件（同判例集550頁）の Sellers 卿判事および *Long* v. *Lloyd* [1958] 1 W.L.R. 753 事件参照）。または(b)当事者が，その相手方を，実質的に契約前の状態に戻すことが，もはや不可能である場合（*Spence* v. *Crawford* [1939] 3 All E.R. 271 事件と前出 *The Lucy* [1983] 1 Lloyd's Rep. 188 事件を参照）。または(c)善意の第三者が，一方において契約の目的につき権益を取得している場合（*Clough* v. *L. & N.W.R.* (1871) L.R. 7 Exch. 26 事件参照）。または(d)善意の不実表示については，最初から解除権を有する当事者

が，長期間その権利を行使しない場合（*Leaf* v. *International Galleries*［1950］2 K. B. 86 事件参照）。契約解除権を喪失した場合，不実表示法第2条第2項の損害賠償を裁定する権限は行使できない（第2条第1項に基づく損害賠償請求は可能であるが）と今まで考えられていた。しかしその場合でも契約解除は可能であると第1審で判示された（*Thomas Witter* v. *TBP Industries*（1994）（未報告）事件参照）。

不実表示に基づく損害賠償

以下のような場合に不実表示をされた相手方は，損害賠償を請求することができる。

84 (1) 詐欺的不実表示

詐欺的不実表示を信頼して損失を被った当事者は，契約を解除する権利だけでなく（前出参照），詐欺による不法行為として損害賠償請求権をも有する。詐欺的不実表示というものは，*Derry* v. *Peek*（1889）14 App. Cas. 337 事件における Herschell 卿によれば，「(1)故意に，または(2)その真実性に確信なく，または(3)真実か虚偽かに注意を払わずになされたものである」。

(2) 不法行為となる過失による不実表示

過失による不実表示をされた相手方は，不法行為による損害賠償を請求することができる。*Hedley Byrne* v. *Heller*［1963］1 Lloyd's Rep. 485 事件参照。しかし，それには不実表示がなされた状況が，不実表示をなす当事者に注意義務を負わせるような状況であったことを要する。どういう場合にそのような義務が生じるかは完全には明確ではない（*Esso Petroleum* v. *Mardon*［1976］2 Lloyd's Rep. 305 事件および *Spring* v. *Guardian Assurance*［1994］3 W. L. R. 354 事件参照）。契約の当事者により，契約前，過失による不実表示がなされた場合で，1967年不実表示法第2条第1項が適用されないような不実表示は考えられない。そして請求者は，挙証責任が相手方に転換しているから，同条に基づき勝訴することの方がどの場合でも容易である。それゆえ不法行為の原則による救済の重要性は，現在，ほとんどないように思える。ただし，不実表示が契約の当事者とならない者によってなされた場合，あるいは契約が後に至っても結ばれていない場合は別である。

(3) 不実表示法第2条第1項における過失による不実表示

不実表示がなされた後，契約が締結され，その結果損害を被った者は，不実表示をした当事者に対し損害賠償を請求することができる。ただし，不実表示者が，「表示事実が真実であると信ずる相当の根拠を有し，かつ契約締結時まで，そのように信じていたことを立証した」場合は，この限りではない（1967年不実表示法第2条第1項）。艀の船主による載貨重量の不実表示が合理的な根拠を有していないと判示された（しかし相手側が過失を挙証できたのか明らかではない）事件について，*Howard Marine* v. *Ogden*［1978］1 Lloyd's Rep. 334 事件参照。

本人のみが，同法第2条第1項に基づき責任ありとされる。同条の言い回しは代理人を含むとはされない（*The Skopas*［1983］1 Lloyd's Rep. 431 事件）。しかし代理人は前出(2)同様に過失につき責任ありとされた。

(4) 付随契約の違反となる不実表示

時には，表示は別個の「付随 collateral」契約の部分として取り扱われ——表示の真実性は相手側の主契約の締結に対する見返りとして約束される。この場合には，約束は通常絶対的

なものとして取り扱われる。そして不実表示に基づく責任は過失の挙証に依存しない。しかし，時には表示者は表示をなすときに，あるいはそれに先立つ調査に，相当の注意を尽くすことのみを約束するものとして取り扱われる。そういう場合には，その責任は過失についての責任と（表示者が契約の当事者となることが要求されないことを除いては）1967年不実表示法第2条第1項に基づく責任に非常に類似している。この二つの責任がガソリン精油所の生産額の
85 予報に関して存在するとした *Esso Petroleum* v. *Mardon* [1976] 2 Lloyd's Rep. 305 事件を参照。

（モータークルーザーの「予想速力」に関する）表示は約束にはならないと判示した事件の例として，*Savage* v. *Blakney* (1970) 119 C. L. R. 435 事件参照（付随契約はないとした前出 *Howard Marine* v. *Ogden* 事件も参照）。

前出すべての状況の下で，主たる契約の期待利益の喪失は，契約違反の訴訟のみで回収できるから，不実表示を信頼したことで被った損失については，一般的に相手側に対する補償が裁定される。しかし，主たる契約の期待利益の喪失は，補償を裁定されないのが一般である。しかし詐欺に基づく損害賠償額は，特定の事件での過失に基づく損害賠償額よりいくぶん大きい（*Doyle* v. *Olby* [1969] 2 Q. B. 158 事件を参照）。そして1967年，不実表示法第2条第1項の特別な文言のために詐欺についての規則はその条項に基づく損害賠償額の計算にも適用されると判示された（*Royscot Trust* v. *Rogerson* [1991] 2 Q. B. 297）。

(5) 1967年不実表示法第2条第2項に基づく損害

裁判所あるいは仲裁人はこの条項に基づき不実表示による契約解除を否認し（前出参照）代わりに損害賠償を裁定することができる。第2条第3項は，損害の計算方法に関するものではない。ただし，その損害額の計算が第2条第1項と同じではないことを意味していることを除く。もっと限定された裁定が意図されているように思える（*William Sindall* v. *Cambridgeshire C. C.* [1994] 1 W. L. R. 1016 事件で本件が別の背景で検討された問題を参照）。

不実表示の責任を排除する条項

契約締結前の不実表示の責任または救済策を制限または排除する規定が，契約中に定められていても，その規定は，1977年不公正契約条項法（The Unfair Contract Terms Act 1977）第8条第1項により修正された1967年不実表示法第3条第3項によって，無効とされる。ただし，契約締結時，当事者が認識し，認識すべきであった状況を斟酌して，かかる規定を定めることが，公正かつ妥当なものであると判断された場合はこの限りではない。不公正契約条項法自身と異なり（第27条と第2付帯条項参照），1967年不実表示法は傭船契約と他の海事国際契約に適用される。したがって，傭船契約のプロパー・ローが英国法である場合には同法が適用される（傭船契約のプロパー・ローについては，後出508頁を参照）。表示を信頼してはならないことを意味する条項は，同法第8条第1項により無効とされた（*Cremdean Properties* v. *Nash* (1977) 244 E. G. 547 事件と *Smith* v. *Eric S. Bush* [1990] 1 A. C. 831 事件）。しかし代理人が表示をする権限を否定する条項は，*Overbrooke Estates* v. *Glencombe Properties* [1974] 1 W. L. R. 1335 事件で同法により無効となった。*Walker* v. *Boyle* [1982] 1 W. L. R. 495 事件も参照。修正前の多少異なる同法の規定が適用された海運事件は *Howard Marine* v. *Ogden* [1978] 1 Lloyd's Rep. 334 事件である。

契約の一部となる不実表示

通常，不実表示は契約締結前になされ，契約までの時間的隔たりのゆえに，あるいは口頭証拠は書面契約の条件を否定したり変更できないという法則（口頭証拠の法則）のゆえに不実表示が契約の中に摂取されたとみなすことはできない。しかし，時には交渉の過程で不実表示は繰り返され，最後には契約の一部となることもある。また，契約は一部書面で一部口頭によると判示されるので，時には不実表示は契約の一条件として取り扱われ，口頭証拠の法則は適用されない。*The Ardennes*（1950）84 Ll. L. Rep. 340事件と *Evans v. Merzario*［1976］2 Lloyd's Rep. 165事件を参照。さらに，不実表示は付随契約の一側面として取り扱われることもある（前出134頁参照）。その場合，訴訟は（書面の主契約との不一致にかかわらず）付随契約ではなく主契約によって維持される（*City and Westminster Properties v. Mudd*［1959］Ch. 129事件参照）。

不実表示が契約に摂取される場合に，契約違反の通常の救済手段（後出137頁参照）が与えられ，通常それは十分である。しかし，不法行為に基づいて訴訟を提起する権利は残ると思われる。しかも，その権利は過失の挙証を条件とするが，時において例えば損害の査定，裁判管轄，出訴期限等に関して，有利となる（*Henderson v. Merrett Syndicates*［1994］2 Lloyd's Rep. 193事件と *Midland Bank Trust v. Hett, Stubbs and Kemp*［1979］Ch. 384事件参照）。さらに，不実表示が契約条件になるという事実は，不実表示を受けた当事者により契約解除を妨げないと，1967年法第1条で規定している。例えば，傭船契約の当該特定条項は条件ではないという事実にもかかわらず，また不実表示の違反は傭船契約の根源に達するほどに重大ではないという事実にもかかわらず，交渉の過程で船主が本船名を不実表示したために，傭船者は，傭船契約を放棄することができるかも知れない。しかし，仲裁人あるいは裁判所は実務上第2条第2項に基づく裁量権を旨く行使し，契約解除の代わりに損害賠償を裁定してもよいであろう。詐欺的不実記載の場合に，傭船者は傭船契約への不実表示の摂取にかかわらず傭船契約を放棄する権利を前出のように持つ。そして第2条第2項は適用されない。

契約の条項

傭船契約のある条項は明確に，あるできごとが発生することの約束である。例えば，ニューヨーク・プロデュース書式の第1条から第5条はこの種類の約束である。他の条項は，約束として表現されていないが，同書式の4行から11行のような表示として書かれている。しかし，表示者は表示が真実であると約束するとみなされるかも知れないという点で，この条項はそれでも契約上の約束として扱われることもある。したがって，例えば「この傭船契約に基づく船積準備完了見込」は *The Mihalis Angelos*［1970］2 Lloyd's Rep. 43事件で，その見込は妥当と考えられる（その条項の違反による損害賠償を計算する方法に疑問あるが）約束を含むと判示された。

"De minimis" の原則（「些細なことを問わない」という原則）

商事契約における契約上の義務に違反があったか否かを考察する場合，契約上要求される履行行為からの取るに足らない程度の逸脱は無視される（*Margaronis Navigation v. Peabody*［1964］2 Lloyd's Rep. 153）。

同事件で，Sellers卿判事は，「すべての事件において，裁判所に求められるのは，物事の本

質を考慮することであり，裁判所から見て，疑うまでもなく，些細な，取り上げるに足りない，無視してもよい事柄を考慮したり，取り上げたりすることではない」と述べた。Diplock卿判事は，「一定数量の物品を引き渡すか，船積する旨の契約において，現実に引き渡し，船積された数量が，取引実務上，避けられない誤差の範囲内であれば，その契約の履行があったと法はみなしてきたと思われる」と述べた。

87 契約違反の救済方法

損害賠償

英国法において契約違反に基づく基本的救済方法は損害賠償請求の訴訟である。

特定履行命令と差止命令

　船舶賃貸借契約の事件では見解は異なるが，定期傭船契約の特定履行は通常認められない（*De Mattos* v. *Gibson* (1858) 4 De G. & J. 276 事件と *The Scaptrade* [1983] 2 Lloyd's Rep. 253 (同判例集256頁) 事件を参照。*The Stena Nautica* (*No. 2*) [1982] 2 Lloyd's Rep. 336 事件を比較)。
　さらに，裁判所は，船主が定期傭船契約の引揚条項に基づき，傭船者の役務からの本船引揚権の行使を抑止する差止命令を付与する裁判権を有しない。船舶賃貸借契約の場合の見解はこれと異なる。Diplock卿は貴族院の *The Scaptrade* [1983] 2 Lloyd's Rep. 253 事件で傍論として，権利喪失についての衡平法上の救済方法は定期傭船契約の引揚条項に基づく本船の引揚には適用されないと判示した。後出317頁参照。同卿は報告書の256頁で次のように言った。「今回関係のない船舶賃貸借契約でない限り，定期傭船契約は，船舶の所有権あるいは占有権を傭船者に譲渡するものではない。定期傭船契約は，船主自身の被用者，船長と乗組員による船舶の使用を通じて船主により傭船者に提供される役務の契約であり，傭船者は，傭船契約書の条件により引き受けられた貨物積込と航海に関する指図を彼らに与えることができ，彼らはその指図に従って行動しなければならない。形式上否定形ではあるが，傭船者の役務から本船を引き揚げる権利を船主が行使するのを抑止する差止命令を付与することは契約履行についての船主への肯定的命令を含む。法律上，それは役務を提供する契約の特定履行の判決と区別がつかない。契約のこの範疇に関して違反がある場合でさえ，これが英国の裁判所がいつも付与する裁判権を否認してきた救済方法である」。
　それでも，傭船契約の履行を妨げるような方法で船主または本船のその他の利害関係者による本船の使用を抑制する仮差止命令を付与する慣行には長い歴史がある（*De Mattos* v. *Gibson* (1858) 4 De G. & J. 276, 299 事件，*Sevin* v. *Deslands* (1860) 30 L. J. (Ch.) 457 事件と *Whitwood Chemical Co.* v. *Hardman* [1891] 2 Ch. 416, 431 事件と後出146頁を参照)。そこで，船主が傭船契約から本船を引き揚げた，あるいは引き揚げると脅かし，傭船者が船主の引揚権を争ったときに，船主は傭船契約に従うのとは別の方法で本船の使用を抑制された。そういう事件では，紛争が審理に付され決定されるまでの間，仮差止命令が出された。目的は紛争が解決するまで現状を保持することである（*The Georgios C* [1971] 1 Lloyd's Rep. 7 事件，*The Oakworth* [1975] 1 Lloyd's Rep. 581 事件，*The Balder London* (*No. 2*) [1983] 1 Lloyd's Rep. 492 事件を参照)。この条件で仮差止命令を付与する権限が前出 *The Scaptrade* 事件でのDiplock卿の判決により影響を受けるとは思われない。しかし，「船主が傭船者の役務から本船

を引き揚げるのを抑止する」(例えば *The Chrysovalandou Dyo* [1981] 1 Lloyd's Rep. 159, 162 事件参照) との表現による差止命令は現在では裁判所が付与する権限ではないと思われる。

契約を消滅したものとして扱う権利

　契約違反が十分に重大な場合に，善意の当事者は「契約を消滅したものとして扱い」あるいは「契約を否認として扱い」，履行を拒否しあるいはそれ以降の履行を拒否し，支払った金額を，または譲渡した財産を回収するために出訴することができる。この過程は時に，契約の
88 「終了 termination」「解約 cancellation」あるいは「解除 rescission」としても言及される。しかし，これは契約の交渉過程の不実表示に基づく契約解除と同じではない (前出参照)。善意の当事者の権利が一般原則ではなく契約自身の厳密な条項に拠る場合に，それは契約上合意されかつ契約により与えられた特定の権利に沿った終了または解約と同じではない (傭船契約上の解約の権利については，後出419頁を参照，傭船引揚条項については後出314頁参照)。

　契約を消滅したとみなす権利は契約違反に基づく損害賠償の権利を損なわないことに注目すべきである。支払われる損害賠償額は，実際，契約を消滅したとみなす権利の行使により増大する。支払われる損害賠償額は，契約のすべてあるいは契約の残りの部分の損失を塡補し，契約が継続していれば，契約違反により生じたであろう損失を単に塡補するものではない。法律上契約違反が，善意の当事者にその権利を与えるほどには十分に重大ではない場合に，善意の当事者が契約を消滅されたとみなそうとするならば，善意の当事者は履行の拒絶という契約違反に自らを置き，広範囲な損害賠償責任に曝される。後出148頁の *The Hongkong Fir* [1961] 2 Lloyd's Rep. 478 事件参照。相手側が履行するあるいは履行を継続することができるか不確かであるという理由だけで，履行を停止する権利はコモン・ロー上一般にはない。しかし，特別条項は，履行を停止する権利を与えるかも知れない。後出427頁のオフハイヤー条項を参照。そしてある事件では契約が当事者に履行を留保する権利を与えると純粋に確信して，かつ当事者には自己の義務の拒絶の意図が全然なく当事者は履行を留保することがあるかもしれない (*Woodar* v. *Wimpey* [1980] 1 W. L. R. 277の建築事件を参照。しかし後出306頁の *The Nanfri* [1979] 1 Lloyd's Rep. 201 の傭船契約事件比較)。

契約条件 (contractual terms) の分類

　善意の当事者が契約を消滅されたものとして扱う権利を持つか否かを決定する際に，違反を生じた契約条件 (contractual terms) の性質に最初に注意を払われなければならないように思われる。*Bunge* v. *Tradax* [1981] 2 Lloyd's Rep. 1 事件参照。このために違反を生じた条件 (the breached term) は3個の範疇のどれかに分けられる。つまり，条件 (*conditions*)，担保 (*warranties*)，および中間的条件 (*intermediate or innominate terms*) である。この分類は，具体的事件で生じたその条件 (that term) の違反の重大さを考慮するよりも，外観上の契約と個別の条件 (the particular term) を解釈して行われる (前出 *Bunge* v. *Tradax* 事件参照)。

条件 (conditions)

　ここでいう条件 (a condition) (この言葉の他の用例は後出参照) とはいかなるその違反も，善意の当事者に全契約を消滅したとして扱う権利を与えるほど重要な契約条件 (a term of the contract) である (*Photo Production* v. *Securicor* [1980] 1 Lloyd's Rep. 545 (同判例

集553頁）事件における Diplock 卿の発言によれば「契約違反から事実上，結果として生じるできごとの重要性にかかわらず……当事者の一方による特定の……義務の**いかなる**不履行も，もう一方の当事者に両者の未履行のあらゆる……義務を終わらせることを選択する権利が生じるものとすることを法の黙示によると，あるいは法の明示の文言によるとを問わず，契約の当事者が合意した」場合に，この条件が生じる。契約条件（the contractual terms）が分類される状況に関する注釈については後出参照）。

担保（warranties）

ここでいう担保（この言葉の他の用例は後出参照）とは，そのいかなる違反も，善意の当事者に全契約を消滅したとして扱う権利を与え**ない**ほどに重要でない契約条件（a term of the contract）である。この条件（a term）の違反に対して善意の当事者は損害賠償請求をすることができるだけである。条件（the term）のこの使用は1893年動産販売法（現在では1979年動産販売法）の後で重要となった。

中間的（または無名の）条件（intermediate or innominate terms）

条件（a condition）あるいは担保（warranties）として分類できない契約条件（any term of the contract）は中間的（または無名の）条件（intermediate or innominate terms）として分類される。この条件（a term）の違反により，善意の相手方が契約を消滅したものとして扱うことができるかできないかは発生した個別の契約違反の性質と，結果次第である。裁判所は，前出 *Photo Production* v. *Securicor* 事件の報告書553頁で，Diplock 卿の言葉によれば，「その結果として生じるできごとが……当事者たちの意図であったが，契約から獲得しようとした**すべての利益を実質的に**相手方から奪う効果を持つ」かどうかを調査するであろう。そのできごとがこの効果を持つならば，善意の当事者は契約を消滅したものとして扱うことができる。さもなくば損害賠償請求ができるに過ぎない。しかし，違反の結果は後出148頁の *Hongkong Fir* 事件の事実に示されるように大変に重大でなければならない。

「条件 condition」という語の他の使用法

前出説明のように，個別条件（a particular term）の表示として「条件（condition）」という語の使用は，英国法の特別の用法としてよく確立しているが，それは「約束（promises）」と「条件（condition）」の一般概念を混同するのでいくぶん不十分であることが注目される。契約を着手する他方の当事者の義務の条件（the condition）は，実際に契約上の約束（promise）の履行（あるいは約束を履行する自発性）である。

「条件（condition）」という語は他の意味で使用されるので，その語を使う判決や契約は注意して読むことが重要である。契約条件（a contractual term）は語のより正確な意味で「条件（a condition）」として存在するので，このことは格別にそうなのである。すなわち，ある事象が起こるとの約束（promise）はされていないが，それが起こらなければ，行為の原因は生じない。しかし相手側に契約の自分側の約束（bargain）を履行する義務は生じない。さらに他の意味は，「細目を条件として」傭船する事例のように，契約実行の停止条件の意味である（前出102頁参照）。

「担保」という語の他の使用法

ここに使用される意味では担保は単に重要でない契約上の約束（promise）を意味する。海上保険契約ではその使用法はまったく異なる。「担保」は，この方法で確かに分類されない契

約上の義務を記述するために，また特に昔の事件で使用される」。堪航性に関する条件（terms）はこの文脈では中間的（または無名の）条件（intermediate or innominate terms）であるゆえ，「堪航性の担保」の表現は，特に誤解を招いている（The Hongkong Fir [1961] 2 Lloyd's Rep. 478 事件と The Ymnos [1982] 2 Lloyd's Rep. 574 事件と後出148頁参照）。

　担保の分類を中間的（または無名の）条件（intermediate or innominate terms）から独立して維持することにほとんど価値がないという議論があるかもしれない。なぜなら，契約条件（a contractual term）の違反は，善意の当事者が契約を消滅したものとすることを正当化するには十分に重大でないことが前もって決せられる場合に，その条件（that term）は担保ではなく，中間的（または無名の）条件（intermediate or innominate terms）と分類されても正当な結果が同様に旨く達成されるであろうからである。The Hansa Nord [1975] 2 Lloyd's Rep. 445（同判例集466頁）事件で，Ormrod 卿判事の判決は，担保の独立分類は実際色あせていると言った。しかし Bunge v. Tradax [1981] 2 Lloyd's Rep. 1 事件で貴族院は，この独立分類の存在を当然のことと考えた。この文脈で「担保」の語に帰属する意味を評価することは依然として重要である。

90　商業的確定性の欲求と公正の欲求との間の衝突

　The Honkong Fir [1961] 2 Lloyd's Rep. 478 事件から Bunge v. Tradax [1981] 2 Lloyd's Rep. 1 事件までの指導的先例から裁判所は，商業契約の当事者の関係に確定性があるべきであるという原則と，当事者間の公正は過度に厳格な規則に妨げられてはならないという原則のときに，相反する原則の均衡をとろうとしているように見える。契約のある条件（certain terms）のいかなる違反も，善意の当事者が契約を消滅したものとして扱うことを許容するという（事前に入手可能な）知識は，その違反またはその結果の重大性についての結果の検証の必要がない場合には，確定性を促進し，条件（conditions）の概念を維持することを正当化する。

　一方，違反は厳密な法解釈によるものであり，かつ，実際には当事者に損害を与えていないという事実にもかかわらず，条件（a condition）が破られたがゆえに当事者は不利な契約であると判明したことから逃れるという事実から，より多くの条件（many terms）は，条件（conditions）としてではなく中間的条件として分類されることが示されている。The Hansa Nord [1975] 2 Lloyd's Rep. 445（同判例集457頁）事件で Roskill 卿判事が述べたように，「原則的として，契約が締結されるのは履行のためであり，気まぐれな市場の変動に応じて回避されないためである」。この考え方は，違反の結果がそれを正当化するほどに重大でないならば，契約から逃れることを許容しない。適用される基準（前出138頁参照）は，契約を消滅したものとして扱うことに全然好意的ではない。したがって24ヶ月の定期傭船契約の The Hongkong Fir 事件（後出148頁参照）において，本船を，不堪航の理由で最初の6ヶ月の内のある20週間を傭船者は使用できなかったが，違反は傭船契約の消滅を正当化するほどに重大ではない（その期間の終わりに不堪航は修正された）と判示された。この考え方は，違反は契約消滅を許容するほどに重大であるか否かはしばらくの間判らないとの批判をも免れない。事実が明白なときでさえ，仲裁または訴訟の長い過程は善意の当事者の権利を決定するために必要であるかも知れない。

　裁判所が現在求めているこの二つの原則の均衡は，Bunge v. Tradax [1981] 2 Lloyd's Rep. 1 （同判例集14頁）事件の Roskill 卿の解説で説明されている。「簡単に言えば，近代的考え方を認識し，かつ契約が裁判所にそうすることを明らかに要求しない限り，条件（terms）を条件（conditions）としてあまりにも容易に解釈しがちであるというのではなく，それにもかか

わらず特定の条件（a particular term）が条件（a condition）であるか否かを決定するための解釈の基本原則は以前と同じである。常に一方で確定性の必要を留意し、また他方で訴えられた契約違反はあまりに厳密な法解釈によるものであり、かつ損害賠償が十分な救済手段であることが明白である場合には、契約解除を合法であっても認めないことが望ましい、と常に銘記している」。

条件（terms）が条件（conditions）として扱われるとき

前出 Bunge v. Tradax 事件で、貴族院は6頁の Wilberforce 卿の言葉で「裁判所は契約条項を条件（conditions）として解釈しがちであってはならない」ことを明らかにした。しかし条件（terms）は次の事例に分類される

1. 義務が制定法に条件（a condition）として指定されている場合。これは定期傭船契約法には関係ない。しかし実例として1979年動産販売法の13、14および15条を参照。
2. 義務が契約に条件（a condition）として明確に指定されている場合。しかしこれは決定的ではない。全契約の文脈が、「条件 condition」という言葉はその厳密な法解釈の意味で読まれてはならないことを示すこともある。Wickman v. Schuler [1973] 2 Lloyd's Rep. 53 事件参照。
3. 義務が他の事案では条件（a condition）であると判示された場合。The Mihalis Angelos [1970] 2 Lloyd's Rep. 43事件では、航海傭船契約の「積込準備完了予定」の条項は部分的にはこれを根拠としての条件（a condition）であると判示された。しかし The Diana Prosperity [1976] 2 Lloyd's Rep. 621（同判例集626頁）事件で Wilberforce 卿は、動産販売の過去の事件のいくつかは再考を必要とすると提言した。そして同卿は契約の他の類型に触れなかったが、この点に関する初期の判例法の確定性が必ずしも当然のことと思われないことは明白である。
4. 契約の条件（the terms）と一般的背景から示唆されるように、当事者の想定される意図がそう示す場合、前出 Bunge v. Tradax 事件で、Wilberforce 卿は、これは通常「商業契約の期間条項」の事例のそれであると示した。そして Roskill 卿は「他の条件（another term）を他方の当事者に履行可能ならしめる停止条件として、ある条件（a term）（その事件では船積港を指定する販売業者の義務の停止条件として f.o.b. 購入業者が本船の U. S. Gulf の到着予定時間を表示すること）が一方の当事者により履行されねばならない場合、」同じことは真実であると言った。The Mavro Vetranic [1985] 1 Lloyd's Rep. 580 事件（「到着予定時間より20日早く」運送契約に基づき船舶の指定がなされる）と Gill & Duffus v. Société pour l'Exportation des Sucres S. A. [1986] 1 Lloyd's Rep. 322事件（船積港が「遅くとも at latest」という所与の日付までに特定される）参照。他の契約の履行は（「連鎖」販売のように）考慮中の契約の履行に拠るという事実は、今一つ別の示唆である。

The Hongkong Fir 事件に先立つ事件で、（傭船者の本船使用目的に関連して、非常に重要な）タンカーの貨油管や加熱管の個々の明細が、船主によって「保証された guaranteed」場合、この部分の表示は、傭船契約の条件（conditions）であると判示された。

タンカー Vendémiaire 号は、7月15日を解約期日として、12ヶ月間傭船された。契約交渉過程において本船の貨油管の直径および加熱管の位置が表示され、それは、船主が「保証した」ものとして、傭船契約にもりこまれた。これらの事項は、糖蜜輸送という本船の使用目的に照らして、傭船者にとっては、非常に重要であった。6月11日および12日、本船の貨油管および加熱管は、傭船者の監督

により検査され，表示に合致していないことが発見された。そこで，早速，傭船者は，本船を受領する義務はないが，船舶が表示どおりとなれば，引渡を受ける用意がある旨，船主に通告した。船主は，改装を実施することなく，6月25日引渡を申し出た。傭船者は，本船が表示に合致していないという理由で，これを拒絶した。船主は，（改装工事をせずに，）傭船者に対して，本船の引取を主張し続けたが，傭船者は6月30日傭船契約を解約した。

Branson 判事は，傭船者が解約の権利を持つと判示した。同判事は，「『保証（guarantee）』という文言は，……この条項から発生する契約上の義務を特別強調し，これを単なる担保（warranties）と区別して，契約の条件（conditions）として取り扱う意思を示したものと考えられる」と述べた。

Pennsylvania Shipping v. Cie Nationale de Navigation (1936) 55 Ll.L. Rep. 271.

今日，同様な事件が裁判所に出されるようなことがあれば，結論が同じであろうことに疑問はないが，Pennsylvania Shipping 事件で条件（conditions）として分類された本船の貨油管と加熱管の保証された明細を含む条項は中間的条件（intermediate terms）として分類されてもよいであろう。本船は傭船者のコンテナサービスに定期傭船された The Ymnos [1982] 2 Lloyd's Rep. 574 事件で，傭船契約には「船主は船舶の安定性に問題なく……コンテナの積取を保証する」との条件（a term）があった。実際には安定性に問題があったが，問題は船積の最終段階または揚荷の最初の段階に関係しており，それは実際，軽微であり，或いは重大であるのかも知れない。その問題は陸上起重機の使用で救済されるか，あるいは起重機が手に入らなければ，多少のコンテナの積取を取り止める結果となろう。The Honkgkong Fir 事件を先例として，Robert Goff 判事は，その条件（the term）は，ことの重大性如何を変更する違反の一つであるので，条件（a condition）として分類するのは適当ではないと判示した。「保証」という語の使用はコンテナの契約本数の積込作業中の安定性の問題が，船主による契約違反となるということを，問題の条項で意味するに過ぎない。それは条項が中間的条件（an intermediate term）としてより，条件（a condition）として解釈されることにはならない。

一方の当事者が契約を終了することを許容する条項（a clause）（例えば，引揚条項，解約条項）により契約条項（stipulation）が強化されるという事実によって，契約条項（stipulation）が条件（a condition）であることをどの程度意味するのか明確ではない。The Mihalis Angelos [1970] 1 Lloyd's Rep. 118 の第1審事件で，Mocatta 判事は，解約条項の存在を，「船積準備完了見込」条項は条件（a condition）では**ない**という結論に近いものとして扱った。この決定は，控訴院により逆転された。しかし，原則として，そういう解約条項は受益当事者のための特別条項であり，契約義務の基準を黙示的に限定しないことは明白である。The Heron II [1967] 2 Lloyd's Rep. 457（同判例集486頁）事件参照（航海傭船契約の解約条項は合理的な早出しの義務を排除するような時間の尺度を設定していない）。定期傭船契約の引揚条項の性質については後出327頁参照。

条件（the term）が破られ，大きなさまざまな変化の結果が生じる場合，その条件（the term）が条件（a condition）として解釈されることはありそうにもない。The Hongkong Fir 事件の指導的判例では，定期傭船契約の堪航性に関する条項はそういう根拠で，中間的条件（an intermediate term）として解釈された（後出148頁参照。そして Toepfer v. Lenersan-Poortman [1978] 2 Lloyd's Rep. 555（原審維持 [1980] 1 Lloyd's Rep. 143）事件によるこの判例の説明参照）。

権利放棄と確約

相手方の契約違反により，契約を消滅したものとして扱う権利のある当事者は，その違反を

「無視 waives」する場合，その権利を喪失することになるかも知れない。例として，The Aegean Dolphin [1992] 2 Lloyd's Rep. 178 事件を参照。船舶は想定された航海を履行するのに必要な速力を出すことができないにもかかわらず，本船は「傭船契約上の義務の履行のための条件を完全に満している」という書面を定期傭船者が受諾していたがために，速力を出せないことは契約の根幹にかかわることであったが，傭船者は後刻本船の引渡を拒否することはできなかった。これは違反に基づき権利を付与する特定の契約条件（contract terms）の放棄にも適用される。したがって，傭船者が期日に傭船料を支払えなかったがゆえに，ニューヨーク・プロデュース書式の第5条により本船を引き揚げる選択権を行使できることとなった船主は，船主がその権利を放棄したと判示されれば，引き揚げる権利を喪失する。後出319から322頁参照。

善意の当事者が契約を消滅したものとして扱う権利と同様に違反に基づく損害賠償の権利を放棄することも可能である。原則として，このような権利の完全な放棄を，拘束力あらしめるためには，約因，つまり見返りとして何かがなされるか，あるいは何かが約束されることを必要とする。しかし，善意の当事者が違反した当事者に，自分はこの権利を行使しないと表示した場合には，いわゆる「衡平法上の禁反言」または「約束に基づく禁反言」という異なる理由に基づき，裁判所は「当事者間で行われた交渉に注目してそれが不公平である場合に」善意の当事者がこの表示に戻ることを妨げる（Hughes v. Metropolitan Railway (1877) 2 App. Cas. 439（同判例集448頁）事件の Cairns 卿による。Birmingham & District Land v. L. N. W. R. (1888) 40 Ch. D. 268 事件も参照）。The Kanchenjunga [1990] 1 Lloyd's Rep. 391（同判例集399頁）事件で Goff of Chieveley 卿は，このことを役に立つ形で次のように説明している。「衡平法上の禁反言は，他者に対して法的権利を持つ者が自らはこの法的権利を強く主張しないことを明白に（言葉あるいは行動で）表示する場合に，生じる。その状況の下で相手方がその表示を信頼して行動する，あるいは行動を思い止まるならば，表示者は，その後で表示者が自分の法的権利を表示と矛盾して主張することは，不公平であるという効力の範囲で，権利を主張することを妨げられる。表示者の側の個別の知識についての疑問は生じないし，かつ禁反言は中止的効力を有するに過ぎない」（The Post Chaser [1981] 2 Lloyd's Rep. 695（同判例集701頁）事件も参照）。

違反の当事者がこれまで考えていたこと以上に限定的な主張，つまり，善意の当事者は（損害賠償を請求する権利を未決定のままとして）契約を消滅したとして扱う権利のみを放棄した，あるいは（違反に際して生じるかどうかにかかわらず）ある契約条項に基づき契約を終了する権利のみを放棄したと主張する場合，裁判所が違反の当事者に要求することはより少ない。このより制限された意味で放棄は「確約」つまり契約の継続的存在の確約，しかし損害賠償請求の権利の放棄を伴わないものとして言及される。この種の放棄は契約を維持するか終了させるかの「選択」から生じると考えられ，いったん放棄されれば撤回することができない。The Mihalios Xilas [1979] 2 Lloyd's Rep. 303（後出322頁参照）事件で，Scarman 卿はこの方法で船主が傭船料の不払に対してボルタイム傭船契約書式の第6条に基づく本船を引き揚げる権利を放棄したかどうかの問題に対応した。「本事件は，選択の過程に関係がある。それが立証されるのであれば，選択の結果は放棄である。つまり，権利の放棄……二者択一で相互に排他的な行為の方針に直面した人は，一つを選択し，彼が選択したことを関係者に信じさせるような方法で関係者に自己の選択を通知したときに，彼は選択を完了したことになる」。前出 The Kanchenjunga 事件で Goff 判事はさらに「一度行われた彼の選択は最終的なものである。それは相手側がそれを信頼したかどうかにはかかっていない」と指摘した。

しかし，契約が消滅したとして扱う権利を持つ者は，彼が違反についての実際の知識や（た

ぶん）選択の権利についての知識を持っていない限り，権利を放棄することを選択したと判示されることはないであろう。Peyman v. Lanjani [1985] Ch. 457 事件と The Uhenbels [1986] 2 Lloyd's Rep. 294（同判例集298頁）事件を参照。しかし，それにもかかわらず禁反言は関連し，自分の権利を知らなかった者が自分は選択しなかったと主張することは禁じられる。困難でかつ議論の多い（Panchaud Frères v. Etablissements General Grain [1970] 1 Lloyd's Rep. 53 事件と前出 Peyman v. Lanjani 事件参照）。これにはもちろん，前出の衡平法上の禁反言の事件の場合と同じように，信頼が要求される。

個々の記載事項

本船が表示を遵守すべき時期

　全般に，傭船契約中の本船についての表示は，傭船契約締結時点で正しい内容でなくてはならない。ただし，速力については，本船は引渡のときに表示どおりでなければならないと言われている（後出「速力と燃料消費」参照）。船主の義務は，契約締結時に表示どおりの特性を持った本船を提供することであるという見解の方が妥当であると言われている。しかし，そこには，船主が契約締結時以降，本船の特性を変更して，傭船者に提供する役務を約定と違うものにしたり，より不利益なものにしないという黙示的条項があると言うべきである（(1921) 6 Ll.L. Rep. 289 と後出147頁の Isaacs v. McAllum 事件参照）。

表示に合致しない本船の引渡

　本船が傭船契約書に船主により不実記載されるとか，引渡前または引渡時に不実記載が発見された場合に，引渡を拒絶されるのか，傭船者は引渡を受けて，不実記載の結果として被る損害を賠償請求しなければならないのかという問題が生じる。回答は，不正確な表示の要素と不実記載の重要性しだいであると思われる。

　後出の The Diana Prosperity [1976] 2 Lloyd's Rep. 60 および621事件で，事実関係をある種の動産販売契約から類推して本船の表示のどの部分の不正確さにより傭船者は引渡を拒絶することができ，契約を消滅したものとして扱うことができるかということが論じられた。この類推により，表示の各要素は重要であると考えられ，ゆえにそれは，その違反により（違反の重大さにかかわらず）傭船者がその違反を拒絶できる契約の条件（a condition）であるに違いない。

94　控訴院での記録長官 Denning 卿も貴族院で，Wilberforce 卿もこの弁論を受け入れなかった。（Simon 卿も Kilbrandon 卿も同意したが，）Wilberforce 卿は，動産販売の過去の事件は再検討されなければならないことであろうが，ともかく過去の事件は定期傭船契約には応用されないという意見を表明した。その見解では，本船の表示の中で本船の「同一性確認」の「実質的要素」であると言える部分のみが契約の条件（conditions）であるとみなしうる（[1976] 2 Lloyd's Rep.（同判例集626頁）参照。「条件（conditions）」の意味については前出138頁参照）。

　本船の表示の要素が条件でない限り，下記のいずれかの場合には，傭船者は引渡を拒絶し，契約を終了したものとして扱う権利のみを持つように思える。

(1) 不実記載の全体の効果は重大で，契約の根本を揺るがし，契約の全利益を実質的に傭船者から奪う（The Diana Prosperity [1976] 2 Lloyd's Rep.（同判例集72頁と627頁）事件と

Cargo Ships El-Yam v. *Invotra* [1958] 1 Lloyd's Rep. 39（同判例集52頁）事件参照)。
(2) 船主が本船を表示に合致するような手段を講じることを拒絶するか,またはその履行ができず,そしてその拒絶または不履行により,契約に拘束されない意思を示し,傭船契約の拒絶となる（後出150頁参照）。
(3) 不実記載は,船主が解約期日までに解約条項の目的のための準備または適合性の要件を満たせないほどのものである。それにより,傭船者は解約する（後出151頁参照）。

船　　名

傭船契約は表示された船名の船舶のみを目的としており,たとえ同一の特性を持っていても,船名の異なる船の受取を傭船者に要求することはできない。しかしその傭船契約がこれから建造され命名される船舶に対するものである場合,引渡のため提供された船舶は,船舶を特定するために傭船契約に用いられた文言と番号から,契約の目的物になるべき船舶を特定することができれば,契約に合致しているとみなされる。

　　建造予定の船舶の管理船主 (Disponent owners) が同船を Shelltime 3 書式により定期傭船に出し,傭船契約書に,その船舶を「大阪造船株式会社によって建造されるものとし,命名まで,Hull No. 354と称する」と表示した。傭船者は同じ書式でその船舶を再傭船に出し,再傭船契約書に「大阪造船で Yard No. 354と呼ばれる新造モータータンカー」として記載した。大阪造船は帳簿上その番号の船を有していたが,事実は,大阪造船にとって,この船舶は大き過ぎて建造することができず,日本の別の造船所,大島造船に下請に出された。この造船所は300マイル離れていたが,大阪造船とは実質的な財政上および経営上の関係を有し,大阪造船はこの船舶の建造を指揮する立場にあった。この取決めは日本における慣行に従ったものであった。船舶は依然大阪造船の帳簿上 No. 354であったが,大島造船の No. 004 も付されていた。貴族院は,原傭船者,再傭船者のいずれも,その船舶の受取を拒否することはできないと判示した。たとえそれが,船舶は表示に厳密に合致すべしという条件であった（多数意見はそうではないと判断したが）としても,この二つの傭船契約書における当該文言は,船舶の表示の本質的部分としてではなく,船舶を識別する手段としてのみの意味を持っていた。Wilberforce 卿は次のように述べた。「問題は単に,特定の手段として,その船舶が,事実上,大阪造船 Yard No. 254とか『大阪造船株式会社により建造され,命名まで Hull No. 354』と言いうるかどうかに過ぎない。……事実,同船は大島 No. 4 でもあったが,終始大阪 Hull No. 354であったし,その建造の設計,手配,指揮は大阪造船株式会社がやっており,同社によって,『建造』されたということは明らかである。……識別条項として,当該文言は事実を十分示しており,他の船舶を示すことはあり得ず,まさに当該船舶を示す適当な文言である」。
　　The Diana Prosperity [1976] 2 Lloyd's Rep. 621.
　　(*Sanko Steamship* v. *Kano Trading* [1978] 1 Lloyd's Rep. 156 事件参照)

95 代　　船

他の船舶あるいは複数の船舶が当初特定された船舶の代わりに提供されることに合意するかどうかは当事者が決定する問題である。

　　タンカー *Driade* 号は約13ヶ月の期間,履行可能な限りの多くの連続航海のために傭船され,船主は「この傭船契約開始前またはその期間,いつでも同じような大きさで同じような位置にいるコイル付きの船舶を代船とする……」自由を持っていた。船主は第1航海の開始前に,*Driade* 号の代わりに似た姉妹船 *Nayade* 号を提供した。その後傭船期間中 *Nayade* 号は修理を行うことが必要となり,

船主は Driade 号を代船として提案した。傭船者は，自由条項は1回のみの代船を許容するものと主張し，代船受入を拒絶した。Devlin 判事と控訴院は，次のように判示した。自由条項は傭船契約の長さと当該条項の商業目的のいずれかに注目して解釈されるけれども，船主には都合の良いときにいつでも代船を提供する権利があるという意図は明白である。

Société Anonyme Maritime et Commerciale v. Anglo-Iranian Oil [1953] 2 Lloyd's Rep. 466 および [1954] 1 Lloyd's Rep. 1 (C. A.).

(Société Navale de L'Ouest v. Sutherland (1920) 4 Ll. L. Rep. 58, 185 事件――傭船の代わりに「相当程度類似の」船舶を代船として提供する義務)

当事者は，また傭船期間開始前，期間中，指定船舶または代船の滅失後のいずれのときでも代船の提供に合意しうる。しかし，船舶滅失後の代船提供の権利を確保する目的のためには，特別に明白な語が使用されねばならない。さもなくば，傭船契約は本船の滅失により履行不能となったと判示され，代船の権利は傭船契約の終了と共に終了するであろう。

Badagry 号は8年間傭船された。傭船契約の第33条は「船主はこの傭船契約期間中類似の種類・大きさの船舶を代船とする選択権を有する」と規定していた。傭船契約書はさらに第3条(d)項に「……本船は推定全損となれば，傭船料の支払はその滅失に帰した海難事故の発生時点から止まる……」と規定していた。Badagry 号は，9月27日頃に推定全損となった。10月17日に船主は Badagry 号の代船として Bonny 号を提供しようとした。控訴院は，第3条(d)項は推定全損後の傭船契約の継続と一致しない，傭船契約は10月17日以前に履行不能となり，傭船契約の終了とともに代船の権利は消滅したと判示した。

The Badagry [1985] 1 Lloyd's Rep. 395.

(「傭船者の承認を条件として」代船を提供する権利に関する事件については，[1961] 2 Lloyd's Rep. 496 と後出464頁の Niarchos v. Shell Tankers 事件参照)

売　船

Sorrentino v. Buerger [1915] 3 K. B. 367 (C. A.) 事件と Isaacs v. McAllum (1921) 6 Ll. L. Rep. 289 事件から，傭船期間中に船主が本船を売却することはそれだけでは傭船契約違反ではないように思われる（結果として起こる国籍変更の効力については後出147頁参照）。ただし，原船主は傭船契約上負っているあらゆる義務の履行につき傭船者に対して継続して責任を負う。

本船の購入者が傭船契約の存在を実際に知りながら，本船を取得した場合，傭船者は傭船契約以外の方法による購入者の本船の使用を抑制する差止命令の権利を持つかもしれない。Lord Strathcona v. Dominion Coal (1925) 23 Ll.L. Rep. 145 事件におけるこの効力についての枢密院の決定は，Port Line v. Ben Line [1958] 2 Q. B. 146 事件における Diplock 判事により，誤りであると言われている。しかしごく最近の事件である Swiss Bank v. Lloyds Bank [1979] Ch. 548事件で，Browne-Wilkinson 判事は枢密院は正しいという見解を表明した。ただし同事件に関する彼の判決は控訴院（[1982] A. C. 584 (C. A. and H. L.)）により他の理由で破棄された。De Mattos v. Gibson (1858) 4 De G. & J. 276 事件（本船の担保権者による傭船契約への介入を抑制する差止命令を付与することに関する事件）で次のように述べた（同判例集282頁）。勲爵士 Bruce 卿判事が設定した原則を Browne-Wilkinson 判事は，特によりどころとした。

「道理と公正は，先行する契約の存在を知りながら合法的に第三者に約因の対価として，特別の方

法により特別の目的で財物を使用するためにある者が贈与または購入により他者から財物を取得する場合には，少なくとも一般的規則は取得者が第三者に実質的損害を与えて先行する契約に反したり，矛盾して，贈与者または販売者が認めない方法で財物を使用してはならないことを規定するように思われる」。

 Browne-Wilkinson 判事はこの衡平法の原則を，契約上の権利への故意の介入という不法行為によく似たものであるとみなした。その原則は，購入者側に単に契約についての知識があると推定されるのではなく，現実の知識を要求する。したがって傭船契約を履行せよという購入者への命令に肯定的には繋がらないが，継続している傭船契約の違反を引き起こすような方法で購入者が船舶取引をするのを抑制する差止命令に繋がる。この見解は，前文の二つの制限を常に条件として将来の事案において守られそうに考えられる。前出 *Port Line* v. *Ben Line* 事件で Diplock 判事が述べたが，この二つの制限は前出 *Strathcona* 事件が正当に判決されたとしても，適用されたであろう。またこの二つの制限は前出 *Swiss Bank* v. *Lloyds Bank* 事件の Browne-Wilkinson 判事が依拠した判例により支持された。この結論は傭船者が定期傭船の船舶に何らかの権利を持つこと（傭船者は持たないことについて，前出137頁と後出612頁参照）には基づいておらず，したがって多くの正当な批判に曝されてきた *Strathcona* 事件の枢密院の論法が取る手法を避けていることが注目される。

国　籍（flag）

 船舶の国籍に関する表示は通常中間的条件（an intermediate term）（これについては前出139頁参照）であると言われている。しかしその国籍が本船の安全，または就航区域に重大な関係を持つ場合，——船舶の国籍がその船舶が中立であるか否かを決定する戦時におけるように——その違反は傭船者が契約を消滅したものとして扱うことを許容するような条件（a condition）（前出138頁参照）として表示は扱われる。

 一般的に，傭船者の同意なしには，本船の国籍を変更しないという黙示条項が認められている。

> *City of Hamburg* 号は，12ヶ月間定期傭船された。本船は英国船であったが，この事実は傭船契約に記載されていなかった。傭船期間開始後間もなく本船は売船され，国籍が変った。本船の国籍が条件であれば，傭船者は傭船契約を終了できたはずであるが，傭船者は異議を唱えたものの，本船の使用を継続したので本船の国籍が条件か否かを判断する必要は生じなかった。しかしながら，傭船者の損害賠償の請求に関して，Rowlatt 判事は，(1)売船それ自体は傭船契約の違反ではないが，(2)本船の傭船期間中，その提供する役務が傭船者に実質上不利益になったり，約定と異なるものとなるように変更されてはならないという黙示の条項があり，国籍の変更は，そのような黙示条項の違反となると判示した。
> *Isaacs* v. *McAllum*（1921）6 Ll.L. Rep. 289.

船体，機関および装備を完全な稼働状態に保持すること

 この文言は堪航性の絶対的担保約束であり，傭船契約締結時の本船の状態に適用される。引渡時，本船は「堅牢強固であらゆる点において輸送業務に適す」べきであるという要件で，堪航性のさらなる絶対的担保約束がニューヨーク・プロデュース書式22行にある。ボルタイム書式にも，引渡時の堪航性の絶対的担保約束がある。第1条は，引渡時に船舶は「あらゆる点に

おいて通常の貨物運送業務に適して」いることを規定している。それは、本船はもっとも広い
97 意味で堪航性がなければならないことを意味すると The Madeleine [1967] 2 Lloyd's Rep. 224
事件（後出151頁参照）で判示された。

　引渡時の堪航性の明示の担保約束がない場合，堪航性の担保約束は黙示的である（Giertsen
v. Turnbull, 1908 S.C.1101)。これも本性において絶対的である。

　しかし引渡時のこの堪航性の担保約束は，それ自体としては，継続する義務ではない（前出
Giertsen v. Turnbull 事件参照）。しかしながら，ニューヨーク・プロデュース書式第24条によ
るようにヘーグ・ルールが傭船契約に摂取された場合，（明示であれ黙示的であれ）引渡時の
堪航性の絶対的義務は傭船契約による各航海発航前，および発航時，本船の堪航性を確保する
ため，相当の注意を払うという担保約束に取って代わられるように思われる。これは，593か
ら598頁で述べる。

　「堪航性」の意味に関する以下の Carver 著『海上運送』（Carriage by Sea）の記述は F. C.
Bradley & Sons v. Federal Steam Navigation (1926) 24 Ll.L. Rep. 446 事件で Scrutton 卿判事
により是認された。「通常の注意力ある船主が本船に航海の開始時にあらゆる状況に留意して
具有することを要求する程度の適合性を本船は具有していなければならない。船主が知ってい
たのであれば，思慮分別のある船主であれば本船を海に差し向ける前に本船を修復すべきこと
を要求したであろうか」。

　運航中，本船を完全な稼働状態に維持することに関する別個の規定が，ニューヨーク・プロ
デュース書式の37および38行と，ボルタイム書式の24および25行にあり，それは明らかに継続
的な義務である。これに関する所見は267頁に述べる。

条件（conditions）にならない堪航性担保義務

　傭船契約締結時における堪航性担保約束も，引渡時における堪航性担保約束も，条件（con-
ditions）ではない（それらについては138頁参照）。それらは中間的条件（intermediate
terms）であり，その違反が，傭船者が傭船契約を消滅したものとして扱うことを許容するか
どうかは，違反の性質と重大さに左右される。堪航性担保義務は非常に広範に及ぶものである
から，比較的些細な点で違反しやすいものであり，したがって，軽微な違反を理由にして傭船
者が契約を終了させる権利をも有するというのは不当である。

　　Hongkong Fir 号はボルタイム書式に基づき，24ヶ月間プラスマイナス1ヶ月で傭船された。本船
　の機関は，引渡の時点でまずまずの状態であったが，船齢のゆえに慎重な取扱が要求された。引渡時
　に船主が雇用した機関士は，人数が足りず能力も欠いていた。その結果，まさに最初の傭船航海で，
　重大な機関故障が続発した。その航海は Liverpool から大阪までであったが，航海中修理のため5週
　間オフハイヤーとなり，引き続いて大阪で15週間の修理が行われた。本船が再び航海の準備を整える
　前に，傭船者は傭船契約を拒絶し，船主はその拒絶が違法であるとの理由で損害賠償を求めた。
　Salmon 判事ならびに控訴院は次のとおり判示した。
　(1) 船主は，機関室要員の能力不足の点で，堪航性担保義務に違反している。
　(2) 機関室要員の能力不足は，その選任にあたって船主自身が相当の注意を払わなかったためである
　　から，船主はボルタイム書式第13条の免責条項により保護されない。
　(3) 堪航性は条件（a condition）ではなく，堪航性担保義務違反はそれ自体傭船者に契約を拒絶する
　　権利を与えるものではない。
　(4) 堪航性担保義務違反が，契約の根本に及ぶ場合にのみ，傭船者は契約の拒絶を正当化できる。
　(5) その担保義務違反の結果，相当の遅延をもたらしたが，その遅延が契約を履行不能とするほどの
　　ものではない限り，義務違反が契約の根本にまで及ぶとか，傭船者の契約上のすべての利益を実質
　　的に奪い去るものとはみなされない。

98 (6) 傭船契約の期間（24ヶ月）の長さ、およびオフハイヤー期間が約定により傭船期間に延長加算される事実を考慮すると、遅延は傭船契約を履行不能にするほどのものではなく、それゆえ、傭船者の拒絶は違法である。
The Hongkong Fir [1961] 1 Lloyd's Rep. 159 および [1961] 2 Lloyd's Rep. 478（C. A.）。

不堪航船の引渡

傭船者は不堪航が発見された本船の引渡を受ける義務はない。傭船者は最初に関連の欠陥を修復することを要求できる。

前出 The Hongkong Fir 事件において、Sellers 卿判事は、「［ボルタイム］傭船契約第1条により、船主は、本船を Liverpool において、「あらゆる点において通常の貨物輸送業務に適する状態」で、引き渡すことを契約した。引き渡されたとき、同船は通常の貨物の輸送に適合していなかった。なぜなら、機関室要員は数が足りず能力も欠いており、航海が進むに従いこの点が露呈したからである。ありきたりの表現であるが、本船は機関室内の能力不足という理由で不堪航であったと言える。……もし本件で機関室要員の不足や能力不足が分っていたならば、傭船者は Liverpool において、傭船契約の第1条に従って本船を提供しなかった船主の怠慢に異議を申し立て、本船をそのままの状態で受け取ることを拒否することができたはずである」と述べた。本船がボルタイム傭船契約の第1条が要求する「あらゆる点において通常の貨物輸送業務に適する状態」になるまで、傭船者は引渡を受けるのを拒否することができたはずである。さらにこの要件が解約条項（後出419から424頁までを参照）の定める時期までに満たされなければ、傭船者はこの条項により傭船契約を終了させる権利を有したことであろう。

解約条項とはまったく別に、本船が引渡時に不堪航で、傭船契約が履行不能に至らない間に堪航性を回復できない限り、傭船者はコモン・ローに基づき、傭船契約を消滅したものとして扱う権利を有する。航海傭船の指導的先例である Stanton v. Richardson (1875) 45 L. J. C. P. 78 事件で、本船は契約貨物を受け取るのに適しておらず、陪審員が認めたように海運事業の目的が履行不能となる以前に修復されず、したがって傭船者は本船に貨物を積み込むあらゆる義務から解放されると、貴族院により判示された。その後の定期傭船契約についての Tully v. Howling (1877) 2 Q. B. D. 182 事件の同旨の Brett 判事の判決も参照。しかし苦情のあった不堪航性が、傭船者から実質的に契約のあらゆる利益を奪って契約の根本にまで至るほど重大ではないか、または契約が法律上履行不能にならないうちに堪航性を回復できない限り、傭船者は傭船契約を継続し損害賠償による救済を求めざるをえない。前に説明したように、堪航性保持義務は条件（conditions）ではなく、記載された結果を生じる堪航性担保義務違反がある場合のみ傭船者は契約の自己の部分の履行拒否を認められる。The Hongkong Fir [1961] 2 Lloyd's Rep. 478（同判例集495頁）事件で Diplock 卿が説明したように、

「……提供されたときに船舶はある点で不堪航であったという、あるいはその不堪航により傭船契約の履行にある程度の遅延が生じたという事実が発生したということだけで、契約当事者の意図であった傭船者の契約上の義務の履行により傭船者が得るあらゆる利益を傭船者から奪うものではない。なぜならば、契約の履行不能までに達しないならば、そういうできごとが発生しようとも傭船者は義務の履行継続を担保するから。……」。

（Photo Production v. Securicor [1980] 1 Lloyd's Rep. 545（同判例集553頁）事件と前出139頁参照）
したがって、本船が引渡時または引渡前に不堪航であることが発見されるが、不堪航が契約

の根本にまで影響を与えない場合には，傭船者は（後出の履行拒絶がない限り）引渡を拒否し契約を消滅したものとみなすことはできない。傭船者は，傭船契約の要件に本船を合致させ引き渡すように船主に求めることができるだけである。船主が解約日までにそうする場合，傭船者は本船を受け取らねばならない。

堪航性回復の拒絶あるいは回復不能

不堪航それ自体は傭船者に傭船契約を消滅したものとして扱うことを認めるほど重大ではないが，船主が堪航性の回復あるいは傭船契約の要件に本船を合致させ引き渡すのを怠ったり，拒否したりすれば，それはもはや傭船契約に拘束されたくないという意思を示したことになる。そこでは，船主の欠陥の回復の拒絶あるいは回復不能は，おそらく傭船者に契約を終了する権利を認める履行拒絶となる。*The Hongkong Fir* 事件において，Sellers 卿判事は前出149頁引用の判決文に続けて，次のように述べた。

「船主が機関室要員を十分な人数と能力に改善することを怠ったり，拒否したりした場合，不堪航それ自体ではなく，船主のそのような行為が傭船契約の履行拒絶となり，したがって傭船者はその履行拒絶を認め，契約を終了したものとして扱うことができたであろう」。

しかしながら，この説示は注意して扱われなければならない。既述のように，船主の行為は，ある種の状況下においては，自己が契約に拘束されたくないという意思を明確に表示したのと同じことになり，履行拒絶を構成することにもなろう。しかし違反状態の修復を怠っても，その違反自体が，契約の根本に関するものでない限り，履行拒絶とはならない。ただし，違反状態の修復の単なる懈怠どころではない別の要因がある場合は，別である。

  Hermosa 号はある状況の下4ヶ月の期間延長の選択権付で2年間ニューヨーク・プロデュース書式により傭船された。本船は原傭船者から同様の期間同一書式で再傭船された。1974年12月の引渡の後，第1航海での輸送貨物に不堪航の結果として重大な損傷が発生した。本船修理は1975年1月中旬から3月末まで行われたため，再傭船者は本船の使用ができなかった。その後の4月の空船航海で，本船は衝突しCuraçaoに修繕のため入港した。船主は，再傭船者が第1航海の後，本船を検査することを許可しなかったが，再傭船者は，再修理の完了期間と修理の効果に十分な確信を得られなかったので，1975年8月9日に本船検査の裁判所命令を入手した。この検査により，第1航海の貨物損傷の原因である艙口蓋の欠陥がなお未修理で，本船は他の点でも状態不良であるということが明らかとなった。これらの欠陥は満足いくように処理されるとの明確な保証を（船主から知らされていなかった）原傭船者から受けなかったので，再傭船者は1975年8月29日に，再傭船契約の終了を目論んだ。再傭船者の知らないところで，船主は8月29日前にこれらの欠陥の修理を手配し，修理は10月22日に適切に完了した。Mustill 判事と控訴院は以下のように判示した。
(1) 再傭船者が，本船の不堪航を理由に傭船契約は消滅したとすることは正当化されない。なぜならば，残存した欠陥は比較的短期間に矯正されうるし，その後に再傭船期間はまだ16-17ヶ月残されている。
(2) 原傭船者による傭船契約の履行拒絶は存在しえない。なぜならば，原傭船者の行為は分別ある者として原傭船者は契約の義務を遂行する意思がないと結論づけさせるようなものではない。再傭船者が艙口蓋が適切に修理されていないと疑うのはもっともだが，傭船契約を終了させるには十分ではない。再傭船者の行為は時期尚早である。
 The Hermosa [1980] 1 Lloyd's Rep. 638 および [1982] 1 Lloyd's Rep. 507.
  （履行拒絶に関し，一般的に *Decro-Wall v. Practitioners in Marketing* [1971] 1 W. L. R. 361 事件および *The Nanfri* [1979] 1 Lloyd's Rep. 201 事件および *Woodar v. Wimpey* [1980] 1 W. L. R. 277 事件参照）

The Hermosa 号事件の控訴院は、さらに次のように判示した。本件のように問題が原傭船者と再傭船者との間の契約が拒絶されたか否かという場合、考慮されるべきは原傭船者の行為であり、原傭船者が傭船契約にもはや拘束されないという意思の表示があったかどうかということである。船主の行為は必ずしも原傭船者の行為としてみなされるわけではない。

100 契約を履行不能にする不堪航

船主が航海始期の不堪航を、傭船契約の取引上の目的が達成不可能となる以前に修復できないか、あるいは修復しない場合、傭船者は契約を消滅したものとして扱うことができる。

Yuri Maru は9ヶ月間定期傭船された。本船は引渡時、通常貨物の運送にあらゆる点で適していた。本船は新造船であったが、その推進器は強度が不足し、傭船契約後3ヶ月にならぬうちに推進器の羽根が欠損し始めた。船主はこの欠陥を直そうと2ヶ月以上を費やしたが成功せず、傭船者は傭船契約を解約した。控訴院は、本船の不堪航が契約の根本を破壊するほどの期間その履行を妨げたものであり、傭船者は解約の権利がある、と判示した。Bankes 卿判事は次のように述べている。

「本件のような定期傭船の事案において、オフハイヤーだからというだけで、傭船者は限りなく長時間（もし、この表現を使うことが許されるなら）本船を使用することなく待つ義務があり、そして本船を使用することがまったく不可能になるだけではなく、約定時点で両当事者が意図した目的のために将来も本船を使用できないことが決定的になった状態で、なお、傭船者には傭船契約を終了する権利がないとの主張はできないと思われる」。

Snia v. *Suzuki* (1924) 18 Ll.L. Rep. 333.

Salmon 判事は、*The Hongkong Fir* [1961] 1 Lloyd's Rep. 159 事件で、この件に言及し、「この事件の事実関係は例外的なものであって、堪航性の保持に船主が再々努力して失敗した後、傭船者は、船主が本船に堪航性を具備させることはできないと信ずるに足る相当の根拠を持つに至った」と述べた（*Stanton* v. *Richardson* (1874) L. R. 9 C. P. 390 事件と前出 *The Hermosa* 事件も参照）。

解約条項

また一方、傭船者が一般原則に基づいて契約を消滅したものとして扱えるほど十分に重大な不堪航がなくても、欠陥または異常が解約日までに修復されない場合、傭船者はこの解約条項にしたがって解約できる。ニューヨーク・プロデュース契約書式の第14条に基づき、傭船者は、本船が解約日前に書面による準備整頓の有効な通知を発行しなかった場合には、解約できる。ボルタイム書式の第1条と第22条に基づき、本船が期日までに「通常の貨物の運送業務にあらゆる点で適合し」て引き渡されない場合には、解約権が生じる。この言葉は、本船が引渡時に最も広い意味で堪航性を持ち、傭船契約の役務を履行できなければならないことを意味する。

Madeleine 号はボルタイム書式に基づき定期傭船された。同船は鼠族駆除免除証明書なしに、引渡のため提供された。燻蒸を行おうと試みられたが、解約日前に証明書を取得できなかった。傭船者に解約権があると判示するにあたって、Roskill 判事は、「このように、明示の堪航性担保の義務が定められているのであるから、港湾衛生当局からの必要な証書を含め、本船が堪航状態で期日までに引き渡されない限り、傭船者は解約権を有する」と述べた。

The Madeleine [1967] 2 Lloyd's Rep. 224.
（この事件の事実関係に関するより詳細な要約は、後出420頁）

解約条項は契約違反の有無によらない。本船が期日までに準備整頓できない場合に，傭船者は，本船の準備不能が船主側の傭船契約違反（それが傭船者に責任がある何事かに帰さない前提で）によらないとしても解約できる。

本件の詳細の議論は解約条項に関する章（419頁）および船積準備に関する章（206頁）を参照。履行不能の原則については461頁で述べる。

10 堪航性担保義務に関する至上条項の効果

後出593頁から598頁参照。

船級に関する表示

船級に関する表示は，通常は条件（a condition）であると思われる（前出138頁参照）。したがって契約締結時に本船が表示どおりの船級を保有していない場合，傭船者は傭船契約を消滅したものとして扱う権利を有する（*Routh* v. *MacMillan* (1863) 9 L. T. 541 事件および *The Apollonius* [1978] 1 Lloyd's Rep. 53（同判例集61頁）事件参照）。

傭船契約に表示された船級が，契約締結時点で船級協会の登録簿に記載されていれば，その表示は正当である。船級の表示は，本船が正当に船級を有していることもそれを将来に亘って維持していることも保証するものではない。

9月4日 *William Jackson* 号は New Orleans で綿花を積むため傭船された。本船は，「A1 1/2. Record of American and Foreign Shipping Book」として，傭船契約に記載されていた。傭船契約締結時，本船はその船級を保持していた。本船が11月 New Orleans に到着した際，8月の船級検査時において，船体外板は，最近の張替であると考えられたものが誤認であると判明したため，その船級が取り消された。傭船者は傭船契約の履行を拒絶したが，控訴院は契約当時，本船は表示どおりの船級を保持していたのだから，傭船者の履行拒絶は違法であると判示した。

French v. *Newgass* [1878] 3 C. P. D. 163.

さらに，船主が船級を記載しても，その船級維持に必要な行為を怠らないことまでも担保するものではない。*Hurst* v. *Usborne* (1856) 18 C.B. 144 事件において，Crowder 判事は，「*Elizabeth* 号が A.1. であるという傭船契約中の記載は，契約締結時まで適用されるだけである，と考えられる。それは傭船契約の定める傭船期間中船舶が A.1. を保持すること，または船主がその船級保持に必要な行為を怠らないことまで保証するものでないことは明らかである」と述べた。

（ニューヨーク・プロデュース書式の37行のように）大抵の定期傭船契約は，船級維持義務を船主に課している。そのような明示の条項がない場合，傭船開始後，結果として船級を失うような本船の変更を船主は行わないという黙示的条項があるものと思われる（類似の事例として，*Isaacs* v. *McAllum* (1921) 6 Ll.L. Rep. 289 事件参照）。

ベール容積と載貨重量

ベール容積と載貨重量の表示は通常は中間的条件（intermediate terms）を構成する。したがって，前出139頁で説明したように，不実記載の結果は，その違反の性質と違反の結果如何による。*Cargo Ships El-Yam* v. *Invotra* [1958] 1 Lloyd's Rep. 39 事件で，Devlin 判事は，傭船者が不実記載を理由に傭船契約を消滅したものとして扱うには，原則として不実記載が，

「それにより，当事者が契約上得るはずのものと根本的に異なったものを得ることとなるようなもの」でなければならない，と述べた。

載貨重量トン数は，通常理論的積載能力を示す数値である。

 Freden 号は，とうもろこしを満載するため航海傭船された。傭船契約には「船主は本船の載貨重量トン数が3,200トンであることを保証し，運賃はこの数量に対して支払うものとする」と規定されていた。控訴院は，本条項を本船の理論的積載重量に関するものと解釈し，容積不足のため，とうもろこし3,081トンしか積載できなかった点について，契約違反とはならないと判示した。
 Millar v. *Freden* [1918] 1 K. B. 611.

|102| 時々見られることであるが，船舶が特定の表示貨物の輸送に，1航海定期傭船される場合がある。このような場合，傭船契約の載貨重量トン数は，解釈の問題として，特定の貨物に関連するものと判断されるであろう。しかし，一般にニューヨーク・プロデュース書式やボルタイム書式のような定期傭船契約書式では，載貨重量が特定貨物のそれを指していると解釈されることはあまりない。これらの書式には，載貨容積と載貨重量が別々に記載されているからである。

ニューヨーク・プロデュース書式の載貨重量トン数は，「貨物，燃料，本船載貨重量トン数の1.5パーセント以下で最低50トンの清水・船用品を含む」と定義されている。これは清水，船用品の合計が50トン，または載貨重量トン数の1.5パーセントの，いずれか大なる方を超えてはならないことを意味すると言われている。

ある航海傭船の事案において，載貨重量トン数の保証は，船主が貨物の適切な積付に使用せざるを得ない荷敷の重量を含むと判示された。

 Benledi 号は，「特に問題のない商品を満載」するため傭船された。傭船契約には，「船主は造船所の図面通り，載貨重量5,600トン，ベール容積300,000立方フィートを傭船者の使用に供することを保証する」との規定があった。Atkin 判事は，船主が貨物の適切な積付に使用せざるを得なかった荷敷のため，貨物の実積込量が保証重量より少なくても，それは載貨重量保証の違反とはならない，と判示した。
 Thomson v. *Brocklebank* [1918] 1 K. B. 655.

「約 about」

ニューヨーク・プロデュース書式，ボルタイム書式共に載貨重量トン数に「約」という文言が付いている。これは正確度についての許容限度を船主に与えている。その数値が許容範囲内であれば，載貨重量トンに関する契約条項の違反とはならない。

「約」という文言の示す許容限度を，一般論として定義付けることはできない。許容限度は事実問題であり，載貨重量の測定精度にもよるし，特定の運送において，どの程度が妥当と考えられるかにもよる。類似の例として，後出「速力と燃料消費」で要約されている *The Al Bida* [1986] 1 Lloyd's Rep. 142 および [1987] 1 Lloyd's Rep. 124 (C. A.) 事件参照。5パーセントの余裕が認められた事例があるが，それは初期の小型船に関するものであって，今日，はるかに大型の船についての依拠すべき指針とは考えられない。このような大型船について，裁判所または仲裁人は，比較的小さな許容限度しか認めないのではないかと思われる。

 Resolven 号は，「2,000トンまたはそれに近く」を運送するために傭船された。Francis Jeune 卿は判決を下すにあたって，次のように述べた。「それに近く thereabouts」という文言は，積高2,000ト

ンという数字にある程度の幅をもたせるものと解すべきと考える。……融通性のある文言は、まさに弾力的に解すべきで、これは本件の問題にも当てはまる。本件の場合、5パーセントが妥当な許容限度と考えられる……」。
　The Resolven（1892）9 T. L. R. 75.
　（約1,100トンの貨物に3パーセントが許容限度とされた――Morris v. Levison（1876）1 C. P. D. 155事件――「約80,000グレン立方フィート」の能力に3パーセントが許容限度とされた――Rederi-aktiebolaget Urania v. Zachariades（1931）41 Ll. L. Rep. 145事件参照）

　「約」として限定された数字が測定値ではなく推定値である場合の事件の判断は許容限度に関する助けになるが、その適用は能力の表示に関する事件に対して注意深く行われるべきである。*The Pantanassa* [1958] 2 Lloyd's Rep. 449 事件で、定期傭船契約には、本船引渡時において予定積載燃料「約6／700トン」と規定されていたが、それは575トンと725トンの間を意味すると考えられた。

103　*Dominator* 号は、「船長が宣言する10,450トン以下8,550トン以上積高船主任意の満船撒積小麦」運送に航海傭船された。船長は、本船の概算積載量を10,400トンと宣言した。控訴院は、「概算（approximative）」は「約」と同じことを意味し、10,400トンの貨物のうち331トン不足（3パーセント強）しても、10,400トン積載するという本船の義務を果たしたことになると判示した。Seller 卿判事は次のように述べた。「10,400トンの貨物のうち331トンの不足は、3パーセントを少し超える不足であるが、約10,400トンを船積する義務を果たしたとみなされる。Morris v. Levison（1876）1 C. P. D. 155事件および *The Resolven*（1892）9 T. L. R. 75事件参照。具体的取引実例の証拠がない本件において、それは、その種貨物に関して妥当な許容限度内にあると考える」。
　Dreyfus v. *Parnaso* [1960] 1 Lloyd's Rep. 117.

　ニューヨーク・プロデュース書式による、傭船契約上のベール容積に関する次に示す事案において、取引関係の証拠が重要であることが再度強調された。

　Tel Aviv 号はニューヨーク・プロデュース書式に基づき傭船され「ベール容積約478,000立方フィート……」として表示された。実際には本船の総ベール容積は484,000立方フィートであり、表示数値を1.2パーセント超えていた。「約」という文言の持つ意味について、Devlin 判事は次のとおり述べた。「1.2パーセントの許容範囲が、『約』という文言の範囲内かどうかを決定しなければならないとしたら、それは手持証拠を慎重に検討しなければならない問題である。一見したところ、1.2パーセントというのは、僅かなものであり、十分『約』という文言の範囲内にあるとも言える。しかも［傭船者側弁護人］は、この点に関する証拠に正しく依拠して、1,000立方フィートまたはその近辺が、本件取引上の問題として、『約』……という文言に認められる許容範囲であることを立証した」。
　Cargo Ships El-Yam v. *Invotra* [1958] 1 Lloyd's Rep. 39.

　本件の場合、裁判所は結局、許容限度が何であるべきかを最終的に決定する必要はなかった。しかし、この判決の説示は、大きな数字を扱う現在、「約」という文言で許容される範囲は、昔の事件で認められた率より、はるかに小さいものになることを示している。

損害賠償の基準
　船舶載貨容積の不実記載の損害賠償の一応の基準は、約定傭船料と現実の載貨容積を有する本船に支払われるであろう傭船料との差である。

　Tibermede 号は、一定の載貨重量トン、一定の容積トンを保有するものと定期傭船契約に記載され

た。実際には本船の載貨重量トン数は表示より多く、容積トン数は少なかった。傭船者は、約定傭船料と、実際の容積トン数を有する船に支払うであろう傭船料との差額を基に、容積トン数不足の損害賠償を請求した。この損害査定の方法に対し、船主は傭船者がその実損を立証すべきであると主張して争った。Shearman 判事は、傭船者の主張を支持して、次のように述べた。「一定の容積トン数の船舶を購入するにあたり、容積トン数が約定より小さい船舶が提供されれば、約定価格からその分を差し引くことができる。傭船の場合もこれと異なるとは考えられない」。

Tibermede v. *Graham* (1921) 7 Ll. L. Rep. 250.
(*Sterns* v. *Salterns* (1922) 12 Ll. L. Rep. 385 事件も参照)

しかしある事件の一応の規則は損害を被った当事者を償えないが、載貨重量または容積トン数が違っていたために、傭船期間中に損失を被ったことを傭船者が立証できる場合、傭船者は、選択的にその損害を基準として賠償の請求をすることもできる(*The TFL Prosperity* [1982] 1 Lloyd's Rep. 617 事件参照)。

速力と燃料消費

速力および燃料消費に関する表示は、通常は中間的条件(intermediate terms)を構成すると思われる。それで、不実記載の結果は、前出139頁で説明した契約違反の性質とその重要性如何による。通常、速力不足または燃料消費過大の問題は、損害賠償という方法だけで補償することができる。しかしながら、いずれかに関して、契約の基礎に関わるような重大な差異があれば、傭船者は契約を消滅したものとして扱う権利を取得することがある。例えば、船舶がエクスプレスコンテナサービスを補充するために傭船された場合のように、速力が当事者の意図する配船の基本的要素となっている場合である。*The Aegean Dolphin* [1992] 2 Lloyd's Rep. 178 事件で、定期傭船者は、もし権利放棄していなければ(前出143頁参照)、「良好な気象条件下で18ノットの速力を基準として」傭船されながら、特定の種類の巡航の履行に必要な速力が不足する船舶を拒否できたであろうと判示された。

速力保持の時期

いつの時点で本船が表示どおりの速力を保持しているべきか、契約締結時か、引渡時か、さらに速力が継続する担保であるかどうかの問題については、意見が分れている。

Adderstone 号は、7ないし9ヶ月間定期傭船され、満載、良好な気象条件の下において、最上級燃料約13トンの消費で約10ノットの航海能力があるものとして、傭船契約に記載された。傭船契約開始1ヶ月後、船主は、本船を売却した。傭船者は買主に対し速力不足と燃料消費過大を理由にクレームを提起した。原船主／買主間紛争の法律問題を判断する中間判決手続において、船舶が表示どおりの性能を出すことができなかったことを前提として、原船主に責任があるかどうかの問題が生じた。Atkinson 判事は(傍論であるが)速力および燃料消費に関する担保は、傭船契約日に本船が表示された性能を出すことができるという担保であり、本船がそのような性能を維持しなければならないということではない、と述べた。
Lorentzen v. *White Shipping* (1943) 74 Ll. L. Rep. 161.

The Apollonius [1978] 1 Lloyd's Rep. 53 事件で、Mocatta 判事は、*Lorentzen* v. *White Shipping*事件の Atkinson 判事の意見に従うことを拒否し、定期傭船契約における速力についての表示は、引渡日のそれであると判示した。

Apollonius号はボルタイム書式により1航海定期傭船された。傭船契約に本船は「……満載状態で燃料油約38トンの消費で良好な天候と平穏な海上において、約14.5ノットの航海が可能」と記載されていた。定期傭船契約は8月28日に締結され、本船は9月25日以降引渡予定、解約期日は10月15日であった。その後の追加条項により、解約期日は10月31日に延期された。数多くの追加条項の中で、第50条は、「船主には、引渡前に船舶を入渠させる自由がある」と定めていた。9月7日から10月26日までの間、本船はWhampoaで揚荷をしており、その間、船底がひどく汚損した。したがって本船は日本からアルゼンチンへの傭船契約航海において、平均10.61ノットしか出なかった。船主は引渡時本船が表示速力を出せなかったことを認めたが、船主の義務は引渡時ではなく、傭船契約締結時にのみ関係を有すると主張した。

　Mocatta判事は、Lorentzen v. White事件におけるAtkinson判事の判断に賛成せず、速力に関する義務は、引渡時に適用されるという傭船者の主張を支持する「有力な商業上の事情」があったと考えた。同判事は、それが引渡時以前または以後の時期にも適用されるか否かについては、触れなかった。

　The Apollonius [1978] 1 Lloyd's Rep. 53.

　しかし、Lorentzen v. White事件で表明された見解は、多年にわたり一般的に受け容れられてきており、本船が、記載された特徴を、将来の引渡時に保有するであろうというのではなく、契約締結時に保有しているという、傭船契約書前文の文言に合致するものと思われる。前出The Apollonius事件で、Mocatta判事が重視した、商業実務上の配慮については、あらゆる点で運航に適する船を引き渡すという明示の義務および契約締結以降、船主は速力の減少、燃料消費の増加をもたらすような変更をしない、という黙示の条項により、大抵対応しうると思われる。類似の事件として、Isaacs v. McAllum (1921) 6 L1.L. Rep. 289事件と前出147頁およびKarsales v. Wallis [1956] 1 W. L. R. 936事件でDenning卿判事が示した黙示条項参照。Robertson v. Amazon Tug (1881) 7 Q. B. D. 598事件の控訴院の判決も参照。

[105]　The Al Bida [1986] 1 Lloyd's Rep. 142（同判例集150頁）事件でEvans判事は、速力担保が、本船の要目は変更されないという黙示の保証から生じる場合を除いて、速力担保は継続する担保であるか疑わしいと言った。担保速力と燃料消費を「維持する能力」の言葉の意味について控訴院 [1987] 1 Lloyd's Rep. 124（同判例集129頁）のParker卿判事の見解も参照。

　さらに、効率的稼働状態に本船を維持すべき義務は、引渡後、初めて適用されると思われるが、その稼働状態の基準は、速力および燃料消費に関する限り、前文中の記載により定められるべきである。

「約 About」

　速力に関する担保を規定するときの「約」という語は表示の速力の両側の限度を認める。限度の範囲は事実問題であって法の問題ではない（The Al Bida [1987] 1 Lloyd's Rep. 124（同判例集129頁）（C. A.））。

　The Al Bida（担保速力が「約15.5ノット」であった）事件で、「約」という語で認められるただ二つの可能な限度、0.5ノットと5パーセントがあると主張された。控訴院は、この主張を退け、限度は「船舶の構造、大きさ、喫水、船首尾の喫水の差等で調整される」という仲裁人に同意した。当事者が、「約13ノット」の担保速力の「約」で認められる限度は0.5ノットであることに合意したThe Ioanna [1985] 2 Lloyd's Rep. 164事件も参照。

平均速力と燃料消費

　平均速力の査定と損害賠償の結果として生じる計算または傭船料の調整に関する問題は、後

出の *Al Bida* と *The Didymi* の各事件で検討された。

　Al Bida 号は，Standtime 書式のタンカー定期傭船契約に基づき2回連続で1年間傭船された。両傭船契約書は前文で，本船は満載時平穏な気象で通常の稼働状態の下約15.5ノットの平均海上速力を維持することができ，……24時間当たり満載で53メトリックトン IFO 1500，空船で50メトリックトンの平均燃料消費」と規定した。その傭船契約に添付され契約の一部を構成する書式 C. Gas は，次のように規定していた。「1年間の保証海上速力約15.5ノット。**燃料消費**。海上。満載で IFO 53メトリックトン……空船で50メトリックトンの平均消費……」。

　仲裁人は，引渡時に船底が牡蠣，海草で汚れていたことと，引渡後，船底清掃が施工されるまでの期間，およびさらに次の入渠までの期間，船主が消費量担保を満たさなかったことを裁定した。これは，船主が引渡時本船を適合させず，船舶修繕義務に従わなかったためである。しかし本船は1年間の平均速力に関する書式 C. Gas の保証条件を満たした。船主は，本船が前文に定めた消費量担保に違反した期間，過剰消費であったのに対して，過小消費の期間は，金銭を受け取る権利があると主張した。換言すれば，全1年の期間の消費が考慮されるべきであると主張したのである。

　Evans 判事と控訴院は次のように判示した。前文が要求しているのは，引渡時と，船主が船舶を前文の要求する状態に維持したかどうかの問題が生じるその後の期間の本船の平均能力の評価である。Parker 卿判事は129頁で次のように述べた。「前文は傭船期間中または実際にどの期間についても現実の平均を要求していない。傭船期間の初期の実際の性能が，引渡時に本船が必要能力を持っているかどうかについての良い証拠であるかもしれないが，それだけのことである。必要能力の不足量は，他の方法で例えば引渡の3週間前に理想的状態で『約』15.5ノットの範囲に含まれる最低速力を出すには表示の数字以上を消費しなければならないという事実により簡単に証明されるかもしれない」。あるときには本船が傭船契約違反で，定められた平均消費量を維持できなかった。そして他のときには過剰性能にもかかわらず同じことがあった。書式 C. Gas が「1年間」保証速力を要求することは前文のこの解釈を裏付けた。消費量に関する類似条項の欠落は，当事者が平均1年間で速力を計算することを意図したが，燃料消費量についてはそうではないことを意味していた。

106

　The Al Bida [1986] 1 Lloyd's Rep. 142 および [1987] 1 Lloyd's Rep. 124（C. A.）。

　Didymi 号はニューヨーク・プロデュース書式で5年間定期傭船された。追加条項に，本船は「良好な気象（平穏な海上，ビューフォード風力階級3以下）で15.5ノットの保証平均速力を1日当たり35ロングトンの保証燃料消費量で」傭船期間中維持でき，かつ維持すべしと規定されていた。同条項にはまた，本船がこの保証に従って履行できない場合には，傭船者は傭船料を減額でき，さらに，本船がより良好な速力かつ・または燃料消費量を維持する場合には，船主は同じ方法で補償されると規定されていた。

　Hobhouse 判事は，平均実績を評価することが最初に必要であると判示した。このために，定義されているように良好な気象の期間中のみの本船の実績を注目しなければならない。5年の傭船期間中，平均実績を評価するに十分な回数と期間の幅がある。こうして到達した平均実績は，傭船料の減額・増額を決定するために，良好な気象の期間だけでなく海上全航海に費やした全時間に適当に適用される。Hobhouse 判事の決定と根拠は，控訴院が承認し採用するところとなった。

　Didymi Corporation v. *Atlantic Lines and Navigation* (*The Didymi*) [1987] 2 Lloyd's Rep. 166 および [1988] 2 Lloyd's Rep. 108（C. A.）。

　（保証以上の良好な実績のために傭船料は「船主と傭船者の間で相互に合意された金額だけ」公平に増額されるというこの事件の条項の考察は，前出99頁参照）

　（Diamond 判事と控訴院は，後出710頁にその事実関係を述べた *The Gas Enterprise* [1993] 2 Lloyd's Rep. 352 事件で，Beepeetime 2 書式付属の改訂第5条のいくらか類似の条項に基づく計算の中に *The Didymi* 事件で採用されたのと同じ手法を取り入れた）

　Shelltime 3 タンカー定期傭船契約書式の第24条の傭船料増額条項を燃料消費へ適用した2つの事件については，*The Evanthia M* [1985] 2 Lloyd's Rep. 154 事件（船舶が貯蔵庫として

使用された期間に改訂第24条を適用）および *The Larissa* [1983] 2 Lloyd's Rep. 325 事件（船舶の現実の最大消費量を超えた数字で第24条に挿入された最大保証燃料消費）を参照。後出711頁参照。

NYPE 93

ニューヨーク・プロデュース書式の1993年改訂版は，「良好なる気象の下で」の文言を「最大風力……ビューフォート風力階級（を含む）までの良好なる気象の下で」の文言に入れ替えた。18行から19行について，前出8頁と53頁参照。

本船の動静

ニューヨーク・プロデュース書式11行，ボルタイム書式8行の「現在 now」という文言の後に，本船の動静が表示される。この表示がときに条件（a condition）となるように思われる。*Bentsen* v. *Taylor* [1893] 2 Q. B. 274. *Behn v. Burness* (1863) 3 B. & S. 751 事件において，「現在，Amsterdam 港に」と記載された船舶が，実際には，Amsterdam 到着がその4日後であった場合，傭船者は積込拒否の権利があると，財務裁判所（Exchequer Chamber）は判断した。しかし，*The Diana Prosperity* 事件において，控訴院の Denning 卿および貴族院の Wilberforce 卿は所見を述べており，その所見からみると，今日その判決を，依拠しうる先例とみなすことができるかどうか疑問である。〔1976〕2 Lloyd's Rep. 73および626頁参照。今日では，船舶の引渡港到着予定時間の計算に関連するとの見地で船舶の所在についての表示を行うので，その表示が「期間条項」（これについては前出141頁参照）を構成するときにのみ条件である（a condition）と，おそらくは考えられる。

「船積準備完了見込」

一方，船主が本船を「就航中 trading」と記載し，一定期日またはその頃「船積準備完了見込 expected ready to load」と表示した場合，それは，おそらく条件（a condition）であると考えられる。その表示が，真実であるとの確信がなく，または妥当な根拠もなく，なされた場合，傭船者は契約を消滅したものとして扱うこともできる。もちろん，この種の条項は，定期傭船契約より航海傭船契約の方に多く見られるが，その効果は，どちらにおいても同一とみられる。見込を表示する場合，それは，正直にかつ妥当な根拠に基づいて表示しなければならない義務がある。

Mihaliss Angelos 号は「現在，就航中，1965年7月1日頃，本傭船契約で船積準備完了見込」と航海傭船契約に記載された。実際は，その年の5月25日，傭船契約を締結する時点で，7月1日頃本船が船積準備を完了すると期待できる理由はなかった。控訴院は動産販売の先例に従い，この条項は条件（a condition）であり，その違反は，傭船者に傭船契約を消滅したものとして扱う権利を与えると判示した。

The Mihalis Angelos [1970] 2 Lloyd's Rep. 43。

108 米　国　法

　米国判例の形成過程において，傭船契約書前文にある本船の特徴に関する各表示に，適切な法的位置付けを与えようとする努力が払われてきた。その結果，各表示は，「表示 representations」，「担保 warranties」，または「条件 conditions」と区別して呼ばれている。本船の不適合に対して，傭船者が契約を終了する権利を取得するか，あるいは違反の結果生ずる損害に対し単に賠償請求権を取得するだけなのかの基本的な論点は，その使用された用語で片づかない。適切な用語法に焦点をあてるよりも，問題となっている保証や表示の隠れた実体，違反や懈怠が生じたときの問題，およびそれらが傭船契約に及ぼす影響の重要性を考察する方が有益である。

　米国の判例では，不実記載が，本船引渡前に判明した事案と，引渡後に明らかになった事案とを区別することが大切である。前者の場合，表示された特徴との差異が比較的少なくても，本船の受取拒否は正当であると判断されてきた。The Maria Lemos, SMA 74 (Arb. at N.Y. 1963) 事件において，本船が，引渡準備完了の状態で提供されたとき，手持燃料油が，傭船契約で定められた最少量に満たず，かつNo.3ディープタンクに，バラスト用水が張られていたという理由により，傭船者は本船受取を拒否する権利を有すると判示された。The Augvald, 1965 AMC 1614 (Arb. at N.Y. 1965) 事件と The Grand Explorer, SMA 551 (Arb. at N.Y. 1963) 事件参照。

　しかし，一度本船の引渡を受けた後は，傭船契約の本質的目的の達成を妨げるような，船主の重大な違反がある場合にのみ，傭船者は，傭船契約の履行を拒否することができる (Aaby v. States Marine Corp. (The Tendo), 181 F. 2d 383, 1950 AMC 947 (2d Cir. 1950)，裁量上告拒否 340 U.S. 829 (1950); United States v. The Marilena P, 433 F. 2d 164, 1969 AMC 1155 (4th Cir. 1969); Petroleum Export Corp. v. Kerr S.S. Co., 32 F. 2d 969, 1929 AMC 905 (9th Cir. 1929); Massari v. Forest Lumber Co., 290 F. 470, 1923 AMC 1111 (S.D. Fla. 1923); Davison v. Von Lingen, 113 U.S. 40 (1885); Romano v. West India Fruit and S.S. Co., 151 F. 2d 727, 1946 AMC 90 (5th Cir. 1945); The Leslie, SMA 1341 (Arb. at N.Y. 1979); The Eastern Street, SMA 1352 (Arb. at N.Y. 1979) 各事件参照)。

　次に示す二つの最近の仲裁事例は，これら諸点を示す例である。The Fu Chiao, SMA 1089 (Arb. at N.Y. 1977) 事件において，仲裁審は，全員一致で，船主が本船の特徴について，不実記載したのであるから，傭船者の傭船契約解約は正当であると判断した。傭船契約には，本船が上下方向に換気されるということは，定められていなかったが，傭船者は，その旨の保証を，成約に至る交渉過程で得ているし，また，その保証がなければ，傭船者は契約を締結しなかったと思われた。仲裁審によれば，

　　善意，悪意を問わず，本船の特徴に関する不実表示があり，それがもとで，傭船者が，傭船契約を締結するに至り，その不実表示のために，傭船者の意図する船舶使用の目的がまったく達成できなくなるか，著しく阻害される場合，傭船者は契約を解約し，損害があれば損害賠償を請求しうるというのが仲裁審の全員一致の見解である。

　The Tordenskjold, SMA 1091 (Arb. at N.Y. 1977) 事件において，本船は「U.S. コーストガード規則に適合し，有効なU.S. コーストガード適合証書を常に保有すべきもの」と傭船契約に規定されていた。本船が3航海を完了したとき，船主は，Houstonでプロピレンを積む場

合には，フランジを3組取りかえなければならない，というコーストガードの勧告を受けた。本船は，その修理に要した3日間オフハイヤーとなった。修理完了後，コーストガードは承認 109 を与えたが，傭船者は傭船契約の解約を決め，本船の積荷準備が整っていなかったことを理由に，傭船契約は，取引上履行不能となったと主張した。それだけでなく，本船は傭船契約の当初からコーストガード適合証書を保有していなかった。しかしながら，仲裁審は，これらの状況は解約を正当化するものではなく，「契約の商事目的を達成不可能にするほどの根本的かつ広範囲な傭船契約違反」ではないと裁定した。仲裁審によると，

　　この法の原則は，一度本船が引き渡されて，部分的にでも契約が履行されれば，たとえ傭船者が傭船契約の解約を望んでも，傭船者は引渡時とは異なった負担をしなければならないとする一連の判例と一致し，比較的明解で説得力があるものと思われる。

タンク塗料の約30パーセントが劣化した事実は，タンク塗料は自然損耗するものであり修理可能であるとの理由で，傭船者が本船を拒否するのは正当ではないと仲裁審が判定した The Ficus, SMA 2473 (Arb. at N. Y. 1988) 事件および，船舶は「……あらゆる点で通常貨物の役務に適し」ていないと判断され，船主は傭船契約違反と判定された (The China Trident, SMA 2756 (Arb. at N. Y. 1991) 事件を，一般に参照)。

船　　名

米国法は，もちろん船主が傭船契約上の船名を有する船舶を引き渡すことを要求する。Compania Naviera Asiatic v. Burmah Oil, 1977 AMC 1538 (S. D. N. Y. 1977) 事件で，裁判所は「Hull ＃2283」の傭船契約はまさにその船舶の引渡を要求すると解釈し，船主の義務は，「Hull ＃2284」と指定された姉妹船の引渡で果たされなかった。「CHRISTINA PEZAS 号またはいかなる航海においても同一場所で Liberty 型代船を投入できる船主権利付」の連続航海傭船契約下で，船主は自由に Liberty 型代船投入の権利があるとの仲裁裁定に関して The Christina Pezas, 149 F. Supp. 678, 1958 AMC 240 (S. D. N. Y. 1957) 事件を比較参照。

国　　籍（flag）

米国の裁判所または仲裁人は，船舶国籍の不実記載が傭船者に契約を終了する権利を与えるか，単に損害賠償請求権を与えるのみか，いずれの契約違反を構成するかを決定するにあたって，その重要性という判断基準に従うと思われる。

The Penta, 1981 AMC 532 (Arb. at N. Y. 1980) 事件で，船主は傭船者の同意を得ずにリベリア船籍からフィリピン船籍に変更したことにより傭船契約違反を犯したと仲裁審は全員一致で裁定した。船籍変更は船舶を傭船者に引き渡した数ヶ月後に行われた。しかし，傭船者に傭船契約を解約する権利を与えるほどに違反は本質的なものではないとも，仲裁審は裁定した。

The Syra, SMA 297 (Arb. at N. Y. 1968) 事件において，本船は，当初，ギリシャ国旗を掲げると表示された。船主は，傭船契約に署名すると同時に，本船の国旗をギリシャからリベリヤに変更した。傭船契約書は，その後，傭船者に送付され，傭船者は国籍の変更に抗議することなく，契約を締結した。その後，同船は，リベリヤ国籍であったため，穀類積載設備の追加を要求されたが，傭船者は，傭船料からその費用を差し引いたうえ，国籍の不実表示を理由

に，船主が責任を持つべきであると申し立てた。仲裁審は，契約締結前，傭船者はその変更を知っていたから，不実表示にはならないと認定し，船主に有利な裁定を行った。傭船契約の明示の条項に従って，船主は船舶の国籍を変更する権利を有すると裁定された事案である（*The Stolt Pam,* SMA 1026（Arb. at N. Y. 1976）事件を比較参照）。

⑩船体，機関および装備を完全な稼働状態に保持すること

　米国の判例は，傭船契約のこの文言を，傭船契約の締結時と傭船者への船舶引渡時の両時点で，本船が充足していなければならない明示的堪航性担保約束とみなしている。*The Caledonia,* 157 U. S. 124（1895）；*The Carib Prince,* 170 U. S. 655（1898）；*The Toledo,* 30 F. Supp. 93（E. D. N. Y. 1939），原審維持122 F. 2d 255（2d Cir.1941），裁量上告拒絶314 U. S. 689. 22行および38行の追加文言は，さらに船舶の堪航性に関する明示的保証を構成しているが，その詳細は，以下に述べる。堪航性について明示的担保がない場合，米国の判決は，傭船契約に別段の規定がないかぎり，堪航性の黙示的担保があると判示している。*Work v. Leathers,* 97 U. S. 379（1878）；*The Edwin I. Morrison,* 153 U. S. 199, 210（1893）；前出 *The Caledonia.*

　傭船契約中に限定的文言，または海上物品運送法の摂取がない場合，堪航性の黙示的担保は絶対的担保である。最高裁判所は，*The Caledonia* 事件において，この点を明らかにした。

　　船主が担保しているのは，本船が，航海中曝される海の危険や，それに付随する危険に耐える能力を具備するために，単に，船主が最善を尽くすこと，そしてそれを尽くしたということでなく，本船が現実にかかる能力を具備していることであると考える。したがって，船主は，その能力の欠如が潜在瑕疵によってもたらされたものであっても，その担保義務を免れるものではない（157 U. S. at 131）。

　船主は各航海開始時に傭船の堪航性を黙示的に担保すると判示された（*Coca-Cola Co. v. The Norholt,* 333 F. Supp. 946, 1972 AMC 388（S. D. N. Y. 1971））。
　黙示的担保は，傭船者が本船を良好な状態として受け取った後でも認められることがある。例えば，*Thomas Jordan, Inc. v. Mayronne Drilling Mud Chem. & Eng'r Serv.,* 214 F. 2d 410（5th Cir.1954）事件において，傭船契約には，本船が傭船者の検査を受け，「第一級の状態」と認められたという規定があったが，その規定は，傭船者が，堪航性に関する黙示的担保を追求する権利を放棄したことを意味しない，と判示された。この事案は，貨物を積載した艀が，傭船者が検査したとき発見できなかった水面下の瑕疵により，沈没したものであった。
　The Carib Eve, SMA 2749（Arb. at N. Y. 1991）事件では，本船は，単一周波数無線が作動せず，安全無線電信証書は更新されていなかったという理由で，担保に適合していないと判示された。

堪航性担保義務違反の結果

　堪航性担保義務違反により，傭船者が契約を拒絶されたものとして扱うことができるのは，その違反が重大である場合でなければならない（前出 *Aaby v. States Marine Corp.* 事件参照）。同事件で，第2巡回区控訴裁判所は，不堪航と言うだけで，傭船者が解約権を取得するものではなく，不堪航が契約の基本的な目的を達成不能にする場合にのみ，拒絶は正当と認められる

と判示した。その事案において，傭船期間開始時における 2 日間の遅延を理由として12ヶ月間の傭船契約を拒絶することは，正当と認められないと判示された。

The Pacsea and The Pacsun, SMA 746（Arb. at N.Y. 1972）事件において，仲裁人は，船舶や乗組員の外見上の欠陥，船主の修理懈怠を理由とする傭船者の傭船契約終了は，正当化されないと裁定した。仲裁審は，この瑕疵は，「傭船契約の終了を是認するほど重要」ではないと認定している。仲裁審によれば，

　　当審は，口頭および後日提出された書面による有力証拠に基づき，傭船者が荷受人から，船舶の定時到着を確実にするよう厳しい圧力をかけられていたこと，また，6 月に，両船が天候のため遅れて，他船にバースを取られてしまった時点で，傭船者が，自己の直面している事態の重大性，それまで，些細ではあるが，さんざん悩まされてきた様々な事態のすべてが，自己と顧客との間の障害の原因と考えるに至ったことは，これを認める。しかし，既に述べたように，個々の事態を取り上げてみても，また些細な迷惑を連続して被ったという事情を取り上げてみても，それは，当審の見解では，契約期間の終了を待たずに，傭船者が船主との約定を終了することを認めるには十分ではない。

傭船者は，乗組員の技量，船舶の性能および船主の非協力等から，不履行の継続が予想できるし，このことは，自己の顧客との業務協定を，まったく実行不可能にするであろうと主張した。また傭船者は，このことを本船傭船契約終了の第一の理由として主張したが，やはり仲裁審の多数意見は，この主張を推測にすぎないとして，その結果は期限前の契約違反となるとした。

The Serena, SMA 1159（Arb. at N.Y. 1977）事件は，本船が航海中，乗組員の過失を主たる原因とする汽罐の不調により遅延した事件であるが，傭船者は，その遅延を生じた航海の後に，5 年間の定期傭船を解約し，その解約の正当性を主張した。傭船者の主張は，傭船契約中の履行担保（performance warranties）についての違反は，いかなる場合でも解約を正当化するというものであったが，仲裁審は，この主張を退け，遅延および本船の欠陥に関する傭船契約条項から考え，解約は不当であるとして次のように裁定した。

　　履行することが，船主の約束の根本であり，本契約の本質であると当事者間で合意しているのであるから，その合意に違反した場合には，解約が認められると，傭船者は主張した。しかし，引渡時，船齢17年近い本船が，担保約束にまったく違反していないなどということを，両当事者が信じていたとは認め難い。契約それ自体には，担保違反に対処する詳細かつ包括的対処方法が定められていた。……傭船者の主張する不履行が，本契約に基づく本船の現実の運航中に生じたとは考えられないし，また，運航を継続していたとしても，契約の根本的違反となり，解約を認められるような重大な不履行が生じたとは考えられない。

「傭船契約の解約権は，義務違反があれば発生するというものではなく，傭船契約解除を正当化するには，違反の性格が契約目的を達成不可能にするようなものでなくてはならない。そうでなければ，補償は被った損害の賠償に限定される」と判示した Hildebrand v. Geneva Mill Co.（The Edward R. Smith）32 F. 2d 343, 348, 1929 AMC 962, 972-973（M.D. Ala. 1929）事件，「不堪航は傭船者に傭船契約拒絶権を与えない」と判断した The Navigator, SMA 287（Arb. at N.Y. 1968）事件，本船は，傭船契約に合致していないけれども，「不一致の程度が，取引上航海を継続できないほどではない」と判断した The Angelica, SMA 504（Arb. at N.Y. 1970）事件，船主の曳船機関修理義務の不履行に対し，傭船者の契約解約が正当であったと裁定した Tug Diane, SMA 819（Arb. at N.Y. 1973）事件，船主が傭船者の離路の指図を拒絶したとの理由では，傭船者は傭船契約解約権を有しないと裁定した The Warm Springs, SMA 134（Arb. at N.Y. 1966）事件参照。

海上物品運送法とハーター法

　傭船契約に海上物品運送法またはハーター法が摂取されると，船主と傭船者は，各々の権利と義務を，傭船契約で明示的に修正しない限り，この両法の条項により制限されることを合意したことになる (*Hartford Fire Insurance Co.* v. *Calmar S. S. Corp.*, 404 F. Supp. 442, 1976 AMC 2636 (W. D. Wash. 1975))。傭船契約に海上物品運送法が摂取された事案で裁判所が判示したように，「適用される海上物品運送法の条項は通常の契約条件と同じ効力と効果で当事者の契約の一部となる」(1976 AMC at 2639) (*The Westmoreland*, 86 F. 2d 96, 1936 AMC 1680 (2d Cir. 1936) 事件も参照)。しかし傭船契約条項と海上物品運送法とが抵触する場合，後者が優先すると判示した *Bunge Corp.* v. *Republic of Brazil*, 353 F. Supp. 64, 1973 AMC 1219 (E. D. La 1972) 事件を参照。

112　傭船契約に海上物品運送法が摂取された場合の最も重要な効果は，黙示の堪航性担保が制限され，絶対的な担保は，本船の堪航性につき相当の注意を尽くすという担保に軽減されることである (*Horn* v. *Cia de Navegacion Fruco S. A. (The Heinz Horn)*, 404 F. 2d 412 (5th Cir. 1968), 裁量上告拒絶 394 U. S. 943 (1969), *Iligan International Corp.* v. *John Weyerhaeuser*, 372 F. Supp. 859, 1974 AMC 1719 (S. D. N. Y. 1974), 原審維持 507 F. 2d 68 (2d Cir. 1974), 裁量上告拒絶 421 U. S. 956)。

　しかし，傭船契約が明示の堪航性の絶対的担保を含む場合には，傭船契約に海上物品運送法を摂取してもその担保は廃止されないと判示された。前出 John Weyerhaeuser 事件で，本船は Weyerhaeuser により New York Navigation にニューヨーク・プロデュース書式に基づき傭船された。今度は New York Navigation が，Iligan International Corp. と契約を結んだ。その契約で，本船は機械と鉄鋼工場の部品の輸送を行うこととなっていた。航海で貨物は損傷し，Iligan は New York Navigation と Weyerhaeuser に対して損失につき訴訟を提起した。

　Iligan と New York Navigation の間の契約は，明示の堪航性担保を規定した海上物品運送法の条項に言及することにより，これを摂取していた。裁判所は，Iligan には New York Navigation との間に有効な二つの義務があったと判示した。それは，一つは明示の担保の下，堪航性のある船舶を提供する絶対的義務，そして二つ目は，堪航性については海上物品運送法により相当の注意を尽くす義務に軽減された黙示の担保であった。裁判所は，New York Navigation は，明示の担保に基づき貨物に責任を負うが，相当の注意を尽くす義務違反については責任がないと判示した。

　同じ分析が Weyerhaeuser と New York Navigation との間の傭船契約に適用された。裁判所は，Weyerhaeuser の本船を「堅牢，強固に，あらゆる点で役務に適合する」よう装備するとの明示の合意は海上物品運送法により修正されない堪航性の絶対的担保であると判示した。この明示の担保はその及ぶ範囲において，黙示の担保に取って代わり，また傭船契約が本船を堪航性ある状態に維持する継続的絶対的担保を課していない場合には，引渡時までに限って有効である。裁判所は，傭船契約が本船を堪航性ある状態に維持する継続的義務を規定しておらず，明示の担保が引渡時に無効となった場合には，その時黙示の担保が出航時に作動すると判示した。

　John Weyerhaeuser 事件で裁判所は，Weyerhaeuser は，貨物積載前に相当の注意を尽くすだけにまで海上物品輸送法により軽減された義務を構成する黙示の担保にはもちろん明示の担保の両方に違反したと判示した。

船級に関する表示

　傭船契約の船級に関する表示が，担保を構成するかどうかの問題について，米国の判例は見当らない。傭船者が，その船舶によって取引ができるかどうかという点から見て，船級は重要であるから，その表示は担保を構成すると判断されるであろうし，その違反は，傭船者に損害賠償請求権を与え，違反が契約目的を達成不能にするほど重大な場合，おそらく，傭船者に傭船契約の解約権を与えるものと思われる。

ベール容積と載貨重量

　傭船契約の，本船の載貨重量と容積に関する表示は，その事件の状況にもよるが，一般に担保（warranties）であると判示されている。*Romano* v. *West India Fruit & Steamship Co.*, 151 F. 2d 727, 731 (5th Cir. 1945)事件において，裁判所が述べているように，

[113]　重要なことは，担保が積極的かつ明白に事実の表示としてなされたか，またはその表示が，その本船を傭船するよう仕向けるような言い方で，なされたかどうかである。

　載貨重量に関する担保は必ずしも，本船が実際にその特定のトン数を積載する担保ではない。したがって，傭船契約が，本船は貨物「5,500MT 積載」の能力があると規定し，本船がその第3航海で5,500MT 積載の能力を証明した場合に，仲裁審は，傭船者の先の2航海の載貨重量不足の損害賠償請求を否定した（*The Robertina*, SMA 1151（Arb. at N. Y. 1977））。
　しかし，特定の表示を，「担保 warranty」または「保証 guaranty」と解すべしという当事者の意図が明らかな場合，傭船契約で，改めて，そのことを明示する必要がないということは，判例上，確立されているところである（*Denholm Shipping Co.* v. *W. E. Hedger Co.*, 47 F. 2d 213, 1931 AMC 297 (2nd Cir. 1931); *Metropolitan Coal Co.* v. *Howard*, 155 F. 2d 780, 783 (2d Cir. 1946)）。
　担保約束違反により，傭船者は本船受取前に，契約を解約することができるが，それと選択的に，本船を受け取り，不実記載から生じた損害賠償を請求することもできる（*Dominica Mining Co.* v. *Port Everglades Towing Co.*, 318 F. Supp. 500, 1970 AMC 123 (S. D. Fla. 1969); *The Aghia Marina*, SMA 1236（Arb. at N. Y. 1978））。*The Atlantic Glory*, SMA 76（Arb. at N. Y. 1962）事件で，仲裁審は，本船の載貨重量トンが，傭船契約に表示されたものより少ないため，傭船者は不足分の載貨重量トンについてまで，傭船料を支払わねばならぬという不利益を被ると判断した。しかし，いったん傭船者が本船を受け取った場合，不実表示がその本船により意図された取引に重大な影響を及ぼさない限り，傭船者は，傭船契約を拒絶する権利を有しない。
　Watts v. *Camors*, 115 U. S. 353 (1885)事件において，本船は，「登録測度積載重量1,100トン，またはそれに近く」と記載された。傭船契約には，傭船者が「満載貨物，撒積小麦大体約11,500クォーター……」を提供するとの規定があった。本船が傭船者に引き渡されたとき，本船のトン数は1,100トン以上であり，事実1,203トンあったため，傭船者は本船の受取，または貨物の提供を拒否した。しかしながら，本船の実際の積載能力は，小麦11,500クォーターであった。船主は，本船の受取拒否から生じた損害賠償請求の訴えを起した。裁判所は，傭船者が期待していたのは小麦11,500クォーターを積載できる船舶であり，傭船者は期待どおりの船舶を取得した，つまり本船は，期待量の積載能力があるから登録屯数の不実記載は重大ではな

く，傭船契約の終了は正当化されないとして，船主勝訴と判断した。
　The Neptune Kiku, SMA 2102（Arb. at N. Y. 1985）事件で，傭船者は船主が本船を「すべての船艙と甲板の全面的利用を妨げるあらゆる障害物」を含めて完全に表示しなかったために生じた損害を回収する権利があると判示された。本船上には，カーデッキがあり，そのためコンテナの甲板積載能力は低下した。甲板上に積載できなかったコンテナは陸路で代替港へ輸送され，揚荷港へ他船で輸送された。船舶の傭船契約上の表示はカーデッキの存在についてまったく触れていなかった。仲裁審は，船主は交渉の過程で説明がなく，傭船契約に記載のない甲板上の障害物のために，船主は傭船契約違反を犯していると認定した。
　傭船料は船主の船舶の表示と比較した運送能力の低下に比例して減額されると判示された *The Treasure Island*, SMA 1898（Arb. at N. Y. 1983）事件と同じ趣旨の *The Coastal Corpus Christi*, SMA 2828（Arb. at N. Y. 1992）事件参照。載貨重量は輸送貨物の種類により実質的に変化する製品タンカーと原油輸送タンカーとして設計された船舶の航海傭船を含む *The Danita*, SMA 2514（Arb. at N. Y. 1988）事件も参照。仲裁審は，傭船者が本船の不実記載により傭船契約を解約するのは不当であると裁定した。

総／純トン数

　船舶登録トン数についての不実記載があっても，極端な不一致がある場合を除き，傭船者は，本船受取を拒否する権利を有しない。しかし傭船者は，不一致を理由に損害賠償請求を提起することができる。前出の *Watts v. Camors*, 115 U. S. 353（1885）。本船の登録トン数に関する傭船契約の表示は，「担保」ではないと判示した *Ashburner v. Balchen*, 7 N. Y. 262（1852）事件，本船の輸送量を推定する傭船契約条項は，担保ではなく，たとえ本船の積載量が記載より相当少ない場合でも，船主は傭船契約に定められた傭船料全額に対し権利を有すると判示した *The Emily S. Malcolm*, 278 F. 943（3d Cir. 1922）事件，当事者が，本船の紙の輸送能力に関して，相互に誤りを犯した場合，船主は，傭船契約を解除する権利を有すると判示した *Ontario Paper Co. v. Neff*, 261 F. 353（7th Cir. 1919）事件，相互に事実誤認のあった本船のベール容積に関する陳述は，担保ではなく，単に推定量を意図したものにすぎないと判示した *S. O. Stray and Co. v. Trottier, Ide and Co.*, 280 F. 249（D. Mass. 1922）事件参照。

「約 about」

　載貨重量トンが，「約」として規定される場合，プラスマイナス5パーセントの余裕が許容される（*J. E. Hurley Lumber co. v. Compania Panamena Maritima San Gerassimo S. A.*, 1958 AMC 2502（Arb. at N. Y. 1958）事件および *The North Hills*, 1973 AMC 2318（Arb. at N. Y. 1972）事件参照）。しかし，本船の載貨重量を記載する際に「約」という語を使用しても傭船契約に限定する文言がない場合には，傭船者が取引し，対価を支払った本船の実際の運送能力に相当程度の余裕を認めることにはならない。*The Aghia Marina*, SMA 1236（Arb. at N. Y. 1978）事件で，本船の載貨重量を，「約17,593ロングトン」として，船主は，船用品と清水は300トン以下であることを担保した。仲裁審は，「約」の規定は船用品と清水分を差し引いた実際の運送能力に適用されるという船主の主張を退けた。傭船者は16,800トンの貨物の積載を要求した。16,467.78トンだけが積載されたので，傭船者はその航海の適用期間内の293.92トンの積み残しに対して傭船料減額の権利があると判示された。

速力と燃料消費

　本船の速力と燃料消費についての表示は，本船が表示の天候条件において，約定の燃料消費率で表示速力を出せることを，船主が担保（warranty）したことを意味する。その表示が担保を構成するものであることが，傭船契約に明示されていなくても同様である（*Denholm Shipping Co. v. W. E. Hedger Co.*, 47 F. 2d 213, 1931 AMC 297 (2d Cir. 1931)）。米法に基づき，本船は傭船者への引渡日において，約定燃料消費率で表示速力を達成することができなければならない。しかし，それは継続的担保ではない。裁判所は *Denholm Shipping* 事件で次のように述べている。

　　しかしながら，担保の意味するところは，また別の問題である。すなわち担保は引渡時からのことを表示しており，本船がそのときに約定条件に基づく表示速力を出すことが「可能」であれば，担保は充足される。したがって，本船が約定速力を，一定不変に出すことまでも，意味するものではない。けだし，速力担保の前提条件が満たされていても，本船の使用状態，船底の汚損によって，速力は変化し，さらに本船が航行不能になることがあるからである。一方，傭船者は，担保が自己にとって，実際上，役立つものと考えることもできる。すなわち，担保が通常の海上航海のことを述べているということである。この点で，後日船主が行ったテストで，約定速力を現実に出しても，そのこと自体は，担保とは関係のないことである。検討しなければならないのは，予定どおりの貨物を積載して，天候良好，海上平穏な状態で，本船が約定速力を出せたかどうかということとである。そして，約定速力が出なければ，傭船者は，違反を立証したこととなる。この点に関する最善の判断基準は，当該航海に，速力担保の前提条件を満たす状態において，本船が現実に出した速力である（47 F. 2d at 215）。

　契約に別段の定めがない限り，担保ということは，全傭船期間を通じて，本船が約定速力を平均して維持することを，船主が保証することではない（*Cargo Ships El-Yam Ltd. v. Stearns & Foster Co.*, 149 F. Supp. 754, 770 (S. D. N. Y. 1955)；*The Ceres*, 72 F. 936 (2d Cir. 1896)，裁量上告拒絶 163 U. S. 706 (1896)；*The Astraea*, 124 F. 83 (E. D. N. Y. 1903) 各事件参照）。悪天候下において，または本船が，港湾や河川のような制限水域にいる場合には，この担保は適用されないことは明らかである（*The Mini Lap*, SMA 1077 (Arb. at N. Y. 1976) 事件および *The Medita*, SMA 1150 (Arb. at N. Y. 1977) 事件を参照）。また，傭船者が良好な気象での船主の履行担保違反につき損害賠償請求を認められたが，荒天時傭船契約上の担保に応じることが不可能であることに考慮は払われなかった *The Drosia*, SMA 1303 (Arb. at N. Y. 1979) 事件も参照。ある傭船契約では，この担保は傭船期間中通して維持されねばならない継続的担保であると明示されることがある。例えば，*The Ionic*, SMA 2519 (Arb. at N. Y. 1988) 事件を参照。

　しかし，本船が担保速力に合致しているかどうかを決定するにあたって，仲裁審が一般的に従う実務は，全傭船期間を通しての本船の実績を考慮することである。仲裁審は *The Seamaid*, 1967 AMC 1362, 1364-1365 (Arb. at N. Y. 1966) 事件で，次のように述べた。

　　速力不足に対する求償（speed claim）を決定するのに，次の二つの確立された方法がある。第1は，……もっぱら良好な天候状態の日に，本船が傭船契約上の担保速力を出したか。
　　第2は，……海流と同様天候条件を考慮に入れて，本船が全航海で出した平均速力が傭船契約上の表示に照らして妥当であったか。

仲裁審の多数意見は，通常，両基準共使用すべきであるという見解である。

The Stove Vulkan, SMA 292（Arb. at N. Y. 1968）事件において，仲裁審は，速力担保義務違反が存在したかどうかを決定するにあたって，従うべき方法は，次のとおりであると判断した。

船舶が，満載状態で，風力5－6の追風の日を2－3日含んだ風力4以下の気象条件の日に出した平均速力が，当該傭船期間内で明らかになった本船の能力を真に示すものとすべきである，と仲裁審は判断した。

The Penta, SMA 1603（Arb. at N. Y. 1981）事件で，傭船契約はボルタイム1939書式で，「そして満載して良好な気象，平穏な海上を条件に約16 1/2ノットで航走可能」と記載されていた。仲裁人は，傭船者の速力クレームを評価する際に，使用される基準は約定の気象条件で本船の実際の成績を吟味することであると裁定した。仲裁人は，本船はこのときに担保された速力を実際に満たし，速力担保に応じる能力を証明したと認定した（*The Mount Athos*, SMA 1570（Arb. at N. Y. 1981）事件も参照）。

船舶の実績を，航走距離を航海所要時間で割って評価する「距離／速力」論は，仲裁審において，速力不足かどうかの決定方法として，幾度かその適用を拒絶されている（*The Bedeburn*, 1931 AMC 1678（Arb.）; *The Cape Palmas*, SMA 440（Arb. at N. Y. 1964）各事件参照）。

一度速力不足が決定された場合，傭船料減額は，速力が欠くことのできない要素であった期間についてのみ行われる。この考えは *The Olympic Garland*, SMA 1209（Arb. at N. Y. 1978）事件で表明された見解である。この事件では，本船は穏やかな気象で15.75ノットの保証平均速力を維持できなかった。その結果，傭船料減額は港での碇泊期間も含めた全期間に基づくのでもなく，穏やかな気象の航走期間のみに限定されるわけでもなく，穏やかな気象で本船が実際に出した14.83ノットの速力で傭船契約の距離を航走するのに必要と思われる期間に基づいて計算された。*The Mangalia*, SMA 2839（Arb. at N. Y. 1991）事件で，仲裁人は，全航海の実績は穏やかな気象の期間の平均速力に基づいて評価されると裁定した。

速力担保条項は，第1条における傭船期間中，本船を十分な稼働状態に保つという第1条に基づく船主の保証（undertaking）との関連でも，また考慮されなければならない。この条項における保証は，船舶の性能担保に関する限り，本船は，傭船期間中，傭船開始時と実質上同一の状態を，維持していなければならないことを要求している。引渡後，船体機関または装置に故障が生じ，船舶の速力や燃料消費に不利に影響した場合，たとえ傭船者が引渡時の速力担保違反を実際上立証することができなくても，本条項を根拠として，傭船者は船主に対し求償権を主張できる（*Hellenic Bulk Transport S. A.* v. *Burmah Oil Tankers Ltd.*, SMA 1086（Arb. at N. Y. 1976）; *Compania Venetico de Navegacion S. A.* v. *Presthus Chartering A/S*, SMA 1110（Arb. at N. Y. 1977）; *Romano* v. *West India Fruit & S. S. Co.*, 151 F. 2d 727（5th Cir. 1945）; *The Astraea*, 124 F. 83（E. D. N. Y. 1903）各事件参照）。

The Grace V, SMA 1760（Arb. at N. Y. 1982）事件で，仲裁審は気象航路選定サービスの用意した報告に基づく傭船者の速力クレームを認容することを拒否した。

仲裁審は，信頼度の低い出所から得た想定気象条件で調整した航海について実使用時間に基づく速力クレームは，認められないと長年一貫して裁定してきた。

さらに，契約の文言と商業的解釈では，荒天期は考慮の対象からはずされるのに使用された気象

サービスの調査結果に基づく速力クレームの申立の中で傭船者が用いた方法によれば，傭船契約に基づく速力評価は全天候計算に有効に換算されることになる（強調は原典による）。

仲裁審は独立系の気象航路選定サービス業者の用意した報告よりも本船の航海日誌に拠るのを良しとした。仲裁審は，本船の記録は「考えられる普通の状況と一致せずに，統合性がないか，あるいはいかなる信頼性もない」ことが証明されない限り，大抵の場合本船の記録に頼る（*The Manila Enterprise*, SMA 2060（Arb. at N. Y. 1983）事件．*The Nilam*, SMA 2705（Arb. at N. Y. 1990）事件，*The Georgios*, SMA 2005（Arb. at N. Y. 1984）事件，*The Trade Endeavor*, SMA 1916（Arb. at N. Y. 1983）事件および *The Spray Cap*, SMA 1706（Arb. at N. Y. 1982）事件参照）。ある事案では，気象航路選定サービスの報告は本船の日誌より信頼性があると認定された（例として後出413頁で議論される *The United Bounty*, SMA 2040（Arb. at N. Y. 1984）事件を参照）。

「約」

速力表示は，通常，「約 about」という文言を付して示される。これは，表示の速力以下0.5ノットの余裕を船主に与えると，繰り返し判断されている（例として *The Northern Clipper*, 1967 AMC 1557（Arb. at N. Y. 1967）事件，*The Ghikas*, SMA 686（Arb. at N. Y. 1972）事件，*Byzantine Maritime Corp.* v. *Matthew Shipping Co. Ltd.*, SMA 972（Arb. at N. Y. 1975）事件，*The Skadi*, SMA 789（Arb. at N. Y. 1973）事件，*Hellenic Bulk Transport S. A.* v. *Burmah Oil Tankers Ltd.*, SMA 1086（Arb. at N. Y. 1976）事件，*The Panagiotis Xilas*, SMA 1035（Arb. at N. Y. 1976）事件，*The Grand Integrity*, SMA 671（Arb. at N. Y. 1971）事件，*The Stove Vulkan*, SMA 292（Arb. at N. Y. 1968）事件，*The Aghia Marina*, SMA 1236（Arb. at N. Y. 1978）事件，*The Argo Master*, SMA 1489（Arb. at N. Y. 1980）事件，および *The Astro Energy*, SMA 2771（Arb. at N. Y. 1991）事件参照）。しかし，「約」という文言の解釈は，それぞれの場合の事実関係にもよるし，また全傭船契約書中に示された当事者の意思によっても変わる（*Cargo Ships El-Yam Ltd.* v. *Stearns & Foster Co.*, 149 F. Supp. 754, 1957 AMC 668（S. D. N. Y. 1955）事件参照）。したがって，0.5ノット以上または以下の許容限度を採用するというのが，当事者の意図したところであると仲裁審が判断することもありうる。例えば *The Seamaid*, 1967 AMC 1362（Arb. at N. Y. 1966）事件では，「約10ノット」の速力を出せると傭船契約で表示された船齢20年の船舶にとって，9ノットは妥当な[117]平均全天候速力であると判示された。*The Adelfoi*, 1972 AMC 1742（Arb. at N. Y. 1972）事件では，本船が，「約」による0.5ノットの余裕に，必ずしも常に満載ではなかった事実に対する0.1ノットを加え，12.6ノットを出していた場合には，表示された燃料消費26トンで速力13ノットという担保条項を満たしていると，仲裁審は裁定した。*The Chris*, SMA 199（Arb. at N. Y. 1958）事件では，「約」は，「約10ノット」の担保に対し，0.33ノットの余裕を許容すると裁定された。

「約」という語が削除されて，担保の変更が認められなかった傭船契約の事例として，*The FFM Matarengi*, SMA 2592（Arb. at N. Y. 1988）事件を参照。

「良好な気象 Good weather」

「良好な気象」は，一般にビューフォート風力階級上風力4以下を意味する，と判断されている（前出の *The Astro Energy* 事件，前出 *The Northern Clipper* 事件。*The Miami*, SMA 240（Arb. at N. Y. 1967）事件；*The Costa Rican Trader*, SMA 203（Arb. at N. Y. 1967）；*The*

Argo Sky, SMA 627 (Arb. at N. Y. 1971);*The Adelfoi*, 1972 AMC 1742, 1743 (Arb. at N. Y. 1972); *The Alma*, SMA 261 (Arb. at N. Y. 1964); *The Union Mariner*, SMA 89 (Arb. at N. Y. 1960))。*The Stove Vulkan*, SMA 292 (Arb. at N. Y. 1968)事件で,「良好な気象」は,「風力4を含み,風が追手または正横後45度より後方から吹く場合には,風力5および6を含めることができる」と,仲裁審は裁定した。

FFM Matarengi, SMA 2592 (Arb. at N. Y. 1988)事件で,仲裁審は「穏和な気象 moderate weather」は風力4を含む4までの風の状態で測定されるべきものであると裁定した。*The Leonidas Glory*, SMA 2753 (Arb. at N. Y. 1991)事件で,ニューヨーク・プロデュース書式を一部修正して「良好な気象」は逆潮またはうねりがない風力3までと修正・規定した。船主が全気象の下での性能保証を傭船契約に定めた事例として *The Ypapadi*, SMA 2814 (Arb. at N. Y. 1991)事件参照。

船底汚損

速力担保と,本船を完全な稼働状態に保持するという付随的約束に関して生ずる共通の問題は,本船の速力を低下させる船底汚損である。誰がこの危険を負担するのか。

初期の事案では,入渠させる船主の義務との関連で,この問題を検討していた。したがって,傭船者が,入渠条項を定めなかった場合,通常の熱帯航路での船底汚損は,第15条の意味する故障または船体の瑕疵ではないと判示された (*Glasgow Shipowner's Co.* v. *Bacon*, 139 F. 541 (2d Cir. 1905); *Damps. Norden* v. *Isbrandtsen-Moller Co.* (*The Katonia*), 43 F. 2d 560, 1930 AMC 1441 (S. D. N. Y. 1930))。*The Katonia* 事件で述べられたように,

> 傭船者は,本船の配船先および航海水域を知っているのであるから,貝藻による船体汚損の結果から,自己を守りたいのであれば,このような事態に対処する特別の条項を定めておくべきである。貝藻繁殖の危険を承知していながら,後日,船体汚損とはまったく異なる事態に対処するための一般的性能保持に関する規定を持ち出して,船主に責任を負わせようとすることは認められない (43 F. 2d at 562)。

傭船契約が入渠条項を含む場合,船底汚損を容易に認識できるなら,船主は,船底貝藻を除去するため,本船を入渠させる義務があると裁定されてきた。このようにして,*The Praxiteles*, SMA 104, 600 (Arb at N. Y. 1964)事件では,貝藻繁殖が発見されたのに,船主が本船を入渠させなかった場合,船主は船底汚損から生ずる速力不足に責任があると裁定された。ニューヨーク・プロデュース書式の第21条は,船底の貝藻繁殖がないことが明らかであり,入渠が不必要であると思われる場合ですら,熱帯航海の場合には,6ヶ月毎に,入渠することを要求している (*Munson S. S. Line* v. *Miramar S. S. Co.*, 166 F. 722 (2d Cir. 1908),裁量上告拒絶 214 U. S. 526; *Noyes* v. *Munson S. S. Line*, 173 F. 814 (S. D. N. Y. 1909); *Falls of Keltie S. S. Co.* v. *United States & A. S. S. Co.*, 108 F. 416 (S. D. N. Y. 1901)。*The FFM Matarengi*, SMA 2592 (Arb. at N. Y. 1988)事件も参照)。

いくつかの事案は,船底汚損の責任問題を無視する傾向にあり,船底汚損の結果の速力低下を,オフハイヤー条項に基づき,他の諸事項と同様に,単なる欠陥 (deficiency) の問題として取り扱っている (*The Northern Clipper*, 1967 AMC 1557 (Arb. N. Y. 1967)事件および *The Panagiotis Xilas*, SMA 1035 (Arb. at N. Y. 1976)各事件参照)。447頁のオフハイヤー条項に関する議論参照。

船底汚損が引渡前に存在する場合,船主は,もちろん責任を負わなければならない。*The*

Atlanta, 82 F. Supp. 218, 1948 AMC 1769 (S.D. Ga. 1948). 同様に，*The Pomona*, SMA 118 (Arb. at N. Y. 1966) 事件で，船主は，長期のオフハイヤー期間中に進行した船底汚損により生じた遅延に対し，責任があると判断された。

一方，傭船期間中における船底の貝藻繁殖は，傭船者の責任であると裁定されてきた。*The Stove Vulkan*, SMA 292 (Arb. at N. Y. 1968) 事件では，傭船者は，傭船契約期間中，船底貝藻繁殖に起因する往復航海の速力不足に寄与しているとして，責任ありと裁定された。仲裁審は，速力不足に対する裁定額から，その25パーセントは，船底の貝藻繁殖のためであるとして，その分だけ差し引いた。*The Mount Athos*, SMA 1570 (Arb. at N. Y. 1981) 事件で，仲裁人は速力算定で船底の貝藻繁殖の存在により生じた速力低下分を差し引いた。

The Milly Gregos, SMA 2190 (Arb. at N. Y. 1986) 事件で，仲裁審はフィリピンで本船が長期滞船期間中に船底に貝藻が繁殖したことによる速力不足についての傭船者の請求を否定した。仲裁審は，傭船者は自らの費用で船底清掃をしてその問題を解決する権利を持っていると述べた。同様に，*The Mykali II*, SMA 2240 (Arb. at N. Y. 1986) 事件で，仲裁審は Durban に長期滞船中に船底と推進器に貝藻が繁殖するのは「船舶が傭船者の指示に応じた自然なかつ予見できる結果である」と裁定した。仲裁審は，燃料過剰消費についての請求とともに，本船はオフハイヤーであるとの傭船者の請求を否定した。

The Happy Empress, SMA 2599 (Arb. at N. Y. 1989) 事件で，船体外板清掃費用についての船主の請求は，傭船契約は傭船者が船体外板清掃に責任ありとの文言を含んでおらず，船主は本船をその航海にあらゆる点で装備せしめる義務を履行できなかったという多数意見に基づき認容されなかった。この事案は，混成の航海が関わっており，定期傭船契約は海上備蓄の条項を設けていた。備蓄を許容するよう修正された航海傭船契約が関わっている *The Grand*, SMA 2548 (Arb. at N. Y. 1989) 事件と比較。傭船者は，貨物荷役ホースの損傷を防ぐために揚荷ターミナルの要求により船舶の外板からフジツボを除去する費用につき責任があると裁定された。

燃料消費

表示速力を維持するための燃料消費量が，速力の表示のすぐ後に記載される。この表示もまた傭船者への船舶引渡時，充足されなければならない担保である。速力と燃料消費の担保は，別個の保証ではなく，まとめて解釈されるべきであると，仲裁審が裁定した。仲裁審が，*The Vendelso*, SMA 663 (Arb. at N. Y. 1971) 事件で述べているように，「適合するということは，両方の担保を満足させなければならず，一方のみを尊重するということではない」。しかし，*The Olympic Garland*, SMA 1209 (Arb. at N. Y. 1978) 事件で仲裁人は，違う裁定をした。ディーゼル燃料油と高粘度燃料油の消費の組み合わせが船主が責任を負う純消費を決定すると述べ，かつまた，ある燃料油を過剰消費し，他の燃料油を過小消費する組み合わせは純過小消費となるとの見解を指摘した上で，仲裁審は過小消費の燃料油の純差額の価値は速力不足の損害賠償から差し引かれるべきであるとの船主の要請を拒否し，「契約の速力と消費の保証は互いに独立して，他方の価値を調整するのに使うことはできない」ときっぱり裁定した。

しかし，*The Panamax Venus*, SMA 1979 (Arb. at N. Y. 1984) 事件で，仲裁審は過小消費についての船主の請求は速力不足の傭船者の請求と相殺できると認定した。

速力担保と同様，「約」という文言の許容限度は，各事案の事実関係によるが，船主の義務を緩和するものである。*The Medita*, SMA 1150 (Arb. at N. Y. 1977) 事件で，本船は傭船契約に記述のある「約」という文言に3パーセントの許容限度を与えられた。同じ許容限度が

The FFM Matarengi, SMA 2592 (Arb. at N.Y. 1988) 事件で適用された。しかし, *The Astro Energy*, SMA 2771 (Arb. at N.Y. 1991) 事件で, 仲裁審は,「約」という文言についての業界の標準許容限度は5パーセントであると裁定した。*The Areti S*, 1965 AMC 2116 (Arb. at N.Y. 1965) 事件で, 本船が平均燃料消費24.35トンで9.5ノットを出した場合について, 仲裁審は, 表示された燃料消費26/27トンで速力10ノットという担保条項に違反していないと判断した (*The Atlantic Master*, SMA 510 (Arb. at N.Y.) 事件, *The Panagiotis Xilas*, SMA 1035 (Arb. at N.Y. 1976) 事件, *The United Bounty*, SMA 2040 (Arb. at N.Y. 1984) 事件参照)。

速力担保と同じく, 燃料消費量担保は, 外海における本船の実績に対してのみ適用される (*The Eurytan*, SMA 289 (Arb. at N.Y. 1968))。しかし, *The Alma*, SMA 261 (Arb. at N.Y. 1964) 事件では, 碇泊中の燃料消費が異常に大きく, 担保義務違反であると判断された。

The Maro, SMA 2533 (Arb. at N.Y. 1988) 事件は, 南アフリカから前ソビエト連邦への航海の「遅い航行」についての請求であった。傭船者は傭船契約に言及のない文言である「経済速力」の航海を本船に指示した。これに応えて本船は8.25ノットの平均速力でゆっくりと航走した。仲裁審は, 結果は全速力航海の際に担保されていた12トン以上の燃料消費であり, 航海期間は12日延びたと認定した。傭船者は, 全速力航海として計算された費用を超えた金額の支払を裁定された。

本船の動静

船舶の動静に関する表示は, その表示状況における表示の重要性しだいにより, 担保となることもある (*Davison* v. *Von Lingen*, 113 U.S. 40, 41 (1885) 事件 (担保) と *Lovell* v. *Davis*, 101 U.S. 541 (1879) 事件 (非担保) を比較されたい)。

Davison 事件において,「本船がいつ, どこにいるかが, その契約の重大かつ本質的部分である」と裁判所は認定した。したがって, 裁判所によれば, 本船の動静に関する表示は担保であり, その違反は, 解約または損害賠償請求を正当化するものである。裁判所によれば,

> 本船は,「Philadelphia向け貨物を積載して, Benizafから現在出帆したか, 出帆しようとしている」という傭船契約書の表示が, 担保または停止条件であることは明白であると考える。それは, 契約中の単なる表示ではなく, まさに契約の本質部分をなすものである。また, 損害賠償請求の根拠としてのみ役立つ, 独立の合意事項でもない。そこに表示されたとおり履行がなされなかった場合, それが一部の不履行であっても, それにより不利益を被る者は, 相手方の担保違反を追及して, 契約を正当に拒絶することができる (113 U.S. at 49-50)。

St. Lawrence 水路凍結時期が近づきつつあるときに, 船舶の現在位置は重大問題であるという理由で, 本船の位置に関する船主の善意の不実表示が解約を許容すると判示した *Himoff Indus.* v. *Seven Seas Shipping Corp.*, 1976 AMC 1030, 1032-33 (N.Y. Sup. 1976) 事件も参照。

[120] 一方, *Lovell* 事件において, 裁判所は, 傭船者が本船の動静に関する表示が正しくないことを知っており, したがってこの表示をまったく頼りにしなかった場合, かかる表示は担保ではなく, 単なる事実の表示にすぎないと判示した。同傭船契約上, 本船は New Orleans 港に碇泊中と表示されていたが, 実際は洋上にいた。本船の New Orleans 到着は遅延し, 傭船者は傭船契約を解約した。裁判所は, 本船の動静に関する表示は, 傭船者がそれに依拠しなかったのであるから, 重要性を認められるべきものではないとして, 船主勝訴を言い渡した。

しかしながら，傭船者が，本船の真の動静を知らずに，本船の動静に関する船主の不実表示を基礎として，契約するに至ったとしたら，*Lovell* 事件は，まったく異なった結果となっていたと思われる。このような状況において，傭船者は，契約法の一般原則に従い，損害賠償の請求原因を有することになったと思われる。

傭 船 期 間

"13. Witnesseth, That the said Owners agree to let, and the said Charterers agree to hire the said vessel, from the time of delivery, for
14. about ...."

「上記船主が，上記船舶をその引渡のときから，向う，約...............の期間，上記傭船者に貸し渡し，上記傭船者がこれを借り受けることに合意した旨の証となるものである。」

「賃貸」と「賃借」

ニューヨーク・プロデュース書式，その他類似の定期傭船契約書式で使用されている，「賃貸 let」と「賃借 hire」の文言は誤解を招く。この文言や「引渡」「返船」という文言があるにもかかわらず，船主は本船を賃貸するわけではなく，また本船の占有を手放すわけでもない。しかし，「引渡」「返船」の表現は，傭船期間の開始，終止時点を記述するのに使われてきた（*The Peonia*［1991］1 Lloyd's Rep. 100（同判例集107頁）事件と *The Berge Tasta*［1975］1 Lloyd's Rep. 422（同判例集424頁）事件を参照）。この契約形式における船主の義務は，船舶，船長および乗組員による約定役務を傭船者に提供することである（後出612/613頁参照）。

引　　　渡

傭船期間は「引渡」をもって始まる。この文言自体は，本船および乗組員を，18行に表示の場所で，傭船者の使用に委ねることしか意味しない。*The Madeleine*［1967］2 Lloyd's Rep. 224（同判例集238頁）事件で，Roskill 判事は，次のように判示している。「船主は，この傭船契約書式（ボルタイム）に基づき，船舶および船長，乗組員の役務を，傭船者の使用に委ねることにより，船舶を定期傭船者に引き渡したこととなり，それ以降，傭船者は，船舶使用に関して（傭船契約条項の範囲内で）船長，乗組員を指図することができるし，船主は自己の船長，乗組員が，このような指図に従うべきことを約定している」。

傭船期間開始前に備えるべき要件については，後出205から213頁参照。傭船料の支払のための計算開始時期については，後出341から342頁参照。

傭船期間（期間超過・期間不足）

次の章で，法が明示あるいは黙示する傭船期間の許容期間に関する効果（後出178頁から180頁参照）と傭船契約上の最終航海の指図に関する傭船者の義務，および実際の返船が遅過ぎる（期間超過），あるいは早過ぎる（期間不足）場合の効果を取り扱う。

最終航海

傭船期間満了までに返船を可能とするような最終航海の指図が当然に予想されるとの意味

で，その最終航海の指図が有効であろうとなかろうと，傭船者が，最終航海の指図を出し，それが結局明示または黙示の許容期間を含めた傭船期間を超過する場合，傭船者は契約違反となる（The Peonia［1991］1 Lloyd's Rep. 100（同判例集107頁）事件と The Berge Tasta［1975］1 Lloyd's Rep. 422（同判例集424頁）事件参照）。

122 The Peonia 事件の判決までは，判例により，最終航海の指図が有効あるいは「適法」である場合には，傭船期間の満了後に返船することは契約違反ではないと一般的に理解されていた（The Dione［1975］1 Lloyd's Rep. 115（同判例集117頁）事件で記録長官 Denning 卿が表明した見解を参照）。

後出 The London Explorer 事件で，貴族院は，最終航海は傭船期間満了前の返船を可能にすると当然に考えられたが，船舶が現実には傭船期間満了（明示または黙示の許容期間を含めて）までに返船されなかった場合に，市場料率が約定料率より低い場合でも，傭船者は返船日まで傭船契約上の約定料率を支払わなければならないと判示した。ニューヨーク・プロデュース書式では，そういう状況の下で約定料率により傭船料を支払うという義務の継続は54行（第4条）の「傭船料は返船日の時間まで継続する」という文言で強調されている。

 London Explorer 号は，ニューヨーク・プロデュース書式で，14行の「約 about」という前置印刷文言を削除して，期間「12ヶ月プラスマイナス15日傭船者任意」で傭船された。本船は，期間内に十分返船できると考えられる最終航海に配船されたが，予見できなかったストライキにより，返船は期間満了時よりかなり遅延した。運賃市況が下落して，傭船者は，傭船者自身が契約に違反したので，したがって，その期間中，傭船契約で約定した（市況より高い）料率で，傭船料を支払い続けるのではなくて，その時点での市場料率で，「超過期間」の損害賠償を支払うべきであると認定させようとした。貴族院は，この傭船者の論議を退けて，次のように判示した。傭船契約期間満了までに返船できない場合に傭船者に契約違反が存するか否かにかかわらず，第4条に従い，傭船料を支払う傭船者の義務は，本船の返船日時まで，継続しかつ存在する。
 The London Explorer［1971］1 Lloyd's Rep. 523.
 （Hector v. Sovfracht（1945）78 Ll.L. Rep. 275 事件も参照）

 The London Explorer 事件についての貴族院の発言は，市場料率が約定料率を下回らず約定料率を上回った場合にどうなるのかという点に，疑問を残す。船主は，前述の意味で最終航海の指図が適法であるとしても，傭船期間満了後，損害賠償として高い傭船料を請求できるのであろうか。Cross 卿が同意した Reid 卿の発言は，この疑問に否定的答えを示しているが，Guest 卿と Donovan 卿が同意した Morris 卿の発言は，次の1節を含んでいる。「たとえ傭船契約に設定された日時が本質的なものとは考えられず，約定日時後の本船の継続使用は即時にその継続使用が契約違反であるという結果とならないとしても，返船は妥当な時間内であることが必要である。したがって，第4条に似た条項で傭船者は現実の返船時に約定料率で傭船料を支払い，（市場料率が約定料率を超えるなら）加えて妥当な時間以内に返船できないことに関して損害賠償金を支払う責任があるというのはもっともなことであろう」。
 後出 The Peonia 事件で，控訴院は，傭船者が事実として傭船期間満了までに返船できなかった場合，傭船者の最終航海の指示の適法性は傭船者が損害賠償を支払う妨げにならないと判示した。後出 The Gregos［1995］1 Lloyd's Rep. 1 事件で，貴族院は The Peonia 事件の控訴院の判決の正当性を前提に手続を進めた。

 Peonia 号は「最短約10ヶ月，最長約12ヶ月の定期傭船，正確な期間は傭船者任意」のニューヨー

ク・プロデュース書式で傭船された。15行に「傭船者は後述の就航区域内で最終航海を完了する追加選択権をも持つ」と追記された。本船は1987年6月11日に引き渡された。1988年5月6日に傭船者は，7月19日前に返船できなくなると思われる航海を決めた。船主は抗議し，6月25日（「約」という語につき14日の余裕期間を付けて）までに返船となる航海指図を要求した。そのような指図は出されることなく，結局船主は要求を取り下げた。

傭船者は，15行に追記の「追加選択権」により傭船期間内の返船となると予想しえない最終航海を本船に指図する権利があると主張した。その主張は，たとえそのときまで市場料率が上回ったとしても傭船者は適法な最終航海の超過期間につき約定料率で支払う権利があるので，傭船者の「追加選択権」は，追加の権利，つまりこの権利がない場合には，傭船期間内の返船となると予想しえないので，違法となる最終航海に本船を配船する追加の権利をもたらす，ということであった。

[123]

この主張は，商事裁判所のSaville判事と控訴院により否定された。The London Explorer 事件とThe Dione 事件の適正な解釈に基づき，傭船者が（船主側の過失という理由以外の他の理由で）傭船期間満了までに返船できない場合には，傭船者は最終航海指図の適法性にもかかわらず契約違反であり，市場料率が約定料率より高いなら，それ以降市場料率を支払う責任がある。本事案では，15行の追加選択権により，傭船者が主張する広い権利は傭船者に与えられず，傭船者は損害賠償の潜在的責任から保護された。

Hyundai Merchant Marine v. *Gesuri Chartering* (*The Peonia*) [1991] 1 Lloyd's Rep. 100.

返船遅れの結果

返船にとり時間が契約の本質的なものであり，そうしてその違反が船主に契約を終了したものとして扱う権利を与えるような条件（a condition）であるのかという問題が，後出 *The Gregos* 事件で生じた。Templeman卿は，返船にとり時間はまさに本質的なものであると判示した。しかしながらAckner卿，Slynn卿とWoolf卿も同意したように，Mustill卿は，この問題の確固とした結論は不必要であると考え，時宜を得た返船は「無名の」条件（term）（前出139頁参照）であり，短期の返船の遅れは契約終結の正当事由とはならないという見解に与したいと思うと述べた。本問題に関してMustill卿が表明した見解は，むしろ支持されるべきものと思われる。

ボルタイム第7条

ボルタイム書式（前出22頁）第7条第2節の効果については後出635頁参照。

最終航海の指図

最終航海の指図の有効性または適法性は第1に，指図が遂行される時期に判定されるべきである。

傭船者はいくらか事前に最終航海の指図を発するかもしれないし，通常そうするであろう。その指図が出されたときに，指図されたその本船の使用は傭船期間満了（明示または黙示の余裕期間を含め）までに返船となると合理的に予測できるという意味で，その指図は有効であると思われる場合には，船主に指図を拒否する権利はない。しかし，前もって出された最終航海の指図の有効性は一時的なものに過ぎない。指図が結果として有効でなくなるような状況変化があれば船主は通常その航海を履行する義務を免除される。

Gregos 号は，ニューヨーク・プロデュース書式で「約50日，最高70日間」，返船は1988年3月18日以前という条件で傭船された。2月9日にFosへ向けて最終航海の指図が出された。その時点では，指図は期限内返船を可能としていた。しかし，2月12日に他船が座礁し，最後から2番目の航海

の揚荷港と最終航海の積荷港のある Orinoco 河は数日間に亘り塞がれた。したがって Gregos 号は2月25日にやっと積荷港に到着した。その時点で，Fos までの最終航海は3月18日までに完了できず，2日から4日の期間超過が予想された。2月25日に船主は傭船者に，Fos 向けの最終航海の履行を拒否し，そして適法な最終航海の修正指図を出すよう傭船者に要請したが，要請が受け入れられない場合には，傭船者は契約を拒否したものとして取り扱い，それに従って本船を引き揚げると通知した。傭船者は元の指図を変えず，修正指図を出すことを拒否した。

124　貴族院は全員一致で，控訴院の決定を覆し，仲裁裁定と第1審の Evans 判事の判決を支持して，傭船者は傭船契約を拒否したので，船主は契約を解消したものとして扱うことができると判示した。冒頭陳述で Mustill 卿は次のように述べた。

(1) 傭船者の指図の有効性を判断する日時は最終航海の履行時であり，本件では2月25日である。もともと有効であった指図はそのときまでに無効となった。
(2) 最終航海の指図を含めて定期傭船本船の使用に関する無効な指図を発することはたとえそれ自身が傭船契約違反（判決の目的にとり正確であると想定されるが，決定していない）であるとしても，船主が主張しているようにその違反は必ずしも傭船契約の拒否とはならない。
(3) 傍論であるが，期限内に返船する傭船者の義務は条件（a condition）（前出138頁）というより無名の条件（an innominate term）であり，短期の超過期間では船主は契約を解消したものとして扱うことを正当化できないし，このことは，超過しそうな航海の指図は必ず傭船契約の拒否となる（Templeman 卿の発言に反する）という船主の主張にたぶん致命的となろう。
(4) しかし，Gregos 号の傭船者は最終航海の有効な指図を出す継続する基本的義務を負っており，元の指図が，無効となったので，傭船者は傭船契約の第11条に基づき，有効な指図を出す義務がある。傭船者が無効な指図に固執して，契約にもはや拘束されないという意思を明確にしたので，傭船契約の拒否に至った。

　　Torvald Klaverness v. *Arni Maritime*（*The Gregos*）[1992] 2 Lloyd's Rep. 40, [1994] 1 Lloyd's Rep. 335（C. A.）および [1995] 1 Lloyd's Rep. 1（H. L.）.

Mustill 判事の発言からすると，ある状況下では，最終航海が開始した後でさえ，船主は傭船者の指図に従った最終航海を完了する義務から解放されることになるようである。彼は，報告書の7頁に次のように述べた。

「……傭船者が履行時期について指図を前もって出せることが実際上双方の当事者の利益のためには，必要であるが，これは少なくとも指図の有効性に関する取り敢えずの判断を伴うに違いない。指図に従えば船主が引き受けていない役務を求められることになることが早期の段階で判るならば，船主は即時にそのように言い，指図を拒否できる。しかし指図が外見的に有効である場合，約束した役務のとおりであるかは役務の性質が決定的に知られるまで，判明せず，その有効性は一時的なものに違いない。そしてこの役務の性質は役務が開始するまで判らず，ある場合には事態が進展した後となる。したがって，求められる役務が，船主が前もって提供することを約した役務である場合およびその限りにおいて，特定の指図は然るべきときに役務を履行する特定の義務を生み出す。しかし，そのような状態が持続する限りである。状況が変化し，指図に応諾することが原契約で船主が決して引き受けなかった役務を求めることになる場合には，応諾義務は消え去らねばならない。私が見てきたように，事前の傭船者の指図は継続する要件となり，その有効性は時の経過と共に変化する」。

もちろん，船主はある状況では，傭船者の指図を応諾して，したがってそれ以降の指図への応諾を拒否する権利を放棄するかもしれない。しかし，応諾の方法が返船の遅れにつき損害を回収する船主の権利を妨げるようなものであることは滅多にあるまい（後出参照）。

The Democritos ［1976］2 Lloyd's Rep. 149 事件で，Bridge 卿判事は，妥当性の判断基準となる，最終航海とは何であるかを決めることの困難な事件もあることを予測している。同判事は，The Dione 事件における控訴院は最終航海をヨーロッパから River Plate の往復航海であると解釈しているが，この点についての議論が聴取されていないと指摘している。記録長官 Denning 卿は「最終全航海」と言っている。

　船舶の最終航海とみなされるものが適法か否かは，傭船者が実際に本船に何を指図したかによっても，また判断されるべきである。The Mareva A. S. ［1977］1 Lloyd's Rep. 368 事件では，本船が最後に返船地域への積荷航海を行うという暗黙の了解ないし共通の期待があったのだが，その積荷航海を行う前段階の最終航海が，船主の責めに帰すべき事由により遅れ，そのため，返船区域への積荷航海の機会を奪われたと傭船者は主張した。しかし，積荷航海の指図を，それが出た時点で船主が拒否すれば，船主の義務違反となったと言うのであればともかく，そのような積荷航海の指図は，出されていなかったのであるから，かかる最終積荷航海の機会を奪われても，傭船者は損害賠償を請求できない，と判示された。Kerr 判事は次のように認めている。すなわち，もし，最終航海の指図と同時に，返船地域への積荷航海の指図が出されていたら，難しい問題，特にその指図が広義の最終航海のためのものか，あるいは，最終航海およびその直前の航海という実質的に二つの航海のためのものかという問題が生じたであろうと述べた（［1977］1 Lloyd's Rep. 368（同判例集379頁）参照）。

無効な最終航海指図

　返船が明示あるいは黙示の許容期間を含む傭船期間満了までに合理的には予見できないという意味で，無効な最終航海の指図を，傭船者が行った場合，あるいは出されたときには有効な指図が後で無効になった場合，船主はその指図を拒否し，新たな適法な最終航海の指図を要求できる。前出 The Gregos 事件参照。

　有効な指図が出されなかったり，傭船者が例えば無効な指図に固執するように，言葉あるいは行動で，傭船契約上の義務を履行する意思がないことを示す場合，船主は，傭船契約が終了したものとして，他に傭船を求め，損害賠償を請求できる。前出 The Gregos 事件（報告書9頁）で Mustill 卿はその見解を次の文で説明している。

　　「原指図が無効になったので，傭船者は第11条［「……傭船者は船長に時に応じてあらゆる必要な指示と航海指図を与える……」］により傭船者の権限に裏付けられた指図と取り替える義務がある。解約のときにこの義務の現実的な違反をしたかどうかは論議の余地がある。しかし，あらゆる事情により傭船者が最終日前に返船区域に本船を空船航海で返すことができない，あるいは修正した積荷航海の指図を出すことが，考えられる限りで，できないならば，時間があったのだから，いずれにしてもその違反は最終的なものではない。しかし，傭船者にはこれをしようという意思がなく，そして有効な指図が出されずに，重大な時が過ぎたことは，仲裁人が述べた事実から明白である。これが，原指図を無効とした状況の変化の意義である。指図自体は拒否とはならないが，指図が無効となった後で，傭船者が固執すれば，傭船者には傭船契約上の義務を履行する意思がないことを意味することになる。つまり，傭船者は「傭船契約にもはや拘束されないとの意思を表明した」。これは，期限前の契約違反であり船主には契約を終了したものとして扱う権利が生じる」。

　無効な指図に単独1回きり応諾したからといって，その後の指図への応諾の拒否あるいは違反について損害賠償請求する船主の権利を放棄することとはたぶんならない（The Kanchenjunga ［1987］2 Lloyd's Rep. 509,［1989］1 Lloyd's Rep. 354（C. A.）事件と［1990］1 Lloyd's

Rep. 391 (H.L.) 事件と *The Batis* [1990] 1 Lloyd's Rep. 345 (同判例集351頁) 事件と後出246頁参照)。しかし, 諸事実と指図の当然の違法性のすべてを知って, 船主が本船の航海の続行を許容した場合には, 船主は契約違反につき損害賠償請求を行う権利を, 放棄したことにはならないであろうが, その後の指図に従うことを拒否する権利についてはこれを放棄したものと通常判示される。前出142頁の権利放棄の一般的解説を参照。本船が違法な航海を引き受けるが, 契約違反につき損害賠償請求する船主の権利を放棄しない場合には, 傭船期間満了までは約定料率で, それ以降, 市況が約定料率を上回っている場合には, 返船まで船主は市場料率での傭船料を取得する権限を有する (*The Dione* [1975] 1 Lloyd's Rep. 115 事件, 特に記録長官 Denning 卿の見解 (同判例集118頁) 参照)。約定料率から市場料率への変更は早期返船の場合には生じないことに注目されたい (*The Black Falcon* [1991] 1 Lloyd's Rep. 77 (同判例集80頁) 事件参照)。傭船期間満了時の市場料率が, 約定料率を下回っている場合は, 船主に対し, 約定料率での傭船料を, 返船まで引き続き支払うべきであると言われている。これは, 特にニューヨーク・プロデュース書式の第4条のような条項を傭船契約書が含む場合, 傭|126|船者の違反に関係なく, 傭船料は, 54行の規定どおり実際の返船まで継続するという前出 *The London Explorer* 事件での貴族院の判例に従った見解である。

傭船期間の真の範囲

前出の法則に従い傭船者の最終航海の指図の有効性または無効性を決定するために, 傭船期間が追加余裕期間まで延長されるか否かを知ることが必要である。これは, 当事者が傭船期間を定める文言しだいである (*The Dione* [1975] 1 Lloyd's Rep. 115 事件の記録長官 Denning 卿の判決を一般的には参照)。

(1) 黙示の許容期間のある場合

傭船契約が, 「6ヶ月」あるいは「2年」というように, 許容期間を定めずに期間を単純に約定した場合には, 妥当な許容期間が黙示的に認められると思われる。これは, 最終航海が終了し, 本船が返船準備となる日を, 傭船者が航海計画策定にあたり, 正確に算定することは, 商業的に言って実行できるものではないという認識の結果である。黙示の許容期間がある場合には, 前述のように約定期間が規定の傭船期間を超過しても, 黙示の許容期間内に終了すると当然に予見しうる最終航海に傭船者が, 本船を配船することは, 契約違反ではない。

Blytheville 号が, 1880年6月26日から3暦月傭船された。傭船者は, 9月26日の4日後に返船できると考えて, 最終航海を指図した。Mathew 判事は, 傭船者はその指図において契約違反ではないと判示した。
Gray v. *Christie* (1889) 5 T. L. R. 577.

傭船期間を――「4ないし6ヶ月」というような――幅のある期間で約定する場合や, 返船時を期間をもって定める場合にも, 許容期間は黙示的に認められると思われる。

Democritos 号が1航海,「期間約4ないし6ヶ月」ニューヨーク・プロデュース書式で傭船された。控訴院は, 6ヶ月を超えても, 許容期間を認めるべきであると判示した。仲裁人が認めた許容期間は, 5日であった。
(約定期間に「約 about」という語が附されていなくても, 許容期間はやはり認められると思われる)。
The Democritos [1976] 2 Lloyd's Rep. 149.

次の事案では，本書の追加文言がなければ，許容期間は開始日付・終了日付の期間に追加して認められたであろう。

*Hugin*号が「1912年5月15/31日から1912年10月15/31日まで」の間，定期傭船された。傭船契約には，ニューヨーク・プロデュース書式54/55行同様の印刷文言で，「本船を英国東海岸の港で返船するまで，（滅失しない限り）引き続き傭船料を支払う」と規定されており，さらに「1912年10月15日から31日までの間に」と加筆されていた。1912年10月18日に，傭船者は10月31日までに返船できないような航海を指図した。10月31日以降の傭船料につき，市場料率で請求がなされたが，Atkin判事は次のように判示した。
(1) 手書の追加文言がなければ，10月31日以降も妥当な許容期間が認められたであろう。
(2) 手書の追加文言は10月31日までの返船義務を傭船者に課している。したがって船主はその日以降市場料率を請求できる。

Atkin判事は，次のように述べている。「〔当事者が〕10月31日以降の契約継続の権利を明白に否定しようとして，言い換えれば，傭船契約書に記載した月日を契約の要素として，傭船料は10月31日で終了すべきであり，本船はその日までに返船されるべきであるということを明確にする目的で，この文言を使用したと推定するのが適当であると思う」。
Watson Steamship v. *Merryweather*（1913）18 Com. Cas. 294.

127 ニューヨーク・プロデュース書式の14行のように，傭船期間の前に，「約」という文言が付される場合，黙示の許容期間を支持する推定は補強される。

(2) 黙示の許容期間のない場合

当事者が傭船期間を，ある最短期間とある最長期間の間の期間であると傭船契約書に明示した場合，裁判所は規定の最長期間を超える許容期間を，認めないと思われる。

*Mareva A. S.*号は，ニューヨーク・プロデュース書式により，1航海傭船された。追加協定書(1)で傭船期間を「5ヶ月プラスマイナス20日傭船者任意」と定めた。その後，さらに追加協定書で「傭船者は，本船を5ヶ月20日間の全傭船期間満了後，引き続き最短2ヶ月最長3ヶ月の期間傭船する」と定めた。Kerr判事は，この3ヶ月をさらに超える許容期間は，認められないと判示した。
The Mareva A. S.［1977］1 Lloyd's Rep. 368.
（最短／最長期間については，［1977］2 Lloyd's Rep. 1および後出636頁の*The Johnny*事件と*The Gregos*［1992］2 Lloyd's Rep. 40（同判例集41頁）事件を参照。そこでは，「約50日最長70日傭船者任意とする期間の定期傭船」の文言は，70日を超えて許容期間を認めないという仲裁人の見解が控訴院で両当事者に受け入れられた）

同様に，傭船期間を規定するのに当事者が例えば基本の許容期間に，「プラスマイナス20日」を追加して許容期間を明示する場合には，追加の許容期間は黙示されない。*The London Explorer*［1971］1 Lloyd's Rep. 523事件での，貴族院の判決の一部分から判断して，こういう場合に，それを超えてさらに妥当な期間が認められるとも考えられたが，この点は，次の事件で，控訴院の多数意見で否定された。

*Dione*号は，ボルタイム書式で「6ヶ月プラスマイナス20日傭船者任意の期間」，定期傭船された。引渡からの6ヶ月は，1970年9月8日で終わり，20日プラスした日は9月28日であった。7月24日Anconaで揚荷中，傭船者は，合理的に考えて約73日を要するRiver Plate往復航海に，配船の意思を表明した。船主が抗議したにもかかわらず，傭船者は8月2日本船をRiver Plateに配船し，本

船は10月7日まで返船されなかった。仲裁人は，事実認定において，6ヶ月20日間をさらに超えて，許容期間を認めることができるならば，実際の8.4日間の超過は妥当であると判断した。控訴院は多数決で次のように判示した。
(1) 契約条項は，許容期間を「プラスマイナス20日」と明示しており，それ以上許容期間を認める余地をまったく残していない。したがって，
(2) 傭船期間は9月28日で満了し，傭船者が8月2日に，本船をPlateに航行するよう指図したことは，傭船期間内に航海が終了するとは考えられないという点で，不当であり，
(3) 傭船者は，9月28日以降10月7日まで，高い市場料率を本船傭船料として支払わねばならない。

The Dione [1975] 1 Lloyd's Rep. 115.

傭船契約印刷書式の傭船期間の表示（ニューヨーク・プロデュース書式の14行を参照）の前にある「約」という文言を当事者が削除する場合，裁判所が黙示の許容傭船期間を認めるのかどうか，最終的な決定をみていない。前出 The London Explorer 事件で，Reid卿は，当事者自身が起案した原案の文言の削除はともかくとして，標準印刷書式からの「約」という文言の削除については，考慮を払うべきであるという明確な見解を持っていた。しかし，その点に関しては，争われなかったので，同卿は最終意見の表明を差し控えた。

傭船期間が12ヶ月「プラスマイナス傭船者任意45日」であると明示された The Matija Gubec [128][1983] 1 Lloyd's Rep. 24 事件で，Staughton判事は「約」という文言がもともと傭船契約の印刷書式にあったのか，削除されたのか，あるいは「約」という文言はまったくなかったのかが問題であるとは考えなかった。いずれの場合でも明示の許容期間により黙示の許容期間はなくなる。しかし，印刷書式から「約」という文言を削除することは，不明確な文言の解釈に影響を及ぼす。標準書式の削除に関する一般的問題については，Drefus v. Parnaso [1959] 1 Lloyd's Rep. 125 事件でのDiplock判事の判決（同判例集130頁）および Punjab Bank v. De Boinville [1992] 1 Lloyd's Rep. 7 (C. A.) 事件のStaughton判事の判決（同判例集32頁）参照。

原許容期間が「傭船者任意プラスマイナス3ヶ月付き5年間の定期傭船」と明示されている場合，返船の許容期間を狭める契約上の権利（義務でもあると判示された）を遅れて行使した事案について，The Didymi and The Leon [1984] 1 Lloyd's Rep. 583 (C. A.) 事件参照。

裁判所が黙示する許容期間の範囲

裁判所または仲裁人が前出(1)で黙示する許容期間の範囲は，個々の事案の状況しだいである。しかし，その範囲は基本的な傭船期間の長さに多分に影響を受けるようである。The Democritos [1975] 1 Lloyd's Rep. 386 事件で，Kerr判事は，「約4ないし6ヶ月」の傭船契約事案における仲裁人の事実認定について，次のように言っている。「……おそらく『約』という文言があるために，また，一般に当然のこととして，定期傭船契約の返船期日は，おおよその目安に過ぎないものであり，ある程度妥当な超過は許されるものとみなすべきであるという理由で，仲裁人は，6ヶ月の期間をさらに5日間延長した。私も同じ結論をとるか，あるいは，より大きな許容を認めるかどうかは，本裁判の問題ではないので，ここでは言及しない。仲裁人は，仲裁人が妥当と認めた期間を加算している。……」。

The Berge Tasta [1975] 1 Lloyd's Rep. 422 事件で，Donaldson判事は，1969年4月25日以降30ヶ月の連続航海傭船に対し，1971年10月25日前後10ないし11日間以内の返船を，まさしく妥当な許容期間内のものと考えたし，また The Dione [1975] 1 Lloyd's Rep. 115 事件で，Londonの仲裁人は，6ヶ月20日間の期間に対する8.4日の超過を（超過が認められるとすれば）妥当であると考えた（Meyer v. Sanderson (1916) 32 T. L. R. 428 事件も参照）。

「最終航海」条項の効果

　船舶が傭船期間満了時に最終航海途上にある場合に，発生しうる事態に備え傭船契約に特別条項を設定することがある。それは Shelltime 3 書式の第18条のような標準印刷条項であることもあれば，あるいは特別な追加条項であることもある。

　適法な最終航海が傭船期間を超過したときに傭船者を損害賠償の責任から保護する条項と，その条項がなければ，違法となる最終航海の指図を有効に適法とする大きな権限を裁判所が認める条項とは区別しなければならない。

　前出174頁の *The Peonia* 事件で，傭船期間は「最低約10ヶ月最高12ヶ月の定期傭船，正確な期間は傭船者任意」と定められた。その後に続く文章「傭船者は後述の就航区域内で最終航海を完了する追加の選択権を有する」は，基本的な傭船期間内に返船できると当然には予見できない航海の指図を認めないが，適法な最終航海が偶々超過した場合に，単に傭船者を損害賠償請求から保護するのみであると控訴院は判示した。

　同じ結論が，ニューヨーク・プロデュース書式の *The Black Falcon* [1991] 1 Lloyd's Rep. 77 事件でも得られた。この傭船契約は，「約9ヶ月間，3ヶ月の傭船者選択権付，さらに3ヶ月の傭船者選択権付，最終期間にプラスマイナス15日」と明示された。次の文章が続く。「傭船者は，傭船契約料率で引渡前に履行中の，最終往復航海を完了する選択権を持つ」。商業裁判所の Steyn 判事は，「商業常識」に反するとして，違法最終航海が傭船期間を超過した場合にこの文章が傭船者を守る，という傭船者の主張を否認した。文字どおり解釈されれば，この文章により，「まったくばかげた見解であるが」返船の最終日直前に発せられた長い最終航海指図は有効となろう。

　しかし，続く *The World Symphony* 事件では，控訴院は，当事者の意図であったことが十分に明確な文言からなる，異なる最終航海条項に基づき傭船者が，この自由を享受できることを認めた。

　World Symphony 号は Shelltime 3 書式で定期傭船された。第3条は「6ヶ月プラスマイナス15日の期間の傭船者任意」を定めていた。最終航海を取り扱う第18条は未修正で，次の文章を含んでいた。「この第3条にかかわらず，本船がこの傭船期間満了時に航海途中にあるならば，現に従事している往復航海の終了と傭船契約書指定の返船港への回航に必要な延長期間について同一料率と条件で傭船者は本船を使用するものとする」。傭船者は15日の選択権を行使して，基本的な傭船期間は1988年12月24日に満了した。1988年10月4日に傭船者は満期日までに明らかに完了しない最終航海の指図をした。結局，返船は1989年1月18日であった。船主は12月24日を超過した期間について市場料率に基づく損害賠償請求をした。控訴院はこの請求を退けた。「その第3条の条項にかかわらず」という文言で始まっていなければ，第18条は *The Peonia* 事件と *The Black Falcon* 事件の紛議となった文章の限定的効果のみを持ったことであろう。しかしこの「決定的」文言は起草者が二つの条項の間に矛盾点を認識していたことと，この矛盾点はしたがって裁判所が最優先効果を与えた第18条に有利に解決されることを示す。傭船者の指図は第18条により適法であり，傭船者は基本的傭船期間内に返船する義務はない。そういう印刷条項は世界中で同じように解釈されるのが望ましい。英国裁判所は Texacotime 2 書式の非常に類似している第11条についての New York 仲裁人の処理を認めるべきである（*The Pacific Sun* 事件と後出188頁の *The Narnian Sea* 事件参照）。

　記録長官 Donaldson 卿は，188頁で次のように述べた。「他の条項を限定する条項と，他の条項と矛盾しかつ他の条項に優先する条項の間には基本的差異がある。誰の責任によるわけではないが，傭船期間が超過する場合に，どうなるかを規定する条項は，免責条項に過ぎない。比較対照によれば他の条項の条件に優先する条項は——本事案では，……1往復航海の傭船契約を固定期間のある契約として『結ぶ』——明白に矛盾点を含む。矛盾点を認め，どちらが優先するかを特定する前置き文言を

要求するのは後者の種類の条項のみである」。
　The World Symphony [1991] 2 Lloyd's Rep. 251 および [1992] 2 Lloyd's Rep. 115 (C. A.).

　ボルタイム傭船契約の第7条については，前出21，64頁と後出635頁を参照。この条項により「傭船契約の終了を定めた大体の時間に」返船できる最終航海が適法となる。しかし，市場料率が約定料率を上回るなら市場料率で実際の超過期間についての支払を要する（Shelltime書式の最終航海条項についての解説は，後出693頁を参照）。

ニューヨーク・プロデュース書式第13条との関連

　傭船契約期間を超過することが，明示的に許容されている場合であって，さらに，傭船者が，ニューヨーク・プロデュース書式第13条による傭船期間の延長権を持つ場合，最長傭船期間の算定について問題が起こりうる。415頁参照。

期間満了前返船

　傭船期間満了以前に，傭船者が船主に返船するという反対の状況において，船主は返船を拒
130否し，傭船料を請求し続けうるかという問題がある。契約の一般原則では，不履行がある場合，善意の当事者は不履行に応じ損害賠償を請求するか，不履行を拒否し相手方に契約を履行させるかのいずれかを選ぶことができる（White & Carter v. McGregor [1962] A. C. 413 事件参照）。しかし，この事案で Reid 卿は，善意の当事者が履行を継続する際に「適法な利益」を有する場合の状況を例外とする。The Puerto Buitrago [1976] 1 Lloyd's Rep. 250 事件（後出295頁参照）で，控訴院は，損害賠償により十分救済され，返船を拒否することがまったく不適当である場合，船主は，損害賠償を請求し，返船に応じなければならないと判示している。しかしながら，一方 The Odenfeld [1978] Lloyd's Rep. 357 事件で Kerr 判事は，同事件の状況下において，船主は，一定期間，本船を傭船者に使用させて，傭船料を請求する権利があると判示した（もっとも，時の経過とともに，船主は，契約が継続しているとみなす権利を喪失するであろうと言っている）。傭船者に意思変更の余地がないことが明白になった場合，裁判所が，損害賠償が適切な救済策であると考えれば，船主に返船に応じさせ，損害賠償請求を行わせるものと思われる。

　Alaskan Trader 号はニューヨーク・プロデュース書式で24ヶ月傭船され，1979年12月に引き渡された。1980年10月に本船は修理に数ヶ月を要することがはっきりしている甚大な機関損傷を被った。傭船者はもはや本船を使用しないと仄めかしたが，それにもかかわらず船主は修理を進めた。修理は1981年4月に完了したが，傭船者は船長への指図を発することを拒否し，傭船契約は終了したとみなすと述べた。船主は傭船者の行動を履行拒絶として扱わず，1981年12月の傭船契約満了まで船員を乗せ出航準備状態において本船を傭船者の自由に委ねた。それから本船はスクラップ売船された。傭船料は，権利を損なわない条件（on a without prejudice basis）でその間傭船者により支払われ続けた。船主は履行拒絶を受け入れ，損害賠償請求すべきであったとの理由に基づき，傭船者は，支払った傭船料の回収請求をした。仲裁人は，船主は1980年10月に傭船者の履行拒絶を受諾する義務はないが，傭船者が本船の受取を最終的に拒否したことで「傭船契約は死滅したことが明白」となったので1981年4月にそうすべきであったと裁定した。仲裁人はさらに，船主は傭船料を継続請求する正当事由があるとの主張についての多様な根拠（銀行の要件，損害査定の困難さ，他の使用方法を見つける困難さ）を否定し，船主は損害賠償請求を行わず傭船者に契約履行を迫ることに適法な利害を有しないと判示した。

Lloyd 判事は裁定を確認し,仲裁人の法的手法に落ち度はなく,事実問題は仲裁人が判断する問題だと述べた。
   The Alaskan Trader (NO. 2) [1983] 2 Lloyd's Rep. 645.

 The Alaskan Trader 事件で,定期傭船契約は当事者間に役務契約の性質以上の協力を要求する契約(その違反は損害賠償という救済を生じるだけ)であるとの主張もまた傭船者のために行われた。主人に不当に解雇された被用者のように船主は傭船者の使用に自らを委ねることで契約上の報酬を請求できないが,その救済は損害賠償に限定される。Lloyd 判事は,本問題を決定するのを拒否しながら,**表面上**,その主張には指摘されるべきことが多いと考えた。しかしながら,類似の主張は The Odenfeld [1978] 2 Lloyd's Rep. 357 事件で Kerr 判事の心証を揺さぶるものではなかった。374頁で彼は述べた。「運賃市況が現在のような低迷時には,商事裁判所に傭船者と船主の間の厳しい紛争が多く出される。しかしこの紛争は傭船契約に基づく本船の運航の障害にはならない」。
   (傭船契約中に,傭船料支払は,明白に傭船契約満了日まで継続するという特別の規定があり,期間前の返船日以降,期間満了日まで傭船料を支払うべきとされた事件として Reindeer Steamship v. Forslind (1908) 13 Com. Cas. 214 事件参照)
   本船の期限前返船が受諾されたが,本船の状態が悪化し,航行できないほどであった場合に,傭船料の代わりに請求できる損害賠償の金額について, The Griparion [1994] 1 Lloyd's Rep. 533 事件参照。

131 特定航海の継続期間をもって定める傭船期間

 傭船期間を月数や日数で定めず,特定航海の期間を尺度として定め,定期傭船することも慣行となっている。後出613頁参照。その場合には,その約定航海は,単に傭船期間の尺度を示すだけではなく,傭船者が本船をその特定航海に配船しなければならないということが契約の主要事項になると思われる。

 Temple Moat 号は,ボルタイム(1920年改訂)書式で, Bristol Channel 引渡, Capetown/Laurenço Marques 間返船として「Kara Sea への周航航海の期間」傭船された。傭船契約は,英国を含め一定の航路定限内に本船を使用できることも定めていた。本船は空船で(Kara Sea の)Igarka へ航行し,1930年8月,そこで, Durban 向け木材を積み取った。しかし本船は,ロシア政府によって, Murmansk へ行き,そこで木材を揚荷するよう命じられた。その命令に傭船者は従わねばならなかった。Murmansk で事情不明の遅延を生じた後,本船は Garston 向け坑木を積載し, Garston で英国政府に徴用された。本船が南アフリカへ直航していれば, Garston での徴用は考えられなかった。船主は,本船が Murmansk で遅延し,南アフリカではなく, Garston 向に再度積荷をし,そこへ向ったことは,傭船者の義務違反であると主張した。傭船者は,約定航海の期間は,どのくらいの間,本船を認められた航路定限内の航海に使用できるかを決定する唯一の方法であり, Kara Sea の後,本船を大体において南アフリカの方面へ航行させなければならないとしても,その大体の航路上の他の場所へも配船することが認められていると反論した。
 貴族院は,約定航海は契約上最優先事項であるとして,傭船契約は,まず Kara Sea に行き,それから南アフリカに行く航海のためのものであり,契約上の航路定限は,当該航海の限度を拡大するものではなく,むしろ制限するものである。それにゆえに,傭船者は契約違反であり,本船徴用により船主が被った損失に対し損害賠償の責任があると判断した。
 (船長がこれらの指示に従ったことは,8条に定められた本船使用についての傭船者の指図に従ったものとして,船主の請求権を害さなかった)

Temple Steamship v. *Sovfracht*（1945）79 Ll.L. Rep. 1.

傭船契約の期間を定めるこのような方法の多様性のゆえに問題が生じる。*The Democritos* [1976] 2 Lloyd's Rep. 149 事件では，ニューヨーク・プロデュース書式に基づき，傭船期間は「太平洋経由で，1港ないし数港経由の1航海，期間約4ないし6ヶ月」と約定された。傭船者側は，この文言があるので，契約は1航海用の定期傭船，少なくとも，1航海用の定期傭船と通常の定期傭船の混成したものとなっており，したがって船主は，前述のような通常の原則に基づいて，6ヶ月を超える部分に対する損害賠償を請求できないと主張した。控訴院は，契約はこのように表現されていても，明らかに定期傭船契約であるとして，傭船者の主張を退けた。しかしながら，実際に使用された非常に曖昧な文言ではなく，意図された航海が正確に定義されていたならば，異なる判例が得られたであろうという意見がある。その意見は，当該傭船契約が定期傭船契約ではなくなるという理由ではなく，約定航海が最優先事項と認められ，表示された月数は，当該約定航海所要期間の大体の目安でしかないということを理由とするものである。しかし，航海の定義が精密になされている場合，期間の表示は，通常，余分なものであると考えられるので，訴訟は起こりえないであろう（*The Aragon* [1975] 1 Lloyd's Rep. 628 事件参照）。

The Lendoudis Evangelos II（1988）事件（未報告だが，1995年6月25日のLMLN 408で言及された）で，Leggatt 判事は次のように判示した。ニューヨーク・プロデュース書式上の定期傭船航海の表示「安全バース／港経由……保証なしで約40/120日の期間」は，期間は誠実に予測されることを求められるが，傭船者に最低期間本船を使用する義務を課すものではない。それにもかかわらず傭船契約は他の条項で傭船者に「返船予定日について15/10日以上前の概算通知および7日前の確定通知」を求めた。その中で，Leggatt 判事は，航海は最低15日間であることが推測されると判示した（*Japy Frères* v. *Sutherland*（1921）26 Com. Cas. 227 (C.A.)（「保証なし」）事件も参照）。

132 米 国 法

期間超過／期間不足：黙示の許容期間

　米国も，傭船契約が「単純 flat」期間のものである場合には，妥当な期間超過を認める英国の原則と一致する。したがって，予期される期間超過がその航海をしないで返船した場合の期間不足より短いならば，たとえ返船が遅れても，傭船者は，傭船契約の範囲内で，本船を商業上実行可能な最短航海に就航させることができる。期限前返船，すなわち期間不足は，不足期間より短い超過期間でもう1航海できると考えられる場合には，傭船契約違反となろう。この原則は「最終航海原則」としてときどき言及される。

　指導的判例である *Straits of Dover Steamship Co.* v. *Munson*, 99 F. 690 (S. D. N. Y. 1899)，原審維持 100 F. 1005 (2d Cir. 1900) 事件で，裁判所は，傭船期間満了後2ヶ月23日遅れの返船を，許容されるものと判示した。傭船契約は，引渡後3ヶ月の単純期間を約定していた。本船は傭船者に責任のない事由により遅延した。裁判所は，一定期日の返船を約束できないことは，当事者も判っていたはずであり，傭船者は，その遅延がなければ3ヶ月以内に終了する妥当な航海に本船を就航させたのであるから，契約違反とはならないと判示した。最終航海の妥当性は，航海開始時点で合理的に予期される期間超過をもとにして判断されるべきであるという，原則が明言されている。

　Anderson v. *Munson*, 104 F. 913 (S. D. N. Y. 1900) 事件で，「約 about」という文言が削除されていたにもかかわらず，49日遅れの返船が認められた。*Trechman S. S. Co.* v. *Munson S. S. Line*, 203 F. 692 (2d Cir. 1913) 事件では，傭船者は，契約期限の29日前に返船したが，相応の期間超過でもう1航海できたという理由により，その返船は認められなかった。しかし裁判所は単純期間の満了までしか船主の損害賠償請求を認めなかった。

　Britain S. S. Co. v. *Munson S. S. Line*, 31 F. 2d 530 (2d Cir. 1929) 事件では，傭船契約上の期間は「引渡以降**約**2ないし**約**3連続暦月間」であった。本船は，3月20日キューバで引き渡された。本船は Hatteras 岬以北の米国大西洋岸の港で，返船されることになっていた。傭船者は，引渡日から2ヶ月満了までに13日早い5月7日に，New York で返船すると申し出た。裁判所は，本船はキューバ／New York 間をもう1航海行うに十分な余裕があり，「約3ヶ月」の期間内で返船できたのであるから，この返船は時期尚早で無効であると判示した。裁判所は次のように述べている。

　　「約 about」という文言を使用しているのは，本船を返船すべき日に関し，傭船者に相応の余裕を与える意思を表わすものと解釈される。……したがって，航海が約定期間満了前に返船港で終了する場合には，たとえ約定期間を超過することが明らかでも，傭船者は，本船に「妥当な」もう1航海を要求できる。しかし，約定期間満了までの残存期間が，さらに1航海行うことを「不当なもの」にするほど短かければ，傭船者は，返船することができるが，また船主も，本船を引き揚げることができることとなり，したがって，期間不足が認められる (31 F. 2d at 531)。

　しかしながら，裁判所は，さらに次のように判示している。傭船者は，5月20日に有効に返船できるのであるから，船主の損害賠償請求は，それに応じて判断される。裁判所は，傭船者は5月20日以降も本船を使用する選択権を有するが，船主はその選択権の実行を要求できないと論断した。

[133] 最短／最長

　傭船契約が最短／最長期間を規定している場合，その間のどの時点での返船も正当である（*Tweedie Trading Co.* v. *Sangstand,* 180 F. 691（2d Cir. 1910）事件）。返船日が最短／最長期間で定められる場合，文言「約 about」が削除されるのは慣習であり，論理上当然である。この場合，期間超過は認められない。したがって傭船契約が「最短」「最長」という確定期間で定められているか，返船日が期間でもって決められている場合，前述のような期間不足／期間超過の原則は当てはまらない。

　The Romandie, SMA 1092（Arb. at N. Y. 1977）事件で，ニューヨーク・プロデュース書式の印刷文言「約 about」が削除され，最短35ヶ月最長38ヶ月の期間傭船者任意と規定されていた。本船は，38ヶ月の約定最長期間を8日超えて返船された。仲裁人は，船主に返船遅延に起因する損害賠償を認めた。裁定は次のようなものであった。

　最短／最長の文言を使用すると共に，ROMANDIE号の傭船期間の前にある，「約 about」という文言を削除しているのは，当事者が明確な最短／最長返船日を期待する明白な意思の表現であると判断する。その他に，この文言の条理に適った解釈は，ありえない。航海の不確実性や，船舶がレールの上を走るのではないという主張に考慮を払ったけれども，当事者が選んだ取決めや，適当であると考えた意思を表現する権利を無視することはできない。
　この傭船契約は，まさしくその条項により，期間超過を許さない，期間が完全に確定している傭船契約である。35ヶ月より前および38ヶ月より後の返船は，契約違反となろう。そして，その違反が船主に起因するものでない限り，傭船者は損害を賠償する責任がある。成功の可能性は，ほとんどないと思われるけれども，本件で傭船者は，返船までの最長期間内で，企画した航海を完了できると計算して危険をおかした。船主の過失によることなく，それが失敗したのであるから，傭船者は，妥当かつ予見できる船主の損害を賠償する責任がある。

　The Scaldia, SMA 905（Arb. at N. Y. 1975）事件でも，同様の結論が出されている。仲裁人は「最短6ヶ月最長7ヶ月」と約定した傭船契約で，「7ヶ月の最長傭船期間は，固定的かつ絶対的なものである」と裁定した。また *The Elizabeth Entz,* SMA 588（Arb. at N. Y. 1971）事件では，「14ヶ月プラスマイナス1ヶ月」と約定されていた場合につき，期間超過も期間不足も許されないと裁定された（*The Themis,* 244 F. 545（S. D. N. Y. 1917）*Schoonmaker-Conners Co. Inc.* v. *Lambert Transp. Co.,* 269 F. 583（2d Cir. 1920）各事件参照）。

　しかし *Ropner* v. *Inter-American S. S. Co.,* 243 F. 549（2d Cir. 1917）事件で，裁判所は，最長期間を単純期間（flat period）とみなすべきであるとして，相応の期間超過を認めた。しかしながら，前に引用した事例が示すように，本判例は，その後の仲裁々定では採用されていない。

　The Arctic Confidence, SMA 2987（Arb. at N. Y. 1992）事件は，「最低30/35日保証なし」の傭船期間を定める1航海の定期傭船契約が関係していた。仲裁人はこの文言は，傭船者が少なくとも30日の期間を保証するが現実の使用期間を約束するものではない，と裁定した。

　The Handy Leader, SMA 3140（Arb. at N. Y. 1995）事件は，「65/75日保証なし」という期間の1航海の傭船が関係していた。仲裁審は，傭船者は最低65日間本船の使用を約束し，期間満了前の返船があるなら船主は不足期間につき損害賠償請求できると裁定した。しかし，結果として延長期間内に本船がオフハイヤーとなる特別な状況が存したがゆえに，実際に不足期間は存しなかった。

134 明示の許容期間

　傭船契約が返船の許容期間を明示している場合，それ以上の期間超過は認められない。The Themis, 244 F. 545 (S.D.N.Y. 1917) 事件で，傭船契約は，「12月15日から１月５日まで」傭船者任意の返船を規定していた。裁判所は，この条項は，傭船者に１月５日以前に返船する義務を課すと判示した。裁判所は次のように述べている。

　　16日間という期間は，航海計画に取引上十分な余裕を与えると考えられた。また，予期しない非常事態に対する備えは，後日検討されるべきものとして，免責条項に十分規定されていた。この16日間という期間は，傭船者に通常の状況変化に対する十分な余裕を与える「重複」あるいは「過渡的な」期間であり，傭船者自身，その期間を超えないと約束したものである。このような約定は，まったく妥当である（244 F. at 552）。

　Tweedie Trading Co. v. Sangstand, 180 F. 691, 692 (2d Cir. 1910) 事件で，裁判所は，明示の許容期間を規定する傭船契約を，単純な期間による傭船契約と区別した。本件傭船契約では，「期間約12ヶ月，傭船者は，この期間プラスマイナス３週間で本船返船を保証する」と規定していた。裁判所は，この条項により，傭船者は11ヶ月と１週間か12ヶ月と３週間，本船を使用する権利を有すると同時に，明記された期日内に返船する義務もあると判示した。

　*Tweedie*事件では，傭船者は，傭船期間をさらに延長する選択権を持っており，それは，確定許容期間により，４月９日に終了することになっていた。３月28日，本船は Hampton Roads に碇泊していた。傭船者は，船長に砂糖積取のためキューバに向け出港するよう指図したが，船主は本船を引き揚げ，傭船者が支払った３月29日から４月６日までの傭船料を返還した。傭船者は，不法な引揚であるとして，損害賠償の訴えを提起した。裁判所は，傭船者は４月９日まで本船使用の権利があるから，引揚は船主の契約違反であると判示した。しかしながら，同時に裁判所は，いずれにせよ本船の航海の終了と返船は，４月９日までに間に合うものではなかったのであるから，船主の補償は，その期間の傭船料の返還および傭船者が船積した燃料油の支払に尽きると判断した。

　The Medita, SMA 1150 (Arb. at N.Y. 1977) 事件で，船主は超過期間について市場料率に基づく損害賠償を裁定された。仲裁審は次のように述べた。

　　簡単に言えば，傭船者は最長許容期間内に確実に返船する絶対的義務を負う，あるいはある料率で存在する超過期間に比例して１日当たりの傭船料を支払わねばならない。本仲裁審は，最終航海実績が大変に悪いかあるいは悪い何らかの証拠があって，適用されるべき所定の規則が不適用となるかを注意深く検討した。事実は，本船の「不履行」に起因する不当な遅延を示す証拠はない。遅延は全天候に関係する……傭船者は，本船の最終航海を決めるときに，そして最終航海が当然に引き受けられるかどうかを決めるときにあらゆる事態を検討しなければならない。最長期間内に返船という絶対的義務は，まさにその検討事項である。この絶対的義務には，高い傭船料を支払うからといって僅か数日といえども傭船者がこれを超過する選択権があるとは考えられない。

　The Har Rai, SMA 1868 (Arb. at N.Y. 1983) 事件で，傭船者は規定された範囲の返船日（その日は既に１度延長された）以前に当然には完了できないような航海に本船を取り決めようとした。仲裁人は，傭船者はその行為により傭船契約の期限前の違反を犯した，そして船主は，最長傭船期間を超過するような傭船者による本船の使用を拒否できると裁定した。しかし，傭船料は本船が引き揚げられた後の期間も前払されていたので，船主に本船を引き揚げる

権利はなかった。

　Texacotime 2 書式は，第11条で次のように規定している。

[135]　……この傭船期間満了時に本船が航海中の場合，この傭船契約の定める返船港に帰着するまで本船が従事する往復航海の完了に必要な超過期間についても，傭船者は同料率，同条件で本船を使用するものとする。

　The Narnian Sea, 1991 AMC 274（Arb. at N. Y. 1990）事件において第11条の目的について「往復航海」の定義に関する紛争が生じた。傭船契約は1年の期間を定めた。傭船者は空船航海を「往復航海」の最初の片航海として取り扱うことができ，それから1年の期間が満了後，貨物を積み取ることができると主張した。仲裁審は，前出解説の最終航海規則に拠るのであれば，傭船者の主張は正しいと裁定した。しかし，第11条は「最終航海理論の主観的合理性の基準」を否定し，それを傭船期間満了時の本船の状態に基づく客観的基準に置き換えていると，仲裁審は結論を出した。この客観的基準を適用して，仲裁審は，「指図」を待てと言う以外に実際の航海指図が本船に発せられなかったので，本船は傭船期間満了時に往復航海に従事していなかったと裁定した。

　The Pacific Sun, SMA 1789（Arb. at N. Y. 1983）事件も参照。

「約 about」

　傭船契約が，一定の期間を「約」という文言付で表示している場合，許容期間の程度は各事案の事実関係によるが，許容期間が認められる。*Britain S. S. Co.* v. *Munson S. S. Line*, 31 F. 2d 530 (2d Cir. 1929) 事件で，裁判所は，次のように述べている。

　　傭船契約が「約6ヶ月」の期間に亘る場合，……「約 about」という文言は，返船日について，傭船者に相応の余裕を認める意思を表示するものと解釈される（31 F. 2d at 531）。

　指導的な米国の判例である *The Rygja*, 161 F. 106 (2d Cir. 1908) 事件では，傭船期間は「約6ヶ月」であり，さらに「約6ヶ月」の期間を延長する選択権を，傭船者に与えていた。本船は1905年7月13日に引き渡され，1905年12月12日，傭船者は，さらに6ヶ月の選択権を行使した。傭船者は，ヨーロッパで本船を返船するという意思表示を，1906年6月12日に行った。しかし，船主は船長に命じ，その航海遂行を拒否させた。傭船者は損害賠償の訴えを起こした。問題となった点は，いつ2回目の6ヶ月が始まるかであった。最初の6ヶ月の期間に基づく最終航海は，1906年3月4日に終了しており，延長期間が始まるのはその時点であると，傭船者は主張した。船主は1月13日，すなわち引渡から6ヶ月後に始まると主張した。裁判所は傭船者の意見を採用し，次のように述べた。

　　この傭船契約での期間は，完全な確定期間ではなく，「約6暦月」である。地方裁判所は，「約 about」という文言の効果を，期間不足の場合にのみ限定した。第4項のような条項を規定する傭船契約にあっては，その条項自体，期間超過を含んでおり，したがって，「約」という文言を必要としないことは明白である。しかし「約」という文言は，6暦月を超過しても不足しても適用できると考えられ，最終航海が，約定期間満了近くで終了し，さらにもう1航海行うことが不適当と思われる場合，傭船者は返船できるし，また船主は本船を引き揚げることができる。また，正当にもう1航海できるような場合には，傭船者は，約定料率で航海することを要求できると思われる。これでは期間不

足の場合において，どんな航海が正当であるかについて紛争の余地を残すが，それは確定期間が合意
されていなければ避けえない問題である。本件において，2回目の期間の問題がなければ，傭船契約
が3月4日に終了したことに問題はないと思われ，傭船者が2回目の期間に対する選択権行使の意思
表示をしたのであるから，2回目の期間は，3月4日から開始すると考えられる（161 F. at 108)。

Prebensens Damps. A/S v. *Munson S. S. Line*, 258 F. 227 (2d Cir. 1919) 事件で,「約 about」
により36ヶ月の傭船期間には1ヶ月の期間超過が認められると判示された。ただし，36ヶ月を
超える期間超過に対しては，傭船者は約定料率ではなく，市場料率での傭船料の支払を求めら
れた。

しかし，*The Adelfoi*, 1972 AMC 1742 (Arb. at N.Y. 1972) 事件では，傭船者が誠実に計
算して計画する期間超過が，現実の期間不足より大きくない場合，もう1航海行うことが許さ
れるという原則を認める一方で，仲裁人は許容しうる期間超過を14日に限定した。本船は「約
21ないし約24ヶ月，傭船者任意の期間」傭船された。傭船者は，24ヶ月の期間を選んだ。裁定
は次のとおりであった。「このような事情で終了した2ヶ年の傭船契約で使用された『約
about』という文言に対して，許容される通常の期間超過は，単純期間（flat term）満了以降
約2週間のみである」（1972 AMC at 1745)。

The Derrynane, 1954 AMC 1015 (Arb. at N.Y. 1954) 事件において仲裁審は，「約6ない
し8暦月，傭船者任意の期間」と規定するニューヨーク・プロデュース書式の傭船契約に基づ
き，広い航路定限のゆえに，傭船者には最低2週間のプラスマイナスの余裕があると裁定し，
また傭船者は，2週間を要すると合理的に考えられる航海に，返船前，本船を配船できると裁
定した。

The Federal Voyager, 1955 AMC 880 (Arb. at N.Y. 1953) 事件では，7ヶ月の傭船契約
での「約 about」は，11日間の期間超過を許すものと裁定された。本件での傭船契約期間は，
「約4ないし約7暦月，期間傭船者任意」であった。船主は，傭船契約は2つの「約 about」
を付した期間を約定しているから，期間超過や期間不足についての通常の規則は適用できず，
期間超過は許されないと主張した。仲裁審はこの申立を退け，傭船者は正当な期間超過で収ま
る航海を行うことが許されると裁定した。

The Trade Yonder, SMA 2435 (Arb. at N.Y. 1987) 事件で，傭船契約は「約80日間保証な
し」の定期傭船航海を求めていた。仲裁審は97日経過した航海の後の返船では船主の超過期間
についての損害賠償請求は発生しないと裁定した。

傭船契約によっては，「約 about」を付した約定期間の規定に，さらに，傭船者に認められ
る余裕期間の合意を明記して限定を付すことがある。*The Aretusa*, SMA 835 (Arb. at N.Y.
1973) 事件では，仲裁審は，「約18ヶ月プラスマイナス15日」という文言を，傭船者に18ヶ月
の前後15日の間で返船する権利を与えるものと裁定した。

妥当な許容期間の範囲

期間超過や期間不足が，正当であるかどうかの判断基準は，*Britain S. S. Co.* v. *Munson S.
S. Line* 事件で述べられている（前出185頁参照)。

傭船期間満了後の返船

傭船料支払は返船までか,傭船期間満了までか

　ニューヨーク・プロデュース書式には,傭船料は返船まで継続すると規定されているが,New Yorkの仲裁人は,許容期間後に返船された場合には,船主は市場料率を基準に損害賠償を求めることができる,という原則に従っている（*Constantine & Pickering S. S. Co.* v. *West India S. S. Co.*, 231 F. 472 (S. D. N. Y. 1914)；*Munson S. S. Line* v. *Elswick Steam Shipping Co.*, 207 F. 984 (S. D. N. Y. 1913), 全員一致で原審維持, 214 F. 84 (2d Cir. 1914))。

　一般的に,期間超過や期間不足の場合の損害賠償は,市場料率を基準にする。博識な Hand 判事が,前出 *Constantine & Pickering S. S. Co.* 事件で,書いているように,船主は,本船が傭船契約に定められた時間と場所で返船されたように,「金銭で処理できる限りは,同じ結果をもたらす」基準で損害賠償を査定される。すなわち,期間不足の場合,損害賠償は,不足期間に対し約定料率と低い市場料率との差額を基準とし,期間超過の場合は,超過期間に対し高い市場料率と約定料率との差額を基準とするのが普通である。しかし,これら一般原則の適用は,常に問題とされる個々の事実関係しだいである。

[137]　傭船契約が明示の許容期間を約定していた *The Jagat Padmini*, SMA 1097 (Arb. at N.Y. 1977) 事件で,仲裁審は,本船は,1973年5月11日に船主に返船されるべきであったと判断した。本船は,現実には6月1日に返船された。したがって,船主に5月11日から6月1日までの間,事実上高い市場料率を基準とした損害賠償が認められた。しかし仲裁審は,期間超過の原因となった最終航海の前の,本船を返船できた日からの損害賠償が認められるべきだという船主の主張を退けた。

　船主の損害賠償を決定するこのような方式は,*The Julia*, SMA 552 (Arb. at N. Y.) 事件や *The Romandie*, SMA 1092 (Arb. at N. Y. 1977) 事件で,仲裁審により適用された。後者の事件では,傭船者は「最短／最長」返船条項に違反していた。同事件で,船主が,返船の遅延がなければ行えたという,利益の多い大西洋横断航海を基準とした「特別損害」の賠償を求めたことは注目に値する。仲裁審は,「特別損害」に対する請求を認める証拠はないと判断したが,「傭船者が,最長期間38ヶ月を超過することによる収支結果を,事前に知らされていたか,あるいは独自に知っていたこと」を,船主が立証していれば,特別損害の賠償が認められていたであろうと明白に指摘した。

　The Thorgerd, 1926 AMC 160 (Arb. at N. Y. 1925) 事件では,返船遅延の結果解約された傭船契約のもとで得たであろう利益を,船主に補償する一種の特別損害の賠償が認められた。本件では,傭船者は,新しい傭船契約の解約日を通知されていた。

　なお,*The Rygja*, 161 F. 106, 107 (2d Cir. 1908) 事件参照。同事件で,傭船契約に明示の許容期間が約定されている場合の損害賠償の計算方法について,Ward 判事は次のように言っている。

> 確定期限のある傭船契約は,航海時間が不確実であるために,必然的に相当の困難を伴うものである。確定期間満了時には,傭船者は,もはや船を使用する権利がない。傭船者が,期間を超過して本船を使用したときは,超過期間に対して約定料率を支払わねばならないことは明白であり,市場料率が上っていたら,市場料率と約定料率の差額も,追加して支払わねばならない。最終航海が,あと1航海行えないほど確定期間満了近くに終了した場合,傭船者は期間満了までの時間をまったく喪失するか,あるいは超過期間に対して市場料率の高騰についての責任を賭して,本船をあと1航海使用するかのいずれかである。

The Scaldia, SMA 905（Arb. at N.Y. 1975）事件では，仲裁人は，市場料率を期間超過に対する損害賠償の基準とすることを拒否した。本件で，傭船者は，返船遅延により，管理船主（disponent owner）との傭船契約に違反したと裁定された。管理船主は，返船されると同時に，原船主に返船した。管理船主は，原船主から何ら期間超過の違約金を要求されなかった。しかし，期間超過は，わずか10日間であった。仲裁人は管理船主がその10日間に実際に有益に本船を使用できたかどうか疑問とした。しかし，傭船者は，10日間の期間超過の間，再傭船により利益を得ていた。仲裁人は，これらの事情に鑑み，管理船主に市場料率を基準として損害賠償を認めるのは非現実的と思われるが，管理船主は，その超過期間中傭船者が得た利益を回収しうるとするのが公正に適うものであると裁定した。

　この問題は，*The Hans Sachs,* SMA 1493（Arb. at N.Y. 1980）事件でも検討された。本船は許容期間を8日と20時間超過して返船されたと傭船者は認めた。仲裁審に出された唯一の問題は船主が回収できる損害の程度であった。船主は，超過期間中の傭船市場料率に基づいた損害賠償を求めた。一方，傭船者は損害の適正な計算は，約定の傭船料率と，船主が許容期間を超過する航海の開始前に決めた傭船契約に基づく次の使用料率との差であると主張した。傭船者の主張によると本船の返船時に船主が他の傭船契約を決めたので，その約定料率を超過する市場料率に基づいた船主の損害賠償は不適当である。仲裁審は，傭船者に同意し，船主が現存する約定料率と現行の市場料率の差に基づいて損害賠償を裁定される法則は一般に期間超過の場合に行われるが，船主は実際には市場に入ることができないのだから，適用されないと判示した。仲裁審によると，本船は以前特別な傭船契約を約束していたので，船主の損害の基礎を構成するのは，その傭船契約と現存の傭船契約との料率差である。

最終航海は適法な航海か

　最終航海が合法的なものであるかどうかの判断基準は，*Britain S. S. Co. v. Munson S. S. Line,* 31 F. 2d 530（2d Cir. 1929）事件で述べられている。しかし，米法の下では，この問題は傭船契約に単純期間（flat period）が記載されている場合や，期間に「約 about」という文言が付せられている場合に，考慮されるに過ぎない。明示の許容期間や「最短／最長」期間が定められている場合で，返船が満了日以降になされた場合には，最終航海が妥当であるかどうかということは，通常問題とならない（前出 *The Romandie*, *The Scaldia*, *The Elizabeth Entz* 各事件参照）。

期間満了前返船

　期間不足の場合，船主は最短傭船期間満了までの逸失利益に基づく損害賠償請求権を有する。例えば，*The Itel Taurus,* SMA 1220（Arb. at N.Y. 1977）事件で，傭船者は傭船契約で許容された最短期日の10日前に本船を返船した。仲裁審は，船主は10日間の証明可能な損害額を回収することができると裁定し，次のように述べた。

　　特に船主は，この損失を軽減すべく受領した収入金額を控除した傭船料について権利を有する。

　もちろん船主は，期間不足の場合に損害額を軽減する義務がある。したがって，船主は不当な返船を拒否できず，本船を引き取り，不足期間についての代替傭船を探さねばならない。*The Lamyrefs,* 1970 AMC 1966（Arb. at N.Y. 1970）事件で，本船は4日早く返船された。仲

裁人は，傭船者が通告していた返船日より早い返船は，傭船契約違反であると裁定した。しかし船主は，ほぼ直ちに，本船を新しい傭船に出した。新しい傭船は損害の軽減であり，船主の損害賠償は，返船後本船が再び傭船に出された日までに得たであろう傭船料のみであると仲裁審は裁定した。

返 船 場 所

　船主は傭船契約に記載された場所あるいは区域で船舶の返船を受けることができる。しかしながら，船主は，望むならこの権利を放棄することができる。例えば，*Munson S. S. Line* v. *Elswick Steam Shipping Co.*, 207 F. 984 (S.D.N.Y. 1913)，全員一致で原審維持 214 F. 84 (2d Cir. 1914) 事件では，定期傭船契約は欧州の港における返船を求めていた。本船は揚荷港 Buenos Aires への途上で連続する予期せぬ遅延により大変な日数を費やし，傭船期間満了後 3 週間経過しても揚荷役を完了できなかった。この状況で，船主は Buenos Aires で本船の返船を主張できると判示された（後出201頁参照）。

　もちろん，傭船者は特定の区域の中のどこででも返船できる。*The Federal Voyager*, 1955 [139]AMC 880 (Arb. at N.Y. 1953) 事件で，傭船者は連合王国，欧州大陸，米国メキシコ湾，米国 Hatteras 岬以北，または英領北米を含む区域内で本船を返船する選択権を持っていた。傭船期間満了時期近くに傭船者は，米国 Hatteras 岬以北で返船を求める再傭船契約を締結し，その旨を船主に通知した。そこで船主は，米国 Hatteras 岬以北での返船を想定して，本船の次の使用契約を結んだ。その後，再傭船契約は破棄され，傭船者は実際にはオランダで返船した。仲裁審は，傭船者はオランダで返船でき，かつ船主は米国 Hatteras 岬以北の返船を自己の責任で想定し将来の傭船契約を手配したと裁定した。

返 船 通 知

　The Procyon, SMA 2674 (Arb. at N.Y. 1990) 事件で，事実上，地震で酷い災害の発生した地域に本船が着岸しており，傭船者が返船の確定通知を 7 日前に船主に出すのが困難であったために，おそらく「日時が経過」したにもかかわらず，仲裁審は，傭船者は返船の確定通知を 7 日前に船主に出すという付属協定上の義務に違反したと裁定した。傭船者は要求された通知期間につき船主に支払うよう指示された。

航路定限

"15. .... within below mentioned trading limits."

「下記航路定限内で」

航路定限の目的

　往復航海のための定期傭船契約の事案であった *Temple Steamship* v. *Sovfracht* (1944) 77 Ll. L. Rep. 257 事件で, Scott 卿判事は定期傭船契約の航路定限条項について, 次のように述べている（同判例集265頁）。「航路定限条項は, 純粋の定期傭船契約から生成し, 性質上, その一部分を成す。純粋の定期傭船契約において, 傭船者は配船の自由を有し, その航海に地理的制限はない。すなわち, 傭船者は,（航海, 航行の危険を別として）可航水域であれば, 世界中どこでも望む所に配船しうる。この点が, それ自体地理的に限定された船舶使用を定める航海傭船契約との根本的差異である。定期傭船契約の航路定限条項の目的は明らかである。それは配船上の自由を与えるのではなく（上記の考え方から見ると傭船者には既にその自由があるのだから），航路定限がなければ, 無制限かつ万能である傭船者の配船上の自由を減じ, 一定範囲を除外することによって限定ないし制限を加えることである」（本件貴族院判決については, 後出参照。定期傭船契約と航海傭船契約との相違に関する解説は後出612頁から613頁参照）。

定限外航海の指図

　傭船者が約定定限外に船舶を配船することは契約違反であり, 船長は傭船者の定限外航行の指示を正当に拒否することができる。Devlin 判事は, *The Sussex Oak* (1950) 83 Ll.L. Rep. 297 事件で, 次のように述べている（同判例集307頁）。「船舶使用に関する傭船者の指図に船長を従わせる旨の定期傭船契約条項は, 傭船者が, その権限外の指図を出した場合にまで船長が従わなければならないと解されるとは思えない」。また船長は, 航路定限外の揚荷港が記載された船荷証券の署名を強要されるものではない。*Halcyon Steamship* v. *Continental Grain* (1943) 75 Ll.L. Rep. 80 事件で, Mackinnon 卿判事は次のように言っている。「航路定限は, ……ロンドン保険者協会担保航路定限であるが, オランダより北は含まれていない。傭船者が, 米国で貨物を積み, 船長に Copenhagen ないし Danzig で荷渡するという船荷証券を呈示した場合, 船長が署名を拒否することは正当であろう……」。

航路定限より狭められた航海を対象とする定期傭船契約

　航海が指定されており, その航海より広い航路定限も併せて明記されている場合, 航海に関する記載は契約上最優先事項であるとみなされるべきであろう。

　Temple Moat 号は, ボルタイム（1920改訂）書式で, Bristol Channel 引渡, Cape Town/Lourenco Marques 間返船として「Kara Sea への往復航海の期間」傭船された。傭船契約は, 英国を含め一定

の航路定限内に本船を使用しうることも定めていた。傭船者の主張は，約定航海の期間は，航路定限
内で本船を使用し得る期間を決定する一方法に過ぎず，またKara Seaの後，本船を実質上南アフリ
カ方面へ航行させなければならないとしても，その返船海域へ向かう途上他の場所へ配船することも
認められるというものであった。

貴族院は，約定航海が契約上最優先事項であると判示した。「Kara Seaへの往復航海」の意味につ
いての事実認定で（これを「往復航海」の意味についての先例とみなすべきではない），傭船契約
は，Kara Seaとその後の南アフリカへの航海のためのものであるとし，本傭船契約における航路定
限は，当該航海の限度を拡大するものではなく，むしろ制限するものであるとした。
Temple Steamship v. *Sovfracht*（1945）79 Ll.L. Rep. 1.
（1航海の定期傭船契約に関する追加説明については，前出183頁と後出613頁参照）

傭船者の指図に従うことの効果

傭船者の航路定限外航海の指図に1度従っても，それが必ずしも，その後従うことを拒絶す
る船主の権利を放棄したことにはならないし，また傭船者の違反につき損害賠償請求する権利
を放棄することになるわけでもない。類似の事件として，*The Kanchenjunga*［1991］1 Lloyd's
Rep. 391（H. L.）事件と後出246頁参照。船長は船舶使用に関する傭船者の指図と指示に従う
ことになっているので，船長が航路定限外航海に従うことによって権利放棄とはならない。

前記（前出183頁も参照）*Temple Steamship* v. *Sovfracht*（1945）79 Ll. L. Rep. 1事件で，
傭船者のGarstonへの指図を船長が受諾し，船主も抗議しなかったのは権利放棄であると傭船
者は主張した。Porter卿は11頁に次のように述べて，この傭船者の主張に対処している。「本
船はMurmanskで5週間以上も抑留されており，船主が傭船者のより悪質な約定外航海の実
施を恐れて，Garstonへの出港に抗議しないことが得策であると考えたとしても当然である。
かかる状況の下で抗議しなかったことは，容易に理解できるし，傭船料を受け取ったからと
いって，約定外航海を認めたものとは判断されない。また約定外航海か否かは別としても，船
長には第8条の要求する航海を極力迅速に遂行し，本船を南アフリカに直行させる義務違反の
問題が残る。船長が，Garstonへの出港につき，傭船者の指図に従ったことは明らかである
が，傭船契約第8条に基づき，本船使用に関する傭船者の指図に従わねばならず，*Tyrer* v.
Hessler, 7 Com. Cas. 166事件で採用された原則に従えば，船長が指図に従ったからといっ
て，船長を雇用している者の権利放棄とはならないと思われる」。

しかし，前出 *Temple Steamship* v. *Sovfracht* 事件よりも普通の状況で，かつ違反を十分承知
している船主が，航路定限外へ船舶が航行するのを許容する場合には，船主は必ずしも損害賠
償請求の権利を放棄してはいないが，その後の指図に従うことを拒否する権利を放棄したもの
とおそらく判示されるであろう。一般的に権利放棄に関するさらなる解説は前出142頁に述べ
られている。

定限外航海に対する損害賠償の程度

傭船者が航路定限外航海を船舶に指図し，船主はこれに抗議しながらも，船長に対しその指
図に従うよう指示した場合，船主は，約定傭船料率と航路定限外航海の市場料率（高ければ）
との差額が当該航海に実際に要した追加費用を上回るとしても傭船者にこれを請求できると判
示された（*Rederi Sverre Hansen* v. *Van Ommeren*（1921）6 Ll. L. Rep. 193）。

航路定限外航行に関する協定

　傭船者が特定の航路定限外航海を本船に指図をし，傭船者がそれにより船舶保険者の要求する追加保険料を支払うことを傭船契約で当事者が合意するのはよくあることである。追加保険料の支払を引き受けたからといって，その指図により本船が立ち寄る航路定限外の港の安全性に関する義務から傭船者が解放されるわけではない。

　Helen Miller 号のニューヨーク・プロデュース傭船契約書式には，航路定限を「Montreal までの St. Lawrence 河を含み，キューバ……ギニアとすべての非安全港を除外するロンドン保険者協会担保航路定限内の安全港の間，ただし傭船者は必要あれば追加保険料を支払って航路定限を越える裁量を有する」と規定する追加条項があった。傭船者はロンドン保険者協会担保航路定限外の港へ本船の航行を指図し，その時期には非安全であると考えられた港への航海で本船は氷により損傷を被った。Mustill 判事は，傭船者は，この損害に責任ありと判示した。船主は定限外の航行に一般的同意をしたが，それが安全港を選択する傭船者の義務を軽減するものではなく，また傭船者が追加保険料を支払うことでこの傭船者の義務が影響されるものではない。「保険料の支払がなければ船主は本船の航海遂行を許容しないが，保険料の支払により傭船者は，その航海に本船を配船できるという恩典を得る。しかし，これは，傭船者がそれによって本船を定限外の航海に危険の負担なしで配船する権利を得るということとはまったく異なる」。
The Helen Miller [1980] 2 Lloyd's Rep. 95.

　The Evia (No. 2) [1982] 2 Lloyd's Rep. 307 事件で，貴族院はボルタイム書式の第21(A)条に言及されている戦争危険に関して傭船者は第2条の安全港の義務から解放されると判示した。しかし，この判決に到達する際に，Roskill 卿は第21条のいくつかの特殊性に注意を促した。*The Concordia Fjord* [1984] 1 Lloyd's Rep. 385（同判例集387/388頁）事件で Bingham 判事が強調したように，すべては，特定の傭船契約の詳細な条件の解釈しだいである。この事案で，Bingham 判事は，改訂ニューヨーク・プロデュース書式に基づき，当該港に課せられた追加戦争危険保険料を傭船者が支払うとする条項があったが，傭船者は戦争のため非安全である港で本船が被った損害につき責任ありとの仲裁人の裁定を支持した。前出 *The Helen Miller* 事件で傭船契約の諸条項は，*The Evia (No. 2)* 事件の契約の諸条項と一様に異なっており，事実関係はさらに異なっていた。したがって，ボルタイム傭船契約の第21(B)(1)条により傭船者は船主が支払う戦争保険料を償還するから，それでも第2条の安全港条項に基づき戦争危険保険者の代位求償に傭船者が曝されるのは不当であるとの Roskill 卿の漠然とした解説によるものでない限り，*The Helen Miller* 事件の判決の有効性が *The Evia (No. 2)* 事件により損なわれると推定する理由はないと思われる。Roskill 卿のこの解説について，Bingham 判事は前出 *The Concordia Fjord* 事件で，傭船者が関連損傷に対して付保する財源につき船主の肩代わりをする契約上の義務を負ったという単にそれだけの理由で，本船に対する責任から傭船者を免除するというどんな漠然とした原則をも，仲裁人が否定したことに賛意を表した。そういう一般原則はないように思われる。

　航路定限の範囲の不実表示に関する事案について，*The Lucy* [1983] 1 Lloyd's Rep. 188 事件と前出132頁参照。

144 米　国　法

航路定限

　広範囲の航路定限は傭船契約の特徴の一つである。航海傭船契約では船舶は通常一つ，あるいは複数の場所への1航海の傭船であるが，定期傭船では船舶が就航する港について船舶は傭船者の指図に従う。定期傭船契約に通常示される地理的限界は安全性または政治的な事項により規定される。

　傭船者が，船舶に特定された航路定限外への航行を指図した場合には，傭船者は傭船契約上の義務違反となる。船長にはそのような航路定限外の指図を拒否する自由がある。傭船者が，本船に合意済みの定限外に就航するようにとの要求を続けるならば，実際，船主には傭船者の役務から本船を引き揚げる正当な事由が存すると判示された。The Central Trust, 1971 AMC 200 (Can. Exch. 1970) 事件で，裁判所は，傭船契約が許容就航区域から「共産国と共産衛星国港」を除外しているのに，傭船者が揚荷にユーゴスラビア港を指定したとき，船主は本船を引き揚げる権利があると判示した (The New Way, 1977 AMC 88, 95 (Arb. at N.Y. 1976) 事件と後出261頁に解説の The Arietta Venizelos, 1973 AMC 1012 (Arb. at N.Y. 1972) 事件の比較参照)。

　The Andros Mentor, SMA 2125 (Arb. at N.Y. 1985) 事件で，傭船契約はロンドン保険者協会担保航路定限区域に航路を明白に限定していたが，傭船者は航路選定指図で，本船にロンドン保険者協会担保航路定限外のベーリング海への航行を求めた。仲裁審は船長は傭船者の指図に拘束されないと裁定し，次のように述べた。

　　　船主は，指示どおりに航行すれば，米貨約15,000ドルの追加保険料が発生したであろうと主張した。傭船者は，その前に船主の許可を得たであろうと主張した。仲裁審はベーリング海経由の航行を追加保険料なしで保険会社がしばしば許可していることに注目したが，申請に応じて，必ずしも自動的とは言えないが（追加保険料の有無もある）保険会社の許可は，下されている。本事案では，そういう許可申請が行われたとか，あるいは討議さえされたというその時の証拠はなかった。

　Texacotime書式の紛争である The Universe Explorer, 1985 AMC 1014 (Arb. at N.Y. 1984) 事件で，仲裁審は，船主は南アフリカに船用品の積込のため寄港したので，世界中の航路に就航できる船舶の適格性を間接的に制限したと述べた。仲裁審はナイジェリア政府が南アフリカ寄港のゆえに積取を拒否した期間につき傭船者はオフハイヤーとする権利があると裁定した。

　The Mana, SMA 2669 (Arb. at N.Y. 1990) 事件で，単一仲裁人は傭船者が台湾の台中から中華人民共和国の上海に直航するよう船舶に強要できるか否かの裁定を求められた。船主は，直航は台湾法に違反し，直航すれば船舶はブラックリストに掲載され，2度と台湾寄港ができなくなると主張した。船主の主張の根拠は次の条項であった。

　　　船舶が中華人民共和国に寄港する場合には，中華人民共和国と台湾の間を直航しない。

　仲裁人はこの文言は本船に対する台湾から上海への航行の指令を傭船者に禁止していないと裁定した。仲裁人は，傭船契約が起草されたときに，船主はブラックリストに掲載される可能性を承知しており，そのときに直航航海を制限する特別条項に固執できたであろうと裁定し

た。

　The Jerom, SMA 2790（Arb. at N.Y. 1991）事件は，Mobiltime書式の傭船契約で，船主 [145] がイラン・イラク戦争のため本船のペルシア湾の航行の許可を拒否したという紛争であった。この事件では戦争条項の制限以外に傭船契約上航行制限はなかった。仲裁審は，船主は傭船契約違反であると裁定した（後出662から663頁の解説参照）。

再傭船自由

"16. Charterers to have liberty to sublet the vessel for all or any part of the time covered by this Charter, but Charterers remaining responsible for
17. the fulfillmment of this Charter Party."

「傭船者は，本契約期間の全部または一部につき，本船を再傭船に出すことができる。ただし，その場合でも，傭船者は，本傭船契約の履行義務を免れない。」

再傭船の効果

16行により，傭船者は定期傭船期間中本船を再傭船に出す明示の権利を持つ。再定期傭船契約（または再航海傭船契約）それ自身だけでは船主と再傭船者の間に契約関係を生じない。したがって本傭船契約または再傭船契約に基づき，または同契約によって船主が再傭船者を訴えることも，また逆に再傭船者により訴えられることもない。これは，契約の当事者でない者に契約は一般的に権利を授けることも義務を課すこともできないという原則に沿うものである（*Dunlop* v. *Selfridge* ［1915］A. C. 847 事件参照）。

しかし，船主と再傭船者の双方が再傭船契約に基づき発行した船荷証券の当事者である場合，再傭船者はその船荷証券に基づき船主と直接的な契約関係に入る。この状況では，船主には再傭船契約に基づく権利または義務はなく，再傭船者に対して原傭船契約の条件を強制はできないが，船主は船荷証券に基づき訴え（かつ訴えられ）ることができる。

Bombay 号は再傭船の選択権付で6ヶ月間定期傭船され，往復航海に再傭船された。原傭船契約は，船荷証券は傭船者またはその代理人が指示した運賃率で原傭船契約の権利を損なわずに，署名されると規定していた。原傭船契約はさらに，船主は「この傭船契約の運賃または傭船料につきすべての貨物に」リーエンを有すると規定していた。船荷証券は再傭船者に対して発行された。船主は原傭船契約に基づく傭船料につき再傭船者の貨物にリーエンを行使しようとした。船主は定期傭船料につきリーエンの権利はなく，リーエンは原傭船契約に基づく傭船者に対してのみ行使しうる権利であると判示された。船主と再傭船者の間の契約を構成する船荷証券に基づき船主はその船荷証券の運賃のみにリーエンを有するとされた。
Turner v. *Haji Goolam* ［1904］A. C. 826.

船主が，被用者または代理人を通じて再傭船者の貨物を占有している場合にも，船主はまた再傭船者に対し受寄者として不法行為責任を負うことがある（*The Termagant* (1914) 19 Com. Cas. 239 事件と *Lee Cooper* v. *Jeakins* ［1964］1 Lloyd's Rep. 300 事件を参照）。しかし，船主は貨物運送契約の免責条項とその他の条項に拠る権利がある（後出395頁参照）。

船長に代わって再傭船者が船荷証券に署名する権限

原傭船契約に再傭船の自由が認められている場合に，再傭船者は船主を拘束する方法で船荷証券に（本人または代理人が）署名することを一般に授権されている。*The Vikfrost* ［1980］1

Lloyd's Rep. 560 事件で Browne 卿判事は次のように述べた（同判例集567頁）。「……傭船者は再傭船に出す選択権を持ち，再傭船契約条件について何の制限も課されていない。私の考えでは，再傭船されれば，再傭船者は船長に船荷証券に署名することを求めうる，かつそれゆえ148に船荷証券に自ら署名でき，船主と船荷証券所持人の間に契約関係を創造できると船主は考えたに違いない」。

ノルウェー法とノルウェーの管轄に従う定期傭船契約に基づき航行している本船の船主は，再傭船者の復代理人は，船長に代わり英国管轄条項を持つ船荷証券を発行する権限はないと主張した。原傭船契約によれば，再傭船の選択権があり，船荷証券にデマイズ条項の摂取を認めているので，再傭船者とその代理人は船荷証券を発行する黙示の権限を持つと判示された（船荷証券の問題については，385から400頁参照）。

再傭船契約に基づく運賃の支払

船主が再傭船契約に基づき船積された貨物に関する船荷証券の運賃に対して権利を有する場合については，後出558頁参照。

149 米　国　法

再傭船の自由

　ニューヨーク・プロデュース書式の下で，傭船者は本船を再傭船に出す権利を持つ。しかし，傭船者は原傭船契約に基づく義務の履行につき引き続き責任がある。再傭船によって船主と再傭船者の間の契約責任は生まれず，原傭船契約に基づく船主に対する傭船者の義務は軽減されない。

　この原則は *Dampskibs Akt. Thor.* v. *Tropical Fruit Co.*, 281 F. 740 (2d Cir. 1922) 事件の判決に示されている。原傭船契約は「約3年間」で，返船は「大西洋またはメキシコ湾の米国港で」行うとあった。再傭船契約は原傭船契約と同一の条件ではなく，「米国大西洋岸Hatteras岬以北の港で」返船を行うとなっていたが，傭船者は再傭船者にその権利を行使した。

　原傭船契約は1915年5月11日に開始した。必然的に傭船契約は1918年5月11日に満了となる。1918年5月10日に，本船は空船状態で New Orleans にいた。しかし，返船する代わりに傭船者はキューバ向け航海に引き続き New York 向け航海を認めたが，航海は1918年5月24日に終了した。そこで，船主は市場料率（原傭船契約に基づく約定料率より高い）による5月11－24日間の傭船料の請求を行い，その請求は認められた。裁判所はキューバへの航海は不合理な超過期間であり，法律の問題としては，原傭船契約は New Orleans で1918年5月11日「頃」に終了していると判示した。再傭船契約により船主と再傭船者との間の契約関係は生じていないし，原傭船契約に基づく船主の権利はまったく変わらないと判示した。

　The Banes, 221 F. 416, 418 (2d Cir. 1915) 事件で，裁判所は，本船が不堪航であるとの理由で，再傭船者は貨物損傷につき船主から直接回収する権利はないと判示した。裁判所は次のように述べた。

　　原傭船契約と同じ契約条件であっても再傭船契約は再傭船者と船主との間の契約関係を構成しない。

　Saxis S. S. Co. v. *Multifacs International Traders Inc.*, 375 F. 2d 577, 582 n. 7 (2d Cir. 1967) 事件も参照。同事件で，裁判所は，「再傭船契約は再傭船者に本船の一般船主に対する権利を与えるものではない……」と述べた (*Flat-Top Fuel Co. Inc.* v. *Martin*, 85 F. 2d 39, 1936 AMC 1296 (2d Cir. 1936); *Perez* v. *Cia Tropical Exportadora*, 182 F. 2d 874, 1950 AMC 1264 (5th Cir. 1950))。

　たとえ再傭船に出す権利を傭船者に与える明示の条項がなくとも，原傭船契約でその旨を特別に禁止していない限り，傭船者は本船を再傭船に出すことができる (*The Ely*, 110 F. 563, 570 (S. D. N. Y. 1901), 原審維持 122 F. 447 (2d Cir. 1903), 裁量上告拒絶 189 U. S. 514 (1903)(「再傭船契約自体は合法的であり，原傭船契約の条件に違反していない。原傭船契約には再傭船を禁止する約定はない。したがって再傭船契約は有効である。」), *Hyundai Corp.* v. *Hull Insurance Proceeds of The Vulca*, 800 F. Supp. 124, 127 (D. N. J. 1992), 原審維持 54 F. 3d 768, 1995 U. S. App. Lexis 11714 (3d Cir. 11 April 1995) 事件も参照 (第3巡回区控訴裁判所の命令は非公開の意見として本事案の引用を制限するかもしれない))。

　再傭船者は状況如何では本船に対しリーエンを有することがある。後出583頁の解説を参照。

150 船長に代わって船荷証券に再傭船者が署名する権限

後出401頁の解説参照。

期間の計算開始の時

ニューヨーク・プロデュース書式の第5条の解説は341頁から344頁を参照。

引　渡　地

|151|

"18. Vessel to be placed at the disposal of the Charterers, at ....
19. ....
20. in such dock or at such wharf or place (where she may safely lie, always afloat, at all times of tide, except as otherwise provided in clause No. 6), as
21. the Charterers may direct. If such dock, wharf or place be not available time to count as provided for in clause No. 5 ...."

「本船は，...............所在の（別に第6条に定める場合を除き，本船が，潮時に関係なく，常時浮揚状態で安全に碇泊しうる）傭船者が指図するドック，埠頭，またその他の場所において，傭船者の使用に供されるものとする。かかるドック，埠頭，またはその他の場所が使用できないときは，第5条の規定により期間の計算を行う。」

常に浮揚状態で安全に碇泊

第6条は，本船を，浮揚状態で安全に碇泊しうるドック，埠頭，その他の場所で，傭船者の使用に供するという義務を修正して，「同じ寸法の船舶が慣例として，座洲状態で安全に碇泊する場所での」座洲を認めている。第6条それ自体は，傭船者が選んだ上記同様のドック，埠頭その他の場所で，貨物の積揚が行われるべきことを規定している。27行は，傭船契約上の本船の使用を，各地域の「安全な港／諸港間の適法な航路」に限定している。これらの条項の合体した効果は後出231頁から254頁で取り扱い，251頁の解説は特に18行から21行と関連する（米国法については255頁を参照）。

期間の計算開始の時

ニューヨーク・プロデュース書式の21行が参照する第5条の部分というのは，明らかに同条の最初の節の最後の文章，すなわち62行から64行の文章である。

期間の計算は，傭船者またはその代理人が午後4時までに書面による準備完了の通知を受け取った日に続く作業日の午前7時から開始する。ただし，傭船者は要求すれば，直ちに本船を使用する権利を有し，その使用時間を傭船期間に算入するものとする。

21行と62行/64行の関係に関する解説について後出341頁を参照。

引渡時の本船の状態

153

"21. .... Vessel on her delivery to be
22. ready to receive cargo with clean-swept holds and tight, staunch, strong and in every way fitted for the service, having water ballast, winches and
23. donkey boiler with sufficient steam power, or if not equipped with donkey boiler, then other power sufficient to run all the winches at one and the same
24. time (and with full complement of officers, seamen, engineers and firemen for a vessel of her tonnage),"

「本船は，引渡時において，船艙を清掃して貨物積取の準備を整え，船体堅牢強固で，水バラスト，ウインチ，十分なる蒸汽力ある補汽罐，補汽罐のないときは，すべてのウインチを同時に運転するに足りる他の動力（および，本船のトン数相応の航海士，甲板員，機関士，機関員の全定員）を備え，あらゆる点において運送業務に適していなければならない。」

一 般 原 則

　本船がニューヨーク・プロデュース書式21行から24行が要求する状態にない場合，第14条の解約条項に基づく準備完了の有効な通知を出すことはできない。95行で許容された期間満了時に傭船者は傭船契約を解約する選択権を行使することができる。合意期日の終わりまでに，本船が第１条16行の要求する「あらゆる点において通常の貨物の運送業務に適する状態で」引き渡されない限り，傭船者はボルタイム書式第22条に基づく同じ権利を持つ。傭船者のこの権利は，船主の契約違反または過失にかかわらず生じる（この点について後出419頁から424頁で詳細に解説する）。
　船主に堪航性義務違反があるか，または本船が傭船契約上の船舶の表示に合致しない場合には，船主は本船を引渡に必要な状態に保つことができないため，解約条項を適用する場合とはまったく別の結果を生じることになる。
　したがって，本船を引渡に必要な状態に保つことができない結果をここに要約することは有益であろう。
(1)　傭船者は解約条項に基づき傭船契約を解約する権利を持つ（前記と後出419頁参照）。
(2)　傭船料支払のための時間が開始しない。ニューヨーク・プロデュース書式第５条の下で時間の開始は，準備完了の（有効な）通知の発行時点如何にかかっている。後出206頁を参照。そして，ボルタイム書式に基づく時間は本船が後出の第１条16行に基づく「あらゆる点において通常貨物の運送業務に適する状態に」なるまで，開始しない。
(3)　本船の状態が傭船契約上の船主義務違反により，傭船者が結果として損失を被ったならば，傭船者には通常損害賠償請求の権利がある（*Thomas Nelson* v. *Dundee East Coast Shipping*, 1907 S.C. 927事件と *The Democritos* [1975] 1 Lloyd's Rep. 386 事件参照）。
(4)　欠陥が修復されるまで，傭船者は引渡の受諾を拒否できる（前出149頁参照）し，修復のために契約の目的を挫くほど遅延が生じる場合には，傭船者は傭船契約を解消されたものとして扱うことができる（前出139頁と151頁参照）。
(5)　本船の状態が船主の条件（condition）違反を構成するとか，または本船の状態が傭船者

から契約の全利益を実質的に奪う違反になる場合には，傭船者には，また契約を解消されたものとして扱う権利がある（前出137頁から140頁参照）。

154 あらゆる点において運送業務に適合し船体堅牢強固

ニューヨーク・プロデュース書式22行の「船体堅牢強固」と「あらゆる点において運送業務に適して」の文言は，個別にあるいは共に明示の堪航性義務を構成する。ボルタイム書式第1条の「あらゆる点において通常の貨物運送業務に適する」という単独の文言も，引渡時の明示の堪航性義務を負わせる（*The Hongkong Fir* [1961] 2 Lloyd's Rep. 478 事件と *The Madeleine* [1967] 2 Lloyd's Rep. 224 事件と前出147頁から152頁参照）。引渡に際しての堪航性担保（undertaking）が明示されていなくとも，そうした担保（undertaking）は黙示的に合意されている。*Giertsen* v. *Turnbull*, 1908 S. C. 1101. これら堪航性義務は，解約条項を適用しようとする場合の準備完了と適合性の要件とは区別される必要がある。ヘーグ・ルールの摂取による堪航性義務の効果については，後出593頁から602頁を参照。

NYPE 93

ニューヨーク・プロデュース書式1993年改訂版は，ボルタイム書式第1条の文言「あらゆる点において通常の貨物運送業務に適する」を採用した（前出8頁の英文書式の34/35行と53頁を参照）。

解約条項を適用しようとする場合の準備

解約日以前に準備完了通知を出すことを要求しているニューヨーク・プロデュース書式（第14条）の解約条項は，21行から24行の要件に言及していない。しかし，21行から24行の要件に適合しない限り，この条項の適切な解釈に基づいて，第14条による準備完了の有効な通知を出すことはできない（419頁を参照）。ボルタイム書式では，解約条項は第1条を明示的に参照している。運送業務に「あらゆる点で適合する」という要件は，本船は広義では堪航性がなければならないことを意味する。前出の2事件 *The Hongkong Fir* 事件と *The Madeleine* 事件と *The Derby* [1985] 2 Lloyd's Rep. 325 事件を参照。しかし，堪航性と運送業務への適合性の概念は，必ずしも同意義ではない。不堪航性の本船はほとんど運送業務に適していないが，堪航性がある本船であっても適合していないこともある。前出 *The Derby* 事件（同判例集333頁）で Denys Buckley 卿の判決と *The Arianna* [1987] 2 Lloyd's Rep. 376（同判例集390頁）事件の Webster 判事の判決を参照。

準備完了と適合性の要件の絶対的性質

（ボルタイム書式の類似の要件と同様に）ニューヨーク・プロデュース書式の引渡時の準備完了と適合性の要件は，傭船契約書の解約条項を適用しようとする場合に，絶対的要件であると考えられている。不堪航に起因する滅失損傷の責任についてのみ規定するニューヨーク・プロデュース書式第24条に摂取された米国海上物品運送法第4(1)条により，この要件が修正されることはない。後出593頁から598頁参照。したがって船主は本船が準備完了し，あるいは適合していることに相当の注意を尽くすというだけでは十分ではない。本船は実際に準備完了し，適合していなければならない（前出151頁および後出420頁参照）。

155 NYPE 93

ニューヨーク・プロデュース書式の1993年改訂版は，37行38行に「船主は傭船者に引渡予定日の……日以上前に通知をしなければならない」と規定している。

清掃した船艙での貨物受取準備完了

貨物受取の準備完了は，航海傭船契約，特に碇泊期間開始に関する事案で，非常に発展した概念である。『航海傭船』(*Voyage Charters*) の283頁から287頁参照。航海傭船契約事案で発展した一般的命題は，引渡時に本船が積取あるいは積付の準備が整っていること，または貨物運送に適していることを要求するが，このことはニューヨーク・プロデュース書式のような定期傭船契約にも，また当てはまると考えられる。

このような考え方での準備完了の意味を，航海傭船契約に関する Groves, Maclean v. Volkart (1884) C. & E. 309事件で，Lopes判事は次のように定義している。「積荷準備の整った本船であるためには，貨物のために使用可能な部分を完全に使用できるように，……すべての船艙に亘って準備が完了していなければならない」。

船艙は，本船引渡時に，貨物積載に適した状態でなければならない。

> Tres Flores 号は航海傭船契約に従い準備完了の通知を出した。そのとき，本船船艙に害虫が棲息していた。地方当局により燻蒸消毒が指示された。燻蒸消毒は数時間で完了する事柄に過ぎなかったが，本船は，碇泊期間開始のための有効な「準備完了」の通知が出せるほど，準備ができていなかったと判示された。
> *The Tres Flores* [1972] 2 Lloyd's Rep. 384 および [1973] 2 Lloyd's Rep. 247 (C. A.).

貨物荷役機器と装置

航海傭船契約の場合，船艙の準備完了の状態と荷役装置の準備完了の状態とは区別される。解約条項を適用しようとする場合にも，荷役装置は必ずしも船艙と同じ準備完了状態にあることを要求されないと判示されている。

> *San George* 号は，Centrocon 書式で，穀物輸送に航海傭船された。同書式上，傭船者は貨物を船側まで運び，船主はそれを積む義務があった。本船が12月27日午後6時までに積荷準備が整わない場合，傭船者は解約権を有していた。本船は，12月27日午前10時30分準備完了の通知を出したが，そのとき本船にはメインマストも後部デリックもなかった。しかし袋入貨物を艀から積み取らない限り，本船荷役装置は必要でなかったし，艀から積み取る（「可能性がほとんどない」状態であったが）場合でも，応急の機具を工夫できると考えられた。傭船者は解約したがそれは不当であると判示された。Devlin 判事は次のように述べている。「傭船者には，最も都合のよい積荷方法を選び，これを実施するに際し船主に相応の協力を求める以上の権利はない。傭船者には，本船装置の欠陥のため，荷役開始時になっても，そのとき決める妥当な方法による積荷の準備ができないとか，不可能であるとかを立証する責任があるが，メインマストと後部デリックがないというだけでは，その挙証責任を果たしたとは言い難い」。控訴院はこの判決を支持した。
> *Noemijulia Steamship* v. *Minister of Food* (1950) 83 Ll.L. Rep. 500 および (1950) 84 Ll.L. Rep. 354 (C. A.).

Devlin 判事は，前出の事案で，本船の荷役装置が船艙の状態とは別個に扱われるべき理由

を説明した。彼は，507頁に次のように述べた。「本船の荷役機器は異なる。ある物はまったく必要ではない。また他の物は，積荷役が進んだ段階まで必要とされない。最初から機器を常時準備し整えておくことは，不必要な労働力と費用を要することになろう。*Vaughan and Others v. Campbell, Heatley & Co.*, 2 T. L. R. 33 事件と *Grampian Steamship Company v. Carver & Co.*, 9 T. L. R. 210 事件と *Armement Adolf Deppe v. John Robinson & Co. Ltd.* [1917] 2 K. B. 204 事件が，例証として挙げられる。どれも直接に問題点を突いていないが，それぞれが[156]それなりに，船艙の状態についての明確な規則とは別に，ある融通性が認められることを示す……船艙の場合について妥当な結果をもたらす基準も，荷役機器についてはうまく作用しないのかも知れない」。

しかし，本船の引渡時に，あらゆる点において運送業務に適していることを明示の要件とするニューヨーク・プロデュース書式や類似の書式による定期傭船契約では，このような区別はないと思われる。Devlin 判事自身，通常書式の定期傭船契約に自分の判決の適用を修正していると思われる次のような意見を付言している（83 Ll. L. Rep. 507頁）。「本件では，傭船者に本船の荷役装置を使用する権利を明示的に与えている傭船契約を扱う必要はないが，そのような場合，約定の荷役装置すべてが準備完了していなければならないと十分主張できるであろう。また特定の積荷方法を約定したり，積荷方法の選択を傭船者に委ねている傭船契約を扱う必要もないが，そのような場合にも，約定の積荷方法に必要な本船の荷役装置の準備を整えていなければならないと主張できるであろう」。

しかし，あらゆる点において運送業務に適合していることが明示的に要求されている場合でさえ，ある程度の自由が許されているように思われる。*The Derby* [1984] 1 Lloyd's Rep. 635（原審維持 [1985] 2 Lloyd's Rep. 325）事件で，Hobhouse 判事は，準備完了と適合性の関係を考慮して，次のように述べた（同判例集641頁）。「傭船契約が相当な期間機能する場合に，船主に対して発する指示について傭船者が広い選択権を有する傭船契約について，今回のように準備完了と適合性の関係が関与する場合，船主が引渡時にあらゆる事態をどの程度予想し前もって備えることを要求されるかという問題が生じる。ボルタイム傭船契約は，『通常の貨物運送業務』と言及してこの問題から逃れている。『準備完了』の文言に関連して，裁判所は（例えば *Noemijulia Steamship Co. Ltd. v. Minister of Food* (1950) 84 LLL. Rep. 354），準備完了はあらゆる貨物に対して直ぐに準備完了にすることを要求しているのではない。ニューヨーク・プロデュース書式で使用されている『運送業務に適合している』との文言に関して，適合性を不公平に狭く解釈すれば，船主は将来の偶発的事態如何によって相矛盾する義務を果たさねばならない状態にその身を置くことになるので，適合性は公平に広く解釈されなければならない。それで，私は，不適合であるがゆえに，本船は元々傭船契約の義務を適切に遂行できないようになっている（例，*Ciampa* 事件と *The Nizeti* [1960] 1 Lloyd's Rep. 132 事件）との船主の主張を受け入れないが，本船あるいは装置等を変更する必要性，あるいはその結果生じる遅延のゆえに，すなわち適合性が最初からなかったことを示すとの傭船者の主張もこれを容認することができない」。

商業的に判断される準備完了

（少なくとも本船の船艙の状態以外の事柄に適用される）準備完了と適合性の問題は商業的感覚で観察されねばならない。したがって，長期間の定期傭船との関係で，全然問題を生じないか，またはごく稀れにしか問題を生じる——生じたとしても，それは些細な問題に過ぎないのだが——タンク清掃器具に欠陥があり，その欠陥が傭船契約の明示の条件（terms）の一つの違

反となって，それで本船が準備未完了や不適合になるものではない。

　Arianna 号は，一般製品の世界規模での輸送に Essotime 書式で10年間定期傭船された。傭船契約は追加条項に，6個のタンク清掃器具は所与の温度と圧力で同時に作動できると定めていた。本船が解約日までに準備完了し，あらゆる点で運送業務に適した状態にならない場合，傭船者は，解約する権利を持っていた。現実には，本船は在港中に他港揚貨物を同時に加熱しながら，6個のタンク清掃器具を同時に作動できなかった。しかし，傭船契約上の輸送形態は，そういう事態を想定していなかった。仮にそういう事態となった場合でも，本船はいつでも4個の清掃器具を作動でき，欠陥ゆえの遅延は些細な遅延に過ぎなかったであろう。
　本船が傭船契約の要件に合致しないという理由で，傭船者は解約しようと目論んだ。仲裁人は，タンク清掃器具に関する傭船契約条件の違反であるが，本船は運送業務に適していたし，解約する正当な事由はないと，裁定した。Webster 判事は，裁定を支持した。本船の安全性または貨物の安全と保全に影響を及ぼさない欠陥は，法の問題として，必ずしも本船を不適合にするものではない。それは，欠陥の重要性次第である。仲裁人が商業的感覚で本案の欠陥を現実的には意味がないものとみなしたことは仲裁人の裁定に暗示されている。
　The Arianna [1987] 2 Lloyd's Rep. 376.

　さらに，商業的感覚で問題を見てみると，準備完了の通知や本船引渡の申出とまったく同時に，傭船者が本船の船艙に直ちに立ち入りできるように，本船が準備を整えている必要はない。

　航海傭船契約の下で，*Elizabeth Van Belgie* 号は揚荷港に到着したが，バースがなく，ブイに係留して待機した。艙口を開け揚貨装置を準備する以前に準備完了の通知が出され，その有効性が問題となった。控訴院は，本船は実務的意味で準備が整っており，ブイでの艙口の開放や揚貨装置の準備は「無用の形式 idle formality」であると判示した。
　Scrutton 卿判事は212頁で次のように言っている。「本船が碇泊した場所で実務上揚荷が行われないことが確かである場合に，碇泊期間開始のためには揚荷の段取りおよび揚荷要員の配置が必要であると考えられてきたとすれば，それは妥当ではあるまい。そのような要求は，実務とかけ離れている」。
　Armement Adolf Deppe v. *Robinson* [1917] 2 K.B. 204.

　同様に，積荷役の遅延を起こさない，出航前に復旧できる意味のない欠陥は時には無視される。欠陥が現実に相当な程度であった次の事案で，Greer 判事は無視できると考えられる種類の欠陥を提示した。

　Waco 号は航海傭船され，その傭船契約は次のように規定していた。本船は「船体堅牢強固で，あらゆる点において予定の航海に適しているべきであり」また「1920年11月25日午後6時までに積荷準備が整わない場合，傭船者は本傭船契約の解約権を有する」。船長が積荷準備完了の通知を出した11月25日午後4時，本船ボイラーは最低10日間を要する修理が必要であった。Greer 判事は，堪航性担保は明示されており，本船が準備完了の通知を出した時点では不堪航であり，したがって傭船者は解約権を有すると判示した。
　Greer 判事は次のように述べている。「本船は積荷場所への到着，積荷，航行，揚荷からなる傭船航海を開始するに適していなければならない。本船が事実上浮揚碇泊し，貨物の積取に適しておれば，些細な欠陥はあっても，積荷中に正常の積荷作業を妨げることなく修復できることが確実である場合，本船は，そのような些細な欠陥があっても，あらゆる点において予定の航海に適していると判断される。しかし本船が解約期日までに準備が完了しない状態である場合や（本件のように）積荷終了時までに準備が整う相当の確実性がない場合，本船は『船体堅牢強固で，あらゆる点において予定

の航海に適し」ているとは言えない」。
New York and Cuba Mail Steamship v. Eriksen & Christensen (1922) 27 Com. Cas. 330.

前出207頁に示された The Tres Flores [1972] 2 Lloyd's Rep. 384 事件で，本船の船艙の燻蒸は短時間で完了するため，欠陥は「些細なことは問わないという原則」に基づいて無視されるべきであるとの主張が船主のために行われた。しかしこの主張を Mocatta 判事は退け，第1審の事案の報告書の394頁に次のように述べた。

　本船を貨物輸送に適するようにするのが船主の義務であると考える。船主がこれを行わず，本船が不適合である限り，船主は準備完了の有効な通知を出すことはできない。もちろんある事実の場合には，法のあらゆる部門におけると同様，「些細なことは問わない原則」が適用されるであろうが，私は本事案の事実はこの法諺の範囲内にはないと考える。

本事案は，準備完了と適合性の厳密な解釈が本船の船艙の状態に適用された具体例である。前出207/208頁参照。

158 特別な装置

一般原則は，その船型の本船が通常行う荷役作業に適していなければならないが，船主は，傭船契約の下で傭船者が積む権利を有する，いかなる貨物をも取り扱いうるように準備を整えておく必要はないということである。

　Rowland Hill 号の航海傭船契約は，「袋入小麦および（または）小麦粉および（または）その他の適法な貨物」の満載を約定していた。傭船者には，本船が指定日の日没までに Portland で「貨物受取準備が完了」しない場合，解約権が与えられていた。指定時に本船は Portland に到着していたが，小麦や小麦粉積込に必要な荷敷をしていなかった。控訴院は，傭船者は解約できないと判示した。記録長官 Esher 卿は明らかに，傭船契約は本船に積荷「準備完了」を要求しているが，積込を「直ちに開始することに適している」ことを要求していないということであった。しかし他の2人の裁判官は，傭船契約は傭船者に対し傭船者が希望するいかなる種類の貨物をも積む権利を与えているが，傭船者が積む多種類の貨物については，荷敷が要求されていないということも理由としていた。
Vaughan v. Campbell, Heatley (1885) 2 T. L. R. 33.

前出 Noemijulia Steamship v. Minister of Foods (1950) 84 Ll.L. Rep. 354 事件で，Tucker 卿判事は，上記判決の後者の理由を「荷役装置に関する限り，傭船者が傭船契約に従って船積を要求できるいかなる種類の貨物をも扱える準備を，船主は最初から整えていなければならないという考えを否定する見解」と論評した（初期の定期用船契約書式での仕切板を準備する義務に関する二つの事案，「あらゆる点で撒荷および一般貨物の運送に適合す」と規定する Rederi Unda v. Burdon (1937) 57 Ll.L. Rep. 95 事件，および「あらゆる点で通常貨物の運送業務に適合す」と規定する Skagerak v. Saremine (1939) 64 Ll.L. Rep. 153 事件を参照。陸上から提供される装置に関する事案については，The Demosthenes V [1982] 1 Lloyd's Rep. 275 事件参照）。

しかし，特殊な貨物が傭船契約に特に記載され，その貨物のために本船が特別な荷役装置を要する場合，問題が生じると思われる。そのような荷役装置がなくては，本船が「あらゆる点において運送業務に適合し」ているとは言えず（ボルタイム書式の要求する「あらゆる点にお

いて通常貨物の運送業務に適合し」ているとの要件を，十分満たしていても），船主の義務違反であると考えられる。一方ニューヨーク・プロデュース書式の45, 46行は船主をかかる義務から救済しているように思える。傭船契約に特定貨物についての特別な記載がある場合，この義務は船主に残り，45, 46行は，傭船者が傭船契約に明示的に約定していない特別な航海や特殊な貨物を積む場合にのみ適用されると言われている。

あらゆる点で適合した；本船の物理的状態を超えて

　ニューヨーク・プロデュース書式の「船体堅牢強固で，あらゆる点で運送業務に適した」，そしてボルタイム書式の「あらゆる点で，通常の貨物運送業務に適した」という文言は，第一義的には本船の物理的状態に関係するが，少なくとも二つの例で，その範囲はもっと広がる。これら文言は，本船はある種類の書類を保有していなければならないという要件を含むが，また本船は十分な数の能力ある乗組員を配乗していなければならないという要件にも及ぶ。

書　　類

　The Derby [1985] 2 Lloyd's Rep. 325 事件で，Kerr 卿判事は，331頁で次のように述べた。「本船は傭船契約に定める運送業務遂行のために堪航性または適合性を示すある種類の書類を携行しなければならない。本船が時に応じて指図される航海に必要な，航海の海図は明確な実例である。しかし，ここでは本船の堪航性を示す証書にわれわれは関心がある。こういう証書の性質は，船籍国の法の要件によって変化し，本船が配船を指図された国において有効な法と規則の要件によって変化し，または本船の寄港地での有効な法に従って，その地の行政または他の機能を果たす当局が，合法的に要求する要件によって変化する」。したがって，*Levy v. Costerton* (1816) 4 Camp. 389 事件で，次のように判示された。本船が「堅牢強固で……かつ，そのような船舶が必要とするすべてのものを具備する」ことを要求する航海傭船契約の下で，船主は，契約に違反していると判示された。なぜなら，その航路に従事する人たちにはよく知られていることであるが，サルディニア法が要求する「衛生証書」（英国法は，それを要求しない）を本船は所有していなかったからである。*Ciampa v. British India Steam Navigation* [1915] 2 K.B. 774 事件も参照（本船は燻蒸されておらず，伝染病汚染港に寄港の後で非汚染を証する衛生証書を携行せず，不堪航と判示された）。
　同様な結論がボルタイム書式の事案で示された。

>　Madeleine 号はボルタイム書式で3ヶ月定期傭船され，Calcutta での引渡に際し「あらゆる点で通常貨物の運送業務に適し」ていることを要求されていた。Roskill 判事は，本船は駆鼠証明書を持っておらず，その証明書がなくてはインド以外の港へは出港できないから，Calcutta での引渡は有効ではないと判示した。そして傭船者は，傭船契約の解約条項を行使する機会を与えられた。
>　Roskill 判事は次のように言っている（同判例集241頁）。「本件では明示の堪航性担保があり，本船が港湾保健当局の必要証明書を含め，堪航性のある状態で約定時までに引き渡されなければ，傭船者は解約権を有する」。
>　*The Madeleine* [1967] 2 Lloyd's Rep. 224.

　しかし，*The Madeleine* 事件の判決の及ぶ範囲は当初よりも狭くなると思われる。後出 *The Derby* 事件で，Hobhouse 判事は，本船は関連証書がないことよりも燻蒸を必要とするとの理由で，本質的に *Madeleine* 号は適合していなかったと指摘した。

さらに，公の証明書や許可証の取得が単なる形式的なものであり，そのような証明書や許可証がなくても，本船の傭船契約の役務遂行が妨げられない場合，それらがないからといって，航海傭船契約における本船の「準備完了」ができていないということにはならないし，定期傭船契約における「あらゆる点で運送業務に適し」ていないことにはならない。

Aello 号は，寄港地の法律に従い，警察許可証を保持することが要求されていたが，それは「形式以上のものではなく」，かつ，それがないからといって本船の積荷を遅延させることはないとの理由で，警察許可証取得前の準備完了の通知は有効であると貴族院は判示した。
The Aello [1960] 1 Lloyd's Rep. 623.

Delian Spirit 号は，航海傭船契約の下で，準備完了の通知をしたが，そのとき，検疫証書を取得していなかった。控訴院は，本船がバース到着時，検疫証書を取得するのに困難や遅延が生ずるとは考えられないから，検疫証書を取得していないからといって，「準備完了」であることを妨げないと判示した。
The Delian Spirit [1971] 1 Lloyd's Rep. 506.

Pencarrow 号は英国から，Baltic 海往復航海のため，ボルタイム書式で定期傭船された。本船は「あらゆる点で通常貨物の運送業務に適し」ていなければならなかったが，スウェーデンの積量測度証書を持っておらず，Stockholm に揚荷のため到着したとき，傭船者はこの証書を収得し料金を支払った。ところで，この証書は Baltic 海往復航海の出航前に取得されるのが通常であるという証拠もなく，本件において，それがないために，本船が Stockholm 港ないし港外で遅延したという証拠もなかった。Acton 判事は，航海の開始時にこの証明書を保持していなくとも，船主に契約違反はないと判示した。
Chellew Navigation v. Appelquist (1933) 45 Ll.L. Rep. 190.
(Wilson v. Rankin (1865) L.R. 1 Q.B. 162 事件も参照)

前出 The Delian Spirit 事件で，記録長官 Denning 卿は，The Austin Friars (1894) 10 T.L.R. 633 事件を「きわめて特別な事件」として区別した。同事件では，傭船者は，航海傭船契約に基づき，本船が10月10日の真夜中までに積荷港に到着の上，積荷準備が完了しない場合，160解約権を持っていた。本船は10月10日23時に到着したが，検疫官は翌日まで訪船せず，したがって傭船者は，まったく本船に出入りできなかった。傭船者は解約できると判示された。

後出 The Derby 事件で，国際運輸労連（ITF）の青色カードまたは証書は，船籍国の法律，本船の寄港地の政府もしくは，地方当局の法律，規則または合法的な行政実務が要求する書類ではないとの理由で，ニューヨーク・プロデュース書式による傭船契約の下で，「あらゆる点で，運送業務に適し」ているために本船は，国際運輸労連の青色カードまたは証書を持つ必要はない，と判示された。さらに，国際運輸労連の青色カードまたは証書を入手することが船主の慣行であるとの証拠は存在しなかった。

乗　組　員

The Hongkong Fir [1961] 2 Lloyd's Rep. 478 事件で控訴審は，機関部職員の無能力と員数不足が確認された事案において，ボルタイム書式の下で，本船は「あらゆる点で通常貨物の運送業務に適し」ていないと判示した。本事件の全解説については，前出148/150頁参照。後出 The Derby 事件で控訴審は，ニューヨーク・プロデュース書式の「あらゆる点で運送業務に適した」との文言は，この点においてボルタイム書式のこの文言と同じように解釈されるべきことを，認めた。

しかし、この文言によって船主は乗組員の賃金率や雇用条件が、国際運輸労連 (ITF) のような自認かつ超法規的組織の要求に適合することを保証 (undertake) するものではない。

　　キプロス船籍の *Derby* 号は、ニューヨーク・プロデュース書式で11ヶ月から13ヶ月定期傭船された。本船には、ITF の承認基準には適合しないが、通常の条件でフィリピン人乗組員が配乗された。ITF の活動が特に活発な国として知られているため、傭船契約の航路定限から除外されている諸国があった。国籍、乗組員、乗組員の賃金を理由とする労働争議により本船が遅延する場合、喪失時間は船主負担となることが追加条項に定められた。傭船期間中に、本船は前出航路定限から除外されていないポルトガルの Leixoes に寄港した。しかし当地の ITF 代表者は調査の上、本船の ITF 青色カードの不所持を暴露し、荷役人夫は揚荷を拒否した。ITF と解決のために交渉し、荷役作業復帰までに合計21日を喪失した。船主は、追加条項の規定により、この21日間の本船のオフハイヤーを認めたが、傭船者はさらに、当然に発生した再傭船契約の解除により生じた損害賠償を請求する権利を有すると主張した。

　　Hobhouse 判事と控訴審は、21行から24行の義務は堪航性の担保となり、傭船契約業務の適切な遂行のための必要な諸書類を所持し、有能で十分な数の乗組員を配乗する義務を含むが、ITF 青色カードの携帯、ITF の配乗要件または乗組員賃金要件への合致までを含まないと判示した。ITF の介入は荷役人夫の荷役作業に悪影響を及ぼすが、それは傭船者の責任範囲である。船主の方には、履行義務ある役務についての不履行は存しない。さらに船主が ITF の青色カードを入手するのが慣行であるとの証拠も存しない。それゆえに、船主は傭船者のいかなる損害賠償請求についても責任がない。
　　The Derby [1984] 1 Lloyd's Rep. 635 および [1985] 2 Lloyd's Rep. 325 (C. A.).

推定的 (*prima facie*) 事実問題

　　本船が運送業務に「適合し」ているかという問題は、推定的事実問題である。*The Arianna* [1987] 2 Lloyd's Rep. 376 事件で Webster 判事は、法の問題であるとの傭船者の主張を390頁に取り上げて、結論を次のように要約した。「最初に、堪航性や適合性等の問題は、推定的事実問題である。第２に、堪航性の問題を決定するに際しての事実の要素は大きく減少するが、堪航性と適合性は必ずしも同意義ではない、そして適合性の問題の決定に重要な事実の要素が残る。第３に、本船の安全性や貨物の安全と保全にまで効果が及ばない本船の欠陥は法の問題として、必ずしも本船を不堪航または不適合にしない。第４に、本船が堪航性を有するのか、適合しているのかという問題は、欠陥の効果の重要性如何に依拠する事実問題である」。

本船の受取

　　傭船者が、受取拒否、解約、あるいは契約を解消されたものとして扱うことができる状況であるにもかかわらず、本船を受け取った場合、抗議をせずに受け取ったとしても、傭船者は船主の義務違反に対する損害賠償請求権を必ずしも喪失するものではない。*The Democritos* [1975] 1 Lloyd's Rep. 386 (後出422頁に事実関係を紹介) 事件で、Kerr 判事は次のように述べた (同判例集397/398頁)。

　　「損害賠償請求を放棄したかどうかの問題は、事実関係と法の両方の問題が混在しているが、圧倒的に事実関係からの推論により決定される問題である……本船を受け取ったという単なる事実は解約権の放棄に過ぎないと考える。事実関係だけを切り離して考えて、本船の受取が損害賠償請求権の放棄となるはずがないし、またはともかくもなんとしても放棄とはならないものである。このような損害賠償請求権の放棄は、潜在的な損害賠償請求を断念するという傭船者の側の何か承諾めいたものからのみ暗示

されうることである」。

　(傭船契約上の権利が放棄される状況の全解説は，*The Kanchenjunga* [1990] 1 Lloyd's Rep. 391 (H.L.) 事件と前出143頁参照)。

　契約違反を構成する欠陥が引渡時に相当に明らかであると認められないか，引渡後まで明らかとならない場合，損害賠償請求権は消滅しない。そんな状況下で，違反が傭船契約の全利益を実質的に傭船者から奪うようなものであれ，引渡を受けたからといって傭船者がその後に契約を解消されたものとして扱うことが妨げられることはない (*Snia* v. *Suzuki* (1924) 18 Ll. L. Rep. 333 事件，*The Hongkong Fir* [1961] 2 Lloyd's Rep. 478 事件，*The Hermosa* [1980] 1 Lloyd's Rep. 638，[1982] 1 Lloyd's Rep. 570 事件および前出148頁と151頁参照)。

NYPE 93

　ニューヨーク・プロデュース書式の1993年改訂版は，引渡時，返船時の「船上の燃料の量と本船の状態」を確認する傭船開始時検査とオフハイヤー開始時検査を定める特別条項を含む(前出9頁の英文書式の40行/47行，第3条と53頁参照)。

損害賠償の算定

　The Fanis [1994] 1 Lloyd's Rep. 633 事件で，Mance 判事は，仲裁人は法的な誤りを犯していないと判示した。仲裁人の裁定は，*Fanis* 号を引渡できず，傭船者が代船を傭船しなければならなかったときに，定期傭船者の損害賠償は，(代船の傭船契約が必要とする以上の燃料を船上に保持して返船したことにより) 代船の傭船契約の下で得た予想もしなかった利益を差し引かれるべきではないというものであった。

162 米　国　法

積荷準備完了

　積荷準備完了というためには，全船艙がすべての点で準備を完了していなければならない。*Crow* v. *Myers*, 41 F. 806 (E. D. Va. 1890). *Rudolf A. Oetker* v. *Koninklijke Nederlandsche Stoomboot-Maatschappij N. V.*, SMA 508 (Arb. at N. Y. 1970) 事件で，船主も知らなかったが，本船を傭船者に引き渡すときに，ヒメアカカツオブシムシが棲息していた。仲裁審は，船主がこの状態を知らなくても，「堪貨性」のある船を引き渡す義務に違反していると裁定した。仲裁審によれば，「船主は，傭船契約上の運送貨物の受取に本船船艙を適合させなければならない」。一度，そのような状態が発見されれば，船主は本船を燻蒸消毒しなければならず，燻蒸が行われている間，オフハイヤーになると裁定している。傭船者が本船受渡証を受け取ったのであるから，船主は燻蒸義務を免れるという船主の主張は否定された。

　The Endeavor, 1978 AMC 1742 (Arb. at N. Y. 1977) 事件で，仲裁審は，船主は豪州の産業別組合の特定地方の要求を満たすために，新しい梯子を取り付ける義務があると裁定した。傭船者には，本船を豪州へ配船する権利があった。もし本船が特別な梯子を装備していないならば，この豪州へ配船する権利は妨げられたであろう（後出271頁の追加解説を参照）。

　しかし船艙は通常，貨物積載の準備がされておればよく，傭船契約上これに反する明示の規定がない限り，船主は特別な扱いを要する貨物のために，船艙を準備する必要はない。*Disney* v. *Furness*, 79 F. 810, 815 (D. Md. 1897) 事件参照。本件は「必要とする準備は相応の準備であり，［傭船者］が定める特定の要求を満たす特別な準備ではない」と判示された。同じように *Greenwell* v. *Ross*, 34 F. 656 (E. D. La. 1888) 事件で，裁判所は次のように判示した。本船が，傭船契約上要求されている「適法な貨物」の積荷準備を，すべての点で行っている場合，傭船者は積込貨物を事前に船主に通知しておらず，本船は簡単にその準備を行えるのに，特別な準備を要する貨物の積荷準備を本船が行っていないとの理由で，傭船者が傭船契約を解約するのは不当である。*The Stolt Lion*, SMA 1118 (Arb. at N. Y. 1977) 事件も参照。

　The Emmanuel C, SMA 1575 (Arb. at N. Y. 1981) 事件で，仲裁審は，National Cargo Bureau の検査員による通常の積込前検査で，すべての貨物艙に錆が見つかったときに，傭船契約の21/22行が意味する範囲で，本船は準備完了していないと裁定した。傭船者が積もうとした貨物は傭船契約の許容する貨物で，撒積のリン安であった。その貨物は錆に曝され汚染したであろう。したがって，本船は許容されている貨物の受取の準備を完了していなかった。本船は，錆の除去に要した期間，オフハイヤーとなると裁定された。

　腐敗しやすい貨物のように，特別な管理を要する貨物を本船で運送しようとする場合，船主は本船をそのように装備しなければならない。指導的な米国の判列は *Martin* v. *The Southwark*, 191 U. S. 1 (1903) 事件である。同事件において，船荷証券は Philadelphia から Liverpool 向け食肉につき発行されたが，Philadelphia 出港前から，本船の冷凍装置が故障したため，食肉は到着時腐敗していた。裁判所は，船主が，本船発航時において，堪航性を保持するために相当の注意を尽くさなかったと認定し，荷主有利に判示した。

　Martin v. *The Southwark* 事件における船荷証券はハーター法に準拠していた。裁判所によれば，堪航性の判断基準は本船が食肉運送に適していたか否かであった。

163
　堪航性は，本船が海上危険に遭遇した際，強固で，かつ適合しているか否かのみで判断されるので

はなく，特定運送貨物に対応する本船の特性についても判断されるものである。したがって，本船が，運送に適しているとされる貨物を運送できなければならないし，そうでなければ，その貨物に関しては堪航性がないものとされる。本船が提供する特別の装置がなければ，精選牛肉のような腐敗しやすい貨物を高温気象下の長期航海で船積することはできない（191 U.S. at 9）。

重大な欠陥があれば，引渡の有効性は妨げられる。*Oneida Nav. Co.* v. *L. Richardson & Co.*, 282 F. 241（2d Cir. 1922）事件で，本船は，補助機関付スクーナー帆船と傭船契約に表示されていた。解約日に補助エンジンは作動不能であり，修理期間は不明であった。裁判所は，その時点で修理期間が8ないし9日間であると分かっていたら，おそらく解約は認められないだろうとしながら，傭船者の解約を妥当なものと判示した。裁判所によれば，解約日には「補助機関付スクーナー船として傭船された本船は補助機関付スクーナー船ではなかった……」というのである（前出159頁の解説を参照）。

船艙を清掃して

The Van Hawk, 1975 AMC 254（Arb. at N.Y. 1975）事件において，ニューヨーク・プロデュース書式の傭船契約により，本船船艙の「清掃」が要求されており，傭船者は受渡検査の上本船を受け取っていた。仲裁審は，傭船者が硫黄の積荷準備のため船艙を追加清掃した費用について，船主に責任はないと裁定した。

なお，*The Augvald*, 1965 AMC 1614（Arb. at N.Y. 1965）事件も参照。同事件において，船主は「コクゾウムシ駆除証明書」を取得しておらず，したがって，本船はあらゆる点において積荷準備が完了しているとは言えないとの理由で，傭船者は本船受取を拒否できると裁定された。船主は，傭船者が穀物を積もうとしていることを知っていた。仲裁審は次のとおり述べている。

船主は傭船者に本船のすべての貨物積載場所を撒荷かつ／または袋入穀物を受け取るために，清潔にし，かつ準備を完了して，提供しなければならないというのが仲裁審の意見である。仲裁審の見解では，すべての本船貨物積載場所を，穀物を害するコクゾウムシやその他の害虫を駆除した上で，提供することは船主の義務である（1965 AMC at 1616-1617）。

船体の堅牢強固

この文言は本船が傭船者への引渡時に堪航性あることの明示的担保を規定する（*Work* v. *Leathers*, 97 U.S. 379（1878）；*Munson S. S. Line* v. *The Miramar S. S. Co.*, 166 F. 722, 724（2d Cir. 1908）；*Iligan Int'l. Corp.* v. *The John Weyerhaeuser*, 372 F. Supp. 859, 1974 AMC 1719（S.D.N.Y. 1974），原審維持507 F. 2d 68（2d Cir.1974），裁量上告拒絶421 U.S. 956）。本船を堪航性ある状態に保持する継続的義務を船主に課すニューヨーク・プロデュース書式第1条に含まれているような文言がない場合，引渡時の本船に堪航性があれば，担保は満たされる。

The Captain John, 1973 AMC 2005（Arb. at N.Y. 1973）事件で，傭船契約に，本船は「相当の注意を尽くすことにより，できる限り堅牢強固で」あることと規定していたが，船主は全傭船期間を通して，相当の注意を尽くす義務があると裁定された。仲裁審は次のように述べている。

この文言は，本船を各航海の開始にあたり，堪航性あるものとするために相当の注意を尽くすという明示の担保であると解される（1973 AMC at 2009）。

The Grand Explorer SMA 551（Arb. at N.Y. 1963）事件で，仲裁審は，傭船契約の要求どおりに，5番船艙が砂糖積用荷台で張りつめられていなかったとの理由で，傭船者の本船受取拒否を認めた。同じように *Coca-Cola Co.* v. *The Norholt*, 333 F. Supp. 946, 1972 AMC 388（S.D.N.Y. 1971）事件で，裁判所は次のように判示している。

傭船契約では，本船のディープタンクが乾貨ならびに液体貨物に適合していることを船主が担保すると明示している。船主という者は，傭船船舶の各航海の開始時における堪航性を，黙示的に担保している者である。本件船主は，各種貨物の安全な保管と運送のための装置とタンクのある本船を提供しなければならず，そうでなければ，担保義務違反となる（333 F. Supp. at 948-949）。

本船は，通常または合理的に予期しうる状況において，貨物を安全に輸送するための適切な装置がなければ，堪航性がない，すなわち運送業務に従事するには不適であると思われる。*Demsey & Assoc.* v. *The Sea Star*, 461 F. 2d 1009（2d Cir. 1972）事件で，裁判所は，鋼材運送のため傭船された本船の中甲板艙口蓋が貨物の重量を十分に支えることができないとの理由で，堪航性がないと判断した。

The Golden Dolphin, SMA 2797（Arb. at N.Y. 1987）事件で，仲裁審は，船主は能力があり十分に訓練された乗組員を提供する注意を尽くしていないと裁定した。傭船者に帰属する船上の燃料は，本船が爆発し沈没したときに滅失したが，船主は，その燃料の滅失につき責任ありと裁定された。

適法な貨物

"24. .... to be employed, in carrying lawful merchan-
25. dise, including petroleum or its products, in proper containers, excluding ....
....
26. (vessel is not to be employed in the carriage of Live Stock, but Charterers are to have the privilege of shipping a small number on deck at their risk,
27. all necessary fittings and other requirements to be for account of Charterers), in such lawful trades,"

「本船は適切な容器に入れた石油または石油製品を含み，...............を除外する適法な貨物の運送に（家畜の運送は除外する。ただし，傭船者は，自己の危険において少数の家畜を甲板積とする権利を有するが，これに要する造作その他の必要整備は傭船者の負担とする）適法な航路において使用されるものとし，」

違法な貨物

適法な貨物には，軍需品や弾薬も含まれる。船積が積地の法律に違反する場合や，指定の揚荷港で合法的に揚荷できない場合，その貨物は適法な貨物とはいえない。貨物は，船籍国の法律，傭船契約のプロパー・ローの下でもまた，適法でなければならないと思われる。外国法の下での違法性の効果について，Dicey & Morris の『法の抵触』 *The Conflict of Laws*（12th edn）（1259頁から1264頁，1280頁から1284頁および1410頁から1413頁）を参照。

Dodecanese 号は，「適法な貨物の輸送のため，適法な航海に」就航するとして，ボルタイム1920年書式に基づき傭船された。傭船者は，地中海諸港において弾薬その他の爆発物を積載し，エジプトの Adabiya で英国軍向けに，これを揚荷することを指図したが，傭船者は，この揚荷がエジプト当局により禁止されていることを知っていた。この指図に従ったため，本船は，エジプト当局のブラックリストに掲載された。その後本船は Port Tewfik において，Aqaba 向け軍需物資をさらに積載したが，出港前，故障を起こした。本船がブラックリストに挙げられていたため，当局は，本船の修理を遅延させ，そのため本船は通常の予定より26日間遅れた。Pilcher 判事は，Adabiya 向け貨物は，揚地で合法的に荷役できないものであるから，「適法な貨物」とはいえず，したがって，傭船者は，それによって生じた遅延損害を賠償する義務がある（26日間本船をオフハイヤーとされたことから生ずる船主の損害を回収させることになる）と判示した。
Leolga v. *Glynn* 〔1953〕2 Lloyd's Rep. 47.
（上記事件において，Pilcher 判事が「その特定事件の事実関係にのみ適用される『用法』の先例として」掲げた *Vanderspar* v. *Duncan* （1891）8 T.L.R. 30 事件も参照）

傭船契約上除外された貨物の船積

傭船者が，傭船契約によって除外された貨物を船積することは，契約違反であり，船長はそのような貨物の船積指図を，当然拒否することができる。*The Sussex Oak* (1950) 83 Ll. L.

Rep. 297事件において，Devlin判事は，「船舶の使用に関する傭船者の指図に船長を従わせる旨の定期傭船契約条項は，傭船者がその権限外の指図を出した場合にまで船長が従わなければならないと解されるとは思えない」と述べた（同判例集307頁）。

除外された貨物の船積により，船主が傭船契約を解消されたものとして扱うことができる状況もありうる。

*Evgenia Chandris*号は，1航海傭船され，傭船船契約には，「適法な雑貨よりなる貨物，ただし酸類，爆発物，武器，弾薬その他の危険貨物を除く」と規定されていた。傭船者は，危険物のテレピン油を船積し，その結果揚荷が遅延した。この貨物は，上記の規定によって除外されており，したがって，傭船者は，「基本的条項」に違反していると判示された。しかしながら，船主は，契約を追認していたから，遅延損害金ではなく，滞船料のみ請求する権利があると判示された。Devlin判事は，滞船料条項が許容貨物と同様除外貨物にも適用されると解釈した。
Chandris v. *Isbrandtsen-Moller* (1951) 1 K.B. 240.
（「基本的契約違反」という時代遅れの原則に関する解説については，後出495頁参照）

Chandris v. *Isbrandtsen-Moller*事件では，除外貨物を船積した場合，（取るに足らぬ程度の極少量の場合は別として）その量の多少を問わず，船主は，傭船契約が破棄されたものとして扱うことができるという主張がなされた。Devlin判事は，このような主張には問題があることを認め，「航海の終りに船主が（上記極少量というには多過ぎる）少量の除外貨物を発見した場合に，船長がその船積を知っていたにもかかわらず，船主は契約全体を破棄しうるというのが法の原則であるとすれば，実務的に不都合が生じうる。本件では，船主が契約追認の道を選択したのであるから，検討の対象として，そのような問題は生じない」と述べた（同判例集251頁）。

契約の基本的条項の違反については，船主に対して，契約が解消されたものとして扱う権利を与えるのであるが，現在の裁判所は，除外貨物に関する条項を，そのような基本的条項とみなさないのではないかといわれている。除外貨物に関する条項の違反も，それが契約の根本にまで影響するほど重大である場合に限り，そのような結果が認められるべきである。

除外貨物引受の効果

傭船者が船長に除外貨物の船積を指図し，船主がこれをまったく知らなかった場合または船長に対し異議を申し立てた上で引き受けることを指示した場合，船主は，損害賠償，あるいは，傭船者の黙示の約束を根拠として，除外貨物輸送につき，現市場料率に基づく追加報酬を受ける権利を有すると思われる。

*Strathcona*号は，スティールビレットを積むため1航海再傭船された。再傭船者は，同船に一部スティールビレットを積み，一部，運賃の市場料率が高い雑貨を積んだが，管理船主（disponent owners）は，この事実を知らなかった。船長は雑貨を引き受けたけれども，原傭船契約を変更する権限を有しないから，管理船主（disponent owners）は，（傭船契約の解除を要求していなかった）雑貨の市場料率運賃を受け取る権利を有すると判示された。除外貨物を積み込むことにより，再傭船者は，それが運送された場合，相当の報酬を支払うという黙示の約束をしたことになる。
Steven v. *Bromley* [1919] 2 K.B. 722.

危険貨物

　ニューヨーク・プロデュース書式には，危険貨物の船積を禁止する条項はない。それに対比して，ボルタイム書式の21/22行には，「家畜または有毒性，発火性もしくは危険性のある貨物（酸類，爆発物，カルシウムカーバイド，珪素鉄，ナフサ，ガソリン，タール，およびその製品のような）を船積してはならない」とある。しかし，ニューヨーク・プロデュース書式25行の空欄にそのような除外貨物について，当事者が合意するのが通常である。

NYPE 93

　ニューヨーク・プロデュース書式の1993年改訂版には，特別な危険貨物条項がある。「あらゆる種類の家畜，武器，弾薬，爆発物，核物質および放射性物質」を除き，特定の国家当局の要件に従う限りにおいて危険貨物の輸送を，危険貨物条項の最初の部分は許容している。次[167]に，輸送されるIMO分類貨物の量を制限し，傭船者がIMO諸規則に合致する証拠を合理的に要求される範囲で提示する義務を定めている。前出9頁の第4条49行から69行までと54頁を参照。

傭船者の黙示の義務

　ある特定の貨物が危険貨物として分類されていないという事実にもかかわらず，その貨物の包装の適否を含めた当該貨物の特異な性質により船舶もしくは船上の他貨物を危険に曝す場合には，その貨物は危険貨物である。

　傭船者が貨物の特異な性質を通知せずに当該貨物を積み込む場合には，傭船者はコモン・ロー上の黙示の保証（undertaking）に違反したことになる。ただし，船主もしくは乗組員が貨物の性質を知っているか，もしくは当然に知っているべきであった場合はその限りではない。この規則は公運送人（common carrier）に対する荷送人の義務を取り扱った先例に端を発する。しかし，The Athanasia Comninos [1990] 1 Lloyd's Rep. 277 事件で Mustill 判事は，次のように述べた。「運送契約の当事者である荷送人には，積込貨物の運送への適合性に関して，および貨物の危険性に関する警告通知に関して，ある種の契約上の義務があるということは1世紀以上の間に亘って，確立されてきた（Williams v. East India Co. (1802) 3 East 192; Brass v. Maitland (1856) 6 E. & B. 470）。この義務は貨物が公運送人（common carrier）に委託される事案に限らず，特定の状況下では海上輸送のあらゆる契約について当てはまる」。したがって，定期傭船契約の下で，このコモン・ロー上の義務は傭船者の負担として降りかかると思われる。Mustill 判事は続けて，先例の影響力により荷送人の義務が絶対的であるとの命題は，裏づけられている，つまり，荷送人の義務は荷送人が当該貨物の危険性を知っていたか，知っているべきであったということとは関係がない，という見解を表明した。さらに，この義務が傭船者の負担とされる場合にも，このことはまた真実であるように思われる。

　上記で解説した原則は，関係する貨物の種類を「危険」あるいは「安全」と簡単に分類できない場合には，適用するのがより難しくなる。The Athanasia Comninos 事件で Mustill 判事が，指摘したように，石炭は危険貨物か安全貨物であるかを抽象的にいうことはできない。石炭からメタンガスが発生し，メタンガスが空気と混じって爆発性の混合物が発生することは周知である。しかし，船主はこの危険性を認識し，適切な用心をしたが，特定の積荷が予想外にまったく異常なほどにガスを発生するという危険性を予測することを船主自身について期待することはできず，その危険性を引き受けることを期待することもできなかったと船主は主張す

るかも知れない。Mustill 判事は，本事案において，次のように述べた。「私は危険貨物の船積について黙示の担保から始めて，その中に事実を当て嵌めるのは正しくないと考える。しかし，契約と事実を一緒に読みとるよりも，契約の本当の解釈に基づいてこの個別の船積に関連する危険は，［船主］が自らその負担を約した危険であるか否かを問うのが正しいと考える」。判事は，更に続けて提言した。「船主が負担を約したとみなされるべき危険は，関連する種類の貨物輸送の適切な方法──専門的化学者の知識の習得ではないが「船主は正当な方法により時代に即応すべく相応の対策を取るものと期待された。」──によれば，その危険性は避けられたであろう」。「この手法は危険貨物に関する大抵の問題を処理するのに十分である。なぜなら，大半の貨物について『通常の』用心によって十分に契約記載の明細を持つ通常貨物の輸送の危険を取り除くことができるのである。完全に外的な諸原因による災害は別として，適切な輸送と『危険な』性質はコインの表裏の関係であると言われる」。もちろん，適切なまたは「通常の」輸送方法は，貨物の通常性にもかかわらず事故を防ぐには実際には不適当であることもあるが，Mustill 判事が考えたこの危険性は，船主の負担する所となった。しかし，特定の貨物がもたらす危険性が，「記載貨物の輸送に付随する危険性と（性質または程度の如何を168問わず）まったく異なる種類」である場合，危険は船主ではなく，荷送人または，傭船者の負担となる（The Atlantic Duchess［1957］2 Lloyd's Rep. 55 事件も参照）。

　ニューヨーク・プロデュース書式上の傭船者のコモン・ロー上の義務は，米国海上物品運送法の条項により補われる（または，取って代わられることもある。後出593頁参照）。

米国海上物品運送法

　プロデュース書式第24条に摂取された1936年米国海上物品運送法は，第4条6項で次のように規定している。

　　「引火性・爆発性または危険性のある貨物については，運送人・船長または運送人の代理人が，その性質や特性を知りながら船積に同意した場合を除き，運送人は，揚荷前，いつどこでも，陸揚・破壊あるいは，無害にすることができ，その処分の代償を支払う必要はない。そのような貨物の荷主は，その船積から，直接または間接的に生ずる，または結果として生ずるすべての損害と費用に責任を負わなければならない。このような性質を承知の上で，船積された貨物が，船舶または他の貨物に危険を及ぼす場合，運送人・船長または運送人の代理人は，同様の方法で，どこででも陸揚し，破壊し，あるいは無害にすることができ，これにつき運送人は，何ら責任を負わない。ただし，共同海損となる場合を除く」。

　第4条6項は，3款に分かれる。**1款**は，引火性・爆発性または危険性のある貨物について，運送人・船長または運送人の代理人が，その性質や特性を知りながら船積に同意した場合を除き，船主が，陸揚・破壊あるいは，無害にすることを許容する。**2款**は，その船積から生ずるすべての損害額と費用につき「荷送人」に責任を負わせる。**3款**は，船主がその性質を承知の上で，船積した貨物が，船舶または他の貨物にとり危険となる場合には，船主に，最初に掲げた陸揚・破壊・無害化の権利を持たせる。

　後出594から601頁に解説されている原則を適用すれば，第4条6項の最初の部分と3款が，ニューヨーク・プロデュース書式の下での船主と傭船者との間で完全に有効といえない理由はない。2款は「荷送人」を「傭船者」と読み替えたからといって，同じように有効であるかということは，はっきりしていない。しかし，ニューヨーク・プロデュース書式の文脈において，これは正確な手法であるといわれている。したがって第4条6項2款はこの文脈で有効で

あるといわれている。

　例えば危険品を仕向地の手前で陸揚するような場合，船主に提起される損害賠償請求に抗弁する際，船主が第4条6項に依拠できることは，明白である。危険貨物によってもたらされた損害に関して船主が提起する賠償請求を支持するために船主は，2款に依拠することもできるであろう。後出357頁の The Athanasia Comninos［1990］1 Lloyd's Rep. 277 事件で，Mustill 判事は，この点について見解を保留したが，この船主の賠償請求の主張は，The Fiona［1993］1 Lloyd's Rep. 257（この点について控訴されてない）事件での Diamond 判事の判決，The Giannis N. K.［1994］2 Lloyd's Rep. 171 事件，後出228頁に引用の米国判例，カナダ判例の The Irwin Schroder［1970］Ex. C. R. 426 事件により支持されている。

　第4条6項が，危険貨物の船積に関して，前出221頁で検討した荷送人のコモン・ロー上の黙示の義務に取って代わって，どの程度に徹底した規定になるのかはまだはっきりしていない。前出 The Athanasia Comninos 事件で，Mustill 判事はこの点に関して立場を保留したが，前出の The Fiona 事件で Diamond 判事は，徹底した規定はヘーグ・ルール第4条6項の同様の条項により創造され，さらに，船主がその条項に基づき救済されない場合には，船主は，危険貨物を船積しないという黙示のコモン・ロー上の保証（undertaking）に後戻りすることは169できないとの見解をとった。しかしながら，傭船契約の特定の条項が効果を持つ余地は残っているように思われる（後出 Chandris v. Isbrandtsen-Moller 事件の Devlin 判事の見解を参照）。

　一部貨物の荷送人に対する船主の賠償請求に関する The Giannis N. K. 事件で，Longmore 判事は，第4条6項は，物理的損傷をもたらしやすいという点で，危険である貨物に限定されると考えた。本件で，同判事は，ヒメアカカツオブシムシのついた南京豆は，船舶にとって危険ではないが，他の貨物にとっては危険であるので，第4条6項の危険な性質を有する貨物であると，判示した。仮にその貨物は物理的に危険ではないので，第4条6項にいう意味の貨物に該当しないとすれば，同判事は，荷送人は船舶の遅延をもたらしがちな貨物（Mitchell v. Steel［1916］2 K. B. 610 事件のように）を積み取らないというコモン・ロー上の別個の，しかし関係ある（厳格）責任に違反していると判示したことであろう。

　The Fiona［1994］2 Lloyd's Rep. 506 事件で，控訴院は，Diamond 判事の判決を支持して，不堪航が危険貨物の船積から生じた損害の唯一の寄与原因であり，船主が，船舶を堪航性があり，貨物輸送に適するように注意を尽くす第3条1項の重要な義務に違反している場合には，第4条6項に基づく船主の賠償請求は，容れられないと，判示した。

　第4条6項の2款で荷送人に課せられる船主に対する責任は，絶対的義務から同法第4条3項の相当の注意を尽くす義務に減じられると，考えられてきた。第4条3項には，「荷送人は，本人，代理人，被用者の行為，過失，懈怠なくして何らかの原因で生じた運送人もしくは船舶が被った滅失損傷には責任がない」と規定されている。後出228頁に引用の米国判例は，義務がそのように小さくなることを示唆しているが，同じ結論が英国法で得られるかは，非常に疑問である。The Athanasia Comninos 事件で，Mustill 判事はこの点に関しても見解を保留したが，前出の The Fiona 事件で Diamond 判事は，荷送人は義務がそのようには減縮されるものではないことを正当に認めたという見解を表明した。彼は，次のように言った。「荷送人側の過失もしくは，懈怠によるものであるか否かにかかわらず，危険貨物の船積は明らかに荷送人の行為である」。前出 The Giannis N. K. 事件で，過失の問題がコモン・ロー上の責任に関連して提起されたにもかかわらず，この点は論議されなかった。

　第4条6項の「貨物の特性を知って」という文言は，船主や乗組員が仮に事実として知らなかったとしても，知っているのが相当であるという知識を含む。前出 The Athanasia Comninos 事件および後出357頁で，Mustill 判事は傍論により，次のように言った。「ヘーグ・ルール第

4条6項が，いやしくも運送人に対するよりも，運送人による賠償請求に関与している場合に，引用された文言は，運送人や乗組員が実際に持っている知識はもちろん，持っているべき知識をも含む。そうでなければ，無知に不当な価値を与えることになろう」。The Fiona 事件で Diamond 判事は，この見解に全面的な同意を表明した。

　第4条6項2款は，（貨物の性質や特質を承知していない）最初の部分に適用され，船長が同意した危険貨物の船積から生じる損害に荷送人は責任を負わないとする（貨物の性質や特質を承知している）3款には適用されない。Devlin 判事は，*Chandris* v. *Isbrandtsen-Moller* [1951] 1 K. B. 240 事件（前出220頁）のこの議論を拒否した。その事件で船長は禁止された危険貨物の船積に同意したが，それに関する船主の権利は放棄していなかったと判示された。同判事は，荷送人（すなわち同法の摂取により，航海傭船者）の責任に関して第4条6項3款が何ら触れていないからといって，そのことが傭船契約上の明示の除外貨物条項に違反した航海傭船者に対する船主の賠償請求についての抗弁とはならないと指摘した。同法は，運送契約にまったく取って代わる包括的な法典として意図されておらず，むしろ，同法は，ある問題に170ついては規制するが，船長の同意を得て貨物を船積した場合の結果のように，当事者が契約条件により当事者自身で自由に自律するその他の問題については何らの規制も加えなかった。

ニューヨーク・プロデュース書式第8条に基づく船主に対する補償

　船主は，危険貨物の積込指図によって生じた損害につき，ニューヨーク・プロデュース書式第8条の下で黙示されている補償に基づいて傭船者を訴えることができる。後出353頁参照。この訴えは，傭船者側の過失の有無に関係がなく（後出356頁参照），この訴えにより船主は，安易な方法で，コモン・ロー上および米国国際海上物品運送法第4条6項2款に基づく傭船者の黙示の義務は一種の注意を尽くすということであり，絶対的なものではない（前出222および223頁の解説参照）と判示される可能性を避けることができよう。さらに，自動的に危険貨物として分類されない種類の貨物の場合に第8条のこの補償に基づき船主が成功するためには，船主は特定の貨物が異常であることを必ずしも証明する必要はない（後出357頁参照）。

警告の欠如

　一般貨物でも，船長に貨物に関する情報を与えていない場合には，危険物となりうる。

　　Agios Nicolas 号は「危険品」の船積を除外して，ボルタイム書式により傭船され，貨物として微粉鉄鉱石が積載された。船長は，（当然必要な質問をしたにもかかわらず）含水量につき誤った説明を受け，含水量が仕切板を必要とするほどのものであることを知らされなかった。仕切板は設置されず，その結果貨物が移動し，本船は避難港に入港せざるをえなかった。定期傭船者は，危険貨物を船積した点で義務違反があると判示された。
　　Donaldson 判事は次のように述べた。「一言で言えば，『船長』に提示されたものは，乾いた羊の皮を被った濡れた狼であった。貨物は外観とは根本的にまったく異なるものであることが船長に通知されていない。そういう状況では，とても議論できないほど貨物は危険なものであると思われる」。
　　Micada v. *Texim* [1968] 2 Lloyd's Rep. 57.

ボルタイム書式

　ボルタイム書式21から22行には，次のように定められている。「家畜または（酸類・爆発

物・カーバイド・珪素鉄・ナフサ・ガソリン・タールおよびその製品の如き）有毒性・発火性もしくは危険性を有する貨物を船積してはならない」。「如き」で始まる括弧の中の文言は，括弧の後の文言の完全かつ自然な意味を制限するものではなく，「如き」は「例示」であり，「言い換え」ではない（*Micada* v. *Texim*（[1968] 2 Lloyd's Rep. 57 と前出）事件を参照）。

特 別 報 酬

　前出 *Steven* v. *Bromley*［1919］2 K.B. 722 事件において，Atkin 卿判事は，船舶を危険性のない傭船に出したところ，危険な仕事に自己の船舶が使用されたことを知った船主が，契約違反に基づき，その損害賠償の一部として，危険な仕事に対する特別な報酬を要求することの可能性を論じたが，その結論を出さなかった。

[171]適法な航路において

　「適法な航路」は，「適法な貨物」と同様に解釈されなければならないと考えられる。航路は，指図された積揚荷港の法律により不法となる場合だけではなく，船籍国の法律または傭船契約の準拠法のいずれかによる場合も，また不法となると思われる。

172 米 国 法

適法な貨物

　傭船契約に運送貨物の種類に関する条項を含めるのは，普通のことである。そういう条項が含まれている場合，船主は，規定された種類の貨物のみを積み取ればよい。除外貨物の規定がない場合に，貨物を積む傭船者の権利を制限できるのは，「適法な貨物」でなければならないということだけである。

　The Wismar, SMA 1454 (Arb. at N.Y. 1980) 事件で，傭船契約には除外貨物条項があり，次のように関連する箇所を規定していた。

第45条A項：除外貨物

　撒積アスファルトとピッチ，酸類，核物質・放射性物質，動物，原皮，旋盤とエンジンブロックのスクラップ。武器，弾薬と爆発物，他の有毒な，発火性ある危険な貨物，ただし，IMCO規則・米国コーストガード規則に従って包装，表示，積込，積付，揚荷される場合を除く。

　船舶は同一条件で再傭船され，再傭船者は，船長にペレット状の直接還元鉄（DRIP）の積取を指図した。DRIPは水と接触すると水素ガスを発し，熱を生じるので，前述引用の除外貨物条項の意味の範囲で危険であるとの報告によって，船主はその貨物の積取を拒否するように船長に指示した。仲裁審は多数意見として，DRIPが本当に危険貨物であるかを決定するに際して，IMCO（現在ではIMO）および米国コーストガードが傭船契約に取締機関として明示されているので，IMCOおよび米国コーストガードの規則が特に関係すると裁定した。DRIPは当時のIMCO危険貨物規定に表示されておらず，米国コーストガードは，DRIPの積込に注意するように規定していたが，同貨を危険貨物として分類していなかった。さらに，カナダ・コーストガードはある種の指針に従うことを条件として積取を承認していた。貨物は公式には，「危険貨物」として分類されていないので，仲裁審は多数意見として，当該物質は水のある所では，爆発性があり発火性があるという趣旨の多数の専門家団体の証言にもかかわらず，傭船契約第45条A項にいう危険貨物ではないと裁定した。

　The Witfuel, SMA 1381 (Arb. at N.Y. 1979) 事件で，船舶は，「原油および／または黒物石油製品」の運送のためタンカー定期傭船書式により傭船された。仲裁審は，傭船者は白物または精製製品を積み取ったゆえに，傭船契約に違反したと裁定し，修理費および汚染罰金を含む，それにより生じた損害につき傭船者は責任があると裁定した。貨物が傭船契約において除外されているか否かの判断は「船舶運航や傭船に携わるものが通常ほとんど知らない基準による精密な定義ではなく，白物と黒物製品，つまり一方で精製品，他方で原油または残滓油という業界における一般的な理解により左右される」と裁定した。

　The Maria K., SMA 1324 (Arb. at N.Y. 1979) 事件では，石油コークス（「ペットコーク」）が除外貨物かということが問題となった。傭船契約は，ニューヨーク・プロデュース書式に拠っており，その22行には，ペットコークが明示されていなかった。仲裁審は，ペットコークは適法な貨物であると裁定し，船主の積取拒否は傭船契約違反であると裁定した。船主のペットコーク積取の不法な拒否による傭船者の損害を査定した*The Pacduke*, SMA 2586 (Arb. at N.Y. 1989) 事件も参照。「脂肪を除去した魚粉・魚蛋白濃縮品」は，傭船契約によ

り許容された非危険貨物であり適法な貨物であると判示した The Sarah, SMA 2671 (Arb. at N. Y. 1990) 事件参照。後出291頁で解説の The Fernglen, 1971 AMC 213 (Arb. at N. Y. 1970) 事件参照。

The Mercandiam Supplier II, SMA 2509 (Arb. at N. Y. 1988) 事件で、仲裁人はマリファナは、適法な貨物ではないと言った。

73 麻　　薬

1986年に海事麻薬法施行法 46 USC (合衆国法典) §1901-1904が立法化された。とりわけ、同法は、米国籍船もしくは米国法を準拠法とする船舶のいかなる乗船者も麻薬を製造し配布することを非合法とする。刑罰には麻薬が発見される船舶の差押え、没収を含む。46 U.S.C. §1904.

危 険 貨 物

一般海事法の下で、貨物の所有者は、自らが知っているか、または知っているべき、また運送人が知らないか、あるいは知っていると当然には予見できない、貨物の危険性を運送人に通知する義務がある。International Mercantile Marine Co. v. Fels, 170 F. 275, 277 (2d Cir. 1909). しかしながら、貨物所有者は貨物に隠れた危険がないことを絶対的に担保するとは考えられない。むしろ、貨物所有者の義務は、危険を実際に知っているか、知っているとみなされるのか、いずれかに基づく。Sucrest Corp. v. Jennifer, 455 F. Supp. 371, 1978 AMC 2520 (D. Me. 1978) 事件, William J. Quillan, 180 F. 681, 682-684 (2d Cir. 1910), 裁量上告拒絶 218 U. S. 682 事件, Akt. Fido v. Lloyd Brasileiro, 267 F. 733 (S. D. N. Y. 1919), 原審維持 283 F. 62 (2d Cir. 1922), 裁量上告拒絶 260 U. S. 737 (1922) 事件参照。

前出の Sucrest Corp. v. Jennifer 事件で、船舶は砂糖の船内移動のため大変な傾きを生じ、船舶と貨物の安全のために意図的に座礁した。砂糖の移動は、生物学的品質低下により生じた。裁判所は、当事故は、「海運界と科学界が原糖の擬液性の経験を得た最初の事例」であると認めた。砂糖は航海備船者の所有物であり、船主は座礁により生じた損害につき航海備船者に責任ありと申し立てた。しかしながら、裁判所は、貨物所有者は、貨物の隠れた危険について実際に知っているべきでも、知っているとみなされるべきでもなかったゆえ、事故について責任はないと判示した。

積荷は運送に相当程度に適しており、安全であるという貨物の荷送人による黙示の担保があるとも判示された (Pierce v. Winsor, F. Cas. Nos. 11, 150 and 11, 151 (D. C. D. Mass. and C. C. D. Mass. 1861))。この事案では、運送人は、他貨を溶解した撒積マスティク樹脂による損害の補償を受ける権利があると判示された (The Santa Clara, 281 F. 725, 736 (2d Cir. 1922) 事件も参照。Luckenbach S. S. Co. v. Coast Mfg. & Sup. Co., 185 F. Supp. 910, 1960 AMC 2076 (E. D. N. Y. 1960) 事件を比較参照)。特に傭船者が貨物を所有している場合には、この担保は、定期傭船の傭船者にも適用されるのが正しいと思われる。

黙示の担保は、船主が貨物の危険性を知っていたり、または知っているべき場合には、適用されない (Westchester Fire Insurance Co. v. Buffalo Housewrecking & Salvage Co., 40 F. Supp. 378, 381-382, 1941 AMC 1601 (W. D. N. Y. 1941), 原審維持 129 F. 2d 319, 1942 AMC 1052 (2d Cir. 1942))。本事案では、裁判所は、船主が積込前に貨物を観察する十分な機会があったので、金属旋盤・ボーリングスクラップの荷送人による黙示の担保は、適用され

ない，と判示した。

　Pitria Star Navigation Co. v. *Monsanto Co.*, 1986 AMC 2966 (E.D.La. 1984) 事件で，賠償請求は船主により航海傭船者と，毒物で液体殺虫剤であるパラチオンの製造者および荷送人に対して行われた。貨物は55ガロンの鉄製ドラムに入っており，各ドラムには，目につきやすい警告表示の札が貼ってあった。パラチオンが船舶のビルジを汚した結果発生した事故により航海中に３人の乗組員が死亡した。揚荷役業者がドラムの扱いを誤り，パラチオンのドラムのいくつかから漏れが生じた。パラチオンは船舶のビルジへ続く所に発見された。航海傭船者が返船した後，ビルジを清掃するときに３人の乗組員がパラチオンに曝されることとなった。裁判所は，殺虫剤の製造または包装に何らの過失は認められないので乗組員の死亡は貨物製造者に対する賠償請求とはならないと判示した。裁判所は，また，死亡の直接的原因は，揚荷港の荷役業者の過失であり，航海傭船契約上，その過失は船主が負うものであるとの認定に基づき，傭船者に対する船主の請求も却下した。裁判所は貨物の危険性につき必要な警告を与えることに，被告の側に過失がないことも認めた。傭船者と荷送人の警告義務について，裁判所は，*Restatement (Second) of Torts* 第388条を適用した。

　　第388条意図された用途の危険が知られている動産
　　　直接または第三者経由で他人の使用のために動産を提供する者は，他人の同意を得て動産を使用すると思われる者に対して，もしくは，その使用により危険に陥ると思われる者に対して，動産が提供される方法で，かつその使用のために動産を提供される者による動産の使用により生じた物理的損害につき責任を負う。ただし，提供者が次の場合に限る。
　(a)　使用のため提供される動産は，危険であるかまたは危険であるように見えることを知っているか，知っている理由がある。
　(b)　使用のため動産を提供される者が，危険な状態を認識していると信じる理由がない。
　(c)　危険な状態もしくは危険であるらしいことを示唆するような事実を被提供者に知らせる相当の注意を尽くすことができない。

　船主がパラチオンは毒物であることを知っていたので，裁判所は被告が船主と乗組員が貨物の危険な状態を認識していないと「信じる理由」はなかったと認定した。

　Serrano v. *U. S. Lines Co.*, 238 F. Supp. 383, 1965 AMC 1038 (S.D.N.Y. 1965) 事件で，裁判所はこの黙示の担保は，米国国際海上物品運送法が適用される所では効力を有しないと判示した。裁判所によると，米国国際海上物品運送法の第1304(3)条が荷送人の責任を律する。この条文は次のとおり規定する。

　　荷送人は荷送人，その代理人または被用者の行為，過失あるいは懈怠なしに，何らかの原因により生じた運送人または船舶が被った減失または損傷につき責任を負わない。

　Serrano 事案は，米国国際海上物品運送法の及ぶ範囲がどの程度かを例証している。本事案は，船舶上に積載されたトレーラのタイヤの爆発により引き起こされた人的損傷についての損害賠償請求であった。船主は，スペース傭船者とトレーラ所有者により負傷した請求者に支払われるべしと判示された金額につき補償を得る権利があると主張した。裁判所は，船主の補償請求は米国国際海上物品運送法を準拠法とすると判示した。請求は貨物損傷についての請求ではなかった。「米国国際海上物品運送法は，権利と義務関係とりわけ貨物運送から生じる関係を［規定］する」。荷送人の側に実際の過失がないので，船主の請求は退けられた。

　The Stylianos Restis, 1974 AMC 2343 (S.D.N.Y. 1972) 事件で，魚粉の荷送人に対する火

災損害についての船主の請求は,荷送人の側の実際の過失を証明することができず,第4条3項により否定された(*Williamson v. Compania Anonima Venzolana de Navigacion,* 446 F. 2d 1339, 1971 AMC 2083 (2d Cir. 1971) 事件も参照)。

ニューヨーク・プロデュース書式のように,傭船契約が米国国際海上物品運送法を摂取している場合,貨物の欠陥または隠れた危険から生じた損害についての,船主に対する傭船者の責任は,米国国際海上物品運送法の第4条3項に準拠する。

米国国際海上物品運送法の第4条6項も,傭船者の責任に影響を及ぼす。同項は,次のとおりに規定する。

「引火性・爆発性または危険性のある貨物については,運送人・船長または運送人の代理人が,その性質や特性を知りながら船積に同意した場合を除き,運送人は,揚荷前,いつどこでも,陸揚・破壊あるいは,無害にすることができ,その処分の代償を支払う必要はない。そのような貨物の荷主は,その船積から,直接または間接的に生ずる,または結果として生ずるすべての損害と費用に責任を負わなければならない。かかる性質を承知の上で,船積された貨物が,船舶または他の貨物に危険を及ぼす場合,運送人・船長または運送人の代理人は,共同海損の場合を除き,運送人は,何らの責任を負うことなしに同様の方法で,その貨物をどこででも陸揚し,破壊し,あるいは無害にすることができる」。

第4条6項に基づき傭船者から補償を得るために,船主は,貨物が米国国際海上物品運送法が意味する範囲内で危険であることを示さねばならない。

当該貨物が危険であるかという基本的問題は,事実問題であり,当該事案が生じた状況に全面的に左右される。例えば,前出 *Westchester Fire Ins. Co.* v. *Buffalo Housewrecking & Salvage Co.* 事件で,貨物である旋盤・ボーリングスクラップが過熱し,艀は火災により破壊された。貨物の性質のすべてを書面で艀船主に対して顕示しない限り,貨物が危険な場合,荷送人に責任があるとの条項を,その積荷の船荷証券は記載していた。貨物が「危険」であるか否かの入口問題を扱う際に,裁判所はそのような旋盤スクラップは爆発物ではなく危険貨物でもないと述べた。しかしながら,裁判所は,過剰な水分または油状の廃棄物やぼろのような廃物を含んだ場合,旋盤スクラップは危険となることに着目した。提示された事実に基づいて,裁判所は,旋盤スクラップは積込のときに,乾いており,廃物もなかったので,「危険」ではないと判示した。

航海傭船契約に絡んだ,*The Kapetan Antonis,* 1989 AMC 551 (Arb. at N. Y. 1988) 事件で,傭船者は旋盤スクラップ貨物の火災から生じた損害に責任あると判示された。仲裁人は,傭船者は船主に「安全で運送可能な貨物を提供する」(1989 AMC at 561) 義務があるが,危険な旋盤スクラップを不注意にも積載したことによりその義務に違反したと裁定した。しかし,船長が船積前に旋盤スクラップが有する危険を承知しており,米国国際海上物品運送法第4条6項の下で,旋盤スクラップ貨物の荷送人は,船主に対して責任を負わないと判示された *The Gyda,* 1971 AMC 2070, 406 F. 2d 1039 (6th Cir. 1969) 事件も参照。

Poliskie Line Oceanic v. *Hooker Chemical Corp.,* 499 F. Supp. 94, 1980 AMC 1748 (S. D. N. Y. 1980) 事件で,塩化スルフリルの貨物の荷送人は,船主に対して,危険物質を,政府規則に合致せずに封印コンテナ内部へ不適当に積み付けることにより生じる損害につき責任ありと判示された。

前述 *The Wismar* 事件で,仲裁審は,多数意見として,米国またはカナダのコーストガードあるいは IMCO (現在では IMO) により公式に危険品として分類されていないので,ペレット状の直接還元鉄は「危険」ではないと裁定した。

石鹸から発するガスにより生じた爆発が絡んだ *International Mercantile Marine Co.* v. *Fels*, 170 F. 275 (2d Cir. 1909) 事件も参照。裁判所は，石鹸は通気性の悪い所に蔵置され，危険であるが，傭船者は貨物の性質について必要なすべての通知を行ったので，船主に過失ありと判示した。

前出 The Stylianos Restis 事件で，魚粉の自然発火により船艙に火災が発生し，船舶は損害を被った。裁判所は貨物の自然発火しやすさは貨物の固有の瑕疵であると認定した。魚粉が貨物であり，その船積可能状態に関する保証（warranties）を含むと明示した航海傭船契約に基づき貨物は船積された。裁判所は，船長は魚粉の固有の性質を十分承知していたと判示した。さらに，船長は船主の明示の承認を得た上で，貨物の積載に同意したのであるから，裁判所は，米国国際海上物品運送法第4条6項の下で，荷送人または航海傭船者が責任ありとする根拠はないと判示した。

貨物が安全に運送されうるか否かは，船長の健全な判断に委ねられた問題である。安全運送の責任は船長にかかっている。*Boyd* v. *Moses*, 74 U. S. 192 (1869)。*A & D Properties Inc.* v. *The Volta River*, 1984 AMC 464, 471 (E. D. La. 1983) 事件に見られるように，

|176| 「船長が，あらゆる状況を十分に考慮した上で，正当な理由のある船舶の安全に関する懸念に基づいて貨物を拒否する場合，船長の決定は，後知恵で判断されない」。

同旨について，*Drummond Coal Co.* v. *Interocean Shipping Co.*, 1985 AMC 1152, 1162 (S. D. Ala. 1985) 事件も参照。

The Kartini, SMA 1958 and 2196 (Arb. at N. Y. 1984 and 1985) 事件で，傭船者は石炭の自然発熱と発火から生じる損害に責任ありと判示された。傭船者は，正規の石炭と共に，可燃性の高い石炭の副産物，乾燥泥炭 (pond solid) を大量に積み込んだ。しかしながら，船長は乾燥泥炭 (pond solid) の性質について警告を受けていなかった。仲裁審は，貨物は船舶の安全性と堪航性に影響を及ぼすから，船長は，貨物に関して船主のために行為したという傭船者の主張を却下した。代わって，仲裁審は，傭船者は積込に責任があり，この点について船長が遂行した行為は傭船者の代理人としてであると判示した（第8条に関して後出376頁の解説を参照）。

米国の他の法規制

「爆発物または危険物の運送規則」46 U. S. C.（合衆国法典）§170 (1970) は，1983年に Pub. L. 98-89，§4(6), 97 Stat. 600-605 により廃止された。§170の廃止は，多くの海事法の総点検の一部であった。新条項は，危険物質の運送を対象として採択され，45 U. S. C. §§ 2101, 3101-3718に法典化された。

加えて，コーストガード規則は，危険性貨物および有毒性貨物の船積に適用される。46 C. F. R.（合衆国連邦規則集）§§ 30-40, 98, 146-154, 171-176参照。コーストガード規則は，広範なものであり，船舶による軍用爆発物の輸送と貯蔵，船用危険品の使用，撒積危険性固体および危険性液体，気体貨物を規制している。

安全港と安全バース

"27. [Vessel .... to be employed] ....
   between safe port and/or ports in British North
28. America, and/or United States of America, and/or West Indies, and/or Central America,
   and/or Caribbean Sea, and/or Gulf of Mexico, and/or
29. Mexico, and/or South America ....
   and/or Europe
30. and/or Africa, and/or Asia, and/or Australia, and/or Tasmania, and/or New Zealand, but
   excluding Magdalena River, River St. Lawrence between
31. October 31st and May 15th, Hudson Bay and all unsafe ports; also excluding, when out of
   season, White Sea, Black Sea and the Baltic,
32. ....
33. ....
34. ....
35. as the Charterers or their Agents shall direct, on the following conditions:"

「英領北アメリカ，アメリカ合衆国，西インド諸島，中央アメリカ，カリブ海，メキシコ湾，メキシコ，南アメリカ，............欧州，アフリカ，アジア，オーストラリア，タスマニアおよび／またはニュージーランド（ただし，Magdalena河，10月31日から５月15日までの St. Lawrence 河，Hudson湾および一切の非安全港，および季節外の白海，黒海，バルチック海，............を除外する）の，傭船者またはその代理人が指示する，安全な一または数港間に配船されるものとし，その他以下の条項によるものとする」。

一般原則

傭船者の第一義的義務は，本船に指図を出した時点で，安全であると予見される港へ向かうのをただ指図することである。安全性の要素は本頁と後続の頁で検討され，予見される安全性の概念は後出242頁で検討する。

NYPE 93

ニューヨーク・プロデュース書式の1993年版は，航路が「安全な港および場所の間」であることを要求しながら，1946年版の27行から31行のいくぶん時代遅れとなった許容地域と除外地域の表を当事者が記入する空欄で置き換えている。前出９頁の英文書式の第５条の72行から76行と54頁を参照。

安全性の要素

安全性の古典的定義は，*Leeds Shipping* v. *Société Française Bunge* (*The Eastern City*) [1958] 2 Lloyd's Rep. 127 事件における Sellers 卿判事の定義である。すなわち「……港は，特定の船舶が，特に異常事態が発生しない限り適切な操船航海技術をもって避けることのできない危険にさらされることなく，当該期間中，入港し，使用し，出港することができない限り

安全とは言えない。……」(同判例集131頁)。

Roskill卿判事は，*The Hermine* [1979] 1 Lloyd's Rep. 212事件の控訴院で，この見解に同意して，次のように述べた。「……これらの非安全港または非安全バースの事案で，多数の昔の判決を参照するのは今やまったく不必要である。……明確に述べられた判例法がある。各事案で，法廷 (tribunal of the fact) が何を決定しなければならないかは，特定の事実に基づいて，安全性という特定の担保が壊れるか壊れないかである」。しかし，*The Mary Lou* [1981] 2 Lloyd's Rep. 272事件で，Mustill判事は，何がSellers卿判事の規定した一般原則により扱えないのかという法の問題点が生じるという事実と，その法の問題点に関する法廷の結論はその一般原則に矛盾しないが，先例に拠ることはそのとき有用であるという事実に注意を喚起した。

当該期間

港の予見される安全性は，傭船者がその港を指図した時点の安全性で判断される。*The Evia (No. 2)* [1982] 2 Lloyd's Rep. 307事件と後出242/243頁を参照。港が安全であると予見される当該期間というのは，当該船舶が，そこを使用する（またはそこに近づき，出港するまでの期間，後出234/235頁参照）期間である。港は特定船舶にとって常に安全でないことがあるし，また，ある特定の時期のみ安全でないこともある。

> *Eastern City*号は「モロッコの1ないし2の安全港」から日本向けの冬期航海に傭船された。傭船者はMogadorでの積荷を指示した。本船は同地に12月26日到着し，錨泊した。2日後天候が悪化し，船長は走錨を心配して，沖出ししようとしたが，強風にあおられ，錨地近くの岩礁に乗り揚げた。
> 　控訴院は，同港は冬期予見することのできない南寄りの突風に曝されており，狭くて錨かきのよくない錨地において，突風が走錨の原因になりやすく，したがって安全港ではないと判示した。
> *The Eastern City* [1958] 2 Lloyd's Rep. 127.

潮流気象その他の理由によって，船舶がしばらく入港を待たなければならないこともありうるが，そのこと自体によって，港が非安全港とはならない。例えば，船が港に接近するに際し，洲をかわすために満潮を待たなければならないこともあるし，また，入港するにあたって暴風が凪ぐのを待たなければならないこともある。Devlin判事が*The Stork* [1954] 2 Lloyd's Rep. 397事件で述べているように「法は，港が本船到着時に安全であることを要求していない。風や気象状況によって積荷港向け航海は遅れる。これと同様の状態に遭遇して，入港もまた遅れる。そして傭船者が，その一方に責任がないというのは，他方にもまた責任がないというのと同じことである」（同判例集415頁）。

入港中の本船が特定の時期に，特定の状況において，安全のため沖出ししなければならないことがあっても港は安全港と言いうる。

> スペインのBurrianaの港外泊地で積込する本船は，特定の気象条件の場合，沖出しできるように常に蒸気を上げておかなければならなかった。しかし同港は事実問題として安全な船積場所であると判断された。
> *Smith* v. *Dart* (1884) 14 Q. B. D. 105.

一時的危険

　まったくの一時的危険では，非安全港とはならないといわれることがある。しかし，一時的危険は，特に船長がその存在を知らない場合には非安全の重要な要素となる。すなわち港内における燈台，ブイ等の航行支援施設の一時的不足，あるいは不存在は，その欠陥が一時的なるがゆえに，船長がその事実を知らない場合には非安全の理由となる（この点に関して The Mary Lou ［1981］2 Lloyd's Rep. 272（同判例集279頁）事件で Mustill 判事の判決を参照）。この意味で，安全が判断される時点が特に重要であるが，これに関して後出242から244頁参照。

　天候状態による危険も，それが短期間であっても港は非安全となる。例えば予想しえない荒天によって本船が港内に立往生し，損害を被りやすい場合には，その荒天が仮に短期間であっても港は非安全となる。前出 The Eastern City 事件参照。

　したがって，一時的危険は港を非安全にしないとの命題は，本船の出入港，碇泊を遅らせる衆知または明確な一時的危険があっても，非安全港にはならないという限られた意味においてのみ正しい。

179 遅　　延

　しかしながら，明白な危険または障害による遅延が，かなりの期間継続すれば，港は非安全となる。

　Knutsford v. Tillmanns ［1908］A. C. 406 事件が例としてあげられる。同事件において本船は，Middlesbrough からの航海において，Vladivostock から40マイルの地点で氷に妨げられた。本船は氷を通り抜けようとしたが，結局3日後に長崎に行き，そこで揚荷をした。船主は，氷のため入港できない場合または船長が安全でないと認めた場合には，船長は他の安全港または場所において揚荷をする権利があると認めた船荷証券上の約款を主張した。Loreburn 卿は「非安全」の意味を論じて，非安全とは，「そのときにおいて非安全という意味ではなく，極端な遅延をもたらすような長期間安全ではないという意味である」と判示した。そして貴族院は，本件のような長期航海において，わずか3日の遅延の後に代替港で揚荷をした船主の行為は，妥当でないと判断した。

　The Sussex Oak (1950) 83 LLL. Rep. 297 事件では，Sussex Oak 号が Elbe 川を遡って Hamburg へ向かう航海において遭遇した異常に強度な結氷でも，一時的危険に過ぎないという議論が持ち出された。この事件における傭船契約はボルタイム書式であった。Devlin 判事は，この点に関する傭船者の主張を退けた仲裁人の判断を支持して，「航海と契約の性質から考えて，極端な遅延をもたらす程度の期間，危険が存続しなければならないというのが法の示すところである。この点，特に S. S. Knutsford Ltd. v. Tillmanns & Co. ［1908］A. C. 406 事件参照。……結氷による危険状態の継続期間と傭船契約の期間および Hamburg までの航海が短いことを比較検討すると，〔仲裁人〕の結論は正しい」と述べた。本船は London からの航海途上であった。仲裁人はその冬の Elbe 川の氷の状況は異常に厳しく異常な期間継続したと認めた。

　「極端な遅延」の意味は，後出 The Hermine 事件の控訴院で説明された。それは傭船契約を履行不能にするほどの遅延期間でなければならない。短期間本船の遅延となる危険または障害では，港は非安全とはならない。

　傭船契約は，ボルタイム書式Cで，U. S. Gulf から北欧州に3航海，本船は，後で特定するという条件で成約した。Hermine 号はその中の1航海に指名され，Mississippi 河の海上から140マイル上流の港，Destrehan へ航行を指図された。Destrehan へ安全に航行し，積込の上，何の損害もなく出港

したがi, *Hermine* 号は，南西水路で沈泥でふさがれ，Destrehan から下流約115マイルのところで止められた。通常のときなら Destrehan から海上まで約10/12時間で到達するが，沈泥のため本船は約30日止められた。

控訴院は，Destrehan から100マイル以上離れた障害（未確定のままの問題である）のゆえに港は非安全とみなされるとしても，障害により生じた遅延は，契約を履行不能にするほどに長期間の場合のみ，非安全を構成すると，判示した。*Hermine* 号が被った遅延は履行不能になるにはまだ不十分であると認定された。

Unitramp v. *Garnac Grain*（*The Hermine*）[1979] 1 Lloyd's Rep. 212.

（履行不能の問題については，後出461頁および479頁参照。港から長距離のところの障害の問題に関しては [1981] 2 Lloyd's Rep. 272 事件と後出238頁の *The Mary Lou* 事件参照）

特定の船舶

港が大きさや特性の異なった船舶にとって安全であっても，それは問題にならない。港は傭船された特定の船舶にとって安全でなければならない。

Sagoland 号は航海傭船契約に基づき Londonderry での揚荷を命ぜられた。本船は同港に入る今までで一番大きな船であった。本船は港の入口が狭くて曲りくねっているので，曳船なしには入港できなかった。しかし Londonderry には曳船がなかったので，船主は Clyde から曳船を呼ばねばならなかった。船主は傭船者に対して曳船費用の支払を請求した。Roche 判事は曳船費用の支払を命ずるにあたって，Londonderry が当該船舶にとって安全ではないという仲裁人の判断を肯定した。しかし同判事は，それにつけ加えた。

「仲裁人の判断を誤解してはならない。仲裁人は同港に行こうとする船舶の100隻中99隻あるいはそれ以上の船舶にとって決して安全ではないと判断したわけではない。ただ問題の船，すなわち *Sagoland* 号にとって，その港が安全でないと判断しただけである」。

Brostrom v. *Dreyfus*（1932）44 Ll.L. Rep. 136.

また，港は特定の船舶がその積み込んだ状態で問題に関係する時期に安全でなければならない。上記 *Brostrom* v. *Dreyfus* 事件において Roche 判事は次のように述べている。「港が物理的，または政治的意味において安全かどうかの基準は，特定の船舶が（問題の特定の運送契約に基づき積込を予定されている，または実際に積み込んだ状態で）問題のその港に入港し，積荷または揚荷するにあたって，安全かどうかという点に求められる」（*Hall* v. *Paul*（1914）19 Com. Cas. 384（積荷状態）および *Limerick* v. *Stott*（1921）5 Ll.L. Rep. 190（空船状態）各事件参照）。

接近時の安全性

本船はその港に安全に到達することができなければならない。

Sussex Oak 号はボルタイム書式によって傭船され，1947年1月 Hamburg に配船された。Elbe 河を遡行中，氷に遭遇したが，水先人は続航することが安全と考えた。本船が Hamburg 付近まで来たとき，巨大な流氷のため停船を余儀なくされた。本船はその後，回頭，後進，碇泊すら安全にできない状態で，河の中に立往生した。そして水先人の助言に従い氷を強行突破し，その結果損害を被った。事実認定において砕氷船の援助なく航行した船長の行為は妥当であり，Hamburg はその当時非安全港であるという理由をもって，傭船者の損害賠償責任が認められた。Devlin 判事は，次のように判示した。「本船が安全に到達できないような港に配船された場合，第2条の違反となる。法律上

は危険がどこにあろうとも問題ではなく，ただ事実として危険が港から離れていれば航海の安全を妨げる度合が少ないことが明白であるというに過ぎない。傭船者は直行航路あるいは特定の航路が安全であるということを保証しないが，傭船者が指図した航海は通常の慎重さと技術をもった船長ならば，安全に到着しうるものでなければならない」。
 Grace v. General Steam Navigation（The Sussex Oak）（1950）83 Ll. L. Rep. 297.

したがって，本船の構造物の一部を取り外さなければ安全に港に着けないような接近航路がある場合，その港は安全ではない。

 Vanduara 号は英国の安全港に向かう航海に定期傭船された。本船が Manchester へ行くには同港から24マイル離れた Runcorn 橋をかわさなければならず，そのためにはマストを取り外さなければならないという理由をもって，控訴院は，Manchester は Vanduara 号にとって非安全であると判断した。
 Re Goodbody and Balfour, Williamson（1899）5 Com. Cas. 59.

入港のために積荷の一部を瀬取しなければならない場合，その港は非安全であるとする判例もある。

 安全港において揚荷すべき旨を定めた Peerless 号の航海傭船契約において，本船は King's Lynn において揚荷を命ぜられた。しかし本船の喫水が深かったため，メイズ満船状態で同船は干満の如何にかかわらず同港に入港できなかった。この件において Sankey 判事は，同港が本船にとって安全ではないこと，したがって船主は，艀費用を回収することができると判示した。
 Hall v. Paul（1914）19 Com. Cas. 384.
 （The Alhambra（1881）6 P. D. 68 事件参照）

指定港に向かう途中敵国の拿捕または攻撃の危険がある場合，その港が安全港ではなくなることがある。

 Frankby 号の定期傭船契約には同船が特定区域内の安全港間に使用されるべき旨の定めがあった。同船は Newcastle へ配船されたが，その当時ドイツ政府は英国周辺において交戦国船舶を撃沈することを宣言していた。判決は Newcastle が安全港がどうか定めるにあたって潜水艦による撃沈の危険を考慮すべきであるとしたが，全事実を検討した結果，同港は当時安全であったと判断した。
 Sankey 判事は「……港は物理的かつ政治的に安全でなければならず，自然現象でも，人為的行為によってでも港が非安全となる」と述べた。
 Palace Shipping v. Gans Line ［1916］1 K. B. 138.
 （The Teutonia（1872）L. R. 4 P. C. 171 事件も参照）

しかし，分別のある船主または船長が港に航行するのを思いとどまらせるほどに攻撃の危険は十分に現実的なものでなければならない。傭船者は絶対的な政治的安全を保証するものではない。

 Saga Cob 号は，Shelltime 3 書式で定期傭船され，Assab から Massawa に1988年1月から8月の間石油製品を積載した20航海を安全に遂行した。8月26日に本船は再び Massawa への航行の指図を受けた錨地で碇泊中に，モーターボートに乗ったエリトリアのゲリラに攻撃され損害を被った。4月以来，Massawa で散発的なゲリラ砲兵隊の攻撃があり，その月の間，Assab 近くの石油精製基地はゲリラボートからの砲弾で攻撃された。5月に Massawa から65マイル離れていた Saga Cob 号を含

めた船団をゲリラが攻撃するという異常事態が生じた。戦争保険の保険者は1990年1月に当該地域の船舶に追加保険料を課徴した。2月にはゲリラは, Massawa そのものを占領した。控訴院は傭船者は契約に違反していないと判示した。1988年8月の時点でそのような攻撃の危険は, Massawa 港の通常の特性ではなかった。Parker 卿判事は, 裁判所の判断として,「普通の船主,または普通の船長がそこへ本船を入出港させるのを拒否するほどに『政治的危険』が大きくない限り,港は現在のような状況の下では,非安全とみなされない」と判示した。

The Saga Cob [1991] 2 Lloyd's Rep. 398 および [1992] 2 Lloyd's Rep. 545 (C. A.).

使用上の安全性

港は, 自然条件および人工的側面からみて, その立地, 大きさ, 構造にわたり, 当該船舶にとって, 使用時に物理的に安全でなければならない。安全に入港できるだけでは不十分であって, 当該船舶がそこにとどまることが安全でない場合にも, 非安全港となる。

Saxon Queen 号は,「Hamburg, Brest および英国の安全港間」の航海に定期傭船され, 英国の Craster に配船された。同船は当時の天候状況下においては安全に入港できた。しかし, 風が変わり状況が変化すると危険になりがちな港であった。結局同船は非安全港と判断された。

Johnston v. Saxon Queen Steamship (1913) 108 L. T. 564.

港は, そこが危険になった場合, 安全に出港することができさえすれば, 安全な使用が中断されても必ずしも非安全港とはならない。Smith v. Dart (1884) 14 Q. B. D. 105 事件で, スペインの Burriana 港は特定の気象条件の下において, 沖出しのため蒸気をあげておく必要があったにもかかわらず, 安全港と判断された。しかしこのような場合, 出港の必要性が予見でき, 本船が安全に余裕をもって必要な手段を取ることができるということが前提となる。

Eastern City 号は「モロッコの1ないし2の安全港」から冬期航海に傭船され, Mogador に配船された。同港は, 錨かきが悪く, 冬期の特定の気象条件になると, 同船程度の大きさの船は安全に碇泊できず, また出港することも危険であった。しかもその襲来は突然であり, 予想できないものであった。同港を非安全港と判断するにあたって, Pearson 判事は次のように述べた (172頁)。「特定の気象状況が切迫した場合に本船が港を離れなければならないとしても, 港はその船にとって安全たりうる。しかしそのためには, そのような天候状態の切迫を余裕をもって認識でき, 本船が安全に港を離れることができるという相当の保証がなければならない」。

The Eastern City [1957] 2 Lloyd's Rep. 153 (控訴院にて支持 [1958] 2 Lloyd's Rep. 127).
(後出 The Khian Sea [1979] 1 Lloyd's Rep. 545 事件参照)

[182] Pearson 判事は The Eastern City 事件の判決において,「ある種の傭船契約においては, その正当なる解釈として, 港が, 積荷中, 中断することなく継続して安全であるべきことを必要とする場合もある」と所見を述べた (同判例集172頁)。

気象警報

荒天に際し沖出しを必要とする場合, 船長に対して十分な気象警報を提供する手配がなければならない。

Dagmar 号はボルタイム書式によってカナダからイタリアに向けての1航海の間傭船された。同船は St. Lawrence 河の小港 Cape Chat にて製材の積込を指示された。同船の着岸した岸壁は, 風浪を

遮るものがほとんどなく，したがって天候状況によっては安全のため，沖出しする必要があった。荒天の際の気象警報はその地方で入手できたが，傭船者はその気象警報を船長に知らせる手配もしなかったし，また，無線当直を手配しおくことは船長の責任であることを船長に対して明確にしてもいなかった。

　Mocatta 判事は同港が非安全港であり，荒天が突然襲来し係船索が切れて座礁した結果，本船に生じた損害につき傭船者に責任があると判示した。
　The Dagmar [1968] 2 Lloyd's Rep. 563.

　荒天に際し，沖出しすべき警報が適切になされても，沖出し操船に十分な水面の余裕がなく，本船が立往生した場合，その警報だけでは不十分である。

　Khian Sea 号はニューヨーク・プロデュース書式によって Valparaiso を含む安全港を経由した1往復航海に傭船された。本船は Valparaiso の防波堤外のバースを指定された。荒天に際し船長は沖出しを通告された。しかし水先人と曳船はすぐ到着したが，付近に錨泊中の2隻の船舶が動くまで数時間の間，本船はバースを離れることができなかった。そうしているうちに同船は広範囲の損害を被った。Donaldson 判事と控訴院は，傭船者に本船損害の賠償責任があると判示し，荒天襲来に際し緊急待避しようとする本船のために，その待避行為に十分な水面を確保する制度ができていないという点においてこのバースは安全ではないと述べた。
　記録長官 Denning 卿は，次のように述べた（547頁）。「……本船がバースを離れなければならない場合，次の要件が満たされなければならない。第1に適当な気象予報システムがなければならない。第2に水先人と曳船が十分に利用できねばならない。第3に操船に十分な海面スペースがなければならない。そして第4に操船に必要な海面および空間のスペースをいつも利用可能にする適当なシステムがなければならない」。
　The Khian Sea [1979] 1 Lloyd's Rep. 545.

着岸，繫船設備

　港はその地理的性質あるいは気象条件以外の理由によっても非安全となることがある。繫船設備が不十分であったり，あるいは本船が指示された港内の岸壁に何か障害物があって危険な場合もある。このような要素が本船の使用時に存在すると，その本船にとって，港は安全ではなくなる。

　Houston City 号は航海傭船契約に基づき，西オーストラリアの1ないし2の安全港において指定される安全な岸壁での貨物の積込を命ぜられた。Geraldton で本船はある岸壁を指定された。その岸壁は北寄りの風に曝されていたが，同船程度の大きさの船にとっては通常は安全なものであった。北風による危険を少なくするために，沖出しブイが2個あり，岸壁にはフェンダーがあった。しかしブイのうち1個は，間もなく復旧されると船長は知らされていたが，修繕のため撤去されていた。また，フェンダーも50フィートにわたる区画がなくなっていた。沖出しブイおよびフェンダーがなかったために本船は北寄りの強風の最中に損害を被った。本件につき，枢密院は，Geraldton はこれらの欠陥のゆえに同船にとって安全ではないと判示した。
　Reardon Smith Line v. *Australian Wheat Board*（*The Houston City*）[1956] 1 Lloyd's Rep. 1.
　（本船が欠陥あるフェンダーにより損傷した *The Carnival* [1992] 1 Lloyd's Rep. 449, [1994] 2 Lloyd's Rep. 14（C. A.）事件も参照）

183 航行支援（水路標識等）

　港の安全性は，水先人，ブイおよび灯台を含む有効な水路標識等の航行支援手段の有無にかかっている。ある航行支援手段がなければ，航行が危険となるが，その航行支援手段が十分に

危険を緩和できる場合，その航行支援手段の存在により，その港は非安全であるとはみなされない。ゲリラ船からの危険に対抗するべく港へ近づく本船のための護送船団方式の設置に関連して，The Saga Cob [1992] 2 Lloyd's Rep. 545 (C. A.)（同判例集550頁）事件における Parker 卿判事の解説参照。

十分でなければならないのは，組織である。十分な組織の下での能力ある個人による過誤について傭船者には責任がない。The Evia (No. 2) [1982] 1 Lloyd's Rep. 334 事件の記録長官 Denning 卿の判決と後出239頁の「異常事態」の解説を参照。

政治的危険

物理的原因以外の理由で生ずる危険，例えば政治的危険（後出危険の項参照）に本船が曝される場合，港は非安全港となり得る。乗組員に対する危険もまた港が，本船の使用に関し，安全かどうかを決定するに際して関連する要素となりうる。

出港時の安全性

出港のとき，本船が危険に曝されるような場合，港は安全とは言えない。

> *Innisboffin* 号は積載状態で運河を通って無事 Manchester に到着した。しかし揚荷後喫水が浅くなったため，出港するにあたって橋をかわすことができなかった。Manchester は同船にとって非安全港であると判断された。
> Limerick v. Stott (1920) 5 Ll.L. Rep. 190.

> Elbe 川を遡って Hamburg に行く航海の途中（前出234頁参照），結氷に遭遇した *Sussex Oak* 号は，川を下って出港するときに異常な結氷のためにさらに損害を被った。傭船者はこの損害にも責任があると判示された。
> The Sussex Oak (1950) 83 Ll.L. Rep. 297.

> (The Eastern Star [1958] 2 Lloyd's Rep. 127 事件および The Khian Sea [1979] 1 Lloyd's Rep. 545 事件も参照)

安全の担保が，本船が出港した後どこまで及ぶのかは判例では明らかではない。The Hermine [1979] 1 Lloyd's Rep. 212（前出233頁参照）事件で，3人の控訴院の判事全員が，本船は遅延なく安全に入港し，出港したが，海洋への航路途上で100マイル下流の障害物に遭遇した場合に，上流の港が非安全とみなされるかどうかの疑問を表明した。

しかし，安全に港へ到達し，出港を可能にする代替の航路がない場合には，論理的には，上流の港と非安全の状況が存在する場所との間の距離には関係がない。

> Mary Lou 号の航海傭船契約は，「New Orleans/Ama/Reserve/Myrtle Grove/Destrehan を1港として勘定する米国ガルフの1安全港（Brownsville を除く）」に積荷のため配船すると定めていた。傭船者は New Orleans 地区を指名した。この大きさの船舶にとり New Orleans から海洋への通路は，Mississippi 河と New Orleans から約100マイルの距離にあって正確に予測しにくい沈泥状態になりやすい川の南西水路以外にはない。同水路を外へ出ていくときに，Mary Lou 号の喫水は水先人が当時勧告した最大喫水よりわずかに浅かったのだが，本船は，座洲し，損傷を生じた。仲裁人はその当時，Mary Lou 号のような船舶が同水路で座洲するほどの大きな危険があり，座洲は本船の操船上の水先人もしくは船長の側の過失によらないと裁定した。つまり，喫水の選択に関して船長は水先人の勧告に従って合理的に行動したと裁定し，水先人が自己の推奨が最新であったか（例えば，陸軍工兵

隊による最新の水路測量を吟味する方法で）をさらに確認すべきではなかったかということを裁定しなかった。

　Mustill 判事は，傭船者は契約に違反していると判示した。彼は，次のように言った（283頁）。「私の判断するところでは，（河川水先人が勧告した最大喫水という）方式が当時現実に有効に作動していない限り，その可航水路の危険は，そのゆえに，港が担保の意味の範囲内で安全ではなくなるような特性となっている。今回は，その方式は有効に作動していなかった。仲裁人がこれは船主の被った滅失損傷をもたらした（事実認定に基づく）契約違反になると判断したのは正当であると私は考える」。同水路は遠距離すぎるので New Orleans を非安全港ではないとする傭船者の主張を退け，彼は次のように言った（280頁）。「ほぼ100マイル離れたところの危険をその港の特徴として取り扱うという考えを，一回だけ見て認めることは確かに容易なことではない。しかし，障害が遠距離にあるほど，本船を安全に港に到達させる代替航路がなくなる可能性は少なくなるけれども，論理的には距離の長短は問題とはならない。しかしながら，今回の事案では，代替航路はなかった。南西水路が唯一の接近航路であった。The Hermine 事件で控訴院がためらいがちに表明した疑問にかかわらず，私は，同水路の非安全な特徴を担保違反とみなす」。

　The Mary Lou ［1981］2 Lloyd's Rep. 272.

　（The Evia（No. 2）事件で Mustill 卿判事が，傭船者の安全義務は絶対的で，継続すると言った判決の一部に貴族院は，同意しなかったことに注意すべきである。後出242頁を参照）

異常事態

　本船の損害が，特定の港において当時存在する特質と無関係に発生した場合，傭船者はその損害について責任がない。したがって港内の本船が，全く異常な荒天あるいは他船の航行上の過失のため損害を被った場合，港は非安全とはならない。このような原因は港の特質それ自体から発生したものではない。The Evia（No. 2）［1982］2 Lloyd's Rep. 307（同判例集317頁）事件で Roskill 卿は，港は「本来的に非安全」ではないと，述べた。控訴院［1982］1 Lloyd's Rep. 334 での同事案で記録長官 Denning 卿は，次のように言った。「港の設備は，良好であるが，それにもかかわらず，設備と関係ない異常事態または異異なできごとのために本船が損傷を被った場合，傭船者は担保違反とはならない。有能なバースマスターが一度だけ過失を犯した場合，あるいは他の船舶が衝突してくる場合がそうである……」。The Saga Cob ［1992］2 Lloyd's Rep. 545 事件で，Parker 卿判事は，次のように言った（同判例集550頁）。「さらに，例えば，危険なものが的確に照らし出されていたが，電源供給が突然ゲリラ活動により切断されたというようないくぶん異異な理由により，灯火が消える場合，その港は予見するところ非安全であり，もしくは，無灯火の下での危険がその港の通常の特性であると，判決で，言うことはできない」。

　The Mary Lou ［1981］2 Lloyd's Rep. 272 事件で，Mustill 判事は，非安全という特定の原因はこの意味において，港の全歴史について見たときに異常であったというだけでは，異常とはみなされないと指摘した。彼は，次のように言った（同判例集278頁）。「新しい環境が港の特性であるとみなされる場合，変化した環境は港を非安全とする」。前出 The Houston City ［1956］1 Lloyd's Rep. 1 事件を引用して，彼は次のように言った。「この種の欠陥をこうむりやすいからではなく，欠陥が十分長く継続した結果当面港の特質となっているので，港は非安全である」。

　したがって，異常事態が港を非安全としないということは，危険が港自身の特質，特性から生じる場合のみ，港は，非安全であるということを別の方法で表現しているものと思われる。

185　後出242頁に事実関係が示されている The Evia（No. 2）事件で，本船がボルタイム傭船契約の下，Basrah で揚荷中のその地域での戦争の勃発は，港の特性であるのか，もしくは，さも

なくば対照的に安全港における異常事態であるのかという問題を生じた。Robert Goff 判事の判決を破棄して，控訴院（記録長官 Denning 卿，Sebag Shaw 卿，ただし Ackner 卿判事は反対）は，戦争の勃発は，港の特性あるいは特質とは関係がなく，まったく別個の異常事態であり，傭船者はそれにより安全港担保義務に違反したことにはならない，と判示した。記録長官 Denning 卿は，次のように言った。「全面戦争が1980年9月22日に勃発したときに，それはまったく異常で異質なできごとであった。それは港を非安全にしたが，この非安全性は，『安全港』の担保義務違反ではない。本船が破裂弾により攻撃された場合，船主は船主自身が損害を負担しなければならず，保険者から損害を回収する。船主は傭船者から回収することはできない。本船は出港を妨げられたとき，——出港しないよう指図されたとき——それは，完全に異常な異質なできごとである」。貴族院は，本事案のこの局面に同じ考え方をした。貴族院が判決を下したときに，Roskill 卿は，次のように言った。「Basrah は，指定時に予見するところ安全であったゆえに（後出242頁参照），かつ非安全は到着後発生し，予見できなかった異常事態に起因しているがゆえに，その指定時点では（傭船者）による第2条の違反はない」。

本船が異常事態によって損害を受ける可能性は，船主が傭船者からの特定の港に行くようにとの指図を受諾せねばならないかを検討するときに，当然考えなくてもよいことである。前出 The Mary Lou 事件で Mustill 判事の判決を参照。The Evia (No. 2) 事件で，Ackner 卿判事は次のように言った。「その状況では，港が安全か否かの基準の構成は，常態を想定し，したがってある異常事態に起因する危険性を除かねばならない」。常態と言うからには，十分な安全体制を作動させる際に関与する関係者による適切な履行がなされることも含まれている。前出 The Saga Cob 事件で，Parker 卿判事の判決を参照。傭船者は適切な体制がうまく作動すると考えることができる。

しかし，ある港へ配船を指図された時点で，その港がある状況に起因する危険のため非安全である場合に，その状況が悪化しただけで危険が増大したというのでは，異常事態とはならない。因果関係の観点から見れば，危険の範囲と重大性は順次増大したのだが，本船の損傷は，そこへ行けとの指図の時点でその港を非安全にした同じ危険から生じた結果である。損傷が質的に別の危険から生じたのであれば，異常事態の概念があるいは該当したのかも知れない (The Lucille [1983] 1 Lloyd's Rep. 387 および [1984] 1 Lloyd's Rep. 244 (C. A.) 事件を参照)。

定期傭船契約の下で，安全であると予見される港への指図が出された後で，本船が当該港の手前で停船したり当該港を出港して危険を避けうる時点で，当該港が（異常事態の結果として）非安全となった場合，傭船者には本船に停船・出港を指図する新しい義務が生じる（後出243頁の The Evia (No. 2) 事件参照）。

危険と政治的非安全性

最も一般的危険は，浅瀬，砂洲などの地形上のもの，および強風，うねり，氷など特定の気象条件に曝されるということである。しかし港は政治情勢あるいは戦争状態によって生じた危険によっても非安全となり得る。

|186| 航海傭船契約には本船が積荷の上，チリーにおける1安全港に行くことが定められていた。傭船者は Carrisal Bago で揚荷を命じた。チリ一政府は当時反乱のために同港の閉鎖を宣言していた。Carrisal Bago は海事的特性に関する限り安全であったが，そこに行けば没収される危険があった。Blackburn 判事は同港を非安全港と判示するにあたり次のように述べた。「先例のまったくない本件

において，私は次のように考える。この傭船契約の解釈として，傭船者は，その指定時において，船長が安全に船を入港させうるような状態の港を指定する義務がある。しかし，港が自然条件上は安全に入港できたとしても，そこに入港すれば，政治的あるいはその他の理由から，その地の政府によって没収されるようなことがあれば，その港はこの傭船契約の意味において安全港とは言えない」。

Ogden v. Graham（1861）1 B. & S. 773.

（前出 Palace Shipping v. Gans Line［1916］1 K. B. 138事件，The Teutonia（1872）L. R. 4 P. C. 171事件，The Lucille［1984］1 Lloyd's Rep. 244事件，The Saga Cob［1962］2 Lloyd's Rep. 545事件および The Chemical Venture［1993］1 Lloyd's Rep. 508事件参照）

The Evaggelos Th［1971］2 Lloyd's Rep. 200事件で，本船は紅海での航海に傭船された。そこは傭船期間中ずっと戦争地域であった。傭船契約は安全に関する明示の義務を含まないが，裁判所は安全に関する条件は，傭船契約に黙示されていると判断した。

後出 The Evia（No. 2）事件で，貴族院は，ボルタイム書式の第2条が物理的非安全性のみに適用されるとの傭船者の主張を退けた。つまり安全性担保義務は政治的非安全性にも適用される。The Chemical Venture［1993］1 Lloyd's Rep. 508事件で，Gatehouse 判事は，Shelltime 3傭船契約の第3条について，同じ判断を下した。

適切な航海操船技術により回避可能な危険

適切な航海，操船技術によって避けることのできる危険があっても，港は非安全とはならない。The Eastern City［1958］2 Lloyd's Rep. 127事件で，Sellers 卿判事は，次のように指摘した（同判例集131頁）。「すべてではないにせよ，大抵の可航河川，水路，港，碇泊所，**繋留地**には，潮，潮流，うねり，浅瀬，砂洲，護岸の危険がある。こういう危険は，灯台，浮標，信号機，警報およびその他の航海補助手段により緩和され，通常適切な航海操船技術により克服される」。しかし危険を避けるために通常の技術以上のことが要求される場合には安全港とは言えない。

タンカー，Polyglory 号は定期傭船期間中，Port La Nouvelle に配船された。バラスト張水中，風力が増大してきたため，船長と強制水先人は岸壁を離れることを決定した。離岸は本船が未だ喫水が浅かったので困難であった。そして錨が引けて海底のパイプラインに損傷を与えた。船主はパイプラインの損害を支払い，傭船者に対して非安全港を理由として求償を図った。船主の請求を認める仲裁裁定を下すにあたり，仲裁人は，(1)港は安全ではなかった，(2)パイプラインの損害は水先人の過失が原因であった，しかしながら，(3)この過失があったとしても，その港へ行けと命令したことと損害との間の因果関係が切れるものではないと判断した。Parker 判事はこの仲裁判断を支持して，港が安全か否かを決定するにあたって適用さるべき原則は，「問題の船と大きさも種類も同じで，適切な装備と乗組員を有する本船が直面する唯一の危険が，通常の合理的注意と技術とによって避けることができる性質のものである場合には，法律的に言って港は安全である。そしてかかる港に配船することは契約違反とはならない」ということであると述べた。

同判事は，仲裁人が，(1)危険が高度の航海操船技術によってのみ避けうる性質のものであったがゆえに，港は非安全であると判断したこと，(2)水先人の過失，それがたとえ時間的にみて直接の原因であったとしても主要原因ではなかったがゆえに，水先人の過失は因果関係の中断をもたらさないと判断した点で正当であると判示した。

Kristiandsands Tankrederi v. Standard Tankers（Bahamas）（The Polyglory）［1977］2 Lloyd's Rep. 353.

本船の職員が相当な技術と注意を行使したにもかかわらず，本船が損傷を被ったとの証明に

より，必ずしも港が非安全ということにはならない。*The Mary Lou* [1981] 2 Lloyd's Rep. 272 事件で，Mustill 判事が，指摘したように，「……注意と安全は必ずしも同じコインの表と裏の関係にはない。第3の可能性が考慮されねばならない。つまり，事故は単なる不運の結果であった」(*The Apiliotis* [1985] 1 Lloyd's Rep. 255 事件も参照)。

187 港またはバースが他と関係なく非安全である場合には，他船の操船の過失が事故の直接の原因であるという事実により，傭船者が責任を免れることにはならない。*The Carnival* [1992] 1 Lloyd's Rep. 449 事件で，本船は，係留されていたときに，通行船の操船上の過失により，本船は欠陥あるバースフェンダーに押しつけられて，船体に穴があいた。海事法廷で，Sheen 判事は，通行船と航海傭船者の双方が全損傷につき責任ありと判示した。その判決は控訴院 [1994] 2 Lloyd's Rep. 14 で支持された。たとえ操船上の過失がなくともフェンダーは危険であるので，航海傭船者は，安全バース義務に違反していた。1978年民事責任（寄与）法に基づき，両者の間の責任負担が，命令された。

事実と法律

安全ということは，事実問題である。例として *The Apiliotis* [1985] 1 Lloyd's Rep. 255 事件を参照。しかし，港が「安全港」かどうか判断するのに適用されるべき基準は，法の問題である。*The Polyglory* [1977] 2 Lloyd's Rep. 353 事件を参照。

傭船者の第一義的義務は，本船に配船を指図するときに生じる

定期傭船契約か航海傭船契約に基づき，配船を指図する港の安全性に関する傭船者の義務は，指図したときに生じる。義務に適合していることを判断するのは，指図したときである。将来適当なときに，本船が到達し，使用し，出港するために，そのときに，港が，安全であると予見できることが必要なだけである。したがって，非安全の状態が，本船の到着前に治癒される予定である場合，指図したときに非安全であるからといって，安全義務を破ることにはならない。港は指図の時点で安全であると予見できるが，指図の後で，発生する予定外の異常なできごとから，結果として非安全状態が生じる場合にも，安全義務を破ることにはならない。この意味で，義務は継続的義務ではない。

Evia 号は，ボルタイム書式で定期傭船され，Basrah で揚荷するためキューバで貨物を積むよう1980年3月に指図された。本船は，7月1日に Shatt-al-Arab に到着し，8月20日に着岸し，9月22日に揚荷を完了した。その日に，イランとイラクの間で戦争が勃発した。本船は，Shatt-al-Arab 川を航行する危険のために出港できず，傭船契約を履行不能にするほどに（後出461頁参照）長い期間閉じこめられた。審判人は次のように認定した。「Basrah は本船にとり，そこへ配船を指図されたときと，そこへ到着したときに，安全であった。港は9月22日まで非安全ではなかったし，そのときまでに本船が出港するのは，不可能であった」。

船主はこの状況の中で傭船者は「本船は良好で安全な港の間で……使用される……」との第2条の安全港担保義務に違反している，と主張した。この点は，Robert Goff 卿により容認されたが，控訴院の多数と貴族院の全員一致により退けられた。貴族院は，傭船者が配船指図したときに，Basrah は安全であると予見されたのであり，非安全状態は本船の到着後，予想外の異常なできごと，つまりその地域の戦争の勃発のために非安全状態が生じたのだから，傭船者は第2条に違反していないと，判示した。

貴族院の判決に際して，Roskill 卿は，次のように言った。「私が考えるところでは，傭船者の契約上の約束は問題の港または場所の特質に関係しているに違いなく，指図が出されたときに，本船が到着し，必要な時間滞在し，適当なよい時機に出港するために港または場所が安全であると予見されることを意味する。しかし，その特質のゆえにこのようにその港または場所を安全であると予見できる場合，それにもかかわらず安全状態であったところに非安全状態を醸成するある予見できない異常なできごとが，その後急に生じ，その結果として本船が遅延し，損傷し，または破壊された場合，契約上の約束により，結果としての物理的，金銭的滅失損傷につき傭船者に責任があると私は考えることはできない。傭船者に責任があるとすることは，傭船者を，予見できない異常危険の保険者とすることになろう。その異常危険は当然に保険証券に基づく本船の保険者の負担となるべきである。もちろん船主が，この点で自家保険を選択しない限り第3条の船主責任により手配される。法の見解では，指定したときに Basrah が安全であると予見されたのであり，そして非安全が異常な事態により到着後に発生したのであるから，前の段階において被告側に第2条の違反はなかった」。

Diplock 卿は，次のように言った。「契約上の約束と関係するのは，本船が積荷役，揚荷役のためにそこにいた時点での，港の予見された安全性である。傭船者が船長または，船主の代理人に積荷，揚荷港に航行するよう指図した時点で，契約上の約束がなされた」。

貴族院の判決の別の根拠は，たとえ仮に傭船者が第2条に違反していたとしても，ボルタイム傭船契約の戦争条項，第21条（後出657頁参照）が，第21条(A)項にいう戦争危険から生じる非安全のあらゆる危険を船主に固定していることである。この危険について，第21条は第2条に取って代わる。その地域戦争の結果として，さもなければ第2条により課せられる責任について本事案では，傭船者は第21条により免除される。

Roskill 卿は，次のように言った。「第21条が完璧な規則であり，こうして船主の権利の問題をきわめつくしているかは，全体としての定期傭船契約の解釈しだいである。船主が，正しくて，第21条が，第2条に基づく定期傭船者の義務を全面的に有効とするならば，一つの注目すべき結果となる。定期傭船者は，追加戦争危険保険料を含む追加保険料を船主に支払う立場にある。しかし，支払う保険料の対象である危険が，本船に滅失損傷をもたらすならば，戦争危険保険者は関連クレームの支払に際して，第2条の違反につき定期傭船者に対する船主の権利を代位求償することになる。この結果は，疑いもなく，戦争保険者にとっては非常に魅力あるものであるが，定期傭船者は自己の利益のためでなく，第21条は別として，第2条が課する責任を何ら切り捨てることなく保険料を支払う不運となろう」（しかし，傭船者に戦争保険料を支払わせる条項すべてがこの効果をもたらすわけではない。*The Concordia Fjord* [1984] 1 Lloyd's Rep. 385 事件，*The Chemical Venture* [1993] 1 Lloyd's Rep. 508 事件と後出727頁参照）。

The Evia (No. 2) [1981] 2 Lloyd's Rep. 613, [1982] 1 Lloyd's Rep. 334（C. A.）および [1982] 2 Lloyd's Rep. 307（H. L.）。

指定した後に港が非安全となる。傭船者の第二義的義務

傭船者が安全であると予見される港へ本船を配船指図する義務を果たしたが，その後，本船がそこへ向かう途上で，港が非安全となる場合，傭船者には原指図を破棄する新たな義務を生じる。航海の継続を望む場合には，傭船者はその時点で，安全と予見される他の港への新しい指図を出さねばならない。同様に，本船が港にいるときに，その後非安全の状態が発生し，出港することで危険を避けうる場合に，傭船者に本船に出港の指図をする新たな義務が生じる。航海の継続を望む場合には，傭船者はその時点で，安全と予見される他の港への新しい指図を出さねばならない（前出 *The Evia (No. 2)* 事件の Roskill 卿の発言参照）。戦争が勃発し，本船が危険に陥ったときまでに，Basrah を出港し危険を避けるには遅すぎたのであるから本事案の特定の事実関係によれば，そのような新たな義務は発生しなかったのである。しかし，*The Lucille* [1983] 1 Lloyd's Rep. 387 事件および [1984] 1 Lloyd's Rep. 244（C. A.）事件では新たな義務が発生したのであるが，履行されなかった。指定時には，安全と予見された港

が，非安全になった。その間に傭船者が指図を破棄する時間の余裕があった。

The Evia (No. 2) 事件で，貴族院は，指定された港が，指定後，非安全となったときに，同様な新たな義務が，航海傭船者に課せられるかどうかを，検討することを拒否した。

前出235頁と後出677頁の The Saga Cob [1992] 2 Lloyd's Rep. 545 事件で，控訴院は，傭船者の指図の後に続いたできごとは，以下のことを判断することに関連していると考えた。
(a) Massawa は，安全と予見される港であるか
(b) 傍論ではあるが，傭船者は Shelltime 3 傭船契約の第3条に基づくこの点について，相当の注意を尽くしたか

The Chemical Venture [1993] 1 Lloyd's Rep. 508（同判例集519頁）事件で Gatehosue 判事は，この手法を問題とした。後出678頁参照。

189 傭船者の知らない非安全性

港またはバースが非安全であることを傭船者が知らない場合でも，傭船者は義務違反となる。

> ボルタイム書式で定期傭船中の Terneuzen 号は Leningrad のバースで座礁した。傭船者，その代理人，さらには本船乗組員もその結果を予想しなかった。特に本船は同じ傭船中の前航海において，同じ場所で安全に積荷を行ったという事情があった。この件で傭船者が安全でないことを知らなかったにもかかわらず，控訴院は傭船者が損害につき責任があると判示した。
> Lensen Shipping v. Anglo-Soviet Shipping (1935) 52 Ll.L. Rep. 141.

前出 The Evia (No. 2) 事件に関する，貴族院の法のリステートメントが，少なくとも傭船者の第一義的義務に関する限りにおいて，この原則を変更したことは，考慮されていない。傭船者が指図する港は，非安全であると予見し，確信する理由のない港ではなく，事実上安全であると予見される港でなければならない。しかしながら，港の指定後非安全と予見されるに至った場合の傭船者の第二義的義務に関して，見解は異なってくる。Roskill 卿は，第二義的義務を説明するときに，この区別をしなかったが，傭船者が非安全の状態が発生した事実を知った場合にのみ第二義的義務が生じるのであればそれは同判事が第二義的義務を述べた方法とより一致するように思われる。しかしながら，第二義的義務の発生以前に知っていることが必要な場合，法廷が実際に知っていたことと同様に知っていたと擬制されることで十分であるか否かを決定することが，結局のところ必要となろう。

「相当の注意」条項

ある傭船契約には，傭船者の安全港義務を相当の注意義務のみに明示的に軽減するものがある。例えば，Shelltime 3 の第3条は次のように定める。

> 傭船者は，本船が安全港間で使用されることを確実にするために相当の注意を尽くす……傭船者は，港の安全性を担保するとはみなされない……相当の注意を尽くすことができないことにより生じた滅失損傷を除いて，責任を負わない……

こういう条項が適用されるときに，傭船者は，港またはバースが安全であることを確証することに相当の注意を払わなかったときにのみ，本条項に違反することになる。政治的に非安全

であることが明白になった港の場合に，傭船者が熱心に質問をし，外観上の危険の程度は非安全とはならないという妥当な結論に達するならば，傭船者はこういう条項の違反とはならないはずである。傍論だが，The Saga Cob ［1992］2 Lloyd's Rep. 545（同判例集551頁）事件と後出677頁で Parker 卿判事の解説を参照。

次の事案で，傭船者は相当な注意を尽くす義務に違反していると判示された。

リベリア籍船のタンカー Chemical Venture は，Shelltime 3 書式で傭船され，イラン／イラク戦争期間中，Mina Al Ahmadi での積込を指図された。その少し前に，イランはサウジアラビアとクウェートのターミナルを使うタンカーを空襲した。最初に船長と乗組員は，航行を拒否したが，テレックスを交換の後，船主の助力により，傭船者は戦時ボーナスの支払により結局乗組員を説得した。

本船が Mina Al Ahmadi につながる海峡を通行中に，イラン空軍機のミサイルにより重大な損傷を被った。その海峡で3隻のタンカーが11日前から同じように攻撃されていた（そこでは各種船籍の11隻のタンカーが，その後5ヶ月の間に，攻撃された）。

商事裁判所で，Gatehouse 判事は，次のように判示した。
(a) 第3条は物理的危険と同様に政治的危険の場合にも適用される。
(b) イランの空襲は，異常または予想外の出来事というよりもタンカーが港へ接近する航海に付随する通常の特性であるので，Mina Al Ahmadi は非安全である。
(c) 関連の事実を知っている傭船者は，相当な注意を尽くすことができなかった，そして第3条に違反している。しかし，
(d) 乗組員のボーナスが手配された間に，傭船者とテレックスを交換して，船主が言ったこと，言わなかったことは，船主は Mina Al Ahmadi への指図を第3条の違反として扱わないということの明確な表示となる。これは，船主が，その後傭船者に賠償請求をする場合の妨げとなる。
The Chemical Venture ［1993］1 Lloyd's Rep. 508.
（本事案と前出 The Saga Cob 事件の全容は，後出677頁参照）

非安全と予見される港への配船指図の結果

傭船者が本船を非安全と予見される港に配船すれば，契約違反である。前出 The Evia （No. 2）事件，The Stork ［1955］1 Lloyd's Rep. 349 事件，および The Batis ［1990］1 Lloyd's Rep. 345 事件参照（The Gregos ［1995］1 Lloyd's Rep. 1（同判例集 9頁）事件で，Mustill 卿が無効な指図を発しただけでも傭船契約違反であるという譲歩を受け入れた表現は，この命題についての疑問が完全には解消していないことを示唆しているが）。船長が傭船者の非安全港への配船指図に合理的に従い，その港の非安全性のために本船が滅失しあるいは損傷を被った場合，船主は損害賠償の権利を取得する（The Houston City ［1956］1 Lloyd's Rep. 1 事件参照）。

一般的に言って，船主と船長は傭船者が港の指定をする際に，契約上の義務に従って指定すると想定する権利を取得する。指定の港へ航行する前に港の安全性を船主または船長が調査する義務は通常存しない。The Stork ［1955］1 Lloyd's Rep. 349（同判例集372頁）事件の Morris 卿判事の判決を参照。The Kanchenjunga ［1987］2 Lloyd's Rep. 509（後出参照）事件で，Hobhosue 卿は，次のように言った（同判例集515頁）。「一般的に言って，人は，契約の一方の当事者が，契約上の自己の役割を適正に遂行することを信用して行動する権利がある。たとえ，契約違反が明確であっても，関係当事者が，違反は重大ではないと考える場合，損害補償を受ける権利を犠牲にすることなく，物事を進めることができるということは，商取引の適正な処理にとり重要である。しかし，このことは，船長が明白に非安全な港に入港し，傭船

者に損害を請求できるということにはならない。被害者が合理的に行動し，損害の極小化に努めなければならないこともまた法則である」。

しかし，非安全港へ航行という指図が「非契約的」であるゆえ——後出 The Kanchenjunga 事件の Goff 卿の言葉では，指図は「契約条件に合致」しない「履行の提供」である——，そして，非安全港に行くことは，船主が合意した本船使用の範囲外に本船をもって行くことになり，したがって，船主または船長はかかる指図を拒絶できる。Lensen Shipping v. Anglo-Soviet Shipping (1935) 52 Ll.L. Rep. 141 事件を参照。上記事件の Greer 卿判事の判決中に反対と推定される文言があるにはあるが，傭船契約上，本船の使用につき，船長が傭船者の指図に従うべきであるとされていても，船長はこのような指図を拒絶しうると思われる。Grace v. General Steam Navigation (The Sussex Oak) (1950) 83 Ll.L. Rep. 297 事件において Devlin 判事は「本船の使用に関する傭船者の指図に船長を従わせる旨の定期傭船契約条項が，傭船者がその権限外の指図を出した場合にまで船長が従わなければならないと解されるとは思えない」と述べている（同判例集307頁）。

船主または船長は港が明白に非安全であることを知っている場合，船主または船長は，指図に従うのを実際，拒絶しなければならない。そうでなければ，損失を引き起こしたと判示される。さらに，他の契約違反と同様に，傭船者に港またはバースの安全性に関する義務違反があった場合，船主はその被りつつある，または被るであろう損害を軽減するための合理的な手段をとる義務がある。前出 The Kanchenjunga 事件の Hobhouse 判事の判決の抜粋参照。しかし，船主が傭船者の非安全港への指図を拒絶する権利を承知の上で放棄し，非安全の程度が変化しない場合，船主は，その港を使用する義務から逃れるために損害を軽減するという考え方を其後活用できることには必ずしもならない。貴族院の Goff 卿の解説（401頁）を参照。船主または船長が傭船者の指図に最初に従った後のある段階で，港が非安全であることを発見した場合，港への入港を拒絶すべきであり，もしくは入港中であれば，出港すべきである。

船主またはその船長が，港の非安全性から生ずる結果を回避または軽減するため，適切な処置をとった場合，傭船者に対して，その費用を請求しうる。曳船費用の例が，Brostrom v. Dreyfus (1932) 44 Ll.L. Rep. 136 事件，および瀬取費用の例は，Hall v. Paul (1914) 19 Com. Cas. 384（前出235頁）事件参照。

船主は，非安全であると予見される港への指図を無効として扱うことができるが，非安全性とこれにより船主に与えられる権利（その要否にかかわらず）を承知の上で，なお船主が指図を有効として，それに従うことを明白に示す場合に，船主は指図を無効として扱う権利を放棄したものと判示されるであろう。

Kanchenjunga 号は，傭船者の選択権付で「Fao と Abadan を除くアラビア湾の 1 ないし 2 の安全港」から連続航海に Exxonvoy 書式で傭船された。印刷書式の第20条(vi)項に次のとおり定められていた。「(b)戦争，交戦，軍事行動のゆえに……積荷港へ入港……積込……船長または船主の判断で危険と考えられる港で貨物の……の場合に，他の安全港で……貨物の積込を……指図する権利を傭船者は有する……」1980年11月20日にイランとイラクの間の全面戦争が始まって間もなく，傭船者は本船に Kharg Island への航行を指図した。戦争のために Kharg は非安全であると承知していたにもかかわらず，船主はこの指図に従った。本船は，Kharg に投錨し，11月23日に積込準備完了通知を発した。その後，優先バース着を要請し，碇泊期間の経過に言及した。バースは11月30日に空いたが，着船前の12月 1 日 Kharg は空襲を受け，船長は，本船をそこから脱出させた。12月 2 日船主は傭船者に対し他の積港を指定するように要請した。しかし，傭船者は本船は Kharg で積み込むべく帰港するように要求し続けた。ロンドンの仲裁人は，傭船者が11月21日に指図を発した時点で，Kharg は安全であるとは予見されなかった，と認定した（非安全性は，12月 1 日の空襲によって変化しなかった，と

認定した)。

商事法廷で，Hobhosue 判事は，次のように判示した。船主は，指図を拒否する権利を放棄したが，第20条(vi)項により，Kharg で積込を拒絶したことについての損害賠償の責任を免れる。判事の判決は，2つの点で，控訴院と貴族院により支持された。船主は，非安全であるので，Kharg での積込の指図を拒絶する権利があることを知っていたが，準備完了通知を発することで指図を明白に受け入れ，優先バース着を要請し，碇泊期間の進行に言及した。こうして，船主は Kharg の指定を拒絶する権利を放棄した。しかしながら，第20条(vi)項は，そこで結果として積込を拒絶したことについての損害賠償の責任から船主を守った。

Goff 卿は次のように言った (399頁)。「拒絶する権利を生ぜしめる事実を承知した上で，なお，船主がそうしないことを明白に選択する場合，船主の選択は，最終的で，確定的であり，船主は，非契約的として申込を拒絶する権利を放棄したことになろう」。

The Kanchenjunga [1987] 2 Lloyd's Rep. 509, [1989] 1 Lloyd's Rep. 354 (C. A.) および [1990] 1 Lloyd's Rep. 391 (H. L.)。

船主が放棄したものは，指定港へ行く指図を拒絶する権利であり，船主が指図に従い，本船が港の非安全により損害を生じた場合，損害賠償を傭船者から回収する追加の権利ではないと *The Kanchenjunga* 事件で強調された。Goff 卿は，港の指定によって傭船者は黙示的に港が安全であることを約束したと (同判例集397頁) 言った。「したがって，指定を拒絶する権利を有しているにもかかわらず，船主は指定に応じ，その結果として本船に滅失損傷を生じた場合，船主は，契約違反により傭船者から損害賠償を回収する権利がある。……」。Brandon 卿は，「船主が放棄した唯一の権利は，指定を……非契約的であるとして……拒絶する権利である」と付言した (*The Batis* [1990] 1 Lloyd's Rep. 345 事件も参照)。

前出 *The Chemical Venture* [1993] 1 Lloyd's Rep. 508 事件で，Gatehouse 判事は，本事案の事実に基づいて，船主は関連の港へという傭船者の指図を安全港担保義務の違反として扱わないという明白な表示をし，したがって，その義務違反につきその後の損害賠償請求を控えた，と判示した。

192 非安全港に配船することは，それに固執する場合には，ある状況の下では船主に傭船契約を終了させる権利を与えることになるかも知れない。例として，前出 *The Kanchenjunga* 事件の Hobhouse 判事の判決参照。無効な指図に傭船者が固執する結果について，*The Gregos* [1995] 1 Lloyd's Rep. 1 (H. L.) も参照 (違反の各種効果についての解説は137頁参照)。こういう指図はまた，ニューヨーク・プロデュース書式61行にある「本傭船契約の違反」という文言の意味する違反行為となり，船主に対し，第5条により本船を引き揚げる権利を与えるものと思われる ([1977] 1 Lloyd's Rep. 397. および後出325頁の *The Tropwind (No. 1)* 事件参照)。

船長または乗組員の過失の効果

港は非安全であるが，船主の被った損害は，船長，乗組員の過失によりまたは過失が寄与して生じたと傭船者が主張することがしばしばある。船長は自分で危険性を確認し，入港を拒否すべきであったと言うこともできる。損害は港の非安全性に起因したものではなく，そのときの船長，乗組員の操船上の過失が原因である，またはこの損害は，部分的に非安全性によるが，かつ部分的には操船上の過失によると主張することもできる。

因 果 関 係

損害の主要な原因が，傭船者の安全に関する条件の違反ではなく船長の過失である場合，傭

船者に責任はない。傭船者の指図から始まる因果関係は，船長の行為または怠慢が介在した場合に中断されると言われている。例として，The Dagmar [1968] 2 Lloyd's Rep. 563（同判例集571頁）事件と The Polyglory [1977] 2 Lloyd's Rep. 353 事件と The Mary Lou [1981] 2 Lloyd's Rep. 272 事件の Mustill 判事の判決参照。しかし主要な原因を決定するにあたっては，船長がしばしばジレンマに陥っていること，およびその原因は傭船者が最初に契約違反を犯したためであることを考慮に入れなければならない。船長がその直面した状況下において合理的に行動していれば，間違っていたとしてもその行為が損害の主要原因と判断されることはあまりないと思われる。例えば，The Stork [1955] 1 Lloyd's Rep. 349 事件における Sellers 卿判事の判決（同判例集363頁）参照。The Houston City 事件において Geraldton は，沖出しブイおよび本船が着岸している岸壁のフェンダーの一部がなかったという理由で非安全港と判断されたが，オーストラリア高等裁判所の控訴院において Dixon 主席判事は反対意見の中で（後に枢密院において支持された），船長の行為によって因果関係が中断されたとする主張に対して次のごとく論じている（[1954] 2 Lloyd's Rep. 148（同判例集158頁）参照）。「本船の損傷はバース指定の自然的蓋然的な結果ではなく，船長が良好な気象条件に頼ろうとしたこと，ストリームアンカーを出さなかったことが介在して因果関係が中断されたとの主張がなされた。さらに船長はそのバースが安全でないことあるいは気象の変化によって安全ではなくなることを知っていたとも主張され，さらにそれを知りながら着岸した船長の行為こそが，損害の真の原因であったと主張された。私はこの見解が支持されるとは思わない。傭船者に安全港または安全バースを指定することを要求する目的は，本船に対する危険を避けるためである。非安全バースを指定することによって，傭船者は船長をジレンマに陥れる。そして船長が傭船者の指図に黙従したとしても，それは，傭船者をその責任から免れさせる理由とはならない。もしそれが重要な問題であるならば，傭船者は船長と同様にその問題を知っているものとして扱われる。傭船者には積込を管理し，状況を知るのに船長と同様の機会を持っている代理店がある。船長は港長である水先人に導かれたのであるが，水先人は何ら他の方法を助言しなかった。このような事情を考えると，発生した事実の経過が，Geraldton で問題のバースを指示したという傭船契約違反の直接，かつ主要な原因ではないと考えるのは困難である」。

　船長が港の安全性に不安を持ちながら，結局入港し，あるいはそこに滞まっていることを決意した場合，その後に発生した船体損害は，なお，傭船者の指図から発生した自然的蓋然的結果——そして傭船者の指図が原因であるとみなされることがある。この点は，船長の不安を傭船者またはその代理店がなだめたような事情がある場合，特にそう判断される。

　　Stork 号は Newfoundland から木材輸送の航海に傭船された。傭船契約には「指図どおりに2箇所以内の認められた積込場所」にて積込を行うと規定していた。傭船者が指図した場所はトミーの腕と称される小さな岩の多い入り江で，非常に狭く，走錨を防ぐために十分な錨鎖を出すことができなかった。そしてその季節にその地方に定期的に発生する暴風のため，本船は損傷を被った。最初到着したとき，船長は本船の安全性につき重大な不安を表明したが，傭船者が同船を迎えにやった経験豊かな地元の水先人の説得でなだめられた。控訴院は Devlin 判事の判断を支持して，当該場所は非安全であり，本船の損害は，傭船者がそのような場所への航行を本船に対して指図したために発生したと判示した。Sellers 卿判事は船長に関して言及し「船長は時に進退極まることがあるが，重要なことは船長の行為が適切であったか否かであると信ずる。法に明るい Devlin 判事は説得を受けた時点での船長の行為は適切であったという意見であったが，私もそれと同意見である」と述べた。
　　The Stork [1954] 2 Lloyd's Rep. 397 および [1955] Lloyd's Rep. 349 (C. A.).

　たとえ傭船者によって支払われようとも，水先人は，通常，船主の被用者とみなされる（後

出279頁参照)。したがって水先人の過失は，傭船者の指図と損害の間の因果関係の連鎖の中断を構成する。しかし，ある場合には，港での水先人の手配は，港の特性と見なされ，水先人の無能力または過失は，港の非安全性を構成する要素の一つであると判示されよう。前出 The Stork 事件と The Mary Lou [1981] 2 Lloyd's Rep. 272 事件参照。The Evia (No. 2) [1982] 1 Lloyd's Rep. 334 (同判例集338頁) 事件も参照。

傭船者の違反は，滅失損傷の確定されたある部分の主要な原因であり，船長または乗組員の過失は，他の明白で別個の部分の主要な原因であると判示されるかも知れない。

1945年法改革（寄与過失）に関する法に基づく損害の分割

非安全港事案において，1945年法改正（寄与過失）に関する法に基づく損害の分割がありうる場合があると思われる。後出369頁参照。例えば，定期傭船契約で，一方の当事者が特定の港の安全性に関する情報，または助言の提供につき特別の責任を負うが，その点で過失があった場合に1945年法は，定期傭船契約に基づく損害賠償に適用される。その場合，他方が，提供される情報，または助言に依拠することが予想され，事実依拠した場合，後出370頁で言及した事案から，傭船契約の有無にかかわらず，不法行為の責任があることになるように思われる。1945年法は，契約が不法行為責任を除外しておらず，かつ両当事者に過失がある場合に，適用される。

しかし，港の安全性に関する事案には1945年法を注意深く適用するのが，正解である。なぜなら，この領域の法はまだ十分に発展していないのだから。

194 安全に関する黙示の条項

傭船者が本船を配船する港の安全性について明文の規定がない場合，裁判所はある状況の下ではその安全性に関する条項が黙示されていると認定するように思われる。

　1968年11月タンカー Evaggelos Th 号が紅海その他の海域への航海に傭船された。当時，その付近は戦争地帯であった。傭船者は船主の戦争保険料の一部を支払うことに合意した。傭船契約には本船が配船される可能性のある港の安全性についての規定はなく，揚荷または積込は，本船が「安全な浮揚状態で常に碇泊」しうる場所にて行う旨の規定があった。傭船者は本船にスエズ向け航海を命じた。この時点において，スエズは休戦状態であった。しかし本船到着後再び交戦状態となり，砲撃のため本船は推定全損となった。判決は，次のとおり下された。
(1) 「安全な浮揚状態で常に碇泊（always lie safely afloat）」という文言は揚地の海事的性質にのみ関係する（後出252頁参照）。
(2) 安全性に関する黙示の約定があると考えるべきであるが，そこでいう安全性は揚荷港が指定された時点において安全であり，かつ本船到着から出港までの間安全であると予想しうるという程度に限られるべきである。
(3) スエズは指定されたとき安全であったし，また，その時点において危険になるとは予想できなかった。したがって傭船者は黙示の安全性に関する条項に違反していない。
The Evaggelos Th [1971] 2 Lloyd's Rep. 200.
(使用および補償条項に基づく船主の選択的請求については後出253頁参照)

　前出 The Evia (No. 2) 事件で，Roskill 卿は，The Evaggelos Th 事件の判決に同意したが，論拠には，疑問を示した。

　裁判所は，傭船契約に商業上の効力を与えるのに必要であるという見解をとらない限り，安全性に関する条項が黙示されているとは認めない。

A. P. J. Priti 号は，イラン・イラク戦争中に Damman からイラクの3個の指定港の中の1港の「1ないし2」のバースまで航海傭船契約された。傭船者は，Bandar Khomeini を選択した。港の安全性に関する明示の条項はなかった。工夫された戦争危険条項で，本船が戦争により危険となった場合に，船長には航海を中断する権利があった。Bandar Khomeini へ接近する途中で，本船は，戦闘ミサイルによる損害を受けた。

　控訴院は，揚荷港の安全性に関する約束が黙示されていることを求めるのは不適当であるとの船主の譲歩を認めた。Bingham 卿判事は，次のように言った。「よく熟慮の上で，明示担保を落としてあり，黙示条項は傭船契約の商売の効力にとり必要ではなく，そのような黙示条項はせいぜい傭船契約の明示担保があってこそ，そのそばに窮屈そうに位置するであろうから，宣言された港が安全である予見されることの担保を黙示するとの根拠はない」。

　裁判所は，続けて，代わりにバースの安全性の条項に依拠することができるという船主の主張を退けた。安全港条項のないところで，安全バース担保義務は，港への接近航路にまで拡張できず，港域内の移動に限定される。さらに，それは，必ずしも全体としての港または，港の中の全バースに影響を及ぼさない危険からの安全のみに関係する。Bingham 卿判事は，次のように言った。「指定のバースが非安全であると予見されても，全体として全バースまたは，港が同じように同じ規模で非安全であるならば，傭船者の側に違反は存しない」。

　The A. P. J. Priti [1987] 2 Lloyd's Rep. 37.

明示された港

　傭船契約に明示されているか，あるいは明示された港のリストの中から傭船者が選んだ港の非安全性につき，傭船者に責任があるかについては明確には決まっていない。傭船契約に港の安全性に関する明示の条項がない場合，傭船者はその港の非安全性に一般的に責任がないと考えられている。港の安全性に関して明示の条項がある場合，その条項が指定港に適用されるか，あるいは傭船契約に基づく，本船の使用中に傭船者が指定する港のみに，適用されるかは，特定の傭船契約の解釈の問題であると思われる。

[195]　*The Houston City*（オーストラリア高等裁判所）［1954］2 Lloyd's Rep. 148 事件——航海傭船の事案——で，Dixon 主席判事は次のように述べている。「傭船をするとき，傭船者が貨物の積込地または引渡地を特定する用意がある場合，船主はその地が安全に碇泊できる場所か否かを確認する義務があり，またその確認について責任を持たねばならない。船主がその地を同意した場合，免責危険の場合を除外して，当該本船をその地にもってゆくことは，船主の絶対的責任である」（同判例集153頁）。この論理は，*The Stork* [1954] 2 Lloyd's Rep. 397 事件において，Devlin 判事によって採用された（同判例集415頁）。しかし，*The Helen Miller* [1980] 2 Lloyd's Rep. 95, 101 事件で，Mustill 判事は，安全性の明示の担保は，港または領域を指定することで，ある程度限定されるということが，その命題の根拠であるかは疑問であるとした（しかし，*The Mary Lou* [1981] 2 Lloyd's Rep. 272（同判例集280頁）事件の同判事の解説参照）。

　当事者が引渡港，返船港を合意し，ニューヨーク・プロデュース書式の18行と55行の空欄に書き入れることがある。このように明示された港の安全性についての傭船者の責任の有無にかかわらず，引渡港内で，傭船者が選定したバースの安全性については，傭船者に責任があるようである（ニューヨーク・プロデュース書式20行および21行，ボルタイム書式15行）。返船場所についても，そのバースが積荷関係の目的のために使用された場合，その理は同じである（ニューヨーク・プロデュース書式第6条，ボルタイム書式第2条）。いずれにせよ，傭船者に責任があろう。後出参照。上記のような場合において，碇泊場所の安全性に関する責任は，その碇泊場所の発着に直接繋がる接近水路にまで拡大されると思われる。この点は *Stag Line* v.

Ellerman & Papayanni Lines（1949）82 Ll.L. Rep. 826 事件において議論されたが，判断をみなかった。同事件は，傭船契約上明記された返船港内において，傭船者が指定したバースの非安全性の主張に関するものである。しかし，*The A. P. J. Priti*［1987］2 Lloyd's Rep. 37事件の控訴院の判決からは，安全バース義務は，港域内移動を対象としうるが，港の発着のための接近水路にまで拡大されないことは明白である（前出250頁参照）。

バースの安全性

　傭船者は，安全港担保義務がある場合，傭船者は，その寄港を指示した港の中におけるドック，岸壁，バースその他の場所の安全性についても責任がある。このことはニューヨーク・プロデュース書式第6条（68～70行）にあるように，本船が「常に浮揚状態で安全に碇泊」できる場所において積込，揚荷するという義務が定められなくても同様の解釈になると思われる。

　ボルタイム書式によって定期傭船された *Terneuzen* 号は，Leningrad において指定されたバースの非安全性のため損害を被った。そこで傭船契約第1条の文言により傭船者に課せられた義務の範囲について問題が生じた。すなわち第1条の文言は「本船は以下の範囲において，常に浮揚状態で安全に碇泊しうるか，あるいは，同様の大きさ，喫水の本船が通常座洲状態で安全に碇泊している場所で，かつ本船も座洲状態で安全に碇泊しうる良好かつ安全な港またはバース間の合法的航海に使用さるべきこと」と定められていた。控訴院は多数意見をもって，上記文言は，それ自体から，本船が港内の安全バースを指定されなければならないと解されるのか，あるいは，この文言があることによって，これと同様の効果を持つ条項が傭船契約に黙示的に含まれていると解すべきか，そのいずれかであると判示した。Slesser 卿判事は「本件における第1条の規定は，そこに取引通念上良好安全であるとされている港に船を差し向けるという船主の権利を含み，したがって港または場所というのは，その範囲内で良好かつ安全なバースを含むことを要求している」と述べた。
　　Lensen Shipping v. *Anglo-Soviet Shipping*（1935）52 Ll. L. Rep. 141.
　　（前出 *Stag Line* v. *Ellerman & Papayanni Lines*（1949）82 Ll.L. Rep. 826 事件参照）

　「安全バース」に関する傭船者の義務は「安全港」に関するものと同様である。*The Stork*［1955］1 Lloyd's Rep. 349 事件参照。壊れたフェンダーが傭船の船体に穴をあけたとき，航海傭船者が，安全バース義務違反と判示された *The Carnival*［1992］1 Lloyd's Rep. 449 および［1994］2 Lloyd's Rep. 14（C. A.）事件参照。

196 港の安全性に関して明示または黙示の条項が存在せず，港の全バースが同じ方法で，同じ程度に非安全であると予見される場合に，バースの安全性に関する明示の条項が，船主を利することはない（［1987］2 Lloyd's Rep. 37 と前出250頁の *The A. P. J. Priti* 事件を参照）。本事案で，控訴院は，こういう傭船契約の安全バース条項を，港内の指定バースから・への移動に対立するものとして港への接近水路の安全性を対象とするために使用とすることはできないと判示した。
　港の場合と同様に，バースの予見される安全性は，指定バースの指図の時点で判断されるべきである。ある港への航海が決定される前に，この指図が出される必要は通常存しない（前出 *The A. P. J. Priti* 事件の控訴院の判決参照）。
　傭船者は，次の場合に，代理人が代わりに出した非安全バースの指図につき責任がある。(a) あらゆる状況で指図は傭船者の指図とみなされて，代理人は傭船契約上の明示また黙示の安全バースの義務に違反した場合か，または(b)真の代理人であり，独立の契約者ではない代理人に，過失があった場合。その場合，傭船契約上の安全バース担保義務の無視につき，傭船者が

代位責任を負う。しかし，港内の特定のバースまたは場所への航行を本船に指図するすべての者が，傭船者に責任をもたらすわけでは決してない。

　Mediolanum 号は，ニューヨーク・プロデュース書式で傭船された。傭船期間の途中，傭船者は代理人を通じて，本船にとり安全港である Las Minas で本船に燃料油を支給した。燃料油を支給するときに，傭船者は暗黙裡に燃料油供給業者に本船に燃料油を支給する正確な場所を選択することを授権した。燃料油供給業者が実際に選択した場所は砂州が海図に記載されていないゆえに非安全であり，その結果本船に損害を生じた。

　控訴院は，燃料油供給業者は実際に燃料油の積込場所の選定に際して，実際に傭船者の代理人として行動したか否かということに重大な疑問を表明した。判決を下すときに，Kerr 卿判事は，*The Isabelle* [1982] 2 Lloyd's Rep. 81 事件の Robert Goff 判事の判決に従って，供給業者は港長または港湾局と類似の機能を代わりに果たすとみなし，港長または港湾局の行為は傭船者の行為ではない，と言った。

　供給業者が，この目的のために傭船者の代理人であることは，「大きな疑念があり」想定できぬとして，裁判所は，安全港の約束の違反はないので，傭船者に責任はないと認定した。さらに，供給業者が独立の契約者としてよりむしろ本船に指図する代理人として真に行動したと，たとえ想定したとしても傭船者が代位責任を負う供給業者の側に過失はなかった。
　The Mediolanum [1984] 1 Lloyd's Rep. 136.

　控訴院における，前出 *The Mediolanum* 事件で表明された注意にもかかわらず，さらに *The Isabelle* 事件で Robert Goff 判事の判決を裁判所が採用したにもかかわらず，Staughton 判事は，*The Erechthion* [1987] 2 Lloyd's Rep. 180 事件において，Dawes 島の錨地で生じた本船の損害についてそこでの瀬取を命じた Port Harcourt 港長の指図は，ニューヨーク・プロデュース書式上の傭船者の指図として考えるべきである。即ち，その指図は，これに従う船主に対し傭船者が補償する黙示の義務により裏付けられていると判示した（その義務については後出353頁参照）。しかしながら，判事は，代理の問題としてではなく，港長が指定する Port Harcourt の揚荷場所への航行が傭船者の指図であることを根拠として，むしろ，事件を扱うのを好むと表明したことは，注目されよう。

NYPE 93

　ニューヨーク・プロデュース書式の1993年改訂版の第12条は，「本船は，傭船者またはその代理人が指示するいかなる安全なドック，安全なバースまたは安全な場所においても船積および揚荷を行う。ただし，それらは，潮時の如何を問わず本船が常時浮揚して，安全に到着し，碇泊し，発航できるところでなければならない」ことを要求して，バースの安全性に関する担保義務を強調している。

[197] 常に浮揚状態で安全に碇泊

　The Evaggelos Th [1971] 2 Lloyd's Rep. 200 事件において Donaldson 判事は「本船は安全な浮揚状態で常に碇泊することができる」という文言について，それはバースの純粋な海事的性格に限ると解釈した。しかし，同判事はこの文言が，ボルタイム書式やニューヨーク・プロデュース書式に使われているものと異なることをはっきりと認めている。したがってこれらの文言は，同判事のように制限的に解釈すべきではなく，そこで検討されたすべての側面に関する安全性の規定であると読むべきである。

航海傭船契約と定期傭船契約

　一般に，航海傭船に適用される基準は定期傭船にも適用される。枢密院は，*Reardon Smith Line* v. *Australian Wheat Board（The Houston City）*［1956］1 Lloyd's Rep. 1 事件で，次のとおり判示した（同判例集9頁）。「定期傭船契約において，……傭船者が本船を良好，安全な港の間の航海に使用すべきことを約束した場合，傭船者の責任は，少なくとも通常の状態においては，航海傭船契約において傭船者が『安全港』を指定することを約した場合と同様である」（前出 *The Stork* 事件の控訴院判決と *The Batis* ［1990］1 Lloyd's Rep. 345（同判例集350頁）事件参照）。

　しかし，*The A. P. J. Priti* ［1987］2 Lloyd's Rep. 37（同伴例集40頁）事件で Bingham 卿判事が指摘したように，積荷港または揚荷港が明示されるかまたは記載されている航海傭船契約の下での，運航時よりも，船主が世界の諸港へ行くことを要求される定期傭船契約の下での運航時に，本船の船主は安全港の約束に基づく保護をより多く必要としている。*The Evia（No. 2）*事件の弁論の中で，Roskill 卿は，多くの航海傭船契約の下で再指定する権利の欠如を含めて定期傭船と航海傭船とのこの分野の区別を念頭に置いて，指定港が指定後に非安全となったとき，定期傭船者に課せられる第二義的義務は，等しく航海傭船者にも適用されるか否かを示すことを拒否した。前出243頁参照。

使用条項による選択的請求

　第8条により，船長は本船の使用に関し，傭船者の指揮命令に従わなければならないとされる。裁判所は船長が傭船者の指揮に従った結果発生した問題につき傭船者は船主に補償するという条項が，この中に含まれていると通常考えるであろう（この点に関し後出353頁参照）。したがって，船長が傭船者の命令どおりに，ある港に向けて出帆した結果，本船が損傷し，あるいは船主が何らかの損害を被った場合，船主は傭船者から補償を請求しうる。この場合前に述べたような因果関係の問題が発生する。

　港の安全担保義務につき傭船者が違反した場合には，第8条に基づく請求は通常無効であると思われる。ニューヨーク・プロデュース書式においては，港の安全担保義務違反に基づく請求が成立しない場合（例えば船長の過失により因果関係が中断された場合），第8条に基づく請求も同様の理由で通常成立しないと思われる（*The Lucille* ［1983］1 Lloyd's Rep. 387 事件参照）。*Stag Line* v. *Ellerman & Papayanni Lines*（1949）82 Ll.L. Rep. 826 事件においては，ボルタイム書式の使用補償条項に基づく選択請求が成立しなかった。Morris 判事は「本件において第1条（本船は常時浮揚状態で安全に碇泊）違反が立証されない場合，原告は，第8条（使用補償条項）に基づいて，被告に対し請求することができない。本件において，事故は，本船が浮揚状態で安全に碇泊できたバースを離れた後に発生している。このような事故は，51番バースに行けという命令から生ずる責任またはその命令の結果とみなすことはできない」と述べた（同判例集836頁）。

198　しかし，安全港に関する傭船者の責任が，制限されている場合，――傭船契約にその旨明示されているか，あるいは裁判所が限定責任だけ黙示した場合――，安全港に関する責任に基づく請求ができなくても，第8条に基づく請求をすることができる。前出249頁の *The Evaggelos Th* ［1971］2 Lloyd's Rep. 200 事件で，Donaldson 判事は，傭船者に安全性に関する黙示義務違反はないと判断したが，さらに続けて，それにもかかわらず，傭船者の命令に従ったことが，船体損傷の原因であると仲裁人が認定した場合には，傭船者は使用補償約款に基づいて責

任があると判断した。同判事は「船主が，本船滅失の近因は，船主または船主の船長が本船の使用に関する傭船者の命令に従った結果であることを立証した場合にのみ，船主は本条により求償することができると考える」と述べた。同事件において，使用補償約款は，ボルタイム書式と同様の文言で作成されていた。そして両者とも，傭船者の命令に従った結果につき船主に補償する明示の規定を含んでいた。

　The Erechthion [1987] 2 Lloyd's Rep. 180 事件で，仲裁人は，傭船者は，安全港またはバースの担保義務に違反はないにもかかわらず，瀬取錨地へ向かえとの傭船者の指図に応じた際に水中物体により本船が被った損傷につき，ニューヨーク・プロデュース書式第8条に基づき船主に補償する責任があると裁定した。Staughton 判事は，損害は傭船者の指図を近因として生じたという仲裁人からの確認を条件としてのみこの裁定を支持した。

戦争条項との相互作用

　同じ傭船契約で安全港条項と戦争条項の間に相互作用があることは異常ではない。その結果生じるいくつかの問題は，後出658頁と722頁で取り扱う。

[199] 米　国　法

非安全港またはバースの指定

　安全港と安全バースの担保は、定期傭船契約に必須の部分である。傭船者は積荷港や揚荷港を指定する際に、広範な自由を与えられているので、この担保は傭船者の指定した港とバースが傭船契約を履行する際に傭船された船舶にとり安全であるとの担保を提供する意味で船主にとりたいへん重要である。

　本船が非安全港または非安全バースを指定したがゆえに損傷し、または遅延した場合に、船主は傭船者から損失を回収する権利を有する。さらに、船主には、非安全港または非安全バースへの傭船者の航行指図の受諾を拒絶する正当な事由がある。

常に浮揚状態で安全に碇泊

　「常に浮揚状態で安全に碇泊する」という文言は、安全港および安全バースの明示の担保となる（例えば、*Cities Service Transp. Co.* v. *Gulf Refining Co.*, 79 F. 2d 521, 1935 AMC 1513 (2d Cir. 1935) 事件参照）。同事件では「傭船契約は、それ自体、本船が『指定されたバース』において、『常に浮揚状態で』碇泊できると保証したものであり、船長はその保証に頼る権利がある」と判示された（なお、*Park S. S. Co.* v. *Cities Service Oil Co.*, 188 F. 2d 804, 1951 AMC 851 (2d Cir. 1951)、裁量上告拒絶 342 U. S. 802 (1951) 事件も参照）。

安全港間

　英米の判例は、この文言が、傭船者による安全港の明示の担保となるという点で一致している。その構成要素は *Leeds Shipping* v. *Societe Francaise Bunge (Eastern City)* [1958] 2 Lloyd's Rep. 127. 事件の中で説明されている（前出231頁参照）。米国裁判所の多数が従う法則の下で、この担保は、傭船者指定の港またはバースは、特定の船舶にとり完全に安全でなければならず、物理的損害の危険に曝されることなく通常の運航で入港、出港ができることを意味する (*Venore Transportation Co.* v. *Oswego Shipping Corp.*, 498 F. 2d 469, 1974 AMC (2d Cir.)、裁量上告拒絶 419 U. S. 998 (1974))。

　The Oceanic First, SMA 1054 (Arb. at N. Y. 1976) 事件において、仲裁審は、安全港担保を次のとおり要約している。

　　両傭船契約とも本船が「安全港」間のみに使用されること、「安全バース」においてのみ積揚することの担保約束を含んでいるという点について争いはない。この担保は次の点を保証したものと一般的に考えられている。すなわち、それは、本船が揚荷のためその港に入港し、出港できるということであり、さらに予見できない異常事態がない限り、適切な航海操船技術により、本船に物理的損傷を与える過度の危険をもたらすことなく、そうすることができるということである。この担保は、本船が新潟にて揚荷を指図された各期間につき、明文をもって与えられており、当該船舶の、同港寄港の各期間中存在する、合理的に予想できる状態に照らして、検討されなければならない。

　安全港と安全バースを提供する傭船者の義務は、転嫁できない。前出 *Venore Transportation Co.* v. *Oswego Shipping Corp.*, 498 F. 2d at 472. この原則は、安全港条項の商業目的から

まったく自然に生じる。前出 Park S. S. Co. v. Cities Service Oil Co. 事件で, Swan 判事は, 次のように書いた。

　　傭船者は, 貨物の揚荷の方法および場所を管理することを望んでいる。……それで, 傭船者は揚荷の正確な場所を選定する権利につき交渉し, 本船は選択の危険を傭船者が受諾する代わりにその権利を放棄する (188 F. 2d at 806)。

200　27行の文言は, 安全港を単に明示的に言及しているだけであるが, 担保は, 安全港とともに安全バースを含むと広く判示されている (The Mozart Festival, SMA 2393 (Arb. at N.Y. 1987) 事件参照)。

安全港担保の確立した水域の解釈は, Orduna S. A. v. Zen-Noh Grain Corp., 913 F. 2d 1149, 1991 AMC 346 (5th Cir. 1990) 事件に関する第5巡回区控訴裁判所 (Louisiana 州, Mississippi 州と Texas 州を含む) の判決により混乱した。

Orduna 事件で, 第5巡回区裁判所は, 一般原則を拒否して, 傭船者による安全港の担保はないと判示した。同裁判所によると,

　　……傭船者に選択したバースの安全性を担保させることで, どんな正当な法的または, 公的政策も, 促進されない。もしそのような担保があれば, 現場で船長がバースの安全性を決定する際に最善の判断を行使することに水をさすだけであろう。さらに, 厳格責任を無効にすることで, 危険は増大しない。なぜなら, 安全バース担保義務条項それ自身に, 船長が本船を非安全港にいれない自由があるのだから。
　　結論として, 傭船契約の安全バース担保義務条項は, 傭船者を安全バースの担保者にしない。代わりに, 安全バース条項は, 傭船者に安全バースを選択する際に相当の注意を尽くす義務を課すると, 判示する (1991 AMC at 356.)。

われわれは, 第5巡回区裁判所の特に, 「法的または公的政策」を重要視することに同意しない。安全な港または, バースを提供する傭船者の担保は, 契約問題であり, 長らく海運界では船主にとって非常に重要な業界の習慣として広く受け入れられてきた。港または, バースを選択するのは船主ではなく傭船者であるというあるがままの商業の現実に立脚すれば, 通常の場合, 独立当事者間の交渉以外の別のものから安全港担保が生じるとは到底言えないのだから, いかなる政策が安全港担保により, 破綻するのかを理解するのは困難である。

文言の挿入により相当の注意を尽くすという基準にまで押し下げたり, または指定港を船主が受諾して, 担保を完全に放棄する効果をもたらすことにより, 安全港／バース担保は, 契約によって修正しうるし, しばしば修正されている。さらに, 裁判所および仲裁人は, 安全港／バース担保義務は, 船長を本船の操船に相当の注意を尽くす義務から解放しないことを一致して判示・裁定してきた。

第5巡回区裁判所は Orduna 事件において Atkins v. Fibre Disintegrating Co., 2 Fed. Cas. 78 (E. D. N. Y. 1868) (No. 601), 原審維持 85 U. S. (18 Wall.) 272 (1873) 事件に依拠したが, それは不首尾に終わっている。第5巡回区裁判所の Atkins 事件の見解に反して, Benedict 判事は, その事案で, 安全バース担保があるが, 船長に入港を拒絶する権利がある場合, 抗議なしに, 船長が港を受諾したことにより安全バース担保は放棄されたと認定した。安全港担保に関して Benedict 判事は次のように書いた。

　　「2番目の安全港」という語は, 本船は法的制限なしにかつ海の通常の危険の範囲で本船が入港お

よび出港できる港であることを暗に意味する。
　(2 Fed. Cas. at 79. Atkins 事件のこれ以上の検討は，後出の「指定港またはバースの受け入れ」という表題の下で行う)

　Orduna 事件で，述べられた安全港担保と相当なる注意義務との差異は，何であろうか。ある仲裁裁定が，一つの解説を提供している。The Mercandian Queen, SMA 2713（1990）事件を参照。傭船契約はニューヨーク・プロデュース書式であった。本船はペルーの Ilo の新 ro/ro バースで鉄道トレーラーを揚荷した。そこは今までその大きさの本船が使用したことはなかった。揚荷中，本船の船底は，大きな岩にぶつかり，船体に破孔を生じた。この岩は，どの海図にも記載なく，この事件の前には当地の水先人も港長も知らなかった。仲裁審は，傭船者に安全バース担保義務による損傷につき責任ありと裁定した。仲裁審は，傭船者も船主も当地の水先人も海図にない岩を知らなかったし，傭船者は「まったく善意で非安全バースを指定」したことを確信すると述べた。仲裁審は安全港担保のゆえに傭船者に責任を課したが，仮に Orduna 事件に基づけば，傭船者に責任なしとされたであろうことは，もとより明らかである。傭船者は，バースを指定する際に，過失はなかった。実際，仲裁審は，傭船者は，結局は非安全港であった港を指定する際に，「善意で」行動したと特別に認定した。

特定の船舶

　米国の判例もまた，港が傭船契約に示された特定の船舶について安全でなければならないという原則を採用している（The Zaneta, 1970 AMC 807（Arb. at N.Y. 1968）事件参照）。例えば The Pyrgos, SMA 896（Arb. at N.Y. 1974）事件で，本船は，Delaware 川の Mantua Creek 錨地にて座礁した。仲裁人は船主に有利な判断を下して，次のように述べている。すなわち「Mantua Creek 錨地は，小型の喫水の浅い船舶にとっては，安全な錨地であるけれども，Pyrgos 号の長さおよび深さの船舶にとって安全ではない……」。

接近および出港時の安全性

　一般に，傭船の期間，特定の傭船が異常気象や他のできごともなく適切な航海操船技術によって回避できないような危険に曝されることなく，入港し，使用し，出港ができるのであれば，港またはバースが安全港条項の目的から見て安全であるということは，十分確立されている。所与の港またはバースがどの所与の船舶にとり安全であるかを決定する「黒白」判定の基準はないが，問題はいつも個別的に解決されなければならない。裁判所または仲裁人は各事案の事実を吟味しなければならず，本船は適切に配乗され，装備され，管理され，操船されると想定して港またはバースが傭船にとり安全であるかを決定しなければならない。適切な航海操船技術により避けることのできる危険では港は「非安全」とは言えない。
　安全港担保は，港の直近の地域だけでなく，本船が入港または出港するために通航を余儀なくされる隣接地域も安全でなければならないことを意味する。
　The Gazelle, 128 U.S. 474（1888）事件において，裁判所は入江の入口に砂洲があるため Gazelle 号が，空船でも積荷を積んでも通過できないことを理由として，傭船者は安全港担保条項に違反したと判断した。裁判所は次のとおり述べている。

　傭船契約の明示の条項により，傭船者は当該船舶を「安全な，直航できるノルウェーまたデンマー

クの港，またはその最寄りの安全に到着し常に碇泊し浮揚状態で揚荷のできる場所にのみ」配船する義務があった。この文言の明確な意味は，当該船舶が積荷状態で安全に入港できる港，あるいは少なくとも，港外に碇泊でき，浮揚状態で積荷のできる安全な錨泊地を持っている港にのみ配船されなければならないということを意味する。……傭船者は，この傭船契約の要求する港に配船することを拒絶し，それと異なった港に行くべきことを固執した点において債務不履行があり損害賠償の責めに任じなければならないとまさしく判断された……（128 U. S. at 485-486）。

Crisp v. *United States & Australasia S. S. Co.*, 124 F. 748 (S. D. N. Y. 1903) 事件で，裁判所は次のとおり述べている。

安全な積荷または揚荷場所の約定は，傭船者が指定する港に当該船舶が全積荷を持って安全に入港でき，船底を接触することなく全貨物を揚荷することができることを含み……，さらに，当然ではあるが，いかなる潮汐においても障害に曝されないことをも含む……（124 F. at 750）。

Crisp 事件において，裁判所は，「常に安全に浮揚状態で碇泊し」という文言は，傭船者に安全港の危険を負わせることであり，傭船者は，強制水先人の監督の下にある本船に損害が発生しても，その損害について責任があると判示した。

Carbon Slate Co. v. *Ennis*, 114 F. 260 (3d Cir.1902) 事件で，裁判所は，不積運賃を請求する権利があると認定して次のように述べている。

[202] ……契約は，その法的効果において，当該船舶が Bilbao またはその最寄りの安全に到達できる場所に向い，積荷後そこを出港し，Philadelphia へ向かうというものであった……。事実は，本船が積込を指示された場所は，そこで全量の積込をすれば，潮の状態如何にかかわらず，港の入口の浅瀬を越えられなくなる場所であった（114 F. at 261）。

The Silvercove, SMA 813A (Arb. at N. Y. 1976) 事件では，水中障害物がバースあるいはそれに隣接する場所にあり，本船の安全なる出港を妨げていた。その水中障害物と接触したために本船の舵に与えた損傷につき，傭船者は責任があると裁定された。

なお，Brooklyn 橋上流の碇泊場所が，マストが高くてその橋桁の下を通れない本船にとって非安全であると判断された *Mencke* v. *A Cargo of Java Sugar*, 187 U. S. 248 (1902) 事件，および仲裁審が「この担保条項は，港およびその付近が，傭船者の要求どおり本船がそこに行ったときに，当該船舶にとって安全でなければならないことを意味すると判断する」と述べた *The Caroline Horn*, SMA 649 (Arb. at N. Y. 1971) 事件および *The Magdalene*, SMA 579 (Arb. at N. Y. 1957) 事件各参照。

安全港担保義務は，地理的範囲においてかなり遠くまで及ぶものであると判示されている。*The Tropical Veneer*, SMA 1172 (Arb. at N. Y. 1977) 事件において，本船は Montreal を出港後，St. Lawrence 河を下ったときに，氷により損害を被った。仲裁審は，全員一致で，傭船者は損害に責任があると判示し，安全港担保義務が Montreal 港から225マイル下流まで延びることは意図されていないという傭船者の主張を退けた。仲裁審は，次のように述べた。

仲裁審は，傭船者が船主と本船に付与した安全港担保義務の必須の部分として本船の出入のための安全な接近水域に関して確立した法および習慣を無視すべしという傭船者の見解を受け入れることはできない。Amazon 河であれ，Mississippi 河であれ St. Lawrence 河であれ，各々の港の法的または地理的限界への接近の可能性に関する限り，すべては接近水域が港の奥または中間点に繋がる港の直

接の延長範囲である。われわれは，接近水域と港域を分離して，接近水域を無視することは安全港担保義務をまるで「そこへ行き，そこから出るために障害を克服できるならば，それは安全港である」という気分でまったく空虚な企てに化してしまうことであると考える。

そこでも，The Ross Isle, SMA 1340（Arb. at N.Y. 1979）事件で，仲裁審は，本船がMississippi河の港に転じた場合に，同河それ自身が安全港担保義務の範囲であると裁定した。

同様に，The Naiad, SMA 1177（Arb. at N.Y. 1977）事件で，仲裁人は，Mississippi河の南西水路の季節による喫水制限の結果，積込停止された貨物につき不積運賃を回収する権利があると判断した。仲裁審は，安全港の担保は，本船が積込をした河の中のバースだけでなく，河の入口をも含むものであると裁定した。

The Eastern Eagle, 1971 AMC 236（Arb. at N.Y. 1970）事件で，仲裁審は，本船をAmazon河のMacapaに配船する傭船者の命令を船主は拒絶する正当な理由があったと裁定した。当該船舶は同じ傭船契約による前航海の途次，そこで座礁したことがあった。さらに仲裁人は，その付近の正確なる海図がなく，航海支援設備は「不足し，その機能も不十分であり，そこにはブイもなく，Macapa付近の水深の変化を実際に知っているものがいないため，有効な水先案内も存在しない」と認定して，港は当該船舶にとって安全ではないと判断した。

しかしながら，安全港担保義務は「ありとあらゆる接近水域に危険がない」ことまでを意味しない（H. Schuldt v. Standard Fruit & Steamship Co., 1979 AMC 2470, 2477（S.D.N.Y. 1978））。本事案で，裁判所は，バースに通じる接近水域が安全である限り，バース近くの浅い水域の岩の多い浅瀬があっても，港は非安全とはならないと判示した（Trade Banner Line Inc. v. Caribbean Steamship Co., 521 F. 2d 229, 1975 AMC 2515（5th Cir. 1975）事件も参照）。その事件では，本船は安全に着桟した後に係船設備が壊れ，近くの浅瀬に座洲したので，バースは非安全ではないと判示された。

氷

現実のまたは予想される氷の状況により，港またはバースは非安全となるかもしれない。The Banja Luka, SMA 1293（Arb. at N.Y. 1979）事件で，氷の状況により港に接近できないのでバースは非安全であると判示された。The Bennington, SMA 940（Arb. at N.Y. 1975）事件で，氷の状況のゆえに，港は非安全であると判示された。前出解説の The Tropical Veneer 事件も参照。後出619頁の解説参照。

使用上の安全性

安全バースの担保は，要するにバースが当該船舶にとって安全であるという約束である。この担保条項での最も重要な要素は，傭船者が当該船舶に対してその積荷状態において十分な水深のあるバースを提供するという義務であると思われる。そしてThe Harding, SMA 959（Arb. at N.Y. 1975）事件では，船積バースの水深が足りなかったために当該船舶に生じた損害につき傭船者に責任があると判示された。本船がバースの水深不足のため船底接触したThe Federal Calumet, SMA 1667（Arb. at N.Y. 1982）事件で，同じ結論となった。Appeal of U.S. Lines Inc., 1977 AMC 318. 338（A.S.B.C.A. 1976）事件では，岸壁は明らかに破損状態にあり，垂直杭も横桁もなくなっていたため，本船がその岸壁にぶつかって損害を被ったのであるが，このようなバースへ配船したことによって，傭船者は，担保義務に違反したと判示さ

The Oceanic First, SMA 1158（Arb. at N. Y. 1977）事件で，同様に，仲裁人は，水中に没しているコンクリート台とともに，突堤の北東の角のむき出しで鋭利なコンクリート強化用鋼製角棒のためにバースは非安全であると裁定した。仲裁審は次のように注釈をつけた。

　　　本船が着桟する際の通常の推奨される手順により，本船が揚荷用の斜面台の中央線に入ったならば，本船は損害を被らなかったであろうという傭船者の主張は，幾分的をはずれている。傭船契約の安全バース条項は傭船者に安全なバースで，かつ安全に入出できるバースを提供する義務を負わせる。バースの物理的性格と Ocean First 号のような，そこに入る船舶の大きさを考慮して，状況如何では，ある船舶は，突堤の北東端において休止し回頭するためにそこを使わざるをえないと結論づけることは妥当と思われる。隣接の水中コンクリート台と同様に，この角の威嚇するような側面に対して何らかの保護装置がなければ船舶がそこに着桟するのに重大な危険となる。

　　ドック自体良好な状態であり，本船が強風下にドックの隔壁に接触した結果損害を生じた場合，傭船者はかかる損害につき責任はないと判断されている。これは損害がバースの非安全性によるものではなく，船主がその危険を負担する航海上の危険によるものであるという理論に基づいている（The Schiffbek, 1934 AMC 713, 716（Arb. at N. Y. 1934））。
　　一般的にいって，不良な気象条件は，港とかバースとかを，傭船者の担保条項の趣旨の上で非安全にはしないものである（Esso Standard Oil S. A. v. The Sabrina, 154 F. Supp. 720, 1957 AMC 691（D. C. Z. 1957）事件参照）。同事件で裁判所は，次のとおり判示している。

　　　当裁判所は，バースが契約条項に違反して非安全であったことが立証されたとは思わない。むしろ申立人の8吋パイプに損害を与えたのと同じ海上の危険の一つである自然現象たる暴風，すなわち不可抗力的できごとのために，当該船舶の損傷が生じたと考える……（1957 AMC at 700）。

204　The Stadt Schleswig, 1971 AMC 362（Arb. at N. Y. 1970）事件で，船主は，本船が揚荷完了後 Grindstone 港のバースから出るときに生じた本船損傷について傭船者は責任があると主張した。船主は損傷が傭船者の安全港担保義務違反の結果生じたものであると主張した。荷役中風力6・7程度の風に見舞われ，本船が岸壁を離れようとしているうちに係船索が切れた。仲裁審は傭船者の主張を受け入れた。当該船舶および同程度の大きさの他の多くの船舶が，以前何回も事故なく当該港に碇泊している。また，船長も数回当港に寄港している。さらに暴風は，数時間にもわたって発達しており，船長は暴風が最強に達する以前に岸壁を離れる十分な余裕があった。仲裁審はこの点につき次のとおり述べている。

　　　当仲裁審の意見では，世界中の最も安全と思われる港ですら，常時安全というわけではない。ほとんどの港が，暴風雨，ハリケーン，高波等の自然現象により一時的に非安全となりうる。このこと自体，港を非安全とするものでもなく，またいかなる時点でも，その港が非安全であると決め付けてしまうわけでもない。本傭船契約の意味する範囲内で，当仲裁審の関心があるのは，Stadt Schleswig 号と大きさおよび形状において同型とされる船舶にとっての Grindstone 港の安全性である。記録および証拠によれば，本傭船契約におけるように同船主の20回以上の寄港も含め Stadt Schleswig 号と同様の大きさ，喫水の船舶が数えきれないほど航海可能な期間 Grindstone 港に寄港している。そして港の記録は，当仲裁審がこの季節において港が非安全であると認定するに足るものではない。風が出るというような一時的現象は，予見しうる危険であり，慎重な対処と最悪の場合荒天を凌ぐために避難錨地に早期に船舶を出港せしめることを要するものにすぎない（1971 AMC at 365-366）。

一般原則として，港またはバースの通常のうねりや潮は安全港条項の目的から見て非安全な状態とはみなされない。したがって，The Maria G. L., SMA 2506（1988）事件で，仲裁人は，韓国のPohangでうねりによって切断された係船索についての船主の請求を退けた。仲裁審は，バースのうねりの状態はそこでの通常予想されるうねりと異ならず，港は非安全とならないと認定した。The Nea Tyhi, SMA 2571（1989）事件で，水深が全体的に減少した場合，「通常状態」の下で傭船契約の水深10.5メートルという安全バース担保は，違反とはされなかった。

危　　険

The Arietta Venizelos, 1973 AMC 1012（Arb. at N.Y. 1972）事件では，本船はTexacotime書式により傭船された。傭船者がリビアにおける積荷港を指定したところ，船主は本船を引き揚げた。その港はゲリラがタンカーを攻撃するおそれがあるという理由で，船体保険者の戦争保険における協会担保約定限外の場所とされていた。仲裁審は多数決をもって傭船者が指定した積荷港は危険地帯にある，したがって船主は，傭船者の安全港担保義務を理由として本船を引き揚げる正当な事由があると判断した。仲裁審は次のとおり述べている。

　　本傭船契約第3条に基づき，傭船者は「本船を安全港間および安全港においてのみ使用するべく相当の注意を払わなければならない」基本的義務がある。そして本船を非安全港に配船することが，傭船契約の基本的義務に違反することは疑う余地がない。……傭船者の契約違反に応じて，船主がとることのできるさまざまの方法を検討することは適当ではない。その一つの選ばれた方法，すなわち本船の引揚は認められるものであり，正当であった（1973 AMC at 1021-1022）。

The Amoco Texas City, 1979 AMC 690（Arb. at N.Y. 1977）事件も参照。

政治的危険

Pan Cargo Shipping Corp. v. United States, 234 F. Supp. 623, 1965 AMC 2649（S.D.N.Y. 1964），原審維持323 F. 2d 525, 1967 AMC 850（2d Cir. 1967），裁量上告拒絶389 U.S. 836 （1967）事件で，船主は，担保条項は傭船者によって指示された港が物理的にも政治的にも安全でなければならないことを意味していると言って争った。イスラエルに寄港した船舶に対するアラブのボイコットの結果，本船はRas Tanuraにおいて貨物油の積込を妨げられた。裁判所は，船主の立場を認める判例があることを認識しながら，「政治的に『安全でない』港において，本船について懸念される危険は，拿捕のようなもの，あるいは『没収の危険』のようなものと思われる」と判断した。裁判所はこのことを踏まえて，安全港の担保は，航海喪失の責任を傭船者に課するほど拡張させることはできないと判示した。裁判所は次のとおり述べた。

　　本件を取り巻く状況において，「安全港」というのは「アラブのボイコットによる積荷妨害の危険なく」という意味に捉えられるべきではない。当事者はそのような意味付けを考えていなかった。すなわち海軍はMemory I号のイスラエル向け航海をまったく知らなかったし，またHoustonでの税関申告の記入によってそのことを通知されてもいなかった。「安全」という文言は，傭船契約の成立した時点において海軍が同意した条項の中には含まれておらず，申立人の仲立人によって追加されたものであって，船主から傭船者への危険の移転のような効果を与えるべきものではない。傭船契約の他の部分は「安全」なる文言が単に物理的安全性の意味のみで使われていることを示している。海軍がイスラエル向けの航海の事実を知らなかったという点も含めてすべての事実を認識した上で，申立人も同船船長もRas Tanuraの指定を受け入れ，何ら抗議することなくそこに向かったのである（234 F. Supp. at 638）。

港が非安全であるとの請求が The Universe Explorer, 1985 AMC 1014 (Arb. at N.Y. 1984) 事件で提起された。船主は，傭船者がナイジェリアで貨油の積込を本船に指図したときに，傭船者は政治的に非安全な港を指定したと主張した。本船は，南アフリカの Cape Town 沖で，船用品を積み込んだため，寄港の6週間前に，南アフリカとの接触を禁止するナイジェリア法に基づきナイジェリア入港を拒絶された。船主と傭船者の双方は，ナイジェリアの規則を承知していた。しかし，船主だけが，南アフリカ寄港の事実を知っていた。仲裁審は，船主のみが南アフリカ寄港を知っていたのであるから，船主はナイジェリアが積込許可を拒絶する危険を負担すると裁定した。

適切な航海操船技術による回避可能性

船長の適切な航海操船技術により危険を回避できるのであれば，港またはバースは非安全ではない。有能な船長がその状況において適切な注意を払って，港またはバースに存する危険を避けると期待されるかどうかが，その基準である。

裁判所や仲裁人は，港またはバースが非安全であるとの理由で，そこへ入るのを拒絶する船長の決定に非常に大幅な自由を広く認めてきた。前出 Atkins 事件で，裁判所は，自らの判断で本船にとり非安全港への入港を拒絶する船長の権利を重要視した。他に例として，The Regent Ranger, SMA 1564 (1981) 事件で，仲裁人は，船長は岸壁側の水深が十分でなく，岸壁の長さも当該船舶に不十分であり，風に曝され岩に接触すると判断したので，船長は St. Croix のバースに着くのを拒絶する正当な事由があると裁定した。The Omina, SMA 3116 (Arb. at N.Y. 1994) 事件も参照。

しかし，損害が港またはバースの非安全な状態ではなく船長の過失により生じた場合，船主には責任がある。座礁はその港の非安全な状態ではなく航海過失の結果であると判示した The Cepheus, 1990 AMC 1058 (Arb. at N.Y. 1990) 事件を例証として参照。非安全港またはバースの状態と船長の過失が損害または賠償される損失の共同原因である場合，責任は船主と傭船者の間で，分担される。

過度の速度と曳船なしで着桟を船長が決定した結果，岸壁と衝突したと判示された The Maryland Trader, SMA 849 (1974) 事件を参照。The Michael C. Lemos, SMA 1906 (1983) 事件では，水先人契約に従って船主に帰すべき水先人の過失により水路の外で座礁したと多数意見で判示された。

206 The Medita, SMA 2347 (Arb. at N.Y. 1986) 事件で，仲裁審は，肥料の揚荷中に大きなうねりにより突堤に本船がぶつかり生じた船体損傷についての船主の損害賠償請求を否定した。仲裁審は，問題の突堤は，安全バースであり，船体に生じた損傷は，いずれも船長が，錨地へ移動して本船を保護する適切な手段をとらなかったためであると認定した。

船長が座礁をおそれて積込を拒否する理由は，合理的でなければならない。The Konkar Victory, SMA 1798 (Arb. at N.Y. 1983) 事件で，仲裁審は，港長，利害関係のない者，公平な者によるバースの安全性の保証にもかかわらず，船長は積込拒否の際に不適切に行動したと判示した。仲裁審は，船長は，自らの主張と懸念を裏付けるため，独立の検査人を招喚すべきであったと述べた。

指定港またはバースの受入れ

「安全港」の担保にもかかわらず，船主または船長が，当該航海において，港が非安全にな

る地方の事情をすべて知った上で積地または揚地の指定を受け入れた場合，傭船者は免責されることがある（*Tweedie Trading Co.* v. *New York & Boston Dyewood Co.*, 127 F. 278 (2d Cir. 1903)，裁量上告拒絶，193 U.S. 669 (1903))。

　例えば，自らが非安全と考えた港へ抗議せずに入る船長の行為は，安全港担保を放棄する結果となる。たぶん，この点に関する古典的判例は，前出 *Atkins* v. *Fibre Disintegrating Co.* 事件である。傭船者は，「……2番目の安全港へ配船する権利」を持ち，この選択権を行使した。傭船者の選択した港は Port Morant であった。裁判所は，珊瑚礁が延びて港の狭い入口を横切っており，*Elizabeth Hamilton* 号の大きさの船舶は，強い一様に吹く風があるときのみ通過できたので Port Morant は安全ではないと認定した。事故発生時，本船は安全に Port Morant に安全に入港したが，出港時に珊瑚礁にぶつかり，結果として，船体に損害を生じた。港は非安全であったがゆえに，Benedict 判事は，船主にはそこへ行く義務はなかったし，「船長には，傭船契約上の権利の範囲内でそのような港の指定を拒絶する正当な事由が存したことと思われる」と記した（2 Fed. Cas. at 79)。

　しかし，決定的事実は，船長は港の安全性につき抗議しなかったということであった。裁判所によると，船長は自らの行動により，Port Morant を安全として受け入れ，安全港を提供する傭船者の保証に依拠する権利を放棄した。Benedict 判事は，次のように述べた。

　　そのとき，指定港は，この本船にとり非安全港とみなされ，傭船契約上の特権の範囲内ではない場合，そのとき船長の異議を知らしめることは，船主の唯一の代表者としての船長の義務であった。船長は異議を申し立てなかったので，船長は拒絶する権利を放棄したとみなされなければならない。そして，条件が放棄されたのであるから，その違反に対する訴訟はいまや維持できない（2 Fed. Cas. at 79)。

　Bunge Corp. v. *The Furness Bridge*, 588 F. 2d 790, 1977 AMC 2109 (5th Cir. 1977)，裁量上告拒絶 435 U.S. 924 (1978) 事件，*Delta Commodities Inc.* v. *The Jo Oak*, 1990 AMC 820, 826 (E.D.La. 1989) 事件も参照。

　The Zoe Christina, SMA 2777 (Arb. at N.Y. 1991) 事件で，傭船契約は，傭船者の安全港・バースの担保を傭船者の過失により生じた損失に制限した。さらに，傭船契約は，傭船者は「船長または船主の側の相当の注意の行使により避けられたであろう」損失につき責任はないと定めていた。仲裁審は，船主が本船を座礁したと申し立てた時間に，および場所で本船が座礁したという証拠がないという理由で，損害に関する船主の請求を却下した。しかし，仲裁審は，たとえ本船がその場所で座礁したとしても，(1)傭船者の指示は，「過失」に至らない，(2)水先人と船長の双方は港の正確な喫水と港の特質を知って，留保または異議なくそこへ航行したとの理由で，傭船契約に従って傭船者には，座礁についての責任はないであろうと認定した。

　The Eva Borden, SMA 219 (Arb. at N.Y.) 事件では，仲裁審は，錨地が安全でないという船主の主張は，「船長が傭船者の碇泊指示を完全に受け入れたという理由があれば，」その根拠を失うと裁定した（前出 *Pan Cargo Shipping Corp.* v. *United States* 事件と *The Breynton*, 1934 AMC 1473 (Arb. at N.Y. 1933) 事件も参照）。

　傭船契約が一つの指定港への1航海である場合，船主は当該港は安全であるとして受け入れたと見なされる（*The Naiad*, 1978 AMC 2049, 2056 (Arb. at N.Y. 1977) 事件と *The Challenger*, 1978 AMC 2037, 2044-2045 (Arb. at N.Y. 1978) 事件を参照）。

過失の介在

　船長の過失の介在によって事故が発生したことを傭船者が立証した場合、傭船者は安全港担保義務違反を免れることがある (*American President Lines Ltd.* v. *United States*, 208 F. Supp. 573, 1968 AMC 830 (N. D. Cal. 1961))。

　Venore Transp. Co. v. *Oswego Shipping Corp.*, 498 F. 2d 469, 1974 AMC 827 (2d Cir.), 裁量上告拒絶 419 U. S. 998 (1974) 事件では、船主は、荒天下、錨地に向け沖出しをしようとして岸壁に衝突し発生した損害につき、その請求を認められた。傭船者は、衝突が船長の過失の介在によるものであると主張して責任を免れようとした。船長は着岸前に岸壁を検査しており、1個のポンツーンが欠けていても着桟は安全であるということを傭船者の代理店から保証されていた。ポンツーンは、船舶がコンクリートの岸壁に当たるのを防ぐためであった。裁判所は、「港内の諸条件に詳しくない船長は、傭船者代理店の為した保証に頼る権利があり」傭船者は、安全バース担保義務違反の責任があると判示した。

　しかしながら、*The Sabrina*, 1957 AMC 691, 695 (D. C. Z. 1957) 事件において、裁判所は、座礁の原因は、船長が正しく投錨し繋船しなかった過失にあると判断した。同様に、ハリケーンの間に繋船索が切れた際、本船が損傷を被った *Trade & Transport Inc.* v. *Caribbean S. S. Co.*, 384 F. Supp. 782, 1975 AMC 1065 (S. D. Tex. 1974) 事件で、船主の航海傭船者に対する損害賠償請求は否定された。裁判所は、損害の原因は、岸壁所有者の助言に基づいてなした船長の、本船を守るに不十分な、別のバースに移動するという誤った判断によって生じたものであると判示した (*Nassau Sand & Gravel Co.* v. *Red Star Towing and Transp. Co.*, 62 F. 2d 356 (2d Cir. 1932) 事件も参照)。

　The Roman Bernard, SMA 1202 (Arb. at N. Y. 1978) 事件は、荒天の中、突堤から本船が突然離れた後、本船の座礁により生じた損失についての船主の請求が関係していた。問題となったバースは、ニカラグアの東海岸に位置する直接外洋に面した碇泊地の突堤であった。仲裁審は、バースは外海に面した碇泊地突堤として、「風、海、うねりの自然力」とよくある気象の急変に「危険なほどに曝される」ことに注目した一方で、多数意見で、バースは非安全ではないと裁定した。それどころか、多数意見は次のように述べた。

　　……そこで係船した本船の船長は、本船が適切に固縛され、Puerto Isabel 地区にとり非日常的できごとではない気象の急変があった場合に備え即刻出港可能な状態にしておくことを保証する特別な責任を負う。雨を伴う激しい突風の間、比較的浅い水面は風で悪化し、うねりを生じて、本船のそばで波うち、しばしば索を切断するので、Puerto Isabel 突堤の周りの地区は急速にかなりの影響を受ける。そういう事態となった場合、船長の責任は即時にバースを離れて、本船にとり深くて広い水域の安全な退避所を目指し、機関を操作して、嵐を無事に乗り切ることである。

　しかし、仲裁審は、多数意見で、右舷の錨の位置を適切に定めなかったので、船長はその過失により確実かつ迅速な離岸方法で、突堤に本船を係留することができなかったと、認定した。さらに、暴風が生じた場合、船長はバースから即時離岸せずに、着埠のままで、無事に乗り切ろうとした。突堤に留まるという船長の誤った決定と適切な投錨をできなかったことが、損失を惹起したと判示され、傭船者は責任を免れた。

　The Zaneta, 1970 AMC 807 (Arb. at N. Y. 1970) 事件において、1回目の座礁により、碇泊場所が安全でないということを認識すべきであったにもかかわらず、積込を続け、2回目に座礁した事件につき、船主は、一切の損害賠償請求を否定された。

　The Pyrgos, SMA 896 (Arb. at N. Y. 1974) 事件で、Pointe-a-Pierre における座礁の結果

生じた損害の回復請求を,船主はやはり否定された。仲裁審は碇泊場所が安全であり,そして座礁は船長の過失によって生じたものであると判断した。仲裁審は次のとおり述べている。

　当仲裁審の意見では,船長は,PYRGOS 号の積込および低潮時の離岸を安全に行うために,もっと多くのことができた。船長は港に精通しており,船長に提示された Texaco 海図は,操船区域が限られていることと,バースの西側に危険な洲があることを示していたし,船長は自分で測深をすることもできた。船長は低潮時に離岸する必要はなかった。この点はまったく船長の自由裁量に任されており,船長の全権限下にあった。

　裁判所は本船の損害は,バースを離れるにあたって,船長および水先人の過失の結果生じたものであり,ターミナル自身は安全であったと判示した Cook Inlet v. Amer. T. & P., 1976 AMC 160 (S. D. N. Y. 1976) 事件も参照。

　同じように,The Itel Taurus, SMA 1220 (Arb. at N. Y. 1977) 事件で,船主はバースでの本船の座礁により被った損傷の賠償請求を否定された。仲裁審は,座礁は非安全状態で生じたのではなく,船長が当局から受け取った水深の表示を超えた喫水で本船の着桟を選択したとき,適切な航海操船技術の原則を無視したことにより生じたと,認定した (The Caribbean Nostalgia, SMA 1788 (Arb. at N. Y. 1983))。

　前出引用事案は,船長または水先人が完璧な水準を求められることを意味するわけではない。むしろ,船主に責任を負わせる過失の介在の事実がなければならない。仲裁審は,The Oceanic First, SMA 1158 (Arb. at N. Y. 1977) 事件で,バースの角の防舷材のない角棒に本船が接触した際に,被った損害につき傭船者に責任ありと判示し,次のように述べた。

　われわれは,完璧な過失のない着桟の努力により接触を避けえたことを否定できないが,操船上の過失が事故に大いに寄与しているとは考えない。しかし,そのような余裕のない水準が,船長または,水先人に要求されているわけではない。

　The Solomon, SMA 3107 (Arb. at N. Y. 1990) 事件で,仲裁審は,傭船者の非安全バースへの航行の指図に適合しようと努力して船長が取った行動は不適当ではなく,過失の介在を構成しないと判断して,傭船者は航海傭船契約のバース安全担保に違反したと判示した。

寄与過失

　船長および傭船者双方に過失がある場合,その過失の割合に応じて損害を分担することもあり得る (United States v. Reliable Transfer Co. Inc., 421 U. S. 397 (1975) ; Cities Service Transp. Co. v. Gulf Refining Co., 79 F. 2d 521 1935 AMC 1513 (2d Cir. 1935) ; Paragon Oil Co. v. Republic Tankers S. A., 310 F. 2d 169, 1963 AMC 158 (2d Cir. 1962) ; Ore Carriers of Liberia, Inc. v. Navigen Corp., 332 F. Supp. 72, 1971 AMC 505 (S. D. N. Y. 1969), 原審維持 435 F. 2d 549, 1971 AMC 513 (2d Cir. 1970) 各事件参照)。

　The Oceanic First, SMA 1054 (Arb. at N. Y. 1976) 事件で,仲裁審は,本船がその第 9 回目の新潟寄港の際に被った損害について,船主,傭船者共に責任があり,その損害を 50:50 で分割すべきであると判断した。すなわち,同港に以前寄港しているのであるから,船主,傭船者共に,同港において通常予想することができる状態を,知り,かつ知るべきであった。ところが両者共,船長からの引き続いて寄港することに対する抗議を無視することにしたのである。仲裁審は次のように述べた。

両者共に計算された危険を冒し，失敗したという点で責任がある。船主が，契約上の安全港，安全バース担保に依存できるといっても，それは，明らかに存在するであろうと思われる非安全性あるいは危険状態を無視した場合にまで，及ぶものではない。同様に，このような担保を与えることは，かかる明白な非安全あるいは危険状態が存在せず，また将来も存在しないであろうということを，保証していることを意味する。当該損害は，両当事者が，この季節に新潟に寄港することによって発生するであろう危険を，相互に評価しなかったために，発生したものである。

Appeal of U. S. Lines Inc., 1977 AMC 318, 343（A. S. B. C. A. 1976）事件の連邦上訴裁判所においても，同様の結論が出された。同事件は，明らかに岸壁が不良状態になっており，風浪が予想されることを十分知っているにもかかわらず，本船が着桟したというものであった。

Board of Commissioners v. *The Space King*, 1978 AMC 856（E. D. La. 1978）事件で，本船は，川の水面が低下したため積荷バースで座礁した，そして川底から離れたときに，隣接のドックに損傷を与えた。裁判所は，本船を座礁させる結果となる方法による貨物の積込を阻止するのは船長の責任であるから，船主は過失で70パーセントの責任があると判示した。さらに，船長は変化する川の状態により引き起こされる本船に対する危険を承知しているべきだった。川の状態に関する入手可能な情報を傭船者の代理店は取得できなかったので，傭船者は，30パーセントの責めを負うべしと判示された。

保 守 条 項

"36. 1. That the Owners shall provide and pay for all provisions, wages and consular shipping and discharging fees of the Crew ; shall pay for the
37. insurance of the vessel, also for all the cabin, deck, engine-room and other necessary stores, including boiler water and maintain her class and keep
38. the vessel in a thoroughly efficient state in hull, machinery and equipment for and during the service."

「1．船主は，乗組員の一切の食料品・給料・乗船地および下船地における領事館費を準備して，その費用を支払い，船舶保険料，ならびに船室・甲板・機関室その他に必要なすべての船用品（罐水を含む）の費用を支払うほか，本船の船級を維持し，傭船期間中，船体・機関および装備を完全な稼働状態に置くものとする。」

給　　料

この文脈での「給料」は，乗組員が自己の役務につき合法的に権利がある報酬を意味する。The Manhattan Prince [1985] 1 Lloyd's Rep. 140事件で，Leggatt 判事は，国際運輸労連（I.T.F.）がボイコットによって船主に押しつけようとした高い賃金を支払わないことで，船主はこの条項に違反しているとの傭船者の主張を Shelltime 3書式第5条の類似の条項に基づいて退け，乗組員の給料は合法的な権利がある報酬を意味すると判示した。この事案の事実関係の全要約については，後出438頁参照。

船舶の保険

船主が船舶保険を支払うとのニューヨーク・プロデュース書式の36/37行の条項は，保険につき「自己の計算において航海する場合と同一の」責任を船主に課する第26条で強化されている。後出614頁に述べているように，これらの条項は，船主に船体保険同様に戦争保険も付保することを要求している。

傭船者が船主にある種の保険料を償還することを定める追加条項の効果に関する解説は，後出614頁から618頁を参照。

保 守 条 項

この義務は，全傭船期間継続し，5行，22行記載の傭船始期における堪航性担保義務を補っている（この点，前出147頁参照）。

本条における船主の義務は，絶対的なものではない。点検，検査，新替，修繕等を慎重に計画し，遂行することを怠った結果，船舶，機関または装備が不調となった場合に船主の義務違反となる。しかし，故障の発生や不堪航になったということだけでは，義務違反にはならない。Tynedale Shipping v. Anglo-Soviet Shipping (1936) 41 Com. Cas. 206事件で，Roche 卿は，かかる保守義務は「なんらかの危険や原因が介在して，本船が航海目的に沿った性能を出

せなくなるようなことがあっても，船主は，本船を保守し続けるという絶対的な約束，あるいは担保をしたことにならない」と述べている（*Giertsen* v. *Turnbull*, 1908 S.C. 1101 事件を参照。保守義務条項の他の類型に関しては，後出参照）。

傭船期間中に，船舶，機関または装備が不調となった場合，船主は，本条項によって，相当[212]の時間内に船舶を修復するため合理的措置を講ずる義務を持つ。Greer 判事は，*Snia* v. *Suzuki* (1924) 17 LLL. Rep. 78 事件で（同判例集88頁），「船主の義務は，就航中の本船を恒常的にかかる状態に置くということではなく，本船の船体および機関が十分に稼働しない状態になった場合，相当の時間内に，本船を元の状態に修復する合理的処置を講ずることである」と述べた。

傭船始期の堪航性担保と同様に，本条項に基づく船主の義務は，条件（a condition）ではなく，中間的義務である。したがって，傭船者は，この義務の違反すべてにおいて，傭船契約を解除されたものとして扱う権利を有するわけではない（*The Hongkong Fir* [1961] 1 Lloyd's Rep. 159 事件での Salmon 判事の判決参照。この判決は控訴院で認められた，[1961] 2 Lloyd's Rep. 478 と前出148頁から150頁）。船主の違反が契約の全目的を実質的に傭船者から奪うほど重大であること——例えば，機関故障の修復が，単に不合理な期間を要するというだけではなく，契約を履行不能にするほど長くかかるか，または，かかる見込であること——，を立証できないならば，保守に関する義務の違反に対して傭船者は，損害賠償で救済されるだけである（*The Hongkong Fir* [1961] 2 Lloyd's Rep. 478 事件における控訴院 Sellers 卿判事の判決（同判例集489頁）参照）。この事件において，Salmon 判事は，修理の遅れた理由として，傭船者の契約解除を認めるには，修繕期間の長さよりむしろ修繕による遅れが契約目的を達成不能にするほど重大でなければならないとする見解によって *Snia* v. *Suzuki* (1924) 18 Ll. L. Rep. 333 事件での判決（前出151頁）と調和をとっている。同判事は，「その事件の事実関係は例外的なものである。傭船者は，船主が堪航性回復に再三失敗したことから，船主が回復に成功する見込がまったくないと信ずるに足る根拠を持つに至った」と述べた（[1961] 1 Lloyd's Rep. 159（同判例集174頁）。[1982] 1 Lloyd's Rep. 570 と前出150頁の *The Hermosa* 事件も参照）。

保守条項のその他の類型

ニューヨーク・プロデュース書式の保守条項は，絶対的義務よりは軽度の義務を船主に課しているけれども，その義務が（免責条項が適用される場合は別として），絶対的であると規定することもできる。例えば，*The Saxon Star* [1957] Lloyd's Rep. 271 事件で，「堅牢強固であらゆる点で運送業務に適し，海上の危険を除き，航海を通じて，そのような状態を維持すること」という記載条項は，絶対的義務を生ずると，控訴院は判示した。この保守条項は，傭船始期の堪航性担保の一部として，記載され，また，それ自体に，保守義務に対する海上の危険免責の文言を含んでいた。絶対的義務より軽度の義務を課すつもりであれば，保守条項免責文言は，不要であったと思われる。Parker 卿が述べているように（同判例集280頁），「保守義務の性質は使用文言どおりに解釈しなければならない」。

（*Adamastos Shipping* v. *Anglo-Saxon Petroleum*（*The Saxon Star*）[1957] 1 Lloyd's Rep. 271 (C.A.) および [1958] 1 Lloyd's Rep. 73 (H.L.) の事実関係は，後出594頁に詳述されている）

NYPE 93

　ニューヨーク・プロデュース書式の1993年版は，船主の第1条の義務を再編成し，「職員および部員からなる全定員を維持する」という明示の義務を追加している。前出9頁の英文書式の第6条78行から82行と54頁参照。

213 米　国　法

　保守条項は，前文中に規定された堪航性の明示的担保を補強し，傭船契約期間を通して，本船を堪航状態に維持する義務を船主に課するものである。この担保は，傭船契約における各航海の発航時に本船が堪航性を有するか，あるいは傭船契約に規定があれば，船主が，各航海前に船舶の堪航性につき相当の注意を尽くした場合にのみ，充足される（*Luckenbach* v. *McCahan Sugar Co.*, 248 U.S. 139（1918））。この事件において，最高裁は，この担保を次のように解明している。

　　船主と Insular Line との関係では，本来の堪抗性担保義務は，本船を傭船者に引き渡したときに終り，傭船者が問題としている保守条項は，各航海の始期における堪航性担保義務を課すものではなく，単に傭船期間中，船体，機関の修繕費用支払義務を定めたものであるという主張がなされた。しかしこの条項の文言や定期傭船契約の性格から見て，この主張は支持できない。傭船契約には，本船が「引渡時，堅牢［かつ］強固である」こと，船主は，――本船の保守費用を支払うのではなく――「運送業務のため，傭船期間中，船体，機関を十分な稼働状態に維持する」と明白に表示されている。本船を稼働状態に維持する義務が，契約によって課せられているのは，定期傭船契約が単一航海の傭船契約と同様，船舶の賃貸借ではないからである。いずれの契約においても，保守修繕は，傭船者が管理しうる問題ではない。運航中，船主が相当の注意を尽くせば発見しえた不堪航によって，損失が生ずれば，傭船者は荷主に対し無制限の責任を負う。そこで傭船者は，自己防衛のために，各航海の始期における無制限の堪航性担保を要求するのである（248 U.S. at 149-50）。

The Fort Gaines, 21 F. 2d 865, 1927 AMC 1778（D. Md. 1927）；*Strong* v. *Unites States*, 154 U.S. 632（1878）；*Mondella* v. *The Elie V.*, 223 F. Supp. 390（S. D. N. Y. 1963）；*The Captain John*, 1973 AMC 2005（Arb. at N. Y. 1973）各事件参照。
　貨物に関する限り，船主は相当の注意を尽くすという他に転嫁できない義務を課せられているが，貨物以外の事項については，保守条項が，同様の義務を課しているとは，通常解釈されない。すなわち，*The Bjorneford*, 271 F. 682, 683（2d Cir. 1921）事件では，本船が入渠中，プロペラに亀裂が発見されその取付中，造船所の不注意で，取り替えようとした予備のプロペラに損傷が生じ，新しいプロペラの鋳造を必要とした。そのため，本船は2週間遅延した。この不稼働期間の損失を回収しようとする傭船者の訴えは，不稼働が造船所の不注意によるものであって，船主は傭船契約に違反していないという理由により棄却された。傭船契約の義務履行にあたって，船主に要求されていることは，「船舶を運送業務に十分な稼働状態に戻すべく，合理的かつ当然の配慮を払うことである」。裁判所によれば，信用のある十分設備の整った造船所を使用することで，船主は，この義務を果たしたことになると言うのである。
　The Argo Leader, SMA 2065（Arb. at N. Y. 1985）事件で，5年間の定期傭船契約の4年目に，本船はオフハイヤーとなる機関故障を生じた。検査人の報告書に基づき，傭船者は，船主は本船の堪航性を回復できない，または回復しようとしないとの結論を出し，本船がまだ修理作業中に傭船契約を破棄した。仲裁審は，契約破棄は時期尚早で不適当であると裁定した。仲裁審は，船主は堪航性と準備完了の要件に応じる機会の権利があり，本船の状態を確認する検査を遂行する前に船主が準備完了通知を出すまで，傭船者は待たねばならないと述べた。
　船舶が，船級を保持しているというだけでは，堪航性があることにはならず，船主が，船級
214 協会から堪航証明を得たというだけでは，相当の注意を尽くしたことにはならない（*Ionian S. S. Co.* v. *United Distillers of America, Inc.*, 236 F. 2d 78（5th Cir. 1956）；*Petition of South-*

ern Transp. Co., 211 F. Supp. 940 (E. D. Va. 1963) 各事件参照)。

　船級協会の証書は，堪航性の「一応の prima facie」証拠として認容されてきており，それは，COGSA が適用されない場合，不堪航の立証の負担を傭船者に転嫁している。*The Seaford*, 1975 AMC 1553 (Arb. at N. Y. 1975) 事件は，COGSA が傭船契約中に摂取されていない場合における，この立証の負担のもたらす困難性に，傭船者が直面した極端な例である。同事件で，荷主は，Gencon 書式による航海傭船契約に基づき，鋼材輸送のため本船を傭船したが，本船は座礁した。仲裁審は，COGSA の不適用を認めて，傭船者は，座礁が「船主自身相当の注意を尽くすことを怠った」ために生じたことを立証しなければならないと判断し，さらに，仲裁審は，船級証書の存在は，堪航性の決定的証拠ではないが，その反証の負担を傭船者に負わせるに足る一応の証拠となると述べた。傭船者は，座礁が，船主の不適当な配乗と無線方向探知器の調整不十分により生じたことを立証しようとした。仲裁審は，傭船者の主張を裏付ける証拠はなく，座礁の近因は，船主に責任のない航海過失であると裁定した。

船艙清掃費用の責任

　傭船契約の期間中，船主は各航海の開始時点で船舶と貨物艙を堪航性ある状態にする義務がある。船舶のある状態のために必要な船艙清掃費用は，船主の負担である。例えば，錆片や塗料片を除去して船艙を清掃しなければならない場合，船主は生じた費用と喪失時間につき責任がある (*The Bjorn Ragne*, SMA 1298 (Arb. at N. Y. 1979), *The Pacsea & Pacsun*, SMA 746 (Arb. at N. Y. 1972) 各事件参照)。しかし，傭船者の積んだ前航荷の残滓のために船艙を清掃する必要がある場合，その費用と時間は傭船者の負担である (*The Long Hope*, SMA 2664 (Arb. at N. Y. 1990) 事件参照)。

変化する法的要件

　長期傭船契約の場合に生じるたいへん困難な問題は，旗国または航路定限内の諸国の法的要件の変化に従って船舶の保守を行う船主の義務である。新しい要件を課する法律が傭船期間中に施行となる場合，船主と傭船者との関係にどんな影響があるのだろうか。新しい要件に応じるため船舶に巨大な費用または大きな資本的改善を必要とする場合，特に，この問題は難しくなる。

　この問題が関与する事案は，常に関与する個別の事情しだいである。ある場合には，契約履行不能の原則が適用されよう。当事者が個別の要件の危険を予想もしておらず，また当事者間でその危険の負担を配分しておらずに，傭船契約を継続履行するための費用があまりにも巨額で航海が商業的に実行不可能となる場合，この原則が適用されよう (後出480頁の解説参照)。

　関与する要素により傭船契約が履行不能にならない場合，考慮すべき主な要素は，変化した法の要件が一方ではかなりの資本的改善を，または他方では，傭船期間中要求されるかも知れないと船主が通常予期する保守項目を要求しているか否かということである。資本的改善を要求する例では，判決が出されたいくつかの事案から船主には応じるべき傭船契約上の義務はないと思われる。これは，船主が船舶を保守すべく相当の注意を尽くす義務を有する場合に，特に真実であるように思われる。保守項目の事例において，船主の船舶保守義務は明白であろう。

　The Endeavor, 1978 AMC 1742 (Arb. at N. Y. 1977) 事件で，傭船者は，豪州航路に必要な船艙内への特殊な梯子の据付義務が傭船契約に基づき船主にあるという要求を実現した。傭

船契約は，ニューヨーク・プロデュース書式で，5年間であった。本船は1973年6月に傭船者に引き渡された。1977年5月に傭船者は，船主に豪州港湾労組の要求する「WWF梯子」の設置を要求した。仲裁審は，多数意見で，傭船者の要求に正当事由があると裁定し，次のように述べた。

この論争は，人命の安全と環境保全に関する不断の技術革新と世界的関心の時代に船主と傭船者の間の義務と責任の分離という微妙なとはいえ多様な主題に言及している。この書面の裁定は，審問期間の最終段階の決定を正式のものとし，純化するために，そのときに要請された決定であった。

仲裁審の多数意見は，次のように考える。「WWF梯子の要求により *Endeavor* 号に既設の艙内梯子の形，意匠，おそらく場所の修正・変更が明確に必要となる。しかしながらこの仕様変更は構造的変更ではない。船主には傭船契約が要求する方法で履行する本船の能力をそのままに保守する義務が残る」。この点に関して，本船は傭船契約上の地理的許容範囲内で航行し，この契約により許容される適法な貨物を運送することができなければならない。WWF梯子の要求は，それが無視された場合，WWFがいる豪州港で，艙内にWWF港湾労働者の存在を必要とする貨物に制限を加えるものである（1978 AMC at 1764-1767）。

船主は保守項目として消火装置の費用を負担すべきであると判示した *The Guldborg*, 1932 AMC 1206（S. D. N. Y. 1932）事件も参照。船主は船積港の規則の遵守に必要な本船の巻き上げ装置の修理費用に責任があると判示した *The Amerocean*, 1952 AMC 1559（Arb. at N. Y. 1952）事件も参照。

The Stolt Lion, SMA 1188（Arb. at N. Y. 1977）事件で，傭船者は，船主はIMCO（現在のIMO）推奨によるオランダの省令が求める高度な音声警報装置を装備しなければならないと主張した。傭船者は，次の傭船契約の条項に基づいて要求した。

本船は，国または国際機関等により示された化学溶剤の輸送の要件をいつも満たさなければならない……。船主は，通常の経年劣化・損耗を免責とするが，船舶と属具をこの傭船契約による引渡時と同様に保守するため，相当の注意を尽くさなければならない。

しかし，仲裁審は，全員一致で，この条項により船主は，オランダでの本船の使用に必要な事実上資本的改善である費用の負担を要求されないと判示した。仲裁審によると，

定期傭船契約の諸条項に基づき，船主は傭船者に特定の船舶，すなわち傭船者が想定している特定の航海に適している船舶を提供する契約上の義務を受け入れた。船舶の図面による事前承認と関連して，本定期傭船契約に基づき本船を受け取る際に，傭船者は引渡時に予定航海に本船が適合していることと，傭船のための交渉での仕様と要件に本船が合致していることを確認した。「この傭船期間中そういう状態で，本船を保守する」という船主の担保は，継続的な担保であるが，仲裁審は音声警報装置の装備と購入がこの担保に分類されるとは考えなかった。仲裁審の意見によると，本船の状態に関連したすべての他の条項を注意深く読むと，船主に音声警報装置のような備品を設置する責任を配分していない。そういう装置の購入と装備は，たとえ政府間規則により要求されようとも，その性質上，資本的改善であり，船舶の質の格上げであって，保守項目ではない。

[216] *The Angantyr*, 1971 AMC 2503（Arb. at N. Y. 1971）事件では，本船は1960 SOLAS（海上人命安全）条約の要求する承認済穀物積込図を所持しておらず，本船に穀物を積載するには，1番艙に追加隔壁の構築が必要であった。仲裁審は，船主はこの費用につき傭船者に対して責任がないと裁定した。

傭船者が果たしていない損害の立証責任の問題はまったく別として，本船にSOLAS規則に基づく積載許可に適合した書類の不提供につき，船主に責任ありとするために，傭船者が根拠とするものは何も当該定期傭船契約に含まれていないということが問題の核心である。仲裁人は，他の定期傭船契約では明確にこの要件を記載する場合があることを承知している。当該傭船契約を成約した時点で，傭船者（または，船主）は穀物を想定していなかったという単なる事実によって，傭船契約にその点についての記載がないとき，どう考えても撒積穀物積載用装備の負担が傭船者から船主に転嫁することはありえない（1971 AMC at 2507）。

この問題は，また The Ultramar, 1981 AMC 1831（Arb. at N. Y. 1981）事件で取り上げられた。本船は，1973年建造，米国籍，約82,000DWTの鉱油兼用船であった。1973年に，本船はMobiltime書式で10年間傭船された。傭船契約の履行期間中，「港とタンカーの安全に関する法」（米国）が発効した。同法に基づき，本船はとりわけイナート・ガス（不活性気体）設備を1981年6月1日までに装備するように要求された。仲裁人は，「港とタンカーの安全に関する法」が要求する変更を履行することを船主が要求されるか否かを裁定するように求められた。仲裁審は，多数意見で，船主は原油タンカーとして航行する能力のある本船を提供し保守する義務があるとの理由により変更を履行しなければならないと判示した。仲裁審は，多数意見で，本船が「港とタンカーの安全に関する法」に適合することを要求する明示の文言は傭船契約にないが，傭船契約条項に基づき，船主は，傭船期間中本船を「原油かつ・または黒物石油製品の輸送にあらゆる面で適合した」状態に保守するのに相当の注意を尽くす義務があることに注目した。本船が「港とタンカーの安全に関する法」に適合しない場合，本船は原油を輸送することを許可されないので，装備できなければ，船主は本船を保守する義務に違反していることになる。

傭船者の手配および費用負担

"39. 2. That the Charterers shall provide and pay for all the fuel except as otherwise agreed, Port Charges, Pilotages, Agencies, Commissions,
40. Consular Charges (except those pertaining to the Crew) and all other usual expenses except those before stated, but when the vessel puts into
41. a port for causes for which vessel is responsible, then all such charges incurred shall be paid by the Owners. Fumigations ordered because of
42. illness of the crew to be for Owners account. Fumigations ordered because of cargoes carried or ports visited while vessel is employed under this
43. charter to be for Charterers account. All other fumigations to be for Charterers account after vessel has been on charter for a continuous period
44. of six months or more.
45.   Charterers are to provide necessary dunnage and shifting boards, also any extra fittings requisite for a special trade or unusual cargo, but
46. Owners to allow them the use of any dunnage and shifting boards already aboard vessel. Charterers to have the privilege of using shifting boards
47. for dunnage, they making good any damage thereto."

「2．傭船者は，すべての燃料費（別段の定めがある場合を除く）・港費・水先料・代理店料・仲介手数料・領事館料（乗組員に関するものを除く），その他一切の通常費用（前記のものを除く）を手配して支払うものとする。ただし，本船の責任に帰すべき事由で入港した場合は，上記費用は，船主の負担とする。乗組員の発病のため，命じられた燻蒸消毒の費用は船主の負担とする。運送品，またはこの契約により本船を使用中の本船の寄港地のゆえに，命じられた，燻蒸消毒の費用は，傭船者の負担とする。その他一切の燻蒸消毒費は，本船を連続6ヶ月以上の期間傭船した場合において，爾後，傭船者の負担となる。

　荷敷・仕切板，および特殊な航海または特殊な貨物のために必要な艤装品は傭船者が供給するものとする。ただし，船主は既に本船にある一切の荷敷・仕切板の使用を認めなければならない。この場合，傭船者は仕切板を荷敷に代用する権利を有するが，これによって生ずる一切の損害を賠償しなければならない。」

傭船者の手配義務の一般的性質

　ニューヨーク・プロデュース書式の39行40行や，ボルタイム書式の第4条により，傭船者に課される義務は，傭船者が手配のために相当の注意を単に尽くせばよいというのではなく，そこに明記された項目を実際に手配しなければならないという意味で，一般に，絶対的義務である。例えば，航海傭船契約で，傭船者は，本船が結氷のため積荷港に入港できないときは，砕氷船を手配することを引き受けていた事案において，貴族院は，傭船者に砕氷船手配の絶対的義務があると判示した（*Anastassia* v. *Ugleexport* (1934) 49 Ll. L. Rep. 1 事件）。本件でWright卿は次のように言っている。「傭船者は砕氷船の提供を約定している。それは，傭船者自身が提供するか，第三者に提供させることを意味し，したがって，傭船者は，砕氷船が自己の管理下になかったとか，これを管理する者からの提供を得られなかったという口実で，砕氷船を手配できなかった責任を免れることはできない。その意味で，この義務は絶対的なもので

ある。傭船者はこのような義務と危険を負っており、そこで、傭船者の義務は、提供のために最善を尽くすことだけには限定されないということになる」。

しかし、ある状況では、傭船者が適切な手配ができるような情報を傭船者に提供する義務が船主にありながら、その情報が不正確なために傭船者が手配できない場合には、船主は損害賠償の訴えを申し立てることはできない（それについては、後出参照）。

燃　　料

引渡時に船舶上の燃料を傭船者が購入し、返船時に船主がこれを購入する規定は、ニューヨーク・プロデュース書式の第3条、ボルタイム書式の第5条にある。それについては、後出218 285頁参照。傭船者が引渡時に購入した燃料は、傭船契約期間中に傭船者が手配した燃料とともに、傭船者の資産である（後出277頁参照）。

量

傭船者は、消費実績と現在の消費に関する情報の提供をほとんど船主とその職員に頼らざるを得ないのだから、当然のことながら、傭船者が、正確な量の燃料を本船に手配するためには、船主とその職員（乗組員）の協力を必要とする。船主とその職員は、傭船者の指図した航海を安全に完了するために必要な追加量も示すことができるであろう。傭船者が必要量の燃料に関する船主側の情報に適切に基づいて処理したが、その情報が間違っていることが判明したとしても、傭船者がその結果として生じる損失につき責任があることにはなりえない。

　Patapsco号はLiverpool/River Plate往復航海に定期傭船された。本船機関士の計算誤りのため、本船は復航第1段階の燃料炭を十分に積み取っておらず、その補給のため、離路しなければならなかった。傭船契約上、傭船者は「すべての石炭を手配し、代金を支払う」べきであるから、発生した追加費用は傭船者の責任であると船主は主張した。しかし、控訴院は、Kennedy判事の判断を支持して、傭船者に石炭を手配する義務があるからといって、往復航海の各段階において十分な石炭を準備する義務を含め、船主の発航時の堪航性担保責任が軽減されるものではないと判示した。Vaughan Williams卿判事は、次のように言っている（128頁）。「傭船契約の本規定に基づく主張は、傭船者がすべての石炭の『代金支払い』だけでなく『手配』をも約定しているのであるから、補炭の全責任は傭船者にあり、船主は、本規定がなければ自己が負担する、燃料炭に関する本船の堪航性保持義務を免れるというものである」。

　「この主張は、傭船者が『すべての石炭を手配し、代金を支払う』という文言にあまりにも広範囲な効果を与えようとするものと思われる。この文言は本船の航海各段階の発航時に本船使用の石炭が十分に船積されていることを確認して、本船の堪航性を保持する船主の義務に影響するとは思われない」。

　　MacIver v. Tate（1903）8 Com. Cas. 124.

The Captain Diamantis [1977] 1 Lloyd's Rep. 362事件で、前出事案の解説をして、Ackner判事は、次のように言った（同判例集367頁）。「『燃料を手配し、支払う』との条項は、燃料支給に関する船主の堪航性確保の責任を軽減するものではない……よって、傭船者が必要な量の燃料を手配するために傭船者に正確な情報を提供するのは、船主の義務である……」。

MacIver v. Tate事件で控訴院は、船主は傭船者の燃料の手配、支払義務により堪航性に関する義務を免れないことをその判決の根拠としたが、堪航性担保義務が、最優先するわけではない。したがって、堪航性担保義務があるからといって、傭船者の賠償請求に対抗して、傭船者はその義務に違反しているとの抗弁を、船主が申し立てることができないことはないであろ

うと思われる。Kennedy 判事の *MacIver v. Tate* (1902) 18 T. L. R. 379 事件の第1審判決を，控訴院が支持したが，同判事は，船長が傭船者に石炭をもっと要求し，これを傭船者が提供しなかったのであれば，見解は違っていたであろうとの意見を述べている。船主が，（例えば，出港前に必要な燃料を自身で手配するとか，手配できない場合には中間港で手配するとかにより）堪航性担保に関する義務を免れる場合，傭船者は船主がそれによって被った損失または追加の出費につき責任ありと考えられる。

質

傭船者は，適切な一般的に良質な燃料で，かつ特定の船舶に装備された機関の型に適合する燃料を手配しなければならない。前もって船主が，機関の特殊な要件に傭船者の注意を喚起していない限り，傭船者はその型の機関に予想される以上の異常な要件に応じる義務はない。燃料の質が一般に悪化しているという観点から，傭船契約に提供される燃料の類型と格についての明示の要件を含めることは現在ではだんだん普通になっている。燃料のこの明示の要件を定めた条項が傭船契約に含まれている場合，傭船者はその条項に従わなければならない。

傭船者が提供した燃料の火災に関する事案について，(1922) 13 Ll. L. Rep. 197 と後出442頁の *Nourse v. Elder Dempster* 事件参照。

NYPE 93

ニューヨーク・プロデュース書式の1993年改訂版の第9条(b)項により，傭船者は本船の機関，補機に適合し，合意された仕様明細に合致する質の燃料を提供することを明示的に要求される。傭船者がこれに応じなかった場合，船主は機関または補機の損傷につき損害賠償請求でき，速力減少や燃料消費増加や期間喪失，または，その他の結果についての傭船者の損害賠償請求から保護される（前出10頁の英文書式の117行から124行と55頁参照）。

燃料の所有権

The Saint Anna [1980] 1 Lloyd's Rep. 180 事件で，Sheen 判事は，Shelltime 3 傭船契約書式に基づき傭船者は，自らが提供し，支払った，船上の燃料の所有権を保持していると判示した。傭船者が，「（調理室用燃料を除き）すべての燃料を手配し，支払う」という同傭船契約第6条の条項を参照して，同判事は，次のように言った。「傭船者が燃料を購入する場合，両当事者がその所有権は船主に帰属する旨を明々白々に合意しない限り，燃料は傭船者の所有物であると思われる」。*The Saint Anna* 事件の判決は，*The Span Terza* [1984] 1 Lloyd's Rep. 119 事件で，その見解はニューヨーク・プロデュース書式に拠っても同じであると判示した控訴院により支持された。ボルタイム書式の第4条に類似条項がある。傭船契約終了時の燃料の所有権に関する効果について，後出285頁の「燃料」以降を参照。

燃料補給場所の安全性

燃料供給業者が燃料供給のための傭船者の代理人である場合，または，傭船者の燃料補給の指図が，燃料供給業者が指示するような場所での燃料補給の指図として適切に解釈される場合に，燃料供給業者により指示された燃料補給場所が安全でなかった結果として本船に生じた損傷に対して，傭船者が（前出251頁参照），責任を持つ場合が限られてはいるが存在する（*The Mediolanum* [1984] 1 Lloyd's Rep. 136 事件と *The Erechthion* [1987] 2 Lloyd's Rep. 180 事件参照，さらにこの2事件を解説している前出252頁参照）。

港　費

　港費とは船舶が出港以前に支払わねばならないすべての費用であるが，出港後発生する船舶の便益に関するものも含まれる。

　*Apex*号の傭船者は，特別な条項により，甲板積貨物を Deptford で揚荷する場合，その港費を支払う義務があった。そして，Deptford で揚荷をしたが，支払うべき港費の中に，艙内積貨物を揚荷する Leith までの残余の航海中に通過する灯台の分の英国水路協会（Trinity House）の灯台料が含まれていた。それは本船が，Deptford に寄港せずに Leith に直行していたら，船主が支払うべきものであった。Mathew 判事は，この料金は傭船者が支払うべきものであると判示した。「この文言の通常の意味は，船舶が出港以前に支払わねばならない費用を示すものと思われる」と同判事は述べている。
　Newman & Dale v. *Lamport & Holt* [1896] 1 Q. B. 20.

[220]　しかし傭船者が責任を負う費用は，傭船期間中に支払うべきであった費用のみである。したがって本船引渡港における灯台料を引渡直前に支払った場合にはボルタイム書式に傭船者が「港費」および「灯台料」を手配し負担すると規定してあるにもかかわらず，船主は傭船者からその灯台料を回収できなかった（*Scales* v. *Temperley Steam Shipping* (1925) 23 Ll. L. Rep. 312 事件参照）。

ボルタイム書式

　ボルタイム書式に関しては，第4条に明白に，傭船者は「引渡港，返船港におけるすべての岸壁料，港税および屯税（ただし本船引渡前または返船後に運送した貨物について生じたものを除く）」を支払う，と規定していることに注意すべきである。すなわちこれら特定費用は一般規則の例外であり，引渡前や返船後に発生したり，支払われるとしても，傭船者が支払うべきである。この文言は，傭船期間外において，発生したか支払った費用について傭船者に支払義務を課すものであるから，狭義に解釈されるべきである。そのような事情で，上記 *Scales* v. *Temerley Steam Shipping* 事件において，Roche 判事は，この文言が同条項の前の方に掲げられている灯台料をも含むものとは解釈しなかった。これに該当する文言はニューヨーク・プロデュース書式にはない。

水　先　料

　地域の規則に応じるため，または船舶の安全性を確保するために水先人が必要な場合，傭船者はニューヨーク・プロデュース書式の39行，またはボルタイム書式の29/30行に基づき，水先人を手配し，支払わなければならない。

　前出275頁に述べた一般原則に従って，水先人が手配されなければならないと思われる。傭船者が水先人を手配しようとしたが，できなかった場合，傭船者は水先人の手配義務不履行を免れないと思われる。それは，傭船者の望み通りには動かない当局に水先人の手配を頼らざるをえないところでさえ，言えることである。手配された水先人が，妥当な能力に欠ける場合，傭船者は契約違反になると思われる。傭船者指名の荷役業者の能力に関する事案について *The Sinoe* [1972] 1 Lloyd's Rep. 201 事件参照。傭船者が，水先人を手配し，水先料を負担したが，水先人が傭船者の被用者になるわけではないから，傭船者が水先人の過失についての船主に対する代位責任を負うことにはならないと判示された。

Sir Bevis 号の定期傭船者は水先人を手配し，料金を支払うことを約定していた。傭船者が手配した水先人の1人の不注意によって，本船は座礁し，損傷を受けた。船主は，水先人は傭船者の被用者であるから，傭船者は水先人の過失につき責任を持つべきであり，したがって傭船者は修理期間中の傭船料支払をオフハイヤー条項によって免れることはできないと主張した。Mathew 判事はこの「法外な主張」を退け，「傭船者が水先料を支払ったからといって，水先人が傭船者の被用者となるものではない」と述べた。

Fraser v. Bee (1900) 17 T.L.R. 101.

前出 Fraser v. Bee 事件で，Mathew 判事が，短い判決で退けた「水先人は傭船者の被用者であった」という船主のはっきりした主張は，注意されるべきである。水先人は傭船者の被用者ではないが，水先人の仕事の責任は船主と傭船者の間で傭船者に転嫁されていたと言う船主のための別の主張がありえた。この主張は，Brys v. Drysdale (1920) 4 Ll. L. Rep. 24 事件の，Greer 判事の「傭船者は，……船長の指揮のもとで貨物積付を行う荷役業者を手配し，費用を負担する」という航海傭船契約の条項の効果について，「その条項がなければ船主に存する適切な貨物積付の義務と責任を，傭船者に転嫁する」ものであるという判決と一致するであろう。Greer 判事の判決は，Court Line v. Canadian Transport (1940) 67 Ll. L. Rep. 161 事件（後出366頁参照）で貴族院により是認され引用されて，権威あるものとみなされるに違いない。それにもかかわらず，Fraser v. Bee 事件の判決は，正しく，今日先例として扱われることになると思われる。類似の事実ではあるが，しかし Brys v. Drysdale 事件に踏襲された前者（Fraser v. Bee 事件）と似たような主張に直面した場合でも，裁判所が，後者の事案（Brys v. Drysdale 事件）を識別する可能性はある。そのことは水先人の仕事とそれに伴う危険は不可避的かつ直接的にその義務と関係があるが，後出366頁で要約されている Court Line v. Canadian Transport 事件で解説された例外的状況を除けば，船主の堪航性担保義務に影響しない荷役業者の仕事とそれに伴う危険の転嫁を Brys v. Drysdale 事件の裁判所が取り扱ったという理由に基づいている。

さらに，「自己の計算で航行するときと同じように……船主は船舶の航行につき責任がある」と定めたニューヨーク・プロデュース書式の170行から171行に，水先人の過失の危険を傭船者へ転嫁することへの反対支援の論点が規定されている。

NYPE 93

ニューヨーク・プロデュース書式の1993年改訂版の282行は，船主が1946年版の第26条に基づき「責任がある」事項に「水先人と曳船の行為」を追加している。前出14頁と58頁参照。

代 理 人

ニューヨーク・プロデュース書式の39行，またはボルタイム書式の34行により傭船者は，代理人を手配し，支払わねばならない。少なくとも有能な企業または人が特定の港または地域にいる場合には，能力ある代理人を選定しなければならないと思われる。傭船者が船主に対して，傭船者が指定した一般に有能な代理人の過失につき責任があるか否かは，明確ではないが，それは代理人が遂行した仕事の種類によるのであり，また少なくとも本船の貨物ではなく本船自体にかかわる程度如何による。

Beepeetime 2 書式の第20条の類似条項を熟慮して，Staughton 判事は，The Sagona [1984] 1 Lloyd's Rep. 194 事件で次のように言った（同判例集199頁）。「……傭船者が指定し，費用を支払った代理人は，船主と傭船者の間で，港での船舶のすべての通常業務について傭船者の

代理人と考えられる。そのような解決法を取れば，傭船者が能力のないまたは怠慢な代理店を指定する場合に生じる困難は生じない。しかし，船主と傭船者の間には，船長自身が行うべきであって，代理人に委任すべきでない業務がある。それにもかかわらず，船長がそういう業務を敢えて代理人に委ねる場合，そのときの代理人の受託業務の履行懈怠は，船主の代理としてのものであり，傭船者代理としてのものではないことがありうる」(*Strathlorne Steamship* v. *Andrew Weir*（1934）49 Ll. L. Rep. 306（同判例集310頁）事件参照)。

その他一切の通常費用

ニューヨーク・プロデュース書式の40行のこの文言が適用されるものに関しては裁判の先例がない。しかしながら，ボルタイム書式の第4条に傭船者が手配し・支払う諸項目の目録中にある「曳船支援」をこの文言が，含めることはありうる。傭船者が曳船を手配する義務があるとすれば，その義務の範囲は前出で解説した水先人に関する範囲と類似していると思われる。ニューヨーク・プロデュース書式の1993年改訂版に関しては，前出を参照。

222 オフハイヤー期間

この条項に基づく傭船者の義務は，反対の明示文言がある場合を除き，全傭船期間を通じて継続する。したがってボルタイム書式における同種の条項（第4条）に基づき，傭船者は，オフハイヤー期間中でさえ使用燃料費負担の義務がある。

> *Arild* 号は修理期間中オフハイヤーであった。燃料炭はこの期間も使用された。傭船者は，傭船契約により「すべての石炭，燃料を手配し，代金を支払う」義務を有しているが，オフハイヤー中は，この義務が中断されるべきであると主張した。McCardie 判事は傭船者の義務を継続すると判示した。
> *Arild* v. *Hovrani*［1923］2 K. B. 141.

ニューヨーク・プロデュース書式においても，反対の明示規定である第20条133行と134行がなければ，オフハイヤー期間中の使用燃料に関する立場は，39行の規定に従って前示同様となる。ボルタイム書式においても，第4条冒頭に，よく使われる「オンハイヤーの間 Whilst on hire」という文言を挿入すれば，ニューヨーク・プロデュース書式と同様になる。この文言の挿入により，使用燃料と同様，第4条に記載された他の事項に対する責任も船主に転嫁される。燃料に関する限り，傭船者を保護するためにニューヨーク・プロデュース書式の39行冒頭に同様の文言を挿入する必要はないが，39行，40行に記載された他の事項に対する責任を，船主に転嫁するためには「オンハイヤーの間 Whilst on hire」と同様の文言を挿入する必要がある。

傭船者の義務は，本船受取以前には開始しないし，返船以降にまで継続しない。ただし明示の規定のある場合（ボルタイム書式第4条におけるように）は別である。なお前出の港費の項参照。

NYPE 93

ニューヨーク・プロデュース書式の1946年版の第2条に相当する1993年改訂版の第7条は，「傭船者は，本船の稼働中，手配し，支払う」で始まる。「オンハイヤーの間 Whilst on hire」を1946年版の39行に挿入した効果について前出の解説参照。1993年改訂版の第7条は，1946年版の文言に細目を追加している（9頁の84行から98行と54頁を参照)。

223 米 国 法

傭船者が手配し,支払う

　前に述べたように,第2条は,燃料,港費,水先料,代理店料のような項目につき,本船に責任がある原因によって諸項目の費用が発生しない限り,傭船者に支払う義務を割り当てている。傭船契約が有効である限り,傭船契約のどこかに特別の免責条項が定められていなければ,傭船者は,この諸項目の支払に責任がある。例えば,ニューヨーク・プロデュース書式の第20条に基づき,傭船者はオフハイヤー中の燃料代を支払う義務を免れる。

　傭船者の傭船契約上の重大な違反を理由として,本船上に貨物を積載したまま,本船が引き揚げられたとしても,傭船者には,この諸費用を支払う責任が残る。The Athenian Horizon, SMA 1197 (Arb. at N.Y. 1977) 事件は,この状況であった。本船が揚荷港へ向かう途上で,傭船者は傭船料の支払を怠った。そこで船主は,傭船者に本船の引揚通知を送付した。仲裁人はこれを正当な事由があると裁定した。しかしながら,通知が送付された時点で,本船は,貨物を積載していた。仲裁人は,貨物が揚荷されるまで傭船契約は有効であると裁定した。船主の引揚通知にもかかわらず,傭船契約は有効であるので,傭船者は揚荷港の港費を支払う責任があった。

　同じように, The Arizona, SMA 1259 (Arb. at N.Y. 1978) 事件で,傭船者は,引揚通知が出されてから,貨物が揚荷されるまでの期間に消費された燃料も支払う責任があると判示された。

燃　料

量

　燃料を供給し支払うのは傭船者の責任である。しかしながら,燃料の供給量を決定するのは船長の責任である。さらに,傭船者が船長に配船を指図する航海の燃料の適切な供給を確実にすることが,船長の義務である。

　The Venetia, SMA 1351 (Arb. at N.Y. 1979) 事件で,本船は燃料油を積み込むためにCape Townに離路し寄港に要する航海の喪失時間は,オフハイヤーであると判示された。船長が,本船の速力と消費能力でその航海に必要な燃料を誤って計算したため,予定外の寄港が,必要となった。傭船者は,航海の始期に船長の要請する量を供給した。仲裁人によれば,傭船者は,船長の誤った計算による喪失時間の傭船料を支払う責任があるとは裁定されなかった。

　同じように, The Argentine Transport, 1956 AMC 1772 (Arb. at N.Y. 1956) 事件で,船主は,船長が注文した余分の燃料の費用につき責任ありと判示された。本船は,当該航海で,493トンを消費し475トンの燃料を残して揚荷港に到着した。仲裁審によれば,船長が要求するほとんど100パーセントの安全率は,過度であった。それどころか「25パーセントの安全率が,公平な安全要素として通常認識されている」。揚荷港よりも船積港の燃料が高いので,船主は価格の差額を支払う責任があると判示された。

　The Silver Hawk, SMA 1857 (Arb. at N.Y. 1983) 事件で,仲裁審は,傭船者は本船に燃料をとんでもなく過剰な供給をしたと裁定した。しかしながら,燃料引渡時に船長が抗議しなかったので,船主には傭船者に対する実務上の償還請求の道がなかった。それにもかかわら

ず，仲裁審は，傭船者は船主に資金繰上の損失により損害を与えたと裁定した。

224　*The Mandolyna*, SMA 2115（Arb. at N.Y. 1985）事件で，仲裁審は，引渡時に傭船契約の規定量を超えた燃料を傭船者が，受け入れ，支払ったが，傭船者は，同じ超過量を積載して返船する必要はないと判示した。

The Zannis, SMA 2074（Arb. at N.Y. 1985）事件で，傭船者は傭船契約の規定量を超えた燃料とともに船舶を返船した。仲裁審は，船主が購入を強いられた過剰燃料の市場価格と傭船契約上の価格差を船主の損害と査定した。

The Packing, SMA 2858（Arb. at N.Y. 1992）事件で，傭船契約は傭船者が本船の引渡時と「ほぼ同じ量」の燃料とともに返船することを求めた。仲裁審は，傭船契約規定の予測を約112トン超過する燃料の船主による引渡が不当ではないように，約158.6トン超過する燃料を残油とする傭船者の返船は，適当かつ予見できる基準を超えるものではない，と裁定した。

The Northern Light, SMA 2645（Arb. at N.Y. 1990）事件で，傭船者は本船を傭船契約の規定より少ない量の燃料で返船した。その後，船主は自身で燃料を購入したが，傭船者が供給すべきであった量を超えて購入した。したがって，仲裁審は，傭船者が供給すべき量に船主の損害回収を限定した。

質

ニューヨーク・プロデュース書式には，傭船者が傭船期間中供給する燃料の質に関して「最良格」でなければならないという文言を除いて，明示の条項がない。燃料の規格に関して詳細な条項がない場合には，傭船者が燃料として一般に受け入れられる標準に合致する燃料を供給する限り，仮に燃料の質のために問題が生じたとしても，船主には傭船者に対し損害賠償を請求する根拠がないであろう。同時に，当事者が使用する燃料の種類または質に関して傭船契約に規格を含めることに同意する場合，傭船者は，傭船契約の表示に合わない燃料の使用により生じるいかなる損失にも責任があると思われる。欠陥燃料から生じる問題は，たいへん重大であり，機関の物理的損害，傭船契約履行の水準低下，喪失時間も問題に含まれる。

The Royal Prince, 1927 AMC 62（S.D.N.Y. 1926）事件で，Augustus Hand 判事は，市場向きの品質を有する燃料炭を自分が供給できないことから生じた損失につき傭船者は，責任があると判示した。

The Maro, SMA 2533（Arb. at N.Y. 1988）事件で，傭船契約には傭船者が提供する燃料は中間燃料油（IFO）1550 SECS と舶用ディーゼルオイル（MDO）と記載されていた。船主は，傭船者の提供した燃料は，傭船契約書の規格と異なり，不適切な混合油で，過剰に異物が混入している，と主張した。仲裁審は，傭船者には，傭船契約の規格に合致する燃料を提供する，他に転嫁できない義務があるとの船主の主張に同意した。

> 傭船契約に合致する燃料を支給する責任を負うのは，燃料業者ではなく傭船者であることは明らかである。本来，傭船者が燃料注文の手配と支払を行うものである。それは，船主に対する義務である。燃料業者は，燃料が特定の船舶の機関に適合しているかを保証せず，業界の基準と傭船者の指示にそった燃料を支給することを引き受ける。燃料購入注文書に記載の粘性に合致することに加えて，燃料はまた現在の標準の適合性を満たし，危険な異物を過剰に含有していないことが必要である。

しかしながら，仲裁審は，傭船者供給の燃料が機関損傷を引き起こしたことを立証する責任を船主は果たすことができなかったと認定した。

The Leslie, SMA 1341（Arb. at N.Y. 1979）事件で，船主は規格と異なる燃料による機関損傷と速力減少につき損害賠償請求をした。傭船契約の前文は，本船の燃料消費に言及し，次

225のように記載している。「……中間燃料油最高レッド粘度300秒約9トンの消費で」。船主は本船から取り寄せた見本から傭船者が供給した燃料油は，粘度750秒であることを証明した。仲裁人は，全員一致で，「この規格と異なる油を使用したので本船が損害を被ったことを船主が証明できる限り，傭船者はそれによる相当な費用につき責任がある」と判示した。

　船主の立証責任は，重いものである。*The London Glory*, SMA 1771 (Arb. at N.Y. 1982) 事件は，たぶんこのことのいちばん良い例証であろう。そこで，仲裁審は，本船の主機ディーゼル機関は，燃料システムを通して機関に入った助燃剤を含む異物に起因する異常損耗を被ったと認定した。しかしながら，仲裁審はさらに，異物は本船が以前使用した燃料ではなく，傭船者が支給した燃料の中に存したことを，確固たる証拠で立証する責任を船主は果たしていないと裁定した。

　Antilles Shipping Co. Ltd. v. Texaco Inc., 321 F. Supp. 166, 1971 AMC 1291 (S.D.N.Y. 1970) 事件で，船主は，機関故障が船舶の潤滑油の不適合により生じたことを立証できなかった。裁判所は，船主がその主張を立証するためには，燃料を適切に使用し，乗組員の過失はなく，損傷は本船の潤滑油システムの中の他の異物により生じたのではないことを証明しなければならないと言及した。

　ある事案では，仲裁人が船主と傭船者の双方に機関故障の責任を配分した。*The Hoegh Mallard*, SMA 2679 (Arb. at N.Y. 1990) 事件で，仲裁人は，本船の機関故障は傭船者が支給した欠陥燃料のみにより引き起こされたことを，船主は揺るぎない信憑性のある証拠を挙げて証明しなかった，と裁定した。しかし，仲裁審は，支給された燃料は，「その質は疑わしく」，まさしく機関損傷に部分的に寄与したと裁定したので，傭船者は船主に支払った傭船料の85パーセントだけを裁定された。

　The Lumber Carrier, SMA 252 (Arb. at N.Y. 1955) 事件で，仲裁人は過剰に水分を含有する燃料から生じた損失について傭船者と船主の双方に責任があると裁定した。船長と機関長には，燃料に欠陥があることを知る判断力がありながら，その状況を是正する手段を講じなかったので，船主は責任があると裁定された。仲裁人は，過剰に水分を含有する燃料を支給した傭船者の違反により直接的に生じた損傷につき傭船者は責任があると裁定した。

　傭船者は，「最良格」の燃料を要求されるだけでなく，船主の異議を制して「最良格」の燃料油を支給する権利がある。*The Derrynane*, 1954 AMC 1015 (Arb. at N.Y. 1954) 事件で，最終航海に，傭船者は，石油会社が「中等舶用ディーゼル」と記載する高値の燃料を支給した。船長は異議を申し立てずにこれを受けた。本船が返船されたときに，当該船舶の機関に使える「舶用ディーゼル」という名の格下の安い値段で残置燃料を傭船者に支払えば十分であると船主は主張した。しかし，仲裁審は傭船者は最良質の燃料油を購入する十分な正当事由があり，船主は返船時の船上残留燃料量の実費を支払う義務があると裁定した。

　The Derrynane 事件の状況が，傭船者が船主の異議を無視して低品質の燃料を支給したいというのであれば，船主が入手可能な最高の品質または「最良格」の燃料に固執する権利を有することには，先ず疑問の余地がない。

水　先　料

　傭船者が水先料を支払う義務があるからといっても，定期傭船契約に基づき本船に乗船する任意手配の水先人は，船主から借りた被用者であり傭船者の被用者ではない（*H. Schuldt* v. *Standard Fruit & Steamship Co.*, 1979 AMC 2470, 2478 (S.D.N.Y. 1978)；*California* v. *The Norfolk*, 435 F. Supp. 1039, 1046 n.2, 1978 AMC 144, 153 n.2 (N.D. Cal. 1977)）。水先人を

[226]雇う決定は，船主の責任である。しかし，傭船者には，特定の任務に適し有資格の水先人を手配することに相当の注意を尽くす黙示の義務がある。前出 *California* v. *The Norfolk* 事件。

　水先人を手配し，料金を支払うという傭船者の義務があるからといって，傭船者には，水先契約の条件に船主を拘束する権限はない。Acadia 号が2隻の曳船により曳航される途中，他船および桟橋に衝突した事例である *A/S Acadia* v. *Curtis Bay Towing Co.*, 304 F. Supp. 1050 (E.D.Pa. 1967) 事件で，船主は水先人の過失が事故の原因であると主張して，曳船会社と水先人に対し訴えを提起した。曳船会社は係留契約中の「水先条項」に基づいて抗弁を提出した。この条項は，水先人が本船に乗船したとき，水先人は本船の被用者となり，曳船会社，曳船，水先人いずれも水先人の本船取扱から生じる損害に責任はないと実質的に規定していた。係留契約は傭船者が曳船会社と締結したものであった。本船船主は，傭船契約は単に傭船者が「水先人を手配し，……水先料を支払う」と約定していると主張し，傭船者が係留契約条項で船主を拘束する権限はないという理由で，曳船会社の抗弁に反論した。裁判所は船主の主張を認め，本傭船契約条項は，船主に関係のない係留契約の水先条項によって，船主を拘束する権限を傭船者に与えていないと判示した。

船艙清掃費用

　傭船期間中積載された前航貨物の残滓を清掃する費用と時間は傭船者負担となる（前出271頁の解説参照）。

燃　　料

"48.　3. That the Charterers, at the port of delivery, and the Owners, at the port of redelivery, shall take over and pay for all fuel remaining on
49. board the vessel at the current prices in the respective ports, the vessel to be delivered
with not less than .... tons and not more than
50. .... tons and to be re-delivered with not less than .... tons and not more
than .... tons."

「3．傭船者は，引渡港において，また船主は，返船港において，本船内の一切の残留燃料を引き取り，それぞれの港における時価で，その代金を支払う。ただし，引渡の際，最低............トン以上，最高............トン以下，返船の際，最低............トン以上，最高............トン以下を，本船が保有していなければならない。」

引渡時および返船時の量

時には本条項に，本船引渡時における燃料の推定積載量が記載される。推定量が「予定量，約」何トンと表示される場合，船主はそれを正直に表示するだけでなく，責任ある職員が当然持つべきあるいは持っている情報を考慮しつつ，合理的な根拠に基づく推定量を示す義務があると判示されている。これは，前出158頁で述べた「積荷準備完了予定日」条項に関する判例からの類推である。

　　Pantanassa 号が1航海定期傭船された。その傭船契約では，本船は，「艀代を含む，門司での現行料率による価格の積載燃料『予定量，約6/700トン』と共に引き渡され，傭船者は引渡時の積載燃料代金を支払う」と規定していた。引渡時，本船積載量は936トンであった。ロンドンの船主代理人は，正直に傭船契約に数量を記載していたが，それは，本船からの電報により伝えられた誤った数量に基づいたものであった。Diplock 判事は船主の契約違反であると判示した。同判事は，数量が正直に記載されたことを認めた上で，次のように言っている。「(船主が) 推定量を出す合理的根拠を持っていたかどうかを検討するにあたっては，推定量を提示したのは船主であるから，船主の責任ある職員が当然持つべき知識は船主の知識であるとみなすべきものであろう」。
　　The Pantanassa ［1958］2 Lloyd's Rep. 449.

傭船者が燃料を手配し，代金を支払う（前出275頁参照）約定があるからといって，傭船者は，傭船期間中に必要としないことが明らかな燃料を，船長に積み取らせることはできない。

　　Captain Diamantis 号はニューヨーク・プロデュース書式で3ないし4ヶ月定期傭船され，第3条は次のように修正されていた。「傭船者は引渡港で，また船主は返船港で，本船積載燃料全量を引き取り，IFO 1ロングトン当たり85米ドル，ディーゼル油1ロングトン当たり120米ドルを支払う。本船は，そのときの積載燃料と共に，引渡・返船される。ただし近接主要補油港まで，航行するに十分な量の燃料であること」。
　　本船が返船港に近づいたとき，残りの傭船期間と近接主要補油港までの航行には十分な燃料を保有していたが，傭船者は，1ロングトン当たり IFO は56米ドル，ディーゼル油は103米ドルで手配できたので，返船前に本船の可能積載量一杯までの補油を本船に指示した。船長は，自己の船主の指令に

基づいて，傭船者の指示を拒否したため，傭船者は修正された第3条に基づき逸失利益の賠償を求めて訴訟を提起した。Ackner判事は傭船者に「傭船契約遂行上必要ではない」燃料積載を指示する権利はないと判示した。彼の判決は，控訴審により支持された。
　　The Captain Diamantis〔1977〕1 Lloyd's Rep. 362 および〔1978〕1 Lloyd's Rep. 346（C. A.）．

228 燃料の所有権

　傭船者は燃料を手配し支払うという（前出275, 277頁参照）ニューヨーク・プロデュース書式の第2条は，傭船者は引渡港ですべての燃料を引き取り，支払うという第3条の規定と相俟って，傭船者に傭船期間中の燃料の所有権を与えることとなる。船主は受寄者として燃料を単に占有するに過ぎない（*The Span Terza*〔1984〕1 Lloyd's Rep. 119事件参照）。傭船契約の第4条と併せて読むときに，返船港ですべての残置燃料を船主は引き取り，支払うという第3条の条項は，返船区域内の港で傭船期間の終了時の返船の際に傭船者から船主に燃料の所有権が移転する効果をもたらす。しかし，特定の事件が発生した際に傭船契約解約の選択権を与える条項に基づき，傭船者が傭船期間中に傭船契約を解約する場合，第3条は適用されない。その場合，解約後も燃料の所有権は傭船者に残る。船主は受寄者のままであるが，船主が傭船者に対して有する契約上の占有権は終了する。しかしながら，本船が海上にある期間，または本船が貨物を船上に保有したままで傭船契約が終了する場合には，船上の燃料を継続使用する船主の権利に関する条項が黙示されているに違いない（前出 *The Span Terza* 事件の貴族院の判決参照）。

　Shelltime 4書式の第15条は船主は「返船時（傭船期間の満了時または傭船契約の早期終了時であれ）」残置の燃料を受け取り，支払うものとすると明示的に規定するので，同条はニューヨーク・プロデュース書式の第3条と異なる。*The Saetta*〔1993〕2 Lloyd's Rep. 268事件で Clarke 判事は，次のように判示した。Shelltime 4書式の第15条の括弧の中の文言はニューヨーク・プロデュース書式の第3条のさらに制限された文言に関する前出 *The Span Terza* 事件の判決と本件を区別するので，傭船料の不払を理由として，船主が本船を引き揚げる場合，Shelltime 4書式に基づき傭船者の燃料所有権は船主に移転する（後出690頁参照）。

　しかしながら，燃料供給業者が代金未払のため権利を保持し，支払が行われていないため，傭船者が当該燃料の所有権を有しない場合，船主は傭船契約の終了時に燃料の所有権を自動的には取得できないし，代金未入金の供給業者が，その結果所有権を主張し，自らのために燃料を使用する場合，船主は燃料の所有権の移転につき供給者に対して責任がある（前出 *The Saetta* 事件参照）。

価　　格

　ニューヨーク・プロデュース書式またはボルタイム書式と異なり―傭船契約に引渡時に傭船者が支払い，返船時に船主が支払う燃料の価格に関する条項がない場合，もともとの購入者が実際に支払った価格を無視してその時点の市場価格が使用される（*The Good Helmsman*〔1981〕1 Lloyd's Rep. 377（同判例集419頁）事件参照）。

NYPE 93

　ニューヨークプロデュース書式の1993年改訂版は，第9条(a)項に空欄があり，引渡時，返船時の燃料価格を当事者が挿入することとしている（前出10頁の英文書式の110行から115行と54

頁参照)。

質

　前出277頁参照。

²²⁹米　国　法

量

前出281頁の解説参照。

価　　格

船主と傭船者が引渡時や返船時の燃料の価格を傭船契約に特定する習慣がある（*The Efplia,* SMA 1359（Arb. at N. Y. 1979）事件参照）。

ニューヨーク・プロデュース書式の下で，引渡時に傭船者が燃料につき支払う燃料の価格や，返船時に船主が支払う燃料の価格はその時点，その場所の市場価格である。しかしながら，傭船契約に価格の定めがない場合，市場価格が実際に支払われた価格と異なっていても，同じ法則を適用するのが正しいと思われる。

質

前出282頁の解説参照。

期間の計算

"51. 4. That the Charterers shall pay for the use and hire of the said Vessel at the rate of ....
52. .... United States Currency per ton on vessel's total deadweight carrying capacity, including bunkers and
53. stores, on .... summer freeboard, per Calendar Month, commencing on and from the day of her delivery, as aforesaid,and at
54. and after the same rate for any part of a month; hire to continue until the hour of the day of her re-delivery .... "

「4．傭船者は，本船の使用ならびに用役に対し，夏期乾舷..........における本船の総載貨重量トン（燃料・船用品を含む）につき，1暦月毎トン当たり....................米国ドルの割合で，上記引渡の日から支払をなすものとする。1ヶ月未満の期間についても，同一の料率による。傭船料の支払は....................返船する日の返船時間までとする。」

地方標準時または経過時間

本船引渡地と返船地に時差のあることがしばしばあるが，傭船期間は引渡港および返船港の地方標準時で計算されるべきか，あるいは引渡時と返船時のグリニッジ標準時の経過時間で計算されるべきかという問題が生ずる。

The Arctic Skou [1985] 2 Lloyd's Rep. 478 事件で，この問題はニューヨーク・プロデュース書式による傭船契約に基づき，判断が下されねばならなかった。この傭船契約書の53/54行の「暦月当たり」と「1ヶ月未満はその割合で」という印刷書式の傭船料の支払に関する言及を削除して，代わりに「1日当たり」と「1日未満はその割合で」と挿入された。Legatt 判事は，傭船料の支払は地方標準時ではなく経過期間で行われねばならないと判示した。同判事は，次のように言った（同判例集480頁）。「人が定期傭船に関係する場合のどんな思慮分別のある商業的考え方によっても，この基本的問題は本船はどれくらいの間，傭船されたかということであるに違いないと思われる。それは，どんな傭船者でも支払うつもりである期間，どんな船主でも支払ってもらうつもりのある期間であるに違いない。弁護士の巧妙さにより，期間の計算は代わりに地方標準時で計算されるべきであるとの意思が当事者にあるとする議論が可能となる。本事案のような定期傭船契約を調べるときには，目前の意思が間違いなく当事者のものであることを指摘し，または確認する明確な文言がなければならないように思われる」。

同判事は，傭船契約中の時間についての各種の言及，その中で特に54行の傭船料に関する「返船の日の返船時間まで」を検討したが，これは返船地の時計が示す時間ではないとの見解を取った。それは実際の返船時間に言及しただけである。したがって同判事は，傭船料が地方標準時間で計算されるべしと結論づけさせるようなものは何も傭船契約にはないと断定した。逆に使用されている文言により，特に「暦月」の代わりに「日」と書くことにより，傭船期間を計算する際，経過した現実の期間の計算は妥当なものとなった。

The Arctic Skou 事件で当事者が印刷書式に重要な変更をしたが，本事件の判決は少なくともその変更に部分的に基づいていたので，書式が無修正の場合も，経過期間に関連して計算が

行われるべきかという問題は残っている。前版で指摘したように,「暦月当たり」は(ボルタイム書式の「30日当たり」と比較して)変動する期間であるので,53行に傭船料は「暦月当たり」で支払われるとある以上,経過日数と時間の正確な数字に固執する意思が示されているも232のではない。しかし,将来裁判所は Legatt 判事の判決の最初の前提を採用するであろう。すなわち定期傭船契約に基づく傭船料の計算で経過期間に有利な推定があり,傭船契約の文言が,地方標準時が好ましいとの明確な意思を示さない限り,経過期間が優勢である。

NYPE 93

ニューヨーク・プロデュース書式の1993年改訂版は,傭船料計算の為に関連する時間は「グリニッジ標準時に調整するものとする」と規定することで,経過期間としてこの時間を解決している(前出10頁の英文書式137/138行と55頁を参照)。

③③ 米 国 法

　米国判例の大半は，傭船契約に基づく期間の計算は，経過期間ではなく，引渡地と返船地の各地方標準時で計算されると判決してきた。
　The Fernglen, 1971 AMC. 213 (Arb. at N.Y. 1970) 事件で，仲裁審は次のように述べている。「傭船期間計算の方法として認められているのは」，引渡港および返船港の「各地方標準時の差である。」「傭船者が，期間算出の方法として，グリニッジ標準時を使うことを意図したのであれば，傭船者は傭船契約書に明示すべきであった」(1971 AMC. at 215)。
　The Bordatxoa, SMA 891 (Arb. at N.Y. 1974) 事件も参照。同事件は，「契約上，グリニッジ標準時を使用することが明示されていなければ，ニューヨーク・プロデュース書式の下では，引渡時刻および返船時刻はその地の標準時によるものと考えられる」と裁定された (*The Toxotis*, SMA 855 (Arb. at N.Y. 1974); *The Haverton*, SMA 743 (Arb. at N.Y. 1973); *The Thunderhead*, SMA 617 (Arb. at N.Y. 1971); *The Argo Sky*, SMA 627 (Arb. at N.Y. 1971))。
　しかしながら，この見解は *The Pacglory*, SMA 2737 (Arb. at N.Y. 1990); *Probulk Carriers Ltd. & Pacific Commerce Line*, SMA 2817 (Arb. at N.Y. 1991); *The Packing*, SMA 2858 (Arb. at N.Y. 1992); *The Constellation*, SMA 3012 (Arb. at N.Y. 1993); *The Pollux I*, SMA 3004 (Arb. at N.Y. 1993); *The North Hills*, 1973 AMC 2318 (Arb. at N.Y. 1972) 各事件では否定されている。仲裁審は，本船は米国太平洋岸で引き渡され，タイ国で返船されたが，だからといって船主に，時間帯の差異により附加された14時間の傭船料は与えられないと裁定した。仲裁審は次のように言っている。

　　2隻の船舶が，引渡港で倉庫代わりに使用できる選択権付で，西海岸の同じ港で，太平洋横断航海のため同じ傭船者に同時に引き渡された場合を考えると，両船共，同じ太平洋標準時で引き渡され，1隻だけが太平洋を横断した場合，その土地の標準時が両船の返船に適用されるなら，傭船者は，極東で返船した船舶に，14時間多く傭船料を支払わねばならず，不合理であろう。
　したがって，仲裁審は全員一致で傭船者有利に認定して，船主の訴えを認めなかった (1973 AMC at 2320)。

　The Atlantic Glory, SMA 76 (Arb. at N.Y. 1962) 事件では，仲裁審は多数意見で，その地の標準時の使用は不公平であると裁定している。理由として，傭船者は本船を使用できない時間の傭船料を控除する権利を有しており，本船は，米国東海岸と返船地，日本との時間差の14時間については，傭船者の使用に供せられていなかったとしている。多数意見は次のように結論を出している。「『暦月』に基礎をおく定期傭船契約のニューヨーク・プロデュース書式は経過時間の使用を表示しており，したがって，傭船料支払のために，その土地の標準時ではなく，定期傭船の経過期間が使用されるべきである」。仲裁審が地方標準時での取扱を否定している *The Doros*, SMA 616 (Arb. at N.Y. 1971) 事件も参照。
　Steamship Co. Gorm v. *United States Shipping Bd. Emergency Fleet Corp.* (*The Knud II*), 285 F. 142 (2d Cir. 1922) 事件では，傭船契約が，1ヶ月未満の端数部分の傭船料支払について，次のような明示条項を規定していた。

　　傭船者は，1ヶ月未満の端数期間については，その割合で傭船料を支払う（日数は30日を1ヶ月と

して、その端数とする)。

　裁判所は、傭船契約中の上記引用の当該条項は、オフハイヤー期間も含め、1ヶ月未満の端数期間についての傭船料算出の実務処理方法を規定しているものと判示した。裁判所は次のように言っている。

234　定期傭船契約の理論は、船主は本船を傭船者の業務に継続提供し、傭船者はその役務提供時間に対して傭船料を支払うということである。もし役務提供に中断があれば、傭船料は支払われない。そして本船がどれだけの期間、役務を提供したかすなわち、どれだけのオンハイヤー期間に対し傭船料が支払われるかが問題となる。本条項は1ヶ月未満の端数部分についての計算方法を規定しており、それは超過期間と同様に、傭船期間途中の傭船料停止にも適用できる (285 F. at 144)。

返　　　　船

〔Clause 4 continued〕
"54. .... hire to continue until the hour of the day of her re-delivery in like good order and condition, ordinary
55. wear and tear excepted, to the Owners (unless lost) at ....
....
56. .... unless otherwise mutually agreed. Charterers are to give Owners
not less than .... days
57. notice of vessel's expected date of re-delivery, and probable port."

(第4条の続き)

「傭船料の支払は，通常の損耗を除き，本船を同様に良好な状態で...............において船主に返船する日の返船時間までとする（滅失の場合を除く）。ただし，別段の合意があるときは，この限りでない。傭船者は，船主に対して，返船の予定日および予定港を少なくとも，その.........日以前に通知しなければならない。」

傭船期間終了時の返船

これは，前出173から184頁でニューヨーク・プロデュース書式の13行から14行で検討された。

傭船料の支払は返船まで継続する

本船が傭船期間終了後に返船される場合の54行の文言の関連性については，前出174頁を参照。

同様に良好な状態での返船

傭船者の傭船契約義務違反の結果，通常の損耗を除き，引渡時より悪い状態で本船を返船すれば，傭船者は損傷に対し責任を負う。

返船時の状態が傭船契約義務違反によるものではない場合でさえ，傭船者が責任を負うこととなりうる。しかし，これには疑問がある。この疑問は主として，傭船期間を通じて本船を稼働状態に保ち（前出267頁参照），付保する（後出614頁参照）という船主の義務があるので，引渡時と同じ状態で本船を返船するという「厳格な」または絶対的な義務を傭船者に適用することの困難さによる。

Limerick v. *Stott* (1921) 7 Ll. L. Rep. 69 事件で，Scrutton 卿判事は，上記の困難性を論じたが，同様に良好な状態での返船義務を「どうしても傭船者の責任に帰せられない損傷」についてまで，適用できるかどうかについての見解の表明を留保した。

保守条項（clause）の下で船主は傭船期間中に発生した損傷のほとんどを修復せざるを得ないが，船主が損傷は傭船者の責任事由により生じたと立証できるときは，傭船者から修復費用を回収できる。返船直前に発生する損傷とか，傭船契約の下で従事している航海において，本

船の稼働に影響のない損傷が発生するだろうが，その場合，船主には保守条項（clause）による修理施行の義務はない。

傭船期間中発生した修理費は，損傷が傭船者によるものである場合のみ傭船者が負担し，傭船終了時は，損傷が傭船者によるか否かを問わず，残っているすべての修理費を傭船者が負担[236]すべきであるというのは，非論理的であるように思われる。しかし，万一傭船者の返船義務は厳格に解釈されるべきであるということであれば，このような立場となるだろう。

さらに，まったく傭船者が関与しない保険危険による損傷の賠償請求から傭船者を保護するものでない限り，船主が海上および戦争危険に対し本船を付保することを求める付保条項（terms）はほとんど効果がないであろう。

したがって，付保条項は，同様に良好な状態で返船する傭船者の義務を，傭船契約の他の義務違反により生じた損傷のみに，あるいは使用条項（clause）あるいは補償条項（clause）の下で傭船者が責任を負う損傷のみに制限するものと解釈するべきであろう（後出461頁参照）。

しかしながら，Acton 判事は，傭船者の義務について，より厳格な見解を下記のように下した。もっとも同事件は，審判人の事実認定が不十分であるばかりでなく，通常ボルタイム書式では船主の義務とされている本船付保義務が，船主にあるのかどうかについても言及がない点で，不満足な先例である。

Pencarrow 号は，英国からボルティック海往復航海にボルタイム書式で傭船された。本船は往航で石炭，復航で鉄鉱石を運送した。鉱石の積揚荷役の間に船艙に損傷が発生した。船主は，傭船者の過失を立証することなく，傭船者が本船を「（正当な自然損耗を除き）引渡時と同様に良好な状態で」返船しなかったとして，損害賠償を請求した。審判人は，この損傷は「正当な自然損耗」ではなく，傭船者が修理費用を支払うべきであると認定した。傭船者は，本船を約定航海で使用して，使用するに際して過失がなかったならば，損傷が発生しても，それは「正当な自然損耗」であると高等法院で主張したが，Acton 判事はこの主張を退け，船主有利に判示した。同判事は次のように述べている。

「賃貸物件の損耗は誰の過失でもなく発生することもあるだろうし，また，当事者間の契約上考慮された範囲内の事柄で，賃借人がそれをなしても賃貸借契約に違反したことにはならない事柄もありうる。そして，そのような結果がすべて『正当な自然損耗』という文言に含まれるわけではない」。
 Chellew Navigation v. Appelquist（1933）45 Ll. L. Rep. 190.

損傷を受けた本船の返船

傭船期間終了の際，傭船者の契約義務違反により発生した損傷があっても，傭船者は損傷のある本船を返船できる。したがって，傭船料支払義務も終了する。船主は返船を拒否できず，損害賠償請求のみが残される。

Wye Crag 号は，傭船契約終了時点で，「引渡時と同じ良好な状態で」返船されることとなっていた。本船船底の損傷は，傭船者の責めに帰すべきものであったので，船主は修理が完了するまで，返船を拒否した。McCardie 判事は返船は有効であり，本船の状態にかかわらず，傭船料支払義務は終了するとし，一方で損害賠償は請求できると判示した。
 Wye Shipping v. Compagnie du Chemin de Fer Paris-Orleans（1922）10 Ll. L. Rep. 85.

裸傭船契約の事案において，控訴院は上記事案と同様に判示している。その傭船契約の文言は，あるいは反対の結果をもたらすかとも考えられていたにもかかわらず，本事案の損傷は例外的なほどに重大で修理を行うのは無駄であった。

Puerto Buitrago 号は，17ヶ月裸傭船された。本船は「引渡時と同様に良好な状態で」返船されることとなっており，さらに「傭船者は返船前に，傭船者の費用と時間で修理を行う」ということが合意されていた。それにもかかわらず，控訴院は，傭船者は傭船期間終了時点で本船を返船できる。ただし船主は損害賠償請求ができると判示した。損傷の程度は，必要な修理が修理時の船体価格を大幅に超えるものであった。

 The Puerto Buitrago [1976] 1 Lloyd's Rep. 250（本件のうち，期間前返船に関する考察については前出182頁参照，また The Odenfeld [1978] 2 Lloyd's Rep. 357 事件および The Alaskan Trader (No. 2) [1983] 2 Lloyd's Rep. 645 事件も参照）.

237 損害賠償の基準

返船時の本船の状態に返船条項に基づく傭船者の義務違反が存する場合，船主が回収できる損害の通常の基準はそれによる本船の価値の減少である。その状況で修理費が商業的に妥当である場合，欠陥状態の修復費用という別の基準によって船主はそれを回収できる（前出 The Puerto Buitrago 事件および The Alecos M [1991] 1 Lloyd's Rep. 120 に依拠する The Rozel [1994] 2 Lloyd's Rep. 161 事件における Phillips 判事の判決参照）。同判事は The Alecos M 事件について，次のように指摘している（168頁）。「商業的な観点からは，その欠陥が本船の価格減少に及ぼす影響と比較して修復費用が不均衡である場合，原告は『修復費用』を基準として損害の賠償を受けることはないことを本判決は実証している」（なお Ruxsley Electronics v. Forsyth [1995] 3 W. L. R. 118（H. L.）事件も参照）.

通常の損耗

損傷が「通常の損耗」であるかどうかを決定する場合，本船が傭船された特定の航海の性質が，その関連要素となる。

 Empress of Britain 号が第一次世界大戦中，兵員輸送に傭船された。定期傭船契約第5条で，「支払の基礎は，（正当な自然損耗および減価を除き）本船を徴用時と同じ状態に修復する費用，本船運航に通常発生するもの以外の船主の支払金の補償，および船体，機関の減価償却費，運航費，管理費を差し引いた後適正な海運業利益をもたらすに十分な傭船料である」と規定していた。
 大戦後，本船は修理の上，定期船として改装された。その費用分担をめぐって，国の責任についての紛争が生じ，仲裁に付託された。損傷は，兵員輸送中に，「通常に発生したもの」として，仲裁人は申し立てた費用を認めなかった。これにつき貴族院も同意した。
 Buckmaster 卿は次のように述べている。「被申立人が国から補償をうけようとする費用が当然に自然損耗とされる費用であると認められるとして，かつ，その文言を本船使用目的と関連させて考えてみると，残された問題は第5条の解釈にあたり本船の使用目的を考慮に入れるべきか否かの判断のみである。本船傭船契約が兵員輸送ないしそれと同様の目的のためであることが明白に規定されていることを考えれば，何が運航中に発生する費用であるかを検討するにあたり，その使用目的を考慮の範囲から除外するとは判断しがたい。したがって仲裁人の裁定に全面的に同意する」.
 Canadian Pacific Railway v. Board of Trade (1925) 22 Ll. L. Rep. 1.

期限前早期返船

期限前早期返船の判例は前出182頁参照。本船が航海に従事できないほど不良の状態で期限前に早期返船される場合，傭船料の代わりに請求できる損害額について The Griparion [1994] 1 Lloyd's Rep. 533 事件参照。

約定以外の場所での返船

　傭船者はニューヨーク・プロデュース書式の55および56行に表示した港または場所で，またはボルタイム書式の第7条に表示した港または場所で本船を返船しなければならない。この義務に違反して傭船者が他の場所で返船する場合，船主は損害賠償を請求できる。その請求は，表示の港または場所への本船の航海を傭船者が指図したと仮定する理論上の航海から船主が得る純利益に通常基づくが，理論上の航海の期間に別途就航により稼ぐ純利益を差し引いたものとなる（*The Bunga Kenanga* [1981] 1 Lloyd's Rep. 518 事件と *The Rijin* [1981] 2 Lloyd's Rep. 267 事件を参照）。後者の事案で，Mustill 卿は次のように述べた（同判例集270頁）。船主は「役務終了まで約定傭船料率で本船の使用を継続する契約上の権利を有する。本船が返船区域に到達するまで役務は終了しない。その区域までの航海は傭船役務の部分を構成する。したがって，本事案のように返船終了の申出が間違った場所だけでなく間違ったときに行われれば，その違反についての全面的な補償は，航海が実際に履行された場合，得られたはずの傭船料の返還を傭船者が船主に対して求めることによる」。本事案で返船は極東諸港区域であり，Mustill 判事は，損害を査定する目的からは理論的最終航海は損害を最小限にする航海，すなわち返船区域内の最短距離にある安全港への空船航海であると判示した。

239 米　国　法

同様に良好な状態での返船

　The Jarmar, 1969 AMC 354 (Arb. at N.Y. 1969) 事件は,「同様に良好な状態で」返船するというニューヨーク・プロデュース書式の傭船者の義務に関連する事案であった。引渡時の共同検査では,「貨物積載場所はすべて清掃されている」と認定していた。一方,返船時の検査では,船艙は清掃されていないことが示されていた。したがって船主は,船艙清掃を指示するとともに,清掃費用および所要時間の補償を求めて仲裁に付託した。傭船者は清掃費用に責任があることを争わなかった。仲裁審は,本船が清掃され,引渡時と同様の良好な状態になるまで,船主は傭船料受取の権利があると裁定した。

　約定の船舶業務から燻蒸消毒の必要性が発生した場合,傭船者は燻蒸費用と所要時間を負担しなければならない。*Dampskibs etc.* v. *Munson Line S. S. Co.*, 20 F. 2d 345 (2d Cir.), 裁量上告拒絶 275 U.S. 561 (1927); *The Muggenburg*, SMA 898 (Arb. at N.Y. 1974) 事件では,傭船者は穀類貨物固有の瑕疵に起因する燻蒸費用および遅延に対し責任があると判断された。*The Ellen Klautschke*, SMA 361 (Arb. at N.Y. 1965) 事件では,熱帯地域諸港を航海後,New Orleans Board of Trade が害虫棲息を発見し,その後傭船者が本船を燻蒸せずに返船した場合につき,船主は燻蒸が完了するまでの傭船料および燻蒸費用の請求権があると裁定された。

　傭船者が,構造上の損傷を未修理のまま,船主に返船を申し出た場合,「その損傷のため本船が不堪航となり,船主が直ちに本船を使用できない場合を除き」,船主は返船を拒否できないと裁定されている (*The Chris*, SMA 199 (Arb.at N.Y. 1958))。

　本船を「同様に良好な状態で」返船するという傭船者の義務のなかには,ニューヨーク・プロデュース書式第16条に記載されているような,相互免責事項に起因する本船損傷は含まれない。例えば,*The Lysland*, SMA 419 (Arb. at N.Y. 1969) 事件では,航海過失による船体損傷に対する船主の訴えは認められず,また *The Napier*, SMA 525 (Arb. at N.Y. 1970) 事件では,乗組員の過失を原因とする爆発による損傷に対し,傭船者は責任がないと裁定された。

　船主は,第4条の下で傭船者から損害を回収する立場を確立するために返船後修理を直ちに行う必要はない。*The Prometheus*, SMA 1154 (Arb. at N.Y. 1977) 事件で本船が第4条が求めると同様に良好な状態で返船されない場合,傭船者は遅延した修理の確認された費用につき責任があると判示された。損傷が修理されない場合,船主の損失の計算に使用される通常の方法は,本船の価格の減少,すなわち良好な状態と損傷状態の本船の価格を比較し決定することである (*The Arizona*, SMA 1259 (Arb. at N.Y. 1978))。

　The Theofilos J. Vatis, SMA 1994 (Arb. at N.Y. 1984) 事件で,暖かい撒積セメントを輸送後,本船の船艙がセメントの堅い膜で覆われた。傭船者は「通常の損耗を除き,同様に良好な状態で」返船できなかったと裁定された。しかしながら,仲裁審は,その後の船主による清掃と修理により船艙は傭船契約が求める以上に良好な状態になったと裁定した。したがって仲裁審は,船主に価値の上昇した額だけ差し引いた船艙の清掃・修理費用を裁定した。

　Zidell Inc. v. *Pacific Northern Marine Corp.*, 1990 AMC 922 (D. Or. 1990) 事件で,裸傭船契約は,本船は……「通常の損耗を除き……引渡時と同様に良好な状態で」本船を保守することを要求していた。本船の正式返船前に返船検査が行われ,通常の損耗を超える本船の外観構造を修理するようにとの勧告がなされた。傭船者は,修理の代わりに船主に対し現金精算がで

きると主張した。さらに、傭船者は修理期間中の傭船料につき自らの責任を容認したが、傭船契約の損害賠償予定額条項は違約金としては無効であると主張した。仲裁審は、傭船契約の条項と業界の習慣に基づいて船主は現金精算を受け入れる必要はなく、通常の損耗を除く良好な状態で返船を受ける権利があると裁定した。さらに、仲裁審は1日につき1,100米国ドルの傭船者の損害賠償予定額は実際の損害の妥当な予測と認定し、したがって船主に対してその損害の裁定を行った。

通常の損耗を除く

「通常の損耗」は、Moran Towing Co. v. Gammino Constr. Co., 363 F. 2d 108, 1966 AMC 2263, 2271-72 (1st Cir. 1966) 事件で、次のように定義されている。

損耗とは、通常の価値低減のことである。何が「通常」であるかは、本船が使用された業務の実態に対応して、考慮されるべきであることは、明らかである。過失によるものは損耗ではなく、また単に、その結果が予想しえたというだけで損耗とはならない。

The Managua, SMA 352 (Arb. at N.Y. 1966) 事件で、仲裁審は次のように述べている。

海事検定人2人の証言で確認されているように、船艙、艙口蓋、甲板の金属部分のかき傷、刻み傷、えぐり傷、凹損、曲損、剪断変形は、グラブ・バケット、ブルドーザー、ペイローダー、その他の機械装置を使う、大抵の撒積貨物の通常の揚荷方法では不可避のことであり、そして、そのような損傷が重大なものでなくて、船艙、艙口蓋、隔壁、甲板の構造材の強度や機能に影響を与えない場合、「通常の損耗」と考えられることは、よく知られていることである。

スクラップ貨物の荷役による損傷は、この「通常の損耗」の範囲内であると裁定した The Mare Feliz, SMA 1954 (Arb. at N.Y. 1984) 事件と同旨。

相当の注意を尽くしたにもかかわらず損傷となったことを傭船者が証明しない限り、本船の損傷に対する責任は、傭船者に課せられると判示した Neubros v. Northwestern Nat. Ins. Co., 359 F. Supp. 310, 320 (E.D.N.Y. 1972) 事件で同じ解決法が取られた。

同様に、Hudson Valley Light Weight Aggregate Corp. v. Windsor Bldg. & Supply Co., 446 F. 2d 750 (2nd Cir. 1971) 事件では、船舶賃貸借に基づき運航中の艀が、重い砕石を運送中に損傷を受けた。裁判所は、船主が艀を良好な状態で引き渡し、損傷状態で返船されたことを立証したときは、船主は、傭船者の過失を一応証明していると判示した。そこで、傭船者は、事故が傭船者の過失によるものではないこと、傭船者は艀の取扱に際して相当の注意を尽くしたことを立証しなければならないと判示された。

Otto Candies Inc. v. McDermott Interantional Inc., 600 F. Supp. 1334 (E.D. La. 1985)、原審維持 785 F. 2d 1033 (5th Cir. 1986) 事件で、2隻の艀が被告に裸傭船され、その管理下で大規模の損傷を被った。傭船契約は、傭船者が引渡時と同じ船級で同じ状態に保守することを求めた。傭船者は引渡時と同じ船級、同じ状態で艀を返船することができず傭船契約に違反したと判示された。裁判所は、傭船者が主張するように構造的損傷と損耗を同一視することは、当事者の意思であるとの証拠は存しないと認定して、傭船者が損耗に頼るのを否認した。したがって、裁判所は船主に傭船契約の条項に従って、両艀の修理費、修理期間中の未払傭船料、雑費、予め設定した利子および妥当な弁護士費用を認定する裁定を出した。

The Matter of Hygrade Operators Inc. and Leevac Marine Inc., SMA 2851 (Arb. at N.Y.

1992）事件で，「通常の損耗」の意味するところが何であるかに関する重要な特性が傭船契約に挿入されておらず，共同検査を実行する業界の慣習に当事者が依存することにより，検査人[241]が確定した基準を適用するという当事者の意思が証明されていると，仲裁人は裁定した。通常の損耗を除き，傭船開始時の検査時に明らかとなった損傷については傭船者に責任があると裁定した The Plod and The Voce, SMA 2719 (Arb. at N.Y. 1990) 事件も参照（B. H. Inc. v. Anthony M. Meyerskin, Inc., 149 F. Supp. 219 (E.D.N.Y. 1957); The G. G. Post, 64 F. Supp. 191, 195 (W.D.N.Y. 1945); Wilson Shipping Corp., Ltd. v. Tamarack Corp., SMA 645 (Arb. at N.Y. 1971); The Elna II, SMA 576 (Arb. at N.Y. 1957); The Theokeetor, SMA 604 (Arb. at N.Y.); The North Man rchioness, SMA 77 (Arb. at N.Y. 1962); The Stavros Commantaros, 1961 AMC 370 (Arb. at N.Y. 1961) 各事件参照）。

「通常の損耗を除き」という文言は，本船の清掃状態には適用されないと裁定されている（The Argo Sky, SMA 627 (Arb. at N.Y. 1971))。

約定以外の場所での返船

傭船者は傭船契約に記載された特定の場所または区域内で本船を返船しなければならない。アイルランドの Limerick での返船は，連合王国の安全港で返船するという傭船者の義務違反であると判示された The Trafalgar, 1938 AMC 463 (Arb. at N.Y. 1938) 事件を参照。仲裁審によると，アイルランド自由州の港は連合王国ではない。The Severoles, 1935 AMC 1135 (Arb. at N.Y. 1935) 事件と The Gerdt Oldendorff, SMA 1981 (Arb. at N.Y. 1984) 事件も参照。

傭船契約に記載された以外の他の場所での返船により，船主は傭船者の契約違反により生じた損害につき賠償を請求する権利を有する。その損害は求められる返船地へ向けた仮定の航海中の船主の逸失利益から構成される。もちろん，船主は損害を極小化する義務がある。本船が仮定の航海に必要な期間に別途就航する場合，船主の損害はこの代替使用から得られる収入で縮小される。

The Christin T, SMA 2527 (Arb. at N.Y. 1988) 事件で，傭船者は傭船契約に記載された以外の場所での本船の返船につき傭船契約違反と判示された。しかし，船主は被った損害の証明ができず，いかなる損害回収も認容されなかった。

The New York Getty, SMA 2200 (Arb. at N.Y. 1986) 事件で，傭船契約は米国ガルフ諸港で返船と定めていたが，本船が Jacksonville で修理のため，入渠したとき，船主は返船を受け入れた。傭船者は本船が米国ガルフ諸港で返船されると想定して傭船料を前払していたので，傭船料の返済を求めた。仲裁審は傭船者は返済を求める権利があると裁定した。

傭船者が傭船契約に記載された場所で返船を用意しているのに対して，船主が記載の場所の手前で返船を受けるのを選択する場合，反対の特約がなければ，実際の返船が行われる場所を超えての追加傭船料や追加燃料の支払を傭船者が要求されることはない。

前出192頁の解説参照。

荷　敷

The Milly Gregos, SMA 2190 (Arb. at N.Y. 1986) 事件で，傭船者は最後の貨物を揚荷し

た後で船上にかなりの量の荷敷を持ったまま本船を返船した。船主は荷敷を取り除く際に発生した費用と時間に相当する傭船料を請求した。傭船契約には，船艙を清掃せずにその代わりに一括金額を支払って，本船を返船することを傭船者に認める条項があった。しかし仲裁審は，この条項はかなりの量の荷敷を除去する費用を含んでいないと裁定した。船上に残った量は荷敷約250/300トンであった。仲裁審はこれは船上に残置するには不当な量であると判示した。

242 船上の残置量がわずかな量であれば，船艙清掃の一括金額支払条項ですまされるとの仲裁審の裁定が出たように思われる。仲裁審は消費燃料と他の処分費用と共に船艙清掃に必要な時間の傭船料の喪失を含めて船主に有利に損害を裁定した。

傭船料の支払と本船の引揚

"58.　5. Payment of said hire to be made in New York in cash in United States Currency, semi-monthly in advance, and for the last half month or
59. part of same the approximate amount of hire, and should same not cover the actual time, hire is to be paid for the balance day by day, as it becomes
60. due, if so required by Owners, unless bank guarantee or deposit is made by the Charterers, otherwise failing the punctual and regular payment of the
61. hire, or bank guarantee, or on any breach of this Charter Party, the Owners shall be at liberty to withdraw the vessel from the service of the Char-
62. terers, without prejudice to any claim they (the Owners) may otherwise have on the Charterers."

「5. 前条の傭船料の支払は，New York において現金（米国通貨）により，毎半月分を前払するものとする。最終の半月，またはこれに満たない期間に対する傭船料は，概算額によるものとし，その概算額が，実際の期間に及ばない場合においては，傭船料の不足額につき，その弁済期の到来する毎に，船主の要求により，連日これを支払わなければならない。ただし，傭船者が銀行の保証を受け，または供託をしていた場合は，この限りではない。傭船料を遅滞なく定期に支払わない場合，銀行保証がない場合，もしくは本契約に違反した場合，船主は自由に傭船者の運航から本船を引き揚げることができる。この場合，船主が傭船者に対して有すべき他の一切の請求は妨げられない。」

一般原則

定期傭船書契約の標準書式は船主にとり傭船料の定期的受領が重要であることを認識し，ニューヨーク・プロデュース書式の60行から62行のような条項を含んでいるが，傭船者が特定の日毎にその日以前に支払うべき傭船料を支払うことができない場合，その条項は船主が傭船契約を終了するのを認めている。

Tankexpress v. *Compagnie Financière Belge des Pétroles* (1948) 82 Ll. L. Rep. 43 事件で，Wright 卿は，次のように言った。「傭船者の義務である傭船料前払が重要であるというのは，それが，船主の提供する本船，乗組員の使用と役務に対応して，船主に与えられる対価そのものだからである。傭船契約が存続する限り，船主は，履行に先立って，約定どおり，傭船料を定期的に受け取る権利を有する。この理由により，傭船契約を解約する船主の権利には，説得力がある」。

なぜならコモン・ローの下では傭船料の支払の単なる遅滞は船主に損害賠償請求の権利をもたらすが，必ずしも船主が本船を引き揚げるのを容認しないので，引揚条項がなければ，船主はそういう権利を通常有しない。あらゆる状況の中で，傭船者が支払おうとしない態度をとるとか，支払えないという態度をとる場合のみ，あるいは期限どおりの支払の不履行が傭船契約の拒絶に至る場合に，船主は傭船契約を終了させることができる（後出346頁参照）。事実上，引揚条項は前述の状況で傭船契約を終了する契約上の選択権を船主に認める。引揚条項が契約の選択権以上のものを認め，傭船料が期限どおりに支払われないことを（損害賠償の問題に影響する）条件（condition）の違反として船主が取り扱う権利があるかどうかの問題について，先例は分かれている（後出327頁参照）。しかし，引揚権を行使する法的効果がどんなもの

であれ，船主はその権利を行使するためには，受け取るべき傭船料が特定の日にあるいはその前に支払われていないことを証明すれば足りる。傭船者が期限どおりに支払えない理由は，船主には関係のないことである（後出312頁参照）。

現　　金

本文における「現金 cash」には，支払の取消が不能で，かつ船主が傭船料を直ちに無条件で使用しうる，商業実務上現金と等価値となる支払方法を含む。銀行内振替，銀行為替，ま
[244]た，*The Georgios C.* [1971] 1 Ll. L. Rep. 7 事件において使用された「銀行支払伝票 banker's payment slip」は，これに含まれる。さらにロンドン通貨決済方式における「支払指図 payment order」をも含むと思われる（*The Laconia* [1977] 1 Lloyd's 315 事件参照）。

The Brimnes [1972] 2 Lloyd's Rep. 465 事件で，Brandon 判事は，「現金での……支払」という文言の意味について，「この文言は，現代の商業実務に照らして解釈されなければならない。そうすれば，この文言が，ドル紙幣その他の米国法定貨幣での支払だけを意味すると解しえない。船主が主張したとおり，この文言は，より広い意味を持ち，送金の結果，受取人が資金を直ちに無条件で使用しうることになる商業上確立されている送金方法も，この文言に含まれていなければならない」と判示した（同判例集476頁）。

本件の控訴院の判決 [1974] 2 Lloyd's Rep. 241 で，控訴院の Edmund Davies 判事は，上記定義に明確な賛意を表した（同判例集248頁）（*The Laconia* [1976] 1 Lloyd's Rep. 395 事件での Lawton 卿判事の判決も参照（同判例集402頁））。

送金された資金を即時に船主が使用できる権利は，「無条件」でなければならない。

Chikuma 号は，ニューヨーク・プロデュース書式で傭船され，傭船料は Genoa の船主の銀行に支払うと定められた。毎月の傭船料は期日にその銀行に支払われた。しかし，同じく Genoa にある支払銀行は，テレックス送金に4日後の「有効日」を含めていた。イタリアの銀行実務上この規定によると，船主は銀行から即刻資金を引き出すことができるが，資金につきそのときから「有効日」までの利子を支払わねばならなかった。船主は第5条により本船を引き揚げた。

貴族院は控訴院の判決を覆し，Robert Goff 判事の決定に戻り，船主は引き揚げる権利があると判示した。送金資金の利子を払う義務により，船主には即時使用を要求する「無条件」の権利がないので，支払は「現金」になっていない。Bridge 卿は前出 *The Brimnes* 事件の Brandon 判事の言説に言及し，次のように付言した。「基本的概念は，間違いなく，こういうことである。支払が文字どおり現金以外の別の方法，つまりドル紙幣，またはその他の法定通貨（誰も期待していないが）で，銀行に対して行われるときに，債権者が受領するものが現金と等価物または現金も同然の……ものでない限り，第5条の意味での『現金による支払』ではない。船主の銀行の帳簿上の1月22日付船主勘定記載事項が現金と等価物でないことは明白であった。実質的に，銀行には当座貸越と同価値のものを利用できるようにする義務があった」。

The Chikuma [1981] 1 Lloyd's Rep. 371.

銀行為替と支払指図

傭船者の銀行が，船主の銀行に銀行為替あるいはそれと同等の書類を引き渡せば，傭船契約上の支払は，その引渡のときに完了する（*The Brimnes* [1974] 2 Lloyd's Rep. 241 事件参照）。船主の銀行が，現実に船主の口座に入金するまでに，内部処理に時間がかかるが，それでも上記の結論が変わるわけではない。*The Laconia* [1977] 1 Lloyd's Rep. 315 事件で，Salmon 卿が指摘しているように，傭船者が現金で傭船料を支払った場合でも，それが船主口座に入金されるまで，若干の事務手続が必要である。

傭船者の銀行が，船主の銀行に対し，ロンドン通貨決済方式による「支払指図 payment order」を出した場合でも，事情は同じであると思われる。事務手続のため，船主の銀行が「支払指図」を受領してから24時間以内に，船主口座に入金されないとしても，この点は変わりがない。この点は，The Laconia 事件で問題となったが，貴族院は，別の理由からこの問題を処理した。同事件において，傭船料は，「船主に対し, 34, Moorgate, London E.C.2 所在の First National City Bank of New York の船主口座の貸方，O.F.C.口座番号705586に振り込み支払うとされていた。この点につき，貴族院の3名の裁判官が意見（tentative view）を表明したが，そのうち2名が，船主の銀行に対して，「支払指図」を引き渡した時点で，支払は有効に成立していると考えた。この見解は，控訴院の判決と一致している。Salmon 卿は，「ドル紙幣による支払と，支払指図による支払との間に，実質的差異はない。支払指図は，銀行業界で，一般に現金として受け入れられている」と述べた。Russell 卿は次のように述べている。「支払指図は，——私の理解では取消不能で，かつ『確実である』——銀行間に関する限り，現金と同価値のものであるから，期限どおりの支払としては，かかる現金同様のものが，指定口座の貸方に計上されるよう，指定銀行に期限内に提供されれば，それで十分である。私は，今述べられた上記のような見解に強く傾いている。本件で定められていたのは，かかる支払方法であった。現金を提供しても，現金同様のものを提供しても，いずれにせよ，口座に『直接』払い込むことはできないのである」。Fraser 卿は，反対の見解を示し，支払は期日までに船主口座に入金できるよう，十分な時間的余裕をもってなされなければならないと述べた。

　上記貴族院の多数意見に従うのが商業実務上，合理的確実性を増すのに役立つと言われている（The Laconia 事件の控訴院における記録長官 Denning 卿と Lawton 卿判事の判断と The Afovos [1980] 2 Lloyd's Rep. 469 事件の Lloyd 判事の判決を参照）。

テレックスによる口座間の振替

　The Brimnes [1974] 2 Lloyd's Rep. 241 事件（同判例集257頁）で Megaw 卿判事は，次のように述べた。「一方で現金または小切手（小切手が支払方法として許される場合）の引渡による支払と他方でテレックスによる支払指示との間に有用な類似性はない。小切手の受領は単なる指示の受領ではない。小切手の所持人は，その証書を所持するおかげで，ある金額に対する合法的権利——必要なら訴訟で彼が執行できる合法的権利を取得するので，小切手の受領は固有の価値を持つ法的文書——無体動産——の受領である。口座間の振替の指示を含むテレックスの受領はそのテレックスの所有者にそういう権利を与えない。それは支払指示であるが，支払ではない」と指摘した。

　The Afovos [1983] 1 Lloyd's Rep. 335 事件で貴族院は，支払がテレックスによる口座間の振替による場合，どの段階で支払がなされたとみなすべきかを判示するのを拒否した。Diplock 卿は単に（同判例集342頁で）それはたいていの事案について法の問題としての判断ではなく問題の時期において普及している銀行の実務の証明に拠るべきであるとの所見を述べるにとどめた。

　傭船者の銀行が傭船契約に指定された受取人の銀行に，口座を有し，受取人銀行に対して，必要な金額を自己の口座から船主の口座に振り替えるよう指示した，The Brimnes 事件で，控訴院は，傭船契約上要求されている支払方法は，「Morgan Guaranty Trust Co. of New York の船主口座に，米国通貨により現金で」支払うというものであったが，この支払がなされたのは，Morgan に対して，テレックスによる口座間の振替を指示した時点ではなく，そのテレックスの行内処理過程で，Morgan Guaranty が，船主口座に入金する有効な決定を行った時点であると判示した（The Zographia M [1976] 2 Lloyd's Rep. 382 事件参照）。

The Afovos〔1980〕2 Lloyd's Rep. 469 事件の第1審で，Lloyd 判事は次のように述べた。「支払が顧客の口座のある銀行から他の銀行へテレックスで振替が行われるときに，受取銀行がテレックスを受領し確認する時点で支払は完了すると私は判断する。そこで，仮に船主が銀行に照会すれば，『はい，お金はあなたの口座に入金しました』と言われる。資金が船主の口座に貸方計上されるべきであったということは余計なことである。まして船主が資金を口座から移すことができるということは必要ではない。船主の口座の**ために**銀行が資金を受領したと言うことで十分である」。その事案では，傭船契約に傭船料は「London の First National Bank of Chicago の……（船主の）口座に入金として」支払うものと規定されていた。入電テレックス振替支払の受領の際の銀行の手続について証拠が提供されたが，入電テレックスの確認の完了と受取人の口座に貸方計上の決定が同時であったのか，またはテレックスの確認の完了がそのような決定に先行したのかは，その判決からは明らかでない。

船主の銀行が傭船者の銀行に口座を持つ場合，傭船契約に基づく支払は，船主の銀行が傭船者の銀行にある自分の口座にこのように入金したという通知を受領するまで完了しない。

Effy 号の傭船料は，「22 St. Mary Axe, London E. C. 3 所在の Williams Deacon's Bank Ltd. にある A. M. Nomikos 商会の米貨ドル口座7450に支払うべきこと」となっていた。傭船者は，その通常の実務に従って，傭船料の特定期分の支払として，イスラエルの銀行に対し，必要金額を振り替えて，それが日曜日である満期日までに船主の銀行に着くことを確実にするよう指示した。イスラエルの銀行は，同様の指示を New York の銀行に対して与えた。New York の銀行は，New York の慣行に従って月曜日まで待ち，同銀行にある Williams Deacon's 銀行の口座に船主の勘定として入金した。この入金についての電信通知は，火曜日の早朝になって Williams Deacon's 銀行に着いた。Mocatta 判事は，電信が Williams Deacon's 銀行に着くまでは，傭船料の支払がなされていないことになると判断した。New York に入金があったという確認を船主が銀行から入手しうるのは，電信が着いた後であり，その確認なしには，船主は傭船料を引き出すこともできない。つまり電信を受け取るまでは，支払も支払の提供もなかったことになる。

The Effy〔1972〕1 Lloyd's Rep. 18.

NYPE 93

ニューヨーク・プロデュース書式の1993年版の146/147行には，傭船料は「支払期日に船主が使用可能なように」支払われることを求めている（前出11頁と55頁参照）。

船主が合意した支払方法の変更

船主が，傭船料支払につき特定の方法を承認し，その方法を用いたため，支払が遅延するに至る情況についての検討は，後出314頁参照。

支払傭船料の不足

傭船料が支払われない場合だけではなく，また支払が遅滞した場合にも，船主は本船を引き揚げることができる。期限内に支払はあったが，その金額が正当な金額に満たず，期日までに残額が支払われない場合にも，船主は本船を引き揚げることができる（*The Agios Giorgis*〔1976〕2 Lloyd's Rep. 192 事件と後出 *The Mihalios Xilas* 事件参照）。両事件で傭船者の法廷弁護人は期日どおりであっても，支払不足により本船を引き揚げる権利が生じることを認めた。

Mihalios Xilas 号は，ボルタイム書式で傭船された。追加第39条に毎月の傭船料の支払について規定していた。さらに，「最終月の傭船料は，本船が返船されると予想される期日までの燃料費および船主のための立替費用，船主負担となる他の項目を差し引いて算定し，前払とする」と規定していた。9ヶ月目の傭船料の支払期限は，3月22日であった。3月21日に傭船者は1ヶ月分の満額よりかなり少ない金額を支払った。傭船者の代理人は船主に対して今回の傭船料の支払は本船契約に基づく最後の支払とみなしていることを明らかにし，前渡金と返船時の残油や立替金を控除したので不足になっていると説明した。仲裁で審判人は，9ヶ月目の月末で本船が返船となるとの傭船者の予測は妥当ではなく，控除額はいずれにせよ不当であり，極端であると裁定した。

Kerr 判事は，この状況で船主は本船を引き揚げる権利があると認めた。同判事は次のように述べた。「結果として傭船者は9ヶ月目の傭船料につき不足となった。この支払不足が，確認された事実に基づき，本船引揚権を含む第6条第2節の『支払不履行』を構成することは，議論の余地がない」（結局，貴族院まで行った裁判所の判決の問題は，その後船主は本船引揚権を放棄したかどうかという事実であった。これについては，後出322頁参照）。

The Mihalios Xilas [1976] 2 Lloyd's Rep. 697, [1978] 2 Lloyd's Rep. 397 (C. A.) と [1979] 2 Lloyd's Rep. 303 (H. L.) 事件（The Lutetian [1982] 2 Lloyd's Rep. 140（同判例集154頁）事件も参照）。

247 本船の使用が妨げられた場合の傭船料の支払

本船の使用が妨げられている間に，定時の傭船料支払期日が到来した場合，傭船者は，やはり，支払期限のきた傭船料を支払わなければならないと思われる。ただし，(a)オフハイヤーを含め，傭船契約上特に規定する金額，(b)傭船料支払期日以前の一定期間本船使用が不当に妨げられたことによる損害（前出参照）に限り，傭船料から差し引くことができる。

Tankexpress v. Compagnie Financière Belge des Pétroles (1946) 79 Ll. L. Rep. 451 事件で，Atkinson 判事は，傭船料支払期日に，船長が船主の命令に基づき，傭船者の船積指示に従うことを不当に拒否していた事情の下では，傭船者が傭船料を支払わなくても，それは，傭船契約違反とならないと判示した。貴族院は，他の根拠に基づいて判決した——(1948) 82 Ll. L. Rep. 43——のではあるが，Porter 卿も，du Parcq 卿も，ともに傍論として，Atkinson 判事の見解は誤っており，傭船料支払義務は継続している（もちろん，船主の行為が契約全体の履行拒絶にまで達し，傭船者が，それを受けて，契約を消滅したものとして扱うことに決した場合は別であるが）という見解を表明した。Porter 卿は，この点に結論を出す必要があるとは考えなかったが，「履行拒絶を受け入れることと，傭船料の支払を続ける義務を結果において伴う傭船契約の継続との間に妥協点があるか疑わしい」と述べた。du Parcq 卿は，「船主が履行拒絶をしようとしているわけではないのに，傭船料支払日の直前・直後数日間，本船が事実上，傭船者の自由にならなかったという理由で，1ヶ月の傭船料前払に合意した傭船者が，傭船料支払の責任を免れる」という議論は納得できないと述べた。

The Charalambos N. Pateras [1971] 2 Lloyd's Rep. 42 事件，および Halcyon Steamship v. Continental Grain (1943) 75 Ll. L. Rep. 80 事件で MacKinnon 卿判事が述べた（同判例集84頁）後出308頁に詳説した原則をも参照。

支払期日に本船がオフハイヤーとなっているときの傭船料の支払

The Lutetian [1982] 2 Lloyd's Rep. 140 事件で，Bingham 判事は，ニューヨーク・プロデュース書式の下で，第15条は，列挙原因による時間喪失の場合，「傭船料の支払は停止する」と規定しているので，本船が傭船料支払期日にオフハイヤーとなっている場合，傭船者は

支払期日にその時点での傭船料の支払をする必要はないと判示した。同判事は，こういう状況では本船が傭船者の役務に再び就く直前まで，前払で翌月の傭船料の支払をする傭船者の義務は中断するという主張を認めた。この判決を本章の最初のところで述べた一般原則と調和させるのは困難であるように思われ，実務上重大な不確実性をもたらすかも知れない。上級審による検討が行われるまで注意して取り扱われるべきものと思われる。

傭船契約の条項により許容される傭船料からの控除

傭船者は，傭船契約上特に許容された金額を傭船料から控除することができる。したがってニューヨーク・プロデュース書式の65/66行の本船の費用の立替は「傭船料から控除されるものとする」(Seven Seas v. Atlantic [1975] 2 Lloyd's Rep. 188 事件における Donaldson 判事の判決参照)。同書式の99/101行で喪失時間および消費燃料と船体，機関または属具の欠陥または故障により生じる速力の低下の結果として生じる費用に関して同じように規定されている。ニューヨーク・プロデュース書式第15条97/99行のオフハイヤー・クレームに関して控除が認められるか否かは，明確に述べられていない。そこで関連する文言は「時間を喪失したときは，傭船料の支払はその期間停止するものとする」である。しかし，The Lutetian [1982] 2 Lloyd's Rep. 140 (同判例集149頁) 事件で法廷弁護士と裁判所は，翌月の傭船料支払から過去のオフハイヤー期間に関して支払った傭船料の控除は許容されることを認めた。後出 The Nanfri 事件に関する控訴院判決でボルタイムの第11条(A)項（「喪失した一切の時間に対しては，傭船料の支払を要しない。傭船料の前払があったときは，これをその時間に応じて精算しなければならない」）に基づくオフハイヤーは，次の傭船料支払から控除できることが判示された。しかしながら，予想されるオフハイヤー期間についての控除は許されない（前出 The Lutetian 事件参照）。ニューヨーク・プロデュース書式133/134行にある船内消費の燃料費も傭船料から控除できよう (Seven Seas v. Atlantic [1975] 2 Lloyd's Rep. 188 事件における Donaldson 判事の判決参照)。

たとえ控除額が前もって仲裁人により決定されておらず，あるいは，船主と合意に達していなくとも，許容された控除は，次の傭船料支払から行いうる。それとは反対の船主の主張は後出 The Nanfri 事件で，Kerr 判事と控訴院により却下された。記録長官 Denning 判事は，次のように述べた。「傭船者が控除できることは疑いない。しかし問題はその時期である。控除を行う前にそのことについて合意されるか，あるいは確証されねばならないか。その趣旨の先例を私は知らない。傭船者は誠実になされた妥当な評価により損失を算定し，その金額を傭船料から控除する権利があると思われる」。The Kostas Melas [1981] 1 Lloyd's Rep. 18 (25頁) 事件も参照。

> 1974年11月に Nanfri と Benfri, Lorfri 号は，同じ傭船者相手に三つの別個の，しかし実質的には同一のボルタイム契約書で約6年間の契約が締結された。通常のボルタイム書式のオフハイヤー条項第11条(A)項および(B)項に加えて，第11条(C)項としてニューヨーク・プロデュース書式のオフハイヤー条項の一部が追加された。その条項は次のとおりであった。「機関……の欠陥により航海速力が低下する場合，喪失時間，その結果として発生する追加消費燃料は……傭船料から控除する」。1977年7月と9月に傭船者は各傭船契約の傭船料の支払から控除を行った。傭船者は1975年のある航海の機関故障による速力低下を申し立て，その関連で第11条(C)項に基づき1977年10月1日の Nanfri 号の支払傭船料から47,122米ドルを控除すると通告した。船主は抗議をし，実行された控除のいくつかに関連して傭船者が前もって有効であると合意していない金額を傭船料から控除する権利が傭船者に一方的にあるかどうかの問題につき仲裁に付託すると通告した。

後出393頁で検討される別個の問題につき、本事案は、法廷に持ち出され貴族院まで行った。貴族院は次の点につき、意見を述べる必要はないと判断した。一方控訴院では、
(a) 全員一致で第11条(A)項および(C)項により有効な請求は次の傭船料の支払から控除できるという見解であった。
(b) 記録長官 Denning 卿と Goff 卿判事は（Cumming-Bruce 卿判事は意見が異なるが）次のように述べた。本船の使用期間につきその全部または一部を船主が傭船者から奪い、傭船契約に違反した場合、傭船者はその損害賠償請求額を傭船料から控除できる。
(c) 傭船者が上記(a)(b)に関して控除する金額につき記録長官 Denning 卿は、その金額は「誠実になされた妥当な評価により算定された金額」でなければならないと判示した。しかし、Goff 卿判事は控除を決定する際に、傭船者は自分の責任で行動するという別の根拠に基づき判断を下した。
The Nanfri [1978] 1 Lloyd's Rep. 581, [1978] 2 Lloyd's Rep. 132 (C.A.) および [1979] 1 Lloyd's Rep. 201 (H.L.)。

損害賠償請求金額の控除：衡平法上の相殺

一　般

現在、先例を綜合すると、船主の契約違反により、傭船者の本船使用が、一部または全部阻害された場合、傭船者は、その阻害期間に関する損害賠償額を傭船料から控除できるという見解が支持されると思われる。The Nanfri [1978] 2 Lloyd's Rep. 132（同判例集140頁）事件で記録長官 Denning 卿は、相殺できる損害賠償請求は「同じ取引から生じる、またはその取引と密接に関連する」損害賠償請求であり、また「原告の請求を直接非難することになる、即ち原告の請求とあまりに密接に関連している故反訴請求を考慮せずに請求の強行を原告に認めることは明らかに不公正となる」損害賠償請求であると述べた。Denning 卿のこの定義の第二点を解説して、Saville 判事は、The Aditya Vaibhab [1991] 1 Lloyd's Rep. 573 事件で次のように述べた。「しかしながら、傭船料が支払われる期間に関して船主が役務を提供する場合、そのような明らかな不公正は生じない。なぜなら、船主が提供していない役務に対して何らかの意味での支払を求めていることを指摘することによって、そのような船主が役務を提供した期間についての傭船料請求を問題にすることはできないからである」。

貨物の損傷に関するようなクレームは、控除できないであろう（The Nanfri [1978] 2 Lloyd's Rep. 132事件（同判例集141頁））が、一方、船主が満船貨物を積み取らなかった場合や（The Teno [1977] 2 Lloyd's Rep. 289 事件）、傭船契約速力担保違反は、この概念（控除可能な損害賠償請求）に含まれると判示された（The Chrysovalandou Dyo [1981] 1 Lloyd's Rep. 159 事件）が、どの種類の損害賠償請求がこの概念に含まれるかは、必ずしも明白ではない。

この問題は、次にさらに詳細に検討される。

本船使用の阻害

この問題に関する法は、未だ最終的に決着を見ていない。この概念に対決する事案が貴族院で取り上げられるまで、歴史的根拠に基づいて問題を扱うのが最良と思われる。

Naxos Shipping v. Thegra Shipping (The Corfu Island) (1973) 事件（未報告事件）では、Ackner 判事は、傭船者は、速力担保違反に関する損害賠償額を傭船料から控除する権利があると判示した。Seven Seas v. Atlantic Shipping [1975] 2 Lloyd's Rep. 188 事件で、Donaldson 判事は、運賃に対して、損害賠償請求額を相殺する権利は認められないが、傭船料と運賃とで異なった取扱をする理由はなく、したがって、損害賠償請求額をもって相殺する一般的権利はないと判示している（The Brede [1973] 2 Lloyd's Rep. 333 事件および The Aries [1977] 1

Lloyd's Rep. 334 事件と *The Dominique* [1989] 1 Lloyd's Rep. 431 事件参照)。しかし，Donaldson 判事は，上記の見解と，*Halcyon Steamship* v. *Continental Grain* (1943) 75 Ll. L. Rep. 80 事件における MacKinnon 卿判事の次のような見解（同判例集84頁）との調和をはからねばならなかった。すなわち「本法廷における最近の事案で，このような定期傭船契約において，傭船者は，次の二つの場合にのみ，約定傭船料を継続して支払う義務を免れることができるということが指摘された。第一は，傭船料停止条項が当該事案に適用される場合であり，第二は，船主の傭船契約違反により，傭船者が被った損害の求償の全部または一部として，一定期間の傭船料相当分と相殺するか，または反対請求できる場合である」(MacKinnon 卿判事が参照していた最近の事案というのは，おそらくは *Sea & Land Securities* v. *William Dickinson* (1942) 72 Ll. L. Rep. 159 事件のことと思われる)。Donaldson 判事は，上記引用文中の「一定期間の」傭船料という文言を強調して，例外となるのは，特定期間内の時間が全面的に奪われた事案に限られると述べた。

Parker 判事は，これらの判決を前にして，*The Teno*, [1977] 2 Lloyd's Rep. 289 事件で，ボルタイム書式による傭船契約において，本船の使用が全部または一部差し止められた場合，傭船者は，その阻害期間に対する損害賠償請求をもって，傭船料と相殺する権利があると判示した。本件において，Parker 判事が扱ったのは，船主の傭船料請求に対し，本船が満船貨物を積み取らなかったことを理由として，傭船者が提起した抗弁であった。Parker 判事は，相殺の権利が，貨物損害賠償のような，その他の賠償請求にも及ぶかという問題については未解決のまま残した。同判事は，その判決の補強として，*Sea & Land Securities* v. *William Dickinson* (1941) 71 Ll. L. Rep. 166 と (1942) 72 Ll. L. Rep. 159 事件，*Halcyon Steamship* v. *Continental Grain* (1943) 75 Ll. L. Rep. 80 事件および *The Charalambos* v. *Pateras* [1971] 2 Lloyd's Rep. 42 事件における各説示を援用した上，さらに続けて「前記諸判例は，船主の契約違反が，とにかく一定期間の不法な本船引揚にあるような場合には，その損害賠償請求権と定期傭船料請求権とを相殺できることが，1941年以来引き続き認められてきたことを示している」と述べた。

同判事は，ついで，相殺という衡平法上の権利の性質を検討し，それは単に，本船使用の全面的引揚の場合だけではなく，部分的引揚の場合にも適用されるべきであるという結論を出した。同判事は，*Hanak* v. *Green* [1958] 2 Q. B. 9 事件に言及し，次のように述べている。「この判決から得た結論は，反訴請求が，単に本訴請求権と同一の契約から生じただけでなく，本訴請求権と直接関係があり，反訴を考慮せずに本訴請求権者の求償を認めることが明らかに不公正をもたらすような場合には，不確定損害賠償額についても，衡平法上相殺の権利があるということである。船主が，その本船をまったく提供しなかったにもかかわらず，その期間の傭船料を請求する場合には，この要件は，明らかに満たされている。本件におけるように，船主が，契約に違反して，本船の部分的使用しか提供しなかったにもかかわらず，その間の傭船料を請求した場合にも，その要件を等しく満足していると考える。反訴請求が，例えば，貨物損害の求償のようにまったく異質のものである場合は，前記要件を充足していないのかもしれない。しかし，それは当面，判断を要する問題ではない」。

The Nanfri [1978] 1 Lloyd's Rep. 581 事件（前出248事件）で，速力不足による傭船料の控除に関する争点について，法廷弁護人は，Kerr 判事に対し，*The Teno* 事件に至る最近の一連の事件において，商事関係の法曹が一般に理解してきた法理を，陳述するよう求めた。これに対し，Kerr 判事は，反訴請求をもって航海傭船運賃や定期傭船料と相殺する権利はない，また，定期傭船料について，特定項目につき傭船料からの控除を認める明示の条項がほとんどの定期傭船契約にみられるが，その条項は，それ自体完結しているとみるべきであるから，相殺

する権利はないと一般的に考えられてきたと述べた。同判事は、さらに次のとおり述べた。「請求や反訴請求が、それら［明示をもって控除を認められた項目］に該当しなければ、傭船料は、継続して全額支払われるべきものであるというのが一般的見解である。控除項目に該当しないものは、金銭債務としてまたは損害賠償として、まったく別個の交叉請求としてのみ持ち出すことができる。傭船料支払の継続性と安全性は、明示の控除項目で制限されてはいるが、航海傭船における運賃に関する場合と同様の意味で、定期傭船契約上の船主に必須の安全保障と考えられている。これが一般的にとられている見解であると信ずるが、だからといって、特に *Gilbert-Ash (Northern) Ltd.* v. *Modern Engineering (Bristol)* Ltd. [1974] A.C. 689 事件の貴族院判決もあること故、*The Teno* 事件の結論を非難するものではない」。

The Nanfri 事件の控訴院（[1978] 2 Lloyd's Rep. 132）において、記録長官 Denning 卿とGoff 卿判事は、*The Teno* 事件の Parker 判事の判決は正しく、船主が不当に本船使用の全部または一部を阻害した場合には、傭船者は、傭船料から控除することができると判示した。Cumming-Bruce 卿判事は、この点につき反対の判決をした。記録長官 Denning 卿は、次のように言った。「前払された傭船料の対価の一部を定期傭船者から奪う契約違反を船主が犯している場合、傭船者は、翌月支払うべき傭船料から同額を控除できる。……したがって定期傭船では船主が不当に、かつ契約に違反して本船の使用を一時阻害する場合、傭船者は喪失時間の傭船料と同額を控除できる」。この事案について貴族院の判決は、別の根拠に拠っており、この論題に何らの指針を示すものではなかった。

Chrysovalandou Dyo [1981] 1 Lloyd's Rep. 159 事件で Mocatta 判事は、衡平法上の相殺権に基づいて、傭船契約の速力担保義務の不履行について、傭船料からの控除を認容した（*The Kostas Melas* [1981] 1 Lloyd's Rep. 18 事件の Robert Goff 判事の判決参照）。

The Leon [1985] 2 Lloyd's Rep. 470 事件で、Hobhouse 判事は、先例を引用して次のように述べた（同判例集475頁）。「商法の領域では、契約上の権利と救済の確定性が最も重要である。法の確定性が存在しなければならない場合、定期傭船料の支払を受ける権利と支払を止める権利は特に明白な例である。控訴院は、根本原理の適切な適用を表す簡単な規則を明確に述べた。その規則を再び用いることができるのであれば、私が関わった本事案よりも良い判決ができるに違いない。第１審裁判所がこの仕事を引き受けるのは、適当ではない。……この事件との関連では、一連の先例があり、われわれはこの指針を受け入れなければならない」。

傭船者のその他の請求

記録長官 Denning 卿は、前出 *The Nanfri* 事件の判決で、相殺する権利は「船主が、傭船者の本船の使用を不当に阻害した場合、または本船の使用に関して傭船者の権利を侵害した場合に」限定されると述べた。同判事は、「私は、その権利を他の違反、または乗組員の過失から生じる貨物損傷のような船主の過失にまで拡大しない」、と続けた。Goff 卿判事は、貨物損害賠償請求を除外するのに同意した。1979年の *The Lok Manya* 事件で Mustill 判事は、この先例に従って、貨物損害賠償請求を相殺する権利を否定し、損傷貨物を海上投棄する費用とその作業に要した３日間を貨物損害賠償請求の構成要素として扱った。しかし、1980年の控訴院で記録長官 Denning 卿は、傍論ではあるが、浪費した３日間の傭船料を相殺する権利を結果的に否定することについて疑問を投げかけた。さらに *The Sargasso* [1994] 1 Lloyd's Rep. 412 事件で、Clarke 判事は、定期傭船者は、船主の契約違反の結果として汚損を生じた貨物をどこかで処分するために本船が契約上の揚荷港を離れねばならず、そのために喪失した時間と傭船料を相殺する権利を有すると判示した。

The Aliakmon Progress [1978] 2 Lloyd's Rep. 499 事件（後出599頁参照）で、主張された

桟橋と本船の接触は乗組員の過失により引き起こされ，本船に損傷を生じた。必要な修理のため，予定していた貨物を確保できず他の貨物を求めて，39日間滞船しなければならなかった。記録長官 Denning 卿は，次のように述べた。「このような請求が衡平法上相殺できるものとして認容されるか疑わしいと思う。この事案［前出 The Nanfri 事件］でわれわれが示したように，衡平法上の相殺は，傭船者が船主の過失により，本船の使用を阻害される場合のみ可能となる。今回，傭船者は本船を使用できたが，貨物を積むことができなかった」（ともかく船主は米国海上物品運送法に基づく抗弁に拠ることができたので，傭船者の請求は，控訴院により無効と判示された。後出599頁参照）。

The Leon ［1985］ 2 Lloyd's Rep. 470 事件で，Hobhouse 判事は，衡平法上の相殺する権利は，次の点に関する数々の違反から生じるという請求を退けた。(a)正確な日誌を記録できなかった。(b)船長は燃料供給者による不正書類作成の関係者である。(c)傭船者の燃料の受寄者としての船主の義務違反。同判事はこの数々の違反について次のように述べた（同判例集474頁）。「これらの違反は本船の使用に関連していない。今回の事案で傭船者は，直接であれ間接であれ，この違反の結果として本船の使用時間を僅かでも喪失したと思わせるものはない。また，何らかの違反の理由で本船の船艙等のすべてが傭船者の自由に委ねられていなかったときがあるとか，または船長は迅速に航海を遂行しなかったとか，または船長は本船の使用に関して傭船者の指図に応じなかったと思わせるものもない」。

The Aditya Vaibhav ［1991］ 1 Lloyd's Rep. 573 事件で，船主は Shelltime 3 に基づく請求の中で未払傭船料のある部分について略式判決を得ることができないことを認めた。船主が船艙清掃義務を適正に遂行できなかったため，本船を傭船者が利用できなかった約14日間の傭船料がそれであった。

252 傭船者が控除できる金額

傭船契約が明示的に控除を許容している（前出306頁）がゆえに，または衡平法上の相殺する権利のゆえ（前出307頁）に傭船者が控除できる権利を有するとした場合，傭船者がどの程度減額できるかという問題が残る。傭船者は，自己の責任において，許容された控除額の計算をするのか。その結果，何らかの理由で後日妥当と判断される金額を超えて控除していた場合，船主は本船を引き揚げるかもしれない。The Nanfri ［1978］ 1 Lloyd's Rep. 581 事件で，Kerr 判事は，認容された控除につき，「傭船者が善意で主張し，合理的根拠に基づき算定した金額」を傭船料から控除した場合には，傭船者は債務不履行とはならないという傭船者に有利な見解を正式に採用した。控訴院 ［1978］ 2 Lloyd's Rep. 132 で，記録長官 Denning 卿はこの手法をとり，次のように述べた。「傭船者が誠実に行われた妥当な査定により自己の損失を算定して，その額を控除しても，傭船者は債務不履行とはならない。船主は傭船料の不払を理由として本船の引揚を行うことはできないし，その点に関して何らかの契約違反のかどで傭船者を有罪と考えることはできない。傭船者が控除しすぎたと結果的に判明する場合，船主はもちろん，差額を回収できる。しかしそれだけのことである」。しかし Goff 卿判事の判決はより厳しい見解で続いた。すなわち，どの程度控除するかを決定する際に，傭船者は危険を覚悟して行動することになる（Cumming-Bruce 卿判事も貴族院も，この点につき何の指針も出していない）。The Chrysovalandou Dyo ［1981］ 1 Lloyd's Rep. 159 事件で，誠実で妥当な査定の控除が行われたが，後で過剰と判明した問題に直面した Mocatta 判事は，この対立する見解の間で選択を余儀なくされたが，「私には商業的配慮から必要なことに一致していると思われる」との記録長官 Denning 卿の見解を選んだ（同じ趣旨で The Kostas Melas ［1981］ 1

Lloyd's Rep. 18 事件の Robert Goff 判事の判決も参照)。

　今日までの先例は，傭船者が誠実に行われた妥当な査定を基準として控除する場合，傭船者は契約に違反していないという見解に有利であるが，この論題に関する法は，最終的に確定したとみなすことはできない。

　しかしながら，傭船者が本船の使用を阻害された期間について支払った，または支払うべき傭船料の金額以上に傭船者は控除できないことが判示されている。The Aditya Vaibhav [1991] 1 Lloyd's Rep. 573 事件でSaville 判事は，Shelltime 3 の傭船契約に基づき定期傭船者は，船主が船艙清掃義務を適正に遂行できなかったということにより本船に遅延を生じ，傭船者の業務に利用できなかった14日間に支払われるべき傭船料を超えた損失と費用は控除できない，と判示した。

控除する権利を誠実に信じることでは十分ではない

　傭船契約，または (前出の) 衡平法上の相殺に基づく控除の権利がない場合，傭船者が控除する権利を持っていると誠実且つ当然に信じるとしても，それは傭船料の不払や支払不足に対して船主による本船の引揚権の行使を妨げることにはならない (The Lutetian [1982] 2 Lloyd's Rep. 140 (同判例集154頁) 事件参照)。

　しかし船主が，傭船者の計算に異議はないと傭船者に誤って信じさせるような態度をとれば，船主が，控除の不正確さに拠るのは禁反言となる (前出305/306頁の The Lutetian 事件参照)。

半月毎に

　ニューヨーク・プロデュース書式58行のこの語は，当事者により「月毎に」としばしば変更される。ここでいう月は暦月を意味する。月毎の傭船料支払は，各暦月の同じ日付に支払期日となる。Freeman v. Reed (1863) 4 B. & S. 174 事件でCockburn 主席判事は，次のように言った。「最初の月の所与の日付から開始し，大小の月如何を問わず，翌月の応答日に1 暦月は完了する」。その月に応答日がない場合，傭船料はその月の最終日が支払期日となる。この問題の最新の見解につき Dodds v. Walker [1980] 1 W. L. R. 1061 事件参照。そこでは，控訴院の多数意見は，「応答日」規則に従い，期間はある月の最終日に開始し，4 ヶ月目の最終日前に終了したにもかかわらず，9月30日からの4暦月は1月30日に期限切れとなると判示した。この判決は貴族院 [1981] 1 W. L. R. 1027 により維持された。

　ボルタイム書式は，傭船料は，「30日毎に」支払われると49/50行に規定して，長い月，短い月の障害を避けている。この計算のためには月は無視される。

前払にて

　傭船料は，「前払 in advance」されるべきものである。そこで，傭船者は，各単位期間の傭船料を，その支払期日前か，その当日に支払わなければならず，支払期日後であってはならない。Tankexpress v. Compagnie Financière Belge des Pétroles (1948) 82 Ll. L. Rep. 43 事件で，Wright 卿は，次のように述べた。「傭船者の義務である傭船料前払が重要であるというのは，それが，船主の提供する本船，乗組員の使用役務に対応して，船主に与えられる対価そのものだからである。傭船契約が存続する限り，船主は，履行に先立って，約定どおり，傭船料

を定期的に受け取る権利を有する」(同判例集53頁)。例えば，ニューヨーク・プロデュース書式102/103行に従って，本船の滅失といったある状況では，前払傭船料のすべて，または一部が傭船者に返却されねばならないかも知れないが，傭船料は，供託金であるとか，または当該日が必ずしも完全には「支払期日と」ならないという意味において，単に「条件付」または「暫定的」であるというものではない (*The Trident Beauty* [1993] 1 Lloyd's Rep. 443 と [1994] 1 Lloyd's Rep. 365 事件の控訴院と貴族院の判決および後出323頁参照)。

明示の協定または確立した慣習がない場合，傭船料を支払う義務は，傭船期間の最初に開始した時間に関係なく，傭船者には各支払期日の真夜中までの時間がある (*The Afovos* [1982] 1 Lloyd's Rep. 562 および [1983] 1 Lloyd's Rep. 335 (H. L.) 事件参照)。

傭船料前払の義務は，傭船開始後の各期傭船料についてと同様，最初の傭船料にも等しく適用される。Branson 判事は *Kawasaki* v. *Bantham Steamship* (1938) 60 Ll. L. Rep. 70 事件で，その旨判示した。したがって，傭船者は，ニューヨーク・プロデュース書式第5条の通告期間満了前か，同項に従い本船を使用する前に傭船料を支払わねばならない。後出342頁に示されている見解に反して，傭船者が指示した場所での本船引渡時に，契約書第5条に関係なく，傭船期間が開始するのであれば，問題が生じよう。傭船者が，予期せぬ早期の引渡の提供を受け，61行によって，本船が即時引き揚げられるという事態を避けるためには，裁判所が (*Budd* v. *Johnson, Englehart* (1920) 2 Ll. L. Rep. 27 における Roche 判事の不満足な判決に従って) 最初の傭船料は前払の要なしとするか，船主が，本船引渡時期について適切な通告を出すべきであるという黙示条項を認める必要があると思われる (*The Zographia M* [1976] 2 Lloyd's Rep. 382 事件において出された提案)。

船主に前払された傭船料は，ある状況では返金されなければならないことがあるが，融資貸付に基づき，傭船料が船主が譲渡した者に支払われた場合に，譲受人からも同じように返金されるべきであるということにはならない ([1993] 1 Lloyd's Rep. 443 (C. A.), [1994] 1 Lloyd's Rep. 365 (H. L.) および後出323頁の *The Trident Beauty* 事件参照)。

254 支払期日が銀行休日にあたる場合

支払期日が日曜日，その他の銀行休日にあたる場合，傭船者は，その休日前の銀行取引日に支払を行わなければならない (*The Zographia M* [1976] 2 Lloyd's Rep. 382 事件での Ackner 判事の判決参照)。同様に，*The Laconia* [1977] 1 Lloyd's Rep. 315 事件 (同判例集323頁) で，Salmon 卿は，次のような所見を (傍論として) 述べている。「支払期限経過後の支払は，期限どおりの支払とはいえない。しかし本件において，期限どおりの支払を期限前に行うことが出来ない理由が私には分らない。傭船料は船主の銀行へ半月毎に前払されるべきものであって，傭船料の支払期日が，銀行休日の日曜日にあたる場合，銀行は土曜日も閉店だから，支払は，その前日の金曜日になされるべきものである。これが前払である。月曜日になってからの支払提供は，対応する傭船期間に対しての前払とはならない」。

絶対的義務

支払期日までに傭船料を支払う義務は，「絶対的」なものである。Porter 卿は，*Tankexpress* v. *Compagnie Financière Belge des Pétroles* (1948) 82 Ll. L. Rep. 43 事件で，次のように言っている (同判例集51頁)。「履行を免除する特別の事情がある場合は別として，支払がなされなかったという事実だけで，債務不履行を構成し，そこに故意，過失による不履行という要件を

必要としない」。

最後の半月分の傭船料

ボルタイム書式

傭船契約に反対の規定がない限り，1ヶ月分または半月分の前払傭船料は，本船が1ヶ月または半月以内に返船されることが明らかであっても，全額支払わなければならないと思われる（Tonnelier v. Smith（1897）2 Com. Cas. 258 事件参照）。過払金額は，返船後，精算の上，船主が返済すべきものと思われる（Stewart v. Van Ommeren ［1918］2 K.B. 560 事件参照）。Tonnelier v. Smith 事件のこの一般原則は，ボルタイム書式に適用される。

ニューヨーク・プロデュース書式

ニューヨーク・プロデュース書式は，それとは反対に58/60行に「最終の半月，またはこれに満たない期間に対する傭船料は，概算額によるものとし，その概算額が，実際の期間に及ばない場合においては，傭船料の不足額につき，その弁済期の到来する毎に，船主の要求により，連日これを支払わなければならない。ただし，傭船者が銀行の保証を受け，または供託をしていた場合は，この限りではない。……」と規定している。したがって，半月以内に返船が行われる場合，半月分の傭船料より少ない金額の前払が可能であることになる。傭船者は，返船のありうる日についての予測に従って計算された金額のみを前払で支払う義務を負うのみである。しかし傭船者は返船予定日までの全期間の傭船料を支払わなければならない。したがって，Mocatta 判事は，The Chrysovalandou Dyo ［1981］1 Lloyd's Rep. 159 事件で，傭船者は自ら予測した返船日の3日前までの期間の傭船料を傭船者が支払ったときに，契約に違反したと判示した。さらに，傭船者の予測は妥当な根拠に基づいて行われなければならない。誠実に予測されたに違いないというだけでは不十分である（The Mihalios Xilas ［1978］2 Lloyd's Rep. 397 と ［1979］2 Lloyd's Rep. 303 事件参照）。そこでは，関連する条項は「最終月の傭船料は，本船の返船予定時までの燃料費を控除して，予測され，かつ前払され……」と規定していた。ニューヨーク・プロデュース書式の文言は，The Mihalios Xilas 事件の文言といくぶん異なるが，この点に関する限りは，同じように解釈されるものと予想される。

253 傭船契約の文言が最後の傭船料の支払から特定の項目を控除するのを許容する場合，そのような控除の額は，客観的に妥当な根拠に基づいて算定されなければならない（前出 The Mihalios Xilas 事件参照）。

NYPE 93

ニューヨーク・プロデュース書式1993年版第11条(c)項は，1946年版の58/68行の規定を拡張して，返船港への最終航海の途上で，支払が行われる場合，最終と想定される支払と同様，その直前の期間の支払を含み返船時の残存の燃料と船主負担となる立替費用を勘定に入れることを求めている（前出11頁の英文書式の168/174行と55頁参照）。

履行拒絶

度重なる傭船料支払遅滞があっても，それ自体は必ずしも，船主が明示の本船引揚権に依拠することなく，本船を引き揚げて契約を終了する権利を船主に与える傭船者の履行拒絶となるものではない（The Brimnes ［1972］2 Lloyd's Rep. 465，および ［1974］2 Lloyd's Rep. 241

(C. A.) 事件参照。詳細は後出327頁の「本船引揚と損害賠償請求権」参照)。

本船引揚の権利

傭船者が，傭船料を期限どおり，すなわち支払期日までに支払わなければ，船主は，本船引揚条項により就航している本船を引き揚げ，傭船契約を終了させる権利を有する。

従前承認された支払方法に起因する支払の遅滞

しかしながら，傭船契約どおりの支払方法に代えて，船主承認の下に，傭船者が従前の傭船料支払に利用してきた特定の支払方法を用いたことにより，支払の遅滞が生じる場合には，船主は，本船を引き揚げることができない。ただし，傭船者に対して，今後は契約どおり支払うべきこととする相応の通知がなされた場合，その通告以降の支払は別である。このように両者が認めた支払方法が有効である限り，傭船者は，通常の状態であれば，期限内の支払が期待される然るべき時点で，支払手続を開始すればよい。

　　Petrofina 号は，1937年から7年間，ノルウェーの船主からベルギーの傭船者に定期傭船に出された。契約書第11条により傭船料は，毎月 London において前払されるべきものとなっていた。また，「そのような支払がない場合，船主は，本船を引き揚げる権利を有することとなっていた。実際には，傭船者は，きまって，当該金額の小切手を Brussels から London の Hambro's 銀行宛投函すると同時に，在 Oslo の船主および在 Paris のブローカーへ，その旨通知することとしていた。問題の小切手は，通常の郵便事情を勘案して，傭船料支払期日の2日前に投函された。これは，「当事者間において容認された方法」になっていたと事実認定された。1939年9月末までは，いつも定時に銀行に到着していた小切手が，郵送中，戦争の勃発によって遅れた。支払期日の翌日，船主は，この小切手による支払を受け取っておらず，船主は，本船を引き揚げた。貴族院は，船主は本船を引き揚げる権利を有しないと判断した。
　　傭船者が船主の承諾を得て採った支払方法は，当事者間の合意ある業務協定となっており，それゆえ，船主は，突如として，また，相手に何ら通知をせず，その支払方法に代えて契約条項に完全に合致した支払を主張できない。Uthwatt 卿は，次のように述べている。「支払協定がある限り，それは，傭船契約の条項を変更する合意とは異なり，傭船契約上の支払義務の実施につき合意された方法を示している。協定がある限り，船主は，業務協定に反する支払を要求できないし，傭船者もまた，業務協定に反する支払を主張できない」。
　　Tankexpress v. Compagnie Financière Belge des Pétroles (1948) 82 Ll. L. Rep. 43.

256　上記判例において貴族院は，傭船者に対して適当な通告をすれば，船主は，かかる業務協定を終了させうることを認めた。これにより，傭船者が，傭船契約どおりに支払義務を履行しなかった場合の船主の本船引揚権が復活するものと思われる。Wright 卿は，次のように述べている。「それゆえ，控訴人である船主は，将来の傭船料について，第11条の条項に，より合致すると思われる履行方法を要求し得るが，それは，船主が，その意思を傭船者に然るべく通知してからできるのであって，その通知が効力を生じるまでは，本船を解約することはできない」(The Effy [1972] 1 Lloyd's Rep. 18 事件参照)。
　　それ以前の支払時において，傭船料の支払が遅れ，異議の申立なしに受領されたという単なる事実は，傭船者がさらに期限どおりに支払わない場合に，船主が本船を引き揚げるのを妨げることにはならないように思われる。貴族院の前出の判決に傭船者が拠ることができるためには，傭船者は支払の遅滞は従前承認された支払の**方法**，または手順の運用から生じたことを証

支払遅滞の事前の承認

しかしながら傭船料の支払の遅滞に直面した場合，船主の態度によっては，その後の支払の遅滞につき本船引揚権を，行使しないことを傭船者に明白に表示したことになることがある。船主がその後の支払の遅滞に関して不意にその権利を行使しようとする場合，裁判所が衡平法上の禁反言の原則をいつでも進んで発動すれば，船主はその権利を行使できない。

The Scaptrade [1983] 1 Lloyd's Rep. 146 事件で Robert Goff 卿判事は，控訴院の判決で，次のように述べた。「衡平法上の禁反言の原則に拠るには，傭船者は最初に，船主が本船引揚の厳密な法的権利を実行しないと明確に表示したことを立証しなければならない。2番目に，当事者間に行われた取引に関して，船主が権利を実行することは不公平であることを立証しなければならない」。しかしながら，1番目の要件は，理性のある傭船者であれば，船主の態度から船主はそういう表示をしていると推論する場合には，満たされる。そして，2番目の要件については，傭船者は実際に船主の表示により左右されたことが証明されるか，または推論できなければならない。問題の事案では，一連の支払の遅滞を船主が受け入れてきたことから，または1回の支払の遅滞の利子の請求から，衡平法上の禁反言を生じさせるに十分な表示が存したことを推論できないと判示された。さらに，傭船者は船主の態度を信頼していなかった。

本船引揚は最終的なものでなければならない

「本船引揚」は，最終的に本船を引き揚げることを意味する。船主は，本船の役務の提供を一時的に差し止める権利を有しない。また，船主は，他のいかなる根拠によっても，そのような権利を有するものではない。ただし，例えば，第18条リーエン条項の場合のように，契約により，明白に認められている場合を除く。ボルタイム書式の *International Bulk Carriers* v. *Evlogia Shipping* (*The Mihalios Xilas*) [1978] 2 Lloyd's Rep. 186 事件で，Donaldson 判事は次のように言った。「傭船料不払についての，一時的本船の引揚は，特に定期傭船契約の条項により船主に認められた場合にのみ，存在しうる権利である。そのような権利は本傭船契約により認められていない」。

Agios Giorgis 号は，韓国から Charleston および Norfolk 向けの航海期間ニューヨーク・プロデュース書式により定期傭船された。本船が，Charleston に到着する頃，月払傭船料の支払期限が到来したが，傭船者は，その傭船料から，速力担保違反相当分を差し引いた。しかし，その減額が，過度であったことが後日判明した。船主は，そのような減額に異議を唱え，本船 Nofolk 到着時，船長に対し Norfolk 向け貨物の揚荷停止を指示した（Norfolk 向け貨物は，傭船者のものではなかった）。船主が，減額分の傭船料を支払うよう傭船者を説得するまでの間，船長は揚荷を停止させ，そのため，揚荷は2日間近くも停止した。傭船者は，船主が航海を極力迅速にし，慣習上なすべき助力を提供するという第8条の義務に違反していると主張し，その主張は認められた。Mocatta 判事は，次のように判示した。

(1) 傭船者には，自己の損害賠償請求を傭船料から減額する権利はなく，かつ，いずれにしても傭船者は，あまりに多額を減額し過ぎているのであるから，傭船料を「遅滞なく定期に支払」わなかったことになる（前出304頁/309頁参照）。
(2) このことは，第5条により，船主に，その本船を傭船者から最終的に引き揚げる権利を認め

る。しかし，船主は，第5条あるいは他のいずれの条項によろうと，第18条（リーエン条項）を適用しない限り，一時的本船の引揚や，本船の運送業務提供を中止する権利を有しない。
 (3) リーエンを行使したという貨物が，傭船者のものではないのであるから，第18条は適用されない。

The Agios Giorgis [1976] 2 Lloyd's Rep. 192.
 （しかし，また The Aegnoussiotis [1977] 1 Lloyd's Rep. 268 事件および International Bulk Carriers v. Evlogia Shipping（The Mihalios Xilas）[1978] 2 Lloyd's Rep. 186 事件および The Cebu [1983] 1 Lloyd's Rep. 302 事件およびリーエン条項の効果に関する後出556頁も参照）

遅滞した傭船料の支払：引揚権の効果

　船主が通知を出す前に，傭船者が期限を徒過した傭船料を申し出ても，それだけでは，船主の本船引揚権は消滅しない。傭船者が，期限を徒過すれば，それだけで債務不履行となるのであるから，徒過後，支払の申出をしても，不履行の事実は変らない。ボルタイム書式による傭船契約に関する，これとは反対の控訴院判決（The Georgios C. [1971] 1 Lloyd's Rep. 7）は，ニューヨーク・プロデュース書式の傭船契約を扱った The Laconia [1977] 1 Lloyd's Rep. 315 事件の貴族院判決によって，明白に覆えされた。

ボルタイム書式；「支払懈怠」

　ボルタイム書式の51/54行の文言は，ニューヨーク・プロデュース書式のそれと多少異なっていることに注意しなければならない。ボルタイムは「傭船料支払の懈怠」の場合の本船引揚の権利を規定している。The Georgios C. 事件で，控訴院は，この文言は，「支払の懈怠があり，懈怠の状態が続く限り」ということを意味し，期限に遅れた支払，または支払の提供がなされた場合，そのような支払や支払提供前に船主が引揚権を行使しない限り，本船引揚権は消滅することになると判示した。この解釈とそれから導き出された判決は，ニューヨーク・プロデュース書式に関する The Laconia 事件において貴族院の判決によって覆えされた。
　同事件において Wilberforce 卿は，「支払の懈怠」の文言は，ボルタイム書式50行の毎期傭船料の「前払」の義務と関連するものでなければならないことを強調し，「控訴院は，事実上『支払懈怠』を『前払金の支払懈怠』と解さずに，『前払であろうとなかろうと，とにかく本船の引揚がある以前における支払の懈怠』と解したのであるが，これは，本条項の解釈というより，構成のやり直しともいうべきものである」。貴族院の本判決によって，ボルタイム書式の当該文言についてニューヨーク・プロデュース書式の当該文言の「傭船料を遅滞なく定期に支払わない場合」と同一の意味が与えられることとなった。

258 本船引揚の通知

　本船引揚の通知は，傭船者に対してなされなければならない。船長への通知は，傭船者に対しては効力を有しない。The Georgis C. [1971] 1 Lloyd's Rep. 7 事件で，記録長官 Denning 卿は，船主について，次のように述べている。「船主は，自己の船長に通知を出しただけだった。それでは不十分と思われる。本船を引き揚げる権利を行使するためには，船主は，傭船者に通知しなければならない。本船引揚は，傭船者が通知を受け取ったときから効力を有する」。
　船主は，本船引揚の権利を行使することを，明瞭に示さなければならない。船主が契約を終了したものとして扱うことを意味するのか意味しないのか，曖昧な書き方では不十分である。Donaldson 判事は，The Aegnoussiotis [1977] 1 Lloyd's Rep. 268 事件で，次のように述べ

た。「用語や通知について特定の形式は不要である。しかし，船主は，傭船料不払を傭船契約の終了として扱うことを，はっきりと傭船者に示さなければならない」。船主の本船引揚決定についての傭船者への明確な表示の効力は，例えばその後，本船が貨物を積載し，かつ仕向地へ運送を続行したとしても損なわれない（*The Tropwind (No. 2)* [1981] 1 Lloyd's Rep. 45事件（同判例集52頁）の Robert Goff 判事の判決参照）。それは記録長官 Denning 卿の反対の解説（傍論として）[1982] 1 Lloyd's Rep. 232 にもかかわらず，この点において正しいと考えられる（反厳格解釈条項に基づく通知に関して，317頁参照）。

権利消滅（forfeiture）に対する衡平法上の救済

船主の本船引揚権は傭船者にとり非常に厳しく作用する。傭船者は自己，または銀行側の些細な過失の結果として価値ある傭船契約を失い，重大な損失を被るかも知れない。このことは，何人かの判事に，*The Laconia* [1977] 1 Lloyd's Rep. 315 事件についての Salmon 卿のある見解を踏襲した権利消滅に対する衡平法上の救済の権限，借地契約の権利消滅条項の厳しい効力を軽減するために発展した権限に訴えることを検討させることになった。しかしながら，*The Scaptrade* [1983] 2 Lloyd's Rep. 253 事件で，貴族院は控訴院の判決を維持し，定期傭船契約に基づく本船引揚の場合，衡平法上の救済を認める裁判所の権限はないと判示した。

Diplock 卿は，他の貴族院議員も同意したが，定期傭船契約は賃貸借傭船（デマイズ）契約ではなく，傭船者に本船の占有の権利を譲渡しないと指摘した。それは，本船および乗組員の使用を通して船主が傭船者に提供する役務の契約である。裁判所は，役務契約の特定履行命令を出すのをいつも拒否してきた。「権利消滅に対する救済」をするのに必要である本船引揚権を船主に行使させない差止判決を出すことは，傭船契約の特定履行命令を出すのと事実上同じことである。これは，権利消滅に対する衡平法上の救済の原則が，定期傭船契約の本船引揚条項に基づく厳格な契約上の権利を船主に行使させないことにまで拡張されうるとの考えを拒否するのにそれ自身で十分な理由である。Diplock 卿は，明示的にその判決をデマイズではない定期傭船に限定して，付言した。「同じ考え方は裸傭船契約には適用されない。私の考えでは，裸傭船契約についての見解を表明するのは賢明なことではない」。

控訴院（[1983] 1 Lloyd's Rep. 146 事件（同判例集153頁））で Robert Goff 卿判事は，この困難な問題を取り扱い，次のように言った。「傭船料の不払に対して，船主が定期傭船者の役務から本船を引き揚げる機会を摑む可能性は，海運界ではよく知られている。そのような事態を防ぐのに有効な反厳格解釈条項が利用できる事態はよく知られている。定期傭船者となろうとする者が傭船契約書の中に，そういう条項を含めようとする場合に，交渉することが可能である。そういう条項を含まない傭船契約に同意することが必要，または望ましいと考える場合には，傭船者は会社の関係課，または銀行に期限どおりの支払実行の重要性を知らせればよい」。

反厳格解釈条項（NYPE 93の第11条(b)項を含む）

反厳格解釈条項は，本船引揚条項の厳格さを修正するよう工夫された条項である。反厳格解釈条項は，乾貨船の定期傭船で，支払不履行の後，本船引揚前に船主が傭船者に48/72時間前の通知をすることを通常規定している。

ニューヨーク・プロデュース書式1946年版やボルタイム書式には，この種類の印刷条項はないが，当事者はしばしばタイプ挿入により反厳格解釈条項を追加している。第11条(b)項は，

ニューヨーク・プロデュース書式1993年版に「猶予期間」の標題を付して挿入された。これは，遅滞のない定期の支払がないことが「傭船者側の，または傭船者の銀行の見落とし，過失，誤り，または不作為による」場合に作動する。船主は，そのとき，合意済みの「正味の銀行取引日」の日数以内に支払うよう通知することを要する。そして猶予期間満了前には，本船を引き揚げることはできない。その後本船の引揚権を有することに加えて，船主は傭船料は未払であるが，傭船料が発生し続ける間は，自らの義務の履行を差し控える権利を認められる（前出11頁の英文書式の160-166行と55頁参照）。タンカー契約書式は，通常 STB 書式の第3条(f)項の次のような印刷条項を含んでいる。「ここに規定する期限どおりの定期の支払が遅滞したときに，船主は……所在の……に通知をする。この場合傭船者は船主からの通知受領後10日以内に満期の傭船料の支払をしなければならず，これを怠った場合，船主は，……本船を傭船者の業務から引き揚げる権利を有する」。

そのような反厳格解釈条項に基づく有効な通知は，傭船者が不履行となった期日の真夜中まで発することはできない。後出 The Afovos 事件で貴族院がこの点につき，判示した（The Lutetian [1982] 2 Lloyd's Rep. 140 事件も参照）。The Pamela [1995] 2 Lloyd's Rep. 249 事件で Gatehouse 判事は，傭船料が金曜日に支払期日となる場合，当日の真夜中前の船主のテレックスによる通知は時期尚早であると判示した。通知は傭船者が読んではじめて「有効」となる。仲裁人は，これは翌月曜日前に予想されることではないと裁定した。しかし，この判決は実際に The Afovos 事件と一致するとの上級審による承認があるまで注意を以て取り扱われるべきものと思われる。

そのような反厳格解釈条項に基づく傭船者への通知文言は，その表現が絶対的でなければならない。傭船料が，遅滞なく支払われなかったことと，船主は，48時間（また，個々の条項では別の特定期間）以内に支払われなければ，本船を引き揚げるとの最後通告を発することをその文言は明確にしていなければならない（記録長官 Denning 卿の The Rio Sun [1981] 2 Lloyd's Rep. 489 事件の判決および後出 The Afovos 事件，The Pamela [1995] 2 Lloyd's Rep. 249 事件を参照）。

　Afovos 号は，追加反厳格解釈条項付きのニューヨーク・プロデュース書式で傭船された。その条項（第31条）は，次のように規定していた。「傭船料が支払期日までに受領されない場合，傭船契約から本船引揚権を行使する前に，船主は，傭船者に土・日・休日を除く48時間の猶予期間付通知を発する。この48時間以内に傭船料が支払われる場合には，本船を引き揚げない」。傭船料は，6月14日が支払期日であった。イタリアの傭船者の銀行は，London の船主の銀行にテレックス送金で，十分な余裕時間を見て送金しようとした。船主の銀行のテレックス番号が通知なく変更され，傭船者の銀行がアンサーバックの点検をしなかったために，テレックス送信は船主の銀行に届かなかった。6月14日の16時40分に船主の代理人は，傭船者にテレックスを発した。「本日支払期日となる傭船料の受領がない場合，本船を役務から引き揚げるため，傭船契約第31条により傭船者に通知するように船主は，われわれに指図した」。控訴院は次のように判示した。
　(1) 支払期日の真夜中を過ぎるまで，傭船者の傭船料支払の不履行はない。
　(2) 第31条の正しい解釈では，48時間猶予通知は，支払期限の最後の時点を過ぎるまで発することはできない。
　(3) ともかく，通知は，その表現が条件付なので正当な通知ではない。
　貴族院は，控訴院の判決を支持した。
　The Afovos [1982] 1 Lloyd's Rep. 562 (C. A.) および [1983] 1 Lloyd's Rep. 335 (H.L.)。

本船の引揚前に船主が通知する必要性を，傭船者が放棄したと，船主が主張した（結果として認められなかった）事案につき，The Rio Sun [1981] 2 Lloyd's Rep. 489 と [1982] 1 Lloyd's

Rep. 404 事件参照。

本船引揚権の放棄

　本船を引き揚げる権利を持つに至っていながら，船主が自らの態度により，傭船者の所定の期限どおりの傭船料支払の不履行を主張しない場合，船主は引揚権を失うかもしれない（権利放棄の一般については，The Kanchenjunga [1990] 1 Lloyd's Rep. 391 (H.L.) 事件と前出142/143頁の解説を参照）。この文脈で権利放棄の法理は選択という言葉でもっともうまく表現される。傭船者が期日どおりに支払わない場合，船主は引揚権を行使するか，または引揚を控え，傭船の継続を許容するかのいずれかを選択する道がある。船主が傭船者に傭船継続を選択したことを示すような方法で行動する場合，船主は然るべき選択をして，したがって引揚権を放棄したと判示されるであろう。The Mihalios Xilas [1979] 2 Lloyd's Rep. 303（同判例集314頁）事件で，Scarman 卿は，次のように言った。「二者択一で互いに排他的な行動方針に直面した際，人はその一つを選択し，関係者に選択の結果を信じさせるような方法で，関係者と交信をした場合，その人は選択を完了したこととなる」。そして，「そのことが立証される場合，選択の結果は，権利の放棄（abandonment），ここの文脈では引揚権の権利の放棄（waiver）である」。引揚権が放棄されたことが論議された具体的事案は，次に述べる。

遅滞した支払の受領

　船主は，傭船料が期日に支払われたのと同様に，期限徒過後の支払提供を受け取ることができる。船主が期限後支払を受け取ったと判断される場合には，船主は，本船を引き揚げる権利を放棄したと判示されるであろう。The Brimnes [1974] 2 Lloyd's Rep. 241 事件で，Cairns 卿判事は，次のように述べている。「……1ヶ月分の前払傭船料が，期限後，本船引揚前に提供され，船主がそれを無条件で受け取った場合，それは当該月の傭船料として受け取ったものと解され，その受領は，船主が本船引揚をしないことを決したものとして，引揚権の放棄となると思われる」。

　船主が，このようにして，期日徒過の支払を受け取ったか否かは，事実問題であり，裁判所は，船主が受け取ったか否かを決定するため，すべての関連事情を審理する。

　本船引揚の通知を出さずに，船主またはその銀行が，提供された傭船料を合理的期間を超えて保持している場合には，船主の受け取り，したがって，本船引揚権の放棄と認め得る。しかし，船主の銀行が傭船者から傭船料を受け取り，その行内処理に着手したという事実だけでは，船主が受け取ったと認定するに足りない。

　Laconia 号は，ニューヨーク・プロデュース書式により傭船され，傭船料は，First National City Bank の London 支店の船主口座に，半月毎に前払されることとなっていた。支払期日が日曜日にあたっていたところ，傭船者の銀行は，翌月曜日の15時頃になってはじめて，当該金額の「支払指図」を船主の銀行に出した。その後間もなく，船主の銀行は，支払指図書の行内手続を始めた。その指図書は，銀行間においては，現金と等価物とされていたが，通常，その受取後，約24時間は，顧客の口座の貸方に計上されない性質のものであった。一方，船主の銀行は，前もって，傭船料の受取時，電話をするよう依頼されていたので，船主の London 代理店にその旨電話をした。ところが，船主の銀行は，船主代理店から，傭船料の受取を拒否し，かつ返還するよう要請を受けた。その翌朝，船主の銀行は，傭船者の銀行に対して，同額の支払指図をした。一方，船主は，月曜日夕刻18時55分，傭船者に対して本船を引き揚げる旨の通告をした。

　貴族院は，船主は本船を引き揚げる権利を有し，かつその権利行使は有効であると判示した。そし

て貴族院は，期日徒過後の傭船料の支払は，船主がそれを受領し，本船引揚の権利を放棄したと認められる場合にのみ，適切な支払となるのであって，船主の銀行が支払指図を受け取り，その行内処理に着手したからといって，船主の権利放棄とはならないと判断した。

Salmon 卿は，次のように指摘している。「傭船料全額が，翌日 Midland Bank に返金される以前に，支払指図の行内事務処理が完了し，全額船主の口座に計上されていたとしても，それをもって船主の権利放棄と認定するのが正当かどうか疑問である。銀行が顧客の指示を待たずに，顧客に代わって，期限徒過の傭船料支払の受取または拒絶という商業上の決定をなすことは，明らかに銀行に与えられた明示または黙示の権限の範囲を越えている。銀行は，船主に対し指示を求めたが，支払の受取を拒絶するよう命じられた。銀行は，支払の受取を拒絶し，その翌日，それを傭船者に返金した。それは，どうみても合理的時間内になされていたといえる。もし銀行が，不当に長い時間，その傭船料を手元に止めていたとすれば，傭船者は，船主が傭船料を受け取ったと信じるに至ったとしても無理からぬところであろう。このことで，船主は，本船引揚権を放棄したことになる。しかし，本件において，かかる事態は発生していない」。

The Laconia [1977] 1 Lloyd's Rep. 315 (H. L.).

船主が，有効な本船引揚の通知を出した以上，傭船料をその後引き続き保持していても，本船引揚または引揚権行使を放棄して，傭船契約の存続を確認したものと考えられることはない。後出 *The Mihalios Xilas* [1979] 2 Lloyd's Rep. 303 事件で，Scarman 卿は，次のように述べた。「船主は，期日どおりの支払がなかった後，本船の引揚の通知を適当な期間内に出さなければならない。船主がそうしない場合，船主は権利を放棄したと判示されるであろう。3月26日の午後に船主はその通知を出した。その時点における傭船料の保持が傭船契約の継続を選択したとして扱われない限り，その通知は妥当な期間内に出されたので（審判人が裁定したように）有効である。私の判断では，何らかの他の選択をするという示唆がないままで前払傭船料を保持することは法の求める明白な行為ではなく，自動的に引揚権放棄を選択したこととはならない」。行為が明白でなければならないという要件について，*The Kanchenjunga* [1990] 1 Lloyd's Rep. 391 (H. L.) 事件参照。

特定の状況下では，有効な本船引揚が行われた後も，傭船料を保持しておけば，原傭船契約と同じ条件で，新しい契約を締結したことにもなりうる。Brandon 判事は，*The Brimnes* [1972] 2 Lloyd's Rep. 465 事件で，この可能性を十分検討した。もっとも同判事は，船主代理人および弁護士が，傭船料を保持しているのは，傭船料としてではなく，反対請求の担保としてであることを明らかにしたので，双方当事者に，新しい契約を締結しようとする共通の意思は推定されえないと認定した。

期日どおりであるが，不足支払の受領

傭船者が，傭船料を期日どおりに支払ったが，不足払の場合，支払の単なる受領は，その不足分が期日までに支払われない場合には，本船の引揚権を船主が放棄したことにはならないと思われる。船主は通常，金額不足の傭船料を保持し，傭船者が残額を期限内に支払うかどうかを注目し，見守る権利がある。後出 *The Mihalios Xilas* 事件で貴族院は，不足払が行われるとの通知を支払期日の2日前に受領した船主は，銀行にその不足払を受け付けないように指図せず，その金額は，翌日実際に受領されたがゆえに，船主は引揚権を放棄したことになるという主張を退けた。Scarman 卿は，次のように言った。「（支払期日）3月22日までは支払の不履行はないので，この主張は「事前の放棄」という考え方である。私が思うに，それは理論的には可能ではあるが，そうなることは滅多にない。支払の最終日前に不足払であるとしても，支払の最終期日まで，本船の引揚権を有するか否かを船主は知りえないという Kerr 判事の見解に賛成する」。もちろん，船主が自らの発言，または積極的態度で不足払を全額払として，ま

たは引揚権を見合わせるとして，受諾する道を選択したと傭船者に信じさせる場合には，見解は異なるかもしれない。

傭船者が，期日どおりに支払ったが，不足払の場合，船主は本船の引揚を決定する前に，傭船者の控除の正確さを調査するために適当な時間をかける権利を有する（後出322頁参照）。

262 本船引揚権行使の遅滞

船主は，本船引揚権行使の通知を合理的期間内に出さなければならない。通知の不合理な遅延は引揚権の放棄となる。船主は，通常敏速に行動するものと期待される。Wilberforce 卿は，The Laconia 事件 [1977] 1 Lloyd's Rep. 315 事件で，次のように述べた。「船主は，傭船者の債務不履行の後，適当な時間内に，傭船者に引揚の通知を出さねばならない。何が適当な時間であるかは――本来，仲裁人が認定すべき事項であるが――，事情如何による。事情によっては，ほとんどの場合，それは短い時間である。すなわち，船主が（相手方の）債務不履行を知り，指示を発するのに合理的に必要とされる最短の時間である（The Mihalios Xilas [1979] 2 Lloyd's Rep. 303 事件（312/316頁）および The Antaios (No. 2) [1983] 2 Lloyd's Rep. 473 (Q. B. and C. A.) と [1984] 2 Lloyd's Rep. 235 (H. L.) 事件も参照)。

債務不履行があったと思い，金額が確かに受領されていないことを，銀行に照会し，確認するのに手間取る場合，船主に，不当な遅滞があったとは判示されないであろう。

 Balder London 号の傭船料は，New York の銀行にある London の銀行の船主の口座に支払われた。……10ヶ月目の支払は，4月17日が期日であった。傭船者の当該事務の担当者の異動のため，この支払の手続が行われなかった。Oslo の船主は，4月18日（金）の真昼に London の銀行に電話をして，New York からの支払はないと告げられた。船主は，New York の銀行に確認のため照合し，折り返し電話をくれるよう依頼した。4月21日の朝，船主は再び London の銀行に電話したが，何らの情報もなく，支払は London でまだ受領されていないことを確認して，New York に再度照合をするように要請した。午後，船主は London から New York の銀行は，入金していないことを確認したと告げられた。その後，すぐに船主は本船引揚通知を出した。Mocatta 判事は次のように判示した。「船主は4月18日に銀行をもっと強硬に攻め立てていたとしても，船主の行為が不当とみなされることはない。したがって，船主の引揚は有効である。船主は（上記引用の）Wilberforce 卿の判決からの抜粋の最初の文の条件を充足しており，その3番目の文は，『多くの事案で適用されるであろうが，あまりにも厳格に述べられている』」。

 The Balder London [1980] 2 Lloyd's Rep. 489.

さらに，船主が引揚を決定する前に自らの立場を熟慮したり，法的助言を求めたりする時間を費やすのは，特定の事案の状況によっては妥当なことであろう。Wilberforce 卿の上記見解を解説して，The Scaptrade [1981] 2 Lloyd's Rep. 425 事件（同判例集429頁）で，Lloyd 判事は次のように述べた。「しかし，合理的に必要とされる最短の時間とは，当該事案の全体の状況如何である。ある場合には，定期傭船契約に基づく引揚は，軽々しく行われるべきではなく，重大な処置であるので，船主が自らの立場を熟慮するのに時間をかけるのは妥当なことである。他の場合には，船主が法的助言を求めることが，妥当であるのかもしれない。Wilberforce 卿が，『不履行を知り，指示を発するのに合理的に必要とされる最短の時間』と言及した際考慮したことからこういう事柄を排除しようとしていたとは，私には考えられない」。

 Scaptrade 号は，Shelltime 3 書式で傭船され，New York で傭船料が支払われることになっていた。傭船料は，7月8日（日）が支払期日であったが，支払われなかった。傭船料受領担当の船主の被用者は，銀行の傭船料支払の確認を待ったが，7月12日（木）になってはじめて専属ブローカーに

照会をした。それからその被用者は，上司に話し，再びテレックスを出し，弁護士に相談した後で，同じ7月12日に本船は引き揚げられた。Tyrer v. Hessler (1902) 7 Com. Cas. 166事件の控訴院の判決によって，Lloyd判事は，本船の引揚は妥当な期間内に行われたと判示した。
   The Scaptrade [1981] 2 Lloyd's Rep. 425.

　引揚通知が出される前の遅滞期間が不当ではないにしても，船主がとかくするうちに傭船契約を肯定した場合には，引揚は無効である。傭船料支払期日と引揚日との合間で船主が，支払不履行を承知して傭船者に言葉，または行動で傭船契約の継続を船主は選択したと傭船者に信じさせる場合には，その後の本船引揚は不当となる。船長が次港で貨物が用意されているかについて，電報を出して費やした7日間の遅延は，本船引揚を正当化する期間とはならないと判示されたTyrer v. Hesslar (1902) 7 Com. Cas. 166事件の控訴院判決と，期日後だがその2日後の引揚通知前の貨物積込に際して，船長の行動は，引揚権の放棄となると判示されたNova Scotia v. Sutherland (1899) 5 Com. Cas. 106事件を比較されたい（前出The Scaptrade事件におけるTyrer v. Hesslar事件の見解およびThe Antaios (No. 2) [1983] 2 Lloyd's Rep. 473事件（同判例集475頁）のStaughton判事の見解参照。前出319頁と権利放棄の問題一般について，前出142頁参照）。
　さらに，傭船料が期日内に支払われたが不足する場合，船主は本船引揚を決定する前に傭船者の控除の正確さを調査するための妥当な期間につき権利を有する。

　Mihalios Xilas号は，ボルタイム書式で傭船された。追加第39条に毎月の傭船料の支払と「最終月の傭船料は，本船が返船となると予想される時点までの燃料費と船主負担となる諸立替費用と船主の責任となる他の諸費用を差し引いて，見積りを出し，前払いされる」旨の規定があった。9ヶ月目の傭船料は，3月22日が支払期日であった。3月21日に傭船者は，1ヶ月の満額傭船料から相当な額を差し引いて支払った。傭船者の代理人は，船主に今回は傭船契約上の最終の支払とみなすことを示して，不足分は，前渡金，返船時の推定燃料および立替金に関して傭船者が控除したため，生じたと説明した。3月22日(金)午後，船主は前渡金の控除を証する書類を傭船者に要求し，返船予定日の算定，および返船時の燃料および諸経費の控除額について争った。続いて船主は3月25日に再度要請をした。しかし，詳細な説明は与えられず，船主は3月26日(火)正午過ぎに，直ちに，本船を引き揚げた。
　仲裁で，審判人は，(a)本船が9ヶ月目の最後に返船されるという傭船者の予測は妥当ではない。(b)控除額はともかく不当である。(c)船主の引揚決定は妥当な時間内に行われたと裁定した。
　貴族院は，船主は有効な引揚をしたと判示した。貴族院は，船主は遅延により，引揚権を放棄したという主張を退けた。Diplock卿は次のように述べた。「権利を放棄するには情報が必要となる。船主は引き揚げるか否かを選択する前に傭船者と本船の船長に，［傭船者の見積は妥当な根拠に基づく］かを確認する目的で照会をするのに（実際にそうした）妥当な期間の権利を有するという審判人の見解に私は同意する。事態は正にそのとおりで，3月21日から3月26日の正午までは，照会のための妥当な期間であるという審判人の認定は侵し難い事実の一つである」。
   The Mihalios Xilas [1979] 2 Lloyd's Rep. 303 (H. L.).

本船引揚の効果

船主により有効な本船引揚が行われた時，傭船契約は終了する。
　傭船契約から本船を引き揚げた後，船主が傭船者の要請でさらに役務を履行する場合，船主は新しい傭船契約に基づきその役務の報酬を得る権利がある。Robert Goff判事は，The Tropwind (No. 2) [1981] 1 Lloyd's Rep. 45事件において，船主のこの報酬の権利の性質を議論した。同判事は，同判例集53頁に次のように述べた。「問われるべき第1の問題は，船主が提供

した役務が傭船者の（明示または黙示の）要請で提供されたかどうかである。その場合，傭船者は，提供された役務に妥当な報酬を通常支払う責任があり，その責任は契約上の責任としておそらく分類することができる。しかしながら，そのような要請がない場合，傭船者の側に契約上の責任はない。そして提供された役務の報酬を支払う傭船者の責任（仮に責任ある場合）は，原状回復の法の原則のみに基づくことができる」。その事案で同判事は，傭船者は，本船が貨物を積み込み仕向地まで運送することを要請したと判示した。この要請に応じたので，船[64]主は当時の市場料率で報酬を受ける権利があった。

　控訴院（1982）1 Lloyd's Rep. 232 は，本船は有効に引き揚げられたという第1審の判決を覆した。したがって判事が決定すべき，引揚後の報酬の問題は生じなかった。しかし，記録長官 Denning 卿は，引揚通知のときに，本船上に貨物があり，船主が貨物を仕向地へ運送する場合，船主は傭船者の新しい要請に応じてではなく，原傭船契約，または船荷証券の履行として，運送を行ったとの見解を表明した。それ故，船主は，提供役務相当額の請求，または他の方法いずれでも市場料率を回収できなかった。Dunn 卿判事は，この問題が判決について生じる場合，この点についての Denning 卿の見解に必ずしも同意しないことを表明したに過ぎなかった。

　原定期傭船者の役務から本船が引き揚げられた後で，本船の使用を継続する再傭船者は船主に妥当な報酬を同じように支払わなければならない（The Lakatoi Express（1990）19 N. S. W. L. R. 285 事件（同判例集304頁）の Carruthers 判事の判決を参照）。

　傭船者は，本船の引揚後の期間について支払った傭船料の返済を受ける権利を有する（Wehner v. Dene Steam Shipping [1905] 2 K. B. 92 事件と The Mihalios Xilas [1979] 2 Lloyd's Rep. 303 事件参照）。しかしながら，だからといって傭船料が船主に支払われずに，融資貸付に基づき譲受人に支払われた場合，傭船者が譲受人から返済を受ける権利を有するということにはならない。

　Trident Beauty 号は，ニューヨーク・プロデュース書式で，傭船された。傭船料は毎月15日間毎にに前払で支払われ，第57条で，本船が連続して12日間オフハイヤーとなる場合，傭船者は傭船契約を解約できると定めていた。船主は，船隊の各船の運航に融資を付けるために融資貸付契約を結んでいた。船主は，この融資貸付に基づき，この傭船契約に基づく傭船料を含む収入を融資者に譲渡することを保証した。譲渡された収入は，一切の相殺，控除，または課徴と無関係であり，「不確定でまたは争いのある」ものであってはならなかった。譲渡通知が傭船者に与えられる以前に，既に傭船者は傭船料を2回船主に支払っていた。本船は Singapore で修理を待つ間，数日間オフハイヤーとなった。譲渡通知に従って，傭船者は3回目の傭船料を全額，融資者に支払った。本船は翌1ヶ月間 Singapore でオフハイヤーのままであり，そこで遂に傭船者は傭船契約を解約した。船主は，破産し，船主の反対給付が全然ないので，傭船者は融資者に3回目に支払った傭船料の返還を求めた。傭船者勝訴の Diamond 判事の判決は，控訴院で覆された。請求が船主に対して行われた場合，傭船者と船主の間の立場がいかなるものであれ，傭船者は融資者から支払を回収する権利はない。前払傭船料の返還は，ある状況では，船主から回収可能であるが，前払傭船料は，ただ単に「条件付き」支払ではなく，本船がオフハイヤーのままである場合，融資者は返還という負担を条件に傭船料の支払を受けているのでもない。

　Beldam 卿判事は次のように述べた（453頁）。「そういう信用供与を提供する者が，自らの安全を頼ることができない場合，船主や傭船者は一様に，自らの商業活動を追求するのはさらに困難と判断することになると思われる」。

　この判決は貴族院で確認された。Gott 卿と Woolf 卿は，傭船者に反対給付のない傭船料を返還する責任があるのは，船主であり，その譲受人である融資者ではないことを強調した。
The Trident Beauty [1993] 1 Lloyd's Rep. 443（C. A.）および [1994] 1 Lloyd's Rep. 365（H. L.）．

しかし，船主は傭船契約存続期間中に発行された船荷証券に基づき，荷主に対し責任を持ち続け，船荷証券に拘束され続けることとなる（後出385/400頁参照）。
　船主が船荷証券に拘束されない場合でも，船主には貨物を合理的に管理する受寄者としての義務がある（Hayn v. Culliford (1878) 3 C.P.D. 410と (1879) 4 C.P.D. 182 (C.A.) 事件と後出 The AES Express 事件参照）。
　さらに，New South Wales 州の海事法廷で本船の引揚に「必然的に付随するできごと」として，船主は，船主の権限に基づき傭船者が発行し署名した船荷証券に基づいて，運送される
265 貨物に関する傭船者の義務を負うと判示された。後出 AES Express 事件参照。このような広い命題は英国の法廷では受け入れられがたいが，船主が自らの意思で仕向地まで，貨物を運送することを決意し，運賃が荷送人により傭船者に対し既に支払済の場合には，船主は，荷受人に運賃の支払を要求できないという，その事案の実際の判決を英国法廷は受け入れるであろう。

　　AES Express 号の管理船主は，傭船者自身が破産寸前にあると通知してきたので，ボルタイム書式の傭船契約から本船を引き揚げた。そのとき，本船は Norfolk から Auckland, Sydney, Melbourne への航海途上で，傭船者が署名し発行した運賃前払の船荷証券に基づき Melbourne 向けコンテナ 8 本のペーパーボードを含む貨物を積載していた。本船の Auckland 到着前に船主は傭船料の不払に基づき本船を引き揚げた。しかし船主が，本船を引き揚げ，貨物を Melbourne へ運送し，そこで引き渡し，引替に運賃を受け取るとの通知をこれらのコンテナの受取人に出したのは，本船が Auckland へ寄港した後であった。受取人が Melbourne への運送を，または Auckland 引渡を要請する時間はなく，受取人はまさしく Melbourne で貨物引渡の際の船主の運賃請求に異議を申し立てた。
　　New South Wales の海事法廷で，Carruthers 判事は，次のように判示した。
　(a) 本船引揚後も，船主には受寄者として貨物の合理的な管理を行う義務が残る。
　(b) 船荷証券は傭船者のものであるが，船主は引揚に必然的に付随する事柄として 6 本のコンテナを Melbourne まで運送する義務を含む，船荷証券に基づく傭船者の義務を負っている。
　(c) この船荷証券の運賃は本船引揚前に，荷送人により，傭船者に支払われたので，船主は荷渡時に運賃収得の権利はない。
　(d) 仮に上記(b)は，間違いであり，船主が Auckland で 8 本のコンテナを揚げる権利があるとした場合，ともかく Melbourne への寄港を意図していたと判事に判定された船主が，追加運送を引き受けるにあたって自発的に行為したのであるから，船主は現状回復の原則，または不当利得の法に基づき Melbourne へ貨物を運送したことに対して報酬を得る権利はない。
　　The AES Express (1990) 20 N.S.W.L.R. 57.

　しかしながら，船主が貨物の引渡時に収得した航海運賃を保持する権利を有することはありうる。Wulsfberg v. Weardale (1916) 115 L.T. 146 (C.A.) 事件の Reading 卿の判決参照。

「あるいは，本傭船契約の違反により」

　ニューヨーク・プロデュースの引揚条項のこの文言は，文字どおりの意味――傭船契約の条件のわずかな違反につき，本船引揚を許容する――を与えられる場合，潜在的影響力はきわめて苛酷で，仲裁人や判事は適正な正当化事由をより限定的に解釈出来るか否か注意深く考慮しなければならなかった。The Athos [1983] 1 Lloyd's Rep. 127 事件で Purchas 卿判事が述べたように（日判例集143頁），裁判所は次の厳しい選択に直面する。「当該条項は，その効果を軽減されないまま認めるべきか，または，裁判所は，その効果が裁判所の見解に従って実務家に合理的に受け入れられるように書き直すべきか」。
　この文言の適切な解釈に関して先例となる判決はない。そして，第 1 審や控訴院の相矛盾す

る判決や付随的意見があるが，The Antaios (No. 2) [1984] 2 Lloyd's Rep. 235（同判例集241と243頁）事件では貴族院の見解が，明確に表明されている。この文言は，文字どおりに解釈されるべきではなく，商業的常識で，履行拒絶の違反に限定される――つまり傭船者の行為により傭船契約を解除されたものとして取り扱う権利を船主に与えるほど，重大な違反である（前出137頁参照）。

後出 The Tropwind (No. 1) 事件で Kerr 判事は，この文言は，期日が到来した支払の不当な拒否を含み，非安全港への指図や，危険品や除外貨物の積込指図を含むが，傭船料以外の他の項目を遅滞なく支払えないことだけによる違反は含まないと判示した。

　Tropwind 号は，ロンドン保険者協会担保航路定限内の，全世界を航海区域として，9ヶ月から12ヶ月間，ニューヨーク・プロデュース書式により傭船された。傭船者は，適当な追加保険料を支払うことを条件に，これらの定限外に配船することができた。本船は，航路定限外に配船され，追加保険料が支払われることになった。船主は，傭船者が「支払期限までに」追加保険料を送金しなかったと主張して本船を引き揚げた。船主は，傭船契約上，追加保険料の支払期限の規定はないものの，相当の期間内に支払われるべきであり，本件の事情の下では，その相当の期間は14日間であり，そのような支払がなかったことは，傭船契約違反となるから，本船を引き揚げることができると主張した。

　Kerr 判事は，「あるいは，本傭船契約の違反により」という文言は，傭船料以外の支払遅滞を対象としていないとして，次のとおり指摘した。「傭船料以外の支払でも，それが単なる遅滞ではなく，傭船者が不当に支払拒絶をした場合には，上記文言の適用が考えられる。また，本件契約書の他の条項に規定されている非安全港への入港指示や，危険品または傭船契約上除外されている貨物の積取というような違反に対しては，確かにこの文言を適用することができると思われる。しかし，本条を読む実務家は，当然，傭船料の支払遅滞が，本船引揚権を発生させるということは理解しても，傭船料以外の支払期限が到来している支払の遅滞に対してまで，この一般的文言が適用されると聞けば驚くことと思われる。これが当事者の意思であれば，傭船料の支払に対すると同様に，期限どおりの支払という要件を，支払期限が到来する他のすべての費目に拡大させておくことは容易であった」。Kerr 判事はまた，追加保険料支払時期に関する船主の主張を退け，相当の期間内に支払が行なわれる要があるという船主の主張は正当であるが，本件の状況下において，14日間というのはあまりに短か過ぎると判示した。

　The Tropwind (No. 1) [1971] 1 Lloyd's Rep. 397.

後出 The Athos 事件の第1審で，Neill 判事は The Laconia (1979) 1 Lloyd's Rep. 315 事件では，Simon 卿ははっきりと Kerr 判事の判決に明白な賛意を表しているが，Kerr 判事の判決を踏襲することはできないと考えた。しかし，控訴院は Neill 判事の判決を承認しつつも，「他の一切の違反」の語句の解釈については多数意見によって反対を表明し，上記 The Tropwind (No. 1) 事件の Kerr 判事の採った解釈を支持した。

　Athos 号のニューヨーク・プロデュース書式による傭船契約書は，次の追加条項を含んでいた。「35. 戦争危険保険は常時付保されるものとする。船主の戦争危険保険の保険者の指図に常に従うものとする。傭船者は，請求書と証拠書類を受領の上，次の傭船料の支払時に割増戦争保険料について，……船主に償還するものとする」。前払の毎月の傭船料は各月の25日が支払期日であった。

　1980年の2月に傭船者は，当時危険水域であったイランへ行くように本船に指図した。その結果，船主は戦争危険協会に追加保険料を支払わねばならなかった。この保険料は，中古船舶市場価格の大幅下落にもかかわらず，数年間同じ金額であった付保価格に基づいて算出された。さらに支払保険料を算出する付保価格に乗ずる百分率は，本船がイランで「封鎖される trapped」危険につき協会の追加担保付保を船主が決定したので，上昇した。追加保険料を聞いて，傭船者は，付保価格と適用百分率の両方に異議を唱えた。この問題について交信の後，3月末に船主は傭船者に保険料の協会請求書

を送付し，次回傭船料支払日以前に支払うことを要求した。4月18日に傭船者は4月25日が期日となる月次の傭船料を支払ったが，要求のあった保険料は支払わなかった。船主が抗議すると傭船者は仲裁をほのめかした。5月22日に傭船者に届いた書状に，船主は保険料の回収の主張を詳細に述べて，割引後の正味保険料の貸し票を封入した。一方，傭船者は5月25日（日）に期日がくる月次傭船料を5月20日に支払った。船主は休日の5月26日の後で，銀行に照会の上，保険料に関する支払がないことを確認し，5月29日に本船を引き揚げた。

Neill 判事は次のように判示した。

267
1. 保険塡補範囲は，慎重な船主の基準により，行使される船主判断の事項である。本事案では，船主は中古船舶市場価格の下落にもかかわらず，船体付保価格を維持し，「封鎖」担保を含めることを選択できる権限を有していた。
2. 傭船者は協会の割引率を控除の上，正味保険料のみを第35条に基づき支払う義務がある。したがって書状同封の伝票が受領されるまでは，「請求書と証拠書類一式の受領」とはならないので，当該本項に基づく支払義務は，5月22日に書状が傭船者に届くまで，発生しない。傭船者は割引の利益や請求書および証拠書類受領の権利を放棄していない。
3. 第35条に基づく支払うべき金額を遅滞なく支払えない場合，それは，船主に本船を引き揚げる権利を与える第5条に基づく「本傭船契約違反」となる。
4. しかし，傭船者は5月22日より前に，当月の傭船料を支払っているので「次の傭船料支払時」の第35条に基づく保険料の支払は6月25日が支払期日となる傭船料の支払と共に行われる。したがって5月29日に船主に本船引揚権はなかった。
5. 上記4と異なり，船主に第5条に基づく本船の引揚権があるとしても，船主は，銀行に照会する一方5月29日まで，本船引揚を遅らせることにより引揚権を放棄したことにはならないであろう。

控訴院は，上記2および4の点につき，Neill 判事の判断を承認したが，多数意見（Kerr 卿判事，Stephenson 卿判事，Purchas 卿判事は意見を異にするが）は，傍論として，上記3で Neill 判事の第5条の文字どおりの解釈は間違っており，さらに The Tropwind (No. 1) 事件で Kerr 判事の採った限定的解釈を選ぶべきであるという見解を表明した。

The Athos [1981] 2 Lloyd's Rep. 74 および [1983] 1 Lloyd's Rep. 127 (C. A.).

The Athos 事件に関する控訴院の多数意見の傍論は，第5条の意図は Kerr 判事が述べた（同判例集137頁）ように「支払に関連する決定的な義務として支払期日までに傭船料の支払を選び出し，しかも一方で傭船料以外の支払と他方で性質の異なる違反とを区別すること」であった。しかし，その見解では，支払が関与する違反以外の他の違反に関して，些細な違反でさえ第5条に基づき，船主が本船を引き揚げることができる可能性を残した。貴族院がこの文言は，履行拒絶の違反のみに言及しているとの強固な見解を表明した後出 The Antaios (No. 2) 事件の後では，既に述べたように，些細な違反による本船引揚の可能性は，今では割引して考えることができよう。

The Antaios (No. 2) [1984] 2 Lloyd's Rep. 235 事件（仲裁人の裁定に対して訴える許可を与える根拠に関連した）において，貴族院での Diplock 卿は同判例集238頁に仲裁人の裁定の理由を，次のように要約した。「もしくは本傭船契約の違反」の語句の「違反」は「履行拒絶の違反」である，つまり傭船者により不法に履行拒絶されたとして船主が契約を取り扱う選択の権利を船主に与えるような無名の条件の根本的違反，または条件（condition）であることを明示された条件（term）の根本的違反である。仲裁人は，この文言は，言葉どおりの意味であるとの船主の解釈を，それは「ニューヨーク・プロデュース定期傭船書式の全体の目的にとっては，まったく不当で，まったく非商業的で，全面的に矛盾する」との理由で退けた。貴族院の他の判事も同意したが，Diplock 卿と Roskill 判事は，「仲裁人が，『履行拒絶の違反』としたその裁定は明らかに正しい」と述べた。

NYPE 93

ニューヨーク・プロデュース1993年版で、61行と関連するところは、「もしくは本傭船契約の根本的違反でも」と修正された（前出11頁の英文書式の150行と55頁を参照）。これは前出 *The Antaios* (*No. 2*) 事件で、貴族院が承認した1946年版の文言の解釈を反映している。

268 本船引揚と損害賠償請求権

本船の引揚に際して、船主の有する損害賠償の問題に影響を与える引揚条項の性質に関して、先例は分かれている。有効な引揚のときに傭船料が未払であれば、船主は引揚時に傭船者が支払うべき他の金額とともに未払傭船料を請求する権利を明らかに有する。しかし、市場傭船料率が約定傭船料より低いために被る損失について、船主が傭船者に対して追加の損害賠償を請求する権利を有するかという問題が生じる。

履行拒絶に至る傭船料の支払不履行

船主は、傭船者の契約の履行拒絶を立証できる場合に限り、そのような損害を請求することができることは、明白である。

当事者の行為が、契約により拘束されない意思を示すか、あるいは、履行ができないことを示し、その不履行のおそれが、傭船契約の全利益を実質的に船主から奪う効果をもたらすほどのものである場合、当事者の行為は、履行の拒絶となるであろう（Diplock卿による *The Afovos* [1983] 1 Lloyd's Rep. 335（同判例集341頁）事件参照）。

しかし、支払期日に傭船料を支払わないからといって履行の拒絶にはならないし、また、単なる誤りで支払わないとしても、まず履行の拒絶とはなりえない（*The Georgios C.* [1971] 1 Lloyd's Rep. 7事件における記録長官Denning卿の所見（同判例集14頁）と *The Tropwind* (*No. 2*) [1982] 1 Lloyd's Rep. 232（同判例集237頁）事件参照。前出 *The Afovos*（同判例集341頁）事件のDiplock卿の所見も参照）。支払がしばしば遅滞したとしても、履行の拒絶とはならないと思われる（*Decro-Wall v. Marketing* [1971] 1 W. L. R. 361 および *The Brimnes* [1972] 2 Lloyd's Rep. 465、さらに [1974] 2 Lloyd's Rep. 241 (C. A.) 各事件参照）。しかしながら、傭船者の行為を通じて、傭船者が傭船料を支払う意思がないことや、支払不能であることが合理的に推定される場合、履行拒絶が成立すると思われる。*Leslie Shipping v. Welstead* [1921] 3 K. B. 420事件で、傭船者は、1ヶ月間の傭船料として自ら振り出した手形の引受を拒絶し、さらに、その次の傭船料も支払わなかった。Greer判事は、船主は、傭船契約を終了したものとして取り扱うことができるし、また損害賠償をも請求することができると判示した。

履行拒絶に至らない傭船料の支払不履行

実状が通常そうであるように、期日までの傭船料不払が、傭船契約の拒絶に至らない場合、傭船料の支払と本船引揚に関する規定が契約の基本的条項（essential term）、または「条件（condition）」になる場合には（前出138頁参照）、やはり傭船契約上の損失についての損害賠償は、回収可能であろう。

The Brimnes [1972] 2 Lloyd's Rep. 465事件でBrandon判事は、ニューヨーク・プロデュース書式の関連規定は、基本的条件になると考え、次のように述べた（同判例集482頁）。「……当事者の意思が傭船料の期限通りの支払義務を契約の基本的条件としたことを明白に示す文言は、第5条には何ら存しないとの結論に私は達したつまり、それ（第5条）は、その違反のゆ

えに本船を引き揚げる明確な権利が認められる条件とは異なるものである」。([1974] 2 Lloyd's Rep. 241 掲載判決で) 控訴院はこの点につき Brandon 判事の判決を維持した (特に同判例集252頁 Edmund Davies 卿判事の所見の注を参照)。同じような見解が, *The Georgios C.* [1971] 1 Lloyd's Rep. 7 (同判例集11および13頁) 事件について第1審と控訴院で表明された。*Leslie Steamship Co.* v. *Welstead* [1921] 3 K.B. 420 事件参照。

United Scientific v. *Burnley Council* [1978] A.C. 904 事件で, Diplock 卿は反対の見解を表明した。同判事は, 924頁に次のように述べた。「物品販売の商業契約において, 一応の引渡時期は欠くことができないが, 一応の支払時期はそうではない……傭船契約において傭船料の支払時期は, 欠くことができない」。*The Afovos* [1983] 1 Lloyd's Rep. 335 事件 (同判例集341頁) でニューヨーク・プロデュース書式第5条について特に触れて, Diplock 卿は, 次のように述べた。同条項の二番目部分は「傭船者が, 期日どおりの支払という第一義的義務に違反した場合に, 船主の権利は何であるかを明白に規定するものである。船主には傭船者の役務から本船を引き揚げる自由がある。換言すれば, 船主には生じた違反を条件の違反 (a breach of condition) として扱う権利があり, 傭船契約に基づくすべての第一義的義務を終了させ, 不履行のままとしてその違反を扱うことを選ぶ権利を船主に与える」。Roskill 判事もまた *Bunge* v. *Tradax* [1981] 2 Lloyd's Rep. 1 事件 (同判例集12頁) で条件 (conditions) として定期傭船の引揚条項に言及した。

電算機貸借契約に基づく請求をめぐる *Lombard North Central* v. *Butterworth* [1987] Q.B. 527 事件で, 控訴院は賃借料の期限どおりの支払は「その本質である」と規定する条項は, 条件 (a condition) であり, その違反は貸主に借主から賃料の将来に亘る残額金すべてを回収する権利を与えるが, ただし, 回収した電算機の再販価格の控除を条件とするだけである, と判示した。この判決の正確さは問題となった (Treitel [1987] LMCLQ 143 参照)。しかし, ともかくニューヨーク・プロデュースおよびボルタイム書式の本船引揚条項の文言は, *Lombard North Central* 事件の条項の文言とは, 後者には時期が「その本質である」という明示的言及がある点で区別できる。これは, 相互に依存する義務 (前出 *Bunge* v. *Tradax* 事件参照) がある場合, 重大な区別とはならないかも知れないが, 支払期日までに傭船料を支払う義務は, この範疇に入らないものと思われる。

前出 Diplock 卿と Roskill 卿の言説は, 傭船料の支払と本船引揚条項はその文言の完全な意味で条件 (a condition) を構成するものと理解されるべきかという問題が残る。条件を構成するとすれば, 下落する市場で船主が, 傭船料の支払がわずかに遅れたという理由で本船を引き揚げても傭船契約の損失について損害賠償を続けて回収できる結果, たとえそれは明らかに米国法 (後出337頁参照) に基づく立場であるとしても, 驚くべき結果となろう。しかしながら, この三つの見解のいずれもが引揚後の損害賠償の問題には向けられなかった。さらに, 二つは傍論である。第三番目の Diplock 卿の *The Afovos* 事件の解説は同判事の判決理由の一部を構成するが, さらに直接的な理由で同じ結論に至ったであろうと指摘された (Reynolds [1984] LMCLQ 189 参照)。それが意味するすべてのことは, いずれにしても傭船料支払義務に本船引揚の選択権を追加することにより, 当事者がその義務に真の条件, すなわち基本的条件という一つの性格を与えること, つまり違反は, 善意の当事者に契約を解消したものとして扱う権利を与えることであった。

要するに定期傭船契約の通常の傭船料支払と本船引揚条項は, 傭船料の支払遅滞の際に何が起こるかをその条項に明白に規定する場合, 僅かな違反に対して傭船契約の損失を損害賠償請求する権利を船主に与えるような, 厳密な意味での条件 (a condition) として扱われる必要はないと思われる。傭船料の期日までの不払が, 拒絶的である場合のみ, 傭船契約の損失の損

害賠償は可能でなければならないと考えられる。しかし，この重要な問題には貴族院がもっと光をあてるまで，不確実な点が残る。

差止命令

　船主が本船を引き揚げる，または引き揚げるおそれがある場合，裁判所が差止命令を出す状況について前出137頁参照。

270 米 国 法

現　金

　厳密に言えば，米国における「現金」とは，現実の通貨，または，連邦準備基金（Federal Reserve funds）のいずれかである。しかし，幅広い商業実務上は，通常の小切手や，支払指図書（payment orders）や，テレックスによる送金が，「現金」と同じものとして認められている。仮に，船主の銀行が，傭船者からの小切手や送金を「入金完了」し，船主が，その資金を無条件に使用するのに，1日あるいは，それ以上要するにしても，そのような支払方法が認められていることに変わりはない。The Penta, SMA 1603（Arb. at N.Y. 1981）事件で，こういう実務が問題とされた。そこでは，仲裁審は全員一致で，期日後に精算される普通小切手で傭船者が傭船料を支払ったのは，「現金」払いをする義務に違反していると裁定した。

　仲裁審によると，

　　「現金」の語は，受領者が無条件に資金を使用できるようにする義務が支払者にあることを意味する。「傭船者」は，電信為替で，支払をすべきであった。または，仮に小切手の支払を選択した場合，小切手は連邦準備基金に呈示するか，または小切手の精算に時間の余裕があるように十分前もって呈示することができたであろう。

　本事案では，本船の引揚は関与していないが，「現金」を正当に定義していることには疑問の余地がない。そして，New York のある商業仲裁人は，遅滞ない傭船料支払の要件について厳密な英国の規則に同意することを示唆している。

傭船料満額以下の支払／控除

　支払傭船料から，いかなる控除が認められるかの問題は，煩わしい問題である。ニューヨーク・プロデュース書式の下で，傭船者に，傭船料の支払を差し止める権利はない。ただし，オフハイヤー，または前払金に関して，傭船契約に明示ある場合を除く。それゆえ，The Uranus, 1977 AMC 586（Arb. at N.Y. 1977）事件で，仲裁審は，傭船者が，申し立てられた貨物損害賠償請求に対する引当として傭船料の支払を留保した場合には，傭船契約違反になると全員一致の裁定を下した。仲裁審によると，

　　係争中の貨物損害賠償請求の引当として，傭船料の支払を差し止めれば，傭船者は，傭船契約の支払条項に違反したことになるという点で，仲裁審は，意見が一致した。ニューヨーク・プロデュース書式の下では，第5条，第15条，その他の明示の規定により，控除が認められていない限り，傭船料は全額支払われなければならない。船主が認めない貨物損害賠償請求を傭船者が追及する手段は，仲裁に持ち込むしかない（1977 AMC at 590）。

　傭船者が船主の承認がないのに傭船料を過度に控除する場合，本船は引き揚げられると仲裁審が裁定した The Katina, SMA 1310（Arb. at N.Y. 1979）事件で同じ結果となった。同様に，The Myriam, 1952 AMC 1625（Arb. at N.Y. 1952）事件で，オフハイヤー，およびこれに関連する諸請求を過度に控除した場合，船主は，傭船料の不払を理由に，本船を引き揚げる

ことができると裁定された。The Brookhurst, SMA 87 (Arb. at N. Y. 1960) 事件で，傭船者には，その主張する速力不足および立替支出相当分を，最後の傭船料から減額する権利がないこと，また，期限が到来し，支払義務の生じた傭船料を傭船者が支払わない場合には，ニューヨーク・プロデュース書式第5条により，船主は本船を引き揚げる権利があることが認められた。

　The Aetolia, SMA 1993 (Arb. at N. Y. 1984) 事件で，仲裁審は積荷の少ない船艙に貨物を固縛するのに使用した時間を傭船者が傭船料から差し引くのを許容する傭船料支払中断条項はニューヨーク・プロデュース書式にはないと裁定された。仲裁審によると，この固縛作業は，貨物の積込，積付，荷均という傭船者の義務の一つである。さらに，仲裁審は貨物の滅失，損傷の損害賠償請求によって，傭船者が傭船料支払を保留する権利は生じないと裁定した。

271　傭船者は，争いのあるオフハイヤーにつき，傭船料の支払を止めることはできないと言われてきた。ところが一方，オフハイヤー条項（第15条）それ自体の趣旨から見ると，傭船料は，そもそも無条件で獲得されるものではなく，現実の機器の障害や速力不足があれば，その限度で傭船料の支払義務はないとも考えられる。したがって，オフハイヤーが発生すれば，船主の同意がなくても，傭船者は，オフハイヤー分を減額できるという傭船者の議論には説得力がある。もちろん，傭船者は自己の主張の根拠に確信がなければならないことに**注意すべき**である。したがって，傭船料から減額した場合，後日，その正当性が立証できない限り，超過部分について，傭船者は支払を怠ったことになり，船主の本船引揚は正当化される。同時に，オフハイヤーによる傭船料の減額について争っていることを理由に，本船を引き揚げる船主は，同様に，自らの主張の根拠に確信を持つべきである。けだし，その減額が，後日正当であると認定されれば，本船引揚は不法と裁定されるからである。この問題については，ちょっとした誤ちが重大な危険に結びつくので，善意の当事者間に紛争が生じた場合，当事者は，早急に紛争を仲裁に付託することを前提とした供託の取決めをなすべきであるといわれている。

　傭船者が，予想されるオフハイヤー分を控除することができるかという問題も同じようにやっかいな問題なのだろうか。例えば，本船が翌月に入渠予定である場合でも，傭船者は，1ヶ月分全額の傭船料を支払わねばならないのか。The Noto, 1979 AMC 116 (Arb. at N. Y. 1976) 事件は，支払う必要がないと思わせるが，先例は分かれており，全額を「前払」しない場合，傭船者は本船引揚の危険を冒すこととなる。

　傭船料について担保を提供することそれ自体，困難な問題を生ずる。The Mare Felice, 1974 AMC 2150 (Arb. at N. Y. 1971) 事件において，傭船者は，第2回目の傭船料支払に合わせて，最後の傭船料に充当すべき担保として，米貨5万ドルを支払った。傭船者は，3回目の傭船料を期日に支払わなかったので，船主は，本船を引き揚げた。傭船者は，第1次的抗弁として，支払遅滞分は，提供してある担保金から充当しうるのであるから，船主の傭船契約解約は正当ではないと主張した。これに対し，仲裁審は，傭船契約上，傭船料支払遅滞があった場合，船主は，本船を引き揚げる権利を明確に与えられているのであるから，船主の本船引揚は正当であると判断し，提供した担保金について，仲裁審の多数意見は，次のように述べている。

　　提供した担保は，返船と同時にその金額を精算するためにだけ使用できるものであり，したがって，その担保の対象となるのは日割計算した最終傭船料のみであるというのが多数意見である（1974 AMC at 2152)。

　ほぼ神聖な船主の傭船料に対する権利は，The Dagny Skou, SMA 2416 (Arb. at N. Y.

1987)事件の仲裁裁定によって実証されている。本船は5年間の定期傭船で運航された。傭船期間中に，アルゼンチンの会社である傭船者は，船主の債権者の申請によりアルゼンチン裁判所の出した仮差押え命令の送達を受けた。裁判所の命令に従って，傭船者は資金を裁判所に供託したが，その後，傭船料から供託金額を控除した。仲裁審は，傭船料からの控除は不当であると裁定した。

The Thekos, SMA 2253（Arb. at N.Y. 1986）事件で，仲裁審は，返船後の速力，または性能クレームおよび弁護士費用は第5条および15条に基づき控除を許容されないと裁定した。

The Treana, SMA 2929（Arb. at N.Y. 1992）事件で，仲裁人は，速力と性能の保証に基づき傭船者は傭船料からギアの不具合と他の小さな差異について控除したが，正当化されないとした（*The Karin M*, SMA 2869（Arb. at N.Y. 1992）事件も参照）。その事案では，傭船者は船主に種々雑多なクレームを主張してそれを傭船料から控除したが，不法であると裁定された。

272 *The Hamlet*, SMA 2780（Arb. at N.Y. 1991）事件で，仲裁人は，ニューヨーク・プロデュース書式には，傭船者が傭船料でクレームを相殺するのを許容する規定はないと裁定した。

The Solar, SMA 2666（Arb. at N.Y. 1990）事件で仲裁審は，船主への再運送賃の譲渡は，傭船料全額払いの傭船者の義務を解除しないと裁定した。

The World Aegeus, SMA 2488（Arb. at N.Y. 1988）事件で，傭船者の本船使用を阻害しない次の傭船契約が最初の傭船契約の期間満了前に遡って，傭船料と燃料の支払を規定していたが，傭船者は全傭船期間につき傭船料の支払を求められた。

The Ocean Advance, SMA 1677（Arb. at N.Y. 1982）事件で，仲裁審は，傭船者にはニューヨーク・プロデュース書式に基づき，本船を再傭船する権利があるが，再傭船者が，傭船者に再傭船料を支払わないからといって船主への傭船料の支払を傭船者が保留することを許容する規定はないと述べた。

傭船料の支払不履行

傭船料の支払不履行が，一般免責条項に列挙された事由により生じる場合，船主には傭船者の役務から本船を引き揚げる権利はない（*Clyde Commercial S. S. Co. v. West India S. S. Co.*, 169 F. 275 (2d Cir.)，裁量上告拒絶 214 U.S. 523 (1909)）。

「前払にて」

ニューヨーク・プロデュース書式第5条の支払期限までに傭船料の支払がない場合，船主は，傭船者が運航している本船を引き揚げることができると裁定した多くの事案がある（例えば *The Admiralty Flyer*, SMA 349（Arb. at N.Y. 1967）事件参照）。同事件で，船主は，傭船者が第5条どおりに傭船料を支払わなかった場合，傭船者が運航している本船を引き揚げることができると裁定された。*The Egle*, SMA 815（Arb. at N.Y. 1973）事件で，船主は，38回目の傭船料支払期日経過後9日経って，即時支払わなければ本船を引き揚げる旨の通告をなした後，本船を引き揚げたのであるが，仲裁審は，第5条に基づいて，返船日より約5ヶ月前のこの本船引揚を認容した。

最初に決定しなければならない問題は，毎期の傭船料がいつ支払期限になるかということである。例えば，3月1日月曜日の午前5時に傭船が開始すれば，もちろん，次の傭船料支払期日は3月15日となろう。3月15日に支払期限がくる傭船料は，たとえ半月決め期間の始期が午

前5時であっても、その応当日の取引時間内のいつでも、これを支払うことができることは、New York において広く認められているように思われる。The Penta, SMA 1603 (Arb. at N. Y. 1981) 事件参照。しかし、傍論ではあるが、これと反対の見解がある (The Vermont I, SMA 747 (Arb. at N. Y. 1970) 事件参照)。

　傭船料支払期限が、土曜日、日曜日あるいは休日にあたる場合は、さらに面倒である。英国の原則によれば、支払は、それに先行する取引日になされなければならない。しかし、The Maria G. Culucundis, 1954 AMC 325 (Arb. at N. Y. 1952) 事件のニューヨーク仲裁では、これと反対の原則が採用された。本件において、傭船料支払期限は、12月23日土曜日であった。傭船者は、12月26日火曜日午後2時になって、傭船料支払のため小切手を提供した。船主は、本船を引き揚げたが、その後における傭船者の損害賠償請求に関する仲裁において、本船引揚は不当と裁定された。この結果は、ニューヨーク法解釈一般法25条 (New York General Construction Law §25) と合致している (McKinney Supp. 1974)。現在、同法は、土曜日、日曜日および休日に期限が到来する支払は、次の取引日にこれを行うことができると規定している。

船主の態度による変更

　支払時期および支払方法に関する規定は、共に船主の一連の態度如何により変更されることがある。それで、The Spyros Lemos, 1967 AMC 2357 (Arb. at N. Y. 1967) 事件で、傭船者の電信送金による方法は、毎回支払期日の1日か2日後になって船主口座の貸方に入金されていた。船主は、これにつき従来異議を申し立てていなかったが、その後、傭船料の支払遅延を理由として、本船引揚の通知をなしたところ、仲裁審は、この本船引揚を不当と判断した。The Pandra, 1973 AMC 1561 (Arb. at N. Y. 1972) 事件でも、結果は同様であった。船主は、支払の遅滞に抗議しなかったことによって、事前の警告なしに本船を引き揚げる権利を喪失したと裁定された。The Essi Gina, SMA 534 (Arb. at N. Y. 1970) 事件でも同様であって、以前の支払記録によれば、その傭船契約の下で7年間、船主は、支払の遅れに抗議することなく、18回も、1日から5日遅れで支払われた傭船料を受け取っていた。この記録により、仲裁審は、船主は、傭船料の支払の遅滞を理由として、本船を引き揚げることはできないと裁定した。仲裁審によれば、次のとおりである。

　　仲裁人は、本傭船契約第5条の文言を慎重に検討した。文言は次のようなものである。「……傭船料を遅滞なく定期に支払わない場合、銀行保証がない場合、あるいは、本傭船契約の違反がある場合、船主は、自由に傭船者の運航から本船を引き揚げることができる。……」その文言は、明瞭であり、曖昧なところはない。それは「遅滞のない定期的支払」と述べているが、遅滞のない定期的受取とは言っていない。したがって、仲裁人は、船主の疑義や抗弁を受けることなく、傭船者が7年間にわたり傭船料を支払ってきたという歴史が、傭船者側から見れば、期限遵守および規則性の一つの典型を築き上げたといえるのであり、それは、特に例外ともいえない唯1回の事例で無視できるものではないと確信する。

　The Proton, SMA 160 (Arb. at N. Y. 1966) 事件では、船主は、支払の遅滞を認める「実務処理方式を、通信文等のやりとりの中で築きあげていた」という理由で船主の本船引揚を認めなかった。この原則は、Cochin Refineries v. Triton Shipping, 1978 AMC 444 (Arb. at N. Y. 1978) 事件で支持された。同事件で、仲裁審は、船主が支払遅滞を長らく黙認したことが証拠により確認されたので、運賃不払を理由に運送契約から本船を引き揚げるのは、正当化さ

れないと裁定した（*The Robertina*, SMA 1151（Arb. at N. Y. 1977）事件も参照）。

しかしながら（上記 *Cochin Refineries* 事件で強い反対意見があるように）以上の事例から，船主は，支払の遅滞に当初異議を唱えなくても，将来，本船引揚条項を厳格に適用する意思を明白に通知することにより，期限どおりの支払を受ける権利を回復することができると思われる。さらに，船主が，従来の支払遅滞に対し異議を唱えていなかった事例についてさえ，傭船料支払遅滞のゆえに，本船引揚が認められた裁決例もある（*The Vermont I*, SMA 747（Arb. at N. Y. 1970）；*The Orient Lakes*, SMA 181（Arb. at N. Y. 1964）各事件参照）。したがって，いつも支払を遅滞し，それを異議なく船主が受領している傭船者は，だまされて安心してしまうかもしれない。

The Pergamos, SMA 3090（Arb. at N. Y. 1994）事件で，傭船者は何回も期日に遅れて傭船料を支払った。船主は，支払遅滞に異議を申し立てたが，本船引揚の権利を行使することはなかった。7ヶ月目の支払について，船主は，傭船者に最終の期限延長を認めた。傭船者の支払は，この最終期限に間にあったという事実にもかかわらず，船主は当事者間で別途の解決をしようとしていた他の係争中の費用を傭船者が支払わなかったとの理由で，本船を引き揚げる権利があると主張した。最終期限の延長により，船主は傭船料支払についての新しい条件を定めたが，係争中の費用の支払はその新しい条件による期限までに，必要ではなかったと仲裁人は考え，船主にはもはや引揚権はないと裁定した。

警告が必要なのか

実際の引揚通知が出される前に警告が必要か否かを船主はしばしば法律顧問に照会する。英国ではそういう原則はないように思われる。しかし，New York の仲裁人は，本船の引揚を判断する際に，より自由寛容な手法に伝統的に従ってきた。したがって，警告により傭船者に支払を実行させ，不履行を矯正させるとしても，警告は賢明なことである。前出 *The Noto* 事件で，ある著名な仲裁審は，本船引揚は思い切った救済であるので，最初に警告が発せられる必要があると思うと言った。

しかしながら，New York の仲裁人の相対的な寛大さは，警告なしでは本船の引揚の有効性が，支持されないことを意味すると理解されるべきではない。*The Athenian Horizon*, SMA 1197（Arb. at N. Y. 1977）事件で，傭船者が傭船料を送金したにもかかわらず，単に銀行の営業時間が終了し，所与の最終期限内に船主がそれを受領しなかったことで，本船引揚は数日間の支払遅滞を理由に支持された。仲裁審は，次のように述べた。

> 傭船者には，前払で傭船料を支払う絶対的義務があった。しかし，その前払がなかったので，船主には本船を引き揚げる契約上の権利が生じた。

The Admiralty Flyer, SMA 349（Arb. at N. Y. 1967）事件も参照。*The Egle*, SMA 815（Arb. at N. Y. 1973）事件で，仲裁審はニューヨーク・プロデュース書式の本船引揚条項を根拠として返船日の約5ヶ月前に本船の引揚権を認める裁定をした。船主は38回目の支払期限の9日後に，支払が即時になされなければ，本船を引き揚げるとの通知を発して，本船の引揚を行った。

本船引揚の通知

　英国法の場合と同様に，傭船料不払を理由に傭船契約を解約しようとする船主は，直ちにこのことを傭船者に通知しなければならない。通知は，特別の文言を要しない。慣用的文言は「貴殿は，支払期日に傭船料を支払わなかったので，船主は，ここにこれ以降の本船運航を取り止め，本船を引き揚げる。ただし，損害賠償請求権を留保する」という趣旨のものである。

遅滞した傭船料支払の受領

　米国の判例には，英国の判例に引用されているこの問題の特異性をまともに取り扱ったものはない。*The U.S. 219 (No. 11)*, 21 F. Supp. 466 (E.D.Pa. 1937) 事件で，裁判所は，期日遅れの傭船料を受領すれば，本船引揚権を喪失すると判示した。これは，将来の本船使用の対価を受領することと，本船を引き揚げることとは，両立しないのであるから，原則として正しいと思われる。さらに，*The San Juan Venturer*, 1974 AMC 1053 (Arb. at N.Y. 1974) 事件において，仲裁人の多数意見は，期限遅れの傭船料が，本船引揚通知発信前に送金され，船主がこれを受領した場合，その傭船料が，本船の過去の運航に対するものであったとしても，解約権の放棄となると裁定した。
　The Shimone, SMA 3092, (Arb. at N.Y. 1994) 事件で，仲裁人は全員一致で，船主が支払遅滞の傭船料を受け取った場合，船主は本船引揚の権利を放棄したことになると裁定した。船主の本船引揚は不法であると裁定されたが，傭船者は傭船契約の残りの期間を履行することで損失を被ったであろうとして，傭船者の損害は裁定されなかった。

期限遅れの支払提示

　第2巡回区控訴裁判所は，初期の判例つまり，*Luckenbach* v. *Pierson*, 229 F. 130 (2d Cir 1915) 事件で，期限遅れの傭船料支払の申出が拒否された後に行われた本船引揚を支持する判決を下している。その後で，New York の仲裁審は，傭船者が期限遅れの支払を申し出る前に，本船引揚通知を受領しない限り，支払申出が拒絶されても本船引揚は有効とはならないと裁定した (*The Noto*, 1979 AMC 116 (Arb. at N.Y. 1976))。しかしながら，船主が期限遅れの支払に対して，引揚権を放棄しない限り，傭船者が，期限遅れの支払により，船主のこの権利を無視することは許容されない。*Luckenbach* 事件で裁判所が，判示したように，こういう場合，期限遅れの支払を拒否するか，受領するかは船主の一存である。

275 船上に貨物がある場合の引揚

　傭船料不払時に，本船が航海中であれば，航海が完了し貨物全量が陸揚されるまで，本船引揚の通知は本当の意味で効力を生じない (前出 *Luckenbach* v. *Pierson*; *Diana Compania Maritima S. A.* v. *Sub-freights of the Admiralty Flyer*, 280 F. Supp. 607, 1968 AMC 2093 (S.D.N.Y. 1968). *Antria* v. *Triton*, 1980 AMC 681 (E.D.Pa. 1978) 事件も参照)。この事件で裁判所は，次のように判示した。船主は貨物を積んだ本船を引き揚げ，貨物を仕向地まで運送したがゆえに，船荷証券上の運賃の支払期日前に本船が引き揚げられる場合のみ，船荷証券上の運賃に「衡平法上」の請求権を持つ。しかしながら，たとえ，貨物の揚荷完了まで，引揚は有効ではないとか，貨物関係者に対して定期傭船者としての義務を船主が負うことで，即時に引揚は

効力を生じるとの見解が聞かれるにしても，船上に貨物があるからといって，有効な本船の引揚が阻害されるものではない（前出 The Noto 事件参照）。

Finora Co. v. Amitie Shipping Ltd., 852 F. Supp. 1298, 1995 AMC 607 (D. S. C. 1994), 原審維持54 F. 3d 209（4th Cir. 22 May 1995）事件参照。この事件で，裁判所は，船主が航海開始後，傭船者から本船を引き揚げようとしたが，その貨物が揚荷されるまで，再傭船者に関して，その引揚は，効力を生じないと判示した（前出334頁にて解説した The Athenian Horizon, SMA 1197（Arb. at N. Y. 1977））。

銀行の過誤

銀行の過誤に関する限り，New York の規則は，英法ほど厳しくはない。The Pandora (No. 2), SMA 755-A（Arb. at N. Y. 1973）事件において，傭船料は，傭船者の銀行から中継銀行を通じ，船主指定の銀行へ送金された。中継銀行の過誤のため，傭船料は，船主銀行に入金しなかった。船主が，傭船者に傭船料の未受領と，本船の引揚を通告したので，傭船者は，その銀行に照会した。しかし，過誤の原因を発見し，遅滞傭船料を送金するのにさらに5日ないし6日の遅れを生じた。本船引揚を肯定するにあたって，仲裁審は，傭船者には，船主の通知を受けた後，傭船料不払を是正する機会があったことに注目した。したがって，仲裁審が，いくらか躊躇しつつも，本船引揚の権利を肯定するに至ったのは，傭船者側が傭船料不払を早急に是正しなかったからである。

The Pandora 事件の非常に興味深い脚注は続いて提起された銀行に対する訴訟である。傭船者は，傭船者側の銀行 Continental Illinois と船主への支払の中継となったその取引銀行 Swiss Bank Corp. を相手に訴訟を提起した。Evra Corp. v. Swiss Bank Corp., 522 F. Supp. 820 (N. D. Ill. 1981), 再審理673 F. 2d 951（7th Cir. 1982）事件で，裁判所は次のように判示した。Continental Illinois から Geneva の Swiss Bank Corp. にテレックス支払指示が送られたが，受信テレックスが紛失したのか，Swiss Bank Corp. の機械の紙がきれたのか（Continental Illinois のテレックス機械は，通信の電子的受信を確認する「アンサーバック」を受信した）の理由で，Swiss Bank Corp. はこのテレックス支払指示に気づかなかった。それにより，肝腎要の傭船料の支払を完了できない事態となった。次のように判示された。(a)Illinois 州法の下，Swiss Bank Corp. は，傭船者に対して配慮する義務がある。(b)Swiss Bank Corp. は，受信テレックスの記録をとれなかったことと，機械の紙の確保に過失があった。(c)解約された傭船契約に関する逸失利益米貨2,000,000ドルを超える傭船者の損害賠償額は，予見可能で Swiss Bank Corp. から回収可能である。しかしながら，損害賠償額は回収可能となるには遠因すぎて間接的であると判示した Hadley v. Baxendale 事件で確立した原則に拠って，上訴裁判所は判決を覆した。

この点に関する今一つの New York 裁決例は，The Essi Gina, SMA 534（Arb. at N. Y. 1970）事件である。同事件で，小切手は，船主指定銀行へ郵送された。しかし，傭船料支払期限日の2日後に，銀行は，小切手が未着であることを通知してきた。翌日，本船は引き揚げられ，傭船料支払のために提供された代わりの小切手は受取を拒絶された。数日後，銀行は，紛失小切手を発見した。もっとも，小切手が銀行に到達した日時について，裁定は何も触れていなかった。仲裁人は，過誤は，一に銀行側に存するから傭船者に責任はなく，したがって，本船引揚は不法であると裁定した。

同様に，The Meltemi, SMA 491（Arb. at N. Y. 1970）事件で，傭船契約は，傭船料の「遅滞のない」支払を規定していた。船主は，満1年にあたる当日の取引時間終了までに，New

York の船主銀行が，傭船料を受領していなかったとして本船を引き揚げた。しかし，同日の朝，Canada の銀行は，New York の銀行に傭船料支払の授権をしたが，テレックスの故障のため，支払が遅れ，翌日の朝になった。この事実に基づき，仲裁審の多数意見は，船主に本船を引き揚げる権利はなく，傭船料の支払は，容認された慣行と傭船契約の明示の条項に従ってなされていると裁決した。

これらの裁定は，a）傭船者自身，その支払の遅れを生じたことについて責任がない限り，また，b）傭船者が傭船料の不払に気づきしだい，それを早急に是正する限り，銀行の過誤による支払遅れの是正を傭船者に許すものと解釈できるといわれている。また，これらの裁定は，誠実に行動した当事者に対する過酷な結果を避ける傾向にある New York 仲裁の伝統的な衡平の観念と軌を一にしているともいわれている。

New York の裁決例では，銀行の過誤による傭船料の支払遅滞の問題を，明白に代理の原則に基づいて取り扱ったものはないと思われる。銀行が，傭船料の受取に関し，船主により指定されれば，その銀行は，船主の代理人となるから，船主の口座に入金するについて銀行に手落ちがあれば，それは，船主の責任に帰せられるべきものであると思われる。The Erie, SMA 497 (Arb. at N. Y. 1970) 事件では，5月19日を支払期限とする傭船料の支払について，小切手がその日に郵送され，船主銀行は，その翌朝，これを受け取った場合，船主は，本船を引き揚げる権利を有しないと裁定された。その傭船料は，5月21日まで船主の口座に入金されなかった。しかし，仲裁審は，これは，船主が，その銀行に，傭船料の支払について，銀行の役割を適切に通知していなかった結果であると判断した。

同様に，傭船者が傭船料を送金するに際して利用する銀行は，傭船者の代理人あるいは復代理人である。したがって，傭船者銀行あるいは，中継銀行の過誤は，傭船者の責任に帰せられるべきものである。The Pandora (No. 2) 事件および The Essi Gina 事件の裁定例は，善意かつ誠実な傭船者は，New York において，有利な仲裁を受けることができると指摘しているが，厳しい危険が伴うことを考えれば，船主銀行が，傭船料を期限どおりに受け取ることを確実にする一種の「安全保障」対策を定めておくことが望ましい。

「あるいは，本傭船契約の違反により」

第5条を文字どおりに読めば，傭船者側のいかなる契約違反を理由としても，船主の本船引揚は認められると思われる。しかしながら，「同種解釈 ejusdem generis」の原則が適用されるべきであり，したがって，傭船料支払不履行と同様の重大さを持つ契約違反の場合にのみ，本船引揚が認められることとなろう。The Arietta Venizelos, 1973 AMC 1012 (Arb. at N. Y. 1972) 事件では，ゲリラにより，タンカーが襲撃されるおそれがあるため，非安全として知られている港を傭船者が指定した場合，本船引揚は有効であると裁定された。この裁定は，Texacotime 書式の下におけるものであったが，しかし，ニューヨーク・プロデュース書式についてもこれを類推することができる。

本船引揚の効果

米法と英法との間の，一つの重要な差異は，本船引揚の結果に関してである。英法の考え方は，本船引揚権を，ある要件事実，すなわち傭船料の支払遅滞（前出329頁参照）という事実が発生した場合に行使できる解約「選択権」として扱うものである。この見解によれば，船主は，本船の引揚はできるが，傭船者の履行拒絶による損害賠償は，本船引揚条項と無関係に，

傭船料の支払に関する傭船者の態度が契約の履行拒絶となるほど重大な場合に限られ，そうでない場合は，認められないと思われる。それゆえ，実際問題として，本船引揚は，傭船市場が堅調な場合に行われるだけであろう。

しかし，米法の考え方によれば，傭船料の支払が単に遅れただけで，船主は，傭船者が傭船契約を履行拒絶したものとして取り扱う権利を有する。それゆえ，「本船引揚」条項は「期限がその本質をなす」規定と同等のものとして解釈され，その違反は，解約の根拠として扱うに十分である。それゆえ，New York においては，船主が単に1回だけ傭船料の支払が遅延した後，軟調市場で本船を引き揚げようとすれば，傭船者は，船主の損害につき責任を負うとの裁定を受ける危険を冒すこととなる。

有効な引揚は再傭船者の権利に影響を及ぼすこともある（*Cardinal Shipping Corp.* v. *The Seisho Maru*, 744 F. 2d 461 (5th Cir. 1984) 事件参照）。同事件で，傭船者の傭船料不払により，原傭船契約の下で船主の引揚権と再傭船者のリーエンは抵触するので，再傭船者は，本船に海事リーエンを行使できないと判示された。

The Shena and The Ave, SMA 2893 (Arb. at N.Y. 1992) 事件で，仲裁人は，傭船者の遅滞した傭船料支払のため，船主が本船を引き揚げた後に再傭船者が支給した燃料につき傭船者は船主から償還を受ける権利があるとの傭船者の請求を退けた。損害額を軽減するために燃料を再傭船者から船主が直接購入することを，仲裁人は容認した。

不法な引揚または解約の際の損害賠償

契約上の損害賠償の目的は，損害を被った当事者が，契約が履行された場合には，置かれたであろう金銭的に同様な立場を回復することである。このようにして，損害を被った当事者の「期待利益」は，保護される（*Restatment, Second Contracts*, §347参照。例として *Sofia Shipping Co.* v. *Amoco Transp. Co.*, 628 F. Supp. 116, 1986 AMC 2163 (S. D. N. Y. 1986) 事件参照）。しかしながら，損害賠償額は，契約が締結された時点で予見可能なものに限定される。契約法は，違反そのものから自然に生じる直接損害賠償額と直接損害を超える損失である間接損害賠償額を区別する。間接損害賠償の回収は，契約締結時点で，当事者たちが，その損失または損傷が契約違反について生じ得る結果として想定していたと判断されない限り，容認されないであろう（*Hadley* v. *Baxendale* (1854) 9 Ex. 341, 156 E. R. 145)）。

本船の不当な引揚，または傭船契約の解約についての直接的損害賠償額の適正な計算は，原傭船料率と同等の商売の契約違反時における支配的な市場料率との差である（*Orion Shipping & Trading* v. *Eastern States Petroleum Corp.*, 312 F. 2d 299 (2nd Cir.), 裁量上告拒絶373 U. S. 949 (1963))。このような手法の目的は，違反した当事者が傭船契約に基づく義務を履行した場合に，非違反者がいたであろう同じ立場に非違反者を置くことである。市場料率は，通常，違反当日ないしその前後の時点に同じ，または匹敵する取引で，匹敵する他の本船の傭船契約を参照して認定される（*United Transp. Co.* v. *Berwind-White Coal Mining Co.*, 13 F. 2d 282 (2d Cir. 1926) 事件参照，*Liberty Navigation and T. Co.* v. *Kinoshita & Co. Ltd.*, 285 F. 2d 343 (2d Cir. 1960)，裁量上告拒絶366 U. S. 949 (1961), *McNear* v. *Leblond*, 123 F. 384 (9th Cir. 1903)）。

The Moshill, SMA 2069 (Arb. at N.Y. 1985) 事件で，傭船者の定期傭船契約の不履行に対する船主の損害賠償額を決定するために仲裁審は，獲得したであろう傭船料，すなわち残余傭船期間に支払われるべき傭船料と，不履行のときから傭船契約の最低期間の満了時までの代替航海の実収入，または代替航海の費用を比較する方法を採用した。

[278] 違反の時点で,同等の取引が市場に存在しない場合もあろう。これは,本船を対象とする取引の性質,または単に市況の変動によるかも知れない。この場合,裁判所や仲裁人はそれでも入手可能な情報に基づき市場料率を決定すべきである。

間接損害賠償額の「本質的実例」は,利益の喪失である (*Nyquist v. Randall*, 819 F. 2d 1014 (11th Cir. 1987) 事件参照)。この問題を含む海事事案の例に次のものがある。*Vitol Trading S. A. v. SCS Control Services*, 874 F. 2d 76, 80-82 (2d Cir. 1989); *Evra Corp. v. Swiss Bank Corp.*, 673 F. 2d 951, 955, 956 (7th Cir. 1982), 裁量上告拒絶 459 U. S. 1017 (1982); *Gardner v. The Calvert*, 253 F. 2d 395, 399-400 (3d Cir.), 裁量上告拒絶 356 U. S. 960 (1958); *Polar Steamship Corp. v. Overseas S. Corp.*, 136 F. 2d 835, 840-842 (4th Cir.), 裁量上告拒絶 320 U. S. 774 (1943); *Czarnikow-Rionda Co. v. Federal Sugar Refining Co.*, 255 N. Y. 33, 41-42, 173 N. E. 913, 915-916 (1930); *The Elbe Ore*, SMA 2561 (Arb. at N. Y. 1989), 追認 1989 AMC 2874 (S. D. N. Y., 1989); および *McAllister Brothers Inc. v. A & S Transportation Co.*, SMA 1989 (Arb. at N. Y. 1984)。

The Independence, SMA 3049 (Arb. at N. Y. 1994) 事件で,管理船主 (disponent owner) は,傭船者の5年間の傭船の拒絶による逸失利益を回収しようとした。仲裁審は,再傭船契約が締結されたときに,傭船者は原傭船契約の条件を承知していたと判断した。二つの傭船契約間の傭船料率の相違により管理船主が得たと思われる利益を傭船者は知っていた。したがって,仲裁審は,管理船主に,原傭船契約を履行した費用と,傭船者が履行した場合に管理船主が得たであろう収入との差を裁定した。

The Boni, SMA 3053 (Arb. at N. Y. 1994) 事件で,本船は火災で被った重大な損傷のため,傭船航海を続けることができなかった。仲裁審は,原油取引の逸失利益は契約時に運送人により合理的に予見できない特殊な損害賠償金額であると判定して,損害賠償額の中に原油取引の逸失利益を含めるべきであるとの再傭船者／貨物所有者の要請を退けた。仲裁審は,さらに貨物所有者の原油相場の掛けつなぎの損失の請求についても退けた。しかしながら,その際に,これらの損失は,特殊な損害額であるとの被告の主張も仲裁審は退けた。代わりに仲裁審は,貨物所有者の原油相場の掛けつなぎは,所定の手続,または一般に認められる業界標準に沿った掛けつなぎ取引ではないことを理由として,その請求を退けた。

The Montecristo, SMA 2941 (Arb. at N. Y. 1993) 事件で,仲裁審は,航海傭船契約の締結時に,航海傭船から生じた損失は予見できたと判定して,貨物を提供できなかったことによる間接損害賠償額を裁定した。

定期傭船または航海傭船契約に基づく事案で,被害者は,損害額を軽減するために合理的な方策を講じる義務がある (*Aaby v. States Marine Corp.*, 107 F. Supp. 484 (S. D. N. Y. 1951))。しかしながら,軽減する義務は長期の運送契約の違反の場合には,生じない。*Orion Shipping & Trading v. Eastern States Petroleum Corp.*, SMA 573 (Arb. at N. Y. 1962) 事件を *McAllister Bro. Inc. v. A & S Transp. Co.*, SMA 1989 (Arb. at N. Y. 1984) 事件および *Alumina Transp. Corp. v. Occidental Chemical Co.*, SMA 2136 (Arb. at N. Y. 1985) 事件と比較。

一般に *Arbitration between Guinomar and Martin Marietta Aluminium Inc.*, SMA 2534 (Arb. at N. Y. 1988) 事件を参照。

一般に,善意の当事者が損害を避けるために合理的に行動しなかったことを証明する挙証責任は,違反した当事者側にある (*Federal Insurance Co. v. Sabine Towing & Transp. Co.*, 783 F. 2d 347, 350 (2d Cir. 1986)。一般に *The Oak Pearl*, SMA 2427 (Arb. at N. Y. 1986) *The Mermaid I*, SMA 1836 (Arb. at N. Y. 1983); *The Captain Demonsthenes*, SMA 1569 (Arb. at N. Y. 1981); *Eddie S. S. Co. Ltd. v. Eastern Development Inc.*, SMA 1051 (Arb. at N. Y.

1976）各事件参照）。

合理的に損害賠償額を軽減する義務を果たすにあたって，船主は「そのときに誠実に合理的な注意を尽くすことだけを求められる。最善の判断を下すことや後知恵なら指令できるような279賢明な道を取ることまで求められない」(*Ellerman Lines Ltd.* v. *The President Harding,* 187 F. Supp. 948, 951 (S. D. N. Y. 1960)，原審維持 288 F. 2d 288 (2d Cir. 1961))。

Aaby v. *States Marine Corp.,* 107 F. Supp. 484 (S. D. N. Y. 1951) 事件は，船主が損害賠償額を軽減する合理的な方策をとれなかった事案の例である。傭船者の違反の後で，船主は傭船者が提案した軽減策を拒否した。裁判所は，傭船者はその当時の市場料率を表示したと判定した。裁判所は「申立人は，市場の上昇を待つことを決意したときに，自らの判断で賭けをした」と述べた（107 F. Supp.（同判例集485頁））。

前出 *The Independence* 事件で仲裁審は，市場情勢が改善したときに，管理船主は，単に現物市場で取引を継続するのではなく，傭船者が5年間の定期傭船を拒否したことにより生じた損害賠償額を軽減するために本船の別の長期傭船を求めるべきであったと裁定した。

傭船者が本船を使用するのを船主が拒否する権利

The Dominique, SMA 2535 (Arb. at N. Y. 1989) 事件で，傭船者が傭船料の支払を遅滞したので，船主は支払を受領するまで，本船の使用を保留した。仲裁審は，支払を遅滞したとの理由で，船主は本船引揚の権利を有するが，船主には，傭船者が本船を使用するのを一時的にだけ拒否する権利はない，と裁定した。仲裁審は，その裁定の際に，裁定は *The Agios Giorgis* [1976] 2 Lloyd's Rep. 192 事件と *The Helindas,* SMA 1589 (Arb. at N. Y. 1981) 事件に則っていると述べた。

The Koycergiz, SMA 2700 (arb. at N. Y. 1990) 事件で，仲裁審は，船主は二つの理由で本船を錨地に繋留する権利があると裁定した。第1に，船主は傭船者に傭船料の支払の遅滞の通知を行い，船主が引揚権の行使を望むのであれば，厳密には本船を引き揚げる権利を行使できるところである。第2に本船の遅延は，傭船者の要請で傭船者の貨物であるアスベストスを乗組員が除去することによって実際に生じたということである。

The Karin M, SMA 2869 (Arb. at N. Y. 1992) 事件で仲裁人は，船主は傭船料の支払の遅滞を理由として，貨物の揚荷の遅延を正当化することはできないと裁定した。傭船者は，揚荷遅延の期間につきオフハイヤーとなるとの裁定を得た。

期間の計算を開始する時

[Clause 5 continued]

"62. .... Time to count from 7 a.m. on the working day
63. following that on which written notice of readiness has been given to Charterers or their Agents before 4 p.m., but if required by Charterers, they
64. to have the privilege of using vessel at once, such time used to count as hire.
65.   Cash for vessel's ordinary disbursements at any port may be advanced as required by the Captain, by the Charterers or their Agents, subject
66. to 2 1/2% commission and such advances shall be deducted from the hire. The Charterers, however, shall in no way be responsible for the application
67. of such advances.
68.   6. That the cargo or cargoes be laden and/or discharged in any dock or at any wharf or place that Charterers or their Agents may
69. direct, provided the vessel can safely lie always afloat at any time of tide, except at such places where it is customary for similar size vessels to safely
70. lie aground.
71.   7. That the whole reach of the Vessel's Hold, Decks, and usual places of loading (not more than she can reasonably stow and carry), also
72. accommodations for Supercargo, if carried, shall be at the Charterers' disposal, reserving only proper and sufficient space for Ship's officers, crew,
73. tackle, apparel, furniture, provisions, stores and fuel. Charterers have the privilege of passengers as far as accommodations allow, Charterers
74. paying Owners .... per day per passenger for accommodations and meals. However, it is agreed that in case any fines or extra expenses are
75. incurred in the consequence of the carriage of passengers, Charterers are to bear such risk and expense."

[第5条続き]

「期間の計算は，傭船者またはその代理人が，午後4時前に書面による準備完了の通知を受け取った日に続く作業日の午前7時から開始する。ただし，傭船者は，要求すれば本船を即時に使用する権利を有し，その使用時間を傭船期間に算入するものとする。

傭船者またはその代理人は，船長の求めにより，2.5パーセントの手数料を徴して，いずれの港における通常の諸掛に必要な現金を，立て替えるものとする。立替金は，傭船料から控除する。ただし，上記の立替金の使用について，傭船者は，一切責任を負わないものとする。

6．貨物の船積または揚荷は，傭船者またはその代理人が指示するドック・埠頭またはその他の場所で行う。ただし，本船が潮時の如何を問わず，常時浮揚状態で安全に碇泊できることを要するが，同じ寸法の船舶が，慣習上座洲状態で安全に碇泊できる場所を含む。

7．本船の区画は，本船の職員・部員，揚貨機，装具，備品，食料品，船用品および燃料のための相当かつ十分な船腹を除き，本船の船艙・甲板，その他通常の積付場所の全容積（本船が合理的な積付および運送をなしうる限度を超えない），および上乗人が同乗する場合，その居住区を含めて，すべて傭船者の使用に委ねなければならない。傭船者は乗客設備の収容限度まで，乗客を乗せる権利を有する。傭船者は船主に対し，乗客設備の費用ならびに食費として，乗客1人当たり1日.........を支払う。ただし，旅客運送の結果，負担金または特別の費用を生ずるときは，傭船者がその危険と費用とを負担するものとする。」

傭船期間の開始

ニューヨーク・プロデュース書式第5条62／64行は18／21行に参照されている。18/21行で，本船は……………所在の「傭船者が指図するドック，埠頭，またはその他の場所において，」傭船者の使用に供されるものとすると規定され，さらに，「かかるドック，埠頭，またはその他の場所が使用できないときは，第5条の規定により期間の計算を行う。」と続く。

傭船者が選んだドック，埠頭，その他の場所が使用可能である場合には，本船がそこに到着し，傭船者の使用に供されたときから傭船料は支払われるべきであり，第5条は当該ドック，埠頭，その他の場所が使用不可能な場合の傭船料支払開始時点の決定にのみ適用されるという議論がある。この点については，判決を待たねばならないが，第5条は傭船期間開始に関しての唯一の条項であるとするのが，当該文言のより妥当な解釈であり，21行は，本船到着時，ドック，埠頭，その他の場所が直ちに使用できない場合でも，第5条が適用されるとすることによって，この見解に矛盾することなく，むしろこれを補強しようとしているものであると言われている。第5条は第14条の解約条項の文言と密接に関連している。解約条項は第5条の準備完了通知の提出を前提としており，傭船期間が第5条のこの通知規定以外の方法で開始するのであれば，解約条項はほとんど満足には作用しないことは明らかであろう。

282 この解釈は，*Kawasaki* v. *Bantham Steamship* (1938) 60 LL.L. Rep. 70事件で，第5条の作用について，Branson判事が表明した見解（傍論）と一致する。同判事は次のように述べている（同判例集77頁）。「準備完了の通知提出後午前7時までは傭船期間が開始しない，というのが第5条の最後の文章の正しい解釈であるという主張には従いかねる。『ただし，傭船者の要求があれば，積荷を直ちに開始し，その使用時間を傭船期間に算入する』という文言は，通知の提出に代わる方法として傭船契約に定められたものと思われる。その実務は次のようなものである。本船が到着したとき，通知を提出することにより，傭船者に受取の義務を課すことができる。午後4時に通知を出したならば，傭船者の受取の有無を問わず，翌作業日の午前7時に傭船期間は開始する。一方傭船者には，本船使用を希望する場合，それを要求する権利があり，要求した場合には本船が直ちに引き渡され，積荷が直ちに開始されるべきである。積荷開始をもって当然傭船期間が開始し，傭船料支払の義務も開始する」。

この見解においては，傭船開始のための本船引渡は，傭船者が本船を受け取り，使用を開始したときか，通知期限満了のいずれか早い時点で行われる。

一度，傭船者の要求により本船が使用されたならば，傭船者が本船を，その時点以降，継続して使用しても，断続的に使用しても，64行に従い傭船期間は開始する。したがって，一度傭船期間が開始すれば，「その使用時間」という文言の不明瞭さにかかわらず，あたかも通知期限の経過後のようにすべての時間が算入される。航海傭船契約における碇泊期間に関する事案で，Donaldson判事は，「使用しなければ」という文言は傭船者により実際に使用された時間のみを使用碇泊期間に算入することを認めるものであると判示したが（*The Helle Skou* [1976] 2 Lloyd's Rep. 205)，定期傭船と航海傭船とは本質的に性格が相違するのであるから，64行に関する限り異なる結果を生じて当然である。

第5条は通知を作業日に提出することを要求していないと思われる。63行の代名詞「that」は「作業日」よりも，むしろ「日」を指していると思われる。

62/64行と94行（「傭船者の要求があるときは，……傭船期間は……より前には開始しない………」）の間の潜在的矛盾について，後出419頁参照。

前渡立替金

66行は，傭船者が傭船契約から65行に述べられている前渡立替金を控除することを許容している。傭船料から許容される控除について前出306/311頁参照。

常に浮揚状態で安全に碇泊

傭船者の選択したバースの安全性の解説について前出251/252頁参照。

傭船者が貨物積載可能な船艙

「本船が合理的な積付および運送をなしうる限度を超えない」
The Roman Karmen [1994] 1 Lloyd's Rep. 644 事件で Mance 判事は，ニューヨーク・プロデュース書式の第7条のこの文言の意味するところは，「物理的な安全と堪航性の配慮」に限定されず，「運航中の本船の物理的な安全という一般的状況の下で貨物の積付と配置に関する船級協会の合理的規則に少なくとも船主を適合させる」ことまで拡大される。

283 甲板積貨物

甲板積貨物に関する解説について後出368頁参照。

NYPE 93

ニューヨーク・プロデュース書式1993年版は，第13条(b)項に傭船者は「甲板積貨物の運送の結果本船に生じたいかなる種類の滅失および・または損傷および・または責任および甲板積貨物を積まなかったならば生じなかったはずのいかなる種類の滅失および・または損傷および・または責任についても船主に対して補償する」ものとすると規定している。前出12頁の英文書式の188/190行と56頁参照。

284 米 国 法

期間の計算を開始する時

　ニューヨーク・プロデュース書式第5条の下では，準備完了の通知を午後4時までに傭船者に提出すれば，提出後の作業日の午前7時に傭船は開始する（*The Hopeville*, 1968 AMC 2650（Arb. at N.Y. 1968）事件参照）。21行に基づき，第5条に規定されているように，たとえ碇泊場所が使用不可能であっても傭船期間は開始する。しかし準備完了の通知を提出したとき，ドックや埠頭が直ちに使用可能である場合でも傭船は翌作業日まで開始しない（*The Alexandros Koryzis*, SMA 271（Arb. at N.Y. 1968）事件参照）。傭船者は通知受取後，翌作業日以前に本船を使用することもできる。その場合，傭船者は当然，使用期間につき傭船料を支払わねばならない。しかしながら，一度傭船者が積荷その他の本船使用を開始すれば傭船期間は継続するという英国の見解に反し，米国法の原則は，傭船者は実際に使用した時間に対してのみ傭船料を支払えばよいというものである（*The Antonis*, SMA 273（Arb. at N.Y. 1959）事件参照）。

極 力 迅 速

"76.　8. That the Captain shall prosecute his voyages with the utmost despatch, and shall render all customary assistance with ship's crew and
77. boats."

「8．船長はその航海を極力迅速に遂行し，本船の乗組員および端艇をもって，慣習上なすべき一切の助力を提供するものとする。」

航海の遂行

本船が必要もないのに避難港に入港したり，避難港で時間を取る場合（*Istros（Owners）* v. *Dahlstorm*（1930）38 Ll. L. Rep. 84, 後出638頁），あるいは船長が，傭船者の指示した港への入港を不当に拒否したり（*The Charalambos N. Pateras*［1972］1 Lloyd's Rep. 1, 後出640頁），あるいは，貨物の積揚を不当に妨げたりした場合（*The Agios Giorgis*［1976］2 Lloyd's Rep. 192, 前出315頁），船長は，その航海を，極力迅速に遂行したことにはならない。

NYPE 93

ニューヨーク・プロデュース書式1993年版は，「極力迅速」の代わりに「相当な迅速」という文言を使用している（前出10頁の第8条（英文書式100行）と54頁参照）。この変更は重要であるとは思われない。

機 関 士

文言は，特に船長となっているが，機関士が，その航海を極力迅速に遂行しない場合をも含む（*The Apollonius*［1978］1 Lloyd's Rep. 53 事件参照）。

免責条項に従って

しかしながら，その義務は，傭船契約中の免責条項により制限される。

　　Keifuku Maru は，6ヶ月間定期傭船された。傭船契約書の第9条は，「船長は，その航海を極力迅速に遂行するものとする……」と規定しており，さらに，第14条は，「本傭船期間を通して，下記事由により発生せる損害，損失は，それが，運送品あるいは運送予定品に関するものであろうと，その他の事項に関連するものであろうと，一切免責されるものとする。……すなわち，その免責事由とは，本船の管理，あるいは航海に関する水先人，船長，乗組員の怠慢，過失，あるいは判断の誤りである」。
　　審判人（umpire）の事実認定によれば，石炭は十分あったのに，これを十分使用しなかったため，航海が遅延したというものだった。Bailhache 判事は，この事実認定は，船長の過失を認定したものであると判断した。そして同判事は，第9条の違反があり，第14条は，第9条の船主義務を「除去する」ものとは解釈できないから，船主は，第14条によって保護されないと判示した。

控訴院は、仲裁人に再度の事実認定を求めた結果、速力減は、「一般的綱紀弛緩」のためであって、過失によるものではないとされた。控訴院の多数意見は、この事実認定の結果、第14条を考慮する必要はないと判断した。しかし、Scrutton 卿判事は、第14条に全面的効力を認めても、なお第9条を適用する問題が依然としてあるのであるから、第9条と第14条が競合する場合には、第14条が優先するとの見解をとった。

286　貴族院の多数意見は、審判人の事実認定が、傭船者の勝訴の決め手になったという、控訴院の判断に同意した。第9条と第14条との関係について、3人の裁判官は、Scrutton 卿判事の意見に同意して、過失の場合は、第14条が第9条に優先するとの意見を表明した。他方、Cave 子爵大法官は、反対の見解をとる Bailhache 判事の考えが正当であるとした。
　　Suzuki v. Beynon（1924）18 Ll. L. Rep. 415, 20 Ll. L. Rep. 179（C. A.）および（1926）24 Ll. L. Rep. 49（H. L.）.
　　（Istros（Owners）v. Dahlstorm（1930）38 Ll. L. Rep. 84 事件における Wright 判事の判決、および後出638頁を参照）

　それゆえ、ニューヨーク・プロデュース書式76行に定める、極力迅速に航海を遂行する義務の違反を追及された場合、船主は、第24条により摂取されている、米国海上物品運送法上の抗弁を、援用することができると考えられる。特に、同法第4条第2項(a)により、「本船の取扱、または航海に関する過失や懈怠……」という抗弁を援用できる。同法の関係条項は、第2条により、貨物の「積込、取扱、積付、運送、保管、管理、および揚荷に関して」のみ適用される。しかし、Adamastos v. Anglo-Saxon Petroleum [1958] 1 Lloyd's Rep. 73 事件では、連続航海傭船上、本船が予定航海数を達成できなかったため、傭船者が被った損失は、第2条の文言に含まれると判示された。定期傭船契約上、極力迅速に航海を遂行する船長の義務不履行による、類似の損失についても、おそらく同じことが言えると思われる。したがって、同法上の抗弁は、傭船者の損失が、貨物の物理的損失、損害以外に起因していても可能な場合がある。
　船長の義務は、103行から106行の一般免責条項により、さらに限定される。これらの免責条項に関する所見については、以下後出489頁を参照。米国法の摂取については、以下593頁を参照。極力迅速に航海を遂行する義務に関するボルタイム書式第13条の効果については、後出638頁を参照。また航海傭船の事案である The Takafa [1990] 1 Lloyd's Rep. 536 事件の Hirst 判事の「最適速力」（all convenient speed）に関する解説を参照。

慣習上の助力

　特定の役務が、「慣習上」のものであるかどうかは、事実問題である。その他の関連要素の中で、特に旗国、乗組員が署名した雇入契約、本船の就航航路などが問題となる。
　塩化カリウム、燐鉱石およびマンガン鉱運送後、穀物船積前の空船航海中の船艙の錆取りに関し、ある London の審判人は、次のような事実認定を行った。それは、Splosna Plovba v. Agrelak Steamship [1975] 1 Lloyd's Rep. 139 事件における、Donaldson 判事の判決の中で、次のように記録されている。

　　浮いている程度の錆を除去するのは、乗組員の職務である。それは、Bela Krajina 号程度の大きさの船では、困難ではあるが、時間と天候に恵まれれば、いつでも乗組員ができることである。
　　堅く固着した錆を除去するのは、大作業であり、空船航海中、乗組員がそれを行うことはできない。足場を築き、動力錆打装置が必要である。Bela Krajina 号程度の大きさの船では、乗組員がその

作業を，効率的かつ完全に行うことはできない。
　船艙の清掃というのは，船殻鋼材の錆打を含まない，しかし，接近できる場所の，大きい浮いた錆の断片を取り除くことは，含まれている。慣習上の協力とは，圧縮空気錆打機，高水圧噴砂機のような，複雑な道具の使用を要する錆取作業まで，含むものではない。

287 米 国 法

極力迅速

　第8条の目的は，状況と安全が許す限り間断なく，迅速に傭船者の指図する航海を遂行する義務を船長に課するものである。

　Lowber v. *Bangs*, 69 U.S. 728 (1865) 事件では，傭船契約が，「本船は，MelbourneからCalcutta向け，極力迅速に航行すること」と規定していた。裁判所は，「(この) 文言は，本船が一地点から他の地点へ直航すべきこと，したがって，その限りで，**少なくとも時間を契約の要素とすること**を目的としていると解する以外に，解釈のしようがない」と判示し，さらに裁判所は，本規定は，「契約の本質そのもの」にまでかかわっており，したがって，本船がCalcuttaへの途中，Manilaに離路し，そのため，離路しなかったときより3ヶ月以上も遅れてCalcuttaに到着したのであるから，傭船者は契約から解放されると認定した。

　しかしながら，極力迅速に航海を遂行する船長の義務は本船と乗組員と貨物の安全に備える最高の義務との均衡を保たねばならない。航海は本船と乗組員と貨物の安全のために遅延の要があると決断する，特定の状況で，船長が，誠実かつ妥当な判断により行動する場合，その遅延は傭船契約の違反とはならないであろう。さらにその状況は航海の離路または航海の一時的中断の正当な事由となろう。

　The Styria, 101 F. 728 (2d. Cir. 1900) 事件は，186 U.S. 1 (1902) において他の理由で修正されたが，本船は New York 向けに Sicily で硫黄の船積をした。Sicily を出港する前に船長はスペインと米国の間で戦争が勃発したのを知った。硫黄が禁制品なので，船長は揚荷して Sicliy の倉庫へ入れた。船長はこのことを受荷主へ書面により「戦争という事実のため，現に硫黄を積んだ New York 向け航海は危険であると判断して」貨物を揚荷していると通知した (186 U.S. at 10)。裁判所は，「船長の行動は，本船と貨物に関するあらゆる利益に十分な配慮をした」という点で，船長の行動はこの状況で正当化されると判示した (186 U.S. at 20)。後出662頁の議論も参照。

　The Robertina, SMA 1151 (Arb. at N.Y. 1977) 事件で，傭船者は傭船料の支払を滞らせているので，船主は船長に Cristobal で本船を停め置くように指示した。運賃前払の船荷証券により船積されていたので，船主は，貨物にリーエンを行使できなかった。さらに船主は過去何度も支払遅延を容認してきたので，船主は傭船料の支払遅延につき，本船の引揚を実行できなかった。仲裁人は，本船の拘留は船主が，貨物にリーエンを行使できないときに，傭船者に傭船料を支払わせようと圧力をかける戦術に過ぎないと判断した。この状況の下で仲裁人は，船主は第8条に基づく極力迅速に航海を遂行する義務に違反したと裁定した。

　The Medita, SMA 1150 (Arb. at N.Y. 1977) 事件で，荒天を避けるために船長が進路から離路した場合に，仲裁人は，船長は，極力迅速に航海を遂行する義務に違反していないと裁定した。

　The Karin M, SMA 2869 (Arb. at N.Y. 1992) 事件で仲裁人は，強風の通過を待つために揚荷港の一つからの出港を遅らせた船長の判断を承認した。

　船長は，例えば，危険品を積んでいて，その積付の安全を確認するために，船長が専門家の救援を求めるような場合，すなわち，本船が危険であると船長が信じるに足る十分な理由がある場合，船長は，航海を遅らせることができると思われる。*The Fernglen*, 1971 AMC 213 (Arb. at N.Y. 1970) 事件で，仲裁審は，旋盤屑鉄 (steel turnings) を含んだスクラップ貨

物の適切な積付について，専門家を呼び，その助言を得ている間，8日間投錨していた船長の行為は，正しいと裁定した。

The Continental Trader, SMA 1503（Arb. at N.Y. 1980）事件で，本船は，揚荷完了後，政治的不安と港湾当局，曳船，水先人を巻き込んだ港のストライキのため，Bandar Shapourで遅延した。船長は港湾当局の正式の出港許可証なしに，あるいは水先人なしで出港するのを拒絶した。本船がほとんど清水や燃料を使い果たした時点で，遂に水先人の助力がないまま，ただし出港許可書の交付を受け，曳船を横付して本船は出港した。仲裁審は，船長は極力迅速に航海を遂行することができなかったという傭船者の主張を全員一致で退けた。仲裁審は次のように述べた。

　　……仲裁審は，本船の船長は，本船の安全性に悪影響を与える事象につき最終決定者であるという海の古い規範を最後の拠り所とする。本船船長は，水先人なしの理想的状態とは程遠い状態で航行して，本船を無用の長物にしたり，大損害を与えるのを防いだ。船長はその後この自制と妥協せざるを得なかったが，船長は，水先人も，曳船も出港許可書もないときに思慮深い抑制と注意の下で行動する権利および，実際のがれることのできない義務の範囲内で行動した。

The Lelaps, SMA 2840（Arb. at N.Y. 1992）事件で，仲裁審は，「本船が，積荷・揚荷できるように早く」という慣用句により修飾された「慣習的に速やかな早出し」（customary quick despatch）という文言は，傭船者は，本船の到着時に積荷バースの提供を求められることを意味するという船主の主張を退けた。なぜなら「慣習的に」という用語を追加することにより，傭船者は，この義務（本船到着時の積荷バースの提供）を免れるからである。

慣習上の助力

The Andros City, SMA 1156（Arb. at N.Y. 1977）事件で，船主は傭船者の要請により行った船艙の掃き掃除および水洗いにつき乗組員に支払った金額の償還を請求した。傭船契約には，ニューヨーク・プロデュース書式にタイプ追加条項で，乗組員の時間外手当は一括定額で傭船者が支払うことと定めていた。本事案で問題となった点は，第8条の慣習的助力の規定により傭船者は乗組員が通常の清掃および船艙の水洗いを行うことを要求できるかということであった。さらに要求可能な場合に，傭船者が支払う毎月の時間外手当の定額が，この作業の報酬の限度であるのかということであった。

仲裁審は，貨物艙の清掃，水洗いは本船乗組員の通常の慣習的業務の一つではないと裁定した。その際，仲裁人は，本船の労働協約が船艙清掃に関与した乗組員に特別手当を与える作業として船艙清掃を取り扱っていることに言及した。仲裁人は，その時間外規定は，入港（渠）・出港（渠）時や，傭船者の使用に供する際の乗組員の通常の義務の履行に関連していると述べた。しかしながら，仲裁審は次のように述べた。

　　第8条の解釈がこの紛争の中心である。したがって注意深くその解釈は吟味されねばならない。そのためには，同条項の最初の部分と二番目の部分を分離することが必要である。「船長はその航海を極力迅速に遂行し，本船の乗組員および端艇をもって，慣習上なすべき一切の助力を提供するものとする」ことを求める最初の部分は，可能な限り効率的に迅速に遂行するためにあらゆる可能な努力をするという本質的に船舶の義務の認定である。それは，同条項や他の条項で別途特に規定されている責任を移転するものとして，文脈で理解，または空虚に解釈できないし，されてはならない。第8条の後半は，貨物の積込，積付，荷均，揚荷の費用を傭船者に割り当てるもので，この点につき仲裁

審は貨物引渡後の船艙清掃機能と船艙の保守または本船の堪航性維持に関与しない船艙清掃機能は，傭船者の勘定となると判断した。

|289| 第8条の「慣習上の助力」は適当な状況下で，空船航海時に貨物の残滓を掃き，水洗いすること，または傭船者のために船長および乗組員が通常船主のために行う他の業務を遂行することを船長および乗組員に求めていると理解されるであろう。しかし，船主の費用で傭船者の使用のために船舶の労働力の使用を指図する無制限の権利は，傭船者に許容されておらず，むしろ船主はそれに協力すべきであるが，この義務の基本的要旨は，船主の不当な協力義務拒否の可能性から傭船者を保護することである。

本船使用条項

[Clause 8 continued]

"77. .... The Captain (although appointed by the Owners), shall be under the orders and directions of the Charterers as regards employment and
78. agency;"

[第8条続き]

「船長は（船主により任命されたことにかかわりなく）本船の使用および代理業務に関しては、傭船者の命令、指示に従わなければならない。」

傭船者の指図に服従

船長には、本船の使用に関する傭船者の指図の妥当性を必要以上に問題とする責任はない。*Portsmouth Steamship* v. *Liverpool & Glasgow Salvage Association* (1929) 34 Ll.L. Rep. 459事件で、Roche判事は、船長は「明らかに重大な危険がない限り」、この指図に従って差し支えないと指摘した。船長は、傭船者の指図を拒否する権利を有するだけではなく、これを拒否しなければならないのは、これらの指図が、本船の安全性や貨物を危険に曝す場合であると考えられる。またすべての指図が、まさしくすべて「本船使用に関する」指図でないことを銘記すべきである（後出所見を参照）。

船長は、傭船者の指図に従って、自らの船舶を就航させる義務を有するけれども、必ずしも傭船者の指図に、直ちに従う必要はない。指図を受領した状況、またはその指図の性質によっては、船長がそれ以上の検討または調査をせずに応じることを不当とする。指図への応諾を相当の時間遅延させる船長あるいは船主の権利は、事案の分野如何で異なるものではない。各事案で決定を要する問題は、合理的な思慮のある者であれば、その状況でいかに行為したかということである（後出 *The Houda* [1994] 2 Lloyd's Rep. 541事件の控訴院の判決を参照）。例えば、船舶または貨物を潜在的な危険に曝す可能性のある指図に直面した場合には、遅延は正当化されるだろう。そして、戦争の場合には、たとえ、貨物または船舶に物理的な直接の脅威がないとしても、受け取った指図の出所と有効性につきさらに情報を求めるために遅延する権利と義務の両方がありうる（後出 *The Houda* 事件参照）。

Anastasia 号は、ニューヨーク・プロデュース書式に基づいて、1航海定期傭船された。本船は、Chalnaでのジュート積取を指示された。同地の傭船者代理店は、船長に対して、積荷は、欧州向けであるが、港湾当局には、船荷証券上の仕向地であるSingapore向けと申告するように依頼した。Chalna出港直後、傭船者は、船長に対し、Chalnaに引き返し、ジュートの増積をするよう、電信で指示した。船長は、しばらく傭船者と交信し、(a)本船の真の仕向港が航海日誌に記入されてしまっているにもかかわらず、傭船者がChalnaに引き返すことを希望していること、(b)砂洲の水深が十分であることを確認してから、傭船者の指示に従った。Donaldson判事は、船長が傭船者の指示に従うのが遅れても、それは正当であると判示した。船長の職務上の責任を説明した後、判事は、次のように指摘した。「そのような背景の下での船長の義務は、指示を受け取りしだい、合理的に行動することであると思われる。指示の中には、性質上、直ちにこれに従わなければ、適切な行動をとったといえ

ないものもあるが，十分な思慮を払い検討した上で従うことが，船長の適切な行動となるものもある」。

Midwest Shipping v. *Henry* [1971] 1 Lloyd's Rep. 375.

(*Pole* v. *Cetcovitch* (1860) 9 C.B. (N.S.) 430事件と *The Teutonia* (1872) L.R. 4 P.C. 171事件の航海傭船の事案も参照)

292　Houda 号は，クウェートの傭船者に Shelltime 4 書式を修正して定期傭船された。本船に与えられていた常備の行動指図は，すべての航海指図はクウェートから出されるとしていた。イラクがクウェートに侵攻後，傭船者の事務所は London に移転し，航海指図が発せられたのは London であった。船主は，その指図は合法的なるものかは疑問とし，さらに侵攻後に当該船荷証券が紛失し，船荷証券なしで Ain Sukhna で貨物を揚荷するようにとの傭船者の指図に応じることを拒否した。Phillips 判事の見解を覆して，控訴院は次のように判示した。

(1) 指図は通常即時の応諾を要求するが，指図が受領される状況または指図の性質により，船長がそれ以上の検討または調査をせずに応諾することは妥当ではないこともある。各事案で決定を要する問題は，合理的な思慮のある者であればその状況でいかに行為したかということである。問題の事案の状況は，応諾の遅延の妥当な根拠とすることができる。

(2) たとえその揚荷が実際問題として貨物の所有権を有する当事者の権利を侵害しないとしても，契約規定がない場合――そして，修正された Shelltime 4 傭船契約書にはそのような規定がなかった――(航海傭船者と同様に) 定期傭船者は船主または船長に船荷証券の呈示なくして貨物の揚荷を求めることはできない。

The Houda [1993] 1 Lloyd's Rep. 333 [1994] および 2 Lloyd's Rep. 541 (C.A.). (本事案の更なる詳細と Shelltime 4 傭船契約書の修正について後出688頁参照)

船長は，傭船者が傭船契約上権限のない指図を与えても，それに従う義務はない。非安全港への配船指示に関する *The Sussex Oak* (1950) 83 Ll.L. Rep. 297事件で，Devlin 判事は，次のように指摘した (同判例集307頁)。「本船使用に関する傭船者の指図に，船長を従わせる旨の定期傭船契約条項は，傭船者が，その権限外の指図を出した場合にまで，船長が従わなければならないと解されるとは思えない」(本件の事実関係については，前出234頁参照)。

したがって船長は貨物を受領する権利のない者に貨物を引き渡すようにとの傭船者の指図に従う義務はない。Staughton 判事による *The Sagona* [1984] 1 Lloyd's Rep. 194事件参照 (同判例集205頁)。

たとえ傭船者の指図に従った貨物の引渡が，貨物を適正に受領する権利のある者の権利を実際に侵害しないとしても，船長は，船荷証券の呈示なしでの貨物の引渡という傭船者の指図に応じる義務はない (前出 *The Houda* 事件参照)。この事案で，定期傭船契約に基づき本船および船長は傭船者の一般的命令と指図を受け，傭船者が貨物の占有権を持つ，または貨物の真の所有者としての処分権限を持つ状況なので，傭船者には船荷証券の呈示なしで貨物の引渡につき合法的命令を出す権利があった，と主張された。この主張を，第1審で Phillips 判事は，容認したが，控訴院は，退けた。控訴院で，Neill 卿判事は，次のように言った (同判例集552頁)。「貨物が船荷証券を呈示しない者に引き渡される場合，船主は契約責任を遂行しないことになるという一般原則から離れる十分な理由はない。……Denning 卿は，*Sze Hai Tong Bank* v. *Rambler Cycle Co. Ltd.* [1959] A.C. 576事件で (同判例集586頁) 次のように言った。『……船荷証券の呈示なく引渡をする船主は，自らの危険でそれを行う。』これは単純な実務上の習慣である。もちろん，補償状である程度保護されると判断し，船荷証券なしで貨物の引渡をするのは，船主の勝手であるが，私の判断では，指図を出す定期傭船者の権利があるからといって，傭船者には，貨物を船荷証券の呈示なしで揚荷すべきであると主張する権利はない」。

船主が傭船者の無効な指図に応じることを拒否した後で，傭船者がそれをあくまで主張した結果について，前出177頁参照。

しかしながら，傭船者の指図に応じ，船主が結果として損害を被る場合，船主は通常，補償という方法で傭船者から損害を回収する権利がある（前出248頁の *The Stork* [1955] 1 Lloyd's Rep. 349事件と後出354頁の *The Sagona* 事件参照）。さらに *The Kanchenjunga* [1987] 2 Lloyd's Rep. 509事件で Hobhouse 判事は次のように述べた（同判例集515頁）。「一般的に言って，人は契約の相手側の当事者は，適正に契約を遂行すると信じて行動する権利がある。たとえ，契約違反が明白であっても，関係者が，その違反は些細であると判断するならば，補償されるべき権利を犠牲にすることなく続行できることは取引のあるべき行為にとり重要である。しかし，このことは，船長が明らかに非安全な港に入り，傭船者に対し，それにより被った損害を請求できることを意味しない。それは，侵害された者は合理的に行動し，その損害を極小化しなければならないという法則でもある」。

船長は，傭船者の指図命令に従うが，船長の過失については，免責条項適用の場合を除き，依然として，船主に責任がある。*Raynes* v. *Ballantyne* (1898) 14 T. L. R. 399事件では，定期傭船されていた船舶が，船長の過失で，傭船者所有の埠頭に損害を与えた。貴族院は，(傭船契約上の免責条項は別として) 船主に責任があると判示した。Herschell 卿は，次のように言った。「船長は，船主が任命しているが，傭船者の指示に従うべきものである。傭船契約の効果として，本船は，契約が規定する制約内で，傭船者の全面的使用に委ねられることとなる。そして，船長が依然として，船主の被用者であることについて疑問はないけれども，上記制約内で，船長は，傭船者の指図に従わなければならない。したがって，その条項［免責条項］は別として，船主は，傭船者の指図を実行している船長に対し，発言権はないが，船長の過失に対して責めを負うことになる」。

Aquacharm 号の船長は，ニューヨーク・プロデュース傭船契約書に基づきパナマ運河を通行許可となる喫水を維持して積み込むことを傭船者に指図された。船長は，過ってその喫水を越えて積み込んでしまった。Lloyd 判事は，仮に第24条により傭船契約に摂取された効果的な抗弁（抗弁については，後出599頁参照）がなかった場合には，船主は派生的損害に責任があったであろうと判示した。彼の判決は，控訴院で承認された。
The Aquacharm [1980] 2 Lloyd's Rep. 237 および [1982] 1 Lloyd's Rep. 7 (C.A.).

しかし，傭船者の指図に従う船長の義務は絶対的ではなく，相当な技術と注意を行使するだけである（前出 *The Aquacharm* 事件を参照）。

黙示の補償

ニューヨーク・プロデュース書式では（ボルタイム書式と異なり），船主に対して明示の補償が認められていない。しかし，傭船者の指図や命令に従った結果，船主が負う責任に対しては，おそらく，黙示の補償が認められていると考えられる。船主は，いかなる貨物を積載し，本船をどこへ航行させるかを，だれが選択できるか(合意の範囲内で)につき，本船を傭船者の自由な決定に委ねる。傭船者がその選択の結果を負担するのが妥当である。Mustill 判事による *The Georges Christos Lemos*（第三者訴訟）[1991] 2 Lloyd's Rep. 107 事件参照。*The Athanasia Comnions* [1990] 1 Lloyd's Rep. 277（同判例集290頁）事件と *The Island Archon* [1993] 2 Lloyd's Rep. 388（同判例集404と407頁）と [1994] 2 Lloyd's Rep. 227 (C. A.)（同判例集237頁）事件参照。

Strathlorne 号は，定期傭船者され，傭船契約によれば，船長（船主が任命したものであるけれども）は，本船の使用，代理，その他の手配につき，傭船者の指図や命令に従うべきものとなっていた。また，傭船契約には，明示の補償条項が含まれていた。本船は，Rangoon から Swatow 向け米輸送のため，1 航海の再傭船に出された。船長は呈示された船荷証券に署名した。Swatow で，傭船者の代理店は，船長に，自己が貨物の引渡に責任を持つといって，事実，その代理店は，船荷証券の呈示なしに，貨物の引渡を行わせた。実際には船荷証券は，それを保持していた銀行から買い取られていなかった。結局，船主は銀行に対し，誤って引き渡された米の価格について，責めを負うと判示された。Roche 判事および控訴院は，次のように判示した。すなわち，明示の補償規定（その範囲については疑問がある）の存否にかかわらず，船長が傭船者の指図に従った結果生ずる船主の責任に対しては，コモン・ロー上，船主は黙示的に補償されるべきである。

控訴院は，Roche 判事の判決を支持して，Toplis v. Grane 事件で Tindal 主席判事が，判示し，Dugdale v. Lovering （1875）LR. 10 C. P. 196 事件に引用されている原則を適用した。

「……被告の明白な指示による原告の行為が，第三者の権利を害する場合，その行為自体が明らかに違法ではなく，被告の指示どおりに，正直かつ誠実になされたものであれば，被告は，その結果につき，原告に対し補償する義務を負う」。

Strathlorne Steamship v. Andrew Weir（1934）49 Ll.L. Rep. 306 と（1934）50 Ll.L. Rep. 185 （C. A.）.

したがって，そのような状況下で，船主は，傭船者の指図または命令に従っている船長の行為が，上記に引用した判決文に説明されているような意味で，明らかに違法でまたは「明らかに不法行為」でないかぎり，補償を受ける権利を有することとなろう。補償請求の権利行使の資格を失う行為は，常に「卑劣な要素を伴っていなければならない。そしてその行為は，行為の真の本性を明白にした者を行為者が不注意にも調査しなかった事案，あるいは行為者が，自らの調査でふらちにも，しかし無謀でもなく誤った推論をした事案には及ばない」（The Nogar Marin ［1988］1 Lloyd's Rep. 412（同判例集 417 頁）事件の Mustill 卿判事による）。

Sagona 号は，Beepeetime 2 で定期傭船された。その契約書の第 20 条に，船長は本船の使用につき傭船者の指図命令に従うものと規定し，傭船者またはその代理人の指図に従って船荷証券に署名することから生じる責任につき船主への補償を組み入れていた。傭船者は，本船に Nordenham で Mabanaft にガスオイルの引渡を指図した。その当時（1978 年）の油輸送の一般の実務（世界的ではないが）に従い，船長は貨物の引渡前の船荷証券または補償状の呈示に固執しなかった。Mabanaft は，実際には当該貨物に対して権利を有せず，本船は，差押えられた。船主は結果として損害を被り，船主はその損害を補償の方法により傭船者から回収しようとした。Staughton 判事は，前出 Strathlorne v. Weir 事件を適用して，船主の損害は，その当時に一般的であった実務──船荷証券の呈示なしの貨物の引渡という船長の行為は明らかに不法であるとか，船長の疑念を引き起こすようなものでもない──の観点から傭船者の指図に応じたことにより生じたと判示した。したがって，船主は黙示の補償により損失を回収できた。

The Sagona ［1984］1 Lloyd's Rep. 194.
（The Nogar Marin ［1988］1 Lloyd's Rep. 412 事件も参照）

たとえ，傭船者の指図が合法的であり，傭船契約上傭船者が発する権利を有する（そして船主が従う義務がある）指図であるとしても，補償を受ける損失が，傭船契約の真の解釈に基づき船主自身が負担を同意した危険から生じないかぎり，補償は通常黙示されている。

Island Archon 号は，ニューヨーク・プロデュース書式により 36 ヶ月間傭船された。傭船期間中，本船はイラクの港へ貨物を運送するよう指図された。貨物損害賠償請求が船主の当地代理店に出され，その応諾を強く迫られた。仲裁人は，損害賠償請求は信頼のおけない不足揚・損傷証明書に基づ

いていると考えた。それでもこの証明書はイラクの裁判所に決定的証拠として承認された。船主は止むなく応諾した貨物損害賠償請求を傭船者に補償請求をした。イラクで揚荷する指図は，有効であり，傭船者の側に傭船契約違反はないので補償の権利は生じない，と傭船者の代理人は主張した。Cresswell 判事と控訴院は，疑わしい貨物損害賠償請求の責任を発生させる危険（傭船契約の日付時点で，その危険は周知されていないと思われた）は，傭船契約に基づき船主が負担を同意していない危険であり，かつ仲裁人の判断によれば，責任はイラクに貨物を運送せよとの傭船者の指図から直接に生じたものゆえ，補償は黙示されていると判示した。

The Island Archon [1993] 2 Lloyd's Rep. 388 と [1994] 2 Lloyd's Rep. 227 (C.A.).

黙示の補償は，ボルタイム書式の明示の補償の場合と同様，船主が負う責任に対するだけではなく傭船者の指示で仕向けた非安全港で本船が受けた損害のようなその他船主が被る損失，295損害（前出253頁参照），または，防訴の妥当な費用（The Caroline P [1984] 2 Lloyd's Rep. 466 事件（同判例集476頁）参照）にも，また適用がある。しかし，航海の危険について補償はない（前出 The Island Archon 事件参照）。さらに，補償の請求が行われるあらゆる事案で，船主は被った損害と傭船者の指図との間の中断のない因果関係を示さなければならない。後出358頁の「因果関係」を参照。船荷証券に関連した黙示の補償につき後出386頁参照。

定期傭船契約に基づき補償の権利があるという事実は，必ずしも同じ状況で補償の権利が，航海傭船に基づき生じることを意味しない（The Georges Christos Lemos（第三者訴訟）[1991] 2 Lloyd's Rep. 107 事件と The Island Archon [1994] 2 Lloyd's Rep. 227 事件（同判例集236頁）と後出359頁参照）。

他の条項との関係

黙示の補償が傭船契約の明示の条件と矛盾する場合，黙示の補償は，傭船契約の明示の条件によって排除されよう（The Berge Sund [1993] 2 Lloyd's Rep. 453 (C.A.) 事件（同判例集462頁）参照）。しかし，それは他の傭船契約条項の範囲外の事柄に限定されない（Royal Greek Government v. Minister of Transport (1949) 83 Ll.L. Rep. 228（同判例集234頁）事件参照）。そしてそのような明示の条項と主題の事項とが重複していることで，必ずしも矛盾が生じるものではない。したがって，オフハイヤー条項の適用により船主の損失傭船料が黙示の補償に基づき回収できる（The Berge Sund [1992] 1 Lloyd's Rep. 460 事件（同判例集467頁）の第1審の Steyn 判事の判決を参照。傭船者の安全港担保義務に関して前出231頁参照）。

明示の補償

上記 Strathlorne Steamship v. Andrew Weir 事件，およびボルタイム書式（71行から73行）の場合のように，ある種の定期傭船契約では，船長が傭船者の命令に従う結果，あるいは命令に従うことから生じる責任につき，船主は，傭船者から補償を受ける明示の権利を認められている（388頁参照。また明示の補償条項に基づく求償の事例については，Portsmouth Steamship v. Liverpool & Glasgow Salvage Association (1929) 34 Ll.L. Rep. 459. 参照，その事実関係は，359頁に要約）。

船荷証券の署名から生じる補償

船長は，傭船者により船荷証券への署名を求められるか，あるいは代理人による署名の許可

を求められ、船主は、傭船契約に基づき負う責任よりも大きな責任を課される場合、船主は追加の責任について通常傭船者により補償される権利がある（後出385/386頁参照）。

傭船者の過失によらない補償

傭船者の指図に応じた結果に対する船主のための補償は、傭船者の側の過失にまったく無関係に作用する。後出357頁の *The Athanasia Comninos* [1990] 1 Lloyd's Rep. 277 事件でMustill 判事は、ヘーグ・ルールの第Ⅳ条3項はニューヨーク・プロデュース書式の黙示の補償に基づく責任から、傭船者を保護するという傭船者の主張を退けて、次のように言った。「今までなかったことであるが、船主の黙示の補償に過失の考えを導入するには、傭船者はこれよりもっと明確な文言を使用する必要があろう」。

296 使　用（Employment）

本文での「使用」とは、「船舶の使用」を意味し、人の雇傭を意味するものではなく、また、貨物積込のための特定の港への配船指図を含むが（前出253頁参照）、その配船指図を航行上の見地から実行する方法は、常に船長に一任されているから、これに関する指図は含まないと貴族院は、判示している。

> *Roman de Larrinaga* 号は、T.99A 定期傭船契約書式の条項に基づき、徴用された。その書式は、ボルタイム書式の本船使用補償条項と、事実上同一の条項を含んでいた。1939年10月、本船は、Newport から St. Nazaire に行き、さらに返船前の共同検査のため、Cardiff に行くよう指図された。St. Nazaire で揚荷後、本船は、悪天候ではあるが、直ちに Quiberon 湾に行き、Cardiff 向け船団に参加するよう、同地の海上輸送係官からの指図を受けた。本船は出帆したが、その後、座礁し、損害を受けた。船主が国に対し、補償を請求した根拠の一つは、本船の損害は、船長が傭船者の指図に従ったことにより生じたものであるというものであった。
>
> 貴族院は、次の理由でこの主張を退けた。St. Nazaire に行き、さらに Cardiff へ行けという指図は、船舶の使用に関する傭船者の指図であるが、いつ、どのように Cardiff へ本船が航行すべきかについての海上輸送係官の指図は、船舶の使用に関するものではないし、いずれにしても、損害は、傭船者の指図が実行されている間に発生したものではあるが、傭船者の指図により惹起されたものでないというのである。
>
> Wright 卿は、「船長宛出されたものと、本件控訴院判事が認定した（海上輸送係官の）出港指図は、Cardiff 向け航行するようにという［傭船者の］指図を実行するための、航海の問題を取り扱っているに過ぎない。そのような航行上の問題を判断するのは、船長の義務である」と指摘した（173頁）。
>
> *Larrinaga Steamship* v. *The Crown* (1944) 78 Ll.L. Rep. 167.
>
> （*Weir* v. *Union Steamship Company* [1900] A.C.525 と *Stag Line* v. *Ellerman & Papayanni Lines* (1949) 82 Ll.L. Rep. 826 事件も参照）

航行と船舶取扱の問題が、常に船主およびその被用者たる船長の責任であることは、ニューヨーク・プロデュース書式170/171行の文言により強調されている。後出 *The Erechthion* [1987] 2 Lloyd's Rep. 180 事件で Staughton 判事は、瀬取のため、錨地へ航行せよとの港長の命令は、本船の使用に関しており、水先人による本船の正確な錨泊地についての助言は、航行に関する事項であると判示した。

ニューヨーク・プロデュース書式で定期傭船された *Erechthion* 号は，傭船者に Port Harcourt で揚荷するよう指図された。本船の喫水はあまりに深かったので，本船は港長により河の錨地へ行き瀬取するよう指図されたが，そこで座洲した。Port Harcourt へ行けとの傭船者の指図に応じた結果につき船主に補償する義務は傭船契約に黙示されているというのは共通の根拠であった。Staughton 判事は，傭船者の指図は港長が指図すべき揚荷場所へ行けという指図としてみなされると判示した。同判事は，港長の指図は本船の使用に関する指図であると判示し，さらに同判事は，航行の問題に過ぎない本船が錨泊すべき錨地内場所についての水先人の助言よりも，この港長の指図が座洲の近因であるか否かの問題を仲裁人に委ねた。

The Erechthion ［1987］ 2 Lloyd's Rep. 180.

(*The Isabelle* ［1982］ 2 Lloyd's Rep. 81 事件と *The Mediolanum* ［1984］ 1 Lloyd's Rep. 136 事件と両事件を論議した前出252頁参照）

本船がある港へ航行すべきか，ある港に碇泊すべきか，という傭船者の指図は，「船舶の使用に関する」指図である。それゆえ，*Temple Steamship* v. *V/O Sovfracht*（1945）79 Ll.L. Rep. 1 事件において（131頁参照），船長は，船舶の使用につき傭船者の指揮下にあるのだから，Murmansk で本船を遅らせたうえ，Garston に航行を命じた傭船者の違法な指図に船長が従ったからといって，傭船契約（修正ボルタイム書式）に基づく船主の傭船者に対する補償請求権を，船主が放棄したことにはならず，船主は，これを傭船者に請求することができるとされた（なお，上記 *Larrinaga Steamship* v. *The Crown*（1944）78 Ll.L. Rep. 167および *The Eugenia* ［1963］ 2 Lloyd's Rep. 381 参照）。傭船者の指図した特定の港で貨物を単に揚荷することで船主がほとんど不可避的に支払わねばならない貨物損害賠償に関しては，まさしくこの理由で傭船者が船主に補償する義務を有する（［1994］ 2 Lloyd's Rep. 227（C.A.）と前出355頁の *The Island Archon* 事件参照）。

同様に，特定貨物の積取指図は，「船舶の使用に関する」指図と判断されてきた。その貨物を積むようにとの指図が，船主に損失をもたらすものであれば，傭船者に補償を求める権利が生じる。

Ann Stathatos 号は，ボルタイム書式の戦時版に基づき，定期傭船された。それには，現行書式の第9項にあるように，船長は，「船舶の使用に関し，傭船者の指図に従う」という記載が含まれており，また船長が，そのような指図に従った結果に対する補償も明示されていた。傭船者は，メタンガスの発生している石炭の積取を本船に指図した。本船の属する船団の出帆を待って，中甲板の water tank の修理を行っているときに，一連の爆発が生じ，本船に損害を与えた。仲裁人は，爆発の直接の原因は，爆発性の気体に，修理の火花が引火したものであると認定した。船主は傭船者に対して，船舶の損害を補償すべきであると主張した。

Devlin 判事は，次のように判示した。「特定の貨物を積むようにとの指図は，船舶の使用に関する指図であり，補償条項の範囲内に属する。しかし，仲裁人の認定した事実によれば，貨物の積取が損失の直接の原因ではないから，補償を求める権利は発生しない」。

Royal Greek Government v. *Minister of Transport*（1949）83 Ll.L. Rep. 228.

Athanasia Comninos 号と *Georges Chr. Lemos* 号はニューヨーク・プロデュース書式で同じ傭船者に傭船された。両船は，傭船者により，Nova Scotia の Sydney で Birkenhead 向け石炭を積み込むよう指図された。各船は出港後，間もなく空気とメタンガスの混合気体の発火で生じた爆発によって損傷を被った。メタンガスは積込後の石炭から発した。船主はこの損害につき傭船者から回収しようとした。たとえ船主が積み込んだ石炭は他の石炭と比べて異常に危険な性質を持つことを証明できないとしても（船主は公判でできなかった），傭船者は，石炭の積込の指図は第8条に黙示される補償の範囲内であると渋々認めた。しかし，傭船者は当該石炭の積込指図と爆発の因果関係の連鎖を断ち切

る船主そして・または乗組員による過失があったと主張した。Mustill 判事は，*Georges Chr. Lemos* 号に関しては，そのような過失はなかったが，*Athanasia Comninos* 号のガスと空気の混合体の発火は船首楼で乗組員が煙草にマッチの火をつけたことで生じたと判断した。したがって，同判事は，傭船者は *Georges Chr. Lemos* 号の船主に責任があるが，*Athanasia Comninos* 号の船主には責任がないと判示した（*Georges Chr. Lemos* 号に関して，同判事は，ヘーグ・ルールの第Ⅳ条3項に基づいて傭船者が提出した抗弁を退けた。それについて前出222頁と後出600頁参照）。

　Mustill 判事は次のように言った。「たとえ問題の貨物の性質が同じ種類の他の貨物の性質と異ならないとしても，ある性質を持つ貨物の船積により生じる損害があることは私には完全にありうることのように見える。今回の事案では，『なぜ爆発があったのか』と尋ねる（船主側の過失の可能性を排除して）場合，回答は『なぜなら船艙にメタンガスがあったから』である。そして『なぜメタンガスが船艙にあったのか』と尋ねると，回答は『なぜなら定期傭船者は本船に石炭の積載を要求したので』である。この回答は私の意見では，当該石炭がいずれにしても異常であることについての証明がなくても補償の根拠を説明するには十分である」。

The Athanasia Comninos [1990] 1 Lloyd's Rep. 277.

因 果 関 係

　船主が傭船者から補償を獲得するためには，傭船者の指図と被った損害との間の，中断事由のない因果関係を立証しなければならない（前出 *Royal Greek Government* v. *Minister of Transport*（*The Ann Stathatos*）事件と *The Athanasia Comninos* 事件参照）。Donaldson 判事は，*The White Rose* 事件（後出）で，次のように指摘した。「定期傭船者の指図に従う過程で，損失が生じることは十分あり得る。しかし，この事実だけでは，その損失が，船主が傭船者の指図に従ったことにより生じたものであり，また，法律上，船主が傭船者の指図に従った結果であることの立証にはならない。その間の因果関係についての証明がない場合，船主が補償を受ける権利はない。」（*The Erechthion* [1987] 2 Lloyd's Rep. 180 事件，*The Berge Sund* [1992] 1 Lloyd's Reo. 460（同判例集467頁）と [1993] 2 Lloyd's Rep. 453（C. A.）（同判例集462頁）事件，*The Island Archon* [1993] 2 Lloyd's Rep. 388 と [1994] 2 Lloyd's Rep. 227（C. A.）事件参照）。*The Aquacharm* [1982] 1 Lloyd's Rep. 7 事件（その事実経緯は後出599頁に述べられている）で Griffiths 卿判事は次のように言った。「船主は接続費用が傭船者の指図に応じた直接の結果として生じたことを示すことができなかった。……傭船者の指図が損害を引き起こしたことを立証する義務は補償を請求する船主側にある。船主は立証できず，したがって接続費用を補償させることができなかった」（後出「通常費用と航行危険」の項も参照）。直接結果を示す必要につき *The Berge Sund* [1993] 2 Lloyd's Rep. 453（C. A.）（同判例集462頁）事件での Staughton 卿判事の警告を参照。

　ボルタイム書式に基づき傭船された *White Rose* 号は，Duluth で穀物を積むよう指図された。第4条に従い，傭船者は，現地の水準から見て，平均的能力を持つ会社を，積荷役業者として指定した。荷役人夫の一人が，私用のため持場を離れて，中甲板船艙の安全柵のないところから落ちた。人夫は，Minnesota 州裁判所で，自身の傷害についての損害賠償を請求して，船主を訴えた。船主は，訴訟費用の出費を余儀なくされ，解決のため，人夫の賠償請求に応じざるを得なかった。船主は，第9条に基づき，傭船者に補償を求めた。Donaldson 判事は，船主の要求を，次の理由により退けた。事故すなわち船主の損失は，安全柵がなかったこと（そのことにつき，傭船者に責めはない）および，負傷した人夫自身の過失により生じたものであって，Duluth で穀物を積むようにとの傭船者の指図に，船主が従ったことにより生じたものではなく，傭船者が，能力のない荷役業者を，選択したことにより生じたものでもない。

The White Rose [1969] 2 Lloyd's Rep. 52.

　Hillcroft 号は，Cape Verde 諸島沖で座礁した *West Hesseltine* 号の瀬取のため，傭船された。傭船契約上，船長は，「傭船者の指示に従う」ことを義務づけられていた。その傭船者は，よって「生じうる結果あるいは責任につき，船主に補償する」こととなっていた。傭船者は，椰子油入樽を *Hillcroft* 号へ積み替えるよう指図したところ，慎重な荷扱いをしたにもかかわらず，漏れが生じ，同船の船艙に損害を与えた。同船は，大きなマホガニー材を積み替えたことによっても，また損害を受けた。Roche 判事は，次のように判示した。傭船者は，両方の事故について，船主に対して補償する責任がある。しかし，傭船者は，フォアピークタンクからの油漏れによる損害に対して，船主に補償する責任はない。なぜなら，この油は，傭船者の指示により積み込まれたけれども，その油漏れは，そのタンクに連結しているパイプが，後になって破損したため生じたものだからである。
　Portsmouth Steamship Co. Ltd. v. *Liverpool & Glasgow Salvage Association* (1929) 34 Ll.L. Rep. 459.
　(*Larrinaga Steamship* v. *The Crown* (1944) 78 Ll.L. Rep. 167 事件における Porter 卿の判決（同判例集176頁）参照)

通常費用と航海危険

　さらに広い意味で，通常の費用と航海上の損失は傭船者の指図に従った結果として発生したという事実にもかかわらず，船主は傭船者の補償に基づき傭船者から通常の費用と航海上の損失を回収する権利はない。これは，*The Aquacharm* [1980] 2 Lloyd's Rep. 237 事件で Lloyd 判事により，次のように表明された。「船主が傭船者の指図に従う直接の結果として黙示の補償に基づき回収できるということはもちろん十分に確立されている。しかし，回収できるのは航海の途中で発生するあらゆる損失ではない。例えば，傭船者が違う航海の指図を出していれば，荒天に遭遇しなかったであろうという理由だけでは，船主は荒天による損失を回収できない。その関連性は希薄に過ぎる。たとえ，ある意味で通常の航行の途中で発生する費用，例えばバラスト調整費用が傭船者の指図に応じる結果として発生するとしても，同じように船主は，それを回収できない。*Weir and Others* v. *Union Steamship Co. Ltd.* [1900] A.C. 525事件参照。本事案にも同じ考え方が適用される。接続費用は航行の途中で発生する通常の費用である」。
　The Aquacharm 事件 Lloyd 判事の判決の抜粋を含む上記1節は，*The Island Archon* [1994] 2 Lloyd's Rep. 227（同判例集235頁）事件についての控訴院の Evans 卿判事の同意を得て，引用された。他の先例に言及して，Evans 卿判事は次のように言った（同判例集236頁）。「したがって，たとえ傭船者が指図を出す権利があり，船長が従う義務があるとしても，先例によると，定期傭船者は明示の補償に基づき特定の貨物の積込または表示の港への航行を傭船に指図した結果につき責任がある。しかし，傭船者が責任を負うその結果は二つの範疇の損失を含んでいない。一つは，続いて起こったできごと，または介在するできごとにより法律上，生じたと見なされる損失である。過失ある行為はこの意味で因果関係の連鎖をしばしば，しかしいつもではないが，切断する（*Portsmouth Steamship Co. Ltd.* V. *Liverpool & Glasgow Salvage Association* (1929) 34 Ll.L. Rep. 459事件（Roche 判事）と *The White Rose* 事件 (59頁) 参照)。2番目に「広い意味」での結果は，船主が冒すことを同意した危険から生じるが，それゆえに航海の危険を含んでいない。そしてまた定期傭船契約と航海傭船契約の間には差異があると判示された（Devlin 判事による *The Ann Stathatos* 事件と Mustill 判事による *The Georges Christos Lemos* 事件（第三者訴訟）[1991] 2 Lloyds' Rep. 107 事件)」。

しかしながら，Evans卿判事は，この点につき航海傭船契約と定期傭船契約の間に厳格な区別をすべきではないと強調した。補償は特定航海，または「1航海」の期間の定期傭船契約の事案では，それほど容易に黙示されていることはないのかも知れない一方で，傭船者に広い選択権がある航海傭船契約では補償はもっと容易に黙示されているのかも知れない。

同判事は，続けて次のように言った（同判例集236頁）。「船主がどのような危険負担を同意したのかは，傭船契約の正しい解釈にかかっているに違いない。したがって傭船契約が締結された当時の状況にかかっている。仮に『イラク・システム』は，1979年3月に傭船契約を締結した時点で，評判が悪いということが，本事案で認定されたのであれば，船主が意向しだいで航路定限から除外できたはずであるから，船主はイラク港で揚荷することを本船に指図した結果を負担することを合意したとの傭船者の主張に意味があることになろう」。

Donald Nicholls副大法官はまた次のように強調した（同判例集238頁）。黙示の補償は，傭船者の指図に船主が応じた結果のある一部だけを償うだけである。損失はその指図から直接的に生じたものでなければならず，「かつ傭船契約の公平な解釈に基づき船主が容認したとはみなすことができないもの」でなければならなかった。

代　　理

この条項により，傭船者には，各港の船務を行う代理店を選任する権利（そして，おそらくは義務）がある。

Wright卿は，*Larrinaga Steamship* v. *The Crown*（1944）78 Ll.L. Rep. 167事件で（同判例集172頁），「船主は，通常，傭船契約の期間中，船舶の代理業務を各港のどの会社または人物に委託するかを決定する権利を有するが，本件では，その選択が，傭船者に委ねられている」と指摘した。

「代理店……を手配し，支払う」と傭船契約に要求するニューヨーク・プロデュース書式の39行も参照。適切な代理店を選任する傭船者の責任と代理店の行為または懈怠の責任の範囲と歩金に関する解説は，前出279頁にある。

300 米　国　法

使用条項

　船長および乗組員が船主により雇用され，傭船期間中被用者であるのは定期傭船契約の基本的要素である。同時に船主は傭船者の指図・命令を遂行しなければならない。しかしながら船長に指図を出す傭船者の権利は決して無制限・絶対的なものではない。例えば，船長は非安全バースに着岸せよとの傭船者の指図を遂行することを正当に拒否できる。あるいは，船舶の航行または取扱に関する限り，船長は傭船者の指図に従うものではない。船長は船舶の堪航性を損なういかなることに関しても非常に広い権限を有する。さらに，状況により定められた航海から離路する必要がある場合には，船長は離路できる（例として The Medita, SMA 1150 (Arb. at N.Y. 1977) 事件参照）。この事案では荒天のため，船長は避難港へ入る正当な事由があると裁定されたことに加えて，仲裁人は12月に予想される悪天候の下で，北大西洋を確実に安全に横断できるように，船長は傭船者に燃料の追加手配を要求できると裁定した（前出348頁の議論参照。The Andros Mentor, SMA 2125 (Arb. at N.Y. 1985) 事件参照）。

　傭船契約が，米国海上物品運送法を摂取していれば，船長が傭船者の指図から逸脱して離路することも，同法第4条第4項により認められる。

　　海上において，人命または財産を救助し，または救助しようとするための離路，あるいはいかなる合理的な離路も，本条あるいは運送契約の違反とはみなされない。それゆえ，運送人は，その結果生ずる滅失または損傷につき責めを負わない。**しかしながら，離路が貨物または旅客の積卸を目的とするものである場合，当該離路は，一応，不合理なものと推定される** (46. U.S.C§1304(4))。

　傭船者の指示に対して，船長が，事故発生前に異議を唱えていれば，船長の側に過失があっても，船主は責めを免れうる (*Mackenzie McAllister* v. *United States*, 1942 AMC 1215 (E.D.N.Y. 1942) 事件参照)。しかし，事情によっては，傭船者の指示が軽率なものであっても，船長の過失で，船主が責任を負う場合もある。例えば，船長が安全でないことを知っている港への入港に同意することは，過失の介在となり，傭船者は，安全港担保義務違反の責任を免れうると判示されている (*American President Lines Ltd.* v. *United States*, 208 F. Supp. 573. 1968 AMC 830 (N.D.Cal. 1961))。さらに，船長が，傭船者が指定した港の港湾事情を知りながら，入港に同意すれば，船長は，安全港の担保に依拠したわけではないから，傭船者は，安全港担保義務につき，責任を負わないと判示されている (*Tweedie Trading Co.* v. *New York & Boston Dyewood Co.*, 127 F. 278 (2d Cir. 1903)，裁量上告拒絶 193 U.S. 669 (1903); *Pan Cargo Shipping Corp* v. *United States*, 234 F. Supp. 623, 1965 AMC 2649 (S.D.N.Y. 1964)，原審維持 373 F. 2d 525, 1967 AMC 850 (2d Cir. 1967)，裁量上告拒絶 386 U.S. 836 (1967)。前出262頁参照)。

　傭船者は，傭船契約が許容する貨物を運送するために本船を使用するけれども，船長は他の点で，本船の安定性または堪航性を損なう指図を拒否する権限を有する。

　例えば The Aetolia, SMA 2157 (Arb. at N.Y. 1985) 事件で，仲裁審は，船長は出港前に積荷の少ない船艙内の貨物をしっかり固縛することを強く主張する正当な事由があると裁定した。仲裁審によると，船艙内に貨物を固縛せよとの船長の要求は分別あるもので，本船の安定性の要件に合致する。艙内で固縛する間の喪失時間につき本船はオンハイヤーであると裁定さ

れた。仲裁審は，さらに他の船主は公表喫水を超えている証拠があるが，広く認められている
301最大安全喫水32フィートを超えて本船に貨物を積載しないようにとのBuenos Airesの代理店
の助言に船長が従うことには正当な事由があると裁定した。したがって，傭船者は積込拒絶さ
れた貨物の損害賠償を請求できなかった。

The Union Harvest, SMA 2626（Arb. at N.Y. 1989）事件で，仲裁審は，傭船者は船長が
貨物を追加して固縛せよと指図したことにより生じた遅延につき本船をオフハイヤーとするこ
とはできないと裁定していた。仲裁審は船長が貨物の適正な積込と積付のために有する広い自
由な管理と権限に基づいて，しかしながら，同時に荷送人は，船長の指図に従うのを拒否した
のでオフハイヤーと追加発生費用を傭船者に償還するよう裁定した。

同じように，*The Athanassia*, SMA 2752（Arb. at N.Y. 1991）事件で仲裁審は，本船の堪
航性の配慮のために積付計画図を船長が変更，修正した結果として発生した遅延および予見で
きなかった追加費用につき，傭船者は管理船主が申し立てた損害賠償を回収できないと裁定し
た。傭船者は実際の積荷役の間，船長の能力について異議を申し立てなかったし，貨物の積込
支援のため，上乗人を使用しなかった。

船主と傭船者との間の補償の権利

船主は，傭船者の指図を遂行する際に生じた責任につき傭船者から補償を受ける権利があ
る。*Nissho-Iwai Co. Ltd.* V. *The Stolt Lion*, 617 F. 2d 907, 913, 1980 AMC 867, 874（2d
Cir. 1980）事件で，裁判所は，「他方が，本来責任ある過失につき一方も責任ありと裁定され
る場合，船主と傭船者との間の補償の権利は存する」という基本的法則を述べた。

The Adventure, SMA 3161（Arb. at N.Y. 1995）事件で，船主の補償請求行為に対する傭
船者の主たる抗弁は，本船をリーエンに曝す権限のない再傭船者に定期傭船されることをあら
ゆる物品供給業者に船長が一般に公告できないわけではなかったのであれば，本船に対する物
品供給業者のリーエンは効力を有しないということであった。仲裁審は，たとえ公告が行われ
ていたとしても，それは物品供給業者に適正に公告することを法的に委任された文言を含んで
いないので，それはリーエンを打破するのに無効であると裁定した。さらに，傭船契約に従っ
て船長は傭船者により借用された被用者として行為していた。傭船者と再傭船者の双方は，
各々傭船契約に違反したと仲裁審は判断し，船主は船主自身への対人的および本船への対物的
請求につき全面的補償を裁定された。順繰りで原傭船者は再傭船者に対する全面的補償を裁定
された。

補償の権利を含む係争は，船主と傭船者の双方に対する貨物および人身傷害の損害賠償請求
の関連で頻繁に生じる（後出の376/383頁の議論を参照）。

貨物の積込，積付，荷均および揚荷

[Clause 8 continued]

"78. .... and Charterers are to load, stow, and trim the cargo at their expense under the supervision of the Captain,"

[第8条続き]

「傭船者は，自らの費用により，船長の監督の下に，積込・積付および荷均を行う。」

傭船者への責任の転嫁

　明示の規定のない場合，貨物を積込，積付，荷均，および揚荷する義務は，コモン・ローでは，船主にある。*The Filikos* [1983] 1 Lloyd's Rep. 9 事件参照。ニューヨーク・プロデュース書式78行は，貨物の積込，積付および荷均に対する本来の責任を，船主から傭船者へ転嫁する効果を有する（*Court Line* v. *Canadian Transport* (1940) 67 Ll.L. Rep. 161 事件と後出366頁参照）。

NYPE 93

　ニューヨーク・プロデュース書式1993年改訂版は，103/105行で，「すべての貨物の取扱」は，傭船者の費用をもってかつ，傭船者の「危険」においてなされると規定し，この基本的な責任の転嫁を強調している（前出10頁と54頁参照）。

揚　　荷

　よくある例であるが，「そして揚荷する」という文言が，ニューヨーク・プロデュース書式の78行に「荷均する」という文言の後に付け加えられる場合，揚荷に関する本来の責任もまた傭船者が持つこととなる。

　「そして揚荷する」という文言が加えられていない場合，この責任関係は，あまり明確ではない。しかしながら（最近の定期傭船契約の取決めでは，ほとんどがそうであるが），傭船者または傭船者に代って責任を有するものが揚荷港で揚荷業者を手配し，荷役賃を支払うことが，取引上通例となっている場合には，その関係は，「そして揚荷する」という文言が，第8条に付加されたのとまったく同様に解されると言われている。

　ニューヨーク・プロデュース書式第2条では，傭船者は，「前述の費用を除き，その他通常費用を生じる一切の事項の……手配を行ない，支払う」ものとされている。揚荷港の荷役費は，それが，通常傭船者の負担とされている場合，「その他の通常費用」に含まれると考えられる。さらに，航海傭船契約における積付の責任に関する *Brys & Gylsen* v. *Drysdale* (1920) 4 Ll.L. Rep. 24 事件で，Greer 判事は，「傭船契約に，（『荷役業者を』）『手配し支払う』または『雇傭し支払う』という文言が使用されている場合，この条項は，さもなければ船主が負う義務と責任を，傭船者に転嫁する効果があると思われる。……」と述べている。

NYPE 93

ニューヨーク・プロデュース書式1993年版は，傭船者が，揚荷を含むあらゆる貨物取扱作業
304 を遂行することを明確にしている。第8条(a)項に，「傭船者は，自己の危険と費用により，船
長の監督の下で，船積，積付，荷均，ラッシング，固縛，荷敷，アンラッシング，揚荷および
検数を含む貨物のすべての取扱を行うものとする」と規定している（前出10頁の英文書式の
103/105行と54頁参照）。

航海途上での揚荷

揚荷に関する傭船者の義務は，通常，指定の揚荷場所で揚荷することのみに適用される。航
海の途上で揚荷が必要となる場合，その揚荷費用は，一応傭船者ではなく船主の負担となる。
その揚荷が傭船者の違反により，必要になるとか，傭船者の命令の当然の結果であることを，
証明できる場合には，事情は異なってくる。傭船者の違反による場合，船主は損害賠償として
揚荷費用を回収する権利を有することになろう。傭船者の命令の当然の結果である場合，使用
条項に基づき，補償の道がある（前出353頁参照）。

Aquacharm 号は，ニューヨーク・プロデュース書式で，1 航海の定期傭船に出された。その第8条
は，「そして揚荷する」と追加修正された。パナマ運河通過の最大喫水まで積込を指図された船長
は，同運河の一部である淡水湖通過時に本船の船首喫水が増大することを計算に入れるのを不注意に
も忘れた。結果的に本船はパナマ運河に入るのを拒否され，貨物の一部は揚荷され，他船でパナマ運
河を通って運送され，再び本船に積み込まれなければならなかった。控訴院は，揚荷費用は，揚荷港
における揚荷のみに適用される第8条によって，回収できず，そして補償請求は船長の過失によるも
のゆえ，できない，と判示した。

The Aquacharm [1982] 1 Lloyd's Rep. 7.

Pythia 号は，ニューヨーク・プロデュース書式で，Shatt-al-Arab へ 1 航海定期傭船された。第8
条は「そして揚荷する」と追加修正されていた。貨物の一部は，Shatt 川の入口の錨地で瀬取しなけ
ればならなかった。残りの貨物は，約60から70マイル上流の Khorramshahr で揚荷予定であった。錨
地で瀬取後，本船は衝突し，Khorramshahr 向け貨物の揚荷のため，錨地へ引き返さなければならな
かった。錨地（傭船者が新しい揚荷場所として指定したのではない）における Khorramshahr 向け貨
物の揚荷費用は，第8条に基づき傭船者の責任ではないと判示された。

The Pythia [1982] 2 Lloyd's Rep. 160.

(*The Hellas in Eternity*, LMLN 221, 23 April, 1988 事件も参照)

前出 *The Pythia* 事件で，Robert Goff 判事は，次のように述べた（同判例集164頁）。「定期
傭船者が，本船に他港向けの運送のため，ある港で貨物の積込を指図する場合，その指図に従
うこと，つまり，傭船された本船で指定の揚荷港へ向けて貨物を運送することは，船主の義務
である。本船が途中で障害に遭遇した場合には，船主は傭船契約上の免責条項により，その結
果についての責任を免れるかも知れない。しかし，船主が適当な方策によりその障害を克服で
きるのに，その方策を取らなかった場合，結果として生じた遅延が免責危険により生じたとは
主張できない。その適当な方策に費用が発生する場合，船主が負担しなければならない。」

海上物品運送法の効果

第24条により，米国海上物品運送法が傭船契約に摂取されても，第8条による荷役の責任区
分は，英国法の下では影響を受けない。同法第3条第2項により，運送品を適切，慎重に積

込，積付，揚荷する義務が，運送人——この文脈では，船主（The Khian Zephyr ［1982］1 Lloyd's Rep. 73）——に課せられているが，それでも第8条による責任区分は変わらない。当事者間で，貨物関係諸業務の分担区分を，適当に定めるのは自由である。同法は，作業の実施方法を規定しているにすぎない。Pyrene v. Scindia Navigation ［1954］1 Lloyd's Rep. 321 事件において，Devlin 判事は，1924年海上物品運送法第2章第3条にある同様の規則を検討して，次のように述べた。「『適切，慎重に積み込む』という文言の意味は，運送人に積込をする義務があり，その積込を適切，慎重にしなければならないというのか，あるいは，運送人が積込を行うかぎり，その積込を適切，慎重にしなければならないというのか，いずれかである。前者は，文言の意味により近い解釈であるが，後者の方が同規則の目的に合致する。同規則の目的は，……契約業務の範囲を定めることではなく，契約上遂行すべき業務の条件を定めることにある。運送人が引き受ける積荷役の範囲は，法制度の相違だけでなく，港の慣習や実務，また貨物の性質によって定まる。同規則が，この点について，普遍的硬直性を押しつけることや，運送人の契約の自由を否定することを目的としているとは考えられない。運送人は，実際上，積揚作業において，何らかの役割を果たさざるをえない。したがって，両作業は，運送契約の範囲内に当然含まれる。しかし，各当事者が，自己の果たすべき役割を契約による自由な決定に委ねることまで，同規則が否定しているとする理由はない。この観点に基づき，運送契約の全体は，同法の適用を前提とするが，積揚作業のどこまでを，運送人の義務の範囲内とするかは，当事者間で決定されるべき問題である」。

この解釈は，Renton v. Palmyra ［1956］2 Lloyd's Rep. 379 事件で，貴族院により承認された。

ヘーグ・ルールのこの解釈から推せば，英法の下では，米国海上物品運送法第3条第2項が傭船契約に摂取されている場合でも，傭船契約の他の条項が，貨物の積込，積付，揚荷を，傭船者の義務として定めていれば，そのような義務が傭船契約上，運送人としての船主にあるとされることはない。

（米国海上物品運送法を，傭船契約に摂取することの効果に関する一般的見解については，後出594頁参照）

滅多にないことであるが，ニューヨーク・プロデュース書式の規定が，明確に船荷証券に摂取され，その船荷証券が船主を拘束しヘーグまたはヘーグ・ヴィスビー・ルールを準拠法とする場合，興味ある，しかし未解決の問題が生じる。すなわち傭船者に対する貨物所有者の契約上の権利が欠けているように見えるが，積付不良の貨物クレームについて貨物所有者が船主を追及することは，第8条により阻害されるのだろうか。The Coral ［1993］1 Lloyd's Rep. 1 （C. A.）事件参照。

ボルタイム書式

ボルタイム書式の第4条は，34/35行で，傭船者が積込，荷均，積付，揚荷を「手配し支払う」ものとすると規定している。この文言は，ヘーグ・ルールの傭船契約への摂取如何にかかわらず，この荷役作業の責任を傭船者へと同様に転嫁するのに十分であると言われている。後出632頁と The Filikos ［1981］1 Lloyd's Rep. 555 と ［1983］1 Lloyd's Rep. 9（C. A.）事件参照）。

船長の監督の下に

「船長の監督の下に」という文言の有無にかかわらず，特に船舶安全性の観点から，船長は，荷役作業を指揮監督する権利を有する。しかし，安全性の配慮はさておき，船長は傭船者に対し監督する義務はない。*The Panaghia Tinnou* [1986] 2 Lloyd's Rep. 586（同判例集591頁）事件の航海傭船の事案のSteyn判事の解説参照。

この文言は，ニューヨーク・プロデュース書式が貨物の積込および積付につき傭船者に課した本来の責任を緩和している。すなわち，

306 (a) 例えば，船舶の復原性のような，特に船長の職責内の事項に関する不注意が原因で，損失や損害が生じた場合，または，

(b) 船長が実際に荷役作業を指揮監督し，損失や損害がその指揮監督に起因する場合。

Ovington Court号は，ニューヨーク・プロデュース書式により，北太平洋と英国または欧州大陸の往復1航海に定期傭船された。傭船期間中，船主は小麦の積付不良による損害を荷受人に賠償する責任を負った。船主の求償請求に対して，傭船者は，積付が船長の責任であることを主張した。貴族院は，積付不良は傭船者の責任であり，船主は求償権を有すると判示した。

「船長の監督の下に」という文言が，船長に積付の責任を課するという主張を退けて，Atkin卿は，次のように述べている（166頁）。

「船長が積付の監督をするのは，いかなる場合でも当然のことである。船長は，いずれにせよ，船舶が不堪航にならないようにする責務がある。堪航性以外の点についても，提示された積付が船主に責任を負担させるおそれがあると思えば，船長は，当然積付に介入できる。積付不良が，船長の命令によって生じたこと，傭船者の提示したとおりの積付をしていれば，損害が発生しなかったことを傭船者が立証できれば，傭船者が責任を免れることは当然である。船長の監督権は，明示の留保がなくても存在すると思われるが，留保があっても，安全な積付という傭船者本来の義務を免除する効果はまったくない。この点は，建築業者が，建築契約上，建築士の監督の下で工事をすることを定めていても，そのことによって，建築業者が，契約条項を正しく履行する義務を免除されないのとまったく同様の問題である」。

Wright卿は，また次のとおり述べた（168頁）。

「本傭船契約の第8条の下では，傭船者は，貨物の積込，積付および荷均を自己の費用によって，行わなければならない。この文言は，必然的に傭船者が，積込，積付義務を引き受けたことを意味すると思われる。傭船者は，本船の積込，積付の義務を免除するだけではなく，傭船者と船主間における，『船主』の積付不良の責任をも免除する。ただし，「船長の監督の下に」という文言により制限される場合は別である……。この文言は，傭船者の積込，積付作業と監督する権利を船長に明示的に与えたものであるが，かかる権利は，いずれにせよ船長が持っているものである。しかし，この権利が明示的に約定されている理由は，単に権利の存在を明らかにするためだけではなく，特に積付を支配する傭船者の権利を制限することにある。したがって，船長が，監督権を行使し，積付についての傭船者の支配を制限する場合，その程度に応じて，傭船者の責任も限定されると思われる」。

Court Line v. *Canadian Transport* (1940) 67 Ll.L. Rep. 161.

荷役作業において，船舶が荷役業者の過失により損害を受けた場合，船主は，この条項により，傭船者に求償することができると考えられる。ただし，この損害が，実際に船長の監督に起因する場合は別である（ニューヨーク・プロデュース書式1993年版は，荷役業者による損傷を扱う特別条項を含んでいることに注意。前出16頁の英文書式の419/432行の第35条と60頁参

照)。

「および船長の責任」

　当事者が，78行に規定された荷役作業の責任を，船主に負わせようとする場合，「監督」という文言の後に，「および責任」（and responsibility）という文言を，挿入するのが普通である。傭船者が介入し，その際に滅失・損傷を引き起こしたことが証明されないかぎり，この語句の追加により，積込，積付，荷均および（傭船契約が然るべく修正される場合には）揚荷に関する責任を傭船者から船主に一応再転嫁する効果があると判示された。船主への責任の一応の転嫁は，貨物の滅失・損傷だけでなく，本船の損傷にも及ぶ。それは，さらに本船のギアや貨物を取り扱う機械的過程に限らず，貨物の荷役計画にも及ぶ。

　次の三つの各事案で，傭船契約はニューヨーク・プロデュース書式78行に「揚荷」を含み，「監督」の後に「および責任」が挿入されていた。各傭船契約には，また，次のような些細な修正追加条項もあった。「船長は貨物の積付を十分に監督し，すべての積込，取扱，（積付），揚荷を職員に管理させるものとする」。

　Shinjitsu Maru No. 5 号は，管理船主によりニュージーランドから西アフリカに1航海定期傭船された。本船は，ニュージーランドでパレット貨物の船積を指図された。（パレットに適した形ではない）船艙に箱を作ることを計画し，パレットを5段積し，フォークリフトで残りの貨物を積み込めるように，その上に木製の床を作ることとした。箱が完成する前にパレットの積込を開始したが，その積付は，しっかりしていなかった。さらに荷送人は，積み付けた貨物の損傷を恐れ，計画された木製の床の上でフォークリフトを運転することを拒否した。したがって床は作られなかった。船長は積付に不安であった。船長は，荷役業者に抗議したが，無視された。荷役業者が手配した検査人は，船長に「積付は，追加ラッシングで安全である」と助言したが，仲裁人が判定したように，事実上本船は出航時に不安定な積付のため，不堪航であった。出航後，間もなく貨物が移動し，本船は貨物の再積付のため，引き返さねばならず，余計な時間と出費がかかった。仲裁人は，船長に過失あるも，責任は60パーセントを船主に，40パーセントを傭船者に分割されると裁定した。Neill卿判事（彼はそれから，貴族院議員になった）は，第1審で次のように判示した。

(1) 「および責任」の語句の追加は，積付不良の責任を船主に一応転嫁した。船主は，傭船者の介入，または干渉（この修正のない場合と逆の状況）により関連する損害が生じたことを証明するだけでこの責任から免れる。
(2) 傭船者の干渉の証拠がない。かつ傭船者が荷送人の行為に責任があることが，認められているが，傭船者に責任を生じさせるのに，損害の原因となるに十分な，または禁反言に根拠を置くのに十分な荷送人の干渉がない。
(3) 荷役業者およびその指定の検査人は，傭船者の代理人としてみなされない。
(4) 損害の主要な実質的原因は，この傭船契約に基づく船長の積付責任と本船の堪航性についての船長の全体責任に関係がある船長の過失である。
(5) 1945年法改革（寄与過失）に関する法は，適用されず，過失の配分は，ありえない（当然の結果として控訴院が本事案の判決に同意しないであろうということにはならないけれども，*Forsikringsaktieselskapet Vesta* v. *Butcher* [1988] 1 Lloyd's Rep. 19事件についての控訴院はNeill卿判事の1945年法の適用問題の議論に同意しなかった。後出369頁参照)。

A. B. Marintrans v. *Comet Shipping* (*The Shinjitsu Maru No. 5*) [1985] 1 Lloyd's Rep. 568.

　Argonaut 号は，1航海定期傭船され，2港揚で御影石を積んだ。両方の揚荷港で，荷役業者が非安全な作業方法を採った結果として，および（最初の港のみで）不適当なフォークリフトを使用した結果として本船のタンクトップに損傷を生じた。損傷は，（本船に持ち込まれた荷役業者の不適当な

道具）「船長の職分」外の事由に主として帰すべきであり，船長が荷役業者の作業の管理を適切に行えなかったわけではないのであるから，仲裁人は，船長は最初の港で生じた損傷について責任を負わないと判示した。しかし，仲裁人は最初の港の損傷の経験に基づいて，船長は2番目の港でより良い防止策に固執すべきであり，2番目の港で被った損傷には責任があると判示した。

Legatt 判事は，「および責任」の追加語句の効果に関して，*The Shinjitsu Maru No. 5* 事件の Neill 卿判事の判決に従った。同判事は，修正された第8条は，本来的義務を船主に課し，そして傭船者の実際の介入がない場合には，それが「船長の職分内」如何にかかわらず，船主は貨物の全荷役に責任があると判示した。傭船者は，したがって，いずれの港のタンクトップの損傷にも責任はない。

The Argonaut [1985] 2 Lloyd's Rep. 216.

308 3番目の事案であるニューヨーク・プロデュース書式傭船契約が同じように修正された *The Alexandros P* [1986] 1 Lloyd's Rep. 421 事件で，Steyn 判事は，*The Shinjitsu Maru No. 5* 事件と *The Argonaut* 事件の判決に従った。この事件も，荷役業者による船舶の損傷に関連していた。Steyn 判事は，傭船者から船主への責任の一応の転嫁は，第8条に関連するあらゆる作業および，そして作業自体の機械的遂行と同様，作業計画上の荷役業者の過失にまで及ぶと強調した。

NYPE 93

ニューヨーク・プロデュース書式の1993年改訂版では，「船長の監督の下で」の語句は，105行に出てくる。「および責任」の語句の追加により，上記趣旨を確実にするには，改訂版の同じ行の前にある「危険および」の語句を削除するのが賢明である（前出10頁と54頁参照）。

禁　反　言

傭船者，または傭船者が責任を負う者の介入が，実際に関連する滅失・損傷を引き起こしたとは言えないが，しかし船長に過失ありとの主張は，傭船者，またはその代理人（例えば上乗人または傭船者の指名した検査人）の行動により，禁反言であると判示されるかも知れない状況は，考えられる限りでは，ありえよう。Neill 判事は，前出 *The Shinjitsu Maru No. 5* 事件でこういう論点を考察したが，仲裁人による事実認定には，こういう結論を支持するものは存しないとして，これを退けた。しかし，航海傭船の事案である *Ismail* v. *Polish Ocean Lines (The Ciechocinek)* [1976] 1 Lloyd's Rep. 489 事件で，控訴院は傭船者が指名した代表が積込に立ち会い，貨物の包装につき確約し，積付につき指示を発した場合，荷送人が，貨物の積付に欠陥ありと主張するのは，禁反言であると判示した。

甲板積貨物

甲板積貨物に関する一切の責任を傭船者のものとする追加条項を定期傭船契約に含めるのは，異常なことではない。傭船契約の他の条項とその条項の間の相互作用は，複雑である。「傭船者の危険において」という普通に用いられる表現は，船主またはその乗組員に過失ある場合に，船主から傭船者に責任を転嫁するには，通常有効ではない（例として *The Fantasy* [1991] 2 Lloyd's Rep. 391 事件参照。*The Dannah* [1993] 1 Lloyd's Rep. 351 事件も参照）。そこでは，問題の特別条項の語句表現は，本船から海中に落下した甲板積コンテナのクレームに関する全責任を船主から傭船者に転嫁すると判示されたが（船主側の過失という上記の問題を取り除く「何が起ころうとも」との追加語句を使用した。*Joseph Travers* v. *Cooper* [1915] 1 K.B. 73 (C.A.) 事件），しかし，海中に没したコンテナは有害であるとの確信により，それ

を捜索し，何本かを引き揚げた地方当局のクレームについては，船主に責任が残ると判示された。

NYPE 93

ニューヨーク・プロデュース書式の1993年改訂版は，「甲板積貨物の運送の結果本船に生じたいかなる種類の滅失，および・または損傷および・または責任，および甲板積貨物を積まなかったならば生じなかったはずのいかなる種類の滅失および・または損傷および・または責任についても」船主は傭船者により補償されると第13条(b)に規定している（前出12頁の英文書式の188/190行と56頁参照）。

1945年法改革（寄与過失）に関する法

先例によれば，原告の被った損害の法的原因として原告自らの過失が部分的に寄与している場合に，過失の責任割合を規定する1945年法改革（寄与過失）に関する法は，契約関係如何にかかわらず，被告が不法行為により注意義務に違反しており，同時に契約の存在かつ・または契約条件が，原告の不法行為に基づく請求を排除していない場合のみ，契約の当事者間の請求に適用される。

Forsikringsaktieselskapet Vesta v. *Butcher* [1986] 2 Lloyd's Rep. 179 および [1988] 1 Lloyd's Rep. 19 (C. A.) 事件——顧客に対する専門家としての再保険仲立人の不法行為による注意義務違反と認めた事案——で，Hobhouse 卿判事は，過失請求に1945年法の適用が，考えられる契約について3類型の範疇を確認した（これにつき控訴院も同意した）。この範疇とは次のとおりであった。
(1) 被告側の過失に左右されないある契約規定から被告の責任が生じた場合。
(2) 注意を尽くすとの文言（または同等のもの）により表現される契約上の義務であるが，契約と関係なく所与の事案に存する注意を尽くすとのコモン・ローの義務に該当しない契約上の義務から被告の責任が生じた場合。
(3) 被告の契約上の責任が契約の存在と無関係に過失による不法行為責任と同じであった場合。

前出 *The Shinjitsu Maru No. 5* 事件で，Neill 卿判事は，1945年法は，契約上の請求にはまったく適用されないと一般的に結論づけた。その判決の趣旨が上記(3)の範疇に入る事案に1945年法の適用を排除した限りにおいて，*Vesta* v. *Butcher* 事件について Hobhouse 判事と控訴院は Neill 卿判事は間違っており，さらに本事案を含むそのような事案で，同法は適用され，損害賠償請求額の配分を行いうる，と判示した。Hobhouse 判事は，*The Shinjitsu Maru No. 5* 事件はたぶん(1)の範疇であっても，せいぜい(2)の範疇であり，(1)の範疇に関しては「同法の適用がない多くの紛争があるとは予想されない」との見解を表明した（[1986] 2 Lloyd's Rep. 179 (同判例集197頁)）。1945年法が(2)の範疇に適用されるか否かを決定する必要はないが，控訴院は，ニュージーランドの事案である *Rowe* v. *Turner Hopkins & Partners* [1980] 2 N. Z. L. R. 550 事件において，被告に不法行為責任があり，契約上同時に併存する責任が取るに足らない場合のみに，過失割合の配分権限を生じるという趣旨の Pritchard 判事の採った1945年法の解釈に賛意を表明した。

以前，Paull 判事は，*Quinn* v. *Burch* [1966] 2 Q. B. 370 事件で(1)の範疇か(2)の範疇として分類される事案に同法は適用されないと判示した。その後で，Brabin 判事は，*De Meza* v.

Apple［1974］1 Lloyd's Rep. 508事件の第1審で同法は(2)の範疇の状況に適用されると判示したが，控訴院は，この問題に見解を表明するのを拒否した（［1975］1 Lloyd's Rep. 498)。

しかしながら，Tai Hing v. Liu Chong Hing Bank［1985］2 Lloyd's Rep. 313事件で枢密院が提起した，不法行為と契約上同時に併存する責任がありうるかという疑問が存するとの意見は，当事者が契約関係にある場合に1945年法が適用できるかという問題を再燃させた。この意見については，Superhulls v. Cover［1990］2 Lloyd's Rep. 431事件でPhillips判事が考察した。その事件では，義務に違反して，不利な条件で再保険を手配し，保険填補の不足を助言せ|310|ず，不利益を救済する手だてを取らなかったブローカーに保険者が損害賠償請求した。同時に競合する責任原則を認めたVesta v. Butcher事件に倣い，Phillips判事は，ブローカーは契約と不法行為法上の双方の義務に違反した，そしてさらに本事案は，(3)の範疇に入るが，寄与過失が存するゆえに保険者の損害賠償額を軽減することにつき，同法が適用される，と判示した。

最近では，貴族院は，不法行為と契約の競合する責任の問題について，および契約の当事者には不法行為の他方の当事者に対する独立の注意義務がある場合について，他方の当事者は契約の存在の有無にかかわらず，義務違反につき出訴できるという権威ある判決を出した。Henderson v. Merret Syndicates［1994］3 W.L.R. 761事件で貴族院は，Lloydの管理代理人は，Lloydの保険会員に保険の引受やクレーム処理を通知する責任を負うので，会員に対し不法行為の注意義務を負い，不法行為の注意義務の存在は契約関係により排除されないと判示した。Hedley Byrne v. Heller［1963］1 Lloyd's Rep. 485事件で貴族院が制定した原則を適用して，Goff卿は，次のように述べた（同判例集789頁）。「……付随的な信頼と結びついた責任の引受は，当事者間の契約関係の有無にかかわらず，不法行為の注意義務を生じさせる。その結果として，契約により原告が排除されない限り，契約および不法行為で競合する救済を利用できる原告は，もっとも有利と思われる救済を選ぶ」。

Hedley Byrne v. Heller事件で，銀行は顧客の1人について身元照会の回答を提供する際の彼らの技能と判断に原告が拠っていることを知っていたか，知っているべきであった，そして原告は実際それに頼り，結果として経済的損失を被ったが，そのとき銀行が原告に誤って有利な照会の回答を提供したことに対する訴訟は原則として，不法行為に基づくと判示された。被告の「責任の引受」と被告の「特別な技能」への信頼が強調された。Henderson v. Merret Syndicates事件で，Goff卿は，「特別な技能」の概念は，「特別な知識」を含むほどに，広く適用されることに疑問の余地はないと解されねばならないと説明した。さらに同判事は，その原則は他の役務の遂行を含む情報と助言の提供を越えるとも指摘した。

したがって，定期傭船の下で貨物の積込，積付および揚荷に関連して1945年法が適用される状況が生じることはありうるように思われる。しかし，関連する法が十分に発展するまで，注意すべきである。

1945年法が，ある非安全港の事案に適用される状況について，前出248頁参照。

ニューヨーク・プロデュース書式に関するP&Iクラブ間の協定

船主と傭船者間で貨物損害賠償クレームの責任を配分することにつき，ニューヨーク・プロデュース書式に明確な指針がないので，主要P&Iクラブ（船主と定期傭船者の両者の貨物に対する責任の保険者である）は，協定に参加するクラブ間で，このクレームを円滑に解決する協定を起草することとなった。

船主と傭船者は，参加P&Iクラブの会員であるからという理由のみで協定に拘束されない

が，参加P&Iクラブは，協定の条件に従って紛争を解決するのに同意するよう各会員に推奨することを保証している。時には，この協定は，明示的にニューヨーク・プロデュース書式に[11]よる傭船契約に摂取される。その場合に，その効果は，「クラブ間協定を傭船者と船主の間で直接に適用する」ことである（*The Ion* ［1980］2 Lloyd's Rep. 245（同判例集248頁）事件参照。*The Strathnewton* ［1983］1 Lloyd's Rep. 219事件および後出373頁も参照）。

クレーム通知の2年の期限を含む現行版（1984年）の協定は次のとおりである。

ニューヨーク・プロデュース書式に関するP&Iクラブ間の協定
（1984年5月改訂）
(Inter-Club New York Produce Exchange Agreement)

前　文

ニューヨーク・プロデュース書式に基づき発生する貨物クレームの責任の分担に関してAssuranceforeningen Gard, Assuranceforeningen Skuld, The Britannia Steam Ship Insurance Association Ltd., The Liverpool and London Steamship Protection and Indemnity Association Ltd., The London Steam-Ship Owners' Mutual Insurance Association Ltd., Newcastle Protection and Indemnity Association, The North of England Protecting and Indemnity Association Ltd., The Standard Steamship Owners' Protection & Indemnity Association Ltd., The Standard Steamship Owners' Protection & Indemnity Association (Bermuda) Limited., The Steamship Mutual Underwriting Association Ltd., The Sunderland Steamship Protecting & Indemnity Association, Sveriges Angafartygs Assurans Forening,The United Kingdom Mutual Steamship Assurance Association (Bermuda) Limitedと The West of England Ship Owners Mutual Protection and Indemnity Association (Luxembourg)（以降まとめて「クラブ」と称する）の間の協定の覚書（以降「本協定」と称する）．

(1) 本協定の適用と解釈

下記条件を条件として，(2)に規定の方式は1984年6月1日以降締結されたニューヨーク・プロデュース書式の傭船契約に関して適用される。

(i) 一切の法務費用を含む貨物クレームは適正に解決または和解され，貨物はヘーグ・ルールまたはヘーグ・ヴィスビー・ルールを摂取している船荷証券またはこれらの規則より運送人に不利でない船荷証券に基づき運送されたことが本協定上の精算の停止条件とする。クレームを支払う法的責任はないが，商売のためにまたはその他の理由で，好意による解決が行われる場合，支払をしたクラブが全額負担するものとし，そのような支払に対して本協定の目的のために何の配慮もなされないものとする。

(ii)

(a) 本協定の適用のためには，ニューヨーク・プロデュース書式による傭船契約の貨物責任条項は実質的に修正されてはならない。実質的修正とは，船主と傭船者の間の貨物クレームの責任を明確にする修正である。特に，第8条への「および揚荷」の語句の追加は実質的修正とはみなされないものとする。

(b) しかしながら，第26条の第2番目の文に「貨物クレーム」の語句を追加すると共に，第8条の「監督の下で」の語句に関連して「および責任」の語句を追加する場合，本協定は効力

がないものとする。傭船契約の他の一切の重要な規定なしに，この2個の追加修正または第26条への「貨物クレーム」の単なる追加は，海損バース基準条項／傭船者分担条項（1971）に基づく傭船者の分担が適用可能な場合には，船主がすべての貨物クレームを負担するものとすることを意味する。

(c) 修正が第8条の「監督の下で」の語句に関連して「および責任」の語句の追加だけの場合，第2条に規定する貨物クレームの分担は次の方式で変化することを意味することにクラブは合意する。

不堪航より発生した貨物の滅失・損傷のクレームおよび単に通風不良により発生した結露損傷クレーム……………………………………100%　船主

積付不良または荷扱いにより発生する（漏損を含む）損傷クレームおよび通風不良以外により発生した結露損傷クレーム………………50%　船主　　50%　傭船者

第2条第2節の規定を除き，（抜荷を含む）不足損害クレームと誤揚げのクレーム
……………………………………………………………………50%　船主　　50%　傭船者

(iii) 本協定は仲裁地，または管轄地にかかわらず，および傭船契約にヘーグ・ルールまたはヘーグ・ヴィスビー・ルールかつ，または海損バース基準条項（クレームの一般基準条項／傭船者分担条項（1971）としても知られている）を摂取している至上条項を含むか否かにかかわらず，適用されるものとする。

(iv) 本協定に基づいて傭船者または船主のいずれかにより，または傭船者または船主に代わって追及されるクレームは，可能な限り早く，ただし揚荷の日または揚荷されるべきであった日より2年以内に書面により相手方に通知されるものとする。期限内に通知なき場合は，回収を放棄し，期限は経過したものとみなされる。通知には船荷証券の明細とクレームの種類と金額を含めるものとする。

(v) 傭船契約が海損バース基準条項／傭船者分担条項（1971）を含む場合，事情しだいで責任が(2)または(1)(ii)(c)項に従って配分された後で海損バース基準条項／傭船者分担条項（1971）が適用され，同条項に別の規定が存したとしても傭船者の負担は船荷証券毎あるいは貨物1個毎ではなく貨物運送航海毎とする。

(vi) クラブが特定の事案で別途合意していないかぎり，再傭船者が関与する場合，本協定は最初に貨物クレームを解決したクラブの段階において初めて適用されるものとする。例えば，再傭船者が一人の場合，貨物クレームを再傭船者が解決した場合，そのクレームは再傭船者と傭船者の間で本協定に従って配分され，この目的のために傭船者が「船主」であるが如くに扱われ，傭船者負担となった部分はその後で本協定に従い傭船者と船主の間で配分されるものとする。

(vii) 本協定は組合員を拘束しないが，すべての案件についてクラブは組合員が本協定を採用するよう無条件で勧告する。

(2) 貨物クレームの配分

本協定が適用される場合に，貨物クレームは以下のように配分されるものとする：

不堪航による貨物の滅失損傷のクレーム………………………………100%　船主

積付不良または荷扱いによる（漏損を含む）損傷のクレーム……100%　傭船者

本条の次の節で規定されているものを除き，（抜荷を含む）不足損害クレームと誤揚のクレームと結露損傷クレーム…………………50%　船主　　50%　傭船者

不足損害または誤揚が事情により船主または傭船者の被用者または代理人の側の懈怠または

過失によることが明白で反駁できぬ証拠がある場合，不足損害または誤揚クレームに関して，被用者または代理人に過失ある側のクラブが，クレームの全額を負担するものとする。このように不足損害が荷役業者の抜荷によるとの確証ある目撃証人がある場合，クレームは100％傭船者の負担となるが，乗組員による抜荷の場合に，海損バース基準条項／傭船者分担条項（1971）に基づく傭船者の負担を条件として100％船主負担となる。

結露損傷クレームは本条の第1節に規定されているように配分されるものとする。ただし，損傷が積付不良のみによることの明白な証拠がある場合を除く。その場合には，100％傭船者の負担とする。しかし損傷が通風不良のみによる場合には，100％船主負担とする。

313 **(3) 本協定の拡張**

本協定が(1)に規定されている事由を理由として厳密に適用されない場合にもかかわらずクラブが望む場合，本協定の全部または一部を適用することはクラブの自由とする。

(4) 期　　間

本協定は変更または停止のときに至るまで有効である。いかなる変更も全クラブの承認を得て初めて発効するが，いずれのクラブも少なくとも3ヶ月以前に他のクラブすべてに宛てた書面による通知をもって協定より脱退することを得る。脱退はこの（3ヶ月）期間満了により効力を生じる。協定は，この通知期間の満了後も，通知を出したクラブ以外の全クラブ相互間で効力を有し，通知を出したクラブも，同通知期間の満了前に締結した傭船契約より発生する貨物クレームについてはこの協定に従い，またその利益に与るべきものとする。

例えば，The Standard Associationが1985年1月1日に本協定から脱退の書面による通知を出した場合，1985年3月31日以前に開始した傭船契約から生じる貨物クレームに関して本協定を適用する義務がある。

(5) 実施：本協定は，本協定のクラブ間で既に決定した解決には影響しないものとする。

クラブ間協定と海上物品運送法の摂取

ニューヨーク・プロデュース書式による傭船契約は通常，米国海上物品運送法の摂取の結果として貨物クレームの1年の期限に従うが（*The Agios Lazaros* [1976] 2 Lloyd's Rep. 47（C. A.）事件参照），当事者がクラブ間協定の原版（1970年）を明示的に摂取した傭船契約では，傭船者から船主に対する貨物クレームの1年の期限は適用されない（*The Strathnewton* [1983] 1 Lloyd's Rep. 219（C. A.）事件参照）。その事案で，Kerr卿判事は，本協定は，「ヘーグ・ルールに基づく機能と責任の配分をして」そして「義務の基準からまったく独立した経済的責任の大方の機械的分担を規定する」と述べた（同判例集225頁。*The Benlawyers* [1982] 2 Lloyd's Rep. 51事件も参照）。しかし，上記の協定の現行版（1984年）は揚荷された日から，または貨物が揚荷されるべきであった日から，2年以内のクレームの通知を要件としている。それがない場合には，一切の回収は放棄され，期限は経過したものとみなされる。協定の(1)(iv)項参照。協定に言及し，摂取している場合，この期限は，傭船契約のどこかにタイプ条項によりクレームに関する別の期限を挿入すれば，無効とすることができる（未報告のEvans判事判決 *The Mary L*（1990）事件）。

傭船契約の中に，本協定を摂取する個別の追加条項により，貨物クレームを解決する一方の当事者が，他方の当事者の承認を得た上で解決するものとするということが，この協定に基づく回収の明示の前提条件となる。これが，後出 *The Holstencruiser* 事件で検討された傭船契約の事例であった。

The Benlawyers [1982] 2 Lloyd's Rep. 51 事件で，Hobhouse 卿は，貨物クレームは本協定の(1)(ii)(c)に基づき全面的に船主負担となるか否かを考察する際に，貨物損傷の実際の原因を配慮すべきで，請求者がクレームを系統立てて述べた方法のみに配慮すべきではない，と判示した。同じことが，不堪航による損傷についての(2)に基づくクレームにもあてはまる（後出 *The Holstencruiser* 事件の報告（389頁参照）。後出その事案の判決の第7を比較参照）。

　The Holstencruiser [1992] 2 Lloyd's Rep. 378 事件で，Hobhouse 卿は，コンテナ航路で運航している複数の船主と傭船者の間の多数の友誼的訴訟で，本協定の範囲と解釈について出された一連の問題に答えた。本協定は，ニューヨーク・プロデュース書式による該当傭船契約に明示的に摂取されていた。同判事の結論は次のとおりである。

1．本協定は，定期傭船契約に基づき適切に発行された船荷証券に従い，支払われまたは解決されたクレームのみに適用される。
2．第8条は，船主に代わって発行される船荷証券を，船長が「メーツ・レシートまたはタリー・レシート」に従って貨物の受取を認め，署名した船荷証券に限定している。選択的に，傭船者は，さもなくば船長が船主の代行として適切に署名したかも知れない船荷証券に署名する黙示の権限を行使できるが，その権限自身は，船主（または，その被用者または権限ある代理人）が実際に受領した貨物についての船荷証券だけに限定する。
3．実務上，これは，「コンテナが船側または船上に到着したときに，貨物がコンテナの内部に存在したことを証明しないかぎり，傭船者がコンテナ貨物に関して本協定に拠れないことを意味する。船荷証券が，裏書により貨物の実際の船積を認めたものである場合，傭船者は実際に船積されたときに貨物がコンテナの中に存在したことを証明する用意がなければならない」。
4．通しまたは接続船荷証券は「他者により提供される役務に全部または一部関係している」ので，本協定は，通しまたは接続船荷証券に基づくクレームには適用されない。
5．本協定の(1)(i)項の範囲内で「法務費用」は，貨物賠償請求者がクレームの回収のために使用した費用を含むが，船主または傭船者がクレームを処理するために要した費用を含まない。
6．傭船者が税関当局に支払った罰金は，本協定に基づく何らの権利も生じさせない。
7．関連する傭船契約に本協定を摂取する追加条項により要求されているように，傭船者が船主の承諾に基づき結露損傷クレームを解決した場合，たとえ船主が，結露による損傷はありえないと後で証明できるとしても，船主は(2)に基づき50パーセントを支払わねばならない。(2)に基づく「結露クレーム」の場合，問題となるのは「クレームの性質」であるので，傭船契約が承認を要求しておらず，船主がクレーム解決を承認していない場合でも結果は同じであろうと思われる（(1)(ii)(c)項と第2条の他の部分が貨物損傷の実際の原因を非常に強調していることを比較。前出参照）。(2)に基づき，当該条項のただし書きを利用し，負担を拒否することができるのは，船主が結露クレームは「積付不良」のみによることを証明できる場合だけである。結露損傷が明らかに甲板積されたコンテナ内の貨物の積付から生じたことを証明できる場合は，これに該当しよう。
8．(2)のただし書きに基づく挙証責任は刑事裁判で要求されるものほど厳しくはない。「明白で反駁できない証拠」の要件は商業的文脈で理解されなければならない。

NYPE 93

　ニューヨーク・プロデュース書式1993年版は，第27条に貨物クレームはP&Iクラブ間協定1984年版またはその改訂または補充に従って，船主と傭船者の間で解決されると規定している

（前出14頁英文書式の285/287行と58頁参照）。

315 海損バース基準条項

ニューヨーク・プロデュース・クラブ間協定に言及され，定期航路の定期傭船契約にしばしば摂取される，この条項は次のとおりである。

　本船がバースで船積し，および・または雑貨を船積する場合，船主と傭船者の間で船主の側に責任が在るかも知れない，積込および揚荷中の荷扱いの不良，積付不良，不足渡（抜荷であれ，他の一切のいかなる原因かを問わず），または誤揚から貨物運送航海に生じるクレームにつきおよびそのようなクレームを避けるため，または軽減するために発生する一切の荷直し費用につき本船の登録総トン数当たり，……に同額まで傭船者は負担するものとする。最初に船主が一切のこのようなクレームを支払う場合，上記範囲にて傭船者はこれを償還する。

　海損バース基準条項を考察した事案として，*Clan Line* v. *Ove Skou*〔1969〕2 Lloyd's Rep. 155 事件と *The Filikos*〔1981〕2 Lloyd's Rep. 555 と〔1983〕1 Lloyd's Rep. 9（C. A.）事件参照。

傭船者は船主の P&I 補償の利益を受ける

　傭船者が，船主の P&I 補償の利益を享受することを規定して，しばしば追加約定される条項に関する判決として，*Court Line* v. *Canadian Transport*（1940）67 Ll.L. Rep. 161 事件参照。

316 米　国　法

　貨物の積込と積付に対する，船主と傭船者のそれぞれの義務に関する米国の指導的判例は，*Nichimen Company* v. *The Farland*, 462 F. 2d 319 (2d Cir. 1972) 事件である。この事件で，貨物側は，船主 A/S Vigra と定期傭船者 Seaboard Shipping 両者に対して，鋼材貨物の損害賠償請求の訴えを起こした。裁判所は，貨物側が損害を回収する権利を有すると判示したが，船主 Vigra と傭船者 Seaboard とのいずれが，その損失に対する最終的責任を負うかは，後日の判断として残した。裁判所は，「特別な約定や事情がなければ，積込，積付，揚荷の義務は，——適切にこれらを履行しないための結果を含めて——船舶およびその船主に課せられる」(462 F. 2d at 330) という，永い間認識されてきた原則をまず認めた。次いで裁判所は，ニューヨーク・プロデュース書式の第8条が，積付の責任を傭船者に転嫁していると判断した。

　……第8条により，積付の安全は，貨物の損害に関する限り，一般的に，傭船者本来の責任である (462 F. 2d at 332)。

　しかし，さらに裁判所は，船長が積込や積付に関与しなくても，船主が貨物の損害につき，責任を負う場合がありうることを認めた。貨物の損害が，船主が船舶の堪航性を維持すること，または航海の間，船舶を「十分稼働状態」に保持することに相当の注意を尽くさなかったことのために生じた場合，船主は責任があると思われる。

　本船船長が，発見しなかったり，修復しなかった本船の欠陥のために，貨物損害が生じた場合，その本来の責任は，船主にある。この種の損害原因は，第8条が，船主から傭船者に転嫁しようとしている責任の範囲を超えている。……同様に，本船に隠れた瑕疵があり，それを船長，船主が，傭船者またはその荷役業者に示さなかった場合，その瑕疵のため，元来，適正であった積付が，危険になったという事情があれば，貨物に対する船主本来の責任が，第8条により，免除されるか疑問である (同上)。

　The Farland 事件における判決は，先の *The Nidarholm*, 282 U.S. 681 (1931) 事件の，最高裁判決に従っている。同事件では，第8条と同様の条項を含む定期傭船契約により，木材貨物が甲板上に船積された。積荷直後，本船は5度傾斜し，甲板貨物を支持している「丸太の柵」が倒壊し，大量の貨物が舷外に落下し滅失した。裁判所は，安定性とトリムを適切に保つことは，本船の堪航性を維持すべき船主責任の一部であるから，甲板積貨物の倒壊の原因となった船体傾斜は，船主の責任に帰すべき過失であると判断した。しかし，裁判所は，「丸太の柵」は積付のためであり，5度傾斜の場合の貨物の圧力を持ちこたえるべきであったという点で，傭船者にもまた過失があると認め，損害賠償は均等に分担すべきであると認定した。

　早い時期の判決である *The Santona*, 152 Fed. 516 (S. D. N. Y. 1970) 事件で New York の地区裁判所は，次のように判示した。

　本船は船主の船舶である。本船の航行と管理のすべてにつき船長と乗組員は船主の被用者である。しかし，貨物の受取と引渡と，傭船者の財布に入る本船の収益に関するあらゆる事柄について船長と乗組員は傭船者の被用者である。事実（法の他の部門からたとえを借りるとすれば）本船から切り出し，傭船者に特定の条件で手交された財産がある。その財産は，積荷を運送し，運賃を稼ぐ能力と，

傭船者の収益促進のための本船，船長および乗組員の使用から構成される。

　Nissho-Iwai Co. Ltd. v. *The Stolt Lion*, 617 F. 2d 907, 1980 AMC 867 (2d Cir. 1980), 破棄 1979 AMC 2415 (S.D.N.Y. 1979) 事件で，裁判所は，*The Farland* 事件で裁判所が明立に発表した法則——負担を傭船者に転嫁するのに役立つ「第8条」の傭船契約の規定がない場合，または当事者の行為がない場合，または当事者間の習慣がない場合，貨物の揚荷の責任は船主にある——を繰り返して言った。

　The Farland 事件を，*Seguros Banvenez S. A.* v. *The Oliver Dreshcer*, 761 F. 2d 855, 1985 AMC 2168 (2d Cir. 1985) 事件は踏襲した *Nitram Inc.* v. *The Cretan Life*, 599 F. 2d 1359, 1366 (5th Cir. 1979) 事件も参照。*Demsey & Assoc. Inc.* v. *The Sea Star*, 461 F. 2d 1009, 1972 AMC 1440 (2d Cir. 1972) 事件参照。*Assoc. Metals & Minerals Corp.* v. *The Arktis Sky*, 978 F. 2d 47, 1993 AMC 509 (2d Cir. 1992) 事件同旨。*The Tulsa*, SMA 2794 (Arb. at N. Y. 1991) 事件も参照。*Tulsa* 号事件で，仲裁審は，不適当に積付し，固縛した貨物が船外に落下したことにつき船主に補償する責任が傭船者にあると判示した。

　The Caribbean Sky, SMA 2827 (Arb. at N.Y. 1992) 事件で，傭船者は貨物損失クレームに関連して，船主からの補償および他の損害賠償を追及した。船主は傭船契約の第8条に従い損失について傭船者に責任があると主張した。仲裁審は，船主の提供義務があった不適当な固縛器具のために本船に積載された最初のフラットベッドが離れたことについて船主に過失ありと全員一致で認定した。これが，本船の損傷と同様に他の貨物の滅失および・または損傷に繫がる一連のできごとを引き起こした。仲裁審は，「どちらの当事者が固縛器具を支給し，または積付作業費を支払うという傭船契約上の責任を伴うかは別として，本船，乗組員，貨物の安全性について究極的責任は船主にある」と述べた。船長は「航海のあらゆる点で本船が適合することを確実にするために相当の注意を尽くす義務」を怠ったと認定して，仲裁審は船主のクレームを認めず，傭船者に損害賠償請求額全額を認める裁定をした。

　一般に *Thyssen Inc.* v. *The Fortune Star*, 777 F. 2d 57, 1986 AMC 1318 (2d Cir. 1985) 事件を参照。この事件で，法廷は甲板積貨物のための離路に関する第8条のタイプ規定に基づき責任ある傭船者は懲罰的損害賠償につき責任を負うと判示することはできない旨傍論として述べた。

船長の監督の下に

　第8条の下で，最も困難な問題は，船長の役割に関する問題である。船長が，積極的に積込および積付に関与した場合，事実上船主に責任をとらせる英国の見解は，New York では，一般的に支持されていない。むしろ，New York でのこの問題の取り上げ方は，船長が関与したかどうかではなく，いかなる資格によって関与したかを考えるべきであるとしている。したがって，船長は，「2つの帽子を着用する」，または二重の代理の役割を果すということが言われる。船長が，伝統的観念で堪航性（例えば水密性，安定性，適正トリム，構造上の堅牢性）のある船舶を提供すべき船主の責任を果している範囲では，船長は船主の代理人として行為する。しかし，（貨物利害関係人に対して，近代的観念での「堪航性」をも意味する）適切な積込，積付，揚荷を遂行すべき傭船者の責任の範囲では，船長は，傭船者の代理人として行為している。だから，傭船者が，船長，乗組員を使用する場合，その船長，乗組員は，第8条の傭船者の責任を果すため，傭船者によって「借り受けられた被用者」となる。この法理は，*The Farland* 事件で，次のように表明されている。

......積付不良による貨物損害について船主が負う責任は，本船の安全と海の危険に耐える能力を保持するため，船長が積付に介入した場合に限定されると考える。単に貨物を保護するため，船長が関与する範囲では，傭船者が責任を負うべきである（462 F. 2d at 333）。

The Agios Panteleimon, SMA 1477 (arb. at N. Y. 1980) 事件も参照。その事件で，仲裁審は，船長は貨物の適正な積付，適性な喫水計画を含む本船の安全で適正な航海に責任があると結論づけた。航海士として積込を実施し，トリム係数を満たす計画を立てるときに，本船がサグになるという事実を考慮に入れることは，船主と船長の責任であった。The Drosia, SMA 1303（Arb. at N. Y. 1979）事件で，仲裁審は船長が誤って満載喫水線を超えて積込を許容してしまい，燃料と清水を卸すために喪失した時間は，船主の負担であり，傭船者はオフハイヤーとする権利があると裁定した。しかし，The Robertina, SMA 1151 (Arb. at N. Y. 1977) 事件で仲裁審は，船長は船舶の安全と安定性の点で船主の被用者であるが，本船の利用可能な能力の使用については傭船者の被用者であると判示した。積付不良または荷均のために特定の量の貨物を積載できない危険は，傭船者の負担となる。

Spence v. Mariehamns R/S, 766 F. 2d 1504, 1986 AMC 685 (11th Cir. 1985) 事件で，裁判所は，「船長の監督の下に」の語句は貨物の船積および揚荷の荷役業者の作業を監督する義務を船主に課するものではないと判示した。この事案で，船主は揚荷中，荷役作業員が被った傷害につき責任を免れた。

The Aetolia, SMA 2157 (Arb. at N. Y. 1985) 事件で，仲裁審は，貨物の固縛を要しない方法で貨物の積付計画図を船長が用意できないため生じた貨物の固縛費用について船主に責任はないと裁定した。仲裁審によると，これは貨物を積込，積付そして荷均する傭船者の義務の範囲内である。

The Carib Eve, SMA 2749 (Arb. at N. Y. 1991) 事件で，傭船者は船外に落下した貨物につき船主の責任を追及した。船主は，傭船者が貨物を適正に積み付けなかったと主張した。仲裁審は，傭船者と乗組員の間の契約に基づかない手配に従って，乗組員が貨物の積込に参画したという事実にかかわらず，これは，傭船契約外のことであり，船主を拘束するものではないと，裁定した。さらに，傭船契約の第8条に従って，傭船者は貨物の積込，積付および揚荷に責任があり，乗組員と船長がその作業に参画する範囲において傭船者により借り受けられた被用者としてそのような行為をしたものであると裁定した。

The Labrador Rex, SMA 2472 (Arb. at N. Y. 1988) 事件で，仲裁人は，積込，積付および揚荷の責任と費用を傭船者に配分している第8条と同様の文言を含む傭船契約で貨物損傷についての傭船者の請求を退けた。傭船者は，本船，または船主側の過失を立証できなかった。

The Ocean Prince, SMA 2517 (Arb. at N. Y. 1988) 事件で，貨物損傷は包装不良と積込不良，積付不良および揚荷不良により実際に生じたと断定した後に，仲裁審は，船主はこれらの損傷危険に責任はないと判定した。仲裁審は船主に貨物損傷クレームについて傭船者による補償を認めた。仲裁審はまた，荷均の目的で貨物を固縛することにより発生した費用は第8条に基づき傭船者の負担であると裁定した。The Unibulk Fir, SMA 1505 (Arb. at N. Y. 1980); The North Emperor, SMA 1284 (Arb. at N. Y. 1978); The Dorothea Bolton, SMA 1211 (Arb. at N. Y. 1978); Int'l Produce, Inc. v. The Frances Salman, 1975 AMC 1521, 1523-24, 1554 (S. D. N. Y. 1975); A/S Brovanor v. Central Gulf S. S. Corp., 323 F. Supp. 1029, 1032 (S. D. N. Y. 1970); Isbrandtsen Co. v. George S. Boutwell, 1958 AMC 351 (S. D. N. Y. 1957); Socomet v. Sliedrecht, 1975 AMC 314 (S. D. N. Y. 1975); The Mesologi, 1971 AMC 2498 (Arb. at N. Y. 1971); Interstate Steel Corp. v. The Crystal Gem, 317, F., Supp. 112 (S.

D. N. Y. 1970); Yeramex International v. The Tendo, 595 F. 2d 943, 1979 AMC 1282 (4th Cir. 1979), 破棄 1977 AMC 1807 (E. D. Va. 1977); Board of Commissioners of the Port of New Orleans v. The Space King, 1978 AMC 856 (E. D. Va. 1978) 各事件参照。

よくあるように、「そして船長の責任」という文言が、第8条の末尾に付記された場合、さらに困難な問題が生ずる。英国では、この文言によって、積付不良の責任が、事情しだいで船主に再転嫁されるのであるが、米国ではどうであろうか、たぶん再転嫁されないと思われる。Coca-Cola Co. v. The Norholt, 333 F. Supp. 946, 1972 AMC 388 (S. D. N. Y. 1971) 事件で、紅茶の荷主は、船主および定期傭船者に対して、訴訟を起した。荷主は、両当事者と示談で解決したが、その後、両当事者は、いずれが損害を負担すべきかを決めるため裁判を受けた。裁判所は、貨物の損害は、一部不堪航状態により、一部積付不良によって生じたと判示した。後者の原因に関して、傭船者は、傭船契約第8条により、船主が積付に対する責任を負っていると主張して、船主に責任を転嫁しようとした。傭船契約書式は修正されており、その第8条は、次の文言を含んでいた。

傭船者は自己の費用で、船長の監督の下に、**船長の責任において**、積込、**揚荷**、積付および荷均作業を行うものとする。

第8条が修正されているにもかかわらず、事実審の判事は、「当事者の種々の行為を補足的に考慮に入れ、第8条を全体として解釈すると、傭船者は、細部にわたる積付を、事実上、自己の手中に確保すべく苦心したと結論せざるをえない」と述べた。傭船者は、事前に積付計画を立てていたが、船長の抗議を受けて計画を変更し、第1番艙の有毒クレジリック酸の真上に、紅茶を積み付けた。「および責任で」という文言は、船貨双方を保護するという船長の基本的責任を単に強調し、拡大しているのみであると解しうるから、この判決は正当と思われる。つまり、事故の発生により、潜在的に極端な結果を**船主**が認めざるをえないような責任転嫁をしようとすれば、より明確な文言を用いなければならないということである。例えば、第8条の末尾に「ただし、貨物の積込、積付、揚荷を援助するにあたっての、船長、乗組員の作為、不作為につき、船主は責任を負う」というような文言を入れば、この目的を達成するのに十分であると思われる。

The Trust 38, SMA 2911 (Arb. at N. Y. 1992) 事件で、原傭船契約は、ニューヨーク・プロデュース書式で、再傭船契約は Stemmor 書式であった。原傭船契約には、船主は「船長の監督と責任の下に適正な積付に関する責任」を明白に負うとする追加条項とともに標準第8条があった。積荷役中に貨物の一部に雨濡れ損傷が生じ、多数の袋物貨物が破れ、裂けた。損傷貨物は、船上に残され、無故障のメーツ・レシートと無故障の船荷証券が発行された。船主は船荷証券の当事者ではないので、責任がないという船主の主張を退けて、仲裁人は、両傭船契約の条項に従って、船主は積込と積付を含む荷役の監督に責任があると裁定した。したがって、傭船者も貨物の滅失・損傷に責任ありと裁定されたが、傭船者には船主から全損害額の回収が裁定された。

The Holland, SMA 2114 (Arb. at N. Y. 1985) 事件で、傭船契約は「甲板積の場合は、傭船者の危険と責任において、かつ船長の裁量により」というタイプ条項を含んでいた。本船は、ロール状のライナーボードペーパーを船積し、艙内と甲板に積み付けた。しかし、甲板積の量が多すぎて、本船は不安定であった。本船が不安定であった結果として、船体は大きく傾斜し、甲板積貨物は舷外へ落下し、艙内の貨物には濡損が生じる事態となった。仲裁審は、船主が貨物損傷にすべての責任を負うと裁定した。仲裁審は、本船の堪航性と安全に関する限

り，船長は船主に代わり本船の安定性を保証する責任があると述べた。船長が適正な安定性の計算をしなかったために貨物損傷が生じたのだから，船主は損害に責任がある。仲裁審によると，甲板積貨物の船積に関する傭船契約の修正は，責任を傭船者に転嫁するものではなかった。

第8条の下で生ずるさらなる問題は，積付不良に対する傭船者の責任範囲に関するものである。大多数の事案において，もちろん，損失は貨物に限定されている。しかしながら，不適当な積付が船舶自体または第三者に損害を与える場合がある。傭船者の責任が，貨物の事案を超えて拡大されることもありうることが，*The Farland*事件で特に言及されたが，この問題は，この事件の争点ではなかった。しかしながら，*Fernandez v. Chios Shipping*, 71 Civ. 2786（S. D. N. Y. 1976），原審維持 542 F. 2d 145（2d Cir. 1976）事件で，この問題が争点として，真正面から取り組まれた。裁判所は，この事件で，揚荷作業中の荷役作業員の負傷による損害賠償に関し，船主が定期傭船者から，補償金を回収することを認めた。この判決は，第8条による定期傭船者の責任に基づくものであった。裁判所は，次のように述べている。

　……日綿事件は……貨物の損害の場合，船主は，傭船者の直接の，あるいは，制定法上の過失，または，その他の過誤が損害の原因であることを立証して，はじめて定期傭船者に対して，求償権を有するという狭い解釈を代表するものと解することもできる。……しかし，そのように制限された解釈は，正当ではないと思える。

　より妥当な解釈は，船主，傭船者間においては，定期傭船契約第8条により，貨物の積込，積付，荷均，揚荷に対する責任が傭船者に転嫁されており，したがって，傭船者は，約定荷役作業が不適当であったため生じた損害を船主に補償しなければならないという考え方である。この見解に従えば，荷役作業を履行する義務は，かかる損害を船主に補償する絶対的義務を伴っていることになる。この義務は，傭船者側の「過誤 fault」の有無や定期傭船契約上の義務の履行のために，定期傭船者が雇用した者と定期傭船者との代理に関する法律上の関係如何にかかわらず適用される。

　裁判所は，後者の見解が正しいと考える。……前述したように，船主と傭船者の間では，船主が傭船者に対して貨物損害を求償することが，この条項（第8条）の解釈として，妥当，公正と思われる。傭船者は，積付および揚荷に「本来の責任を負うべき」であるし，船長の監督の役割が，船舶の堪航性を害する計画を拒否することに軽減されているのであるから，（おそらく，荷役には，信用ある荷役業者を雇っていると思われる）傭船者の過失を，後日直接立証した場合にのみ，補償を認めるとするのは，公正と言いがたく，また，荷役業者は，代理……関する法律の下では，独立した請負人でもあるから，荷役業者の過失につき，傭船者が責任を負うと判断されてはならないというような主張を，傭船者に許すことも，公正を欠くものと思われる。

　日綿事件で，控訴院により判断されたように，第8条が，荷役作業を積極的に管理する本来の責任を傭船者に転嫁する意味を有することは，本裁判所にとって明らかである。……さらに，本件のように，船主に不利な不堪航という事実認定が，船主が創り出した状態によって生じたというより，荷役業者や荷主が創り出した安全でない状態によって生じた場合，傭船契約により，本船船長の荷役作業に対する責任が限定されていることもあり，傭船者に対する求償を拒絶する衡平法上の根拠はないと思われる。

Fernandes 事件の判決は，第9巡回区裁判所における *Turner* v. *Japan Lines Ltd.* 651 F. 2d 1300, 1981 AMC 2223（9th Cir. 1981），裁量上告拒絶 459 U. S. 967（1982），修正 702 F. 2d 752, 1984 AMC 2703（9th Cir. 1983）事件により追従された。

Haluapo v. *Akashi Kaiun, K. K. S. A. M. Inc.*, 748 F. 2d 1363, 1985 AMC 1107（9th Cir. 1984）事件では，第9巡回区裁判所は，*Turner* 事件の判決を当該事案と区別するために幅広く説明した。*Haluapo* 事件で，本船は，裸傭船の後，定期傭船され，その上で，航海傭船され

た。原告は，揚荷中に傷害を被った荷役作業員であった。傷害は，船上の故障した巻揚げ機により生じた。原告と同一の裁判管轄に服する唯一の関係者は，定期傭船者であった。裁判所は，定期傭船者が，本船上の欠陥についての知識もなく，乗組員の行動を管理する能力もなく，定期傭船者は本船の運航や，貨物の船積に関与していないという理由でこの訴訟を却下した。Turner 事件では定期傭船者が実際に荷役業者を雇ったと判決して，裁判所は，Turner 事件を区別した。さらに，裁判所によると Turner 事件の状況と異なり定期傭船者には，乗組員の行動を管理する権利も能力もなかった。裁判所による後者の指摘が有効な区別かどうかは，疑問である。裁判所は，定期傭船者の提出した矛盾のない宣誓供述書に基づいてこの結論に到達した。Turner 事件で，裁判所は，本船の船長は貨物の船積および揚荷に関する確かな目的のために定期傭船者の代理人であると考えた。

同様に The Mount Athos, SMA 1570 (Arb. at N. Y. 1981) 事件で，荷役業者の過失により鋼鉄スクラップの積荷役中に本船の外板に刺し穴があいた。仲裁審は，損傷は傭船者の責任であると裁定した。仲裁審によると，船長が個人的に積荷役に関与しているという事実は，損傷の責任を傭船者から転嫁するものではなかった。

対照的に，Desormeaux v. Oceans International Corp., 1979 AMC 1962 (W. D. La. 1979) 事件で裁判所は，傭船者が独立の契約者であれば傭船者側に責任を生じるような種類の積荷役の監督および管理をしたという証拠がない場合，第8条に基づき，定期傭船者は傷害を受けた荷役作業員に対する損害賠償にも，船主に対する補償にも責任はないと判示した。このように判決を出して，裁判所は，D/S Ove Skou v. Hebert, 365 F. 2d 341, 1966 AMC 2223 (5th Cir. 1966)，裁量上告拒絶 400 U. S. 902 (1970) 事件が指摘するような第5巡回区裁判所の第8条の解釈に賛成する Fernandez 事件を退けた。Ove Skou 事件で，裁判所は傭船者からの補償を求めた船主の請求を次の理由で退けた。

> 船長は「使用と代理に関して」傭船者の指図の下にあり，「傭船者が貨物を積込，積付および荷均する」と規定する典型的な条項は，定期傭船者にこれらの作業の管理を委ねるものではない。この傭船契約規定は，これらの行為のいずれかの最終的経済的費用を負担する当事者——船主または傭船者——を特定することがその本質である。
>
> 傭船者は，貨物の船積や揚荷の手配のみならず，水先人，曳船を確保し，港湾を使用し，港湾当局に支払うが，これらを本船または乗組員が行う場合，定期傭船者は作業上の責任を負担するものではない。……独立の契約者——ここではそういう者は存在しないが——の行為に責任を生じる状況がない場合，定期傭船者は船主，または荷役作業員を含む第三者に対して荷役業者による不作為，または作為につき責任がない。

Bourgeois v. Bergen Juno, 1979 AMC 1396 (E. D. La. 1978)；Warnock v. Daiichi Chuo Kisen Kaisha, 1983 AMC 1463 (E. D. Ore. 1981)；Shaw v. South African Marine Corp., 1983 AMC 1578 (E. D. Va. 1982)；Roby v. Hyundai Merchant Marine, 700 F. Supp. 316, 1989 AMC 1126 (E. D. La. 1988) 各事件参照。Irby v. Tokai Lines, 1990 AMC 1042 (E. D. Pa 1990)；Harris v. S. P. Shipping, 818 F. Supp. 149, 1993 AMC 1538 (E. D. Va. 1993)；Hines v. British Steel Corp., 907 F. 2d 726, 1990 AMC 2986 (7th Cir. 1990) 各事件同旨。

Hayes v. Wilh. Wilhelmsen Enterprises Ltd., 818 F. 2d 1557, 1988 AMC 259 (11th Cir. 1987) 事件で，裁判所は定期傭船者に対して主張された人身傷害賠償請求を却下した。原告は，本船の水圧運転の貨物室扉から漏れた水圧液体に足を滑らせて，負傷した荷役作業員であった。裁判所は，ニューヨーク・プロデュース書式の第8条は荷役の責任を定期傭船者に転嫁するが，本船の貨物室扉の保守は第8条に基づき定期傭船者が負う責任の範囲内ではないこ

とに注目した。裁判所によると，甲板の状態は，本船の堪航性を損なっており，船主の責任範囲である。船主は，船長と乗組員が，問題の液体を掃除し，警告をしていなかったという過失について責任があった。そういう判決を出す際に，裁判所は，*Fernandez* v. *Chios Shipping* 事件の第2巡回区裁判所の判決に拠ったと思われる。同じ論拠が *American Home Assur. Co.* v. *Sletter M/V*, 43 F. 3d 995 (5th Cir. 1995) 事件でも採用された。その事件で，傭船者は密航者による本船の貨物損傷に対し責任があると判示された。

322 *Torres* v. *Cool Carriers*, 26 Cal. App. 4th 900, 31 Cal. Rptr. 2d 790, 1994 AMC 2690 (1994) 事件同旨。*Cooper* v. *Offshore Express*, 171 F. Supp. 1180, 1990 AMC 666 (W. D. La. 1989), 理由を付さず原審判断維持 915 F. 2d 1569 (5th Cir. 1990) 事件も参照。その事件で，傭船者は本船の航行について運航管理をしていないとの理由で，船主は本船が据付乗降階段と衝突したときに生じた人身傷害に100パーセント責任があると判示された。

The Reliant, SMA 3077 (Arb. at N. Y. 1994) 事件で，船主は，貨物の積込中に生じた人身傷害に関する荷役作業員のクレームの解決に支払った金額の補償を第8条に従って傭船者に求めた。傭船契約は New York の仲裁を規定していたが，準拠法を示していなかった。船主は，第2巡回区裁判所の問題の解釈に賛成と論じた。傭船者は，第5巡回区裁判所の方法を踏襲すべしと主張した。仲裁審は，New York で仲裁に付すとの当事者間の合意に基づいて，第2巡回区裁判所の解釈が適用されるべきであると裁定した。

Padro v. *Vessel Charters Inc.*, 731 F. Supp. 145, 1990 AMC 1664 (S. D. N. Y. 1990) 事件も参照。その事件で，裁判所が当事者の意図の証拠であるとした傭船契約には，船主は乗組員の被った一切の人身傷害に責任があるとの規定があった。

クラブ間協定

クラブ間協定は，傭船契約に摂取される場合，当事者間の契約上の合意として強制できる。

Siderius Inc. v. *The Amilla*, 880 F. 2d 662, 1989 AMC 2533 (2d Cir. 1989) 事件で，傭船契約は，ニューヨーク・プロデュース・クラブ間協定を摂取していた。第2巡回区裁判所は，本船の不堪航により船主が運送貨物の損傷に責任があると判断したが，裁判所による本協定の適用により損害賠償額の50パーセントにつき傭船者が船主に補償することを求めた地方裁判所の判決を維持した。Pratt 判事の反対意見は，傭船者は補償問題に関するその事案を提起する正当な機会を退けられたというものであるが，これは留意されるべきである。

The Finnfalcon, SMA 2873 (Arb. at N. Y. 1992) 事件で，仲裁審は全員一致で，クラブ間協定に述べられた配分に従った傭船者の分担請求を退けた。その際，仲裁審は，第8条には「船長の監督の下に」の語句に加えて「および責任」の語の特別追加はないので，固縛不良から生じる損害賠償額は，100パーセント傭船者の負担に帰すると裁定した。

The Trade Yonder, SMA 2435 (Arb. at N. Y. 1987) 事件で，傭船契約は，1970年2月のクラブ間協定を摂取していた。仲裁審は，不足損害，物理的損傷，しみ汚れの貨物クレームの解決に関して傭船者の補償請求の大半を退けた。仲裁審は，傭船契約の第8条に「責任」の語の追加修正がなかったので，クラブ間協定の下で責任は傭船者にあると裁定した。しかしながら，仲裁人は，傭船者と船主の間の不足損害責任をクラブ間協定に従い，50/50で配分した。

船主と傭船者は，荷受人によって結露クレーム，不足損害クレーム，荷扱い損傷につき訴えられた。公判の前に船主が解決し，船主が，クラブ間協定に沿って傭船者の分担を要求した。傭船者は，船主の要求を拒否し，仲裁に付されることとなった。仲裁審は，結露損傷につき傭船者は50パーセントの責任があると裁定する際に，372頁に引用のクラブ間協定の第2節を適

用した。仲裁審は，問題の結露損傷は，通風不良のみの結果でもなく，それは積付不良のみにより生じたのでもないと裁定した。仲裁審は，通風不足が結露の主要原因であると思われ，船主の過失の方が程度が大きいとあるいは結論できるかもしれないと述べたが，クラブ間協定の下では，一方が「単独で」過失あるとの「明白な証拠」がない限り，その損害賠償額は同じ分担とされる。仲裁人は，結露損傷は通風不良か，積付不良のいずれかの単独の過失のみによるのではないと考え，クラブ間協定に規定のとおり損害賠償額の同等配分が適用されねばならないと裁定した。

訴訟告知（Vouching-in）

「訴訟告知」は，コモン・ローの訴訟手続である。これによって訴訟での被告は，訴訟が係属していることを非当事者に告知し，事案の抗弁を非当事者に対し提示する。そして非当事者がその抗弁を引き継ぐことを拒否し，被告が責任ありと認定される場合，被告は，被告知者の補償を求めることを期待する。非当事者が抗弁の提示を拒否すれば，非当事者は裁判所の判決によって拘束され，その後における補償のための訴訟において第1次訴訟の決定事項を再度争うことを認められない（*Humble Oil & Refining Co.* v. *Philadelphia Ship Maintenance Co.*, 444 F. 2d 727, 735 n.14 (3d Cir. 1971))。「訴訟告知」は，第三者引込訴訟規則に広く取って代わられており，第三者を第1次訴訟で訴追できるのであれば，「訴訟告知」は，一般に利用できない。*Atlantic Richfield Co.* v. *Interstate Oil Transp. Co.*, 784 F. 2d 106, 111 (2d. Cir.)，裁量上告拒絶 479 U. S. 817 (1986) 事件を引用している，例えば *Farrell Lines* v. *Nalfleet Bull & Roberts Inc.*, 1995 U.S. Dist. Lexis 1091 (S.D.N.Y., 31 January 1995) 事件参照。対人裁判権または承諾を得られない，または第三者引込訴訟を利用できなくするその他の制限がある場合には，訴訟告知は一つの選択肢として残る。

SCAC Transport (USA) Inc. v. *The Danaos*, 845 F. 2d 1157, 1163, 1988 AMC 1827 (2d Cir. 1988) 事件で，裁判所は，「荷役業者が傭船者の賠償者である場合，権利毀損の詳細な証明なしに，荷役業者は傭船契約に基づく仲裁に［荷役業者の承諾なしに］傭船者により訴訟告知される」と判示した。さらに，裁判所は，訴訟告知を無視した荷役業者は，傭船者がその後の訴訟手続で補償を追求する事故は荷役業者の過失に起因するという仲裁人の裁定に拘束される，と判示した。

Universal American Barge Corp. v. *J-Chem. Inc.*, 946 F. 2d 1131, 1993 AMC 1888 (5th Cir. 1991) 事件参照。その事件で，被賠償者が賠償者の利益を有効に表示するのを妨げる賠償者と被賠償間の利害の対立のゆえに賠償者が訴訟告知される以前の訴訟手続で決定された問題に賠償者は拘束されないと判示された。*Marathon Int'l Petroleum Supply Co.* v. *I. T. I. Shipping S. A.*, 740 F. Supp. 984 (S.D.N.Y. 1990) 事件で，非当事者だけが原告に対して責任があるという被告の見解は，被告が仲裁で非当事者の利益を適切に保護したという被告の主張を妨害するので，裁判所は，仲裁で裁定された問題は，仲裁で被告の抗弁を引き継がなかった非当事者に対する賠償を求めるその後の訴訟で排除的効果をもたらさないと述べた。*Jamaica Commodity Trading* v. *Connell Rice & Sugar*, 766 F. Supp. 138 (S.D.N.Y. 1991) 事件で，裁判所は，「Danaos」基準を適用し，被告は，原告の賠償者ではなく，原告は仲裁で被告の利益を正当に申し立てなかったので，被告，商品販売者は，原告と海上運送人の間の仲裁の結果に拘束されないと判示した。

船荷証券（B/L）の署名

[Clause 8 continued]

"78. .... the Captain, who is to sign Bills of Lading for
79. cargo as presented, in conformity with Mate's or Tally Clerk's receipts."

[第8条続き]

「…………船長は，船荷証券の呈示がなされた場合，メーツ・レシートまたはタリー・シートの記載に基づいて，これに署名しなければならない。」

呈示された（As presented）

ニューヨーク・プロデュース書式で傭船された船舶の船長は，傭船者やその代理人により「呈示された」船荷証券に，通常署名しなければならない。

　Ellen 号は，Cardiff から Bilbao まで，コークスを運送するため傭船された。傭船契約書によれば，船長は，呈示された船荷証券に署名することとなっていた。6月30日以降到着するコークスには，輸入税の増税が予想され，船主は，この増税分が，貨物引渡時の支払運賃残額から差し引かれることを心配した。船長は，通常の書式の船荷証券に署名することを拒否し，「7月1日以前に到着しないことによって生ずる積荷関税につき，本船は責任を負わない」旨の文言を挿入することを主張した。傭船者は，そのような船荷証券を拒否し，船荷証券の署名・発行なしに，本船は出帆した。結局，増税課徴の心配は，根拠のないものと分った。船長は，通常の書式の船荷証券に署名することを拒否した点で，契約に違反していると判示された。Bramwell 卿判事は，次のように言っている。「船長は，船荷証券に署名する義務がある。ここでいう船荷証券は，通常の書式の船荷証券であり，通常の書式と異なる船荷証券まで含まない。ただし，署名を拒否する，特別の理由がある場合は別である。しかし，本件の場合，何ら特別の理由はない」（124頁）。しかしながら，傭船者は船長の船荷証券署名拒否による損害を立証することができなかったので，名目的損害賠償額が認められるにとどまった。
　Jones v. *Hough*（1879）5 Ex. D. 115.
　（*Hansen* v. *Harrold*［1894］1 Q. B. 612, *The Anwar Al Sabar*［1980］2 Lloyd's Rep. 261 と *The Garbis*［1982］2 Lloyd's Rep. 283 各事件も参照）

　しかし，どのような事情があれば，定期傭船契約に基づき船長は，船荷証券の署名を拒否できるのか，また，船長が署名を拒否できるような船荷証券に署名した結果について，裁判所は包括的な判断を下していない。
　Jones v. *Hough* 事件と前出引用の他の先例は，すべて航海傭船に関連する事案であった。定期傭船者は，船長に署名を要求する船荷証券の書式と内容を決定する大変広い権能を有する。これは，*The Nanfri*［1979］1 Lloyd's Rep. 201（同判例集332頁と486頁）事件で Wilberforce 卿により明らかにされた。その事案では，ボルタイム書式で傭船された船舶の船主たちは船長たちに「運賃前払」と記載された船荷証券に署名するのを拒否するよう指示し，すべての船荷証券に定期傭船契約の条項を摂取する条項を取り入れることに固執した。同卿は，次のように言った（同判例集206頁）。

「現在の傭船契約が定期傭船契約であると，留意することはこの点で重要である。定期傭船契約の性質と目的は，いかなる方法であれ，傭船者が適していると考える航路に傭船期間中傭船者が船舶を使用できるようにすることである。特定書式の船荷証券の発行は，傭船者の商売にとり，不可欠であり，そして実際c.i.f.またはc.&f.契約を伴う，この商売の継続には，運賃前払船荷証券の発行が不可欠である。さらに定期傭船契約については常にそうであるが，第9条は，船長が船荷証券に署名することから生じるあらゆる結果または責任に対する補償条項を含む。このことは，本船を利用する過程で，どんな船荷証券が商売にふさわしいかを決定し，船主は補償条項により保護されているとして，船長にそういう船荷証券の発行を指図する傭船者の権能を強調する」。

傭船契約以上の責任を船主に課する船荷証券

船荷証券の約款が，定期傭船の船主に定期傭船契約上の責任以上の加重された責任を課している場合でも，その船荷証券が呈示されれば，当然船長は一般的に署名を拒否できないということになる。しかし，船主は，加重された責任について（明示または黙示の）補償により傭船者に求償する権利がある（*The Island Archon* [1994] 2 Lloyd's Rep. 227（C. A.）事件参照）。

契約違反

傭船契約条項と船荷証券の約款との間の不一致に関する指導的判例は，大部分航海傭船に関するものである。傭船契約上船主が認めている責任を加重するような船荷証券に署名することを，傭船者が船長に要求すれば，それは傭船者の契約違反になるという見解が，指導的判例の多くによって支持されている。傭船契約より重い責任を船主に課す場合とは，例えば，傭船契約上免責されている特定の危険について，船荷証券上免責が規定されていないような場合をいう。

  Invermore 号の船主は，傭船契約を締結したが，その契約に基づき，船主は，船長の過失に対する責任を免除されていた。傭船契約は，さらに，船長は，「この傭船契約の条項に反することなく，積荷に対する無故障船荷証券に署名すべきものとする」と規定していた。傭船者は船荷証券を呈示し，船長は，これに署名した。当該船荷証券は，傭船契約条項を摂取しているかに見えたが，過失条項を有効に摂取していなかった。船長の過失により，本船，積荷共に滅失したが，その結果，船主は，船荷証券に過失条項が摂取されていれば免責される責任を，船荷証券所持人から追及された。控訴院および貴族院は，「船主は，船荷証券所持人に支払った金額を傭船者に対して求償する権利を有する」と判示した。
  Kruger v. Moel Tryvan [1907] 1 K.B. 809 (C.A.) および [1907] A.C. 272 (H.L.).

控訴院および貴族院が，船主の傭船者に対する求償を認めるに際して，もっとも重視した根拠は，傭船者は，そのような船荷証券を呈示した点で，契約に違反しており，それゆえ，船主は，損害賠償の権利を有するというものであった。同様の見解は，その後における航海傭船に関する判例によって明らかにされている。それらの判例の中には，*Elder Dempster* v. *Dunn* (1909) 15 Com. Cas. 49（不正確な荷印を表示した船荷証券）事件の貴族院の事案や，*Dawson Line* v. *Adler* (1931) 41 Ll.L. Rep. 75（船荷証券が，現実の貨物の重量より少ない重量を示しており，運賃は，その少ない重量により支払われた）事件の控訴院の判決がある。

黙示の補償

  上記諸判例が，選択的にまたは，それ自体を根拠としたもう一つの理由は，傭船契約と船荷証券との間に矛盾があれば，黙示の求償権が生じるということである。Bingham判事は，*The*

C. Joyce [1986] 2 Lloyd's Rep. 285 事件で，上記二つの貴族院事案の判決の根拠に決定的であることは，「傭船者が傭船契約に基づき呈示の権限を有する船荷証券と，実際に呈示した船荷証券の相違を発見することであった」との見解を表明した。それは，控訴院が *The Nogar Marin* [1988] 1 Lloyd's Rep. 412（同判例集420頁）事件で支持した。Bingham 判事は，続けて次のように述べた。「この認定から自然に結論が導かれる。船主が，損害補償がその算定基準である契約違反の損害賠償を請求するのか，あるいは船主が，傭船契約上の義務ではない傭船者の要求に応じたため生じた損失による損害補償を請求するのかは，重要な問題ではない」。

この解説は，航海傭船契約の事案に適しているが，定期傭船契約の事案では，必ずしも適しているとは言えないとされる。船長が呈示した船荷証券に署名するのを求める定期傭船契約の通常の書式の場合では，傭船者が，傭船契約より負担が大きい約款を有する船荷証券を，船長の署名のために呈示しても，一般的には契約違反とはならない。署名のためにそのような船荷証券を呈示することで，「傭船契約に基づく船主の義務ではないことをすることが」船主の義務となるということはできない。それは，（傭船契約の明示の条件の範囲内で）「いかなる方法であれ，傭船者が適していると考える航路に傭船期間中船舶を傭船者が使用できるようにすること」(*The Nanfri* [1979] 1 Lloyd's Rep. 201 事件の Wilberforce 卿（同判例集206頁））である通常の定期傭船契約の目的にまったく反している。さらに，それは良識に反している。ヘーグ・ルールまたはその国内法を摂取していない標準傭船契約書式の場合を考えて見ると，傭船契約に基づき発行される大抵の船荷証券は，明示的にヘーグ・ルールを摂取している点で，またはその船荷証券は，船積国または予定仕向国の国内法によりヘーグ・ルールに強制的に従わせられるので，その船荷証券は傭船契約条項と相当に異なるものとなることは避け難い。そうなると，契約違反の観点から，または契約に基づかないまたは不適切な船荷証券の呈示の観点から，この問題を捉えることは正確であるとは言えない（*The Paros* [1987] 2 Lloyd's Rep. 269（同判例集273頁）事件参照）。本書の旧版で表明されたこの見解は，前出355頁に事実経緯が述べられている *The Island Archon* [1994] 2 Lloyd's Rep. 227 事件で控訴院が支持した。控訴院は，補償は法の問題としてまたは商業上の効力の問題としてそのような状況では黙示されていると判示した（Staughton 判事による *The Nogar Marin* [1987] 1 Lloyd's Rep. 456 事件（同判例集460頁））。前出引用の *The Nanfri* 事件の Wilberforce 卿の弁論の一節に言及して（同判例集233頁），Evans 卿判事は，次のように続けた。

「傭船契約と異なる運送の契約条件を含む船荷証券に署名を求めて呈示することによって傭船者が契約違反となるということではなく，船荷証券は，積込貨物の外観状態については正確であるものの，傭船契約に従って考えられる範囲外であると言いうる条件を満たしていないという前提で，船長が署名を拒否するなら，船長は船主を契約違反にするであろうという状況は，したがってしばしば生じる。そういう場合に補償を受ける黙示の権利は生じるのか。私の判断では，*Sheffield Corporation v. Barclay* [1905] A.C. 392 事件で創設された一般法則に沿って黙示の権利が生じないという理由は原則として存在しない」。

これが，ニューヨーク・プロデュース書式の定期傭船契約に基づく見解であるということは，*The Caroline P* [1984] 2 Lloyd's Rep. 466（後出388頁参照）事件の関係者に受け入れられたが，Neill 卿判事は当事案が，契約違反に基づいて扱われる可能性を拒否した（同判例集475頁参照）。船荷証券は，傭船契約以上の面倒な責任を船主に課するので，船主は黙示の補償の利益を受ける権利があるというのは，関係者の間の共通の意見であった（船主は大きく修正したGencon傭船契約に基づき補償を受ける権利がないと判示された航海傭船の事案 *The C. Joyce* [1986] 2 Lloyd's Rep. 285 事件を比較）。しかしながら，問題は貴族院でなお検討され

なければならない。

Kruger v. *Moel Tryvan*〔1907〕A.C. 272事件で，大法官Loreburn卿は，次のような言葉で，黙示の補償を説明した。すなわち，「船主は，船長の航海過失免責という立場で，貨物の運送を引き受けたが，傭船者は，船荷証券により，船主が責任を負うべきものとした。したがって，船主に適当な補償を与える義務が，傭船者に生じる」。

明示の補償

定期傭船契約が明示の補償規定（ボルタイム書式71行から74行参照）を有する場合，その効果は，一般的にいって黙示の補償がある場合と同様である。

328　*Port Victor*号の定期傭船契約は，船長，船員の過失免責任を定めていた。さらに，「船主は，傭船者，その代理人が定めた運賃率の船荷証券に，本傭船契約の権利を害することなしに署名しなければならず，傭船者は，船長が傭船者の指示に従ったことおよび船荷証券に署名したことから生じる結果につき，船主に対し補償することを合意する」との規定もあった。過失免責約款のない船荷証券が呈示され，船長が署名した。そのため，船主は，船長の過失により生じた衝突の結果発生した共同海損分担金を荷主から回収することができなかった。控訴院は，船主は，共同海損分担金回収不能による損害を，傭船者から回収する権利を有すると判示した。

Milburn v. *Jamaica Fruit*〔1900〕2 Q.B. 540.
(*The Nanfri*〔1979〕1 Lloyd's Rep. 201事件も参照)

状況如何によっては，黙示の補償の範囲のほうが，明示の補償の範囲より，事実上広いことがあり得る（*Strathlorne Steamship* v. *Andrew Weir*（1934）50 Ll.L. Rep. 185事件と前出386頁参照）。しかし，また，より狭くなる状況もあり得る（*The Island Archon*〔1994〕2 Lloyd's Rep. 227（C.A.）（同判例集230頁）事件参照）。

NYPE 93

ニューヨーク・プロデュース書式1993年改訂版の第30条(b)項は，「いかなる船荷証券または海上貨物運送状も，本傭船契約を侵害してはならず，傭船者は，本傭船契約と自己またはその要請により船長が署名した一切の船荷証券または海上貨物運送状との間の不一致から生じるすべての結果または責任について，船主に補償する」と規定している。前出14頁の英文書式311/314行と58頁参照。

補償請求が生じるとき

補償請求の開始時期を知ることは，請求期限がいつになるかを知る意味で重要である。請求が定期傭船契約に基づく船主の黙示の補償のような黙示の一般的補償に基づく場合，開始時間は裁判所の判決またはその他により責任の確定があって，はじめて開始する。補償請求開始時間如何は請求が明示の補償に基づく場合，補償を責任に対する補償（その場合，開始時点は責任が発生する時点である）として解するのかまたは一般的補償として解するのかに拠るであろう。

*Caroline P*号は，ニューヨーク・プロデュース書式で傭船された。第8条は，積込や積付と同様に揚荷について傭船者に責任ありと修正された。船荷証券が呈示され，船長に代わって署名された。これにより，船主は船荷証券の譲受人にこの荷役作業につき責任を負うこととなった。譲受人がイラク

裁判所で提起した訴訟で船主はこの作業中に生じた貨物の減失損傷につき,責任ありと判示された。船主の傭船者に対する補償請求につき責任が最初に発生した揚荷時から時間が開始するのか,責任が最初に確定したイラク裁判所の最初の判決の日から開始するのかという問題が生じた。この状況では,船主のための補償は,傭船契約に黙示されているということが当事者間の共通の意見であった。Neill 判事は,黙示の補償は船長が船荷証券に署名した結果に対してであるが,一般的補償である補償は,責任がイラク法廷で最初の判決により確定するまで,強制できないと判示した。
The Caroline P [1984] 2 Lloyd's Rep. 446.
(ボルタイム書式の第9条に基づく明示の補償につき,後出640頁参照)

異常な性質の条件または傭船契約と「明らかに矛盾している」条件

異常な性質の条件または傭船契約と「明らかに矛盾している」条件を含む船荷証券に船長が署名する義務はないと言われている。Halsbury 卿が,*Kruger* v. *Moel Tryvan* [1907] A.C. 272事件で次のように述べた(同判例集282頁)。「船長は呈示された一切の船荷証券に署名しなければならないと言われることには,私は同意できない。呈示された船荷証券が,明らかに傭船契約と不一致である場合に,私は……拒否するのが船長の義務であると考える」。Dunedin 卿は,*Tillmanns* v. *Knutsford* [1908] A.C. 406事件で,「異常な性質」を有する規定について次の一節で述べた(同判例集410頁)。

「船長が署名を拒否するほどの異常な性質の規定を船荷証券が記載している場合,傭船者の署名が船主を拘束するかという問題に関する抗弁は船主と傭船者に等しく開かれている」。

(後出395頁参照。*The Berkshire* [1974] 1 Lloyd's Rep. 185 (同判例集188頁), *The Vikfrost* [1980] 1 Lloyd's Rep. 560 (同判例集567頁), *The Garbis* [1982] 2 Lloyd's Rep. 283 (同判例集287頁) 各事件も参照)

船荷証券の条項が傭船契約の条項と異なるという事実は,それ自身少しも重要ではない。船長が署名を拒否できるのは,船荷証券の条項が傭船契約で禁じられているか,または傭船契約の大意に反しているとの意味で,船荷証券の条項が異常,または傭船契約と「明らかに矛盾している」場合のみである。

傭船契約と「明らかに矛盾」しているので,船長が船荷証券に署名拒否できる場合に,傭船者もその代理人も船長に代わり署名する権限を持たないことは,*Tillmanns* v. *Knutsford* 事件から引用された一節と *The Vikfrost* 事件(後出397頁参照)における Browne 卿判事の判決からも黙示されている。しかしながら,ある状況では,彼らは船荷証券署名のための表見代理権を持つと見なされることもある(前出119頁および後出399頁参照)。

仕向港が傭船契約の航路定限外にある船荷証券

船長は,傭船契約上の航路定限外にある港を仕向港として指定した船荷証券に署名することを拒否する権利を有するが,おそらく,拒否する義務もあると思われる。MacKinnon 卿判事は,*Halcyon Steamship* v. *Continental Grain* (1943) 75 Ll.L. Rep. 80 事件で,次のように指摘している。「航路定限は,……保険協会担保航路定限であって,オランダより北は含まない。傭船者がアメリカで貨物を船積し,Copenhagen あるいは Danzig で貨物を引き渡す船荷証券を船長に呈示した場合,船長が,……その署名を拒否することはもちろん正当である」。

傭船契約により要求される条項を摂取していない船荷証券

　定期傭船契約が明文をもって，その傭船契約に基づき発行する船荷証券に摂取されるべきものと規定している条項が，呈示された船荷証券に摂取されていない場合，船長は，おそらく，その署名を拒否できると思われる。例えば，ニューヨーク・プロデュース書式の第24条により要求される条項が，同書式に基づき発行される船荷証券に含まれていない場合である。

　しかし，船荷証券が，リーエン条項のような定期傭船契約の他の条項を摂取していない，または定期傭船契約の条項を全般的に摂取していないという理由で，船長は，署名を拒否できない。*The Nanfri* [1979] 1 Lloyd's Rep. 201 事件で，Wilberforce 卿は，次のように述べた（同判例集206頁）。「船主が船荷証券に定期傭船契約の条項を摂取するように記載することを要求できないのは，明らかであるに違いない。そのような要求は，傭船契約の商業的全目的に反する」（後出「運賃前払船荷証券」の項をさらに参照）。

貨物の状態につき不実記載のある船荷証券

　船長は，現実に損傷のある（あるいは，受領していない）貨物について，外観上良好な状態でこれを受け取ったことを認める船荷証券に，署名することを拒否する権利と義務を有する。

330　貨物を検査し，船荷証券が確実に船積時の外観状況を反映するようにする船長の義務からして，傭船者が損傷貨物に無故障船荷証券を呈示し，船長，または船主の代理人が署名する場合，通常，船主のための黙示の補償はないということになる。

> *Nogar Marin* 号は，Gencon 書式で1航海，傭船された。コイル状の鉄棒を積載完了して，船長が署名した無故障メーツ・レシートが，傭船者により，または傭船者の代理人により呈示された。実際には，コイルのいくつかは，錆びており，積込前に貨物を検査した船長は，錆に言及せずに署名した点で，過失があった。その結果，本船の代理人は，無故障メーツ・レシートの効力を頼って，船長に代わって無故障船荷証券に署名した。それゆえに，船主には船荷証券に基づく荷受人に対する責任が生じた。船主の傭船者に対する補償の請求について，控訴院は，請求は，認められないというStaughton 判事と仲裁人の決定を維持した。その理由は，次のとおりであった。
> (1) 傭船者は，傭船契約の黙示の条件に違反していない。貨物を適切に検査し，その外観状態をメーツ・レシートまたは船荷証券に記録する責任は船長にあるので，傭船者またはその代理人が貨物の状態を正確に記載しているメーツ・レシートまたは船荷証券を呈示しなければならないという黙示の条件はない。
> (2) いずれにしても，たとえ傭船者がある黙示の義務に違反したとしても，貨物の状態を適正に点検し，メーツ・レシートに制限を付け，船荷証券への書き入れ要求することを船長が怠慢により履行しなかったことにより，因果関係の連鎖は充分に断ち切られた。
> (3) 船主のための補償は黙示されていない。船荷証券に署名する前に貨物の状態を確認する船長の義務は，業界で周知されており，傭船者の無故障船荷証券の船長への呈示を，将来発生しうるクレームに対する補償と引換に船荷証券に無故障で署名することを求める黙示の要請と解釈することはできない。
> *The Nogar Marin* [1988] 1 Lloyd's Rep. 412.

　ニューヨーク・プロデュース書式の下では，船荷証券は，メーツ・レシートに記載された，外観上良好な状態を根拠とする免責約款を，必ず含んでいなければならない。しかし，メーツ・レシートに損傷の記載がないからと言って，船長は，損傷貨物に対する無故障船荷証券に署名することを要求されるものではないと言われている。なぜなら，船長の一般的義務は，そ

れが船荷証券の善意の譲受人の権利に強く影響するものだけに，優先すべきだからである。日付違い船荷証券の事案である The Almak [1985] 1 Lloyd's Rep. 557 事件で，Mustill 判事は，「呈示された船荷証券に署名する義務は，もちろん虚偽記載の船荷証券に船長が署名することまでも要求できるものではない」と述べた（同判例集561頁）。

補償を受ける権利の喪失

船長が，貨物の損傷を知りながら，傭船者の求めにより，無故障船荷証券に署名した場合には，船主は，その船荷証券の譲受人に対して負うべき責任に関し，傭船者から受けなければならない補償の権利を喪失するものと思われる。後出 Brown Jenkinson 事件を参照。そして，船長が船積時の状態を検査するのに不注意であり，損傷貨物について無故障船荷証券を発行するのに注意深い判断を欠くときにも，船長はその権利を喪失することがある。というのは，船長の過失が船主の損失の近因であると判示されることがあるからである。前出 The Nogar Marin 事件参照。しかし，貨物の状態につき真性な紛争がある場合，または外観上の欠陥が些細である場合には，船長は，無故障船荷証券への署名を正当化できるかも知れない。

Titania 号の船主代理人は，明らかに欠陥のある樽に入った貨物について，外観上良好な状態で船積された旨の無故障船荷証券に署名した。その無故障船荷証券は，荷送人の補償状と引換に発行された。船主は，受荷主からのクレームを支払い，補償状に基づき補償を求めた。控訴院は，船主は，代理人を通して，荷送人と結託し詐欺を行ったものであるから，その補償状は，荷送人に対して強制力がない，と判示された。この船荷証券は，虚偽の表示がなされており，その船荷証券を手中にしたもの（受取人や銀行）が，その虚偽の表示を信頼することを知りながら発行された。

(裁判所は，補償状との引換の無故障船荷証券の発行も，例えば，貨物の状態，包装について善意の争いがあるか，欠陥が微々たるものである場合のような特定の限定された情況の下では，妥当であることを認めている)

Brown Jenkinson v. *Percy Dalton* [1957] 2 Lloyd's Rep. 1.

不正確な日付の船荷証券

The Almak [1985] 1 Lloyd's Rep. 557 事件で，Mustill 判事は，船長は不正確な日付の船荷証券に署名する義務はないという確固たる見解を表明した。同判事は，次のように述べた（同判例集561頁）。「船長は，日付の相違に気がついた場合には，いつでも拒否する権利がある。相違に気がついたが，それでも署名するのを選択した場合，船主は，次の理由で補償の権利を喪失するであろう。(i)真実を知りながら，不正確な船荷証券に署名する決定は署名の要請とその結果生じる損失との間の因果関係の連鎖を断ち切る。または(ii)署名行為は「コモン・ロー上の補償」という……黙示の権利の対象から本事案を外すほどに「それ自身明らかに不法」である（前出 The Nogar v. Marin 事件参照）。

船積貨物の数量または性質を誤表示している船荷証券

船荷証券は実際に船積された物品を記載すべきであり，不正確と判る貨物の明細を含むべきではないというのが，黙示の要件である（後出 The Boukadoura 事件参照。前出 The Almak と The Nogar Marin 事件参照)。

Boukadoura 号は，STB 航海傭船書式で航海傭船された。傭船契約の第20条(a)項（STB 定期傭船契

約第20条(a)に類似している)は、「船荷証券は、呈示された船長が署名し、……傭船者は傭船者またはその代理人の提供した書類の不備……から生じる……あらゆる結果につき船主に補償するものとする。」と規定していた。船長が実際に船積した量よりも多いと主張した（結局正確であると判明した）ある量の石油の船荷証券を傭船者は、呈示した。船長は船荷証券の署名について責任を限定する留保を付けようとした。しかし、傭船者はこれを受諾するのを拒否し、本船は貨物を再検量する間、遅延した。Evans 判事は、船長は船荷証券の署名を拒否する権利がある、積み込んだ量に関する船荷証券の不正確さは、第20条(a)項の意味の範囲で「不備」であり、船主は傭船者から遅延の結果発生する損失を回収できると判示した。

The Boukadoura ［1989］1 Lloyd's Rep. 393.

艙内積と誤って表示する船荷証券

船長は、貨物が艙内積ではないことを知っているときは、艙内積を表示する船荷証券に署名してはならない義務がある。

NYPE 93

ニューヨーク・プロデュース書式1993年版第30条(c)は、「甲板積貨物に対する船荷証券には、『傭船者、荷送人および荷受人の危険、費用および責任で甲板上に船積した。それによって生ずる一切の滅失、損傷または遅延につき、本船または船主の側に責任を課さない』旨の条項が挿入されねばならない」と規定している（前出14頁の英文書式の315/317行と58頁参照）。

デマイズ条項（demise clause）を含む船荷証券

The Berkshire ［1974］1 Lloyd's Rep. 185 事件で、船荷証券上のデマイズ条項（demise clause）は「異常な条項」（前出389頁参照）であって、傭船者が、かかる条項を記載した船荷証券を署名のため、船長に呈示すること自体、違法であるから、かかる船荷証券に署名したからといって、船主自身拘束されることはないという議論が展開された。これに対して、Brandon 判事は、次のように言っている。「率直に言って、この議論は理解し難い。デマイズ条項（demise clause）が果たす役割は、その船荷証券が船主の船荷証券であることを明白な文言で書き記すことに尽きる。傭船契約は、傭船者がその種の船荷証券を船長に対して呈示し、船長に船主の代理人として署名させるか、傭船者自身が、船主の代理人として署名する権限を傭船者に与えている。どうして、デマイズ条項（demise clause）が、……異常な条項であるということができるのか。それは、異常どころか、きわめて当たり前の条項である」。

The Vikfrost 事件（後出参照）で、船舶の再定期傭船者の代理人は、デマイズ条項を含む船荷証券を発行する権限を黙示したと判示された。原定期傭船契約は原傭船者に再傭船する選択権を与え、同じような形式でデマイズ条項付きの船荷証券を発行するのを許していた（The Jalamohan ［1988］1 Lloyd's Rep. 443 事件参照）。

「運賃前払」船荷証券

船長は、「運賃前払」船荷証券に署名するのを通常拒否しないし、傭船契約に基づき支払うべき金額につき運賃または再運送賃上に船主がリーエンを有する権利を有効に表現するために傭船契約のリーエン条項を船荷証券に摂取することを要求しない。

Nanfri 号は，他の2隻とともにボルタイム書式に類似の傭船契約に基づき，同じ傭船者と契約された。傭船者は，傭船料からある控除をしたが，船主は傭船者に控除の権利はないと主張した。船主が抗議し，紛争を仲裁へ付託すると言及したにもかかわらず，傭船者はさらに控除をした。それについて船主は3隻の船長に次のように指示した。(a)船長に代わって船荷証券を発行・署名する権限を引き揚げること。(b)呈示された「運賃前払」船荷証券に署名するのを拒否すること。(c)リーエン条項を含む定期傭船契約の条項を摂取する条項を付加してすべての船荷証券が裏書されることに固執すること。傭船者は，五大湖の穀物取引に船舶を使用しており，その取引では定期傭船契約の条項に言及せずに「運賃前払」と船荷証券に記載するのが通常であった。しかしながら，船主は，船長に船荷証券に署名するのを拒否するよう指示する権利があると主張した。その署名はボルタイム書式第18条の「本契約に基づく一切の請求権につき，定期傭船者のすべての積荷，再傭船料，および船荷証券上の運賃に」リーエンを有する船主の権利を損なうかも知れないのである。

貴族院は，控訴院と Kerr 判事（この点において）を支持し，傭船契約の（第9条）使用条項に基づき，傭船者は，船長が定期傭船契約の条項につき，一言も触れない「運賃前払」船荷証券に署名するのを要求できると判示した。船主はリーエンの権利を否定されるかも知れないが，補償の権利により保護された。

The Nanfri ［1979］1 Lloyd's Rep. 201.
（前出385頁と後出563頁も参照）

外国の裁判管轄条項を含む船荷証券

傭船契約が契約上の紛争をある国の仲裁に付すことを求める裁判管轄条項を含むという事実のゆえに，紛争を異なる国の仲裁または法廷に持ち込むことを求める裁判管轄条項を含む船荷証券に，船長が署名するのを拒否する権利を持つことにはならない。そういう船荷証券は，傭船契約に「明らかに矛盾する」ものではない。傭船者またはその代理人は，そういう条項を含む船荷証券を発行する権限を黙示的に持っている。

Vikfrost 号は，傭船契約上の紛争はノルウェー法に従って，仲裁により Oslo で決定されると規定する原定期傭船契約に基づき貸船された。本船は，London 仲裁条項を含む再傭船契約で再傭船された。英国法に準拠し，紛争は他の一切の国の法廷の管轄を排除して英国の高等法院に付託されると規定する船荷証券を，再傭船者の代理人は船長に代わって，署名発行した。控訴院は，再傭船者の代理人は，そういう船荷証券を発行署名する権限があると判示した。Brown 卿判事は，次のように述べた（568頁）。「……傭船契約の裁判管轄条項と船荷証券の裁判管轄条項に矛盾はない。傭船契約は，傭船契約に基づく船主と傭船者間の紛争は，Oslo で仲裁に付託されると規定している。このことは，異なる契約に基づく異なる当事者間——船主と船荷証券所持者——の紛争は当地の高等法院で決定されるという船荷証券の規定と矛盾しない」。

The Vikfrost ［1980］1 Lloyd's Rep. 560.
（本事案の詳細について，後出398頁参照。*The Paros* ［1987］2 Lloyd's Rep. 269事件も参照）

傭船契約上の権利を侵害することなく

定期傭船契約の中には，船荷証券は，「傭船契約上の権利を侵害することなく」署名されなければならないと規定するものがある。この文言は，船長に傭船者が呈示した船荷証券に船主が署名する義務に影響を与えるものではない。それは，傭船契約に含まれる船主と傭船者間の契約は（たぶん）異なった条件の船荷証券の署名により影響を受けないままであることを意味しているに過ぎない（*Hansen* v. *Harrold* ［1894］1 Q. B. 612事件，*Turner* v. *Haji Goolam* ［1904］A. C. 826事件，*The Nanfri* ［1979］1 Lloyd's Rep. 201 事件（同判例集206頁）参照）。

NYPE 93

ニューヨーク・プロデュース書式1993年版第30条(b)項は、「いかなる船荷証券または海上貨物運送状も、本傭船契約を侵害してはならず、傭船者は、本傭船契約と自己またはその要請により船長が署名した一切の船荷証券または海上貨物運送状との間の不一致から生じるすべての結果または責任について、船主に補償する」と規定する（前出14頁の英文書式の311/314行と58頁参照）。

署名の効果；船主のあるいは傭船者の船荷証券

船長自身が署名した船荷証券

傭船契約が本船の賃貸借（デマイズ）にならない場合は、通常（後出611頁参照）、その一般原則は、船荷証券により証明される契約は船主とのものであり、傭船者とではない。Channell判事による *Wehner* v. *Dene Steam Shipping* [1905] 2 K.B. 92事件（同判例集98頁）。

コモン・ローに基づき、船長は、船主に代わって、船荷証券に署名する通常の、あるいは一般的権限を有する。船長が署名する場合、例外的状況を除き、船荷証券は船主を拘束する（*Tillmanns* v. *Knutsford* [1908] 2 K.B. 385, *Wilson* v. *Andrew Weir* (1925) 22 Ll.L. Rep. 521, *The Rewia* [1991] 2 Lloyd's Rep. 325 (C.A.) 各事件参照）。さらに、船主が、船長の一般的権限を制限した場合でも、船荷証券所持人が、その制限を知らない限り、船主は、船長がその一般的権限内で発行した船荷証券に拘束される。

> Boston City 号の定期傭船契約には、「船荷証券に署名するにあたり、船長は、傭船者の代理人として署名するに過ぎないことを、ここに明白に合意する」という珍しい条項が含まれていた。船長が署名した船荷証券は、傭船契約のすべての条項を、明示をもって摂取していた。しかし、船荷証券の譲受人は、傭船契約を見たこともないし、問題の条項も知らなかった。控訴院は、船荷証券によって証される契約は、船主との間に存在する旨判示した。Lopes卿判事は、次のように指摘した。「『非常に明白で誤解の余地のない文言が』、記載されていない限り船荷証券所持人は、船長が、船長の資格において、その通常の権限を行使して船荷証券に署名していると当然信じ、かつ考えるものである」。
> *Manchester Trust* v. *Furness, Withy* [1895] 2 Q.B. 539.

船主と締結する契約は、定期傭船者の利益のために結ばれるのであって、定期傭船者の代理人としての船長および船主と結ばれるものではない。そういう契約に基づき、船荷証券の運賃を回収する権利があるのは、定期傭船者ではなく、当然船主であるということになる。もちろん、船主は、傭船契約に基づく未払傭船料を減額した後で、傭船者に返還する義務がある（後出560頁参照）。

しかしながら、船長の署名で、傭船者が拘束されることもありうる。しかし、それは、船荷証券の文言および客観状況により、船長が、船荷証券に署名するに際して、船主を拘束する自己の一般権限を行使したのではなく、単に傭船者の代理人としてのみ、署名したことがきわめて明らかな場合に限られる。

> Lindenhall 号の船主は、本船を Edward Perry & Co. に定期傭船に出した。その傭船契約には、ボルタイム書式のそれと同じような使用条項および補償条項が含まれていた。米国から日本向け石油運送の船荷証券は "Edward Perry & Co.'s Steamship Line" と頭書のある書式で作成され、貨物の明細および支払われるべき運賃の記載がある、荷送人 Standard Oil Co. と傭船者間の運送契約を引用していた。船長は、この船荷証券に署名した。Walton 判事は、船長の署名にもかかわらず、荷送人の運送契約は、四囲の状況に照らし、本船の船主とではなく、傭船者との間で締結されたと判示した。

船荷証券（B/L）の署名   395

Samuel v. *West Hartlepool Steam Navigation*（1906）11 Com. Cas. 115.

　Harrison v. *Huddersfield Steamship*（1903）19 T. L. R. 386 事件で，船長は傭船者の代理人であり，船長は船主に代わって船荷証券契約を締結する権限はないという協定が船主と傭船者の間で交わされた。船荷証券に印刷してある「船長として as Master」の語句は削除され，代わって「定期傭船者の代理人として」との語句が書き込まれた。船荷証券は，船主を拘束しないと判示された（*Elder Dempster* v. *Paterson, Zochonis*［1924］A. C. 522 事件（後出要約，臨時の傭船の船長により署名された有名な定期船会社の船荷証券に関する事案），*The Venezuela*［1980］1 Lloyd's Rep. 393 事件と *The Rewia*［1991］2 Lloyd's Rep. 325（C. A.）事件参照）。

船荷証券の約款に基づく受託者としての船主
　船長が傭船者の代理人として船荷証券に署名したものとされるからといって，それだけで船荷証券の約款が船主と荷主との間に適用されないというわけではない。

　Elder, Dempster 社は，西アフリカ航路の自社船隊を補強するため，Griffiths Lewis が所有する *Grelwen* 号を傭船した。「African Steamship Company and the British and African Steam Navigation Company. Managers, Elder Dempster & Company」との名前を冠した船荷証券が，やし油に対して発行され，船長は，その船荷証券に「P. Bedford, Agent」として署名した。やし油の樽は，その上積みとなった袋詰めのやし核によって押し潰された。船荷証券上，運送人は，積付不良については免責されていたが，不堪航については免責されていなかった。荷主（Paterson, Zochonis）は，船主，定期傭船者およびその管理する会社2社を訴えた。Rowlatt 判事は，運送契約は，船主との間のものではなく，African Steamship Company との間で結ばれたものであると判示した。(1922) 12 Ll.L. Rep. 69 事件は上級審に持ち込まれたが，この点の判断は争われなかった。
　貴族院は，Rowlatt 判事および控訴院の判決を破棄して，次のように判示した。貨物の損害は，不堪航よりむしろ，積付不良に起因するものであり，したがって，African Steamship Company と本船船主は共に，船荷証券の免責約款を援用する権利を有する。船主は，運送契約の当事者ではないが，そのような権利を有する。
　Elder, Dempster v. *Paterson, Zochonis*［1924］A. C. 522.

　船主は，自らが当事者ではない船荷証券の免責約款を援用する権利を有するとの判決の正当性については，多々議論がなされてきたが，*Midland Silicones* v. *Scruttons*［1961］2 Lloyd's Rep. 365 事件で，貴族院は，上記判決は，船長が船荷証券に署名することにより，船主は，船荷証券の約款に基づき，受託者として貨物を受け取ったことになるという理由でのみ，支持されうるに過ぎないと判示した（*Morris* v. *Martin*［1965］2 Lloyd's Rep. 63, *The Eurymedon*［1974］1 Lloyd's Rep. 534, *The Kapetan Markos N. L.*（*No. 2*）［1987］2 Lloyd's Rep. 321. 各事件参照）。

335　上記事案は，*The Pioneer Container*［1994］2 A. C. 324（件名別称 *The K. H. Enterprise*［1994］1 Lloyd's Rep. 593）事件で，枢密院が検討した。当事案では，貨物は，運送のすべてまたはその一部を「いかなる条件でも」下請契約する権限のある原契約運送人が発行した船荷証券に基づき船積されており，船荷証券の当事者ではないが，貨物の所有者は再受託者としての実際運送人が発行した他の船荷証券の約款に拘束されると判示された。実際運送人が依拠する排他的管轄条項は，原契約運送人に貨物の所有者が与えた広い権限外であると見なされるほどに不当なまたは異常なものではなかった。
　下請契約する権限は，その事案では明示されていたが，それは黙示されたり，または表見的

に授権されることもありうる（Lloyd's Report の602頁参照。Bell [1995] LMCLQ 177 も参照）。

傭船者またはその代理人が署名した船荷証券

船長は使用と代理権に関して傭船者の命令と指図に従うというニューヨーク・プロデュース書式77行と連結して，船長は，呈示された船荷証券（as presented）に署名しなければならないという，78行，79行目の規定は，傭船者またはその代理人に対して，船長の代理人として船荷証券に署名する権限を一般的に認めている。The Berkshire [1974] 1 Lloyd's Rep. 185 事件で，Brandon 判事は，この文言について次のように述べている（同判例集188頁）。「傭船契約における［ニューヨーク・プロデュース書式第8条］のような条項の効果は，既に十分確立されている。すなわち，第1に，同項により傭船者は，船長が船主の代理人として船荷証券に署名するよう船長に対して船荷証券を呈示する権限を取得する。かかる船荷証券は，その中に，異常な，あるいは，明らかに傭船契約と矛盾する約款を含まない限り，荷送人と船主間の契約の証となるか，その契約そのものに相当するものとなる。したがって，かかる船荷証券が呈示されれば，船長は，船主の代理人として署名しなければならない。第2に，傭船者は，船主の代理人としての船長の署名を得るべく船荷証券を船長に呈示する代わりに，傭船者自身が船主の代理人として，船荷証券に署名することができる。船長が傭船者の指示により署名しようと，問題を単純化して傭船者自身が署名しようと，いずれの場合であっても，署名により，船主は，船荷証券に表象されるか，船荷証券によって証される契約の本人として，その契約に拘束される。上記のような解釈の判例は，Tillmanns & Co. v. S. S. Knutsford, [1908] 2 K.B. 385；[1908] A.C. 406事件で示されている」。

The Berkshire 事件において，船長は，事実上傭船者の代理人に対して，船荷証券署名権を明白に与えていた。このように，船主または船長の現実の授権がある場合，その授権が，傭船契約上の特定の条項に基づくものであれ，傭船契約署名後の当事者間の合意によるものであれ，傭船者または，その代理人が船主を拘束しうることについて疑問の余地はない。しかしながら，上記 Brandon 判事の判断は，船長による明示の授権に根拠を置いていない。権限は定期傭船契約の標準の条項に通常黙示されていると思われる。

Knutsford 号は，Watts, Watts & Co. of London へ定期傭船された。傭船期間中に，Vladivostock 向け貨物を Middlesbrough と London で積載した。3通の船荷証券は，10月12日の日付で船長自身が署名した。10月26日付の4通目の船荷証券（たぶん London 積貨物）は，Watts, Watts & Co. が「船長と船主に代わって For the Captain and Owners」署名した。傭船契約には，船長は「使用，代理または他の手配に関して傭船者の命令と指図に従う」と規定され，さらに傭船者は，「傭船者または，その代理人の指示に基づき，船長が船荷証券に署名したことから生ずるすべての結果または責任につき船主に補償する」と規定されていた。

船主は，傭船者の署名した船荷証券に拘束されないと主張したが，控訴院の Channell 判事（Vaughan Williams 卿判事は疑問とはしたが）は貴族院の全員一致で，船主は傭船者の署名した船荷証券に船長自らが署名した船荷証券と同様に拘束されると判示した。Kennedy 卿判事は，控訴院 [1908] 2 K.B. 385（同判例集406頁）で次のように述べた。

「船主と船長に代わってなされたものとしての署名の権限を否定する言辞を［船主］が口にすることはない。船主自身が，船長が傭船者の指図に従って行為することに契約により合意しているからである。したがって，船主と船長に代わって傭船者が行った署名は，貨物を船積した荷送人により船主が訴えられた際には船主が否認できない署名として取り扱わねばならない。なぜなら船主は証券への署名を指示する権利を契約の明白な文言で傭船者に付与していたからである。そして，船主は船長および船主自身の双方に対して，その両者またはその一方に代わって，署名する権限を傭船者に対して

付与していたと暗黙裡に理解されねばならない」。
　　Tillmanns v. *Knutsford*〔1908〕A.C. 406.

　上記事案で船長が自らに代わって船荷証券に署名することを暗黙裡に承認していたのかも知れないというある提言があるが（L.C.（1908）A.C. 408頁の大法官 Loreburn 卿の発言参照），それにもかかわらず，判決の明確な理由は権限は傭船契約の条項から黙示されるべきであるということである。

　傭船契約が再傭船の選択権を含んでいる場合には特に，船長に代わって船荷証券に署名する再傭船者またはその代理人の権限は，また原定期傭船契約の同じような条項で黙示される（*The Vikfrost*〔1980〕1 Lloyd's Rep. 560 事件参照，そして前出392頁と後出398頁参照）。

ボルタイム書式

　ボルタイム書式の第9条に，船長が呈示された船荷証券に署名するものとするという規定はないが，船長は使用と代理に関して傭船者の指図に従い，傭船者は，船長または代理人が船荷証券に署名した結果について船主に補償するものとするということは，明記されている。したがって，前出 *Tillmanns* v. *Knutsford* 事件の先例に基づき，ボルタイム書式の下での見解は，ニューヨーク・プロデュース書式の下と同様である（*LEP International* v. *Atlanttrafic Express Service*（1987）10 N.S.W.L.R. 614 事件の Clarke 判事の判決も参照）。

タンカー傭船契約

　いくつかのタンカー傭船契約において，船荷証券の署名に関する見解は明確に詳細に説明されている。例えば STB 書式の第20条(a)項には，次のように規定されている。

　　「船荷証券は呈示どおりに船長により署名されるものとし，……しかし，傭船者の選択により，傭船者またはその代理人が，船長に代わって船荷証券に署名することもできる……」。

NYPE93

　ニューヨーク・プロデュース書式1993年改訂版第30条(a)項は，「船長は，……船荷証券または海上貨物運送状に署名しなければならない」と規定し，さらに続けて「ただし，傭船者は，事前に船主から書面による権限を受け，常にメーツ・レシートまたは検数人のタリー・シートに従って発行される船荷証券または海上貨物運送状に，船長に代わって署名することができる」と規定している（前出14頁の英文書式の308/310行と58頁参照）。事前の書面による権限という明示の要件は，それがない場合には，こういう権限は黙示されないことを示すものと理解される。

船主を拘束する船荷証券

　傭船者またはその代理人（またはその復代理人：前出 *The Berkshire* 事件および *LEP International* v. *Atlanttrafic Express Service* 事件参照）が「船長に代わって（for the master）」署名した船荷証券は，ほとんど常に船主を拘束するものとみなされる。

337　*Wilston* 号は，傭船者の指示に基づき船長が船荷証券に署名するという規定のある定期傭船契約によって傭船された。「River Plate 向け共同配船，Andrew Weir & Co. 代理店，Turner Morrison & Co. Ltd……」と頭書された船荷証券が発行され，定期傭船者 Andrew Weir の代理店である Turner

Morrison が, 船荷証券に署名した。Andrew Weir は, 船荷証券に基づくクレームを支払った後, 船主に対し補償を求めた。船主は, 船荷証券の当事者は自分であって, 定期傭船者ではないとの理由で, 補償金の支払を拒絶した。船荷証券の本文には, 定期傭船者のことを指していると思われる「The Company」という文言があったが, 他方では, 「本船の船長, 船主あるいは代理店 master, owners or agents of the vessel」という文言もあった。Roche 判事は, 船荷証券は, 「船長に代わって (for the master)」署名されているから, 船主との契約を証するものであり, Andrew Weir との契約を証するものではないと判示した。

Wilston v. *Andrew Weir* (1925) 22 Ll.L. Rep. 521.

(前出 *Tillmanns* v. *Knutsford* 事件および前出 *The Berkshire* 事件, *Kaleej International* v. *Gulf Shipping Lines* (1986) 6 N.S.W.L.R. 569 (C.A.) 事件も参照)

傭船契約の航海で船荷証券は, 船長に代わって傭船者の代理人が署名し, Salen の船荷証券にあるデマイズ約款, または類似のデマイズ約款を含むことができるという条件に基づいて, *Vikfrost* 号は, 船主により Salen に定期傭船された。Salen のデマイズ約款には, 本船が, 船荷証券を発行する会社により所有またはデマイズ傭船されていない場合, 船荷証券は本人としての船主またはデマイズ傭船者と契約した効力を生じるものとすると規定されていた。傭船契約には, また使用と補償条項があり, 船長は呈示された船荷証券に署名しなければならなかった。

再傭船の選択権に基づき, Salen は Lauritzen に再傭船に出した。Lauritzen の復代理人は, 船長に代わって Laurtizen の頭書の入った船荷証券に署名した。この船荷証券には, Salen のデマイズ約款に類似した条件のデマイズ約款があった。

Mocatta 判事と控訴院は, 再傭船者の代理人は, 船主を拘束する船荷証券に署名する黙示の権限を有すると判示した。原傭船契約は, 船荷証券に挿入される条項に何ら制限を課しておらず, デマイズ約款を含める自由を与えていた。さらに原傭船契約は, 明示的に再傭船を許可しており, 船主は, 再傭船者が再傭船契約に基づき, 船長が船荷証券に署名することを要求する権利があること, あるいは, 船長に代わって再傭船者が船荷証券に署名する権利があることを予期していたに違いない。

The Vikfrost [1980] 1 Lloyd's Rep. 560.

(船荷証券に英国管轄約款を挿入することについて, 前出393頁参照)

実際に, Leggatt 卿判事は, 後出 *The Rewia* 事件で次のように判示した。「契約が傭船者のみと結ばれ, 署名する者が署名する権限を有し, かつ船主ではなく傭船者にまさしく代わって署名しない限り, 船長に代わって署名された船荷証券は傭船者の船荷証券ではありえない」。

Rewia 号は, 船長は呈示された船荷証券に署名するものとすると第8条に通常どおり規定されるニューヨーク・プロデュース書式で傭船された。傭船契約にはさらに, 「船長は, 傭船者またはその代理人に船長に代わって船荷証券に署名する権限を授与する」と規定された。再傭船者の名前とその管理者の名前を付けた定期船荷証券が, 再傭船者により, 発行された。船荷証券は「船長に代わって (for the Master)」代理人により発行された。貨物所有者は, 管轄についての紛争で, 船荷証券が定期船形式で傭船者により発行され, 荷送人が本船が傭船されていることを知らない場合, 契約に明確な反対の文言がなければ, 船長の代わりに署名された船荷証券は, 傭船者を拘束する, と主張した。

控訴院はこの主張を退けて, 船荷証券は船主との契約の証拠であると判示した。Leggatt 卿判事は, 次のように言った (333頁)。「正当な解釈によれば, 代理人が……船荷証券に船長に代わって署名したのであり, 船長は呈示された船荷証券に署名することを要求されるのだから, 船長は代理人に署名する権限を授与する権限を与えられており, かつ署名する権限を授与したと理解されなければならない」。

The Rewia [1991] 2 Lloyd's Rep. 325 (C.A.).

時には, Leggatt 卿判事が述べた例外的な方法で船荷証券が署名され, 船荷証券に表象され

る契約は船主ではなく傭船者を相手にしているという異常な結果となることがある。次の事案において，本船は，自社船隊による定期航路のサービスの補充船腹として傭船されたが，再傭船者は「船長に代わって」ではなく，本人として自身のために署名した。

　Ruggiero di Flores 号と *Okehampton* 号とが衝突した。その後の訴訟で，*Ruggiero di Flores* 号の再定期傭船者として，MacAndrews は，本船積貨物に対する船荷証券上の運賃を取得する権限を，有するか否かが問題となった。貨物の果物は，スペイン諸港で積み込まれ，MacAndrews が占有していた。MacAndrews は，自社船によりスペイン諸港からの定期配船を運営していたが，*Ruggiero di Flores* 号は，その定期配船の補強として傭船されていた。MacAndrews は，無条件で自己の名義で船荷証券の署名をした後，その写2通を荷送人に引き渡し，1通を自社の Hamburg 駐在員に送付した。Hamburg 駐在員は，本船から貨物を引き取り，船荷証券の呈示と引替に，その被裏書人に対して，貨物を引き渡すことになっていた。

　控訴院は，船荷証券は，MacAndrews との間の運送契約を証明するものであり，船主との運送契約を証明するものではない旨，判示した。
　The Okehampton [1913] P. 173.

　さらに，特定の船荷証券の明示の条件が（たとえ署名されても）契約は船主以外の誰かが相手であることを非常に明確にしているので，この意図が傭船者またはその代理人が「船長のために」署名する通常の効果を無効にするという事態が時折生じることがある。

　Samjohn Governor 号の船主は，ボルタイム書式で傭船者に本船を傭船に出した。傭船者は，日本から南アフリカへの定期航路を運航している会社に本船を再傭船に出した。日本の再傭船者の代理人は，再傭船者の通常の定期船荷証券を発行した。船荷証券の裏には，再傭船者と共同運航の相手方である他の会社の頭文字があり，どちらであれ「運送人」としての運航者であるという内容の運送人同一性約款を含んでいた。デマイズ約款も，またその他本船が定期傭船されていることを示すものもなかった。「船長により，または船長に代わって署名する（signed by or on behalf of Master）」という印刷語句の下に，代理人はインクで署名した。その署名の下には，印刷された横線があり，それから再傭船者の頭文字と「総代理人および船長の代理人として（general agents and as agents for the Master）」の代理人の名前があった。海事法廷の Sheen 判事は，船主でなく再傭船者が船荷証券の当事者であると判示した。同判事は，仮に誰が契約当事者であるかを示すものが代理人の署名以外に何も船荷証券には存しない場合，前出 *Tillmanns* v. *Knutsford* 事件の先例より，当事者は船主であるということを受け入れるであろうと述べた。しかし，船荷証券の内容から明らかに運送人として契約しているのは再傭船者一人であり，船荷証券に拘束されるのは再傭船者であった。
　The Venezuela [1980] 1 Lloyd's Rep. 393.

船主を拘束する傭船者の表見的権限

　船舶を定期傭船に出している船主が，傭船者またはその代理人に対し，船荷証券を用意することから，それに「船長に代わって（for the master）」として署名することまで委ねることが実務上，現在広く行われている。船主が自己の船舶を定期傭船に出し，傭船者の運航に委ねている場合，現在では明示の規定がなくても，船主は，傭船者やその代理人に対して，自らに代わって船荷証券に表象される契約を締結する権限を与えたものと解されることは間違いない。ただし，船主が，これに反する趣旨の特段の処置を，積極的に取っている場合は事情を異にする。かくして，傭船者や，その代理人は，真実の権限に関係なく，船主を拘束する表見的権限を有することになろう。

　Nea Tyhi 号は，ニューヨーク・プロデュース書式で1航海傭船された。追加条項により，傭船

者，または船長を含むその代理人が船荷証券に署名することによって生じる責任に関して傭船者による船主に対する明示の補償が与えられていた。

本船は，合板を甲板に積載したが，合板に雨水による損傷が生じた。船荷証券は傭船者の代理人が発行し，船長に代わってその代理人が署名した。船荷証券にはタイプで「艙内積」と記載された。傭船者の代理人はその書式で船荷証券を発行・署名する権限を有しないので，この船荷証券に基づく合板の受荷主に対する責任は船主にはない，と船主は主張した。

Sheen 判事は，傭船者の代理人は甲板積貨物について「艙内積」船荷証券を発行し，署名する実際の権限を有しないが，その代理人は表見的権限を有するので，船主は船荷証券に拘束される，と判示した。

The Nea Tyhi [1982] Lloyd's Rep. 606.

上記事案は，次のことを例証している。傭船者やその代理人が，署名のために船長に船荷証券を呈示せず，自らが船荷証券に署名することによって生じる一つの問題は，船長が拒み得たか，あるいは拒むべきでさえあった船荷証券の署名を，傭船者やその代理人はなしうるということである。他の例で言えば，傭船者やその代理人は，傭船契約上の航路定限外の港向けの船荷証券にすら署名することができる。このような署名が，傭船者やその代理人が船主から与えられている実際の権限（明示あるいは黙示の）を超えるものであることに，疑問の余地はない。しかし，よくあるように，傭船者やその代理人が，船主に代わって船荷証券に署名する一般的権限を授けられていると推定される表見上の権限を有する場合には，現実に権限がないことを知らされていない荷送人あるいは船荷証券所持人に対する関係では，船主は当該船荷証券に拘束される。

米 国 法

メーツ・レシート (Mate's receipts)

　貨物積込後に，通常一等航海士が発行するメーツ・レシートは，本船が貨物を受け取ったことを認めるものであり，それにより貨物の管理，注意義務は，運送人へ移転する (*Continental Grain Co.*, v. *American Commercial Barge Line Co.* 332 F. 2d 26 (7th Cir. 1964); *E. T. Barwick Mills Inc.* v. *Hellenic Lines Ltd.*, 331 F. Supp. 161 (S. D. Ga 971), 原審維持 472 F. 2d 1406 (5th Cir. 1973) 各事件参照)。
　メーツ・レシートに合致しない船荷証券の発行の結果を議論する後出事案参照。

船荷証券 (Bill of lading)

　船荷証券は，海上貨物運送に関して，(1)権原証券，(2)物品受取証と(3)運送契約を含む多様な機能を果たす。貨物が傭船者に所有されている場合，傭船契約は運送契約として作用し，船荷証券は権原証券および受取証として機能する (*The Fri*, 154 F. 333 (2d Cir. 1907))。しかしながら，貨物の所有者が，第三者である場合，船荷証券は運送契約の証として作用する。

船荷証券の署名

　一般海事法に基づき，船長は船主を代理して船荷証券を発行し，署名する権限を有する。*The Schooner Freeman*, 59 U. S. 182 (1856) 事件で最高裁は，この基本原則を述べた。

　　海事法に基づき，誠実に，かつ船長としての表見的権限の範囲内で船長と結ばれた運送契約は……そういう契約の履行のために本船を商品に拘束するというのが，われわれの意見である。

　船荷証券に署名する船長の権限は，本船の使用と商売に関した事柄について船主を拘束する船長の権利に由来する (*Pope* v. *Nickerson*, F. Cas. No. 11, 273 (C. C. D. Mass. 1844)。一般に *The Flash*, F. Cas. No. 4, 857 (S. D. N. Y. 1847) 事件を参照。*The Aurora*, 14 U. S. (Wheat. 1) 96 (1816); *Bulkley* v. *Naumkeag Steam Cotton Co.*, 65 U. S. 386 (1860); *Instituto Cubano de Est. Del Azucar* v. *The Golden West*, 246 F. 2d 802, 1957 AMC 1481 (2d Cir. 1957), 裁量上告拒絶 355 U. S. 844 (1957); *Gans S. S. Line* v. *Wilhelmsen*, 275 F. 254, 262 (2d Cir. 1921), 裁量上告拒絶件名別称 *Barber & Co.* v. *Wilhelmsen*, 257 U. S. 655 (1921))。
　しかしながら，異常な明示の指図がない限り，船長の権限は無制限ではない。例えば，船長は故意に偽造船荷証券に署名することによる詐欺に船主を拘束する権限はない (前出 *The Schooner Freeman* 事件，前出 *Pope* v. *Nickerson* 事件参照)。前出 *The Schooner Freeman* 事件で裁判所が注目したように，船長が署名し発行した船荷証券を受け取る当事者は，「署名の真性と署名者は本船の船長であるという事実の真性の危険だけでなく，船荷証券を発行する船長の表見的権限の危険を負担する」。他人の表見的権限に基づいて行為する当事者の事案におけるように，船長から船荷証券を受領する当事者は船長の権限が依拠する事実を確認する義務がある (*Yeramex Int'l* v. *The Tendo*, 595 F. 2d 943, 944, 1979 AMC 1282, 1283 (4th Cir. 1979); *The Senicoll Sierra*, SMA 2966 (Arb. at N. Y. 1993))。

船長自身が署名した船荷証券

　船主の代理人として船長が署名した船荷証券が，船主と船荷証券所持人との間の契約を証するものであることは言うまでもない。Aljassim v. The South Star, 323 F. Supp. 918, 922, 1971 AMC 1703, 1707 (S. D. N. Y. 1971) 事件で次のように判示されている。

　　賃貸借ではなく，傭船された船の船長が発行した船荷証券が証する契約は，本船の契約であり，船荷証券を発行させた傭船者の契約でもあり，また，自己の権限ある代理人としての船長が船荷証券を発行した船主の契約でもある。

　また Gans S. S. Line v. Wilhelmsen, 275 F. 254, 262-263 (2d Cir. 1921)，裁量上告拒絶件名別称 Barber & Co. v. Wilhelmsen, 257 U. S. 655 (1921) 各事件参照。

傭船者またはその代理人が署名した船荷証券

　傭船者は自らのために発行した船荷証券に基づく物品の運送人として責任がある (Mente & Co. v. Isthmian S. S. Co. (The Quarrington Court), 36 F. Supp. 278, 1940 AMC 1546 (S. D. N. Y. 1940)，原審維持 122 F. 2d 266, 1941 AMC 1234 (2d. Cir. 1941). Glynwed Steels Ltd. v. Great Lakes and European Lines Inc., 1979 AMC 1290 (N. D. Ill 1978) 事件も参照)。

　しかしながら，傭船者が，船長の署名もなく，船主名も記載されていない船荷証券を発行しても，船主自身は，その船荷証券につき責任を負わない (United Nations Children's Fund v. The Nordstern, 251 F. Supp. 833 (S. D. N. Y. 1965)；Tube Products of India v. The Rio Grande, 334 F. Supp. 1039, 1971 AMC 1629 (S. D. N. Y. 1971) 各事件参照)。傭船者が，「船長に代わって for the master」として，船荷証券に署名しても，船長または船主が，現実に傭船者に対して署名権限を与えていないかぎり，または契約当事者として船主を船荷証券に拘束する表見的権限を傭船者に付与していないかぎり，船主自身は責任を負わない (前出 Yeramex Int'l v. The Tendo 事件。Demsey & Associates v. The Sea Star, 461 F. 2d 1009 (2d Cir. 1972) 事件参照。Ross Industries Inc. v. The Gretke Oldendorff, 483 F. Supp. 195, 1980 AMC 1397 (E. D. Tex. 1980)；Excel Shipping Corp. v. Seatrain Int'l, 584 F. Supp. 734, 1986 AMC 1587 (E. D. N. Y. 1984)；Pacific Employers Ins. Co. v. The Gloria, 767 F. 2d 229 (5th Cir. 1985)；Commercial Metals v. The Luckyman, 1994 AMC 673 (E. D. Pa. 1993))。

　ニューヨーク・プロデュース書式は，明確に傭船者に船荷証券を発行する権利を付与し，船長が「呈示された」船荷証券に署名することを求めている。米国法の下で，傭船者の呈示した船荷証券に署名する際に，一般的海事法の下で伝統的によくあることであるが船長は船主の代理人としてではなく，厳密に傭船者の代理人として署名することになる。したがって，傭船者の船荷証券に船長が署名することは，傭船者を拘束できるだけでなく，状況如何では単に傭船者だけを拘束することがある。

　前出 Yeramex Int'l v. The Tendo 事件で，貨物の取扱または船荷証券の約款によっても，船主が「船長に代わって for the master」発行された傭船者の船荷証券の当事者であると誤って荷送人またはその他の第三者に無理なく信じさせることができなかったであろうという理由で，傭船者に船主を船荷証券に拘束する実際の権限はなく，また船主を拘束する表見的権限も存在しない場合，船主自身は，契約当事者として対人的責任を負わない，と判示された。

[341] 船長は傭船契約に基づく義務の履行に際し「1人2役を演ずる」との，上記377頁で議論し

た考え方に基づき，裁判所はその決定を下した。傭船契約は船主を船荷証券に拘束する権限を傭船者に与えたと判示し，船長が実際に傭船者に対して，船長に代わって船荷証券に署名する許可を与えたかどうかにつき，事実の再審理を求めて差し戻した Thyssen Steel Co. v. M/V Kavo Yerokas, 50 F. 3d 1349（5th Cir. 1995）事件と，船主は傭船者の船荷証券に拘束されると判示した Pacific Employers Ins. Co. v. M/V Gloria, 767 F. 2d 229（5th Cir. 1985）事件を比較されたい。

Centennial Insurance Co. v. Constellation Enterprise, 1987 AMC 1155（S. D. N. Y. 1986）事件で，裁判所は，船主は船荷証券に基づく「運送人」ではないという理由で船主に対する貨物損傷クレームを却下した。船荷証券は，船荷証券に基づく契約運送人は傭船者であると明示的に規定している，傭船者が用意した書式で印刷された。船荷証券は，傭船者が船荷証券の発行に際して「船長に代わって」代理人として行為すると記載しているが，傭船者が運送人として船主を拘束する権限を有するとの証拠はなかった（Sail America v. The Prosperity, 778 F. Supp. 1282, 1992 AMC 1617（S. D. N. Y. 1991）事件同旨）。

同様に Mahroos v. The Tatiana L, 1988 AMC 757（S. D. N. Y. 1986）事件で，傭船者が貨物のメーツ・レシートとまったく矛盾する船荷証券を発行した場合，船主は傭船者の発行した船荷証券に基づく対人的責任を負う運送人ではないと判示された。メーツ・レシートは，貨物の大半は積込前から損傷していたことを示していたが，船荷証券は貨物が積込前から損傷していたことに触れておらず，「無故障の状態で船積」されたことを記載していた。傭船契約は，傭船者が船主の代わりに船荷証券を発行することを授権されていると明確に規定している特別条項を含んでいるが，その条項はこの権限を「メーツ・レシートに従って」発行される船荷証券に制限していた。裁判所は，傭船者が実際に行った方法で船主の代わりに船荷証券を発行する権限はなく，したがって船主は COGSA に基づき訴えることができる運送人ではないと判示した（Tuscaloosa Steel Corp. v. The Naimo, 1993 AMC 622（S. D. N. Y. 1992）事件同旨）。

The Tulsa, SMA 2794（Arb. at N. Y. 1991）事件で仲裁審は，傭船者は積付が適切でなく，固縛された貨物が舷外へ流失したことに責任ありと裁定した。傭船者はメーツ・レシートに合致しない無故障船荷証券を発行したために，傭船契約に違反した。それゆえに，傭船者はすべての貨物クレームについて船主に補償することを求められた。船荷証券は，(1)貨物の真の状態を記載するメーツ・レシートの注記を摂取しておらず，(2)貨物が「甲板上に」積み付けられたことを表現していなかった。

Procter & Gamble v. The Fraser, 1992 AMC 1575（E. D. La. 1991）事件で裁判所は，傭船契約が傭船者の代理人に船長に代わって船荷証券に署名することを授権していない場合，船主は船長に代わって署名された船荷証券に拘束されないので，船主は COGSA に基づく運送人ではないと判示した。しかしながら，それでも船主の傭船者に対する堪航性の担保違反を理由として，裁判所は貨物の所有者が船主から直接に汚損貨物の損害賠償額を回収することを許容した。

S. A. Cockerill v. The Kyung Ju, 1983 AMC 1517（M. Da. Fla. 1982）事件で裁判所は，傭船者に船主に代わって船荷証券の発行を授権する原傭船契約は，その趣旨の特段の規定がない場合，再傭船者にまでその権限を拡大しないと判示した。

船主は，船長または正当な権限を有する自己の代理人が，現実に署名した船荷証券によってのみ契約上拘束されるのであるが，船舶は，船荷証券が傭船者によって発行されても，貨物損害について対物的責任を負う。British West Indies Produce Inc. v. The Atlantic Clipper, 353 F. Supp. 548, 1973 AMC 163（S. D. N. Y. 1973）事件で，本船がヤムイモを積載し，西インド諸島から New York へ向う航海中，貨物が損傷を受けた。船荷証券は，傭船者が発行した

ものであり，船長の署名は**なかった**。裁判所は，貨物損害につき，本船は対物的責任を負うと判示して，次のように述べた。

　本船が，Atlantic Lines, Ltd. に傭船されていたことは，本船の責任を左右するものではない。また，それは，船長が船荷証券に署名しなかったことの帰結でもない。いったん，汽船 Atlantic Clipper 号が，受荷主の貨物を積んで出帆した以上，その船荷証券は，追認されたこととなる（1973 AMC at 170）。

　しかしながら，本船側は，弁護士費用をも含めた全部の損害額を，貨物の積込，積付を管理していた傭船者から回収できると判断された。
　いったん，貨物が船長了承の下，本船に積まれた以上，本船は対物的責任を負うことになる。この瞬間，本船と貨物が一体化するわけである。さらに船長が傭船者の船荷証券の約款を知らなくても，本船は対物的責任を負う。船長は船荷証券の約款を知っているとの推定を受けるからである。*The G. A. Tomlinson*, 293 F. 51, 52 (W. D. N. Y. 1923). 前出 *Demsey* 事件と *Cactus Pipe & Supply Co.* v. *The Montmartre* 756 F. 2d 1103, 1113, 1985 AMC 2150, 2161-2163 (5th Cir. 1985) 事件も参照。

　Insurance Company of North America v. *The American Argosy*, 732 F. 2d 299, 1984 AMC 1547 (2d Cir. 1984) 事件で裁判所は，船舶の船主または傭船者からの授権なしでは NVOCC（非船舶運航公運送人）が発行した船荷証券に基づいて船舶が対物的責任を負うことはないと判示した。裁判所は，船主が航海に対して自己の船荷証券を発行し，被告の船舶が良好な状態での貨物引渡後の別の運送人による継続運送中に貨物損傷が発生したことに注目した。

中間の定期傭船者

　しかし，それでは，貨物を成約しない，あるいは自分自身の船荷証券を発行しない「中間の」定期傭船者とは何か。中間の定期傭船者は貨物の滅失または損傷について運送人として責任があると判示されるのか。*Thyssen Steel Corp.* v. *The Adonis*, 364 F. Supp. 1332, 1974 AMC 389 (S. D. N. Y. 1973) 事件では，本船は Adonis から Teseo へ定期傭船に出され，Teseo は，Atlantic と再航海傭船契約を締結した。Thyssen は，貨物損害につき，Teseo に対し訴訟を提起した。Teseo は，その貨物につき船荷証券を発行していなかったのであるから，貨物の損害に対し責任がないと判示して，裁判所は，次のように述べている。

　　COGSA の下においては，荷主と運送契約を締結した運送人のみが，運送品の適切かつ慎重な積込，取扱，積付，運送，保管および揚荷の義務を有する。当該船荷証券は，Atlantic の書式に則り，同社の代理人によって発行された。訴訟において，Teseo が Atlantic またはその代理人に，Teseo に代わって船荷証券に署名し，発行することを授権したことを示す証拠は提出されなかった。航海傭船契約上，船長は船荷証券署名権を与えられていたけれども，記録によれば，船長は船荷証券に署名していないし，また，船長が Atlantic や，その代理人に，自らに代わって署名することを授権したことを示す証拠も提出されなかった。したがって，Teseo は，Thyssen と運送契約を締結しなかったのだから，Teseo は COGSA の下における運送人ではない……（1974 AMC at 393）。

　裁判所はまた，荷主は Adonis と Teseo 間の傭船契約の第三受益者として，Teseo に対して求償することができるとの主張を退けた。その傭船契約によれば，Teseo は，積込，積付に対し責任を負うこととなっていた。裁判所は，Adonis と Teseo 間の定期傭船契約の第8条が

「Thyssenを含む海運界の利益のために挿入された」(同上)という証拠はないとした。
　Yasuda Fire and Marine Ins. Co. v. *The Indian City*, 1981 AMC 1451 (M. D. Fla. 1980) 事件で裁判所は*Thyssen*事件を踏襲した。裁判所は誰が船荷証券を発行したのかだけでなく，誰が運送人の義務を履行したのかも考慮すべきであると判示した (*Hyundai Corp. USA* v. *Hull Ins. Proceeds of The Vulca*, 800 F. Supp. 124, 1993 AMC 434 (D. N. J. 1992)，原審維持 54 F. 3d 768, 1995 U. S. App. Lexis 11714, (3d Cir., 11 April 1995) 事件参照。*Joo Seng Hong Kong Co.* v. *The Unibulkfir*, 483 F. Supp. 43 (S. D. N. Y. 1979) 事件同旨)。
　Glynwed Steels Ltd. v. *Great Lakes and European Lines Inc.*, 1979 AMC 1290 (N. D. Ill 1978) 事件でも裁判所は，この責任理論は，COGSAの明白な意図と矛盾すると述べて，荷送人の第三受益者クレームを退けた。裁判所によると，船主ではなく傭船者が運送人であり，かつCOGSAは，運送人は本船の堪航性を維持することに相当の注意を尽くす義務がある当事者であると規定しているので，COGSAは荷送人を船主の傭船者に対する堪航性担保の受益者として扱う第三受益者理論を適用することを排除する。
　United Nations Children's Fund v. *The Nordstern*, 251 F. Supp. 833 (S. D. N. Y. 1965); *The Muskegon*, 10 F. 2d 817 (S. D. N. Y. 1924); *The Blandon*, 287 F. 722 (S. D. N. Y. 1922); The *Poznan*, 276 F. 418 (S. D. N. Y. 1921) 各事件参照。しかし先に論じた*Procter & Gamble* v. *The Fraser*事件も参照。

船荷証券の追認

　ある状況では，船荷証券が船長またはその正当な権限を有する代理人により署名されない場合でもその船荷証券が有効となることがある。*The Blandon*, 287 F. 722, 723-724 (S. D. N. Y. 1922) 事件で裁判所は，いったん貨物を本船に積載して出帆した場合には，船長は傭船者の発行した船荷証券を追認したとみなされると判示した。裁判所によると，いったん本船が抜錨すると「……船荷証券に傭船者だけが署名しているにもかかわらず，船荷証券は船舶の義務と貨物の特権の尺度となる」。
　The G. A. Tomlinson, 293 F. 51 (W. D. N. Y. 1923); 前出 *The Muskegon*; 前出 *United Nations Children's Fund* v. *The Nordstern*; *Tube Products of Indian* v. *The Rio Grande*, 334 F. Supp. 1039, 1041 (S. D. N. Y. 1971); *Cavcar Company* v. *The Suzdal*, 723 F. 2d 1096, 1984 AMC 609 (3d Cir. 1983) 各事件も参照。
　しかしながら，「非船舶運航公運送人」(「NVOCC」) が関与した事案で，いくつかの裁判所は，傭船者とNVOCCを区別し，上記で論じた追認理論は授権されていない船荷証券がNVOCCによって発行された場合には，適用されないと判示した。船舶は授権されていない船荷証券に基づいて生じたクレームについて対物責任はないと判示した前出 *Insurance Co. of N. A.* v. *The American Argosy*事件を引用した *Ultimo Cabinet Corp.* v. *The Mason Lykes*, 1991 AMC 1343 (S. D. N. Y. 1991) 事件を参照。*The Mason Lykes*事件で裁判所は，船荷証券は船主の理解または同意なしで発行されたと判示し，船主および対物的訴訟での船舶に対する貨物損傷クレームを却下した。

不堪航または不法行為について貨物所有者に対する船主の直接責任

　ある事案で船主が運送契約の当事者でない場合に，貨物所有者は不法行為と思われるクレームについて船主側の責任を確定するのに成功した。*The Poznan*, 276 F. 418 (S. D. N. Y.

1921）事件で裁判所は，船主は傭船者が署名した船荷証券に基づく責任はないが，船主が本船に離路を命じ，それによって傭船者の契約履行を妨害した場合，船主は責任ありと判示した。(*Sunil Industries* v. *The Ogden Fraser*, 1981 AMC 2670 (S. D. N. Y. 1981) 事件も参照)。

Siderius v. *The Amilla*, 880 F. 2d 662, 1989 AMC 2533 (2d Cir. 1989) 事件で裁判所は，判例法に具体化された「海事法の確立した法則」に言及して，船主が傭船者に対する堪航性の担保に違反した場合，貨物所有者は船主から直接に回収できると判示した (*Procter & Gamble* v. *The Fraser*, 1992 AMC 1575, 1582 (E. D. La 1991) 事件同旨。*New York Cent. R. R.* v. *New York, N. H. & H. R. R.*, 275 F. 2d 865, 866 (2d. Cir. 1960); *S. C. Loveland Co.* v. *Eastern States Farmer's Exch.*, 92 F. 2d 180, 181 (3d. Cir. 1937), 裁量上告拒絶 302 U. S. 762 (1937); *Davis* v. *Dittmar*, 6 F. 2d 141, 142 (2d. Cir. 1925) 各事件参照)。

船主が貨物運送契約の当事者でない場合，船主は契約に基づき利用できる責任制限の免責を享受できない。例えば，COGSAに規定する責任の抗弁は船主が「運送人」でない限り，利用できない。*Toho Bussan Kaisha Ltd.* v. *American President Lines*, 265 F. 2d 418, 1959 AMC 1114 (2d Cir. 1959) 事件で，COGSAの第3条(6)項に基づき適用される1年の出訴期限は運送契約から生じるクレームに関してのみ作用すると判示された。前出 *Sunil Industries* v. *The Ogden Fraser* 事件で同様に裁判所は，船主は運送契約の当事者でないゆえ，1年のCOGSA制限期間は船主に対するクレームについて適用されないと判示した (*Bunge Edible Oil Corp.* v. *The Torm Rask*, 756 F. Supp. 261, 266, 1991 AMC 1102, 1109 (E. D. La. 1991), 原審維持 949 F. 2d 786, 1992 AMC 2227 (5th Cir. 1992), 裁量上告拒絶 120 L. Ed. 2d 875, 112 S. Ct. 2998 (1992) 事件参照)。船主がCOGSAの「運送人」でなくとも，船主には一般海事法の下で認められている抗弁の利益があり，責任制限法 (46 USC 183等) に基づき責任を制限する権利を有する。

呈示された

船長は「呈示された」船荷証券に署名する義務を傭船者に対して負う。*Field Line (Cardiff) Ltd.* v. *South Atlantic S. S. Line*, 201 F. 301, 304 (5th Cir. 1912) 事件で裁判所は，「船長が船荷証券に署名するものとするとの傭船契約の規定は船長が署名する単なる権限だけでなく，船荷証券に署名しなければならないという合意であり，違反すれば船主に責任が生じる」(*The Misphah*, F. Cas. No. 9648 (D. Del. 1878) 事件 (航海傭船の事案) も参照)。

The Pacbaron, SMA 2660 (Arb. at N. Y. 1990) 事件で仲裁審で，船長には呈示された船荷証券に署名する義務があると裁定した。船荷証券にヘーグ・ルールへの言及がなければ，船主は保険填補を失うと感じたので，ソビエト連邦の海運法典への言及は削除されるべきであると船主は固執したのであるが，仲裁審は，船主が本船を約4日間引き止めたことに正当な事由はない，と裁定した。仲裁審によると，船主には同法典に関する情報を即時に確認する義務，または別途の抗議文を出すとともに，船荷証券に署名する義務がある。

傭船契約以上の責任を船主に課する船荷証券

傭船者が呈示した船荷証券に署名する船長の義務は，仮に船荷証券が傭船契約と矛盾する場合，または船主が傭船契約よりも大きな責任に問われる場合でも，適用される。しかしながら，傭船契約が船荷証券は傭船契約上の権利を毀損してはならないと明示しているか否かにかかわらず，その状況の下で船主は，被った損失について傭船者に対して補償の権利を有する。

例として前出 Field Line (Cardiff) Ltd. v. South Atlantic S. S. Line ; Kennedy v. Weston & Co., 136 F. 166 (5th Cir. 1905) 各事件参照。

しかしながら，傭船者は自分が呈示するいかなる船荷証券にも船長が署名することを要求する絶対的権利を有するということではない。例えば，船長には，実際に積み込まれていない貨物の船荷証券，または許容された航路定限外の揚荷港を指定する船荷証券に署名する義務はない (The Alonzo, F. Cas. No. 257 (D. Me. 1869) ; The Loch Rannoch, 192 F. 219 (D. Me 1911), 原審維持 208 F. 884 (1st Cir. 1913) 各事件参照)。受取の際に貨物が良好な状態でないことを船長が知った場合には，船長は，また「無故障」船荷証券に署名するのを拒否できる。さらに，船荷証券が，第三者を拘束するとされており，船長がその第三者を運送契約の当事者でないと知っている場合には，船長は船荷証券に署名するのを拒否できる (Ramsay Scarlett & Co. Inc. v. The Koh Eun, 462 F. Supp. 277, 286-287 (E. D. Va. 1978) 事件参照)。船長は，また白紙の船荷証券に署名する権限を有しない (The Joseph Grant, Fed. Cas. No. 7538 (D. Wis. 1857) 事件参照)。

The Ocean Dove, SMA 2750 (Arb. at N. Y. 1991) 事件で仲裁審は，不一致点が小さなものであれ，メーツ・レシートと矛盾する船荷証券に署名することを船長が拒否することは不当ではないと判示した。したがって，遅延期間についての傭船者のオフハイヤー請求は否定された。

The Hans Leonhardt, SMA 2820 (Arb. at N. Y. 1991) 事件で，単独仲裁人は，船長は当該貨物であるプラスティック箔の紙の一部のみが積み込まれたに過ぎないことに気づいたので，船長が無故障船荷証券に署名するのを拒否したことは，正当であると裁定した。

The Exi, SMA 2709 (Arb. at N. Y. 1990) 事件で仲裁審は，船長は貨物に虫がついているのを記載していない無故障船荷証券の発行を強制されることはありえないと裁定した。

The Phassa, SMA 2650 (Arb. at N. Y. 1990) 事件で仲裁審は，陸上の測定は，本船に積み込まれた原油の量を正確に反映していないと船長が結論づけるのに十分な理由があるので，疑わしい陸上の測定に基づいた無故障船荷証券に署名するのを船主が拒否したのは適正であると裁定した。

傭船契約上の「権利を侵害することなく」署名された船荷証券

傭船契約が，船荷証券は，本傭船契約の「権利を侵害することなく」署名されるものとすると規定する場合，船主と傭船者両者間の権利と義務は，船荷証券に影響されない。この法則は，Crossman v. Burrill, 179 U. S. 100, 109 (1900) 事件について最高裁で確認された。そこで裁判所は次のように言った。

> ……傭船契約は傭船者の要請に従って船荷証券に署名する義務を船長に負わせているが，「本傭船契約の権利を侵害することなく呈示された船荷証券に署名する」ことを要求する傭船契約の規定は，船荷証券または船荷証券を所持している受荷主が，傭船契約のあらゆる条項に従うことを意味するものではなく，本船とその船主への傭船者の義務は，署名された船荷証券により左右されないことを意味するものに過ぎない。

前出 Field Line (Cardiff) Ltd. v. South Atlantic S. S. Line 事件も参照。その事件で船長は署名のために呈示された船荷証券の内容に対し抗議したが，傭船者の要求に沿って船荷証券に署名した。材木の船積を証する船荷証券に次の規定があった。

共通の安全のための甲板積貨物の投荷（とその運賃）は共同海損として認容されることを除き共同海損は1890年ヨーク・アントワープ・ルールによって支払う。

この規定は、「甲板積貨物の投荷は共同海損として支払われないものとする」と規定している傭船契約と直接的に矛盾していた。その航海で材木を投荷することが必要であった。共同海損が宣言されたときに、船主には投荷材木の費用が生じざるを得なかったが、その航海で船積された他のすべての貨物の船荷証券は傭船契約と一致していたので、船主は共同海損の分担拠出について他の貨物関係者を当てにできなかった。裁判所は、この状況において、傭船者が船長に傭船契約と矛盾し、船主に損害をもたらす船荷証券を発行させたのであるから、船主は補償を得るための傭船者に対する有効な訴訟原因を有すると判示した。

船荷証券発行の際の明示の制限

もちろん、船主と傭船者は望むなら自由に船荷証券の発行につき制限を課すことができる。例えば、*The Scan Venture*, SMA 1627 (Arb. at N.Y. 1982) 事件で、傭船契約はニューヨーク・プロデュース書式に拠っており、追加条項を含んでいた。その一部は次のとおり。

> 船荷証券は傭船契約の権利を毀損することなくメーツ・レシートかつ、または検数人のタリー・シートに一致して署名される。傭船者が定期船船荷証券の発行を望む場合には発行の度毎に船主の権限が要請されるものとする。

346 仲裁人は、この条項は船長が定期船船荷証券に署名するのを要求する傭船者の権利に制限を加えるものであり、したがって船主の事前の承認無しで傭船者が発行した定期船船荷証券は適切ではないと、全員一致で裁定した。

船荷証券を請求する荷送人の権利

一般海事法に基づき、貨物の荷送人は船舶に船積された貨物に対し船荷証券の発行を請求する権利がある。この場合、船荷証券は受取証として機能する（*The Delaware*, 81 U.S. 579 (1872); *Watt* v. *Cargo of Lumber*, 161 F. 104 (2d Cir. 1908); *Akt. Brunsgaard* v. *Standard Oil of N. J.*, 283 F. 106 (2d Cir. 1922); *The Alonzo*, F. Cas. No. 257 (D. Me. 1869) 各事件参照）。

COGSAを準拠法とする船荷証券に基づき外国貿易で米国向けまたはからの船積の事案で、船荷証券の発行を請求する荷送人の権利は第3条(3)項により規制される。

ハーター法は第4条に類似の条項を含み、同法に沿って請求された船荷証券を請求ありしだい、発行することを拒否した船主に米貨2,000ドル以下の罰金を規定している。船荷証券を規制する他の米国法としては、米国港間または米国港から外国への貨物の運送に従事した公運送人により発行される船荷証券だけを規制するポメリーン法49 U.S.C. §§81-124がある。

貨物の引渡前に船荷証券の呈示を請求する船長の権利

船長には揚荷開始前に船荷証券の原本の呈示を請求する権利がある。*The Bless River*, SMA 1889 (Arb. at N.Y. 1983) 事件で、傭船者が船荷証券の原本または補償協定を船長に呈示で

きなかった場合に船主は揚荷の開始の遅れと保証荷役費用の責任を免れた。

運送人の同一性または「デマイズ」条項

多くの船荷証券は，次のように規定した「運送人の同一性」または「デマイズ」条項を含んでいる。

　本船荷証券により証される契約は，商人とここに指定の船舶（または代船）の船主との間のものであり，したがって上記船主だけが，船舶の堪航性の関与如何にかかわらず，……運送契約上の義務違反または不履行による損傷または滅失につき責任あることが合意される。船長のためにかつ船長の代理としてこの船荷証券を作成した会社，代理人は，この商取引の本人ではないので，上記会社，代理人に運送契約上の責任はないものとする。すなわち，これらの者は運送人でもなく，貨物の受寄者でもない。

　貨物の損害についての潜在的責任を船主に転嫁しようとして傭船者が使用するとき，このようなデマイズ条項は法律上無効である（*Epstein* v. *United States,* 86 F. Supp. 740（S. D. N. Y. 1949）; *Blanchard Lumber Co.* v. *The Anthony II,* 259 F. Supp. 857, 865-866, 1967 AMC 103, 120-121（S. D. N. Y. 1966））。裁判所は，デマイズ条項は責任を船主に転嫁しようとする定期傭船者の努力を示しているので，公序良俗の問題として当該条項は無効であると判示した。

　傭船者は責任を船主に転嫁するデマイズ条項に拠ることができないが，貨物利害関係者は同条項に拠ることができると判示された。*Recovery Services International* v. *The Tatiana L,* 1988 AMC 788（S. D. N. Y. 1986）事件で裁判所は，船荷証券に運送人の同一性約款が記載されていることについて荷送人は責任がないので，荷送人は船主に責任を課するために同約款に拠る権利があると判示した。

ボルタイム書式

　後出641頁の議論参照。

航 海 日 誌

"80.　9. That if the Charterers shall have reason to be dissatisfied with the conduct of the Captain, Officers, or Engineers, the Owners shall on
81. receiving particulars of the complaint, investigate the same, and, if necessary, make a change in the appointments.
82.　10. That the Charterers shall have permission to appoint a Supercargo, who shall accompany the vessel and see that voyages are prosecuted
83. with the utmost despatch. He is to be furnished with free accomodation, and same fare as provided for Captain's table, Charterers paying at the
84. rate of $1.00 per day. Owners to victual Pilots and Customs Officers, and also, when authorized by Charterers or their Agents, to victual Tally
85. Clerks, Stevedore's Foreman, etc., Charterers paying at the current rate per meal, for all such victualling.
86.　11. That the Charterers shall furnish the Captain from time to time with all requisite instructions and sailing directions, in writing, and the
87. Captain shall keep a full and correct Log of the voyage or voyages, which are to be patent to the Charterers or their Agents, and furnish the Char-
88. terers, their Agents or Supercargo, when required, with a true copy of daily Logs, showing the course of the vessel and distance run and the con-
89. sumption of fuel.
90.　12. That the Captain shall use diligence in caring for the ventilation of the cargo."

「9．傭船者に，船長・航海士，または機関士の行為を不満足とする相当な理由がある場合，船主は，その苦情の詳細を受け取りしだい，その事実を取り調べ，要すれば，配乗を変更するものとする。

10．傭船者は，随意に1名の上乗人を任命することができる。上乗人は本船と同航し，航海の極力迅速な遂行を確認するものとする。上乗人に対しては，居住設備を無償で提供し，サロン待遇を与えるものとする。この場合，傭船者は1日につき1ドルの割合で，その食費を支弁しなければならない。船主は，水先人・税関吏の食事を供するほか，傭船者またはその代理人の承諾がある限り，検数人・船内荷役フォアマンその他の者の食事を供するものとする。これら一切の食費は，傭船者が，毎食，時価で支払う。

11．傭船者は随時，船長に対し書面により，一切の必要な指図，および航海上の指示を与えるものとする。船長は，傭船者またはその代理人の用に供すべき，または航海に関する完全かつ正確な航海日誌を作成し，傭船者，その代理人または上乗人の要求がある場合には，本船の針路・航海距離・燃料消費高を記した航海日誌の正本を提出しなければならない。

12．船長は貨物の換気の実施に注意するものとする。」

米国法

傭船者の航海指図

　The Andros Mentor, SMA 2125 (Arb. at N.Y. 1985) 事件で，本船は Vancouver からフィリピン諸島へ1航海傭船された。傭船者は船長に気象航路選定業者の指図に従うようにという航海命令を呈示した。しかしながら，船長はこの指図に従うことを拒否し，代わりに船主が雇っていた業者が推奨する南の航路を取った。太平洋横断の以前の経験に基づいて，船長は南航路はより安全で経済的であると信じたので，船主の雇った会社が推奨した航路は里程で約688マイル長かったが，船長は船主の会社が推奨した航路を取った。後刻傭船者は航海の完了に必要な追加期間の傭船料を控除した。

　仲裁審の決定がニューヨーク・プロデュース書式の第11および24条の間の相互作用を解説している。仲裁審は，第11条は船長に書面による指図と航海上の指示を出す義務を傭船者に課すが，第11条は，また船長に指図・指示に従う義務を黙示している，と述べた。定期傭船契約の下で悪天候による遅延の危険は傭船者にあるので，第11条は傭船者が気象航路選定業者を自ら選定し，自らの費用負担での利用を認めている。同時に安全航行の責任は船長にある。

　船長には航路選定業者の助言に従う絶対的義務はない。船主と傭船者両方の最善の利益と本船，貨物および乗組員の安全を考慮に入れて，発航地から目的地へ最良で最も安全な航路を取るのを決定する際，船長は唯一の判断者である。

　仲裁審は，船長は傭船者の航路選定業者の提案する航路選定には従わないという航海開始時点の船長の発表は第11条の厳密な法解釈上の違反であると考えた。しかしながら，あらゆる証拠に基づいて，仲裁審は，船長が船主の航路選定業者が推奨した針路に従うことには正当な事由があると裁定した。

　仲裁審は，第11条の「航海指図」の語句によって，特定の航路選定指図ではなく「傭船者は一般的指図を出す権利を有するだけである」と述べた。仲裁審が挙げた例は，「パナマ運河経由」または「喜望峰経由」であり，本船の航行に干渉するまでには至っていない。

　海上航海の問題についての自己の判断と特権を行使する船長の権利を保持することは，最高に重要である。証拠によりその判断が厳しく無効とされるか，不注意であることが示される場合にのみ，船長は批判にさらされ，あるいは賠償の請求を受けることがある。

　仲裁審は，さらに傭船者は船主の同意なくして協会担保航路定限に違反することを本船に指示できないと裁定した。

　The Agia Skepi, SMA 2891 (Arb. at N.Y. 1992) 事件で，傭船者は，本船が間違った港へ航行したときに，傭船者は喪失時間について12時間本船をオフハイヤーにする権利があると主張した。船主は，船長は書面によるもともと指定された港向け命令にではなく口頭による他の港への航行指図に従ったと述べた。傭船契約には傭船者の航海指図はすべて書面によらねばならないと規定する条項があるので，仲裁審は，船長に対する針路変更の口頭指図ではなく傭船者の書面による指図の方が説得力があると認定した。かくして傭船者は，離路による喪失時間のオフハイヤーを認められた。

航 海 日 誌

　多くの理由で，船長が傭船者の要請により傭船者が利用できるすべての正確な航海日誌を保持することは重要である。正確な航海日誌の書き込みは速力または性能クレームに関して傭船者にとり特に重要である。このクレームは本船が遭遇した気象状況に大いに左右され，信頼のおける航海日誌は，その航海で遭遇した気象状況についてのしばしば唯一容認可能な証拠である。

　The Largo, SMA 1230 (Arb. at N.Y. 1978) 事件で，航海日誌は信頼できないと考えられたときに，生じる問題が解説されている。本船は管理船主により傭船者に1航海の定期傭船のために傭船された。傭船者は速力クレームを提起した。それについて，管理船主は航海日誌に逆風，不利な海象，霧が記載されていることを根拠として抗弁した。しかしながら，仲裁審は本船の性能を評価する際の参考として航海日誌は必ずしも十分に完備したものではないと判断した。管理船主は，管理船主には登録船主の被用者を監督する力はなく，航海日誌の欠陥について責任はないと主張した。しかしながら，仲裁審は，この主張を退け，次のように述べた。

　　船主の被用者と航海日誌に対して管理船主の監督が及ばないという船主の抗弁は，道理に合わない。傭船契約の第11条は明確に次のように規定している。船長は，航海に関する完全かつ正確な航海日誌を作成し，**要求がある場合には**（強調追加），傭船者に航海日誌の正本を提出しなければならない。本船の最初の傭船者としての関係において正確な航海日誌の船主への提出を要請し，これを取得しその提出を確かめるのは管理船主の義務である。

　The Bertina, SMA 3144 (Arb. at N.Y. 1995) 事件で，傭船者は主機の問題について詐欺かつ／または隠匿を主張し，それに基づき船主に損害賠償を請求した。不適切な管理のために潤滑油濾過系に不調が生じ，本船は続けて海上で停船し，何度も危険な難局に立ち至った。仲裁審は，傭船者が500ヶ所以上の書き込みが白く消去されていると主張した航海日誌は「完全に信用を失墜した」と考え，航海日誌に完全な不信を抱いた。仲裁審は，また航海日誌記帳の不正確さから判断を下したが，不正確な管理のゆえに，仲裁審はその航海日誌記帳を永続させることを許されるような「……単なる不備どころではない」と考えた。仲裁審は，傭船者の詐欺のクレームについて証拠不十分として退けたが，傭船者は過失と「不堪航という重大な事実を証明した」と判示した。

　The Golden Shimizu, SMA 2991 (Arb. at N.Y. 1993) 事件で仲裁審は，傭船者が本船は速力および燃料消費担保に違反したとクレームした事案で，本船の航海日誌は信頼できないという傭船者の主張を退けた。仲裁審は，傭船者のクレームは些細であり，「本船の傭船契約との実質的適合性という観点からは認めるに値しない」と述べた。この裁定を行うにあたり，仲裁審は，「明白で故意の間違いであることの否定しがたい証拠をもって反駁されない限り，船長の航海日誌は航海で経験した気象の，正確でかつ信頼できる表示と考えられる」と裁定した仲裁前例への同意を明確に表明した。

　The Konkar Kinos, SMA 2631 (Arb. at N.Y. 1990) 事件で仲裁審は，本船の気象および速力についての航海日誌およびその抄録は十分正確であると考え，航海日誌に拠るべきではないという傭船者のクレームを退けた。仲裁審は，傭船者がある方法で抄録が用意されるのを望むのであれば，本船の職員に特定の指図を出すべきであったということを明確にした。同時に仲裁審は，本船の記録は燃料消費量を計算するには不十分な資料でしかないと考え，実際の消費量を査定するために自らの調査を終了した。

　The United Bounty, SMA 2040 (Arb. at N.Y. 1984) 事件は，正確な航海日誌を作成する

ことの重要性につき他の例証を提供している。この事案は，速力不足に対する傭船者のクレームと過小消費燃料の価格の戻しという船主の反訴が関与している。傭船者のクレームは，航路選定業者により作成された航海分析に基づいていた。航行距離と使用時間に関する限り，本船の航海日誌と航路選定業者の航海分析は，異なっていない。しかしながら，気象状況の報告に２ヶ所の大きな違いがあった。仲裁審は，船長と職員は「その場の実際の状態の最善の判定者であるとみなされる」ので，通常仲裁人は本船の報告を容認することに注目した。航海日誌が信頼できないことを証明するのは，傭船者には重い負担である。仲裁審は，注意深く航海日誌を精査し，ほとんど海上航海の全期間中を通して逆潮と逆風を報告するという明白なやり口が存することに気づいた。仲裁審は，「本船が報告する気象の類型は風向きが極端なまでにしばしばまったく食い違っていることである」と判定した。その見解に基づいて，仲裁審は，航海日誌は信頼できないと裁定し，代わって気象航路選定業者の航海分析に裁決の根拠を求めた。

同様に *The Mangalia*, SMA 2839（Arb. at N.Y. 1991）事件で単独仲裁人は，本船の航海日誌の多様な不整合および脱落のために，本船は「船員の訓練および資格証明並びに当直の基準に関する国際条約」（STCW条約）の要件に適合していないと裁定した。したがって，仲裁人は気象状況の報告のために傭船者が雇った独立会社の分析に拠った。

米国籍船には航海日誌を保持し記帳しなければならないという，米国制定法上の要件がある。46 U.S.C. §§11301-11303. とりわけ，航海日誌の記帳は事象の発生後，可能な限り早急に行い，署名することが要求されている。同法違反は民事罰の対象となる。

傭船契約の継続

"91.　13. That the Charterers shall have the option of continuing this charter for a further period of ....
92. ....
93. on giving written notice thereof to the Owners or their Agents .... days previous to the expiration of the first-named term, or any declared option."

「13. 傭船者は，傭船期間をさらに....................間，継続する権利を有する。その場合，当初定めた傭船期間もしくは明示の選択期間の満了する....................日前に，船主もしくはその代理人に書面でその旨を通知しなければならない。」

傭船契約を継続する選択権の行使

　ニューヨーク・プロデュース書式第13条によって傭船者に認められている選択権を行使するには，傭船者はその旨を明確な言葉で船主に通知しなければならない。The Trado [1982] 1 Lloyd's Rep. 157 事件で，Parker 判事は次のように述べている。「有利な選択権を有する者がその選択権を行使しようとする場合には，疑問の余地のない言葉で行わなければならない」。
　いったん，傭船者が選択権を行使する旨の通知を行えば，その傭船者の決定を取り消すことはできない。同じことは，傭船者が選択権を行使しないことを通知する場合についても妥当することである（なお，上記の The Trado 事件を参照）。

14行の傭船者任意の許容期間についての効果

　14行（前出173頁参照）の傭船契約の基本期間に，傭船者任意でのプラスマイナス何日間との明示許容期間があり，かつ，傭船者が契約をさらに同様の期間継続できるという第13条の選択権を行使する場合，全最長期間を算出するに際して，14行の許容期間は無視される。

　Aspa Maria 号は，「6ヶ月プラスマイナス30日傭船者任意」の期間で傭船された。第13条により，傭船者は，「さらに6ヶ月プラスマイナス30日傭船者任意，ただし，4ヶ月経過時に行使するかどうかの通知を行うことを条件とする傭船契約継続に関する選択権」を有していた。傭船者は，第13条による選択権を行使したが，その結果生じる全最長傭船期間は，12ヶ月と30日か，あるいは12ヶ月と60日のいずれであるかの問題が生じた。控訴院は，前者が正しいと判示した。すなわち，最初の30日の規定は，いったん，傭船者が第13条により選択権を行使した場合，切り捨てられるべき基本期間6ヶ月に対する明示の許容期間に過ぎないと判示したのである。
　Gulf Shipping Lines v. *Compania Naviera Alanje* [1976] 2 Lloyd's Rep. 643.

354 米 国 法

傭船契約の継続

　13条に基づき,傭船者はいかようにも期間を延長する選択権を有すると規定することがある。期間延長の通知を要する時期に加え,許容される追加傭船期間の規定の仕方については,細心の注意を払わなければならない(*The Cielo Rosso*, 1980 AMC 2088 (Arb. at N.Y. 1980) 事件を参照)。例えばこの事件では,傭船期間の継続に関する条項の文言作成に細心の注意が払われなかったことにより係争が生じている。裸傭船契約の事例であるが,*The Gulf Pacific*, SMA 2854 (Arb. at N.Y. 1991) 事件も参照。

　The Santa Katerina, 1974 AMC 1383 (Arb. at N.Y. 1974) 事件は,ニューヨーク・プロデュース書式13条を範とした追加規定の適用に関する争いであった。この事例では,傭船者は「船主に対し書面による通知をすることにより,暦月で3ヶ月間プラスマイナス3週間傭船者任意」という傭船期間を延長する選択権を有していた。延長した3ヶ月間終了後の8月25日以後しか返船できない最終航海について,傭船者がその航海を行うことは許されない,と船主は主張した。仲裁人の判断は,傭船者は確定3ヶ月間のみならずプラスマイナス3週間の期間を自由に使う権利を有するとした。本船はその3週間の期間内に返船されたのであるから,傭船の期間超過は存在しなかったのである。

　The Jagat Padmini, SMA 1097 (Arb. at N.Y. 1977) 事件において,本船は「およそ最短6ヶ月間プラスマイナス15日間傭船者任意――かつ傭船者は本船引渡時から4ヶ月以内に船主へ通告することによりさらに6ヶ月の傭船期間延長の選択権を持つ」との条件で傭船に出された。この事例では,仲裁審は,傭船者が本船を保有できる期間は正確に12ヶ月と15日間であると判定した。返船条項には「およそ」(about) という文言が含まれているが,当事者間で意図された猶予は「プラスマイナス15日間」と判断されたのである。

　もし本船がオフハイヤーされた期間分だけ傭船期間が延長されるとすれば,傭船者が傭船契約継続の選択権を行使する期間もその分延長できると判示されている。*The Tropigas Far East*, SMA 1594 (Arb. at N.Y. 1981) 事件では,傭船契約の当初の期間が3年間で,1年間ずつ延長する選択権が傭船者に認められていた。ただし,傭船者はその選択権を行使するには遅くとも傭船期間満了の6ヶ月前までにその旨を通知しなければならなかった。当初の3年の間に,本船がオフハイヤーとなり,船主と傭船者間で1979年10月15日であった満了日を10月24日に変更することに合意した。その後,傭船者は傭船期間延長の選択権を2度行使したが,いずれも傭船当初の傭船期間満了期間である10月15日の6ヶ月前である4月15日,すなわち当初の期限までにその旨の通知を行った。さらに傭船者は3度目の期間延長選択権を行使したが,その通知は4月22日に行った。その際,船主は,傭船者の選択権行使は時機を失したものであると主張した。しかし,仲裁人は,傭船者有利の裁定を行った,すなわち当初の傭船期間ならびにその後の延長後の傭船期間の満了日が10月15日から10月24日に変更されているとして,選択権行使期間の期限も同様に延びていると裁定したのである。

　The Narnian Sea, 1991 AMC 274 (Arb. at N.Y. 1990) 事件では,仲裁審は,本船の修理のための不就航期間についての傭船者の損失分の回復はオフハイヤーに限定され,傭船者は傭船契約上の法的な権利を勝手に解釈し一方的に傭船期間を延長することは許されないと裁定した。傭船者は,傭船契約の規定する期間延長権を行使しなかったことを理由に,不当な本船引揚であるとする傭船者の主張は認められなかった。

傭船期間の満了日の変更は非常に重要な修正であり，明確に定められなければならない。
The Galahad, SMA 3057（Arb. at N. Y. 1994）事件。

解 約 条 項

"94. 14. That, if required by Charterers, time not to commence before ....
and should vessel
95. not have given written notice of readiness on or before .... but not
later than 4 p. m. Charterers or
96. their Agents to have the option of cancelling this Charter at any time not later than the
date of vessel's readiness."

「14. 傭船者の要求があるときは，傭船期間は........................より前には開始しない。本船が
..............................の午後4時までに書面による準備完了の通知をしないときは，傭船者またはその代理人は，本船の準備完了前ならば，いつでも本契約を任意に解約することができる。」

原　則

　The Democritos［1976］2 Lloyd's Rep. 149 の事件において，記録長官 Denning 卿は同判例集152頁で解約条項に関し次のように述べている。「解約条項の効果は，本船が解約期日までに適切な状態で引き渡されない場合，船主に契約違反がない場合でも，傭船者は自らの利益を守るために傭船契約を解約できる，というものである」。

　解約条項は，ある特定の状況に至れば，自動的に傭船契約を解約する権利を傭船者に付与し，船主の傭船契約違反がなくても，傭船者に付与される。Smith v. Dart（1884）14 Q. B. D. 105事件（同判例集110頁）と以下に引用する The Madeleine［1967］2 Lloyd's Rep. 224（同判例集239頁）の事案を参照。加えて，本船引渡の準備の完了と本船が適切な状態にあるとの要件が，解約条項の目的のため絶対的なものと考えられている。これについては，前出206頁を参照。

　それゆえ，この条項に基づく傭船者の解約権は，船主の契約違反によって傭船者が傭船契約を解除できる権利とは明確に区別されなければならない。この別個の権利が発生する状況を検討するものとして，前出148頁から152頁を参照。

傭船者による約定日以前の使用

　94行の内容と前出342頁で議論した62行から64行の規定の間に矛盾が生じる可能性がある。まず，62行と63行の通知期間条項によれば，94行を無視する場合，94行の規定の日時より以前に傭船料の支払が始まると言える。ただし，この状況では94行が優先し，傭船料の支払は合意した日時までは生じないとされている。次に，傭船者は通知期間の満了前に本船を使用することができ，その場合は直ちに傭船料の支払が始まるという64行の規定が適用される。この状況においては傭船料支払の開始が，94行の規定の日時まで停止されることはない。すなわち，傭船者は本船を直ちに使用することを選ぶことによって（さもなければ94行の規定を選べたのに），94行の規定に拠らないこととした（この立場は，航海傭船契約においては，違ってくることがある。Pteroti v. National Coal Board［1958］1 Lloyd's Rep. 245 事件を参照）。

準備完了の要件

ニューヨーク・プロデュース書式のもとでは、定められた日時までに本船が引渡完了通知を行わないと、傭船者が傭船契約を解約する権利を持つことになる。船主の準備完了の通知は、適切な時期になされなければならず、さらに有効でなければならない。本船が準備未完了であり、21行から24行の要件を満たしていなければ、その通知は有効とはならない。準備完了の要件、およびいつそれが満たされるかの解説については、前出206頁から211頁を参照。

同様に、ボルタイム書式においても、本船が傭船契約第1条で要求されている状態で、すなわち「あらゆる点において通常の貨物輸送に適した状態で」、所定の期日までに引き渡されなければ、傭船者は22条に規定する解約権を有する。

Madeleine 号はボルタイム書式で3ヶ月間傭船された。解約日は、双方合意にて5月10日まで延長された。5月6日に本船の鼠族駆除免除証明書が失効した。5月9日、前貨の揚荷役が完了した。しかし、港湾衛生当局は本船を検査した後、鼠族駆除免除証明書の発給を拒否した。当局は、燻蒸を命じ、燻蒸終了後鼠族駆除免除証明書の発給を行うつもりであった。有効な鼠族駆除免除証明書がなければ、本船は、傭船契約の規定通りの航行ができなかった。燻蒸は5月12日まで終了しなかった。傭船者は5月10日午前8時に船主に対し傭船契約を解約した旨を伝え、同日の午後8時48分に再度解約の通知を行った。証明書は5月12日に発給され、船主は傭船者の解約は不当であると主張した。Roskill判事は次のように判示した。本船は、第1条に要求される条件を満たしたうえで、(すなわち「いかなる点においても通常の貨物輸送に適した状態」、つまり堪航性を有した状態で)傭船者に引き渡されなければならないが、5月10日午後6時の時点で、船主は、堪航性を有する本船を引き渡すことができなかったので、傭船者には解約する権利があった。
The Madeleine [1967] 2 Lloyd's Rep. 224.

解約条項に関し、Roskill判事は上記の報告書（239頁）で次のように述べている。「傭船者が行使しようとする権利は、傭船契約22条により傭船者に認められている明らかな契約上の権利であることを強調することが重要である。傭船者のこの権利は、船主の債務不履行の有無とは関係ない。この解約権が生じるのは、船主の債務不履行により生じるものではなく、船主が第1条に規定された船主の義務を時機を得て履行したかどうかによるものである。」

準備完了の通知

ニューヨーク・プロデュース書式における準備完了を知らせる船主からの通知は、95行で要求されているように書面でなされなければならず、かつ本船は18行が規定する傭船者の使用に委ねられる場所に来ていなければならない。通知が有効となるには、その通知はすべての重要な点で正確でなければならない。

軽微な違反

しかし、解約条項は、性質上、権利喪失規定であるので、裁判所は準備未了が厳密な法解釈上のものであるか、あるいはほとんど重要性のない、かつ船舶または貨物の安全に影響のない装置もしくは機器の欠陥に関するものである場合には、解約権行使を認めることを躊躇する。*Noemijulia Steamship* v. *Minister of Food* (1950) 83 Ll.L. Rep. 500 事件で、Devlin判事は次のように述べた。「例えば、船積作業開始後数日間は不必要なウィンチが、1～2時間ほどの

分解掃除を要するに過ぎない場合,傭船者が解約できるとは到底思えない。これは権利喪失規定であり,それゆえ,軽々しく適用されるべきではないことを,常に銘記しなければならない。その契約において真に重要でない欠陥が,傭船契約を最終段階で放棄させてしまう手段に使われるとすれば,それは不幸なことだと思う」。Devlin 判事は,ここで航海傭船契約における解約条項を論じているが,その見解は定期傭船契約にも等しく適用されるべきであろう。実際,Roskill 判事は, *The Madeleine* [1967] 2 Lloyd's Rep. 224 事件の判決の中で(同判例集237頁),その見解はボルタイム書式の解約条項にも等しく適用されるべきであるとしている。

前出209頁の *The Arianna* [1987] 2 Lloyd's Rep. 376 事件ならびに,本船もしくは貨物の安全に影響のない微小な欠陥に関する前出209頁の *New York and Cuba Mail Steamship* v. *Eriksen and Christensen* (1922) 27 Com. Cas. 330 事件の Greer 判事の判決の抜粋も参照。

しかし,航海傭船契約の事例において,貨物を受ける船艙の状態に関しては,準備完了の要件は厳格に適用される(前出207頁を参照)。*The Tres Flores* [1972] 2 Lloyd's Rep. 384 および [1973] 2 Lloyd's Rep. 247 事件において,第1審の Mocatta 判事および控訴審の Roskill 卿判事は,碇泊期間の問題について厳格に適用される要件が,解約条項発動を考慮する場合にも同様に厳格に適用されるべきかどうかについては,異なる見解を述べている。

Moccatta 判事は第1審の報告書の394頁で次のように言っている。

　　……確かに碇泊期間開始に関する事例と解約条項に関する事例は区別されるべきであろう。解約条項に関する事例では,本船を解約日までに間に合わせないと,傭船者が傭船契約を解消できることになり,その影響はきわめて深刻となる。一方,碇泊期間に関する事案は,準備完了の通知の有効性の決定が,最悪の場合でもせいぜい滞船料もしくは早出料の額に影響する程度である。

控訴審において,Roskill 卿判事は次のように述べている(同判例集252頁)。

　　……もし,この種の法則を非常に厳格に適用することが(些細なことは問わないという問題のみを条件として subject only to questions of *de minimis*)船主に酷すぎるとか,もしくは公平さを欠く結論にしかならないのであれば,当事者はいつでも自由にコモン・ローの原則を修正すればよい。現在の事例においては,その法則は「バース待ちでの時間喪失」条項により修正できたかもしれない。しかし,この種の事例では,碇泊期間や滞船料の問題に対しても,本船を期日までにもってこない場合の傭船者の解約権の問題に対しても,特定の事例の所与の事実について,基本原則を単純に適用できるということがきわめて重要であろう……。この例をとればいいのである。〔法廷弁護士の〕主張が正しいとすれば,本船の到着と解約日との間の時間差が僅少のため,貨物の積込に支障となる本船の特定の瑕疵を僅か数時間で直せると考えて準備完了通知を出したが,結局予想どおり瑕疵を修復できない場合には,どうなるのであろうか。もし瑕疵が結局解約日まで治癒されなければ,各々の当事者の立場はどのようになるのか。法廷弁護人の主張では一応有効と推定される準備完了の通知が,予期せぬ展開によって,突如遡及して無効となるのであろうか。この状況は,際限なく複雑である。そのような複雑さを間違いなく避けるには,絶対確実に適用できる原則を持つことである。

問題の瑕疵が貨物を積み込む船艙の状態に関するものである場合には,碇泊期間のための準備完了と解約権のための準備完了を区別する理由はないのかもしれない。しかし,Devlin 判事が上述の *Noemijulia Steamship* 事件で指摘しているように,解約条項はその性質が権利喪失条項であるだけに,軽々しく適用すべきではない。それゆえ,もし問題となっている瑕疵が本船の安全やすぐさま積み込む貨物の安全に影響を与えなければ,傭船期間の長さ,航路の範囲,貨物選択権に関する事項を考慮すべきであるとされている。「準備完了」は,実務上の良識に従って解釈されなければならない([1987] 2 Lloyd's Rep. 376 と前出209頁の *The Arianna* 事

件を参照)。

準備完了の状態の欠如についての立証責任は，それを主張する傭船者にある（*Noemijulia Steamship* v. *Minister of Food*（1950）84 Ll.L. Rep. 354 事件を参照)。

不実表示（Misdescription）

解約条項に関しては，船舶はニューヨーク・プロデュース書式21行から24行の要件に沿って，準備がなされてさえいれば十分であるとされている。準備完了通知の時点で，船舶が3行から11行の中の船舶の表示に一部合致していないという事実は，必ずしも傭船者に解約権を認めるものではない。例えば，本船が22行の「あらゆる点において，輸送業務に適する」という条項に合致しなくなるほど速力を出せない場合は別として，単に9行または10行の表示速力を出せないという理由だけでは，本条項の解約権は発生しない。傭船者はもちろん，解約条項とは別個の救済手段を有している（これに関しては，前出132頁を参照)。

要件を満たさない準備完了の通知

碇泊期間開始のための準備完了通知に関する航海傭船契約の事例を類推すれば，通知が出されたときに本船の準備が完了していなければ，その通知は無効であり，傭船者が明示または黙示により，あらためて通知の不要に同意しない限り，後刻本船の準備が完了したからといって前の通知が有効になるものではない（*Christensen* v. *Hindustan Steel* [1971] 1 Lloyd's Rep. 395 事件における Donaldson 判事の判決（同判例集399頁）を参照)。同判事は，この事件では，*The Massalia* [1960] 2 Lloyd's Rep. 352 事件とは異なる見解を示した。なお，*The Massalia* 事件は，Diplock 判事の担当であったが，この事件ではこの事件特有の事実に基づき，通知は不要と判断された（*The Tres Flores* [1973] 2 Lloyd's Rep. 247と *The Helle Skou* [1976] 2 Lloyd's Rep. 205，*The Demosthenes V (No. 1)* [1982] 1 Lloyd's Rep. 275 の各事件参照)。準備完了の通知が受領された後，その船が準備未了であったことが判明した場合の効果に関する事例については，*The Shackleford* [1978] 1 Lloyd's Rep. 191 と [1978] 2 Lloyd's Rep. 154（C. A.）事件を参照。

解約期日までに本船を引き渡すことは船主の絶対的義務ではない

船主は，本船を解約期日までに到着させるという絶対的義務を負っていない。*Smith* v. *Dart* (1884) 14 Q.B.D. 105 事件（同判例集110頁）で，A.L. Smith 判事が述べたように，「船主は，ある特定の日までにそこに到着することを約束していない，期日までに到着しなければ，傭船者は解約できるというだけである」。

明文の規定がない場合，船主の義務は解約期日までに本船を航海に適した状態で引渡できるよう，傭船契約締結の日から合理的な注意義務を尽くすというだけである。この義務は，黙示的に認められる。

Democritos 号は1969年11月8日に，ニューヨーク・プロデュース書式により「期間約4〜6ヶ月，太平洋，諸港経由1航海」で傭船された。本船は Durban で引き渡される予定になっており，解約期日は12月20日であった。本船は9月に特別検査のために入渠し，その後 Bombay 向け貨物を積んだ。Bombay での揚荷の過程で2番中甲板の損傷が発見された。本船は12月4日 Bombay を出港し，Durban に12月16日に到着した。中甲板の損傷は，解約期日までに修理できるものではなかったが，傭船者は12月18日にその損傷未修理のまま本船を受け取った。その後，傭船者は，船主は解約期

日までに本船を傭船契約に合致した状態で引渡を行う絶対的な義務があると主張した。控訴院は，そのような絶対的義務はなく，船主の唯一の義務は，解約期日までに本船を航海に適した状態で引き渡すよう，相当の注意を尽くすことであり，この点で船主の義務違反はないと判示した。
　The Democritos [1976] 2 Lloyd's Rep. 149.

　航海傭船契約の解約条項に関する The Heron II [1966] 1 Lloyd's Rep. 595（C. A.）と [1967] 2 Lloyd's Rep. 457（H. L.）事件の判例から次のことを指摘することができよう。すなわち，もし，船主が合理的な注意を尽くさず，その結果本船の提供が遅れる船主の義務違反がある場合，たとえ万が一本船が解約期日に間に合ったとしても，船主は傭船者がそれによって被る損失を賠償しなければならないだろう。Diplock 卿判事は，控訴院の報告書610頁において次のように述べている。「傭船契約で解約期日を定めることは，当日までに本船を到着させなければ荷主に契約を解除されることがあるとの警告を船主に与えるものであり，決してまず第１に適切な速力で積荷港まで本船を航行させる船主の主たる義務，もしその第１の義務を達成できない場合，その結果，荷主が被る損失に対する金銭賠償という第２の義務を免除するものではない」。なお，Upjohn 卿の貴族院報告書486頁における所見も参照。

解約期日前に解約する権利（義務）はない

　たとえ，本船が解約期日後にしか到着しないことが避けられない場合でも，傭船者はこの条項に基づき解約期日前に解約することはできない。The Madeleine [1967] 2 Lloyd's Rep. 224 事件で，Roskill 判事は，ボルタイム書式22条（同書式の解約条項が規定されている）の最初の文章に関し，次のように述べている。「本条に基づく期限前解約権というべきものがあるとすれば，その権利はそのような解釈に必要な意味を22条から引き出せるときにのみ生じるというべきであろう。５月10日（解約期日）までに本船が引き渡されないときに解約できるという明文の規定があるのに，それより早い時点，すなわち約定の解約期日に本船が間に合わないことが不可避となった時点で解約できる暗黙の権利が，同時に存在するとするのは非常に難しい，と私は考える」。
　この見解は，The Mihalis Angelos [1970] 2 Lloyd's Rep. 43 事件における，控訴院の多数意見でも支持された。この事件では，控訴院は，航海傭船契約の場合，解約権は解約期日前には発生しないと判示したのである。
　逆に，解約期日後であっても，本船を傭船者に提供するに先立ち，船主は傭船者に対して，解約権を行使するか否かを明らかにするよう，要求することはできない（Moel Tryvan v. Weir [1910] 2 K. B. 844 事件を参照)。本船が引渡の場所にいるが，引渡の準備ができていない場合にも，同様のことが言える。The Democritos [1975] 1 Lloyd's Rep. 386 事件（同判例集397頁）で，Kerr 判事は次のように述べた。「認定された事実によれば，中甲板の損傷修理が解約期日の12月20日までに行われなかったことは明らかである。一方，傭船者は本船が傭船契約に基づいて，準備完了状態で傭船者に提供されるまで，何もする義務はなかった。12月20日を経過した時点で，傭船者は希望するのであれば，解約することができ，あるいは本船が提供されるまで何もせずに待つこともできた。そして傭船者は，14条に基づき，本船が12月20日以降に準備完了の状態で提供されるまで，解約権を行使するかどうかの選択権を保留した」。このような場合の船主の立場を改善する特別条項につき，後出の NYPE 93 を参照。
　傭船者が，本条項に基づき，解約期日前に解約権を行使できないことは，傭船者が有するコモン・ロー上の権利や，それらの権利の行使時期に影響を与えない。かくして，本条項の解約に

関する選択権とは別に，傭船者はコモン・ローに基づいた契約解除はできるし，その解除権は解約期日前に生じ，行使することができると考えられる。Roskill判事は，*The Madeleine* [1967] 2 Lloyd's Rep. 224事件（同判例集244頁）で，次のように述べた。「……あらかじめ解約する契約上の権利がないからと言って傭船者に解約期日に先立ち契約を解除する権利がないとは言えない。……傭船者は，契約が履行不可能になった，あるいは，傭船者に契約解除の権利を付与する解約期日前の契約違反があったと主張し，それが認められる場合には，傭船者はコモン・ロー上の解除権を持つこととなる」[1967] 2 Lloyd's Rep. 224（同判例集243頁）事件の Roskill 判事の判決で引用されている *Bank Line* v. *Capel* [1919] A.C. 435 事件の Scrutton 卿判事の判決文（未報告）の一部も参照。

NYPE 93

ニューヨーク・プロデュース書式1993年改訂版では，16条の一部に「解約の延長」条項を設けることにより，この潜在的に非常に酷なルールの救済を図っている。すなわち，規定の但し書きによって，解約期日を遵守できないことが予想される場合，船主は傭船者に対し，引渡港への本船の到着が遅延する場合に，解約権を行使するかどうかを，事前に明らかにすることを要求できるようになった（前出12頁の英文書式の210行から218行と56頁を参照）。

解約権の行使

船主が約定日の遅くとも午後4時までに，書面による準備完了通知を出さない場合には，94行から96行の規定により，傭船者は解約権を有する。午後4時というのは63行の規定と一致する。18行から21行により，引渡場所として定めた場所で，本船を傭船者に提供するだけでは不十分で，期限までに書面による通知がなければ，傭船者は解約することができる。

解約選択権とその他の権利

傭船者が解約権を行使したからといって，それが，船主の傭船契約上の義務違反の結果として傭船者に損害を被らせた場合の傭船者の損害賠償請求権を奪うものではない。

航海傭船契約の事案である *Nelson & Sons* v. *Dundee East Coast Shipping*, 1907 S.C. 927事件において，傭船者は解約権を行使したとしても，損害賠償を要求できると判示された。M'Laren 卿は同判例集934頁で以下のように述べている。「……解約の選択権を認める条項の挿入が本船の提供あるいは補償の支払を求めるコモン・ロー上の義務に取って代わるものとの観点から，賠償の要はないと，[傭船者]が申し立てたとされるが，私は，解約選択権条項の挿入は，決してそのような目的のために行われたのではないと思う」。

同様に，解約を行わないことを傭船者が選択したとしても，そのことが契約違反についての通常の法的救済を必ずしも傭船者から奪うものではない（[1975] 1 Lloyd's Rep. 386（同判例集397頁）および前出213頁，422頁の *The Democritos* 事件を参照。一般的な権利放棄の問題に関しては，[1990] 1 Lloyd's Rep. 391 (H.L.) と前出143頁の *The Kanchenjunga* 事件を参照）。

361 米　国　法

解約期日

　船舶の提供が遅れた場合，傭船者は解約権を有し，その権利を行使することも行使しないこともできる。傭船契約に何らかの修正文言がない限り，引渡遅延に基づく傭船者の解約権は絶対的なものであり，遅延の原因が何であれ，行使しうる (*Karran* v. *Peabody*, 145 F. 166 (2d Cir. 1906) 事件を参照)。

　他方，船主には船舶を提供する絶対的義務があり，解約期日を過ぎても本船を提供しなければならない (*The Progreso*, 50 F. 835 (3d Cir. 1892)，*The Samuel W. Hall*, 49 F. 281 (S. D. N. Y. 1892)，*The Orient Point*, SMA 246 (Arb. at N. Y. 1961) の各事件を参照)。

　一般的に，船主による提供の遅延は傭船者に解約権を与えるだけで，船主に対する損害賠償請求権まで与えるものではない (*Sanday* v. *United States Shipping Board Emergency Fleet Corp.*, 6 F. 2d 384 (2d Cir. 1925) 裁量上告拒絶 269 U. S. 556 (1926)；*The Michael L*, SMA 1301 (Arb. at N. Y. 1979)；*The Lucerna*, SMA 2579 (Arb. at N. Y. 1988) の各事件参照)。

　Sanday 事件においては，契約は Galveston から Rio de Janeiro までの航海傭船で，指定された本船が Galveston において1920年11月15日までに積荷準備完了とならない場合に，傭船者に解約権が与えられていた。本船は11月11日に Norfolk におり，解約期日までに Galveston に到着できないことが明らかであったので，傭船者は受取を拒絶し，他の船舶の手配を行った。本船は3日遅れて Galveston に到着し，その時点で一応提供された。一方，傭船者は，本船提供の遅延により生じたとする損害の賠償を請求して，船主に対し訴訟を提起した。その理由は，傭船契約は船主に本船を解約期日までに提供する義務を課しているというものであった。しかし，裁判所はこの訴えを却下し，解約条項の本当の目的は，提供の遅延から生ずる損害の賠償請求訴訟を排除することにあるとして，次のように述べた。

　　傭船契約に引渡期日を明記していない場合，船主の約束は，船舶を合理的な迅速さで提供することであり，そのような約束に船主が違反した場合には，傭船者はもちろん訴えることができる。その場合，船主が船舶を遅滞なく提供するために合理的な注意義務を果たさなかったことを立証する責任は傭船者にある。船主の約束が解約条項の存在によって影響されるものでないことについて，私はまったくの同意見である。この見解は *Nelson & Sons* v. *Dundee East Coast Shipping Co., Limited*, 44 Scottish Law Reporter, 661 (1907, Court of Session) 事件でも支持されていると思う。

　　しかし，解約期日があることが，解約日，またはそれ以前，もしくはその他の確定期日に，本船を提供するとの船主の約束があるということの証拠になる，というわけではない。そのような結果を回避するため，当該文言の言い回しが選ばれていることは，きわめて明らかと思われる。船主には，解約期日後に本船を提供すれば解約されるという危険性があるが，合理的な注意義務をもって本船を目的地に差し向けることより重い義務を引き受けているのではないと思われる。そのような重い義務については，解約期日までに提供することを約束するというように，明文にて規定されなければならず，本条の傭船者の解約権は，いかなる意味においてもそのような義務の存在を意味しているものではない (6 F. 2d at 385)。

　船主が，傭船契約書に本船の動静や引渡の準備完了につき，著しい不実表示をしている場合には，傭船者は損害賠償請求権を取得する (*Davison* v. *Von Lingen*, 113 U. S. 40, 49-50 (1885)，*The Michael L* (前出)，*The Tropez Comfort*, SMA 2616 (Arb. at N. Y. 1989) の各事

件を参照)。さらに，もし船主が本船の引渡に際し「合理的な迅速さ」で本船を差し向ける義務に違反した場合には，傭船者は損害賠償請求権をもつこととなる。例えば船主が不当な中間航海を実施したり修繕のため本船を遅らせるといったような場合に，この損害賠償請求権が発生する (*The Gilia*, 1972 AMC 1738 (Arb. at N.Y. 1972), *The Caribbean Wave*, SMA 278 (Arb. at N.Y. 1961), *The Noto*, 1979 AMC 116 (Arb. at N.Y. 1976) および *The Federal Fraser*, SMA 1804 (Arb. at N.Y. 1983) の各事件を参照)。

|362| *The Marta Z*, SMA 2602 (Arb. at N.Y. 1989) 事件では，積荷港に寄る前に故障した機関の修理ならびに他の傭船者の貨物積取のために，他港に寄る配船スケジュールを組んだ船主は傭船契約違反であると判示された。さらに船主は，本船の機関の堪航性を保つために相当の注意を払う義務，すなわち速やかに機関の故障を修理した上で，航海を遂行する義務にも違反していると判示された。なお，この事件では通常12日間で完遂する修理を57日間遅滞させている。傭船契約上は，前払運賃はいかなる状況下でも払い戻されないと規定されていたが，仲裁審は船主に責任があるゆえ，船主は前払運賃を保持できないと裁定した。さらに，［船主の行為で］傭船契約上の指定期日までに本船を引き渡す見通しについての合理的な根拠が船主にはなかったゆえに，傭船者は傭船者が本船遅延のため顧客に支払った延滞罰金をも船主より回収できるとの裁定を得た。

引渡時の状態

前出159頁の議論を参照。

オフハイヤー条項

"97.　15. That in the event of the loss of time from deficiency of men or stores, fire, breakdown or damages to hull, machinery or equipment,
98. grounding, detention by average accidents to ship or cargo, drydocking for the purpose of
examination or painting bottom, or by any other cause
99. preventing the full working of the vessel, the payment of hire shall cease for the time
thereby lost ; and if upon the voyage the speed be reduced by
100. defect in or breakdown of any part of her hull, machinery or equipment, the time so lost,
and the cost of any extra fuel consumed in consequence
101. thereof, and all extra expenses shall be deducted from the hire."

「15. 人員または船用品の不足，火災，船体・機関もしくは装備の故障または損傷，座礁，本船または積荷の海損事故による滞船，船底の検査または塗装のための入渠，その他本船の完全な稼働を妨げる一切の事由により時間を喪失したときは，傭船料の支払は，それによって喪失した時間について中断する。船体，機関または装備の欠陥または故障により，航海中速力が低下したときは，それによって喪失した時間，その結果余分に消費した燃料費，その他一切の費用が，傭船料より控除される。」

一 般 原 則

　全傭船期間を通じて傭船料を支払い続けることは，傭船者のもっとも基本的な義務であるが，オフハイヤー条項はその義務を免除する条項として機能する。ニューヨーク・プロデュース書式第15条に関し，Kerr判事は，*The Mareva A. S.* [1977] 1 Lloyd's Rep. 368(同判例集381)事件の中で，次のように述べている。「一応正当と推定される傭船料が支払い続けられなければならないことは確立された原則であり，もし傭船者が支払の中断を主張するためには，中断を主張する状況がオフハイヤー条項に明白に該当することを立証しなければならない。この条項には確かに解釈上難しい点があり，また類語反復も含んでいるようである。例えば，『船体・機関もしくは装備の故障または損傷』のあとに『本船または積荷の海損事故』との文言が続く点がそうである。しかしながら，この条項の目的はきわめて明瞭であると思う。船主は，本船とその本船で働く乗組員を提供する。そして，それらが十分に機能し，その時点で傭船者が要求する役務が提供されている限りは，傭船料は支払われ続けなければならない。しかし，何らかの理由で本船が十分に稼働しないで，その時点で傭船者が要求する役務が提供されず，その結果傭船者が時間の喪失を被った場合，その時間の喪失分だけ傭船料の支払は中断する」。
　したがって，オフハイヤー条項が当該事情のもとで適用されるかどうかを立証する責任は，傭船者にある。この点に関し，Bucknill卿判事は，*Royal Greek Government* v. *Minister of Transport* (1948) 82 Ll.L. Rep. 196事件（同判例集199頁）で，次のように述べている。「本件のような傭船契約を解釈するに際しての，……基本原則は，傭船者がオフハイヤー条項に規定された例外に該当することを立証できない限り，傭船者は本船使用の対価たる傭船料の支払を免れないということである。傭船者は，オフハイヤー条項が適用される場合であることを明確に立証しなければならない，と私は思う。当該文言の意味に疑義がある場合は，船主有利に解

釈されるべきである。なぜならば，傭船者は，船主の傭船料債権を減額しようとしているからである」。

債務不履行はオフハイヤーの要件ではない

オフハイヤー条項は，船主の契約不履行とは完全に独立して機能する。もし，傭船者がこの条項を首尾よく援用すれば，その効果としての傭船者の権利は，オフハイヤー条項の文言自体により明確にされよう。また損害賠償請求権は契約不履行に関するコモン・ロー上の別の原則によることとなる。*The Ioanna* [1985] 2 Lloyd's Rep. 164 事件（同判例集167頁）で，Staughton 判事は次のように言っている。「オフハイヤーとなる事由は，必ずしも契約不履行となるものではない。ゆえに，契約不履行による損害賠償請求と，オフハイヤー条項から導かれる答えが異なるものであっても，特段驚くべきことではない」。

364 時間の喪失

例えば機関の故障等のようなオフハイヤー条項に列挙された事態が発生すれば，それにより傭船料支払が当然に中断するわけではない。傭船料支払が中断するためには，結果として傭船者が時間を喪失したことを証明しなければならない。

それゆえ，推進機関の故障の場合，それが積荷・揚荷の期間中に発生しても，修理がその期間内に完了すれば，通常オフハイヤーにはならない。留意すべきは，当該期間中に本船に要求されている業務は何であるかということで，そしてその業務に影響が出てはじめて，オフハイヤーの可能性が生じる。したがって，本船が航行中か，航行することを求められているときには，推進機関の故障によりオフハイヤーになることがあるが，推進機関を必要としない業務に本船が就いたとたんオンハイヤーに戻るのである。

Westfalia 号の定期傭船契約には，次のようなオフハイヤー条項が定められていた。すなわち，「人員または船用品の不足，機関の故障，修理の欠陥または損傷により連続48時間を超えて本船の業務が停止し，時間の喪失が生じたときは，本船がその業務を再開することが可能な状態に復帰するまで，傭船料の支払は停止されるものとする」。この本船はアフリカから Harburg 向け積荷航海中，高圧エンジンの故障で Las Palmas への入港を余儀なくされた。しかし同港では修理ができないので，本船は低圧エンジンを補助としつつ，Harburg に曳航された。Harburg 到着後，有効に稼働していた本船の蒸気ウィンチと荷役機器を用いて揚荷が行われた。この事件につき，貴族院は次のように判示した。すなわち，Las Palmas から Harburg に曳航中は，本船はオフハイヤーの状態であった。なぜなら，貨物は本船に積載されたまま目的港へ運送されたが，本船は曳航中，曳船の援助なしには航行が不可能であり，その点において本船は十分な稼働状態になかったからである。しかし，揚荷が開始されてからは，その時点で本船は要求されている業務を行うことができるようになったのだから，オンハイヤー状態に戻った。Halsbury 卿は，次のように述べている。「その期間中（揚荷期間中），船主は傭船料の支払を請求する権利があると思われる。なぜなら，本船は十分に稼働していたからである。つまり，その時本船は，要求された業務を有効に遂行していたのである」。
Hogarth v. *Miller* [1891] A.C. 48.

したがって，本船が不堪航の状態で航行している事実のゆえに，その不堪航の状態が治癒されるまで必ずしもオフハイヤーとなるわけではない。傭船者は，オフハイヤー条項に列挙された事項の一つに該当することを示したうえで，かつそれが時間の喪失を生じさせたことを示さなければならない。なお，この点に関しては，*The Hermosa* [1980] 1 Lloyd's Rep. 638 事件

(艙口蓋に欠陥がある本船が，空船航海を行った事案）ならびに The Berge Sund [1993] 2 Lloyd's Rep. 453 事件（追加のタンク清掃作業が，傭船者に時間の喪失を生じさせなかった事案）を参照。

「正味喪失時間」オフハイヤー条項と「期間」オフハイヤー条項

　前出 Hogarth v. Miller 事件では，傭船者が要求する業務を本船が遂行できるようになるやいなや，オンハイヤー状態に復すると判示された。この判断は，当該傭船契約のオフハイヤー条項の文言に沿ったものである。一方ニューヨーク・プロデュース書式のオフハイヤー条項は，それと異なる文言になっており，本船が能力を回復した時期に関係なく，「傭船料の支払は，それによって喪失した時間について中断する」と規定している。その趣旨は，列挙された事態の発生によって傭船者が喪失した正味通算時間分をオフハイヤーの時間として傭船者に認めるべきだとの点にあると思われる。一方，Hogarth v. Miller 事件におけるオフハイヤー条項の趣旨は明らかに異なっている。この文言は，オフハイヤーの「期間」を明確に決めることを目的としている。例えば，Tynedale v. Anglo-Soviet (1936) 41 Com. Cas. 206事件（後出432頁）では，そのオフハイヤー条項では「時間の喪失の開始時点から，本船が業務再開可能な状態に復するまでの間，傭船料の支払が停止する」と規定されていたが，Roche 卿判事は，「正味の喪失時間を確定することは，このオフハイヤー条項とは無関係である」と判示している。オフハイヤーの期間は，ある事由の発生によって始まり，他の事由の発生によって終了することとなる。

365　The Pythia [1982] 2 Lloyd's Rep. 160 事件で，Robert Goff 判事は，「期間」オフハイヤー条項と比較して，ニューヨーク・プロデュース書式は「正味喪失時間」オフハイヤー条項であると判示した。この考え方は，既に The H. R. Macmillan [1973] 1 Lloyd's Rep. 27 事件の第一審において，両法廷弁護士によって容認されており，さらに控訴院（[1974] 1 Lloyd's Rep. 311（314頁））においても記録長官 Denning 卿が傍論において採用している。Denning 卿は，オフハイヤー条項に関する上記のような解釈に基づき，本船のクレーンの一つが故障しても，残るクレーンの稼働で必要な作業を行い時間の喪失がなかった場合，傭船料の支払は停止しないと判示した。この点について，ボルタイム書式の文言（「それによって喪失した一切の時間」）は，ニューヨーク・プロデュース書式の文言と類似している。The Ira [1995] 1 Lloyd's Rep. 103 事件で，Tuckey 判事は，そのような正味喪失時間条項のもとでは，傭船者は実際に時間を喪失したことを証明しなければならないとして次のように述べている（同判例集104頁）。「……傭船者が，オフハイヤーの事態の発生と，その継続を示すのみでは，必ずしも傭船者が時間を喪失したことを立証したことにはならない。その立証の内容は，個々の事案の事情によって変わってくる」。

　それゆえに，ニューヨーク・プロデュース書式とボルタイム書式のオフハイヤー条項は，「正味喪失時間」条項であり，そのようなものとして適用されるべきである。しかし，ニューヨーク・プロデュース書式の場合，これまでの判例では，喪失時間の査定に際し本船が稼働能力を回復した後の期間は算入しないという裁量的な例外を認めているようである。ボルタイム書式では，この点は明文で規定されている。ニューヨーク・プロデュース書式の場合，The Marika M [1981] 2 Lloyd's Rep. 622 事件と The Pythia [1982] 2 Lloyd's Rep. 160 事件でのオフハイヤー条項に関し，このような解釈がなされている。

　The Bridgestone Maru No. 3 [1985] 2 Lloyd's Rep. 62 事件において，Hirst 判事は，タンカー定期傭船契約の Shelltime 3 書式におけるオフハイヤー条項は「期間」オフハイヤー条項であり，「正味喪失時間」オフハイヤー条項ではない，と判示した。

傭船料全額の支払義務が再開する時期

「期間」オフハイヤー条項では,明らかに,傭船料の支払義務は,本船が業務能力を完全に回復した時点で再開することになる。

　Carisbrook 号の定期傭船契約には,次のような規定があった。「本船の業務を阻害する損傷によって,時間の喪失が連続24時間を超える場合,本船が業務能力を回復するまで,傭船料の支払は停止するものとする」。本船は座礁し,貨物の陸揚を余儀なくされ,その後本船の修理が行われたという事件が起こった。ここで,傭船料の支払は,修理の完了した10月18日に再開するのか,それとも貨物の再積込の完了した10月30日に再開するのか,という問題が生じた。この問題に対しては,修理完了により本船は業務遂行能力を回復し,傭船料の支払はその時点から再開するとの判断がなされた。Bailhache 判事は次のように述べている,すなわち「確かに,本件事故により,10月30日午前8時30分まで時間が喪失していることは疑いがない。もしオフハイヤー条項が,事故の結果傭船者が喪失した時間のすべてにつき傭船料の支払を要しないと規定していたのであれば,(傭船者の法廷弁護士の)主張は正しかったであろう。しかし,そのような文言は使用されていない」。
　Smailes v. *Evans* [1917] 2 K.B. 54.

　上記事件で Bailhache 判事が指摘したように,「正味喪失時間」条項のある場合では,論理的には,本船が完全に稼働能力を回復した後であっても,オフハイヤー事由により生じた正味の喪失時間分を,傭船者は傭船料から控除する権利があると言える。例えば,本船がオフハイヤー事由の発生した場所に戻る必要がある場合,論理的には,本船が同地点に戻るために喪失した時間分を,傭船者は控除する権利があると言えそうである。

　ところが,この見解は,*Vogemann* v. *Zanzibar* 事件ならびに *The Marika M* 事件(後述)では採用されなかった。少なくとも,ニューヨーク・プロデュース書式第15条に関して言えば,この見解は支持されないようである。*Vogemann* v. *Zanzibar* 事件の事案は次のとおりであった。

　Zanzibar 号の定期傭船契約のオフハイヤー条項は,「船員または船用品の不足,機関の故障または損傷,舵または推進機器の破損または損傷,座礁(河川における場合を除く),本船または貨物の海損事故による滞船,その他船舶の完全な業務(貨物の積/揚も含む)を阻害する事由により時間を喪失した場合,連続24時間を超える喪失時間に対して,傭船料の支払を要しない」と規定されていた。*Zanzibar* 号は,Hamburg から米国へ航行中,海損事故による修理のため Queenstown に回航することを余儀なくされた。本船は,事故発生時から Queenstown を出港するまでの間は,明らかにオフハイヤーであった。さらに,傭船者は,事故が発生した地点に本船が復帰するまで「時間」の「喪失」が継続したのだから,本船が同地点に達するまでオフハイヤーが続いた,と主張した。

　Phillimore 判事は,事故が発生した地点に本船が復帰するまでの時間に対し,傭船料が支払われるべきか否かという問題は,「本船または貨物の海損事故による滞船」の文言の解釈に帰すると述べている(第一審報告書の253頁)。さらに,同判事は続けて次のように述べている。「オフハイヤー条項のもっとも安全な解釈方法は,同条項を免責もしくは権利消滅条項の一つと考えることであると思う。同条項に基づいて,傭船料が支払われる期間から,一定の時間が控除されることとなる。ゆえに,控除となることを望む事由があれば,傭船者はそれを条項中に挿入すべき義務を負っていると思う。本定期傭船契約には,本件で問題とされている時間がオフハイヤーだとする文言はないが,原告は上記オフハイヤー条項の文言を根拠にオフハイヤーになると主張している。しかし,私の見解では,オフハイヤー条項の『滞船』という文言は,本件では適用されない。『滞船』という文言は,例えば『遅滞』ほど強い文言ではない。本船が修理のため,ある港に回航され,そこで繋留されている限り,滞船している。しかし,修理が完了し,航海を再開すれば,もはや滞船しているとは言えないと思う」。

同判事は，さらに，本船が原点に復帰した正確な時間を計算することは，きわめて困難であろう，と付言している。

控訴院は，上記判決を支持した。記録長官 Collins は，Phillimore 判事の判断を支持したが，さらに付け加えて，「本船が完全なる業務能力を回復したとき，傭船料の支払は再開する。これは本条項の自然な解釈で，もしこれと異なる解釈をとれば，喪失時間の計算を複雑にしてしまう」と述べた。

Stirling 判事および Cozens-Hardy 卿判事も同様に上記判断を支持した。特に，Stirling 判事は，「傭船料の支払が停止するには，本船の完全なる稼働状態を妨げる事態の発生がなければならない。本船の修理が完了し，完全なる稼働状態を回復すれば，本船はもはやオフハイヤー条項にいう『滞船』には該当しない」と述べている。

Vogemann v. *Zanzibar*（1901）6 Com. Cas. 253 および（1902）7 Com. Cas. 254（C. A.）。

Vogemann v. *Zanzibar* 事件の判決は，「海損事故による滞船」によって時間の喪失がある場合に，傭船料は滞船期間中だけ停止するという，狭義の命題について，先例としての意義をもつ。しかし，この判決は，問題となっている条項（ニューヨーク・プロデュース書式におけるオフハイヤー条項とすべての点で同一である）において，本船が再び完全な稼働状態に復した後，喪失時間についての傭船料控除は許されないと解釈されるべきである，という広義の命題についての先例であると思われる。

確かに，Roche 卿は，*Tynedale* v. *Anglo-Soviet* 事件（下記参照）において，当該事案のオフハイヤー条項の文言の差異には言及しなかったが，*Vogemann* v. *Zanzibar* 事件の判決は，より広義の原則を示したものと評価し，次のように述べている。「……本航海の途中，業務能力を喪失し避難港に向かった場合，修理を受けた後本船が業務能力を回復してから元の地点に復帰するまでの時間について，傭船者が傭船料を支払わなければならない点で，船主は条項解釈上，有利になったものである。すなわち，傭船料請求を阻止する事由が終了した時点で，傭船料の支払が再開したのであるから，本船の故障によって時間が喪失したにもかかわらず，船主は傭船料の支払を受けたといえる。そして，私はこの解釈が正しいと考える」（(1936) 41 Com. Cas. 206, 220頁）。

Parker 判事もまた，*The Marika M*（後出）事件において，*Vogemann* v. *Zanzibar* 事件の控訴審判決は，より広い原則を示した先例であり拘束力があると述べている。

Marika M 号は，ニューヨーク・プロデュース書式で定期傭船され，7月17日に座礁しなければ，7月18日に Bahrain 港のバースに着岸する予定であった。本船は7月27日に離礁したが，バースに着岸するには8月6日まで待たなければならなかった。傭船者は，本船は7月27日（本船はこの日に離礁し，完全なる稼働状態を回復した）以降も，8月6日まではオフハイヤーであった，と主張した。理由として，本船座礁の結果8月6日まで時間を喪失したため，と傭船者は主張したのである。これに対し，船主は，本船が離礁し，完全な稼働状態を回復した時点以降は，オフハイヤーではないと反論した。Parker 判事は船主の言い分に軍配を上げた仲裁人の判断を支持するとともに，派生的な時間の喪失を査定することの困難さ，ならびに船主が主張した解釈が長年採用されているようにみえる事実を強調した。

The Marika M [1981] 2 Lloyd's Rep. 622.
(*The Pythia* [1982] 2 Lloyd's Rep. 160 事件の Robert Goff 判事の判決も参照)

すなわち，英国法の下では，米国法の考え方とは異なり（この点に関しては，後出447頁を参照），ニューヨーク・プロデュース書式第15条に基づき，本船が稼働状態に復帰すれば直ちに，傭船料の支払が再開すると言えそうである。一方，この例外のために，本船が業務能力を完全に回復するまでは，傭船料の支払は再開されないものと思われる。例えば，全般的な故障

が生じた後，部分的に業務能力を回復しても，この例外を適用するには不十分であり（部分的業務不能の問題については下記を参照），また正味喪失時間の計算は，業務能力が完全に回復するまで継続する。なお，完全な業務能力とは，傭船者がその時々に要求する業務に照らして判断されなければならない（*Hogarth* v. *Miller*［1891］A.C. 48事件参照）。

ボルタイム書式では，この点，付加文言によりその解釈は明瞭である。同書式の第11条(A)には，「それにより喪失した一切の時間に対して，傭船料の支払を要しない」という文言が使用されており，同条項が「正味喪失」条項であることが明らかである。しかし，さらに続けて「本船が即時要求されている業務を行えない期間」という文言が付加されていることにより，（完全な）業務能力の回復後に，傭船料の支払が再開されることは明確である。

NYPE 93

ニューヨーク・プロデュース書式1993年改訂版のオフハイヤー条項は，次の文言が挿入されることにより，上記状況での傭船料支払再開の時期は遅れることとなる。「本船が航海中，傭船者の指図または指示に反し，または貨物の事故もしくは本傭船契約の257行から258行目で容認されている場合以外の事由により離路し，または引き返したときは，本船が離路を開始し，または引き返し始めた時点から，本船が再びその開始地点または目的地から等距離の地点において航海を再開するまで，傭船料の支払は中断する」（前出12頁の英文書式の226行目から230行目と57頁を参照）。

部分的業務不能

本船が業務を再開するのに十分なる稼働状態を回復するまでは傭船料の支払が停止される，と定める条項（「期間」条項）においては，部分的業務不能は，完全な業務不能と同じ効果を有する。いずれの場合も，本船は完全にオフハイヤーとされ，本船の部分的稼働状態に対しては，何らの考慮も払われない。

 Horden 号は，旧版のボルタイム書式により定期傭船された。そのオフハイヤー条項には，「入渠，その他本船の稼働状態を維持するために必要な作業または……船体の損傷その他の事故により連続24時間を超えて本船の業務が阻害された場合，その時間喪失の開始から本船が業務を再開するのに十分な能力を回復するまでの間，傭船料の支払が中断する……」と規定されていた。本船は，Archangelから Liverpool に向け航海中，甲板に積んだ木材の移動により，フォアマストに重大な損傷を被った。Liverpool までの航海には影響なかったが，同港における荷役作業で，後部に積んだ木材は本船の荷役機器を用いて行われたものの，前部に積んだ木材は破損したマストに妨げられて，本船の荷役機器が使用できず，フローティングデリックの使用を余儀なくされた。傭船者は，本船は揚荷期間を通じて不十分な稼働状態にあったから，揚荷の全期間がオフハイヤーになると主張した。一方，船主は，本船が揚荷を行える以上，たとえその作業が遅いといえども本船には業務能力があり，傭船は継続すると反論した。控訴院は，本船の完全なる業務は荷役機器の部分的業務不能により阻害され，その全揚荷期間を通じてオフハイヤーになると判示した。同判決で，Roche 卿判事は，「損傷を被ったマストは，航海を阻害しなかったが，揚荷を阻害した。ここにいう阻害とは，*Hogarth* v. *Miller* 事件で貴族院が示した解釈，すなわち揚荷すなわち傭船契約にしたがって要求される本船の業務の阻害，という意味である」と判示した。
 Tynedale v. *Anglo-Soviet*（1936）41 Com. Cas. 206.

 Hogarth v. *Miller* 事件では，曳航中，本船が低圧機関を補助として使用した点については，まったく考慮が払われなかった。

368 しかし，ニューヨーク・プロデュース書式のオフハイヤー条項（同条項は「正味喪失時間」条項である）のもとでは，部分的業務不能の場合には，それにより現実の時間喪失がある場合に，その範囲でのみ傭船料が控除されることとなる。The H. R. Macmillan〔1974〕1 Lloyd's Rep. 311 事件において，記録長官 Denning 卿はニューヨーク・プロデュース書式のオフハイヤー条項について次のように述べている。「この条項それ自体からすると，同条項は，もしクレーンの1個が破損した場合，それによって時間が喪失したかを検討しなければならないことを意味する。その検討自体きわめて難しいものである。例えば，3個あるクレーンのうち1個が破損し，残り2つが稼働して必要な作業のすべてを処理することができ，実際に処理できた場合には，［破損による時間の喪失］はなく，傭船料の支払は停止しない。しかし，もし3個のクレーンに相当する作業があって，1個のクレーンの破損によって時間の喪失があった場合には，その喪失時間を査定する必要が出てくる。この場合，原審の判事が指摘したように，『2個のクレーンではなく，3個のクレーンが終始稼働能力を有していたならば，本船はどれくらい早く，船積港または荷揚港を出港できていたか』という問題が問われなければならない。原審判事はこの条項を［正味喪失時間］条項と呼んだ」。

傭船開始前に発生した事由

オフハイヤー条項に定める事由により，傭船期間中に時間の喪失があった場合，その時間喪失を生ぜしめる事由が，傭船開始以前に発生したかどうかは重要なことではない。したがって，傭船開始前の座礁によって被った損傷を修理するため，本船が傭船開始後に入渠した場合でも，本船はオフハイヤーとなる（The Essex Envoy (1929) 35 Com. Cas. 61 ならびに The Apollonius〔1978〕1 Lloyd's Rep. 53 の各事件を参照）。同様のことは，ニューヨーク・プロデュース書式99行から101行までの速力の低下について言える。傭船契約に基づく本船引渡時点で存在した本船船体の欠陥により時間を喪失した場合にも，傭船料の控除ができる（〔1985〕2 Lloyd's Rep. 164 および後出446頁の The Ioanna 事件を参照）。

人員の不足

「人員の不足」という規定は，業務を遂行できる職員および部員の十分な定員が乗船しているが，彼らの全部または一部が業務遂行を拒否している場合には適用にならない。

> 1943年12月，Ilissos 号の職員および乗組員は，New South Wales の Newcastle から，護衛つきでなければ出港しないと6日間以上にわたって出港を拒否した。控訴院は，この場合人員の不足ではないから，「人員の不足」という規定の適用はない，と判示した。
> Royal Greek Government v. Minister of Transport (1948) 82 Ll.L. Rep. 196.

たとえ乗組員の人数が不足していても，それが本船の効率的な稼働に影響を及ぼさないのであれば，つまり本船の完全な稼働状態を妨げないのであれば，オフハイヤーにはならない（The Good Helmsman〔1981〕1 Lloyd's Rep. 377 事件（同判例集422頁）を参照）。ニューヨーク・プロデュース書式97行から98行に規定するすべての事由（「人員の不足」も当然含まれる）によりオフハイヤーが生じるには，それによって99行にいう「本船の完全な稼働状態が妨げられた」ことが条件になる（〔1977〕1 Lloyd's Rep. 368 と後出434頁の The Mareva A. S. 事件を参照）。

病　　気

十分な定員の職員および部員が乗船しているが，彼らの大多数が，病気または負傷により業務を遂行できない場合に，それが「人員の不足」に該当するか否かについては，*Royal Greek Government* 事件において議論がなされた。第1審の Sellers 判事は，これを肯定する見解を示したが（81　Ll.L. Rep., 359頁），控訴院の Bucknill 卿判事はその見解に疑問を投げかけた（82 Ll.L. Rep., 199頁）。

369　人員の不足というためには，職員および部員の不足でなければならない。「人員」には，商船を敵の潜水艦から護るために配置する砲兵は含まない（*Radcliffe* v. *Compagnie Général Transatlantique*（1918）24 Com. Cas. 40 事件を参照）。

NYPE 93

ニューヨーク・プロデュース書式1993年改訂版の220行では，1946年版の「人員の不足」という文言から，「職員もしくは部員の不足および・または怠慢および・またはストライキ」という文言に変更されている（前出12頁と56頁を参照）。

故　　障

機関の瑕疵により時間の喪失が発生し，機関の状態がしだいに悪化する場合，「故障」は，修理のため避難港に向かうことが合理的に必要となる時点で生じたと言える（*Giertsen* v. *Turnbull*, 1908 S. C. 1101事件を参照）。

本船もしくは貨物の海損事故による滞船

滞　　船

海損事故による滞船は，海損事故の結果生ずる単なる遅滞以上の意味を有する。以下に紹介する判決で，Kerr 判事が述べているように，滞船は，「傭船契約に基づく本船の業務に関連して，本船の動きに対し，物理的に，もしくは地理的に何らかの制約が加わる」ものでなければならない。

　　ニューヨーク・プロデュース書式に基づいて傭船された本船が，US Gulf から Algiers に向け穀物を運んだ。運送中，艙口蓋の瑕疵により海水漏れを生じ，貨物に濡損が生じた。この濡損で，Algiers での揚荷は，当初予定より15日間余計にかかってしまった。ただし，この期間中本船は，要求されるすべての業務を完全に遂行する能力，特にすべての本船船艙から貨物を揚荷する完全な能力を持ち続けていた。この事案に対し，本船は貨物に対する海損事故によって「滞船」したものではない，ゆえにオフハイヤーにはならない，と判示された。
　　The Mareva A. S. [1977] 1 Lloyd's Rep. 368.
　　（また，*Vogemann* v. *Zanzibar*（1901）6 Com. Cas. 253 および（1902）7 Com. Cas. 254（C. A.）事件も参照。）

海損事故

「海損事故」とは，損傷を引き起こす事故を意味する。「海損事故」が共同海損を引き起こすことはあるが，その「海損事故」は，共同海損事故を意味するものではない（*The Mareva A. S.* [1977] 1 Lloyd's Rep. 368 事件）。

NYPE 93

ニューヨーク・プロデュース書式1993年改訂版には，「cargo」（貨物）の後ろに「unless resulting from inherent vice, quality or defect of the cargo」（貨物固有の隠れたる瑕疵，性質または欠陥による場合を除く）との文言が付加されている．223行と224行を参照．また，同改訂版には，新たなオフハイヤー事由として，「本船のアレストによる滞船」（ただし，そのアレストが傭船者，その代理人または下請業者が責任を負う事由によって生じる場合を除く）が加えられている（本書の12頁の英文書式の同改訂版221行から223行と56頁を参照）．

ニューヨーク・プロデュース書式1993年改訂版はまた，ボルタイム書式11条(B)の一部を次のように取り入れている（後出の642頁を参照）．「本船が，悪天候のため港や錨地への避難を余儀なくされたとき，または水深の浅い港，浅瀬のある河川もしくは港へ就航した場合の滞船および／あるいは，滞船によって生じた費用は傭船者負担とする」（前出12頁の英文書式の231行から233行と57頁を参照）．

70 もしくは本船の完全な稼働を妨げるその他一切の事由によって

本船の完全な稼働を妨げるということ

「本船の完全な稼働を妨げる」との文言は，「その他一切の事由」のみならず，その前の部分すなわち97行から98行にかけて列挙されている「人員の不足」等々の事由のすべてに，かかっている．The Mareva A. S. 事件（[1977] 1 Lloyd's Rep. 368）において，Kerr 判事は次のように述べている（同判例集382頁）．「『その他』『もしくは本船の完全なる稼働状態を妨げるその他一切の事由』という文言は，前の部分で列挙されている多様なオフハイヤー事由についても，それによって本船の完全な稼働が妨げられ，かつその結果傭船者が時間の喪失を被る場合にのみ，オフハイヤーという効果を生ぜしめるものであることを示している，と私は考える」．

Mareva A. S. 号事件において，貨物に対する海損事故は本船の完全な稼働を妨げることはなかったとして，本船はオフハイヤーではなかったと，Kerr 判事は，判断を下した．たとえ，艙口蓋の欠陥による漏れで，貨物の濡損が生じたとしても，本船はその時要求された業務――すなわち揚荷作業――を完全に遂行することができたとして，揚荷作業の期間につき本船はオフハイヤーにはならない，と判示した．Kerr 判事は，同じ判決の中で（同判例集382頁）次のように述べている．「例えば，たとえ貨物が事故の結果損傷を被ったものの，しかし本船の完全な業務遂行能力がそれによって妨げられたり，阻害されない場合，本船そのものはすべての点において完全に稼働しているので，オフハイヤー条項には該当しない，と私は思う」．

「本船の完全な稼働」の意味については，以下の事例で考察し，それに続く項で論ずることとする．

傭船者の要求する業務を有効に遂行する

ニューヨーク・プロデュース書式97行，98行に列挙されている他の事由についても言えるが，「その他一切の事由」によって時間の喪失が生じ傭船料の支払が停止するのは，その事由が本船の完全な稼働を阻害した場合だけである．The Aquacharm 事件（後出）において，記録長官の Denning 卿は，次のように述べている．「まず，最初に問うべき点は，本船の完全な稼働が阻害されたかどうかという点である．それが阻害された場合にのみ，『事由』をまさに考慮することとなる」（なお，The Roachbank [1987] 2 Lloyd's Rep. 498 事件（504頁から507頁）における，Webster 判事の判決を参照）．また，Court Line v. Dant & Russell（後出）事件において，Branson 判事は，河川で障害物に阻まれた本船につき，その本船がまだ完全な稼

働状態であったとして，オフハイヤーにはならないとの見解を示した。

　Errington Court 号は1937年3月にニューヨーク・プロデュース書式にて定期傭船された。本船は，揚子江の上流750kmの位置のWu-huに向かうことを命じられた。本船がそこに到着したときに，日本と中国との間で戦争が勃発し，中国は船を沈めて，日本船が揚子江を遡江するのを阻止するための防材を作った。その結果，*Errington Court* 号は障害物に阻まれた形になった。Branson判事は，傭船契約は履行不能に陥ったと判示したが，付け加えてもう一つの主張，すなわち本船はオフハイヤーになったかどうかという点に関し，次のように述べた（352頁）。「傭船者は第15条を根拠にオフハイヤーになったと主張している。論点は，障害物によって生じた遅滞が，『本船の完全な稼働状態を妨げるその他一切の事由』に含まれるか否かということで，私は含まれないと考える。私は，この結論を出すのに *Hogarth* v. *Miller* の判例に依拠せず，この傭船契約の文言に依拠した。なお，この傭船契約の文言は，*Hogarth* v. *Miller* 事件において裁判所が解釈を行った傭船契約の文言とは根本的に異なっている。本件の傭船契約のオフハイヤー条項の文言は，本船はすべての点において支障はないが，このような事由で航海の継続が妨げられる場合を含んでいない」。
　Court Line v. *Dant & Russell*（1939）44 Com. Cas. 345.
　（また，*The Wenjiang* [1981] 2 Lloyd's Rep. 308 および [1982] 1 Lloyd's Rep. 128（C. A.）事件を参照。この判決では，局地戦争によりShatt川に閉じ込められた本船につき，Shelltime 3書式のもとでオンハイヤーであるとした仲裁人の判断につき控訴院は控訴を許可しなかった。）

[371]　前出 *Court Line* v. *Dant & Russell* 事案では，本船そのものは十分な稼働状態を維持していたが，本船それ自身とはまったく関係のない何か外因的な事由によってのみ，すなわち河川の防護柵のために，傭船者が要求する業務の遂行が制限された。さらに最近の一連の事件で，裁判所は，本船自身または本船に関連した事由が，直接的あるいは間接的に，本船の業務遂行を妨げる状況の事例を扱っている。まず，本船が十分に稼働可能とみなせるかが論点となる。その際，本船は十分に稼働可能であるが，業務の障害を本船の外的な要因によるとみることができる場合（なお，その場合は前出 *Court Line* v. *Dant & Russell* 事件での状況の側面と一致する）がありうる一方で，業務の障害が外的な要因とは到底言えないような場合がある。そこで，その障害が外因的であることが，船主の事案にとって，真に本質的な要素であるのか否か，あるいは，逆に，問題は第1の側面すなわち，本船が所要の業務を遂行するのに十分な稼働能力を有していたのか否かが判断されなければならない。
　前出 *Hogarth* v. *Miller* 事件では，問題に当面した時に傭船者が要求する業務は一体何であるのかを明確にすることの重要性が強調された。主機関が損傷し，航海中には十分な稼働能力がないとしても，揚荷作業中は，その時要求される業務を十分に行うことができるとして，オフハイヤーにならないとされた。同様に，*The Berge Sund* [1993] 2 Lloyd's Rep. 453事件では，原因を特定できない貨物汚損をなくすために特別なタンク清掃が必要となった事件について，傭船者がその時点で要求している業務は，なお一層のタンク清掃であると，控訴院は判示した。そして，本船はその目的のためには十分な稼働状態にあり，オフハイヤーではないと判断された（この事件の詳細は，後出701頁を参照）。
　「本船が十分な稼働状態にあり，傭船者が要求する業務を即座に遂行できる状態」に，本船がないことの立証責任は傭船者が負う。なおこの文言は後出 *The Roachbank* 事件で Webster 判事が使っている。

　Aquacharm 号は，ニューヨーク・プロデュース書式で一航海だけ定期傭船された。パナマ運河を通行できる範囲での最大喫水まで貨物を積むことを命じられたが，船長の不手際でパナマ運河の一部である淡水湖を通る際，船のおもて部分の喫水が深くなることを考慮しなかった。その結果パナマ運河

に入ることを拒否された。結局，かなり遅延したあげく，貨物の一部を下ろし，それを別の船でパナマ運河を通り抜け運んだ後，再び本船に積み込んだ。傭船者は，このとき本船はオフハイヤーであったと主張した。これに対し，Lloyd 判事は正しい基準を次のように表現した。「オフハイヤーかオンハイヤーかを決めるものは，本船そのものが十分な稼働状態にあるのかどうか，つまりその時点で本船に要求される業務を十分に遂行できる能力を持っているかどうかである。もし，そういう能力を持っているのであれば，外因的な事由でその業務の遂行が妨げられたとしても，オフハイヤーにはならない」。結局，Lloyd 判事は，本船はその意味で十分な稼働状態にあったので，オンハイヤーだったと判示したのである。この判断は，控訴院でも支持された。
　The Aquacharm ［1980］2 Lloyd's Rep. 237 および［1982］1 Lloyd's Rep. 7（C. A.）。

　The Aquacharm の事案では，貨物を積みすぎて，それが過度の喫水となり，そのために本船が遅延した。本船自体，機関，装備もしくは乗組員にはなんの欠陥もなかった。記録長官 Denning 卿の言葉を借りれば，「本船は十分に稼働していた，しかし貨物の一部をおろす必要が生じて遅延が生じたのである」。前出 The Mareva A. S. 事件の，Kerr 判事の言葉である「本船自体，あらゆる点で十分に稼働できる状態にあった」も参照。これから紹介する事例は，問題が本船自身の（疑わしい）状態に，より密接に関連しているものである。

　Apollo 号は，ニューヨーク・プロデュース書式により傭船された。Naples 港での揚荷中に2名の乗組員が発疹チフスの疑いで病院に運ばれた。その後，本船は船積のため Lower Buchanan へ向け出港した。Lower Buchanan 港沖に到着すると，検疫官が本船し Naples 港で発生した事件の事情を聴取し，船員および本船を検査した。発疹チフスの形跡は発見されなかったが，検疫済証は，船内消毒が完了するまで出なかった。検査および消毒のため，検疫済証を取得するのが遅れ，傭船者は約30時間を喪失した。傭船者は，「その他一切の事由により」の後に「いかなるものでも」という文言を付して修正された第15条を根拠として，本船をオフハイヤーにする権利があると主張した。Mocatta 判事は，次のように判示した。検疫済となるのが遅れたのは，乗組員が病気（発疹チフス）になったことが原因となっており，本件の状況下では，検疫官の行為は「単なる手続き」を超えて本船の完全な稼働を阻害しているので，本船は喪失時間中オフハイヤーになると。
　The Apollo ［1978］1 Lloyd's Rep. 200.
　（乗組員の1人が逃亡し1人の欠員を生じたが，十分な稼働状態にある本船に入国管理官が乗り込んできたために本船が遅延した場合の事案と比較せよ（The Good Helmsman ［1981］1 Lloyd's Rep. 377（C. A.）事件（同判例集422頁）を参照）。ただし，Ackner 卿判事の判決が正しく報告されているかについては，若干の疑問がある。また，The Roachbank ［1987］2 Lloyd's Rep. 498 事件（同判例集505頁）の Webster 判事の見解も参照）。

　The Aquacharm ［1982］1 Lloyd's Rep.（11頁）事件において，Griffiths 卿判事は，The Apollo 事件の判決に対し次のように述べている。「発疹チフス汚染の嫌疑をうけた本船は，その嫌疑が晴れるまでは，十分なる稼働を妨げられていると言える。と言うのは，責任を伴う人間であればそのような状態の本船を使用しないからである。その場合，本船が荷役をできなかったのは直接的には嫌疑を受けている本船自体の状態に起因している。これは，私の見解では，本件（The Aquacharm 事件）とは明らかに異なるものである」。このような方法は，The Bridgestone Maru No. 3 事件（［1985］2 Lloyd's Rep. 62）にも適用されている。この事件は，本船のブースターポンプがイタリアの規則 Registro Italiano Navale の基準に合致せず，イタリアの港で遅延を生じた事件であるが，Shelltime 3 と同じような文言「本船の十分な稼働状態を妨げる一切の事由……」のもとに，本船は，遅延した期間，オフハイヤーになると判示された。83頁で，Hirst 判事は次のように述べている，「The Aquacharm 事件における Griffiths 卿判事の言葉に合わせれば，本船が揚荷役をできなかったのは，本船自体の嫌疑のためであった。その結

果，乗組員は，機器の一部，すなわちポンプを使用できなかったのである」。

 The Mastro Giorgis 事件（［1983］2 Lloyd's Rep. 66）において，Lloyd 判事はニューヨーク・プロデュース書式の当該条項の適用範囲を拡大している。すなわち，穀物の貨物受取人が航海中に貨物損害があったとして本船をアレストし，それによって本船運航に支障が生じた場合，本船は傭船契約第15条（「その他一切の事由」の後に再び「いかなるものでも」（whatsoever）という文言を付加して修正されている）に基づき本船はオフハイヤーであるとする仲裁人の判断が支持されたのである。Lloyd 判事は69頁で次のように述べている。「本船の物理的状態ばかりではなく，仲裁人の言葉を借りれば，本船の性質ならびに特徴にも注意を払わなければならない。性質ならびに特徴には，本船の歴史，所有関係も加わることになると，私は考える。本船のアレストは，私の見解では，本船の状態そのものが原因でなければ，直接的にその本船の歴史に起因すると考える」。

 しかし，この The Mastro Giorgis 事件の判決が，この条項の解釈の限界点を示しているのかもしれない。例えば，その後難民を洋上で救助した本船の入港を，港湾局が拒否したような場合，本船はオフハイヤーとはされていない。

 Roachbank 号はニューヨーク・プロデュース書式で傭船され，その第15条は「any other cause」の後に「whatsoever」という文言が付加されるという修正がなされていた。東シナ海において，同船は遭難船を発見し，かなりの数のベトナム難民を乗船させた。本船が台湾の高雄に到着したとき，当局は難民の上陸を許可せず，本船に対しては港外にとどまるよう要請した。傭船者は，これによって喪失した時間分，オフハイヤーであると主張した。仲裁人から上訴されたが，Webster 判事は，仲裁人の多数が認定した結論を覆すことを拒否した。仲裁人の多数が認定した結論は，本船上に難民が乗っている事実，またその人数が，本船 Roachbank 号の要求されている業務，すなわち高雄港に入り積荷役を即刻行うことを妨げているとはいえないというものである。すなわち，本船の完全な稼働は妨げられておらず，オンハイヤーの状態が続いたとされた。

 The Roachbank ［1987］2 Lloyd's Rep. 498.

 外部の機関が本船に対してとった行動に関連して（この場合は，国際運輸労連 ITF），Shelltime 3 書式の同様な文言のもと，同じような結論が判示されたケースにつき，以下を参照。

 Manhattan Prince 号は，Shelltime 3 書式で傭船された，そのオフハイヤー条項（第21条）はまったく修正されておらず，次のような文言であった。「本船の完全な稼働を妨げるその他一切の事由……」。ITF のボイコットの脅しに対応して，船主は ITF の条件に合致した乗組員を採用すると約束したが，その後，ITF 料率に合致しない給与の船員に切り替えた。そのため ITF により Oxelsund でボイコットされ，本船に遅延が生じた。Leggatt 判事は，本船はオフハイヤーではないと判断した。同判事は，この状況での「有効に稼働」の文言は，「有効に物理的に稼働した」ことを意味すると判断し，確かに，本船は ITF の行動によって傭船者の望むようには稼働していないが，本船は十分に稼働できる状態であったとされた。

 The Manhattan Prince ［1985］1 Lloyd's Rep. 140.

 The Manhattan Prince 事件では，Leggatt 判事は，Shelltime 3 書式の「有効な稼働」の意味は，実際に，本船の物理的に有効な稼働に限定されるものと解釈した。一方，The Mastro Giorgis 号事件では，Lloyd 判事は，上述のとおり，Shelltime 3 書式と同じ文言をもつニューヨーク・プロデュース書式の当該文言につき，いくぶん広い意味を与えた。現時点では，将来裁判所が，どの程度まで本船の物理的状態から逸脱した広い解釈を行うかについては，はっきりしていない。前に述べたように，今の時点でその解釈の限界点に到達しているのかもしれな

い。

　本船の完全もしくは有効な稼働が妨げられる事態が存する場合，次にはそれが，オフハイヤー条項に列挙された事由によって生じたものか，それとも「その他一切の事由」によって生じたものかを考えなければならない。

「その他一切の事由」と同種解釈の原則

　法律の通常の考え方は，「その他一切の事由」という言葉の範囲は，同種解釈の原則に従って制限されるべきか，あるいは少なくともその意味するところがオフハイヤー条項および傭船契約の文脈によって制限されるとする見解が有力なようである。しかし，「いかなるものでも」(whatsoever)との文言が，「その他一切の事由」(any other cause)という文言の後に挿入されている場合は，同種解釈の原則は排除されることとなる（後述参照）。

　同種解釈の原則は，特定の文言または句に続いて，概括的文言が使われている場合，その概括的文言の広い意味を制限しようとする解釈上の原則である。契約当事者は約定しようとする特定事項を念頭におきながらも，契約文書作成においては，契約当事者が意図していたものよりどうしても広い意味を有する概括的文言を使ってしまうという気遣いから，この原則は生まれたようである。もちろん当事者の真の意図は，契約書の当該部分またはその他の部分で使われている文言または句から明らかに分かる場合がある。そのため，具体的な事案からこの原則をどの場合に適用し，どの場合に適用しないのかの明確な基準を引き出すことは難しくなっている。

　いくつかの事案では，特定事項の列挙に続き概括的文言がある場合に，この原則を自動的に適用すべきではないかと考えられた。そうすると，問題はこの原則を適用すべきか否かといったことではなく，例えば列挙事項すべてがもつ属性を示すことができない場合にこの原則の適用ができるか否かということが問題となる。しかし，Devlin 判事は，*Chandris* v. *Isbrandtsen-Moller* [1951] 1 K.B. 240 事件で，オフハイヤー条項中に使用される概括的文言が限定的意味を有するのだとする旨の何らかの表示が当該傭船契約書の中にない場合は，その概括的文言が通常有する広い意味で取り扱わなければならないと指摘した。同判事は，*Anderson* v. *Anderson* [1895] 1 Q.B. 749事件の控訴院判決に依拠したが，その *Anderson* v. *Anderson* 事件の判決の中で，「……概括的文言は，それが特定列挙事項と同種の事項のみを意味するものとして使用されていることが明白な場合を除き，一般的には，その有する広い意味に解釈されるべきである」と記録長官 Esher 卿は述べている。

　Rigby 卿判事は，単に特定的文言の後に概括的文言が続いているということだけでは，同種解釈の原則が適用されるべきであるとの十分な意図が示されているとは言えない，と付け加えた。この考え方は正しいと言われている。

　この同種解釈の原則が，ニューヨーク・プロデュース書式の概括的文言に適用があるのかどうかについては，これまでのところ判例はない。*Adelaide Steamship* v. *The Crown*（No. 2）(1923) 17 Ll.L. Rep. 324 事件では，この原則が適用されるべきだとして，その試みが行われようとしたが，結局その点は，決定されなかった。*The Apollo* [1978] 1 Lloyd's Rep. 200 事件において，Mocatta 判事は，同種解釈の原則は，「その他一切の事由」の後に「いかなるものでも」との文言を加えたことによって排除される旨を判示したが，同判決は，その文言がなければ，この原則を適用しようとしていたことを示唆しているようである。*The Mastro Giorgis* [1983] 2 Lloyd's Rep. 66 事件において，Lloyd 判事は，同じような結論に到達している。もっとも，この点に関しては船主の法廷弁護人は既に譲歩していた。

　The Aquacharm [1980] 2 Lloyd's Rep. 237 事件において，Lloyd 判事は，この原則が適用

されるかどうかはそれほど重要なことではないとの見解を示しているが，次のようにも付言している（同判例集239頁）。「傭船者の法廷弁護士は，もしこれらの文言がその条項の文脈もしくは『基盤』にしたがって解釈されるのであれば，その広い意味に何らかの制限が加えられてもよいことを承認した。しかし，このことは同じことを別の言い方で表現しただけではないかと思われる。同種解釈の原則は，私にしてみれば，すべての契約の条項は，言葉の上でも，またその背景からも，その文脈に沿って解釈すべきであるとの，より一般的な原則を説明しているに過ぎない」。

The Roachbank [1987] 2 Lloyd's Rep. 498 事件（同判例集507頁）において，Webster 判事は，同種解釈の原則をたぶん適用すべきであると考えた。同判事は次のように述べている。「オフハイヤー条項の文言に修正なく，その条項に『いかなるものでも』との言葉が付加されていなければ，同種解釈の原則が適用できるし，たぶん適用すべきだと思う。そして，もし本船とまったく無関係な事由が，オフハイヤー条項のなかの『その他一切の事由』という言葉の意味に該当しないと認定されたとしても，それは全然驚くべきことではない。もっともこの事例では，私はその点を認定する必要はない」。Leggatt 判事が上述の The Manhattan Prince 事件で，この原則を使用している例も参照。そこでは，未修正 Shelltime 3 書式における「本船の有効な稼働状態」という文言の意味を，本船の物理的状態に限定している。

しかし，この原則を厳格に適用する試みも，先行して列挙された事由が包含する属性を見い出すことができなくて，失敗するかもしれない。この点につき，前出 The Apollo 事件において，当該文言は，本船またはその乗組員の内在的事由に制限され，外部的な障害や遅延を排除すべきである，とする法廷弁護士の議論に対し，Mocatta 判事の示した見解を参照。以上から，概括的文言の解釈にもっとも真実に近い見解を示しているのは，The Aquacharm 事件において上に引用した Lloyd 判事の言葉であるのかもしれない。

ボルタイム書式の文言（「その他の事故」）については，これまで同種解釈の原則の適用はない，とされてきた（後出642頁を参照）。

NYPE 93

ニューヨーク・プロデュース書式1993年改訂版のオフハイヤー条項においては，1946年版の「cause」の後に，「similar」（同様の）との文言が付加されていることにより，同種解釈の原因のみが有効であることを明確にしている（前出12頁の英文書式の225行と56頁を参照）。

「その他一切のいかなる事由」

同種解釈の原則は，「その他一切の事由」の文言の後に，「いかなるものでも」を付加すれば，その適用が排除される。この点に関し，The Apollo 事件の Mocatta 判事と The Mastro Giorgis 事件の Lloyd 判事の判断を参照。また，The Aquacharm 事件で Lloyd 判事が述べた解釈に関する一般的な原則についても参照。

しかし，「whatsoever」（いかなるものでも）を挿入させる当事者の意図は，例えば Court Line v. Dant & Russell 事件における防護柵のように，本船とまったく関係のない事由によってもオフハイヤーとなすべきであるというものでもあるが，まだその意図は達成されていないようである。その理由は，「その他一切の事由」と言っても，まずそれが「本船の十分な稼働状態を妨げる」ことが求められるからである。つまり，この後の句に限定的な解釈が与えられてきたがためである。The Mastro Giorgis 事件において，Lloyd 判事は次のように述べている。「ここに，『whatsover』（いかなるものでも）との文言が付加される場合，物理的であれ，法律上であれ，本船がそのときに要求される業務の完全な遂行を妨げるものであれば，そのす

べての事由が本船をオフハイヤーにするのに十分であるように思われる。ある事由が本船の完全な稼働を妨げたかどうかを決定するに際し，*Court Line* v. *Dant & Russel Inc.* 事件の防護柵のようなまったく本船そのものと関係のない事由と，機関の故障などの本船そのものの状態に帰しうる事由とに区別がなされる」。

前出 *The Roachbank* 事件において，Webster 判事は，「いかなるものでも」（「whatsoever」）との文言が付加される場合の背景にある当事者の意図を否定することに反対すると述べている。すなわち，その文言が付加されれば，本船そのものと関係ない事由とその他の事由を区別するのは不適当であるというのである。Webster 判事は次のように言っている。「問われなければならない点は，判例によれば，本船が十分に稼働可能で，本船自身，その時傭船者に求められた業務を遂行しえたかどうか，という点である。もし，この問いに対する回答が否であり，オフハイヤー条項に『いかなるものでも』（whatsover）との文言が付加されていれば，そして『その他一切のいかなる事由でも』が限定的に解釈されないとすれば（もっとも，限定的に解釈されるようなことはほとんどないと思うが），本船の完全な稼働を妨げた特殊な事由が何であるのかを考える必要はない」。

控訴院は，Webster 判事の判決に対する控訴を却下した。なぜなら，Lloyd 判事との見解の相違は異なる結論をもたらすには至らなかったからである。仲裁人は，*Roachbank* 号は Lloyd 判事の基準を適用して，オンハイヤーであったと判断した。Webster 判事は，オフハイヤーとなる事由を広く解する見解をもつが，その見解のもとでも，その事件をオンハイヤーと判断し，同じ結論になっている（The Roachbank［1988］2 Lloyd's Rep. 337 事件を参照）。このように，Webster 判事の見解と Lloyd 判事との見解の相違は，いまだ解決されていない。

一方，Martin Davies が［1990］1 LMCLQ 107 で指摘しているように，第15条（オフハイヤー条項）の適用を拡大しようと考える当事者は，「その他一切の事由」という文言を修正する方法をとるよりも，「本船の完全な稼働状態を妨げる」という文言を，本船自体が効果的に稼働したかどうかという点を弱め，かつ実際に，傭船者の商取引上の必要を満たすために本船が稼働できたかどうかを示す文言に置きかえるべきである，とする。

オフハイヤー条項の事由は偶発性のものでなければならない

「その他一切の事由」という文言は，また偶発性のある事由に限られ，傭船者が本船を利用することの当然の結果としての事由を含まない。*The Berge Sund*［1993］2 Lloyd's Rep. 453 事件（同判例集460頁）で，Staughton 卿判事は次のように述べている。「もし，傭船者がある航海で本船に撒積の石炭を積むことを命じ，次の航海で撒積の砂糖を積むことを命じた場合，砂糖を積むために必要とされる清掃を船主勘定の時間で行わせることを期待することはできない」。

Rijin 号がニューヨーク・プロデュース書式により傭船されていたとき，貨物の待ち時間およびそれに続く積荷作業の時間が長引き，本船の船底に海の生物が付着して汚れた。そのために喪失した時間につき，傭船者は，船底の汚れが「本船の完全な稼働状態を妨げるその他一切の事由に該当する」として，本船のオフハイヤーを主張し，加えて本船の速力が「船体の瑕疵によって」低下したとして，第15条の後段部分の99行から101行の部分を援用して，傭船料から時間の喪失分を控除できると主張した。Mustill 判事は，この傭船者のいずれの主張も退けた。Mustill 判事は次のように述べている。「傭船契約の作成者は，本船の完全な稼働が妨げられる事態が生ずるすべての場合に，傭船料の支払を停止することを考えていなかったはずである。この読み方は，取引通念上意味をなさず，このオフハイヤー条項の後段部分を冗漫な繰り返しにしてしまう。私の判断では，オフハイヤーかどうかを考慮するに値する事由は，偶発性のある事由に限られ，傭船者の指示に従った本船に必然的に生ず

る事由を含まない。海の生物が付着して船底が汚れた場合については，その海の生物の付着がまったく異常かつ予想し得ない例外的な事件のみ，オフハイヤーとなる要件を満たすのである。*Cosmos Bulk Transport Incorporated* v. *China National Foreign Trade Transportation Corporation* [1978] 1 Lloyd's Rep. 53 [*The Apollonius*] 事件を参照，これは通常とは異なる文言に関する裁定であり，また仲裁人は非常に特殊な事実認定をしている。しかし，大多数の事例では，海の生物の船底への付着増大は，単なる本船運航の当然の結果であるにすぎず，けっして偶発性のものではない。本条項の後段部分に基づくクレームに関し，私は同じ見解をもっている。傭船契約期間中に船底に海の生物の付着が増大することを船体の『瑕疵』とみなすことは非常に難しいと言わざるをえない。しかし，仮にそれが船体の『瑕疵』と言えるにしても，その瑕疵は傭船者がその本船を使用する際の当然の結果として，生起したものである。それゆえ，私は，この場合の時間の喪失は傭船料から控除すべきものではないと考える」。

The Rijin [1981] 2 Lloyd's Rep. 267.

（しかし，一方で，本船の船底が海の付着物で汚れた状態で，傭船者に引き渡された案件に関し，[1985] 2 Lloyd's Rep. 164 と後出446頁の *The Ioanna* 事件を参照）

376 傭船者の義務違反により生じた事由

オフハイヤー条項に該当する事由が，傭船者の傭船契約の明示ないし黙示の条項の違反により発生した場合，裁判所は，次の二つの方法のいずれかにより処理することができる。一つの方法は，本船をオフハイヤーにすると宣言しながらも，損害賠償として船主に傭船者から傭船料を取り戻させることであり，もう一つは，本船がオンハイヤーの状態を保持しているとみなすことである。通常は，どちらを選んでもほとんど差異はないが，ある種の状況下では，どちらを選ぶかが重要な問題となる。

ニューヨーク・プロデュース書式のオフハイヤー条項は，過失については何も規定していないので，発生した事由がその文言に該当するだけで自動的に適用になる，という主張もできるが（前出427頁を参照），いくつかの判例ではこれと反対に，オフハイヤー条項に定める事由が傭船者の契約違反によって生じた場合には，傭船者はオフハイヤー条項の適用を主張できないとする見解を支持している。*Board of Trade* v. *Temperley* (1927) 27 Ll.L. Rep. 230 事件の控訴院判決においては，傭船者が傭船契約上の明示または黙示の条項に違反したため，時間喪失が生じたのであれば，傭船者はオフハイヤー条項の適用を主張できないと考えられたようであるが（詳細は，Scrutton 卿判事の判決，232頁を参照），この事案では契約違反は立証されなかった。*Fraser* v. *Bee* (1900) 17 T.L.R. 101 事件においても同様の推定がなされたが，この事案も参照。以下の判例では，傭船者が傭船契約に基づき提供する義務に関係して，時間の喪失が生じた場合，傭船者はこの条項の適用を主張することができないとされ，いくらかより狭い解釈が支持されていることは明らかである。もっとも，その判断は，単なる条項の解釈だけでも到達できたはずである。

Megna 号は，傭船者が提供した粗悪な燃料炭の危険な燃焼により遅延した。オフハイヤー条項は，次のように規定していた。

「本船の業務を阻害する機関の故障または船体の損傷によって，連続24時間を超えて時間を喪失した時は，本船が業務を再開するのに十分な稼働状態を回復するまで，傭船料の支払は停止する。もし，故障または損傷が海上で発生し，本船が引き返す必要が出てきた場合，それが貨物に起因するものではない限り，傭船料の支払は，本船が原点に復帰するまで停止する」。

この事案に関し，判決は，この条項の前段・後段とも，機関の故障または船体の損傷に限定されており，そのいずれも発生しなかったのであるから，オフハイヤー条項は適用されない，とした。同判決中で，Greer 判事は「傭船者が責任を負う事項」，本件では傭船者提供の燃料によって時間の喪失

が生じた場合には，傭船料の支払は停止しないと述べている。
　　Nourse v. Elder Dempster（1922）13 Ll.L. Rep. 197.

　Lensen v. Anglo-Soviet（1935）52 Ll.L. Rep. 141 事件において，控訴院は，ボルタイム書式の下で，傭船者が安全バースへの配船義務に違反した結果被った船体損傷の修理中に，本船はオンハイヤーである，と述べた。先例となる Greer 卿判事による判決は，一つには傭船契約で合意された就航区域を越えて本船を動かすときは傭船者はオフハイヤー条項を発動できないこと，もう一つは補償約款に基づいているが，同判事はさらに，「厳密な意味では，本船がオフハイヤーであったとしても」，船主には損害賠償による傭船料請求権があることに言及している。この判決は，傭船者の指図によって生じる遅延が，明示または黙示の補償によって担保されている場合は，特に傭船契約上の就航区域の制限を越える運航指図がなされた場合（非安全港，非安全バースへの配船も含む）に限り，先例としての拘束性が認められなければならないが，それ以上に広範な解釈を支持する判決ではないと考えられる。Greer 卿判事が，本船が「厳密な意味では」オフハイヤーとなりうると判断したことは，より一層の注意を要する問題を提起している。とはいえ，前出の判例と併せた効果は，オフハイヤーの事由が，傭船者の契約違反によって生じる場合には，オフハイヤー条項は機能しなくなるということである。

傭船料支払の停止

　The Lutetian [1982] 2 Lloyd's Rep. 140 事件において，Bingham 判事は，ニューヨーク・プロデュース書式の下では，第15条が，列挙された事項によって時間を喪失した場合，「傭船料の支払が停止する」と規定していることにより，その時点で本船がオフハイヤーになれば，支払期日に傭船者は傭船料の支払を行わなくてもよい，と判示した。さらに，オフハイヤーになっている状況下においては，傭船者が次の月の傭船料を前払しなければならないとしても，本船が再び傭船者の業務に復帰する直前まで，その前払を一時停止することができるとする，傭船者の言い分を Bingham 判事は認めている。この判決を，上述の427頁の一般原則と調和させるのは難しく，実務上きわめて不安定な状況を作り出している。この点については，さらに上級裁判所の判断が出るまで気をつけて処理することが望まれる。

オフハイヤー期間中の燃料およびその他の義務

　オフハイヤー条項の適用により傭船料の支払を要しないという単なる事実は，当該オフハイヤー期間中の傭船者のその他の義務を軽減するものではない。したがって，反対の趣旨の明示規定がある場合を除き，傭船者はオフハイヤー中であっても，燃料を供給し，かつ燃料代を支払う義務を継続して負担する（例えば，Arild v. Hovrani [1923] 2 K. B. 141 事件を参照）。ニューヨーク・プロデュース書式では，第20条に，明文でオフハイヤー期間中は，傭船者は消費燃料代の支払義務を免除されているが，この条項は傭船者のその他の義務に及ばないから，もし他の義務についても免除されることを望むならば，それを規定する適当な文言を挿入しなければならない。ボルタイム書式には，燃料代が免除になるという明示の条項がない（この点に関し，前出 Arild v. Hovrani 事件ならびに The Bridgestone Maru No. 3 [1985] 2 Lloyd's Rep. 62 事件を参照）。それゆえ，ボルタイム書式の第4条の冒頭に，「オンハイヤーの間」（While on hire）との文言を付加修正するのが一般的となっている（前出280頁を参照）。

NYPE 93

ニューヨーク・プロデュース書式1993年改訂版では，オフハイヤー時に消費した燃料代は船主の費用，と規定されている（前出12頁の英文書式の230行から231行と57頁参照）。その他傭船者が提供すべき項目に関する限り，84行により，傭船者がその義務を果たすのは，本船がオンハイヤーであることが条件になっている（前出9頁と54頁を参照）。

船主または傭船者のその他の救済手段についての効果

傭船者の賠償請求

オフハイヤー条項は，船主に対する傭船者の損害賠償請求権を消滅させるものではなく，また縮小させるものでもない。このことはオフハイヤー条項が規定する事項に関する損害賠償についても同様である。傭船者が，船主の傭船契約違反の結果，本船の使用ができなくなったこと以上に，またはそれに加えて損害を被ったことを立証できる場合には，傭船者はそれらの損害の賠償を請求することができる。The Democritos [1975] 1 Lloyd's Rep. 386 事件において（同判例集401頁），Kerr判事は「オフハイヤーが船主の契約違反により発生した場合，傭船者がそれによりそれ以上の損害を被ったことを立証すれば，傭船者はオフハイヤー期間分の傭船料の支払義務を免れるとともに，もちろん既払であれば，その分の返還請求もできるが，これとは別にそれ以上の損害賠償を請求できる。この問題は，実際上はめったに生じなかったと思われるので，この見解は共通の認識であることをここに繰り返し述べることとする」旨説明している。たとえば，本船の装置の故障により本船にきわめて深刻な遅延を生じ，その原因が船主による引渡時において本船を運送業務に適した状態に保つ義務もしくは堪航性を保つ義務の違反であり，あるいは引渡後において本船を効率的状態に維持する義務の違反であり，また，万一その遅延が傭船者の航海の利益を大きく損なうようなものであるとすれば，傭船者の船主への損害賠償請求は，オフハイヤー条項による傭船料の払戻の部分に限定されない。もし，得られなかった航海の利益が，傭船料の戻分を上回るとすれば，傭船者は，損害と行為の間の相当因果関係の不存在の問題を条件に，損害賠償請求という形で，利益喪失分を請求することができる。また，オフハイヤー条項に基づく傭船料の取戻の権利も尊重される（本船に特別に備え付けられたガントリクレーンの故障による遅延に関する The H. R. Macmillan [1973] 1 Lloyd's Rep. 27 事件を参照。また，Sea & Land Securities v. Dickinson (1942) 72 L.l.L. Rep. 159 事件も参照。類似の判例として Leslie Shipping v. Welstead [1921] 3 K. B. 420 事件参照。この事件では，Greer判事は，船主の損害賠償請求権は，傭船契約中の船舶引揚条項によって，縮小されない旨判示した）。

船主の損害賠償請求

同様に，もし傭船者による契約違反の結果によって，オフハイヤー条項が適用されることになった場合，船主は傭船者の契約違反により被った損害の全部または一部として，喪失した傭船料を傭船者に対して請求することができる。

　　Dodecanese 号は，ボルタイム書式で傭船され，その傭船契約には「合法的就航区域で，適法な商品の輸送を行う」との規定があった。傭船者は，エジプトにいる英国軍のために，その本船に弾薬とその他火薬を積んだ。もっとも，そのことがエジプト政府当局により禁止されていることを，傭船者は十分知っていた。その結果，本船はエジプト政府当局のブラックリストに載せられ，その後本船の機器が故障したとき，エジプト政府当局はこの船の修理を遅らせ，本来ならば4日間で修理完了するところを30日間をも要した。傭船者はオフハイヤー条項にしたがって，30日間全部をオフハイヤーに

したが，Pilcher 判事は，傭船者は「適法な商品」のみを輸送しうるとの傭船者の義務に違反しており，船主は損害賠償としてオフハイヤー条項に基づき被った損害のうち26日分の傭船料を傭船者から回収する権利がある，と判示した。

　Leolga v. *Glynn*〔1953〕2 Lloyd's Rep. 47.
　(*Lensen* v. *Anglo-Soviet*（1935）52 Ll.L. Rep. 141 事件も参照)

　船主が，オフハイヤー条項の発動で傭船料を喪失したとき，前出355頁で議論した時間の喪失と傭船者の指図に従ったこととの間に強い因果関係の存在の証明が可能であり，黙示の補償が船主に与えられる場合，船主はまた失った傭船料を回復することができる。
　ところが，*The Berge Sund*〔1993〕2 Lloyd's Rep. 453 事件で，控訴院は，Mobiltime 2 書式のオフハイヤー条項の「傭船者の過失によらない」時間の喪失への言及により，傭船者側に過失がない場合，黙示の補償は排除されている，と判示した。

オフハイヤーによる傭船料の控除と本船の引揚

　オフハイヤー期間につき，傭船者が傭船料の控除を行う状況ならびにその控除額の査定については，前出306頁から311頁までの「傭船料の支払と本船の引揚」の項を参照。

ニューヨーク・プロデュース書式99行から101行に規定されている本船速力の低下について

　ニューヨーク・プロデュース書式99行から101行には，「船体・機関もしくは装備の故障または損傷」により，航海中速力が低下したときは，それにより喪失した時間，その結果余分に消費した燃料費，その他一切の費用が傭船料より控除される，との追加規定が置かれている。

船底の汚れ

　前出441頁の *The Rijn*〔1981〕2 Lloyd's Rep. 267 事件において，Mustill 判事は，本船傭船期間中に船体に付着した海の生物の堆積によって，特に傭船者が本船を使用した当然の結果として，船体への付着が生じた場合は，本船の航海速力の低下は，オフハイヤー条項100行の「欠陥」とはならないと判示した。一方，下記の *The Ioanna*〔1985〕2 Lloyd's Rep. 164 事件においては，Staughton 判事は，本船引渡前に既に本船の船底が汚れていたことにより航海期間中に本船の航海速力が低下したのは，100行に規定されている船体の「欠陥」となる，と判断した（*The Apollonious*〔1978〕1 Lloyd's Rep. 53 事件も参照）。

燃料の節約分

　もし，本船の航海速力の低下の結果，ある種の使用燃料油の消費量が減少する場合，その節約分は別の種類の燃料油消費の増加分の費用と相殺できることもある。しかし，ある燃料の節約分が別種の燃料の増加分を超えるような場合に，オフハイヤー条項に基づく請求によっては，船主はその差額を自分のものとすることができない。そのような状況の下では損害賠償の請求という形で請求がなされる場合にのみ，船主はその差額を自分のものと主張することができる。

　Ioanna 号は，1航海だけ定期傭船され，その傭船契約には，本船は「完全な稼働状態と外観の船体，機関，装備を有した」船舶と記載されており，オフハイヤー条項には，「……船体，機関，装備

の欠陥または故障によって，航海中速力が低下すれば，それによって喪失した時間，その結果余分に消費した一切の燃料費用やその他一切の費用が，傭船料から控除される」との規定があった。本船は，船底が汚れたままの状態で，つまり完全な稼働状態とは言えない状態で，傭船者に引き渡された。その結果，本船は契約で保証した速力を出すことができなかった。本船のディーゼル油の消費量は増加したが，燃料油（F. O.）の消費量は減少した。傭船者から提起された時間の喪失分とディーゼル油の消費量増加による追加費用分の回収に関する請求に対し，Staughton 判事は次のように判示した。

(1) もし，傭船者が船主の債務不履行による損害賠償を請求する場合は，船主は燃料の消費で傭船者が利得した部分と傭船者の時間の喪失分を相殺することができる。
(2) しかし，引渡時に船底が汚れており，そのために本船の速力が低下したのは「本船船体……の欠陥により」まさしく生じたものと言えるので，傭船者は，オフハイヤー条項に基づき請求を提起することができる。
(3) 「余分に消費した一切の燃料」との文言は，燃料油（F. O.）のみに限られるのではなく，ディーゼル油（D. O.）と燃料油（F. O.）の消費量の各々の増加・減少分を差し引いた正味の費用増加分を意味するものである。
(4) もし，燃料油（F. O.）の節約分が，ディーゼル油（D. O.）の費用増加分を上回っている場合，傭船者は燃料に関しては何らの請求もなし得ないが，その正味節約分につき船主に返還を要する，ということにはならない。

The Ioana [1985] 2 Lloyd's Rep. 164.
（しかし，傭船中に船底の汚れが生じたケースとして，前出 *The Rijn* 事件を参照）

380 米 国 法

一般原則

　米国裁判所によって採用されている原則は，オフハイヤー条項に列挙された事由の一つが傭船者に時間の喪失をもたらす場合には，船主の過失の有無にかかわらず，自動的に傭船料の支払義務が停止する，というものである。この原則は，指導的判例である Clyde Commercial S. S. Co. v. West India S. S. Co., 169 F. 275, 278 (2d Cir. 1909), 裁量上告拒絶214 U. S. 523 事件に，もっとも上手く要約されている。この判決は次のように述べている。

　　……第15条には，船主の過失の有無にかかわらず，その事態が発生すれば傭船料が停止することを意図した絶対的なカテゴリーが表示されているものと了解されなければならない……

時間の喪失

　傭船者は，傭船料を支払う対価として本船を利用する権利をもつが，オフハイヤー条項にはその事実が反映されている。The Yaye Maru, 274 F. 195 (4th Cir.), 裁量上告拒絶257 U. S. 638 (1921) 事件では，定期傭船された本船がBaltimore港に錨泊し，船積予定貨物である石炭の輸出解禁を待っていたとき，他船に衝突された。Yaye Maru は損傷を被り修理が必要となり修理を行ったが，石炭の輸出禁止は，その修理完了以降までも継続した。その後の訴訟において，船主は，傭船者は修理期間中も錨泊待機以外の目的に本船を利用することはできなかったはずだから，オフハイヤーにはならない，と主張した。しかし，裁判所はこの船主の主張をしりぞけ，修理期間中に傭船者が実際に本船を利用したであろうかどうかは重要ではない。傭船者は本船を使用することができなかったのであるから，傭船者にはオフハイヤーにする権利がある，と判断した。裁判所は，次のように述べている。

　　確かに，さもなければ存在しているオフハイヤーとする権利は，傭船者が本船を使用しないこと（傭船者の権利不行使）によって失われることはない。本船が保持することを約束している「完全に有効な稼働状態」が損なわれて，そのため本船を使用する権限が害される，そのような事態が発生し，それが継続している間は，傭船者は，許容された使用であればその使用の態様如何，あるいは不使用，使用の如何にかかわらず，オフハイヤーとする権利がある。傭船者は，本船を使用する権限を奪われている限り，傭船料の支払を行わなくてもよい (274 F. at 197-198)。

　機関，船体または機器が故障したとしても，それが傭船者の本船使用を妨げなければ，本船はオフハイヤーにはならない。例えば，本船の故障が揚荷または積荷を行っている間に生じて，それがそれらの荷役を妨げないのであれば，傭船者は継続してその間傭船料を支払わなければならない。

　いくつかの事件において，仲裁人は，本船の使用の一部が妨げられた場合，仲裁人は傭船者に対し，その代償として傭船料の減額支払を認めている。The Karen C, SMA 3042 (Arb. at N.Y. 1994) 事件では，本船の15タンクのうちの1個のタンク用の水中カーゴポンプが破損したが，傭船者はそれによる時間の喪失を立証できないままに，本船をオフハイヤーとしたのは不適切であった，と仲裁審は裁定した。傭船者は，タンクが使えなかった時間に比例した傭船料分しか控除できないと判断された。

The Shena and The Ave, SMA 2893 (Arb. at N.Y. 1992) 事件では，仲裁審は，「正味時間喪失の概念」に基づいてオフハイヤーを認めた。それは5本のクレーンのうち2本が故障して積荷作業に使えなかった事案であるが，使えなかった割合に応じた傭船料の控除を認めたのである（後出453頁の議論を参照）。

傭船料の再開

米国の裁判所と仲裁人は，オフハイヤー条項に列挙されたいずれかの事由によって喪失した正味の期間が傭船者に認容されるべきである，との原則におそらく従うものと思われる。*The Chris*, SMA 199 (Arb. at N.Y. 1958) 事件において，仲裁審は，第15条の「広く一般に認められている」解釈として，本船が修理のため当該航路より離路せざるをえなくなったような場合，オフハイヤーの期間は，本船が再び物理的に航行可能になった時点を越えて延長される，すなわち傭船料支払が停止された位置に本船が復帰するに要した時間も含むものと判断した。*The Grace V*, SMA 1760 (Arb. at N.Y. 1982) 事件では，オフハイヤーの期間は，密航者の発見時点から開始するのではなく，本船が密航者を降ろすために積港へ離路した時点から始まり，その最初に離路した位置と等距離を回復するまでの期間であるとされた（*The Chrysanthi G. L.*, SMA 1417 (Arb. at N.Y. 1980) 事件と上記で検討した *The Shena and The Ave* 事件も参照）。

ニューヨーク・プロデュース書式のオフハイヤー条項は，*Dunlop S. S. Co.* v. *Tweedie Trading Co.*, 162 F. 490, 493 (S.D.N.Y. 1908)，原審維持 178 F. 673 (2d Cir. 1910) 事件で問題となったオフハイヤー条項とは違っていた。この事件で問題となったオフハイヤー条項は，故障が生じた場合，傭船料の支払は本船が「業務再開可能な状態に復帰する」まで停止すると規定していた。裁判所は，本船が堪航性のある状態に復帰するまでだけ，傭船者は傭船料の支払を免除されると判断した。この事件の判例に基づけば，傭船料の支払の停止は本船の業務再開可能状態に復帰するまで，と傭船契約に規定してあれば，たとえ本船が修理のために離路しなければならなかったとしても，故障の修理が完了すれば，直ちに傭船料の支払が再開する，と裁判所は判断すると思われる。しかしながら，ニューヨーク・プロデュース書式では，その結論はまったく違ってきて，すなわち傭船者には喪失した正味の時間に照らして，オフハイヤーが認められると思われる（前出 *The Chirs* 事件，*National Transp. Corp.* v. *Texaco*, 1976 AMC 1549 (Arb. at N.Y. 1976) 事件を比較参照）。

The Plod and The Voce, SMA 2719 (Arb. at N.Y. 1990) 事件では，Florida からコロンビアまでの空船航海期間中に，傭船者がオフハイヤーとすることにより，傭船者が節約した時間と，節約した燃料の費用について，船主にはそれらの支払を請求する権利があると判示された。

人員の不足

不適格

米国の判例では，就労する職員および部員の能力に不適格があれば，本船はオフハイヤーになる。前出 *Clyde Commercial S. S. Co.* 事件では，2等機関士と3等機関士が発熱し業務につくことができなかったので，本船は当初 Colon において遅延した。裁判所は，この遅延は人員の不足によって生じたものであり，したがって，本船はその喪失した時間分オフハイヤーになる，と判断した。

同様に，*The Robertina*, SMA 1151（Arb. at N.Y. 1977）事件では，機関長が入院したが，このとき本船は「人員の不足」に陥ったと判断された。仲裁審は，代わりの機関長が本船に到着するまで，本船はオフハイヤーであったと判断した。
　さらに，「人員の不足」には，現実の不足だけでなく，解釈上の「人員の不足」というのも考えられる。*Tweedie Trading Co.* v. *George D. Emery Co.*, 154 F. 472（2d Cir. 1907）事件では，本船は New York 港検疫錨地に約2日間停留した。実際に病気であった乗組員が本船から移送された。代替乗組員が雇い入れられたが，本船の検査が完了するまで乗船を許可されなかった。この事件につき，裁判所は次のように判断した。

　　……本船の検疫錨地到着から，代替要員が実際に乗船するまでの間，人員の不足が［オフハイヤー］条項で意味する本船の業務を阻害した（同上，at 473）。

　このように，船主がいつでも就労できる十分な定員を用意しておきながら，検疫による乗組員の就労不可能から，解釈上の人員の不足が生ずるのである（*Gow* v. *Gans S. S. Line*, 174 F. 215（2d Cir. 1909）事件および *Noyes* v. *Munson S. S. Line*, 173 F. 814（S. D. N. Y. 1909）事件参照）。後者の事件では，本船が検疫上隔離された時は，解釈上の人員の不足になると判断されている。*The Canadia*, 241 F. 233（3d Cir. 1917）事件では，乗組員が酔っぱらいで無法者であったことを理由に，人員の不足があったと判断された。*Northern S. S. Co.* v. *Earn Line S. S. Co.*, 175 F. 529（2d Cir. 1910）事件では，病気による人員の不足があったと判断された。
　The Alcazar, SMA 1512（Arb. at N.Y. 1981）事件でも人員の不足があったとされた。この事件では，8人のポーランド人の乗組員がいることを理由に，本船は Florida 州 Pensacola の米国沿岸警備隊に抑留された。Pensacola は米国海防上，国家機密の領域と考えられており，米国／ソ連の海運協定でもそこへの入港は制限されていた。仲裁審では，8人のポーランド人の職員は Pensacola 港への入港を法律で禁止されて，その分「不足」している本船の状態が本船遅延の原因であるので，本船はオフハイヤーであった，と判断された。
　The Family Anthony, SMA 1820（Arb. at N.Y. 1983）事件でも同様の状況が発生している。本船は，米国のいくつかの港からサウジアラビアに向けて，武器と弾薬を輸送することになっていた。しかし，その本船の乗組員には6人のロシア人機関士が含まれていて，その6人は二つの積荷港で入港を禁止された。*The Alcazar* 事件では，入港を拒まれていた乗組員は本船が積荷港を出港した後，再び本船にもどったが，この事件では事情が異なり，ロシア人職員はその貨物が揚荷港で揚荷されるまで，本船に戻ることを禁止された。その理由は，積荷の一部が非常に高度の国家的機密性があるためであった。ところが，傭船者はそのことを船主に事前に知らせていなかった。この事件に関して，仲裁審は，船主はロシア人船員を米国からモスクワまで移送する費用と Dubai で再び本船に乗船させるために使った費用を傭船者から回収できる，と判断した。
　近年，国際運輸労連（ITF）によって組織されたストライキまたはボイコットの結果，多くのいわゆる「便宜置籍船」が，遅延している。通常の場合，本船が積荷または揚荷のため入港するとき，陸上労働者が ITF によって発表されたピケラインまはたボイコットを承諾することから本船の遅延が生じている。このような遅延は，本船乗組員が自ら就労を拒まない限りオフハイヤーとはならないことは明らかであるように思われる。むしろ，ボイコットは，例えば港湾労働者のストライキに相当するものと考えられるべきである。就航形態を定めるのは，傭船者であるから，本船の運航を阻害し，または遅延をもたらすストライキの危険を負担するのは傭船者である。傭船された本船が「便宜置籍船」として労働組合にねらいうちされるとして

も，この立場を変更するものではない。もちろん解決策は，傭船者が傭船契約に特約を設けて，船主がITFの要請に従うよう要求することである。そのような船主がITFの要請に従う旨を保証する特約の条項がある場合，その義務を怠る場合には，船主は契約違反となり，よって生ずる遅延に対しては責任を負わなければならない。

傭船者が指定した港でITF問題が予想されても，そのようなITF問題の港への就航を排除する条項が傭船契約に書かれていない限り，船主はその港への入港を拒否することはできない。

The United Faith, SMA 1409 (Arb. at N.Y. 1980) 事件では，ITFボイコットが予想されるAntwerp/Hamburg港揚の再傭船者の貨物を積むことを，船主は拒否できるかどうかの問題が，単独仲裁人の判断に委ねられた。傭船契約にも，再傭船契約にも，ITFの行為による遅延は除外されるが，それ以外のボイコットやブラックリストに載ることによる時間の喪失はオフハイヤーになるとのタイプで打った条項が存在した。また，その条項には，本船はITF証書を所有していない旨が書かれていた。仲裁人は，船主はその航海の遂行を拒むことはできないと判断し，次のように述べている。「ITF地域への本船の就航義務を制限する適切でかつもっとも普遍的方法は，傭船契約の就航区域を定める条項で，そのような問題のある地域への就航を排除することである」。この事件では，傭船契約にそのような規定がなかったので，船主にはその航海を遂行する義務があった。

就労忌避

United States v. *The Marilena P.*, 433, F. 2d 164, 1969 AMC 1155 (4th Cir. 1969) 事件では，傭船契約第17条は次の文言を含んでいた。

383　……ストライキを含むが，それに限定されない人員の不足のために時間の喪失があった場合には，傭船料の支払はその時間の喪失分だけ停止する……。

乗組員は，戦争地域への航海に抗議してストライキに入った。裁判所は，傭船契約第17条により人員の不足となり，本船は適当な人員および職員が仕事に戻るまでオフハイヤーであると判断した。ただし，ニューヨーク・プロデュース書式は，乗組員のストライキについてのオフハイヤー条項を含んでいないことに留意すべきで，*The Marilena P.* 事件で発生したようなストライキが，ニューヨーク・プロデュース書式のもとで「人員の不足」とみなされるかどうかは疑問である。*Edison S. S. Corp.* v. *Eastern Minerals*, 167 F. Supp. 601 (D. Mass. 1958) 事件を参照。

The Thunderbird, SMA 54 (Arb. at N.Y. 1964) 事件では，傭船者は労働争議の可能性があることを知りながら，本船をCamdenに配船した。本船は，陸上の労働者がストライキに突入してからちょうど35分経過したところで，バースに着いた。傭船者はWilmingtonに移動するように本船に命じたが，機関士がピケラインに従うことを約束したため，本船は本船自身の機関で動くことができず，また曳船の助力も手配できなかったため，結局ストライキが終わるまでCamdenに留まってしまった。傭船者は，機関士の機関室への就労拒否は，第15条の意味の範囲内で「人員の不足」を構成し，本船はストライキによって喪失した時間につき，オフハイヤーになると主張した。しかし，仲裁審は，船主を支持し，傭船者は労働争議の可能性を知りながら本船をCamdenに向けたのだから，「それにより喪失した時間につき傭船料の支払が免除されるべきだと主張する」ことはできないと判断した。

Montauk Oil Transportation Corp. v. *Sonat Marine Inc.*, 871 F. 2d 1169, 1989 AMC 1147

(2d Cir. 1989) 事件では，傭船した艀が New York 港のストライキのため遅延した。傭船契約には，ストライキに起因する遅延の危険性に言及する条項はまったくなかった。裁判所は，傭船契約に明示の条項によりその危険の分配がなされていない場合，時間を重んじる海事の原則を尊重する，すなわちそのようなストライキによる遅延の不利益は傭船者が負うべきものと判断した。したがって，ストライキによる艀の時間の喪失分につき，オフハイヤーにはならないとされた。もっとも実際には，裁判所は遅延の一部は船主の過失によるものとし，その部分の時間の喪失につき船主の負担とした。

本船または貨物の海損事故による滞船

指導的判例である *Barker v. Moore & McCormack Co.*, 40 F. 2d 410, 1930 AMC 779 (2d Cir. 1930) 事件において，裁判所は，船舶の完全な使用を妨げる予想外の本船の機能的損傷がある場合に，「海損事故」が発生すると判断した。この事件では，悪天候のため本船の燃料消費量が相当増加し，追加燃料補給のため離路が必要となった。しかし，悪天候は「海損事故」ではないと判断された。Chase 判事は次のように述べている。

> たとえ他にどのような考え方があるとしても，「海損事故」という理由でオフハイヤー条項を適用するには，明らかにある種の事故の発生が必要となる。北大西洋の冬季の悪天候は，航海上それに遭遇するか否かは，多少とも偶然性の問題であるという意味で事故である，ということがもっともらしく議論される。しかし，当該時期に荒天で悪名高い海域において，航行不能になるほどではないにせよ，荒天による時間の喪失を「海損事故」として原告負担とする意図があるのであれば，この傭船契約の当事者はその意図の表現に不適切な文言を選んだと言われてもしかたがない。これは航海よりもむしろ期間を基礎とする傭船契約の一般的な目的と正面から矛盾するものである。事故という言葉は，改めて定義づける必要がないほどよく使われてきた言葉のひとつであり，また従来なされた定義づけを，その特定の背景から切り離して一般的に依拠する指針とするにはあまりにも微妙な意味をもっている。本傭船契約の明らかな目的は，被告に迅速な航海の利益を与えることであり，またいかなる状態に直面しても本船がなすべきことをなすに当たってそれを妨げる事態が発生しないことを条件として，航海の遅延の危険を被告に負わせることである。この表現が，同種のものに解釈（ejusdem generis）されるならば，それは「本船の完全な稼働」を阻害するものを意味しなければならないし，そのように解釈されるべきであるとわれわれは考える。それは，地理的進行を妨げるといった類のものではなく，十分な乗組員，設備を有し，運航手段と動力を備えた本船が，自然の力を克服し，風波に抗して航行する時，本船を十分使用できなくする何らかの予想外の機能的損傷である。このような意味に解すると，いかなる種類の事故もなかったことは明らかである。本船は荒天の状況下，期待されるすべてのことを行ったのである（40 F. 2d at 411-412）。

ニューヨーク・プロデュース書式では，「貨物」に対する海損事故によっても本船がオフハイヤーとなる。しかし，この規定はしばしば削除され，その削除により貨物にのみ影響し，本船の運航には影響を及ぼさない事故によって失われた時間は，傭船者の負担になるという結果をもたらしている。

The Andros Oceania, SMA 2012 (Arb. at N.Y. 1984) 事件では，本船甲板上積丸太が崩れた事故が，海損事故と認定された。しかし，仲裁審は，事故は，傭船者がその貨物の積み方・固定の仕方を適切に行っていなかったことにより生じたとして，傭船者の傭船料返還請求を拒否した。

入　渠

　本船が，98行に列挙された目的で入渠している間はオフハイヤーになる。*Munson S. S. Line v. Miramar S. S. Co.*, 166 F. 722 (2d Cir. 1908), 他の理由で修正 167 F. 960 (2d Cir. 1909), 裁量上告拒絶 214 U. S. 526 (1909)：*Falls of Keltie S. S. Co. v. United States & Australasia S. S. Co.*, 108 F. 416 (S. D. N. Y. 1901) 事件。ドックが利用可能になるのを待っている間に生じた遅延では，オフハイヤーにはならないと思われる。*Albis Co. v. Munson*, 139 F. 234 (2d Cir. 1905)。ただし，*Noyes v. Munson S. S. Line*, 173 F. 814 (S. D. N. Y 1909) 事件では，ドック待ちをしている間の喪失時間につき船主が責任を負う旨判断されている。この事件では，本船が傭船契約の条項に従って入渠を必要とした時に，傭船期間は2日間を残すのみであった。船主はその時点では入渠を拒否したが，返船後直ちに修理のために入渠させている。この事実に基づき，傭船者は2日分の傭船料の返還を請求できるものと判断された。

　The Halifax and The White Sea, SMA 2984 (Arb. at N. Y. 1993) 事件では，傭船契約では，1年延長された傭船期間中の入出渠のための航海途中の本船利用については何らの制限もなく，本船を入渠させることが認められていたから，造船所までと造船所から傭船者への業務を再開する港までの航海期間は，本船を使用する権利が船主にあると仲裁審は判断した。

火　災

　直接火災に起因する時間の喪失だけが，オフハイヤーと認められる。*The Canadia*, 241 F. 233 (3d Cir. 1917) 事件では，10月8日に本船が埠頭で火災を発生させたときから，火災が鎮火し10月15日に本船が揚荷を開始するのに適する状態に復した時点まで，傭船料支払が停止すると判断された。しかし，この事件では，碇泊地での遅延により，揚荷作業は12月4日になるまで現に完了しなかったし，また本船は貨物を運送するのに適当ではないと宣言された。しかし，傭船者は10月15日から12月4日まで揚荷作業に本船を完全に使用したのであるから，その間の傭船料については支払義務があると判断された。

船体，機関または装備の故障または損傷

　列挙された原因の一つが生じ，かつそれによる現実の時間喪失がなければ，オフハイヤーは認められないと思われる。この原則は，*Steamship Knutsford Co. v. Barber & Co.*, 261 F. 866 (2d Cir. 1919), 裁量上告拒絶 252 U. S. 586 (1920) 事件において示されている。この事件で裁判所は，火災の後，貨物が検査のため本船より取り出される期間は，オフハイヤーにはならないと判断した。

　　砂糖の検査・再積込に必要な時間は，第16条の意味する「時間の喪失」ではない。その間，必然的に本船の遅延がもたらされるものの，傭船者はなお自分自身の目的のために本船を使用していたのであり，その使用目的は本船の損傷に起因しているものではなかった (261 F. at 868)。

　　同様の理由で，裁判所は船艙の損傷の検査および修理のための喪失時間は，オフハイヤー条項の「時間の喪失」となることを認めた（同上）。

　本船をオフハイヤーとするには，機関の「完全な故障」がなければならない。*American Asiatic Co. v. Robert Dollar Co.*, 282 F. 743, 746 (9th Cir. 1922), 裁量上告拒絶 261 U. S. 615

(1922)。

　本船のウィンチが傭船者の目的に照らし、十分な動力を有していないという事実は、オフハイヤー条項における機械の故障には当たらないと判断された（もっとも、裁判所は、この欠陥により本船は「いかなる点においても業務に適している」とはいえないと判断した）。前出 *Munson S. S. Line* v. *Miramar S. S. Co.* 事件。

　Lake Steam Shipping Co. v. *Bacon*, 129 F. 819（S. D. N. Y. 1904）、原審判断維持 145 F. 1022（2d Cir. 1906）事件では、本船が座礁し、再浮揚した後の修理のため離路を余儀なくされている。本船は結局は予定された揚荷港に到着し、同港で揚荷した。この事案では、傭船者は座礁のときから揚荷港に到着するまでの間、傭船料の支払義務を負わないと判断された。

　Temple Steamship Co. v. *Mercator Marine Corp.*, 1959 AMC 641（Arb. at N. Y. 1958）事件では、貨物の金属スクラップを船積中に、電磁石が隔壁と接触したため、本船の羅針儀が動かなくなった。回転羅針儀が本船に設置される間、本船は遅延し、傭船者はこの遅延につき傭船料からの控除の権利があると判断された。

　The Anoula A, SMA 307（Arb. at N. Y. 1967）事件では、悪天候による損傷は、第15条のもとでは「船体の破損または損傷」であり、修理が完了するまで本船はオフハイヤーである、と仲裁審は判断している。

　傭船者が本船の一部を使用できない場合、しばしば仲裁人は、傭船料支払の一部控除を認める。*The Lenoudis Kiki*, SMA 2323（Arb. at N. Y. 1986）事件では、本船の5個のウィンチのうち1個が動かなくなったが、5つの船艙のうち4つの船艙で作業を行った。この場合、仲裁人は、傭船者は傭船料の5分の1の控除とステベの待機費用を船主に請求できる、と判断した。同様に、*The Maria Glyptis*, SMA 2223（Arb. at N. Y. 1986）事件では、本船上の12のウィンチのうち1個が動かなくなり、その結果6個の船艙のうち1個で作業ができなかった。この場合傭船者は傭船料の6分の1を控除できるとされた。また船主は荷役業者の待機費用の6分の1につき責任があるとされた。これ以外の例として *The Mandolyna*, SMA 1967（Arb. at N. Y. 1984）事件がある。この事件では、傭船者はクレーンの故障による時間の喪失を立証できなかったのであるが、傭船者は、5本のクレーンのうち1本の不稼働により、5分の1の傭船料を回収できる、と仲裁人は判断した。

その他の一切の事由

　米国の判例は、オフハイヤー条項を解釈するにつき、同種解釈の原則に従っている。*Edison S. S. Corp.* v. *Eastern Minerals*, 167 F. Supp. 601, 605（D. Mass. 1958）事件において、裁判所は、傭船者の被雇用者を組織しようとしている労働組合の組合員によるピケに同情し、乗組員が行った本船ウィンチ操作の拒絶は、オフハイヤーの事由にはならないと判断した。Wyzanski 判事は次のように述べている。

　　支払拒絶の理由は、定期傭船契約の第15条に明確に特定されている。ストライキ、ピケに関しては何らの言及もない。列挙された理由の類型は、まったく異なる性質のものである。そして、オフハイヤー条項には、そこに列挙された具体的な特定原因に加え、「時間の喪失は……本船の完全な稼働を阻害する他の一切の原因により」という一般的な文言があるが、それはよく知られた同種解釈の原則に照らして解釈されなければならない。そしていかに拡大解釈をしても、本条項は、単に傭船者企業の事情によって生じた労働者の行為に起因する時間の喪失までも含むものではない。一方の包含は、他方の排除（*Inclusio unius exclusio alterius*）。

同旨判例として，*The Sea Ranger*, SMA 1240（Arb. at N.Y. 1978）：*The London Confidence*, SMA 1257（Arb. at N.Y. 1978）；*The Binship*, SMA 1416（Arb. at N.Y. 1980）。

しかしながら，*The Andros Island*, SMA 1548（Arb. at N.Y. 1980）事件では，本船がオフハイヤーとなるかどうかを決めるのに，仲裁人は，より広い基準を採用した。キプロスをめぐるギリシャとトルコの戦闘行為の勃発とトルコ軍のキプロスへの侵攻により，ギリシャ籍本船船長は，ルーマニア揚貨物のための傭船者の着埠指図と積取指図を拒否した。その航海ではトルコ領海域を通過せざるをえなくなることより，船主は船長にその貨物の積込を拒否するよう指示したのである。この事案につき，仲裁人は，船主のとった行為は正当化できないと裁決した。しかしながら，仲裁審は，これが傭船契約の特定の条項に該当し，オフハイヤーになる，とは言えないと判断した。ただし，仲裁審は，「……通常の概念におけるオフハイヤーの状況がいつの時点においても存在しなかったとしても，傭船者はそれにもかかわらず，船主との契約で，本船とその乗組員が提供するはずであった役務を享受する機会を奪われた」とし，それゆえに，傭船者は喪失した時間分の傭船料の払戻を受ける権利があると判断した。

The Hira II, SMA 2246（Arb. at N.Y. 1986）事件では，船長が本船のバース接岸を拒否した結果，船主と傭船者間で論争が起こった。船長は，その港に入るには，本船の喫水が深くなり過ぎている，と主張した。仲裁審の多数意見は，船長の接岸拒否は本船をオフハイヤーにしない，というものであった。仲裁人は，本船は傭船者の指図にすぐにでも，かつ十分に従うことができる状態にあったが，船長は本船の超過喫水の状態で，本船をバースにつける義務はなかったと認定した。この場合，傭船者が取れる代替策は，瀬取して損害賠償を求めること，別の港に本船を差し向けて損害賠償を求めること，もしくは船長の交替を要求すること等である。さらに仲裁人は，船長はそのような状況下で，不合理な行動を取ったことを，もし傭船者が立証できれば，傭船者は立証できた損害の賠償を請求できる，と述べている。しかし，単に損害賠償を求める権利があると主張するだけでは，傭船者の傭船料の不払を正当化することはできなかった。仲裁人によれば，「運賃もしくは定期傭船料という形での収入は，海運業にとってもっとも重要なものであり，それゆえその支払義務を途絶させ，遅らせ，もしくは怠らせるどのような方法も，当事者が合意したまさにその条項がもつ解釈の幅のなかで，狭く考察されなければならない」。

The Kitsa, SMA 3119（Arb. at N.Y. 1994）事件では，同種解釈の原則により，第三者の生命救助のための離路は，本船をオフハイヤーにする事由にはあたらない，と仲裁人は判断した。この判断をさらに支持するために，仲裁人は，米国海上物品運送法（COGSA）では人命救助のための離路につき船主の免責が規定されているが，傭船契約がこの COGSA を摂取していること，また違約金なしに人命救助のために離路できるとする「自由約款」が傭船契約に挿入されていることに，言及している。

傭船者の過失による本船の遅延は，本船をオフハイヤーにはしない（*The Andros Oceania*, SMA 2012（Arb. at N.Y. 1984）事件を参照）。*The Hoegh Mallard*, SMA 2679（Arb. at N.Y. 1990）事件では，本船の物理的欠陥，機関の過度の損耗，部品の問題，拙劣な本船操作や保守管理，異常な配乗方針等の要因が重なり合って，本船の主機関は徐々に劣化し，故障したことを理由として，傭船者は支払済傭船料の払戻を受けることができるとの裁定を得た。この事件では，傭船者は85パーセントだけの傭船料の払戻を受けることができるとされた。というのは，傭船者が提供した粗悪な燃料油が機関故障の原因に15パーセントだけ寄与していると判断されたからである。

387 本船の差押え（アレスト）

　本船がアレストされる場合、オフハイヤーになるであろうか。その疑問は多くの事例において生じるが、以下がその回答となるように思われる。すなわち、船主が責任を負うべき行為の結果アレストされれば、オフハイヤーになるし、反対に傭船者の行為もしくは傭船者に責任ある行為の結果アレストされれば、オフハイヤーにはならない。

　The Wismar, SMA 1454（Arb. at N.Y. 1980）事件では、本船が再傭船者からアレストされた。再傭船者の主張は、船主が不法に再傭船契約上の再傭船者の権利に干渉し、再傭船者の貨物積込を拒否したというものであった。原傭船契約の傭船者は、本船がアレストされたこの事件の当事者ではないが、本船がアレストされた時点から船主がアレスト解除の手段をとるまでの間、オフハイヤーを宣言した。仲裁人は、この傭船者の行為を正当と判断した。アレストによって本船はその業務から離脱し、そのアレストそのものも傭船者の行為の結果生じたものでないことより、本船を使用できない期間については、傭船者は傭船料の支払を要求されないのである。

　The Mesis, SMA 2167（Arb. at N.Y. 1985）事件では、油濁事故の嫌疑をうけ、船主が保証状を差し入れるまで、アルジェリア政府当局により Oran で抑留された本船に関し、傭船者から抑留期間の傭船料払戻の請求につき争われた。本船は、New Orleans からアルジェリアの Oran まで砂糖を輸送した。揚荷役は円滑に行われたが、揚荷役がまさに完了して出港しようとしたその日に、港湾局の官吏が乗船し、船長に油濁を惹起した廉で詰問した。翌日、当局より正式に港を汚染したとの嫌疑を受け、裁判所の調査を条件に10万ディナールの保証の提供を要求された。本船は Oran 港に5日間停められ、その間船主は当局の保証の要求を満足させようと試みた。結局当局の満足すべき保証が提供され、短い審理が行われた後、本船は油濁嫌疑に関して有罪とされた。査定をうけた罰金額が支払われ、結局油濁事故より1週間後、本船は Oran を出港した。この事案で、傭船者はその期間の傭船料の払戻を要求した。一方、船主はアルジェリア裁判所の決定はきわめて信用のおけないものであると主張した。しかし、仲裁審は、この案件を判断する先例はないと述べた上で、当事者はアルジェリア裁判所の決定に従わざるをえない、との判断を示した。さらに加えて、仲裁審は、罰金のために保証を提供するのは、油濁事故の直接的な結果であり、そのために喪失した時間を傭船者に負担させることはできない、との結論を下した。

　The Sea Ranger, SMA 1240（Arb. at N.Y. 1978）事件では、アレスト期間の傭船料につき、傭船者が責任を負うと判断された。このアレストは、Bahrain の荷受人によってなされたが、荷受人の請求は結局裁判所によって却下された。もちろん、傭船者みずからの非行のために本船がアレストされたり、もしくは合法的に拘留された時間について疑いもなく傭船者が責任を負うことは、仲裁審も十分に承知していた。しかし、この *The Sea Ranger* 事件では、傭船者は Bahrain の裁判所より有責だとはされていなかったのであるから、上記とは事情が異なっていた。それゆえ、第三者である荷受人から不当なアレストをされたことにより、本船の使用ができなかった時間につき、傭船者がその間の傭船料を支払わなければならないのか、との問題が出てくる。

　結局、仲裁審は、この場合のアレストの期間につき、オフハイヤーにはならないと判示し、その理由を次のように説明した。

　　一般的に言って、定期傭船者には、その傭船料支払につき、船主の過失もしくは傭船契約の明示の条項によって、その義務が終了するか中断されない限り、その全額の支払義務がある。貨物に関連

した動き，もしくは傭船者のその他の責任を根拠とすれば，第三者の本船アレストの正当性の有無如何にかかわらず，傭船契約の条項には，傭船者の傭船料支払義務を中断させる条項がないことに気がつく。確かに，傭船者は，傭船料支払の対価である本船の利用ができなかったのであるが，もし逆の結果であれば，もっと不公平なものとなるであろう。傭船者に関連した行為に起因した根拠の薄弱な請求を原因としてアレストが行われたとき，船主の傭船料を回収する権利は差し止められるべきであろうか。傭船契約で特にその旨規定していない限り，答えは明らかに否である。

388 仲裁審はまた，同種解釈の原則を適用すれば，アレストおよび拘留が第15条の「その他一切の事由」に当てはまらない，すなわち第15条に明確に列挙された事由と同じ種類のものではない，と判断した。

 The Sea Ranger 事件と The Orient Horizon, SMA 1709 (Arb. at N.Y. 1982) 事件では違った判断がなされている。仲裁審は，後者の事件につき，アレストされている期間につき，オフハイヤーが成立すると判断し The Sea Ranger 事件について次のように解説している。

> The Sea Ranger 事件での仲裁審の判断は，アレストの原因になった請求は根拠のないものとされているものの，傭船者が本船を使用できなかったのは自らの活動が関係したアレストによってもたらされたとの事実に基づき下された。一方，The Orient Horizon 事件でのアレストは，事実は船主の過失がほとんどないことを明らかにするが，明らかに船主が関係した活動に関連していた。しかしながら，もしあるとすれば船主の些細な過失が，本船のアレストを引き起こしたのであり，そこには傭船者は何らの関わりもない状況が存した。すなわち，何らの落ち度もなくあるいは責任もなく，アレストされている間本船の使用を阻害されている傭船者に，傭船料支払の継続を求めるのは，不適当であり，不公平であると判断する。

 The Athenian Horizon, SMA 1197 (Arb. at N.Y. 1977) 事件もまた参照。この事件では，傭船者は船主の本船引揚が不当であると訴えたが，認められず，この訴訟に関連した本船のアレスト中の時間の喪失分の傭船料は，傭船者が支払う責任があると判断されている。

 The Mercandian Supplier II, SMA 2509 (Arb. N.Y. 1988) 事件では，コンテナの中から10,500ポンドのマリファナが見つかり，米国税関によりアレストされたことによる遅延の責任を船主，傭船者のいずれが負うべきかという難しい問題に，単独仲裁人は判断を下した。コンテナはジャマイカで積まれ，本船の Miami 到着時，傭船者が提供したコンテナシールは完全な状態であった。マリファナは，揚荷役中に行われたコンテナ検査で発見された。税関当局は，米貨1,380,800ドルの罰金を賦課し，本船のアレスト解除に10パーセントの保証金を要求した。ところが，船主も傭船者も進んで保証金を提供しようとせず，そのため本船は遅延した。傭船者は遅延した間本船はオフハイヤーであると主張し，その分の傭船料を支払わなかった。単独仲裁人は，船主は傭船期間のすべてについて傭船料の権利があると判断した。仲裁人の事実認定は，コンテナは荷主と傭船者で詰められて本船に積まれ，マリファナは荷主によって不法に本船に持ち込まれたというもので，船主と傭船者の関係では，後者（傭船者）がこれによる喪失時間の責任を負うべきである，と判断した。

 The Omina, SMA 3116 (Arb. at N.Y. 1994) 事件では，船主は傭船者の未払傭船料を被担保債権として，再運送賃にリーエンを行使し，船荷証券にその旨記入した。荷主は，無故障船荷証券を本船が発行しなかったとして，本船をアレストし，その期間につき傭船者はオフハイヤーであると主張した。仲裁人は，船主が貨物にリーエンを行使し，その旨を船荷証券に記入する権利があると判断した。それゆえ，アレストの期間も本船はオンハイヤーの状態にある，と判断した。

The Bergen Bay, SMA 3060（Arb. at N.Y. 1993）事件では，航海中に貨物に損傷を生じたとして本船はイタリアで受荷主により，アレストされた。貨物損傷の原因は，貨物積付の拙さにあった。イタリア法では，船主も傭船者も運送人であると考えられている。受荷主は，船主と傭船者の双方が保証状を発行すれば，本船アレストを差し控えるつもりでいた。船主のP&Iクラブは船主のために単に保証状を発行しただけであるが，傭船者は別途の保証を提供することを拒否した。傭船者は，アレストされた時間分の傭船料を控除し支払わなかった。仲裁人は，船主は本船の解放のため要求されることをすべて行っており，傭船者も自らのための保証を提供する義務があったと判断した。結局，傭船者はアレストの期間につき不当に傭船料を控除したとして，仲裁人は，船主有利の裁定を行った。

　The Jerom, SMA 2790（Arb. at N.Y. 1991）事件では，傭船者は，傭船契約に基づき本船に対してリーエンを行使する権利が完全にあったとして，その結果であるアレストはオフハイヤー条項にいう本船の拘留になる，と仲裁人は認定した。

389 航海中の速力の減少

　この規定がなければ，速力の減少は，たとえ傭船者が損害賠償請求の権利を有するにしても，オフハイヤー事由とは考えられないと思われる（*Steamship Knutsford Co.* v. *Barber & Co.*, 261, F. 866, 870（2d Cir. 1919），裁量上告拒絶 252, U.S. 586（1920）事件を参照）。

傭船者のその他の義務

　米国裁判所は，オフハイヤー条項の適用は，傭船者の傭船契約に基づくその他の義務を停止しないという英国の見解に従ってきた（*Northern S. S. Co.* v. *Earn Line*, 175 F. 529（2d Cir. 1910），*Norwegian Shipping & Trade Mission* v. *Nitrate Corp. of Chile Ltd.*, 1942 AMC 1523（Arb. at N.Y. 1942）の各事件を参照）。

船主と傭船者のその他の救済についての効果

　オフハイヤー条項は，特定の偶発事件により喪失した時間に対する傭船者の損害賠償の唯一の方法を規定している（*Aaby* v. *States Marine Corp.*, 80 F. Supp. 328（S.D.N.Y. 1948），原審維持 181 F. 2d 383（2d Cir.），裁量上告拒絶 340 U.S. 829（1950））。

　*Aaby*事件では，本船が1年間の傭船に出されたものの，引渡直後に故障して，修理に2日半を要した。裁判所は，本件故障は傭船契約の商業上の目的を達成不能にするものではないから，傭船者に解約の権利はないと判断した。裁判所は，傭船者の時間の喪失に関する賠償請求は，オフハイヤー条項に規定されており，その条項によって，傭船者は修理期間中の傭船料の支払を免除されると述べた。

　この原則は，*The Ask*, 156 F. 678, 681（S.D.N.Y. 1907）事件において，Hough判事により非常に明確に述べられている。

　　Ask号が破損して，仮修理が必要となった……。このような偶発事件については，傭船契約が約定損害賠償（すなわち傭船料の喪失）を定めており，その他の手段は許されない……

　しかし，明らかにオフハイヤー条項は，その範囲が限定されている。それは，一定の偶発事

件が発生した場合，傭船者の傭船料支払義務を免除する効力を有するが，傭船者が，例えば機関の故障の結果被る間接損害についての傭船者救済方法が規定されていない。さらに，傭船契約上のその他の担保違反により，損害が発生する可能性もあるが，オフハイヤー条項はそのような担保違反にも適用がない。そのため，オフハイヤー条項は，故障の結果生ずる間接損害に関し，傭船者の救済を制限するものと理解されてはならない。このことは，Aaby事件における地方裁判所の意見のなかで認められている。同裁判所は次のように述べている。

　　しかし，本件において故障が第15条の文言にそのまま該当することはきわめて明白であり，同条項によって通常取り扱われるであろう。それは全部で2日半に満たない時間の喪失を生じただけのまったく小さな故障であった。この時間喪失分につき，被告が傭船料の支払を免除されることは明白であるが，**さらに船主の担保違反の結果，被告が被った特別の損害を訴求する権利を有する**（80 F. Supp. at 333）（強調は追加）。

　The Polyxeni, SMA 1961（Arb. at N.Y. 1984）事件において，船主は The Seafaith, 1955 AMC 2062, 2063（Arb. at N.Y. 1954）事件を引用して，オフハイヤー条項に何らの規定もないので，傭船者の回復分は傭船料の払戻に限られ，間接損害は回復できないと主張した。仲裁審は，The Seafaith 事件の判例の内容に同意せず，判断の根拠に本書の初版を引用して，間接損害分も回復できると判示した。

　The Captain John, 1973 AMC 2005（Arb. at N.Y. 1973）事件では，本船は糖蜜を積んで Hamburg に向かう途中，大規模な修理を行うために Lisbon 港への入港を余儀なくされた。貨物は揚荷され，別の船で目的地向け運送された。加えて傭船者は，Captain John 号の修理中，他の契約を履行するため，代船を傭船した。仲裁審は，本船は修理期間中オフハイヤーであると判断した。傭船契約には，傭船者は本船がオフハイヤーとなった期間を傭船契約に付加し延長させる権限があった。しかし，この権限があるにもかかわらず，多数意見は傭船者は Captain John 号を使用すれば生じていた傭船料および燃料費を控除し，さらに期間延長による節約分を差し引いた上で，代船の傭船費用を回収できると判断した。

　The Tordenskjold, SMA 1091,（Arb. at N.Y. 1977）事件では，仲裁審はオフハイヤーに加えて，傭船者はオフハイヤー期間中に被った損害につき，それが立証できるのであれば回収できると判示した。この事案では，本船は船主がプロピレン運送に関する米国コーストガードの規則に適合するようフランジを取り替える間，オフハイヤーとなった。しかし，この事件では仲裁審は，傭船者は何らの損害も立証できなかったと認定した。Fort Morgan S. S. Co. v. Baltimore & Jamaica Trad. Co., 284 F. 1, 4（4th Cir. 1992）事件を参照。この事件では，オフハイヤー条項は，「本船を座礁させた当直の航海士の過失によって発生した……損害とは関係がない……」と判示している。The Ask, 156 F. 678, 681（S.Y.N.Y. 1907）事件では，裁判所は，腐敗しやすい貨物に関して，「本船が既知の欠陥を隠して貨物を積み込み，その後港に滞留して修理を行ったことにつき，船主が傭船料支払の一時停止以上の責任を負わないと言う主張は成り立つものではない……」と述べている。

　The Shena and The Ave, SMA 2893（Arb. at N.Y. 1992）事件では，仲裁審は，傭船者の間接損害を含んだオフハイヤーの計算を認めなかった。しかし，次のことは留意すべきである。つまり，傭船者が本船の遅延に何らの責任もなく，本船もしくは船主の故意のあるいは目に余る職務怠慢を示すことができる場合には，仲裁審はより広い傭船者の救済を判断したであろうと思われる。

　The Intermar Progress, SMA 2468（Arb. at N.Y. 1988）事件では，仲裁審は，傭船契約の

規定に従い，本船が原油清浄装置と不活性ガス装置を装備する期間については，傭船者は本船をオフハイヤーにできない，と裁定した。しかし，そのシステムを装備せずに本船を使用すれば，傭船者はオフハイヤー以上に損害を被るのであるから，船主には傭船者が控除したオフハイヤー分の傭船料を回収する権利はなかった。

いくつかの事例では，より制限的な手法が採用されてきた。例えば，*Cia Estrella Blanca Ltda* v. *The Nictric*, 247 F. Supp. 161（D. Ore 1965），全員一致で原審維持 368 F. 2d. 575（9th Cir. 1966）事件では，本船荷役機器の欠陥のために積荷作業が妨げられ，定期傭船者が締結している航海傭船契約上取得できる滞船料が少なくなったにもかかわらず，船主により定期傭船者に認められる唯一の救済策は，オフハイヤー条項に基づくものであると判断されている。

The Largo, SMA 1230（Arb. at N.Y. 1978）事件では，本船は，船長が最後に通報した到着予定時間から数時間遅れて港に到着したが，当初その本船に割り当てられていたバースは他船に使われることとなり，バース待ちが発生したため，その待ち時間につき傭船者はオフハイヤーを主張した。仲裁審は，その請求された遅延損害は本質的に間接的損害であり，傭船者が契約に基づき損害を回復する手段はないとの結論を出して傭船者の主張を拒絶した。しかし，その決定には，ある面では，傭船者がすでに到着遅れとなった航海について速度クレームを認められた事実が一部影響していることを，仲裁審自身が示唆している。

The Stolt Capricorn, SMA 2359（Arb. at N.Y. 1987）事件では，本船がアレストされ，揚荷港での長期間の遅延により，傭船契約は商売上履行不能に陥ったと判断された。履行不能により傭船契約が解約したとみなされるまで，本船は喪失時間すべてについてオフハイヤーとされた。傭船者は，もし本船の抑留がなければ得た再傭船契約上の喪失利益を，回収しようと試みた。仲裁審は，確かに傭船者は再傭船契約上で利益を得るはずであったことを認定したが，「傭船者は，傭船契約上喪失した時間すべてを傭船料の払戻という形で取り戻しているから，もし，傭船者がまさしくその条件下の利用できる時間の枠組で実現しなかった利益分を取り戻すのであれば，それは『二重取り』になってしまう」との結論を示した。

The Universe Explorer, 1985 AMC 1014（Arb. at N.Y. 1984）事件では，本船がその前に南アフリカ共和国に寄港したことにより，ナイジェリアでバースへの接岸を阻まれたことによる時間喪失を，傭船者が回収する唯一の方法は本船をオフハイヤーにすることだけである，と仲裁人は裁定した。傭船者は代船を傭船するために追加運賃を支払わなければならなかったが，仲裁審は，傭船者の損害賠償の請求を拒絶した。仲裁審は，オフハイヤー条項の特定の事由に該当する時間喪失に対する傭船者損害の救済は，オフハイヤー条項が規定する傭船料支払の停止だけであるとの立場に固執した。さらに，仲裁審は，一般相互免責条項によって，「統治者，支配者あるいは人民の抑留」による損害は，いずれの当事者も相手の当事者から損害を回収しえない，と述べている。

傭船者に解約の選択権を付与する条項

本船のオフハイヤー状態がある一定期間続いた場合，傭船者に解約選択権を付与する旨の印刷条項が，傭船契約に盛り込まれていることは，まれというわけではない。そのような条項は，ニューヨークの仲裁審によって適用されてきた。例えば，*The Argo Leader*, SMA 2065（Arb. at N.Y. 1985）事件を参照。この事案では，傭船期間が12ケ月以内で，物理的な故障により合計36日間のオフハイヤー事態が続いた場合，傭船者は傭船契約解約の権利を得る，となっている。また *The Theodora*, SMA 2333（Arb. at N.Y. 1985）事件では，本船が連続30日間以上オフハイヤー状態を続けた場合，傭船者は解約権を有することになった。

傭船契約の履行不能

"102.　16. That should the Vessel be lost, money paid in advance and not earned (reckon-
　　　　ing from the date of loss or being last heard of) shall be
103. returned to the Charterers at once."

「16. 本船が滅失したときは，反対給付が得られなかった前払金（滅失または最後の消息があった日から起算する）を，直ちに傭船者に返還しなければならない。」

本船の滅失

　定期傭船契約における本船の滅失は，その滅失の状況やその原因により異なる結果を生じる。滅失は，傭船契約当事者のいずれかによる債務不履行にその原因を帰せしめることができる場合がある。例えば，船主が傭船契約条項に基づき責任を負う本船の不堪航が原因で本船が滅失する場合も考えられる（前出147頁，206頁，後出593頁を参照）し，傭船者の安全港配船義務違反で生じる場合も考えられる（前出231頁を参照）。このような場合には，債務不履行の当事者は相手方の損害に責任があるが，傭船契約に本船滅失後の効果的な代船提供の規定がなければ（後出464頁を参照），義務履行の手段である本船の滅失によって，両当事者は，それ以上の義務の履行を免れる。

　本船の滅失もしくはそれを生ぜしめる事由を，傭船契約で完全に規定しておくことができれば，本船滅失という事態が生じた場合の当事者の権利は傭船契約によって決められることとなる（後出469頁を参照）。しかし，傭船契約には不十分な規定しかなく，本船滅失がいずれの当事者の責めにも帰することができない場合，各当事者は履行不能の法理により，以後それ以上の履行義務を免除される。ニューヨーク・プロデュース書式の102行，103行は不完全な規定である。したがって，そのような場合には，履行不能の法理が適用となり，当事者は自動的に履行義務を免除される。ただし，傭船料の払戻の条件については，1943年法改革（履行不能により消滅する契約）に関する法によって修正されるかもしれない（後出478頁を参照）。

　この章で，本船の滅失とは別に，履行不能の法理によって傭船契約の当事者が自動的にその後の履行義務を免除されるその他の状況にも触れておくこととする。ニューヨーク・プロデュース書式第16条とボルタイム書式第16条はともに，本船が滅失した場合，傭船料の支払が停止すると規定する。さらに，その他当事者の合意や権利行使がない場合に，自動的に傭船契約が終結する状況もある。

履行不能の法理

　契約のいずれかの当事者の債務不履行によらずにある事態が発生し，そのために傭船契約の同一性が失われるか，あるいは履行することが，取引上の観点からみて契約の枠組をはずれたまったく異質のものとなる場合，その契約は法の作用により終結する。このような結果をもたらす事態には，定期傭船船舶の全損，もしくは取引の通念上全損とみなされる場合，もしくは極端に長期にわたる徴用や抑留，履行行為の本質部分が中断または破壊されるため定期傭船契

約の履行行為が違法もしくは不可能になる場合等が考えられる。*Davis Contractors* v. *Fareham U. D. C.* [1956] A.C. 696 事件で，Radcliffe 卿は次のように述べている（同判例集729頁）。「ある特定の事態が発生し，その状況下で履行することが，当初約定した履行行為と極端に異なるものになる場合，法は，いずれの当事者も債務不履行に陥らせることなく，契約上の義務履行が不可能になったと認める。この場合に履行不能が生じるとする。*Non haec in foerdea veni*. すなわち，これは自分が履行することを約束したものではないというのである」。

この法理については，*National Carriers* v. *Panalpina* [1981] A.C. 675 事件で，Simon 卿が次のような言葉で述べている（同判例集700頁）。「傭船契約の当事者が締結当初合理的に考えていた契約上の権利や義務の性質（費用や負担に限らない）をまったく異なるものにする不測の事態が発生し，そのような新たな状況下において，傭船契約の条項を文言どおり履行することが不公正であると判断される場合に（いずれの当事者にも何らの債務不履行なく，傭船契約にもその場合に備えた規定がない場合），契約の履行不能が生ずる」。そういう場合法は両当事者を以後それ以上の履行義務から解放することを宣言する。「不測の事態」の意義については，*The Super Servant Two* [1989] 1 Lloyd's Rep. 148 事件における Hobhouse 判事の判決ならびに後出476頁を参照。

Roskill 卿は，*Panalpina* 事件において（同判例集712頁），履行不能の効果は，当事者を履行義務より自動的に解放するものであることを強調した。「その法理の適用は，当事者の作為もしくは不作為にかかわりなく行われる」。ゆえに，履行不能をもたらす事態の発生に備えた後，当事者が契約を継続させるような扱いをしても，それがこの法理の適用を妨げることにはならない。

> *Singaporean* 号は1916年に10ヶ月の期間定期傭船された。本船は1917年3月に傭船者の使用に提供される予定であったが，引渡前に徴用された。船主は，徴用期間は短いものと思い，傭船者に徴用解除後に本船を使用することの確認を行った。傭船者は使用するとの回答を行ったが，徴用は1919年3月まで続いた。
> 　枢密院は，本船の徴用により傭船契約は履行不能になっており，その後当事者間で何らかのやり取りがあったとしても，当事者は各々自らの履行義務から解放されている，と判示した。当事者間に新たな契約の締結はなく，当事者同士で契約がまだ存在しているかのように考えていたという事実も，履行不能の原則が適用されることに影響はなかった。
> *Hirji Mulji* v. *Cheong Yue S. S.* [1926] A.C. 497.
> （さらに，*B. P. Exploration* v. *Hunt* [1981] 1 W.L.R. 232, 241 事件を参照）

同様に，履行不能となる事由が発生した後，傭船者が傭船料を支払おうとしたこと，もしくは支払い続けようとした事実があっても，それで船主がこの原則に依拠することを妨げられることはない（後出 *Bank Line* v. *Capel* [1919] A.C. 435 事件を参照）。

事実問題と法律問題

ある契約が履行不能となっているかどうかを決定した仲裁人の判断が上訴される場合，裁判所により，その判断のどの部分が事実問題として扱われ，どの部分が法律問題として扱われるかは，きわめて重要な問題となる。というのは，通常，裁判所は，仲裁人の裁定のうち法律問題のみを再吟味し，事実問題には干渉しないのが通例だからである。近年，裁判所は，履行不能の事例で，その区別をはっきりさせようとしている。

Universal Cargo Carriers v. Citati [1957] 1 Lloyd's Rep. 174 事件で，Devlin 判事は次のように述べている（同判例集192頁）。「履行不能の法理の適用は法律問題であるが，どの程度の遅延期間によって履行不能となるかは，事実問題である」。一方，The Angelia [1972] 2 Lloyd's Rep. 154 事件において，Kerr 判事はこの Devlin 判事の言葉は，Davis Contractors v. Fareham U. D. C [1956] A. C. 696 事件における Radcliffe 卿の見解と調和させることが難しいとの注釈をしている。なお，Radcliffe 卿は，「履行不能の原則が適用される状況の記述と，それに続きある特定の事件で，そのような状況が存在するかどうかの決定は，必然的に法律問題となる」と述べている。さらに，Devlin 判事の意見は，Re Comptoir Commercial Anversois and Power [1920] 1 K. B. 868 事件における控訴院の決定とも，また Tsakiroglou v. Noblee Thorl [1961] 1 Lloyd's Rep. 329 事件における貴族院の決定とも一致していない，と Kerr 判事は考えている。

395 The Nema 事件（後出参照）の控訴審判決において，Templeman 卿判事は，Citati 事件における Devlin 判事の主張と Davis Contractors v. Fareham U. D. C. 事件の Radcliff 判事の見解には矛盾はないと述べている。Templeman 卿判事によれば，前者の事件は「その事件において履行不能となるにはどの程度の遅延が必要であるのかという狭い問題を扱っており，遅延という事態が履行不能に繋がるかどうかの問題を扱っているのではない」という。Roskill 卿は，The Nema 事件の貴族院判決において，The Angelia 事件が正しく判断されたかについて疑問を呈しつつ，次のように述べている。「究極的には，契約が履行不能になっているかどうかの分析は，法律問題であるけれども，一方 Radcliffe 卿がこの件について124頁で，『結論は，商売上確認される扱い方と商人の理解によってほとんど完全に決定される』と述べているように，Tsakiroglou & Co. Ltd. v. Noblee Thorl G. m. b. H. [1962] A. C. 93 事件で，同判事は，自らの見解として次のように判断した。すなわち，筋の通った裁定により，起用された仲裁人たちが正しい法律上の基準を適用したことを認定できるとき，道理をわきまえた人間がその正しい法律上の基準を適用された事実に基づいては，到達できない結論の場合に限り，裁判所は干渉すべきである。裁判所は，その事実に基づきその基準を適用すれば，同じ結論に自ら到達しないもしくは到達しないかもしれないというだけの理由で干渉してはならない。というのは，そうすれば仲裁法廷の独占的な機能である事実認定を裁判所が覆す結果になるからである」。

結局，問題は事実と法律が混交しているように思われる（National Carriers v. Panalpina [1981] A. C. 675（同判例集688頁）事件を参照）。遅延が，すなわち遅延あるいはどの類型の遅延が，ある特定の事件で，契約を履行不能とする可能性があるかどうかは法律問題であるが，その遅延がどの程度継続すれば契約を履行不能にするかは，事実問題である。したがって，仲裁人の履行不能の法律的基準の理解とその基準の適正な適用に裁判所が満足している場合，事実がその基準を満たしているかどうかに関する仲裁人の判断を，裁判所は容易に変えようとはしない。後述の The Nema 事件において，Roskill 判事は次のように述べている。「将来のため，私は次のように考える。すなわち，他の点においては控訴が適切である事例につき［控訴に関しては後出515頁を参照］，履行不能を争っている事案で仲裁人に論断された裁定に現れている種々の問題の結論に関し，仲裁人が法の適用を誤って，正しい法の基準を適用していない場合と，正しい法の基準を適用しているといいながらも仲裁人が認定した事実に立脚すれば，道理をわきまえた人間が到達できない結論を仲裁人が出している場合にのみ，裁判所は，その結論に干渉すべきである」。

Nema 号は，連続6回から7回，St. Lawrence 河の Sorel から Calais もしくは Hartlepool に向けて

チタニウム滓を輸送する航海のために，1979年の4月から12月までの期間，傭船された。傭船契約の第5条では，ストライキによる時間の喪失が碇泊時間より除外されることが規定され，第27条では，「ゼネスト」により船積が妨害される場合，傭船契約解約の選択権が船主に認められていた。最初の航海の後，Sorelのチタニウム工場ではストライキが勃発し，Nema号が1979年6月20日にSorelに到着時，船積ができなかった。結果，追加の取決めが行われ，2番目の航海はある条件の下で延期されるとともに，船主は1980年さらに7回の航海を行う旨合意した。しかしながら，ゼネストには発展しなかったが，ストライキはその後も続き，1979年9月時点で，ストライキの終息の見通しもなく，本件傭船契約の履行不能の成否につき，仲裁に付託されることとなった。

仲裁人は，1979年の季節用航海の傭船契約と1980年の季節用航海の傭船契約は分離できるものと考え，1979年の傭船契約は1979年9月26日までに履行不能になったと判断した。この件は商業裁判所に控訴されたが，そこでRobert Goff判事は，本件の傭船契約は期間が2つの季節にまたがる分離できない1個の傭船契約であると判断した。さらに，同判事は，仮に1979年の季節が分離できるとしても，ストライキは，1979年の季節用傭船契約を履行不能にするほど極端に影響を及ぼしてはいない，と判示した。

控訴院の判断は，本件の傭船契約は1979年と1980年の別々の季節に分離できるとする仲裁人の判断を支持して，仲裁人の決定を復活させた。この控訴院の判断は，貴族院でも支持された。控訴院は，さらに次のとおり判示している。もし，仲裁人が法の要点につき誤りを犯していない限り，もしくは彼の判断が，合理的な仲裁人であれば誰しも到達できない判断でない限り，履行不能の問題に関する仲裁人の結論は容認されなければならない。

The Nema [1980] 2 Lloyd's Rep. 83 と 339 (C. A.) および [1981] 2 Lloyd's Rep. 239 (H. L.)。
（分離可能，不可能な契約に関しては，*Larrinage* v. *Soc. Franco-Americaine des Phosphates* (1923) 14 Ll.L. Rep. 457（輸送契約，COAに関するもの）と *Dominion Coal* v. *Roberts* (1920) 4 Ll.L. Rep. 434（定期傭船契約に関するもの）を参照）

396 傭船船舶の喪失による履行不能

本船の現実の全損だけでなく，ひどく損傷をうけ事実上商船としての機能を破壊された場合にも定期傭船契約は履行不能となる。*Blane Steamships* v. *Minister of Transport* [1951] 2 Lloyd's Rep. 155 事件の船舶賃貸借の事案を参照。

代船条項

傭船船舶が滅失し，その結果傭船契約が履行不能となる場合，当該傭船契約中の代船を認める条項も無効となる。もし，本船滅失後であっても代船を認める意図があれば，特に明確な文言を用いて，滅失により当該傭船契約が履行不能になるのを阻止しなければならない。

World Sky 号の7年間の定期傭船契約には，同船より大型船を代船として提供する権利を船主に認めている条項があった。この傭船契約期間中に，同船は座礁し，全損となった。McNair判事は，World Sky 号の全損により定期傭船契約は履行不能になったのであるから，船主は代船提供の権利（あるいは義務）も喪失したと判示した。

Niarchos v. *Shell Tankers* [1961] 2 Lloyd's Rep. 496.
（また [1985] 1 Lloyd's Rep. 395 と前出146頁の *The Badagry* 事件も参照）

遅延による履行不能

どのような遅延であれ，それが履行不能となるには，その遅延の結果が極端なものでなければならない。この点に関し，*Tatem* v. *Gamboa* (1938) 61 Ll.L. Rep. 149 事件で，Goddard判

事は次のように述べている（同判例集156頁）。「契約の目的物が破壊された場合，あるいは長期の中断や遅延のために履行することがまったく別の契約の履行となる場合，契約の基礎が失われる。ただし，当事者はこのような場合に対処する規定を予め設けることができるし，事実設けていることが多い。しかし，そのような規定を設けていない場合，契約の履行は不能になったとみなされる。」（しかし，The Nema [1980] 2 Lloyd's Rep. 339 事件（同判例集346頁）において，記録長官 Denning 卿が「少しばかりより自由な考え方」を支持していることに留意すべし）。

傭船始期の遅延

契約始期が遅れることが見込まれる場合，その予想される遅延により，契約の履行が当初定められていた履行行為と極端に異なるものになると考えられれば，そのような遅延が見込まれるだけで，契約が履行不能と判断されることも十分にありうる。

1915年2月 Quito 号は，期間12ヶ月，解約期日4月30日の約定で傭船された。本船は4月30日までに引き渡されなかったが，傭船者は解約しなかった。5月11日本船は徴用されてしまい，船主は5月，6月と徴用の解除を試みたが，成功しなかった。1915年8月，船主は政府からの徴用解除を条件として本船の売却に合意した。徴用の解除は，船主が代船を提供する条件で認められ，本船は9月に徴用解除となり売却された。そこで，傭船者は本船の引渡義務の不履行に基づく損害賠償を船主に請求した。貴族院は多数意見をもって，傭船の始期が，長期にわたると予想される不特定期間延期された場合には，傭船契約は履行不能となる，と判示した。Sumner 卿は次のような意見を述べている（460頁）。「Quito 号の徴用は，傭船役務の同一性を破壊するものであり，実務上傭船契約はまったく別物になったと言うのが私の意見である。徴用により契約の履行は，まったくの不特定期間かつ多分かなりの長期間，遅延している。また徴用が解除されるかどうかは，両当事者の認識できないあるいは管理の及ばない問題に左右されていた」。

Bank Line v. Capel [1919] A.C. 435（本件のその他の点の検討は，後出469頁を参照）。

397 Jackson v. Union Marine Insurance (1874) L. R. 10 C.P. 125 事件という古い事件において，財務裁判所は，Newport から San Francisco にレールを運送する傭船につき，1月初旬に提供されるべき本船が座礁し，修理に8月下旬までを要した場合に関し，傭船者はこの本船に対する船積義務を免れる，と判示した。本件の判断の理由を現代の状況に当てはめるには，若干の注意を要する。もっともこの問題に対する初期の考え方を知ることは，興味あるものである。それは，傭船者が船積義務を免れた理由は，傭船契約の履行不能ではなく，船積義務の前提条件が満たされなかったという点であった。その場合の前提条件とは，本船が傭船航海を遂行するために，約定時間までに Newport に到着することというものであった。Bramwell 男爵は，次のように述べている。「船主は，本船の積地到着にあらゆる可能な手段を尽くすことを引き受けており，かつ取引上の見地から船主と傭船者が行った商売上の投機が終わっておらず，まだ続いているとみなされる時期までに，本船が積地に到着すべきことに合意している。この後者の合意もまた前提条件である。このような時期までに本船が到着していなければ契約は終結する。もっとも，遅延が免責危険によって発生した場合には，それは訴訟提起の理由とはならない」。

上記の理由付けでは，どんなに遅れても，傭船者は船主に船積のため本船の提供を要求できないことはない，という結論となるが（もっとも，本件ではこの問題は生じていないが），現代の理由付けでは，履行不能となり両当事者は契約上の義務を免除されるものとして扱われる

こととなる。

航海のための傭船期間の延長

　傭船契約を履行している期間中の遅延，例えば船舶の損傷，運河の閉鎖等によって生じる航海の延長は，十分に履行不能の理由となると思われる。しかし，裁判所は，遅延という事態が履行不能の効果をもたらすとの判断を行うのに，これまで消極的であった。この態度は，以下に要約する貴族院の *Davis Contractors* v. *Fareham U. D. C.* [1956] A.C. 696 事件の判決に従っているものである。しかし，ここで留意すべきは，この論点に関する海事の指導的判例は，いずれも腐敗しやすい貨物に関するものではなかったこと，また航海傭船，定期傭船のいずれについてもその当事者である船主と傭船者に余分の出費がかかったというだけの事例であったことである。

　　建築業者が，地方公共団体と一定敷地内に 8 ヶ月間以内に92,425ポンドで78軒の家を建てることに合意した。ところが，熟練労働者の不足，天候不順等を含むさまざまな理由により，建設は22ヶ月間を要し，また費用も115,233ポンドに達した。建築業者は，長期遅延の結果，契約は履行不能となり，契約上の固定価格ではなく，実価格相当の支払を受ける権利があるとして，その費用を請求した。貴族院は，遅延およびその結果によって建築業者に余分な費用が発生したにもかかわらず，契約は履行不能とはなっておらず，建築業者は固定価格のみ請求できると判示した。
　　Reid 卿は次のように述べている（724頁）。
　　「遅延は，契約で意図していたものを変質させ，契約を終結させる性質を持つものもある。しかし，本件では単に遅延の程度が予想より長期化しただけで，その遅延は予期できなかった原因や事情で発生したわけではない。建設作業そのものの負担が増大したことは明らかであったが，それはけっして契約で意図していたものとまったく異なる性質のものに変質したわけではない」。
　　Davis Contractors v. *Fareham U. D. C.* [1956] A.C. 696.

　　Eugenia 号は，Genoa から黒海を経由してインド向け航海にボルタイム書式で定期傭船された。傭船条項を確定する前に，スエズ運河閉鎖の危険を了知していた両当事者は，このような事態に対処するための特別の条項を検討した。結局，特別条項については合意に達しなかったが，傭船契約には通常の印刷された戦争条項21条が含まれていた。本船は黒海において鋼材を積み込み，Port Said へ向かった。Port Said 到着時には，エジプトの対空砲火が始まっており，運河地域は裁判所の判断によると，戦争条項で定める「危険」の状態となっていた。1956年10月30日，船主代理店は傭船者代理店に対し，戦争条項に従って本船が Port Said あるいはスエズ運河に入らないような手段をとることを要求した。しかし，そのような手段はとられず，Port Said の傭船者代理店は運河に入る手続を行い，1956年10月31日本船は運河に入ってしまった。同日夕刻，エジプトはスエズ運河を閉鎖した。そして，*Eugenia* 号は1957年 1 月北航路が開通するまで，そこに停留されてしまった。南側は1957年 4 月まで開かれなかった。本件において，控訴院は次のとおり判示した。
1．傭船者は，本船を運河に入れてしまった点において，戦争条項に違反した。
2．本船が停留させられたのは，傭船者自身の過失であり，したがって履行不能の理由として運河の中に閉じ込められた事実を持ち出すことはできない。
3．本船が仮に停留されていない場合には，喜望峰回りでインドに向かわなければならなかった事実は，傭船契約の履行不能をもたらすものではない。というのは，貨物は腐敗しやすいものではなく，またその程度の期間延長（引渡から返船まで，スエズ経由なら108日に対し，喜望峰経由なら138日）では，喜望峰回りの航海を極端に異質なものにするものでもなく，唯一の実際上の差はそれが非常に費用がかかったという点だけである。そして，このことは契約を履行不能とみなす理由とはならない。

Ocean Tramp Tankers v. *Sovfracht* (*The Eugenia*) [1963] 2 Lloyd's Rep. 381.

 Captain George K 号はメキシコから Kandla, Bombay 向け撒荷姿の硫黄輸送のために傭船された。その当時スエズ運河は開いており，その閉鎖を予想すべき理由もなかった。しかし，本船が運河の北端に到着したとき，船長は地域で最近勃発した戦争のため運河が閉鎖されていることを知らされた。そこで船主は本船を，地中海，喜望峰回りで目的地に向かわせた。結果として，運河が開通していれば9,700マイルで済んだところを，18,400マイルの航海を行った。船主は，現傭船契約は無効になったとして，余分に要した費用米貨67,690ドルを請求した。Mocatta 判事はこの請求を退けたが，その理由は控訴院の前出 The Eugenia 事件の判決に拘束される，ということだけであった。そして，その先例がなければ同判事は「実際の航海は，傭船契約で明確に意図された航海と根本的に異なる種類のものであると判断したものと思われる」。
The Captain George K [1970] 2 Lloyd's Rep. 21.

 Dunolly 号はバルト海往復（イギリスからバルト海諸港を経てイギリスに帰る）航海のために傭船された。本船は1914年7月初旬に引き渡され，バルト海に向かって出港した。そして8月上旬フィンランドで積荷をしている最中に戦争が勃発した。本船はロシア官憲の命令によりフィンランドから出港することができなかった。控訴院は，傭船者が不特定の期間，本船の使用を妨げられたとして傭船契約の履行不能を認めた。
Scottish Navigation v. *Souter* [1917] 1 K.B. 222.

約定された航海航路のみが不可能になった場合

 The Eugenia 事件（前出）において，傭船契約上で定められた唯一の航路がスエズ運河経由であったとしたら，傭船契約は履行不能の成立を認められたことと思われる。

 第1審の Megaw 判事は以下の言葉によって，その可能性を論じている。「傭船契約上，当事者が特定の航路のみを航海すべきことを明示または黙示により合意している場合には，当該本船が商業上の見地からその航路を使用できないのであれば，裁判所が商業上の見地から他の航路をとることが実務上適しているか否かを検討する必要はないと思われる。契約上の義務は，当事者が合意した特定の航路を使うことのみによって履行することができるのである」（[1963] 2 Lloyd's Rep. 155 174頁）。

 The Eugenia 事件で，控訴院は *The Massalia* [1960] 1 Lloyd's Rep. 594 事件における Pearson 判事の判決を覆した。*The Massalia* 事件では，「船長はスエズ運河通過時に『Maritsider Genoa』で電報を入れること」との条項があったため，インドからイタリア向けの傭船航海でスエズ経由の航路を通る義務があった。しかし，このように傭船契約上唯一の航路を通るべきことが明示され，しかもその航路が通行不能になったにもかかわらず，裁判所はこの問題に何ら言及しないで，傭船契約は履行不能にはならないと判示した。

 ただし，定期傭船契約では，特定航路の予定期間をもって傭船契約の期間を定めることはあるが，その場合でも特定航路を定めることは稀であるから，この問題は実務上は，それほど頻繁に重要問題となることはないようである。

傭船期間内に業務を中断させるもの

 1航海の定期傭船契約と異なり，月または年単位で定める定期傭船契約に関する限り，この種の遅延がもっとも通常の形である。

 当該船舶が徴用や物理的な封鎖などの理由によって，定期傭船の業務の履行が相当の期間中断されるような場合に，定期傭船契約は履行不能になると判断されることがある。

判例によれば，傭船契約が履行不能とされるには，その中断がかなり長期に，特に履行不能を主張する時点での残存傭船期間との関係において，十分に長期に亘るものでなければならない。その時点の予想で，中断事由が終了した後，残りの傭船期間がかなりあると思われるような場合，裁判所は履行不能と判断するのを躊躇する。しかしながら，もちろん，状況によっては当然裁判所が履行不能と判断する場合もありうる。例えば，ある緊急性のある特殊な航海のための傭船の場合とか，あるいは傭船期間内の遠い将来に航海が再開されることがあっても，全体の傭船期間から見れば，本船を使用できない期間が，不釣り合いに長くなりそうな場合がそうである。*The Wenjiang (No. 2)* [1983] 1 Lloyd's Rep. 400 事件（同判例集408頁）と *National Carriers* v. *Panalpina* [1981] A.C. 675 事件（同判例集697, 707頁）を参照）。

さらに，仲裁人が履行不能に関する正しい法律的基準を適用して，具体的な事件の事実が，その基準を満たすと判断したような場合，裁判所は，たとえ自らは違う結論に至るであろうと思う場合でも，その仲裁人の判断に干渉することを渋るということに留意しなければならない。[1981] 2 Lloyd's Rep. 239 と前出464頁の *The Nema* 事件を参照。また *The Wenjiang* [1982] 1 Lloyd's Rep. 128 事件を参照。少なくとも1人のロンドンの仲裁人は，この分野では，「少しばかりより自由な考え方」を取るべきであるとする見解に立っているゆえ，このことは重要な意味をもっているのかもしれない。この見解は，*The Nema* [1980] 2 Lloyd's Rep. 339 事件（同判例集346頁）で，記録長官 Denning 卿によって採用された。

タンカーの *F. A. Tamplin* 号は1912年12月から5年間定期傭船に出された。1914年12月本船は短期間徴用され，その後1915年2月に再度徴用された。さらに本船は兵員輸送船として改装された。船主は，徴用および改装によって，傭船契約が履行不能になったと主張した。貴族院において本件が審理された時点で，傭船期間はまだ19ヶ月残っていた。裁判所は3対2の多数決をもって，傭船契約は履行不能にはなっていないと判示した。すなわち，徴用期間は不特定であったが，契約終了までに本船が再び傭船に提供されうる機会は十分にあったとされた。Loreburn 伯爵は，405頁で次のように述べている。

「5年間の傭船期間が終了するまでに，本船は相当の期間商売上の目的に使用できる可能性がある。その期間につき，規定の傭船料で当該本船を使用できることは，傭船者にとって貴重な権利である。傭船者がその権利を奪われる理由があるのであろうか」。

Tamplin Steamship v. *Anglo-Mexican Petroleum* [1916] 2 A.C. 397.
（前出本書465頁の *Bank Line* v. *Capel* [1919] A.C. 435 事件の要約参照）

Tamplin 事件の扱いは注意を要する。すなわち，傭船契約が履行不能になったと主張しているのは船主であり，傭船者は，当時海軍省が約定傭船料率よりも高い料率の補償を行っているのを奇貨として，当該船舶を利用できなかったにもかかわらず，傭船契約が継続していることに満足していた。ところで，この事例で，もし海軍省の補償が傭船料よりも低く，傭船者が傭船契約の継続を拒否したならば，貴族院の判決内容も違っていたのではないかと想像される。*Metropolitan Water Board* v. *Dick, Kerr* [1918] A.C. 119 事件の Dunedin 卿の見解（同判例集129頁）を参照。

1937年3月 *Errington Court* 号はニューヨーク・プロデュース書式により，1937年12月15日から1938年1月末までの間にオーストラリアで返船との条件付で傭船された。本船は，1937年7月 Oregon 州 Portland において積荷を行い，同年8月7日揚子江を750マイル上った Wu-hu に到着した。日中戦争が8月13日に勃発し，中国は日本軍が川を遡江するのを阻止するために船舶を沈めた。証拠では，本船が立ち往生した時点（9月3日揚荷を完了したとき）で，川を下ることのできない状態が無期限に続くと予想された。Branson 判事は，本件傭船契約は履行不能になったと判決するにあたり

次のように述べている。「本船に対する両当事者の管理支配が物理的に奪われない限り，定期傭船に履行不能の原則の適用はない，と船主は主張した。しかし，本件の航海が，Bank Line 事件の航海よりも履行不能となる阻害程度が小さいとはとても思えない。航海を継続するに必要な能力が，一方の事件では徴用により，他方の事件では防御柵の構築によって奪われている」。
    Court Line v. Dant & Russell (1939) 44 Com. Cas. 345.

　Silveroak 号はニューヨーク・プロデュース書式で，30ヶ月の定期傭船に出された。傭船開始後17ヶ月めに，本船は，君主大権（王国の防衛のために必要とされるかぎり王室に占有の権利が認められる大権）に基づき，英国政府によって徴用された。徴用時において，その徴用は 3 ないし 4 ヶ月続くと予想され，事実そのとおりであって，したがって本船は10ヶ月の傭船期間を残して返船された。この事件では，Diplock 判事は傭船契約は履行不能にはならないと判断した。
    Port Line v. Ben Line [1958] 1 Lloyd's Rep. 290.

　Breconian 号は15ヶ月の期間で傭船に出され，1914年12月に引き渡された。1915年10月に英国政府により徴用された。この時点において，傭船期間はあと 4 ヶ月半残っていた。船主は，徴用によって傭船契約は履行不能になったと主張し，この船主の主張は控訴院によって（船主側の法廷弁護士の弁論を求めるまでもなく）認められた。
    Heilgers v. Cambrian Steam Navigation (1917) 34 T.L.R. 72.
    （後出470頁の Pacific Phosphate v. Empire Transport (1920) 36 T.L.R. 750事件，後出660頁に要約されている The Evia (No. 2) 事件を参照）

当事者が考慮した事態もしくは契約に規定された事態

　契約締結時に，当事者が特定の事態を考慮あるいは予期していたとしても，履行不能の原則の適用は排除されない。しかし，当事者がその旨を示す条項を作成し，かつその文言が現実に発生した事態にも及ぶように表現されている場合，履行不能の原則の適用は排除される。

考慮された事態

　Molton 号は，1937年 7 月 1 日から30日の期間，スペインの共和党政府の代理人に傭船された。明文の規定で，傭船目的は北スペインからフランスに難民を疎開させることと定められていた。本船は 1 航海を実施したが，その後，7 月14日国民党の船舶によって拿捕され，9 月 7 日まで抑留された。Goddard 判事は，「当事者が契約締結時に，船が拿捕されるかもしれないあるいはされるであろうことを予期していても，本件の傭船契約は履行不能となる。なぜならば，本件の傭船はごく短期間の非常に高い運賃による限られた地域内での特定の目的のためであって，拿捕により傭船契約の基礎が破壊されている」，と判示した。
    Tatem v. Gamboa (1938) 61 Ll.L. Rep. 149.

　前出 Ocean Tramp Tankers v. Sovfracht (The Eugenia) 事件では，当事者がある特定の事態に備える規定の作成を検討したが，合意することができず，結局かかる事態が発生した場合には「弁護士の解決に委ねる」ことになった。実際，その事態（スエズ運河の閉鎖）が現実に発生した。記録長官 Denning 卿は，本件に履行不能の原則が適用されなかったのは，このことを理由とするものではない，と述べている。

規定された事態

　ある事態について，傭船契約中に明文の規定が定められ，実際その事態が発生した場合，まず問題になるのはその規定が完全なものかどうかということである。Bank Line v. Capel

401 [1919] A.C. 435 事件（前出465頁）の場合，傭船契約には「本船が傭船期間内に政府によって徴発された場合」，傭船者は解約権を有する旨の明文の規定があり，実際に本船は徴発（もしくは徴用）された。結局，この規定があっても傭船契約は履行不能になると判断された。Finlay 卿は解約の選択権を認めたこの規定は，「本船が徴発された場合，傭船者は徴発状態が判例の示すごとく契約を終了させるほど長期間続きそうであることを立証しなくても，直ちに傭船契約を解約できることを意味するに過ぎない」（同判例集443頁）と判示している。

Haldane 子爵は同判例集445頁で，「契約の義務の履行が可能になるためには，契約の目的物の継続使用が前提となる契約が締結され，その目的物の使用が船主が制御できない事情のために予期せぬ結末で終了した場合，船主は，特にその場合でも船主は契約に拘束されると契約に規定がない限り，契約の拘束から免れることは明白である」と述べている。

同様に，履行の遅延や中断を理由とする履行不能が主張される場合，傭船契約の条項のなかに，その文脈に照らして，新しく発生した事態に十分対応すると解されるものがないかを検討しなければならない。実際実務においては，履行不能をもたらすような極端な事態に対応しうる規定はほとんど見当たらないが，そのような規定がないことは，履行不能を成立させる障害にはならない。*Fibrosa* v. *Fairbairn* [1943] A.C. 32 事件で，Simon 子爵は次のように述べている。「当事者の懈怠によってではなく，後発の事態発生により履行が無期限に不可能となり，何れにしても契約には拘束されるとの特別の規定がない場合，たとえ当事者がある限られた期間の中断の場合の明文規定を設けていても，それは契約の履行不能の成立を妨げるものとはならない」。

1913年8月に被告は，原告に対し，Ocean Island/Nauru からヨーロッパ向けの燐鉱石を毎月輸送するため，1914年から1918年まで毎年12隻の特定のタイプの船を提供することを約束した。契約には，英国が参戦しこの輸送に危険をもたらす戦争がおきた場合，両当事者は戦争が終結するまで契約を中断する選択権を有するが，その中断期間を契約の終期に加算する旨の規定があった。被告は，1914年8月に契約の中断を主張した。1919年6月に被告は自ら所有する全船舶が徴用下にあることを理由に，契約の全部が履行不能になったと主張した。Rowlatt 判事は，被告の船舶提供義務がその所有船舶に限られているわけでもないにもかかわらず，また上記戦争を念頭に入れた条項があるにもかかわらず，被告の主張を認め，本事件では履行不能が成立していると認定した。同判事の判決内容（の一部）は次のとおりである。

「……ある種の戦争が考慮されていることは事実であるが，それが現実に発生した戦争と合致するかということだけでなく，当事者がその戦争の結果まで認識していたか，ということの検討も必要である。同判事は，事実関係を検討した結果，当事者は多少の危険のある戦争状態を考えていたが，実際に発生した戦争は，海運業の混乱，政府の海運管理，その結果船主の自由の事実上の剥奪をもたらした。そして当事者はこのような戦争およびその結果まで考慮に入れていなかった，と認めたのである」。

Pacific Phosphate v. *Empire Transport* (1920) 36 T.L.R. 750.

（その他，「官憲の抑留による免責」につき *Tamplin* v. *Anglo-Mexican* [1916] 2 A.C. 397 事件，「ストライキ条項」につき *The Penelope* [1928] P.180 事件と [1980] 2 Lloyd's Rep. 339 と前出464頁の *The Nema* 事件，「本船が徴用された場合における選択権なしの解約を規定した傭船契約」につき，*Capel* v. *Soulidi* [1916] 2 K.B. 365 事件を各々参照）

中断の程度の評価

評価を行うときの基準時点

中断の長さおよびその影響は，後知恵の要素を入れずに，その中断が発生した時点におい

て，評価されなければならない。Anglo-Northern v. Jones [1917] 2 K.B. 78 事件において，Bailhache 判事はその原則を次のように述べている（同判例集85頁）。「履行不能を主張する当事者は，その主張の根拠となる事態が発生すると同時に傭船契約が履行不能により終了したと主張する権利を有する。そこで問題になるのは，海運業に従事する合理的な実務家がその時点で，本船を使用できない期間がどの程度続くと考えるかであり，当事者の予想が，その後の事態に照らして，正しかったか否かは重要な問題ではない」。

(1939) 44 Com. Cas. 345 と前出468頁の Court Line v. Dant & Russell 事件では，予想遅延期間については，1937年9月初旬の時点において根拠となりえた証拠のみで，判断された。この事件は，結局12月9日に日本軍によって中国の防御柵が破壊され，本船は12月17日揚子江を下って出港できたのであるが，その時点で本船は傭船期間内にオーストラリアで返船するのに十分な時間を残していた。しかし，判決ではこの点は重要ではないと判断された。本船が防御柵のために封鎖された9月初旬時点での証拠によれば，無期限の停留が予想された。それが，後日間違いであるとわかったとしても，それは問題とはならない。Branson 判事は「当事者は，履行不能の原因となる事実が発生した時に問題を考慮しなければならないのであるから，裁判所もまた当事者と同様の立場に立って，その事態がどの程度継続するかを最善を尽くして判断しなければならない。すなわち，重要なのは，そのときに中断期間がどの程度の長さになるかとの予測であり，事件後に判明した事実ではない」と述べた。実際に生じた結果は，当事者が履行不能が成立するかどうか決定を要したときの予測の合理性を考えるひとつの補助資料に過ぎない（Denny, Mott & Dickson v. James B. Fraser & Co. [1944] A.C. 265 事件（同判例集277, 278頁）と National Carriers v. Panalpina [1981] A.C. 675 事件（同判例集707頁）を参照）。

上述の The Nema [1980] 2 Lloyd's Rep. 339 事件では，Templeman 卿判事は，仲裁人が傭船契約が履行不能に陥ったとの裁定を出した後，予想外にも，僅か9日後にストライキが終了した事実につき，それは履行不能の判断に影響を与えるものではない，と判示した（同判例集349頁）。

ストライキ

ストライキは，性質上，不確定期間継続するが，いずれは終了するのであるから，それが傭船契約を履行不能にすると判断されるのは，例外的な事情のある場合のみである（Reardon Smith v. Ministry of Agriculture [1961] 1 Lloyd's Rep. 385 事件（同判例集404頁）の Sellers 卿判事の判決を参照）。もちろん，それでも，相当な状況がある場合には，ストライキにより傭船契約の履行不能の成立が妨げられるものではない。Sellers 判事は，上記事件の判決中に下記事件を引用しているが，その判決の趣旨に反対しているのではない。

> Penelope 号は South Wales からイタリア向け石炭の輸送のために1926年5月20日から6月20日の間のいずれか特定した日から12ヶ月間，連続航海傭船された。5月1日に炭坑のゼネストが発生し，その結果6ヶ月間すなわち1926年11月まで石炭の輸出ができなくなり，さらにその状態は政府の輸出禁止のため12月末まで続いた。当事者の合意により，本船は2回ほど代替航海に就航したが，9月初旬，本来の目的どおりの履行ができなくなったとして，傭船契約は履行不能になったと判断された。
> The Penelope [1928] P. 180.

The Nema [1981] 2 Lloyd's Rep. 239 事件では，控訴院も貴族院も，ストライキが3ヶ月間続き，契約期間を3ヶ月残すのみとなり，かつその時点でストライキの終息の見通しが立たない状況下，連続航海傭船契約は履行不能になった，とする仲裁人の裁定を覆そうとはしな

かった（前出464頁にこの事件のより詳細な事実関係の説明あり，参照）。Roskill 卿は，同判例集255頁で次のように述べている。「仲裁人が認定した事実に基づけば，仲裁人はその結論に到達すべきではなかったとは，私にはまったく言うことができない。ストライキが，履行不能を生じさせることはない，というわけではない。しかし，過去において，ストライキを履行不能の原因として援用するほとんどの試みは失敗したことが指摘されている。The Penelope [1928] P. 180 事件がほとんど唯一の成功例であるが，その事例につき，判決の結論は十分正しいのかも知れないが，その基本となる判決理由には踏襲しがたいものがある。どうして，原則として，ストライキが，遅延による履行不能を生ずるものでない，とされるのか，私にはその理由が分からない。遅延の原因をいくつかの種類に分類し，ある種の遅延は履行不能となり，ある種の遅延は履行不能を生じさせない，とするのは正しくない。重要なのは，遅延の原因の性質というより，その遅延の原因が契約の当事者が各々他方の当事者に負っている義務の履行にどのように影響しているかである」。

戦　　争

前出 The Nema 事件で Roskill 卿が表明している理由により，戦争の影響に関し何らかの推定が存在するのかどうかにつき，疑問が出されている。戦争の場合，戦争状態は無期限に続くと推定され，したがって戦争が原因で，その戦争中ずっと続きそうな遅延は，通常商事契約の履行不能をもたらすものと推定される。Geipel v. Smith (1872) L. R. 7 Q. B. 404 事件は，フランス軍による Hamburg の封鎖で航海が妨害された事件であるが，Lush 判事は「戦争状態は，本件におけるように長期間継続して商業活動を妨害し，商取引の目的を無為に帰し，破壊すると推定しなければならない」と述べている（同判例集414頁）。以来，この判決はしばしば支持され，引用されている。例えば，Horlock v. Beal [1916] 1 A. C. 486 事件の Atkinson 卿（同判例集501頁）。なお，Denny, Mott and Dickson v. James B. Fraser [1944] A. C. 265 事件の Wright 卿は，やはりこの判決を支持し，引用している。ただし，彼の説明は以下のとおりである（同判例集278頁）。

「確かに，Lush 判事はその判決のなかで，単一の明確な商売について言及しているが，継続する商売には言及していない。しかし，商業上の責任に関する事案に適用される真の原則は，商売人は不確定な中途半端な立場に立たされるべきではない，ということである。もし，その中断の性質から判断して，その期間が不確定であるとの見通しにならざるを得ないのであれば，商人は自らの資産，施設や装備，事業活動を他の可能性に向ける自由があり，またこれからの不確かな期間，不毛な事態に縛られる約束からは自由であるべきである」。

しかし，Akties. Nord-Osterso Rederiet v. E. A. Casper, Edgar (1923) 14 Ll.L. Rep. 203（同判例集206頁）事件において，Sumner 卿は，（違法行為の事案は別として）戦争の勃発だけで履行不能をもたらすかどうかは，その事態の傭船契約への影響しだいであることを強調する。戦争と言っても，その激しさ，地理的範囲は戦争毎に大きく違ってくる。傭船契約にきわめて甚大な影響を与える戦争もあるし，一方でほとんどあるいはまったく影響を与えない戦争もある。それ以上に，戦争状態は無期限に続くものだとする推定も，ある特定の事案では反駁される余地がある。いずれにしても戦争状態が，必ずしも無期限に続き，契約の履行に影響を与えるとは限らないのである。

The Chrysalis [1983] 1 Lloyd's Rep. 503 事件において，Mustill 判事は，判例を検討した上で，戦争につき，次のような結論を出している。「(1)続発する違法行為の場合を除いて，傭船契約の当事者同士が敵・味方に別れる場合でも，宣戦布告は契約の履行を妨げない。履行を妨

げるか妨げないかは，個々の事案の事情に応じて，その後の戦争の進展で，どのような行為が行われるかである。(2)もし何らかの推定があるとしても，それは戦争の継続期間に関わるものであり，戦争が契約の履行に与える影響に関わるものではない。戦争そのものと戦争が契約に及ぼす影響は，必ずしも同一延長線上にはない。(3)戦争のもつ無期限の継続期間に関する推定は，反駁されることがありうる」。

1980年に始まったイランとイラクの戦争が原因の事案において，裁判所は，特定の傭船契約が，戦争の影響で，いつの時点から履行不能になったかについての仲裁人の決定を再検討することを求められた。実質的に同じような事実関係を有する一連の事件において，履行不能となった日をいつにするかについて，仲裁人によって結論が違った。しかし，The Nema [1981] 2 Lloyd's Rep. 239 事件と The Evia (No. 2) [1982] 2 Lloyd's Rep. 307 事件で，貴族院は次のような判断を示した。すなわち，控訴された特定の事案で，統一をはかるため，裁判所が他の事案の仲裁人の判断に干渉することは許されない，とした。裁判所は，仲裁人が法の適用を誤っているか，道理をわきまえた仲裁人であれば決して到達しない結論を出している場合にのみ，干渉できるのである。

Evia 号は，ボルタイム書式に則り，18ヶ月間プラスマイナス2ヶ月の傭船期間で傭船され，選択権行使があればそれに従うが，一応1981年5月20日に返船の予定であった。1980年9月22日にイラン・イラク戦争が勃発したとき，本船はBasrahにいて，Shatt-al-Arab川地域での戦闘行為により本船は航行を妨げられた。10月1日に，本船には最小限の人員のみ残して，乗組員は本国に送還された。当初，戦闘行為は，短期間に終わるものと考えられていた。しかし，10月4日までには両国の戦闘員が激しく交戦し，Shatt-al-Arab地域は主戦闘地域になったことが明らかになった。控訴院は，本傭船契約は10月4日に履行不能になったとする審判人の判断を支持した。貴族院もこれを支持した。

The Evia (No. 2) [1981] 2 Lloyd's Rep. 613 [1982] 1 Lloyd's Rep. 334 (C. A.) および [1982] 2 Lloyd's Rep. 307 (H. L.)。

一方，The Wenjiang (No. 2) [1983] 1 Lloyd's Rep. 400 事件で，仲裁人は，期間12ヶ月で，返船の予定が1981年の3月もしくは4月の予定であった傭船契約の同様な事案で，その契約が履行不能になったのは1980年の11月24日と判断した。控訴院は控訴を認めて（[1982] 1 Lloyd's Rep. 128)，十分な審理をした上で，10月の初旬に履行不能になったとするのがより適切であったかもしれないと述べたが，Bingham 判事は，仲裁人の判断に干渉する理由はない，と判示した。The Chrysalis [1983] 1 Lloyd's Rep. 503 事件では，同じような状況において，Mustill 判事も同様に，1航海のための定期傭船契約は1980年11月24日までに履行不能になったとする仲裁人の判断を覆すことを拒否している。

遅延が当初短期間で終了するように思われるが，その後その遅延が無期限に続きそうであると予想される場合は，その時点で契約は履行不能になる。Bank Line v. Capel [1919] A.C. 435 事件で，Sumner 卿は，「履行不能の原因が長期間続いたか，あるいは状況が変化して無期限の遅延を推定させるような状態になった場合，その時点で契約の運命を決定すべき時期がきたことになる」と述べている（同判例集455頁）。

経済的損失

契約の一方の当事者に予想以上の経済的負担をもたらす事態が発生しても，契約が履行不能となるとは限らない。履行不能となるには，経済的損失が異常なものでなければならない。

Davis v. *Fareham U. D. C* [1956] A.C. 696事件では,貴族院のRadcliffe卿は次のように述べている。「苦境,不都合,重大な損失は,それだけでは履行不能の原則を適用する原因にはならない。履行不能になるには,これに加えて,もし約束されたことが履行されれば,約定されたこととは違ったものになるような,債務の性質そのものの変化が必要となる」(同判例集729頁)。

同様に,記録長官Denning卿は *The Eugenia* [1963] 2 Lloyd's Rep. 381事件で次のように述べている(同判例集390頁)。「一方の当事者にとって思った以上に負担が重くなるとか,より費用がかかるからと言って,それだけで履行不能になるものではない。履行不能となるには,単に負担が重くなるとかより費用がかかることだけでなく,それ以上の事態でなければならない。それは当事者に契約を履行させることがきわめて不公平となる事態である」。

さらに,*Larrinaga* v. *Société Franco-Américaine des Phosphates* (1923) 14 Ll.L. Rep. 457事件において,Sumner卿は,「商事契約における不確定要素は,必ずしも正確とは言えないまでも,結局のところ金銭に換算でき,その契約の一方当事者に損失あるいは経済的苦境をもたらしても,それが履行不能の原因になることはきわめて稀である」と述べている(同判例集464頁)。

それゆえ,例えば,予想できなかった燃料油の暴騰,あるいは断続的な運賃市場の変動によって,傭船契約の一方の当事者に損失が生じても,そのことは傭船契約の履行不能の原因にはならない。*Occidental* v. *Skibs A/S Avanti* [1976] 1 Lloyd's Rep. 293事件で,Kerr判事は,以上のような考え方に関し,さらに次のような論評を行っている。「これらの本船が傭船料の高いいわゆるにわか景気のときに傭船され,その後傭船期間中に不況におそわれたという事実は,タンカー市場が時折経験する通常の変動現象である。傭船料は,傭船期間中固定しているので,それ自体船主の利益にはならなかったが,傭船者に損失を生じた。もし,市場が下降しないで,1973年当時のように上昇しておれば,傭船者は利益をあげたことであろう。しかし,この場合にも履行不能になるとの考え方には根拠がない」(同判例集325頁)。

過失の効果

契約違反

履行不能を生ぜしめる事情が,一方当事者の契約違反に起因する場合,その当事者は履行不能の原則に依拠することができなくなる。厳密に言えば,それは履行不能の状況といったものではまったくなく,むしろ契約違反による契約の解消という状況である。この場合,契約違反の当事者に対する損害賠償には,さもなければ,契約の履行不能の基礎とみなされた事由に起因する損失を含むことがある。

Monarch Steamship v. *Karlshamns Oljefabriker* [1949] A.C. 196事件で,Wright卿とPorter卿は,堪航性担保義務に違反した船主は,それが明らかに意図的でないとしても,履行不能を持ち出して荷主からの請求に対抗することはできないとの見解を示した。*The Eugenia* [1963] 2 Lloyd's Rep. 381事件でDonovan卿判事は,戦争条項に違反してスエズ運河に本船を入れた傭船者が,そこで本船が立ち往生しても,それを理由に履行不能を主張することはできないのは当然であると判示した。同事件につき,記録長官Denning卿はもっと単純に,「運河内に本船を立ち入れた点で,傭船者は戦争条項に違反しており,このように自ら招いた事態を理由として履行不能を主張することはできない」と述べている。

しかしながら,履行不能の法理を妨げるような契約違反があっても,それを免責する適切な条項があれば,履行不能の法理を妨げる効果を避けることができると思われる。例えば,船主

の被用者の航海過失によって本船が沈没し，その過失が履行不能の法理の適用を妨げるに十分であっても，契約上船主はその過失責任を免れることになっている場合，船主は履行不能の申立を行うことができる。後出の Constantine v. Imperial Smelting 事件で，Wright 卿は，次のように述べてこの見解を支持している。「しかしながら，一般免責条項は重要な問題である。なぜなら免責条項がなければ，契約違反を追求できる事情から履行不能が生じた場合，免責条項によってその過失を免責してしまうからである」。この見解は一般原則に合致しているように思われる。Jackson v. Union Marine (1874) L.R. 10 C.P. 125 事件では，Bramwell 男爵は，「ところで，海上の危険の免責およびそれによって生じる遅延の効果はどのようなものであろうか。この点について私は，それは船主を免責するものであるが，船主に権利を認めるものではないと考える」（なお，The Super Servant Two [1989] 1 Lloyd's Rep. 148（同判例集 156頁）事件の Hobhouse 判事の判断も参照）。

意図的な行為または選択

さらに，傭船契約の履行不能をもたらす事態が，一方当事者の意図的行為あるいは選択によって惹起された場合，それ自体が契約違反ではない場合でも，その当事者が自己を守るために履行不能の原則に依拠することはできないと思われる。

1928年トロール船 St. Cuthbert 号は，12ヶ月の期間で傭船された。契約にはいずれかの当事者に対する3ヶ月前までの通告により終結されない限り，期間満了後も契約は毎年自動的に更新される旨の規定があった。また，同船は漁業にのみ使用されるとの明示の定めもあった。1932年には，傭船料の減額とともに傭船契約の更新が合意された。この新しい合意が成立したとき，オッタートロールの無免許使用を禁止する法律が可決されたことを両当事者は知っていた。本船は，オッタートロール装備船で，それにしか使用できないものであった。傭船者はオッタートロールを備えたトロール船を本船の他に4隻運航しており，その5隻の船舶について免許を申請した。結局免許は3隻にしか認められなかった。傭船者は3隻をオッタートロール船として指定したが，その中に St. Cuthbert 号を含めなかった。傭船者は傭船契約に認められた唯一の目的（漁業）に使用することが違法になったので，その後の履行義務を免れると主張した。これに対して，枢密院は履行不能は「自ら招いたもの」であり，St. Cuthbert 号を免許保有船として指定しなかったのは傭船者の怠慢であって，傭船者は自己の怠慢を理由に契約上の義務を免れることはできない，と判示した。
Maritime National Fish v. Ocean Trawlers (1935) 51 Ll.L. Rep. 299.

枢密院での判決にあたり，Wright 卿は次のように述べている。「重要な点は，傭船者がその気になれば，St. Cuthbert 号に免許を付与させることができたという点である。本件を St. Cuthbert 号が免許船から除外された事件として構成すると，その原因は控訴人（傭船者）にある。というのは，控訴人（傭船者）の申請に従って，所轄大臣は免許を発行し，その結果 St. Cuthbert 号が除外されたからである。『履行不能』の本質は，それが当事者の行為または選択に起因するものであってはならない，ということである」。

自力推進ができる艀 Super Servant Two 号の船主が掘削機を日本から Rotterdam 向けに輸送することを約束した。契約では，Super Servant Two 号かその姉妹船（艀）である Super Servant One 号のいずれかを使用することとなっていた。結局船主は Super Servant Two 号の使用を決めたが，その艀は，輸送に取りかかる前に，別の掘削機を輸送中に沈没し，全損になった。姉妹船艀は，すでに他の仕事の予定が入っていたので，Super Servant Two 号の滅失により，その契約は履行不能になったと，船主は主張した。予審裁判の Hobhouse 判事と控訴院は，もし主張されているとおりに，揚荷役

の際,船主の被用者の不注意な監督が原因で艀が沈没したのであれば,船主は履行不能を主張できない,と判示した。この原則の適用如何は,「外部のできごともしくは外生的な事情の変化」の生起にかかっている。もし,主張されているとおり,艀の滅失が,「履行不能の原則に依拠しようとする当事者が阻止する手段と機会をもっていたにもかかわらず,生起させてしまったか,生起を許した」できごとであれば,その艀の滅失は,「外部のできごともしくは外生的な事情の変化」とは言えない([1990] 1 Lloyd's Rep. 1 (10頁)のBingham卿判事による)。またさらに船主は,他の艀を使用すれば,その契約を履行できたはずである。履行が不可能になったのは, Super Servant Two 号の滅失が理由ではなく, Super Servent One 号を使用しないと決めた自分自身の決定によるものである。それゆえ,船主の不履行は,「自ら招いた」のである。Hobhouse判事は,「契約者が契約を履行する複数の方法を持っていて,そのうちのひとつが不可能になった場合も,それにより契約者が契約の履行ができなくなるわけではない。もし,契約の履行不能が,契約者がある選択をするが故に生じるに過ぎないものであれば,申し立てられた履行不能の原因をなすものはその選択であって,先行するできごとではない。

The Super Servant Two [1989] 1 Lloyd's Rep. 148 および [1990] 1 Lloyd's Rep. 1 (C. A.)

過　失

履行不能となる事件が,不注意な行為,と言ってもそれ自体契約違反とは言えない行為によって引き起こされた場合にも,同じことが言えるであろう。The Super Servant Two 号事件のHobhouse判事と控訴院は,その艀の滅失に関わる事情が船主の支配の及ぶ範囲にあったとすれば,艀の船主はその艀の滅失をこれから開始する運送契約が履行不能となる理由にはできないと判示した。すなわち,そのような状況下で,適切な技量を発揮しなかったことは,契約違反ではなく,あるいは,その他の注意義務違反でもないが,それ(技量の発揮がない)が故に,履行不能の原因を艀の滅失に帰することはできないのである。

Constantine v. Imperial Smelting 事件(後出)において, Wright卿とSimon子爵とは,単なる過失が「債務不履行」とみなされ,自己の招いた履行不能とされるかどうかについては,疑問を表明した。Simon子爵はこの点につき,次のように述べている。「履行不能の申立を無効にする要素である『債務不履行』の範囲は,未だ厳密に判決をもって示されているとは思えない。二つの先例判決に示された『自己の招いた』履行不能は,意図的に選択した行為に関するものであった。そこに示されているのは,意図的な行為によって履行不能を発生せしめた者は,その結果発生した履行不能を理由として免責を主張できない,というに等しい。『債務不履行』というのは,より広い意味を持ち,履行不能が問題とされる多くの商事事件において,過失と同じように扱われている。しかし,商事事件とは範疇を異にする個人的な履行を目的とする契約の履行不能の事件においては,不注意が原因でその個人の履行能力が欠ける場合,履行不能の申立が却下されるとは判断されていないと思われる」([1942] A.C. 154, 166頁)。Wright卿はこれに加えて,「この点に関し,単なる過失のみで『債務不履行』を構成するのに十分であると提言されたことはないように思われる」と述べている (195頁。The Evia (No. 2) [1982] 1 Lloyd's Rep. 334 事件をも参照)。前出 The Super Servant Two 事件で, Hobhouse判事はこれらのコメントに言及して,次のように述べている (同判例集156頁)。「一方の当事者が無理なく管理できる事実が契約を履行不能にすると考えられるのであれば,それは良い方法ではない,と私は考える」。控訴審で, Bingham卿判事は,次のように示唆している (同判例集10頁)。「本当の問題」は,「履行不能を惹起した事由が,真に外部のできごともしくは外生的な事情の変化と言えるかどうか,もしくはそれが,履行不能の原則に依拠しようとする当事者が阻止する手段と機会をもっていたにもかかわらず,生起させてしまったか,生起を許したのかどうか」ということである。これは正しい考え方で,上記のWright卿とSimon子爵の懸念にも答えるものである,と言われている。しかし,その点に関しては,多少の注意が

必要であるのかもしれない。[1989] LMCLQ 3 の Hobhouse 判事の判決と [1989] LMCLQ 153 控訴院の決定に関する McKendrick の意見を参照。

立 証 責 任

自己が招いた履行不能であることの立証責任は，履行不能の原則の適用を否定する側にある。したがって船主が傭船契約の履行不能を一応証明（*prima facie*）すれば，その事態が船主によって引き起こされたものであるという点の立証責任は傭船者側にある。

Kingswood 号はその航海傭船期間中，補機関の爆発によりかなりの損害を被り，その修繕期間（当事者に争いのない）は，その航海の商業目的を無に帰するほどに長期にわたった。しかし，傭船者は，船主が自己の責めに帰することのできない事由で爆発が生じたことを立証しない限り，船主は貨物不積の責任を免れないと主張した。事件は，仲裁に付託され，仲裁人は証拠上爆発原因を判断することができなかった。仲裁人は，爆発が船主被用者の過失により発生した可能性を否定することも，また過失なしに発生した可能性も否定できなかった。問題は，かくして船主の債務不履行の存在の立証責任が傭船者側にあるのか，あるいはその不存在の立証責任が船主側にあるのかの問題となった。貴族院は，立証責任は傭船契約が履行不能にならないと主張する傭船者側にあると判示した。
Constantine v. *Imperial Smelting* [1942] A.C. 154.

履行不能に伴う義務

コモン・ローの立場

コモン・ロー上，履行不能は契約および契約当事者の義務を直ちに終了させる。履行不能が生じたときに存在する権利はそのまま存続し，その当時存在しない権利がその後生じることはありえない。したがって，契約上支払時期が到来していないものは支払う必要はなく，その反対に，支払時期の到来している前払金は全額支払義務があり，もしそれが支払済の場合は，返還の必要はないと思われる。例えば，*Lloyd Royal* v. *Stathatos* (1917) 34 T.L.R. 70 事件の場合，控訴院は傭船者の前払傭船料返還請求を退け，傭船者は傭船契約のいずれかの条項によってのみ返還を受けることができるが，傭船契約が履行不能となったのであるから，そのすべての条項もまた失効してしまったと判示した。1943年以来，前払金に関するこの原則は一部変更され，前払金の対価となる約因全部が失われた場合には，前払金は返還されるとされている（*Fibrosa* v. *Fairbairn* [1943] A.C. 32事件）。しかし，そのためには，その約因はすべて失われなければならず，そういう事例はあまりないと思われる。

1943年履行不能により消滅する契約に関する法（Frustrated Contracts Act 1943）によるコモン・ローの変更

上記のコモン・ロー上の原則は，1943年法改革（履行不能により消滅する契約）に関する法によって変更された。この法律は，契約が履行不能になるかどうかの問題を扱っているのではなく，前述の原則に従って契約が履行不能になったと判断される場合，その契約の当事者の立場を扱ったものである。この法律は，定期傭船契約に適用される。しかし，航海傭船契約または船荷証券については適用されず，それらについては，古いコモン・ローの原則が適用される。したがって，履行不能となった傭船契約が定期か航海であるかは，重要な問題である。

Eugenia 号はボルタイム書式によって傭船された。その期間は「……Genoa……から黒海経由インドまでの1航海」と表示され，傭船料は月払，就航区域は，「Genoa，黒海経由インド」とあった。

Megaw 判事は，これを定期傭船契約と判示した。控訴院は契約が履行不能になったという Megaw 判事の判断を覆したが（この点は前出466頁），定期傭船の点は肯定した。
　Ocean Tramp Tankers v. *Sovfracht*（*The Eugenia*）[1963] 2 Lloyd's Rep. 155 および 381.
　（*Temple Steamship* v. *Sovfracht*（1945）79 LLL. Rep. 1 事件および *The Democritos* [1976] 2 Lloyd's Rep. 149 事件参照）

　この法律は「英法を準拠法とする」契約，すなわち英法により解釈されるべき契約にのみ適用される。この法律の第1条(2)，(3)および第2条(3)が，*B. P. Exploration Co.* v. *Hunt* [1979] 1 W. L. R. 783 および [1981] 1 W. L. R. 232（C. A.）事件で概括的に考察されている。

　履行不能と帰した定期傭船契約の当事者の権利に関するこの法律の効果は，次のとおりに要約できる。

1．履行不能発生以前に支払った金額は返還しなければならず，また，それ以前に支払義務が発生した金額については支払義務がなくなる。しかし，かかる金額の支払を受け，または，支払を受けるべき者が，契約履行過程において，または，履行のために出費している場合，裁判所は，その裁量により，かかる金額の全部または一部を，その出費した者に受領させることができる（本法の第1条(2)を参照）。

　したがって，半月毎の前払傭船料は，その半月間の何時の時点に履行不能になったとしても返還しなければならない（例えば，*The Eugenia* [1963] 2 Lloyd's Rep. 155（同判例集177頁）事件を参照）。しかし，履行不能以前に船主が支出した履行のための運航費については，裁判所はこれを船主が受領することを裁量により許すと決めることができる。これに加えて，もしくはこれと選択的に，船主は第1条(3)により支払を求めることができる。それ以前の定期的支払分に関しては，下記の3．を参照。

2．履行不能以前に，一方の当事者が相手方のなした契約履行過程の，または，履行のための行為によって利益を受けた場合，裁判所は，裁量により，その利益を受けた者に対して適当な支払をなすべきことを要求することができる。その支払われるべき正当な金額を査定するために，裁判所は次の要素を考慮に入れなければならない。(a)受益者の支出した費用，これには本法の第1条(2)の下で支払った額もしくは支払うべき額を含む，(b)履行不能を生じせしめた状況からどのような利益を得たか（第1条(3)を参照）。

　第1条(2)は，上記のとおり，前払傭船料が支払済であるかあるいは支払時期が到来している場合に，船主にその受領権限を，裁判所が裁量をもって与えることを規定したものであるが，この項は，裁判所にさらなる裁量権を与えるものである。第1条(2)は，支出した費用に（たぶん運航費に）限られるが，第1条(3)は，実際上，裁判所に相当日数分の傭船料全額の支払を命ずることも認めるものである。

3．裁判所が，履行不能になった契約の一部が，他の部分と適当に「分離」可能と判断した場合，例えば特定部分は履行不能以前に完全に履行し終わったという場合，この分離可能部分は，履行不能が発生しなかったと同様に扱わなければならない（第2条(4)を参照）。

　したがって，月払傭船料の定めのある定期傭船契約が，例えば7ヶ月目に履行不能になった場合，裁判所は「分離」させて，前6ヶ月分の各傭船料の支払義務をそのまま残すことができ

るし，たぶんそうするであろうと思われる（*The Eugenia* [1963] 2 Lloyd's Rep. 155 事件では，履行不能が発生した当該半月間以前の各半月ごとの傭船料について本法が適用される，とは言っていない。また，船主はボルタイム書式第5条により，本船引渡時に本船が持っていた燃料油の費用を回収する権利があるとも判断されている）。

「履行不能により消滅する契約に関する法」の効果の排除

この法律の第2条(3)は次のように規定している。「本法が適用になる契約が，履行不能となる状況もしくはその条項がなければ履行不能となる状況において，その契約を真に解釈すれば，ある効果を意図する何らかの条項を有している場合，あるいは，契約を履行不能とする状況の発生如何にかかわらず，ある効果を意図した条項を有している場合，裁判所は，その条項の効力を認めるが，この法律の前述の規定に関しては，その条項と矛盾しないと思われる範囲にその効果を制限するものとする。」

本船が全損になった場合の傭船料の扱いを定めたニューヨーク・プロデュース書式の102, 103行および，ボルタイム書式119行から122行の規定は，いずれもこの法律の第2条(3)が適用される規定であると考えられている。

傭船者の財産

定期傭船契約が履行不能となった場合，傭船者は傭船契約に従って支払った燃料油，他の船用品に対する権利を有する。*The Eugenia* [1963] 2 Lloyd's Rep. 155 事件において，Megaw判事は次のとおり述べた。「かかる事情のもとでは，船用品は傭船者の財産である。つまり傭船者は船用品代金を支払ったか，あるいは支払義務があるが，船主はその船用品をもはや当該傭船者の目的のために使用する義務はないからである」（同判例集177頁）。

（一方，傭船者はボルタイム書式第5条により，本船引渡時の燃料油，炊事用燃料，水の代金を支払う義務があると判示された。上記3参照）

⌊410⌋ 米　国　法

反対給付が得られなかった前払金

相互免責条項の直前には，次の文言が置かれている。

本船が滅失したときは，反対給付が得られなかった前払金（滅失または最後の消息があった日から起算する）を，直ちに傭船者に返還しなければならない。

引用された文言は，起案の仕方としては，後に続く相互免責の文言と分離された条項に置かれなければならない。なぜならば，その文言には，相互免責規定の適用がないからである。本船が滅失した場合とオフハイヤーになった場合に，前払傭船料の払戻を受ける傭船者の権利は，払戻をする船主の義務が独立の義務であるように，独立の権利である。その義務履行は，通常の場合，相互に免責された危険のいずれによっても不可能になることはない（*Clyde Commercial S. S. Co.* v. *West India S. S. Co.*, 169 F. 275 (2d Cir. 1909)，裁量上告拒絶214 U. S. 523 (1909) 事件を参照）。この事件では，君主による抑留の遅延が生じても，傭船者は傭船料を支払う義務があると裁判所は判断した。

傭船契約の履行不能

米国法においては，予期せざるできごとによって傭船契約の履行が不可能あるいは「商業的に実行不可能」になった場合，船主，傭船者ともに傭船契約上の義務を免れる。しかし，履行不能の原則が適用されるには，厳格なる基準がある（一般的には，*Restatement 2d Contracts* §261 *et seq*. を参照）。

傭船契約の履行不能に関する米国法上の指導的判例は，*Transatlantic Financing Corp.* v. *United States*, 363 F. 2d 312, 1966 AMC 1717 (D. C. Cir. 1966) 事件である。この事件において，*Christos* 号の傭船船主は，米国からイラン向け貨物運送航海に際して，スエズ運河閉鎖の結果生じた余分な費用を航海傭船者から回収しようとした。船主の主張は，航海傭船契約の規定は，航海が「通常かつ慣習的」航路，すなわちテキサスからスエズ運河経由イランに至る航路によるべきことを定めており，スエズ運河の閉鎖は傭船契約の履行を不可能にしたというものである。船主は喜望峰経由での航海を行って貨物を引き渡し，それによって生じた余分な費用の回収を求めた。

船主の不可能の主張を検討するに際して，裁判所は履行不能が発生したかどうかを決定するために考慮すべき要素を次のごとく示した。

この理論は，結局商業実務および一般社会的慣習に対応すべく裁判所が画す一線を示すものであるが，それは常に変化する。その接点は，契約はその条項に従って強制されるべきであるという一般社会の要求より，その履行を要求することが商業上意味を持たなくなるということのほうが強くなるところに求められる。問題が起きた場合，裁判所は変化した状況をもとに履行の条件を組み立てることを要求されるが，その過程は，少なくとも三つの段階に分けるのが合理的である。第1は，偶発性，すなわち予期せぬ事態が発生しなければならないこと。第2は，発生する危険の分担が，合意または慣習によって，定められていないこと。最後は，その偶発事態により，契約の履行が商業的に実行不可能となったことである。裁判所が，以上の三つの基準を満たしていると判断しない限り，履行が不可能であるとの申立は成立しない（363 F. 2d at 315-316）。

この三つの基準に照らして、事実関係を検討した結果、裁判所は最初の二つの基準は事実上満たしていると判断した。すなわちスエズ運河の閉鎖は、予期しなかったものであり、そのような偶発事件の危険分担については、当事者間に取決めはなかった。しかし、裁判所は、スエズ運河閉鎖のために航海費用は増加したが、その増加は傭船契約の履行を商業的に不可能ならしめるほど極端なものではない、したがって、履行不能は成立しないとの結論を下した。

事態は予見不可能であることを要する

　履行不能の第1の要件は、それが予見しえない事態によって生じるということである。第2巡回区控訴裁判所が判示しているように、「この原則により、契約の義務から解放されるのは、まったく予期できない大変動が発生し、契約が一方の当事者にとって無価値なものになった場合に限られる」(*United States* v. *Gen. Douglas MacArthur Sr. Vil. Inc.,* 508 F. 2d. 377, 381 (2d Cir. 1974). *United States* v. *Buffalo Coal Mining Co.,* 345 F. 2d 517, 518 (9th Cir. 1965) 事件も参照)。この事件では、裁判所は次のように判示している。

>　……まったく予期できない原因によって契約の目的が破壊されない限り、当事者は契約に拘束される。この予見可能性の基準は、客観的なものであって、当事者の心理状態まで立ち入る主観的なものであってはならない。

　予見可能性の概念は、*The Poznan,* 276 F. 418, 425 (S. D. N. Y. 1921) 事件で示されている。この事件では、Havana において貨物を引き渡すという約定に違反したという理由で、船主に対し訴訟が提起されたが、船主は、本船が10月から11月にかけ6週間 Havana に錨泊中、船込みのためバースも艀も確保できず、したがって貨物引渡が不可能であったという理由で、契約は履行不能になったと抗弁した。裁判所は、9月に傭船契約が締結されたとき、すでに同港が船込み状態であることは明らかであった、という理由で船主の抗弁を退けた。つまり裁判所の判断では、10月、11月の遅延は予期せぬ事態とみなすことはできない、というものであった。

　この事件が履行不能の事件でないことは明らかである。たぶん繰り返すまでもないが、契約の履行を不可能にする後発的事態のなかには、契約者の履行義務を免除するのが妥当と言えるほど、まったく予期できず、かつ当事者の期待をまったく裏切るものもありうる、という一般原則を示したにすぎない。それでも、契約者は、契約履行にはそれを妨げるある程度の危険がつきものであることを認識していなければならず、約定する際に、そのような危険を引き受けていると了解されなければならない。履行義務を免除し、その結果相手方が被る損害を救済せず放置するにあたり、裁判所は、その厳格さの程度は異なるが、常に次の点に留意してきた。すなわち、履行を阻害する事情は起こりうべからざる事態であり、そのような事態のもとでは当事者はとうてい履行することに合意しない、というものでなければならない。……ただし、それがいかに不可能であっても、履行者は、一応履行義務に拘束はされるが……(276 F. at 425)。

　The Kronprinzessin Cecilie, 244 U. S. 12, 22 (1917) 事件で、連邦最高裁判所は、金を積んで英国に向かうドイツ船の船主は、独英間の戦争が勃発した場合、ニューヨークに引き返す権利があると判示した。連邦最高裁判所は、戦争の勃発によって拿捕される危険が発生したが、その危険は「履行の相手方がその危険を冒せと要求し、履行者がそれを引き受けるものとは考えられない」性質のものであり、それゆえ、契約の履行は免除された、と判示した。

しかしながら，*Madeirense Do Brazil S/A* v. *Stulman-Emrick Lumber Co.*, 147 F. 2d 399 (2d Cir.), 裁量上告拒絶 325 U.S. 861 (1945) 事件において，材木の売主は，1940年10月に締結された契約に基づき，材木を New York で買主に引き渡すため，ブラジルからの材木の輸送契約を運送人と締結する義務があった。買主からの契約不履行に基づく請求に対して，売主は，船腹の不足のため履行が不可能になったと抗弁した。裁判所はその抗弁を退け，次のとおり述べた。

　[売主は]，さらに契約不履行の責めを免れるため，船腹不足のを理由として，商品を要求どおり引き渡すことができなかったと主張した。[買主]はこの主張について争わなかったが，本件ではこの事実関係を判断する必要はない。というのは，船がなかったとしても，[売主]は，本件の状況下において，その履行義務を免れないからである。すなわち，[売主]の手紙によると，売主は第2の契約を締結した当時，船舶がプレミアム付であったことが明らかであり，実際売主は，追加船積を行えば，船腹の確保が容易になると考えたから，第2の契約の締結を急いだのである。そこにはそんなに驚くべき状況の変化はない。欧州での戦争はすでに1年以上も続いており，真珠湾は未だ先のことであった。さらに，米国や南米諸国が戦争に参加したのは，契約が締結されてから1年あるいはそれ以上もたってからのことであった。このことから1941年1月における船舶の不足は，[売主]が当然負担すべき予見可能な危険であったということになる。このような状況下においては，不可抗力の主張は成立しない。……（147 F. 2d at 403）。

　Glidden Co. v. *Hellenic Lines Ltd.*, 275 F. 2d 253 (2d Cir. 1960) 事件では，「予見可能性」の基準に関する最後の例を提供している。事件は，スエズ運河の閉鎖によって発生した。船主は，スエズ運河の閉鎖のため，インドから米国向けの傭船航海が不可能になったと主張した。その傭船契約には，船主にはスエズ経由，喜望峰経由，パナマ運河経由の選択権が与えられていた。それゆえ，裁判所は，当事者がスエズ運河経由以外の航路による契約の履行も考えていたとして，航海は履行不能にはならないと判示した。

危険の分担

　履行不能の第2の要件は，傭船契約の文言あるいは慣習によって，船主と傭船者との間に危険の分担が定められていないことである。この原則は，抗弁の要素である予見可能性と密接な関係がある。と言うのは，契約において，危険の分担が定められている場合には，明らかに「予期できなかった」と主張することはできないからである。

　The Ocean Commander, SMA 2930 (Arb. at N.Y. 1992) 事件は，乗組員の過失でパイプラインからの漏れが起こり，その修理のために航海に遅延が生じた事件である。傭船者は，引渡時に本船は不堪航であり，パイプラインに関して船主は十分な注意義務を尽くしていないと主張した。傭船者は，貨物を積むのが間に合わなかったことで，傭船者が売買契約の義務を果たすことができなかったことより，航海傭船契約が解約された事実の承認を要求し，航海は履行不能になったと主張した。仲裁人は，傭船者は本船が不堪航であったことを立証していない，と判断した。さらに傭船者が遭遇した問題は，傭船契約自体にとって本質的なものではないことを根拠に，傭船者の履行不能の主張は否定された。パイプラインからの漏れは，決して予見できないものではなかった。本船装備の故障による遅延の危険は，当事者間で分担されており，さらに傭船契約は，なかんずく乗組員の過失による損害について，それが船主自らの故意または過失でなければ，船主の責任を排除している。さらに仲裁人は貨物の揚荷に関し，傭船契約には特定の履行日が書かれていなかったと認定し，その遅延は履行を不可能にしないと

判断した。

商業的に実行不可能な履行

　履行不能の事件において最も困難な問題は，履行が不可能，あるいは，Transatlantic 事件で示されたように，「商業的に実行不可能」にならなければならないという要件から必然的に発生する。Cameron-Hawn Realty Co. v. City of Albany, 207 N.Y. 377, 381, 101 N.E. 162, 163 (1913) 事件において，裁判所は，不可能に関する法の古典的記述として，次のように述べている。

　　当事者は，契約上の義務を果たされなければならないというのは，確立した法の原則である。約定したことが，可能かつ合法であるならば，履行義務を果たさなければならない。約定した義務の遂行が困難であるとか，できそうにもないということは，履行義務者が主張できる問題ではない。いかなる手段をもってしても遂行できないということを立証しなければならず，その立証を欠いた場合，不履行の責めを免れることはできない。

　「商業的に実行不可能」という基準は，不可能というより若干緩やかではあるが，それでも履行不能を主張する当事者にとって非常に重い立証責任を課している。ゆえに，傭船契約の履行は，それがより困難になったとか，より経費がかかるとかという理由では，商業的に実行不可能となったとはみなされない。American Trading & Production Corp. v. Shell International Marine Ltd., 453 F. 2d 939 (2d Cir. 1972) 事件で，本船が Texas からインドに向け大西洋上を航海中，中東戦争が勃発しスエズ運河が閉鎖された。船主は本船を喜望峰経由として航海を完了させ，傭船者に対し余分にかかった費用を請求して訴訟を起こした。その理由として，傭船航海は履行不能となったのだから，積荷は提供役務相当額の運賃を受けることを条件として引き渡されたというものであった。裁判所は，Transatlantic 事件に示された三つの基準を採用して，最初の二つの条件は満たしていると判断した。しかし，それに引き続いて，スエズ運河の閉鎖によって傭船航海が商業的に実行できなくなったわけではない，と判断した。喜望峰回りによる追加出費は，当初の航海の約33パーセント増にのぼったが，裁判所は，履行不能の主張を正当化するためには，余分の費用が「極端でかつ合理性を欠く」ところまで達しなければならないと述べ，本件において船主の出費はこの要件を満たしていないと判断した。

　The Paros, SMA 1025 (Arb. at N.Y. 1976) 事件でも，同様の結論が出された。本件では，傭船者が積地における長期の遅延を予期して，傭船契約を解除したことは不当であると判断された。履行不能の抗弁を退けるにあたって，仲裁審は次のとおり述べた。

　　3ヶ月と予想された船積の遅延は「極端に不合理」な出費をもたらすとは思われない。実務感覚のある船主および傭船者ならば，この事態は不幸なできごとではあるが，世界の各地において決して異常なできごとではないということを認識しているはずである。

　The Mermaid I, SMA 1836 (Arb. at N.Y. 1983) 事件は，航海傭船の事件であるが，有益な類似例を提供している。この事件は，本船が傭船者に受け取られた直後に，衝突に巻き込まれた事件である。本船が錨地でバース待ちをしているときに，衝突された。仲裁審は，全会一致で，そのような衝突は「予測できない事故」ではなく，それゆえ，第1の要件を満たしていない，と判断した。「傭船契約中の碇泊期間の進行に関する条項によって，生じた遅延の危険は分担されている」ことにより，第2の基準についても，それを満たしていないと判断され

た。さらには、仲裁審は、第3の基準を満たしていることが、立証されていないと判断した。というのは、「本船 Mermaid I に積載すれば、遅延により若干余分の費用がかさみ、スケジュールに不都合が出たかもしれないが、傭船者には、多くの別船に積む機会があった。」

The Gulf Sea, SMA 3095 (Arb. at NY 1994) 事件では、本船は修理のために11日間滞留し、傭船者はそれを理由に残りの傭船期間を履行不能と宣言した。傭船者の主張は認められず、傭船者は傭船者が不当に解約した傭船契約の期間につき、傭船料を船主に支払うよう命じられた。

The Intermar Progress, SMA 2468 (Arb. at NY 1988) 事件では、船主は、米国港とタンカーの安全に関する法(「PTSA」)と船舶による汚染防止のための国際条約(「MARPOL 73/78」)に従って、原油洗浄装置と不活性ガスシステムの装備を求められた。船主は、傭船者に対し、その経費の分担を求めた、すなわち提供役務相当額(*quantum meruit*)を要求し、商業的に実行不可能の原則を援用した。仲裁人は、PTSA や MARPOL 73/78の要求は、定期傭船契約を履行不能にするものではないと判示し、船主がそれらの経費の分担を求める交渉を傭船者と行ったときに、一度も商業的な履行不能や実行不可能の問題を提起していない点を、仲裁人は重要視した。

The Turmoil, SMA 2842 (Arb. at N.Y. 1992) 事件では、受入可能な信用状を傭船者が提供するのが遅れ、そのために貨物が間に合わなかったのであるが、その事実によっては傭船契約は履行不能にはならない、と判示された。碇泊期間をちょうど使い果たし、僅か1日間だけ超過碇泊期間に入っただけで、船主が傭船契約を拒絶するのは、不合理であると判断されたのである。

[414] 契約の履行を妨げる第三者の債務不履行

特に航海傭船においてしばしば起こる問題は、荷送人あるいは荷受人との契約上の障害を理由に、傭船者が契約の履行を免れうるかということである。一般原則は、傭船契約の本質にかかわらない問題については、履行義務を免れることはできない。例として、*Krulewitch* v. *National Importing & Trading Co. Inc.*, 195 A.D. 544, 186 N.Y.S. 838 (1921) 事件がある。この事件では、National は Krulewitch に対してタピオカの粉を売却する契約を結んだ。その契約には、商品は「2・3月 Java より」積込と規定されていた。Java 政府当局の New York 向け船積を禁止する措置により、New York 向けの直接輸送は停止した。これを理由に National は履行義務を免れたと主張した。裁判所は、この主張を退けて、禁止措置があっても、経費をかけさえすれば、商品は中間港経由で New York に運送することができたと判断した。さらに、裁判所は貨物輸送の手配をするについて National が直面した障害は、Krulewitch との契約の履行義務を免れさせるものではないと判断した。

> 運送手段を確保することは、この契約の付随的問題である。このこと自体原告に何らの関係もない。原告は New York のドックで商品と引換に金を支払うと約定したのであって、その輸送方法は原告の関知するところではない (186, N.Y.S. at 840)。

Bardons & Oliver, Inc. v. *Amtorg Trading Corp.*, 123 N.Y.S. 2d 633 (Sup. Ct. 1948)、理由を付さず原審維持 275 App. Div. 748, 88 N.Y.S. 2d 272 (1st Dep't 1949)、原審維持 301 N.Y. 622, 93 N.E. 2d 915 (1950) 事件において、Aはある機械をBに売ることに同意した。Bはそれを米国からソビエトに輸出しようと考えた。Bは米国政府の輸出許可を得ることがで

きず，そのためにAとの契約は履行不能になったと主張した。裁判所はBの抗弁を退けて次のとおり述べた。

　契約には，その効力や履行が輸出許可証の取得にかかっているいることについて何ら言及がない。契約は，両当事者の義務を明確に定めている。この契約において，両当事者とも国外向け出荷について，何らの義務も負っていない。同契約上の引渡は「F. O. B. cars, Cleveland, Ohio……」条件となっていた。したがって，売主が引き受けたことと言えば，適当な荷印をつけて，適当なB/Lと引換に商品を貨車に積み込むことだけであった。積替はまったく被告のみ関係する問題であった。被告は，その履行を輸出許可証の取得の有無にかからしめる意思があれば，そのことを契約の条件として，その旨を契約に記載することができたのである。被告はそれをしなかったのであるから，その主張がとおるとは思えない（123 N. Y. S. 2d at 634）。

　The Erisort, SMA 1022（Arb. at N. Y. 1976）事件において，この点がとりあげられている。この事件では，航海傭船者は，約定のスクラップ貨物の提供ができなかった点に責任があると判断された。仲裁審は，貨物に対するガテマラ政府の輸出許可が発給されず，貨物供給者が傭船者との契約を履行しなかったことを理由として履行ができなかったとする傭船者の選択的抗弁を退けた。同様の事件として，Econolines Inc. and Mohammed Al-Haddad, et al., 1980 AMC 424（Arb. at N. Y. 1979），この事件では，アスファルト貨物の買主が購入契約を拒絶しているが，傭船者の傭船契約が履行不能になったとする主張が否定された。さらに，The Ocean Commander 事件（前出）も参照。

　なお，これに反する意見については，Tradax International S. A. v. Government of Pakinstan, 1973 AMC 1609（Arb. at N. Y. 1973）事件参照。

過失の効果

　履行不能となる事態は，契約当事者の一方によってもたらされたものであってはならない。Gemini Shipping v. Seas Shipping, SMA 1253（Arb. at N. Y. 1978）事件では，タイ国政府が船積契約による亜鉛鉱の輸出を許可しなかった。その理由は，傭船者がタイ国に亜鉛精錬所を建設する特許契約に従わないため輸出停止の一因を作ったという点に存した。そのような場合，傭船者は，不可抗力や履行不能の抗弁を援用することはできない，と判示された。

法律の変更

　傭船契約の履行に影響を与える契約成立後の法律の変更を理由とする履行不能の主張がなされた事件が数多くある。この点に関して，もっとも重要なことは，契約履行を律する米国法の変更と，外国法における同様の変更とを区別することである。その理由は，国内法における禁止規定は，履行不能の理由となるが，外国法の場合は，原則がその反対になるからである。したがって，米国法下における一般原則は，外国法の変更のため履行が不可能になっても，契約上の義務の不履行の責めを免れることはできないということである。J. Zeevi & Sons Ltd. v. Grindlays Bank（Uganda）Ltd., 37 N. Y. 2d 220, 371 N. Y. S. 2d 892, 裁量上告拒絶423 U. S. 866（1975）；Central Hanover Bank & Trust Co. v. Siemens & Halske Akt., 15 F. Supp. 927（S. D. N. Y.），下記理由にて原審どおり維持84 F. 2d 993（2d Cir.），裁量上告拒絶299 U. S. 585（1936）；Gonzalez v. Industrial Bank, 12 N. Y. 2d 33, 234 N. Y. S. 2d 210（1962）。

　この問題の論点が，Tweedie Trading Co. v. James P. McDonald Co., 114 F. 985（S. D. N. Y. 1902）事件で説明されている。同事件において，TweedieはMcDonaldとの契約により，

その所有船によって労務者をBarbadosからColonまで4航海輸送することを約束した。2航海の後，Barbadosの植民地政府は労務者の乗船を禁止する命令を公布した。その結果McDonaldは第3，第4航海に労務者を提供することができなかった。Tweedieは最後の2航海分の得べかりし運賃の請求を求め訴訟を起こし，裁判所はTweedieを勝たせた。裁判所の判示は次のとおりである。

　　契約は，その締結地および履行地のいずれにおいても，締結当時有効であった。また当事者が契約当時考慮しなかった事態によって妨げられるまで，契約の履行は可能であった。この種の事件において，履行不能が自然的原因に起因している場合には抗弁としては認められないが，政府の行為によって履行が違法となるような場合には，抗弁が成り立つというのが，確立された原則のようである。しかし，本件においてTweedieは，履行は法律によって妨げられたが，その法律は外国法であるがゆえに事実の問題であり，そのために抗弁とはなりえず，本件には一般原則の適用があると主張した。これに対して，McDonaldは，履行地法が契約の準拠法であり，その法律の変更が履行を不可能にしたのであるから，契約は消滅したと主張した。真に問題となる点は，外国政府当局の法的な行為が，この種の契約の完全なる履行を妨げる場合，その法的な行為が当事者の権利を左右するかどうかである。契約当事者は，自国の法律の変更という偶発的措置にも従わなければならず，そのため契約の履行が妨げられれば，その結果を負担しなければならない。しかし，それは不可能という理由によるものではなく，違法となったという理由によってである。約定行為が，契約締結地の法律上有効であったのであれば，たとえ外国法によって妨げられても，その外国法は免責事由にならない。まして，本件では契約締結当時，履行地においても適法であったのであるから，免責は問題とはならない。この契約は履行されるべきである，と明らかに約定されていたと言える。特に，反対の意思が証明されない限り，契約履行地の法律が通常，履行に付随する問題を律するものである。

　　前出 Krulewitch v. National Importing & Trading Co. Inc. 事件を参照。そこでは，裁判所は，外国の通商禁止措置は，契約不履行を免責しないと判断している。P. N. Gray & Co. v. Cavalliotis, 276 F. 565 (E.D.N.Y. 1921), 理由を付さず原審維持 293 F. 1018 (2d Cir. 1923) の事件では，「外国の通商禁止は通常契約不履行の免責事由とはならない」，とされた。Richards & Co. v. Wreschner, 156 N.Y.S. 1054, 1057 (1915)，原審維持 174 A.D. 484, 158 N.Y.S. 1129 (1916) 事件では，「外国の戦争は不可能の言い訳にはならない」，とされた。Glynn v. United Steel Works Corp., 160 Misc. 405, 289 N.Y.S. 1037 (1935) 事件では，ドイツにおける支払猶予令は New York で支払うべきドイツ紙幣による支払を禁止するものではない。Sokoloff v. National City Bank, 239 N.Y. 158, 145 N.E. 917 (1924) 事件では，ロシアが出した New York 銀行 Petrograd 支店口座の接収命令は，銀行の原告に対する預金返還義務を免除しないとされた。

　　しかしながら，一方で，外国の行為によって契約履行が不可能になったことを理由に，当事者が傭船契約上の義務を免れた事件もある。その指導的判例は，Texas Co. v. Hogarth Shipping Co., 256 U.S. 619 (1921) 事件である。その事件では，航海傭船中の英国船が英国政府によって戦争目的のために徴用された。最高裁は，このような国家の行為は船主の履行義務を免除すると判断した。

　　本件では，本船は実在し完全な堪航性を備えていたが，徴用のため，傭船契約の履行にはまったく使えなかった。言い換えれば，国の行為によって傭船契約を履行することが不可能となり，傭船者は本船を使用できず，船主は約定運賃を取得できなくなった。この状況，すなわち航海開始前の徴用という予期しない後発事態の発生で，本船が使用不能になった場合は，契約は終了し，当事者は履行責任を免れるという契約の黙示の条件を満たしたとみなすべきである (256 U.S. at 629-631)。

輸出禁止令

　一般原則では，外国政府の行為は，通常，契約を履行不能とする理由とはならないが，いくつかの事件において，商業実務人の仲裁人が外国政府の輸出禁止令が不履行を免責すると判断している。*The Caliopi Carras*, SMA 1111（Arb. at N. Y. 1977）事件において，リビアの石油輸出禁止令が，約定された米国への石油の輸送を不可能にしたと判断された。同様に，*The Gota River*, SMA 1241（Arb. at N. Y. 1978）事件では，エクアドル政府が傭船者の原油供給を差押えたことにより，エクアドルからの船積契約が履行不能になったと判断された。

　The Orduna, SMA 2967（Arb. at N. Y. 1993）事件では，イラクのクウェート侵攻により，指定された積荷港が閉鎖され，イラク原油の輸出禁止が実施された。傭船者は代替貨物を探すべく合理的な努力を行ったとして，仲裁人は，傭船者の傭船契約の解約は不当なものではなく，クウェートへの侵攻は不可抗力の事態であった，と判断した。

　しかしながら，仮に輸出禁止や外国政府その他の干渉により，履行が不可能もしくは商業的に実行不可能になったとしても，履行不能とはならないとされる。例えば，*The Corona*, SMA 961（Arb. at N. Y. 1975）事件では，アラブ原油の輸出禁止により，オランダへの船積ができなくなった。しかし，傭船者は揚荷港に関し，広範囲の選択肢をもっていたことにより，契約の履行不能は否定された。同様に，*Retla Steamship* v. *Canpotex*, 1977 AMC 1594（Arb. at N. Y. 1977）事件では，傭船者は，東南アジアでのリン鉱石市場の崩壊，インドネシア政府のリン酸肥料の輸入禁止に続いた，陸上施設の過度な混雑のゆえに Singapore でのリン鉱石の揚荷は不可能になったと主張した。仲裁審では，これらの状況は，合意された中継港である Singapore での揚荷が，本件契約を履行不能とするほど，困難なものにはなっていなかった，と判断した。

　The Tore Knudsen, SMA 1108（The Arb. at N. Y. 1977）事件でも同じような結果となっている。この事件ではトルコ政府が石油製品の輸出を禁止したが，傭船者はその他にも積荷港の選択肢をもっていた。また，*The Thomas A & Thomas Q*, 1979 AMC 202（Arb. at N. Y. 1978）事件では，リビアの輸出禁止令は，傭船者の北アフリカのその他の諸港から積荷を行うという選択肢に影響を与えていない，と判断された。

　同様に，*The Energy Explorer*, SMA 3033（Arb. at N. Y. 1993）事件では，イラクの輸出禁止令によっても，航海傭船契約の傭船者がその他諸港で積荷を行うことは排除されていない，と判断された。傭船者はまた，本船を再傭船に出す選択肢があり，それにより，その当時 ULCC を埋めるほどの貨物を見つけるのは難しかったが，その代わり VLCC 用の貨物を得ることはできたのである。

　The Golden Gate, SMA 2188（Arb. at N. Y. 1986）事件もまた参照。この事件では，コスタリカとガテマラ間の通商海域が閉鎖されたが，傭船者は別の海域で通商を行う選択肢を持っていたとして，仲裁審は，傭船契約が履行不能になったと判断することを拒否した。

全損の効果――代船条項

　Niarchos（London）Ltd. v. *Shell Tankers Ltd.* [1961] 2 Lloyd's Rep. 496 事件の英国の判例では，本船の滅失により傭船契約は終結し，それにより船主の代船提供の選択肢も消滅すると，判断されている。New York での仲裁事件 *The Mary Ellen Conway*, 1973 AMC 772（Arb. at N. Y. 1973）事件も，この判例に従っている。しかし，それに続く New York での仲裁案件の *The Giovanna Lolli-ghetti*, 1974 AMC 2161（Arb. at N. Y. 1974）事件において

は，仲裁審は，前出 Niarchos 事件の理由付けに従うことを拒否した。この事件では，本船が定期傭船者に引き渡される前に，滅失した。傭船者が，船主が指定した代替船の受取を拒否したため，船主は期限前の傭船契約違反であると主張した。仲裁審の多数は，「もし，選択権が強制の場合しか実行できないのであれば，それはもはや選択権とはいえない」との船主の主張を認め，当該定期傭船契約は本船滅失によって履行不能にはなっておらず，船主は代船提供の特権を行使できると判断した。

同様に，*The Grand Zenith*, 1979 AMC 2179 (Arb. at N.Y. 1979) 事件では，本船が傭船期間中に滅失したにもかかわらず，仲裁人は，傭船契約上，船主には代船提供の選択権があると判断した。そして船主がその選択権の行使を望んでいるのだから，傭船契約に名前が書かれている本船の滅失があっても，傭船契約は履行不能にはなっていない，と判断した。この *The Grand Zenith* 事件での損害賠償の問題に関する仲裁審の判断に関しては，SMA 2186 (Arb. at N.Y. 1986) に報告されている。

推定全損

Asphalt Int'l v. *Enterprise*, 514 F. Supp. 1111 (S.D.N.Y. 1981)，原審維持 667 F. 2d 261 (2d Cir. 1981) 事件で，裁判所は，本船の損傷が修理後の本船価値を上回る場合傭船契約は履行不能となるかどうかの問題を，判断している。本船は長期の定期傭船契約の下での運航時，衝突事故により損傷を受けた。衝突前の本船の公正な市場価格は米貨75万ドルで，修理費用は少なくとも米貨150万ドルと見積られた。本船の船体保険付保額は米貨250万ドルであったから，保険という観点からすれば，推定全損とは言えなかった。しかし，船主は，本船はもはや修理する価値がないとして，スクラップにした。これに対し，傭船者は，船主は修理をすべきであった，もしくは代船を提供すべきだったと主張して，傭船契約違反として，船主を訴えた。裁判所は，修理費用が本船の公正な市場価格を超えており，傭船契約は，それでも修理を強制する，過度で，不合理な義務を船主に負わせてはおらず，契約の履行は，「商業上不可能になった」という理由で免除されている，と判断した。さらに，裁判所は，船主には代船を提供する義務もない，と判示した。

一般免責条項

[Clause 16 continued]

"103. .... The act of God, enemies, fires, restraint of Princes, Rulers and People, and all dangers and accidents of the Seas,

104. Rivers, Machinery, Boilers and Steam Navigation, and errors of Navigation throughout this Charter Party, always mutually excepted."

(第16条続き)

「本傭船期間中，天災，公敵，火災，君主・統治者および人民による抑留，海上，河川，機器，汽罐および汽船航海の一切の危険および事故，ならびに航海上の過誤について，当事者は相互に免責されるものとする。」

一般原則

これらの行は，ニューヨーク・プロデュース書式の免責条項の主要な部分を構成する。しかしながら，この免責条項がもたらす保護はきわめて限られている。特に，過失の免責が含まれていない。傭船契約の第24条により摂取されている，米国海上物品運送法が，船主により広い保護を与えている。これらの行で認められている保護は，船主だけでなく傭船者にも及ぶ。

本船滅失に限らない

103，104行の免責条項は，全般的に適用されるのであり，第16条冒頭の文章のすぐ近くにあるからといって，本船の滅失の場合だけに適用されるのではない。*The Oliva* [1972] 1 Lloyd's Rep. 458 事件において，Mocatta 判事は，上記の行の限定的適用の主張を退けた。

米国海上物品運送法

ニューヨーク・プロデュース書式第24条が修正されることなく，米国海上物品運送法が傭船契約に摂取されていると，第16条中の免責事由は，(a)当該責任が物品の「積込，取扱，積付，運送，保管，管理および揚荷」あるいは，傭船契約に基づき船主が果たす他の契約上の行為と関連のない問題で生じた場合（後出599／600頁参照）か，(b)または列挙された免責事由を船主だけでなく傭船者にも及ぼす場合にだけ，適用がある。米国海上物品運送法第4条(2)項の免責は，その適用がある場合は，第16条の免責よりその範囲が広い場合がほとんどである。そのうえ，第4条(2)項(a)には航海または船舶取扱上の過失に関する免責が設けられているが，第16条は航海過誤に対する免責のみで，航海過誤に関する一般的な免責は含まれない（後出参照）。

よくあることであるが，至上条項，すなわち米国海上物品運送法が，第24条より削除されていると，残りの免責条項はきわめて限られたものになる。ただし，その一方，後出597頁でも述べているように，各航海ごとに堪航性に関し，相当の注意義務を尽くさなければならない義務は生じない。

420 天　災

　Nugent v. *Smith*（1876）1. C. P. D. 423事件で，Cockburn卿判事は，「運送人に要求されることは，物品の安全を図るために，合理的かつ実際的に可能な手段を尽くすことである。つまり経験ある慎重な運送人が通常用いる手段を尽くせば，運送人はその要求されているすべてを適切に行ったことになる。そういう事情があれば，嵐その他の自然現象に圧倒されても，天災という不可抗力だったとして免責される」と述べている（同判例集437頁）。

　風あるいは海の異常な事態のほか，落雷や凍結（*Siordet* v. *Hall*（1828），4 Bing 607事件）も「天災」となりうる。この免責は米国海上物品運送法第4条(2)項(d)にもある。

公　敵

　これは，本船の船籍国の敵方の行為，あるいは傭船者や船主が会社組織であれば，登録国の敵方の行為を指し，当事者が個人であれば，その国籍のある国の敵も含まれる（*Russell* v. *Niemann*（1864）34 L. J. C. P. 10事件を参照）。

　米国海上物品運送法第4条2項(f)にはおそらく海賊を含む「公敵の行為（Act of public enemies）」の免責条項が含まれている。この免責条項は，事態が過失によって生じた場合には，何らの保護も与えない。

火　災

　この免責条項に該当するのは，過失に起因しない火災のみであることを再度述べておく。

　　*Thrasyvoulos*号は定期傭船契約のもとで，相当量の酒類を運んでいたが，揚荷の際，傭船者の荷役業者の過失により，厚板が本船船艙に落ちた。それが原因となって火花が飛び，火災が生じ本船は焼失した。定期傭船契約書には，「火災による滅失，損害は常に相互に免責される」と規定していたが，控訴院は，傭船者はその免責条項を援用できないと判示した。その理由として，火災は傭船者の被用者の過失によるものであり，しかも過失の場合につき傭船契約に特に言及がない場合は，火災免責条項は，過失ある場合には適用されないことをあげている。
　　Polemis v. *Furness Withy*（1921）8 Ll.L. Rep. 263および351.

　ニューヨーク・プロデュース書式第24条が修正されず，その結果米国海上物品運送法が摂取されていると，火災に関する免責条項は第4条(2)項(b)により拡張され，「火災が運送人自らの故意，過失により生じたものでない限り」船主は免責されるということになる。ただし，船主が発航前，発航時の堪航性に相当の注意を払うことを怠り，しかも火災原因が不堪航によるものである場合は，第4条(2)項(b)の適用による保護を受けられない（*Maxine Footwear* v. *Canadian Government*［1959］2 Lloyd's Rep. 105事件を参照）。

　本船が英国船の場合，船主，傭船者は1958年商船（船主等の責任）法により改訂された1894年商船法第502条による保護も受ける。この法律によれば，英国船の船主，傭船者は，

　　「次のような場合，自己の故意，過失により生じたものでない限り，滅失，毀損について一切の責任を負わない。すなわち，(i)物品，商品，その他のいかなるものであれ，船内や船上に積まれたものが本船の火災により滅失または，毀損した場合……」。

この法律による保護は，船主や傭船者の故意，過失によるものでない限り，たとえ不堪航により火災が発生しても失われない。

421　第502条(i)での「火災による損害」とは煙，消火に使用された水による損害を含む (*The Diamond* [1906] P. 282 事件参照)。「火災」には現実の燃焼のない発熱を含まないとされた (*Tempus Shipping* v. *Dreyfus* [1930] 1 K. B. 699 事件を参照)。

君主，統治者および人民による抑留

これは貿易上の制限，税関や検疫規則による処置，貨物に関する政府自身の所有権保護行為，あるいは政治的理由による処置のような傭船契約の遂行を妨げる政府あるいは国家による強制的な干渉をさす。

抑留が現に行われており，対抗手段を取らなければ，傭船契約の遂行に影響を与える場合の強制的な干渉の**危険**をも，この文言は含んでいる。この判断基準は，分別のある人間が契約の履行が抑留により影響されると考えるか否かである (*Watts* v. *Mitsui* [1917] A. C. 227 事件，*Phosphate Mining* v. *Rankin* (1915) 21 Com. Cas. 248 事件，および *Nobel's Explosives* v. *Jenkins* [1896] 2 Q. B. 326 事件を参照)。

現実の物理的強制は必要要件ではない。*Rickards* v. *Forestal* [1942] A. C. 50 事件で，Wright 卿は，「抑留というのは，当該国による物理的強制が現存しなくてもよい。その国の国民に対して強制力があり，絶対的服従を強い，物品を有効に抑留するような行為をとることを要求する国家の命令があれば十分である」としている（同判例集81頁。*Miller* v. *Law Accident Insurance* [1903] 1 K. B. 712 事件と *The Bamburi* [1982] 1 Lloyd's Rep. 312 事件を参照)。

本船が，抑留を行っている国家の司法管轄の外にある場合でも，船主が（おそらく運航者としての傭船者も）国家内におり，その管轄下にある場合は免責条項が適用される。

> スウェーデンの船主が，1916年に *Zamora* 号を英国の傭船者に6ヶ月間の傭船に出し，就航区域は「英国，ヨーロッパ大陸 (Dunkirk, Sicily 島を限度とし)」と定められた。本船は英国からイタリアまでの航海を終えたが，船主は傭船者の次の航海を拒んだ。傭船契約には，君主による抑留の免責条項があり，船主の主張は，スウェーデン緊急令 (Swedish Emergency Regulations) のため自国水域外の航行は許されないというものであった。Bailhache 判事は船はスウェーデン司法管轄内になかったが，船主は管轄内におり，したがって，免責条項が適用されるとした。
> *Furness, Withy* v. *Banco* [1917] 2 K. B. 873.

しかし，次の場合には免責事由の適用はない。

(a) 国の統治権を有していない者の行為 (*Nesbitt* v. *Lushington* (1792) 4 T. R. 783 事件を参照)。したがって，反乱軍やゲリラの行為には適用されない。
(b) 通常の司法手続のもとでのアレストあるいは留置 (*Finlay* v. *Liverpool* (1870) 23 L. T. 251 事件を参照)。*The Anita* [1970] 2 Lloyd's Rep. 365 事件で，Mocatta 判事は，船が国家の官吏により押収された場合は，非常時軍事裁判所の干渉がましい判決によっても，その押収が国家による抑留であることに変わりないと判示した（同判事の判断は，控訴院 [1971] 1 Lloyd's Rep. 487 事件において，別の見地から破棄された)。しかし，米国海上物品運送法第4条(2)項(g)では，君主，統治者および人民による抑留に関する免責条項は，明文で「法的手続による差押え」にまで拡張されている。
(c) 傭船契約締結時にすでに発生していた状態から生じた抑留で，しかも免責条項を援用しよ

うとしている当事者が抑留理由の根拠法を知っていた場合（*Ciampa* v. *British India* [1915] 2 K.B. 774 事件を参照）。この事件は，ペスト汚染港から船に対する法令上の薫蒸消毒の例である（*Induna* v. *British Phosphate Commissioners* (1949) 82 Ll.L. Rep. 430 事件も参照）。これは夜間作業が禁止されていたことを傭船契約の両当事者が不知だった事件（さらに，*Reardon Smith* v. *Ministry of Agriculture* [1959] 2 Lloyd's Rep. 229 および [1961] 1 Lloyd's Rep. 385 事件（ストライキ）も参照）。

(d) 過失による抑留。

米国海上物品運送法第4条2項(g)では，より広い免責条項を設け，「君主，統治者および人民による抑留，アレストあるいは法的手続による差押え（seizure）」としている。

海洋，河川の危険および事故

これは，海洋，河川に固有の危険，あるいはそこを航行することについての固有の危険で，相当の注意を尽くしても避けられないものを指す。したがって，異常な強風によって生じた損害は，過失がなければ免責条項の適用範囲内である。しかし，浸水の場合には悪天候でなくても適用範囲内と思われる。したがって，過失なしに氷山や暗礁あるいは漫然と航海している他船と衝突した結果，あるいはねずみが鉛管をかじった結果浸水した場合は，免責条項が適用される（*The Xantho* (1887) 12 App. Cas. 503 および *Hamilton, Fraser* v. *Pandorf* (1887) 12 App. Cas. 518 各事件を参照）。

また，嵐による浸水を防ぐため，通風口をしめることなど，海洋や河川の危険および事故に備える必要かつ相当な処置により生じた損害にも適用される（*Canada Rice Mills* v. *Union Marine* [1941] A.C. 55 事件参照）。

しかし，免責条項は，海上の（on the sea）危険というより，海の（of the sea）危険や事故に関するものであり，したがって例えば，火事や落雷はこれに含まれない（前出 *Hamilton, Fraser* v. *Pandorf* 事件参照）。前出 *Canada Rice Mills* v. *Union Marine* 事件で，Wright 卿は，「雨は海の危険（a peril of the sea）ではなく，いうなれば海上の危険（a peril on the sea）である」としている。

米国海上物品運送法第4条(2)項(c)では，「海およびその他航行水域での危険および事故」が除外されている。

機関，汽罐，蒸気航海

Mercantile Steamship v. *Tyser* (1881) 7 Q.B.D. 73 事件で，Coleridge 卿主席判事は，「蒸気航海の危険」について，「この危険とは蒸気機関で動く船に免れがたい物理的危険である。機関の故障，スクリューの破損等の類のものであり，それが，穏やかな好天の時に発生してもそうである。……」と述べている。

しかし，それが過失に起因しているのであれば，免責条項の適用はない。

航海上の過誤

この免責文言は，反対の意思が明示的に示されていない限り，過失に起因する場合には適用されない，という免責文言の解釈の原則により，適用が制限されうる。この文言は過失ある航

海には適用がないが，航海上の過誤が過失に至らない場合もある。*The Satya Kailash* [1984] 1 Lloyd's Rep. 588 事件を参照，この事件で，控訴院は Staughton 判事の決定（[1982] 2 Lloyd's Rep. 465 事件）を支持しており，また Bingham 判事の下した同趣旨の裁決（*The Emmanuel C* [1983] 1 Lloyd's Rep. 310 事件）を是認した。

より広い免責条項となっている米国海上物品運送法第4条(2)項(a)については，次に続く本文を参照。

423 常に相互に免責される

この文言により，免責条項は船主のみならず傭船者にも適用される。そして，火災に関する免責条項のように過失があれば，船主は責任を免れず，また免責条項は相互的なものであるから，傭船者およびその被用者に過失があれば，傭船者も免責条項の保護を受けることはできず，責任を免れることができないのである（前出の「火災」の項に引用した *Polemis* v. *Furness, Withy*（1921）8 Ll.L. Rep. 263 and 351 事件および *Fagan* v. *Green* [1926] 1 K.B. 102 事件（同判例集108頁）を参照）。

米国海上物品運送法における免責条項

第4条2項

米国海上物品運送法第4条2項で規定され，ニューヨーク・プロデュース書式第24条により傭船契約に摂取される（これについては，後出593頁から602頁を参照）免責条項の全項目は以下のとおりである。

(a) 船長，海員，水先人または運送人の被用者の航海，船舶の取扱に関する行為，過失，怠慢
(b) 火災，ただし運送人自らの故意，過失による場合を除く（前出参照）
(c) 海上あるいはその他可航区域での危険（前出参照）
(d) 天災（前出参照）
(e) 戦争
(f) 公敵の行為（前出参照）
(g) 君主，統治者および人民による抑留あるいはアレスト，または法的手続による差押え（seizure）
(h) 検疫上の制限
(i) 荷送人もしくは運送品の所有者またはその代理人の作為または不作為
(j) 原因，規模の如何を問わず，ストライキ，ロックアウト，作業の停止あるいは制限。ただし，運送人自身の行為による責任まで免除されるとは解釈されない。
(k) 暴動および内乱
(l) 海上における人命や財産の救助ないしは救助のための行為
(m) 物品固有の瑕疵や性質，あるいは品質不良に起因する容量，重量の減少，その他の減失や損害
(n) 荷造りの不完全
(o) 荷印の不完全あるいは不適当
(p) 相当の注意を払っても発見できない潜在瑕疵

(q) その他,運送人の故意または過失およびその代理人や被用者の過失に起因しない原因。ただし,この例外規定の利益を主張するものには,運送人の故意または過失あるいはその代理人とか被用者の過失により滅失や損害が生じたものでないことの立証責任がある。

米国海上物品運送法第4条3項

米国海上物品運送法第4条3項は,次のように規定する。「荷主,その代理人,被用者の行為,過失,あるいは不注意に起因しない運送人あるいは本船が被った滅失または損傷について荷主は責任を負わないものとする」(前出353頁参照)。

|424| この条項を使って,ニューヨーク・プロデュース書式第8条により生ずる黙示の補償に基づく船主からのクレームを退けようとした傭船者の試みは,*The Athanasia Comninos* [1990] 1 Lloyd's Rep. 277 (前出357頁と後出601頁を参照) 事件において,Mustill 判事によって拒絶されている。Mustill 判事は,定期傭船契約の文脈においてこの条項は,何らかの意味をもっているかどうかに疑問を呈している。

免責条項および102行と103行の第1文

第16条の第2文すなわち103行から104行に含まれている免責条項は,第1文たる102行と103行に述べてある状況での傭船料返還を妨げるものではない。*The Oliva* [1972] 1 Lloyd's Rep. 458事件で Mocatta 判事は,この旨の論議を退けて,第2文の免責の文言は「第1文の反対給付の得られなかった傭船料を払い戻すという(船主の)義務には適用されない」と述べている。

免責条項の解釈に関する一般的解説

免責条項は,慣例上,厳密に解釈されてきた。免責条項の文言が,当該契約違反にあてはまらないということが,慎重な検討の結果明らかになれば,免責条項は適用されないし,曖昧な点があれば,その文言に依拠しようとする者に不利に解釈される。したがって,売買契約における「明示または黙示の担保義務違反」を免責している条項は,条件違反の責任までも免除するものではない,と貴族院により判示された (*Wallis* v. *Pratt & Haynes* [1911] A.C. 394 事件を参照)。

さらに,その免責文言に該当する行為や事件があっても,免責することが契約の趣旨と矛盾すると判断される場合には,免責を主張する者を保護しない。*Glynn* v. *Margetson* [1893] A.C. 351 事件で,貴族院は,積荷のオレンジを目的地に直送しなかった船主が,船荷証券上許容されていた航海自由条項(この条項はまさに船主の行った行為を許容していた)に依拠することを認めなかった。Herschell 卿は「既に述べたように,この傭船契約の主目的および趣旨は Malaga から Liverpool までのオレンジの運送である。これが,荷送人が非常に懸念していたことである。したがって,船主の恣意により,どこへでも好きな方法で行き,オレンジの揚地にいつ着いてもよいというような権限が船主にあると解釈するのは,契約の主たる目的と意図に反するように思われる」と述べている (同判例集355頁)。

Halsbury 卿も,また「契約書全文に目を通し,その主目的とみなされなければならないものを以下に述べる理由から検討し,契約の主目的とされるものに合致しない部分は,それが数語であろうと全条項にわたろうと無効にしなければならない」としている (同判例集357頁)。

同様に,船荷証券を回収せずに,受領権限のない者に引渡を行った船主は,揚荷後の免責を

定める条項によっては保護されない，との判決を枢密院は下している（*Sze Hai Tong Bank* v. *Rambler Cycle* [1959] 2 Lloyd's Rep. 114 事件）。Denning 卿は，枢密院による判決を下すにあたり，その条項は「少なくとも船会社が引渡義務を意図的に無視することがないように限定しなければならない」としている。

これらの原則は，それに相応しい状況下で適用され，ニューヨーク・プロデュース書式の103行，104行の免責条項もしくはハーター法と米国海上物品運送法の摂取により傭船契約に持ち込まれた免責条項に，契約違反の当事者が依拠できない場合が出てくる。

425 これらの原則に対する最近の修正

しかしながら，最近の事例では，ほぼ同等の交渉力を持つ当事者間の契約における免責条項に対しては，裁判所が反感をもつことが明らかに少なくなってきたことに留意すべきである。このことは，以前に比べ，免責条項をより厳格には解釈しない方向に向かわしめているようである。*Photo Production* v. *Securicor* [1980] 1 Lloyd's Rep. 545（同判例集554頁）事件における Diplock 判事の次の見解は，特に意義深いものがある。「主に，今日消費者契約とか附合契約と呼ばれている契約の免責条項に関し，非常に無理な解釈を行った例が多数存在することが報告されている。Wilberforce 卿が指摘しているように，言葉の意味を司法が歪める必要性は，議会がこの種の契約を1977年不公正契約条項法によらしめるようにすることにより，なくなった。自らの利益を保護し様々な種類の契約の履行に内在する危険をどのようにすればもっとも経済的に負担させることができるか（通常は保険による）を決定できる商人間で交渉された商業上の契約においては，私の見解では，明らかに一つの意味にしか解されないような免責条項の文言に関し，解釈でその意味を歪めてしまうのは間違いではないかと思う」。

ほとんどの傭船契約は，明らかに上記で述べられている Diplock 卿が考えた契約類型に属する。それゆえ，前出 *Glynn* v. *Margetson* 事件のような船荷証券の善意の所持人に対する船主の権利に関する伝統的な指導的判例の妥当性は，少なくとも傭船契約において，船主もしくは傭船者が傭船契約の相手方に対し免責条項を主張する場合，その免責条項に対する厳しい解釈に関する限り，将来否定される可能性がある。もちろん，曖昧さの事例に関しては，「起草者不利の」解釈の原則が適用になろう。

根本的な契約違反

免責条項は，「根本的な」契約違反をした当事者には適用されない，とかつては解釈された。「根本的な」契約違反とは，(a)契約条項の一つ以上に違反し，それが契約の根本にまで達するほど重大で，契約関係そのものを拒絶するような違反，もしくは(b)契約条項のなかでも非常に重要なもので，傭船契約の根本条項とみなされる条項の違反を，言う。

時として，これは単なる解釈上の規範（非常に強い規範だが）に過ぎない，と説明されることがあった。*U. G. S. Finance* v. *National Mortgage Bank of Greece* [1964] 1 Lloyd's Rep. 446 事件で，Pearson 卿判事は「……通常，契約書中の免責，除外規定ないしは類似の規定は，根本的な契約違反によって作られた状況には適用がないと解されるべきである，というのが解釈の規範である」と述べている（同判例集453頁）。しかし，別の事例では，この原則は，解釈上の指針というだけではなく，根本的違反があった場合には，はっきりと免責条項に依拠できなくなるという特別な法の原則として捉えられているようである。*Suisse Atlantique Société d'Armement Maritime* v. *N. V. Rotterdamsche Kolen Centrale* [1966] 1 Lloyd's Rep. 529 事

件では，貴族院は，そのような法の原則は，存在しないし，これまでの事例のすべては，問題となっている条項の厳格な解釈に基づけば，説明できると判示した。しかしながら，離路の説と融合したさらなる理論が，次のように展開されている，すなわち契約が違反によって解除された場合，その契約が終了し，契約に含まれている免責規定が排除される結果となるのである。この考え方は，Harbutt's Plasticine v. Wayne Tank and Pump [1970] 1 Lloyd's Rep. 15 事件の控訴審で採用された。この事例では，工場に設置された設備に欠陥があり，その欠陥が工場そのものを全焼させる火災を引き起こしている。裁判所は，責任制限条項の文言はその起こった事象に適用されるに十分なものであったが，過失ある契約者は，その責任制限条項に依拠できないと判断した。

426 Photo Production v. Securicor [1980] 1 Lloyd's Rep. 545 事件で，貴族院は，明確に Harbutt's Plasticine 事件の判決を覆すとともに，免責条項の有効性は，契約の全体ならびに生じた契約違反とに関連する免責条項の適切な解釈によって決まることを明確にした。続いて，George Mitchell v. Finney Lock Seeds [1983] A. C. 803 事件において，貴族院は，重大なる契約違反の原則は，すでに Securicor 事件で法の原則としては拒絶されているが，解釈の規範として生き残るかのかという論点につき，消え残る疑問を払拭した。その原則は今や，完全に効力をなくしたと言えそうである。裁判所は，これからも免責条項に関しては厳しい解釈を続けるだろうし，免責条項を適用するには，生じた事態に該当する明確な文言が引続き要求されるであろうが，もはや免責条項に適用される特別な原則は何もない。

重大なる契約違反の原則は，個々の消費者が，大会社の標準書式契約の広範かつ綿密に作成された免責条項に脅かされた事件などにより発展したものである。Reid 卿は，Suisse Atlantique 事件において，同じような政策的考慮は，船主と傭船者間のように，同等な契約上の力関係を有する当事者間の契約には，必ずしも適用されないと指摘している。また特に1977年の不公正契約条項法等の，消費者に有利な新法の制定があってからは，裁判所が一般原則を持ち出す必要性は少なくなりつつある。上記の Photo Production v. Securicor 事件では，Scarman 卿は，次のように言っている。「MacKenna 予審判事が，同等の交渉能力を有する当事者間の商業上の紛争につき，不公正契約条項法の施行前に，精巧なこじつけの理論を駆使することを拒絶し，消費者を護る判決を出す方向に裁判所を向かわしめなかったことを賞賛した。本件の如き状況では，当事者が何を合意したか（明示ないしは黙示の）が重要なのである。裁判所の義務は，彼らの契約をその趣旨に従って，解釈することなのである」（同判例集549頁の Wilberforce 卿の見解ならびに同判例集554頁の Diplock 卿の見解を参照）（同判例集555頁）。

（なお，1977年不公正契約条項法は，通常，傭船契約や海上物品運送契約には適用されない。したがって，ここでは扱わないこととする）

米　国　法

相互免責条項

　相互免責条項の目的は，明示された除外事由が原因で発生した損害の賠償責任から船主あるいは傭船者を保護することにある。この条項が適用された米国の指導的判例は，前出の *Clyde Commercial S. S. Co.* v. *West India S. S. Co.*, 169 F. 275 (2d. Cir. 1909), 裁量上告拒絶 214 U. S. 523 (1909) 事件である。そこでは，この条項の機能を裁判所は以下のように説明している。

　　相互にということにより，当事者は，除外事由が原因で契約条項の履行が遅れたり，妨げられたりした場合，一方が他方に負うべき責任から保護する趣旨の免責規定を意図したと解せられる。船主が免責事由のいずれかにより，本船を適切な状態に維持すること，契約上のスペースの提供，極力迅速に航海すること，積荷の通風を適度にすること，船底の掃除，等々のことができなかった場合，船主は傭船者に対して責任を負わないし，他方において傭船者も同様に，石炭の提供，港費の支払，水先人の提供，期日までの傭船料の支払等々ができなくても船主に対するそれに伴う責任を免れ，しかも傭船料を支払わなかった場合にも，船主は第6条の規定に従っても本船を引き揚げることはできない (169 F. at 277)。

　The Marine Sulphur Queen, 460 F. 2d 89, 1972 AMC 1122 (2d Cir. 1972), 裁量上告拒絶 409 U. S. 982 (1972); *The Toledo*, 122 F. 2d 255 (2d. Cir. 1941), 裁量上告拒絶 314 U. S. 689 (1941); *The African Glen*, 1969 AMC 1465, 1467 (A. S. B. C. A. 1969); *Gans Line* v. *Wilhelmsen* (*The Themis*), 275 F. 254 (2d Cir. 1921), 裁量上告拒絶 257 U. S. 655 (1921) 等の各事件も参照。

　相互免責条項は，免責事由により実際その履行が妨げられた場合は別として，各当事者の傭船契約上の多くの独立した義務の履行を免除するわけではない。免責条項は，多くの場合船主の利益に作用することが多いが，それによって船主の堪航性担保義務が緩和されるわけではない。不堪航によって生じた損害，または堪航性担保義務が傭船契約上緩和されて，堪航性の維持につき相当の注意を尽くせばよい場合の，その相当の注意を尽くさなかったことによる損害は，この第16条によって免責とされることはない (*The Caledonia*, 157 U. S. 124 (1895); 前出 *The Marine Sulphur Queen*)。また，船主が留意しなければならない点は，この条項が船主自身の利益のために傭船契約に挿入されているとの理論から，通常の場合，船主に対して厳しく解釈されるということである (*Compania de Navegacion La Flecha* v. *Brauer*, 168 U. S. 104, 118 (1897) 事件を参照)。

　相互免責条項が，第15条のオフハイヤー条項に規定してある当事者双方の権利，義務に影響を及ぼさないということは確立されている。したがって，相互免責条項中に規定されている原因により本船が故障しても，傭船者は傭船料支払を免れるし，その間の前払分傭船料の払戻を請求することができる。この原則は，前出 *Clyde Commercial S. S. Co.* v. *West India S. S. Co.* 事件に，以下のように述べられている。

　　第15条は，船主の過失の有無を問わず，傭船料の支払が停止されるべきであるという当事者の意図を述べた絶対的な規定と解されるべきである。したがって，第17条（一般免責条項）は，第15条の問題に関し，まったく適用されない (169 F. at 278)。

上記事件において，本船はまずパナマで乗組員の不足のために遅れたが，この点につき傭船者は喪失時間分の傭船料の支払義務が免除されると判断された。同船は航海を続けたが，パナマを出てきた本船に対する検疫命令のために遅れた。この後者の遅延に関し，裁判所は，これは君主の拘束に当たり，第16条の相互免責条項に該当するとして，傭船者はその間の傭船料の支払義務を免れないとした。

[428] 天　　災

この概念に該当するのは，その事件が「人的介在のない自然的原因によるもの」でなければならない。*Gans S. S. Line* v. *Wilhelmsen*。したがって，パナマ運河拡張工事に起因する土砂くずれのため同運河が通行止めになった場合，傭船者が期日に本船を返還できない責任を免除する理由としての天災にはならないと判示された。

さらに，これに該当する事態というのは，「運送人が委託された財産の保護を為すにあたり，このような事態から財産を守りえずに損害を与えた場合に，その責任を免除することが妥当であると言うほどの」抗しがたくかつ予測不能な事態でなければならない (*Compania de Vapores Insco S. A.* v. *Missouri Pacific R. Co.*, 232 F. 2d 657, 660 (5th Cir. 1956), 裁量上告拒絶 352 U. S. 880 (1956) 事件。*New Rotterdam Insurance Co.* v. *The Loppersum*, 215 F. Supp. 563, 567 (S. D. N. Y. 1963) 事件，*The Hsing May*, SMA 3019 (Arb. at N. Y. 1993) 事件も参照)。

その事態によって生じた損害に過失が寄与している場合は，天災は免責事由とはならない。*Sidney Blumenthal & Co.* v. *Atlantic Coast Line R. Co.*, 139 F. 2d 288 (2d Cir. 1943), 裁量上告拒絶 321 U. S. 795 (1944)。また天災という免責事由は，荷送人の財産を救助し，損害の拡大を防止するために相当の注意を尽くすべき運送人の義務を免除するものではない (*McNeil Higgins Co.* v. *Old Dominion S. S. Co.*, 235 F. 854, 857 (7th Cir. 1916))。

火　　災

The Buckeye State, 39 F. Supp. 344, 347 (W. D. N. Y. 1941) 事件で，「火災」は次のように定義されている。

「火災」は，発火または燃焼によって起こり，かつ視認できる熱または光の観念を含む。

したがって，熱と煙のみで，燃焼や炎を伴わなければ「火災」ではない，と判示されている (*Western Woolen Mill Co.* v. *Nothern Assurance Co. of London*, 139 F. 637, 639 (8th Cir. 1905), 裁量上告拒絶 199 U. S. 608；*Cargo Carriers* v. *Brown S. S. Co.*, 95 F. Supp. 288, 290 (W. D. N. Y. 1950))。英国の判例と同じように，米国の判例も，火災損害は，煙または消火に用いられた水その他の物質から生じた損害も含むとしている (*American Tobacco Co.* v. *Goulandris*, 173 F. Supp. 140, 177-178 (S. D. N. Y. 1959), 原審維持 281 F. 2d 179, 1962 AMC 2655 (2d Cir. 1960), 他の理由で修正, *Lekas & Drivas Inc.* v. *Goulandris*, 306 F. 2d 426 (2d Cir. 1962))。この事件では，裁判所は，貨物であるタバコの損害の一部は貨物の固有の欠陥から生じた自然発熱のため，実際の火災以前に生じていたと認定した。この「実際の火災以前の損害は連続した一連の過程の中の主要な部分である」として，船主の責任を免除した。

後出522頁と523頁で議論される米国海上物品運送法の火災に関する広範な免責規定に加えて、「火災法 Fire Statute」として知られる責任制限法の第1項は、船主に対して一般免責規定よりもさらに広範な免責を認めている。火災法は次のように規定している。

　　船主は、火災が自己の故意または過失により生じた場合を除き、本船であるいは本船上で生じた火災により、本船に積み込まれ、船艙や甲板上におかれた物品がどのような損害を被っても、その損害を賠償する責任を何人に対しても負担しない（46 U.S.C §182）。

火災が船主の「故意や過失＝design or neglect」に起因しない限り、船主の責任を免除しているこの法律の最後の文言は、米国海上物品運送法の火災免責の要件である「その者自身の故意または過失＝actual fault and privity」と本質的に同じ意味であると判示されている（*Ta Chi Navigation（Panama）Corp.（The Eurypylus）*, 677 F. 2d 225（2d Cir. 1982）の訴訟事件, *Asbestos Corp. Ltd* v. *Compagnie de Navigation Fraissinet（The Marquette）*, 480 F. 2d 669, 672, 1973 AMC 1683, 1686,（2d Cir. 1973）事件を参照）。これらの2法のもとでは、船主は自らに過失がなければ、火災によって生じた損害の責任は負わない（*Walker* v. *Transp. Co.*, 70 U.S. 150（1866）；前出 *The Marquette*, 1973 AMC at 1687 n.7）。したがって、船長や乗組員の過失によって生じた火災は船主の責任ではない（*Consumers Import Co.* v. *Kabushiki Kaisha Kawasaki Zosenjo*, 320 U.S. 249, 1943 AMC 1209（1943）；*Earle & Stoddart Inc.* v. *Ellerman's Wilson Line*, 287 U.S. 420, 1933 AMC 1（1932）；*American Tobacco Co.* v. *The Katingo Hadjipatera*, 81 F. Supp. 438, 446（S.D.N.Y 1948）、他の理由で修正 194 F. 2d 449（2d Cir. 1951））。船舶所有者が法人の場合は、船主の過失とは経営に当たっている管理職か代理人の過失である。

火災法もしくは米国海上物品運送法の火災に関する条項を援用するためには、船主は訴えられた貨物の損害が火災に起因したことを立証しなければならない。そうすると、立証責任が貨物の所有者に移り、出火もしくは消火が妨げられたのは、船主自らの故意または過失にあることを立証しなければならなくなる（前出 *The Eurypylus* 事件を参照）。留意すべき点は、火災ではない事件に一般的に適用される場合と比べて船主と貨物の所有者との間の立証責任の分配方法が違うということである。火災ではない事件では、本船が堪航状態を維持するために船主が十分な注意義務を尽くしたかどうかの立証責任は船主側にある。ところが、火災の免責条項は、その立証責任を荷主側に移転させている（前出 *The Eurypylus* 事件と *The Marquette* 事件を参照）。かくして、火災の原因が船主の過失に存したもしくは船主が不堪航の状態を是正するために十分な注意義務を尽くさず、しかも火災原因がその不堪航によるものであったか、消火作業がその不堪航により妨げられたことを立証する責任は貨物の所有者にあることになる。*The Boni*, SMA 3053（Arb. at N.Y. 1994）事件では、再傭船者／貨物所有者が火災法および米国海上物品運送法上、立証責任があると判断され、救助費用ならびにその利息併せて米貨3,400,000ドル以上を負担すべきである、との判断が下された。しかしながら、*Sunkist Growers Inc.* v. *Adelaide Shipping Lines Ltd.*, 603 F. 2d 1327（9th Cir. 1979）、裁量上告拒絶 449 U.S. 1012（1980）事件では、*The Eurypylus* 事件や *The Marquette* 事件と反対の結論が採られ、火災法や米国海上物品運送法第4条(2)項(b)の火災免責を利用するには、堪航性のある本船の提供につき、相当の注意義務を船主が尽くしたことの立証責任は船主にあると判断された。

火災原因が不明な場合、船主は火災法により責任を免れる、というのは、船主の過失により損害が生じたことの立証責任は貨物の所有者にあるからである。*Re Caldas*, 350 F. Supp. 566, 1973 AMC 1243（E.D.Pa. 1972）, *Re Anderson, Clayton & Co.* 名義で理由を付さず原

審判断維持485 F. 2d 678（3d Cir. 1973）。同様の結論は，米国海上物品運送法が適用される訴訟においても，導き出せると思われる（前出 The Marquette 事件を参照）。

君主，統治者および人民による抑留

　君主による抑留は，主権の作用により傭船契約の履行が妨げられる場合を含む。*Baker Castor Oil Co.* v. *Insurance Co. of North America*, 60 F. Supp. 32 1945 AMC 168（S. D. N. Y. 1944）事件，原審維持157 F. 2d 3, 1946 AMC 1115（2d Cir. 1946），裁量上告拒絶329 U. S. 800（1947）事件では次のように述べられている。

　　君主による抑留は，主権国家の立場で，権力の行使による主権の作用を意味する……。

　この抗弁には，戦時封鎖により，実際に本船の航行禁止となったことにより生じた不履行（*Olivera* v. *Union Insurance Co.*, 16 U. S. 183,（1818）事件）ならびに交戦国の巡洋艦による拿捕のおそれが十分に根拠ある場合における本船の引渡の遅延（*The Styria*, 101 F. 728（2d Cir. 1900），他の理由で修正，186 U. S. 1（1902）事件）を含む。*The George J. Goulandris*, 36 F. Supp. 827, 1941 AMC 1804（D. Me. 1941）事件参照。この抗弁は，平和時における本船の公的検疫にまで拡大されるが（*Clyde Commercial S. S. Co.* v. *West India S. S. Co.*, 事件），政府役人が自己の権限を越えて行った本船の抑留にまで拡大されることはない（*Northern Pacific R. Co.* v. *American Trading Co.*, 195 U. S. 439（1904）事件参照）。

　「君主による抑留」というには，正式なる政府の行為が必要である。例えば，*The Andros Island*, SMA 1548（Arb. at N. Y. 1980）事件では，キプロスを巡るギリシャとトルコ間の戦闘行為の勃発に続いて，ギリシャの商船省がギリシャ船に発したある指示が一般免責条項に該当する，と船主は主張した。しかしながら，仲裁人は，その指示は，政府の命令とは言えず，船主の服従を要求しない単なる警告であり，予防的な勧告に過ぎないと判断した。それゆえ，船主は，一般免責条項の保護を受ける権利がない，と判断された。

　The Otelia, 1980 AMC 424（Arb. at N. Y. 1979）事件では，単独仲裁人は，イラク政府の小さな部局が，本船がイラクの揚荷港への入港許可を脅すように拒絶したことは，君主による抑留には該当しないと判断した。理由として，その部局の行為は，正式なイラク政府の行為とはみなせない，というものであった。同時に，仲裁人は，正式な政府による入港禁止の措置は，君主による抑留に該当すると明確に認識した。

　通常の法的手続に沿った裁判所の命令による本船の抑留は，君主による抑留ではない，と裁定された（*The Gabriele Wesch*, 1981 AMC 1324（Arb. at N. Y. 1981）事件）。

　The Universe Explorer, 1985 AMC 1014（Arb. at N. Y. 1984）事件では，本船は，ナイジェリアにおいて1979年9月18日から10月8日まで原油の積込をナイジェリア政府から許可されなかった。理由は，その本船が以前，南アフリカ共和国の Cape Town において，ヘリコプターを使用して船用品を積み込んだためであった。ナイジェリアは，ナイジェリア到着6週間以内に南アフリカ共和国に寄港した船の入港を禁止する規則を実施していたが，政府はその規則に沿った行動をとったのである。傭船契約には，政府の干渉により時間の喪失を生じたときは，その間傭船料の支払は中断すると規定されており，仲裁審は，その傭船契約に従って問題となった期間すべてをオフハイヤーと判断した。傭船者はオフハイヤーの他に，損害賠償を要求した。しかし，仲裁審は，一般免責条項の君主による抑留の条項により，損害賠償の請求は妨げられると判断した。

The Bright Evelyn, SMA 2914（Arb. at N.Y. 1992）事件は，航海傭船の事案であるが，中国とルーマニア両国間の肥料20万トンの売買契約を遂行するための輸送に携わる船へバース優先権を付与するとのルーマニア大統領令と称する「布告」がなされたとして，本船のバースへの接岸が遅れた。自らの貨物が約6週間は遅れるだろうとの情報を得た傭船者は，不可抗力を宣言し，傭船契約を解約した。この案件に関し，仲裁人は，傭船契約を否認した傭船者の行為は正当化できず，傭船契約を履行不能にするような不可抗力の事態は生じていない，と判断した。問題の「布告」は公布されておらず，単に非公式に知られていただけであるから，政府の正式な行為は何らなされていない，と仲裁人は判断した。加えて，本船の滞船料が発生した後では，傭船契約の免責条項は適用されない，と判断した。最後に，仲裁人は，遅延は履行を商業上実行不可能にするほど，また傭船契約を履行不可能にするほど，極端なものではなかったと判断した。

The N'tchengue, SMA 2665（Arb. at N.Y. 1990）事件では，ナイジェリアの石油エネルギー大臣が貨物の一部積込を禁止する規則により，本船がナイジェリアで原油を積み込むことを許可しないことを理由として，「君主による抑留」の条項と履行不能の原則により，自らは履行義務を免れる，と傭船者は主張した。これに対し，仲裁人は，両当事者は契約締結時にこの規則の存在を知っており，また両当事者とも，この規則を強制しないとする「実際のやり方」を，ナイジェリアの大臣がいつ何時，その裁量権を行使して，変更するかも知れないという危険を十分に承知していたとして，この傭船者の主張を否認した。さらに加えて，仲裁人の多数は，大臣の決定が「傭船契約の履行可能性をまったく破壊してしまった」との結論を導いた，とする傭船者の主張の努力が，十分ではなかった，と判断した。

海洋，河川の危険および事故

海の危険の適用範囲は，「天災」における適用範囲よりも広く，自然の力だけによる損害以外も含むのである。The Majestic, 166 U.S. 375（1897）事件を参照。

「海の危険」は The Rosalia, 264 F. 285, 288（2d Cir.1920）事件において，非常に劇的に次のように表現されている。すなわち，「海の危険とは，有能で慎重な船員が，本船と貨物を安全に目的港へ到達させるために通常用いる，あらゆる安全手段を打ち破るほどきわめて異常の事態である」（Duche v. Thomas and John Brocklebank, 40 F. 2d 418, 1930 AMC 717（2d Cir.1930）；The Warren Adams, 74 F 413, 415（2d Cir.1896），裁量上告拒絶163 U.S. 679；The Giulia, 218 F. 744, 746（2d Cir.1914）の各事件を参照）。The Rosalia 事件以降の各事件においては，免責の範囲はいくぶん広げられており，The Philippine Bear, 1960 AMC 670, 677（A.S.B.C.A. 1959）事件では次のように記されている。「最近，しだいに『海の危険』の異常性や破滅的な性質が強調されることは少なくなってきている」。Davison Chemical Co. v. Eastern Transp. Co., 30 F. 2d 862, 1929 AMC 161（4th Cir.1929）事件においては，嵐は激しかったけれども時期的には珍しいものではなかったと認定されたにもかかわらず，貨物の損害は海の危険が原因であると判示された。Parker 判事は，次のように言及している。

「猛烈な嵐であっても，ある時期のある海域においては予測可能である。しかし，だからと言って，そのような嵐が海の危険の分類から排除されるならば，船荷証券からその海の危険の条項が削除されたのと同じになってしまう」（30 F. 2d at 864）。

Gerber & Co. v. The Sabine Howaldt, 437 F. 2d 580（2d Cir.1970）事件において，裁判

所は，海の危険が認定されるのは，風力や海象の激しさ厳しさ如何によるが，それについては正確な定義をなしえない程度の問題であると述べている。地方裁判所は，*Sabine Howaldt* 号が遭遇した海と風は，海の危険ではないと認定したが，控訴裁判所は地方裁判所の認定を覆す判断を行った。同裁判所は，*Sabine Howaldt* 号は，出港時は堪航性を保持していたし，航海の全般を通じてきちんとした操船方法で運航されており，本船側に何の落度もなかったと判断した。かくして，船主は責任を免除されたのである。

Thyssen Inc. v. *The Eurounity*, 21 F. 3d 533, 1994 AMC 1638 (2d Cir. 1994) 事件では，裁判所は上記の *The Sabine Howaldt* 事件に従って，海の危険というには，事故が生じた時と場所に鑑みて，気象の条件が予見しえなかったものでなければならないことを強調した。この事案では，*Eurounity* 号が遭遇した気象の条件は，波高が10メートルから11.5メートルもあるような厳しい嵐であったが，冬場の北太平洋ではけっして異常ではないので，海の危険にはならない，と裁判所は判断した。

Taisho Marine & Fire v. *The Sea-Land Endurance*, 815 F. 2d 1270, 1987 AMC 1730 (9th Cir. 1987) 事件では，地方裁判所は，本船が激しく叩きつけられ，40度以上横揺れを起こす異常な風と波があったこと，本船には不堪航の要素ならびに船長や乗組員の操船に不味い点が一切なかったことを認定し，それを理由に本船貨物は気象のみの理由で失われたと判示した。第9巡回区控訴裁判所も地方裁判所のこの判断を支持している。

Nichimen Co. v. *The Farland*, 462 F. 2d 319 (2d Cir. 1972) 事件では，傭船者は，米国海上物品運送法1004条(2)(c)の海の危険の免責条項により，貨物損傷につき責任がない，と主張した。裁判所は，貨物の減失は不適切な積付が原因だとして，傭船者の過失によって生じたと判断した。裁判所は，船内での貨物の移動は海の危険によって生じたとする被告の主張を拒絶し，そのとき運送人が自らの技術と注意によって，減失を避けることができたのであれば，運送人は，海の危険による免責は主張できず，減失の責任を負わなければならないと判示した。

|432|同趣旨の判決として，*Royal Insurance Co.* v. *The Maracaibo*, 488 F. Supp. 521 (S.D.N.Y. 1980) 事件がある。この事件では，裁判所は，本船が非常に厳しい気象に遭遇し，それが米国海上物品運送法が意味する海の危険を構成するものと認定したが，船主に有利の判決を下さなかった。貨物の積付方法に過失があったと裁判所が判断したからであった。

Re Complaint of Tecomar S. A., 765 F. Supp. 1150, 1991 AMC 2432 (S.D.N.Y. 1991) 事件は，本船と27名の乗組員と米貨22,000,000ドル相当の貨物が一挙に失われた摩訶不思議な事件であったが，裁判所は，この事故の原因は，本船の不堪航によるもので，海の危険によるものではないと判断した。すべての状況に鑑み，予見可能性が，海の危険があるかどうかの決め手になることを強調し，本船は非常に厳しい気象に遭遇しているが，「それでも2月中旬の北大西洋では，『起こりうることを予想し得た』ものである」と裁判所は認定した。

Quigley Co. v. *The Safir*, 750 F. Supp. 790, 1990 AMC 2104 (S. D. Tex 1989) 事件では，本船は積荷港に向け出発前は堪航性をもっており，非常に厳しい気象に遭遇し，それで通風口のカバーが破れ，さらにいくつかの空気パイプが破損し，それによって海水が本船の船艙に浸水した。裁判所は，この事実により海の危険の抗弁を援用できると判断した。

機　　関

ニューヨーク・プロデュース書式第16条の「機関」とは，本船の機関の全般を言う。

The Toledo, 30 F. Supp. 93 (E.D.N.Y. 1939)，原審維持 122 F. 255 (2d Cir. 1941)，裁量上告拒絶 314 U.S. 689 事件では，本船のクランク軸綱の折損が，「機関の事故」と判断され

た。裁判所は，相互免責条項を全面的に適用して，本船の故障による貨物の他船への積換を要した傭船者の損害に関し，傭船者にその損害賠償を要求する権利はない，と判断した。そのクランク軸網の折損は，本船の潜在瑕疵により生じたもので，相当の注意を尽くしても発見できなかったと，裁判所は判断した。しかしながら，その欠陥は，傭船契約締結時および傭船者への本船引渡時の両方の時点において，本船を不堪航とするものである。それにもかかわらず，裁判所は，傭船契約締結時以後に生じた機関の事故による相互免責条項の利益を，船主は享受することができる，と判示した。

航海上の過誤

この免責の効果は，本船乗組員側の航海上の過誤の結果傭船者が被った損害に関し，船主の賠償責任を免除するものである。この免責条項は，船主側に，航海の過誤もしくは傭船者の損害の原因となり，あるいはそれに寄与するような，本船の堪航性担保責任の違反がないときにのみ適用になる（*The Binship*, SMA 1416（Arb. at N.Y. 1980）事件）。

米国海上物品運送法における免責条項

米国海上物品運送法には，船主ならびに荷送人双方を利する免責条項がある。船主は，米国海上物品運送法第4条(2)項のすべての条項の利益を享受することができる。米国海上物品運送法第4条(2)項は，次のように規定している。

(2) 運送人，本船とも以下の事由により生じた滅失もしくは損害に関し，責任を負わない。
 (a) 船長，海員，水先人または運送人の被用者の航海，船舶の取扱に関する行為，過失，怠慢
 (b) 火災，ただし運送人自らの故意，過失による場合を除く
 (c) 海上あるいはその他可航区域での危険
 (d) 天災
 (e) 戦争
 (f) 公敵の行為
 (g) 君主，統治者および人民による抑留あるいはアレスト，または法的手続による差押え（seizure）
 (h) 検疫上の制限
 (i) 荷送人もしくは運送品の所有者またはその代理人の作為または不作為
 (j) 原因，規模の如何を問わず，ストライキ，ロックアウト，作業の停止あるいは制限。ただし，運送人自身の行為による責任まで免除されるとは解釈されない。
 (k) 暴動および内乱
 (l) 海上における人命や財産の救助ないしは救助のための行為
 (m) 物品固有の瑕疵や性質，あるいは品質不良に起因する容量，重量の減少，その他の滅失や損害
 (n) 荷造りの不完全
 (o) 荷印の不完全あるいは不適当
 (p) 相当の注意を払っても発見できない潜在瑕疵
 (q) その他，運送人の故意または過失およびその代理人や被用者の過失に起因しない原因。ただし，この例外規定の利益を主張するものには，運送人の故意または過失あるいはその代理人や被用者の過失により滅失や損害が生じたものでないことの立証責任がある。

傭船契約に米国海上物品運送法やハーター法を摂取したとしても，それがニューヨーク・プロデュース書式第16条の免責条項を破壊したり弱めたりすることはない（*The Toledo*, 30 F.

Supp. 93, 96 (E. D. N. Y. 1939), 原審維持 122 F. 2d 255 (2d Cir. 1941), 裁量上告拒絶 314 U. S. 689 事件を参照)。したがって, 船主は, 免責条項の抗弁に加え, 米国海上物品運送法ならびにハーター法のもとで利用できる抗弁の利益を有することとなる (*The Westmoreland,* 86 F. 2d 96, 97, 1936 AMC 1680 (2d Cir. 1936) 事件も参照)。

米国海上物品運送法は, 荷主の責任に影響する条項も含んでいる。第4条(3)項は以下のように規定している。

「運送人や本船が被った損害でも, それが荷主やその代理人や被用者の過失に起因しないものについては, 荷主が責任を負うことはない。」

傭船者が積荷の荷主ではない場合, 傭船者が上記の条項の利益を享受できるかどうかは疑問である。特に, 傭船者が米国海上物品運送法上, 「運送人」とされる場合はなおさらである。

解釈の規範

前出106頁の議論を参照。

自 由 条 項

[Clause 16 continued]

"105. The vessel shall have the liberty to sail with or without pilots, to tow and to be towed, to assist vessels in distress, and to deviate for the
106. purpose of saving life and property."

[第16条の続き]

「水先人を同乗させまたは同乗させずに航行すること,曳航しまたは曳航されること,遭難船舶を救助すること,人命・財産を救助する目的で離路することは,本船の自由とする。」

離　　路

　離路の概念は,ある種の航海の傭船契約(trip charters)の場合には適用があるかもしれないが,厳密な意味においては,それは,期間の定期傭船契約には適用がない,と考えられる。前出184頁を参照。したがって,この章で検討する「自由」は,主にニューヨーク・プロデュース書式第8条の義務である航海を極力迅速に遂行することと,本船の使用に関し傭船者の命令に従わなければならないことに関連してくる(前出345頁と351頁を参照)。
　ニューヨーク・プロデュース書式第24条により傭船契約に摂取した米国海上物品運送法は,本条項(105行,106行)の後半部分を修正する。この傭船契約の規定(前出593頁から602頁)を補足する米国海上物品運送法の規定は,次のような規定(第4条4項)を含んでいる。

　　海上において人命または財産を救助し,または救助しようとするための離路あるいは合理的ないかなる離路も,本条あるいは運送契約の違反とはみなされない。それゆえ,運送人はその結果生ずる滅失または損傷につき責任を負わない。しかしながら,離路が貨物または旅客の積卸しを目的とするものである場合,当該離路は,一応,不合理な離路と推定される。

「合理的な離路」という文言が米国海上物品運送法に含まれていることで(*Stag Line* v. *Foscolo, Mango & Co.* (1931) 41 Ll.L. Rep. 165 および *The Daffodil B* [1983] 1 Lloyd's Rep. 498 事件),105行および106行の自由は,この傭船契約が米国海上物品運送法を摂取していることにより,そこまで拡がっていることがわかる。しかし,同条の但し書文言(それは英国法には見あたらない)の存在に留意すべきである。
　離路の効果については,Cooke, Kimball 他著の『航海傭船契約』(*Voyage Charters*) (Lloyd's of London Press, 1993)の185頁から202頁を参照。

仲　裁

"107.　17. That should any dispute arise between Owners and the Charterers, the matter in dispute shall be referred to three persons at New York,
108. one to be appointed by each of the parties hereto, and the third by the two so chosen; their decision or that of any two of them, shall be final, and for
109. the purpose of enforcing any award, this agreement may be made a rule of the Court. The Arbitrators shall be commercial men."

「17. 船主と傭船者との間に争いが生じたときには，その係争事項を New York において，3名の仲裁人に付託するものとする。この場合，双方の当事者が各々1名を選定し，選定を受けたこれら2名が共同してさらに第三の者を選定する。これら仲裁人全員もしくはいずれか2名の裁定を終局のものとして，これに従う。仲裁判断の執行については，前記の合意をもって裁判所の命令とみなす。仲裁人は，実務家に限る。」

この章の範囲

　この章は，仲裁に関する英国法のすべての点を扱う意図もないし，注釈のために仲裁に関する論点を十分に論じようとする意図もない。その代わり，特にニューヨーク・プロデュース書式第17条で使われている文言と仲裁法との相互作用に注意を払いながら，仲裁に関する概要を述べることとする。仲裁に関する米国法に関しては，より詳しく述べる（後出518頁を参照）。なお，この問題に関する英国法の十分なる解説については，Mustill & Boyd 著の『商業上の仲裁』（*Commercial Arbitration*）を参照。

仲裁の場所

　傭船契約書の当事者が自らの係争を London の仲裁で解決したいと望めば，ニューヨーク・プロデュース書式107行の New York を London に変更すればよい。ボルタイム書式174行では，係争は London か当事者が合意したその他の場所で仲裁に付託されると規定されている。

仲裁人によって適用される法律の選択

　仲裁人は，付託される係争について，傭船契約の準拠法あるいはプロパー・ローを適用しなければならない。
　1991年4月1日以降に締結された傭船契約の場合は，準拠法は，契約の責任に適用される法律に関する条約（「ローマ条約」）ならびにその条約を国内法化した1990年契約（適用）法によって決まる。しかし，まだ多くの係争が1991年4月1日前に締結された傭船契約より発生しているので，法律の選択を規制するコモン・ロー上の法則がまだ適用されている。

1991年4月1日以前に締結された傭船契約

　当事者が傭船契約の中で，準拠法を明確に示しているときは，コモン・ロー上，その法律が契約のプロパー・ローになる。
　そのような法律の選択に関する明示の文言がない場合，当事者の意図を示唆する文言がないかが検討される。当事者が使用している文言で，当事者がどの法律を適用したいかという共通の意図を示すものがあれば，それが裁判所によって尊重されることとなる（*Amin Rasheed* v. *Kuwait Insurance* [1983] 2 Lloyd's Rep. 365（同判例集368頁）事件での，Diplock 卿の発言を参照）。

438　傭船契約の当事者がある特定の法律を明示的にも黙示的にも選択していない場合，プロパー・ローは，その傭船契約が最も密接かつ実質的な関係を持つ法体系またはその国の法律となる。

　　チュニジア国の傭船者は，Paris でフランスの船主と英国タンカー航海傭船書式に基づき，チュニジア国の2港間石油輸送のための「船腹契約」を結んだ（チュニジア国の民法は，フランスのナポレオン法典に基づいている）。運賃は Paris にてフランス・フランで支払われることとなっていた。船主は，自己が所有しているか，支配しているか，傭船している船を指定すべきことになっていた。船主が所有している船はすべてフランス国籍だった。仲裁人の事実認定によれば，両当事者は，契約履行のため「少なくとも，先ず第1に」船主の所有船舶を使用することとなっていた。
　　傭船契約第13条は，「本契約は，物品を輸送している本船の旗国法に準拠する。ただし，海損または共同海損の場合には，1950年のヨーク・アントワープ・ルールによる」と規定していた。
　　さらに第18条では，「この傭船契約の履行中に生ずるすべての紛争は London において解決される」と定められていた。
　　貴族院は，この契約のプロパー・ローはフランス法であると判示した。多数意見は第13条を根拠としてこの結論に達した。すなわち，船主のフランス国籍船が「少なくとも，先ず第1に」使用されるという両当事者の意図を考慮して読めば，第13条はフランス法を選択することを示している，と判断したのである。さらに，全員一致の意見で，仮に第13条がフランス法を選択することを示していないとしても，契約のプロパー・ローは，フランス法であるとされた。その理由は，フランス法がこの取引に最も実質的な関係をもつ法体系だからであるとされた。
　　Compagnie Tunisienne v. *Compagnie d'Armement Maritime* [1970] 2 Lloyd's Rep. 99.

　London が仲裁地として指定されていれば，通常は，当事者が英国法をその契約のプロパー・ローと考えているとみなされる可能性が大きい。しかし，必ずそのようにみなされるとは限らない，というのは上記の *Compagnie Tunisienne* 事件のように，反対の指標が非常に強いような事案もあるからである。この事件で，Wilberforce 判事は，114頁で次のように述べている。「仲裁条項は，契約の他の条項や関連する四囲の状況とともに検討されるべき一つの判断指標として扱われなければならない。それは，常に有力な指標であり，特に，当事者の国籍が異なる場合や，契約から生ずる取引形態が様々である場合には，唯一の明白な指標であろう。しかし，他に明白な指標がある場合には，その明白な指標に判断の基準を譲ることになる」（*The Parouth* [1982] 2 Lloyd's Rep. 351 (C. A.) 事件，*The Komninos S* [1991] 1 Lloyd's Rep. 370 (C. A.) 事件を参照）。また一般的なコモン・ローにおける法の抵触の問題について，Dicey & Morris 著の『法の抵触』（*The Conflict of Laws*）（第11版）1161頁他を参照。

1991年4月1日以降に締結された傭船契約

　ローマ条約の基本原則は、第3条1項に、次のように規定されている、すなわち「契約は、契約の当事者が選択した法律により律せられる」。次に、黙示的に選択された法律が準拠法ということになるのであるが、それは次の文言に表されている。「法の選択は明示的に、もしくはその契約の条項か事案の状況により合理的な確かさをもって示されていなければならない」。しかしながら、ローマ条約についての権威のある注釈書には、もっとも明確に準拠法として示されているもの、管轄条項、仲裁条項が、法の黙示的選択の問題に答えるものであると特に書かれてはいるが、これらの文言によって、以前の英国法と同じくらい容易に、裁判所が黙示的な法の選択を認めるようになったかどうかはよく分からない（その権威ある注釈書とは、Giuliano-Lagarde Report をいうが、これをローマ条約の条項の解釈のため参考にすることが、1990年法によって認められている）。

　さらに、ローマ条約は最後の拠り所として、「契約にもっとも密接な関係をもつ国の法律」を挙げている（第4条1項）。しかし、適用される法をどのように決定するかは、ある仮定によって規制されているが、それには難しい問題があり、この本の範囲を越えるものである。Dicey & Morris 著の『法の抵触』（第12版）1187頁等が参考になるであろう。

439　しかしながら、上記で示したように、どの法を選択しているかは、当事者が合意した仲裁条項によって、黙示的に示されているように思われる。このことにより、条約のより難しい規定は、ほとんどの傭船契約の下では空論と化し、上述の1991年4月1日以前に締結された契約に適用されるコモン・ローの法則と同じ結果を生じることとなる。

仲裁合意，管轄および仲裁手続を規制する法律

　ローマ条約は、仲裁合意および裁判所の選択についての合意には適用がない（第1条の1）。まず、仲裁合意に関する限り、ローマ条約の適用が排除されるのは、その手続だけではなく、仲裁合意の形式、有効性および効果に対してもである。確かに、交渉において、そのような合意がなされたという事実は、傭船契約のプロパー・ローの決定の決め手になると思われるが、合意がなされたかどうか、もしくはその合意が契約の一部となっているかどうかという現実の問題は、少なくとも理論上は、条約とは関係がない。それでも、それは推定上のプロパー・ローによって律せられ、そのような合意の有効性を律する法が、通常、その合意ないし合意が含まれる契約を律する法とみられているようである（*The Heidberg* [1994] 2 Lloyd's Rep. 287 事件（303から308頁）参照）。

　英国法が、契約のプロパー・ローであるか否かにかかわらず、London が当事者によって仲裁地に選ばれていれば、その従うべき仲裁手続はほぼ確実に英国法によって律せられる（*James Miller* v. *Partners* v. *Whitworth Street Estates* [1970] A.C. 583 事件ならびに *Naviera Amazonica Peruana* v. *Compania Internacional de Seguros del Peru* [1988] 1 Lloyd's Rep. 116 事件を参照）。

米国海上物品運送法第3条6項の出訴期限の摂取

　航海傭船に関する *The Agios Lazaros* [1976] 2 Lloyd's Rep. 47 事件で、控訴院は、ヘーグ・ルールを摂取することにより、当事者は、第3条6項の出訴期限の規定を含めヘーグ・ルールのすべての規定を、傭船契約の中に取り入れることになると判示した。また、この出訴

期限の規定は，裁判所の訴訟手続と同様に仲裁手続にも適用されると判示した。*The Merak* [1964] 2 Lloyd's Rep. 527 事件を参照。

ヘーグ・ルール第3条6項と同じ規定が，米国海上物品運送法の第3条6項に規定されている。この規定は，ニューヨーク・プロデュース書式第24条によって，傭船契約に摂取されている。

その効果は，「運送人および船舶」は，「貨物が到着した日，または到着すべかりし日から1年以内に訴訟が提起されない限り，貨物の滅失または損害に関し，すべての責任から免れる」というものである。これは，明らかに，傭船者が船主に対して訴訟提起を行う場合を含んでいる。しかしながら，船主が傭船者に対して訴訟提起を行う場合を含んでいない。確かに，傭船者が船荷証券の上で運送人となる場合，米国海上物品運送法第1条(a)では，「荷主と運送契約を締結する傭船者」も「運送人」の定義に含めてはいるが，傭船契約という関係の中では，「運送人」とは船主を意味し，「傭船者」を意味していないから，上記のように言えるのである（*The Khian Zephyr* [1982] 1 Lloyd's Rep. 73 事件を参照）。

米国海上物品運送法のこの規定の適用は，運送品の物理的滅失や損傷だけでなく，運送品に関連した滅失や損傷にも及んでいる（*The Ot Sonja* [1993] 2 Lloyd's Rep. 435 (C. A.) 事件，*The Standard Ardour* [1988] 2 Lloyd's Rep. 159 事件および後出の600頁を参照）。なお，もし，傭船契約にヘーグ・ルールもしくはヘーグ・ヴィスビー・ルールの第3条6項が摂取されていても，同じこととなる（*The Stena Pacifica* [1990] 2 Lloyd's Rep. 234 事件と後出716頁440を参照）。補償を求めるクレームの出訴期限を扱っているヘーグ・ヴィスビー・ルールの第3条6項の効果については，後出716頁を，またニューヨーク・プロデュース書式に基づく貨物クレームの扱いに関するPIクラブ間の協定を摂取している場合の出訴期限については，前出373頁を参照。

仲裁における「訴の提起」の時期

米国海上物品運送法第3条6項は，1年以内に「訴訟が提起」されない限り，請求を失効させてしまう。仲裁においては，一方の当事者が相手方に，書面で仲裁人の選任要求を送達したとき，もしくは仲裁人の選任に関する同意を求める要求を送達したときに，「訴訟が提起」されたことになる（後述の*The Agios Lazaros* [1976] 2 Lloyd's Rep. 47 事件を参照）。

1950年仲裁法第27条における仲裁開始のための期限の延長

1950年仲裁法第27条の規定により，裁判所は「事件の状況に鑑み，そうしなければ不当に困難なことが生ずると認める」場合，裁判所は仲裁手続を開始する期限を延長する権限を有する。この権限は，期限徒過の前後にかかわらず存在する。しかし，期限がすでに徒過してしまっている場合は，申立人は迅速に行動しなければならない（*The Eurotrader* [1987] 1 Lloyd's Rep. 418 事件を参照）。

ヘーグ・ルールやそれを国内法化した法規，例えば米国海上物品運送法などが摂取された傭船契約の出訴期限に関しても，裁判所はこの仲裁法第27条の権限を行使することができる。*The Virgo* [1978] 2 Lloyd's Rep. 167 事件における控訴院の決定を参照。

何が「不当な困難（undue hardship）」であるかに関する裁判所の見解については，*The Pegasus* [1967] 1 Lloyd's Rep. 302, *The Simonburn (No. 2)* [1973] 2 Lloyd's Rep. 145, *The Bratislava* [1977] 2 Lloyd's Rep. 269, *The Aspen Trader* [1981] 1 Lloyd's Rep. 273, 前出 *The Eurotrader* の各事件を参照。

仲裁人の選任

　仲裁合意が，各当事者による仲裁人の選任を規定している場合，仲裁人は次のように選任される。(1)ある仲裁人に，係争事件の仲裁人の引受を依頼し，(2)その者の同意を取り付けた上で，その者を仲裁人に任命し，(3)係争の相手方に，仲裁人を選任したことを通知する（*Tradax Export* v. *Volkswagenwerk* ［1970］1 Lloyd's Rep. 62 事件を参照）。

仲裁の開始

　1980年出訴期限法の第34条(3)(a)は，1939年出訴期限法第27条(3)をほとんど修正しないで受け継いでいるが，次のように規定している。「……仲裁の一方の当事者が，相手方に仲裁人の選任を要求するもしくは選任した仲裁人に合意することを要求する通知を送達したときに，仲裁が開始されるものとして扱う……」。

　この規定は，ヘーグ・ルールの第Ⅲ条，規則6の1年の出訴期限の規定にも，類推適用される（*The Agios Lazaros* ［1976］2 Lloyd's Rep. 47 事件を参照。さらに，1950年仲裁法の29条(2)，33条，44条(3)と *The Rimon* ［1981］2 Lloyd's Rep. 640 事件を参照）。

　相手方への通知は，直接に，もしくは手紙やファックスやテレックスにより行うことができる。しかし，出訴期限が切れる以前に相手側に到達しなければならない。*The Pendrecht* ［1980］2 Lloyd's Rep. 56 事件において，Parker 判事は，「この規定は，当事者を，高等法院に訴訟を提起したのとほとんど同じような地位に立たせることを意図しているものと，私には思われる。期限の進行を止めるような正式な行為を当事者は何も取ることができないので，当事者は，相手方に通知を送付するか，それによって相手に到達すると予想される場所に通知を送達しなければならない」と述べている（同判例集65頁。*The Sargasso* ［1994］1 Lloyd's Rep. 162 事件を参照）。

仲 裁 法

　もし，傭船契約に，仲裁は London で行うと規定されている場合，仲裁の手続はほとんど確実に英国法により律せられる（上記を参照）。そのような仲裁には，司法の運営に関する法律（1981年版，1982年版および1985年版）と1990年裁判所および法的サービス法等で修正された1950年仲裁法，1975年仲裁法，および1979年仲裁法が適用される。修正された3つの仲裁法の当該部分については，原書の付録C（省略）に掲載している。

　（省略）

「3人の（仲裁人）」に関して

　1950年仲裁法第9条のもとでは，仲裁合意が3人の仲裁人を予定している場合は，その仲裁合意は3番目の仲裁人を選任するのではなく，審判人を選任する旨を規定しているのと同様の効力を有する。しかしながら，1979年仲裁法第6条(2)は，3人の仲裁人に関しての完全な効果を付与しており，1950年仲裁法第9条に代えて次のような条項となっている。

　　3人の仲裁人が選任される場合，仲裁合意のなかで明らかに反対の意図が示されていない限り，3人の仲裁人うちのいずれかの2人が合意した裁決が拘束力をもつ。

実際的には，最初に選任された2人の仲裁人が反対しなければ，当事者はしばしば，事案が正式な審理の段階に達するまで，3番目の仲裁人を選任しないことを当事者間で合意している。

仲裁人の数が特定されていない場合

もし，仲裁合意が紛争を審理する仲裁人の数を定めていない場合は，仲裁付託は単独仲裁人に対するものとみなされる（1950年仲裁法第6条参照）。

実務家（Commercial men）

商事事件を扱っている弁護士は，ニューヨーク・プロデュース書式の109行の意味における「実務家」ではない。しかし，仲裁を専門的に職業にしている仲裁人は，実務家である。

> North Duchess 号の航海傭船契約中の仲裁条項は，「仲裁人は実務家でなければならない」と規定していた。一方の当事者は専任の職業仲裁人を選任した。その人物はもともとは弁護士の資格を有していたが，そのときは弁護士の職務から離れていた。Donaldson 判事は，専任の職業仲裁人として商事および海事の紛争に携わっている限り，その人間は実務家の範疇に属すると判示した。しかし，傍論で，弁護士の業務を行っている者は，たとえ商事の分野で仕事をしていても，実務家とはみなされないと述べている。
>
> Pando v. Filmo ［1975］1 Lloyd's Rep. 560.

仲裁人によって選任される審判人も「実務家」でなければならない。もし，審判人が実務家でない場合，その瑕疵ある選任は，仲裁人や当事者の法廷弁護人が，その審判人の面前に出頭しても，治癒されない（Rahcassi v. Blue Star ［1967］2 Lloyd's Rep. 261 事件を参照）。

[442] 仲裁付託の場合の訴訟手続の停止

仲裁合意の一方の当事者が，裁判所に訴訟を提起した場合，もう一方の当事者は仲裁結果が出るまで，訴訟手続の停止を裁判所へ申し立てることができる。仲裁合意の両当事者あるいは仲裁地のいずれかが英国々内であれば（「国内の仲裁合意」），1950年仲裁法の第4条(1)により，裁判所はその裁量を行使して，訴訟手続を停止させることができる。

> しかし，仲裁合意が「国内の仲裁合意」ではない場合，裁判所は，1975年仲裁法の第1条で，訴訟手続を停止しなければならない。
> ……もし仲裁合意が無効であるか，履行できない場合か，もしくは当事者間に仲裁に付託するとした合意事項に関する争いが事実上存在しないと判断されない限り……
>
> (Nova (Jersey) Knit v. Kammgarn Spinnerei ［1977］1 Lloyd's Rep. 463 事件，The Rena K ［1978］1 Lloyd's Rep. 545 事件，The Cleon ［1983］1 Lloyd's Rep. 586 事件を参照）

当事者が仲裁人を起用しない場合

1950年仲裁法第7条は，2人の仲裁人を選任する場合，すなわち当事者が各々1人ずつ仲裁

人を選任する場合で，一方の当事者が仲裁人の選任を怠っている場合，既に仲裁人の選任を終えているもう一方の当事者は，選任している仲裁人をその係争事件の単独仲裁人とすることができる，と規定している。しかし，そのような手段をとるには，仲裁人の選任を怠っている当事者に，まず正味7日間の時間が与えられなければならない（*The Bengal Pride*［1986］1 Lloyd's Rep. 167事件を参照）。

　3人の仲裁人を選任する場合，まず各々の当事者が1名ずつ仲裁人を選任するが，一方の当事者が仲裁人の選任を拒絶しているか，合理的な時間内に（もしくは，仲裁合意にその時間が定めてあれば，その時間内に）仲裁人の選任を行わないとき，もう一方の当事者は，通知を行った後に，(a)裁判所に仲裁人の選任を求めることができる（1985年司法の運営に関する法律によって加えられた1950年仲裁法第10条(3)，そして現在では，1990年裁判所および法的サービス法の下で，新設された1950年仲裁法の10条(3)，（3A），（3C)），あるいは(b)1991年4月1日以降に締結された仲裁合意については，自ら選任した仲裁人を単独仲裁人とすることができる（裁判所と法的サービス法101条により追加となった1950年仲裁法10条(3)（3A)（3B)（3D)）。

仲裁を行う際の仲裁人の権限

　仲裁の当事者は，仲裁の進行過程を当事者自身決定できる。例えば，訴答書面交換の有無を，当事者間の相互の文書開示手続の有無，口頭審理の有無，提出書面のみによる係争案件裁決申立の有無を決めることができる。もし，当事者がそれらの事項に合意しない場合には，仲裁人に決定を求めることができる。これら事項すべては，コモン・ロー上も，制定法上も，仲裁人の権限の範囲内のことである（*Bremer Vulkan* v. *South India*［1981］1 Lloyd's Rep. 253事件を参照）。審理の延期についての仲裁人の権限に関する事案につき，*The Jhansi Ki Rani*［1980］2 Lloyd's Rep. 569事件も参照。

　1950年仲裁法第12条(1)は，反対の意思がなければ，仲裁合意の当事者は，「仲裁に関する手続の進行中は，仲裁人や審判人が要求するすべてのことを」なすべき旨を，規定している。また当事者の別途合意なしには，仲裁人は訴訟費用の担保に関する命令を出すことはできないし（*Re Unione Stearinerie Lanza and Wiener*［1917］2 K.B. 558事件），さらに，仲裁人は，当事者が仲裁人の命令に従わないことを理由に，請求や抗弁を却下することはできない。もっとも，そのような状況では，命令に従わない当事者に適切な注意を与えた上で，審理にそのまま入ることとなる（*Crawford* v. *A. E. A. Prowting*［1973］Q.B. 1事件を参照）。さらに，仲裁人は，当事者の合意がなければ，2つの仲裁の併合を命じる権限はない（*The Eastern Saga*［1984］2 Lloyd's Rep. 373事件を参照）。また，1950年仲裁法12条(1)のもとでの，仲裁人の権限の行使に関する指針につき，*The Peter Kirk*［1990］1 Lloyd's Rep. 154事件を参照。

　つい最近までは，仲裁手続が長い間何らの進展もない場合に，いろいろな問題が生じていた。訴訟追行がない場合でも，仲裁人には，事件を却下する権利がなかったし，裁判所も仲裁に関しては，限られた権限しか有せず（下記を参照），裁判所自体に対し提起された請求案件であれば，訴訟遅延を理由にその請求を却下できるが，仲裁に関しては，裁判所も請求を却下できなかったのである（*Bremer Vulkan* v. *South India*［1981］1 Lloyd's Rep. 253事件を参照）。もっとも，あるケースでは，遅延の状況とその長さにより，裁判所が，当事者の意図として，もはや仲裁合意が破棄されたと認定するか，禁反言を認定したりすることもあった（*The Splendid Sun*［1981］2 Lloyd's Rep. 29（C.A.）事件，*The Hannah Blumenthal*［1983］1 Lloyd's Rep. 103（H.L.）事件，*The Leonidas D*［1985］2 Lloyd's Rep. 18（C.A.）事件および *The Antclizo*［1988］2 Lloyd's Rep. 93（H.L.）事件を参照のこと）。

しかしながら、1992年1月以降は、仲裁合意に異なる意思が表明されていない限り、「請求を申し立てる側に極端でかつ弁解のできない遅延」があり、それによって「その請求の係争を公正に解決することができない十分な危険を生ぜしめる」とか、「深刻な不利益を被告に」及ぼすか、及ぼす可能性がある場合、仲裁人に請求そのものを却下する権限が付与された。1990年裁判所および法的サービス法によって、1950年仲裁法に導入された第13条Aを参照。この新条項は、1992年1月に施行されたばかりだが、「極端でかつ弁解のできない遅延」の有無を考慮するとき、1992年以前の期間も考慮に入れてよいこととなっている（The Boucraa [1994] 1 Lloyd's Rep. 251 (H.L.) 事件を参照）。

裁判所の権限

仲裁人の選任

単独仲裁人による仲裁で、かつ当事者が仲裁人の選任に関し合意できない場合、いずれの当事者も裁判所に単独仲裁人の選任を申し込むことができる（1950年仲裁法10条(1)(a)）。

裁判所は、さらに、申立を受ければ、次のような場合にも仲裁人を選任することができる。第3の仲裁人もしくは審判人の審理を拒否し、審理不能、死亡の場合（1950年仲裁法10条(1)(d)）。当事者もしくは仲裁人が第3の仲裁人もしくは審判人を選任しようとしない場合（1950年仲裁法10条(1)(c)）。仲裁の当事者でも現存の仲裁人でもない者が、仲裁人や審判人を選任することとなっているが、その者が選任を怠っている場合（1950年仲裁法10条(2)）。3人の仲裁人を選任する事案で、一方の当事者が仲裁人の選任を拒否しているか、規定の時間内の選任を怠っている場合（1985年司法の運営に関する法により追加された1950年仲裁法第10条(3)）。上述の最後の場合で、仲裁合意が1991年4月1日以降になされた場合、選任を怠っている当事者が、選任実施の要請通知を受けて、7日以内に選任を行わないときには、もう一方の当事者は、裁判所に選任を申請するか、自ら選んだ仲裁人を単独仲裁人として起用することができる（1990年裁判所および法的サービス法にて追加された第10条(3)、(3)(A)から(3)(D)）。

1950年仲裁法のもとでは、仲裁人は、自らが選任されたらすぐにも審判人を選出する必要があった（1950年仲裁法第8条）。もっとも、仲裁人が審判人を選任しなかったとしても、2人の仲裁人が合意した裁決を出せば、自らの管轄権を奪われることはなかった（The Dalny [1979] 2 Lloyd's Rep. 439 事件を参照）。しかし、1979年仲裁法第6条(1)により1950年仲裁法第8条(1)が改正された。これによれば、現時点では、2人の仲裁人が合意できない場合、仲裁人は直ちに審判人の選任を要する但し書が条件にはなるが、審判人の選任は、いつの時点でもできるようになった。

仲裁の実施

1950年仲裁法第12条(6)により、裁判所は、訴訟費用の担保、証拠の提出、財産の保全と調査、ならびに差止命令に関する命令を出すことで、仲裁を規制する権限がある。

ただし、この裁判所の権限は、上記事項に関する命令を出すことができるという仲裁人の権限を害するものではない、しかし、通常、仲裁人の権限は、裁判所の権限に比べるとかなり制限されたものとなっている（上記を参照）。

1979年仲裁法第5条(1)と(2)において、もしどちらか一方の当事者が仲裁人もしくは、審判人の命令に従わない場合、仲裁人、審判人あるいは当事者のいずれかは裁判所に仲裁人もしくは審判人の権限の拡大を申請することができ、それを受けて裁判所は、同じ様な状況で高等法院の裁判官が課すことができる制裁の権限と同様の権限を仲裁人や審判人に付与する命令を発す

仲裁　　　　　　　　　　　　　　　515

ることができる（*Waverly v. Carnoud Metalbox Engineering* ［1994］1 Lloyd's Rep. 38 事件を参照）。この事件は，当事者が文書の証拠開示に関する仲裁人の命令に従わなかった場合で，第5条に従って，命令が発せられた。

1979年法の下での裁判所への上訴

　1979年法第1条の下では，仲裁判断から生じた法律問題に関し，次の条件を満たせば，高等法院に上訴する権利がある。
- (a) 仲裁判断に理由が付されていること。もしくは，もし理由が付されていない場合は，仲裁判断が出される前にそのような理由付の仲裁判断を求めたか，なぜ理由が要求されなかったかの特別の理由が存すること（第1条(6)。*Hayn Roman v. Cominter* ［1982］1 Lloyd's Rep. 295 事件を参照）。
- (b) 法律問題をどう決定するかが，「実質的に一方のもしくは双方の当事者の権利に影響を与えうる」と，裁判所が考えて，上訴の許可を与えること（第1条(3)(b)と(4)。後出 *The Nema* ［1981］2 Lloyd's Rep. 239 事件を参照）。

　上記(a)の「理由付きの仲裁判断」といっても，特別な形式をもった裁決である必要はない。事実，そのような仲裁判断とは，1950年法のもとで，仲裁人が裁判所に意見を求める「特別事件」と，同じくらい正式なものであると考えられているわけではない。*Bremer v. Westzucker* ［1981］2 Lloyd's Rep. 130 事件で，Donaldson 卿判事は次のように述べている（同判例集132頁）。「要求されるすべてのものは，仲裁人が，証拠に関する自分の見解に基づき，何が起こり何が起こらなかったかを示し，その起こったことに照らして，自分が下した決定の理由，また決定の内容を簡潔に説明することである。まさしくそれが『理由付きの仲裁判断』を意味するのである。私が言おうとしているのは，1979年仲裁法に沿った理由付きの仲裁判断とは，特別事件の形式の仲裁判断とは，まったく異なっているということである。それは専門的なものでもなく，到達が難しいものでもない。とりわけ，それは，審理の終結時にすばやく迅速に生み出すことができ，生み出されなければならない」。

　上述の(b)については，貴族院は，*The Nema* ［1981］2 Lloyd's 239 事件において，仲裁判断につき，上訴の許可を求める申請に関し，裁量を行使する裁判官のために，次のような指針を示した。
- (i) その案件に含まれる法律問題が，「1回限りの」条項（定期的に使用されている，すなわち「標準」の条項に相対するもの）の解釈に関するものであれば，仲裁人が明白な誤りを犯していない限り，上訴は許されない。Diplock 卿は，247頁で次のように述べている。「その案件に含まれる法律問題が，『1回限りの』条項の解釈で，本事件の特定の事実に対するその条項の適用が，仲裁において問題となった場合，当事者の主張を聞かずに，理由付きの仲裁判断そのものだけを読んで，仲裁人がその条項に与えた意味が明らかに間違っていると，裁判官が考えない限り，上訴は通常許可されない。さらに，もしその仲裁判断を熟読した結果，裁判官が，その仲裁判断の論理を説得力あるものと再考し，当初の第一印象とは異なり，仲裁人は正しいのかもしれない，との感触を持ったならば，彼は上訴の許可を与えてはならないのである。良きにつけ悪しきにつけ，当事者は，彼らが第1にその案件を解決するために選んだ，仲裁法廷の決定を受け入れるべきである」。
- (ii) 解釈されるべき条項が，「標準」の条項である場合は，上訴を許す基準は，より厳しくない基準が適当である。特に，その条項の意味を裁判所が決定することが，商法上において，

より重大な確実性をもたらすような場合はなおさらである。しかし，Diplock 卿の言葉によれば（同判例集248頁），「もし，仲裁人が解釈を誤っているとの非常に強い推定がなされると担当裁判官が判断しなければ，そのような事案についても，上訴の許可は与えるべきではない。また標準的な条項も，それが特定の仲裁事件に適用された場合，その案件自体は『1回限りの』案件であり，『1回限りの』条項にとって適当な基準として私が指摘しているものと同様の，より厳しい基準がその『1回限りの』案件にも適用されるべきである」（上述の(i)を参照）。

(iii) 決定のための問題点が，あるできごとが契約を履行不能にしてしまうかどうかということであれば（もしくは，一方の当事者が，他方の当事者の契約不履行により，契約上の義務から解放されるかどうかということであれば），一般的には，仲裁人が明らかに法の適用を誤っているか，通常の仲裁人であれば，そのような結論には絶対に到達しない，ということが言える場合にのみ，上訴の許可が付与されるべきである。とくに，検討される案件が，『1回限りの』案件である場合はなおさらそのように言える。しかしながら，検討される案件が，「同じ種類の商取引に従事するその他の多くの者の間の，同じような取引に影響する，一般的性質をもった事案である場合，例えば，スエズ運河の閉鎖，米国大豆の禁輸措置，イラン・イラク戦争等」であれば，Roskill 卿は，裁判官は，仲裁人が誤った結論に達したと考えるならば，上訴の許可を与えるのが，正しいであろうと述べている（同判例集248頁）。

貴族院によって定められたこれらの指針は，下級裁判所にとっての枠組みを提供するものであるが，控訴院（*The Rio Sun* [1981] 2 Lloyd's Rep. 489 事件）においては，それらはあくまで指針に過ぎない旨が指摘されている。記録長官 Denning 卿の言葉は以下のとおりとなっている。「『1979年仲裁法』によって課された足かせは，法の問題点が当事者の権利に実質的に大きく影響を与えなければ，上訴は許されない，ということである」（当事者の権利というのは，一般商業社会のその他の者の権利と言うより，仲裁の当事者の権利である。前出の *The Nema* 事件で，貴族院は，仲裁の当事者の利害に注意を向けているようである）。*The Nema* 事件で定められた指針をさらに検討したものとして，*The Kerman* [1982] 1 Lloyd's Rep. 62 事件の Parker 判事の判決および *The Antaios (No. 2)* [1984] 2 Lloyd's Rep. 235事件の貴族院の裁決を参照。

上訴の許可を与えるに際し，裁判所は許可を申し立てた当事者に条件をつけることができる（第1条(4)と *Mondial v. Gill & Duffus* [1980] 2 Lloyd's Rep. 376 事件を参照）。

もし，仲裁の当事者のすべてが合意すれば，仲裁判断に対する上訴は，行うことができる。この場合，裁判所の許可は要求されない（第1条(3)(a)を参照）。

上訴が決定すれば，裁判所は，仲裁判断を確認し，変更し，もしくは破棄できる。また，法律問題に対する裁判所の意見をつけて，仲裁人に差し戻す（第1条(2)を参照）。

海事仲裁の当事者は，合意することにより，裁判所への上訴の権利を排除することができる。しかし，それは，一つの例外を除き，仲裁開始後の合意によってのみ可能である。第4条(1)(i)を参照。なお，その一つの例外とは，契約が外国法によって律せられ，かつその契約の少なくとも1人の当事者が外国人である場合である（第4条(1)(ii)と3条(6)を参照）。なお，この場合は，仲裁開始前の上訴排除合意も有効とされる（第3条(1)を参照）。

446 控訴院への上訴

仲裁審からの上訴に基づき，高等法院で出した判決に対する控訴院へのさらなる上訴は，高等法院もしくは控訴院の許可が必要で，高等法院が扱っている法律問題が一般的に非常に重要なものであるか，その他の特別の理由によって控訴院での判断が必要であると認定されない限

り行うことができない（第1条(7)と *The Baleares* [1991] 1 Lloyd's Rep. 349（C. A.）事件を参照）。

第1審での，相反する裁決もしくは相反する裁判官の傍論がある場合の上訴の許可に関する指針につき，*The Antaios（No. 2）* [1984] 2 Lloyd's Rep. 235事件と *The Roachbank* [1988] 2 Lloyd's Rep. 337事件を参照。

高等法院が上訴を許可しない限り，控訴院は，仲裁判断に対する上訴を高等法院が許可するか拒絶するかの決定を審理する管轄権を有しない（第6条1(6A)，*Aden Refinery* v. *Ugland Management* [1986] 2 Lloyd's Rep. 336事件ならびに上記 *The Antaios（No. 2）* 事件を参照）。

利子についての仲裁人の権限

仲裁人はその裁定金額に基づき，仲裁判断の日付までの期間について，また仲裁の主題であり，また仲裁判断決定前に支払われる金額の支払期日までの期間について，適当と判断する利率による利子を裁定することができる（1982年司法の運営に関する法律で追加された1950年仲裁法の第19条Aを参照）。しかし，仲裁人は仲裁開始以前にすでに支払済の金額については，それが支払遅帯でも，一般的な損害賠償という形で，利子をつけることはできない（*President of India* v. *La Pintada Cia Navegacion* [1984] 2 Lloyd's Rep. 9（H. L.）事件を参照。この事件の判決により，*Tehno-Impex* v. *Gebr. van Weelde* [1981] 1 Lloyd's Rep. 587（C. A.）事件での判決が覆されている）。仲裁開始前の支払済金額に関しては，仲裁人は，次の場合だけに限り利子をつけることができる。契約の特別条項に基づき，その利子の請求が負債のクレームとして適切に行われうる場合，もしくは *Hadley* v. *Baxendale*（1854）9 Ex. 341事件のルールの第2部に基づく特別損害のクレームとして，その利子の請求がなされる場合（前出 *La Pintada* 事件，*The Lips* [1987] 2 Lloyd's Rep. 311事件と *The World Symphony* [1991] 2 Lloyd's Rep. 251事件を参照）。

暫定仲裁判断

1950年仲裁法第14条によれば，仲裁人は暫定的な判断を下すことができる。したがって，たとえ，当事者間で仲裁に傭船料以外の事案が付託されていても，傭船料金額が正しく満期であることを仲裁人が納得し，傭船者のほうにその支払を差し止める確たる反論がない場合，仲裁人は，支払期日満期の未払傭船料の支払を命じる暫定裁決を下すことができる（*The Kostas Melas* [1981] 1 Lloyd's Rep. 18事件を参照）。仲裁人は，条件が適当であれば，条件付の暫定裁決を出すことができる（*The Angelic Grace* [1980] 1 Lloyd's Rep. 288（C. A.）事件（この案件では，暫定裁決は，交差請求の担保の提供を条件に出された）を参照）。

NYPE 93

1993年改訂版ニューヨーク・プロデュース書式第45条は，仲裁条項であり，仲裁の候補地の選択として New York と London が示されている。同条項では，また小額クレームに関し，各事案毎の採択の問題としてより簡潔で廉価な手続を規定している。すなわち，New York における海事仲裁人協会の短縮された仲裁手続や London における London 海事仲裁人協会による小額クレーム手続などが書かれている（18頁の英文書式の498行から522行と61／62頁を参照）。

447 米 国 法

仲裁の合意

　仲裁は，厳密に言えば，当事者間に生じる紛争を解決するための方法を定めた両当事者の合意の産物である。確かに，New York か London が仲裁地として選ばれ，3人の仲裁人により構成される仲裁審で行われることが慣例となっているが，仲裁の場所や仲裁審の構成如何は，当事者間の決定事項である。その他の標準書式と同様に，ニューヨーク・プロデュース書式第17条も，そのような仲裁に関する合意であり，その合意により船主も傭船者も New York において3人で構成される仲裁審による仲裁に，係争を付託しなければならない。

法 の 選 択

　特定の法律を適用する旨の明示の条項がなければ，New York を仲裁地に選択していることにより，米国の一般海事法が適用されることとなる。一般海事法とは，主に，海事法廷と言われる連邦裁判所の判例からなる。英国の先例や州法（おもに New York 州法）も，連邦裁判所の判例がない場合に考慮される。州法（例えば統一商法典）は，通常海事契約には適用されないが，係争案件に関し，一般海事法の原則がない場合にのみ適用される。仲裁は，契約による創造物であるから，当事者は特定の法の選択条項に合意することができる。

仲裁に関する制定法

　連邦仲裁法，9 U.S.C.§§1-14, 201-208は，すべての海事契約書の中の仲裁合意に適用される。この法律は，仲裁の強制，仲裁継続中の訴訟手続の停止，仲裁判断に対する審査，仲裁の過程に関する連邦裁判所の最終的な監督等々につき，規定している。法と法が抵触する部分については，連邦法が適用されることとなるが，New York 州の裁判所は仲裁を監督する競合管轄権を持っている（New York 民事実務法と規則の§7501）。しかしながら，非常に多くの海事仲裁事件が，連邦裁判所に提起されている。

書面による仲裁合意

　仲裁法では，傭船契約に規定されている仲裁に関する「書面の条項」は有効とされる。9 U.S.C.§2. 口頭での傭船契約も，有効で，強制力もあるが，仲裁法では，口頭での仲裁の合意は，強制力をもたないとされている。もっとも，テレックスやその他書面で，契約の内容が固まったことを確認している場合は，仲裁法上十分に，その仲裁合意に強制力が付与される（*A/S Custodia* v. *Lessin Int'l Inc.*, 503 F. 2d 318, 320 (2d Cir. 1974); *Ocean Industries Inc.* v. *Soros Assoc. Int'l Inc.*, 328 F. Supp. 944 (S.D.N.Y. 1971) の各事件参照）。

　Hart Enterprises Int'l Inc. v. *Anhui Provincial Import & Export Corp.*, 1995 U.S. Dist. Lexis 7432 (S.D.N.Y. 1995) 事件では，もともとの契約には仲裁合意条項が入っており，その契約に関する紛争を解決するための示談合意書には仲裁条項がはいっていない事案であった 448 が，示談合意書に関し，当事者間で紛争が生じた。この場合，裁判所は，示談合意書に関連するクレームはもともとの契約と「切っても切れない密接な相互関係」があるから，両当事者

は，示談合意書に関する紛争も仲裁に付託の要ありと判示した。

仲裁合意は，禁反言の原則，追認の原則に基づいても，強制される（*Deloitte Noraudit* v. *Deloitte Haskins & Sells*, 9 F. 3d 1060 (2d Cir. 1993) 事件を参照）。この事件では，仲裁条項を含んだ契約の署名者の系列会社は，禁反言の原則により仲裁条項に縛られると判断された（*Sunkist Soft Drinks Inc.* v. *Sunkist Growers Inc.*, 10 F. 3d 753 (11th Cir. 1993) 事件も参照）。この事件では，裁判所は，衡平法上の禁反言を理由に，仲裁合意が強制される，と判断した。また *Daisy Manufacturing* v. *NCR Corp.*, 29 F. 3d 389 (8th Cir. 1994) 事件では，当事者の前任者が署名した契約を追認したとして，その当事者は仲裁合意に縛られると判断された。

船荷証券は，しばしば傭船契約の条件や条項を摂取しており，その傭船契約には仲裁条項を含んでいる。このような場合，運送人と船荷証券の所持人との間には，仲裁合意が存することとなる。例えば，船荷証券の所持人から提起される貨物クレームに関しては，船主は，仲裁に付託することを要求できる（*Son Shipping Co.* v. *Defosse & Tanghe*, 199 F. 2d 687 (2d Cir. 1952)；*Lowry & Co.* v. *The Le Moyne d'Iberville*, 253 F. Supp. 396 1966 AMC 2195 (S. D. N. Y. 1966)；*Midland Tar Distillers Inc.* v. *The Lotos*, 362 F. Supp. 1311, 1973 AMC 1924 (S. D. N. Y. 1973)；*Amoco Overseas Co.* v. *The Avenger*, 387 F. Supp. 589, 1975 AMC 782 (S. D. N. Y. 1975)；*Alucentro Div. Dell'Alusuisse Italia S. p. A.* v. *The Hafnia*, 1992 AMC 267 (Fla. 1991) の各事件を参照）。しかしながら，仲裁条項が，より一般的に傭船契約から生じるすべての係争を仲裁に付することを要求するのではなく，明らかに「船主」と「傭船者」間の紛争に限定しているのであれば，船主，傭船者以外の当事者はその仲裁条項には縛られないこととなる（*Otto Wolff Handelsgesellschaft mbH* v. *Sheridan Transportation Co.*, 1992 AMC 2646 (E. D. Va 1992)，別の理由で棄却 800 F. Supp. 1359, 1993 AMC 406 (E. D. Va. 1992) 事件を参照）。

米国海上物品運送法上の船荷証券に記載された外国仲裁条項の有効性については，*Vimar Seguros y Reaseguros S. A.* v. *The Sky Reefer*, 515 U.S. —, 115 S. Ct. —, 132 L. Ed. 2d 462, 1995 AMC 1817 (1995) 事件の画期的な最高裁判決により，支持された。*Indussa Corp.* v. *The Ranborg*, 377 F. 2d 200, 1967 AMC 589 (2d Cir. 1967) 事件の判決では，船荷証券に記載された外国の裁判所に管轄権を与える裁判管轄条項は，米国海上物品運送法上，無効だと判断されていたが，*The Sky Reefer* 事件の最高裁の判決の多数意見は，*Indussa Corp.* v. *The Ranborg* 事件の理由付けをきっぱりと否定したのである。今後，*The Sky Reefer* 事件の判例がどのように適用されていくか，注視していかなければならないが，船荷証券上の管轄条項は，それが外国の裁判所もしくは外国の仲裁地を規定していても，その条項自体が，運送人の貨物滅失の責任を減じるものでない限り，もしくは米国海上物品運送法第3条(8)と抵触しない限り，適用されるであろうことを，多数意見は強く示唆している。

船荷証券が明示的に傭船契約に言及し，船荷証券に傭船契約が摂取されることを，船荷証券の所持人が実際に通知を受けたか，通知を受けたと推定されるならば，船荷証券に，有効に仲裁条項が摂取されることとなる（前出 *Midland Tar Distillers Inc.* v. *The Lotos* 事件を参照）。もし，船荷証券に傭船契約に言及する紙幅が設けられているものの，その紙幅が空白である場合には，通常は，傭船契約の摂取および仲裁条項の摂取はなされていないと判断される（*Southwestern Sugar & Molasses Corp.* v. *The Eliza Jane Nicholson*, 126 F. Supp. 666, 1995 AMC 746 (S. D. N. Y. 1954)，*Tropical Gas Co.* v. *The Mundogas Caribe*, 388 F. Supp. 647, 1975 AMC 987 (D. P. R. 1974)，*Cia Platamon de Navegacion S. A.* v. *Empresa Colombiana de Petroleos*, 478 F. Supp. 66, 1980 AMC 538 (S. D. N. Y. 1979)，*United States Barite Corp.* v. *The Haris*, 1982 AMC 925 (S. D. N. Y. 1982))。もし，船荷証券が曖昧であれば，例えば「傭

船契約」によるとしていながらも，その「傭船契約」自体が特定されていない場合，裁判所は，当事者の意図如何を決定するために，外部的な証拠に目を向けるかもしれない。例えば，傭船契約をめぐる交渉において，当事者が船荷証券に傭船契約を摂取することを意図しており，受荷主がその意図を実際に通知されたか，通知されたと推定されれば，傭船契約の仲裁条項は有効に船荷証券に摂取されたとみなされる。

ただし，*Pacific Lumber & Shipping Co. Inc.* v. *Star Shipping A/S*, 464 F. Supp 1314, 1979 AMC 2137（W.D.Wash. 1979）事件では，船主と傭船者の合意で，船荷証券に摂取された仲裁条項に関し，荷送人の合意を取り付けておらず，そのためその仲裁条項は有効ではない，と判断されている。この事件では，London仲裁条項が1度も荷送人と交渉されていなかったことにより，裁判所は，仲裁条項は船荷証券に有効に摂取されていない，と判断した。

仲裁判断を待って，訴訟手続を停止

請求する当事者の一方は，その請求を仲裁に付託するよりも，訴訟に訴える方法を選択するかもしれない。そうは言っても，そのような場合には，もう一方の当事者は，係争を仲裁に付託させる権利があり，仲裁法第3条により，当該係争の仲裁判断を待つため，訴訟手続きの停止の命令を取得することができる。さらに加えて，訴訟で権利を主張する者自身も仲裁判断を待つために，自らの訴訟追行行為を停止させることができる。

仲裁法第3条の仲裁判断を待つために訴訟手続の停止を求める申立を検討する際，裁判所が考慮すべき唯一の問題は，当事者が係争を仲裁に付託するという合意を作成し，履行したかという点である。もし，係争は仲裁に付託されなければならない，と裁判所が認定すれば，第3条のもとでは，裁判所には，停止命令を出さない選択の裁量権はない。*Seguros Banvenez S. A.* v. *The Oliver Drescher*, 761 F. 2d 855, 1985 AMC 2168（2d Cir.1985）事件では，船主と傭船者間の傭船契約は，いかなる係争についてもLondon仲裁を規定していた。貨物側が，5個のクレーンの滅失に関し，船主と傭船者を訴えた。地方裁判所は，貨物側有利の判決を出した。船主は傭船者に対し，傭船者は船主に対して，補償もしくは分担を求める交差請求をお互いに行った。訴訟経済を考慮し，裁判所は，第3条を根拠とした船主の訴訟手続の停止の申立を拒絶した。控訴裁判所は，地方裁判所には訴訟手続停止の許可を拒絶する裁量権がないとして，地方裁判所の判決を覆した。控訴裁判所は，さらに貨物滅失による損害に関し，傭船者に船主への補償を命じた船主有利の地方裁判所の判決を無効とした。

一方の，あるいは双方の当事者が，当初から裁判手続を利用する方法は，仲裁付託の権利の放棄ではないかとの疑問を生むことが，決して少なくない。単に訴訟を開始しただけでは，権利を主張する者が仲裁付託の権利を喪失しないことは，明らかである。もっとも，権利を主張する者ははっきりと仲裁付託の権利を留保しておくことが必要である。同様に，原告の訴状に対し，積極的防御や反訴（それらは仲裁に付託できるものであるが）を含んだ回答を行っても，また訴外の第三者を訴訟に引き込む訴状を提出しても，そのことで，仲裁付託の権利を放棄したことにはならない。もっとも，訴状への回答や第三者を訴訟に引き込む訴状に，明確に仲裁を要求する権利を留保しておかないと軽率であるとの謗りを免れないと思う。仲裁の権利が放棄されたか否かを決める目安は，仲裁への移行許可により一方の当事者が被る不利益如何である。すなわち，通常，仲裁付託請求の遅延の度合，正式な事実審理前の証拠開示手続の進捗度合による（*Cotton* v. *Sloan*, 4 F. 3d. 176（2d Cir.1993），*Re Ballard Shipping Co.*, 752 F. Supp. 546, 1991 AMC 721（D.R.I. 1991），後訴 772. F. Supp. 721, 1992 AMC 402（D.R.I. 1991），他の理由で修正 32 F. 3d 623, 1994 AMC 2705（1st Cir.1994）。*Carcich* v. *Re-*

deri A/B Nordie, 389 F. 2d. 692, 1968 AMC 299 (2d Cir. 1968); *Demsey & Assoc.* v. *The Sea Star,* 461 F. 2d. 1009, 1972 AMC 1440 (2d. Cir. 1972) の各事件を参照）。*Mages Foundation* v. *Thrifty Corp.,* 916 F. 2d 402 (7th Cir. 1990) 事件と *Commercial Union Ins.* v. *Gilbane Building Co.,* 992 F. 2d 386 (1st Cir. 1993) 事件を比較。この事案では，仲裁に付託する権利は放棄されていない，と判示された。

　仲裁の権利放棄の問題は，上記の *Seguros Banvenez S. A.* v. *The Oliver Drescher* 事件において生じた。裁判所は，当事者が仲裁請求の権利を放棄しているというには，もう一方の当事者の権利が害されていることが必要である，と判示した。この事案では，訴状や交差請求へ回答する初期の段階で，仲裁への付託を要求しているし，証拠開示手続や審理への参加も，ひとえに地方裁判所が London の仲裁判断が出るまで手続停止の申出を許可しなかったからであった。控訴裁判所によれば，「非仲裁の行動をとったからと言って，仲裁付託の権利が放棄されたと推定はできない」(1985 AMC at 2178)。

450 仲裁の強制

　もし，一方の当事者からの仲裁付託の要求に対して，もう一方の当事者が何の返事もしないか，拒否した場合，仲裁の申立人は仲裁法第4条に基づき，仲裁強制の申立ができ，また，第5条に基づき，裁判所に対してそのような返事をしなかった相手方に代わって仲裁人を選任するよう要求することができる。同様に，両当事者によって選任された2名の仲裁人が，第3の仲裁人を合意できない場合には，第5条によって，どちらかの当事者の申立があれば，裁判所はその第3の仲裁人を選任することができる。仲裁の合意の存在が否定された場合には，裁判所は第4条に基づき，その争点についての略式裁判の実施を命ずることができる（*Interocean Shipping Co.* v. *National Shipping & Trading. Corp.,* 462 F. 2d 673 (2d Cir. 1972); *Interocean Shipping Co.* v. *National Shipping & Trading Corp.,* 523 F. 2d 527 (2d Cir. 1975), 裁量上告拒絶 423 U. S. 1054 (1976); *A/S Custodia* v. *Lessin Int'l Inc.,* 503 F. 2d 318 (2d Cir. 1974) の各事件を参照）。*Interbras Cayman Co.* v. *Orient Victory Shipping Co. S. A.,* 663 F. 2d 4, 1982 AMC 737 (2d Cir. 1981)（判事全員の意見）事件において，法廷は，仲裁を拒否している当事者が，仲裁合意の当事者であるのかというまったくの事実の問題に関して，十分な証拠を提出していれば，略式裁判を行う必要が生じると判示した。

　第4条に基づき，強制仲裁の申請が行われたとき，裁判所によって決められるべき唯一の問題は，仲裁合意存在の有無であり，そしてもし存在している場合，もう一方の当事者はなぜ仲裁に応じなかったのか，もしくは拒否し，怠ったのかという点である（*Conticommodity Services Inc.* v. *Philipp & Lion,* 613 F. 2d 1222 (2d Cir. 1980); *Hanskar Shipping Co.* v. *Iron Ore Co. of Canada,* 1980 AMC 1249 (S. D. N. Y. 1980)）。請求の具体的な内容に関する問題は，仲裁人の判断に委ねられている。前出 *Conticommodity Services* 事件において，裁判所は，次のように述べている。

　　第4条における裁判所の権限は，当事者が仲裁を拒否しているか否かを決定するだけに限られ，当事者が十分な理由をもって拒否しているか否かを決定するのは，その権限外となる (613 F. 2d at 1227)。

　それゆえに，例えば，仲裁付託の要求が時機を得て行われた否かの問題は，仲裁人によって決定されなければならない（前出の *Conticommodity Services,* 613 F. 2d 1226 事件，同趣旨の

判例として，*Shearson Lehman Hutton Inc.* v. *Wagoner*, 944 F. 2d 114 (2d Cir. 1991)；*Soares Financial Group Inc.* v. *Nat'l Assoc. of Securities Dealers*, 1994 U.S. Dist. Lexis 8245 (N.D. Cal 1994)；*Mitsubishi Corp.* v. *The Oinoussian Strength*, 1994 U.S. Dist. Lexis 2625 (S.D.N.Y. 1994), *New Zealand Insur.* v. *The Greenland Rex*, 1991 AMC 21 (S.D.N.Y. 1991) の各事件を参照）。

しかしながら，*Smith Barney, Harris, Upham & Co.* v. *Luckie*, 85 N.Y. 2d 193, 623 N.Y.S. 2d 800 (1995) 事件を参照。この事件では，New York 控訴裁判所は，仲裁合意に New York 法選択の条項が含まれていることにより，その仲裁合意は，出訴期限問題でどの法律を適用するか裁判所に決定権限を与えている New York 法が適用されると，判断した。このとき，裁判所は，*Volt Information Sciences* v. *Board of Trustees of the Leland Stanford Jr. University*, 489 U.S. 468 (1989) 事件の判例に依拠した。この事件で，最高裁は次のように述べている。

「当事者は，仲裁に関し州の法則に拠ることを合意した。その結果として，たとえ仲裁を停止させることがあっても，仲裁合意の条項に従って，その法則を強制することは，連邦仲裁法の目的と完全に一致する」。

Gov't of India v. *Cargill*, 867 F. 2d 130 (2d. Cir 1989) 事件，*Son Shipping Co.* v. *De Fosse & Tanghe*, 199 F. 2d 687, 1952 AMC 1931 (2d. Cir. 1952) 事件も参照。この事件では，請求自体が仲裁に付されるのであれば，貨物損害の請求が出訴期限を過ぎたか否かを決定するのは仲裁人であると判断されている。*Trafalgar Shipping Co.* v. *Int'l Milling Co.*, 401 F. 2d. 568, 1969 AMC 1006 (2d Cir. 1968) 事件では，義務懈怠と適時に訴訟が提起されたか否かは，ひとえに仲裁人の問題であると判断された。*World Brilliance Corp.* v. *Bethlehem Steel Co.*, 342, F. 2d 362, 364, 1965 AMC 881, 882 (2d Cir. 1965) 事件では，懈怠もしくは放棄によって仲裁に付する権利が喪失したか否かの判断は，仲裁人が決定するものである，と判断された。

非常に狭い範囲でのみ，裁判所は，仲裁を要求する時期があまりに不適切ゆえに，衡平法上[451]の出訴制限の原則により，仲裁に付すことがもはやできない，と判断することができる（前出 *Conticommodity Services Inc.* v. *Philipp & Lion*, 613 F. 2d at 1226 事件を参照）。これは，裁判所が第4条によって決めることを要求されている問題，すなわち，仲裁の合意はなされたか，仲裁に付託することができなかったか，拒否したか，怠ったかという問題に関連した遅延の論点に限定されるであろう。例えば，もし，一方の当事者が，仲裁の要求に関し，証拠を提出できたという事実が，仲裁の要求を行ったもう一方の当事者の遅延によって害された場合，それでも遅延を生ぜしめた当事者は，仲裁法によって仲裁を強制できるかどうか。それを決定するのは，裁判所の権限となる。*Polar Shipping Ltd.* v. *Oriental Shipping Corp.*, 680 F. 2d 627, 1982 AMC 2330 (9th Cir. 1982) 事件では，当該傭船契約は，Shelldemise 書式に拠っており，その傭船契約には，各々の当事者は London での仲裁を提起することができる，ただし，相手方から係争に関する書面での通知を受け取って21日以内に提起しなければならない，と規定した条項が入っていた。所定の期間内に仲裁が提起されなかったとして，裁判所は，仲裁に付託する権利がなくなったと判断した。

しかしながら，仲裁合意が，ある特定の係争を対象としているかどうかの決定は，裁判所の権限となる（*John Wiley & Sons Inc.* v. *Livingston*, 376 U.S. 543, 546-547 (1964) 事件）。

1988年，米国仲裁法に，仲裁事案の上訴に関する新しい章が設けられ，9 U.S.C. §16とし

て法典化されている。裁判所は，*Stedor Enterprises Ltd.* v. *Armtex Inc.*, 947 F. 2d 727, 729 (4th Cir. 1991) 事件で次のように述べている。「仲裁の強制を求める申立を拒否もしくは是認する命令に対する上訴可能性を規制する法則は，常に，少しばかり錯綜していた」。1988年の改正は，仲裁を好ましい紛争解決手段であると強く考える公の政策に沿うものであった。したがって，16条では，仲裁を強制する最終命令に対しては上訴できるが，仲裁を強制する中間的な命令に対する上訴は許されていない。なお，仲裁を否定する命令に対しては，それが中間的な命令であれ，最終的命令であれ，上訴できる。

　上訴可能性を決めるための，「中間的」命令と「最終的」命令の違いについては，かなり明白である。もし，紛争を仲裁に付する強制的な命令を求めるためだけの目的で申立が行われるのであれば，その申立に対する命令は，「最終的」と言える。というのは，裁判所が判断するのは仲裁に付託させるかどうかだけであるからである。これに対して，もし，例えば契約違反を理由とする損害賠償訴訟という実質的救済を求める請求を含む広い訴訟の一環として，仲裁の要請が出て来た場合に，当事者を仲裁に向かわしめる命令は中間的なものと考えられる。*McDermott Int'l Inc.* v. *Underwriters at Lloyd's*, 981 F. 2d 744 (5th Cir), 裁量上告拒絶 U. S. 113 S. Ct. 2442, 124 L. Ed. 2d 660 (1993), 第5巡回区裁判所の事件では，*Catlin* v. *United States*, 324 U. S. 229, 233 (1945) の判例を引用して，次のように述べている。

　　仲裁に影響を与える命令が，終局的なものか中間的なものかを決める際に，ほとんどの裁判所は，仲裁を求める行為が「独立」しているのか，それとも他のクレームのなかに「埋め込ま」れているのかを区別する。一般的に言えば，もし裁判所が判断すべき問題が，仲裁に付託すべきかどうかだけであれば，その申立行為は独立したものであると考えられ，その問題に関する裁判所の決定は，最終判断と考えられる。

　同趣旨の判例として，*Sphere Drake Ins.* v. *Marine Towing Inc.*, 16 F. 3d 666, 667-668, 1994 AMC 1581, 1583 (5th Cir. 1994), 裁量上告拒絶— U. S. —, 115 S. Ct. 195, 130 L. Ed. 2d 127, 1994 Lexis 6329 (U. S. 1994) 事件と前出 *Stedor Enterprises* v. *Armtex Inc.* 事件および *American Casualty Co.* v. *L-J. Inc.*, 35 F. 3d 133, 135 (4th Cir. 1994) 事件。仲裁判断を承認し，無効にし，修正する地方裁判所の命令は，仲裁法第16条(a)(1)(D)と(E)によって，終局的命令とされ，一般的には上訴可能と判断されている。上訴された仲裁判断を，訂正もしくは修正のために仲裁人に差し戻す地方裁判所の命令を上訴できるかどうかの法則は，それほど明確ではない。この場合，仲裁人が何を要求されるかにもよるが，一般的には，そのような命令は中間的なものとして，上訴できない。*Landy Michaels Realty* v. *Local 32B-32J*, 954 F. 2d 794 (2d Cir. 1992) 事件（この事件では，事件を仲裁に差し戻すとの地方裁判所の命令は，上訴できないとされた），*CSX Transp. Inc.* v. *United Transp. Union*, 950 F. 2d 872 (2d Cir. 1991) 事件（この事件では，仲裁人にそれ以上の権限は存しないと言う理由で，地方裁判所の仲裁への差戻命令は上訴できると判断された）。

　Exportkhleb v. *Maistros Corp.*, 790 F. Supp. 70, 1992 AMC 1804 (S. D. N. Y. 1992), 理由を付さず原審維持 979 F. 2d 845, 1993 AMC 608 (2d Cir. 1992) 事件を参照。この事件は例外的な事案で，船主は，貨物所有者の反訴を仲裁に付託すべしと抗弁する権利を放棄したと判断された。

仲裁の併合

　仲裁手続の併合を命ずる連邦裁判所の権限については，本書の旧版の出版以降に，法律の変

更があった。米国最高裁は，この点について判断を下していないが，地方裁判所は仲裁手続の併合を命じる権限を有しない，と明らかに過半数の連邦巡回控訴裁判所は，判断している。もちろん，別個の仲裁の当事者たちが手続を併合させることに合意することはできるし，多くの事例では手続の併合は奨励されるべき意義のある方法とされる。

法律や事実の問題で，共通のものが扱われている別個の仲裁につき，連邦仲裁法には，地方裁判所にそれらの仲裁を併合する権利を付与する条項はない。むしろ，それは判例で創造された原理である。併合の目的に関しては，Haight 判事は次のように要約している。

　仲裁の併合は，もし別々の仲裁を許せば，矛盾した事実認定や不公平をもたらしてしまう明白かつ現実の危険性をもつ，複数の当事者，複数の契約の事案を取り扱うための，衡平法裁判所の実利的な手続上の道具である。
　Re Transportacion Maritima Mexicana S. A., 636 F. Supp. 474, 476 (S. D. N. Y. 1983).

仲裁の併合が，すべての関係者にとって有益となる古典的な例は，本船が再傭船に出されており，かつある事件の発生により，連鎖しているすべての傭船契約において，クレームが生ずるような事例である。

Government of The United Kingdom of Great Britain v. Boeing Co., 998 F. 2d 68, 1993 AMC 2913 (2d Cir. 1993) 事件の判決が出るまでの，New York における原則は，連邦地方裁判所が，共通の法と事実の問題が絡んだ別個の仲裁を併合させる権限を有する，というものであった。この点に関して，巡回控訴裁判所では判断が分かれており，当事者が締結している仲裁条項に併合に関する定めがない場合は，当事者が仲裁の併合に反対しているのを覆してまで，併合を命ずる権限は地方裁判所にはない，というのが多数の巡回控訴裁判所の判断であった（American Centennial Ins. Co. v. National Casualty Co., 951 F. 2d 107 (6th Cir. 1991) 事件，Baesler v. Continental Grain Co., 900 F. 2d 1193 (8th Cir. 1990) 事件，Protective Life Ins. v. Lincoln Nat'l Life Ins., 873 F. 2d 281 (11th Cir. 1989) 事件，Del E. Webb Constr. v. Richardson Hosp. Auth., 823 F. 2d 145 (5th Cir. 1987) 事件，Weyerhaeuser Co. v. Western Seas Shipping Co., 743 F. 2d 635 (9th Cir.)，裁量上告拒絶 469 U.S. 1061 (1984) 事件を参照）。

Boeing 事件の判決を受けて，第２巡回区控訴裁判所は多数の巡回裁判所が採用している原則を採用するようになった。すなわち，各傭船契約のすべての当事者の合意がなければ，別個の仲裁合意から出てきた複数の仲裁手続の併合を禁止した。もっとも，まだ第１巡回区控訴裁判所は，地方裁判所は仲裁を併合することができるとの見解を変えていない（New England Energy Inc. v. Keystone Shipping Co., 855 F. 2d 1, 1989 AMC 537 (1st Cir. 1988) 裁量上告拒絶 489 U.S. 1077 (1989)）。

多数意見に組することで，第２巡回区裁判所は，実質的に Compania Espanola de Petroleos S. A. v. Nereus Shipping S. A., 527 F. 2d 966 (2d Cir. 1975)，裁量上告拒絶 426 U.S. 936 (1976) 事件の判例を覆している。Compania 事件では，第２巡回区裁判所は，地方裁判所が仲裁を併合する権限をもっていると判断しており，その判決のなかで次のように述べた。「連邦仲裁法の自由な目的に徴すれば，明らかに，併合が適当と思われる事案では，仲裁の併合を許す，もしくは仲裁の併合を奨励しているとさえ言えるようにこの仲裁法を解釈すべきである」(527 F. 2d at 975)。

Boeing の事案では，第２巡回区裁判所は，仲裁の併合を強制すべきであるとの英国政府の申請を認めた地方裁判所の判断を覆した。この判決を出すに際し，第２巡回区控訴裁判所は，

Nereus 事件以後の最高裁の判例を検討した上で，判決を出しているのであるが，最高裁の判例は，仲裁法が意図しているのは，たとえ非効率な点が出てくる可能性があるとしても，厳格に当事者の意思に沿って，当事者間で交渉された仲裁合意が実行されるべきである，としている (*Volt Info. Sciences* v. *Board of Trustees*, 489 U. S. 468, 478-479 (1989) 事件，*Dean Witter Reynolds Inc.* v. *Byrd*, 470 U. S. 213, 217-219 (1985) 事件，*Moses H. Cone Memorial Hosp.* v. *Mercury Constr. Corp.*, 460 U. S. 1, 20 (1983) 事件を参照)。これらの最高裁の事案は，「仲裁法の目的に関するわれわれの解釈の基礎を崩している」 (527 F. 2d at 72) と述べて，第2巡回区裁判所は，もはや *Nereus* 事件は，それが連邦民訴法と，連邦仲裁法の「自由な目的」を土台としている点において，もはやよい法とは言えないとの判断を示した。しかしながら，第2巡回区裁判所は，「裁判所の一般的な公正な権限と契約法の原則に基づく限度において」，*Nereus* 事件の判旨を維持している (527 F. 2d at 74.)。*Boeing* 事件と異なる状況の事案で，裁判所が，将来，この判旨により仲裁の併合を命じることになるかどうかは，まだわからない。

Boeing 事件以後の第2巡回区裁判所の事件として，例えば *North River Ins. Co.* v. *Philadelphia Reinsurance Corp.*, 856 F. Supp. 850 (S. D. N. Y. 1994) 事件 (仲裁判断を破棄している)，*Active Glass Corp.* v. *Architectural and Ornamental Iron Workers Local Union*, 1995 U. S. Dist. Lexis 1500 S. D. N. Y. 8 February 1995 事件 (複数当事者の仲裁要請を拒絶) を参照。

仲裁の併合に代わるものが，*The Kostas Melas*, 1988 AMC 68 (S. D. N. Y. 1983) 事件で用いられている。この案件では，船主と傭船者間で紛争が生じたが，その紛争は海事仲裁協会の規則に従って構成される仲裁審に付託されることとなっていた。さらに，穀物供給契約のもとで，同じ航海において，傭船者と貨物である穀物の供給者との間にも別の紛争が生じた。穀物供給契約には，米国仲裁協会の穀物仲裁審による仲裁が規定されていた。裁判所は，傭船者による仲裁併合の申立を拒絶したが，仲裁の手続は一緒に行うよう指示した。その指示のなかで，裁判所は，将来の仲裁審が審理を行うにあたり遵守すべき手続を示している。

仲裁人，審判人の選任

仲裁法第5条に列挙されている状況においては，裁判所に仲裁人を選任できる権限がある。仲裁合意のなかに仲裁人を選任する方法が定めてある場合，第5条では，裁判所は忠実にその合意に従わなければならないとされている。仲裁人の死亡もしくはその他の理由で，仲裁審に欠員が生じた場合にも，同様のことが言える。仲裁合意が，仲裁人の選任に関してなにも規定しない場合には，裁判所は単独仲裁人を選ぶこととなる (*Ore & Chem. Corp.* v. *Stinnes Interoil Inc.*, 611 F. Supp. 237, 240-241 (S. D. N. Y. 1985) 事件を参照)。

当事者が選任した仲裁人が死亡した場合，特に難しい問題が生ずる。*Marine Products Export Corp.* v. *The Globe Galaxy*, 1987 AMC 2310 (S. D. N. Y. 1987)，後日の訴 1992 AMC 1336 (S. D. N. Y. 1992)，原審維持 977 F. 2d 66, 1993 AMC 190 (2d Cir. 1992) 事件は，各当事者が1名ずつ選んだ「海運実務に経験をもつ仲裁人」による仲裁を規定している傭船契約における係争であった。その条項は，さらに，「選任された2人の仲裁人が合意しない場合には，その仲裁人は海事弁護士を3人目の仲裁人に指名する」と規定していた。さて，係争が生じ，両当事者は1人ずつ自分の仲裁人を選任し，審判人として機能する議長も選任した。仲裁手続を行っている途中で，一方の当事者が選任した仲裁人が死亡した。死亡した仲裁人を選任した当事者は，仲裁法第5条に基づき，各当事者が新しい仲裁人を選任し，まったく最初から

仲裁手続を再開することを求める命令を出すよう，地方裁判所に申立を行った。裁判所は，仲裁法第5条に規定されているように，一方の当事者が選任した仲裁人が死亡した場合，その後どのように対処するかの当事者の合意がないことにより，「欠けた仲裁人を埋める方法」に「誤り」があったとした。裁判所は次のように述べている。

　　当事者は拘束力のある契約で約束していない限り，商事上の係争を仲裁に付託することを強制されない。同じように，当事者の明確な合意に反するようなやり方の仲裁を強制されることはない。

　かくして，地方裁判所は，両当事者に新しい仲裁人を選任させて，最初から仲裁手続を再開させ，「仲裁合意の条件に沿ったかたち」で，手続を進行させた。1993 AMC 192頁，ここで1987 AMC 2314頁を引用している。

　この問題に関する原告の上訴が不成功に終わった後，新しい仲裁審が選任された。被告有利の仲裁判断がなされたが，原告は，地方裁判所に対して，仲裁判断の破棄と生き残った2人のもともとの仲裁人を復職させて，その2人にもう1人の新しい仲裁人を選ばせて，当初の仲裁審によって本件係争を判断させる命令を出すよう，申立を行った。1993 AMC 192頁。

　原告の申立は，主に，その当時の最新判例であった *Trade & Transport Inc. v. Natural Petroleum Charters Inc.*, 931 F. 2d 191 (2d Cir. 1991) 事件の判決を根拠として行われたのである。この判決は次のようなものであった。すなわち，仲裁審が責任の点については，全員一致の判断を下していたが，賠償額については未決定の時点で，仲裁人の1人が死亡した事案で，地方裁判所は仲裁人の交替を認め，そして第2巡回区裁判所もその地方裁判所の判断を支持した。この事件において，死亡した仲裁人の交替に関する規定は，仲裁合意にはなかった。責任の点に関する仲裁判断は，最終判断であると考えられており，第2巡回区裁判所は，「任務完了」の原則に基づき仲裁審のこの点に関する権限は終結した，との結論を出した。それゆえ，このような特別な状況であったから，第2巡回区裁判所は，まったく新しく仲裁人団を選び直して仲裁をはじめから行うよりも，欠員仲裁人の交替の選任を許して，損害賠償額の問題のみを審理させるのに同意したのである。

　Globe Galaxy 事件では，地方裁判所が原告の仲裁人の再任の申立を拒否した案件の上訴について，第2巡回区裁判所は，原告が選んだ仲裁人の死亡後，仲裁のやり直しを要求した地方裁判所は，その権限を逸脱してはいない，と判断した。理由は，*Trade and Transport* 事件の状況と違って，もし，仲裁判断を出す前に，仲裁審の1人が死亡した場合，まったく新しい仲裁審により，新たに仲裁の手続が開始されなければならないという一般原則から外れることを正当化する事由は何もないからである。

　前出 *Globe Galaxy* 事件の問題は，傭船契約書もしくはその他の書面に，仲裁人が欠けたとき，交替の仲裁人を選任する規定を含んだ海事仲裁人協会の規則を挿入しておけば，避けられる。

　Cargill v. *Empresa Nicaraguense Dealimentos*, 25 F. 3d 223 (4th Cir. 1994) 事件を参照。この事件では，第4巡回区裁判所は，当事者相互の合意によって選ばれていない仲裁人が下した仲裁判断を無効とした。

「実務家」

　ニューヨーク・プロデュース書式第17条では，仲裁人は，「実務家」であることが要求されている。他の傭船契約は，ニューヨーク・プロデュース書式ほど制限的ではなく，弁護士の起

用も許している。「実務家」が何を意味しているかの問題は, 予想以上に難しいことが判明している。

　W. K. Webster & Co. v. American President Lines Ltd., 32 F. 3d 665, 1995 AMC 134 (2d. Cir. 1994) 事件で, 裁判所は, ある人物が,「実務家」であり同時に「弁護士」であることも認める, との判断を示した。この判断を示す際, 裁判所は, Aramco Servs. Co. v. EAC Bulk Transp. Inc., 1993 AMC 1885, 1886 (Fla. 1993) 事件の判断に同意しない旨を表明した。この事件の判例は,「実務家とは, 海運業に雇われているか, 精通している人間を意味する」としている。どちらの事案でも, 単に現役の弁護士であるとの理由により, 忌避された仲裁人がその資格なしとはいえないとの結論が出されたのであるが, Webster 事件を扱った裁判所は, Aramco 事件の判決が, 法律の仕事を通して海運業に精通していることが, 十分に「実務家」の資格になると判断した点に, 賛同していない。代わりに, 第 2 巡回区裁判所は, Pando Compania Naviera S. A. v. Filmo S. A. S. [1975] 1 Lloyd's Rep. 560 (Q. B) 事件でなされた識別方法を採用した。すなわち, 後者の事件では, 弁護士としてのみの経験しかない者を排除している。Webster, 32 F. 2d at 668事件。しかしながら, Pando 事件と Webster 事件によれば, 弁護士でも必要とされる海運業の商売上の実務経験を有している者は,「実務家」としての資格を有するとされるだろう。

仲裁開始前の証拠開示手続

　一般的に, 当事者が係争を仲裁に付することを合意しているとき, 裁判所は, 通常, 仲裁開始前の証拠開示手続を行うことを拒否するものである。しかし, 例外的な場合においては, 係争が仲裁に付託されるとしても, 裁判所が仲裁開始前の証拠開示手続を許したことがある。Koch Fuel v. South Star, 1988 AMC 1226 (E. D. N. Y. 1987) 事件で, 傭船者は, 本船船主が貨物として積載している燃料油を横領した, と主張した。傭船契約によれば, 傭船者のクレームは London の仲裁に付託されることとなっていた。まさに本船が出港しようとしており, かつこの横領事件に関し事情を知る乗組員を London の仲裁に証人に召喚することはできないと考えられたことより, 裁判所は, 傭船者が担保を取得するために本船をアレストした際, London での仲裁を助けるために, 乗組員から供述をとることを許可した。裁判所は, このような証人が得られなくなるような状況は, 供述録取を命じる裁判所の介入を認めるのに十分例外的なものであると考えたのである。

　Oriental Commercial & Shipping v. Rosseel N. V., 125 F. R. D. 398 (S. D. N. Y. 1989) 事件と Deiulemar Di Navigazione S. p. A., 1994 AMC 2250 (E. D. La. 1994) 事件も参照。

仲裁付託を条件とした係争

　仲裁に付する権利は, 契約によって創造されるから, 当事者は, 公序良俗の制限に触れさえしなければ, 仲裁の合意を広くも狭くも, 自らの望むものにすることができる。この領域におけるもっとも顕著な事例は, 当事者が, 仲裁合意存在の有無を, 仲裁に付することを合意することである。

　First Options of Chicago Inc. v. Kaplan, 514 U. S.―, 115 S. Ct.―, 131 L. Ed. 2d 985 (1995), 原審維持 19 F. 3d 1503 (3d Cir. 1994) 事件において, 米国最高裁判所は, 個人としての投資家は仲裁に合意していない, また仲裁に参加したからといって, 裁判上で異議を唱える権利を放棄したものではないと判断した控訴裁判所を支持した。控訴審は, 仲裁付託の可

否の問題は，裁判所が独自に考慮すべきものであるとしたが，最高裁判所はこの控訴審の判断を正しいものと考えた。この事案では，係争の理非を仲裁に付託することに合意したかどうかについて，当事者間で，意見が分かれたのみならず，本件係争を仲裁に付するべきかどうかの決定権限を仲裁人が有するか否かについても当事者の意見の一致がなかった。仲裁に付託すべき問題を仲裁に付託することを当事者が合意したか否かを決定するに際して，裁判所は，その旨の合意を示す明らかで間違いようのない証拠がない限り，裁判所は，当事者がそのような合意をしたと考えるべきではない，と警告した。もし当事者が，仲裁に付託すべきかどうかの問題を仲裁に付託することを合意していれば，仲裁人の決定は，「ある特定の狭い状況において」のみ，破棄されるべきである。もし，当事者が，仲裁に付託すべきかどうかの問題を仲裁に付託することに合意していなければ，当事者が仲裁に付託することに合意していない他の問題同様，この問題も裁判所が決めることとなる。仲裁法の基本的な目的が当事者の意図に沿って仲裁契約を強制することにあると再度強調し，裁判所は，仲裁人は当事者が仲裁による解決を合意した係争のみ判断を下すことができるとし，それ以下でもそれ以上でもない，と述べている。

ニューヨーク・プロデュース書式における「船主と傭船者間のあらゆる係争」という文言は，これまで非常に広く解されてきた（*Re Canadian Gulf Line*, 1938 AMC 1123, 98 F. 2d 711（2d Cir. 1938），*Caribbean Steamship Co., S. A.* v. *Sonmez Denizcilik ve Ticaret A. S.*, 598 F. 2d 1264, 1979 AMC 1270（2d Cir. 1979）の各事件を参照）。もちろん，この条項は傭船契約における船主および傭船者の各々の権利と義務に関係する係争に及ぶ。さらに，契約上の係争に加え，この条項は法の適用により生じたその他の係争も対象とするとされてきた。

Boyle v. *Rederij Shipmair VI*, 1979 AMC 2844（E. D. Pa. 1979）事件において，港湾労働者が貨物積載を手助けしているときに，怪我をしたとして船主を訴えた。船主は，傭船者をこの訴訟に巻き込んだが，傭船者は，船主から傭船者に提起されている補償を求める仲裁を先にするため，訴訟手続の停止を求める申立を行った。船主は，傭船者に対して補償もしくは損害の分担を求める請求は傭船契約から発生したものではなく，法の作用により課される義務と責任によって発生したものであるとの理由により，傭船者の仲裁を先に行えとの申立に反駁した。裁判所は，その請求は仲裁によるべきだと判断し，次のように述べた。

　　仲裁条項の広い文言は，本船船主と傭船者の現在の係争を対象としている。その条項は明らかにどのような係争にも適用があるので，仲裁条項は，純粋に契約上の係争のみに限定されるのではなく，法の作用によって生じる係争も対象としているのである（1979 AMC at 2845-2846）。

前出 *Caribbean Steamship Co. S. A.* v. *Sonmez Denizcilik ve Ticaret A. S.* 事件においては，傭船者が自己の親会社の保険者から代位求償貨物クレームを譲渡されたが船主はそれを例外的な状況であるとの理由で，傭船者との仲裁に付託しなければならない，と裁判所は判断した。事実は，次のとおりであった。船主は，本船を Caribbean に傭船に出し，本船は Caribbean の親会社である Reynolds が所有する貨物を積んだ。航海中に，本船が沈没し，貨物は全損になった。Reynolds は船主とは仲裁協定を結んでおらず，裁判所も「Reynolds は自分自身の子会社の法人格を否認」できなかったとし，Caribbean と船主との傭船契約に基づいて，船主との仲裁を求めることはできないと判断した。しかしながら，Reynolds の権利を代位した保険者は，その貨物クレームの権利を Caribbean に譲渡した。この譲渡契約の条項においては，Caribbean による回収は，譲渡人である保険者の収支になるとされていた。この「譲渡」を得た後，Caribbean は船主との仲裁を求め，裁判所も Caribbean にはそうする権利があると判断

した。

　裁判所は，Reynoldsの貨物クレームに関し，傭船者は船主に仲裁を強いることはできないと判断した。裁判所の考えは以下のとおりである。

　　「いかなる係争」という範囲の広い仲裁契約を持っている者に権利を譲渡しても，少なくとも仲裁契約の当事者がそのような結果を意図していたことを示す証拠がなければ，仲裁に付託することのできないクレームを仲裁に付託できるようにすることはできない（1979 AMC at 1273）。

　しかしながら，裁判所は，船主と傭船者間で，仲裁に付託するような「係争」が存するとした。裁判所によれば，保険者からの譲渡を受けたことにより，傭船者は補償を求めるクレームを実際，いくぶん促進させたというのである。傭船者は，貨物クレームに関しては，Reynoldsに対して責任はないが，裁判所は，このような状況では，傭船者の船主に対するクレームは，真の補償を求めるクレームと十分に同類のものであり，傭船者はその係争につき船主に仲裁を提起する権利があると判断した。もちろん，船主は取りうるすべての抗弁を行うことができる。

　Caribbean Steamship Co. 事件は，例外的なケースであり，それゆえに，先例としての価値は限られたものとならざるをえない。しかしながら，この事件には，疑問が生じた場合，裁判所は仲裁を志向するという裁判所の強い意向が示されている。

仲裁の放棄

　仲裁を進めることを怠っていると，仲裁を放棄しているとの理由で請求そのものを却下する判断が下される結果となることがある。The Marathon, SMA 2425 (Arb. at N.Y. 1987) 事件では，仲裁人は，仲裁を提起した当事者が13年間も本件請求の追行を怠っていたことを理由に，その当事者不利の裁決，すなわち仲裁そのものを却下する判断を下した。The Marathon 事件における遅延は極端なものではあるが，この仲裁判断によって確立された原則は適切であり，各々の事案の事情にもよるが，The Marathon 事件より短い期間の仲裁手続追行の遅延にも適用がある。The Agios Nikolaos III, SMA 2540 (Arb. at N.Y. 1988) 事件と The Archangelos III, SMA 2541 (Arb. at N.Y. 1988) 事件では，仲裁手続追行を怠ったとして，クレームもまた却下されている。

利子，報酬，費用に関して仲裁判断を下す権限

　仲裁人には，利息に関し仲裁判断を下すことができる本来的な権限があると考えられており，仲裁人の裁量により，通常の裁判で適用される法律上の最高利率を超える利息を命じることもできる。Finagrain Compagnie Commerciale Agricole et Financiere S. A. v. Federal Commerce & Navigation (1974) Ltd., 80 Civ. 0839 (S.D.N.Y., 3 September 1980) （判決速報）。この事件では，裁判所は，仲裁人が下した利息17パーセントとの裁定は，仲裁人の権限内の裁定であるとの判断を示した。

　Re Telfair Shipping Co. v. Institute Rio, 1978 AMC 1120 (S.D.N.Y. 1978) 事件において，仲裁判断が言い渡された8.5パーセントの利息を裁判所は是認した。Oceania Shipping Corp. v. Thos P. Gonzalez Corp., 442 F. Supp. 997 (S.D.N.Y. 1977) 事件では，8パーセントの利息の裁定が出たが，裁判所はこれを支持している。Peoples Security Life Insur. v. Monumental

Life Insur., 991 F. 2d. 141 (4th Cir. 1993) 事件では、仲裁判断以前の利息につき、7パーセントとの裁定が下されたが、これも是認されている。

仲裁人は、各当事者に対して仲裁手続にかかった費用を負担せよと命ずる権限があり、事件の状況を考えて適当と思われる費用を割り振ることができる。前出 *Oceania Shipping Corp.* v. *Thos P. Gonzalez Corp.* 事件では、仲裁人は一方の当事者に75パーセント、もう一方の当事者に25パーセントを割り振る裁定を下し、裁判所もその裁定を支持した。

しかしながら、各当事者の弁護士費用に関しては、仲裁条項に記載がなければ、仲裁人は判断を下す権限はないようである。*Transvenezuelian Shipping Co. S. A.* v. *Czarnikow-Rionda Co. Inc.*, 1982 AMC 1458 (S. D. N. Y. 1982) 事件では、傭船契約の仲裁条項に、当事者の弁護士費用に関して、仲裁人に判断を下すことができる権限を付与するとの明確な記載がなかった。この事件で、仲裁人は弁護士費用に関し裁定を下したが、裁判所は仲裁人が権限を超えた裁決を下したと判断した。同趣旨の判例として、*Sammi Line Co. Ltd.* v. *Altamar Navegacion S. A.* (*The Maria Sitinas*), 1985 AMC 1790 (S. D. N. Y. 1985) 事件。また、*Federal Commerce & Navigation Co. Ltd.* v. *Associated Metals & Minerals Corp.*, 1979 AMC 1733. 1734 (S. D. N. Y. 1978) 事件を参照。この事件のなかで、裁判所は、仲裁法は「報酬に関する裁定の権限を付与してはいない」と述べている。

同趣旨の判例として、*Menke* v. *Monchecourt*, 17 F. 3d 1007 (7th Cir. 1994) 事件と *Shipping Transportation Enterprises* v. *Transatlantic Petroleum*, 1992 AMC 663 (S. D. N. Y. 1991) 事件がある。しかしながら、*Todd Shipyards Corp.* v. *Cunard Lines Ltd.*, 943 F. 2d 1056, 1992 AMC 328 (9th Cir. 1991) 事件では、第9巡回区裁判所は、「米国規則」に対する不誠実を理由とする例外を認め、弁護士報酬に関し裁定を下す権限が仲裁審にあった、と判断した。さらに *C. T. Shipping Ltd.* v. *DMI Ltd*, 774 F. Supp. 146 (S. D. N. Y. 1991) 事件では、防御的な補償を求める訴訟と仲裁前の差押手続に関連し発生した弁護士報酬に関し仲裁人が下した裁定を、裁判所は支持した。

いくつかの事件においては、たとえ傭船契約に、仲裁審に弁護士報酬に関し裁定を下す権限があると規定されていなくても、当事者の双方が各々の弁護士報酬の支払を求めている事実から、当事者はそのような権限を仲裁人に付与する合意をしたとみなすことができると、仲裁により判断されている。例えば、*The Manila Enterprise*, SMA 2060 (Arb. at N. Y. 1985) 事件、*The Liberian Statesman*, SMA 2092 (Arb. at N. Y. 1985) 事件を参照。これが法的にみて正しい方法かどうかは疑問であるが、仲裁条項自体か仲裁付託合意のなかで、仲裁人が弁護士費用まで裁定できるかどうかの当事者の意図を明らかにすることの重要性を示している。

The China Trident, SMA 2756 (Arb. at N. Y. 1991) 事件においては、当事者の契約に規定されていなかったことにより、法廷弁護人の費用について裁定を下す権限が仲裁人にないことを仲裁人自身認めたが、London での仲裁と差押え手続に関する法廷弁護人費用については仲裁人が裁定を下せるとの、強い反対の立場を仲裁人は多数意見により示した。

懲罰的損害賠償

仲裁が米国連邦仲裁法に準拠するのであれば、懲罰的賠償が適当であると思われる事案では、仲裁人は懲罰的賠償を命ずる権限を有している。ただし、連邦仲裁法自身には、仲裁人に懲罰的賠償を命ずる権限がある、との明確な規定があるわけではない。むしろ、特定の事件において、当事者の仲裁合意が懲罰的な賠償を含むほど広いものであったと、これまで裁判所は判断してきたのである。*Raytheon Co.* v. *Automated Business Systems Inc.*, 882 F. 2d 6 (1st

Cir. 1989) 事件では，一般的な契約上の仲裁条項には懲罰的賠償を命ずる裁定ができるとの明示的な規定はないものの，その仲裁条項に従って商事仲裁人は，懲罰的賠償を命じる裁定を下す権限があるとされた (*Baravati* v. *Josephthal, Lyon & Ross Inc.*, 28 F. 3d 704 (7th Cir. 1994) 事件 (この仲裁は米国仲裁協会の規則に従って行われた)，*Todd Shipyards Corp.* v. *Cunard Lines Ltd.*, 943 F. 2d 1056, 1992 AMC 328 (9th Cir. 1991) 事件，*Bonar* v. *Dean Witter Reynolds Inc.*, 835 F. 2d 1378 (11th Cir. 1998) 事件，*Willoughby Roofing & Supply Co.* v. *Kajima International*, 598 F. Supp. 353 (N. D. Ala 1984) 事件，全員一致で原審維持 776 F. 2d 269 (11th Cir. 1985) 事件を参照)。

一般的な海事法における，海事不法行為に関する事件ならびに，契約違反であってもそれが同時に不法行為でもあるような事件では，懲罰的賠償の裁決がこれまで下されてきた (*Thyssen Inc.* v. *The Fortune Star*, 777 F. 2d 57, 1986 AMC 1318 (2d. Cir. 1985) 事件，*Protectus Alpha Navigation Co. Ltd.* v. *North Pacific Grain Growers Inc.*, 767 F. 2d 1379, 1986 AMC 56 (9th Cir. 1985) 事件，*Muratore* v. *The Scotia Prince*, 663 F. Supp. 484, 1988 AMC 859 (D. Me 1987) 事件を参照)。加えて，米国の法律には，仲裁において，懲罰的もしくは懲戒的な賠償を命ずる規定が存在する。

仲裁合意の当事者は，確かに仲裁人の懲罰的賠償を命ずる権限を制限することができる。しかしながら，印刷されたニューヨーク・プロデュース書式のような広い仲裁条項の場合，請求者の救済の範囲が準拠法自身より狭くなるようなことはない。

The Octonia Sun, 1988 AMC 832 (Arb. at N. Y. 1987) 事件では，単独仲裁人が，「船主が貨物の一部を本船の燃料油に流用する慣行が現存し，事実流用したことを認定して，そのような行為は決して許容される慣行ではなく，実のところ厳しく非難されるべきである」として，請求者に懲罰的賠償の裁定を下した。

The Ellis Pontos, SMA 2116 (Arb. at N. Y. 1985) 事件では，仲裁審は懲罰的損害賠償を命ずることを拒否したが，それを命ずる権限はあると考えているようであった。同様に，*The Kapetan Antonis*, 1989 AMC 551 (Arb. at N. Y. 1988) 事件においては，仲裁人は，自分たちには懲罰的賠償の判断を下す権限があると述べたが，この事件では，その行使を拒否した。

もし仮に，仲裁合意が New York 州法に準拠するものであれば，仲裁人は懲罰的賠償を命ずる判断を下すことは認められていない (*Garrity* v. *Lyle Stuart Inc.*, 40 N. Y. 2d 354, 386 N. Y. S. 2d 831 (1976))。

Fahnestock & Co. v. *Waltman*, 935 F. 2d 512 (2d Cir. 1991) 事件，裁量上告拒絶 502 U. S. 942 (1991)，裁量上告拒絶 502 U. S. 1120 (1992)，後日の訴 792 F. Supp. 31 (E. D. Pa. 1992)，理由を付さず原審維持 989 F. 2d 490 (3d Cir. 1993) 事件ならびに *Barbier* v. *Shearson Lehman Hutton Inc.*, 948 F. 2d 117 (2d Cir. 1991) 事件を参照。どちらの事件も，第2巡回区裁判所は，当事者が New York 州法を選択している状況において，U. S. C. 第10条(a)(4)のもとで，仲裁人が懲罰的賠償を命ずるのは権限踰越である，と判断している。連邦仲裁法と Garrity 事件において宣言された法則との間には，何ら抵触するものはなく，第2巡回区裁判所は，両方の事件において，「懲罰的賠償裁定の妥当性を許容する当事者の合意がなければ，この問題に関し，連邦の実質法が，New York 州法に先んじて適用されることはない」ことを示した (*Fahnestock*, 935 F. 2d at 518 事件および *Barbier*, 948 F. 2d at 121 事件を参照)。

「通常であれば，適切であると考えられている仲裁での懲罰的賠償裁定が，契約による法律選択の条項によって排除されるか否か」の問題に関しては，相反する判例が存することに鑑み，米国最高裁は，*Mastrobuono* v. *Shearson Lehman Hutton Inc.*, — US —, 115 S. Ct. 1212, 131 L. Ed. 2d 76 (1995) 事件で，その問題を検討した。ただし，*Mastrobuono* 事件は証券法

に関するものであるため，それが傭船契約の事件に適用があるかどうかはまだ明確ではない。

Mastrobuono 事件では，申立人は，自分の証券口座が被申立人であるブローカーにより不当な取扱をされたとして訴えた。仲裁審は，申立人のために，米貨400,000ドルの懲罰的賠償と米貨159,327ドルの補償賠償を被申立人に命じた。この仲裁判断を再審理し，地方裁判所と控訴裁判所は，*Garrity* 事件の法則を根拠に，懲罰的賠償を命じた仲裁判断を認めなかった。最高裁は，New York 州法の法選択条項，それ自体が懲罰的賠償を絶対的に排除しているのではない，との理由により，下級審の判決を破棄した（115 S. Ct. at 1212）。仲裁条項ならびにNASD の仲裁手続規定と懲罰的賠償を規定している NASD の仲裁人に与えられている手引書を検討して，最高裁は，当事者が懲罰的賠償を除外することに合意したと結論づけてしまうと矛盾が生じてくる，との判断を示した。それゆえ，最高裁が考えたように，「仲裁条項と法選択条項とをもっとも適切に調和させる方法は，『New York 州法』は New York の裁判所が適用する実質的な原則は包含しているが，仲裁人の権限を制限するような特別な法則は含んでいないと読むことである。かくして，法選択の条項は，当事者の権利義務を規定し，仲裁条項は仲裁を規定し，いずれも他方を侵害するものではないのである」（115 S. Ct. at 1219）。

仲裁判断実現を目的とする担保

米国の海事仲裁法で，より重要と思われる一つの点は，仲裁法第8条に規定されており，それは，被告の船のアレストもしくはその他の財物を差押えることによって，クレームの支払を確保するための担保を取得することを許容していることである。被告の船のアレストもしくはその他の財物を差押えることにより，裁判所は仲裁を命じ，当事者に対する管轄を保持し，仲裁判断に基づいた命令を出したりする。通常の仲裁法第8条の事件では，その行為は「海事差押えの手続」すなわち本船，貨物，運賃のアレストによって開始される。しかし，仲裁法第8条の行為を開始するのに，非海事の差押えの法的救済手段を用いることもできることが判示されている（*Murray Oil Products* v. *Mitsui & Co.*, 146 F. 2d 381（2d Cir. 1944）事件を参照）。このように仲裁法第8条は，二つの目的のために差押えを認めている。一つは権利を侵害された当事者に，その者のクレームの担保を確保させる目的，もう一つは，裁判所に被告に仲裁を進めるよう命ずることができるように，被告に対する管轄権を付与する目的である。*The Anaconda* v. *American Sugar Refining Co.*, 322 U. S. 42（1944）事件，*Schoenamsgruber* v. *Hamburg American Line*, 294 U. S. 454（1935）事件，*The Belize*, 25 F. Supp. 663（S. D. N. Y. 1938），控訴却下 101 F. 2d 1005（2d Cir. 1939）事件を参照。後者の事件で，裁判所は仲裁法第8条の目的を以下のように要約している。

> 仲裁法第8条の目的は，海事関連の紛争において，権利を侵害された当事者に，対物訴訟もしくは外国での差押えでの，管轄権の利益を付与し，同時にその当事者の仲裁に関する権利を保護することにある。……この章では，原告の申立と本船もしくはその他の財物の差押えが，仲裁に関する合意を強制する手続の最初のステップとなりうる。……「通常の海事訴訟手続に沿って，他の当事者を提訴し，その者の本船もしくはその他の財物の差押えを行うことにより」，海事の訴訟を開始した当事者は，決して仲裁条項を否認しているのではないし，後日仲裁を要求することが妨げられるものでもない。この条項は，明白にその旨を規定している（25 F. Supp. at 665）。

同趣旨の判例として，*Mitsubishi* v. *The Oinoussian Strength*, 1994 U. S. Dist. Lexis 2625（S. D. N. Y., 2 March 1994）事件（もっとも，原告の対物訴訟の訴えは，出訴期限徒過と判断された……）。

たとえ，仲裁条項に仲裁地が London もしくはその他の外国の地が規定されていても，仲裁法第8条の差押え (attachment) またはアレストによって，仲裁手続が開始されることがある (*Andros Compania Maritima* v. *Andre & Cie. S. A.*, 430 F. Supp. 88, 1977 AMC 668 (S. D. N. Y. 1977) 事件，*Atlas Chartering Services Inc.* v. *World Trade Group Inc.*, 453 F. Supp. 861, 1978 AMC 2033 (S. D. N. Y. 1978) 事件；*Paramount Carriers Corp.* v. *Cook Industries Inc.*, 465 F. Supp. 599, 1979 AMC 875 (S. D. N. Y. 1979) 事件を参照)。通常，担保請求訴訟提起前に，契約違反が生じていなければならない。実際の係争がなければ，海事リーエンはまだ存在しないし，本船アレストも時期早尚であろう (*Marubeni America Corp.* v. *The Unity*, 802 F. Supp. 1353, 1993 AMC 141 (D. Md. 1992) 事件を参照)。

この状況において，もっとも重要なことは，仲裁法第8条に基づいて本船差押えまたはアレストが行われるということである。*McCreary Tire & Rubber Co.* v. *CEAT S. p. A.*, 501 F. 2d 1032 (3d Cir. 1974) 事件，*Metropolitan World Tankers Corp.* v. *P. N. Pertambangan Minjakdangas Dumi National*, 1976 AMC 421 (S. D. N. Y. 1976) 事件，*Sanko Steamship Co. Ltd.* v. *Newfoundland Refining Co. Ltd.*, 1976 AMC 417 (S. D. N. Y. 1976)，下記理由で原審維持 1976 AMC 417 (2d Cir. 1976) 事件では，州法に基づいて行われた仲裁前の差押えが無効とされた。最初の二つの事件では，差押えが「外国仲裁判断の承認と執行」に関する条約に違反するとの理由で，無効とされた。*Sanko* 事件では，フォーラム・ノン・コンビニエンスの原則により，差押えが却下された。

正しい実践の問題として，本船アレスト訴訟の訴状では，対物訴訟手続の対象となっている財物を特定するだけでなく，その財物の所有者を特定しなければならない。たとえ本船のみが対物訴訟の被告として訴えられていても，仲裁法第8条により，裁判所は船主に仲裁を強制することとなる (*E. A. S. T. Inc.* v. *Alaia*, 1988 AMC 1396 (E. D. La. 1987) 事件を参照。また，*Industrial y Frutera Colombiana S. A.* v. *The Brisk*, 195 F. 2d. 1015, 1952 AMC 738 (5th Cir. 1952) 事件も参照)。

本船の差押えまたはアレスト前に，仲裁を開始したからと言って，担保を要求する権利は影響をうけない。*Unitramp Ltd.* v. *Mediterranean Brokerage*, 1994 AMC 476 (E. D. La. 1993) 事件，*West of Eng.* v. *McAllister*, 829 F. Supp. 122, 1993 AMC 2559 (E. D. Pa. 1993)，無効の申立が拒絶された 829 F. Supp. 125, 1993 AMC 2563 (E. D. Pa. 1993) 事件，*Siderbulk Ltd.* v. *Nagos Maritime Inc.*, 1993 AMC 2566 (S. D. N. Y. 1992) 事件を参照。ただし，*Continental Chartering and Brokerage* v. *T. J. Stevenson & Co.*, 678 F. Supp. 58, 1988 AMC 617 (S. D. N. Y. 1987) 事件では，反対の結論が判示されている。

担保の提供を裁定する仲裁人の権限

仲裁判断の履行のための担保を得るもう一つの方法は，仲裁人に対して，相手方より担保を提供させるための一部終局裁定を求めることである。もちろん，仲裁人は，当事者に対して担保の提供を命じる権限を有する。商業仲裁人の衡平法上の権限が裁判上広範に認められたのは，*Sperry International Trade Inc.* v. *Government of Israel*, 689 F. 2d 301 (2d Cir. 1982) 事件を起源とする。この事件で第2巡回区裁判所は，係争になっていた米貨1,500万ドルの信用状を第三者預託に寄託するよう命じた仲裁人の命令を是認し，裁判所に本来期待出来ない救済方法を命じた仲裁人の権限を是認したのである (同書306頁)。同様に *Compania Chilena de Navigacion Interociania* v. *Norton, Lilly & Co.*, 652 F. Supp. 1512, 1987 AMC 1565 (S. D. N. Y. 1987) 事件では，仲裁人は被告に米貨123,000ドルの保証金を供託することを命じたが，

それは仲裁人の法的な権限を越えていない，と判断した。*Konkar Maritime Enterprises S. A. v. Compagnie Belge d'Affretement（The Konkar Pioneer）* 668 F. Supp. 267, 1989 AMC 182 (S. D. N. Y. 1987) 事件では，船主のクレームの担保のために，利子の発生する第三者預託口座に米貨202,889.29ドルの預入れを傭船者に命じる仲裁人の判断が認められている。*East Asiatic Co.* と *Transamerican Steamship Corp.（The Camara and Cinchoma）* との間の仲裁 1988 AMC 1086 (S. D. N. Y. 1987) 案件では，船主より申し立てられたクレームを担保するために，各々米貨84,183.62ドルと米貨142,584.66ドルを利子を生む共同の第三者預託口座に預入れを命じる仲裁人の予備的な二つの裁定が認められている。さらに，*Blue Sympathy Shipping Co. v. Serviocean International S. A.,* 1994 AMC 2522 (S. D. N. Y. 1994) 事件では，原告のために傭船者に対して米貨194,796.06ドルを第三者預託口座への預入れを命じ，また傭船者のために原告に対して米貨175,000ドルプラス利子分を金額とする保証状の差入れを要求する仲裁人の判断が認められた。*Southern Seas Navigation Ltd. of Monrovia v. Petroeos Mexicanos of Mexico City（The Messiniaki Floga）,* 606 F. Supp. 692, 1985 AMC 2190 (S. D. N. Y. 1985) 事件では，裁判所は，仲裁裁定が「事実上予備的差止命令を認める」ことになることを了解しながら，傭船者に対し本船に対するリーエン・クレーム通知の撤回命令を出した仲裁人の一部終局裁定を承認した。

　本書の執筆時点では，担保要求を裁定する仲裁人の権限の行使についての明確な指針は確立されていない。担保提供を命じる決定は，事件の特徴を考慮に入れた仲裁人の査定しだいである。担保提供を命ずることは例外的な救済であると考える仲裁人もいるが，他の仲裁人は担保提供を正当化する特別な状況がなくても担保提供を命じている。仲裁人に担保提供が必要であると判断させるための立証の度合，ならびに担保の額が適当であるかどうかは，仲裁人の実務家としての健全な判断に委ねられている。例えば，以下の例を参照。*The Hallborg,* SMA 2639 (Arb. At N. Y. 1990), *The Eurogas,* SMA 3005 (Arb. at N. Y. 1993), *The Liberty Bell Venture,* SMA 3147 (Arb. at N. Y. 1992)；*The Lilliana Dimitrova,* SMA 3075 (Arb. at N. Y. 1994)；*The Bermuda,* SMA 3097 (Arb. at N. Y. 1994) および *The Maaslot,* SMA 3074 (Arb. at N. Y. 1994). 担保提供が拒否された裁定としては，*The Enerchem Avance,* SMA 2907 (Arb. at N. Y. 1992) 事件, *The Cheshire,* SMA 3129 (Arb. at N. Y. 1994) 事件を参照。

　担保提供を命ずる一部終局裁定は，自力執行ができず，相手方が自発的に従わない限り，裁定はすぐには有効とはならない。もし相手側が担保提供命令に従うことを拒否する場合，もう一方の当事者は連邦仲裁法第9条に基づき，裁判所に一部終局裁定の承認を求めることができる。*Compania Chilena,* 652 F. Supp. at 1516-1517 事件，*East Asiatic,* 1988 AMC at 1089-1090 事件，*Blue Sympathy,* 1994 AMC at 2522-2524 事件を参照。最後の事件では，仲裁裁定を承認した命令に傭船者が従わない場合には，裁判所は法廷侮辱と判断し，単に，経済的に担保提供ができないという被告の答弁は，法廷侮辱に対する有効な抗弁にはならない，と注意を促している。

仲裁判断の確認

　仲裁法第9条は仲裁判断の確認につき規定している。しかしながら，仲裁判断の確認は，仲裁合意に裁判所が仲裁判断に踏み入ることができるとの明示の規定がある場合に限られる。ニューヨーク・プロデュース書式においては，この要件は，「裁判所の命令とみなされる (may be made a rule of the Court)」という文言があることによって充たされる。仲裁合

意の中に,このような文言あるいは同じ趣旨の文言が入っていない場合には,仲裁判断を執行するのに不必要な困難が生じる。というのは,そのような規定がなければ,裁判所は,仲裁判断に基づいた判決を下すことができないと考えられているからである(*Varley* v. *Tarrytown Associates Inc.*, 477 F. 2d 208 (2d Cir. 1973); *Splosna Plovba of Piran* v. *Agrelak S. S. Corp.*, 381 F. Supp. 1368 (S. D. N. Y. 1974))。なお,明白な文言で示されていないにもかかわらず,当事者の意図は,仲裁合意により,仲裁判断に基づく判決を認めるものであったと,裁判所が認定した事例もいくつかあった(*I/S Stavborg* v. *National Metal Converters, Inc.*, 500 F. 2d 424 (2d Cir. 1974)事件を参照)。

Daihatsu Motor Co. v. *Terrain Vehicles Inc.*, 13 F. 3d 196 (7th Cir. 1993)事件においては,仲裁合意が摂取している日本商事仲裁協会の規則は,仲裁判断の確認に関し明確に規定してはいないが,裁判所は当事者の行為の全体を評価した結果,当事者は仲裁判断を裁判所に確認させることを意図していた,と判断した。同様に,*Rainwater* v. *National Home Ins. Co.*, 944 F. 2d 190, 194 (4th Cir. 1991)事件では,仲裁に付託する合意のなかに,「まず仲裁に付することが,訴訟開始の前提条件である……」との文言があったが,裁判所はこの文言があっても,仲裁判断の拘束力が損ねられるものではない,と判断した。また,「最終的(final)」というような「魔術的文言」が,仲裁判断が連邦裁判所の確認の対象となるためにどうしても必要なものというわけではなく,「AAA仲裁に訴えるということは,当事者が明示的に反対の趣旨を規定していない限り,その仲裁判断は拘束力を持ち,かつ裁判所の審査の対象にもなりうる,と判断されるであろう」。

仲裁法第9条によらずに,仲裁判断を強制執行することも可能である。その通常の手続は,訴訟を提起し,仲裁判断に基づく略式判決を求めることである。

最終仲裁判断のみが,裁判所の確認の対象となる(*E. B. Michaels* v. *Mariforum Shipping S. A.*, 624 F. 2d 411, 1980 AMC 1901 (2d Cir. 1980)事件)。それゆえ,例えば,責任の有無の点だけを扱い,損害賠償額の算定がまだ行われていない中間裁定は,裁判所の確認の対象にはなりえない。

しかしながら,独立したクレームを最終的に,かつ限定的に取り扱った一部終局裁定もしくは中間裁定は,たとえ残りの部分がまだ仲裁審で審理中だとしても,裁判所での確認の対象となりうる(*Eurolines Shipping Co. S. A.* v. *Metal Transp. Corp.*, 491 F. Supp. 590, 1980 AMC 2445 (S. D. N. Y. 1980))。一部のみ有効な仲裁判断は,その有効な部分が有効でない部分と分離できる場合にのみ,その有効な部分のみ裁判所の確認の対象となりうる。「最終的」と言うためには,仲裁判断が仲裁に付託されたすべての争点を解決していなければならない,という一般原則の例外に関し,*Puerto Rico Maritime Shipping Authority* v. *Star Lines Ltd.*, 454 F. Supp. 368 (S. D. N. Y. 1978)事件のなかで,裁判所は次のように説明している。

　　もし,仲裁判断の一部が有効で,一部が有効でなく,かつ有効な部分のクレームが有効でない部分のクレームから「分離され」,それに「左右されない」ものであれば,仲裁に付託されたクレームを最終的にすべて決着するような仲裁判断がまだ出ていなくても,仲裁判断の有効な部分は裁判所の確認の対象となりうる。

463　*Unimarine S. A.* v. *Interessentslskapet Wind Endeavor*, 1984 AMC 405 (S. D. N. Y. 1981)事件および *Marabueno Compania Naviera S. A.* v. *Cayman Caribbean Carriers*, 1984 AMC 1849 (S. D. N. Y. 1984)事件では,保留された運賃に関し,船主に対し出された一部終局裁定が裁判所の確認の対象となっている。同様に,*Southern Seas Navigation Ltd.* v. *Petroleos Mexica-*

nos, 606 F. Supp. 692, 1985 AMC 2190 (S.D.N.Y. 1985) 事件では，傭船者のクレーム額上限設定の，また傭船者が船主のリベリア船籍登記簿に登録したリーエン金額減額要請の暫定裁定は，裁判所の確認の対象となると判断された。

しかし，裁判所が，一部終局裁定を確認することを拒否する場合，その拒否は即時上訴の対象となる終局的判決ではない。*Liberian Vertex Transports Inc.* v. *Associated Bulk Carriers Ltd.,* 738 F. 2d 85, 1984 AMC 2841 (2d Cir. 1984)。

仲裁判断の確認を求める申請は，仲裁判断が下されてから1年以内に行われる（9 U.S.C. §9）。もっとも1年以内に行わなければ明らかに出訴期限の利益を失うわけではない（*Sverdrup Corp.* v. *WHC Constructors,* 989 F. 2d 148 (4th Cir. 1993)。また，*Kerr McGee Refining Corp* v. *The Triumph,* 924 F. 2d 467 (2d Cir. 1991) 事件も参照）。当事者の双方が米国人（米国法人）でなければ，たとえ仲裁判断が米国で下されても，その仲裁判断は外国における仲裁判断の承認と執行に関する条約（9 U.S.C. §201, *et seq.*）が適用されることとなる。それゆえ，仲裁判断が2人の外国人当事者間で下されるときは，その仲裁判断は9 U.S.C. §207に基づき，仲裁判断後3年以内であれば裁判所で確認することができる（*Bergesen* v. *Joseph Muller Corp.,* 710 F. 2d 928, 1983 AMC 1960 (2d Cir. 1938) 事件を参照）。

仲裁審が一旦最終判断を出してしまうと，それにより職務完了（*functus officio*）となり，もはやその決定を見直すことができなくなる（*Ottley* v. *Shwartzberg,* 819 F. 2d 373, 376 (2d Cir. 1987)，*Proodos Marine Carriers Co.* v. *Overseas Shipping & Logistics,* 578 F. Supp. 207, 211 (S.D.N.Y. 1984)）。同じような趣旨のものとして，*Domino Group* v. *Charlie Parker Mem. Foundation,* 985 F. 2d 417 (8th Cir. 1993) 事件（仲裁人が別の損害賠償の救済方法を裁決するために，仲裁判断の内容を仲裁人が明らかにしようとするのは，職務完了（*functus officio*）の原則に反する。ゆえに，仲裁人の権限を踰越するものとされる）；*Colonial Penn Insur. Co.* v. *Omaha Indemnity Co.,* 943 F. 2d 327 (3d. Cir. 1991) 事件（職務完了（*functus officio*）の原則により，仲裁人が最初の仲裁判断の命令を明らかにすることが妨げられる）。

しかしながら，裁判所は仲裁法により，明らかな数字上の誤りを正す権限を持っている（9 U.S.C. §11）。さらに加えて，仲裁人が不明瞭な，もしくは不完全な，あるいは曖昧な判断をしていると裁判所が考えた場合は，裁判所は，明瞭にするためにその事案を仲裁人に差し戻すことができる（後出546頁の議論を参照）。以下に論ずるとおり，最終仲裁判断を覆す裁判所の権限は，仲裁法によりきわめて慎重に制限されている。

仲裁判断の破棄

「最終判断」

仲裁法第10条には仲裁判断が破棄される場合の理由が列挙されている。仲裁法第9条の規定により，最終判断のみが裁判所の確認の対象になるように，「最終判断」のみが第10条により正しく破棄申立の対象になりうる。

E. B. Michaels v. *Mariforum Shipping S.A.,* 624 F. 2d 411, 1980 AMC 1901 (2d Cir. 1980) 事件で，責任の問題だけを判断し，その他の問題についてはまだ判断がすんでいない「決定と暫定判断」を，傭船者は第10条に基づき破棄する申立を行った。この申立に対し，裁判所は仲裁人の決定が「最終的」なものでないから，この申立は時期尚早であるとの判断を行った。裁判所は次のように述べている。

「最終的」というためには，仲裁判断は仲裁人に付託されたクレームのすべての点につき決定され

ていなければならない。
　一般的に，クレームが完全に判断されているというためには，仲裁人がクレームに関し当事者の責任の問題のみならず，損害賠償の額についても判断を行っていなければならない。

464　同様に，*Kerr-McGee Refining Corp.* v. *The Triumph*, 924 F. 2d 467, 1991 AMC 1051 (2d Cir. 1991), 裁量上告拒絶 502 U. S. 821 (1991) 事件も参照（一部終局裁定は，分離した独立のクレームを最終的に処理していなかった），また *Mobil Oil Indonesia Inc.* v. *Asamera Oil (Indonesia) Ltd.*, 43 N. Y. 2d 276, 281-282, 401 N. Y. S. 2d 186, 187-188 (1977) 事件，*Finagrain Compagnie Commerciale Agricole et Financiere S. A.* v. *Federal Commerce & Navigation (1974) Ltd.*, 80 Civ. 0839 (S. D. N. Y. 3 September 1980) （判決速報）事件，*Golden Eagle Liberia Ltd.* v. *Amoco Transport Company*, 1979 AMC 698 (N. Y. County, Special Term, Part I, 1979) 事件も参照。

　仲裁法のもとでは，地方裁判所は仲裁人による中間判断を吟味し，仲裁手続を監督する権限を有しない。*Compania Panemena Maritima San Gerassimo S. A.* v. *J. E. Hurley Lumber Co.*, 244 F. 2d 286, 1957 AMC 1759 (2d Cir. 1957)。それゆえ，証拠開示手続，召喚状の提出，証拠への異議，その他仲裁を行う上で生じる手続上，実体上の様々な事項についての仲裁人の判断は，それらが最終判断を攻撃する理由を提供する場合を除いて，地方裁判所は審査することができない。一般論として，*Complaint of Koala Shipping & Trading Inc.*, 587 F. Supp. 140 (S. D. N. Y. 1984) 事件を参照。案件を処理するのに仲裁人としての資格，公平さにつき問題がないかどうかについてさえも，最終判断がなされるまで，地方裁判所は審査の対象とすることができない（前出 *E. B. Michaels* v. *Mariforum Shipping S. A.*, 624 F. 2d at 414 n. 4 事件を参照）。また，*Florasynth Inc.* v. *Pickholz*, 750 F. 2d 171, 174 (2d Cir. 1984) 事件を参照）。

　Commonwealth Oil Refining Co. Inc. v. *The Grand Commonwealth*, 1978 AMC 975, 976 (M. D. Fla. 1978) 事件において，裁判所は次のように述べている，

　　ある係争事件につき，一旦，地方裁判所が，仲裁人によって解決されるべきであると決めた場合，仲裁手続が継続中であれば，地方裁判所は一切仲裁人の仕事に干渉できない。もし，干渉が許されるとすれば，仲裁「継続中」に，裁判所を仲裁人の行為を審査できる地位に置くことになる。このことは，仲裁手続を遅らせる駆引きのためのパンドラの箱を開けてしまう。原告は，仲裁判断に対する不満を適当なタイミングで十分に吟味する機会が与えられる。仲裁人のあらゆる判断は，法に従ってこの裁判所の再審理に服することとなる。

「期間の制限」

　9 U. S. C. §12 に基づけば，仲裁判断の取消，訂正もしくは修正を求める申立は，仲裁判断が出されてからもしくは送達されてから 3 ヶ月以内に行わなければならない。

　Florasynth Inc. v. *Pickholz*, 750 F. 2d 171 (2d. Cir. 1984) 事件では，裁判所は，3 ヶ月以内に仲裁判断取消の申立を行わなかった当事者は，仲裁判断の確認を求めてきた相手方に反駁した後で救済を求めることはできない，と判示した。仲裁判断が出て 3 ヶ月以内にその確認を求める申立が行われた場合，そしてそれが仲裁判断の取消を求める申立前に行われた場合，もし取消を求める意思があれば，その当事者はすぐに取消を求める申立を行わなければならない（*The Hartbridge*, 57 F. 2d 672 (2d Cir. 1932) 事件，*Munson S. S. Line* v. *North England S. S. Co.* の件名で裁量上告拒絶 288 U. S. 601 (1933) 事件）。3 ヶ月間という期間の制限は，出訴期限制限の規定と解されている。*Foster* v. *Turley*, 808 F. 2d 38, 41 (10th Cir. 1986) 事件

では、裁判所は、12条の期間の制限は、制定法上の出訴期限の規定の性質を有するから、当事者が放棄すれば、その放棄が認められることとなると述べた（さらに、*Domino Group* v. *Charlie Paker Mem. Foundation*, 985 F. 2d 417（8th Cir. 1993）事件も参照）。

「攻撃の理由」

仲裁法第10条には、仲裁判断の取消を求めることができる場合の理由が列挙してあり、1個の例外を除き、そこで列挙してある事由だけが、仲裁判断に挑戦できる理由となる（*Bell Aerospace Co. Division of Textron Inc.* v. *Local 516*, 500 F. 2d 921（2d Cir. 1974））。仲裁を強く支持する連邦国家の意図があり、議会がその過程で形成される仲裁判断を効果的に攻撃する機会を制限したのは、その理由による。なるほど仲裁判断は有効なものであるとの推定を受ける。その推定を覆し、取消の申立のために当事者に求められる説得責任は非常に重い。*McIlroy* v. *Paine Webber Inc.*, 989 F. 2d 817（5th Cir. 1983）事件を参照（この事件では、仲裁判断の取消を求める申立が、9 U.S.C.第10条に列挙された仲裁判断を攻撃するいずれの理由にも該当しないとして、否定されている）。

仲裁判断の妥当性を争う理由には、次のようなものが含まれている。

　　第10条(a)　仲裁判断が、汚職、詐欺もしくは不公正な方法で得られた場合、

この条項の平明な文言が示しているように、この条項は、賄賂、恐喝、脅迫およびその他の汚職的手段によって得られた仲裁判断を取り消すことを意図している。

Bonar v. *Dean Witter Reynolds Inc.*, 835 F. 2d 1378, 1383（11th Cir. 1988）事件で、第10条(a)によって仲裁判断が取り消される場合に関する3個の基準が示された。

1. 申立人が、明白かつ説得力のある証拠をもって、詐欺を立証しなければならない。
2. 仲裁の前もしくは仲裁手続の期間中に、相当の注意を払っても詐欺が発見できない。
3. 仲裁の取消を求める人間は、詐欺が仲裁の問題と実質的に関連あるものであることを示さなければならない。

Bonar 事件は、次の各事件と同趣旨の判決となっている。*Foster* v. *Turley* 808 F. 2d 38（10th Cir. 1986）, *Karpinnen* v. *Karl Kiefer Machine Co.*, 187 F. 2d 32（2d Cir. 1951）; *Mobil Oil Indonesia Inc.* v. *Asamera Oil（Indonesia）Ltd.*, 487 F. Supp. 63（S. D. N. Y. 1980）および *Newspaper Guild of New York* v. *New York Post Corp.*, No. 32 Civ. 7226（DNE）（S. D. N. Y., 14 July 1983）(Lexis, Genfed library の Dist. file で入手可能)。

「不公正な方法」は、より広い意味を有し、それは仲裁における当事者の一方の行為が、現実に「汚職している」とは言えないが、それにもかかわらず相手方を害するような場合に適用されると言われる。*Drayer* v. *Krasner*, 572 F. 2d 348（2d Cir. 1978）, 裁量上告拒絶 436 U. S. 948（1978）事件では、証券会社の元不平従業員が、不法な雇用関係の終了により被ったと主張する損害賠償を求めて訴訟を提起した。その従業員は、証券詐欺に関わる職務怠慢の廉で解雇された。彼は詐欺に関ったとのことで起訴された。しかし、詐欺に関った他の人間は有罪となったが、この従業員は無罪だった。仲裁において、証券会社は起訴状と詐欺に関った他の人間が有罪となった裁判所の判決を証拠として提出した。仲裁人たちは、これらの書類を証拠として採用するのを拒絶したが、明らかに仲裁人の全員もしくは一部の者がそれらの書類を読んだのである。仲裁判断は、その従業員にとって不利な内容となった。そこで、彼は、仲裁人

が起訴状ならびに裁判所の判決を読んだことが彼に不利益をもたらしたとして，それを理由に仲裁判断の取消を申し立てた。

裁判所は，従業員の仲裁判断取消の申立を拒絶し，一方の当事者が相手側にとり不利な証拠を公然と提出することは「不公正な方法」の範疇には入らないと判断した。しかしながら，裁判所は意図的に，その判断はこの特殊な事案にのみ適用されるものだとして，不利な内容の仲裁判断につながるような非常に偏見を抱かせる証拠を仲裁人が受領することが，第10条(a)の「不公正な方法」と見なされる場合がありうることを否定しなかった。

第10条(a)に基づく，仲裁判断への攻撃がかかわる別の事件で，すなわち Catz American Co. v. Pearl Grange Fruit Exchange Inc., 292 F. Supp 549（S.D.N.Y. 1968）事件を担当した裁判所は，申請者の仲裁拒否がかかわる事件と関連を有するある裁判所の判決を証拠として提出することが「不公正な方法」であるとの主張を拒絶した。その判決で，裁判所は，仲裁拒否の抗弁は，「内容がなく」「ごまかし」であると指摘している。

同様に，National Bulk Carriers Inc. v. Princess Management Co. Ltd., 597 F. 2d 819, 825（2d Cir. 1979）事件も参照。この事件では，示談の提案を示す証拠の採用が，仲裁判断の取消を正当化するような偏見を生じさせてはいない，と裁判所は判示した。

|466| 第10条(b) 仲裁人たちに，もしくは仲裁人のいずれかに明らかな不公平もしくは汚職が存する場合，

この条項では，仲裁判断が攻撃の対象となるには，1人もしくは複数の仲裁人に「偏向の様子」があるというだけでは不十分である。むしろ，実際に偏向があったとの立証が必要となる。International Produce Inc. v. A/S Rosshavet, 638 F. 2d 548, 1981 AMC 472（2d Cir. 1981），裁量上告拒絶 451 U.S. 1017（1981）事件では，座礁により本船 Ross Isle 号の船主と傭船者間で係争が生じた。双方が各々1人ずつ仲裁人を選任し，その選任された2人の仲裁人が3番目の仲裁人かつ議長として Hammond Cederholm 氏を選んだ。この仲裁案件では，船主の代理人にはA法律事務所が，傭船者の代理人にはB法律事務所がそれぞれ就任した。Cederholm 氏は，船主とも傭船者とも経済的な利害関係はなかった。しかし，彼は当事者が異なる別の係争事件に直接関わっており，その事件では，A法律事務所とB法律事務所が逆の立場で再度対立していた。Cederholm 氏は，彼が雇われている仲立業会社の顧客のために，第2の事件に直接関わっており，その仲立業会社の法務代理人がA法律事務所であった。その係争事件での彼の役割は，A法律事務所による直接の尋問で証言を行うために召喚され，続いてB法律事務所弁護士の反対尋問を受けることであった。

Ross Isle 事件の仲裁判断は，A法律事務所の依頼人にとって有利なものであった。そこで，B法律事務所の依頼人は，第2の事件での Cederholm 氏とA法律事務所との関係により公平さが担保されていないように思われ，かつその推定が働くとして，その仲裁判断の無効を申し立てた。地方裁判所は，その主張に賛成し，仲裁判断を無効とした。

しかしながら，控訴審はその地方裁判所の判断を覆し，単に偏向の様子があるというだけでは，仲裁判断を無効にするのには十分でない，むしろ実際に偏向があったとの立証が必要であると判示した。

「実際の偏向」があったかどうかの立証責任は非常に重いものである。事実，Merit Ins. Co. v. Leatherby Ins. Co., 714 F. 2d 673, 681（7th Cir. 1983），裁量上告拒絶 464 U.S. 1009（1983）事件において，裁判所は，「もちろん，実際の偏向があるかもしれないが，証明するのは不可能である」と述べている。表向き中立な仲裁人が，一方の当事者に肩入れしているとの

偏向を認めるようなことはほとんどないであろう。偏向の立証は非常に難しいことを認識しながら, *Merit Ins. Co.* 事件で, 裁判所は, 第10条(b)の意味する「明白な偏向」があったというには, 「平均的に正直な人間が偏向があるのではないかと合理的に疑いを抱くような状況であること」を示すことだと, 結論している。しかしながら, 裁判所は「そのような状況であると言うには, 偏向が推論できることを強く示さなければならない」と注意している。

同じような方法が, *Morelite Const. Corp.* v. *New York City District Council Carpenters Benefit Funds*, 748 F. 2d 79, 84 (2d Cir. 1984) 事件でも採用されている。この事件で, 裁判所は「道理をわきまえた人間が, 仲裁人が仲裁の一方の当事者に偏向しているとの結論を出すような場合」には「明白な偏向」がある, と述べている。

Morelite 事件では, 仲裁人が一方の当事者（会社）の副社長の息子であり, この場合, 裁判所は仲裁判断を無効とした。裁判所は, 親子関係のみで,「明白な偏向」を示すのに十分であると判断した。親と子の関係がどれほど緊密であったか, 仲裁に発展した係争について彼らの意見がどの程度違っていたか, といった点をまったく問うことなく, 裁判所は次のように結論を出した。

> それ以上知らなくても, われわれは, 子供は父親に対しより忠実であり, 父親のほうに傾き, また父親のために偏頗であるとの, 強い心証をもつ。われわれは, そのような不公正と考えられる事由に拠った仲裁判断を本当に是認することはできない (748 F.2d at 84)。

同趣旨の判決として, *Peoples Sec. Life Ins.* v. *Monumental Life Ins.*, 991 F. 2d 141 (4th Cir. 1993) 事件。*Standard Tankers (Bahamas) Co. Ltd.* v. *The Akti*, 438 F. Supp. 153, 1978 AMC 181 (E.D.N.C. 1977) 事件もまた参照。この事件で, 裁判所は,「明白な偏向となるには, 明白な非行, 明白な証拠, 明白な不公平が存在することが要求される」と判示している。

Commonwealth Coating Corp. v. *Continental Casualty Co.*, 393 U.S. 145 (1968) 事件では, 仲裁人側に「明白な偏向」があるとして, 仲裁判断が無効とされた。この事例では, 仲裁人は, 勝利した当事者にコンサルト業務を4年以上も提供し, 約米貨12,000ドルの収入を得ており, さらに彼が仲裁を行っている係争事件に関してさえも, コンサルト業務を提供していたのである。これらの事実は敗訴した当事者には開示されていなかった。裁判所は彼がこれらの事実を開示しなかったことにより仲裁判断は無効にすべきだと判示した。この判決から推論できるのは, 仲裁人が仲裁の当事者とかなりの仕事上の付き合いをして実質的な利害関係をもっている場合, その仲裁人はその事実を相手側に開示する義務を負い, もしそれを開示しなければ仲裁判断を出すときに明白な偏向があるとして, 異議を受ける危険があるということである。

Schmitz v. *Zilveti*, 20 F. 3d 1043 (9th Cir. 1994) 事件では, 仲裁人に「明らかに偏向」があるとして, 仲裁判断が無効とされた。申立の無効を判断するに際し, 第9巡回区裁判所は, 同裁判所にとって, まったく初めてとの印象を与える係争問題として開示を行っていない案件, *Commonwealth Coatings* の判例の適用方法を決定する必要があった。開示されていない事実が, 偏向しているとの合理的な印象を与える場合, 明白な偏向があるとする *Commonwealth Coatings* 判例の基準を採用したその他の裁判所と同様に, 第9巡回区裁判所は, 仲裁人の所属する法律事務所が35年間で少なくとも19件以上の事件について, 被上訴人の親会社を弁護していた事実があった場合, 仲裁人自身がその事実をきちんと把握しておくために相当の努力をしておくべきだったという NASD Code（全国証券業協会規約）上の義務を果たしていない, と判示した。仲裁人は実際その事実を知らなかったが, その事実を知っていたとの推定を受けた。その推定および矛盾点の存在により, 仲裁人が仲裁の当事者に知らしめなかったことが明

白な偏向があったとの裁判所の判断をもたらした。*Middlesex Mut Ins. Co.* v. *Levine*, 675 F. 2d 1197 (11th Cir. 1982), *Sanko S. S. Co.* v. *Cook Indus Inc.* 495 F. 2d 1260 (2d Cir. 1973), *Sheet Metal Wkrs. Int'l Ass'n, Local 420* v. *Kinney Air Cond. Co.*, 756 F. 2d 742, 746 (9th Cir. 1985), *Toyota of Berkeley* v. *Automobile Salesmen's Union*, Local 1095, 834 F. 2d 751, 755-756 (9th Cir. 1987), 裁量上告拒絶 486 U. S. 1043, 後に修正 856 F. 2D 1572 (9th Cir. 1988) の各事件を参照。

さらに，*Sun Refining & Marketing Co.* v. *Statheros Shipping Corp.* 間の仲裁，761 F. Supp. 293, 1991 AMC 1874 (S. D. N. Y. 1991), 理由を付さず原審維持 948 F. 2d 1277, 1992 AMC 1216 (2d Cir. 1991) 事件を参照。この事案では，仲裁人の会社がこの事件の当事者と，まだ係争中の別の事件で，仲裁を行っていた。裁判所は，道理をわきまえた人間であれば，その忌避された仲裁人は公平ではなかったと判断するだろうし，それゆえ仲裁判断は無効であるとの結論を出した。

Miseroachi & Co. S. p. A. v. *Peavy Int'l Inc.*, 78 Civ. 1571 (S. D. N. Y. 15 September 1978) 事件では，仲裁人の会社が一方の当事者から合計米貨41,073.33ドルのコミッションを受領していたことより，その仲裁人が下した判断が無効とされた。裁判所は，次のように述べている。

　……仲裁人が仲裁の当事者の一方からこの事件で明らかになったような収入を得ていたとすれば，(1)その事実は開示されなければならないし，(2)もう一方の当事者に不服を申し立てられれば，その不服の申立が放棄されるか，もしくはそれが取るに足らない事項だとされない限り，仲裁人はその資格を喪失する。

また，さらに *Transmarine Seaways Corp.* v. *Marc Rich & Co. A. G.*, 480 F. Supp. 352, 1979 AMC 1496 (S. D. N. Y. 1978), 理由を付さず原審維持 614 F. 2d 1291, 1979 AMC 2906 (2d Cir. 1980), 裁量上告拒絶 445 U. S. 930 (1980) 事件を参照。この事件では，仲裁人のうちの1人を雇っている会社が，この事件とは関係のない案件で一方の当事者を訴えた会社の代理人として行動したことにその当事者が苦情を訴え，仲裁判断の無効を申し立てたが，裁判所はその申立を拒絶した。裁判所は，仲裁人自らのその当事者との関係も，それが当然には仲裁判断の無効には繋がらない，と判断した。

Sunkist Soft Drinks Inc. v. *Sunkist Growers Inc.*, 10 F. 3d 753 (11th Cir. 1993) 事件では，米国仲裁協会の規則を摂取している当事者間の契約では，「中立」な仲裁人と「当事者が選任した」仲裁人の差異を認めている。後者にはより緩和された義務とそれほど厳しくない事実開示規則が適用される。裁判所は，仲裁人は選任してくれた当事者をひいきするかもしれないということは，仲裁判断を覆す十分な理由にはならない，と判断した。さらに，*National Shipping Co. of Saudi Arabia* と *Transamerican Steamship Corp.* 間の仲裁，1993 AMC 684 (S. D. N. Y. 1992) 事件，*Employers Ins.* v. *National Union Fire Ins.*, 933 F. 2d 1481 (9th Cir. 1991) 事件を参照。

　第10条(c)十分な理由が示されたにもかかわらず，仲裁人が審理の延期を拒否したり，論争点に関連のある実質的な証拠の審理を拒否するような不当な管理を行い，もしくは仲裁人が一方の当事者の権利を害するようなその他の不公正を行い仲裁人が有罪となる場合。

　すべての論点に関する当事者の主張を聴き，証拠を提出させる公平かつ十分な機会を双方当

事者に対して与えるような手続を，仲裁人が取り進めなければならない点が，きわめて重要である (*Standard Tankers (Bahamas) Co. Ltd.* v. *The Akti*, 438 F. Supp. 153, 1978 AMC 181 (E. D. N. C. 1977) 事件)。仲裁法第10条(c)では，仲裁の取り進め方により一方の当事者の権利が害される場合，仲裁判断が無効になる可能性があることを規定している。

Totem Marine Tug & Barge Inc. v. *North Amerian Towing Inc.*, 607 F. 2d 649, 1980 AMC 1961 (5th Cir. 1979) 事件では，仲裁人が一方当事者の法廷弁護士だけと一方的な連絡を行い，それが他方の当事者の権利を害したとして，仲裁判断が無効とされた。仲裁人は，傭船者の不当な解約による船主の損害賠償を裁定し，船主の傭船料喪失分を基に損害額の算定を行った。仲裁審理手続の終了近い時点で，傭船者の法廷弁護人に伝えることなく，船主の法廷弁護人に電話で接触し，本船の収入を確認した。電話をした理由は，すべての仲裁人が損害賠償につき了知しているものの，各々の仲裁人がすべて違った数字の賠償額を書いていたためである。船主の法定代理人が示した数字は，仲裁人たちが思っていた数字のどれとも同じものではなかったが，仲裁審は船主の法定代理人の示した数字の賠償額を採用し，それを仲裁判断に挿入したのであった。裁判所は，明らかに損害額そのものが争点になっており，仲裁審が船主の法廷弁護人だけと一方的に接触したことは傭船者の権利を害する不公正なもので，仲裁法第10条(c)により，仲裁判断の無効を正当化するにたる，と判示した。

Cofinco Inc. v. *Bakrie & Bros. N. V.*, 395 F. Supp. 613 (S. D. N. Y. 1975) 事件でも，仲裁判断が無効とされた。この事件は，生コーヒー豆の売買契約のもとでの係争に関連したもので，生コーヒー豆協会の規則に基づき，仲裁に付託された。この規則では，最初に3人の仲裁人による仲裁審で審理され，その仲裁判断はさらに5人の仲裁人からなる仲裁審に上訴できることとなっていた。最初の審理において，申立人はクレームに関する一部の証拠を提出したのみであった。これに対し，被申立人は，本件申立はすでに出訴期限を過ぎていると，入口での反論を行ったが，本案についての証拠は提出しなかった。3人仲裁審は，本案審理を一時中断し，まず出訴期限の点につき審理することとし，後に，被申立人の出訴期限の主張を認めた。そこで，申立人は5人仲裁審に上訴したところ，それは3人仲裁審の出訴期限に関する判断を覆した。さらに本件申立の証明に資する申立人が提出した不十分な証拠のみを使って，5人仲裁審は申立人の主張を認める判断を下した。被申立人は，仲裁判断を無効とする申立を行い，そこで本案審理で申立に対する抗弁の十分な機会を与えられなかったと主張した。裁判所は，被申立人の主張を支持し，仲裁判断を無効とした。裁判所によれば，5人仲裁審が被申立人側の反論に関し，十分にその主張を聴くことを拒否したとして，そのやり方は，9 U. S. C. §10 (c)に抵触し，したがって仲裁審は不公正な行為を行った，という。裁判所は次のように述べた。

　　上訴を受けた仲裁審が，証拠を審理することを明らかに「拒否」したことは，まさに怠慢により無視する行為を行ったと同じである。審理を受けるという基本的な権利が甚だしく完全に妨害された (395 F. Supp. at 615)。

Chevron Transport Corp. v. *Astro Vencedor Compania Naviera S. A.*, 300 F. Supp. 179, 1969 AMC 1582 (S. D. N. Y. 1969) 事件を参照。この事件では，仲裁人が一方当事者から入手した航海日誌を他方の当事者に見せなかったという過ちを犯したとして，仲裁判断は無効とされた。*Katz* v. *Uvegi*, 18 Misc. 2d 576, 583, 187 N. Y. S. 2d 511, 518 (Sup. Ct. 1959)，原審維持 11 A. D. 2d 773, 205 N. Y. S. 2d 972 (App. Div. 1960) 事件では，次のように判示された。

仲裁人は，別段の定めがなければ，一方に偏した審理を行いあるいは各々の当事者が不在の場合証拠を受けることができない。

　前出 Standard Tankers (Bahamas) Co. Ltd. v. The Akti 事件では，船主は，仲裁審が重要参考人への2度目の反対尋問を許可しなかったことは，公正なる審理の機会を奪うものだと主張した。裁判所は，船主の仲裁判断無効の申立を却下し，「仲裁判断を無効にしなければならない手続上の誤りというには，全体としてみて，仲裁審の行動が被申立人の公正な審理の機会を奪うものでなければならない」と述べた (1978 AMC at 185)。
The Konkar Pioneer, 668 F. Supp. 267, 271-272 (S. D. N. Y. 1987) 事件を参照。

　第10条(d)仲裁人が自らの権限を踰越した場合，もしくは自らの権限を不完全に行使した結果，当該事案に対する相互的，最終的，かつ明確な裁定がなされなかった場合，

　第10条(d)に規定されている曖昧な基準は，その基準を解釈した判例である程度平明な意味を与えられている。

「仲裁人が自らの権限を踰越した場合」

　仲裁人に付託されていないクレームに関し，仲裁人が判断を下す場合，その仲裁判断は無効とされる。ただし，この条項のこの部分は非常に厳格に解釈されてきており，仲裁付託合意の範囲につき疑義がある場合は，できる限り範囲内とする方向で決せられている。Andros Compania Maritima S. A. v. Marc Rich & Co. A. G., 579 F. 2d 691, 703 (2d Cir. 1978) 事件において，裁判所は次のように述べている。

　9 U.S.C. 第10条(d)に規定する仲裁人がその権限を越えた場合，特に，まず第1に，適切に付託されたと全員が認める係争問題を正しく判断していないとの疑義を仲裁人が受け，権限踰越というその文言の適用が主張されるような場合において，われわれは首尾一貫して，仲裁判断を無効にする仲裁法の権限をもっとも狭く解釈してきた。

　Peoples Sec. Life Ins. v. Monumental Life Ins., 991 F. 2d 141 (4th Cir. 1993) 事件に関し，仲裁では，3年間はお互いの代理店の引き抜きを禁止するとの合意を破ったとして Monumental は Peoples Security に米貨9,424,651ドルを賠償せよ，との判断が下された。仲裁判断は地方裁判所に上訴されたが，地方裁判所はこの仲裁判断を無効とすることを拒否した。この事件は，その地方裁判所の命令と判決を不服として，控訴裁判所に上訴されたものである。Monumental は，仲裁人たちの1人が「明らかに偏向がある」との理由で，その判断は破棄されるべきであり，Monumental が不公正競争による不法行為の責任を負うべきで，損害の3倍の賠償と仲裁判断までの期間に対する7パーセントの利息をつけた賠償額を命ずる判断を下した仲裁人たちは，仲裁人としての権限を越えていると，主張した。第4巡回区裁判所は，販売代理店を支持する判決を維持した。第4巡回区裁判所は，その判決を出すに際し，以下の4点の認定を行った。すなわち，(1)実際に偏向があったとの証拠がない。(2)仲裁の範囲には，制定法に基き3倍賠償を含むNorth Carolina 州不公正取引慣行法による不公正な競争によるクレームも入っている。(3)仲裁判断は，仲裁および仲裁人の権限の範囲を逸脱していない。(4)仲裁判断の賠償部分のみに裁定前の期間につき，7パーセントの利息が加算されるのは，法律の範囲内であった。

同種の事例として，*Lyeth* v. *Chry isler Corp.*, 929 F. 2d 891, 900 (2d Cir. 1991) 事件がある。

この章の始めの部分でも述べたように，仲裁は当事者間の合意の産物である。そして，*Western Electric Co. Inc.* v. *Communication Workers of America, AFL-CIO*, 450 F. Supp. 876, 881 (S. D. N. Y. 1978)，理由を付さず原審維持 591 F. 2d 1333 (2d Cir. 1978) 事件において，裁判所は次のように述べている。

|470| 仲裁人の権限は当事者の合意によってその範囲が定められる。当事者が提起する問題が仲裁人の管轄権を設定するとともにその限界を画する。仲裁人がその管轄権の範囲内で行動したかどうかの判定の義務は審理する裁判所にある。

仲裁が，付託合意に従って行われる場合，その合意は仲裁審が判断すべきクレームを明示し，仲裁手続の範囲を定めることとなる。New York における海事仲裁では，まず当事者たちが仲裁付託合意書に署名することが慣例となっており，その仲裁付託合意書には係争の概略が示され，傭船契約の仲裁条項が摂取される。しかしながら，傭船契約に仲裁条項があれば，その条項の存在のみで，その条項に規定する係争について，当事者は仲裁に付託しなければならない義務を負っている。この状況では，仲裁人の権限は，仲裁判断を求めて仲裁人に付託されたクレームの陳述書によって決定されることとなる。

Yasuda Fire & Marine Ins. v. *Continental Cas. Co.*, 37 F. 3d 345, 351 (7th Cir. 1994) 事件を参照。この事件で，第7巡回区裁判所は，仲裁審が安田火災に最終仲裁裁定の結果がでるまでの暫定担保として米貨2,549,660ドルの信用状を差し入れるよう命じたことに関し，それを命じた仲裁人の権限は，契約の本旨を源としており，仲裁審に付与された権限を逸脱するものではない，と判示した。*Flender Corp.* v. *Techna-Quip Co.*, 953 F. 2d 273 (7th Cir. 1992) 事件は，販売代理店契約を不法に解約したとして，販売代理店がメーカーを訴えた仲裁を，そのメーカーが止めさせようとして起こした訴訟である。そのメーカーは，その係争が仲裁に付託されるべきかを争い，かつ仲裁判断自体についても争った。地方裁判所は，仲裁条項の広い文言が，販売者の法的組織の変化に関連する係争およびクレームを含んでいると判断したが，第7巡回区裁判所はこの地方裁判所の判断を正しいものと認めた。さらに，*Warth Line* v. *Merinda Marine*, 1992 AMC 1406 (S. D. N. Y. 1991) 事件をも参照。この事件では，裁判所は，航海実績が予定以下であることに関する係争は，適切に仲裁に付託することができ，仲裁人の判断に委ねられるべきものであったし，仲裁人はその問題を判断する際，権限を逸脱していなかった，と判断した。

Totem Marine Tug & Barge Inc. v. *North American Towing Inc.*, 607 F. 2d 649, 1980 AMC 1961 (5th Cir. 1979) 事件では，仲裁人は，Totem が不法に傭船契約を解除した，と判断した。North American は，Totem が合意された港で，本船の返船を怠ったとして，米貨45,000ドルの損害賠償を求めた。このクレームには本船を戻す費用も含まれていた。ただし，このクレームでは，North American は残りの傭船期間の傭船料を損害賠償として請求しているわけではなかった。ところが，仲裁審は，North American がその傭船料までも損害賠償として受領できるとする判断を下した。そこで，Totem は，仲裁人たちは付託されていない事項にまで判断を下すという，自らの権限を逸脱しているとの理由で，裁定の無効を申し立てた。

裁判所は，仲裁人達は自らの権限を逸脱して，未払傭船料に関する損害賠償を命じた，との Totem の主張に賛成した。裁判所は，North American から付託されたクレームの陳述書が

未払の傭船料には何も触れていないし、当事者による摘要書も未払傭船料に関するクレームには何も触れていなかった、と認定した。さらに、損害賠償のクレームは「債務不履行クレームの一般的範囲と当然にからみ合っている」との主張も拒絶した。

The Matter of Cephalonian Shipping Co. S. A., 1979 AMC 1451 (S. D. N. Y. 1979) 事件においても、仲裁人たちは仲裁人の権限を逸脱していると判示された。この事件では、当事者はまず示談合意書の有効性と実効性に特定された問題を仲裁人に判断してもらい、すべての損害賠償の問題はその後の付託に委ねるとの意向であったのだが、仲裁人たちは損害の軽減を怠っているかどうかの問題の判断をしたのである。このような理由で、地方裁判所は、仲裁人たちの暫定判断を無効とした。

しかしながら、もしその問題を判断するのにその他の法律もしくは事実の問題を判断する必要がある場合には、仲裁人は特定の問題を超えて判断を下す権限がある。Federal Commerce & Navigation Co. v. Kanematsu-Gosho Ltd., 457 F. 2d 387, 1972 AMC 946 (2d Cir. 1972) 事件では、主たる傭船契約は10航海を規定していた。最初の2航海が実行されず、係争が生じた。当事者間で、仲裁人には、最初の2航海の不履行に関する争いを判断してもらうのか、それとも主たる傭船契約自体の有効性を判断してもらうのかに関し、合意ができていなかった。結局、最終的には船主のとった様々な行為により主たる傭船契約が無効になったかどうかの争点を仲裁人に判断させることで、当事者間の合意ができた。それにもかかわらず、仲裁人は主たる傭船契約がまだ有効であるかという点と、最初の2航海の取消の効果につき、判断を示した。そこで、船主は、仲裁人が自らの権限を逸脱したとして、仲裁判断の無効を申し立てた。

裁判所は、仲裁判断を支持した。仲裁人に付託された主たる傭船契約の現有効性に関する問題を解決するためには、仲裁人はどうしても船主が最初の2航海の取消に立ち至った事情を考慮せざるを得なかった、と裁判所は判断した。その判断の理由として、裁判所は、仲裁人が主たる問題に判断を下すには、その付属する問題も判断しなければならない事実を、船主は知らされていたことを挙げている。裁判所によれば、「仲裁人は、付託された問題を決定するために必要であれば、いかなる法律もしくは事実問題についても考慮する権限がある」という (457 F. 2d at 389)。

さらに裁判所は、仲裁人の権限を制限することにより、仲裁人がその他の事情を考慮することを排除して、自分に付託された狭い範囲の問題を有か無の問題として扱うことを要求されることは、不適当であるとの見解を示した。そうすることは、取引実務の知識が仲裁人としての資格を与えているのであるから、仲裁人にとり適切かつ公平と考えられる方法による和解の権限を仲裁人から奪うことになろう、との見解を裁判所は示した (457 F. 2d at 390)。

前出 The Matter of Cephalonian Shipping Co., S. A. 事件に関し、次のように言っている。

仲裁判断が、実際にもしくは必然的に仲裁人に付託された問題の解決を示している限り、もしくはそれらの問題の妥協による解決を示している限り、その判断は是認されるに足るものである。

Kerr-McGee Refining Corp. v. The Triumph, 924 F. 2d 467 (2d Cir. 1991) 事件を参照。この事件では、船主が不法な貨物の流用をしたことにつき、仲裁人は RICO に基づき3倍の懲罰賠償の判断を下したが、第2巡回区裁判所は、仲裁人は自らの権限を逸脱していない、と判断した（訳者注：RICO は RACKETEER INFLUENCED AND CORRUPT ORGANIZATIONS ACT の略語）。さらにまた、Kanuth v. Prescott, Ball & Turben Inc., 949 F. 2d 1175 (D. C. Cir. 1991) 事件を参照。この事件では、仲裁人は、雇用者が不法に雇用契約を解約したとして、被雇用者のために米貨38,233,079ドルを支払うべきであるとの判断を下し、それを裁

判所は認めた。

　The Machitis, 1978 AMC 1120 (S. D. N. Y. 1978) 事件では，不可抗力の条項につき，その文言が非常に明白で解釈の必要がないとの主張があったにもかかわらず，その不可抗力条項の解釈を仲裁人が行った。しかしそのことで仲裁人は権限を逸脱してはいない，と裁判所は判断した。

　The Evryalos, 1980 AMC 296 (S. D. N. Y. 1979) 事件では，特別の言葉で表現され，提示された問題に，仲裁人が答を出さなかったにもかかわらず，裁判所は仲裁判断を支持した。

　The Konkar Pioneer, 668 F. Supp. 267 (S. D. N. Y. 1987) 事件では，仲裁人は，傭船者が支払を拒んだ争いのある傭船料分につき，傭船者にその分を利子を生む共同の口座に預けるよう命令したが，裁判所は仲裁人にはそう命ずる権限がある，と判断した。裁判所によれば，仲裁付託合意書には，仲裁人に共同の口座をつくらせる権限があるとの明確な規定はなかったが，仲裁人には共同の口座に金の預託を命ずることができる暗黙の権限がある，という。

　Sun Ship Inc. v. *Matson Navigation Co.*, 785 F. 2d 59 (3d Cir. 1986) 事件では，仲裁人はPennsylvania 州法で規定された法定利息を適用せず，プライムレートを用いて利息の支払を命ずる判断を下したが，このやり方が仲裁人の権限を逸脱しているとの主張を，裁判所は，取るに足らない浅薄な反論として拒絶した。

　Gov't of India v. *Cargill Inc.*, 867 F. 2d 130 (2d Cir. 1989) 事件では，仲裁人が仲裁判断の期日を延ばす裁量権を行使したことに対して，裁判所は，それは仲裁人の権限逸脱ではない，と判示した。

|472| 「……相互的，最終的，かつ明確な仲裁判断」

　もし，付託された問題につき，仲裁判断が「最終的」かつ「明確」でなければ，その判断は無効とされることがある。例えば，*Confinco Inc.* v. *Bakrie & Bros. N. V.*, 395 F. Supp. 613, 616 (S. D. N. Y. 1975) 事件では，仲裁人が明確な金額を示さなかったため，その仲裁判断は無効とされた。仲裁人は，明確な金額を示すことなく，単にいろいろと「発生した費用」と「平均プライムレート」の利息を請求者は回収することができるとの裁定を下した。裁判所は次のように述べている。

　　　仲裁手続の目的は，明確な金額であったし，その金額である (395 F. Supp. at 616)。

　Flender Corp. v. *Techna-Quip Co.*, 953 F. 2d 273, 280 (7th Cir. 1992) 事件を参照。この事件では，裁判所は仲裁人の判断が最終的かつ明確でなかったとの理由からそれを覆すべきだとする主張を拒絶した。その理由は，仲裁人は，「彼に付託されたすべてのクレームに関し結論を出しており，後は販売代理店に払うべき金額の補助的な計算方法のみを地方裁判所に委ねているだけであった」ことを裁判所が認定したからである。

　しかしながら，裁判所は，一般的には，仲裁判断の内容を明確にする機会をつくるために，事件を仲裁人に差し戻す権限を行使することを好む。*Americas Ins. Co.* v. *Seagull Compania Naviera S. A.*, 744 F. 2d. 64, 67 (2d Cir. 1985) 事件では，裁判所は，曖昧な仲裁判断は何を執行してもらいたいのかを裁判所が知ることができるように仲裁人に差し戻すべきであると述べた。同じ理由で，*Olympia & York Florida Equity Corp.* v. *Gould*, 776 F. 2d 42 (2d Cir. 1985) 事件でも，仲裁判断が仲裁人に差し戻されている。しかし，*Ottley* v. *Schwartzberg*, 819 F. 2d 373 (2d Cir. 1987) 事件では，裁判所は，仲裁審監視者に仲裁判断に従わせる目的で仲裁審に差し戻すことは不適当であると判示した。

明らかな法の無視

　第10条の(a)から(d)までに列挙された理由に加え、「明らかに法を無視」しているか、「不合理」的に仲裁判断が下された場合、その判断は無効とされるということは、一般に容認されている原則のようである。裁判所がそのように述べている事例は多い。例えば、*Wilko* v. *Swan*, 346 U.S. 427, 436-437 (1953) 事件を参照。この事件で、最高裁は適用法を「明らかに無視」した仲裁判断は、見直されなければならない旨を示した。その他 *Andros Compania Maritima S. A.* v. *Marc Rich & Co. A. G.*, 579 F. 2d 691, 704 (2d Cir. 1978) 事件、*Sobel* v. *Hertz, Warner & Co.*, 469 F. 2d 1211, 1214 (2d Cir. 1972) 事件および *San Martine Compania de Nav. S. A.* v. *Saquenay Term. Ltd.*, 293 F. 2d 796 (9th Cir. 1961) 事件を参照。しかし、*Robbins* v. *Day*, 954 F. 2d 679 (11th Cir. 1992)、裁量上告拒絶—U.S.—, 113 S. Ct. 201, 121 L. Ed 143 (1992) 事件を参照（この事件では、「明らかなる法の無視」を理由とした仲裁判断無効の申立が拒絶された。第11巡回区裁判所は、いまだこの基準を採用していない）。

　この原則は、*Brotherhood of Railroad Trainmen* v. *Central of Georgia Co.*, 415 F. 2d 403, 411-412 (5th Cir. 1969) 事件の判決で、次のように要約されている。

　　仲裁の関連では、「理由付けと事実に根拠のない」仲裁判断は、権限を逸脱した、あるいは仲裁審の管轄する範囲を逸脱しているものになる。仲裁の結果が「理由付けと事実に根拠」を持たなければならないことは、論理的に言えば、仲裁判断が契約の文言もしくは目的から引き出されなければならないことを意味するものである。

　第2巡回区控訴裁判所は、*Merrill Lynch Pierce Fenner & Smith Inc.* v. *Bobker*, 808 F. 2d 930 (2d Cir. 1986) 事件において、この問題に対する歓迎される明確化の基準を持ち出してきた。仲裁人が証券法を「明らかに無視し」たとして、地方裁判所は、証券の問題に関する仲裁判断を無効とした。控訴裁判所は、その地方裁判所の判断を破棄して、次のように述べた。

　　この理由の範囲については、これまで一度も定義されたことはないが、法律に関する間違いもしくは誤解以上のものを意味していることは明らかである。そして、その間違いは明白で、仲裁人となるべき通常の人間ならば容易にかつ直ちに気づくことができるようなものでなければならない。さらに、「無視する」との文言は、仲裁人が適用される法の原則の存在を十分に認識していながらも、あえてそれを無視すると決意したか、その原則にまったく配慮しなかった、ということを意味している (808 F. 2d at 993)。

　紛争を解決するためのより好ましい方法として、仲裁を尊重していこうという方針がよく言われるが、裁判所は明らかにこの考え方に添おうとしていた。この考え方では、裁判所が再審理する範囲はきわめて限られてくるし、明白な無視を主張する者は、仲裁人が「きちんと定義され、率直で、明確に」適用されるべき法律を無視していることを、証明するという非常に重い立証責任を負うこととなる。808 F. 2d at 934. 後に *Gov't of India* v. *Cargill Inc.*, 867 F. 2d 130 (2d Cir. 1989) 事件で、裁判所は、同じ法則を適用している。

　この理由に基づく異議申立が成功する要件が、いくつかの判例で示されている。例えば、*The Machitis*, 1978 AMC 1120 (S.D.N.Y. 1978) 事件で、裁判所は次のように述べている。

　　当裁判所は、仲裁人が行う契約書の解釈が根本的に合理的なものであったかどうかが、実質的な

問題であると考えている……。結果が非合理的なものでない限り，仲裁人は事実に則して法を自由に解釈することができる。再審理を行う裁判所は，仲裁人がどのように契約を解釈したか，その解釈に縛られることとなる。……そして，裁判所は，仲裁人が付託の範囲を超えていなければ，事実認定や法の適用の間違いもしくは契約の解釈の誤りを理由に，仲裁人の判断を無効にはしない（1978 AMC at 1123）。

I/S Stavborg v. *National Metal Converters Inc.*, 500 F. 2d 424（2d Cir. 1974）事件では，裁判所は，「契約につき，明らかに誤った解釈を行って」，仲裁人は判断を下したと認定したが，その解釈が「不合理的」なものではなかったので，仲裁判断を覆す理由にはならない，と判断した。裁判所によれば，

訂正しなければならない仲裁人の法の誤謬がいかなるものであれ，単純な契約の誤った解釈は，その中には入らない（500 F. 2d at 432）。

W. K. Webster & Co. v. *American Pres. Lines Ltd.*, 32 F. 3d 665（2d Cir. 1994）事件（貨物クレームに関し，貨物の引渡時期を特定していないが，そのことは，仲裁審が明らかに法を無視したことを示すものではない，とされた），*Folkways Music Publishers Inc.* v. *Weiss*, 989 F. 2d 108（2d Cir. 1993）事件，*Advest Inc.* v. *McCarthy*, 914 F. 2d 6, 10-11（1st Cir. 1990）事件，*Elite Inc.* v. *Texaco Panama*, 777 F. Supp. 189, 1992 AMC 698（S. D. N. Y. 1991）事件（この事件では，仲裁人が故意に明らかに適用法規を無視したことを示す立証責任を果たしていない，とされた），*U. S. Offshore* v. *Seabulk Offshore*, 1991 AMC 616（S. D. N. Y. 1990）事件（たとえ，仲裁人が誤りを犯していたとしても，仲裁判断を無効にするほどのものではなかった，とされた）を参照。

しかしながら，仲裁人は，ある特定の紛争を規制する法律を適用すべく努力する義務を負っていることは定着していると思われる。*Sobel* v. *Hertz, Warner & Co.*, 469 F. 2d 1211, 1214（2d Cir. 1972）事件では，裁判所は，「もし仲裁人が単純に適用法を無視した場合，『明白な無視』の基準を文字どおり適用すれば，仲裁判断を無効とせざるをえなくなる」と言った。

また，しかしながら，「仲裁人が到達した結論が，なんとかそれらしい正当化理由をもつ」ならば，仲裁人の判断は妨害されない，と言うことも同じように正しい……（前出 *Andros Compania Maritima S. A.* v. *Marc Rich & Co. A. G.*）。

Finagrain Compagnie Commerciale Agricole et Financiere S. A. v. *Federal Commerce & Navigation (1974) Ltd.*, 80 Civ. 0839（S. D. N. Y., 3 September 1980）（判決速報）事件では，地方裁判所は，法を明らかに無視したとの理由で，あやうく仲裁判断を無効にするところであった。この事案は，滞船料をめぐる紛争で，仲裁人を選任した後，示談にて解決された。ところが，後に，傭船者が再びクレームを蒸し返し，船主はすでに示談が成立しているので傭船者はクレームできない，と反論した。この紛争を解決する際，傭船者は仲裁を申し立てる権利を放棄した，と仲裁審は判断したが，その後さらに仲裁審は，事情が変わったことにより，傭474船者の「権利放棄は有効でなくなり」，傭船者のクレームを申し立てる権利が復活した，との判断を行った。船主は，仲裁判断の無効を申し立てた。地方裁判所は，次のように述べている。

もし仮に，実際の状況に鑑み，仲裁審が正しく Finagrain の示談状を拘束力のある権利放棄書とみなしていると，裁判所が確信したならば，Federal が後に出した折衷案の申込をもとに，仲裁審の多数がその後に出した結論である……仲裁に付託する権利を放棄したことが「もはや有効ではなくなっ

ている」との判断は，「法を明らかに無視している」ということで，十分に仲裁判断の無効を主張できる理由となったはずである。というのは，もし有効で拘束力のある権利放棄があったのなら，それは取り消すことができなかったはずだからである。

しかしながら，裁判所は続けて次のような結論を述べた。仲裁人が「権利放棄」と言っているとき，必ずしもその言葉どおりに意味していたのではなく，すなわち，有効な取消不能の権利放棄ではなくて，「権利を害さないことを条件とする仲裁の取り下げ，もしくは多分条件付きの仲裁付託権利の放棄」であった。

Sun Oil Co. v. Western Sea Transport Ltd., 1978 AMC 1372 (S.D.N.Y. 1978) 事件を参照。この事件では，仲裁審が別の仲裁判断の結果に従わなかったことは，法の明白な無視にはならない，と判断された。Anthony Shipping Co. Ltd. v. Hugo Neu Corp., 482 F. Supp. 965, 1980 AMC 1477 (S.D.N.Y. 1980) 事件では，権利行使を怠っていることを理由に，仲裁人がクレームを却下しているのは，法の明白な無視にはならない，と判断された。

仲裁人が単に仲裁判断の理由を述べていないだけで，その仲裁判断を無効にできることにはならない。United Steelworkers of America v. Enterprise Wheel & Car Corp., 363 U.S. 593, 598 (1960) 事件で，最高裁は，「仲裁人は，仲裁判断の理由を示す義務を裁判所に負っていない」ことを再確認した。

公序良俗違反

法を明白に無視するという判例法が生んだ法理の変更が，Re Sea Dragon Inc., 574 F. Supp. 367, 1984 AMC 699 (S.D.N.Y. 1983) 事件の判例で見られる。地方裁判所は，米国の公序良俗に反するとの理由で，仲裁判断を無効とした。仲裁判断では，傭船者による船主に対する運賃の支払を命じたが，その支払は傭船者の債権者が得たオランダの裁判所の仮差押命令により禁止されていた。仲裁判断に従えば，傭船者がオランダ裁判所の判決に違反することになる，と裁判所は認定した。そのような結果は，傭船者を矛盾する立場に立たせ，さらに重要なことは，国際礼譲の原則に反することになる。仲裁判断は，オランダ法の違反を強制することになるから，米国の公序良俗に反する，と判断された。

外国仲裁判断の承認および執行に関する条約

もし，仲裁合意がLondonもしくはその他外国の管轄で仲裁を行うと定めていても，その仲裁判断は，仲裁法第201-208条により，New Yorkもしくはその他米国のどこでも強制執行ができる。仲裁法のこれらの条項は，外国仲裁判断の承認および執行に関する条約を取り入れており，その中には，権利を侵害された当事者が相手方に外国管轄の仲裁を強制したり，もしくは外国で得た仲裁判断の執行を行いうることを規定した条項も含まれている。米国に加え，英国を含むほとんどの海運国もこの条約の当事者である。

仲裁に付託するとの書面による合意に関し，Sphere Drake Ins. v. Marine Towing Inc., 16 F. 3d 666, 1994 AMC 1581 (5th Cir. 1994) 事件を参照。この事件で，第5巡回区裁判所は，仲裁条項を含んだ保険契約につき，署名はまだされていないものの，当事者間には条約で言うところの「書面による合意」があった，と判断した。Sen Mar. Inc. v. Tiger Petroleum Corp., 774 F. Supp. 879, 882 (S.D.N.Y. 1991) 事件と比較。この事件では，強制できるためには，署名された文書もしくは，書状の交信のなかに仲裁条項の存在が必要であると判断され

た。

　条約に基づいて仲裁を強制する申立に関しては，「条約は，裁判所が非常に限られた質問を意図している」と判断された。*Sedco* v. *Petroleos Mexicanos*, 767 F. 2d 1140, 1986 AMC 706 (5th Cir. 1985) 事件。また，*Ledee* v. *Ceramische Ragno*, 684 F. 2d 184, 185-186 (1st Cir. 1982) 事件では，裁判所は，条約に基づき仲裁を強制する申立を認めるかどうかを決定するための四つの問いを示した。

1．紛争を仲裁に付託するとの書面による合意の有無，換言すれば，仲裁合意の広狭。
2．仲裁合意が規定する仲裁地が，条約締結国であるのか。
3．仲裁合意が，商業上の法律関係から生じているのか。
4．仲裁合意の当事者は，アメリカ市民ではないのか。

　条約によれば，これらの基準に合致する場合，地方裁判所は仲裁を強制することとなる。*Riley* v. *Kingsley Underwriting Agencies Ltd.*, 969 F. 2d 953, 959 (10th Cir. 1992)，裁量上告拒絶－ US －, 113 S. Ct. 658, 121 L. Ed. 2d 584 (1992) 事件を参照。この事件で，第10巡回区裁判所は，上記 *Ledee* 事件で設定された問への肯定的回答により，裁判所は条約に基づく仲裁を命ずることを求められると述べた。同裁判所は，*Rhone Mediterranee Compagnia* v. *Lauro*, 1984 AMC 1575, 1580, 712 F. 2d 50, 53 (3d Cir. 1983) 事件の判例を引用しながら，裁判所が仲裁を強制しなくともよい条約上の「無効」の例外事由は狭く解釈されるべきだとした第3巡回区裁判所の結論の理由付けと同じ見解をとった。

　Brier v. *Northstar Marine Inc.*, 1993 AMC 1194 (D. N. J. 1992) 事件で，原告は，救助業者と結んだ London 仲裁条項を含んだ LOF (救助) 契約は，無効な付合契約であると主張した。さらに，事件が，裁判所が遵守しなければならない条約の範囲外のものであるから，裁判所は外国での仲裁を強制できない，と原告は主張した。裁判所は，LOF 契約は決して無効な付合契約ではないと述べ，原告は，9 U. S. C. §2 に従って，その契約が詐欺，強迫，もしくは「普通法あるいは衡平法により取り消される理由」が存在するとの立証の責任を果たしていない，と判断した。しかしながら，裁判所は，仲裁を行うのに適当な場所は New Jersy であり，London ではないと判断した。前出の *Ledee* 事件で提示された要件の分析をもとに，LOF 契約規定上の場所や法律が外国と何らの関連もないという事実に加え，すべての当事者が米国市民なので，4番目の要件が充たされていないとして，そのように判断されたのである。このようにして，裁判所は，この事件に条約の適用はない，と判断したのである。

　同じ趣旨の判例として，*Jones* v. *Sea Tow Services*, 1994 AMC 1107, 828 F. Supp. 1002 (E. D. N. Y. 1993)，破棄差戻 1994 AMC 2661, 30 F. 3d 360 (2d Cir. 1994) 事件では，地方裁判所は英国での仲裁を命じたが，第2巡回区裁判所は，この事件のすべての当事者がすべて米国市民で，純粋に国内の救助に関する紛争に関わっていること，また条約の管轄となるための外国との関係がまったくない事実を認定して，地方裁判所の判決を破棄した。

　条約に規制される外国での仲裁判断は，米国の地方裁判所において強制執行ができる。条約の目的を促進させるため，9 U. S. C. §208 により，裁判所の確認を得るために，申立の形の略式手続が利用される。このように，多くの仲裁判断が，宣誓供述による申立により，裁判所に確認されてきた。例えば，*Imperial Ethiopian Go'vt* v. *Baruch-Foster Corp.*, 535 F. 2d 334, 335 n. 2 (5th Cir. 1976) 事件を参照。

　第207条では，条約の範疇に入る仲裁判断の強制執行は，判断が出て3年以内に行わなければならない。ただし，米国で強制執行を行う場合は，裁判を提起された米国の裁判所が，被告の対人訴訟を管轄する裁判権を有していなければならない。*Transatlantic Bulk Shipping Ltd.*

v. *Saudi Chartering S. A.*, 1985 AMC 2432 (S. D. N. Y. 1985) 事件では, 裁判所は, 被告が New York の対人裁判管轄権には服さないとの理由で, London での仲裁判断の確認の申立を拒絶した。

　条約は, 米国で出た商法上の仲裁判断にもまた適用される。*Bergesen* v. *Joseph Muller Corp.*, 710 F. 2d 928 (2d Cir. 1983) 事件。この事件で, 裁判所は, 仲裁判断を米国連邦仲裁法のもとでも強制できるという事実は, 全然重要ではない, と述べている。裁判所は, 「米国議会が, 条約と仲裁法の間に, 重複する適用範囲を設けることを意図していないと考える理由はない」と言っている (710 F. 2d at 934)。この点は, 強制執行を求める当事者にとっては, きわめて重要であった。というのは, 仲裁法に基づき仲裁判断の強制執行を行う場合の出訴期限は 1 年で, これは既に経過していたが, 条約に基づく 3 年の出訴期限はまだ過ぎていなかったからである。

　条約が適用される仲裁判断の確認に抗するには, 条約上では, 第Ⅴ条に限定的に規定された理由だけしか利用できない。第Ⅴ条(1)(c)では, 仲裁人が権限を逸脱しているとの抗弁を利用できる。この条項の範囲は, 前に議論した仲裁法第10条(d)に類似している。この抗弁は狭く解釈されるべきではあるが, 当事者が, 「仲裁判断が仲裁付託合意の範囲を超えると反駁する」ことは許される (*Parsons & Whittemore Overseas Co. Inc.* v. *Société Generale de L'Industrie du Papier*, 508 F. 2d 969, 976 (2d Cir. 1974))。

　当事者がその事件を提訴できなかったという抗弁が, 第Ⅴ条(1)(b)により適用になる (*Iran Aircraft Industries* v. *Avco Corp.*, 980 F. 2d 141 (2d Cir 1992) 事件を参照)。この事件では, この理由により仲裁判断の強制執行が拒否された。

　Waterside Ocean Navigation v. *Int'l. Nav. Ltd.*, 737 F. 2d 150, 1985 AMC 349 (2d Cir. 1984) 事件では, London の仲裁判断の確認を否認した当事者は, 第Ⅴ条(2)に規定の公序良俗による抗弁をその否認の理由にした。即ち, その当事者は, 損害賠償を命じたその仲裁判断は偽証証言によったもので, その仲裁判断を確認することは, 詐欺に対する公序に反する, と主張した。裁判所は, この主張を認めなかった。司法制度の廉直さを維持するには, 「訴訟の手続のなかで, 訴訟当事者を『無定見に有利にしたり不利にしたり』しないことが重要である」(737 F. 2d at 152) が, もし, 仲裁人が判断した証拠上の所論の矛盾の意義を決定するために, 裁判所が記録文書を調べるとなれば, それは条約の目的に反することになる, と裁判所は述べた。所論の矛盾した証言の裁判では, それによる瑕疵を修復するためにどのような法的救済が必要かが検討されるべきである, と裁判所は提唱した。*Fotochrome Inc.* v. *Copal Co.*, 517 F. 2d 512 (2d Cir. 1975) 事件では, 「公序良俗の抗弁は狭く解釈されるべきで, その仲裁判断を強制することがわれわれの『最も基本的な道徳と正義の観念』にそむく場合にのみ, 適用されるべきである」として, 裁判所は仲裁人が下した以前の判断に従った (737 F. 2d at 152)。前出 *Parsons & Whittemore Overseas Co. Inc.* v. *Societe Generale de L'Industrie du Papier* 事件, *Fertilizer Corp. of India* v. *IDI Mgt. Inc.*, 530 F. Supp 542 (S. D. Ohio 1982) 事件も参照。

　同趣旨の判例として, *Halcoussis Shipping Ltd.* v. *Golden Eagle Liberia Ltd.*, 1989 U.S. Dist. Lexix 11401 (S. D. N. Y. 27 September 1989) 事件がある。

　前に議論した, 仲裁法のもとで, 判例により認められている仲裁判断の無効を求める「明らかなる法の無視」という理由は, 条約のもとでは適用がない (*Brandeis Intsel Ltd.* v. *Calabrian Chemicals Corp.*, 656 F. Supp. 160, 165 (S. D. N. Y. 1987))。さらに, 裁判所は, この事件で, 法の「明らかなる無視」というのは, 条約第Ⅴ条が意味する公序良俗に反することと同一のものではない, と判断している。前出 *Parsons & Whittemore Overseas Co. Inc.*

v. *Société Generale de L'Industrie du Papier* 事件で、この問題が議論されているが、結論は出されていない。

条約第 VI 条により、仲裁判断の執行を求められる裁判所は、もし仲裁判断の取消もしくは一時停止を求める申立が、その判断が下された国の裁判所もしくはその他正当な当局に対して477なされていれば、その裁量により、執行の延期を決定することができる。

条約の第 VI 条には重要な条項があり、その条項により、裁判所は、仲裁判断の強制執行を求める一方の当事者のために、もう一方の当事者に対して適切な担保の提供を命じることができる。*Spier* v. *Calzaturificio Tecnica S. p. A.*, 663 F. Supp. 871 (S. D. N. Y. 1987) 事件では、イタリアの裁判所に申し立てられた仲裁判断の再審査の結論が出るまで、地方裁判所は第 VI 条に基づき、強制執行の手続を延期した。裁判所は、仲裁判断に基づいて可能な他の判断を下すよりは、強制執行の手続を延期するほうがよいと判断した。ただ、その後その仲裁判断は、その判断が下された国の裁判所で取り消された (663 F. Supp. at 875)。

Fertilizer Corp. of India v. *IDI Management Inc.*, 517 F. Supp. 948, 962 (S. D. Ohio 1981), 再審請求を拒否 530 F. Supp. 542 (S. D. Ohio 1982) 事件も参照。この事件では、裁判所は、インドで下された仲裁判断の強制執行の決定を、インドの裁判所がその仲裁判断を最終的に有効なものであると認めるまで、延期した。裁判所は、インドでの手続の結果がでるまで、第 VI 条に基づく担保の提供を命じた。

条約自体には差押えまたはアレストを授権する明文の規定はないが、米国の裁判所は、第 8 条に基づき、条約に照らして強制執行可能な仲裁合意を助力するための担保取得の行為を認める。*Paramount Carriers Corp.* v. *Cook Industries Inc.*, 465 F. Supp. 599, 1979 AMC 875 (S. D. N. Y. 1979) 事件では、裁判所は、条約上の仲裁に付託されるべき滞船料の紛争に関連して、第 8 条に基づき、海事差押えを支持した。*Polar Shipping Ltd.* v. *Oriental Shipping Corp.*, 680 F. 2d 627, 1982 AMC 2330 (9th Cir. 1982) 事件では、問題は提起されたが、決定はされなかった。

仲裁判断後で、裁判確定前の利息は、条約が対象とする仲裁判断を強制執行する際、地方裁判所が命じることができる (前出 *Waterside Ocean Nav.* v. *Int'l Nav. Ltd.*, 737 F. 2d (at 153-155) 事件)。

Jamaica Commodity Trading Co. v. *Rice*, 1991 U. S. Dist Lexis 8976 (S. D. N. Y., 3 July 1991) 事件では、弁護士費用の支払が命じられた。この事件では、外国での仲裁判断が、条約の第 V 条(2)(b)による公序良俗に反するとして、その判断の無効を求める被告の申立が、裁判所により、まったく理由を欠くものと、判断された。

仲裁判断の第三者拘束力

ある状況では、仲裁判断は、仲裁に参加していなかった第三者を拘束することがある。*SCAC Transport (USA) Inc.* v. *The Danaos*, 845 F. 2d 1157 (2d Cir. 1988) 事件では、荷役業者は、仲裁の手続に適切に訴訟告知された後では、船主と傭船者の仲裁の結果に拘束されると裁判所は判示した。このクレームは、本船への積荷役中に生じたトラックに対する損傷クレームであった。船主が荷主とこのクレームの解決を行い、補償をもとめて傭船者に仲裁を申し入れた。傭船契約には London 仲裁が定められていた。傭船者は、荷役業者に対し、London 仲裁の抗弁を提示したが、荷役業者はそれを拒否した。仲裁は結局、船主を勝たせ、傭船者を負かす結果となった。そこで、傭船者は補償を求め、荷役業者を New York の裁判所に訴えた。抗弁の提出を拒否したことにより、荷役業者はその事故が荷役業者の過失で生じたと

のLondon仲裁の事実認定に拘束されることになる，との判断を裁判所は下した。裁判所は，この種の事件では，仲裁がすべての当事者にとって有効で，効率的な紛争解決をもたらすとの認識を持ち，「特段，荷役業者の権利を害することもなく，荷役業者は傭船者のための賠償者|478|として，傭船者により傭船契約上の仲裁に訴訟告知される」と判断した(845 F. 2d at 1158)。前出383頁の議論を参照。

手続を開始する時期

後述の604頁を参照。

リーエン

"110. 18. That the Owners shall have a lien upon all cargoes, and all sub-freights for any amounts due under this Charter, including General Aver-
111. age contributions, and the Charterers to have a lien on the Ship for all monies paid in advance and not earned, and any overpaid hire or excess
112. deposit to be returned at once. Charterers will not suffer, nor permit to be continued, any lien or encumbrance incurred by them or their agent, which
113. might have priority over the title and interest of the Owners in the vessel."

「18. 船主は本契約上当然受け取るべき一切の金額（共同海損分担額を含む）につき，すべての積荷，再運送賃の上にリーエンを有し，傭船者は反対給付が得られなかった一切の前払金につき，本船の上にリーエンを有するものとする。既払傭船料または供託金の超過分は，直ちに返還されなければならない。傭船者またはその代理人は，船主の船舶に対する権利，利益を害することあるべきリーエンその他の負担の発生，存続を認めないものとする。」

英国法と米国法の重要な違い

この条項によって認められるリーエンの性質は，英国法と米国法とでは大いに違っている。米国法では（後出567頁以下を参照），18条により一般的には，対物訴訟で強制執行可能な海事リーエンが生じる。英国法では，このリーエンは契約上のもののみであり（以下を参照），海事リーエンが生じることはない。

積荷に対する船主のリーエンの性質

英国法上のリーエンには，海事法における海事リーエン，もしくはコモン・ロー，衡平法，法律および契約によって生じるリーエンがある。ニューヨーク・プロデュース書式の110行およびボルタイム書式の126行によって認められる，積荷に対する船主のリーエンは，契約によって生じるリーエンのみである。そのリーエンは，海事法，コモン・ロー，衡平法，制定法上の独立の根拠を持つものではない。その結果，その条項が含まれる契約の当事者間のみでの権利ということになる。したがって，船荷証券の所持人が定期傭船者の場合を除き，船主は船荷証券の所持人の積荷にリーエンを行使することはできないのである。

*Bombay*号は，再傭船の選択権付で6ヶ月間定期傭船され，さらに往復航海の目的で再傭船に出された。最初の傭船契約には，船荷証券は，傭船者またはその代理人がその傭船契約を害さない範囲で指示する運賃率で署名されるものであるとあり，さらに，同傭船契約には，船主は「本傭船契約上支払われるべき運賃，その他の金銭，すべての貨物のうえに」リーエンを有する旨の規定があった。船荷証券は再傭船者に対して発行され，船主は定期傭船契約上の傭船料のために再傭船者の貨物に対してリーエンを行使しようとした。枢密院は，船主は再傭船者の貨物の上にリーエンを有しない，と判示した。Lindley卿は，「運賃または契約上支払われるべき金銭につき，すべての貨物に上にリーエンを与えることに関し」次のように述べている。「この規定は定期傭船者を拘束する規定であり，船主に対して，船主が前払運賃につき有するものより広いリーエンを与えるものである。しかし，この規

定は，異なる運賃額で船荷証券を発行する船長の権限を無効にしたり制限したりするものではなく，また，船主に対して定期傭船者との契約となんの関係もない者の貨物に対しリーエンを行使する権限を船主に与えるものでもない。ある人の負債のため，他の人の品物を留置する権利は，裁判所にそれを識別することを期待するまでもなく，明白に規定されていなければならない」。

Turner v. Haji Goolam [1904] A.C. 826.

このような場合，傭船者が船主に支払を要する金員があった場合，もし船主が積荷を本船から手離すことを拒否してリーエンを行使すれば，船主はニューヨーク・プロデュース書式第8条の「船長はその航海を極力迅速に遂行する」義務の違反を主張する傭船者のクレームに対し有効な防御策を有することになり，傭船料は遅滞の期間も払い続けられることとなる。[1981] 1 Lloyd's Rep. 159 と後出558頁の The Chrysovalandou Dyo 事件を参照。

留　　置

ニューヨーク・プロデュース書式110行およびボルタイム書式126行で船主に認められるリーエンは，留置権付のリーエンであり，傭船者が船主に対して支払を要する金員が支払われるまで，船主は貨物の占有を維持することができる。Hammonds v. Barclay (1802) 2 East 227 事件で，Grose 判事は次のように述べている。「リーエンとは，ある物を占有している者の要求が充たされるまで，他人の所有物であるその物の占有を占有者が保持する権利である」。この文言は，船の上に存在し，船主の占有下にある貨物に対する船主のリーエンの性質を正確に表現している。

リーエンはどの貨物に対して行使しうるか

上述のとおり，船荷証券所持人が傭船者自身でないか，船主の傭船者に対するリーエンが船荷証券に摂取されていない限り，貨物に対する船主のリーエンを船荷証券所持人に対して行使することはできない。しかしながら，そのような場合でも，船主は**船主自身と定期傭船者間**の問題として，貨物を留置することができるかどうかが問題となる。

ボルタイム書式

ボルタイム書式126行により，船主には傭船者に属する貨物にしかリーエンを行使する権利が認められないことは明らかである。「船主は，定期傭船者に属するすべての貨物および再運送賃につき，リーエンを有する」(The Mihalios Xilas [1978] 2 Lloyd's Rep. 186 事件を参照)。

ニューヨーク・プロデュース書式

ボルタイム書式126行の文言と比較すると，ニューヨーク・プロデュース書式110行の文言は，リーエンを行使できる貨物が傭船者の貨物にはっきりと限定されているわけではない。船荷証券に傭船契約のリーエン条項が摂取されていない場合は，船主は貨物所有者に対してリーエンを行使する権利がないにもかかわらず，船主は**傭船者に対して行うように**，本船上にある傭船者に属さない貨物を留置できるかどうかが問題となる。この点に関しては，相矛盾する判決がある。

The Agios Giorgis [1976] 2 Lloyd's Rep. 192 事件（前出315頁を参照）において，Mocatta 判事は，傭船者の傭船料未払により留置した貨物が，傭船者のものでなく傭船者以外の者に属する場合には，船主の差押えは，110行の規定によっては正当化されない，と判示した。しか

し,正反対の結論が,その後しばらくして,Donaldson 判事により,*The Aegnoussiotis* [1977] 1 Lloyd's Rep. 268 事件で出された。

上記の二つの事件では,定期傭船料が未払であり,それゆえ,船主は船長に対して傭船料が支払われるまで揚荷を中止する指示を出した。両事件とも,貨物は傭船者以外の者に属していた。*The Agios Giorgis* 事件で,Mocatta 判事は次のような見解をとった。リーエンが,(リーエンが行使される場所の法ではなく)傭船契約のプロパー・ローによって解釈されるとしても,英国法は,契約上のリーエンの行使の有効要件として,留置されるべき貨物の所有者がその契約の当事者であるべきことを要求している。本件は,それに該当しないから,船主は,揚荷拒否を正当化するリーエンを持っていない。

The Aegnoussiotis 事件では,Donaldson 判事は Mocatta 判事の判決を知ってはいたが,異なった見解を示した。「私の考えでは,第18条はその文字どおり,船主がすべての貨物の上にリーエンを有することに,定期傭船者が合意しているという意味に解されるべきである。貨物が第三者の所有に属する場合,定期傭船者は契約でリーエンを設定し,船主にそれを与える義務を負っている。定期傭船者がそれを怠り,船主が第三者の貨物にリーエンを主張した場合,第三者は船主に対して訴訟を提起することができる。しかし,定期傭船者の立場はこれと異なる。定期傭船者は自らの契約違反を主張し,利用することができないのである。本件で意図されたリーエンの行使は,定期傭船者に対する限り有効である」。

The Cebu [1983] 1 Lloyd's Rep. 302 (同判例集306)事件で,Lloyd 判事は,*Paul* v. *Birch* (1743) 2 Akt. 621 事件で示された法理に,より合致しているとの理由で,*The Aegonoussiotis* 事件の Donaldson 判事の考えの支持を表明した。確かに,Donaldson 判事の処理方法は,船主がすべての貨物の上にリーエンを有するという規定に実際的な効果を与えるものである。また,*Tonnelier and Bolckow, Vaughan* v. *Smith* (1897) 2 Com. Cas. 258 事件の控訴院で採用された考え方により沿うようにも思われる。しかし,法はまだこの点に関して十分な答を示していない。

The Aegnoussiotis 事件の Donaldson 判事の判決が正しいとすれば,場合によっては,傭船者の所有に属しない貨物の留置は傭船者に対しては有効であるが,船荷証券所持人に対しては不法なものになる。ここで,不法に貨物を留置したことにより船荷証券所持人に対して負う損害賠償責任に関し,船主は傭船者に対して補償を求める権利があるかどうかの問題が生ずる。あまり考えられない事例ではあるが,貨物がだれの所有に属するかということを知らずに,あるいは傭船者が発行した船荷証券約款を知らずに船長や船主が貨物を留置した場合は,補償を請求する権利は生ずるように思われる。これとは逆に,実際にあるいは推定によって,貨物の所有者および船荷証券約款を知りながら不法に差し押えた場合には,船荷証券所持人に対する責任につき,船主は傭船者に補償を請求する権利はない。このような行為は明らかに不法である。類似の事例として,*Strathlorne Steamship* v. *Weir* (1934) 50 Ll.L. Rep. 185 事件(前出388頁)参照。また使用補償条項に関する一般的解説については,本書351頁から360頁を参照。

船荷証券が(明示的にもしくは参照によって)傭船契約のリーエン条項を摂取している場合は,上記で議論した問題は生じない。船主は,貨物が傭船者の所有であると否とにかかわらず,貨物に対して契約上のリーエンを有し,それを行使することができるのである。*The Chrysovalandou Dyo* [1981] 1 Lloyd's Rep. 159 事件の Mocatta 判事の判決(同判例集165頁)を参照。

リーエンを行使する場所

船主が貨物に対してリーエンを有していても,一般的にその貨物を積んだ船が,揚荷港に到

着する前に、その船を止めてリーエンを行使することはできない。前出の The Mihalios Xilas [1978] 事件において、船主は船を航海途中の補油港で止めた。Donaldson 判事は「船主が貨物の輸送を途中で拒絶したからといって、貨物にリーエンを行使していることにはならないと思われる。運送航海の完成を拒絶することにより、リーエンを行使することは可能であろう。しかし、これは特別な事情のため仕向港でリーエンを行使することができないか、あるいは運送を継続すれば貨物の占有を喪失してしまうような場合にのみ、認められるべきものと考える」と述べた。

しかしながら、通常は、本船が揚荷港の港外で錨泊していれば十分だといえる。Mocatta 判事は、*The Chrysovalandou Dyo* [1981] 1 Lloyd's Rep. 159 事件において、そのように判示した。上記の Donaldson 判事の判決を理由に、本船が貨物を揚げる場所、岸壁もしくはブイに着いていなければ、船主はリーエンを行使することができないと、傭船者は主張したが、Mocatta 判事は傭船者の主張を退けた。「このことを要求すれば、不必要な費用がかかるし、ある場合には港で船混みが生じる」。

再運送賃に対する船主のリーエンの性質

このリーエンは、上記で議論したように、契約によってのみ生じるという意味で、貨物上のリーエンに似ている。しかしながら、このリーエンは、すでに船主の占有にあるものを留置する権利ではなく、第三者から傭船者に渡される金銭の流れを妨げる権利である。確かに、これが本当に「リーエン」と言えるかどうか疑わしい（後出559頁を参照）。

「再運送賃」の意味

第18条の「再運送賃」が船荷証券や航海傭船の運賃に限定されるのか、それとも再定期傭船料も含んだ、本船の使用から傭船者が得る報酬も含まれるかについて、商業裁判所の判決と矛盾する判決がある。

The Cebu [1983] 1 Lloyd's Rep. 302 事件で、Lloyd 判事は、後出 *Inman Steamship* v. *Bischoff* 事件に続き、広く解釈するのが正しい、と判示した。彼は、さらに、ニューヨーク・プロデュース書式の「再運送賃」は、傭船者に直接支払われるべきもの、そうでないものも含め、すべての再運送賃、それには再々運送賃、再定期傭船料が含まれると判示した（後出561頁を参照）。彼は、「再運送賃」には、定期傭船者による船舶の使用により生ずるとみられるあらゆる金員が含まれると考えた。

> *City of Paris* 号は、月払傭船料で定期傭船され、船主は「未収運賃」に保険をつけた。保険証券上の請求が、「運賃」は定期傭船料を含むという立場で主張され、この見解は貴族院によって認められた。Blackburn 卿は、*Flint* v. *Flemying*, 1B. & Ad. 48 事件における Tenterden 卿の見解を引用して次のように述べた。「『保険証券のなかで用いられた運賃という文言は、船の傭船によって生ずる利益を意味するものである』、それゆえ、その表示は期間中の月々の傭船料を含む」。
>
> *Inman Steamship* v. *Bischoff*（1882）7 App. Cas., 670.
>
> （*Seven Seas* v. *Atlantic Shipping* [1975] 2 Lloyd's Rep. 188 事件、および *The Nanfri* [1978] 2 Lloyd's Rep. 132 事件における控訴院の判決を参照。後者の事案では、運賃からの控除に関する基準の適用の文脈におけるものであったが、「傭船料」は「運賃」と同様に扱われるべきかどうかに関し、異なった見解が表明されている）。

しかし，*The Cebu (No. 2)* [1990] 2 Lloyd's Rep. 316 事件で，同様の定期傭船の再傭船契約関係において，ほとんど同じ種類の紛争が商業裁判所に提起されたとき，Steyn 判事は再考し，この問題に関する Lloyd 判事と異なる結論を出した。Lloyd 判事のときよりもさらに十分な議論を行って，一連の傭船契約の最初のものが締結された1979年までに，海運市場は明らかに「運賃」と「傭船料」を区別しており，「運賃」は船荷証券および航海傭船契約上の運賃に限定され，「傭船料」は定期傭船料に限定されると，Steyn 判事は確信したのである。*Inman Steamship* v. *Bischoff* 事件は，19世紀のより特定されない言葉の使い方を反映していたことに加えて，より重要なことは，海上保険の用語として，その当時より以降「運賃」に与えられたより広い意味を反映していたのである。ニューヨーク・プロデュース書式の他の部分に使われている「傭船料」という文言の統一ある使い方をも念頭に入れて，Steyn 判事は第18条の「再運送賃」は再定期傭船料までは含んでいないとの結論に達した。そうでなければ，再定期傭船契約の傭船者は，定期傭船契約の船主（head owner）に傭船料を支払うことを求められ，一方でそうすることにより再定期傭船契約の船主（disponent owner）から船を引き揚げられる危険に曝され，おそらくどちらが真の権利者かどうかを見極める時間も十分にないであろう。Steyn 判事は，そのような傭船者の負担を考慮することにより，自分の見解がさらに正当化されると考えた。

　第1審において，このように矛盾する判決が存在するので，この問題については現在上訴審の判断が待たれている。

483　NYPE 93

　ニューヨーク・プロデュース書式93年版では，1946年版の「すべての再運送賃」の文言に加えて，「およびまたは再傭船料」の文言が加えられている（前出13頁と57頁参照）。

船主に支払われるべき再運送賃

　もし船主が船荷証券契約の一方の当事者の場合，船主はリーエンの権利を行使する必要はない。なぜならば，船主は，運賃を傭船者に納めることにはなっているものの，傭船者ではなく，船主が運賃を受領する権限を有しているからである。船主のリーエンの権利は，まず第1に傭船者が契約上再運送賃を受領する権利がある場合に問題となる。*Molthes Rederi* v. *Ellerman's Wilson Line* (1926) 26 Ll.L. Rep. 259 事件で，Greer 判事が述べているように，「船荷証券という形の船主がなした契約により，船主に払われるべき債務の上に船主がリーエンを有するというのは，言葉の使い方を誤っているように思われる。傭船契約のリーエン条項は，再運送賃が船主ではなく傭船者に支払われるべき場合に，船主にリーエンの権利を付与するものである……」（同判例集262頁）。

　本船が定期傭船されている場合，船荷証券上の運賃は，通常，傭船者の代理人に支払われる。これは，たとえ貨物が船荷証券契約に基づいて運送され，その契約の一方の当事者が船主である場合も同様である。傭船者の代理人が船荷証券上の運賃を受領する前に，船主が，その代理人に運賃の支払請求を通知した場合には，その代理人は，傭船者のためではなく船主のために運賃を徴収しなければならない。代理人がすでに運賃を受領した後に，船主がこのような通知を行った場合にも，おそらく同じことがいえるであろう。*Wehner* v. *Dene* [1905] 2 K. B. 92 事件では，そのような判決が下された。しかし，それに続く *Molthes Rederi* v. *Ellerman's Wilson Line* (1926) Ll.L. Rep. 259 事件では，この問題は明らかに未解決の問題として残された（後出を参照）。

船主は，自分が受領した船荷証券上の運賃から，定期傭船契約上，自分が受け取るべき金額を差し引いた後，その残額を定期傭船者に納める義務がある。船主は，船荷証券上の運賃が代理人に支払われた時点で，支払時期にきている傭船料の金額のみを差し引くことができる。

 Ferndene 号は定期傭船され，さらに1航海再傭船された。船荷証券は再定期傭船契約に基づいて発行され，船長によって署名された。再定期傭船者は，船荷証券運賃を徴収するための代理人を選任した。12月15日に代理人は荷受人から運賃を受領した。12月16日に船主はその運賃につき，代理人に請求の通知を行った。当時12月9日付の，最初の定期傭船契約に基づく半月分の傭船料のが支払となっており，さらに12月23日に支払期日が到来していた。船荷証券運賃を取得する権限を有するのは，再定期傭船者か，船主かという問題が生じた。Channell 判事は，次のように判示した。
1．船荷証券により表象される契約は船主との間のものであるから，船主は船荷証券運賃を請求する権利がある。
2．再定期傭船者によって選任された代理人は，反対の証拠がない限り，再傭船者の代理人であると同時に，船主の代理人とみなされるべきである。
3．したがって，船主は，12月15日に代理人が受領した運賃を請求する権利があるが，受領の日に船主に支払われるべきであった金額のみを差し引いた上で，再傭船者に残額を納める義務がある。
4．したがって，船主は，12月23日にはじめて支払時期の到来した傭船料については，これを差し引く権利はない。
 Channell 判事は，次のように述べている。「船荷証券により表象される契約は，船主が締結した契約であるから，船主は，船荷証券所持人から船荷証券上の運賃を請求する権利を有するけれども，船主はまた傭船契約により，本船の使用の対価として船荷証券上の運賃と異なった額で満足することに合意しており，その額は多くの場合，船荷証券上の運賃の合計額より少ない。それゆえ，船主が船荷証券上の運賃を要求して受領した場合（船主はそうしようと思えばそれができる），船主は傭船契約上支払時期の到来している傭船料を差し引いた後の残額を，傭船者もしくは場合によっては再傭船者に納めなければならないであろう」。
 Wehner v. *Dene* [1905] 2 K.B. 92.

<u>484</u> 船荷証券上の運賃が支払われる前に，船主は，運賃を徴収するために傭船者が選任した代理人に対し，船主のために運賃を徴収するよう要求することもできる。その場合，その代理人は，船主の代理人として運賃を徴収し，それを船主に支払う義務がある。代理人は，そのようにして徴収した運賃から，傭船者の代理人としての立場から生じた費用を差し引く権限を有しない。

 Sproit 号はボルタイム書式により定期傭船され，さらに再航海傭船された。揚荷港で，定期傭船者は揚荷の手配および運賃徴収のための代理人を選任した。運賃が支払われる前に，船主の代理者はその代理人に，船主の代理人として運賃を徴収するよう要求した。というのは，定期傭船契約上の傭船料のかなりの額が未払であったからである。代理人はこれに同意したが，その後自己に生じた費用が，徴収した額をすでに超過しているということを理由に，徴収した運賃を引き渡すことを拒否した。Greer 判事は，代理人は定期傭船者のための代理人であるけれども，船主は，自己が船荷証券により表象される契約の当事者である場合には，代理人に対し自己のために運賃を徴収するよう要求する権限があり，また，代理人は定期傭船者の代理人としての立場から生じた費用を運賃から差し引く権限を有しない，と述べた。Greer 判事は，船主が請求の通知を出す以前に運賃が徴収された場合に，代理人はそれを船主に渡すべき義務があるかという点（前出 *Wehner* v. *Dene* 事件ではそう判断された）については，意見を表明するのを避けた。同判事は，前出 *Wehner* v. *Dene* 事件における Channell 判事の判決と控訴院の後出 *Tagart, Beaton* v. *Fisher* 事件の判決とを調和させるのは困難であると考えたのである。
 Molthes Rederi v. *Ellerman's Wilson Line* (1926) 26 Ll.L. Rep. 259.

傭船者に支払われるべき再運送賃

　ニューヨーク・プロデュース書式110行によって船主に認められているリーエンは，傭船者が船荷証券上の運賃を受領する権限を有する場合もしくは再傭船契約上で，再運送賃が傭船者に支払われるべき場合にも，行使できる。しかし，このリーエンは，船主が貨物の上に行使するリーエンとは異なっている。後者は，船主の既占有貨物を船主が留置を継続する形で行使するリーエンであり，前者は占有の継続に依拠するリーエンではなく，再運送賃の傭船者への支払前の支払妨害を拠りどころとするものである。The Lancaster [1980] 2 Lloyd's Rep. 497 事件の Robert Goff 判事の判決，および The Vestland [1980] 2 Lloyd's Rep. 171 事件の Mocatta 判事の判決を参照。The Nanfri [1979] 1 Lloyd's Rep. 201 事件で，Russel 卿は船主の再運送賃に対するリーエンに関して次のように述べている。「このリーエンは，荷送人から傭船者に対して支払われるべきものに対する衡平法上の担保として作用し，これが有効に機能するには，（請求の通知によって）再運送賃が荷送人から傭船者に支払われる以前に，その再運送賃の支払を妨害できることが必要である」（同判例集210頁）。また，以下の The Attica Hope [1988] 1 Lloyd's Rep. 439 事件も参照のこと。

　船主の傭船者に再運送賃が支払われるのを妨げるこのリーエンは，運賃を徴収するため傭船者が選任した代理人に対して，一旦運賃が支払われてしまえば，もはや消滅してしまう。Greer 判事は，前出 Molthes Rederi v. Ellerman's Wilson Line (1926) 26 Ll.L. Rep. 259 事件において，再運送賃が傭船者に対して当然支払われることになっている場合，「船主はリーエン条項によって初めて再運送賃に対する権利を取得するが，その再運送賃が傭船者自らに，あるいは代理人を通じて傭船者に支払われ，受け取られてしまった後では，リーエンを行使しようとしても遅すぎる」と述べた。

　これは，以下に要約する控訴院の Tagart, Beaton v. Fisher [1903] 1 K.B. 391 事件の判決の影響である。もっとも，この事件ではなぜ再運送賃が船主にではなく，傭船者に支払われるべきなのかについて，十分説明がなされていない。この点につき，前出 Molthes Rederi 事件において，Greer 判事は，その理由は，この事件での船荷証券は傭船者宛てに発行され，貨物の受取書としての役割しかないが，運賃がその船荷証券で表象される契約上支払われるものではないから，と述べている。すなわち，Greer 判事は，運賃は再傭船契約に基づき支払われたものと推論している。

|485| 　Askehall 号は定期傭船され，その傭船契約書には，船主は傭船契約上支払われるべき一切の金額につき，すべての貨物と運送賃の上にリーエンを有するとの規定があった。定期傭船者のために運賃を徴収する目的で定期傭船者が選任した代理人に対し，荷受人は運賃を支払った。代理人がその徴収した運賃を傭船者に渡す前に，船主は代理人が所持している運賃に対し，リーエンを行使しようとした。控訴院は，定期傭船者の代理人に対する支払は，定期傭船者自身に対する支払であるから，船主のリーエンは消滅する，と判示した。

　Tagart, Beaton v. Fisher [1903] 1 K.B. 391.

再傭船者に支払われるべき運賃

　傭船契約において船主に認められているリーエンと同じような権利が，再傭船契約の条項で，傭船者に認められているとすれば，ニューヨーク・プロデュース書式110行で船主に認められている再運送賃を妨害する権利は，再傭船者に対して支払われるべき再運送賃，すなわち定期傭船者に直接には支払われない再運送賃にも及ぶ。

Cebu 号は，ニューヨーク・プロデュース書式で定期傭船に出され，その傭船契約の傭船者は本船をLamsco に再定期傭船に出し，さらにまた Lamsco は Itex に再々定期傭船に出した。再定期傭船契約も再々定期傭船契約もニューヨーク・プロデュース書式で締結された。船主は，原定期傭船契約上船主に対する傭船料が未払であると主張し，さらに Lamsco より原傭船者に同額の傭船料が未払であることを前提に事案は進んだ。船主は，定期傭船契約第18条のリーエンを行使することを表明する通知を Itex と Lamsco とに行った。この件に関し，Lloyd 判事は次のように判示した。

(1) ニューヨーク・プロデュース書式第18条でいう「再運送賃」は，再傭船契約の傭船料ばかりではなく，再々傭船契約の傭船料も含んでいる（この判断と異なる判決として，*The Cebu (No. 2)* [1990] 2 Lloyd's Rep. 316 事件の Steyn 判事の判断ならびに，前出558頁を参照）。

(2) 船主のリーエンは，衡平法上の譲渡の性質として，原傭船者に支払われるべき再傭船契約上の傭船料のみならず，再傭船契約の傭船者である Lamsco に支払われるべき再々傭船契約上の傭船料にも，及ぼすことができる。傭船契約の傭船者は，再傭船契約第18条のリーエン条項によって，譲受人として，Itex から Lamsco に支払われるべき再々傭船契約の傭船料にリーエンを行使することができ，そのリーエンの権利を原（head）傭船契約第18条によって，船主に正当に移転させていたのである。

The Cebu [1983] 1 Lloyd's Rep. 302.

上記の事件で，Lloyd 判事は，ボルタイム書式で傭船契約が締結されておれば，上記と同じ結論にはならないことを示唆している。というのは，ボルタイム書式では，リーエンが及ぶのは「定期傭船者」に属するすべての貨物と再運送賃に限定されているからである。

請求の優先

傭船者が再運送賃を第三者に譲渡した場合，船主の再運送賃に対するリーエンが優先するのか，それとも譲渡された第三者が優先権をもつのかの問題は，*Dearle* v. *Hall* (1828) 3 Russ. 1 事件での法則に従って，いずれの通知が先に行われたかによって決まる。

Attika Hope 号は1983年11月16日にニューヨーク・プロデュース書式により定期傭船された。12月15日に，定期傭船者は航海傭船契約を結んだ。ほぼ同じ時期に，定期傭船者は航海傭船契約の運賃を第三者に譲渡し，この譲渡の通知を再傭船者に行った。1月13日に，船主は定期傭船契約の第18条のリーエンを行使する旨を再傭船者に通知した。船荷証券発行後20日経過した1月15日が再運送賃の支払期日になっていた。1月17日に譲受人は譲渡契約に基づき，運送賃の支払を要求した。Steyn 判事は，譲渡の通知が船主のリーエン行使通知の1月13日より以前に行われているので，譲渡を受けた第三者が優先すると判示した。船主に再運送賃を支払うことに同意して支払った再傭船者は，運賃債権の譲受人に再び運賃を支払う義務がある，とされたのである。

The Attika Hope [1988] 1 Lloyd's Rep. 439.

486 船主のリーエンが担保権として登記されるとき

もし，定期傭船者が英国またはウェールズで設立された法人である場合，1985年の会社法395条から460条により担保権の創設後21日以内にリーエンの明細が担保権として登記されていなければ，船主の再運送賃上のリーエンは，定期傭船者の精算人もしくは債権者には対抗できなくなる（*The Ugland Trailer* [1985] 2 Lloyd's Rep. 372 事件と *The Annangel Glory* [1988] 1 Lloyd's Rep. 45 事件を参照）。また，定期傭船者が，英国で設立されていなくても英国に営業所を持っている外国法人か（1985年会社法409条参照），1985年会社法と同様の法律を持った国で設立されたか，そこに営業所を有している法人であれば，リーエンを担保権として登記し

ていなければ，上記と同じ結果となる。

　上記の事例では，担保権を創設する手段として，1985年法の395条により（以前は，1948年会社法95条），定期傭船契約を締結するときに，定期傭船契約そのものを登記することができたはずであると判示された。The Ugland Trailer 事件では，395条に基づき定期傭船契約自体を登記することの非現実性が強く強調されたが，Nourse 判事は，法律の明文に規定されていることに鑑み，そのような実際の商売上の斟酌は無視せざるをえないと感じた。The Annangel Glory 事件で，Saville 判事も同様の見解を示した。ニューヨーク・プロデュース書式とボルタイム書式双方の第18条が担保権により将来の再運送賃を譲渡する合意を形成していると言えるとしても，依然として，傭船契約上，実際に定期傭船者から船主に支払われるべき金額が定まるまで，衡平法上の譲渡が有効となるとは言い難い。もし，リーエンの明細を登記する日が，傭船契約に基づく傭船料の船主への支払期日であるとすれば（傭船契約も担保権の創設を証拠立てる手段として登記できるとき），The Ugland Trailer 事件で表明された多くの取引通念上の異論は解決されたであろう（1989年会社法93条により，本項の解説は不適切となった。原著者 Mr. Terence Coghlin による，訳者注）。

運賃前払の船荷証券（B/L）

　運賃前払の船荷証券は，確かにボルタイム書式での傭船契約18条の船主の権利，すなわち「定期傭船者に属するすべての貨物，再運送賃および船荷証券運賃」の上にリーエンを有するとの権利を害するものではあるが，傭船者から要請されれば，船長はそのような船荷証券に署名することを拒むことができない。The Nanfri〔1979〕1 Lloyd's Rep. 201 事件，特に Wilberforce 卿の見解を参照（同判例集206頁）。「9条のみならずこの18条も，契約の全趣旨のなかで読まれなければならず，かつ定期傭船契約に存在する取引通念上の状況に関連していなければならない。リーエン条項は，再傭船契約上もしくは船荷証券上で運賃や再運賃が将来支払われるべきものとなるか，また実際に支払われるべきものになった場合に，船主にそれらの運賃や再運賃に対するリーエンが認められるものとして，解釈されなければならず，またその条項は，本船を使用し，その使用のために船長を指図する傭船者の主たる権利を妨げるものとして読むことはできない」。ニューヨーク・プロデュース書式でも同じ原則が適用される（これ以外の注釈として，前出392頁を参照。また，The Shillito（1897）3 Com. Cas. 44事件も参照）。

本傭船契約において支払われるべきすべての金額

　既に発生している傭船料に関してのみ，再運送賃に対するリーエンを行使することができる。船主が支出したもので，傭船契約上傭船者の責任になる金額が，「この傭船契約において支払われるべき金額」ということになる。

　　Lindenhall 号は，定期傭船に出され，その傭船契約には，船主は傭船契約上支払われるべきすべての金額について，すべての貨物およびすべての再運送賃の上にリーエンを有するとの規定があった。傭船料は前払であった。本船は米国で，日本向けの貨物を積むよう命令された。傭船者は荷渡時に運賃の一部が支払われるとの船荷証券を発行した（船主は，この船荷証券の当事者ではなかった）。航海途中で，傭船者が破産して，船主は燃料代を払い，その他傭船契約上傭船者が負担すべき支払を行わざるをえなかった。揚荷港において，船長は運賃の残額をまとめて徴収し，燃料代，航海中生じた諸費用および船荷証券上の運賃残額の支払後に支払期日のくる傭船料もあわせて相殺しようとした。Walton 判事は次のように判示した。

(1) 船荷証券により表章される契約は，傭船者との契約であって船主との契約ではないから，船長は傭船契約上のリーエンの規定によってのみ，運賃を受領するものである。
(2) 船主の有するリーエンは，燃料代と航海中に生じた費用についても認められる。なぜなら，これらは傭船者の責任であり，したがって「本傭船契約上，支払われるべき金額」だからである。
(3) リーエンは，船荷証券上の運賃残額が支払われるときに，すでに支払期日のきている前払傭船料についてのみ行使することができる。その時点で支払時期のきていない傭船料については，行使することができない。
(4) 船主は，徴収した運賃のうち，上記(2)(3)により有効なリーエンを有する部分の額を超える金額については，これを傭船者に納めなければならない。しかし，船主は船荷証券上の運賃が徴収された後に支払時期の来る傭船料および傭船者が傭船契約を履行しなかったことによる損害賠償を，この勘定と相殺することができる。

Samuel v. West Hartlepool (1906) 11 Com. Cas. 115 および (1907) 12 Com. Cas. 203 (また，The Lakatoi Express (1990) 19 N. S. W. L. R. 285 事件も参照)。

定期傭船者の使用から船主が本船を引き揚げた後，再傭船者に本船の使用の継続を許可するのと引き換えに，船主がその対価としての支払を受ける権利を有するようになった場合，その支払はもはや原定期傭船契約上の「支払われるべき金額」ではない (The Lakatoi Express (1990) 19 N. S. W. L. R. 285 (304頁) 事件を参照)。

本船に対する傭船者のリーエン

ニューヨーク・プロデュース書式の111行によって，相互的に，傭船者には「反対給付が得られなかった一切の前払金につき，本船上にリーエン」が認められている。ボルタイム書式の第18条も同様の権利を認めている。

定期傭船者は裸傭船者と違って本船の占有を得るわけではないので，占有を保持することができないから，傭船者に認められるリーエンは真に留置権を伴う権利ではないが，それと同様の権利を認めると思われる，すなわち傭船期間の終了時に船主が自らの目的のため本船を自分の管理下に戻すことを阻止するのである。Rigby 卿判事は，Tonnelier and Bolckow, Vaughan v. Smith (1897) 2 Com. Cas. 258 事件の多数意見に与みして，次のように述べた。「傭船者が，反対給付を得られなかった一切の前払金につき，本船上にリーエンを有する，という規定は，この規定がなければ必ずしも明白でない点，すなわち，前払金は暫定的なものに過ぎず，最終的なものではないのであるから，傭船者は反対給付を得られなかった前払金が返還されるまで，返船を延期することができるということを明らかにしている」。この意見に対して，Sumner 卿は，French Marine v. Compagnie Napolitaine [1921] 2 A. C. 494 事件で疑問を呈した。Sumner 卿は，「このリーエンの規定を，傭船者は返船を拒絶することができ，また，それ以後の傭船料につき責めを負わないと読むのが困難であることは明白である。また，厳密な意味では，傭船者は本船上にリーエンを有しない……私は，このリーエンと言われるものの意味および効果につき，意見を表明することを保留する」と述べた（同判例集516頁）。しかし，Sumner 卿の上記の評釈を注意深く考察した後，Robert Goff 判事は The Lancaster [1980] 2 Lloyd's Rep. 497 事件で，Rigby 卿判事の見解に従いつつ，それを発展させて次のように判示した。すなわち，傭船者は傭船契約の終了時に自らのリーエンの権利を条件として返船することができた，そして「おそらく差止命令」によって船主が本船使用に関する管理を取り戻すことを阻止できたのである，と。Robert Goff 判事のこの問題への取組み方は，Rigby 卿判事が使った「返船を延期する」という言葉から離れていることが注目される。それは，Sumner

卿が指摘した困難な問題点，すなわち，もし傭船者がリーエンを行使するために返船を延ばせば，傭船者の傭船料を支払う義務が継続する，という問題点に対処するためであった。

488 しかしながら，傭船者に認められるこのリーエンは，本船上に，もしくは本船滅失に対し支払われる保険金の上に，それ以上の権利を傭船者に認めるものではない。前出 The Lancaster 事件において，傭船者はまずこのリーエンは衡平法上の権利であると主張し，ゆえに本船の滅失後，傭船者は船舶保険金を差し押えた。さらに船舶抵当権により銀行に与えられている船舶保険金の受領権より優先する，と傭船者は主張した。Robert Goff 判事は，傭船者の三つの主張のいずれも認容しなかった。最初の主張に関して言えば，Robert Goff 判事は，リーエンの適用は，前の段落で説明されたものに限定されるとし，さらに The Panglobal Friendship [1978] 1 Lloyd's Rep. 368 事件の Roskill 卿判事の判決を援用して，リーエンが何らかの本船の所有権を認めるものであるとの言い分を拒絶した。

一切のリーエンもしくは財産上の負担

ニューヨーク・プロデュース書式112行と113行の効果については，もし傭船者自らの過失もしくは傭船者の代理人の過失によって，本船上に何らかの「リーエンもしくは財産上の負担」が生じ，それが第三者に船主の所有権に優先する権利を認めさせ，そのことによって本船がアレストされるような事態になった場合，傭船者は本船を解放させるために担保を提供しなければならない。このような効果を有するリーエンには，例えば救助や衝突損害のクレームに随伴するコモン・ロー上の海事リーエンが含まれ，請求者は海事法上の対物訴訟を提起することができる。すなわち，いわば本船自身に対する権利であり，善意の第三者に本船が売却されたとしても，その権利を行使できる。1981年最高法院法には，例えば，人命の喪失，怪我，運送物品の滅失／損傷，水先人の費用，共同海損に関する海事クレーム，もしくは「本船による物品運送に関する合意から生じる，または本船の使用あるいは傭船の合意から生じるあらゆる海事クレーム」が列挙されている。それらの海事クレームに関して，英国法は請求者に制定法上のリーエンを認めるが，ここでいうリーエンには，そのような制定法上のリーエン（もっと正確に言えば，「制定法上の対物訴訟の権利」）も含まれているようである。ただし，この制定法上のリーエンは，海事リーエンとは異なり，本船の所有権をまだ有しておりそのクレームにつき対人的に責めを負う者に訴訟が提起される場合にのみ有効となる（The Monica S. [1967] 2 Lloyd's Rep. 113 事件を参照）。そのような制限があるものの，対物訴訟が開始されれば，請求者は担保付きの債権者の地位を得ることとなり，本船に対し船主が有する「権原および権益」に優先する請求を有することとなる（なお，海事および制定法上のリーエンの歴史および効果に関する権威ある概説に関しては，The Halcyon Isle [1980] 2 Lloyd's Rep. 325 事件の Diplock 卿の所説を参照）。

Vestland 号は Linertime 書式で傭船に出され，その傭船契約にはニューヨーク・プロデュース書式112，113行と同じ文言の条項が入っていた（第20条の第2文）。船主が拘束される船荷証券に基づき貨物クレームが提起されたが，この貨物クレームは，傭船者の指示で船荷証券記載の揚荷港と異なる港で貨物を揚げ，その後傭船者代理店の保管上の怠慢で生じたものであった。本船は，英国の1956年司法の運営に関する法律（現在は1981年最高法院法）に規定された法律上のリーエンと同様の規定をもつカナダ海事法上の手続に従い，カナダでアレストされた。傭船者は，本船を解放するために，適切な担保を提供するつもりもなく，また用意することもできなかった。船主も同様に担保の提供を拒否した。その結果，本船がアレストされてから10日後，傭船者は船主に対して，もし船主がただちに本船を解放するためにしかるべき処置を取らなければ，その行為は船主による傭船契約の拒絶とみな

す，と述べた。それでも，船主は拒否の方針を変えず，翌日，傭船者は本船解放に対する自らの利害関係通知を裁判所に行うとともに，船主に対し損害賠償を要求した。それに対して，船主は，傭船者が担保の提供を怠ったこと，本船解放に関する利害関係通知を行ったことは，傭船者みずから傭船契約を拒絶しているものであると，主張した。

Londonでのその後の手続で，仲裁人は，船主が不法に傭船契約を拒絶したかどうかについては，商業裁判所により判断される法の問題であると述べた。Mocatta判事は，船主は傭船契約を不法に拒絶してはいない，と判示した。同判事によれば，本件では傭船契約第20条の第2文の部分が適用され，本船はカナダにおいて対物訴訟を提起されて「財産上の負担」を負ってしまっており，それは法的に船主の所有権に優先する「リーエン」であるが，その「財産上の負担」は傭船者もしくは傭船者の代理人によって「もたらされ」たとの認定をした。その結果，船主は，傭船者に対し，傭船者が必要な担保を提供する義務があると主張できた，と判示した。

The Vestland [1980] 2 Lloyd's Rep. 171.

489 NYPE93

ニューヨーク・プロデュース書式1993年改訂版の第23条のリーエン条項には，次の文言が追加されている。「傭船者は，この傭船契約期間中に，船主の支払いもしくは船主の時間となるような形で，港費や燃料費を含む，船用品，必需品およびサービスを調達しないことを約束する」。

265行から267行および前出13頁と57頁を参照。

490 米　国　法

海事リーエン

　(a)船主が，本船の貨物または運賃の上に海事リーエンを有する場合，もしくは(b)傭船者または貨物所有者が本船自体の上に海事リーエンを有する場合には，その財産に対して対物訴訟を提起することができる。本船であれ，貨物であれ，もしくは運賃であれ，その財物自体に対する権利を付与することが，海事リーエンのまさしく本質なのである。この理由により，リーエンの権利を有することは，航海の事業に従事する海事財物に対して創設される権利によって，一種の担保が船主や傭船者に付与されることになるので，本船を傭船をするに際し，非常に重要な役割を果たすのである。

　海事リーエンに関する古典的な記述として，*The Young Mechanic*, 30 F. Cas. 873, 876 (No. 18, 180) (C. C. D. Me. 1855)事件で述べられたものがあり，裁判所は，海事リーエンの特性を根本的に次のように描写している。

　　債権者は，その権利に基づいて訴訟を提起し，財物の占有者からその占有を奪い，売却によってその債務の弁済に充当することができる。また，その権利は財物に内在しており，売買によってその物が誰の手に渡っても追求しうるし，財物が没収されても，抵当権が設定されても，あるいは債務者が何か他の担保に供しても，単なる個人の権利あるいは特権と対比してその権利を奪われることはない。この権利は，法によって暗黙のうちに創り出され，司法裁判所の助力によってのみ執行が認められ，その結果，司法競売が行われるものであるが，質権者の権利，有償受寄者のリーエンと同様に，財物それ自体に内在する財産権である。当初はどうであったかわからないが，リーエンを強制的に執行する海事訴訟は，特定の者を対象として，その者に何かを強制的になさしめ，あるいは，何かを受忍させる請求ではなく，すべての人に対する請求であり，世界中に対して，原告が，物に対する権利を主張できる対物訴訟である，と長い間考えられてきた。それは物的権利を追求する物的訴訟である。

　海事リーエンは，一般海事法の適用により生じあるいは契約により生じる。もちろん，リーエンは，ニューヨーク・プロデュース書式第18条によって明確に規定されているように，その性質上，契約上のリーエンである。いずれであれ，米国法上は，リーエンは，その物に対する対物訴訟によってのみ，執行することができる。英国法では，状況はかなり異なる（前出555頁参照）。

未履行の契約

　傭船契約の違反による海事リーエンは，契約が単に未履行というのであれば，生じない。*The Schooner Freeman* v. *Buckingham*, 59 U. S. 182 (1856), *The Saturnus*, 250 F. 407, 408 (2 d Cir. 1918), 裁量上告拒絶 247 U. S. 521 (1918)事件, *The Valmar*, 38 F. Supp. 618, 1941 AMC. 872 (E. D. Pa. 1941), *Bunn* v. *Global Marine Inc.*, 428 F. 2d 40, 1970 AMC 1539 (5 th Cir. 1970), *European-American Banking Corp.* v. *The Rosaria*, 486 F. Supp. 245, 255 (S. D. Miss. 1978). 遺憾ながら，定期傭船契約の場合，契約がもはや未履行ではなくなる時点につき，判例は異なっている。これまで，本船が実際に傭船者に引き渡されるまで，傭船契約は未履行であると判断されてきた。例えば，*Rainbow Line Inc.* v. *The Tequila*, 480 F. 2d 1024,

1027 n. 6, 1973 AMC 1431, 1435 n. 6 (2d Cir. 1973) 事件で，裁判所は次のように述べている。

　本船の引渡により定期傭船契約の履行が開始され，これにより契約は未履行の状態を脱するのである。

　同様に，*The Oceano*, 148 F. 131, 133 (S. D. N. Y. 1906) 事件では，裁判所は次のように述べている。

　定期傭船契約の履行開始と同時に，荷主や傭船者のために本船上にリーエンが存在することになり，傭船契約から生じる船長や船主の責任につき，対物訴訟を提起することができる。

491　*E. A. S. T. Inc.* v. *The Alaia*, 673 F. Supp. 796, 1988 AMC 1396 (E. D. La. 1987), 原審維持 876 F. 2d 1168, 1989 AMC 2024 (5th Cir. 1989) 事件で，裁判所は，*The Tequila* 事件の判例に追随して，定期傭船契約違反による海事リーエンの発生は，本船が傭船者の利用に提供された後に生じると判断した (*The Director*, 26 F. 708, 710 (D. Ore. 1886))。
　ある別の事件では，貨物が本船に積まれるまでは，傭船契約は未履行のままである，との判断がなされた (*Belvedere* v. *Compania Ploman de Vapores S. A.*, 189 F. 2d 148, 1951 AMC 1217 (5th Cir. 1951) 事件 (しかしながら，この案件は航海傭船に関連したものである), *Interocean Shipping Co.* v. *The Lygaria*, 1981 AMC 2244 (D. Md. 1981))。
　しかしながら，少なくとも第18条のような傭船契約条項に関わる事件では，船主および傭船者のリーエンは，本船の引渡および履行開始時，執行可能になる権利であるとされている。例えば，傭船料を前払した傭船者は，第18条により，本船引渡の時点から本船に対してリーエンを有することに疑問の余地はない。船主と傭船者のリーエンは性質上相互的なものであるから，第18条に基づく再傭船料に対する船主のリーエンは，貨物の本船への船積如何にかかわらず平等に傭船契約の履行開始時点より作用すべきである。もっとも，通常，貨物が本船に積まれるまでは，再傭船料の債権は発生しないことが，認識されなければならないことはいうまでもない。
　貨物に関するリーエンについての法は，よく整理され確立している。傭船者が所有する貨物に対する船主のリーエンの場合，貨物が本船上に持ち込まれているか，さもなくば本船の管理下に入り本船と貨物が結合している，と言えなければ，船主はリーエンを行使することはできない。同時に，貨物の滅失や損傷による本船に対するリーエンもまた，本船と貨物が結合したと言えなければ，発生しない (*The Keokuk*, 76 U. S. (9 Wall.) 517, 519 (1870)：*Osaka Shosen Kaisha* v. *Pacific Export Lbr. Co.*, 260 U. S. 490 (1923)；*Krauss Brothers Lumber Co.* v. *Dimon Steamship Corp.*, 290 U. S. 117 (1933)；*Diana Compania Maritima S. A. of Panama* v. *Subfreights of the Admiralty Flyer*, 280 F. Supp. 607, 1968 AMC 2093 (S. D. N. Y. 1968)；*Antria Shipping Co. Ltd.* v. *Triton Int'l Carriers Ltd.*, 1980 AMC 678, 680 (S. D. N. Y. 1976))。

船主のリーエン

　米国の裁判所は，傭船契約中に反対の規定がない限り，傭船契約上支払時期の到来している傭船料につき，傭船者自身の貨物の上にリーエンを行使する一般海事法上の船主の権利を認めている。*The Bird of Paradise*, 72 U. S. 545 (1867) 事件を参照。このように，第18条の規定がなくても，船主は傭船契約上，支払時期の到来している金額につき，傭船者自身の貨物の上

にリーエンを有するであろう。Jebsen v. A Cargo of Hemp, 228 F. 143 (D. Mass 1915) 事件を参照。貨物が第三者の所有に属するものである場合、船主は貨物にリーエンを有しないが、傭船契約の第18条に基づき、再運送賃に対してリーエンを有する。

船主のリーエンは、傭船契約の締結と同時に発生するといわれている。しかしながら、リーエンはいまだ不完全であり、貨物が積まれるまで行使することはできない (American Steel Barge Co. v. Chesapeake & Ohio Coal Agency Co., 115 F. 669 (1st Cir. 1902))。

問題になっている条項上の船主の権利は、傭船契約締結の日に遡って発生し、現在、貨物の所有者が考えているように、船荷証券発行の日に発生するのではない。

したがって、海事法の一般的な規則に従い船主はこの運賃の上に傭船契約締結の日に発生したリーエンを有するので、正式な譲渡の方式を要求しない海事法の観点からみれば、船主は、譲渡証書に基づく譲受人のすべての権利を有する (115 F. at 673)。

Luckenbach Overseas Corp. v. Subfreights of the Audrey J. Luckenbach, 232 F. Supp. 572, 1965 AMC 692 (S. D. N. Y. 1963) 事件も参照。同事件で、裁判所は、次のように述べた。

492 傭船契約第18条により、船主は本船が取得するすべての運賃の上にリーエンを認められ、これを有している。このリーエンは、未完成なリーエンとして傭船契約日に発生する……(1965 AMC at 694)。

貨物と再運送賃の上の船主のリーエンの範囲は、The Freights of The Kate, 63 F. 707 (S. D. N. Y. 1894) 事件の判決の中で説明されている。この事件で、裁判所は次のように述べている。

傭船契約により「本傭船契約上支払を受くべき金額について、全ての貨物および再運送賃」にリーエンが認められた。この条項は、定期傭船契約ではありふれたものである。「支払うべき」と「本船契約上」という文言によって、リーエンの範囲が制限される。その文言は、通常の取引上の意味で用いられ、運賃の支払期限が到来し、その回収が可能になった時点での「支払われるべき」金額を意味しており、そして、将来のまたは不確定の責任――その場合、支払うべきではない――と区別される合法的に収受し、「支払期の到来している」傭船者の債務不履行の部分に充当しうる金額、さらには、傭船契約の規定上、支払うべきことになった金額にも適用される。

それゆえ、このリーエンは、本船が傭船者の使用から引き揚げられた時点までの傭船料を含み、また、その時点で現実に傭船者から船主に支払われるべき他の項目、例えば傭船者への立替金・燃料代・食料費・港費などのほか、傭船契約の規定により、傭船者が支払うことになっているその他の金額をも含んでいる。さらに、このリーエンは、傭船契約の規定により、その傭船者が本船と船主に補償する義務を負っている過失によって生じた貨物の不足、損傷のために支払時期が到来し、支払われるべき金額をも含んでいる (63 F. at 722)。

上述のとおり、もし貨物が傭船者の所有ではなく、第三者の所有である場合、船主は傭船契約上、傭船料につき貨物に対するリーエンを有しない。Goodpasture Inc. v. The Pollux, 602 F. 2d 84, 1979 AMC 2515, 再審拒否 606 F. 2d. 321 (5th Cir. 1979) 事件で、この原則が非常に明瞭に説明されている。Goodpasture は Empac と小麦販売契約を結び、その契約によれば売買代金が Empac から Goodpasture に支払われるまで、小麦の所有権は Goodpasture に属するとなっていた。Empac は小麦を運ぶために傭船した。貨物が本船に積載された後、Empac は Goodpasture に対し小麦の売買代金の支払もできなかったし、船主に対し傭船料の支払もできなかった。そこで、船主は運賃前払船荷証券の発行を拒絶し、その後本船を引き揚げ

た。続いて，船主は，未払傭船料を回収するために，貨物に対する対物訴訟を提起した。しかしながら，裁判所は，貨物の所有権が一度も Empac に移転していないことと，船主と Goodpasture 間に一切の契約関係がないことを理由として，アレストはできないと判示した。裁判所は次のように言っている。

> Goodpasture は Negocios とは契約関係はなく，ただ Empac とのみ契約している。Goodpasture は小麦が Colombia に運ばれようが，Timbuktu に運ばれようが，本船上で鼠に食べられてしまおうが関心はなく，その売買代金が支払われさえすればよく，通常，法によって強制されるものを除き，本船や Negocios に対して何らの義務も負うものではない。特に，本船 Pollux 使用の対価の支払分につき，Negocios が傭船者 Empac に対しいかなる権利を有していたとしても，それは Goodpasture やその所有に属する小麦に対して有効ではなかったのである。

船主にとってそれ以上の打撃は，裁判所が，貨物のアレストの根拠がないと判断したことに加え，このようなアレストは不法な貨物の横領であり，船主が責任を負わなければならないと判示したことである。

船主は，第三者所有の貨物に対するリーエンを有しないが，契約によって第三者所有の再運送賃にリーエンの権利を獲得することができる。このようにして，第18条は，船主に，傭船契約上で支払われるべき金額につき，「すべての貨物と再運送賃」の上にリーエンを認めることとなる（*The Kimball*, 70 U.S. 37 (1835) 事件，前出 *American Steel Barge Co.* v. *Chesapeake & Ohio Coal Agency Co.* 事件，*Larsen* v. *150 Bales of Sisal Grass*, 147 F. 783 (S.D. Ala. 1906) 事件，前出 *The Freights of The Kate* 事件，*N. H. Shipping Corp.* v. *Freights of The Jackie Hause*, 181 F. Supp. 165 (S.D.N.Y. 1960) 事件，*The Pandora*, SMA 1466 (Arb. at N.Y. 1980) 事件を参照）。

船主の再運送賃に対するリーエンは，契約によって生ずるとみなされ，したがって，破産法の目的をもつ「差押え，判決，罰金もしくはその他普通法上もしくは衡平法上の過程および手続によって得られる」リーエンではない（*Re North Atl. Gulf S. S. Co.*, 204 F. Supp. 899, 1963 AMC 871 (S.D.N.Y. 1962), 原審維持 320 F. 2d 628 (2d Cir. 1963) 事件）。倒産した定期傭船者が有する再運送賃債権に対する船主の海事リーエンは，統一商法典第9条で要求される登録を必要としない（*Re Sterling Navigation Co. Ltd.*, 31 B.R. 619, 1983 AMC 2240 (S.D.N.Y. 1983) 事件，*Re Pacific Caribbean (U.S.A.) Inc.*, 1985 AMC 2045 (Bankr. N.D. Cal. 1984), *Re Topgallamt Lines Inc.*, 125 B.R. 682, 1992 AMC 2511, 2514-2517 (Bankr. S.D.Ga. 1992), 別の理由で修正 154 B.R. 368, 1993 AMC 2775 (S.D.Ga. 1993), 理由は付さず原審維持 20 F. 3d 1175 (11th Cir. 1994))。

船主のリーエンを行使できる時期

貨物および再運送賃の上の船主のリーエンは，傭船者が傭船料または傭船契約上支払うべき金額の支払を怠った場合にのみ，行使することができる（例えば，*Union Industrielle et Maritime* v. *Nimpex International Inc.*, 459 F. 2d 926, 1972 AMC 1494 (7th Cir. 1972); *Marine Traders, Inc.* v. *Seasons Navigation Corp.*, 422 F. 2d 804, 1970 AMC 346 (2d Cir. 1970) の各事件を参照）。

さらに，このリーエンは，貨物が荷受人に条件付で引き渡された場合にのみ，行使することができる（*United States* v. *Freights of the Mt. Shasta*, 274 U.S. 466, 1927 AMC 943 (1927); *Beverly Hills Nat. Bank & Trust Co.* v. *Compania de Navegacion Almirante S. A.*

Panama (The Searaven), 437 F. 2d 301 (9th Cir. 1971), 裁量上告拒絶 402 U.S. 966 (1971)；*N. H. Shipping Corp.* v. *Freights of the Jackie Hause* の各事件を参照）。船主は，貨物に対する支配を保持している限り，貨物を揚げた後も，なおその貨物の上にリーエンを有する。船主がとりうる様々な手段のうち，次の方法が前出 *The Jackie Hause* 事件で採用された。この事件では，船主は，貨物を引き渡すことに同意したが，条件として，貨物の代わりに再運送賃を第三者勘定に供託させたのである。

船主のために貨物に対するリーエンが規定され，同時に運賃は貨物が揚荷されるまで収受できないと規定された航海傭船契約において，時々困難な問題が生ずる。船主は「二律背反」に陥る可能性がある。何故なら，運賃を収受するには貨物の揚荷を要する一方で，貨物を揚荷すればリーエンを失う懸念があるからである。裁判所は，*Arochem Corp.* v. *Wilomi Inc.*, 962 F. 2d 496, 1992 AMC 2342 (5th Cir. 1992) 事件で，この問題に直面した。貨物は原油で，この貨物が本船から別の艀に揚げられたのである。裁判所は，次のように判断した。すなわち，船主は無条件の揚荷を行ったのではなく，航海傭船者が負担すべき運賃や滞船料のために，艀へ揚荷された貨物に対してリーエンを行使する権利を有する。揚荷は「条件付」で行われ，船主のリーエンはなくなっていない，という裁判所の結論は，傭船契約の分析を基礎としている。傭船契約は，運賃や滞船料のために貨物に対するリーエンを規定している一方で，それら費用の支払時期は貨物の引渡完了まで到来しないと規定していた。裁判所によれば，

> 貨物の引渡後支払時期が到来する費用のために，貨物に対して設定されるリーエンであるのに，そのリーエンを貨物の引渡により消滅させる，そのようなことをする非合理な人間はいない。もしそうであれば，そのリーエンは無益な保全の仕組となってしまう。すなわち，当事者は貨物の引渡後も，リーエンを消滅させない意図であった，と判断せざるをえない。

リーエンは，再運送賃の上に，その総額いっぱいまで行使できるが，それは再傭船者または荷送人が船主のリーエンの通知を受け，かつまだ傭船者に対して再運送賃を支払っていない場合に限られる（*American Steel Barge Co.* v. *Chesapeake & Ohio Coal Agency Co.*; *Akt Dampsk, Thorbjorn* v. *Harrison & Co.* 260 F. 287 (S.D.N.Y. 1918); *Larsen* v. *150 Bales of Sisal Grass*, 147 F. 783 (S.D. Ala. 1906); *The Solhaug*, 2 F Supp. 294, 300 (S.D.N.Y. 1931); *Hall Corp.* v. *Cargo Ex Steamer Mont Louis*, 62 F. 2d 603, 605 (2d Cir. 1933); 前出 *Marine Traders Inc.* v. *Seasons Navigation Corp.*; *Oceanic Trading Corp.* v. *The Freights of The Diana*, 423 F. 2d 1 (2d Cir. 1970) の各事件を参照）。

再運送賃に対するリーエンは，留置権的なものではない。すなわち，リーエンの有効性は，リーエンの所有者が貨物を法的に訴える権利を有しているとか，貨物を占有していることを要件とはしない。それゆえ，船主は，運賃に対するリーエンを行使するために，貨物に対し訴訟を提起することを要求されない。むしろ，リーエンは，それ自身に基づいて，再運送賃を有する当事者に直接主張することができる（*Tarstar Shaipping Co.* v. *Century Shipline Ltd.*, 451 F. Supp. 317, 1979 AMC 1011 (S.D.N.Y. 1978)，原審維持 597 F. 2d 837, 1979 AMC 1096 (2d Cir. 1979) 事件）。

再運送賃に対するリーエンは，再傭船契約上もしくは船荷証券上支払われるべき金額が未確定か，もしくはその額につき争いがあっても，行使することができる（前出 *United States* v. *Freights of the Mt. Shasta* 事件を参照）。

さらに，*Western Bulk Carriers (Australia) Pty. Ltd.* v. *P.S. Int'l Inc.*, 164 B.R. 616, 1994 AMC 1981 (S.D. Ind. 1994) 事件を参照。この事件で，裁判所は，再運送賃に対するリーエ

ンは，再傭船者の銀行口座の預金に対して行使できると判示し，またそのリーエンは銀行口座の預金の源が何であるかには関係なく，唯一関係があるのは，返済されるべき負債がリーエンに拠っているか否かという点である。裁判所は，さらに，船主の海事リーエンは，その銀行口座の預金に対する銀行のUCC担保に優先すると判示した。

船主のリーエンの通知がないまま，あるいは傭船者が債務不履行を犯していない状況でなされた再運送賃の支払は，有効にリーエンを消滅させる。前出の *American Steel Barge Co.* v. *Chesapeake & Ohio Coal Agency* Co. 事件を参照。この事件では，船荷証券所持人が貨物および再運送賃の上に船主のリーエンが存在することを知らないで，支払時期の到来した運賃を船長に支払った場合，その船荷証券所持人は，その支払金額について保護されると判示された。また，前出の *Larsen* v. *150 Bales of Sisal Grass* 事件では，傭船契約の条項を知らないか，あるいは傭船契約上の運賃が支払われたかどうかを知らずに，船荷証券の運賃が支払われた場合に，その支払が傭船者の債務不履行が発生する前になされている限り，再運送賃の上の船主のリーエンは消滅すると判示された。前出の *Akt Dampsk.* v. *Harrison & Co.* (The *Thorbjorn*) 事件においては，傭船料につき一切の貨物と一切の再運送賃の上にリーエンを付与する定期傭船上の規定は，船主に対し，船主からの何らの請求の通知も受けないで傭船料を支払った再傭船者の所有する貨物の上に，リーエンを与えるものではない，と判示された。

前出の *Union Industrielle et Maritime* v. *Nimpex International Inc.* 事件では，裁判所は，「リーエンが発生する以前に，Nimpex により Midland に対してなされた支払は，本件貨物に関する運賃についての Union のすべての請求権を消滅させる」と判示した（*MCT Shipping Corp.* v. *Sabet*, 497 F. Supp. 1078 (S. D. N. Y. 1980) 事件も参照）。

しかしながら，再傭船者または荷送人が二重払を要求された事例もある。すなわち，傭船契約上，傭船料の支払時期が到来しており，かつ，船主のリーエンについて通知を受けていたにもかかわらず，再傭船者が傭船者に再運送賃を支払った場合には，船主は，なお，再運送賃のうえにリーエンを行使することができるのである。

前出の *Tarstar Shipping Co.* v. *Century Shipline Ltd.* 事件では，再傭船者が再運送賃を二度支払わされている。船主は，再傭船者に対して，傭船者が債務不履行に陥った後，再運送賃に対するリーエンの通知を口頭と文書により行った。船主からリーエンの通知を受領する以前に，再傭船者は，傭船者への再運送賃の支払につき自己を代理する会社宛既に再運送賃を支払っていた。しかしながら，再傭船者がリーエンの通知を受領したのは，その代理人が実際に傭船者に再運送賃を支払う前であった，それにもかかわらず，さらに傭船者に対する支払がなされるべきか，その再運送賃を差し止めておくべきかを決断しようとはしなかった。再傭船者には，この場合，代理店の手許にあった再運送賃を確定させるための速やかで，誠実な努力を行う義務があった，と裁判所は判断した。再傭船者は自らの代理人が傭船者に対する支払を止めることができたのだから，船主が傭船者から受領すべきすべての金額につき，再傭船者は船主に対し支払う義務がある，と判断された。

Antria Shipping Co. Ltd. v. *Triton Int'l Carriers Ltd.*, 1980 AMC 681 (E. D. Pa. 1978), 理由を付さず原審維持 609 F. 2d 500 (3d Cir. 1979) 事件も参照。

Jebsen v. *A Cargo of Hemp*, 228 F. 143, 147-48 (D. Mass. 1915) 事件で，Ore Company は船主との傭船契約に基く傭船料の支払を怠った。本船は，Ore から Munson Line へ再傭船に出され，Munson は Ore に対して，Ore との傭船契約上支払時期が来ていた運賃を支払った。にもかかわらず，裁判所は，次のように判示した。(1)船主は，Ore から受け取るべき運賃について，貨物の司法上の差押えを行う権利を有し，その場合(2)その権利に附随して，貨物所有者（Peabody）から Munson に支払われるべき運賃を自らに支払うよう求めることができ

る。

　これは，船主がその運賃の上にリーエンを有しているからではなく，船主が有しているのは，貨物の上のリーエンに過ぎないが，運賃というのは，その貨物の運送のための本船の使用の対価を意味しているからである。船主は，本船の使用を示す傭船料，それが支払われない場合は，荷送人が運賃として約定した金額のいずれかの支払を受けることができる（228 F. at 149）。

　さらに裁判所は，貨物の上のリーエンにより，船主の船荷証券運賃に対する権利は，Munsonのそれに対する権利に対して優先権を持つと判示した。裁判所は，次のように述べている。

　（Munson から Ore に対する）支払が，原告が主張するリーエン実行の意思通知以前になされたか否かの点は，それが重要な事実であるとしても，ここでは明白ではなく，またそのいずれかによって支払の効力に差異をもたらすという問題は，本件においては提起されていない。……Munson Line は，原告たる船主が，船主自身に支払われるべき傭船料につき，貨物の上にリーエンを有することを留保し，その旨を通知したものとして，原告に対処しなければならない。Ore Company が支払不能になったからといって，原告のリーエンが失われるものでもなく，Munson Line が代位，その他の方法で利益をうるものでもない。逆に支払不能は，原告に対し，自己が明示的に留保したリーエンによって確保した担保を実行する機会を与えるものである。そして，船主がこのリーエンを放棄するような行為をしたという主張はなされていない。
　請求者［Munson］が Ore 社に支払うべきものを支払ったという事実は，請求者に有利な衡平法上の権利を与えるものではない……Munson Line は，慎重な取引上の行為として，Ore 社の傭船契約を調べる義務があったし，また同契約中の傭船料につき，船主が「すべての貨物」の上にリーエンを留保している条項に拘束されるものとして，自らを律すべきであった。……Munson Line の Ore Company への支払は，Munson Line が自らの危険においてなしたとみなされるべきであると思われる（228 F. 145-46, 148）。

　Re North Atlantic and Gulf Steamship Co., 204 F. Supp. 899, 904, 1963 AMC 871, 877（S. D. N. Y 1962），原審維持320 F. 2d 628（2d Cir. 1963）事件では，裁判所は次のように判示した。

　……船主は，荷送人による再運送賃の支払前であれば，リーエンの存在を荷送人に通知することにより，自己のリーエンを主張することができる。……このリーエンの通知により，荷送人は，傭船者に対する再運送賃の支払をもって自己の責任が消滅したと主張できなくなる。

　現在，巡回裁判所の間では，船主のリーエンの通知と擬制される事由があれば，再傭船者や荷送人を拘束するに十分となるかどうかに関して，見解を異にしている。最近の判例では，船主が有効なリーエンを有するには，荷主や再傭船者が傭船者に支払う以前に，船主がその者たちにリーエンの存在を知らせる通知を実際に行っていなければならない，とされている（*Finora Co.* v. *Amitie Shipping Ltd.*, 54 F. 3d 209（4th Cir. 1995），原審維持852 F. Supp. 1298, 1995 AMC 607（D. S. C. 1994）事件，また *Berdex Int'l Inc.* v. *The Kapitan Grishin*, 1992 AMC 1559（N. D. Cal. 1992）事件も参照（これらの事件では，リーエンを万全にするには「明白なる通知」が必要である，とされた））。このように判断する際，*Finora* 事件の裁判所は，*The Solhaug*, 2 F. Supp. 294（S. D. N. Y. 1931）事件と異なった判断を行った。なお，後者の事件では，裁判所は，リーエンの通知と擬制される事由で十分であると判示している。
　The Solhaug 事件は，再運送賃が既に傭船者に支払われていた場合でも，その再運送賃の上

の船主のリーエンが有効であると判断された，もう一つの例を提供している。裁判所は，リーエン条項の効果は，原傭船契約が締結された時点からその契約によって発生した債権額につき，すべての再運送賃の上に有効なリーエンが生ずることである，と判示した。裁判所によれば，リーエンは，そのリーエンの通知を実際に受けたもしくは受けたとみなされるすべての当事者に対して行使できる，という。荷送人は，少なくとも原傭船契約に関し通知を受けているため，船主のリーエンについて通知を受けたとみなすことができることから，船主に合理的な質問をすることなく再運送賃を支払ったことは自らの危険で行ったもの，と判断された。

　East Asiatic Trading Co. v. *Navibec Shipping Ltd.*, 1979 AMC 1043, 1046 (S. D. N. Y. 1978) 事件で，裁判所は，再傭船者にリーエンを通知したと言うためには，船主の再運送賃に対するリーエンに関し，再傭船者が復唱する必要も，その存在を認めることさえも必要ではない，と判示した。再傭船契約の中で，原傭船契約（head charter）の傭船者が管理船主の地位にあることに触れていることだけで，原傭船契約（head charter）の存在とその中に規定されているリーエン条項が通知がされていると十分にみなされる，と裁判所は判断した（*Sarma Navigation S. A.* v. *Navibec Shipping Ltd.*, 1979 AMC 1050 (S. D. N. Y. 1979) も参照）。

　なお，*Saint John Marine Co.* v. *United States*, 1994 AMC 2526, 1994 U. S. Dist. Lexis 8334 (S. D. N. Y. 1994) 事件と比較。この事件で，裁判所は，傍論で，再運送賃に対するリーエンを万全にするためにどの程度の通知が必要かという問題については未解決のままである，と述べている。

　Cornish Shipping v. *Ferromet*, 1955 AMC 235 (S. D. N. Y. 1995) 事件では，裁判所は，再運送賃に対するリーエンは，傭船者やその代理人に属する資金には行使できず，傭船者に債務を負担している荷主やその他の者に対してのみ行使できる，と判示した。この事件では，荷主および傭船者とも船主のリーエンの通知を受けた後，荷送人が傭船者の代理人に再運送賃を支払った。荷送人には，まだ船主に対する再運送賃の支払義務が残っていたが，その一方で，裁判所は，リーエンは傭船者自身の財産に対しては行使できないと判示した。というのは，支払分に関しては，それは既に再運送賃ではなかったからである。

「運賃前払」の船荷証券

　運賃前払の船荷証券が船主またはその授権のもとに発行され，第三者に譲渡された場合，船主は再運送賃または貨物の上にリーエンを主張することはできないと思われる。*Beverly Hills National Bank & Trust Co.* v. *Compania de Navegacion Almirante S. A. Panama* (*The Searaven*), 437 F. 2d 301, 304 (9th Cir. 1971)，裁量上告拒絶 402, U. S. 996 (1971) 事件では，船荷証券上に「傭船契約に従い運賃前払」との記載があった。この事件で，裁判所は，「しかしながら，船主の権利の通知がなされずに運賃が支払われている場合には，運賃の上のリーエンは消滅する」と判示した。

　Beverly Hills 事件で，リーエンが行使される前に運賃前払船荷証券が買主に有償で譲渡されたために，荷受人が運賃支払の担保を差し入れていたたものの，船主がそのリーエンを喪失した点は，特記すべきことである。リーエンの通知なしに船荷証券が譲渡された場合，リーエンは消滅し，仮に傭船料に代わるものとして担保の差入あるいはその他の保証がなされていても，リーエンは復活しないのである。

　船主が第三者の貨物にリーエンを行使する場合，荷送人は，傭船者に対する自己の債権をもって相殺することはできない。前出の *American Steel Barge Co.* 事件を参照。

　さらに，船主のリーエンは，傭船契約が効力を生じたときに発生するのであるから，船主

は，傭船者からの再運送賃の譲受人に対し優先権を有する。*Luekenbach Overseas Corp.* v. *The Subfreights of the Audrey J. Luckenbach*, 232 F. Supp. 572, 1965 AMC 692 (S.D.N.Y. 1963) 事件を参照。*Schilling* v. *A/S D/S Dannebrog*, 320 F. 2d 628, 1964 AMC 678 (2d Cir. 1963) 事件では，裁判所は，定期傭船者が傭船契約に違反して早期に返船した場合，船主は支払期限のきている傭船料の金額のすべてにつき，再運送賃の上にリーエンを主張することができる，と判示した。裁判所は，船主は支払期限のきている傭船料を，傭船者による実際の使用期間によって比例按分する義務はない，と判示した。

　一般的には，*Rainbow Line Inc.* v. *The Tequila*, 341 F. Supp. 459, 1972 AMC 1540 (S.D.N.Y. 1972)，原審維持 480 F. 2d 1024, 1973 AMC 1431 (2d Cir. 1973) ; *Diana Compania Maritima S. A.* v. *Subfreights of The Admiralty Flyer*, 280 F. Supp. 607, 1968 AMC 2093 (S.D.N.Y. 1968) の各事件を参照。

　Berdex Int'l Inc. v. *The Kapitan Grishin*, 1992 AMC 1559 (N.D.Cal. 1992) 事件では，定期傭船者は荷送人が支払うべき運賃残額のために海事リーエンを行使しようと試みた。傭船者は，貨物積込時に荷送人が運賃の半額を支払い，残りは本船の揚荷港到着時点での支払を条件とする船荷証券を発行した。その後荷送人は第三者に貨物を売却し，その売却の条件は再運送賃の全額を荷主に支払うことであった。再運送賃の全額を受領し，荷送人は第三者に，運賃前払船荷証券を発行した。後者の船荷証券にはリーエン条項がなく，第三者，すなわち貨物の買主に対し，傭船者が再運送賃につき貨物にリーエンを有しているとの通知もなされなかった。続いて，本船が揚荷港に到着したとき，荷送人は傭船者に支払うべき運賃の残額を支払わなかった。そこで，傭船者は貨物をアレストしたのである。裁判所によれば，「善意の貨物購入者と本船の傭船者とそれぞれ独立別個に契約した第三者が定期傭船者に対する債務不履行に陥った場合，前者と後者の何れが損失を負担しなければならないか」という問題が現出してきた。この場合，裁判所は，傭船者が負担すべしとの判断を下した。裁判所は，貨物アレストの訴えを却下し，傭船者のリーエンの通知を受けることなく善意で再運送賃を支払った第三者が所有する貨物に対して，傭船者はリーエンを主張できない，と判示した。

自　　助

　積荷に関する海事リーエンは，その物品に対し，対物訴訟を提起することにより完璧になる。米国の手続上，そのような行為は「アレスト」として知られている。もし，基本的なクレームが別の方法で解決されなければ，アレストは，物品の司法的競売につながっていく。ある事案においては，貨物の引渡を拒否することによるリーエンの行使が認められてきた。この「自助」の方法は，船主が貨物の上に有効なリーエンを有している場合に認められる。ただし，リーエンを有する者は，貨物を自分の物にする権利を有しておらず，司法的競売を行うには，対物訴訟を提起することが求められる。

　The Lenoudis Kiki, SMA 2323 (Arb. at N.Y. 1986) 事件では，仲裁審は，傭船者に傭船料の最終支払を強制するために，船主が貨物の揚荷を停止したのは正当化される，と判示した。本船は，Texas から Passau に米を運ぶために一航海だけ傭船された。傭船者は傭船料の一回目の支払は行ったものの，それ以後の支払はずっと遅れていた。本船が揚荷港に到着したとき，傭船料はまだ未払のままであった。貨物は，米国政府により運賃が支払われると記載された船荷証券により運送された。この船荷証券の規定のゆえに，未払傭船料につき，貨物に海事リーエンを行使できるかにつき，船主は自信がなかった。傭船者に傭船料の最終支払をさせるために，船主は本船に残っていた貨物の揚荷を中断させた。本船は，傭船料が支払われるま

で，揚荷港に留まったままとなった。仲裁審は，船主の行為を支持し，揚荷を継続しなかったことは本船の引揚になるとの傭船者の主張を認めなかった。仲裁審によれば，「……本船が港にとどまり，貨物の管理を続けている限りにおいて，この行為は本船引揚とみなすのではなく，救済の通知と考えるべきである。揚荷を止めることが，船主にとって唯一の防衛策であった」。

The Sally Stove, SMA 2320（Arb. at N.Y. 1986）事件で，同じような判断が下されている。その事件では，傭船者が傭船料の支払を怠っていたとして，船主は貨物である鉄パイプの揚荷を中止したが，仲裁審は，その船主の行為を正当なものと判断した。

対照的に，航海傭船の事例の The Mistral, SMA 2724（Arb. at N.Y. 1990）事件では，仲裁人たちは，船主および本船船長に対し「直ちに，遅滞なく，また海事リーエンを主張することなく，本船 Mistral 号の貨物である鉄屑の揚荷引渡」命令を出すことを求めた傭船者の申立を認めた。この事件では，仲裁人は，傭船者は既に傭船料の95パーセントを支払っており，残りの傭船料ならびに滞船料は揚荷後に支払時期が到来する，との事実認定を行った。さらに，船荷証券には運賃前払の記載があった。

傭船者のリーエン

　一般的な海事法上では，傭船契約の履行が開始した後で，船主の傭船契約上の債務不履行が生じる場合，傭船者はその債務不履行につき，本船上にリーエンを有することとなる。指導的判例である The Oceano, 148 F. 131, 133（S.D.N.Y. 1906）事件で，裁判所が次のように述べている。

　　傭船契約の履行着手と同時に，荷送人または傭船者の本船に対するリーエンが発生し，船長や船主の責任につき対物訴訟を提起することができる。
　　……傭船契約の違反によって傭船者が被った損害は，本船に対するリーエンの被担保債権になる。

Rainbow Line, Inc. v. The Tequila, 480 F. 2d 1024（2d Cir. 1973）事件で，裁判所は，傭船者は，船主による傭船契約の違反につき本船の上に海事リーエンを有すると判示した。本船は，ニューヨーク・プロデュース書式で6ヶ月間，ただし6ヶ月間を2度更新できる選択権を傭船者が持つとの条件で，傭船された。船主は，早すぎる時期に本船を引き揚げてしまい，仲裁人は傭船者にその本船引揚によって被った損害の賠償を船主に請求できる旨の仲裁判断を下した。続いて，傭船者は仲裁判断に基づき損害を回収するため本船に対する対物訴訟を開始した。裁判所は，傭船者は一般海事法上の海事リーエンを有するとの判断を示し，次のように述べた。

　　米国法では，明らかに，傭船契約の当事者の債務不履行につき，海事リーエンが発生する。そして，［傭船者］によって回復が求められている損害が海事上の性質そのものを有しており，かつ傭船契約の債務不履行により直接的に発生しているのであるから，傭船者は海事リーエンを有する（480 F. 2d at 1027）。

　また，The Schooner Freeman v. Buckingham, 59 U.S. 182, 190（1856）事件も参照。この事件では，「通常の商取引において，傭船契約書は，必ず，傭船契約の履行につき法が本船に対するリーエンを与えるよう作成されなければならない」と述べている。

　E. A. S. T. Inc. v. The Alaia, 876 F. 2d 1168, 1989 AMC 2024, 2035-2036（5th Cir. 1989）

事件では，裁判所は前出の Rainbow Lines 事件の判断を採用し，本船の傭船者への引渡時に，傭船契約上の契約違反のためのリーエンは契約未履行の状態を終え，効力を生じる，としている。

前出の Schilling v. A/S D/S Dannebrog 事件では，返船時の残油の額につき，傭船者は，本船に対して海事リーエンを有しているかどうかの問題が含まれていた。傭船契約第３条は次のように規定していた。「船主は返船港において，船内に残っている燃料油の一切を引き取り，当該港における時価でその代金を支払う……」。裁判所は，船主が第３条に違反した場合には，傭船者は第18条に基づき，本船の上に有効なリーエンを取得することを明白に判示した。その第18条の一部は次のとおりである。「傭船者は反対給付が得られなかった一切の前払金につき，本船の上にリーエンを有する」。しかしながら，裁判所は，本件の事実に基づき，船主は第３条には違反していないと認定し，むしろ船主が支払をしなかったのは，早期返船のため傭船者に対して請求できる，より多額の未払傭船料を有効に相殺したのである，と判示した。

二つの事件で，傭船者は得べかりし利益については，本船に対してリーエンを取得しない，と判断されている。*European-American Banking Corp.* v. *The Rosarid*, 486 F. Supp. 245 (S. D. Miss. 1978) 事件と *Interocean Shipping Co.* v. *The Lygaria*, 1981 AMC 2244 (D. Md. 1981) 事件がその二つの事件である。後者の事件では，傭船者は，本船が再傭船契約を履行できた場合得ていたであろう利益について，海事リーエンを行使しようとした。本船を使用できなかった理由が，船主の本船堪航性維持という傭船契約上の義務違反に存するとしても，運送されるべき貨物がまったく船積されていないので，得べかりし利益について，傭船者がリーエンを有することはない，と裁判所は判示した。

Inter-American Shipping Enterprises Ltd. v. *The T. T. Tula*, 1982 AMC 951 (E. D. Va. 1981) 事件では，傭船者は過払傭船料について，本船に対するリーエンを有しない，と判示された。

傭船者のリーエンの優先権

傭船された本船が担保物受戻権喪失手続の対象となった場合，傭船契約不履行についての，傭船者が本船に対して有するクレームの優先度合いの問題が出てくる。一般的な原則として，船主の傭船契約違反により生ずる海事リーエンは，優先度の低い契約上のリーエンである。*The Bold Venture*, 638 F. Supp. 87, 1987 AMC 182 (W. D. Wash. 1986) 事件では，傭船者は自らのリーエンの請求が，不法行為の地位を有している，と主張した。裁判所はこの主張を退け，傭船契約不履行のクレームは単に契約上のものにすぎない，と判断した。

優先の問題に関する通常の原則は，優先権のある海事リーエンが関わってくる場合，修正をうける。優先権のある本船への抵当設定前に海事リーエンが発生したり，海事リーエン自体が衝突事件のような不法行為によって発生するために優先権をもつのであれば，それは本船への抵当（mortgage）に優先する。ゆえに本船への抵当（mortgage）の登記前に締結された傭船契約の債務不履行による海事リーエンは，その後に設定された抵当（mortgage）にまさる「優先された」海事リーエンとなる（*Rainbow Line Inc.* v. *The Tequila*, 480 F. 2d 1024, 1025-1026 (2d Cir. 1973)）。抵当（mortgage）の登記後に，債務不履行が生じた場合でさえも，この法理が妥当する。この法理は，傭船契約の債務不履行についての海事リーエンは，本船の傭船者への引渡時点で発生し，リーエンが行使できる実際の債務不履行が現出するまで不完全の状態に留まるという原則と合致する（例えば，*Redwood Empire Production Credit Assoc.* v. *Fishing Vessel Owners Marine Ways Inc.*, 530 F. Supp. 75 (W. D. Wash. 1981) 事件を参照）。

しかしながら，もし抵当（mortgage）の登記後に，傭船契約が締結されたとすれば，抵当（mortgage）の方が優先する。例えば，*Kopac Int'l Inc. v. The Bold Venture*, 638 F. Supp. 87, 89 (W. D. Wash. 1986) 事件およびその中で議論されている事案を参照。これらの原則は，以前は船舶モーゲージ法 46, U. S. C. § 953 に規定されていた。この法律は，1988年11月23日の Public Law 100-710 によって改正された。当該条項は，現在，46 U. S. C. §§ 31301(5)(6) と 31321-31330 に存在する。

運賃についての海事リーエンは，同じ担保物権で完全な非海事 UCC 担保権より優先する（*Re Topgallant Lines Inc.*, 125 B. R. 682, 1992 AMC 2511, 2514 (Bank S. D. Ga 1992), 別の理由で修正 154 B. R. 368, 1993 AMC 2775 (S. D. Ga. 1993), 理由を付さず原審維持 20 F. 3 d 1175 (11th Cir. 1994) 事件を参照)。

傭船者発注による物品供給者のリーエン

第18条には，傭船者との契約により，本船に商品や燃料を供給する造船所や納入業者が，その債権につき本船の上にリーエンを取得することを排除するための定めがなされており，この目的のための規定として有効であると判示されている。

前出の *Schilling* v. *A/S D/S Dannebrog* 事件において，裁判所は，第18条は「傭船契約中にリーエンに関するこの規定が存在することを知り，また，知りうべかりし納入業者のリーエンを排除するのに十分である」と判示した (320 F. 2d at 632)。この事件では，返船時の残油燃料の価額につき，傭船者はリーエンを有していると主張した。裁判所は，傭船者の債権は，第三者たる燃料納入業者の権利を代位したものであるが，その納入業者は，その燃料代金につき本船の上にリーエンを有しないのであるから，傭船者も同様にリーエンを有しない，と判示した。

United States v. *The Lucie Shulte*, 343 F. 2d 897 (2d Cir. 1965) 事件も参照。この事件は，「本件傭船契約書中のリーエン禁止条項は，相当の注意を払えば，この条項の存在を確認することができた者のリーエンの主張を否定するに足りる」と判示している (*United States* v. *Carver*, 260 U. S. 482 (1923); *Damps. Dannebrog* v. *Signal Oil & Gas Co.*, 310 U. S. 268 (1940)。一般的に，*Cardinal Shipping Corp.* v. *The Seisho Maru*, 744 F. 2d 461, 1985 AMC 2630 (5th Cir. 1984) 事件を参照)。

The Adventure, SMA 3161 (Arb. at N. Y. 1995) 事件では，リーエンを禁止する傭船者の一般的な通知は，船長が本船上で示すことが要求されていたが，実際示されたとしても，納入業者のリーエンを打ち破ることはできなかった，と仲裁審は判断した。何故なら，その一般的な通知が，納入業者への適切な通知文言を記載していなかったからである。

しかしながら，第18条は，連邦海事リーエン法 (Federal Maritime Lien Act, 46 U. S. C. §§ 971-975) の改正により，大きくその効力が失われている。この法律は，納入業者のリーエンに関する統一的な法を規定するために，1910年に採択され，本船に対するリーエンの発生の問題に関する限り，これまでの一般海事法ならびに州法に置き換わった。1971年に改正され，同法の971条は次のように規定されるようになった。

> 外国船であると国内船であるとを問わず，当該船舶の船主または船主により授権された者の注文により，当該船舶に対し，修繕，供給，曳航をなし，乾入渠または船の引き上げ台の使用をさせ，またはその他の必需品を供給した者は，当該船舶の上に海事リーエンを有し，対物訴訟により強制執行することができ，また，当該船舶を担保として，掛け売りがなされたことを主張，立証する必要はない。

連邦海事リーエン法は，1988年11月23日 Public Law 100-710 によって改正された。46 U. S. C § 971 のなかの「必需品」という文言は，「修繕，供給，曳航および乾入渠，船の引き上げ台の使用」を含む表現に改正された。46 U. S. C. § 31301(4)。「その他の必需品」という文言は削除されたが，立法の変遷の説明では，その削除は実質的な変更を意図したものではない (H. R. Rep. No. 100-918, 100th Cong., 2d Sess. 14, 15, 36 (1988) を参照)。

一連の様々な種類の物品供給業者は，必需品を供給することにより，リーエンを取得できる。一般的には，本船義務に当然必要とされるもの，あるいは本船を危険から守る，もしくは本船から危険を排除するためのものであれば，「必需品」とみなされるであろう。この法律では，「必需品」という文言は荷役業者の提供する業務も含んでいると判断されてきた（例えば, *Bermuda Express N. V. v. The Litsa*, 872 F. 2d 554, 563, 1989 AMC 1537, 1549 (3d Cir. 1989), 裁量上告拒否 493 U. S. 819 (1989) 事件, *Universal Shipping Inc. v. Panamanian Flag Barge*, 563 F. 2d 483, 1978 AMC 1458 (1st Cir. 1976) 事件, *TTT Stevedores of Texas Inc. v. The Jagat Vijeta*, 696 F. 2d 1135, 1138, 1983 AMC 1980, 1982 (5th Cir. 1983) 事件を参照)。

確かに，荷役業者は実際に働いた時間だけでなく，たとえ実稼働はなくても，労働協約によって荷役作業員に支払わねばならない，拘束時間や「保証時間」についても，海事リーエンを主張できると判示されてきた (*Atlantic & Gulf Stevedores Inc. v. The Rosa Roth*, 587 F. Supp. 103, 1985 AMC 718 (S. D. N. Y. 1984) 事件を参照)。

「必需品」にはまた，燃料や潤滑油も含まれる (*Gulf Trading v. Transp. Co. v. The Hoegh Shield*, 658 F. 2d 363, 1982 AMC 1138 (5th Cir. 1981) 事件, *Exxon Corp. v. Central Gulf Lines Inc.*, 780 F. Supp. 191, 1992 AMC 1660 (S. D. N. Y. 1991) 事件, *Re Queen Ltd.*, 361 F. Supp. 1009 (E. D. Pa. 1973) 事件を参照)。その他の「必需品」には，水先料，食料，修理，船員の給与，レーダーおよびその他の装備，入渠や宣伝等が含まれる。たばこでさえも「必需品」と判示されている (*Allen v. The Contessa*, 196 F. Supp. 649, 1961 AMC 2190 (S. D. Tex. 1961) 事件)。

いくつかの裁判所では，リース契約により本船に提供されたコンテナも必需品であると判断している (*Foss Launch & Tug Co. v. Char Ching Shipping U. S. A. Ltd.*, 808 F. 2d 697, 1987 AMC 913 (9th Cir. 1987), 裁量上告拒絶 486 U. S. 828 (1987) 事件およびその中で引用されている事件。それらの事件と *Triton Container Int'l v. Itapage*, 774 F. Supp. 1349, 1350-1351, 1991 AMC 2319, 2320-2321 (M. D. Fla. 1990) 事件を比較)。しかしながら，特定の個々の船に対してではなく，コンテナがまとめてリースされ，船会社に提供される場合には，海事リーエンは発生しない (*Itel Containers Int'l Corp. v. Atlanttrafik Express Service Ltd.*, 982 F. 2d 765, 1993 AMC 608 (2d Cir. 1992), 破棄 1992 AMC 622 (S. D. N. Y. 1991) 事件，およびその事件で判例として挙げられている *Piedmont & Georges Creek Coal Co. v. Seaboard Fisheries Co.*, 254 U. S. 1 (1920) 事件を参照。また，前出の *Foss Launch & Tug Co. v. Char Ching Shipping U. S. A. Ltd.* 事件も参照)。さらに，保険も必需品と判断されており，保険証券の発行者が，保険料の支払につき海事リーエンを有するとされる (*Equilease Corp. v. The Sampson*, 793 F. 2d 598, 1986 AMC 1826 (5th Cir.)（全員一致）, 裁量上告拒絶 479 U. S. 984 (1986) 事件, *Flagship Group v. Peninsula Cruise*, 771 F. Supp. 756 1992 AMC 815 (E. D. Va. 1991) 事件を参照)。しかし *Grow v. Steel Gas Screw Loraine K*, 310 F. 2d 547, 1963 AMC 2044 (6th Cir. 1962) 事件を参照。この事件では判断が異なっている。

「必需品」を広く解釈して，*Chi Sun Hua Steel Co. Ltd. v. Crest Tankers Inc.*, 708 F. Supp. 18, 1989 AMC 2551 (D. N. H. 1989) 事件においては，裁判所は，「必需品」のなかに，債権

者が前港で行った差押え解除の合意も含まれると判断した。裁判所によると，差押えの解除に合意することにより，債権者は本船が航海を継続するために必要なサービスを提供した，としている。

本書旧版で議論した「一般」代理店と「特別」代理店の差異は，米国最高裁の Exxon Corporation v. Central Gulf Lines Inc., 500 U.S. 603, 1991 AMC 1817（1991）事件での判決によって，覆されてしまった。最高裁は，代理店契約それ自体が海事法の管轄にはならないとした Minturn v. Maynard, 17 How. 477（1855）事件の判決を覆して，実際に代理店が提供する業務を見て，それが海事契約かどうかを決めるという柔軟なルールに置き換えたのである。もし，契約に基づき供給される業務が海事の性質をもち，本船にとって必要なものであったのであれば，代理店は海事リーエンを有することとなる。

海事リーエンは譲渡できるし，代位によって取得することもできる。Medina v. Marvirazon Compania Naviera S.A., 709 F. 2d 124, 1983 AMC 2113 (1st Cir. 1983) 事件で，裁判所は，船員の給与に関するリーエンを解除させるため，金員を提供した者には，その者が「本船や船主と緊密な関係にあり，本船を十分に管理していることによりリーエンを付与することが不公平になる」と考えられない限り，その者は船員の権利を取得すると判断した。また，Conti-Lines v. The Baroness V., 1992 AMC 681, 682-684 (M.D. Fla. 1991) 事件も参照，この事件では，本船の修理に必要な資金を提供することにより，外国の傭船者は海事リーエンを獲得すると判示された。

本船のために，必需品の供給者に支払を行った者に関しても，同様の原則が適用されるようである。Tramp Oil and Marine Ltd. v. The Mermaid I, 630 F. Supp. 630, 1987 AMC 129 (D.P.R. 1986)，原審維持 805 F. 2d 42, 1987 AMC 866 (1st Cir. 1986) 事件では，燃料油の仲立人が本船に供給した燃料につき，海事リーエンを行使しようとした。仲立人Aは仲立人Bと契約し，燃料油の納入業者を手配した。裁判所は，仲立人Aはリーエンを有しないと判示した。仲立人Aは納入業者に支払を行っているが，傭船者もすでに仲立人Bに燃料代を支払っていた。仲立人Bが仲立人Aに支払う前に，仲立人Bが倒産した。裁判所は，リーエンを有する者からそのリーエンを代位したり，その権利を譲り受けたりする判例を承知していたが，その原則はこの事件の原告には適用されない，と判示した。裁判所によれば，仲立人Aは仲立人Bの債権を否定したり，燃料油の納入業者にその業者が有するリーエンを譲渡するよう要請することにより，自らの権利を守ることができたはずである。さらに，裁判所は，傭船者は本船のためにすでに燃料代を支払っており，その支払金が仲立人Aに届かなかったことに関し，傭船者に何の落度もないのであるから，仲立人Aが自動的に燃料油の納入業者のリーエンを代位することを許容するのは不公平になる，とした。

第972条は，次のように規定する。すなわち，「供給港において船の運航，管理等をまかされている，運航者（managing owner），船舶管理人，船長，その他の者は」供給品その他を調達する権限を船主から付与されていると推定されるべきである。第973条は，本船を拘束する権限を有するとみなされるべき者には，「傭船者または一時的な（pro hac vice）所有者，もしくは買船に同意して本船を占有している買主，等々の者に選任された職員および代理人を含むものとする」と規定している。

しかしながら，第973条の規定にもかかわらず，納入業者が第18条の通知を受けているか，または，傭船者は本船に対してリーエンを有しないという事実を納入業者が知っている場合には，第972条に規定されている権限の推定は覆される。しかし，船主側の立証責任は重いものであろう。

502　第971条が，納入業者有利の方向で緩やかに，また海事リーエンが存在するという推定を納

入業者が信頼するのを認めるように解釈された事例が数多く存在する。納入業者は，傭船契約の条件を調べたり，本船を拘束する傭船者の権利について質問したりする義務はない。

もし本船の船主が納入業者が「リーエンを許さない条項」を実際に承知していたことを示すことができた場合は，納入業者に有利な推定は覆る (*Marine Fuel Supply & Towing Inc.* v. *The Ken Lucky*, 859 F. 2d 1045, 1989 AMC 390 (9th Cir. 1988) ; *Gulf Oil Trading Co.* v. *The Caribe Mar*, 757 F. 2d 743, 1985 AMC 2726 (5th Cir. 1985) ; *Lake Union Drydock Co.* v. *The Polar Viking*, 446 F. Supp. 1286, 1978 AMC 1477 (W. D. Wash. 1978)の各事件を参照)。裁判所は，これらの事件で，原材料提供者が実際にリーエン禁止条項を知っていた場合に限り，リーエンの主張が妨げられると判示している (*Gulf Trading* v. *The Tent*, 1979 AMC 753 (N. D. Cal. 1979)事件および *Jan C. Uniterwyk Co. Inc.* v. *The Mare Arabico*, 459 F. Supp. 1325 (D. Md. 1978)事件を参照)。

Ramsay Scarlett & Co. Inc. v. *The Koh Eun*, 462 F. Supp. 277 (E. D. Va. 1978)事件は，第971条に関する1971年以降の代表的な判例である。この事件では，管理船主は，荷役業者による海事リーエンの主張を避けようと試みた。その根拠として，管理船主は，荷役業者は本船が定期傭船契約のもとで運航されていることを承知しているので，当然リーエン禁止の条項の存在も承知していると推定される，と主張した。裁判所は，管理船主の言い分を却下し，次のように述べた。

　　裁判所は，1971年以後の法を次のように考えている。本船への必需品の納入業者は，傭船契約の存在について，もしくは既知の傭船契約のリーエン禁止条項について，尋ねる義務はない。納入業者は46 U.S.C. §971条以下の法的推定に依拠する権利がある。ゆえに，実際にリーエン禁止条項を含んだ傭船契約の存在を知らない納入業者に対しては，いかなるリーエン禁止条項も効力がないのである。傭船契約が存在することのみを知っていても，それがリーエンを妨げることにはならない (462 F. Supp. at 285)。

通常，船主は，船長や代理店に対して，荷役業者やその他原材料提供者からの仕入書や注文書には，本船がリーエン禁止条項を含んだ傭船契約のもとで運航されている旨を通知するスタンプを押すよう指示している。このように仕入書にスタンプを押すことにより，傭船者が本船に対してリーエンを創設することができない旨を，十分に納入業者に知らせていると言える。しかしながら，それが有効となるには，納入業者がサービスを提供するときに，リーエン禁止条項を実際に通知しなければならないことは明白である。

ゆえに，*Gulf Oil Trading Co.* v. *The Freedom*, 1985 AMC 2738 (D. Or. 1985)事件で，燃料油の供給者が本船に燃料を供給した後に，その受取書にリーエン禁止の通知のスタンプを押しても，それは有効ではないと判示された。その一方で，燃料油の供給前に，石油会社がリーエン条項の禁止を通知する書状を受領していた事案では，供給した燃料油についての石油会社の海事リーエンが拒否された (*Gulf Oil Trading Co.* v. *The Caribe Mar*, 757 F. 2d 743, 1985 AMC 2726 (5th Cir. 1985))。

納入業者がリーエンを放棄することは可能である。連邦海事リーエン法第974条は次のように規定する。

　　この章のどの部分も，修理，供給，曳航，乾入渠や船の引上台の使用，その他の必需品の提供者もしくは抵当権者がリーエンの権利を，また優先譲渡抵当リーエンを有する場合は，そのリーエンの優先的地位の権利を，どの時点においても，合意もしくはその他の方法で，放棄したものと解釈されてはならない。さらに，この章は，以下の5個の点において，1920年6月5日時点の法の原則に影響を

与えるものではない。その5個の点とは, (1)前払金額について本船に対して訴訟を提起する権利, (2)本船に対するリーエン行使の権利を怠ること, (3)対人訴訟を提起する権利, (4)海事リーエンの中で優先される海事リーエンの順位, (5)優先される抵当を除き, 米国船に対しては, 海事リーエンと抵当の優先順位の諸点である。

しかしながら, 第974条からは, リーエンの放棄は, 納入業者が他の担保権者のために, 明白にリーエンを放棄する意思を明示した場合に限られるようである (*Nacirema Operating Co. v. The Al Kulsum*, 407 F. Supp. 1222 (S.D.N.Y. 1975) 事件, 前出の *Lake Union Drydock Co. v. The Polar Viking* 事件, *Ramsay Scarlett & Co. Inc. v. The Koh Eun* 事件を参照)。*Jones Tug & Barge Co. v. The Liberty Manufacturer*, 1978 AMC 1183 (C.D.Cal. 1976) 事件で, 裁判所は, 納入業者は PI クラブの信用を頼りに役務提供に合意したとき, 裁判所は本船に対するリーエンを放棄した, と判断した。

対照的に, 前出の *Gulf Trading & Transp. Co. v. The Hoegh Shield* 事件では, 燃料油の供給者は, 定期傭船者の信用を明らかに信頼していたと認定されたが, それでも本船に対する海事リーエンを有していた, と裁判所は判断した。裁判所は, 納入業者は傭船者の信用のみを信頼していたのではなく, さらに「本船に対する海事リーエンの放棄を明確に意図していたこと」を示唆するいかなる行為もとっていない, と判断した (1982 AMC at 1145)。

本船の船主と商品もしくは役務の供給者とでは, 前者が, 後者にリーエン禁止条項を伝える積極的な義務があることは明白である。しかしながら, 船主と傭船者では, リーエン禁止条項を伝える義務があるのは傭船者である。第18条では, 傭船者は本船に対するリーエンを発生させない義務を負い, 第18条の文言が納入業者のリーエンをその範囲に含んでいるのは疑いないことである。傭船者が, リーエン条項の禁止の通知を怠っているのは, 傭船契約違反であり, 船主はそれによる損害の補償を傭船者に求めることができる。この文脈で船主の損害の補償を行う傭船者の義務には, 本船がアレストされた場合の本船解放のための担保提供の費用も含まれる (例えば, *The Irene's Grace*, SMA 1213 (Arb. at N.Y. 1978) 事件, *The George Vergottis*, SMA 1214 (Arb. at N.Y. 1978) 事件および *The Scotiacliffe Hall*, SMA 1464 (Arb. at N.Y. 1980) 事件を参照)。

The Pacduke, SMA 2586 (Arb. at N.Y. 1989) 事件は, 船主が原案を作成し, 傭船者が承諾した特別条項をめぐる係争であったが, この条項は, 傭船者が供給品, 必需品もしくは役務の提供者から, 本船への物品ないし役務の提供は傭船者の信用をもとに行われ, 未払の請求書につき本船に対するリーエンを持たないことを認め, 署名済陳述書を取得しなければならない旨を規定していた。船主は, この条項が, 納入業者を代理したブローカーからではなく, 実際の納入業者自身の署名済陳述書の取得を傭船者に義務づけるものであるとの宣言を求めた。仲裁審は, 問題となっている条項が曖昧であるとして, 船主不利の判断を行った。しかし, もし, もっと明確な文言であったら, 船主の意図を充たす条項となったであろうことを仲裁審も認めた。

第三者との関連で, 傭船者が注意しなければならない別の種類のリーエンがある。例えば, 荷受人が, 傭船者の責めに帰すべき貨物損害について, 海事リーエンを行使して, 本船をアレストするような場合はどのように考えれば良いか。もし貨物滅失が傭船者の行為の直接の結果である場合, 傭船者はリーエンを生じさせたことにより, 確かに第18条違反を犯したと言える。*The Peerless*, 2 F. 2d 395, 1923 AMC 236 (S.D.N.Y. 1923) 事件で, 裁判所は, 傭船者が責めを負うべき修理につき修理業者のリーエンを残したまま本船を返船したことは, 重大な傭船契約の違反である, と判示した。

The Three Sisters, SMA 345（Arb. at N.Y. 1969）事件において，仲裁人は多数意見をもって，傭船者は，傭船契約第18条において「傭船者またはその代理人は，船主の本船に対する権利・利益を害することありうべきリーエン，その他負担の発生，存続を認めない」という約束を船主に対して行っているのであるから，その約束違反の結果として，船主が本船を傭船業務から引き揚げたのは正当である，との判断を下した。この事件では，本船は，傭船者が岸壁使用料，貨物保管料，荷役料金を支払わなかったために，荷送人によりアレストされていた。

　The Wismar, SMA 1454（Arb. at N.Y. 1980）事件も参照のこと。この事件では，傭船者は本船をニューヨーク・プロデュース書式に基づき再傭船に出し，再傭船契約は，ほとんど原傭船契約と同様の条項を持つ契約であった。再傭船者は不法に再傭船契約を解約し，登記船主に対するクレームの担保を要求して，カナダで本船をアレストした。仲裁人は，「自らの行為もしくは自分の代理人の行為によって本船をアレストされる」という結果を招いた場合には，定期傭船船主は，第18条の下で，「本船をアレストから解放する」義務を負うと判断した。アレストは，実際，登記船主に対するクレームに関連して再傭船者により執行されたのであるから，仲裁審は，本船を解放する手続きをとるのは登記船主の義務であると，判示した。仲裁審は，また，第18条の解釈で，再傭船者は傭船者の代理人とはみなされない，との見解を示した。

納入業者のリーエンの優先度

　「必需品」の供給に関する海事リーエンは，優先度から言えば，海事契約のリーエンの地位を有する。したがって，通常，そのリーエンは，船員の給与，救助業者，不法行為による海事リーエンの後順位となる。もし，船舶抵当の問題が絡んでくると，納入業者のリーエンは，米国の抵当が登記以前に生じた場合にのみ，優先的地位を得る。米国以外での船舶抵当の場合は，たとえその船舶抵当の登記後に生じたとしても，米国の納入業者のリーエンが優先される（46 U.S.C. §31326(b)(2)）。

　納入業者の海事リーエンは州法のリーエンより優先される。例えば，*Bay State Yacht Sales Inc.* v. *Squantum Engine & Service Co. Inc.*, 117 B.R. 16, 1991 AMC 94（Bank. D. Mass. 1990）事件を参照。この事件では，納入業者の海事リーエンは，善意の購入者のクレームより優先されると判示された。

再傭船者のリーエン

　理論的には，再傭船者は管理船主（disponent owner）の契約違反により本船に対して海事リーエンを取得するはずである。しかし，原傭船契約にはリーエン禁止条項が含まれており，これにより再傭船者のものも含まれるリーエンを本船に創設する契約を傭船者が締結することを制限している。例えば，*MMI Int'l Inc.* v. *Skyros*, 1991 AMC 1264（N.D.Cal. 1990）事件で，裁判所は，原傭船契約にリーエン禁止条項があることで，再傭船者は傭船者の契約違反によるリーエンの行使が妨げられると判示した。再傭船者は，合理的な注意を払えば，本船がリーエン禁止条項を含んだ傭船契約に基づき運航されていると確定できたのであるから，再傭船者は十分にリーエン禁止条項の通知を受けているといえる，と裁判所は判断した（*Cardinal Shipping Corp.* v. *The Seisho Maru*, 744 F. 2d 461, 469, 1985 AMC 2630, 2641（5th Cir. 1984）事件と *United States* v. *The Lucie Schulte*, 343 F. 2d 897, 1965 AMC 1516（2d Cir.

1965）事件も参照）。

アレストから本船を解放する義務

　船主と傭船者間で，いずれが本船をアレストから解放するためのコストを負担すべきか，あるいはいずれが本船を解放する義務を負うかについては，個々の事案の事実により決まる。一般的には，もしアレストが傭船契約の違反により生じたならば，傭船契約に違反した者が，本船を解放させるための費用を負担する義務を有する。

　The Pandora, SMA 1466（Arb. at N.Y. 1980）事件では，傭船者が傭船料の支払を行わなかったため，船主は第18条に基づき貨物に対しリーエンを行使した。仲裁人は，リーエン行使に関する費用をいずれの当事者が負担すべきかにつき第18条は何も規定していないが，リーエン行使の必要が生じたのは，傭船者の傭船契約の不履行が原因であるから，傭船者が，船主のリーエン行使に要した費用のすべてを負担する義務がある，と述べた。

　前出の The Wismar 事件における状況は，きわめて複雑であった。この事件では，船主に向けられた貨物の積荷役の不法妨害を廉に，再傭船者が船主にクレームを提起し，本船をカナダで差し押えた。第18条によれば，定期傭船者が「自らの行為もしくは自己の代理人の行為の結果，本船がアレストされれば，定期傭船者が本船を解放する義務を負う」ことについては，仲裁審も十分承知していた。しかしながら，アレストは，船主に対するクレームに関連して，再傭船者によってなされたので，船主が本船を解放する積極的な義務を有することとなり，この義務を怠った場合，本船は解放されるまで，オフハイヤーになる，と判示された。

　The Scotiacliffe Hall, SMA 1464（Arb. at N.Y. 1980）事件では，仲裁人は，傭船者は第18条に違反しているので，揚荷港で荷受人によってアレストされた本船の解放を行う義務があるとの判断を下した。仲裁審は，貨物の受荷主は傭船者の代理人でないことを承知していた。しかし，本船は傭船者に対するクレームに関連してアレストされたのであるから，本船の抑留は傭船者の行為が原因であると判断されたのである。

　The Ming Belle, SMA 2043（Arb. at N.Y. 1984）事件は，貨物を積んだ本船が座礁した事件である。救助のための曳船が本船を再浮上させるために使用され，続いて救助者は救助費用の担保を求めるクレームを提起した。船主はすぐさま担保を提供したが，貨物側は13日後まで担保を提供しなかった。船主は，傭船者もしくは再傭船者が，貨物が分担すべき分の担保を提供しなかったので，本船が救助のリーエンを満足させる担保不提供のために差し押えられていた時間もオンハイヤーである，と主張した。仲裁人の多数意見は，貨物所有者のために傭船者や再傭船者が救助費用のための担保を提供する義務を負っているとはいえないとして，船主の主張を拒絶した。

　もうひとつの仲裁判断も上記を裏付けている。The Gabrielle Wesch, 1981 AMC 1324（Arb. at N.Y. 1981）事件では，第三者の傭船者に対する貨物クレームに関し，その第三者が担保を要求してガテマラで訴訟を提起し本船をアレストした。貨物クレームそのものは，別の船で生じた関係のない航海でのものであった。船主も傭船者もアレストを解除しようと必死の努力を行ったものの，双方とも解除に成功しなかった。仲裁判断が出たときには，本船はすでに1年以上もアレストされた状態であった。傭船者は，第18条のもとで傭船者自身，アレストに対する責任はないと主張した。傭船者は，本船が傭船者の所有に属するとの虚偽の陳述を基礎に本船はアレストされたので，そのアレストそのものが「違法」であることを，その理由とした。しかしながら，仲裁審の多数意見は傭船者の主張を拒絶した。確かに，ガテマラの裁判所は最終的にはアレストが不適切であったと判断したかもしれないが，ともかくガテマラの裁判所が

許可したアレストだったのだから，アレスト自体が「違法」なものではない，と判断した。仲裁審の多数は，第18条によって，アレストは傭船者の責任であるとした。理由は，アレストが生じた原因は傭船者に帰せられ，船主には何らの落度も存しなかったからであるとした。したがって，傭船者はアレストから生じる傭船料およびあらゆる費用につき責任があると判示された。

Seguros Banvenez S. A. v. The Oliver Drescher, 761 F. 2d 855, 1985 AMC 2168 (2d Cir. 1985) 事件は，とくに貨物クレームの担保を求めての本船アレスト事件であった。船主であるDrescherの要請により，地方裁判所は，船主のDrescherが本船解放のために必要な供託金を提供できるように，傭船者のVenlineに対し十分な担保をDrescherに提供するよう命じた。しかし，第2巡回区裁判所は，この問題に関する地方裁判所の判決を覆した。
理由は以下のとおりである。

　Venlineは本件を裁判所に持ち込むことを要請しなかったし，Drescherに対する責任に関し譲歩していなかった。確かに，その問題はまだ仲裁での結論が出ていなかった。船主は本船をアレストした者に対し，担保を提供することを強制されていない。自発的な担保を提供したことの対価は，本船の解放である。Drescherへの担保をVenlineに強要することによって，同じような対価もなく，当事者各々の権利を吟味することなく，またVenlineの利益と費用を保護する条項もないのに，Venlineからそれ自身の財物を奪ってしまうのは，適正手続に違反している嫌いがある (761 F. 2d at 863-864, 1985 AMC at 2179-2180)。

海事リーエンがついている傭船者の財物

　傭船者の所有に属し，「本船にとって不可欠の部分で，航海や運航にとって必須の」本船上の装備は，本船に対する海事リーエンの対象となる。*The Tropic Breeze*, 456 F. 2d 137 1972 AMC 1622 (1st Cir. 1972) 事件で，撒積セメント運搬船の運航になくてはならない傭船者に属するセメント装備は，海事リーエンの対象になると判示された。その他の事件で，冷凍設備，潜水鐘，エアポンプ，ネット，ネットつり揚げ装置，オイルタンク，漁具，いずれも傭船者所有のものであったにもかかわらず，海事リーエンの対象になると判示された。

海 難 救 助

"114. 19. That all derelicts and salvage shall be for the Owners' and Charterers' equal benefit after deducting Owners' and Charterers' expenses and
115. Crew's proportion." [The rest of Clause 19, up to and including Line 132, concerns general average: it is set out in the full text of the charter at page 4 above.]

「19. 一切の漂流物および救助料については，船主および傭船者の費用と乗組員の分配額を控除した後，船主と傭船者は均等に利益を受けるものとする。」[第19条のこの続きは132行まで共同海損に関するものであり，全文については前出6頁を参照。]

得られた純救助料の分配

ニューヨーク・プロデュース書式114行，115行の「均等の利益 equal benefit」という文言は，救助料から船主，傭船者が支出した費用，犠牲損害を差し引いた残額を均等に分配する意図を示している。

Pocklington 号は，*Dart* 号を救助する際，損傷を被った。その損傷を修理している期間，本船はオフハイヤーとされた。船主は修理代金の他に救助作業に関連して，何がしかを出費した。傭船者は，総救助料の半分を請求した。その根拠は「すべての拾得物および救助料は船主および傭船者の均等の利益とする」という条項であった。Bigham 判事は，分配すべき金額は純救助料であり，それは一方で修理期間中にオフハイヤーで失った傭船料の損失を含む船主の損害出費を減額し，他方で救助期間中，本船を使用できなかった傭船者の損害および余分に消費した燃料費（船主はこの減額を妥当と認めた）の代金を減額した後の残額である，と判示した。同判事は，「船主，傭船者に認めうる『均等の利益』とは，それを得るために両者が使った費用を考慮したものでなければならない。本条における救助料とは，海事裁判所における訴訟によって回収した金額を言うのではなく，その救助行為による純金銭的な結果である」と述べた。

Booker v. *Pocklington Steamship* [1899] 2 Q. B. 690.

この判決は，費用という文言を，狭く解するのではなく，広く解すべきことを示している。すなわち，救助料を分配する前に，救助行為によって生じた船体損傷の修理費，救助行為中および修理中の傭船料および燃料代等を回収することを認めることを示している。本条に該当するボルタイム書式第19条は，この条項よりも詳細に規定しており，上記と同じ結果を明文をもって規定している。

船主負担の燃料

"133. 20. Fuel used by the vessel while off hire, also for cooking, condensing water, or for
grates and stoves to be agreed to as to quantity, and the
134. cost of replacing same, to be allowed by Owners"

「20. 本船がオフハイヤー中に使用する燃料および炊事、造水または暖炉やストーブ用の燃料についても、その使用量を協議するものとし、船主がその補給費用を負担する。」

船主が支払うべき燃料費

　第20条は、オフハイヤー時に本船が使用する燃料は船主負担となることを規定している（前出443頁を参照）。第20条の残りの部分、とりわけ「造水または暖房用の燃料」については、*The Sounion* [1987] 1 Lloyd's Rep. 230 事件で考察されている。控訴院は、Gatehouse 判事の判決を覆して、仲裁人の多数意見である、ニューヨーク・プロデュース書式の様式は、本船の推進および荷役に使用する燃料費は傭船者負担で、船内で乗組員のために使用する燃料費は船主負担である、との見解を支持した。裁判所は、第20条の意図は、乗組員が船内で使用する燃料のすべてにつき、それが照明、暖房、炊事、もしくはエアコンやテレビなど個人使用の電気製品のための燃料であっても、その費用は船主が負担すべきである、と判示した。「暖房やストーブ」との文言は、船主は暖房のみに限定して解釈すべしと主張したが、そのように限定すべきではない、と判示した。

510 米 国 法

　やや古めかしい第20条の文言が，*The Ming Autumn,* SMA 2189（Arb. at N.Y. 1986）事件で考察されている。傭船者は，船内用として消費されたすべての燃料は船主が負担すべきものであり，船員の部屋のエアコンやファンに加え，当時の「暖炉やストーブ」に相当する現在の電気用品やスチームのための燃料もそこに含めるべきだと主張した。日々の予想使用量に基いて計算された，料理用ディーゼル油の費用を，傭船者は船主に請求できることに，仲裁審は合意した。さらに，仲裁審は，本船の部屋の暖房用に使用した燃料費を，傭船者は請求できると判断した。ただし，仲裁審によれば，その他の燃料費用は，傭船者は船主に請求できないとした。たぶん，最も議論になる項目は，エアコンで，仲裁審の見解は，第20条の文言のままでは，エアコンに要した燃料費は第20条の範囲には入らない，とのことであった。この判断に基づけば，もし本船上のエアコンにかかる燃料費を傭船者が請求できるようにするためには，その旨を明確にした本条の修正がなされなければならないこととなる。

　The Mykali II, SMA 2240（Arb. at N.Y. 1986）事件では，傭船者は，本船が港に停泊中の料理用燃料費につき，船主が負担すべしと主張した。しかしながら，仲裁審は，第20条が「数量につき合意されるべし」と規定していることに注目した。傭船契約には，数量につき合意している条項はなく，仲裁でも当事者は合意できなかった。傭船者は本船の1日当たりの船内燃料消費量の計算を示したが，仲裁審は，それをあくまで机上の計算とみなし，港に停泊中の料理用燃料については，傭船者の主張を拒絶し，「このクレームのための数量を決定する適当な場所は，その数量につき合意を模索すべき，成約交渉の場である」と述べた。

入渠と設備

"135.   21. That as the vessel may be from time to time employed in tropical waters during the term of this Charter, Vessel is to be docked at a
136. convenient place, bottom cleaned and painted whenever Charterers and Captain think necessary, at least once in every six months reckoning from
137. time of last painting, and payment of the hire to be suspended until she is again in proper state for the service.
138. ....
139. ....
140.   22. Owners shall maintain the gear of the ship as fitted, providing gear (for all derricks) capable of handling lifts up to three tons, also
141. providing ropes, falls, slings and blocks. If vessel is fitted with derricks capable of handling heavier lifts, Owners are to provide necessary gear for
142. same, otherwise equipment and gear for heavier lifts shall be Charterers' account. Owners also to provide on the vessel lanterns and oil for
143. night work, and vessel to give use of electric light when so fitted, but any additional lights over those on board to be at Charterers' expense. The
144. Charterers to have the use of any gear on board the vessel.
145.   23. Vessel to work night and day, if required by the Charterers, and all winches to be at Charterers' disposal during loading and discharging;
146. steamer to provide one winchman per hatch to work winches day and night, as required, Charterers agreeing to pay officers, engineers, winchmen,
147. deck hands and donkeymen for overtime work done in accordance with the working hours and rates stated in the ship's articles. If the rules of the
148. port, or labor unions, prevent crew from driving winches, shore Winchmen to be paid by Charterers. In the event of a disabled winch or winches, or
149. insufficient power to operate winches, Owners to pay for shore engine, or engines, in lieu thereof, if required and pay any loss of time occasioned
150. thereby."

「21. 本傭船期間中，本船を熱帯水域に使用したときは，適当な場所において入渠させるものとする。船底の掃除および塗装は，傭船者ならびに船長が必要と認めたときに行うほか，前回の塗装から少なくとも6ヶ月を経過する毎に行う。傭船料の支払は，本船が再び適切な稼働状態に戻るまで中止される。

22. 船主は本船装備の設備を維持し，3トン以下の積揚貨物の荷役に堪える（すべてのデリック用の）索具のほか，綱・吊索・スリングおよび滑車を準備しなければならない。本船が前記のトン数以上の重量を有する貨物の荷役に堪えるデリックを装備するときは，船主においてこれに要する索具を準備するものとする。ただし，その装備がないときは上記の重量を有する貨物のための属具および索具は，傭船者の負担とする。船主はまた，本船に夜間作業用のカンテラおよび灯油を準備し，かつ，本船に電灯設備があるときは，これを使用に供するものとする。ただし，船内の灯火以外に増設した一切の灯火の費用は傭船者の負担とする。傭船者は本船上のあらゆる器具を使用することができる。

23. 本船は，傭船者の要求がある場合，昼夜ともに作業に従事するものとし，積荷および揚荷中，全ウィンチを傭船者の使用に委ねるものとする。本船は，艙口毎に1人のウィンチマンを配置し，要求がある場合には，昼夜にわたりウィンチを運転しなければならない。傭船者は本船の諸規定に定められた作業時間ならびに賃率に従い，航海士・機関士・ウィンチマン・甲板員および補汽罐手の時間

外労働に対し支払を行う。港則または労働組合の規約が、乗組員によるウィンチの運転を禁止している場合には、陸上ウィンチマンの費用を傭船者が支払う。ウィンチの運転の不能、もしくはこれに要する動力の不足を生じたときは、船主は陸上の荷役機械、または要求があればこれに代わるその他の機械の費用を支払い、かつ、それによって時間を喪失したときは、その支払を行うものとする。」

第21条に関しては前出169頁、船底の汚染の問題については、前出441頁と446頁を参照。

NYPE 93

プロデュース書式の1993年改訂版では、1946年版135行136行に規定の少なくとも半年毎の入渠の義務を省いている。代わりに、当事者には次の二つの選択権が与えられる。(a)「船級の要求または事情により」、双方が合意した都合のよい時期と場所で入渠を許す条項と、(b)緊急な場合を除き、本傭船期間中の入渠は行わないとする条項のいずれかである（前出13頁の英文書式改訂版の242行から248行および57頁を参照）。

米国海上物品運送法

"151.　24. It is also mutually agreed that this Charter is subject to all the terms and provi-
152. sions of and all the exemptions from liability contained
153. in the Act of Congress of the United States approved on the 13th day of February
154. 1893, and entitled "An Act relating to Navigation of Vessels,
155. etc., "in respect of all cargo shipped under this charter to or from the United States of
156. America. It is further subject to the following clauses, both
157. of which are to be included in all bills of lading issued hereunder;

U. S. A. Clause Paramount

156. This bill of lading shall have effect subject to the provisions of the Carriage of Goods
157. by Sea Act of the United States, approved April
158. 16, 1936, which shall be deemed to be incorporated herein, and nothing herein con-
      tained shall be deemed a surrender by the carrier of
159. any of its right or immunities or an increase of any of its responsibilities or liabilities
      under said Act. If any term of this bill of lading
160. be repugnant to said Act to any extent, such term shall be void to that extent, but
      no furhter.

Both-to-Blame Collision Clause

161. If the ship comes into collision with another ship as a result of the negligence of the
     other ship and any act, neglect or default of the
162. Master, mariner, pilot or the servants of the Carrier in the navigation or in the man-
     agement of the ship, the owners of the goods carried
163. hereunder will indemnify the Carrier against all loss or liability to the other or non-
     carrying ship or her owners in so far as such loss
164. or liability represents loss of, or damage to, or any claim whatsoever of the owners
     of said goods, paid or payable by the other or non-
165. carrying ship or her owners to the owners of said goods and set off, recouped or re-
     covered by the other non-carrying ship or her
166. owners as part of their claim against the carrying ship or carrier."

「24. この傭船契約の下で，米国を仕向地または積地とするすべての貨物については，本契約は1893年2月13日米国連邦議会の承認を経た『船舶の航海等に関する法律』に定める一切の条項・規定および免責条項に従うものであることも，またここに合意する。上記のほか，傭船契約は，本契約の下で発行する一切の船荷証券に挿入されるべき下記二条項にも従うものとする。

米国至上条項

本船荷証券は，1936年4月16日承認された米国海上物品運送法の規定により，その効力を有し，かつ，それらの規定が本証券に挿入されているものとみなすほか，本証券に定めるいかなる事項も，同法に基づく運送人の権利もしくは免責の権利を放棄し，またはその責任もしくは義務を加重しないものとみなす。本証券の文言が，上記の法律と抵触するときは，その文言はその抵触を限度として無効となるものとする。

双方過失衝突条項

相手船の過失と，本船の船長・乗組員・水先人その他運送人の被用者の航海もしくは船舶の取扱いに関する行為・怠慢または懈怠の結果，本船と相手船が衝突し，相手船たる非積載船またはその船主が，本証券記載物品の滅失，損傷，その他貨物所有者の請求一切につき，これを貨物所有者に対して賠償したかまたは賠償義務を負い，かかる損害を衝突損害の一部として，積載船または

運送人に求償し，相殺または回収した場合，貨物所有者は，運送人が被った上記損害を補償するものとする。」

ハーター法および米国海上物品運送法（1936年）の摂取

ハーター法

1893年法はハーター法として知られている。同法および米国海上物品運送法は附録A（省略）に掲げている。

ハーター法は，現在，米国海上物品運送法（1936）によって一部改廃されている。ハーター法は，船積前および揚荷後引渡までの間，運送人が貨物に責任を有する期間につき適用がある。たまに，本契約24条から米国至上条項のみが削除され，他の部分がそのままになっていることがある。このような場合，ハーター法第3条の適用により，第16条の船主免責あるいは，その他の船主の抗弁権が，本船の堪航性を備えるにつき船主が相当の注意を払ったことを条件としてのみ，認められるようになる。そうなると，本船が不堪航であって，船主が堪航性を備えるにつき相当の注意を払ったことを立証できない場合，船主はその不堪航が滅失や損傷と因果関係がないという抗弁を行うことができない。

第24条の151行から153行の明確な文言により，ハーター法は米国向けまたは米国からの積荷に関してのみ適用される。米国海上物品運送法を摂取した場合は，このような限定はない。この点に関する判例として，後出 Adamastos 事件および The Satya Kailash ［1984］1 Lloyd's Rep. 588事件があるが，同法は地域的限定なしに，傭船契約上のすべての航海に適用される。

米国海上物品運送法

米国海上物品運送法を摂取した効果は，次のとおりである。
(1) 傭船契約始期における明示の堪航性担保義務（前出147頁）は，本船に堪航性があるという絶対的責任から，堪航性を備えるにつき相当の注意を尽くすという責任に軽減される（後出597頁参照）。
(2) 同法3条(1)に基づき，傭船契約上の各航海の開始前および開始時に，船主は堪航性を備えるにつき相当の注意義務を尽くすべき義務がある（後出597頁参照）。
(3) 同法のすべての条項が全文，傭船契約に書き込まれているのと同じこととなり，船主・傭船者間の権利義務を律する効果が与えられる。このことは特に，同法に列挙の免責される危険に関して，重要となる（後出597頁を参照）。

Saxon Star 号は，18ヶ月以内で行いうる連続航海傭船に出された。機関室要員の無能力に起因する機関の故障によって，本船は，最初の積地に行く空船航海も含めいくつかの航海において遅延した。船主は，機関室要員の選任にあたって，相当の注意を尽くしていたが，ともかく機関室要員は無能力であった。そのため，本船は不堪航であった。傭船者は，この不堪航のため，傭船期間中の実航海数が予定航海数より少なくなった，と主張した。

傭船契約は「本船は堅牢強固で，あらゆる点で航海に適し，かつかかる状態を航海中維持する。ただし海上の危険は除外する」という文言により堪航性担保の絶対的責任を定めていた。またタイプ打ちされた条項には「ここに添付した至上条項は，本傭船契約に摂取されたものとする」と規定されて

いた。添付の至上条項は，ニューヨーク・プロデュース書式第24条おける米国至上条項と同じものであった。

船主は，米国至上条項が傭船契約に摂取されたことにより，堪航性担保の絶対責任が，堪航性について相当の注意を尽くすという義務に軽減されていると主張した。

貴族院は全会一致をもって次のように判示した。
(1) ヘーグ・ルールを傭船契約に摂取することは，当事者の明白な意思であり，この意思に効果が与えられなければならない。したがって，至上条項中の「本船荷証券」とあるのを「本傭船契約」と読むべきこととなる。
(2) 本法は傭船契約には適用しないものとする，との米国法第5条は，無視するべきである。

また，多数決をもって次のように判示した。
(3) 傭船契約は世界的なものであるから，米国向けまたは米国からの航海のみに適用されるという米国法上の制限は，無視されなければならない。そして航海の起点，終点がどこであろうと，同法が適用される。
(4) 米国法——ヘーグ・ルール——で規定される義務の基準は，空船航海，積荷航海を問わず，すべての航海に適用される。
(5) 米国法第4条(1)における「滅失または損害」に関する船主免責条項には，貨物の物理的滅失または損傷だけでなく，ここで主張されている損失すなわち傭船契約上の航海数が減ったことによる傭船者の損失も含まれる。

Adamastos Shipping v. *Anglo-Saxon Petroleum（The Saxon Star）* [1958] 1 Lloyd's Rep. 73.

Adamastos 事件での貴族院の判断は，ニューヨーク・プロデュース書式による傭船契約にも等しく適用されるべきであると考えられている。むろん，定期傭船契約と連続航海の傭船契約との間には重要な差異がある。「各々の航海での堪航性の義務」における差異については，後出597頁で考察されている。しかし，*Adamastos* 事件における貴族院の考え方からすると，ヘーグ・ルールを傭船契約に適用しようという当事者の意図が契約に示されている場合，裁判所は，できるかぎり当事者のその意思に効果を与えようと努力することが明らかである。この考え方は，連続航海の傭船契約の場合と定期傭船契約の場合とで異なるとは思えず，*Adamastos* 事件以後の裁判所の判決もその結論を支持しているようである（以下を参照）。

ニューヨーク・プロデュース書式の場合，米国至上条項が単に傭船契約に基づいて発行される船荷証券だけでなく，傭船契約自体にも適用されるべきであるということは，*Adamastos* 事件の場合より，一層はっきりしている（153行および154行を参照）。

155行から159行の米国至上条項は，*Adamastos* 事件におけるのと同じ条項である。「船荷証券」という言葉を「傭船契約」と読めば（後出 *The Aliakmon Progress* 事件参照），この条項の文言は曖昧なところがなくなる。すなわち，同法の条項が摂取され，それらは傭船契約の中の既に印字されている同法と矛盾する条項に優先して適用されるというものである。法律の条項が，既に印字されている条項に優先するかどうかは，全体的に契約をどう解釈するかの問題となる。後出「米国法の他の効果について」を参照。ヘーグ・ルールもしくはヘーグ・ルールを国内法化した法律を摂取する条項は，その表題に「至上条項」と銘打っていても，それだけでヘーグ・ルールを他の条項に優先させるものではない（*Marifortuna Naviera* v. *Government of Ceylon* [1970] 1 Lloyd's Rep. 247 事件を参照。この事件では，*Adamastos* 条項のより強い文言が指摘された。なお，*The Agios Lazaros* [1976] 2 Lloyd's Rep. 47 事件における Goff 卿判事の見解（同判例集53頁）を参照）。

1航海のための定期傭船契約に関する事件につき，裁判所は躊躇なく第24条がヘーグ・ルールを傭船契約に摂取していることを認めた。ニューヨーク・プロデュース書式に基づく1航海のための定期傭船契約上の事件である *The Aliakmon Progress* [1978] 2 Lloyd's Rep. 499 事件

で,控訴院は,本船の操船上の過失で埠頭に衝突し,損傷した結果発生した損害賠償クレームに対し,船主の航海過失免責の抗弁を支持した(1936年米国海上物品運送法第4条(2)(a))。記録長官 Denning 卿は,「*Adamastos* 事件における貴族院の判決を基礎として,『本船荷証券は……の効力を有する』ことは明白であるとの条項があるが,実際に意味するところは『本傭船契約は……の効力を有する』であり,ゆえにヘーグ・ルールの規定がこの定期傭船契約に適用される」と述べている。1航海の定期傭船の事案である *The Aquacharm* [1982] 1 Lloyd's Rep. 7 事件でも,控訴院は,船主有利の形で,同じ抗弁の効果を与えた(さらに後出599頁を参照)。

後出 *The Satya Kailash* 事件において,控訴院は再び,*Adamastos* 事件の貴族院の判決を考察した。この事件で,裁判所はニューヨーク・プロデュース書式第24条が,1936年米国海上物品運送法をインドで他船の貨物を瀬取する目的で短期間傭船された本船の傭船契約に摂取する効果をもち,その効果は傭船契約の文脈から言えば,米国行き,もしくは米国向けの航海に限定されない,と判断した。

Oceanic Amity 号は,Tuticorin 沖で傭船者の本船 *Satya Kailash* 号の貨物を瀬取するために,ニューヨーク・プロデュース書式で20日間から40日間定期傭船された。*Satya Kailash* 号は *Oceanic Amity* 号の操船上の過失により損害を蒙った。この場合,*Oceanic Amity* 号の船主は,その損傷の責任につき傭船契約第24条で免責されるのか,それとも第16条の免責条項で免責されるのかの問題が生じた。控訴院(Robert Goff 卿判事と Oliver 卿判事)は次のような判断を示した。
(1) 第24条により米国海上物品運送法は有効に傭船契約に摂取され,その効果は,米国向けもしくは米国行きの航海だけに限定されない。
(2) *Satya Kailash* 号が被った損害は,米国海上物品運送法の第4条(2)(a)が規定する範囲内の航海上の懈怠によって生じる「滅失又は損傷」であるから,*Oceanic Amity* 号の船主はその免責条項により保護される。
(3) しかしながら,船主は第16条の「航海上の過誤」の免責条項では保護されない。なぜならば,その文言は不注意による過失までも含むほど広いものではないからである(前出493頁を参照)。
The Satya Kailash [1982] 2 Lloyd's Rep. 465 と [1984] 1 Lloyd's Rep. 588 (C. A.)。

The Satya Kailash 事件での Robert Goff 卿判事の言葉から推察すれば,彼は,米国海上物品運送法の航海毎の堪航性の義務は,ニューヨーク・プロデュース書式の期間単位の定期傭船契約にも適用があると考えているように思われるが,その問題はこの事件では生じなかった。したがって,期間単位の定期傭船契約において,特に堪航性の問題(後出参照)につき,ヘーグ・ルールがどの程度効果を及ぼすかについては,裁判所によってまだ十分に回答が出されているわけではない。

米国海上物品運送法の摂取の方法

米国法を摂取するには,*Hamilton* v. *Mackie* (1889) 5. T. L. R. 677事件で記録長官 Esher 卿が示した方法によるべきである。同事件は傭船契約の条項を船荷証券に摂取する方法を示したものであるが,この方法は *Adamastos* 事件で,貴族院に支持された。すなわち,「傭船契約の諸条項は,船荷証券中に全文印刷されているかのように文言どおり読まれなければならない。そしてそのように読まれることによって,傭船契約の条件には,船荷証券と矛盾するものもあるが,その矛盾する傭船契約の部分は意味がないので,無視されなければならない」。Simonds 子爵は,*Adamastos* 事件でこの論旨を採用し,さらに続けて「同法中には,本傭船契約に関する限り意味をなさず,あるいはむしろ適用がない,したがって無視しなければならない

規定が多数あることは明らかである」と述べた。[1958] 1 Lloyd's Rep. 73（同判例集81頁）。「それゆえ，同法の規定は，本契約上の規定として**適用することが可能な限りにおいて**摂取されているというべし」と Somervell 卿は述べている（同判例集99頁）。

ニューヨーク・プロデュース書式においては，すべての航海に米国法が適用される

　Adamastos 事件の判決の帰結として，米国法は積荷航海だけでなく，空船航海にも適用があり，また米国を起点・終点としない航海にも適用されることとなる。Simonds 子爵の言葉によれば（[1958] 1 Lloyd's Rep. 73），「契約上の目的は，船が傭船されている全期間であり，私の意見では，当事者はその全期間について，制定法上の義務や免責の基準を適用することに合意しているのである」（同判例集82頁）。そして，ニューヨーク・プロデュース書式の摂取文言は，これと同じ程度の広い意味を持っている（*The Satya Kailash* [1982] 2 Lloyd's Rep. 465 と [1984] 1 Lloyd's Rep. 588（C. A.）事件も参照）。

各航海における堪航性担保義務

　米国法が摂取されていない場合には，ニューヨーク・プロデュース書式上，傭船期間中の各航海の始期における明示あるいは黙示の堪航性担保義務は存在しない。傭船の開始時における堪航性担保義務のみであり，それと37行/38行に定める船舶保守義務がある（前出147頁，267頁を参照）。

　しかし，米国法の摂取により各航海開始前および開始時に，堪航性につき相当の注意を尽くすべき義務が発生すると言われている。この問題は，*Adamastos* 事件の判決ではカバーされていない問題である。すなわち，同事件では連続航海傭船の契約が扱われており，米国法の摂取によって修正されたとはいえ，各航海において堪航性担保義務が既に存在していた。

　The Aquacharm [1982] 1 Lloyd's Rep. 7 事件で，記録長官 Denning 卿および Griffiths 卿判事により，傍論で，ニューヨーク・プロデュース書式第24条は，1航海の，単品の貨物のための定期傭船契約に，航海開始時において堪航性保持のための相当の注意義務を尽くすべきヘーグ・ルール上の義務を摂取する効果をもつと認められた。これもまた，本船引渡時の堪航性の義務の修正に過ぎない。これに対して，期間単位の定期傭船契約の場合，もし提言された効果を有するとすれば，米国法によって，存在する義務が修正されるのではなく，新しい義務が**創り出された**というべきである。しかし，傭船契約中に同法の全文が観念的に書きこまれているとすれば，該当条項である第3条1項を「意味不明」とか「適用なし」として無視する十分な理由はないし，「航海」という文言に通常と異なった意味を与えることも十分な理由はないように思われる。さらに，本船の堪航性保持に関し相当の注意を尽くすべき義務を定めるハーター法第3条が，米国向けおよび米国からの航海に関しては，151行から153行により明白に傭船契約に摂取されている。

　Adamastos 判決がニューヨーク・プロデュース書式の定期傭船契約に与えた衝撃についてのこの見解は，裁判所がこの判決を完全に受け入れるまでは，注意して取り扱う必要がある。*The Hermosa* [1980] 1 Lloyd's Rep. 638 事件で，Mustill 判事は，傍論として次のような解説を行った（同判例集647頁）。「ヘーグ・ルールを定期傭船契約に挿入することにより生ずる困難については，裁判所ではまだ十分に検討されていない。連続航海傭船の場合を類推するのは正確ではない。例えば，傭船者は，本船が傭船されている間は，空船航海も含めてずっと，直

接傭船料を支払っているし，ほとんどの定期傭船契約は，初期の堪航性とその堪航性を維持することに関する明確な規定を有しており，航海ごとに相当の注意義務を創設するヘーグ・ルールの体系とは容易には調和しない。航海傭船に関連した［Adamastos］事件で採用された解釈が，すべての点において，当然にヘーグ・ルールを摂取した定期傭船契約に適用されると考えることはできない。しかしながら，現在の事件でこの問題を取り扱う必要はない。というのは，認定した事実に基づけば，最初の段階で本船の堪航性を維持する担保義務，もしくは（ヘーグ・ルールにより要求される担保義務である）本船の堪航性維持のため相当の注意を尽くす義務に違反していた，と言えるからである」。

米国法のその他の効果

一 般 論

この法律の条項は，観念的に傭船契約に全文書き込まれるので，その文脈上意味不明か，「適用不能」か，あるいは「傭船契約の目的と矛盾する」条項は無視される。Adamastos 事件において，Reid 卿は「この考え方は，米国海上物品運送法の運送人・荷送人の権利義務関係の部分につき，運送人を船主に，荷送人を傭船者と読み替えれば，その部分が傭船契約に摂取でき，傭船契約への適用ができるのではないかとの問題を残している」と述べている（貴族院におけるこの条項を摂取した結果についての判断において，Reid 卿は少数意見であった）。

他の条項との衝突

第24条で傭船契約に摂取された米国法の規定と，傭船契約の他の条項が衝突する場合は，法の規定の方が優先することとなる。衝突がない場合は，法の規定は契約条項を補足するものとなる。The Agios Lazaros ［1976］2 Lloyd's Rep. 47 事件で，Shaw 卿判事は次のように述べている（同判例集59頁）。「契約の条項と，ヘーグ・ルールとが融合し，合体した条項が相互に作用しあう。そして，合体した条項の性質や効果につき，その境界や差異を示すものはない。ただし摂取した文言が至上条項であれば，ヘーグ・ルールは単に契約を補足するものではなく，契約中のヘーグ・ルールと矛盾する条項を修正する効力を有することとなり，事情を異にする」。

The Agios Lazaros 事件は，至上条項がタイプ打ちの追加条項で挿入されている事例であった。最初からの印刷条項である第24条によって，米国法の規定が摂取されている場合とタイプ打された追加条項で米国法の規定が摂取された場合では，事情が異なるかもしれない。The Staya Kailash ［1984］1 Lloyd's Rep. 588 事件では，タイプ打ち追加条項があり，その条項で堪航性の絶対的保証を課していた。控訴院の判決で，Robert Goff 卿判事は次のように述べた。「われわれの判断では，これらの条項が第24条の解釈そのものに影響を与えることはない。これらの条項で最も多く言えることは，タイプ打ち条項は，印刷条項の第24条の至上条項に優先し，その限度において，第24条で傭船契約に摂取された米国法第 4 条(1)項を無効にするのである。タイプ打ちの追加条項で，絶対的な堪航性維持の保証を定めたことを適当と当事者が考えたという事実が，第24条で米国法を傭船契約に摂取したことに影響を与えるものとは考えない。ともかく，そのような考え方の前提は，タイプ打ちの追加条項がなければ，米国法第 3 条 1 項，第 4 条 1 項により認められた堪航性担保義務がそのまま適用されるということである」。

米国法第4条(2)の免責事由

この条項によって，船主，場合によっては傭船者は，傭船契約の103行と104行で認められる免責事由に加え，前出493頁に列挙の米国法第4条(2)に規定されている免責事由による保護を主張できることとなる。

Aliakmon Progress 号の船主は，ニューヨーク・プロデュース書式による1航海の定期傭船契約で支払われるべき傭船料に関し，訴訟を提起した。この訴訟は，傭船者の義務を保証している会社に対して提起された。保証人は，アイスランドの港で生じた事故により発生した損害賠償のクレームと傭船料請求を相殺しようと試みた。本船がバースに接岸するとき，船長の後進の命令が遅れすぎたため，岸壁に衝突し，本船に損傷を与えた。仮修繕が行われ，Antwerp 向け貨物が積み取られた。貨物を揚荷後，Antwerp で本格的な修理が行われたが，この修理のため，傭船者は予定の貨物を積むことができず，代替貨物を39日間待たなければならなかった。この事件につき，控訴院は，船主は米国法第4条(2)(a)の免責事由（「本船の……運航における……船長の行為，懈怠，不履行」）を主張できるから，保証人のこの反対請求は支持できない，と判示した。
The Aliakmon Progress [1978] 2 Lloyd's Rep. 499.

Aquacharm 号は Baltimore から日本まで石炭を輸送するために，1航海だけ，ニューヨーク・プロデュース書式で定期傭船された。パナマ運河を通過できる喫水の限界まで貨物の積取を命じられた船長は，うかつにもパナマ運河の一部をなす真水の湖の部分を通過しなければならないことを考慮に入れず，本船の前部の喫水が大きくなり過ぎた。その結果，本船はパナマ運河への進入を拒否された。貨物の一部を他船に積み替えて，パナマ運河を通過し，通過後に他船に積んだ貨物を再積込したため，本船に大幅な遅れが生じた。控訴院は，米国法第4条(2)(a)で免責と規定されている本船の取扱に関する船長の過失により損害が生じているため，本船はオンハイヤーであったと判示し（前出本書436頁を参照），傭船者が損害賠償として，船主に支払った傭船料の回収を求める代わりのクレームは認められなかった。
The Aquacharm [1980] 2 Lloyd's Rep. 237 および [1982] 1 Lloyd's Rep. 7. (C. A.).

反対に，傭船契約103, 104行に規定の免責は，同法第3条(8)の保護を超える部分につき無効となる。

第2条が貨物の「積込，取扱，積付，運送，保管，管理および揚荷」だけに言及していることより，米国法（上述の第3条(8)も含んで）がどの程度まで適用されるかについては，これまで議論の対象となってきた。Adamastos 事件で，Devlin 判事は米国法第4条(1)と(2)の「滅失もしくは損傷」という文言は，物品の物理的な滅失や損傷に限定されないものの，上記に示した第2条に列挙された作業に「関する」もしくは「関連する」滅失もしくは損傷に限定されるとの見解を示した。貴族院では，多数の判事が Devlin 判事の見解を支持し，「滅失および損傷」は物理的な滅失もしくは損傷に限定されず，ゆえにこの事件のクレーム，すなわち連続航海の傭船契約のもとで航海数が減少したとのクレーム（Somervell 卿が考えたように，このクレームが貨物の積込と運送に関連して生じたか否かにかかわらず）もその範囲に含まれるとされた。しかしながら，The Satya Kailash [1984] 1 Lloyd's Rep. 588（同判例集595頁）事件の控訴院は，この点に関し Adamastos 事件で貴族院が決定したことは，「契約の当該事項が単に海上運送だけでなく航海にも関連しているのであれば，第2条の明白な文言にもかかわらず，第4条の免責は契約上の航海に関連するものにも適用あると読まれなければならない」ことを示したに過ぎない，と述べている。

The Satya Kailash 事件の控訴院は，さらに続けて，ヘーグ・ルールが摂取されている場合は，第2条で言及された事項に関連する滅失や損傷ばかりではなく，傭船契約上履行されるべ

きその他の契約上の行為に関してもヘーグ・ルールは船主に保護を与えるという、より広い原則を定めた。Robert Goff 卿判事は、次のように述べた（同判例集596）。「米国法第2条は、海上運送契約に関して、米国法に規定されている船主が負わなければならない責任と義務、および主張できる権利と免責事由が適用となる、船主の活動を示すものである。この活動の範囲は非常に広い包括的なものであり、米国法が適用される通常の船荷証券契約に関するすべての範囲の行為を含んでいる。それゆえ、そのような契約において、運送人はそのすべての関連行為において、第4条の免責事由の権利を行使できる。しかしながら、傭船契約において（それが定期傭船契約であれ航海傭船契約であれ）、船主は、第2条に規定の行為よりも広い範囲の行為を履行することが求められる。例えば、定期傭船契約では、空船航海を行わなければならないし、航海傭船契約では、契約書に定められたもくしは傭船者に命令された積荷港に向かわなければならない。次のような問題が出てくる。もし米国法が傭船契約に摂取されている場合、船主は広い範囲の行為に関し、第4条の免責事由を援用することができるのであろうか。この問題に対する Admastos 事件の貴族院の多数意見による回答は、これを肯定していると、私は思う」。

したがって、The Satya Kailash 事件では、母船から小麦を積むことは傭船契約上、履行しなければならない契約上の行為であるから、母船を軽くするために起用された船の船主は、その本船が母船（母船は傭船者の所有であった）に与えた損害につき、たとえその行為が米国法第2条の範囲内にない場合でも、その本船の船主は第4条の免責事由を主張することができると判示された（前出596頁を参照）。前出の The Aliakmon Progress 事件、Australian Oil Refining v. Miller [1968] 1 Lloyd's Rep. 448 事件および後者の事件に対する The Satya Kailsh 事件での見解も参照。

ハーター法第3条で認められている免責は、前項で説明された米国海上物品運送法第2条によって課されたと同じような制限に服するものと表示されているわけではない。このことは、傭船契約が単に1936年米国海上物品運送法のみに言及している場合に比べて、ニューヨーク・プロデュース書式の第24条に、より広い適用が認められると言えるのかもしれない。しかしながら、151から153行の文言によるハーター法の摂取は、明らかに米国向けもしくは米国からの「すべての貨物に関して」適用になる事実を考えれば、より広い適用が認められることは疑わしく、やはり同じような制限があることを示しているように思われる。

520 米国海上物品運送法第3条(6)

米国法の摂取により、船主に第3条(6)の1年間の出訴期限を主張する権利が与えられることとなる（前出本書509頁と The Agios Lazaros [1976] 2 Lloyd's Rep. 47 事件を参照）。第3条(6)の「滅失もしくは損傷」という文言は、物理的な滅失および損傷に限定されず、貨物に関連した滅失もしくは損傷にも適用される。The Ot Sonja [1993] 2 Lloyd's Rep. 435 (C. A.) 事件を参照。この The Ot. Sonja 事件では、船主の傭船契約違反により、航海傭船の傭船者が被った、貨物の船積遅延による経済的損失や臨時のタンク清掃や貨物の汲み上げ費用は、貨物に関連する滅失もしくは損傷であると判断され、その費用に関するクレームは米国法第3条(6)を摂取している Asbantakvoy 書式の傭船契約のもとで、出訴期限徒過と判示された。しかしながら、The Standard Ardour [1988] 2 Lloyd's Rep. 159 事件では、Saville 判事は、船荷証券発行の遅れによる傭船者のクレームは積荷に関連するものではないから、第3条(6)の1年の出訴期限にはかからない、と判示した。

ニューヨーク・プロデュース書式の傭船契約に貨物クレームの取扱に関する PI クラブ間協定の出訴期限に関する規定を摂取している効果については、前出の373頁を参照。

米国海上物品運送法第4条(4)と第4条(6)

船主は、また第4条(4)に基き限定された離路の権利及び第4条(6)により認められた危険品に関する権利を得る（前出222頁を参照）。

米国海上物品運送法第4条(3)

この条項の文言については、前出223頁を参照。The Athanasia Comninos [1990] 1 Lloyd's Rep. 277（前出357頁を参照）事件で、Mustill判事は、ニューヨーク・プロデュース書式第8条から生ずる黙示の補償のもとで、傭船者は船主からのクレームに対する抗弁としてこの条項を利用することはできない、と判示した。確かに、同判事は、この条項が傭船契約において何らかの意味を有するものであるかについて、疑問を呈した。彼は次のように言っている。「ここは、ヘーグ・ルールを定期傭船契約の不適切な文脈のなかに摂取することによって生ずる難しい問題を十分に議論する場所ではない。ただ、当事者がヘーグ・ルールを含めることにより当事者がどのような結果を導こうとしても、また、たとえ『荷主』を『傭船者』の意味に読むことができるとした場合であっても、従前、なかったことであるが、過失の概念を船主の黙示の補償に導入するには、これまでになく明確な言葉を使用しなければならないのである。ヘーグ・ルールの第4条規則3［これに相当するのは米国法では第4条(3)である］は、傭船契約の文脈においては、まったく何らの意味も持たないのかもしれない」。

損害の計測

船主が、自身の定期傭船契約中のヘーグ・ルールに違反したことにより、傭船者が自分自身の航海傭船契約の条項に従い、貨物汚損に対する責任を負わなければならなくなった場合、Clarke判事は、定期傭船契約に基づき傭船者が補償を求め得る損害賠償額は、Londonの仲裁人が航海傭船契約に基づき傭船者に支払を命じる額に、付帯費用を加えたものである、と判示した（The Sargasso [1994] 1 Lloyd's Rep. 412事件を参照）。この結論に抗するには、船主は、傭船者が仲裁で自らを適切に弁護しなかったことか、仲裁人の誤った行為、すなわち通常の合理的な仲裁人であれば出すことがない結論を出したことかのいずれかを立証しなければならない。

521 船主と傭船者間の業務の分担

米国法が摂取されても、傭船契約上明文で定められた傭船者が分担すべき業務の責任が船主に移動することはない。例えば、78行で合意されているように、傭船者は貨物の積込および積付に責任があることに変わりはない。米国法の役割は、傭船契約において船主の分担とされている業務の責任基準を定めることである。Pyrene v. Scindia [1954] 1 Lloyd's Rep. 321事件で、Devlin判事は、ヘーグ・ルールに関し、次のように述べている。「ヘーグ・ルールの目的は……契約上の業務の範囲を定めることではなく、その業務遂行の条件を定めるものである。当事者が、その契約で各自の業務分担を定めるにあたって、ヘーグ・ルールがその決定に介入することはない」（同判例集328頁）。

双方過失衝突条項

この条項は、ヘーグ・ルールによって運送船積貨物側による直接の求償からは保護されているものの、運送人が間接的にその貨物の責任を負うこととなる米国法のもとでの特別の状況に

対処するために，船荷証券に挿入されてきた条項である。米国法では，衝突による貨物の滅失および損傷につき，損害を被った貨物側は，その貨物を積載していない船に対して100パーセントの損害賠償を要求することができ，さらにその本船は，相手船積貨物へ支払った賠償につき，衝突に関する過失割合に応じて相手船に補償を求める。双方の船に過失がある場合，運送人は自分自身の貨物に間接的な責任を負うこととなる。双方過失衝突条項は，自船積貨物側に対して求償を求めうる契約上の権利を運送人に認めるもので，これにより有効にヘーグ・ルール上の地位を回復することになる。このことは，米国法の解説の部分の後出607頁でより詳しく説明される。そこではこの条項の有効性も併せて考察される。

NYPE 93

ニューヨーク・プロデュース書式1993年版の第31条は，傭船契約に次の各条項を摂取し，その傭船契約のもとで発行されるすべての船荷証券とウェイビルにその条項を挿入することを要求している。その条項とは，(a)至上条項，(b)双方過失衝突条項，(c)ニュー・ジェイソン条項，(d)米国向け航海・麻薬条項，(e)戦争条項である。第32条は，特別戦争解約条項であり，これは傭船契約のみに適用される（前出14／16頁の英文書式318行から402行および58／59頁を参照）。ハーター法への言及は一切なく，至上条項に関する部分は以下のとおりとなっている。

　　この船荷証券は，米国海上物品運送法，ヘーグ・ルール，ヘーグ・ヴィスビー・ルール，その他船荷証券の発行地または仕向地において強行法として適用されるべき同種の国内法の規定によってその効力を有し，かつ，それらの規定が本証券に挿入されているものとみなし，本証券に定めるいかなる事項も，上記の法に基づく運送人の権利もしくは免責の特権を放棄し，またはその責任もしくは義務を加重しないものとみなす。本証券の文言に，同法と抵触する箇所がある場合，その文言は抵触の箇所に限り無効とするが，それ以上のものではない。

522 米 国 法

ハーター法と海上物品運送法

　ハーター法と米国海上物品運送法はそれ自身の条項によって傭船契約に適用があるわけではないが，傭船契約に全面的あるいは部分的に摂取されてはじめて有効に適用されることとなる (*United States* v. *The Marilena P*, 433 F. 2d 164, 1969 AMC 1155 (4th Cir. 1969) 事件, *The Marine Sulphur Queen*, 460 F. 2d 89, 1972 AMC 1122 (2d. Cir.), 裁量上告拒絶 409 U. S. 982 (1972) 事件を参照)。

　ニューヨーク・プロデュース書式第24条はハーター法を，少なくとも米国発もしくは米国向けの貨物に関して，明らかに摂取している。ただし，単に「米国至上条項」に言及して，それ以上の言及がない場合に，有効に海上物品運送法が摂取されているかどうかについては，まだ結論が出ていない。この問題は，*Nissho-Iwai Co. Ltd.* v. *The Stolt Lion*, 617 F. 2d 907, 913, 1980 AMC 867, 875 (2d Cir. 1980) 事件で取り上げられたが，結論は出なかった。しかしながら，海上物品運送法は，その旨を明確に傭船契約に言及することにより，また明確に摂取を規定する至上条項か，そうでなくとも当事者が海上物品運送法に従う意図が示されている至上条項によって，傭船契約に摂取される。次の二つの判例を比較せよ。*Shell Oil. Co.* v. *The Gilda*, 790 F. 2d 1209 (5th Cir. 1986) 事件（この事件では，至上条項によって海上物品運送法が完全に摂取されている）と *Associated Metals & Minerals Corp.* v. *The Jasmine*, 983 F. 2 d 410, 1993 AMC 957 (2d Cir. 1993) 事件（この事件では，海上物品運送法を摂取するには，傭船契約の文言が不十分であると判示された）である。ニューヨーク・プロデュース書式第24条の，傭船契約は「次の条項に……依拠する」との文言と米国至上条項への言及により有効に海上物品運送法を摂取している (*Hartford Fire Insurance Co.* v. *Calmar S. S. Corp.*, 404 F. Supp. 442, 1976 AMC 2636 (W. D. Wash. 1975)，原審維持 554 F. 2d 1068 (9th Cir. 1977) 事件を参照)。ハーター法と米国海上物品運送法を傭船契約に摂取するもっとも大きな効果は，本船の堪航性の絶対的な担保責任が，本船を堪航状態に保つための相当の注意義務を尽くす義務に軽減されることである（前出270頁の論議を参照）。

　ハーター法と海上物品運送法には重大な差異が存在する。最も重要な差異は，両法とも貨物が本船に積載されたときから，本船より揚荷された時点までの期間につき適用されるが，ハーター法は揚荷後，貨物が適切に荷渡されるまでに生じた損害についても適用される (*Caterpillar Overseas S. A.* v. *The Expeditor*, 318 F. 2d 720, 1963 AMC 1662 (2d Cir.)，裁量上告拒絶 375 U. S. 942 (1963) 事件, *Procter and Gamble Ltd.* v. *The Stolt Llandaff*, 1981 AMC 1880, 1885 (E. D. La 1981)，原審維持 664 F. 2d 1285, 1982 AMC 2517 (5th Cir. 1982) 事件を参照)。

運送人としての船主と傭船者

　海上物品運送法のもとでは，貨物に関する限り，しばしば船主も傭船者も運送人となることが生じる。例えば，船荷証券が傭船者自身の様式で発行され，船長によって署名されているような場合がそうである。一般的な事例として，*Mente & Co.* v. *Isthmian S. S. Co.* (*The Quarrington Court*), 36 F. Supp. 278, 1940 AMC 1546 (S. D. N. Y. 1940)，原審維持 122 F. 2d 266, 1941 AMC 1234 (2d. Cir. 1941) 事件, *Trade Arbed Inc.* v. *The Ellispontos*, 482 F.

Supp. 991, 994 (S. D. Tex. 1980) 事件, *Granite State Ins. Co. v. The Caraibe*, 825 F. Supp. 1113, 1994 AMC 680 (D. P. R. 1993) 事件, *Hyundai Corp. U. S. A. v. Hull Ins. Proceeds of the Vulca*, 800 F. Supp. 124, 1993 AMC 434 (D. N. J. 1992), 原審維持 54 F. 3d 768, 1995 U. S. App. Lexis 11714 (3d Cir. 11 April 1995) 事件を参照。

われわれは、すでに船主および傭船者とも貨物損傷につき責任を負うべき場合の、船主、傭船者間の権利と責任の問題につき、議論を行ってきた。たとえ、船主および傭船者とも運送人であっても、それによって自動的に貨物に対する双方の権利・義務が同一となるわけではない。

Hasbro Industries Inc. v. *The St. Constantine*, 1980 AMC 1425 (D. Haw. 1980) 事件では、本船の機関室から火災が発生し、大きな貨物損傷が生じた。船荷証券は再傭船者が発行しており、貨物所有者は船主と再傭船者に対して訴訟を提起した。公判審理の後、裁判所は、火災は本船の不堪航より生じたもので、このことは船主自身が実際に承知していた事項であり、海上物品運送法第4条(2)(b)により船主が貨物側に責任を負うと認定した。しかしながら、たとえ傭船者および再傭船者の貨物に対する責任はまた海上物品運送法により規制されていたとしても、彼らは免責されたのである。裁判所は、傭船者は本船の運航や管理および乗組員の訓練等に関し、直接の管理を行うものでないことを承知していた。すなわち、傭船者は、海上物品運送法第4条(2)(b)で、運送人の責任を立証するのに必要とされる火災の原因について、傭船者自身が「実際に知りうべき」地位にはないとされた。

裁判所によれば、傭船者の義務は、船主をして本船を「完全に有効な稼働状態にし、もっとも水準の高い船級 Norwegian Veritas を維持させる」ことであった。この義務は、傭船者に「本船が船級の基準を維持するように要求させること、また船級が維持されていることを保証する本船の検査を監視させる」ことによって履行されるものであった。

The St. Constantine 事件は、米国海上物品運送法の火災免責のもとでのクレームに関するものであり、前出の議論で指摘したとおり、貨物所有者に、火災の原因が**実際に**運送人が承知している範囲で生じたことを立証する義務を負わせている。しかしながら、米国海上物品運送法の他の条項での立証責任はそれほど大きいものではなく、通常では、船主が本船の不堪航を是正するのに相当の注意義務を尽くさなかったために、貨物の損傷もしくは滅失の責任があるとされる場合には、傭船者の貨物に対する直接の責任は、船主とのそれと同じものとなる。

手続の開始時期

Son Shipping Co. v. *DeFosse & Tanghe*, 199 F. 2d 687 (2d Cir. 1952) 事件では、裁判所は、海上物品運送法が摂取されても、同法の訴訟提起に関する1年の期間制限の規定が、仲裁手続の開始時期にまで適用されることはないと判示した。同事件において、傭船者が貨物滅失を理由とする請求の申立をしたのは、1年の期間経過後であったので、船主は仲裁申立が時期遅れであると抗弁した。裁判所はその抗弁を退け、次のとおり判示した。

> 運送人が、傭船契約において海上物品運送法上享受すべき権利を留保していても、仲裁申立の時期が遅れたとは言えない。確かに、同法第1303条(6)に定める訴訟に関する1年の期間を経過した後に、仲裁の申立が行われた。しかし、同法でいう「訴訟 (suit)」に仲裁は含まれていないので、仲裁に関しては期間の制限はない。仲裁の申立は、訴訟することなく紛争を解決することを定めた契約の履行にすぎない。……契約によって紛争を仲裁に委ねることに合意した当事者、特に船主にとって仲裁申立の期限は非常に重要な問題である。しかし当事者が明示の期間制限によってその旨の合意を契約の条件としていない限り、本件におけるごとく合理的な期間内に申立を行えば、期間徒過とはならな

い（199 F. 2d at 689）。

　傭船契約に仲裁条項がある場合，請求が期間徒過になるか否かは仲裁人の判断による（*Conticommodity Services Inc.* v. *Phillip & Lion*, 613 F. 2d 1222（2d Cir. 1980），*Office of Supply, Government of the Republic of Korea* v. *N. Y. Navigation Co., Inc.* 469 F. 2d 377, 1973 AMC 1238（2d Cir. 1972））。

524　*National Iranian Oil Co.* v. *Mapco International Inc.*, 983 F. 2d 485, 491（3d Cir. 1992）事件で，裁判所は，仲裁を要求する時期に関しては仲裁人が決め，仲裁を強制する申立の時期に関しては地方裁判所が決定する，と判示した。しかしながら，非常に限られた状況では，裁判所は懈怠を理由に，仲裁の要求が否定されるべきかどうかを決めることができる。上記の *Conticommodity Services Inc.* 事件では，裁判所は，*Reconstruction Finance Corp.* v. *Harrisons & Crosfield*, 204 F. 2d 366（2d Cir.），裁量上告拒絶 346 U. S. 854（1953）事件の裁定を非常に狭く解釈し，次のように判示した。「裁判所は，仲裁法第4条が裁判所で決定することを要求している二つの点，すなわち仲裁合意の成立，仲裁の不履行，拒否もしくは懈怠という二つの点に関連する遅滞の問題ついてのみ決定することができる」（613 F. 2d at 1226）。例えば，もし一方の当事者が仲裁を求める要求を遅らせたことで，もう一方の当事者が仲裁の要求に関連する証拠を提出することが阻害されたことを示した場合，引き延ばした当事者が仲裁法によって仲裁を強要することができるかどうかを決定するのは，裁判所の権限の範囲内である。

　「仲裁」は，海上物品運送法で使われている「訴訟」ではないという意味での，*Son Shipping* 事件判決の言葉にもかかわらず，New York の仲裁人は一般的に英国の法則に追随し，米国法を摂取している傭船契約に基づく貨物損傷についてのクレームの仲裁手続の開始に関しては，海上物品運送法規定の1年の期限を厳守することを要求してきた（*The Osrok*, SMA 654（Arb. at N. Y. 1971）事件を参照。これは後に 469 F. 2d 377（2d Cir. 1972）で原審維持の判断がなされている）。*The Uranus*, 1977 AMC 586, 590-91（Arb. at N. Y. 1977）事件では，仲裁審は「一般至上条項」を取り入れることによって，当事者は少なくとも貨物クレームに関する限り，1年の出訴期限を傭船契約の一部とすることを意図したとの結論を出した。*The Sivlerhawk*, SMA 1041（Arb. at N. Y. 1976）事件および *The Prairie Grove*, 1976 AMC 2589（Arb. at N. Y. 1976）事件でも，同じような結論が出されている。後者の事件では，仲裁審における1年の出訴期限の厳格な適用が地方裁判所によって肯定されている。同地裁は次のように述べた。

　　当事者は契約によって，貨物の滅失・損傷に関する運送人および本船の責任は，貨物引渡後1年以内に訴訟が提起されない限り消滅する旨合意した。そして，1年以内に訴訟も仲裁の申立もなされなかった。仲裁人は，請求が期限を徒過していると判断しているが，その判断は妥当であり，かつそのように判断すべきものであった（1976 AMC at 2594）。

　海上物品運送法を傭船契約に摂取した場合，荷役業者に対する貨物損害の求償も1年の出訴期限の適用を受ける。*United States* v. *The South Star*, 210 F. 2d 44（2d Cir. 1954）事件は，政府の船主に対する貨物損害賠償請求の訴訟であった。傭船契約には，貨物の滅失損害の賠償請求の訴に関する1年の出訴期限を定める海上物品運送法の規定が摂取されていた。訴訟は貨物引渡から1年以上経過した後提起され，船主に対する関係で，訴訟は却下された。しかし船主は，本船の代理店および荷役業者に対して引込訴訟を行っていた。政府は，1年の期限は代

理店,荷役業者には適用がないと主張した。しかし,裁判所はこの主張を退けて次のように述べた。

　　本船および船主は適切な方法で積付を行う義務があるが,その義務の履行は代理店および荷役業者に委託されており,したがって傭船契約上の出訴期限に関する規定は代理店および荷役業者のために適用されるとLeibell判事は判断したが,われわれもその判断に賛成である……(210 F. 2d at 45)。

　　船主または傭船者が,第三者である荷主から貨物に関する損害賠償請求の訴を提起された場合,荷主に払わざるをえない金額を回収すべく,内部求償することがある。このような場合,もととなる貨物損害賠償請求に,海上物品運送法の1年の出訴期限が適用されても,船主または傭船者のそれぞれ相手方に対する求償権には同法の1年の出訴期限は適用されない(*Lyons-Magnus Inc.* v. *American Hawaiian S. S. Co.*, 41 F. Supp. 575, 1941 AMC 1550 (S. D. N. Y. 1941)事件, *Spanish Amer. Skin Co.* v. *Buanno Transp. Co.*, 1975 AMC 910 (N. Y. Civ. 1975)事件, *Francosteel Corp.* v. *The Tien Cheung*, 375 F. Supp. 794, 1973 AMC 2370 (S. D. N. Y. 1973)事件)。この点は,権利行使懈怠の原則(doctrine of laches)の適用をうけ,裁判所または仲裁人は,求償権行使を扱う類似の州法を検討し,訴の提起が期限内になされているかどうかを決定する。New Yorkでは,州法での類似の出訴期限に関する規定により,もととなる貨物クレームの賠償金を支払ってから6年以内に求償権を行使すればよいとされる(C. P. L. R. §213; *St. Paul Fire and Marine Ins. Co.* v. *United States Lines*, 258 F. 2d 374, 1958 AMC 2385 (2d Cir. 1958),裁量上告拒絶 359 U. S. 910 (1959)事件を参照)。

　この原則は,傭船契約が海上物品運送法を摂取している場合にも適用される。前出 *Francosteel Corp.* 事件で裁判所は次のように述べている。

　　いずれにせよ,海上物品運送法の出訴期限は,求償権行使の訴訟には適用がない。求償権行使にこの法律を適用することは,連邦民事訴訟法第14条の目的および近年の判例の傾向と相反する。またこのように解さない限り,原告は出訴期限の巧妙な操作により被告を選択し,その被告が出訴期限徒過のため,第三者への求償ができないような立場に追い込むことができるようになるのである(例えば,原告が,出訴期限の1日前に訴訟を提起するような場合を考えよ)(1973 AMC at 2372)。

　同様に,*Marubeni-Iida (A) Inc.* v. *Toko Kaiun Kabushiki Kaisha*, 327 F. Supp. 519 (S. D. Tex. 1971)事件で,荷主が傭船者と船主に対して貨物損傷による損害賠償の訴を提起した。傭船者は荷役業者に求償の訴訟を提起した。荷役業者は船荷証券上の受益者であるという理論に基づき,米国海上物品運送法上の1年の出訴期限が適用され,求償権行使の訴訟は却下されるべきであると主張した。裁判所は,船荷証券上にその旨が明示されていれば,荷役業者は第三受益者と考えることができるとしながらも,この規定は荷主から荷役業者に対する直接の請求にのみ適用され,傭船者からの求償権行使には適用がない,と判示した。

　本書旧版で,われわれは,求償権が海上物品運送法の1年の出訴期限の適用を受けるという第5巡回区裁判所の異例の判決に言及した(*Grace Lines Inc.* v. *Central Gulf S. S. Corp.*, 416 F. 2d 977 (5th Cir. 1969),裁量上告拒絶 398 U. S. 939 (1970)事件)。しかしその判決は *Hercules Inc.* v. *Stevens Shipping Co., Inc* 事件において第5巡回区裁判所により「海底へ」沈められた。すなわち *Hercules Inc.* v. *Stevens Shipping Co. Inc.*, 698 F. 2d 726, 755, 1983 AMC 1786 (5th Cir. 1983)事件では,求償を求める訴訟の原因は,「貨物クレームとは別に,また貨物クレームに関する責任が確定してから生ずる」(698 F. 2d at 735)ものであり,さらに1年の出訴期限ではなく権利行使懈怠の原則が適用されるとの多数派の法則を採用

するに至っている（全裁判官出席）。

　それにもかかわらず，求償クレームに関する問題の難しさが，The Ruth, SMA 2426 (Arb. at N. Y. 1987) 事件の仲裁人の判断のなかで示されている。この事件では，中間にいる傭船者が，London の仲裁において，貨物汚損につき責任を負うと判断された。この貨物クレームは海上物品運送法によって律せられ，貨物引渡後，1 年以上を経過した後，仲裁に付託されることとなったが，英国高等法院はクレームは出訴期限を経過しておらず，仲裁手続を続行することを許した。London の仲裁で責任を負うと判断された中間の傭船者は，原傭船契約に基づき船主からの求償を求めて New York で仲裁を提起した。しかしながら，New York の仲裁審は，傭船者に対して不利な判断を下した。仲裁審によれば，船主とは New York での仲裁を合意し，また再傭船者とは London での仲裁を合意したことにより，中間の傭船者は英国法と米国法の抵触の危険を負担することとなった。New York の仲裁審は，もし貨物汚損のクレームが New York で提起されていれば，そのクレームは出訴期限徒過で拒絶されていたはずである，との見解を示した。さらに，英国の法廷での判決にもかかわらず，New York では出訴期限徒過である，と仲裁審は判断した。そして，仲裁審は，そのような法の抵触の危険は，この場合，船主ではなく，傭船者が負うべきであるとした。

526 双方過失衝突条項

　「双方過失衝突条項」は，両船に過失あって衝突した場合，その衝突の結果発生した貨物損害に関連して適用される。もし衝突が航海過失によって生じた場合，通常米国海上物品運送法上では，航海過失免責が適用されるので，荷主は当該積載船舶から何らの損害賠償を得ることもできない。しかし，荷主は衝突の相手方である非積載船から全額を回収することができる。(The Atlas, 93 U. S. 302, 315 (1876) 事件)。その結果，非積載船は責任割合に応じて積載船に対して求償することになる (The Chattahoochee, 173 U. S. 540 (1898) 事件を参照)。双方過失衝突条項がある場合，積載船は，貨物クレームの損害賠償として非積載船に支払った金額を，荷主から回収することができる。

　すなわち，A 船と B 船が，両船の過失で衝突した場合，A 船の貨物は B 船から全額を回収できる。そして，B 船が貨物に支払った金額は B 船の損害となり，B 船はその一部を A 船の過失割合に応じて A 船から回収することができる。結局 A 船は自らの船に積載した貨物に対する直接の責任がないにもかかわらず，間接的にその責任の一部を負担することになる。双方過失条項の目的は，この間接責任を回避することにある。

　双方過失衝突条項は，ハーター法もしくは米国海上物品運送法が適用される海上運送契約において，公運送人により使用された場合には無効である，と長い間判断されてきた。United States v. Atlantic Mut. Ins. Co., 343 U. S. 236, 1952 AMC 659 (1952) 事件。この事件で最高裁は，一般貨物運送に従事する船主は，上記二つの法律の下で，自己の過失の責任を免れることはできない，と判断した。

　しかしながら，傭船契約という私的契約において双方過失衝突条項が使用された場合，同条項は有効であると判断されている。American Union Transport Inc. v. United States, 1976 AMC 1480 (N. D. Cal. 1976) 事件。この事件で，裁判所は次のように述べている。

　　私的運送契約の当事者は，損失や損害の危険を自由に調整することができ，過失責任も含めていかなる理由による責任も回避することができる……。

　　また，留意すべきことは，双方過失衝突条項が，本件のように私的運送契約で使用されている場

合,積載船を,航海過失による貨物クレームから実質的に「免責する」わけではないということである。すなわち,貨物のかかる請求から積載船を免責することが,海事法の政策であるからそうするのである。なおまた,同条項によって非積載船の過失責任が免責されるわけでもない。私的運送契約において,航海過失免責という制定法上の条項があるにもかかわらず間接的に一部負担せざるをえなくなった貨物損害を貨物から回収することによって,貨物に対する積載船の航海過失免責という法の規定を意味あるものにすることを求めているだけである。

一般運送に関連する船荷証券上の双方過失衝突条項に対する公序良俗の観点からの配慮がどのようなものであるにせよ,そのような配慮は,私的運送契約における双方過失衝突条項の適法性を認める長い間確立された海事法上の原則を覆す理由とはならない(1976 AMC at 1483-1485)。

Alamo Chemical Transportation Co. v. *The Overseas Valdes*, 1979 AMC 2033, 469 F. Supp. 203 (E. D. La 1979) 事件を参照。この事件でも,私的運送契約において双方過失衝突条項は有効である,と判示されている。

双方過失衝突条項が至上条項と一緒に傭船契約に盛り込まれている場合に,同条項が傭船契約上有効であるかどうかの問題がまだ残されている(*American Union Transport Inc.* 事件における傭船契約はいかなる形においても海上物品運送法を摂取していなかった)。至上条項は,その文言自体により,双方過失衝突条項をも含め,海上物品運送法に反するいかなる条項をも無効にすることを目的とするものであるから,至上条項が同条項を無効にするという点については,議論の余地がある。しかし,上記で示唆したとおり,たとえ海上物品運送法が傭船契約に摂取されていても,双方過失衝突条項が私的契約においては有効である,と結論づける説得力のある理由がある。

Allseas Maritime v. *The Mimosa*, 574 F. Supp. 844 (S. D. Tex. 1983) の事例で,裁判所は,海上物品運送法を特別に摂取している私的運送契約において,双方過失衝突条項が有効で効力を有する条項であると判示した。

裁判管轄条項

船荷証券には,しばしば裁判管轄条項が含まれる。*Indussa Corp.* v. *The Ranborg*, 377 F. 2d 200, 1967 AMC 589 (2d Cir. 1967) 事件では,船荷証券の「管轄」条項は,「本船荷証券に関連して生ずる一切の紛争は,運送人の主たる営業の場所が存在する国において解決されるものとし,本船荷証券中に別段の規定がない場合は,その国の法律が適用される」となっていた。*Indussa* 事件における運送人は,ノルウェー国をその本拠地にし,貨物損傷クレームの抗弁として,「管轄」条項は拘束力を有すると主張した。第2巡回区控訴裁判所は,この抗弁を拒否し,「管轄」条項は海上物品運送法上効力を有しない,と判断した。裁判所によれば,裁判管轄条項は,貨物損傷に対する運送人の責任を軽減する効果を有するので,海上物品運送法第3条(8)に反する,とのことであった。裁判所は次のように述べている。

> 米国向けもしくは米国行き貨物の船荷証券の契約条項が,貨物所有者が運送人に対する米国での裁判管轄を持つことを妨げて,裁判所がその裁判を行えず,議会が定めた実質的な規則の適用もできなくなるのであれば,議会はそのような条項を無効にする意図を有する,とわれわれは考える。

Indsussa 事件の判例は,その他の巡回裁判所でも例外なく遵守され,外国裁判管轄条項は,海上物品運送法第3条(8)により無効であるとの,確固たる基本原則が確立した。

この基本原則の有効性は,たとえこの原則が未だに生き残っているとしても,米国最高裁の

Vimar Seguros y Reaseguros S. A. v. *The Sky Reefer*, 515 U.S. — 1995 AMC 1817 (19 June 1995) 事件の画期的な判決によって,大きく減じられることとなった。この事件では,裁判所は船荷証券のなかの「外国仲裁管轄条項」を有効と判断したのである。そのような判断を行うに際し,裁判所の多数意見は *Indussa* 事件の理由づけをきっぱりと否定したのである。今後,*The Sky Reefer* 事件の判決がどのように適用されていくか見なければならないが,多数意見が強調するところでは,船荷証券の管轄選択条項は,それが外国での仲裁を規定している場合でも,外国の裁判所の管轄を規定している場合でも,その条項自体がとにかく運送人の貨物滅失に対する運送人の責任を減少させない限りにおいて,有効として,強制的に適用されそうである。もっとも,運送人の責任を減少させる場合には,海上物品運送法第3条(8)に反することになる。

傭船契約の性質

"167. 25. The vessel shall not be required to enter any ice-bound port, or any port where lights or light-ships have been or are about to be with-
168. drawn by reason of ice, or where there is risk that that in the ordinary course of things the vessel will not be able on account of ice to safely enter the
169. port or to get out after having completed loading or discharging.
170. 26. Nothing herein stated is to be construed as a demise of the vessel to the Time Charterers. The owners to remain responsible for the
171. navigation of the vessel, insurance, crew, and all other matters, same as when trading for their own account."

「25. 本船は結氷港，もしくは結氷を理由として灯標または灯船が撤去されているか撤去のおそれのある港，もしくは結氷のため通常の方法では本船が安全に入港し，もしくは積荷，揚荷後出港できないような危険がある港には，配船されないものとする。
26. 本契約書記載のいかなる事項も，定期傭船者に対する船舶賃貸借とは，解釈しないものとする。船主は常に本船の航海，船舶保険，乗組員，その他一切の事項につき，自己の計算において航海をする場合と同一の責任を負う。」

氷 条 項

ボルタイム書式第15条，後出654頁を参照。

船舶の賃貸借ではない

ニューヨーク・プロデュース書式の170行は，いずれにしても傭船契約のその他の規定からの結論，すなわち，この契約が「定期」傭船契約であり，「裸傭船」契約ではないことを強調している。170行と同趣旨のものを欠いているボルタイム書式においても，同様のことが言える。定期傭船契約と他の傭船契約との基本的差異は次のとおりである。

賃貸借（demise）契約

賃貸借契約においては，船主は，定期的な傭船料の支払と交換に，合意された期間本船を傭船者に賃貸する。
傭船者は，本船の占有と管理権を取得する。実際，少なくとも第三者との関係においては，傭船者は一時的に本船の船主になる（*The Father Thames* [1979] 2 Lloyd's Rep. 364 事件を参照）。Herschell 卿主席判事は，*Baumwoll v. Furness* [1893] A.C. 8 事件の傭船者につき，「傭船者は，その場限りの，かつ傭船期間中，本船の船主となる」と述べた。
通常，船主は本船の職員および部員をつけることなく本船を傭船者に提供し，傭船者はみずから乗組員を手配し，給与を支払う。このような傭船契約を「裸」傭船契約と呼び，しばしば「賃貸借（demise）」契約と同義として用いられる。ともかく，賃貸借（demise）契約での本船の職員および部員は，ほとんどの目的において，船主ではなく傭船者の被用者としての取扱

をうける。したがって,船長が署名した船荷証券によって拘束されるのは,賃貸借（demise）契約の傭船者であり,船主ではない（*Baumwoll* v. *Furness* [1893] A.C. 8 事件を参照）。同様に,職員もしくは乗組員の過失の結果,本船が衝突した場合の損害に関し,責めを負うのはやはり船主ではなく,賃貸借（demise）契約の傭船者である。*Fenton* v. *Dublin S. S.* (1838) 8 A. & E. 835 事件および結果として本船に対して海事リーエンを設定した事件である *The Father Thames* [1979] 2 Lloyd's Rep. 364 事件での Sheen 判事の判決を参照。

530 定期傭船契約

定期傭船契約では,船主は,定期的な傭船料の支払と交換に,合意された期間,職員と部員をつけた本船を傭船者に提供する。

燃料油については,傭船者が負担するのが通常である。しかし,職員および部員は船主の被用者のままで,船主が本船の航海および本船の全般の管理に関し責任を保持する。船主は本船の占有を手放すものではない。*Port Line* v. *Ben Line* [1958] 1 Lloyd's Rep. 290 事件で,Diplock 判事は,ニューヨーク・プロデュース書式の傭船契約は「定期傭船契約であり,賃貸借（Demise）傭船契約ではない。傭船者は,本船に対する所有権も占有権も取得しない」と言っている。このことがニューヨーク・プロデュース書式の170行で強調されている。

定期傭船契約は,本船のリースでも,賃貸契約でもない。むしろ,業務提供契約,すなわち船主が職員および部員と本船を提供することによって行うサービスを提供する契約であると言える。もっとも標準的な傭船契約に「貸す」「借りる」「引渡」「返還」といった反対の意味を示すような重要語句が使用されてはいるが,定期傭船契約は役務提供の契約である。*The London Explorer* [1971] 1 Lloyd's Rep. 523 事件で,Reid 卿は次のように言っている。「そのような傭船契約では,本当のところ,賃貸というものはない。傭船期間のすべての期間を通じて,本船の占有は船主にあり,船長以下乗組員は,船主の被用者であることに争いはない。傭船者が手にするのは,本船を使用する権利である」（同判例集526頁）。また,前出173頁の「引渡」における *The Madeleine* 事件についての Roskill 判事の見解も参照。

Sea & Land Securities v. *Dickinson* (1942) 72 Ll.L. Rep. 159 事件で,MacKinnon 卿判事は,これらの表現は本船の賃貸借（demise）契約をその起源としていることに言及し,これがより近代的な定期傭船契約においても使われている,と言っている。同判事は,162頁で次のように述べた。「定期傭船契約の最近のものは,本質的には,一定の期間,船主が運送人として船主の被用者および乗組員を使って,定期傭船者が本船に持ち込んだ貨物を輸送する役務を提供するということを,船主と傭船者間で合意したものであるが,その印刷された書式の言い回しのいくつかは,古い賃貸借契約書式で使用されていた言い回しがそのまま引き継がれている。その例として,『船主は本蒸気船を貸すことに合意した』とか『傭船者は本蒸気船を借りることに合意した』という表現がそうである。しかし,そのような本船を「貸す」とか「借りる」というようなことはないのである。「返還する」という言葉は,船主から傭船者に対して引渡があったり,占有の移転があった場合に関連するものである。しかし,そのようなことは何もないのである。本船はいつの時点でも,船主が占有しており,乗組員も船主が提供した上で,傭船者の貨物を輸送する役務を提供することを引き受けているだけである」。

上記で述べたように,この定期傭船契約は,船の賃貸借（demise）契約と対照的なもので,賃貸借（demise）契約は,本質的には船主が本船の占有をまさに手放してしまう契約である。上記で引用されているのと同じ判決のなかで,MacKinnon 卿判事は,船の賃貸借（demise）契約と定期傭船契約間のこの違いを強調して,次のように述べている（同判例集163

頁)。「ボートを借りて，自分自身でそのボートを漕ぐこと，すなわちボートの占有がその者に移転することと，浜辺にいる人間がボートに乗せてもらう契約をすること，すなわちそれは彼をボートに乗せて輸送するという役務を提供することとなるが，との間には大きな差異がある」。

定期傭船契約は，本船が利用される区域と（前出193頁の航路定限を参照），積んではいけない貨物の種類（前出219頁の「適法な貨物」）を特定している。

「1航海のための定期傭船契約」については，以下の「航海傭船契約」を参照。

航海傭船契約

航海傭船契約では，船主が，職員・部員・燃料をみずから供給し，運賃を対価として，合意された航海で特定の貨物を輸送することに合意する契約である。「その運賃は，その航海で単純に積・揚された貨物の数量をもとに計算されること」を特徴としている。

そのような傭船契約は，複数の航海をカバーする場合があり，その複数の航海は，空船航海の必要により分割されるか（「連続航海」傭船契約，例えば [1958] 1 Lloyd's Rep. 73 と後出594頁の The Saxon Star 事件を参照），船主が傭船者以外の者の貨物を運ぶために就航航路を変えることによって（「断続的航海」傭船契約，例えば The Oakworth [1975] 1 Lloyd's Rep. 581 事件と前出464頁を参照）分割される。よくあることであるが，連続航海傭船契約が，特定の航海数を規定しているのではなく，ある一定の期間で行いうる，できる限り多くの航海を行うことを規定している場合は，それは少なくとも幾ばくかの定期傭船契約の性質を有することとなる。The Berge Tasta [1975] 1 Lloyd's Rep. 422 事件の Donaldson 判事の見解（同判例集424頁）を参照。

今日，非常にしばしば使用されるのは，「1航海のための定期傭船契約」である。これは，普通，通常の標準定期傭船契約の書式で作成されるが，特定の航海を明示し，年，月，日といった期間ではなく，その航海を遂行する実際の継続期間を規定する。それにもかかわらず，傭船者の傭船料の支払が，定期的間隔をおいて，なされるとすれば，傭船者は特定された航路に船を就航させなければならず，また当初よりその期間がどのくらいになるか不確かであっても，そのような傭船契約は，やはりほとんどの目的で，定期傭船契約として扱われることとなる（Temple Steamship v. Sovfracht (1945) 79 Ll.L. Rep. 1 事件と前出183と193頁の解説を参照）。

1943年法改革（履行不能により消滅する契約）に関する法は，賃貸借 (demise) 契約，定期傭船契約には適用があるが，航海傭船契約には適用がない（The Eugenia [1963] 2 Lloyd's Rep. 155 and 381 事件および前出479頁で議論した事項を参照）。

航　　海

傭船者が第2条に従い，水先人を提供し，水先料を支払うとしても，水先人は傭船者の被用者となるわけではなく，傭船者が水先人の過失責任を水先人に代わって負うわけではない（(1900) 17 T.L.R. 101 ならびに前出279頁の Fraser v. Bee 事件とその一般的な見解を参照）。

NYPE93

ニューヨーク・プロデュース書式1993年改訂版では，1946年版の第26条で船主が責任を負うべき事項に，「水先人および曳船の行為」を追加している（前出14頁と58頁を参照）。

保険填補の範囲

ニューヨーク・プロデュース書式の第26条は、船主に対して「船主自身の計算において航海をするのと同様に」保険付保の責任を負わせるものであるが、第1条の船体保険料支払義務と合体して、船体および機器の危険と同様に、契約上の航路定限の範囲内の戦争危険に対しても保険を付保することを船主に要求している。*World Magnate Shipping* v. *Rederi A/B Soya* [1975] 2 Lloyd's Rep. 498 事件における Donaldson 判事の判決を参照。第1条の「本船の……」という文言は、狭く解釈してはならず、適切な補助的填補、例えば運賃および支出のようなものの填補が含まれる（後出 *The Athos* [1981] 2 Lloyd's Rep. 74 事件を参照）。

どのような形で保険が付保されるかは、付保される危険の正確な範囲や付保される船体の保険付保額も含めて、船主の裁量事項である。しかし、その裁量は、慎重なる船主が有する基準に従って、行使されなければならない（後出 *The Athos* [1981] 事件を参照）。

532 「船主自身の計算において航海するのと同様に」との文言があるからと言って、傭船契約開始前の航海時と同じ保険填補を、傭船契約期間中も船主は維持しなければならない、ということにはならない（*The Antaios* [1981] 2 Lloyd's Rep. 284 事件と後出の Robert Goff 判事の判決を参照）。

ボルタイム書式

ボルタイム書式第3条は、船主に「本船の保険を、手配し保険料を支払うこと」を要求している。戦争保険に関し、特別に規定している条項が、第21条である。もし、本船がその条項の(A)に定義されている危険水域に就航する場合、船主は、(B)の145行から148行により最終的には傭船者の勘定で、「本船に対する自分自身の権利もしくはそれによって生じうる危険に瀕する傭船料につき、船主が適当と判断する条件で、保険を付保することができる」。STB タンカー書式にも、その501行から508行までに同様の規定があり、それはより特定的かつ限定的なものである。

本船の損傷に関する船主の傭船者に対するクレームの効果

船主が、本船の保険料を支払うべしとする条項は、必ずしも船主が、傭船者またはその被用者による船体損害につき、傭船者に対して損害賠償を行うことができないことを意味しない（*Aira Force* v. *Christie* (1892) 9 T. L. R. 104 事件を参照）。

さらに、船主と傭船者の合意によって、船体保険者が要求する追加の保険料を傭船者が支払うことにより、傭船者が本船を航路定限外の区域に就航させることができると言って、航路定限外での港の安全性に関する傭船者の責任が免除されるわけではない。

> *Helen Miller* 号に関するニューヨーク・プロデュース書式の傭船契約には、就航区域の定義に関し、次のような追加条項が含まれていた。「就航区域は、IWL（協会担保航路定限）の範囲内の Montreal 港を含みかつ同港に至る St. Lawrence 河の安全港間とするが、キューバ……ギニアおよびすべての非安全港を含まない。しかし、傭船者は IWL（協会担保航路定限）の制限を超えることができ、その場合傭船者は追加の保険料を支払うこととなる」。傭船者は、IWL（協会担保航路定限）の制限外の港へ向かうことを命じ、そこへの航海で本船は氷による船体損害を被り、後に、その事故発生時そこは非安全港であったと判断された。Mustill 判事は、傭船者はこの損害につき責任を負うと、判示した。船主は、IWL（協会担保航路定限）の範囲外に本船を就航させることに一般的に合意した、しかしそれによって傭船者の安全港選択義務が減ぜられることにはならないし、その義務は、

傭船者が追加の保険料を支払うことによって影響を受けるものでもない。「追加保険料の支払によって，傭船者は利益を得る。その利益とは，もしその保険料を負担しなければ，船主が許さなかったであろうことを履行させることができたということである。しかし，だからと言って傭船者は，そのことによって，まったく危険なしに，そのような航海に本船を就航させることができるというわけではない」。
 The Helen Miller [1980] 2 Lloyd's Rep. 95.

 しかし，The Evia (No. 2) [1982] 2 Lloyd's Rep. 307事件では，貴族院は，ボルタイム書式第21条の戦争条項により，特に船主はその条項が規定する危険を保険に付保することができ，そのための追加保険料を傭船者に負担させることができるのであるが，その条項は完全な条項として機能し，その条項が規定する危険に関して，船主は他の条項に基づいてクレームを提起することはできない，とされる（前出242頁と後出659頁を参照）。

傭船者による保険料払戻条項

 定期傭船契約には，ボルタイム書式145行から148行のように，既に印刷されている条項か，あるいは，特別の追加条項によって，ある種の保険につき，付保は船主で行うものの，保険料の支払に関しては究極的に一部もしくはすべてを傭船者とすることを規定している。IWL（協会担保区域）の範囲を超えるための追加保険料に関し，前出の The Helen Miller 事件および以下に示した危険水域における戦争危険に対する保険に関する一連の紛争を参照。

533 保険料の割引

 傭船者は，船主が実際に保険者に支払った以上の保険料を負担する義務はない。それゆえ，傭船者は，保険者が船主に与えた総保険料に対する割引を利用することができる。The Athos [1981] 2 Lloyd's Rep. 74 事件を参照。この事件で，Neill 判事は次のように述べている。「一応保険料を払い戻さなければならない義務は，相手方が実際に支払った分を払い戻す義務であって，払い戻す者は，相手方が得た割引の利益を享受することができる，ということを私は確信する」。

戦争保険の保険料

 イラン／イラク間の敵対行為勃発の後，生じた一連のできごとにおいて，傭船者は，戦争保険の保険料の払戻に関し，船主の要求につき争った。ほとんどの事案は通常の標準的な書式の傭船契約によっており，細かな文言は異なるものの，追加条項があり，傭船者による船主への保険料の払戻が定められていた。

 これらの事件の判決から明らかになった一つの原則は，戦争危険の付保に関し，どの程度のものを用意するかは（そしてその保険料は，問題となる追加条項が規定する限度で，最終的には傭船者の負担となる），船主の裁量事項となる。もっとも，その裁量は，慎重な船主の基準に従って行使されなければならない（[1981] 2 Lloyd's Rep. 74 と後出の The Athos 事件を参照）。

 さらに，これらの判決から言えることは，ニューヨーク・プロデュース書式第1条の「本船の保険付保」およびそれと同様なその他一般的表現は，狭く解釈されるべきではなく，ある種の付随的な危険，例えば拘留費用，運賃や船費など厳密に言えば，本船自身の保険とは言えない危険にまで拡張される。

 傭船者が船主に払い戻さなければならない義務は，特定の追加条項の正確な文言に拠る。そ

れゆえ，以下に示した判例が主に問題とするのは，これらの正確な文言の解釈である。

Athos 号のニューヨーク・プロデュース書式の傭船契約には，次のような追加条項が入っていた。「第35条．戦争保険は常時付保されていなくてはならず……追加の戦争保険に関しては，請求書と支払を裏付ける領収証をつけて請求すれば，傭船者は船主に対してその費用を支払わなければならない。」

1980年2月，傭船者は本船にイランに向かうことを命じた。そのときイランは危険地域であった。その結果，船主は，戦争保険協会である The Hellenic に追加の保険料を支払わなければならなかった。The Hellenic からの塡補は以下の部分に分けられていた。

Part A. (i) 船体保険
　　　　(ii) 運賃，保険料，船費
　　 B. 拘留，離路費用
　　 C. P&I 保険料
　　 D. 損害拡大防止費用

追加の保険料は，本船の保険付保額を基礎として計算される。それは運賃や船費の要素を含んでおり，本船の市場価格が大きく下落しても，数年間は同じ水準が維持される。さらに，保険料を算出するために，保険付保額に掛けることになる百分率は，除外することを選ぶこともできた拘留や離路費用の危険も含んだ完全な塡補を維持することを船主が決定したため，大幅に大きくなった。拘留および離路費用の部分の保険塡補は，もし戦争によって拘留されたり，離路したりして，その拘留が90日間以上になった場合，通常の費用を塡補するものであった。それは1年間の拘留で支払われる金額が保険付保額の10パーセントとなるように，実際は拘留されている期間に比例して支払われることとなっていた。傭船者は，船主が傭船契約第35条に基づき傭船者に払戻を求めた保険料の額の大きさに反駁した。傭船者は，船主が運賃や船費および拘留，離路費用の担保を選択したことにより，船主は第1条の「本船」の保険付保以上のものを行ったと主張し，さらに保険付保額そのものも下げられるべきであったと主張した。Neill 判事は，船主が支払ったすべての追加保険料は傭船者から回収できると判示した。同判事は，第1条の「本船の保険」は狭く解釈されるべきではなく，保険付保の範囲は，「船主の裁量事項である。もっともその裁量は慎重な船主の基準に従って行使されなければならない」と述べた。船主により手配された保険付保は，この基準を満たしているし，船主が支払った追加保険料は第35条によって傭船者より回収可能である。特に，同判事は，船主は以下の点に関する権利を有すると判断した。

(a) 本船の付保額に，「本船が実際全損もしくは推定全損になった場合に船主が賠償を求める金額の一部」として，運賃や船費の部分を含ませることができる。
(b) 本船の市場価格が大幅に下落しても，一般的な取引上の慣習により，保険付保額を維持できる。
(c) 慎重なる船主として，イランに封じ込められるという非常に高い危険に鑑み，取捨選択可能な「拘留および離路費用」の保険を付保することができる。

The Athos [1981] 2 Lloyd's Rep. 74, その他の理由で上訴 [1983] 1 Lloyd's Rep. 127 事件。

Antaios 号は四つの定期傭船契約で傭船，再傭船されており，いずれの傭船契約もニューヨーク・プロデュース書式によるものであり，各々に追加として第40条が挿入されていたが，その第40条は次のような文言であった。「本船，職員，船員のための戦争危険保険料の増額は，船主から傭船者に速やかに通知され，本船がその保険料の増加する地域に就航すれば，傭船者はその増額分を支払う。しかし，傭船者が支払うべき増額分は，本船が London のロイズに付保されていれば，そのロイズが提示した額を超えない」。

どの傭船契約も，本船は，IWL（協会担保航路定限）の範囲内で，世界中を就航できる旨が規定されており（傭船者が追加保険料を負担すれば，IWL の範囲を超えることができるとの条項もあった），また P&I 保険の加入も行うよう規定されていた。本船が原傭船契約によって1979年1月に傭船され，本船がアラブの湾岸に入ったとき，その地域はまだ Hellenic War Risks Association より追

傭船契約の性質   617

保険料を要する地域として宣言されていなかった。しかし,再傭船契約に基づき,本船が再傭船者へ引き渡されるときまでに,その地域は追加保険料を要する地域になった。Antaios 号が1981年9月17日に湾岸地域に入ったとき,船主は,「拘留および離路費用」(前出の The Athos 事件を参照)と「運賃,保険料および船費」に関する付保も含んだ,完全付保の保険料を Hellenic Association に支払った。

Robert Goff 判事は,(1)再傭船者は本船引渡時の保険料率からの増額分についてのみ支払う義務があるとし,(2)第40条は,Hellenic Association が提供するすべての付保に適用されることを意図したものであった,と判示した。
The Antaios [1981] 2 Lloyd's Rep. 284.

Oinoussian Virtue 号はニューヨーク・プロデュース書式によりペルシャ湾までの1航海のため傭船されることとなった。第36条(b)は次のように規定していた。「通常の戦争保険料に追加されるいかなる戦争保険の保険料およびもし認められているのであれば,戦争危険の割増賃金は,傭船者が負担するものとする」。Robert Goff 判事は,すべては特別条項の文言に拠るとして,「追加」という言葉は「通常」と対照すれば,本船の戦争保険付保で,追加料率の支払を要する地域に本船が入った場合に,支払われる保険料の追加分を指すのが自然な解釈である,と判示した。同判事はまた,傭船者は,「拘留および離路費用」の保険付保も含め(上記の The Athos 事件を参照),戦争保険協会での全付保分について船主が支払うべき保険料を負担する責任があるとした仲裁人の判断を,支持した。また,仲裁人は,船主がそのような付保をしたことは,合理的であり,かつ第36条(b)の「いかなる(any)」追加の戦争危険保険料に言及していると裁定し,同判事は支持した。
The Oinoussian Virtue (No. 2) [1981] 2 Lloyd's Rep. 300.

Apex 号は,アラビア湾岸への1航海のため,ニューヨーク・プロデュース書式で定期傭船された。追加条項の第53条は次のように規定していた。「船体および乗組員の基本的な戦争保険の保険料は常に船主が支払うべきであるが,定期傭船者の要請により,通常の戦争保険で付保されない地域に本船を進めるときには,このような危険の追加の保険料または乗組員の割増賃金については,船主の保険者やブローカーの原本の請求書の提示に対して,傭船者から船主に支払われるべきである」。
船主は,Hellenic Association に追加保険料を支払うことで,AからDまでのすべての戦争保険付保を維持することができた(上記の The Athos 事件を参照)。そして,船主は,その追加費用を傭船者に請求しようとしたが,A(i),CとD以外の付保については,傭船者はその追加費用の支払義務につき争った。
Mustill 判事は,第53条の「本船の船体および機関」は付保部分を定義していると解釈されるべきではなく,本船に関する通常の戦争危険保険を意味しているに過ぎない。それゆえ,Part A(ii)と Part B の付保部分についても,それが Hellenic Association が提供する保険の必須の部分だとして,傭船者は,追加保険料を負担する義務を負っている,と判示した(上記の The Athos 事件を参照)。
The Apex [1982] 2 Lloyd's Rep. 407.
(同様に,後出 The Agathon 事件も参照。その事件で,Hobhouse 判事は上記の「船体および機関」の解釈を批判した)

535 上述の事案はすべてニューヨーク・プロデュース書式の傭船契約に関するものであった。以下に続く事案は,ニューヨーク・プロデュース書式以外の定期傭船契約に関するものである。

Taygetos 号は Beepeetime 2 書式の定期傭船契約により,1975年から10年間定期傭船された。この傭船契約の第38条は次のように規定していた。「もし本船が戦争状態(事実上もしくは法律上の戦争状態)の地域に就航せざるをえないとき,船主が支払った追加の費用は,その費用を支払う前に,傭船者が同意の意思を示す機会を与えられることを条件に,傭船者が負担する。本船が安全地域の制限を超えることによる,戦争保険の保険者への追加保険料の支払および乗組員への割増賃金は,傭船者の負担とする」(第2文は,第38条の印刷文言に,タイプ打ちで追加したものであった)。1980, 1981

年アラビア湾向け航海に本船が就航したとき，傭船者が船主に追加保険料を支払う義務につき，争いが生じた。本船は Hellenic Association に付保されていた。Bingham 判事は，第38条の第2文は Part B の付保を取り込むほど十分に広いものであり（前出の *The Athos* 事件を参照），合理的で慎重な船主であれば，Part B の付保を選択の対象外にすることはない，と判示した。

The Taygetos [1982] 2 Lloyd's Rep. 272.

Agathon 号は，ボルタイム書式で定期傭船され，第21条（後出657頁を参照）は修正されなかった。12ヶ月の傭船期間内に，本船は Basrah 向け就航を命じられたが，1980年9月に閉塞されてしまった。本船は Hellenic Association の全面填補を付保していた（*The Athos* 事件を参照）。Hobhouse 判事によって次のように判示された。第21条(B)の文言は，船主に「本船あるいは運賃に関し，戦争によって生じうるあらゆる危険に対して，船主が適切と考える保険を付保できる」権利を付与しているが，これは特別な条項で，*The Apex* 事件を除いた過去のあらゆる事件の通常の条項とは区別されなければならない。それでも，これらの文言の適切な解釈により，船主は Hellenic Association が提供する全面填補の付保を申請したのである。

The Agathon (No. 2) [1984] 1 Lloyd's Rep. 183.

El Champion 号およびその他2隻は，各々別の傭船契約で，ペルシャ湾への航海のために，定期傭船された。3個の傭船契約のうち，2個には，第68条として次のような条項があった。「戦争保険の基本保険料は常に船主の負担。本船ペルシャ湾就航による，本船の船体および機関に対する追加の戦争保険料については，傭船者負担とする」。3番目の傭船契約には，「ペルシャ湾」という文言が第68条から削除されていた。傭船契約の締結の日から，本船が湾岸に入るまでの間，戦争危険の料率は，一般の海域でも，湾岸でも引き上げられなかった。それゆえ，ずっと「基本料率」の据置で「追加料率」は存しなかったとして，傭船者は，ペルシア湾岸料率の支払義務はないと主張した。Staughton 判事は，戦争保険料の「基本料率」は一般の海域でのものを対象としており，第68条は「追加料率」の支払を要する海域に本船が入った場合で，船主が実際に追加料率を支払った分を傭船者に支払わせることを要求している条項である，と判示した。これは第68条に「ペルシャ湾」の挿入の有無如何にかかわらず，同じである。同判事は，さらに，もし船主が「増加した評価額もしくは船費，利息の評価分を加えたもの」を基礎として保険証券を手配しても，その保険証券に基づく保険料もやはり「本船の船体および機関に基づいた」保険料である，と判示した。

The El Champion [1985] 2 Lloyd's Rep. 275.

Discaria 号は，カタールからイランまでの貨物輸送のために，航海傭船された。この傭船契約は，第4条で次のように規定していた。「戦争保険料の追加料率分および封鎖・閉塞の場合の保険料および職員や部員に支払うべき戦争危険に対する割増賃金は，傭船者負担とする」。この航海開始前に，船主は収入の喪失分に対する填補を欠いたこれまでの戦争保険を解約し，その填補を含む新しい戦争保険を手配した。Staughton 判事は，この条項では，船主は傭船者から収入の喪失分を填補する保険料を取り戻すことはできない，と判示した。理由として，回収できるのは現行保険での追加料率分に限定されるべきで（危険に直面して付保された追加保険と異なり），それには必ずしも「封鎖や閉塞の場合」は含まれないことを挙げた。

The Discaria [1985] 2 Lloyd's Rep. 489.

536 米　国　法

氷　条　項

　氷条項の下では，船長は氷で凍結した港，もしくは氷の状態により積荷もしくは揚荷役終了後，本船が安全に出港できない恐れのある港に無理に入港することはない (*The Dirphys*, SMA 283 (Arb. at N. Y.) 事件)。しかしながら，その港に接近できないとか，その可能性があると抗議するのは船長の責任となる。船長が抗議を怠れば，氷条項における船主の権利の放棄と同じ結果になる可能性がある（前出の *The Dirphys* 事件および *The Leprechaun Spirit*, SMA 1056 (Arb. at N. Y. 1976) 事件を参照)。

　多くの事案で，氷の状態が港やバースをそれぞれ非安全港，非安全バースとし，前出255頁から259頁で議論した安全港・安全バース担保義務が適用されると判示された。氷条項は，安全港・安全バースの担保義務を修正するものではないから，このことは正しいように思われる。確かに，氷条項は，氷の状態によって危険である港，もしくは氷により危険になると船長が合理的に危惧する港への入港を船長が拒絶できる権利を明示することにより，安全港・安全バース担保義務を強化・拡大しているように思われる。ただし，単に氷の状態が予想されるだけで，港が非安全港とされるわけではない。しかしながら，氷条項の下では，氷のために本船が閉塞されるとか，危険に晒されるといった，現実的な恐れを船長が感じれば，その港への入港を船長は拒絶できるのである（前出の *The Leprechaun Spirit* 事件を参照)。

　The Ming Summer, SMA 2490 (Arb. at. N. Y. 1988) 事件では，仲裁審は，本船が氷のなかで立ち往生し，その結果本船が被った損害は，水先人と船長の過失によるものであると判断した。船主の修理代の請求は却下され，傭船者は修理期間につきオフハイヤーを裁定された。

定期傭船者の本船に対する利害

　定期傭船契約は，単に傭船者に対し傭船期間中，本船を使用する権利を与える契約であり，傭船者に本船に関する財産上の権利を付与するものではない (*Robins Dry Dock & Repair Co. v. Flint*, 275 U. S. 303 (1927); *The Bay Master*, 1969 AMC 359 (E. D. N. Y. 1969); *Mondella v. The Elie V*, 223 F. Supp. 390 (S. D. N. Y. 1963); *Federal Commerce & Navigation Co. v. The Marathonian*, 392 F. Supp. 908 (S. D. N. Y. 1975), 全員一致で原審維持 528 F. 2d 907 (2d Cir.1975), 裁量上告拒絶 425 U. S. 975 (1976) の各事件を参照)。

　Robins 事件において，本船は造船所の被用者の過失で，入渠中に損害を被った。傭船者は，同船の修理中，本船の使用を妨げられた損失を造船所から回収しようとした。しかし，裁判所は，傭船者は本船に対する財産上の利害関係を有しない，したがって傭船者と船主との契約が第三者の過失により妨げられた結果，傭船者が被った損害を回収することはできない，と判示した。

　この原則は，上記の *The Marathonian* 事件において挑戦を受けた。同事件では，傭船者は衝突損害の修理期間中に，本船使用を妨げられた損失について，過失ある相手船から回収しようとした。しかし，*Robins* 事件の判例に従って，この請求は否定された (*Rederi A/B Soya v. Evergreen Marine*, 1972 AMC 1555 (E. D. Va. 1971) 事件を参照)。

　Robins 事件の例外は，*Venore Transportation Co. v. The Struma*, 583 F. 2d 708, 1978 AMC 2146 (4th Cir. 1978) 事件である。この事件で，裁判所は傭船契約の合意の内容により，*Rob*-

ins 事件の判例は適用されない，と判示した。*Oswego Liberty* 号は13年半の期間に及ぶ定期傭船に出された。その傭船期間中に，本船は *Struma* 号と衝突し，修理のために1年間本船は不稼働状態となった。傭船契約の条項により，本船の修理期間中も傭船者は傭船料を支払わざるを得なかった。傭船者は，本船が修理中に船主に支払った傭船料を回収すべく，*Struma* 号に対する訴訟を提起した。

　本船が修理中でも，傭船者の傭船料を支払う義務は中断されなかったのだから，傭船者には訴訟を提起する訴えの利益がある，と裁判所は認定した。厳密な意味では，傭船者は本船に対する単純占有権を一切有していないことは認識しているものの，裁判所は，「船主には傭船料受取の中断がなく，かつ船主は本船不使用についての塡補請求を受けていない場合，傭船者は本船に対する利害関係により，傭船者には支払った傭船料をベースに算定される損害賠償請求を提起する地位が与えられる」と判断した (1978 AMC at 2150)。

　Standard Navigazione S. p. A. v. *The K. Z. Michalos*, 1981 AMC 748 (S. D. Tex. 1981) 事件もまた参照。この事件では，契約上，衝突事件後の修理期間中も傭船料を支払い続けることを義務付けられた定期傭船者は，支払った傭船料の限度において，船主の権利を代位し，それにより衝突相手船の船主に対する訴訟を提起することができる，と裁判所は判示した。

　Robins 事件の効果は，様々な文脈において，大きな意味を持つものである。たとえば，*Riffe Petroleum Co.* v. *Cibro Sales Corp.*, 601 F. 2d 1385, 1979 AMC 1611 (10th Cir. 1979) 事件では，定期傭船者が破産手続 (Chapter XI) の債務者となった。破産裁判所は，債務者に対する一切の訴訟提起を禁ずる一般的な停止命令を出した。停止命令が発せられた後，燃料供給者は，本船にとっての必需品および燃料油を供給したことについての海事リーエンを行使するために，本船に対する対物訴訟を提起した。定期傭船者は，燃料油供給者が本船に対する対物訴訟を提起したことは，裁判所の停止命令に背くもので，法廷侮辱にあたると主張した。裁判所は，この対物訴訟は，債務者の財物に対して提起されたものではないから，破産裁判所の命令に背くものではない，と判断した。裁判所が認定したように，「定期傭船契約では，船主は，傭船者が一切の財産権を有しない本船で物品を運送することに合意している」のである (1979 AMC at 1615)。

「船主は……につき責任がある」

　定期傭船契約の基本的な特徴として，船員配乗，本船保守は，船主の責任である。傭船者は，たとえば燃料油のように，本船使用から生ずるいくつかの費用の支払責任があるが，いかなる意味においても定期傭船契約は，船の賃貸借契約ではない。傭船者は，傭船契約が規定する制限内で，本船を望むとおりに使用する権利を有するとは言え，航海，保険の手配・保守，船員の供給，およびその他の事項はすべて船主の責任である（一般的な例として，*Bergan* v. *Int'l Freighting Corp.*, 254 F. 2d 231, 1958 AMC 1303 (2d Cir. 1958) 事件，および *Riffe Petroleum Co.* v. *Cibro Sales Corp.*, 601 F. 2d 1385, 1979 AMC 1611 (10th Cir. 1979) 事件を参照）。

　H. Schuldt v. *Standard Fruit & Steamship Co.*, 1979 AMC 2470, 2477 (S. D. N. Y. 1978) 事件では，本船が New York の East River の Pier 42 に入渠しようとした際に，ドック水先人の過失の結果，座礁した。船主は，傭船者に水先料金の支払義務が存するゆえ，水先人の過失については，傭船者が責任を負うべきであると主張した。裁判所は，船主の主張に同意せず，デマイズ条項のもとで，船主にドック水先人の過失についての責任が残っていると判断した。

　傭船者の本船に対する利害はそのようなものであるから，傭船者自身に積極的な過失がない

限り，傭船者は不堪航や運航上の過失の責任を，乗組員に対して負うものではない（*Morewitz v. Imbros Shipping Co. Ltd.,* 1979 AMC 1622（E. D. Va. 1978）事件を参照）。このように，傭船者は，通常，乗組員の人身事故に関して責任を負うものではない。それにもかかわらず，もし傭船者が乗組員の管理をする義務を負う立場での業務を行う場合，傭船者はその行為から生じる損失につき責任を負うこととなる（*Mondella v. The Elie V,* 223 F. Supp. 390, 393, 1965 AMC 2672, 2676（S. D. N. Y. 1963））。

538 保　　険

　この条項に基づき船主が本船に「自分自身の計算において航海を行うのと同様の」保険を付保する責任は，第１条規定の船主の本船保険料支払義務を補強している。これらの条項は，傭船の範囲内で，十分に慎重な船主であれば付保するであろう保険の付保義務を船主に負わしているものと思われ，その中にはP&I保険，船体保険および戦争危険保険が含まれる。

　傭船者は，本船には一切の単純占有権を有さないが，対照的に，保険料を船主に補償する責任を負うことがある。この保険料の費用に関する責任の負担は，傭船者が使用する本船の航路で，船主が追加の費用を支払わなければならないときに，しばしば生じる。たとえば，*Seas Shipping Co. Inc. v. United States,* 1951 AMC 503（S. D. N. Y. 1951）事件では，本船が「米国航路定限」の範囲外を航行する場合の海上保険に関する追加保険料は，傭船者が船主に補償することに合意していた（もっとも，この事件では，裁判所は，本船が許容された航路定限を超えて航行していたのではないとして，船主の追加保険料請求は拒否された）（*The Stuyvesant,* SMA 1722（Arb. at N. Y. 1982）事件を参照）。

　The Panagos D. Pateras, SMA 1566（Arb. at N. Y. 1981）事件では，傭船契約に次のようなタイプ打ちの条項が存した。

> 追加戦争保険料ならびに正式に課された乗組員の割増賃金は，傭船者の負担とする。その中には，もしあれば，スエズ運河航行の際の戦争保険料も含まれる。

　船主は，戦争危険のための保険をHellenic Mutual War Risks Association（Bermuda）Limitedに付保していた。この協会の保険付保は，以下の４つの部分に分けることができた。(A)船体と機関，船費，(B)拘留および離路費用，(C) P&I保険料，(D)損害拡大防止費用。この協会の規則では，上記のすべての項目が標準的な付保であった。傭船者は，項目(B)以外のスエズ運河航行に関するすべての追加保険料の支払に関し，自分に責任があることを認めたが，項目(B)に関しては，ニューヨーク・プロデュース書式第１条により，船主の費用であると主張した。傭船者によれば，項目(B)の付保は，実際，「封鎖・閉塞」の保険であり，通常戦争保険では，別の付保形式でのみ提供されている。

　仲裁人は，この傭船者の主張を拒絶し，船主は，項目(B)についても傭船者から回収できると判断した。仲裁人は次のように述べている。

> たとえ，「封鎖・閉塞」が通常の標準戦争保険では別項目として扱われていたとしても，船主が基本的な塡補範囲を変えなければならない理由を見出せない。通常の戦争保険付保をどこから入手するかの選択は，船主に委ねられている。もし，ある特定の保険協会もしくは保険会社を選択することによって，通常何がしかの追加塡補範囲とされているものが，常に塡補に関する規則の範囲内で，公開されている保険証書により，「基本的な」塡補範囲として塡補されていれば，傭船者は船主の最善の利益において，その船主の選択を受け入れなければならない。すべての保険者もしくは保険協会が

まったく同条件の保険証書を用いることは現実的ではなく，傭船契約で，特別に合意していなければ，船主が個々の傭船者の要請に沿うために，保険契約の塡補範囲をわざわざ変更させることはなおさら非現実的である。

The Olympic Armour, SMA 1840（Arb. at N.Y. 1983）事件も参照。この事件では，Hellenic War Risks Club's 2(B)の付保範囲である「拘留および離路費用」に関する追加保険料につき，傭船者に支払義務があると判断された。*The Capetan Costis I,* SMA 1622（Arb. at N.Y. 1981）事件では，船主は傭船者よりスエズ運河通過に関する追加保険料を回収できると判断されている。

The Crane Nest, 1939 AMC 1186（Arb. at N.Y. 1939）事件では，再定期傭船の船主は，再傭船契約における追加保険費用につき，支払義務があるとされた。傭船者は，追加保険料の支払義務を認めたが，その額が大きすぎると反論した。仲裁人は，再傭船者は真摯に最も低い料率を得ようと努力したのであるから，傭船者には支払責任があると判断した。

手　数　料

"172.　27. A commission of 2.5 per cent is payable by the Vessel and Owners to ....
173. ....
174. on hire earned and paid under this Charter, and also upon any continuation or extension of this Charter.
175.　28. An address commission of 2.5 per cent payable to ....
on the hire earned and paid under this Charter.
　　　　　By cable authority from"

　「27. 本船および船主は，本契約およびその継続または延長により受け取り，支払われる傭船料の2.5パーセントを仲介料として...............に支払うものとする。
　28. 本契約により受け取る傭船料のうち，2.5パーセントをアドレス・コミッションとして.........…に支払うものとする。
　　　　　...からの電信による授権によって

　仲立人は，その名前が173行に書き込まれるが，傭船契約の当事者ではない。しかし，その手数料に対する権利については，傭船者が仲立人の受託者として船主に対して強制することができる (*Les Affreteurs Reunis* v. *Walford* [1919] A.C. 801)。もし，傭船者がそうすることを拒否した場合，仲立人自身で，傭船者側に加わって，自己の権利を主張することができる (*The Panaghia P* [1986] 2 Lloyd's Rep. 653事件参照)。
　手数料は，傭船契約またはその延長による，支払受取傭船料に対応する部分についてのみ支払われる。したがって，傭船契約が当事者の合意により終了する場合，そのように契約が終了しなければ支払義務が生じたであろう傭船料に対応する手数料を，仲立人は請求することができない。

　Clematis 号は，18ヶ月間傭船され，仲立人は支払受取傭船料の2.5パーセントの手数料を取得することになった。4ヶ月後，本船は傭船者に売却され，傭船契約は当事者の合意で解約された。仲立人は残存期間14ヶ月の手数料を請求したが，貴族院は仲立人にはその権利がないと判断した。裁判官は，傭船契約中に船主はいかなる事情があっても傭船契約を終了させないという黙示の条項がない限り，仲立人の請求は認められないが，本件の場合そのような黙示条項を認める理由はないと判断した。Buckmaster卿は，「契約はそのような黙示条項を認めなくても十分に機能する。仲立人は，自己の獲得する手数料が，傭船契約解消のため支払われないとなるのを防ぎたかったのであれば，自分と船主との間で，明文の規定をもってその旨を定めておくべきであった」と述べた。
　French v. *Leeston Shipping* [1922] 1 A.C. 451.

　仮装の解約——上記の判決おける Dunedin 卿の言葉で言えば「手数料を免れるためにのみ」解約がなされた場合は立場が違ってくる。しかし，それ以外では，いかなる場合でも——例えば船主の傭船者に対する契約義務違反の場合でも——仲立人には未払傭船料に対する手数料の権利，もしくは得べかりし手数料の喪失に基づく損害賠償を請求する権利はない。*White* v. *Turnbull, Martin* (1898) 3 Com. Cas. 183事件参照（ボルタイム書式での差異については，後出664頁を参照。また，その他の代理店契約においては，本社が主契約を解約し，相手方を

その契約から解放することにより代理店の手数料収入を奪わない旨を黙示していると積極的に考える裁判所の傾向につき，*Alpha Trading* v. *DunnShaw-Patten* [1981] 1 Lloyd's Rep. 122 事件を参照。さらに，この問題に対する一般的な見解として，Bowstead 著の『代理について』(*On Agency*)（第15版）の233から238頁を参照。

542 アドレスコミッション

この手数料に関する通常のやり方に関し，*The Good Helmsman* [1981] 1 Lloyd's Rep. 377 事件を参照（同判例集419頁から421頁）。

～からの電信による授権

前出120頁で引用されている判例を参照。

543 米　国　法

手　数　料

　仲立人が提供する傭船契約を手配する業務は，裁判所の観点では海事関連のものとは考えられていない。したがって，仲立人からのクレームは，通常海事関連の訴訟とはならず，仲立人のための海事リーエンは発生しない (*The Thames*, 10 F. 848 (S. D. N. Y. 1881); *Taylor* v. *Weir*, 110 F. 1005 (D. Or. 1901); *Andrews & Co.* v. *United States*, 124 F. Supp. 362, 1954 AMC 2221 (Ct. Cl. 1954), 原審維持 292 F. 2d 280 (Ct. Cl. 1954); *Marchessini & Co. (New York)* v. *Pacific Marine Co.*, 227 F. Supp. 17, 1964 AMC 1538 (S. D. N. Y. 1964); *European-American Banking Corp.* v. *The Rosaria*, 486 F. Supp. 245, 255 (S. D. Miss. 1978); *Boyd, Weir & Sewell Inc.* v. *Fritzen-Halcyon Lijn Inc.*, 1989 AMC 1159 (S. D. N. Y. 1989) の各事件を参照)。

　しかしながら，*Naess Shipping Agencies Inc.* v. *SSI Navigation Inc.*, 1985 AMC 346 (N. D. Cal. 1984) 事件では，裁判所は，仲立人の手数料に関するクレームに関し，海事裁判所が管轄権を有すると判断した。その事件では，仲立人は4隻のコンテナ船の建造およびそれに続く傭船についての契約を手配した。仲立人の義務は，建造契約の実行期間および傭船契約の期間のすべてに及び，仲立人には契約が存続する14年以上，手数料が入ることになっていたので，海事裁判所の管轄権があるとされた。裁判所は，その他の事件では，仲立人の手数料に関するクレームには，海事裁判所の管轄権はないと判断しているが，この事件については，その契約そのものが海事契約の単なる準備段階のものではなく，むしろ，仲立人の義務は契約の全期間に及んでいるので，その仲立人の契約そのものが性質上海事関連のものとみなすことができるとして，その他の事件とは異なると判示したのである。

　仲立人は，傭船契約の当事者ではないので，傭船契約に基づいて手数料回収を主張する権利はない (*Congress Coal and Transp. Co. Inc.* v. *International S. S. Co.*, 1925 AMC 701 (Penn. 1925) 事件)。さらに，傭船契約に基づく訴訟において，傭船者は仲立人の権利を実現しようとしたが，これを拒絶された。二つの事件で，仲裁人は，仲立人が傭船契約の当事者でないことにより，仲立人の費用に関して判断を下す管轄権は仲裁人にはない，と判断した (*The Caribbean Trader*, SMA 41 (Arb. at N. Y. 1964) 事件と *Jugotanker-Turisthotel* v. *Mt. Ve Balik Kurumu*, SMA 1133 (Arb. at N. Y. 1977) 事件)。

　仲立人の手数料に対する権利は，手数料に関して授権している契約にどのような文言があるかによって完全に左右される。傭船契約に，別の旨が規定されていなければ，仲立人は実際に傭船契約に基づき支払われた傭船料の額に対応する分だけ，手数料を回収することができる (*Lougheed & Co. Ltd.* v. *Suzuki*, 216 App. Div. 487, 215 N. Y. S. 505, 原審維持 243 N. Y. 648, 152 N. E. 642 (1926) 事件; *Caldwell Co.* v. *Connecticut Mills*, 225 App. Div. 270, 273, 232 N. Y. S. 625, 原審維持 251 N. Y. 565, 168 N. E. 429 (1929) 事件; *Tankers Int'l Navigation Corp.* v. *National Shipping & Trading Corp.*, 499 N. Y. S. 2d 697, 1987 AMC 478 (A. D. 1 Dept. 1986) 事件)。

　前出 *Lougheed* 事件では，傭船契約には，手数料は「月毎に支払われる傭船料」に対して生じる，と規定されていた。傭船者は，船主が本船を適時に引き渡さなかったとして，傭船料を一切支払わなかった。裁判所は，仲立人の手数料に対する請求を棄却し，仲立人手数料の条項は，「実際に受領された月々の傭船料に対してのみ，手数料が支払われるとの明確な意図を示

していた」と判断した（216 App. Div. at 492.)。裁判所によれば、「手数料は、本船に対する月々の傭船料が実際に受領されたときにのみ、[仲立人]に支払われるべきものであった……」(同書 at 493)。

　上記 *Tankers Int'l* 事件では、仲立人は、未払傭船料に関する船主のクレームを解決するために傭船者から船主に支払われた傭船料のための資金額について手数料を要求した。手数料支払義務が傭船者の債務不履行に優先するかどうかの実際上の疑問が提起される一方で、法律上は、解決資金の送付は、それ自体まだ傭船契約上の傭船料支払と同一のものではないとの判断を、裁判所は示した。裁判所によれば、

　　仮に、船主自らが要求する傭船料全額を回収している場合でも、仲立人は、ただ単に自分の委託者が、傭船契約が履行されていれば受け取っていたであろう金額と同額を確保しているだけでは、手数料を回収する権利はない、というのが確立された原則である（499 N.Y.S. 2d at 701)。

　Rountree Co. v. *Dampskibs Aktieselskabet Oy II (The Hinnoy)*, 1934 AMC 26 (City Ct. N. Y. 1933) 事件では、仲立人が手配した傭船契約が解約され、その傭船契約上の損害賠償額を小さくするために、傭船者が締結した代替の傭船契約上の収入に基づいた手数料を仲立人は要求したが、その仲立人の要求は却下された。

　もし、傭船契約が締結された時点で、手数料は支払われるべきである、との条項が傭船契約に存する場合には、たとえ傭船料の支払がなくとも、仲立人は手数料を受け取る権利を有することになる（*Vellore S. S. Co. Ltd.* v. *Steengrafe*, 229 F. 394 (2d Cir. 1915) 事件を参照)。

ボルタイム書式

ボルタイム書式

THE BALTIC AND INTERNATIONAL MARITIME CONFERENCE
(Formerly The Baltic and White Sea Conference)
UNIFORM TIME-CHARTER

1 "IT IS THIS DAY MUTUALLY AGREED between .... Owners
2 of the Vessel called .... of .... tons gross/tons net Register,
3 classed .... of .... indicated horse power,
4 carrying about .... tons deadweight on Board of Trade summer freeboard inclusive
5 of bunkers, stores, provisions and boiler water, having as per builder's plan .... cubic-feet
6 grain/bale capacity, exclusive of permanent bunkers, which contain about ...... tons, and fully loaded capable
7 of steaming about .... knots in good weather and smooth water on a consumption of about
8 ...... tons best Welsh coal, or about .... tons oil-fuel, now ......
9 and ....
10 of .... Charterers, as follows: "

ボルティック　アンド　インターナショナル・マリタイム・コンファレンス
（前　ボルティック　アンド　ホワイト　シー　コンファレンス）
統一定期傭船契約書

「本日ここに，船主..........................と，その所有に係る..................号，総トン数／純トン数......トン，船級..................指示馬力，商務省夏期乾舷における載貨重量トン約......トン（燃料，船用品，食料品および罐水を含む），造船所図面上，艙内載貨容積グレーン／ベールにて..............立方フィート（約......トンをいれる常備用燃料庫を除く），燃料消費最良ウェールズ炭にて約......トン，もしくは燃料油にて約......トンの消費量で，天候良好，海上平穏の状態における満載航海速力約..........ノット，現在..................中の船舶に関し，..............の傭船者................との間で，下記のとおり合意した。」

契約の成立：前出97／104頁参照。
契約当事者：前出111／121頁参照。
船舶の表示：一般的には前出131／158頁参照。
　本船が表示を遵守すべき時期：前出144頁。
　船名：前出145頁。
　国籍：前出147頁。
　船級に関する表示：前出152頁。
　載貨重量：前出152頁。

「約」:前出153頁。
速力と燃料消費:前出155頁。

Clause 1 — Period/Port of delivery/Time of delivery
11   "1. The Owners let, and the Charterers hire the Vessel for a period of ....
12   calendar months from the time (not a Sunday or a legal Holiday unless taken over) the Vessel is delivered
13   and placed at the disposal of the Charterers between 9 a. m. and 6 p. m., or between 9 a. m. and 2 p. m.
14   if on Saturday, at ....
15   ... in such available berth where she can safely lie always afloat, as the Charterers
16   may direct, she being in every way fitted for ordinary cargo service.
17   The Vessel to be delivered .... "

第1条 — 期間／引渡港／引渡時

「1. 船主は本船を貸し渡し,傭船者は借り受けることとし,その期間は.........暦月間とする。傭船開始時は(受渡のない限り日曜日または公休日を除く),午前9時から午後6時まで,土曜日ならば午前9時から午後2時までの間に..................における,傭船者の指示する本船が常時浮揚状態で安全に停泊し,利用できるバースにおいて,あらゆる点において通常の貨物運送業務に適する状態をもって本船が引き渡され,傭船者の使用に委ねられたときとする。
本船は,.........................引き渡されるものとする。」

546 **賃貸と賃借**:前出173頁および612頁。
傭船期間(超過／不足):前出173／184頁参照。
傭船者の指示する場所で引渡
  引渡:173頁。
  表示に合致しない本船の引渡:前出144頁。
  不堪航／堪航性ある本船の引渡:前出149頁。
  引渡準備:前出206頁
  解約条項のための準備と適合:前出206／214頁と419／422頁。
  本船の受取:前出213頁と権利放棄について一般的に前出142／143頁。
  引渡のとき:前出419頁。

利用できるバース
  傭船者は,本船が引渡地または引渡港に到着するまでに,本船が遅滞なく碇泊できるバースを指定しなければならない。

  *Golfstraum*号は,ボルタイム書式により,Sfaxにて引渡ということで傭船された。本船が,同港外に到着したとき,船込みがあり,傭船者がバースを確保するまで,4日待たなければならなかった。Mocatta判事は,傭船者は本船到着までに本船を直ちに利用できるバースを指定すべき義務に違反しているのであるから,船主は待ち時間分の傭船料を取得する権利があると判示した。
  The Golfstraum [1976] 2 Lloyd's Rep. 97.

常に浮揚状態で安全に碇泊：前出203頁と252頁参照。
通常の貨物運送にあらゆる点で適合し：前出206頁参照。

Clause 2 — Trade

18 " 2. The Vessel to be employed in lawful trades for the carriage of lawful merchandise only
19 between good and safe ports or places where she can safely lie always afloat within the following
20 limits : ....

21 No live stock nor injurious, inflammable or dangerous goods (such as acids, explosives, calcium
22 carbide, ferro silicon, naphtha, motor spirit, tar, or any of their products) to be shipped."

第2条 — 航　　路

「2. 本船は，適法な貨物の運送のための適法な航路に使用するものとし，その航路は，本船が常時浮揚して安全に碇泊できる下記の区域内の良好かつ安全な港，その他の場所の間に限る

………………………………………………………………………………………

家畜または（酸類・爆発物・カーバイド・珪素鉄・ナフサ・ガソリン・タールおよびその製品のような）有毒性・発火性もしくは危険性を有する貨物を船積してはならない。」

適法貨物：前出219／225頁参照。
危険貨物：
　ニューヨーク・プロデュース書式と異なり，ボルタイム書式は，危険貨物の船積を明示的に禁止していることに注意すべきである。前出221頁参照。

安全港：前出231／254頁参照，後出659頁も参照。
547 **航路定限**：前出193／195頁参照。

Clause 3 — Owners to provide

23 " 3. The Owners to provide and pay for all provisions and wages, for insurance of the Vessel, for all
24 deck and engine-room stores and maintain her in a thoroughly efficient state in hull and machinery
25 during service.
26 　The Owners to provide one winchman per hatch. If further winchmen are required, or if the
27 stevedores refuse or are not permitted to work with the Crew, the Charterers to provide and pay
28 qualified shore-winchmen."

第3条 ── 船主の支給

「3.船主は一切の食料および給料,船舶保険料,甲板および機関室用のすべての船用品を準備して,その費用を支払い,傭船期間中,船体ならびに機関を完全な稼働状態に維持しなければならない。

船主は,艙口毎に,1人のウィンチマンを配置しなければならない。ただし,その増員を要する場合,または船内荷役作業員が乗組員との共同荷役を拒否するか,その共同荷役を認められていない場合,傭船者は資格のある陸上ウィンチマンを配置し,かつその費用を支払うものとする。」

船舶保険の船主支払:前出614/618頁参照。
完全な稼働状態を維持:前出267頁参照。

Clause 4 ─ Charterers to provide

29 "4. The Charterers to provide and pay for all coals, including galley coal, oil-fuel, water for boilers,
30 port charges, pilotages (whether compulsory or not), canal steersmen, boatage, lights, tug-assistance,
31 consular charges (except those pertaining to the Master, Officers and Crew), canal, dock and other dues
32 and charges, including any foreign general municipality or state taxes, also all dock, harbour and
33 tonnage dues at the ports of delivery and re-delivery (unless incurred through cargo carried before delivery
34 or after re-delivery), agencies, commissions, also to arrange and pay for loading, trimming, stowing (includ-
35 ing dunnage and shifting boards, except any already on board), unloading, weighing, tallying and
36 delivery of cargoes, surveys on hatches, meals supplied to officials and men in their service and all
37 other charges and expenses whatsoever including detention and expenses through quarantine (including
38 cost of fumigation and disinfection).
39 All ropes, slings and special runners actually used for loading and discharging and any special
40 gear, including special ropes, hawsers and chains required by the custom of the port for mooring to be
41 for the Charterers' account. The Vessel to be fitted with winches, derricks, wheels and ordinary
42 runners capable of handling lifts up to 2 tons."

第4条 ── 傭船者の支給

「4.傭船者は賄用石炭を含むすべての石炭・燃料油・罐水の費用,港費,水先料(強制水先料であると否とを問わない),運河操舵手賃,通船料,灯台料,曳船料,領事館費(船長・職員および部員

に関するものを除く），運河通航料，桟橋料，その他の税金ならびに料金（外国の一般地方税または国税を含む）のほか，引渡港・返船港における桟橋料，港税およびトン税（ただし本船の引渡前または返船後の運送品について生じたものを除く），代理店料，仲介料をも手配して，これを支払わねばならない。積込・荷均・積付（荷敷・仕切板を含む。ただし，既に本船に在るものを除く）・揚荷・検量・検数・積荷の引渡・艙口検査，就業中の役人，または被用者に支給した食事，検疫（燻蒸消毒・殺菌消毒を含む）による抑留およびその費用も含むその他の諸費用の手配とその支払とは，すべて傭船者の負担とする。

積込および揚荷に実際に使用する一切の綱・スリング・特別の動索および一切の特別の索具（港の慣習により必要とする繋船用の特別の綱・大索・鎖を含む）は，傭船者の負担である。ただし，本船は2トン以下の積揚貨物の荷役に堪えるウィンチ・デリック・滑車および普通の動索を装備するものとする。」

傭船者の手配および費用負担：前出275／280頁参照。
港費：

ニューヨーク・プロデュース書式と異なり，ボルタイム書式に基づき傭船者は（引渡前または返船後の運送品について生じたものを除く）引渡港と返船港におけるすべての桟橋費，港費，トン税を支払うものとするということは注意すべきである（278頁の解説と Scales v. Temperley Steam Shipping (1925) 23 Ll.L. Rep. 312 事件を参照）。

貨物の積込，荷均，積付，揚荷と引渡

The Filikos [1981] 2 Lloyd's Rep. 555 事件で，Lloyd 判事（彼がこの争点につき判決を下す必要はなかったので）は，貨物の積込，積付および揚荷を手配し，その費用を支払うボルタイム書式の第4条の義務は貨物の積込，積付および揚荷の義務と責任を傭船者に転嫁する効力を当然有するものと考えた（同じ事案についての控訴院 [1983] 1 Lloyd's Rep. 9（同判例集11頁）における記録長官 Donaldson の判決も参照）。

548 オフハイヤー期間

この条項に基づく傭船者の義務は傭船契約の期間中継続し，「オンハイヤーの間」の語句が第4条の最初に追加されていない限り，オフハイヤー期間中も継続する（[1923] 2 K.B. 141 と280頁の Arild v. Hovrani 事件参照）。

Clauses 5 and 6 — Bunkers/Hire

43 "5. The Charterers at port of delivery and the Owners at port of re-delivery to take over and
44 pay for all coal or oil-fuel remaining in the Vessel's bunkers at current price at the respective ports.
45 The Vessel to be re-delivered with not less than .... tons and not exceeding .... tons of coal or
46 oil-fuel in the Vessel's bunkers.
47 6. The Charterers to pay as hire: ....
48 per 30 days, commencing in accordance with clause 1 until her re-delivery to the Owners.
49 Payment of hire to be made in cash, in .... without discount, every
50 30 days, in advance.

51　In default of payment the Owners to have the right of withdrawing the Vessel from the service of
52　the Charterers, without noting any protest and without interference by any court or any other formality
53　whatsoever and without prejudice to any claim the Owners may otherwise have on the Charterers
54　under the Charter."

第5条および第6条 ── 燃料／傭船料

「5．傭船者は引渡港において，また船主は返船港において，本船燃料庫内の一切の石炭または燃料油の残高を引き取り，それぞれの港における時価で，その代金を支払う。ただし，最低......トン以上，最高......トン以下の石炭または燃料油を，本船燃料庫内に残置して，返船しなければならない。
　6．傭船者は傭船料として，30日につき......を，第1条による傭船開始のときから，船主に返船するときまで支払うものとする。傭船料の支払は現金により，.....................において，毎30日分を前払するものとし，減額を認めない。
　この支払がないときは，船主は催告，裁判所の介入その他の手続によることなく，傭船者の業務から本船を引き揚げる権利を有する。この場合，船主が傭船者に対して本契約上有する他の一切の請求は妨げられない。」

引渡時および返船時の燃料：前出285頁。
傭船料の支払と本船の引揚：一般に前出301／329頁参照。

傭船契約の条項で許容された傭船料からの控除

ボルタイム書式の第14条に基づき，傭船者またはその代理人は，本船の支出のために船長に必要な資金を前渡し，その前渡金は傭船料から控除することができる。また，第11条A項（85／86行）に基づきオフハイヤークレームは，「傭船料の前払があったときは，これをその時間に応じて精算しなければならない」という語句により，次の傭船料から控除することができる（*The Nanfri* [1978] 2 Lloyd's Rep. 132 事件と前出310頁参照）。しかしながら，そういう控除は誠実に行われる合理的な評価に基づいて定量化されねばならない（前出 *The Nanfri* 事件参照）。

最終日の傭船料

ニューヨーク・プロデュース書式と異なり，返船が次の30日以内と予測されるときに満1ヶ月分に満たない傭船料の支払についての規定はボルタイム書式にはない。それにもかかわらず，満30日の傭船料が支払われなければならない。過払分は返船後に精算される（前出313頁と *Tonnelier* v. *Smith*（1897）2 Com. Cas. 258 事件参照）。

支払懈怠

ボルタイム書式51〜54行の文言は，ニューヨーク・プロデュース書式のそれとは多少異なっていることに注意しなければならない。ボルタイム書式では，支払懈怠（default of payment）がある場合に本船引揚権がある。*The Georgios C.* [1971] 1 Lloyd's Rep. 7 事件で控訴院は，この文言は，「支払の懈怠があり，懈怠の状態が続く限り」ということを意味し，したがって，期限遅れの支払または支払の提供がなされた場合，かかる支払や支払提供前に船主が引揚権を行使しない限り，本船引揚権は消滅すると判示した。この解釈，そしてそれから導

き出された判決は，ニューヨーク・プロデュース書式に関する事件 *The Laconia* [1977] 1 Lloyd's Rep. 315（前出319頁）における，貴族院判決により覆えされた。

同事件において，Wilberforce 卿は，「支払の懈怠という文言は，ボルタイム書式50行の毎期傭船料の「前払」義務に関するものでなければならない」ことを強調し，「控訴院は，事実上 549 『支払の懈怠』を，『前払金の支払懈怠』と解さずに『前払の有無如何にかかわらず，とにかく本船引揚以前における支払の懈怠』と解したのであるが，これは，本条項の解釈というより，再構成ともいうべきものである」と述べた。貴族院における本判決によって，ボルタイム書式の当該文言について，ニューヨーク・プロデュース書式の当該文言と同一の意味が与えられることになった。

Clause 7 — Re-delivery

```
55  "7. The Vessel to be re-delivered on the expiration of the Charter in the same good or-
    der as when
56  delivered to the Charterers (fair wear and tear excepted) at an ice-free port in the Char-
    terers' option in .............................................................................................................
    ..............................................................................
57  between 9 a. m. and 6 p. m., and 9 a. m. and 2 p. m. on Saturday, but the day of re-
    delivery shall not
58  be a Sunday or legal Holiday.
59     The Charterers to give the Owners not less than ten days' notice at which port and
    on about
60  which day the Vessel will be re-delivered.
61     Should the Vessel be ordered on a voyage by which the Charter period will be ex-
    ceeded the
62  Charterers to have the use of the Vessel to enable them to complete the voyage, pro-
    vided it could be
63  reasonably calculated that the voyage would allow re-delivery about the time fixed for the
    termination
64  of the Charter, but for any time exceeding the termination date the Charterers to pay
    the market rate
65  if higher than the rate stipulated herein."
```

第7条 — 返 船

「7．返船は傭船期間の満了と同時に，傭船者が本船の引渡を受けたときと同様の良好な状態で，（正当な自然損耗を除き）結氷していない傭船者任意の港……………………において，午前9時から午後6時（土曜日は午後2時）までの間に行うものとする。ただし，返船日は，日曜日または公休日であってはならない。

傭船者が船主に対して行う返船の予定港および予定日の通知は，その少なくとも10日以前でなければならない。

本船の指示された航海が傭船期間を超過する場合には，傭船者は，本船を使用してその航海を完了することができる。この場合，右の航海については，所定の傭船終了時頃に返船しうる相当の見込があったことを要する。ただし，傭船終了日以後の期間については傭船者は，市場料率が本契約に定めた傭船料率を超える場合，その市場料率を支払わねばならない。」

良好な状態にて返船：前出293／295頁。
傭船期間（超過／不足）：前出173／184頁参照。

最終航海

　The Peonia [1991] 1 Lloyd's Rep. 100 事件の控訴院の判決と The Gregos [1995] 1 Lloyd's Rep. 1（前出175／176頁参照）事件の貴族院の判決に照らして、第7条の最終項の趣旨により、指図が出され、履行される航海が傭船契約の終了日「頃」までに返船が可能であると合理的に計算できる場合、船主には最終航海を履行せよとの指図を拒絶する権利はないと思われる。しかし、指図された最終航海が合理的な計算に基づいて終了日前に返船できる見込があった場合でも、傭船者は実際の超過期間について市場料率で傭船料を支払わねばならない。これは、最終航海の指図が合法的か否かにかかわらず、終了日までに返船できないことは傭船契約の違反であるからである（前出173頁参照）。

　この条項の修正版に関する事案について、Hector Steamship v. V/O Sovfracht (1945) 78 LL.L. Rep. 275 事件と The Peonia [1991] 1 Lloyd's Rep. 100（同判例集110頁）事件の Bingham 卿判事の解説参照。

傭船期間満了後の返船

　第7条の最終項により、傭船者は、合理的に計算して傭船期間を多少超過する航海に本船を市場料率で継続して配船する権利が認められている。この場合、傭船終了時「頃 about」に返船できる相当の見込がなければならない。The Johnny [1977] 2 Lloyd's Rep. 1 事件において記録長官 Denning 卿は、反対意見の中で傍論であるが、63行にある「頃 about」というのは13ヶ月という確定した最長傭船期間より2～3日の超過を認めるにすぎないと述べた。しかし The Bunga Kenanga [1981] 1 Lloyd's Rep. 518 事件において Parker 判事の傍論の解説は、この見解はあまりにも制限的であるという趣旨であった。これは、傭船期間自体を定めるにあたって、「約 about」という文言を使用する場合に、その範囲を定めるにあたって払われた考慮とまったく同じである。この点については180頁参照。しかし63行の文言を検討するにあたっては、全傭船期間を考慮すべきではなく、最終航海に配船する際の残存傭船期間のみを考慮すべきであるという論もある。

市場料率

　適用すべき妥当な傭船料率は、問題の配船航海がなされた現実の定期傭船契約にできる限り近い形で対応する定期傭船の市場料率である、と控訴院は判示している。

　Johnny 号は、ボルタイム書式により、最短11暦月、最長13暦月傭船された。13ヶ月の期間は、11月7日が満期であった。9月19日、傭船者は、英国／欧州大陸から Karachi 向けの航海を決め、本船は、10月2日から18日まで Rotterdam にて積荷を行い、12月7日 Karachi において本船は返船された。船主は、第7条の適用を認め、11月7日から12月7日までの期間、英国／欧州大陸から Karachi までの1航海定期傭船契約の市場傭船料を取得する権利があると主張した。これに対して、傭船者は、適用すべき傭船料は、11／13ヶ月の定期傭船の市場傭船料率によるべきであると主張した。控訴院は、多数意見をもって、第7条の「ここに定める傭船料より高いときは」という文言は、時期を異にする期間傭船料との比較を示しており、期間による料率と航海による料率との比較を示していない。したがって、ここで妥当な市場料率といえば、原傭船契約とほぼ同様の期間の定期傭船契約の現在の市場料率であると判断した。

　The Johnny [1977] 2 Lloyd's Rep. 1.

期限前の返船：前出182頁参照。
特定航海の継続期間をもって定める傭船期間：前出183頁参照。

Clause 8 — Cargo space

66　"8. The whole reach and burthen of the Vessel, including lawful deck-capacity to be at the
67　Charterers' disposal, reserving proper and sufficient space for the Vessel's Master, Officer, Crew,
68　tackle, apparel, furniture, provisions and stores."

第8条 ── 貨物スペース

「8．傭船者が使用できる船腹は，本船の船長・職員・部員，揚貨機，装具，備品，食料および船用品のための相当かつ十分な船腹を除き，本船の区画および全積載力（適法な甲板積載力を含む）に及ぶものとする。」

本船の区画および全積載力

　この語句により，傭船者はその表現の一般に認められる意味での貨物スペースのすべてを使用できる。バラストに要するスペースは含まれない。*Weir* v. *Union S. S.* [1900] A. C. 525 事件参照。この語句は，本船の建造時ではなく，定期傭船契約締結時の本船の構造的能力を指している（*Japy Freres* v. *Sutherland* (1912) 6 Ll.L. Rep. 381. *Noemijulia Steamship* v. *Minister of Food* (1950) 83 Ll.L. Rep. 500と84 Ll.L. Rep. 354)。

Clause 9 — Master

69　"9. The Master to prosecute all voyages with the utmost despatch and to render customary assistance
70　with the Vessel's Crew ...."

[Clause 9 is continued below]

第9条 ── 船　　長

「9．船長はすべての航海を極力迅速に遂行し，本船の乗組員により，慣習上なすべき助力を提供するものとする。」

[第9条は以下に続く]

[551]**極力迅速に航海を遂行**：前出345頁参照。

第13条免責条項の適用

　航海の遅延が船長の過失，怠慢による場合，船主は，一般的に第13条によって保護される。

Istros 号は，ボルタイム書式（1920）により傭船され，Tyne 河からの航海を指図された。航海中，気象は悪かったけれども，船長が避難港3港に入ることを正当化するほどのものではなかった。避難港に入ったのは，船長の過失であり，船長は，極力迅速に航海を遂行する義務に反していると判断された。しかし船主自身が，相当の注意を尽くすことを怠ったかまたは船主の怠慢の立証がないので，船主は，免責条項によって保護されると判断された。Wright 判事は，次のように述べている（当時免責条項は第12条であり，現在の第9条は第8条であった）。

　「本件では，船舶の堪航性，航海適合性を具備するにつき，船主または船舶管理人側に相当の注意を欠いたということはなく，また船主，船舶管理人自身の作為，不作為，怠慢もない。存在した過失といい怠慢といい，船主の被用者の過失であり，怠慢である。仲裁人は，船長の過失，怠慢があり，それが遅延をもたらしたと認定した。このことは，まったく第12条の範囲内の問題であると思われる。船長が，第8条に基づき極力迅速に航海を遂行しなかった場合に，すべて第12条で対処できるかは，ここで検討する必要はない。船長の行為により第8条違反を生じる場合で，第12条があるにもかかわらず，船主が責任を負う具体的事例は今のところ思い浮ばない。しかしそのような事例もあるかも知れない。とにかく，第12条の文言に明白に適合する事例については，第12条の効力が認められるべきであると思われる。その効果が，船長が極力迅速に航海を遂行する義務を怠る場合に，船主は，その結果生じる損失，遅延につき責任がないということであれば，船主には，その条項の全面的利益を受ける権利があると考える」。

　Istros v. *Dahlstrom*（1930）38 Ll. L. Rep. 84.
　（この判決は後出644頁に要約されている The *TFL Prosperity* [1984] 1 Lloyd's Rep. 123 事件の貴族院により同意された）

　機関士が機関を適切に使用しなかったため，遅延した場合でも，船主はおそらく免責されると思われる。

　Apollonius 号はボルタイム書式で傭船されたが，機関士が，特定の期間，機関を全速にかけなかったため，日本から River　Plate 向けの航海で遅延した。Mocatta 判事は，このこと自体，極力迅速に航海を遂行するという第9条の義務違反となるが，第13条により，船主は免責されると判示した。

　The *Apollonius*（1978）1 Lloyd's Rep. 53.
　（本事案の他の側面に関して Mocatta 判事が表明した見解は，前出 The *TFL Prosperity* 事件において貴族院により批判された）

　第9条違反を第13条でどの程度まで救済しうるかについては，未だ裁判所により十分検討されていない。

　Suzuki v. *Beynon*（1926）24 LLL. Rep. 49 事件では，免責条項が極力迅速に航海を遂行する義務を「免除する」のであれば，免責条項に効力を認めるべきではないという見解が表明された。しかし，この事件における意見の重要性は，船長の過失，怠慢はともかくとして，とにかく極力迅速に航海する義務を適用する事態が存する場合には，船長の過失について船主を免責する条項に全面的効果を認めるべきであるという点にあった（本件の要約については346頁参照）。前出 *Istros*　v.　*Dahlstrom* 事件で，Wright 判事は，そのような事態もありうると考えたが，具体例は示さなかった。同判事は，第9条の違反に対して，船主が第13条に基づく抗弁をなしうるとしても，第9条は，その規定のとおり行動する船長の義務を認識することにその実務的な意義があると判示した。

　遅延が，船主の指図に基づくものである場合には，船主は第13条によって保護されない。
　International Bulk Carriers v. *Evlogia Shipping*（The *Mihalios Xilas*）[1978] 2 Lloyd's Rep. 186.

552   Clause 9 continued — Master (employment and indemnity)

70   "...The Master to be under the orders of the Charterers as regards employment
71   agency, or other arrangements. The Charterers to indemnify the Owners against all consequences or
72   liabilities arising from the Master, Officers or Agents signing Bills of Lading or other documents or
73   otherwise complying with such orders, as well as from any irregularity in the Vessel's papers or for
74   overcarrying goods. The Owners not to be responsible for shortage, mixture, marks, nor for number
75   of pieces or packages, nor for damage to or claims on cargo caused by bad stowage or otherwise.
76   If the Charterers have reason to be dissatisfied with the conduct of the Master, Officers, or
77   Engineers, the Owners, on receiving particulars of the complaint, promptly to investigate the matter,
78   and, if neccessary and practicable, to make a change in the appointments."

第9条 続 ── 船長（使用と補償）

「船長は本船の使用，代理店業務，またはその他の手配に関しては，傭船者の指図に従わなければならない。傭船者は船長・職員または代理人が船荷証券その他の証書に署名するか，もしくはかかる指図に従ったため，および本船の書類の不正確または持越貨物によって生ずる一切の結果または責任につき，船主に補償するものとする。船主は荷不足・混合・荷印・貨物の個数，もしくは積付不良その他によって生じる積荷の損害または請求に対しては，その責めに任じない。

傭船者において船長・航海士，または機関士の行為を不満足とする相当な理由があるときは，船主は苦情の詳細を受け取りしだい，直ちにその事実を取り調べ，必要かつ可能の場合，これを交代させるものとする。」

本船使用と補償：一般に前出351／360頁参照。

ニューヨーク・プロデュース書式と異なり，ボルタイム書式は明示の補償を含むことが，注意されるべきである（前出355頁参照）。

代理またはその他の手配

ボルタイム書式の本船使用および補償条項と同様の条項は *Larrinaga Steamship Co.* v. *The Crown* (1944) 78 Ll. L. Rep. 167 事件で，貴族院により検討された。同事件については，356頁に要約してあり，その中で Wright 卿は，この条項につき次のように言及している。「通常，傭船契約の展開過程で，各港において，本船の代理人をどの会社にするか，誰にするかは，船主に決定権がある。ここでは，その選択権は傭船者にある。……『手配 Arrangements』というのはより幅広い意味を持っている。この文言は，本傭船契約書［T. 99 A. ボルタイム書式の戦時方式］の第3条でも使用されているが，ここでは，船舶運航関連の役務につき支払を要する諸経費のことをいっており，第9条と同様の範囲を意味していると思われる」。

前出279頁も参照。

結果または責任

Royal Greek Government v. *Ministry of Transport*（*The Ann Stathatos*）(1949) 83 Ll.L. Rep. 228 事件（前出357頁に要約）では第 9 条の「結果または責任」は，傭船契約の他の条項に含まれる事項についても適用されると判示された。Devlin 判事は，次のように述べている (234 頁)。「本条項が，いわば，それ自体の生命を持ち，他の諸条項からもれた雑事項の引受場所以上のことを意図しているという考え方がまさに調和のとれた考え方であると思われる。危険物，航海，港，場所等は，すべて他の明示の条項で限定することができる。しかし，禁止条項による厳しい枠組に収まらない事態が多く生じうるし，船主が自ら選択できるのであれば，行きたくない場所もあろうし，積みたくない貨物もある。それは，必ずしも，確定的危険を船主が予見しているわけではなく，何か面倒に巻き込まれるという感じを持っているだけのこともある。船主が自らの選択の自由を放棄し，船長を傭船者の指揮下に委ねなければならないとすれば，この見返りとして，完全な補償条項を定めることは全く合理的なことである」。

Bosma v. *Larsen* [1966] 1 Lloyd's Rep. 22 事件で，「一切の結果または責任」を補償するということは，責任の発生に対して補償する義務を傭船者に課するということであり，したがって，船荷証券上の貨物損害責任に関する第 9 条に基づく船主の請求原因は，貨物損害の支払時ではなく，貨物に対する責任が生じた時点で発生すると判示された。しかし *County & District Properties* v. *Jenner* [1976] 2 Lloyd's Rep. 728 事件では，*Bosma* v. *Larsen* 事件は踏襲されず，建築契約上の責任の補償を求める請求の原因は，当該契約の補償条項に基づきその基になる責任が確定してはじめて発生すると判示された。*Green & Silley Weir* v. *British Railways Board* [1980] 17 B. L. R. 94 事件でも，裁判所は *Bosma* v. *Larsen* 事件を踏襲しなかった。*The Caroline P* [1984] 2 Lloyd's Rep. 466 事件（前出388頁参照）で，Neill 判事は，先例を分析し，*Bosma* v. *Larsen* 事件に同意するか否かを述べなかったが，彼は，McNair 判事は第 9 条の補償規定を解釈するにあたって，「一切の結果」の語句を切り離して扱わなかったと述べた。したがって *Bosma* v. *Larsen* 事件の判決は今では大いに疑問のある先例であると見られている。

かかる指図

The Ann Stathatos (1949) 83 Ll.L. Rep. 228 事件では，「かかる指図」というのは，船荷証券その他の書類の署名にのみ関連するものではない，と判示された（「結果と責任」の項参照）。

第13条との関係

傭船者の本船使用に関する指図を船長が不当に拒否する場合，傭船者は損害賠償の請求をできるが，船主は，第13条により抗弁することができる。これは，請求が，貨物の物理的滅失損傷に関するものでなく，傭船期間中の遅延に関する請求である場合も同様である（後出646頁参照）。この請求を遅延の請求とみなすことができるかという問題は，*The Charalambos N. Pateras* [1972] 1 Lloyd's Rep. 1 事件について控訴院により未解決のまま残された。本事案についての控訴院の実際の判決の根拠（つまり第13条の 2 番目の文は，物理的滅失損傷だけでなく経済的損失も扱うということ）は，*The TFL Prosperity* [1984] 1 Lloyd's Rep. 123（後出664頁参照）事件において貴族院により誤っていると判示された。

船荷証券の署名：一般的に前出385頁から400頁参照。
ボルタイム書式が，「呈示された」船荷証券に船長が署名することを明示的には求めていない点を注意すべきである。しかし，傭船契約上のこの語句の有無にかかわらず，状況は変わらな

いと思われる（前出397頁および *LEP International* v. *Atlanttrafic Express Service* (1987) 10 N. S. W. L. R. 614 事件の Clark 判事の判決を参照）。

米　国　法

船荷証券を発行する傭船者の権利

　The Penta, SMA 1603（Arb. at N. Y. 1981）事件で仲裁審は多数意見で1939年ボルタイム書式の第9条に基づき傭船者は船荷証券を発行する権利がない、または船荷証券に署名する代理人として自らに船長が授権することを指示する権利はない、と裁定した。仮に傭船者が再傭船者または荷送人の正体を船長に助言せずに、船荷証券を発行し署名する場合、逆の裁定では再運送賃にリーエンを行使する船主の権利を損なう権限を傭船者に与えることになる、と多数意見は判断した。仲裁審の多数意見によると、船荷証券に署名することによるすべての結果に対して、第9条に基づき船主に与えられた明示の補償は、傭船者自身に船荷証券を発行する権利を認めない。それどころか傭船者がこの権利を望んだのであれば、船主から明示の同意を取り付ける必要があった。

554　**Clause 10, 11 and 12 — Directions and logs / Suspensions of hire etc. / Cleaning boilers**

79　"10. The Charterers to furnish the Master with all instructions and sailing directions and the
80　Master and Engineer to keep full and correct logs accessible to the Charterers or their Agents.
81　11. (A) In the event of drydocking or other necessary measures to maintain the efficiency of the
82　Vessel, deficiency of men or Owners' stores, breakdown of machinery, damage to hull or other accident,
83　either hindering or preventing the working of the vessel and continuing for more than twentyfour
84　consecutive hours, no hire to be paid in respect of any time lost thereby during the period in which
85　the Vessel is unable to perform the service immediately required. Any hire paid in advance to be
86　adjusted accordingly.
87　(B) In the event of the Vessel being driven into port or to anchorage through stress of weather,
88　trading to shallow harbours or to rivers or ports with bars or suffering an accident to her cargo,
89　any detention of the Vessel and/or expenses resulting from such detention to be for the Charterers'
90　account even if such detention and/or expenses, or the cause by reason of which either is incurred,
91　be due to, or be contributed to by, the negligence of the Owners' servants.

92 　12. Cleaning of boilers whenever possible to be done during service, but if impossible the Charterers
93 　to give the Owners necessary time for cleaning. Should the Vessel be detained beyond 48 hours hire
94 　to cease until again ready."

第10，11条および12条 ── 指図と航海日誌／傭船料の支払停止等／汽罐の掃除

「10. 傭船者は一切の指図，および航海上の指示を，船長に与えるものとする。船長および機関士は，完全かつ正確な航海日誌を作成し，傭船者またはその代理人の閲覧に供しなければならない。

11. (A) 入渠その他本船の稼働状態を維持するに必要な処置，人員または船用品の不足，機関の故障，船体の損傷その他の事故により，連続24時間を超えて本船の業務が阻害された場合，本船が即時に提供すべき業務を履行しえないために喪失した一切の時間に対しては，傭船料の支払を要しない。傭船料の前払があったときは，これをその時間に応じて精算しなければならない。

(B) 本船が荒天のため港湾または錨地に避難したとき，水深の浅い湾または沙洲のある河川・港湾に寄港したとき，もしくは本船の積荷に事故を生じた場合，滞船および／またはこれによって生じた費用は，傭船者の負担とする。この場合，滞船および／またはその費用，もしくはその原因が，船主の被用者の単独の過失によるか寄与過失によるかを問わない。

12. 汽罐の掃除は，できる限り業務期間中に行うものとする。これが不可能な場合には，傭船者は掃除に必要な時間を船主に供与しなければならない。本船が48時間を超えて滞船するときは，傭船料の支払は，本船が再び準備完了となるまで中止する。」

オフハイヤー条項：全般的に前出427／446頁参照。
「純喪失時間」条項

「それによって喪失した時間について，傭船料を支払わない」という文言から，この条項は，「期間」条項というより，むしろ「純喪失時間」条項であるといわれている（前出428／433頁の論議参照）。しかし，本船が，そのとき要求される役務を遂行できるようになれば，直ちに傭船料支払義務が生じる（例として，*Court Line* v. *Finelvet*（*The Jevington Court*）[1966] 1 Lloyd's Rep. 683 事件（後出643頁）および Roskill 判事の判決(3)の項参照）。

本船の業務を阻害するその他の事故

上記文言は，同種解釈の原則（*ejusdem generis*）によって制限されないと判断されてきた（前出439頁参照）。したがってこの文言は，文字どおりの意味と含蓄を持つ。例えば，河川での座礁である。*Magnhild* v. *McIntyre* [1920] 3 K. B. 321 およびその控訴院 [1921] 2 K. B. 97 (C. A.) ならびに *Court Line* v. *Finelvet* [1966] 1 Lloyd's Rep. 683. この文言は軟体動物の付着による船底の汚れが予想できない海域で発生した場合をも含むと判断された（*The Apollonius* [1978] 1 Lloyd's Rep. 53. (しかし [1981] 2 Lloyd's Rep. 267および前出441頁の *The Rijin* 事件を参照))。

この文言が適用されるためには，「事故 accident」がなければならない。控訴院は，乗組員が船団を組まずに出港することを拒否した場合には事故とはいえないと判示した（*Royal Greek Government* v. *Minister of Transport*（*The Illissos*）(1949) 82 Ll.L. Rep. 196)。「事故 Accident」とは，ものごとが自然の成行からはずれて発生するできごとをいう（*The Apollonius* [1978] 1 Lloyd's Rep. 53 事件の Mocatta 判事の判決参照)。

連続24時間を超えて継続

一旦，24時間を超過した場合，その24時間も，その余の遅延時間と共に計算される（*Maede-King, Robinson* v. *Jacobs* [1915] 2 K.B. 640。

第11条(B)

第11条(A)は，本船がオフハイヤーとなるべき事由を掲げている。第11条(B)は，その反対に，船主の被用者の過失の有無にかかわらず，本船がオフハイヤーとならない場合を掲げている。第11条(A)の事項と11条(B)が重なり合う範囲で第11条(B)は，実務上，免責条項の例外を定める条項として作用する。

第11条(A)の事由から，第11条(B)の事由が発生することも，また，第11条(B)の事由から，第11条(A)の事由が発生することもある。例えば，「積荷の事故」から「船体の損傷」が発生することがある。本船の滞船が，事実船体損傷のため発生すれば，船体損傷自体，積荷の事故に起因していても，本船はオフハイヤーとなる。これに反して，貨物の損害が原因で船舶が滞船した場合，例えば貨物の事故の結果，移動または加熱した貨物を揚荷するため入港したような場合，本船はオフハイヤーとならない。

Ann Stathatos 号の積荷石炭が爆発し（前出357頁参照），船体と上部構造物が損傷を被り，修理に時間を要した。しかし，石炭自体には大した損害がなかった。したがって，本船の滞船は，船体損傷修理のために生じたが，船体損害自体は，積荷の事故によるものであった。Devlin 判事は，本船の滞船は船体修理のために生じたものであるから，第11条(A)の適用があり，本船は同条によりオフハイヤーとなる，と判示した。
Royal Greek Government v. *Minister of Transport* (1949) 83 Ll.L. Rep. 228.
（移動した甲板積貨物が船舶に損傷を与えた例である *Burrell* v. *Green* [1914] 1 K.B. 293 事件を参照）

第11条(B)の適用を求めるには，船主は，当該滞船または出費と第11条(B)記載の事項との間の因果関係（または近因関係）を主張しなければならない。例えば，事故当時，本船が，洲のある河を航行中であったことを立証するだけでは不十分である。

Jevington Court 号は，一部貨物の穀物を積んで Rosario から出港中，強制水先人の過失および水道の標識の欠陥のため，Martin Garcia Bar という地点に乗り上げた。約6週間後，本船は離礁した。その当時，本船は，航海継続に適した状態であったが，加熱した積荷を，Buenos Aires で揚荷し冷却し，再積込する必要に迫られ，そこでさらに遅延した。当時，本船は，ボルタイム書式で定期傭船されていた。船主は，第11条(B)に依拠し座洲中の傭船料（および若干の出費）を傭船者が支払うべきであると主張した。Roskill 判事は，次のように判示した。(1)「洲（Bar）を伴う」という文言は，「港」および「河」の双方にかかる。(2)船主は，滞船（および出費）の近因は，本船が洲のある河を航行したためであるという因果関係を立証しなければならないが，本件では船主はその立証をなしえなかった。さらに，Buenos Aires における時間について，同判事は，(3)第11条(B)に該当する事故があったけれども，Buenos Aires では本船は，いつでも「そのとき要求されている役務」すなわち加熱した貨物の揚荷やその後の再積込ができたのであるから，本船は再びオンハイヤーとなったと判示した。
Court Line v. *Finelvet* [1966] 1 Lloyd's Rep. 683.

洲を伴う（with bars）

上掲 *Court Line* v. *Finelvet* 事件で，この文言は，「港」にも，「河」にもかかると判示され

た。*Magnhild* v. *McIntyre* [1921] 2 K. B. 97 事件当時使用されていたこの条項の初期の文言（「浅い港，河，洲のある港」）は，前述と異なり，洲は，港にのみかかり，河にはかかっていなかった。前者の事件で，Roskill 判事は，次のように注釈を加えた。「傭船契約の標準書式のある条項を解釈するにあたって，裁判所は，その条項についての他の判決を尊重しすぎないように注意しなければならない。けだし，かかる条項は，ある側面では同様であっても，肝心な点で文言が異なっているからである」。

Court Line 事件の Roskill 判事の判決から，「洲 bar」というのは，水面下の自然の砂堤または沈泥で，両側に深水域があって，船がそこを迂回せずに制限された喫水で横切るような場所をいうようである。それは，必ずしも河口にある必要はなく，また，洲の中を浚渫された水路が通っていても洲であることを妨げない。

Clause 13 — Responsibility and exemption

95   "13. The Owners only to be responsible for delay in delivery of the Vessel or for delay during

96   the currency of the Charter and for loss or damage to goods on board, if such delay or loss has been

97   caused by want of due diligence on the part of the Owners or their Manager in making the Vessel sea-

98   worthy and fitted for the voyage or any other personal act or omission or default of the Owners or

99   their Manager. The Owners not to be responsible in any other case nor for damage or delay whatsoever

100 and howsoever caused even if caused by the neglect or default of their servants ...."

[Clause 13 is continued below]

第13条 — 責任と免責

「13. 本船引渡の遅延，傭船期間中の遅延，積荷の滅失，損傷については，本船を堪航状態におくにつき船主または船舶管理人に相当の注意が欠けていたために生じた場合，もしくはそれが船主または船舶管理人自身の作為・不作為または懈怠から生じた場合に限り，船主はその責任を負担する。これ以外の場合については，船主はたとえ自己の被用者の怠慢または懈怠に起因するいかなる損害または遅延を生じても責任を負わない。」

[第13条以下続く]

第13条の免責

第13条の95／100行の免責は，本船を堪航状態におくにつき船主または船舶管理人自身の相当の注意の欠如，または船主あるいは船舶管理人自身の懈怠に起因しない引渡の遅延および傭船期間中の遅延および船上貨物の物理的滅失損傷の場合に限定される。第13条の第2番目の文（99行と100行）は，他のあらゆる種類の損害に対して船主を免責せず，特に経済的損失にまで免責を広く及ぼすものではない。

TFL Prosperity 号は「ロールオン・ロールオフ」船であり，ボルタイム書式で傭船された。追加タイプ条項（第26条）に，本船のある固定した構造上の特性を詳細に規定していた。特に，メインデッキの高さが6.10メートルと記載された。実際の高さは，6.05メートルに過ぎないため，コンテナ詰め

のトレーラーを 2 段積でメインデッキに積載することはできなかった。傭船者は誤表示により被った経済的損失を請求した。船主は船主自身の懈怠はないとして第13条に拠った。貴族院は控訴院の判決を覆し，The Charalambos N. Pateros [1972] 1 Lloyd's Rep. 1 事件の裁判所の判決をも覆して，次のように判示した。
  (i) 第13条の最初の文 (95行から99行) は，船主が責任を負う事項，すなわち記載の原因による場合，引渡の遅延，傭船期間中の遅延および船上貨物の滅失損傷 (経済的損害ではなく，物理的損害を意味する) だけを，扱っている。
  (ii) 第13条の 2 番目の文 (99行から100行) は，第13条全体の解釈の問題として，最初の文と関連し，最初の文と同じ種類の遅延および貨物の物理的滅失損傷をまた示し，かつそれだけを示す。
  (iii) したがって第13条は，船主の違反により被った経済的損失についての傭船者の請求に対する抗弁を船主に与えない。
  (iv) ともかく，第13条を，表示に関する条件の違反について船主を免責するものと解釈することはできない。
  The TFL Prosperity [1984] 1 Lloyd's Rep. 123 (H. L.).

Westfal-Larsen v. Colonial Sugar Refining [1960] 2 Lloyd's Rep. 206 事件の New South Wales 州の最高裁の Walsh 判事の判決は，McNair 判事が The Brabant [1965] 2 Lloyd's Rep. 546 事件で，Mocatta 判事が The Apollonius [1978] 1 Lloyd's Rep. 53 事件で，正しいとして受け入れたが，The TFL Prosperity 事件の判決に際して，貴族院は意見を異にした。Westfal-Larsen 事件で，船主は傭船者に共同海損分担金を請求したが，傭船者は不堪航を根拠として抗弁した。船主は第13条の免責に拠って傭船者の抗弁を挫くことができると判示された。Roskill 卿は Walsh 判事の判決を批判して，Westfal-Larsen 事件の請求は「貨物の滅失損傷の請求ではなく，機関長の過失と思われる燃料問題により本船が適正な蒸気を維持できなかったために生じた」と述べた。

引渡遅延

  たとえ引渡遅延が船主または船舶管理人自身の相当の注意の欠如，または過失によらないとしても，第13条によって，船主は，本船のあらゆる引渡遅延から保護されているわけではない。特に傭船者が当事者となっているわけでもない従前の契約関係から遅延が生じた場合には，第13条は適用されない。ただし，かかる遅延の危険を傭船者が負担する意図が，傭船契約の全体の趣旨から明らかにされている場合は別である。本条項は，船主のためのものであるから，解釈は，傭船者に有利になされる。

  「後日命名される……建造中の新造機船」と表示された Helvetia-S 号がボルタイム書式で傭船された。第 1 条により，本船は，「碇泊期間，1956年 6 月10日に引き渡される」ものとされており，解約期日 (第22条) は，7 月15日であった。建造が遅延し，6 月12日船主は，傭船者に対し，8 月以前には引き渡せないと通知した。そこで，第13条により船主は，保護されるかの問題が生じた。船主の主張は，95行「引渡遅延」は，「引渡の延期」を意味し，船主の管理が及ばない建造過程で生じた事態により，遅延が発生すれば，その遅延は第13条の範囲内のものであるというものであった。Pearson 判事は，本条は，そのような広い意味を持たず，建造の遅延は，引渡の遅延ではないと判示した。
  The Helvetia-S [1960] 1 Lloyd's Rep. 540.
  (前出 The TFL Prosperity 事件で貴族院は，この判決に賛意を示した)

傭船期間中の遅延

船長が,極力迅速に航海を遂行する義務(第9条)に違反しても,船主または船舶管理人自身が,相当の注意を欠いたり,怠慢であったという事情がない限り,船主は本条により,遅延の責任を免れるのが普通である((1930) 38 LLL. Rep. 84 および前出638頁の *Istros* v. *Dahlstrom* 事件参照。644頁と *The TFL Prosperity* 事件も参照)。

相当の注意の欠如

本条項のもとでは,本船に堪航性を備えさせるにつき船主または船舶管理人自身に相当の注意の欠如,その他船主または船舶管理人自身の怠慢や作為があった場合にのみ船主は責任を負う。したがって,第13条の効果は,傭船の始期における黙示的堪航性担保の絶対的義務違反,または16行の「あらゆる点で通常貨物の運送業務に適する状態で本船を引き渡す」義務違反に対する責任を軽減するものである(前出147頁および206頁参照)。97行の「相当の注意」というのは,ヘーグ・ルールの解釈とは異なり,被用者,代理人,下請業者がこれを欠いた場合を含まず(*The Muncaster Castle* [1961] 1 Lloyd's Rep. 57 事件参照),98行の「自身の personal」という文言で限定されている。

　　Brabant 号は,ボルタイム書式によりウッドパルプの輸送のため,1往復航海に傭船された。傭船契約の印刷された追加条項は,「甲板,船艙,その他の貨物スペースは,船主の危険と費用において船積前に適切に清掃される」と定めていた。スウェーデン諸港において積んだウッドパルプは,前航の石炭貨物の残留物によって損害を被った。船主は,船荷証券の所持人に対して責任を負い,第9条に従って傭船者にその補償を求めた。石炭が残留していたのは,積荷前,乗組員が船艙を適切に清掃しなかったためであることが判明したが,それについて,船主または船舶管理人自身が相当の注意を欠いていたという事情はなかったと認定された。McNair判事は,第13条における船主の責任は,船主自身が相当の注意を欠いていた場合に限られるが,本件の特定の情況の下においては,船主に船艙清掃の危険を課する印刷した条項が第13条に優先すると判示した。
　　The Brabant [1965] 2 Lloyd's Rep. 546.
　　(*Westfal-Larsen* v. *Colonial Sugar Refining* [1960] 2 Lloyd's Rep. 206 事件も参照)

　誰の作為,不作為が船主「自身」の作為,不作為とみなされるのかということは,船主の会社の規則と組織しだいであり,本船の運航が船舶管理人に委ねられる場合には,その会社の規則と組織しだいと思われる(*The Marion* [1984] 2 Lloyd's Rep. 1 (H. L.) 事件と *The Ert Stefanie* [1989] 1 Lloyd's Rep. 349 (C. A.) 事件参照)。Willmer卿判事は,*The Lady Gwendolen* [1965] 1 Lloyd's Rep. 335 (同判例集345頁) 事件で次のように述べた。「船主が株式会社である場合,困難な問題が生じるのはほとんど避けがたい。誰の作為または不作為が会社自身の作為,不作為であると公平にいえるかどうかを判定するには,会社の組織を注意深く見る必要がある」。
　その事案で船主「自身」の故意または過失の問題が1894年商船法の第503条に基づく船主責任制限の権利の文脈について生じた。船主は醸造業の会社であり,その海運活動は主たる業務に従属するものであった。取締役会の構成員ではないが,常務取締役に対して責任を負う管理者により,船舶は管理されていた。Hewson判事と控訴院は,常務取締役は会社の海運部門運営に関する限り,船主の分身であり,彼の過失は,船主自身の過失であると判示した。ところが海運部門の管理者の不作為でも船主自身の不作為として位置づけるという見解が控訴院で,表明された。Willmer卿判事は,次のように述べた(同判例集345頁)。「本事案におけるように,会社に会社の船舶を管理する責任を負う別の運輸部門がある場合,会社の船舶を扱うこと

に関係する限り，取締役ではなくてもその部門の長の行為は会社自身の行為そのものとみなされると私は思う」。

しかし，Diplock 卿は Tesco v. Nattrass [1972] A.C. 153 事件で，会社そのものの権限を委託されていない者が，会社の分身たりうることを示唆する限りにおいてこの見解を踏襲しなかった。誰が業務遂行の行為のために会社として刑事法上の処遇を受けるかという問題は，「会社定款により，または役員による行為の結果として，または定款に従った社員総会により会社の権限の行使を委託される」者を確認することで，答えられると同判事は考えた。同判事は次のように続けて述べている（同判例集200頁）。「H. L. Bolton (Engineering) Co. Ltd. v. T. J. Graham & Sons Ltd. [1957] 1 Q.B. 159, 172, 173 事件の Denning 卿判事の判決から両手と比較した会社の『頭脳と神経中枢』という同判事の生き生きした隠喩を抜粋する傾向が近年みられる。そこでは，制定法が会社に負わせる義務を果たすときに特定の者が法的に会社そのものとしてみなされるか否かの基準を規定するものとして，それが会社定款ではなく，この二分法を論じている。この隠喩が最初に使用された事案で，Denning 卿判事は，会社の権限が会社定款に基づき授与される会社の役員の行為と意図を取り扱っていた。その事案の判決は，会社定款によりまたは会社定款に基づく行為により会社の権限を行使することができる者以外に，会社自身そのものの行為として法律的にみなされる行為者の職階を拡大する先例ではない。The Lady Gwendolen [1965] 事件（同判例集294頁）での逆の傍論がある限り，定款は判決にとっては必要ではないし，私の考えではそれは不適当である」。

しかしながら，The Ert Stefanie [1989] 1 Lloyd's Rep. 349（同判例集352頁）事件で，控訴院の判決を出した Mustill 卿判事は，会社の取締役でない者が委託されていなくとも，取締役権限の範囲内である上級管理者の機能を行使する場合，その者は会社の支配する意思と知力を共に構成する者として扱われることを示唆した。実質上会社そのものの行為をする者にそういう者を追加することは，前出 The Lady Gwendolen 事件の Willmer 卿判事の見解と一致する。それは，少なくとも民事事件で普及している見解であると思われる。しかし Mustill 卿判事は，対照的に，責任問題となる行為を為したときに通常，取締役の権限外の職務を行ったという理由だけで，例外的場合を除いて会社の管理からその者をはずすことはできないと引き続き判示した。1894年商船法の第503条に基づく船主の責任制限の権利に関する The Ert Stefanie 事件で Hobhouse 判事と控訴院は通常，取締役の権限外の機能（特定の貨物の運送のために特別な要件と予防策を船長に助言する）を行った場合，自ら過誤を犯した専務取締役の過失は船主「その者自身の過失」であると判示した。

商船法に基づく船主の責任制限の権利に関する事案で船主またはその船舶管理人自身は，船舶の効率的管理，運航および配乗のための適正な体制を設け維持する責任を負うが，有能な部下を選任するだけでは十分ではないと判示された（The Garden City [1982] 2 Lloyd's Rep. 382 事件と The Marion [1984] 2 Lloyd's Rep. 1 (H.L.) 事件参照)。

もちろん船主自身が雇い入れた乗組員の能力不足で損害が生じた場合，採用にあたり，乗組員の能力を十分調査しなければ，船主自身が相当の注意を欠いたことになるので，船主は第13条の利益を享受しないものと思われる（The Roberta [1938] 60 Ll.L. Rep. 84 および The Hong Kong Fir (1961) 2 Lloyd's Rep. 478)。

立 証 責 任

主張された遅延，滅失，損傷が，いかにして生じたか，さらにそれが第13条に該当することの立証責任は，船主にある。Greer 卿判事は本条（当時の第12条）につき，前出 The Roberta (1938) 60 Ll.L. Rep. 84 事件において次のように述べている。「このことは，船主が相当の注

意を欠いたために滅失，損傷が生じたものではないことを主張した場合に，第12条の適用が認められるのであって，なぜ損傷貨物を引き渡すことになったのかの説明も立証もできない場合，船主は免責条項の適用を受けない」。

第13条と他の条項との関係

上記で検討したとおり，第13条は，通常，極力迅速に航海を遂行するという第9条の義務の違反から船主を保護し，また「通常の貨物運送業務にあらゆる点で適合する」船舶の引渡という義務によって本来課せられる絶対的堪航性担保義務を軽減する。

誤表示

しかし，本条は，通常船舶の誤表示について船主を保護しないと思われる。次の事件は速力の担保に関連してこの問題が生じた事例であるが，まだ判決が出ていない。

Apollonius 号は，1航海，ボルタイム書式によって定期傭船された。傭船契約は，本船は，「満載状態で，気象，海象共良好な場合，燃料消費約38屯で約14.5ノットの速力を出せる」と表示された。第13条は，次のように訂正されていた。「本船の引渡の遅延，傭船期間中の遅延，本船上の貨物の滅失，損傷については，かかる遅延，滅失，損傷が，船主，その被用者，管理人が本船をその傭船期間中の各航海に適合させ，堪航性を備えるにあたり相当の注意を欠いたため，または船主または管理人自身のその他の作為，不作為，怠慢から生じた場合にのみ船主は責任を負う」。極度の船底の汚れ（相当の注意を欠いたためではない）のため，引渡時において，本船は，担保速力を出すことができなかった。その結果，日本からアルゼンチンの傭船航海で時間の喪失が生じた。その航海中，さらに，機関士が機関の全出力を出さなかったことからも，時間喪失が生じた。

Mocatta 判事は，速力に関する担保は，引渡時に適用されるが，その義務違反の責任について船主が第13条によって保護されるかについては判断しなかった。この側面を扱うにあたって，Mocatta 判事は，次のように述べている。

「(傭船者の法廷弁護士)は，本条項中の『遅延 delay』という文言を，速力担保違反の結果，または，機関士が主機を適正に作動させなかった結果から生じた事態に適用するのは不適当であると主張した。しかしこの議論は速力担保違反から生じた遅延に関しては，十分説得力があるとは思えない。また機関士の行為に関しても，この議論が通用するとは考えられない。全体的に見て本文脈中の『遅延』という文言は，上記二つのできごとに適用されると思われる。しかし，……速力担保に関しては，適用されるか否かを決定する必要はないと思われる」。

The Apollonius [1978] 1 Lloyd's Rep. 53.

しかしながら，*The TFL Prosperity* [1984] 1 Lloyd's Rep. 123 事件で貴族院は，当事者が特定の航路のために建造され使用される船舶の明細を傭船契約に記述した場合に，仮に広く解釈したとしても，第13条は不実表示に対する請求について船主を保護しないと判示した（当該事案の事実の要約は前出644頁参照）。Roskill 卿は次のように述べた（同判例集130頁）。貴族院の他の全員が同判事に賛意を表した。「本当に，第13条が約束した第26条の明細に関する担保違反を許容し，または傭船者に対する経済的補償のない本船の引渡不履行を許容すると解釈されるのであれば，傭船契約は定期傭船料の支払の対価として本船の貸渡，船主，船長，職員および部員による役務の履行のための契約では事実上なくなり，船主が明細または引渡に関する約束を遂行できない場合，その見返りとして傭船者が傭船料の方式で巨額を支払う義務があるのであるから，それは，単なる船主の意思表示書に過ぎなくなり，傭船者はそれに代わる何らの権利をも有しない。これが当事者の真の共通の意思と一致しうるとは私は信じることができない。この結論が，本事案の当事者が真の共通の意思を書面で明示したと思われる傭船契約

の正しい解釈と一致するとは，私は思わない」。
　さらに，傭船契約が成約に至るまでの交渉過程で不実表示がなされ，その不実表示が誘因となつて傭船者が傭船契約を締結した状況下で，第13条を適用することが1977年不公正契約条項法（Unfair Contract Terms Act）第8条1項により改正された1967年不実表示法（Misrepresentation Act）第3条に基づき，不適当であると認められる場合には，第13条は船主の利益を保護する役目を果さない（この点に関し前述132頁および1967年法の他の条項を参照）。

免責条項の解釈
　免責条項の解釈に関する注解については，前出494頁から496頁参照。

タイプされた追加条項
　ある特定の事項について船主に責任を課す特別規定がタイプされた追加条項になっている場合には，その追加条項は第13条に優先して適用されるであろう。前出646頁 The Brabant [1965] 2 Lloyd's Rep. 546事件参照，当事件は前出 The TFL Prosperity 事件で貴族院によりこの範囲で承認された。TFL Prosperity 事件で，Roskill 判事はタイプされた追加条項は明確に印刷条項の代用として意図されている場合，タイプされているという理由だけで，タイプ条項が印刷免責条項より必ずしも優先するとはみなされないと考えた。貴族院の他の者も同判事に同意した（本事案の事実経緯の要約について644頁参照）。

至上条項（Paramount Clause）
　ボルタイム書式による傭船契約書中に至上条項がはいっている場合，傭船契約書中の他の条項との関係における至上条項の効果は，至上条項を傭船契約に摂取する文言および，至上条項 561 自体の文言によって決定される。しかし，一般には第13条の規定にヘーグ・ルールが優先する（Adamastos v. Anglo-Saxon Petroleum [1958] 1 Lloyd's Rep. 73事件，Marifortuna v. Government of Ceylon [1970] 1 Lloyd's Rep. 247事件および前出594頁から601頁各参照）。
　しかし，ニューヨーク・プロデュース書式第24条によって（前出593頁参照）摂取されている型の至上条項がボルタイム書式に万一摂取されることがあれば，その一般的効果はニューヨーク・プロデュース書式における場合と同様であろう。第13条の広範な免責は，貨物の物理的な滅失，または損傷に関する限り，米国海上物品運送法第4条2項の狭い免責に代わる。傭船開始時の堪航性の義務は，相当の注意を尽くす義務になり，その義務がおそらく傭船契約の下での各航海に関し課されることになる（前出596頁参照）。
　摂取する条項が単に「至上条項」と述べているだけで，ヘーグ・ルールに制定法上の効力を与える特定の法規を指定していない場合には，ヘーグ・ルール自体が摂取される。

　Agios Lazaros 号は航海傭船され，傭船契約書には次のような規定があった。「ニュー・ジェイソン条項，双方過失衝突条項，P and I 補油条項，英国海運会議所戦争危険条項第1，第2および至上条項が本傭船契約書に摂取されているものとみなされる」。
　この傭船契約の下でのクレームがヘーグ・ルール第3条6項の1年間の出訴期限にかかるかどうかの問題が生じた。至上条項には数多くの異なる書式があるので，単に「至上条項」というだけでは無効であるとの主張がなされた。控訴院は，当事者の意図は「至上条項」と言及したことにより，明らかであるからこの傭船契約はヘーグ・ルールに従うものであり，ヘーグ・ルールがその原型のまま摂取されていると判示した。記録長官 Denning 卿は次のように述べた。
　「海運関係の人間にとって『至上条項』とは何を意味するであろうか。それは船荷証券に適用のあるものである。このような状況においてのその意味は疑問の余地のないほど明確である。それはヘー

グ・ルールを船荷証券により表章される契約に摂取する条項である。またその条項はそれと矛盾するいかなる明示の例外規定や条件にも優先する。……『至上条項』が何らの留保文言なしに（傭船契約書に）摂取されている場合には，ヘーグ・ルールの全条項が摂取されていることを意味している。当事者が単にヘーグ・ルールの一部だけを（例えば第4条）摂取する意図であるか，または強制的に適用される場合のみを意図しているときは当事者はその意思を契約書の中に表示する。そのような事情がなければ『至上条項』はヘーグ・ルールのすべての条項を摂取したものと思われる」。

The Agios Lazaros [1976] 2 Lloyd's Rep. 47.

しかしながら，「至上条項」が，英国法を準拠法とするボルタイム傭船契約に摂取される場合，1971年海上物品運送法が有効となる1977年以降ヘーグ・ヴィスビー・ルールが摂取されているとみなされることになろう。

Clause 13 continued — Strikes etc
100 　　　　　　　　　　　　　　　　　　　　　　　　　　　"...The Owners not
101 　to be liable for loss or damage arising or resulting from strikes, lock-outs or stoppage or restraint
102 　of labour (including the Master, Officers or Crew) whether partial or general."

[Clause 13 continued below]

第13条　続　— ストライキ等

「船主は局地的・全般的の別なく，ストライキ，ロックアウトもしくは労働の停止または制限（船長，職員または部員を含む）から生じる滅失または損傷を負担しない。」

[第13条以下続く]

101行と102行の一般的解説

101行の「損失」は，物理的損失と同様に経済的損失も含む。*The TFL Prosperity* [1984] 1 Lloyd's Rep. 123 事件（同判例集128頁）参照。しかし損害賠償請求が第13条の最初の文章の範囲の遅延に対する請求として分類され，かつ船主または船舶管理人自身の相当の注意の欠如（前出646頁参照）または懈怠がない場合は別であるが，発生した事件が過失による場合（*Polemis* v. *Furness Withy* (1921) 8 Ll.L. Rep. 263 and 351 事件参照），この免責は何らの保護も与えるものではない。

562 ストライキ

「ストライキ」は，*The New Horizon* [1975] 2 Lloyd's Rep. 314 事件で記録長官 Denning 卿により次のように定義されている。「ストライキとは給与または労働条件の改善のため苦情をぶちまけるため，あるいは何かに対して抗議するため，あるいはそのような諸行為により他の労働者を支援し同調するために労働者によってなされる一致協力した仕事の停止である。それは，爆撃のおそれや危険の懸念のような外的要因により惹起された仕事の停止と区別される」。

他の仕事が行われていたり，またはその行動が特定の複数船に限定されていても，またたとえたった1隻の船に関する行動であっても，ストライキを構成する妨げとはならない。

Laga 号は，ストライキ中であったフランス鉱山労働者の支援のため Nantes 港港湾労働者が揚荷および石炭積載船に対する労務提供を拒絶したことにより遅延した。港湾労働者は他の船については通常どおり就労した。McNair 判事は次のように判示した。Laga 号が傭船された航海傭船契約の免責条項中の「ストライキ」は同情ストまたはゼネストを含んでいるので他の仕事が継続されていても本件とは関係がない。Laga 号に関する限り，それはストライキであった。
　　The Laga〔1966〕1 Lloyd's Rep. 582.

同様に，その行動が労働者の雇傭契約に違反していなくても，またその行動が単に労働時間の短縮にとどまるものであっても，ストライキである。

　　New Horizon 号は St. Nazaire 港における一部労働者の夜間就業拒否により遅延した。通常同港は，3交替制の24時間就労であった。しかし契約によれば労働者は夜間就業を強制されていなかった。控訴院は，夜間就業拒否は労働条件改善を目的として行われたものでありストライキになると判示した。
　　Tramp Shipping v. Greenwich Marine (The New Horizon)〔1975〕2 Lloyd's Rep. 314.

乗組員

戦時において，潜水艦による攻撃のおそれを理由とする乗組員一致の航海の拒絶があった場合につき，Sankey 判事は，船主はストライキに対する免責条項によって保護されると判示した。Wiliiams v. Naamlooze (1915) 21 Com. Cas. 253. 他方，船主に対する苦情の表明として荷役業者の揚荷を乗組員が拒絶した場合，それによって生じた損失は傭船契約書にある免責条項の「ストライキまたは労働停止」にあたらないと判示された (Compania Naviera Bachi v. Hosegood (1938) 60 Ll.L. Rep. 236)。同事件で Porter 判事は次のとおり述べている。「ストライキも労働の停止も，損失の原因ではないと思われる。それは，揚荷役に従事する労働者自身が労働を差し控えたというのではなく，それ以外の者が揚荷をしようとする者を妨害したのである」(同判例集243頁)。

停止 (Stoppage)

「停止」は，労働争議に起因する停止のみに限定されない。したがって病気をおそれての就労の拒否はストライキとはならないと判示されているけれども (Stephens v. Harris (1887) 57 L. T. 618) そのような拒絶は「停止」となるであろう。前出 The New Horizon 事件参照。それ自身独立して使用されている場合「停止」という文言は，完全な仕事の停止を意味すると解釈されている。

　　Mercedes de Larrinaga 号は航海傭船契約により傭船され，契約書には「本船の積荷準備完了時点から6連続日以上業務停止が継続した場合には，本傭船契約は無効となる」と規定していた。本船は準備完了であったが，6日以上貨物を受け取らなかった。この期間中鉄道ストが行われ，それは荷役を妨げたが，貨物の積み出しバース搬入が完全に停止したわけではなかった。証拠によるとその全体の期間を通じて，低能率ではあったが他船への積荷は行われていた。Roche 判事は，これは停止ではないと判示した。この見解は控訴院において支持された。
　　Miguel de Larrinaga v. Flack (1924) 20 Ll.L. Rep. 268 および (1925) 21 Ll.L. Rep. 284.
　　(なお，Akt. Adalands v. Whittaker (1913) 18 Com. Cas. 299 事件も参照)

しかし，第13条の「停止」という文言は，「部分的にであれ全体的にであれ」という文言によって修飾されているので，停止が完全ではない場合をも含むと思われる。しかしそれは，

「仕事をゆっくり行うこと go slow」や「順法闘争 work to rule」の場合は，含まないとされている。

Clause 13 continued — Charterers' responsibilities

103　"The Charterers to be responsible for loss or damage caused to the Vessel or to the Owners by goods
104　being loaded contrary to the terms of the Charter or by improper or careless bunkering or loading,
105　stowing or discharging of goods or any other improper or negligent act on their part or that of
106　their servants."

第13条　続 — 傭船者の責任

「本契約に違反して船積した貨物により，または燃料積取・貨物の積込・積付・揚荷の不適当あるいは不注意により，または傭船者もしくはその被用者の怠慢な行為または過失によって，本船もしくは船主に滅失または損傷を生じたときは，傭船者はその責めに任じなければならない。」

本船の滅失または損傷についての傭船者の責任

The TFL Prosperity ［1984］1 Lloyd's Rep. 123 事件（同判例集128頁）で Roskill 卿は，103行から106行の免責は，傭船契約に基づき，またはコモン・ロー上ともかく傭船者が負担するよりも大きな責任を課するのかということを疑問視した。

The White Rose ［1969］2 Lloyd's Rep. 52 事件で，102行から106行に基づいて傭船者から損害の賠償を得るためには，船主は「滅失や損傷」が104行から106行に記載の三つの範疇の事由の一つから生じたことを立証しなければならない，と判示された。「滅失」には，責任を処理することにより生じた経済的損失を含む。Donaldson 判事は前出 The White Rose 事件で，次のように述べた。「本条項により得られる補償の範囲は，十二分に広く，本船の物理的滅失，損傷または経済的損失（例えば本船の不稼働損失）と対照的な意味での潜在的クレームの合理的解決によって生じた損失をも含む。しかし本条項が適用されるのは，当該損失が，(a)積込，積付をなす者の不適当，不注意な行為によって生じた場合であり，それが定期傭船者の選任した独立の契約者または定期傭船者の被用者，代理人によってなされたかを問わない，または(b)定期傭船者またはその被用者側の不適当または過失ある他の何らかの行為により生じた場合に限られる」（同判例集60頁）。

傭船契約に反して積み込まれた物品

非安全港における本船への積荷により損害が生じる場合，本条項により傭船者は責任を負う。

ボルタイム書式により傭船された，Terneuzen 号は，Leningrad 港での積荷を命ぜられたが，バースが安全でなかったため損傷を受けた。控訴院において，Greer 卿判事は次のように述べた。喪失時間につき本船がオフハイヤーとされるならば，船主は本条項に基づき，同金額を損害として傭船者から求償することができる。なぜなら船主の損害は，傭船契約の条項に反して物品が積み込まれたこと

被用者

前出 The White Rose [1962] 2 Lloyd's Rep. 52 事件では，106行の「被用者」とは傭船者がその者に代位して責任を負わなければならないという関係にある階級の者に限るとされた。

危険品：一般に前出221頁から225頁参照。

Clauses 14 and 15 — Advances/Excluded ports

107　"14. The Charterers or their Agents to advance to the Master, if required, necessary funds for
108　ordinary disbursements for the Vessel's account at any port charging only interest at 6 per cent p. a.,
109　such advances to be deducted from hire.
110　15. The Vessel not to be ordered to nor bound to enter: a) any place where fever or epidemics
111　are prevalent or to which the Master, Officers and Crew by law are not bound to follow the Vessel
112　b) any ice-bound place or any place where lights, lightships, marks and buoys are or are likely to
113　be withdrawn by reason of ice on the Vessel's arrival or where there is risk that ordinarily the Vessel
114　will not be able on account of ice to reach the place or to get out after having completed loading or
115　discharging. The Vessel not to be obliged to force ice. If on account of ice the Master considers it
116　dangerous to remain at the loading or discharging place for fear of the Vessel being frozen in and/or
117　damaged, he has liberty to sail to a convenient open place and await the Charterers' fresh instructions.
118　Unforeseen detention through any of above causes to be for the Charterers' account."

第14条および第15条 — 前渡金／除外港

「14. 傭船者またはその代理人は，船長の求めにより，いずれの港においても，通常の船用金として必要な金員を立て替えるものとする。この場合，船主は右の立替金について年6分の利子以外負担しない。立替金は傭船料から控除する。

15. 本船は(a)熱病または流行病の蔓延している場所，もしくは船長・職員および部員が法律の規定により本船と同航する義務のない場所，(b)結氷地，または本船の到着時に結氷を理由として灯火・灯船・標識・浮標が撤去されているか，または撤去のおそれのある場所，もしくは結氷のため通常の方法では到底本船が到着しまたは積取・揚荷の完了後において出港できない危険が現存する場所のいずれに向けても，配船を命ぜられ，もしくは入港の義務を負うことがない。本船には，結氷を強行突破する義務はないものとする。結氷のため船長が積地または揚地に碇泊するときは，凍結およびまたは

損害を被るおそれがあると認めた場合，船長は随意に最寄りの開放地に回航して，新たに傭船者の指図を待つことができる。
　前項の事由による予見しえない滞留は，傭船者の負担である。」

傭船料からの控除：前出306頁参照。

氷　条　項

　Scrutton 卿判事は *Limerick* v. *Stott*〔1921〕2 K.B. 613 事件で次のように述べた。本条項により，「船長は，凍結港への航海を拒否することができるし，また，航海途上で遭遇する氷を強行突破することを拒否することもできる。その拒否は，傭船契約の違反にならないし，また傭船者からの次の適正な指図，または氷海外への航海指図を待つ間，船主は傭船料を請求できる。船長はまた，凍結しそうな港から退去することもできる。しかし，これは義務ではない。すなわち船長が退避することができたのに，その港に留まったからといって船主の傭船料請求権がなくなるわけではない」（同判例集620頁）。

凍結港

　人工的手段を用いなければ，通常1年の内の一定期間凍結港が砕氷船により開港されている場合には，本条項の意味する凍結港ではない。

　　Innisboffin 号は初期のボルタイム書式で「ボルティック1周航海」に傭船された。本船は，冬期，砕氷船により開港されている Abo 港への航海を指図された。そして，Stockholm と Abo 間を船舶が1週間に6航海定期的に航海していたという証拠があった。Bailhache 判事と控訴院は，は Abo 港は，凍結港ではないと判断した。
　　Limerick v. *Stott*〔1921〕2 K.B. 613.

通常

　本船が氷に妨げられることなく通常入出港できる港に配船されても，本条項の違反とはならない。しかし，それでも，その港が結氷のため安全でないことはありうる（後出 *The Sussex Oak*（1950）83 Ll.L. Rep. 297 事件参照。しかし *The Evia*（*No.2*）〔1982〕2 Lloyd's Rep. 307 事件（同判例集321頁）の Roskill 卿の意見を参照）。

本船に砕氷の義務はない

　船長は結氷を強行突破するのを拒否できる。しかし船長が配船港へ到達するために，砕氷航海を選んだ場合，その配船指示自体適切であれば，傭船者は本船が受けた損害につき責めを負わないと思われる。
　前出 *Limerick* v. *Stott* 事件において，本船は Abo 港に至る通常の航路上で厚い氷に遭遇した。そのとき，本船は Abo 港から200マイルほどの距離にいた。砕氷船の救援を待つ代わりに，船長は，砕氷航海を試みることを決定した。船長は，失敗し，本船は氷に閉ざされた。それから，砕氷船が呼ばれ，残余の航海につき，本船は砕氷船の援助を得た。控訴院は，傭船者は，本船が砕氷航海にあたって被った損害に責任はないと判示した。

航海途上の結氷に因る損害

　上に要約した *Limerick* v. *Stott* 事件では，船長が自ら砕氷を試みずに直ちに，砕氷船の援助を求めていたら，本船は，その仕向港たる Abo 港に安全に到達したはずである。しかし，航

海途上の氷のため，本船は，仕向港に安全に到着する可能性がなく，船長が砕氷しなければならないのであれば，傭船者は，その港は安全でないとの理由により，本船の損害につき責任を負うことになろう。

　　Sussex Oak 号は，ボルタイム書式により，傭船され，1947年1月Hamburgへ向けるよう指示された。本船が，Elbe河を遡航する折，氷に遭遇したが，水先人は，遡航は安全であると考えた。しかしながら，本船がHamburg附近まで来たとき，本船は，一大流氷群に遭遇し航行できなくなった。そのとき，本船は，回頭も，後進も，投錨も安全にできない場所にいた。水先人の忠告に従って，本船は氷中を強行突破し，その結果，損害を受けた。船長は，砕氷船の救援を受けなかったけれども適切に航行したと事実認定された。Devlin判事は，Hamburgは当時，非安全港であり，傭船者は，本船に対し，同港への配船指示をする権限はないという理由により，傭船者は，本船に対する損害につき責任を負うと判示した。Devlin判事は，次のように指摘した。
　　「危険が存在する場所が港から離れていればいるほど，航海の安全を害する度合が少ないことは，事実として明らかであるけれども，法律上は重要ではない。傭船者は，港への最短航路または特定航路が安全であることを，保証するものではないが，その命じる航海は通常の慎重にして，熟練した船長が安全に航海し得るものでなければならない。本件において，Hamburgへの唯一の航路は，Elbe河によるしかなかった。そして，仲裁人は，この進入水路は，氷のため，安全ではないと裁定した」。
　　The Sussex Oak (1950) 83 Ll.L. Rep. 297.

　　上記事案で傭船者は，第15条が結氷の危険についての排他的救済策を規定しているので船主は第2条に基づく安全港担保義務に拠ることはできないと，主張した。Devlin判事は，この主張を退けたが，The Evia (No.2) [1982] 2 Lloyd's Rep. 307事件（同判例集321頁）でRoskill卿は，Devlin判事がこの点で正しいか否かという問題について，結論を留保したことは明らかであった。

Clauses 16, 17 and 18 — Loss of Vessel/Overtime/Lien

119　"16. Should the Vessel be lost or missing, hire to cease from the date when she was lost. If
120　the date of loss cannot be ascertained half hire to be paid from the date the Vessel was last reported
121　until the calculated date of arrival at the destination. Any hire paid in advance to be adjusted
122　accordingly.
123　17. The Vessel to work day and night if required. The Charterers to refund the Owners their
124　outlays for all overtime paid to Officers and Crew according to the hours and rates stated in the Vessel's
125　articles.
126　18. The Owners to have a lien upon all cargoes and sub-freights belonging to the Time-Charterers
127　and any Bill of Lading freight for all claims under this Charter, and the Charterers to have a lien on
128　the Vessel for all moneys paid in advance and not earned."

第16, 17条および第18条 ― 本船の滅失／時間外／リーエン

「16. 本船が滅失するか, または行方不明となったときは, その滅失の日から傭船料の支払を中止する。滅失の日が確定しないときは, 本船につき最後の通信があった日から起算して, 仕向地到着を予定された日まで, 傭船料の半額を支払う。前払傭船料は, すべてこれに応じて精算するものとする。

17. 本船は要求がある場合, 昼夜, 作業するものとする。この場合, 傭船者は本船の船員雇用契約に定められた時間ならびに料率に従って船主が職員および部員に支払った一切の時間外労働の費用を償還しなければならない。

18. 船主は本契約に基づく一切の請求権につき, 定期傭船者のすべての積荷, 再運送賃, および船荷証券運賃の上に, リーエンを有し, 傭船者は反対給付が得られなかった一切の前払金につき, 本船の上にリーエンを有するものとする。」

本船の滅失：「履行不能」の場合の本船滅失について全般的に前出461／479頁参照。
貨物に対する船主のリーエン：前出555／566頁参照。

566 **定期傭船者に帰属するすべての貨物および再運送賃**

ニューヨーク・プロデュース書式と対照的なのは, 船主がリーエンを行使できるのは, 傭船者に帰属する貨物についてのみであることがボルタイム書式の第18条によって明らかにされていることである (*International Bulk Carriers* v. *Evlogia Shipping* (*The Mihalios Xilas*) [1978] 2 Lloyd's Rep. 186 事件および前出556頁を参照)。

再運送賃に対する船主のリーエン：前出558／563頁を参照。
本船に対する傭船者のリーエン：前出564頁を参照。

Clauses 19 and 20 ― Salvage/Sublet

129 "19. All salvage and assistance to other vessels to be for the Owners' and the Charterers'
130 equal benefit after deducting the Master's and Crew's proportion and all legal and other expenses
131 including hire paid under the charter for time lost in the salvage, also repairs of damage and coal
132 or oil-fuel consumed. The Charterers to be bound by all measures taken by the Owners in order
133 to secure payment of salvage and to fix its amount.
134 20. The Charterers to have the option of subletting the Vessel, giving due notice to the Owners, but
135 the original Charterers always to remain responsible to the Owners for due performance of the Charter."

第19条および第20条 ― 海難救助／再傭船

「19. 他船に対してなした, あらゆる救助・救援については, 船長および乗組員への分配額, 一切の法定その他の費用 (救助のため喪失した時間に対し本契約により支払う傭船料, ならびに損傷の修理, 消費した石炭または燃料油を含む) を控除した後, 船主と傭船者とにおいて均等の利益を受ける

ものとする。傭船者は，船主が救助料の支払を確保し，かつその金額を定めるためになした一切の処置に従わねばならない。

20. 傭船者は，船主に対し，相当な通知をなして，任意に本船を他に再傭船させることができる。ただし，原傭船者は常に船主に対し，本契約履行の責任を免れない。」

海難救助：前出587頁を参照。
再傭船の自由：前出199／200頁を参照。

Clause 21 — War

136 "21. (A) The Vessel unless the consent of the Owners be first obtained not to be ordered nor
137 continue to any place or on any voyage nor be used on any service which will bring her within a
138 zone which is dangerous as the result of any actual or threatened act of war, war hostilities, warlike
139 operations, acts of piracy or of hostility or malicious damage against this or any other vessel or its
140 cargo by any person, body or State whatsoever, revolution, civil war, civil commotion or the operation of
141 international law, nor be exposed in any way to any risks or penalties whatsoever consequent upon
142 the imposition of Sanctions, nor carry any goods that may in any way expose her to any risks of
143 seizure, capture, penalties or any other interference of any kind whatsoever by the belligerent or
144 fighting powers or parties or by any Government or Ruler.
145   (B) Should the Vessel approach or be brought or ordered within such zone, or be exposed in
146 any way to the said risks, (1) the Owners to be entitled from time to time to insure their interests
147 in the Vessel and/or hire against any of the risks likely to be involved thereby on such terms as
148 they shall think fit, the Charterers to make a refund to the Owners of the premium on de-
149 mand; and (2) notwithstanding the terms of clause 11 hire to be paid for all time lost including
150 any loss owing to loss of or injury to the Master, Officers, or Crew or to the action of the Crew
151 in refusing to proceed to such zone or to be exposed to such risks.
152   (C) In the event of the wages of the Master, Officers and/or Crew or the cost of provisions
153 and/or store for deck and/or engine room and/or insurance premiums being increased by reason of
154 or during the existence of any of the matters mentioned in section (A) the amount of any increase
155 to be added to the hire and paid by the Charterers on production of the Owners' ac-

count therefor,
156 such account being rendered monthly.
157 　　(D) The Vessel to have liberty to comply with any orders or directions as to departure,
158 arrival, routes, ports of call, stoppages, destination, delivery or in any otherwise whatsoever given
159 by the Government of the nation under whose flag the Vessel sails or any other Government or any
160 person (or body) acting or purporting to act with the authority of such Government or by any
161 committee or person having under the terms of the war risks insurance on the Vessel the right to
162 give any such orders or directions.
163 　　(E) In the event of the nation under whose flag the Vessel sails becoming involved in war, hosti-
164 lities, warlike operations, revolution, or civil commotion, both the Owners and the Charterers may cancel
165 the Charter and, unless otherwise agreed, the Vessel to be redelivered to the Owners at the port
166 of destination or, if prevented through the provisions of section (A) from reaching or entering it,
167 then at a near open and safe port at the Owners' option, after discharge of any cargo on board.
168 　　(F) If in compliance with the provisions of this clause anything is done or is not done, such
169 not to be deemed a deviation."

第21条 ― 戦　　争

「21.　(A) 本船は，現実のまたは切迫せる交戦行為，戦争，敵対行為，軍事的行為，私人・団体・国家のいずれによるかを問わず，本船その他の船舶またはその積荷に対する海賊行為または敵対・悪意の加害行為，革命，内乱，暴動または国際法上の行為のため危険となっている区域内航行を必要とする一切の場所または航海につき，配船の指図を受けまたはこれを続行しもしくはかかる業務に使用されることも，制裁権の発動に基づく一切の危険または刑罰に曝されることも，交戦国または交戦団体もしくは官憲による，あらゆる種類の没収・捕獲・刑罰その他の処分を受けるおそれのある貨物の運送も要求されないものとする。ただし，予め船主の承諾を得た場合は，この限りではない。

(B) 本船が，かかる危険区域に近づき，立ち入り，またはその水域へ配船を命ぜられたとき，もしくは前項記載の危険に曝されたときは，(1)これに関連するおそれのある一切の危険に対し，船主自ら適当とする条件により，本船および/または，傭船料に関する自己の利益を，随時，保険に付することができる。傭船者は船主の請求があるときは，その保険料を償還すべきものとする。また(2)船長・職員または部員の死傷，もしくは乗組員がその危険区域への航行，またはその危険に曝されることを拒否したために喪失した時間その他，全喪失時間に対しては，第11条の規定にかかわらず，傭船料を支払わねばならない。

(C) (A)項記載のいずれかの事実が存在するため，またはその存在期間中に，船長・職員および/または部員の給料もしくは食料品および/または甲板および/または機関室用の船用品の費用および/または保険料が増加するに至った場合，船主からこれに関する計算書の提出を受けたときは，傭船者はその増加額を傭船料に付加して支払うものとする。右の計算書は毎月これを提出する。

(D) 本船は，本船の旗国政府その他の政府，もしくはかかる政府の権限を行使するかまたは行使

しているとみられる個人（団体），もしくはかかる本船に関する戦争保険条項により権限を賦与された委員会または個人から受ける発航・到着・航路・寄港地・停船・仕向地・引渡その他一切の事項についての命令または指示に従うことができる。

(E) 本船の旗国に戦争，敵対行為，軍事的行為，革命，または暴動が波及するに至った場合，船主ならびに傭船者は本契約を解約することができる。ただし，特約がないときは，仕向港において返船するものとし，仕向港に到達または入港することが(A)項の規定上許されないときは，本船の一切の荷物を揚荷した後，船主が選定した最寄りの安全な開港において返船するものとする。

(F) 本条項の規定に従ってなした作為もしくは不作為は，離路とみなされない。」

136行の「指図されること」および137行の「使用される」という文言は，積揚港（地）あるいは航海途上の補油地への，傭船者の配船指図に適用されるだけではない。定期傭船が期間によるものであれ，航海によるものであれ，本船は，契約期間中，傭船者の指図に従うものである。慣習的な航路を通る場合にも，傭船者がその航路について十分な知識を有していながら，本船の危険地域への進入を認めた場合，傭船者は暗黙のうちに危険地域への航行を命じたということになる。

136行および137行の「いかなる地点への航海または，いかなる航海をも続行しない」という文言は，「指図に従って航海を継続する」ことを意味するものでなく，本船が危険地域へ進入しようとしていることが明白である場合，傭船者は，航海の継続を許容してはならないことを意味する。

傭船者が第21条(B)項に違反した場合の船主の救済は，同条(C)項および(B)により，船主に付与される権利に限られるものではない。同条(B)項，(c)項は，船主が本船の危険地域内への進入に同意した場合に発動される。しかし，船主がかかる同意をせずかつ，傭船者が同条(A)項に違反している場合，船主は損害賠償の救済を受ける。

Eugenia 号は，ボルタイム書式により，Genoa の引渡時から「黒海経由インドへ至る1航海のため」定期傭船された。傭船者は，インドの東海岸2港で揚荷するため，黒海の2港で積荷をするよう本船に指図した。しかし，傭船者は，航海がスエズ経由か喜望峰経由かについての明白な指図を船長に与えなかった。しかしその当時，スエズ運河は，本件のような航海にとって慣習的航路であった。1956年10月29日，イスラエル軍がエジプトに侵入した。そして，10月30日には，仲裁審の審判人が認定したように，運河は同条(A)項の意味における危険地帯となった。船主は，スエズ運河が危険水域となった後本船がスエズ運河経由で航行すること，運河に入ること，運河内を航行することのいずれにも同意しなかった。10月30日船主は，本船が運河に入ることに反対した。しかし傭船者は何らの措置も講じなかった。10月31日本船は運河に入り，その後そこで立往生した。控訴院は，この点についてのMegaw 判事の見解を支持して，次のように判示した。すなわち，傭船者は，船主の同意なしに，本船が危険水域に進入することを暗黙裡に指図しているか，本船がそのような水域に向けて航行し続けることを許容したという点で，傭船者は，第21条(A)に違反しており，したがって船主の損害につき責任を負う。

The Eugenia [1963] 2 Lloyd's Rep. 381.

船主は本船そして・または傭船料についての自己の利益を付保する権利がある

本船が第21条(A)項に規定する危険水域に近づくか，立ち入るか配船を指図される場合，146行および147行の第21条(B)項に基づき，船主は本船そして・または傭船料の自己の利益を付保する権利がある。そしてそういう状況のもとで，傭船者は保険料を船主に償還する義務がある。*The Agathon* (*No. 2*) [1982] 2 Lloyd's Rep. 183 事件で Hobhouse 判事は，この語句により船主は Hellenic War Risks Association の提供する全面的な保険塡補の保険料を回収するこ

とができると判示した（本事件の事実経緯の要約は前出618頁を参照）。

The Evia (No.2) [1982] 2 Lloyd's Rep. 307 事件で貴族院は，第21条(A)項に言及されている戦争危険に関して傭船者は第2条に基づく安全港担保義務から解放されると判示した。Roskill 判事の理由は，第21条(B)項により傭船者は船主の戦争危険保険料を償還するので，傭船者が第2条に基づき戦争危険保険者からの代位求償に引き続き曝されるのは不当であるということであった（前出243頁と下記参照）。

568 すべての喪失時間の傭船料の支払

149行および150行の第21条(B)(2)項に基づき，本船が第21条(a)項に規定の危険水域に近づくか，立ち入るか配船を指図される場合，オフハイヤー条項の規定にかかわらず，すべての喪失時間の傭船料は支払われねばならない。しかし次の事案ではこの下位条項は履行不能の法理の作用を排除するものではないと判示された。本条項そのものは別として，下位条項は傭船契約を履行不能にする効果のある状況には適用されなかった。

Evia 号はボルタイム書式でプラス・マイナス2ヶ月の傭船者任意付きで18ヶ月間傭船された。本船は1979年11月20日に引き渡された。したがって返船は1981年の3月20日から7月20日までの期日となった。1980年3月1日に傭船者は Evia 号に Basrah 向け貨物の積込を指図した。（揚荷のための待機期間の後で）1980年8月20日に本船は Basrah 港に着岸した。1980年9月20日に Basrah での揚荷を完了したが，この日までにイラクとイランの間に敵対行動が勃発した。戦争により生じた Shatt-al-Arab 水路を航行する危険のため，本船は出港できなかった。仲裁審理で審判人は，傭船契約は1980年10月4日に履行不能となったと裁定した。しかし船主は第21条(B)項は発生した事態の規定であるので，履行不能の法理は適用されないと主張した。Robert Goff 判事と控訴院は，第21条(B)項は履行不能の結果を規定することを意図するものでもなく，履行不能を除外することを意図するものでもないと判示した。すなわち特定の状況で時間が喪失した場合に，オフハイヤー条項にかかわらず，傭船料は継続して支払われねばならないということを単に規定しているだけである。貴族院は，同意した。The Evia (No.2) [1981] 2 Lloyd's Rep. 613, [1982] 1 Lloyd's Rep. 334 (C.A.) および [1982] 2 Lloyd's Rep. 307 (H.L.)。

（安全港担保義務の性質の論議について前出242頁を参照）

他のいかなる政府

Gencon 航海傭船契約の戦争危険条項中のほとんど同一の規定を扱った事件において，159行の「他のいかなる政府」という用語は，傭船契約の準拠法が英法であり，英国政府が事実上も法律上も，問題の政府を承認していなかったにもかかわらず，一定の領土上に排他的な行政権，立法権を行使している国の政府を意味する，と判示されている。

イタリアの国旗を掲げた Marilu 号は，Gencon 書式により，北中国の港から欧州向け航海のため，チェコスロバキアの会社により傭船された。戦争危険条項は，次のように規定していた。
「本船は，出帆，到着，航路寄港地，停船，仕向地，引渡，あるいはその他の事項につき，以下に挙げる者から発せられるいかなる形式の指図あるいは命令にも従う自由を有する。すなわち本船旗国の国家，あるいはその一部門，他のいかなる政府，あるいはその一部門，かかる政府あるいはその一部門から権限を与えられて行為している者または行為していると称する者，本船の戦争危険保険条項に基づき上記指図命令を与える権利を有する委員会や人物……」。

青島で積荷を行い，欧州向け出帆した本船は，その途中，台湾政府の軍艦により拿捕され，基隆へ連行された。そこで積荷を陸揚した後，本船は釈放された。その当時，英国政府としては，台湾政府を事実上も法律上も中華民国政府として承認するのを止めており，また台湾にいかなる政府の存在も認めていない，と英国の外務省は公表した。Seller 判事は，次のように判示した。すなわち，「他の

いかなる政府」という文言は，国家の政府（市当局や県当局というような地方の機関とは異なり）を意味し，一定の領土に排他的な行政権．立法権を行使している政府である。この事実認定によれば，台湾政府は，そのような政府であった。そして法解釈の問題としても，法の原則の問題としても，台湾政府が英国政府により承認されていないということは関係ないことである。したがって船主は基隆に行き，そこで積荷を陸揚するようにとの，台湾政府軍艦の命令に従う権利があったと判示された。
Luigi Monta v. Cechofracht [1956] 2 Lloyd's Rep. 97.

569 戦争条項により，船主や傭船者に認められている裁量権は，合理的に行使されなければならない。

　　Hartbridge 号は，Tyne 河から，スペインの Barcelona を含む指定数港の内の1港向け航海に傭船された。傭船契約の戦争条項は，指定揚荷港が，指定自体適当であっても，封鎖された場合，あるいは，戦争，敵対行為，作戦行動，市民戦争，市民暴動，革命，または，国際法上の軍事行動のため，揚荷港入港が危険もしくは，不可能であると船長または船主が独自に判断した場合において，貨物は他の安全港で揚荷されるべきものとする，と規定していた。傭船契約締結1週間後に，Barcelona や傭船契約書に指定されているその他の港が封鎖されそうな模様が，ラジオを通して放送された。しかし，結局，港は封鎖されることなく，他の船舶は，それらの港を使用し続けた。貨物の積荷以前に，船主は，Barcelona その他指定されているいずれの港向けの配船をも承諾しないことを明らかにした。そして結局，傭船者は，異議を留保した上，代案として Oran を指定した。
　　判決は次のように指摘した。
(1)　「封鎖」は，法律的な意味での封鎖を意味するものであり，Barcelona は決して封鎖されていない。
(2)　戦争危険条項の規定は，貨物が積まれた後にはじめて適用される。そして（傍論として）
(3)　戦争危険条項により船主に認められる裁量権は，合理的に行使されなければならない。
　　Lewis 判事は「裁量権は，独断的，かつ不合理な形で行使されてはならない。本件では，裁量の基となる事実について，検討がなされなかったか，あるいは十分な調査が行われなかったものであるから，本来の意味での裁量権の行使なるものは，事実上なかったことになる」と述べている。
Government of the Republic of Spain v. North of England Steamship (1938) 61 Ll.L. Rep. 44.

　　The Product Star [1993] 1 Lloyd's Rep. 397 事件で控訴院は，船主自らの裁量により戦争のため，危険であると考えた港での積込の指図を拒否する，Beepeetime 2書式の第40条(2)項に基づく権利を船主が独断的に行使するのは無効であると判示した。Legatt 判事は，次のように述べた（同判例集404頁）。「私の考えでは，先例は，裁量権は正直に誠実に行使されねばならぬだけでなく，裁量権を付与する契約の規定に関してそれが独断的に気まぐれにあるいは不当に行使されてはならないことを示している」。裁判所はその事案で，傭船契約を締結した時点で既に存在した危険の程度に関して第40条(2)項を船主は有効に発動できないとも判示した。
　　さらに，船主や傭船者に認められている選択権は，合理的期間内に行使されなければならない。

　　Belpareil 号は，定期傭船契約により，傭船された。同契約によれば，船主および／または傭船者は，中国／日本間に戦争が生じた場合，解約する選択権を有していた。契約の期間中である，1937年9月に日中間の戦争が勃発し，傭船者が傭船契約解約の選択権を行使しようとした1938年4月に至っても，戦争は未だ継続していた。仲裁人は，事実認定として，選択権行使の合理的時期は，1938年4月以前に期限切れとなっていたと判断した。Branson 判事は仲裁人の判断は，正当であり，傭船者は解約権行使を決意するため必要な関連事実の確認に相応の時間のみ与えられていると判示した。

Kawasaki K. K. v. *Belships*（1939）63 Ll.L. Rep. 175.

戦争条項で,「戦争」という文言は普通の法律的意味にではなく, 常識的意味に解釈されるだろう（*Kawasaki K. K.* v. *Bantham*（1939）63 Ll. L. Rep. 155)）。しかし戦争条項の「封鎖」の意味につき, 上記 *Government of the Republic of Spain* v. *North of England Steamship*（1938）61 Ll.L. Rep. 44 事件を対照。

米 国 法

戦争危険条項

　傭船契約が戦争危険条項を規定していなくても, 戦争が勃発し, 本船の航海が, 敵の領域に及ぶ場合, 船主はその航海を放棄することができる（*The Kronprinzessin Cecilie,* 244 U. S. 12 (1917)）。

570　傭船契約が「君主による拘束」条項を含んでおり, 一方の交戦国が積荷を捕獲する危険が存在する場合, 船主は他方の交戦国向けに積み出される戦時禁制品の運送を拒否することができると判示された。*The Styria,* 186 U. S. 1 (1902)；*The George J. Goulandris,* 36 F. Supp. 827, 1941 AMC (D. Me. 1941)；*The Wildwood,* 133 F. 2d 765, 1943 AMC 320 (9th Cir. 1943). これらの事件で裁判所は, 船長が本船とその積荷を護るため, 航海を打ち切ることは適切であると判示した。しかしながら, 本船が捕獲される危険や船体への危険は, 現実のものでなければならない。その可能性が薄く, 非現実的なものである場合, 船主の航海打ち切りは正当ではない（*Luckenbach S. S. Co.* v. *W. R. Grace & Co.,* 267 F. 676 (4th Cir. 1920) 事件参照)。

　The Trade Fortitude, 1974 AMC 2195 (Arb. at N. Y. 1974) 事件において, イスラエルとアラブ諸国間でヨムキプール戦争が行われた1973年10月に, 船主は本船を引き揚げた。その際, 傭船者は, 代替積荷港の指定を拒絶した。その傭船契約は, 海運会議所定の戦争危険条項（タンカー用）1952を含んでいた。敵対行為が中東各地での公然たる戦争へと拡大した際, 船主はペルシャ湾内での戦闘行為がなかったにもかかわらず, 同湾は「危険地域」になったと主張し, 傭船者による湾内の積荷港への配船指示に従うことを拒絶した。しかしながら, イスラエルでの現実の交戦は終息しており, 国連監視部隊が進駐していた。ペルシャ湾の国々は, 公式には, イスラエルと戦争状態にあったが現実の交戦状態は存在しなかった。おそらく, もっとも重要なことは, その前月を通じて, 戦火たけなわだった折にも, ペルシャ湾は, 船舶にとっては安全であったことと思われる。これらの事実に基き, 仲裁審は, ペルシャ湾は,「危険地域」ではなく, したがって船主は, 本船を引き揚げる権利を有しないと裁定した。

　仲裁審は, 船主が本船を正当に引き揚げることができるかどうかを決定するに際して, 考慮すべき要素を次のように要約した。

　　各事件は, その事件固有の具体的事実如何で決まる。しかし, 既決の事件から, 三つの指導原理が明らかにされているように思われる。(1) 戦争危険条項を解釈するに際して, 検討されるべき事実関係は, 問題の時点において, 知られており, また信じられている事実である。それは, 真実の事実ではなくても, また, その後知りえた事実により意義が変ってもよい。(2) 戦争危険条項の規定に依拠してある港へ行くことを拒否する船主は, その条項に示される事実状態の一つ以上が現実に存在する

ことを，信じるに足る相当の根拠を持たなければならない。そして(3) 傭船者が，ある特定の港への配船指図を出した時点で，戦争危険条項に示される事実状態が現実に存在すると信じるに足る相当の根拠がない場合，傭船者は傭船契約に違反したことにはならない（1974 AMC at 2198）。

Clause 22 — Cancelling

170 "22. Should the Vessel not be delivered by the .... day of ...... 19 ....
171 the Charterers to have the option of cancelling.
172　If the Vessel cannot be delivered by the cancelling date, the Charterers, if required, to declare
173 within 48 hours after receiving notice thereof whether they cancel or will take delivery of the Vessel."

第22条 ― 解　　約

「22. 19......年......月......日までに本船の引渡がないときは，傭船者は本契約を解約することができる。

　解約期日までに本船の引渡ができない場合，傭船者は，船主の要求があれば，その旨の通知受領後48時間以内に，解約もしくは本船引取の意思を表示しなければならない。」

解約：前出419頁から424頁を参照。

傭船者の通告

　船主からの通知受領後48時間以内に，解約するか，本船を受取るかの通告をすべしという第22条第2項に基づく傭船者の義務は，解約日到来後はじめて生じる（*The Helvetia-S* [1960] 1 Lloyd's Rep. 540事件におけるPearson判事の判決（同判例集552頁）参照。この事案の事実経緯について前出645頁参照）。

Clauses 23, 24 and 25 — Arbitration/General average/Commission

174 "23. Any dispute arising under the Charter to be referred to arbitration in London (or such
175 other place as may be agreed) one Arbitrator to be nominated by the Owners and the other by the
176 Charterers, and in case the Arbitrators shall not agree then to the decision of an Umpire to be
177 appointed by them, the award of the Arbitrators or the Umpire to be final and binding upon both
178 parties.
179　24. General Average to be settled according to York/Antwerp Rules, 1974. Hire not to contribute
180 to General Average.
181　25. The Owners to pay a commission of .... to ....
182 on any hire paid under the Charter, but in no case less than is necessary to cover the actual expenses

183   of the Brokers and a reasonable fee for their work. If the full hire is not paid owing to breach
184   of Charter by either of the parties the party liable therefor to indemnify the Brokers against their
185   loss of commission.
186   Should the parties agree to cancel the Charter, the Owners to indemnify the Brokers against any
187   loss of commission but in such case the commission not to exceed the brokerage on one year's hire. "

第23, 24条および第25条 ── 仲裁／共同海損／手数料

「23. 本契約に関して生ずる一切の紛争は，ロンドン（または合意により定めたその他の地）において，これを船主・傭船者双方が各々1名宛選任した仲裁人の仲裁判断に付託するものとする。仲裁人の判断が一致しないときは，双方の仲裁人は共同して審判人を選任し，その裁定を求める。両当事者は，仲裁人もしくは審判人の仲裁判断を終局のものとして，これに従う。

24. 共同海損は1950年ヨーク・アントワープ・ルールに準拠して決済するものとする。傭船料は共同海損を分担しない。

25. 船主は本契約により受け取る一切の傭船料につき，…………の手数料を…………に対して支払うものとする。ただし，いかなる場合においても，仲立人の実際に要した費用，およびその業務に相当する報酬を下回らないものとする。当事者の一方の契約違反により，傭船料全額について支払がない場合には，その当事者が仲立人に対し，手数料の損失を塡補する責任を負うものとする。

両当事者の合意により本契約を解約したときは，船主が仲立人に対して手数料の一切の損失を補償する。ただし，その場合でも，手数料の額は1年分の傭船料に対する仲立料を超えないものとする。」

仲裁と準拠法：全般について前出507／517頁を参照。

手数料：全般について前出541頁参照。本書式の下で仲立人の立場は，ニューヨーク・プロデュース書式におけるより三点で大きく改善されている。
(1) 支出費用に加え，提供した業務相応の報酬に見合った最低手数料が支払われる（182行および183行）。
(2) 傭船契約のいずれか一方の当事者の契約違反で，傭船料全額が支払われない場合，仲立人は，塡補を受ける権利を有する（183行から185行）。その請求は，違反をした当事者に対して行われる。その当事者が，傭船者である場合，船主は仲立人の受託者として訴訟を提起するものと思われる。
(3) 当事者間の合意による傭船契約解約の場合，仲立人は，1ヶ年分の手数料を取得する権利を有する（186行および187行）。

船主が，所定の日まで本船を引き渡す義務に違反した結果，傭船契約が解約され，上記(2)により，船主は仲立人に対し，責任を負うと判示された事案につき，[1960] 1 Lloyd's Rep. 540 および前出645頁の *The Helvetia-S* 事件参照。

シェルタイム書式

シェルタイム書式

　本章は，シェルタイム書式と他のタンカー定期傭船契約書式に関して，主に英国裁判所の判例の指針となることを意図している。したがって，タンカー傭船契約の事案は，本書の前章で検討済みのものも再度詳細に取り上げた。本章では骨組としてShelltime 4を取り上げたが，1972年3月改訂のShelltime 3に関する解説も，他の書式に関する事案を参照するとともに，行っている。

"SHELLTIME 4"

```
 1  IT IS THIS DAY AGREED between
 2  of                    (hereinafter referred to as "Owners"), being owners of the
 3  good         vessel called
 4  (hereinafter referred to as "the vessel") described as per Clause 1 hereof and
 5  of                    (hereinafter referred to as "Charterers"):
```

　本契約は，本日，本契約第1条に表示された..........................と称する良好な船（以下「本船」という）の船主である...............所在の......（以下「船主」という）と..............................所在の.................（以下「傭船者」という）との間で合意したものである。

　契約の成立と契約の当事者に関して生じる問題は，それぞれ本書の97／104頁と111／121頁で取り扱われている

Clause 1 — Description and condition of vessel

```
 6   1. At the date of delivery of the vessel under this charter
 7       (a) she shall be classed;
 8       (b) she shall be in every way fit to carry crude petroleum and/or its products;
 9       (c) she shall be tight, staunch, strong, in good order and condition, and in every
way fit for the
10   service, with her machinery, boilers, hull and other equipment (including but not limited
to hull stress calculator
11   and radar) in a good and efficient state;
12       (d) her tanks, valves and pipelines shall be oil-tight;
13       (e) she shall be in every way fitted for burning
14          at sea——fuel oil with a maximum viscosity of Centistokes at 50 degrees Centi-
grade /any
15                     commercial grade of fueloil ("ACGFO") for main propulsion, marine die-
sel oil/ACGFO
17                     for auxiliaries
18          in port——marine diesel oil/ACGFO for auxiliaries;
19       (f) she shall comply with the regulations in force so as to enable her to pass
through the Suez and
20   Panama Canals by day and night without delay;
```

21　　　(g) she shall have on board all certificates, documents and equipment required from time to time by
21　any applicable law to enable her to perform the charter service without delay;
22　　　(h) she shall comply with the description in Form B appended hereto, provided however that if there
23　is any conflict between the provisions of Form B and any other provision, including this Clause 1, of this charter
24　such other provision shall govern.

第1条 ── 本船の表示および状態

1．本契約に基づき，本船の引渡日において，
　(a) 本船は…………の船級を保持すること，
　(b) 本船は原油ならびに・もしくは精製油の運送にあらゆる面で適すること，
　(c) 本船は船体堅牢，水密で良好な状態にあり，その機関，汽罐，船体その他装備（少なくとも船体応力計算機，レーダーを含む）も良好，能率的な状態にして，あらゆる面で航海に適すること，
　(d) 本船のタンク，バルブおよびパイプラインは油密であること，
　(e) 本船は，
　　　航海中：主機に，摂氏50度において最大粘度…………CSの燃料油・市販のいずれの等級の燃料油（ACGFO）を，補機に舶用ディーゼル油（ACGFO）を，
　　　碇泊中：補機に舶用ディーゼル油・ACGFOを，焚くのにあらゆる面で適合していること，
　(f) 本船は，昼夜を問わず遅滞なくスエズ運河およびパナマ運河を通航できるよう施行中の規則に準拠していること，
　(g) 本船には，本契約を遅滞なく履行するために，いずれの適用法によるにせよ随時必要とされるすべての証書類と備品を具備していること，
　(h) 本船は，本契約に添付された書式Bの要目に適合すること，ただし，書式Bの条項と本条を含む本契約の他の条項との間に抵触あるときは，本契約の条項が優先すること。

Shelltime 4 の第1条の(a)/(g)項は，引渡時の本船の状態に関する保証（undertakings）を扱い，(h)項は，本船が添付書式Bに詳述する表示に合致することを要求する。第1条は，本船の表示を構成する。第2条(a)項の乗組員に関する規定と共に3行目に挿入される本船名（新造船の場合には，造船所名とその船台番号。*The Diana Prosperity*［1976］2 Lloyd's Rep. 621 事件参照）も，本船の表示を構成する。本船が不実表示されたり，または不実表示を傭船者が引渡前または引渡時に発見した場合，引渡を受けることを拒否できるのか，または傭船者は引渡を受け損害賠償を請求する他ないのかという問題は，一面では，不正確なのは表示のどの要素かしだいであり，他面では不実表示の重大性の程度しだいである（この問題は，前出144頁で検討した）。この条項の規定は，相当の注意を尽くしたか否かという問題とは関係がないという意味で，現実に絶対的な義務を課す（*The Fina Samco*［1994］1 Lloyd's Rep. 153（同判例集158頁）参照。その事実関係は，後出第3条で詳述する。前出131／158頁の船舶の表示を一般的に参照）。

コモン・ローは定期傭船契約に基づく引渡時の堪航性の絶対的保証（undertaking）あるいは担保（warranty）を黙示する（前出148／151頁参照）。したがって Shelltime 4 傭船契約に基づく明示の保証は，コモン・ローの黙示の保証と同延ではないが，双方とも絶対的保証であるという意味で，似ている。「貨物の滅失損傷または貨物に関する損害」から生じる損害賠償請求は，第27条(c)(ii)項によりヘーグ・ルールまたはヘーグ・ヴィスビー・ルールに従うこととなるが，その損害賠償請求に関する同ルールの第Ⅳ条1項の効果により堪航性義務は絶対的義

務から本船の堪航性保持のため相当の注意を尽くす義務に軽減される。

　Shelltime 3 書式の傭船契約に基づく引渡時の本船の状態に関する明示の保証はとにかく絶対的ではない。船主は引渡時に本船の堪航性を維持し，本船を適合させるために相当の注意を尽くすことだけを要求される。一般的に明示の条件は，黙示の条件に優る（後出第3条に言及されている *The Bridgestone Maru No.3*［1985］2 Lloyd's Rep. 62 事件参照）。

　本船が「船体堅牢で……あらゆる面で航海に適しているものとする」という Shelltime 4 の第1条(c)項の一般的要件は，堪航性の明示の保証を構成する。裁定に影響を与えるとは思われない差異であるが，「fit」の代わりに「fitted」の語が使用されているのを除けば，文言はほとんど同様であるニューヨーク・プロデュース傭船契約の事案で，次のように判示された。*The Derby*［1984］1 Lloyd's Rep. 635（同判例集641頁）事件で，Hobhouse 判事は，ニューヨーク・プロデュース書式の22行の「船体堅牢強固であらゆる点で運送業務に適した」という文言を考慮して，次のように述べた。「今回のように相当な期間継続予定の傭船契約が関係し，その定期傭船契約により船主に傭船者が発する指示に関する広範囲な選択が傭船者に与えられる場合，引渡時に前もってあらゆる異常事態をどの程度予想し，手配するように船主に要求されるかという問題が生じる……。ニューヨーク・プロデュース書式に規定される『運送業務に適合（fitness）』に関して，適合（fitness）は公平に一般的に解釈されねばならない。さもなければ，考慮される異常事態によっては相反し矛盾する義務を遂行しなければならない状態に船主は曝される。そこで私は，適合していないというからには，本船は……傭船契約上の義務を適正に遂行することができないとあらかじめ決まっていなければならないという船主の主張を受け入れないが，他方本船または属具等の改造のためにどれだけ遅れようとも，あるいはその改造の必要性がいくらかでもあれば，それは自動的に一番最初の適合が存在しない状態を示すことになるという傭船者の主張も受け入れない」。同判事の判決は控訴院［1985］2 Lloyd's Rep. 325 事件で支持された。

　こういう考慮すべき問題は Shelltime 4 の第1条で具体的に論じられていない事柄にいちばん関連しているが，対照的に第1条の(d)(e)(h)項で具体的に論じられているような事柄については一般に関連性が低い。しかし，引渡日に本船は「本契約を遅滞なく履行するために，いずれの適用法によるにせよ随時必要とされるすべての証書類と備品を備えおよび装備をしていること」という第1条(g)項のような広範囲の保証が存する場合に，船主はあらゆる異常事態を想定することをどの程度まで求められるかという問題が生じるであろう。この義務に合致するための適合性と船上に装備が求められる証書類に関する判例について，前出206／212頁を参照。

575　適合性の問題は，推定（*prima facie*）上の事実問題である。属具の欠陥が本船の安全性または本船の効率的運航，貨物の安全性または状態に影響を与えず，実際上商業的に意味のない場合，その欠陥のゆえに問題の属具が傭船契約の要件に合致することはないが，本船が運送業務に不適ということにはならないであろう。

　Arianna 号は Essotime 書式で世界就航のために10年間定期傭船された。傭船契約書の第3条は次のように規定していた。「……相当の注意を尽くして得られる程度まで，本船は傭船者の検査員が満足するよう船艙と洗浄し清潔にした貨物タンク，パイプおよびポンプを準備完了し，引渡時に堅牢強固で，『通常の製品貨物』の運送業務に適して，パイプライン，ポンプ，加熱管が良好な作動状態で……本船を傭船者に委ねると……船長が傭船者に書面による通知を発したときに傭船は開始する」。さらに追加条項の第69条は次のように規定していた。「船主はいつもタンク洗浄装置を6個の機械が海水温度180度Fで170PSIの圧力で同時に作動できるように良好な状態に維持するものとする」。

　本船が引渡のため提供されたときに，本船のタンク洗浄装置は傭船契約に合致しないという理由で，傭船者は本船の引取を拒否した。仲裁人は，本船の6個のタンク洗浄機械は第69条の求める温度

と圧力で同時に作動できたが，同条を適正に解釈すると，本船の在港中同時に他港揚貨物を加熱しながら，6個の機械を同時に作動させることを求めているが，本船はそれができなかったと裁定した。仲裁人はさらに，傭船契約に基づく就航様式ではそういう状況（在港中に他港揚貨物を加熱して6個のタンク洗浄機械を作動する）は決して生じないが，仮にそうなった場合，本船は4個のタンク洗浄機械を作動できるので，欠陥の存在は結果的に，いくぶん小さな遅延を引き起こしたに過ぎないと裁定した。仲裁人は，第69条の違反にかかわらず，本船はそれでも「あらゆる点で運送業務に適して」おり，傭船者の引取拒否に正当な事由は存しないと裁定した。

控訴院において，傭船者の代理人としての法廷弁護士はタンク洗浄装置の欠陥に鑑み本船は法の問題として「運送業務に適して」いないと主張した。この意見を拒否して，Webster判事は適合性の問題は一義的に事実問題であると判示した。本船が適しているか否かは，欠陥の重大さ次第である。それは，仲裁人が本事案の欠陥は商業的意味において実際上重大なものではないとみなした仲裁人の裁定に暗示されている。

The Arianna [1987] 2 Lloyd's Rep. 376.

しかしながら，The Arianna 事件の傭船契約書式はShelltime 4とかなり異なり，特に，傭船契約に基づく引渡日に本船は書式Bの要目に適合することという第1条(h)項の明示の要件と同等なものを含んでいないことに注意すべきである。The Arianna 事件は，解約条項と関連して後出第5条でも検討する。

タンカー定期傭船契約の代船条項に関する判例については，Société Anonyme Maritime et Commerciale v. Anglo-Iranian Oil [1953] 2 Lloyd's Rep. 446と [1954] 1 Lloyd's Rep. 1 (C. A.) 事件と Niarcos v. Shell Tankers [1962] 2 Lloyd's Rep. 496 事件と前出145頁参照。

Clause 2 — Shipboard personnel and their duties

25 2. (a) At the date of delivery of the vessel under this charter
26   (i) she shall have a full and efficient complement of master, officers and crew for a vessel of her
27 tonnage, who shall in any event be not less than the number required by the laws of the flag state and who shall be
28 trained to operate the vessel and her equipment competently and safely;
29   (ii) all shipboard personnel shall hold valid certificates of competence in accordance with the
30 requirements of the law of the flag state;
31   (iii) all shipboard personnel shall be trained in accordance with the relevant provisions of the
32 International Convention on Standards of Training, Certification and Watchkeeping for Seafarers, 1978;
33   (iv) there shall be on board sufficient personnel with a good working knowledge of the English
34 language to enable cargo operations at loading and discharging places to be carried out efficiently and safely and
35 to enable communications between the vessel and those loading the vessel or accepting discharge therefrom to be
36 carried out quickly and efficiently.
37   (b) Owners guarantee that throughout the charter service the master shall with the vessel's officers
38 and crew, unless otherwise ordered by Charterers,

39   (i) prosecute all voyages with the utmost despatch;
40   (ii) render all customary assistance; and
41   (iii) load and discharge cargo as rapidly as possible when required by Charterers or their agents
42 to do so, by night or by day, but always in accordance with the laws of the place of loading or discharging (as the
35 case may be) and in each case in accordance with any applicable laws of the flag state.

第2条 ── 乗組員およびその義務

2．(a) 本契約に基づき，本船の引渡日において，
 (i) 本船には，本船のトン数に見合う適正かつ必要な定員数の船長，職員および部員が乗り組むものとし，それらの員数は，いかなる場合においても，旗国法により要求される数を下回ってはならず，また，それらは本船およびその装備を十分かつ安全に操作するよう訓練されていること，
 (ii) すべての乗組員は，旗国法の要求に従い，正当な資格証明書を保持すること，
 (iii) すべての乗組員は，1978年の船員の訓練，資格証明および当直の基準に関する国際条約（STCW条約）の関係条項に従って訓練されていること
 (iv) 本船には，積揚地において荷役が効率的かつ安全に遂行されるよう，また本船と荷送人または荷受人との間の意思疎通が迅速かつ能率よく行われるよう，英語の適切な実用的知識をもった十分な数の船員が乗り組むものとする，
 (b) 船主は，傭船者より別途の指図がない限り，本契約を通じて，船長が本船職員および部員と共に，
 (i) 極力迅速に全航海を遂行すること，
 (ii) 一切の慣習上の助力を提供すること，および
 (iii) 傭船者またはその代理人より要求あったときは，昼夜を問わず，可能な限り迅速に船積および揚荷を行うこと．ただし，積地または揚地の法（その場合による）に常に従い，またそれぞれの場合に旗国のいかなる適用法にも従って船積および揚荷を行うことを保証する．

　引渡日の乗組員の資格適格，適正能力，有効能力に関するShelltime 4の第2条(a)項の詳細な要件は，本船の表示の一部でもあり，現実に絶対的でもある（前出第1条参照）．第2条(a)(i)項は，乗組員に関する限り，コモン・ローが黙示する引渡時の堪航性の保証と同等である（前出212頁参照）．
　Shelltime 4の第2条(a)(i)-(iv)項は，乗組員の資格適格，適正能力，有効能力について船主は何を求められるかを具体的に記載する．一方，Shelltime 3書式に基づく船主の義務は，本船を「このトン数の本船にとり十分かつ有能な定員の船長，職員，部員をもって，……あらゆる点で運送業務に適する」ようにすると一般的文言で表現されるが，それは相当の注意を尽くすことのみに限定される（Shelltime 3の第2条(b)項）．
　Shelltime 4の第2条(b)項の「保証（guarantee）」は第1条および第2条(a)項と異なり引渡日の状態に関係しないが，傭船期間中の本船の職員および部員の義務と関連する．タンカー定期傭船契約の古い判例（前出91頁に事実関係掲載の *Pennsylvania Shipping v. Cie Nationale de Navigation* (1936) 55 Ll.L. Rep. 271 事件）では，本船の貨物管の直径と加熱管の位置に関して「保証した（guaranteed）」という語の使用は，その語句に契約の条件（condition）という位置を与えたと判示されたが，第2条(b)項の「保証（guarantee）」の語の使用は，義務は絶対的であるとの意図であり，この条項は条件（a condition）としてではなく，中間的条件（an intermediate term）として解釈されることを意味するに過ぎないと考えられる（この区別の意義について前出138頁参照）．

極力迅速に全航海を遂行し，一切の慣習上の助力を提供する義務に関する解説については，前出345頁参照。

Clause 3 — Duty to maintain

44　3. (i) Throughout the charter service Owners shall, whenever the passage of time, wear and tear or any
45　event (whether or not coming within Clause 27 hereof) requires steps to be taken to maintain or restore the
46　conditions stipulated in Clauses 1 and 2 (a), exercise due diligence so to maintain or restore the vessel.
47　　(ii) If at any time whilst the vessel is on hire under this charter the vessel fails to comply with the
48　requirements of Clauses 1, 2 (a) or 10 then hire shall be reduced to the extent necessary to indemnify Charterers
49　for such failure. If and to the extent that such failure affects the time taken by the vessel to perform any services
50　under this charter, hire shall be reduced by an amount equal to the value, calculated at the rate of hire, of the time
51　so lost.
52　　Any reduction of hire under this sub-Clause (ii) shall be without prejudice to any other remedy
53　available to Charterers, but where such reduction of hire is in respect of time lost, such time shall be excluded
54　from any calculation under Clause 24.
55　　(iii) If Owners are in breach of their obligation under Clause 3 (i) Charterers may so notify Owners in
56　writing; and if, after the expiry of 30 days following the receipt by Owners of any such notice, Owners have failed
57　to demonstrate to Charterers' reasonable satisfaction the exercise of due diligence as required in Clause 3 (i), the
58　vessel shall be off-hire, and no further hire payments shall be due, until Owners have so demonstrated that they
59　are exercising such due diligence.
60　　Furthermore, at any time while the vessel is off-hire under this Clause 3 Charterers have the
61　option to terminate this charter by giving notice in writing with effect from the date on which such notice of
62　termination is received by Owners or from any later date stated in such notice. This sub-Clause (iii) is without
63　prejudice to any rights of Charterers or obligations of Owners under this charter or otherwise (including without
64　limitation Charterers' rights under Clause 21 hereof).

第3条 — 保船義務

3．(i) 傭船業務を通じて，船主は，時の経過，自然損耗，その他の事由（本契約第27条に該当する

と否とを問わない）により，第1条および第2条(a)に記載された状態を維持または修復する措置をとる必要が生じたときは，相当の注意を尽くして本船の維持または修復を行うものとする。

(ii) 本契約に基づき本船のオンハイヤー中，本船が第1条，第2条(a)または第10条の要件に適合しなくなったときは，傭船料はそのような不適合に対して傭船者に補償するのに十分な金額を差し引くものとする。このような不適合によって，本船の本契約の履行に要する時間が影響されるときは，傭船料は，その喪失時間を傭船料率に基づいて計算された額と等しい額を差し引き減額するものとする。

本項(ii)による傭船料の控除は，傭船者の取りうるその他の賠償請求の権利を損なわない。ただし，その傭船料の控除が喪失時間に関するものである場合には，その喪失時間は第24条に基づく計算から除外されるものとする。

(iii) 船主が第3条(i)項に基づく義務に違反している場合には，傭船者はその旨を船主に書面で通知することができる。船主がその通知を受け取った後30日を経過しても，船主が第3条(i)項で要求される相当の注意を尽くしていることを，傭船者の相応の満足を得るまで行わなかったときは，本船はオフハイヤーとなり，以後の傭船料の支払は，船主がそうした相当の注意を尽くしていることを示すまで中断するものとする。

さらに，本船が第3条に基づきオフハイヤーとなっているときにはいつでも，傭船者は書面による解約通知を発し本契約を終了する選択権を有する。その場合の解約は，そうした通知が船主に受け取られる日またはその通知に記載された日以降より効力を生じる。本第3条(iii)項は，本契約あるいはその他に基づく，傭船者の一切の権利（本契約第21条に基づく傭船者の権利を無条件に含む）または船主の義務を損なうものではない。

(i) 項

Shelltime 4 の第1条，第2条に基づく義務と異なり，第3条(i)項に基づく保守義務は絶対的ではない。船主の義務は相当の注意を尽くすだけである。Shelltime 3 の第2条に基づく保守義務は相当の注意を尽くすことに同じように限定される。傭船契約の他の条件が船主に特定の業務を遂行する義務を課する場合，その義務は絶対的なのかまたは相当の注意を尽くすことに限定されるのかは，全体としての当該傭船契約の解釈しだいである。

Bridgestone Maru No.3 号は，Shelltime 3 で1年間定期傭船された。傭船契約の第2条は，次のように規定していた。「本傭船契約に基づく本船の引渡日およびそれ以前に，船主は……傭船契約の第1条に規定するように本船を保守するために取るべき手続を必要とする……船主がこの傭船契約に基づく運送業務の期間中船主が保証する……完全冷凍のブタンかつ・またはプロパンの輸送にあらゆる点で本船が適し，……あらゆる点で運送業務に適すべく相当の注意を尽くすものとする」。第1条はとりわけ引渡日に本船が船級に適合していることを求めた。追加のタイプ条項でさらに次のように規定した。「船主はブースターポンプが装備される……ことに翌日同意する」。

傭船者は次のように主張した。傭船契約の適正な解釈によると文言は船主に，ブースターポンプは適正に注意深く装備され，船舶船級協会の承認がその装備につき求められ，取得されるという絶対的義務を暗黙に課している。Hirst 判事は，この主張を拒否して，次のように述べた（76頁）。「私の判断では，商業的有効性は相当の注意を尽くすという明示の義務により十分満たされる。装備の方法やブースターポンプの船級の側面に具体的に適用されるさらに厳しい条件を付加する必要はない。したがって，黙示の条件は履行されない，これらの点で被告の義務は第2条に存すると，私は判示する。船級に関連して相当の注意を尽くす義務は所与の装備に必要な船級承認を取得するための相当の注意を尽くす義務を含むものとして適正に解釈されうると私は考えると付言すべきであるが」。

The Bridgestone Maru No.3 [1985] 2 Lloyd's Rep. 62.

The Fina Samco [1994] 1 Lloyd's Rep. 153 および [1995] 2 Lloyd's Rep. 344 (C. A.) 事

件(その事実関係は後出(ii)項に詳述)のShelltime 4の第3条(i)項を検討して,Colman判事は,第1審の報告の158頁で次のように述べた。「その条項は明確に,傭船役務の過程で,時の経過,通常の損耗,その他のできごとにより,本船が引渡時点で要求された状態を維持し,その状態が失われている場合には,修復するために必要とされる措置を船主はとらねばならないことを意味している。本条項は,本船引渡の後に生じる行動の必要性を示している。すなわち引渡の時点で本船は契約上必要とされる特性を保持していたが,本船引渡の後,何らかの状況が発生して,本船の特性の中のどれかが失われ,あるいは船主がそれを維持するための必要な措置をとらない限り,将来失われてしまうことを本条項は考えている。相当の注意を尽くす船主の義務が生じるのはそうした状況である」。

第3条(i)項に基づく船主の義務に違反している場合の傭船者の救済策(それは,有効な通知がなされていることを条件に,本船をオフハイヤーとし,その後傭船契約を終了することである)は,第3条(iii)に含まれている。本第3条(iii)とは別に,船主側が保守義務に従わないために,傭船者が傭船契約を消滅したものとして扱うことができる蓋然性については,268頁参照。

(ii)項および(iii)項

傭船料の減額に関する第3条(ii)項の条項は,本船引渡の時点における第1条または2条(a)の違反を構成する欠陥に適用されるが本船の引渡後に生じる第1条あるいは第2条(a)のいかなる特性の欠陥にも適用されない。また当規定は,いかなる時点であろうと第10条(貨物積載場所)の違反を構成する欠陥にも適用される。

Fina Samco号はShelltime 4により定期傭船された。傭船契約中に本船は,苫小牧および名古屋の内地2港で原油を揚げるよう指図された。本船は,苫小牧に1990年10月21日に入港し,翌22日午前1時12分に揚荷を開始した。揚荷の開始から同日の午前8時48分の間,11回の荷役中断があり,その時間は1回につき6分から36分の間であり,原因は汽罐の故障であった。午前8時30分までの間,中断時間の総計は3時間2分に達した。同22日の午前11時15分,バースマスターは気象および海象の悪化を理由に本船の離桟を命じた。

仲裁人は,たとえ汽罐の調子が良くても,バースマスターはその時点で本船の離桟を命じたであろうと考えた。本船は,その後11月8日まで天候が回復しなかったので再度の着桟ができなかった。その間に故障の原因が見つかり,修理作業が行われた。仲裁人は,本船は傭船者への引渡時点で問題はなかったと考えた。傭船者は,10月22日から11月8日までオフハイヤーであると主張した(本事案のオフハイヤーに関する解説については後出700頁を参照)。傭船者は,傭船契約第1条の要件に本船が適合できなかったことにより時間喪失が生じたと主張し,傭船契約の第3条(ii)項の規定する補償を請求する方法をとった。

Colman判事と控訴院は,第3条(ii)項は第1条,第2条(a)および第10条の違反により傭船者が被った損害のみに,したがって傭船契約に基づく本船の引渡時点で存在した第1条あるいは第2条(a)に規定する特性の欠陥に適用すると判示した。したがって本船引渡の後生じた欠陥について当該規定は適用されず,それゆえに,本件の荷役中に発生した中断の原因となる汽罐の欠陥にも当該規定は,適用されなかった。

The Fina Samco [1994] 1 Lloyd's Rep. 153 および [1995] 2 Lloyd's Rep. 344 (C. A.).

The Fina Samco事件の定期傭船契約第3条の(i),(ii)および(iii)項の作用を説明して,同判事は,第1審の報告書の159頁で,次のように述べた。「[第3条(ii)項]は,定期傭船契約に基づく無限定の諸義務の違反によりオンハイヤー中に被った損害につき補償による救済策を規定している。そう解釈すると本船の引渡の時点において欠陥がないが,本船の引渡後第1条または

第2条(a)項の特性の実際の喪失あるいは後刻の喪失という潜在的な喪失に，［第3条(ii)項］は関係がない。引渡後の喪失は，第3条(i)項の範疇に止まり，そしてそれによりまったく別個の相当の注意義務が生じるし，第3条(iii)項はその義務の補足的な罰則である。第1条，第2条(a)あるいは第10条の義務に不履行のため時間の喪失が生じる場合，第3条(i)項に規定する補償が発生し，さらに本船はオフハイヤー条項によりオフハイヤーとなる。また第3条(i)項の義務の不履行により時間の喪失が生じる場合，第3条(iii)項あるいはオフハイヤー条項に基づき本船はオフハイヤーとなる。しかしながらさらに第3条(i)項の違反に対する諸救済策に加えて，第3条(ii)項は傭船料の控除による補償を規定するだけであると判断する」。

　控訴院は，同判事の第3条(ii)項に関する解釈を肯定する際に，その解釈は，第1条および第2条(a)の「……要件に本船が適合しなくなった時は，……いつでも……」という条項の文言に容易には適合しないことを認めた。しかし控訴院は以下のとおり判示した。すなわち，第3条(ii)が，傭船者の主張のように，本船引渡後の第1条および第2条(a)項の特性の欠陥へ適用されるとすれば，事実上第3条(i)項の保船義務——それは用語で相当の注意義務である——を，本船の引渡時点で求められるべき状態を傭船契約期間を通して維持する絶対的義務へ変形させることとなるであろう。したがって，第3条を全体として解釈すれば，本船の引渡の時点で存在し，その後継続する第1条または第2条(a)項の特性の欠陥，およびあらゆる時点に生じる第10条の違反を構成する欠陥に第(ii)項が制限される場合にのみ，第(ii)項は実務的意味を持つということになる。

Clause 4 — Period and trading limits

65　4. Owners agree to let and Charterers agree to hire the vessel for a period of
66　commencing from the time and date of delivery of the vessel, for the purpose of carrying all lawful merchandise
67　(subject always to Clause 28) including in particular
68　in any part of the world, as Charterers shall direct, subject to the limits of the current British Institute Warranties
69　and any subsequent amendments thereof. Notwithstanding the foregoing, but subject to Clause 35, Charterers
70　may order the vessel to ice-bound waters or to any part of the world outside such limits provided that Owners
71　consent thereto (such consent not to be unreasonably withheld) and that Charterers pay for any insurance
72　premium required by the vessel's underwriters as a consequence of such order.
73　Charterers shall use due diligence to ensure that the vessel is only employed between and at safe places
74　(which expression when used in this charter shall include ports, berths, wharves, docks, anchorages, submarine
75　lines, alongside vessels or lighters, and other locations including locations at sea) where she can safely lie always
76　afloat. Notwithstanding anything contained in this or any other clause of this charter, Charterers do not warrant
77　the safety of any place to which they order the vessel and shall be under no liability in respect thereof except for
78　loss or damage caused by their failure to exercise due diligence as aforesaid. Subject as above, the vessel shall be

79　loaded and discharged at any places as Charterers may direct, provided that Charterers shall exercise due
80　diligence to ensure that any ship-to-ship transfer operations shall conform to standards not less than those set out
81　in the latest published edition of the ICS/OCIMF Ship-to-Ship Transfer Guide.
82　　　The vessel shall be delivered by Owners at a port in
83　at Owners' option and redelivered to Owners at a port in
84　at Charterers' option.

第4条 ── 期間および航路定限

　4．船主は本船を提供することに合意し，傭船者は，本船の引渡日時から開始する…………の期間に，特に…………を含め，あらゆる適法な貨物（第28条には常に従う）を運送する目的で，英国の現行協会担保航路定限およびその後に改正された航路定限に準拠した，傭船者の指図する世界全域で，傭船することに合意する。前記にかかわらず，ただし，第35条に従い，傭船者は，船主の承諾を得て（この承諾は不当に保留されてはならない），かつ傭船者の指図の結果本船の保険者により請求される割増保険料を傭船者が支払うことを条件として，結氷海域または上述の定限外の世界全域に本船を仕向けることができる。
　傭船者は，本船を常時浮揚して安全に碇泊できる安全な場所間および安全な場所（この表現が本契約で使用される場合は，港，バース，埠頭，ドック，錨地，海底油管，他船または艀の舷側，および海上の指定地を含むその他の指定地を含む）においてのみ使用するよう，相当の注意を尽くすものとする。本条または本契約の他の条項の記述にかかわらず，傭船者は，自己が本船を仕向けるいかなる場所の安全性も保証するものではなく，上述の相当の注意を尽くさなかったことにより生じた滅失または損傷を除いては，それに関し何ら責任を負わないものとする。上記を条件として，本船は，傭船者の指示するいかなる場所においても船積し，揚荷するものとする。ただし，傭船者は，船舶間積み替え荷役が少なくとも ICS・OCIMF の Ship-to-Ship Transfer Guide の最新版に記載されている基準に従うよう，相当の注意を尽くすものとする。
　本船は，船主任意の…………にある港において船主より引き渡され，傭船者任意の…………………にある港において船主に返船されるものとする。

　Shelltime 4 の第4条の65行目から72行目までで生じる問題は，本書の前半の次の章，傭船期間（173頁から184頁），適法な貨物（219頁から225頁）および航路定限（193頁から195頁）の章に記されている。68行目にいう航路は，英国の現行協会担保航路定限に制限されているが，それにかかわらず，かつ第35条（戦争危険条項）に従い，船主の承諾と追加の保険料を支払うことにより，傭船者は本船を結氷海域に就航させるだけでなく，現行協会担保航路定限の範囲を越えて「世界中のいかなる地域」へも就航させるべく指図することができる。傭船契約で特定された航路定限を越えて本船を就航させることへの一般的な承諾は，たとえ航路定限を越えるための追加の保険料を支払うとしても，契約により就航する港の安全に関する義務から傭船者を免除するものではない。前出614頁参照。船主が特定の港に本船を就航させることに同意する場合，その見解は，大きく異なる。
　73行目から81行目は本船が安全な港とその他の安全な場所との間のみで使用されることを確実にするため傭船者が相当の注意を尽くす義務について述べている。この義務は，それは大抵のタンカー傭船契約に共通しているが，乾貨物船の定期傭船契約に基づき傭船者が保証する港の安全性の確保に関する一般的な義務より狭いものである。
　第4条に規定する安全な港に関する条項および相当の注意を尽くす義務を含む他の同様の条項を正確に解釈するためには，まず以下の点について考慮する要があると思われる。すなわ

ち，The Eastern City［1958］2 Lloyd's Rep. 127事件および The Evia (No. 2)［1982］2 Lloyd's Rep. 307事件およびその他の関連する判例で規定された基準を適用してその港が安全であるかどうかである（前出231／232頁参照）。もしその基準で，港が非安全である場合，その上で傭船者が相当の注意を尽くしたかどうかの問題が検討されなければならない（The Saga Cob［1992］2 Lloyd's Rep. 545事件および The Chemical Venture［1993］Lloyd's Rep. 508事件（同判例集510頁）参照）。

この文脈における相当の注意（due diligence）とは，妥当な注意（reasonable care）を意味している（The Saga Cob 事件551頁，The Chemical Venture 事件519頁）。The Saga Cob 事件で，控訴院は相当の注意が尽くされていたかどうかについては，言及する必要がなかった。しかしながら，たとえすべての事実が港が非安全であることを示していると傭船者が知っていたとしても，傭船者が相当の注意を尽くさなかったことには必ずしもならなかったとの意見を表明した。仮にすべての事実が港が安全でないことを示していることを傭船者は知っていたが，船主により一般に安全であるとみなされた港へ，傭船者が本船を配船する場合，傭船者は法により保護されると控訴院は考えた。しかし傭船者は，以下のような場合に限り保護されることは明らかである。それは，船主が，港を安全であるとみなし，港が安全でないことを予見させる事実についても知っているような状況に限り，傭船者は守られるということである。これは実際のところ，本件を結審した Parker 卿判事の判決に示唆されている。彼は551頁で，少なくとも次のような強い主張があると述べた。つまり相当の注意を尽くしたかどうかの判断基準は，「相当に注意深い傭船者であれば既知の事実に基づいてその港が非安全であると予測できると結論付ける」かどうかによるべきである。

Saga Cob 号は，傭船契約 Shelltime 3 にて傭船されていた。同傭船契約第3条（それは Shelltime 4の第4条に相当する）は，「傭船者は，本船を常時浮揚して安全に碇泊できる……安全な港の間および安全な港においてのみ使用するよう，相当の注意を尽くすものとする。本条または本契約の他の条項の記述にかかわらず，傭船者は，自己が本船を仕向けるいかなる場所の安全性も保証するものではなく，……上述の相当の注意を尽くさなかったことにより生じた滅失または損傷を除いては，それに関し何ら責任を負うと判断してはならない」と，規定している。

本船は紅海アデン湾およびアフリカ東岸において白物の石油製品の運送のため，傭船されることとなっていた。この傭船契約に基づき本船は，事故なく Massawa への航海に約20回従事した。1988年8月26日本船は再度 Massawa へ向かうよう指示された。しかし，港外錨泊中の9月7日，本船は武装した EPLF（Eritrean People's Liberation Front－反政府団体）のボートに襲撃され，損傷した。それ以前に Massawa の町で散発的な銃撃戦があったが，港が安全でないと判断させるには不十分であった。海上における攻撃に関する限り，1988年5月31日 Saga Cob 号と同じ船団を組んでいた錨泊中の他船が Massawa の南65マイルの海上で EPLF の攻撃を受けている。その後 Saga Cob 号は，適宜海軍の護衛を受けていた。しかし Saga Cob 号の1回を除き，9月7日までこれ以外の攻撃はなかった。その後も，1990年1月まで，これ以外の攻撃は発生していない。

本件は第1審において Diamond 判事が扱った。曰く，8月26日に指示された時点で，Massawa 港は，安全でない港であることが予測された。つまりその日に，EPLF により海上で攻撃されることが予見でき，それは確かに高い可能性ではなかったが，ともかく無視できないほどの危険が存在した。同判事は，さらに，傭船者は，その事実と相当な危険について承知しており，傭船者は相当の注意を尽くすことを怠っていたと判示した。

控訴院は，Diamond 判事の判決を覆し，Massawa 港は8月26日の時点で，安全であり，同判事は，攻撃の危険が予見できたことを考慮する際に間違った基準を本件へ適用したと判示した。控訴院は，同じ年の5月から8月にかけて他の事故が発生しておらず，海軍による護衛体制に何らかの欠陥があったことを示す証拠もなく，その後の1990年の1月までそれ以上の攻撃もなかったことを強調した。Parker 卿判事の判断は，551頁で次のような結論となっている。すなわち「本事案のような状況

において，妥当な判断をする船主または船長が本船をそこへ仕向け，あるいは出航させるのを拒否するだけの「政治的な」危険が，十分でない限り，[ある港]は，非安全であるとみなされない。本事案はそうした状況を示すような証拠は存在せず，その後の経緯も1988年8月26日およびそれ以降長期間，Massawa港が危険であるとは考えられないことを示した」。

The Saga Cob［1991］2 Lloyd's Rep. 398および［1992］2 Lloyd's Rep. 545（C. A.）．（［1993］LMCLQ 150におけるDavenport氏による本事案の解説を参照）

The Saga Cob事件で控訴院は，その後の経過，すなわち本船に対する攻撃の後，18ヶ月にわたりそれ以上の事件が発生しなかったことを以下のように考察した。つまりそれは港の安全を評価するだけでなく，傭船者が相当の注意を尽くしていたかの問題に関連があるとした。Gatehouse判事は，The Chemical Venture事件でこの点につき，特に相当の注意という論点について留保した。その当時，本船にとり非安全と予見された港へ，傭船者が本船に向かうように指示した際に，傭船者が相当の注意を尽くしたかどうかの問題と，引き続いて発生するできごとがどのように関連することがあるのか，同判事は，理解できなかった（［1993］1 Lloyd's Rep. 508（同判例集519頁））。同判事は，またThe Saga Cob事件の控訴院の次の所見も参考とした。港が非安全であることを示すすべての事実を知っている傭船者が，それにもかかわらず本船にその港へ行くことを指示した場合でも，傭船者が相当の注意を尽くすことを怠ったということには必ずしもならないであろう。同判事は，その所見および具体例から二つの結論を導いた。第1は，傭船者が，その指示の正当性を示す証拠を呈示しない限り，本件は，過失推定則（res ipsa loquitur 物自体が，語る）の一例である。次に，意見を述べる資格のある他の利用者が反対意見を呈示した証拠がある場合，その港が安全であるといういくつかの意見を挙げることは傭船者にとって十分なことではない。The Chemical Venture事件の場合，他の船主，傭船者または船長，他の船主から何の証拠も呈示されなかった。しかしそれにもかかわらず同判事は，港が安全でないことを示す事実（それらを傭船者はすべて気づいていた）が自明の理であると考え，さらに傭船者は相当の注意を尽くす義務を怠ったと考えた。

Shelltime 3の傭船契約書により傭船された，リベリア籍タンカーChemical Venture号は，イラン・イラク戦争のとき，Mina al Ahmadiにて船積するよう指示された。その指示が出される少し前にイランは，サウジアラビアとクウェートのターミナルを使用する不特定多数のタンカーに対して航空機による攻撃を行い始めた。当初，船長およびその乗組員は就航を拒否した。しかし，本船と船主のMina al Ahmadi間のテレックスのやりとりの結果，傭船者は最終的に戦争手当を支払うことで乗組員を説得した。11日前までに攻撃を受けた他の3隻のタンカー同様にMina al Ahmadiへ入る航路で（ここで本船の就航後，5ヶ月の間に連続して各国のタンカー11隻が攻撃を受けている），本船は，イラン空軍機のミサイル攻撃を受けて著しく損傷した。

商事法廷において，Gatehouse判事は，以下のとおり判示した。(a)傭船契約書の第3条は，物理的な危険と同じく政治的な危険にも適用される。(b)イラン空軍の攻撃は，異常なまたは予見できない事件というより，むしろ，タンカーの入港航路の通常の性質と言えるので，Mina al Ahmadiは非安全であった。(c)傭船者は，関連する事実を認識していたが，相当の注意を尽くすことを怠っており，第3条に違反した。しかしながら，(d)乗組員の戦争手当を手配して，船主が傭船者とのテレックス交信において言ったこと（および言わなかったこと）は，Mina al Ahmadiへの航海指図を第3条の違反として扱わないという明白な表示となった。したがってこれにより船主はその後傭船者に対して損害賠償の請求をできないこととなった。

The Chemical Venture［1993］1 Lloyd's Rep. 508.

The Chemical Venture事件で次のような傭船者の主張を支持して傭船者に代わって持ち出さ

れた議論の一つは，契約履行のなんらかの局面が，戦争により影響を受け，したがって第3条の安全港条項に頼る必要がない場合，Shelltime 3 定期傭船契約にある戦争条項は，当事者の権利を扱う完全な法典であるということである。傭船者の主張とは，Shelltime の定期傭船契約の書式にある安全港条項は，物理的な危険にのみ適用され，政治的な危険には適用されず，特定の戦争危険に適用されるということであった。これに対し判事は，以下のとおりこの主張を退けた。すなわち Shelltime 3 傭船契約条項は，貴族院が，ボルタイム傭船契約の戦争条項は完全な法典を構成すると判示した The Evia (No.2) 事件の条項とはまったく異なる，と判示された (The Chemical Venture 事件のこの点に関する判決の論拠は，後出728頁を参照)。Shelltime 4 の戦争条項は，Shelltime 3 の戦争条項に似ているが，Shelltime 4 の戦争保険規定と戦争追加費用の規定は Shelltime 3 の規定とは異なる (後出723頁参照)。

引渡と返船は82／84行で取り扱われる。船主がその選択権を行使する際に，特定の引渡港を指定する場合，傭船者はその港の安全性につき義務を免れる。

Clause 5 — Laydays/cancelling

85　5. The vessel shall not be delivered to Charterers before ……… and Charterers shall
86　have the option of cancelling this charter if the vessel is not ready and at their disposal
　　on or before

第5条 — 傭船開始・傭船解約

5．本船は，………日以前には傭船者に引き渡されないものとし，本船が，………日またはそれ以前に使用準備が整わず，傭船者の使用に委ねられないときは，傭船者は本契約を解約する選択権を有するものとする。

本条項は，本船が定められた日までに使用準備が整わず，傭船者の使用に委ねられない場合には，傭船者に解約権を与えるものである。必要とされる準備整頓の状態とは疑いもなく，Shelltime 4 の第1条および第2条(a)項に述べられているものである。解約条項と準備整頓に関する一般的解説については，前出419／424頁参照。

The Arianna [1987] 2 Lloyd's Rep. 376 事件の Essotime 書式の解約条項は，Shelltime 書式にいくぶん似ていた。その傭船契約書は次のように規定していた。

「第3条　相当の注意を尽くして得られる程度において，……本船が……引渡時に準備完了し堅牢強固で……あらゆる点で業務と第57条の輸送に適合し……パイプライン，ポンプ，加熱管が良好に作動する状態であることの通知が書面で行われるときに傭船は開始する……
　第4条　……本船がこの契約の規定に適合して準備されない場合には，傭船者は本傭船契約を解約する自由を持つものとする。……
　第57条A項．　本船は製品タンカーが安全に輸送できるあらゆる液体貨物の一般的製品輸送に使用できるものとする。
　第69条．　船主は，良好な状態にタンク洗浄装置を常に保守し，170P.S.I.の圧力海水温度華氏180度という条件で同時に6台のタンク洗浄機器が作動できるものとする。」

当事案の事実関係は前出第1条で述べられている。生じる問題の一つが，本船が引渡時に第69条に適合できないという事実を理由として，傭船者は解約できるかということである。解約

条項を検討して，Webster判事は，同判例集387頁に次のように述べた。「傭船契約を解約する傭船者の権利は第4条の解釈しだいであるというのが第1審では共通の根拠である。傭船者代理として［法廷弁護人］は，「この契約の規定」という第4条の言及は傭船契約の（第80条に含まれる詳細規定を含む）全条項への言及として理解されると主張した。さらに，特にそれは第69条への言及を構成すると主張した。私はこの主張を退ける。私の見解では，第4条の『この契約の規定に適合して準備』との文言は，第3条の規定への言及として解されるべきであり，したがって第3条の『そのときに準備』に始まり『相当の注意を尽くして達成できる』で終わる文言への言及として理解されるべきである。これが，私が心から同意する……仲裁人の結論であった」。

後で商事法廷に控訴された仲裁裁定で仲裁人は，次のように述べた。「『この契約の規定に適合して準備』という第4条の文言は，提供された本船は引渡日に適用できる傭船契約の各条項を満足させなければならないことを意味すると，傭船者は主張した。われわれは本傭船契約の解約条項のこの広い解釈に同意しない。われわれの考えでは，本解約条項は引渡準備を扱う傭船契約の規定に特に関連する。本船が解約日までに引渡準備できていない場合に，その条項は解約する選択権を与えるのを意図しているだけである。引渡準備に関する特別条項は，第3条であり，われわれの考えでは，本船が第3条の引渡準備に関する規定を満足しない場合，傭船者は第4条に基づき解約する権利を有するだけである」。

本事案の具体的状況の下で，傭船者に解約する権利はないと判示された。前出第1条を参照。

Clause 6 — Owners to provide

87　6. Owners undertake to provide and to pay for all provisions, wages, and shipping and discharging fees
88　and all other expenses of the master, officers and crew; also, except as provided in Clauses 4 and 34 hereof, for all
89　insurance on the vessel, for all deck, cabin and engine-room stores, and for water; for all drydocking, overhaul,
90　maintenance and repairs to the vessel; and for all fumigation expenses and de-rat certificates. Owners'
91　obligations under this Clause 6 extend to all liabilities for customs or import duties arising at any time during the
92　performance of this charter in relation to the personal effects of the master, officers and crew, and in relation to
93　the stores, provisions and other matters aforesaid which Owners are to provide and pay for and Owners shall
94　refund to Charterers any sums Charterers or their agents may have paid or been compelled to pay in respect of
95　any such liability. Any amounts allowable in general average for wages and provisions and stores shall be credited
96　to Charterers insofar as such amounts are in respect of a period when the vessel is on-hire.

第6条 ── 船主負担費目

6．船主は，船長，職員および部員の一切の食料，賃金，乗船および下船費用，その他一切を支給し，その費用を支払う義務を負い，さらに本契約第4条および第34条に規定されたものを除き，本船に係わる一切の保険，すべての甲板，船室および機関室の備品，水，本船の一切の入渠，分解検査，保守および修理，また一切の燻蒸費用および鼠族駆除証明書につき，その費用を支払うことを保証する。本第6条に基づく船主義務は，船長，職員および部員の手回品に関し，また，船主が支給し支払うべき船用品，食料および上述のその他の物に関し，本契約履行中に生じる関税または輸入税についてのあらゆる債務を含むものとし，船主は，傭船者またはその代理人がこのような債務を支払いまたは支払うことを余儀なくされた金額については，傭船者に補償するものとする。賃金，食料および船用品につき共同海損に容認される金額は，その金額が本船のオンハイヤー期間についてのものである限り，傭船者に返還される。

Shelltime 4 第6条に相当する Shelltime 3 第5条は，前者を多少変更したものであることを，留意すべきである。生水を使用していた時期に遡る Shelltime 3 にある「汽罐用の水を除き」との除外規定は，現代のタンカーにとって不適当であるとして削除された。入渠，分解検査，保守および修理についての言及が Shelltime 4 に追加された。

Clause 7 ── Charterers to provide

97　　7. Charterers shall provide and pay for all fuel (except fuel used for domestic services), towage and
98　　pilotage and shall pay agency fees, port charges, commissions, expenses of loading and unloading cargoes, canal
99　　dues and all charges other than those payable by Owners in accordance with Clause 6 hereof, provided that all
100　　charges for the said items shall be for Owners' account when such items are consumed, employed or incurred for
101　　Owners' purposes or while the vessel is off-hire (unless such items reasonably relate to any service given or
102　　distance made good and taken into account under Clause 21 or 22); and provided further that any fuel used in
103　　connection with a general average sacrifice or expenditure shall be paid for by Owners.

第7条 ── 傭船者負担費目

7．傭船者は，一切の燃料（船内用燃料を除く）曳船および水先人を手配し，その費用を支払うものとし，また代理店料，港費，手数料，貨物の船積および揚荷費用，運河通航料，および第6条により船主が支払うべき諸掛以外の一切の費用を支払うものとする。ただし，これらの費用が船主のために消費され，使用され，または生ずるとき，または本船がオフハイヤーにあるとき（そのような費目が第21条または第22条に基づき，提供した業務または短縮された距離が，傭船料からの控除額の算定に際し考慮されることに相当な関係がある場合を除く）は，そのような費目の全費用は船主の負担とし，さらに共同海損犠牲または費用に関連して使用された一切の燃料は船主が支払うものとする。

調理用燃料は現在では船内用燃料の全必要量の中の僅かな部分であるので，Shelltime 3 第6条にある「調理用燃料」という文言は Shelltime 4 で「船内用燃料」と修正されたことが，

留意されるべきである。第21条または第22条に基づき提供した業務または短縮された距離が，傭船料からの控除額の算定にあたり考慮されることに関係がある場合を除き，Shelltime 4 は，傭船者の負担として記載されている費目は本船のオフハイヤー中，船主負担とする旨を規定しているので，Shelltime 3 とは，また異なる。Shelltime 3 の同条項の文言に関する事案について，*The Bridgestone Maru No.3* [1983] 2 Lloyd's Rep. 62 事件を参照。前出673頁も参照。

こうした条項に関する一般的解説について，前出275／280頁参照。Beepeetime 2 傭船契約第20条の傭船者が代理店を提供し代理店料を支払う義務に関する所見につき *The Sagona* [1984] 1 Lloyd's Rep. 194 事件と前出279頁を参照。

Clause 8 — Rate of hire

104   8. Subject as herein provided, Charterers shall pay for the use and hire of the vessel at the rate of
105   .... per day, and pro rata for any part of a day, from the time and date of her delivery (local
106   time) until the time and date of her redelivery (local time) to Owners.

第 8 条 — 傭船料率

8．本条の規定に従い，傭船者は，本船の使用ならびに傭船につき，1 日当たり，また 1 日に満たない部分は按分で，...............の料率で，本船引渡日時（引渡地時）から船主への本船返船日時（返船地時）まで支払うものとする。

傭船料の計算に際して地方時間が使用されるとの表現により，そのような明示の表現を含まない傭船契約の場合に解釈の困難が生じないようにしている。*The Arctic Skou* [1985] 2 Lloyd's Rep. 478 事件と前出289頁参照。「引渡」の定義について前出173頁参照，そして返船に関する解説については前出293／296頁参照。

Clause 9 — Payment of hire

107   9. Subject to Clause 3(iii), payment of hire shall be made in immediately available funds to :
108   Account
109   in ...... per calendar month in advance, less :
110   (i) any hire paid which Charterers reasonably estimate to relate to off-hire periods, and
111   (ii) any amounts disbursed on Owners' behalf any advances, and commission thereon, and
112   charges which are for Owners' account pursuant to any provision hereof, and
113   (iii) any amounts due or reasonably estimated to become due to Charterers under Clause 3(ii) or
114   24 hereof,
115   any such adjustments to be made at the due date for the next monthly payment after the facts have been

116　ascertained. Charterers shall not be responsible for any delay or error by Owners' bank in crediting Owners'
117　account provided that Charterers have made proper and timely payment.
118　　　　In default of such proper and timely payment,
119　　　　(a) Owners shall notify Charterers of such default and Charterers shall within seven days of receipt of
120　such notice pay to Owners the amount due including interest, failing which Owners may withdraw the vessel from
121　the service of Charterers without prejudice to any other rights Owners may have under this charter or otherwise;
122　and
123　　　　(b) Interest on any amount due but not paid on the due date shall accrue from the day after that date
124　up to and including the day when payment is made, at a rate per annum which shall be 1% above the U.S. Prime
125　Interest Rate as published by the Chase Manhattan Bank in New York at 12.00 New York time on the due date,
126　or, if no such interest rate is published on that day, the interest rate published on the next preceding day on which
127　such a rate was so published, computed on the basis of a 360 day year of twelve 30-day months, compounded
128　semi-annually.

第9条 ── 傭船料の支払

9．第3条(iii)項を条件として，傭船料の支払は，直ちに使用可能な資金として，.....................の...
........................にある口座に毎暦月次の費用を控除して前払するものとする。
　(i) 既に支払われた傭船料に対して，傭船者がオフハイヤー期間に関連して正当に見積る一切の金額，
　(ii) 船主のための立替金，前払金およびそれに関する手数料，また本契約の各条項に従って船主負担となる費用，および
　(iii) 本契約第3条(ii)項または第24条に基づき傭船者に支払われるべき，または傭船者に支払われることになる正当に見積られた一切の金額。
その精算については，その事実が確定した後の次回の月例支払期日に行うものとする。傭船者は，期限までに正当に支払を行ったものに限り，船主の取引銀行が船主の口座への入金に際し惹き起した遅延または過失には一切責任を負わない。
期限までに適正に支払がなされなかったときは，
　(a) 船主はその不履行を傭船者に通知し，傭船者はその通知を受け取ってから7日以内に利息を付した相当額を船主に支払うものとする。これを怠ったときは，船主は，本契約またはその他において，船主に存する他の一切の権利を損なうことなく，本船を傭船者の運航から引き揚げることができる，また
　(b) 支払期日に支払われなかった金額に対する利息は，支払期日の翌日から支払のなされる日を含む日までについて発生し，年利は，支払期日のNew York時間正午現在においてNew Yorkのチェイス・マンハッタン銀行が発表する米国プライムレートに1パーセント上乗せしたものとする。その日にレートが発表されない場合には，次に発表された日のレートによるものとし，30日を1ヶ月とする12ヶ月，つまり1年を360日として半年複利で計算する。

備船料の支払と本船の引揚に関する一般的解説は，前出301／329頁にある。

船主が本船の保守義務に違反した場合，第3条(iii)項に基づき傭船者はある状況の下で傭船料の支払を中断することができるが，傭船料の支払義務は，第3条(iii)項を条件とする。傭船料の支払は「即時に使用可能な資金」で行われなければならない。この用語法は先例にある現金送金――すなわち船主に「送金資金を即時使用する無条件の権利」を与える送金――と同価値の
|584|定義を必ずしも正確に反映していない。The Chikuma [1981] 1 Lloyd's Rep. 371 (H. L.) 事件を参照，その事実関係は前出302頁に述べられている。The Chikuma 事件で送金資金は即時に使用可能であったが，無条件ではなく，現金と商業的に同価値ではないと判示された。

たとえ傭船料の支払期日に本船がオフハイヤーであったとしても，「支払済傭船料」に関してのみ控除ができるので，第9条(i)項に基づき，傭船者は予想されるオフハイヤーに関して傭船料の支払から控除することはできない。特定の諸原因から時間が喪失される場合，「傭船料の支払は終止するものとする」というオフハイヤー条項を含む傭船契約に基づき適切であると言われる見解と，これは，異なるものである (The Lutetian [1982] 2 Lloyd's Rep. 140 事件と前出305頁参照)。

しかしながら，第9条(ii)項に言及の船主のための立替金，前払金および費用とは別に，第9条(iii)項の将来の傭船料に関して傭船者が他に控除できる場合があるようである。その下位条項に基づき，傭船者は，第3条(ii)項または第24条に基づき当然支払われるべき金額，あるいは当然支払われるべきものとして合理的に見積った金額を控除できる。傭船者が契約上権利を有する貨物積載場所を傭船者から奪い第10条に違反した場合，第3条(ii)項と第9条(ii)項により前払傭船料から使用不可能の貨物積載場所に相当する金額を傭船者が控除することができるように思われる。

傭船者は船主の銀行側の遅延または過失に責任を負わないと規定する116／117行は，傭船者の銀行側の遅延または過失につき傭船者と船主の間では傭船者が責任を負うことを単に強調しているだけである。「適切かつ時機を得た」支払がないときに，船主は本船を引き揚げる即時の権利を持たず，第9条(a)項に基づき引揚7日前の通知をしなければならない。支払実行場所の時間で支払期日の24時00分後という支払時期が期限切れとなるときまで，船主は有効な通知を出すことはできない ([1983] 1 Lloyd's Rep. 335 (H. L.) と前出318頁 The Afovos 事件を参照)。有効な通知を出した後で傭船者には支払まで7日あるが，支払うべき傭船料に加えて，傭船者は第9条(b)項に従って計算された利子を支払わねばならない。

Clause 10 — Space available to charterers

129　　10. The whole reach, burthen and decks of the vessel and any passenger accommo-
　　　　dation (including

130　　Owners' suite) shall be at Charterers' disposal, reserving only proper and sufficient
　　　　space for the vessel's master,

131　　officers, crew, tackle, apparel, furniture, provisions and stores, provided that the weight
　　　　of stores on board shall

132　　not, unless specially agreed, exceed .... tonnes at any time during the charter period.

第10条 ― 貨物積載場所

10. 本船の全部，積載場所，甲板およびいかなる旅客用船室（船主の室を含む）も，本船の船長，職員，部員，索具，装具，備品，食料および船用品のための適切かつ十分な場所を除き，すべて傭船者

の使用に委ねられる。ただし，船内の船用品の重量は，特に合意のない限り，傭船期間中いかなる時も……トンを超えてはならない。

船主が第10条に違反した場合，傭船者は傭船料の減額につき第3条(ii)項に基づき権利を有するが，その違反につき他の救済手段も有する (*The Fina Samco* [1994] 1 Lloyd's Rep. 153 および [1995] 2 Lloyd's Rep. 344 (C. A.) 事件参照)。傭船者に使用不可能となった貨物積載場所の価値を傭船者は前払傭船料から控除できる (前出第9条(iii)項を参照)。

Clause 11 — Overtime

133　11. Overtime pay of the master, officers and crew in accordance with ship's articles shall be for Charterers'
134　account when incurred, as a result of complying with the request of Charterers or their agents, for loading,
135　discharging, heating of cargo, bunkering or tank cleaning.

第11条 — 時間外手当

11. 本船の就業規則に基づく船長，職員および部員の時間外手当は，それが傭船者またはその代理人の要請に応じて船積，揚荷，貨物の加熱，補油またはタンク清掃を行った結果生じたときは，傭船者の負担とする。

記載された作業を傭船者が求める場合，時間外手当は傭船者が支払う。しかしながら乗組員の過失または義務違反が先行して発生し，その結果として時間外が必要となる場合もあろう。その場合，船主はその過失または義務違反に責任があるか，または船主責任は第27条(a)項の364／365行の「本船の管理……の際の過失……」の免責規定により排除されるかという問題が生じる。後出714頁参照。

Clause 12 — Instructions and logs

136　12. Charterers shall from time to time give the master all requisite instructions and sailing directions, and
137　he shall keep a full and correct log of the voyage or voyages, which Charterers or their agents may inspect as
138　required. The master shall when required furnish Charterers or their agents with a true copy of such log and with
139　properly completed loading and discharging port sheets and voyage reports for each voyage and other returns as
140　Charterers may require. Charterers shall be entitled to take copies at Owners' expense of any such documents
141　which are not provided by the master.

第12条 — 指図および航海日誌

12. 傭船者は，随時一切の必要な指図および航海指図を船長に与えるものとし，船長は完全で正確な

航海日誌を作成し，傭船者またはその代理人が必要に応じ閲覧できるようにするものとする。船長は，要求があるときは，傭船者またはその代理人に同航海日誌の正本および完全な船積港および揚荷港の手仕舞書類，各航海毎の航海報告書その他報告書を提出するものとする。傭船者は，船長が提出しない書類については，船主費用で複写する権利を有するものとする。

本件につき前出351／360頁を参照。前出413頁も参照。

　ある状況では，船主または船長が指図に即時に従わないことが妥当な場合がありうる。事実経緯は次の第13条に述べているが，*The Houda* [1994] 2 Lloyd's Rep. 541 事件で，本船はShelltime 4 で傭船された。常備の行動指図として「貴船の航海に関するすべての指図はクェートの Kuwait Petroleum Corp. より発せられる。」が傭船者により本船に与えられた。イラクのクェート侵攻の後，本船が航海指図を London から受領したときに，指図はクウェート発ではなかったので，指図は適法であるかを疑問とし，船主は指図に従うことを拒否した。控訴院は，船主が指図の合法性に妥当な疑問を抱く場合，原則として船主は傭船契約に基づき指図に従うことの影響を検討するため相当な時間を割く権利があると判示した。Neill 卿判事は549頁で次のように述べた。「もちろん，当裁判所は諸事実に基づき船主に思案する妥当な根拠があるか否かを決定するものではない。しかし私は，たとえ貨物または本船に直接の物理的脅威がないとしても，受領する指図の出所および有効性に関する追加情報を求めるために思案する権利，否，実際には義務が生じうる状況が戦争状態では十分にありうる，と確信する」。

Clause 13 — Bills of Lading

142　13. (a) The master (although appointed by Owners) shall be under the orders and direction of
143　Charterers as regards employment of the vessel, agency and other arrangements, and shall sign bills of lading as
144　Charterers or their agents may direct (subject always to Clauses 35(a) and 40) without prejudice to this charter.
145　Charterers hereby indemnify Owners against all consequences or liabilities that may arise
146　　　　　(i) from signing bills of lading in accordance with the directions of Charterers or their agents, to
147　the extent that the terms of such bills of lading fail to conform to the requirements of this charter, or (except as
148　provided in Clause 13(b)) from the master otherwise complying with Charterers' or their agents' orders :
149　　　　　(ii) from any irregularities in papers supplied by Charterers or their agents.
150　　(b) Notwithstanding the foregoing, Owners shall not be obliged to comply with any orders from
151　Charterers to discharge all or part of the cargo
152　　　　　(i) at any place other than that shown on the bill of lading and/or
153　　　　　(ii) without presentation of an original bill of lading
154　　　　unless they have received from Charterers both written confirmation of such orders and an
155　indemnity in a form acceptable to Owners.

第13条 — 船荷証券

13. (a)船長は（船主により任命されるとはいえ），本船の使用，代理行為その他の手配に関し，傭船者の命令および指図に従うものとし，本契約上の権利を損なうことなく，傭船者またはその代理人の指図のとおり船荷証券に署名しなければならない（ただし，常に第35条(a)および第40条を条件とする）。

傭船者は，
(i) 傭船者またはその代理人の指図に従って船荷証券に署名したことにより生ずる一切の結果または責任のうち，その船荷証券の条項が本契約の条件に反する部分に対し，または（第13条(b)の場合を除き）船長が別途傭船者またはその代理人の指図に従ったことにより生ずる一切の結果または責任に対し，また
(ii) 傭船者またはその代理人が提供した書類の不備により生ずる一切の結果または責任に対し，船主に補償するものとする。
(b) 前項の規定にかかわらず，船主は，
(i) 船荷証券に記載されていない場所において，かつ・または
(ii) 船荷証券の正本の提出を受けることなく，
傭船者からの貨物の全部または一部の揚荷指図に従う義務はないものとする。ただし，船主が傭船者からその指図の確認書と船主が受入可能な補償状の双方を受け取った場合は，この限りではない。

　船長は，傭船者の命令と指図に従うものとするとの規定は前出351頁で扱われている。「本傭船契約上の権利を損なうことなく」船荷証券に署名することについての解説については前出393頁を，船荷証券の署名に関する一般については前出385／400頁参照。
　第13条(a)項に基づき船長は傭船者の命令と指図に従うものとするとの事実は船長または船主は必ずその指図に即刻従わなければならないということを意味するものではない（後出 The Houda 事件を参照）。第13条(a)項は，明示的に補償を含んでいる。あるタンカー傭船契約は明示の補償を含んでいないが，傭船契約が明示の補償を含むと含まないとにかかわらず，傭船者の指図に従う結果に対しては通常船主に有利に補償が黙示されている（前出353頁参照）。しかしながら，補償義務の黙示は自動的なものではない（The Nogar Marin [1988] 1 Lloyd's Rep. 412（同判例集422頁）事件参照）。傭船契約の明示の条項と一致しない補償は黙示されない。

586　詳細な事実関係が後出702頁で述べられているが，The Berge Sund [1993] 2 Lloyd's Rep. 453（C. A.）事件で，傭船契約はタンカー傭船契約の標準書式に共通している多くの条項を含んでいるが，標準書式ではなかった。この事案の傭船契約には明示の補償が含まれていなかった。もっとも共通して見られるように同契約は，「船長は，船主が指名し雇用しその指揮命令の下にあるが，本船の使用，傭船者の代理人または本契約上傭船者の必要とする手配に関して傭船者の指図を遵守するものとする。」と規定していた。さらに，オフハイヤー条項に，「傭船者の過失に拠らない」時間の喪失が多くの記載原因により24時間以上継続する場合，本船はオフハイヤーとなるものとするとの規定があった。規格外の貨物または汚損貨物の輸送によりタンク洗浄に異常な長時間を要し，その間，本船はオフハイヤーとなると傭船者は主張した。船主の提出した主張の一つは，船主または乗組員の側には過失はなく，タンク洗浄に要した異常な長時間は，傭船者の当該貨物の積込指示の結果であるので，船主は，傭船者が（本船がオフハイヤーとなる場合，）オフハイヤーとした金額につき黙示の補償により賠償される権利を有するというものであった。傭船者は，黙示の補償の意味するところはオフハイヤー条項の文言と矛盾すると回答した。仲裁人は傭船者のこの主張を認容した。第1審で Steyn 判事は

（［1992］1 Lloyd's Rep. 460（同判例集467頁））補償の意味するところにつき仲裁人と別の見解を示したが，オフハイヤークレームの主題である遅延が，とにかく傭船者の直接の指図により生じていないと結論づけた。控訴院で Staughton 卿判事は，傍論として次の見解を表明した。本事案の傭船契約の黙示の補償の意味するところはオフハイヤー条項の「傭船者の過失」の免責規定と矛盾する。同判事は控訴院の報告書の462頁で次のように述べた。「傭船者の過失の免責規定の正確な意味がいかなるものであれ，過失免責規定からは傭船者の行為が本船のオフハイヤーを妨げるような状況と明らかに関係があるように私には思える。傭船者に過失がない場合，傭船者の指図に従ったことにより生じる同条項に基づく喪失傭船料につき傭船者が船主に補償するという黙示の条件を免責規定は排除すると思う」。同判事は，遅延が傭船者の指図により直接的に生じた証拠はないとの Steyn 判事の結論にも同意した。

第13条(a)(ii)項に基づき船主は「書類の不備」から生じるすべての結果に対して補償を受ける権利がある。The Boukadoura ［1989］1 Lloyd's Rep. 393 事件で，Evans 判事は船積した油の量を過大表示した船荷証券は，STB Voy 書式の第20条(a)項の類似条項の意味の範囲で「不備」であると判示した。同事案の事実関係のすべてについては前出391頁を参照。

第13条(b)項に基づき船主が求める補償は船主が曝される潜在的な責任に関して妥当な金額でなければならないと思われる。しかし補償状に関する限り，補償状が受け入れられるか否かを判断する際に船主に求められるのは誠実に行動することだけであると思われる（Astra Trust v. Adams ［1969］1 Lloyd's Rep. 81 事件（同判例集87頁），The John S. Darbyshire ［1977］2 Lloyd's Rep. 457 事件（同判例集466頁），B. V. Oliehandel Jungkind v. Coastal International ［1983］2 Lloyd's Rep. 463 事件（同判例集469頁）を参照）。船主は既に第13条(a)(i)項に基づき「傭船者またはその代理人の指図に船長が……従うことから……生じるすべての結果または責任につき」傭船者自身の補償を確保しているので，第13条(b)項に基づき「船主が受け入れられる補償状」は，第13条(a)(i)項に基づき船主が既に持っているよりもより多くの保証を船主に提供できるものでなければならないと思われる。したがって，第13条(b)項に基づき船主は例えば銀行または PI クラブの発行するまたは連署する補償状を要求できると思われる。

第13条(b)項は，船主が傭船者から書面による指図と受入可能な補償状を受け取らない限り，船荷証券に記載のない他の場所で，または船荷証券の原本の呈示のないままに貨物を揚荷してはならないと規定している。次の事案で，Shelltime 4 の第13条(a)項は修正され第13条(b)項は削除された。船荷証券の呈示なしに貨物を揚荷することが，貨物所有権者の権利を侵害しないとしても，契約上の規定がない場合には，船主と船長が船荷証券の呈示なしに貨物を揚荷せよとの傭船者の指図に応じることを拒否できるかどうかという問題が生じた。

Houda 号は，Kuwait Petroleum Corporation に Shelltime 4 書式を修正して定期傭船された。イラクがクウェートに1990年8月に侵攻したときに，本船は Mina Al Ahmadi で積込待ちをしていた。本船は貨物の一部を積んで，積荷港に船荷証券を未完成のまま放置した。この船荷証券は換金されることもなく，流通しなかった。侵攻後，傭船者の経営管理は London に移転し，そこから，Fujairah 沖で錨泊していた本船は紅海に向かい Ain Sukhna で貨物を揚荷するよう指図した。船主は，その指図は権限あるものか疑問とし，指図に応じることを拒否した。本船に与えられていた常備の行動指図書は，航海指図はクウェートから出されるとしていた。

およそ5週間遅延の後で，当事者間で合意に達し，貨物は Ain Sukhna で揚荷された。傭船者は，本船はその間オフハイヤーとなると主張した。(a)船主は London からの指図が適正に授権されたのかを点検する相当な時間をかける権利があり，(b)傭船者は，ともかく船荷証券なしに貨物を揚荷する適法な指図を出すことはできないので，船主の側に指図違反はないと船主は主張した。Shelltime 4 の第13条の重大な規定は次のように修正されていた。「（船主によって指名されてはいるが）船長は本船

の使用につき傭船者の指図と指揮に従うものとする……船長が……傭船者または代理人の指図（船荷証券の呈示なしでの貨物の引渡を含む）に応じたこと……から生じるすべての結果または責任につき傭船者は茲許船主に補償する……船主 PI クラブの文言に従った補償状がこの傭船契約に摂取されるものとする。」

　傭船者は，(a)安全性の問題が関係しない場合適法な指図に応じる際の遅延に正当化の事由はない，かつ(b) London からの指図は権限あるもので，その指図は貨物の所有権を有する当事者の権限と共に与えられるので，指図は適法であり，船主は船荷証券の原本の呈示なくして貨物の揚荷を行う義務がある，と主張した。定期傭船者に貨物の所有権を有する当事者の権限がなかったのであれば，船主には揚荷を拒否する権利があったであろう。

　論議の途中で，修正された傭船契約第13条それ自身により，船荷証券の呈示なしで貨物の引渡を傭船者が船主に指図する権利があると，傭船者の代理人は主張した。しかしながら，Phillips 判事と控訴院は，修正第13条は傭船者が発することのできる指図の種類を定義したり，または拡張すること意味しないと判示した。その指図が適法であるか否かにかかわらず，それは船主が指図に応じることにつき傭船者の補償する義務を規定しただけのことであった。

　2個の主たる係争点につき Phillips 判事の見解を覆して，控訴院は次のように判示した。(1)指図は通常即時応じることを要求するが，指図が受領される状況または指図の性質により，船長が追加の検討または調査をせずに従うことは妥当ではないであろう。指図に応じる前に相当な時間の猶予を持つ船主または船長の権利は事案の特定の範疇に制限されない。各事案で決定されるべき問題は，相応の思慮分別のある者ならその状況でいかに行為したであろうかということである。問題の事案の状況であれば，指図に応じることがいくらか遅れても相応の根拠が存するということができる。(2)たとえその揚荷が貨物の所有権者の権利を侵害しないとしても，契約上の規定がない場合，定期傭船者は船主または船長に船荷証券の呈示なくして貨物の揚荷を求めることはできない。

　The Houda [1993] 1 Lloyd's Rep. 333および [1994] 2 Lloyd's Rep. 541（C. A.）。

　しかしながら，Shelltime 4 の第13条が修正されずに，傭船者が船主に受け入れられる補償状（前出参照）を船主に提供する場合，傭船者の求めにより，船主は，船荷証券の原本の呈示なしで貨物の揚荷をしなければならない。

Clause 14 — Conduct of vessel's personnel

156　　14. If Charterers complain of the conduct of the master or any of the officers or crew, Owners shall

157　immediately investigate the complaint. If the complaint proves to be well founded, Owners shall, without delay,

158　make a change in the appointments and Owners shall in any event communicate the result of their investigations

159　to Charterers as soon as possible.

第14条 ── 乗組員の行為

14. 傭船者が，船長またはいかなる職員もしくは部員であろうとも，その行為に不満を表明した場合，船主は直ちにその不満を調査するものとする。その不満が十分根拠あると認められるときは，船主は遅滞なく任命を変更するものとする。また，船主は，いかなる時にも，調査の結果を可及的速やかに傭船者に通知するものとする。

Clause 15 — Bunkers at delivery and redelivery

160   15. Charterers shall accept and pay for all bunkers on board at the time of delivery, and Owners shall on
161   redelivery (whether it occurs at the end of the charter period or on the earlier termination of this charter) accept
162   and pay for all bunkers remaining on board, at the then-current market prices at the port of delivery or redelivery,
163   as the case may be, or if such prices are not available payment shall be at the then-current market prices at the
164   nearest port at which such prices are available; provided that if delivery or redelivery does not take place in a port
165   payment shall be at the price paid at the vessel's last port of bunkering before delivery or redelivery, as the case
166   may be. Owners shall give Charterers the use and benefit of any fuel contracts they may have in force from time to
167   time, if so required by Charterers, provided suppliers agree.

第15条 ── 引渡時および返船時の燃料

15. 傭船者は, 引渡時, 本船にある一切の燃料油を受け取り, 代価を支払うものとし, 船主は返船時(本契約の契約期間の満了時であると中途での終了時であるとを問わず), 本船に残存する一切の燃料油を受け取り, 代価を支払うものとする。その代価は, 引渡港または返船港それぞれにおけるその時の市場価格によるものとし, その市場価格が利用できないときは, それが利用可能な最寄りの港におけるそのときの市場価格で支払うものとする。ただし, 引渡または返船が港で行われないときは, それぞれ引渡または返船の直前の補油港で支払われた価格で支払うものとする。船主は, 傭船者の要求により, 供給者の同意を得て, 船主が随時有する一切の有効な補油契約を傭船者に利用できるようにし, その便宜を与えるものとする。

Shelltime 3 の第14条に相当する文脈で, 引渡時の船上の燃料を「傭船者は, 受け取り, 支払う」という文言は, *The Saint Anna* [1980] 1 Lloyd's Rep. 180 事件 (*The Span Terza* [1984] 1 Lloyd's Rep. 119 事件で貴族院が効力を認めた) で引渡時に燃料の所有権が船主から傭船者に移転するとの意味として解釈された。その他の点では Shelltime 4 の第15条は Shelltime 3 の第14条と異なるが, この点での見解は Shelltime 4 と同じである。

The Span Terza 事件 (同判例集122頁) で Diplock 卿が説明したように「一旦, 船上に積み込まれたすべての燃料の占有権は疑いもなく受寄者としての船主に授与される。傭船者は傭船契約により本船の使用につき船長に指図を与える権限があるが, その指図を遂行する際に船長が燃料を使用するようにする義務が疑いもなく受寄者としての船主には存する。」けれども, *The Saint Anna* 事件で, Shelltime 3 に基づき傭船契約期間中積み込んだ燃料は通常傭船者の財物であると判示された。

返船時に船主が購入するまで, 燃料の所有権は, Shelltime 3 に基づき傭船者に残る。Shelltime 4 に基づいても見解は同じである (*The Saetta* [1993] 2 Lloyd's Rep. 268 事件参照)。

しかしながら, Shelltime 3 は, Shelltime 4 の160-162行の規定の括弧の文言を含まないので, Shelltime 4 は, Shelltime 3 と異なる。「……船主は返船時 (本契約の契約期間の満了時であると中途での終了時であるとを問わず), 本船に残存する一切の燃料油を受け取り, 代価を支払うものとする。……」*The Saetta* 事件で, 括弧内の文言は返船の契約日前の本船の引揚に

よる傭船契約の終了に対して，引揚時に傭船者に属する燃料の所有権を船主に移転すべく，適用されると判示された。しかしながら，当事案が示すように，燃料の所有権は必ずしも燃料供給業者から傭船者に移転しないので，傭船者が同意しない本船引揚の際に，または傭船契約の他の事由による終了の際に，船主は燃料の権利を取得しないこともある。

    Saetta 号は，Shelltime 4 で傭船された。傭船契約は印刷条項第15条の燃料の価格に関する162／166行を削除し，「引渡時に FO 約250／350トン MDO 約70／150トンを各々米貨80ドルと米貨165ドルで傭船者が支払い……返船時に約同量，同価格で」という追加第53条を含んでいた。
    本事案で原告は，法的権利留保条項付の契約に基づき，傭船契約期間中傭船者に燃料を供給する燃料供給者であった。傭船者は燃料代を支払えず，船主はそれを知っていたが，燃料供給契約の法的権利留保条項を知らなかった。船主は燃料の不払につき本船を引き揚げ，船主は船上の燃料に権利があると主張して，燃料の価格を船主に支払われるべき傭船料の代償とした。Clarke 判事は，次のように判示した。(1)傭船契約の第15条は，傭船契約の早期終了を含む「返船」を定義しているので，本船引揚の際に，傭船者が船上の燃料に有する所有権は，燃料の占有権と共に船主に移転する。(2)傭船者は燃料供給契約の法的権利留保条項の理由で燃料の所有権を有しないので，1979年動産売買法第25条の規定に基づき，船主は引揚時に燃料の所有権を横領し，燃料を消費して，船主は船上の動産領得の罪を犯した。同法は，誠実にかつリーエンまたは原販売者の他の権利についての通知なしで販売または他の処分により動産を受領する当事者に，ある権利を与える。(3)しかし，本船引揚時の傭船者から船主への占有権の移転は，非任意であり，かつ傭船者の側の行為または黙認により達成されたものではなかった。「引渡」は同法の第61条(3)項に「ある者から他者への占有権の任意の移転」として定義されているが，1979年動産法の第25条(1)項に基づく傭船者による船主への燃料の「引渡」はなかった。
    The Saetta [1993] 2 Lloyd's Rep. 268.

    船主が「傭船契約の満期日に」「船上に残るあらゆる燃料と汽罐用水につき支払う」ことを求める Shelltime 3 に基づく場合，裁判所は，*The Span Terza* 事件の傭船期間の満了日前の傭船契約の解約は船上の燃料の所有権を傭船者から奪う効果を有しないという結論に，おそらく同じように達するであろう。*The Span Terza* 事件で貴族院は，本船が港にあって積載貨物がない場合ではなく海上にいて，傭船契約が終了した場合，船主が傭船者の燃料を使用するどのような権利を有するかについての疑問を未解決のままとした。

Clause 16 — Stevedores, pilots, tugs

168   16. Stevedores when required shall be employed and paid by Charterers, but this shall not relieve Owners
169 from responsibility at all times for proper stowage, which must be controlled by the master who shall keep a strict
170 account of all cargo loaded and discharged. Owners hereby indemnify Charterers, their servants and agents
171 against all losses, claims, responsibilities and liabilities arising in any way whatsoever from the employment of
172 pilots, tugboats or stevedores, who although employed by Charterers shall be deemed to be the servants of and in
173 the service of Owners and under their instructions (even if such pilots, tugboat personnel or stevedores are in fact
174 the servants of Charterers their agents or any affiliated company); provided, however,

that
175　　　　　　　　　(i) the foregoing indemnity shall not exceed the amount to which Owners
176　entitled to limit their liability if they had themselves employed such pilots, tugboats or stevedores, and
177　　　　　　　　　(ii) Charterers shall be liable for any damage to the vessel caused by or arising out of the use of
178　stevedores, fair wear and tear excepted, to the extent that Owners are unable by the exercise of due diligence to
179　obtain redress therefor from stevedores.

第16条 ── 荷役業者，水先人，曳船

16. 荷役業者を必要とするときは，傭船者により雇傭され，支払がなされるものとする。ただし，これをもって，船長をしてすべての積揚貨物を常に厳密に計算させ監督をさせるべき船主の適切な積付義務を免除するものではない。船主はこれにより，傭船者により雇傭された者とはいえ，船主の被用者となりその業務に従事し，その指揮下にあるとみなすべき水先人，曳船乗務員または荷役業者（たとえその水先人，曳船乗務員または荷役業者が実際に傭船者，その代理人，またはその関係会社の被用者であっても）の雇傭により生ずる一切の損害，請求，責任および義務に対し，傭船者，その被用者および代理人に補償するものとする。

ただし，
(i) 上記の補償は，船主が自らそのような水先人，曳船および荷役業者を雇傭した場合にその責任を制限する権利を有することになる額を超えないものとする。また
(ii) 傭船者は，自然損耗を除き，荷役業者の使用により本船に生じたあらゆる損害につき，船主が相当の努力をしたにもかかわらず荷役業者からその賠償を得ることができない場合に限って，責任を負うものとする。

明示の表現がない場合，船主は貨物の積込，積付，揚荷に責任を負う。前出363頁参照。しかしながら，傭船者が荷役業者を手配し支払う場合，荷役業者が履行する荷役の責任は傭船者に移転する（『航海傭船（*Voyage Charters*）』の270頁を参照，そこに多数の事案が引用されている）。したがって第16条の最初の文章のみがある場合，船主に積付責任が残る一方，傭船者が起用し，支払う荷役業者が履行する他の作業の責任は傭船者に移転するかとも考えられる。しかしこの最初の文の言外の意味は次の2番目の文の補償条項によりおそらく退けられよう。特に，傭船者が雇用する水先人，曳船または荷役業者が「船主の被用者となりその業務に従事し，その指揮下にあるとみなされる」との表現により退けられる。もちろん傭船者自身がそういう作業に関して過失ある場合には，見解は異なることがあろう。

Clause 17 — Supernumeraries

180　17. Charterers may send representatives in the vessel's available accommodation upon any voyage made
181　under this charter. Owners finding provisions and all requisites as supplied to officers, except liquors. Charterers
182　paying at the rate of …… per day for each representative while on board the vessel.

第17条 — 定員外の乗船

17. 傭船者は，本契約に基づくいかなる航海においても，本船の船室が利用できるときは代表者を乗船させることができる。船主は，酒類を除き，職員と同じ食事および一切の必需品を支給し，傭船者は，本船乗船期間中，代表者１人につき１日当たり..........の..........料金を支払う。

Clause 18 — Sub-letting

183   18. Charterers may sub-let the vessel, but shall always remain responsible to Owners for due fulfilment of
184   this charter.

第18条 — 再 傭 船

18. 傭船者は本船を再傭船に出すことができる。ただし，本契約の正当な履行について常に船主に対し責任を負うものとする。

再傭船の解説については前出199頁参照。

Clause 19 — Final voyage

185   19. If when a payment of hire is due hereunder Charterers reasonably expect to redeliver the vessel before
186   the next payment of hire would fall due, the hire to be paid shall be assessed on Charterers' reasonable estimate of
187   the time necessary to complete Charterers' programme up to redelivery, and from which estimate Charterers
188   may deduct amounts due or reasonably expected to become due for
189   (i) disbursements on Owners' behalf or charges for Owners' account pursuant to any provision
190   hereof, and
191   (ii) bunkers on board at redelivery pursuant to Clause 15.
192   Promptly after redelivery any overpayment shall be refunded by Owners or any underpayment made
193   good by Charterers.
194   If at the time this charter would otherwise terminate in accordance with Clause 4 the vessel is on a
195   ballast voyage to a port of redelivery or is upon a laden voyage, Charterers shall continue to have the use of the
196   vessel at the same rate and conditions as stand herein for as long as necessary to complete such ballast voyage, or
197   to complete such laden voyage and return to a port of redelivery as provided by this charter, as the case may be.

第19条 —— 最終航海

19. 本契約に基づく傭船料支払期日が到来したときに、傭船者が次回の傭船料支払期日の到来前に本船の返船を正当に予測する場合、その支払傭船料は、返船に至るまでの傭船者の計画を遂行するのに必要であると、傭船者が合理的に予測する時間に基づき算出するものとし、傭船者はその算出額から、
　(i) 船主のための立替金または本契約の条項により船主負担となる費用、および
　(ii) 第15条により、返船時本船にある燃料
に対して支払義務のある、または支払義務が生ずると合理的に予想される金額を控除することができる。

返船後、直ちに、支払超過額は船主から返戻され、支払不足額は傭船者から支払われるものとする。

本契約が第4条により終了するときに、本船が返船港へ空船航海をしているか、または積荷航海中である場合には、傭船者は、その空船航海を終了するのに必要とされる期間、または当該積荷航海を終了して本契約に定められた返船港へ回航するのに必要とされる期間につき、本契約に定めるものと同一の傭船料率と条件で本船を引き続き使用するものとする。

定期傭船契約の最終航海の指図が適法か否かの問題は前出173／178頁で検討されている。「最終航海条項」は前出181頁で広く取り扱われている。傭船契約がShelltime 3 書式によったThe World Symphony［1992］2 Lloyd's Rep. 115事件で、記録長官 Donaldson 卿が控訴院で（同判例集118頁で）検討した原則はThe Dione［1975］1 Lloyd's Rep. 115事件（その事実関係は前出179頁に述べられている）とThe Peonia［1991］1 Lloyd's Rep. 100事件（前出174頁参照）の判決から次の表現で抽出されたと述べた。「1．固定期間の傭船契約にはその期間に小さな黙示の許容期間がある。2．明示の許容期間（本事案では『プラスマイナス15日』）付きの固定期間の傭船期間には、黙示の追加許容期間はない。3．上記1.2の事例で『最後の航海』（last voyage）条項がない場合、本船が黙示または明示の許容期間により延長された固定期間の満了後に返船となる場合、引渡遅延が船主有責の原因により生じない限り、傭船者は契約違反となる。4．『最後の航海』（last voyage）条項が必要である。傭船者が、期限どおりに自己の過失なく返船できると合理的に予測できるが、結果的にそういう返船が不可能であると判明するにもかかわらず最終航海を引き受けるよう指図する場合に、傭船者は返船遅延による契約違反から『最後の航海』条項により守られる。5．遅延の結果となりやすい、または遅延の結果となるに違いない航海を傭船者が指図した場合に、『最後の航海』（last voyage）条項が返船遅延による契約違反から傭船者を守るためにあるのであれば、この保護を規定する意図は明確に表現されねばならない」。

Shelltime 3（第18条）の最終航海条項は、傭船者に本船が傭船契約の固定期間（明示または黙示の許容期間を延長した）を超過しそうな最後の航海につき傭船者が指図するのを許容している。しかし、その超過期間中の市場料率が傭船料より高い場合にも、傭船料の損害賠償問題を生じることはない。

World Symphony 号はShelltime 3 書式で定期傭船された。第3条は「傭船者任意でプラスマイナス15日の延長付で6ヶ月」と規定した。第18条は修正されず、次のように規定した。「この第3条の規定にかかわらず、本船がこの傭船期間満了時に航海途上にある場合、傭船者は、本船が就航している往復航海の完了と、傭船契約に定める返船港に帰港するために必要な延長期間中、同一料率と条件で本船を使用できるものとする」。傭船者は15日間の延長選択権を行使し、基本傭船期間は1988年12月24日に終了した。1988年10月4日に傭船者は期日満了までに完了できないことが明らかな最終往復航

海を指図した。結果として返船は1989年1月18日に行われた。船主は12月24日以降の超過期間につき市場料率に基づいて損害賠償請求をした。控訴院はこの請求を退けた。控訴院は多数意見で，第18条が，「この第3条の規定にかかわらず」の文言で始まっていなければ，基本的傭船期間内に返船ができると合理的に予想される最後の航海を許容するだけであったであろうと判示した。多数意見では，この「決定的」文言は，起草者が2個の条項の矛盾を認識しており，第18条に優先権を与えてこの矛盾を解決している，したがって裁判所が第18条に優先権の効果を与えるべきことを示している。傭船者の指図は第18条で適法化されたのであり，傭船者に基本傭船期間内に返船する義務はなかった。そのような印刷条項は，世界的に同じ方法で解決されるべきであり，かつ英国の裁判所はTexaco2書式の非常に類似した第11条についてのNew York仲裁人による取扱を認識すべきことも望まれた。The Pacific Sun, 1983 AMC 830事件と The Narnian Sea, 1990 AMC 274事件を参照。
The World Symphony [1991] 2 Lloyd's Rep. 251および[1992] 2 Lloyd's Rep. 115 (C.A.).

The World Symphony 事件でShelltime3第18条の文言について控訴院が到達した結論に，それとは異なるShelltime4第19条の文言についても裁判所が到達するかどうかは疑わしいようである。第19条の関連規定（194/195行）の冒頭の「本契約が第4条により終了するときに，本船が返船港へ空船航海をしているか，または積荷航海中である場合には，……」この語句が，第19条に優先的効果を与え，かつ傭船者が最後の航海の指図を発したときに基本傭船期間内の返船について無理のない予測が立たない場合，損害賠償請求から傭船者を保護すると裁判所がみなすかどうかは疑わしい。

Clause 20 — Loss of vessel

198 20. Should the vessel be lost, this charter shall terminate and hire shall cease at noon on the day of her loss;
199 should the vessel be a constructive total loss, this charter shall terminate and hire shall cease at noon on the day on
200 which the vessel's underwriters agree that the vessel is a constructive total loss; should the vessel be missing, this
201 charter shall terminate and hire shall cease at noon on the day on which she was last heard of. Any hire paid in
202 advance and not earned shall be returned to Charterers and Owners shall reimburse Charterers for the value of
203 the estimated quantity of bunkers on board at the time of termination, at the price paid by Charterers at the last
204 bunkering port.

第20条 — 本船の滅失

20. 本船が滅失したときは，本契約は終了し，傭船料は本船滅失の日の正午に停止するものとする。本船が推定全損となったときは，本契約は終了し，傭船料は，本船の保険者が本船の推定全損に同意した日の正午に停止するものとする。本船が行方不明になったときは，本契約は終了し，傭船料は最後に本船の消息があった日の正午に停止するものとする。前払傭船料のうち反対給付が得られなかった分は傭船者に返戻するものとし，船主は，本契約終了時の本船の推定燃料油量につき，傭船者が最終補油港で支払った価格で傭船者に返戻するものとする。

定期傭船契約に基づく船舶の滅失は、その発生状況とその原因しだいで異なる結果を生む。特に船舶の滅失、または契約のそれ以上の履行を妨げるかまたは致命的に悪影響を与える他の付随して生じる事件は、履行不能の法理に基づき契約の終了をもたらす。傭船契約の履行不能は前出461／479頁で扱われている。

Shelltime 3 第19条には船舶の推定全損の際に、契約終了の明示の規定がなく、前払傭船料および燃料についての規定を欠く点で、Shelltime 4 の第20条は、Shelltime 3 の相当する条項第19条とは異なる。他のタンカー定期傭船契約は、推定全損の場合に傭船料は本船滅失を生じる事故発生の時点で停止すると定めている（例えばSTB書式の場合、後出750頁参照）。これは代船条項に関連する問題を生ぜしめる（*The Badagry* [1985] 1 Lloyd's Rep. 395 事件参照。その事実経緯は前出146頁に述べられている。また、*Court Line* v. *The King* (1945) 78 Ll.L. Rep. 390 事件と [1961] 2 Lloyd's Rep. 496 と前出464頁の *Niarchos* v. *Shell Tankers* 事件参照）。

推定全損の際に傭船契約は終了し、船舶が推定全損であることに船舶の保険者が同意する日に傭船料は停止するという Shelltime 4 の第20条の規定は、1906年海上保険法の第61条について考慮しているのかも知れない。同条に基づき被保険者は、その任意で本船の滅失を分損、または全損として扱うことができる。船主は同法第62条に基づき保険者に委付の通知をする場合にのみ、一般に推定全損としての保険者の承諾が成立する。したがってある状況の下では、いつ傭船契約が終了するかは船主自身の裁量の問題であるのかも知れない。長期間拘留の場合、この規定は保険者が推定全損に同意する日よりも早い段階で傭船契約は履行不能となるとの主張を退ける。

1943年法改革（履行不能により消滅する契約）に関する法の効果については、前出559頁参照。Shelltime 4 の第20条は同法の第2条2(3)項が適用となる規定であると思われる。

|592|

Clause 21 — Off-hire

205　21. (a) On each and every occasion that there is loss of time (whether by way of interruption in the
206　vessel's service or, from reduction in the vessel's performance, or in any other manner)
207　　　　(i) due to deficiency of personnel or stores; repaires; gas-freeing for repairs; time in and waiting
208　to enter dry dock for repairs; breakdown (whether partial or total) of machinery, boilers or other parts of the
209　vessel or her equipment (including without limitation tank coatings); overhaul, maintenance or survey; collision,
210　stranding, accident or damage to the vessel; or any other similar cause preventing the efficient working of the
211　vessel; and such loss continues for more than three consecutive hours (if resulting from interruption in the vessel's
212　service) or cumulates to more than three hours (if resulting from partial loss of service); or
213　　　　(ii) due to industrial action, refusal to sail, breach of orders or neglect of duty on the part of the
214　master, officers or crew; or
215　　　　(iii) for the purpose of obtaining medical advice or treatment for or landing any sick or injured

216   person (other than a Charterers' representative carried under Clause 177 hereof) or for the purpose of landing the
217   body of any person (other than a Charterers' representative), and such loss continues for more than three
218   consecutive hours; or
219   (iv) due to any delay in quarantine arising from the master, officers or crew having had
220   communication with the shore at any infected area without the written consent or instructions of Charterers or
221   their agents, or to any detention by customs or other authorities caused by smuggling or other infraction of local
222   law on the part of the master, officers, or crew; or
223   (v) due to detention of the vessel by authorities at home or abroad attributable to legal action
224   against or breach of regulations by the vessel, the vessel's owners, or Owners (unless brought about by the act or
225   neglect of Charterers); then
226   without prejudice to Charterers' rights under Clause 3 or to any other rights of Charterers
227   hereunder or otherwise the vessel shall be off-hire from the commencement of such loss of time until she is again
228   ready and in an efficient state to resume her service from a position not less favourable to Charterers than that at
229   which such loss of time commenced; provided, however, that any service given or distance made good by the
230   vessel whilst off-hire shall be taken into account in assessing the amount to be deducted from hire.
231   (b) If the vessel fails to proceed at any guaranteed speed pursuant to Clause 24, and such failure
232   arises wholly or partly from any of the causes set out in Clause 21(a) above, then the period for which the vessel
233   shall be off-hire under this Clause 21 shall be the difference between
234   (i) the time the vessel would have required to perform the relevant service at such guaranteed
235   speed, and
236   (ii) the time actually taken to perform such service (including any loss of time arising from
237   interruption in the performance of such service).
238   For the avoidance of doubt, all time included under (ii) above shall be excluded from any
239   computation under Clause 24.
240   (c) Further and without prejudice to the foregoing, in the event of the vessel deviating (which
241   expression includes without limitation putting back, or putting into any port other than that to which she is bound
242   under the instructions of Charterers) for any cause or purpose mentioned in Clause 21 (a), the vessel shall be
243   off-hire from the commencement of such deviation until the time when she is again

ready and in an efficient state
244 to resume her service from a position not less favourable to Charterers than that at
which the deviation
245 commenced, provided, however, that any service given or distance made good by the
vessel whilst so off-hire
246 shall be taken into account in assessing the amount to be deducted from hire. If the vessel, for any cause or
247 purpose mentioned in Clause 21(a), puts into any port other than the port to which she is bound on the
248 instructions of Charterers, the port charges, pilotage and other expenses at such port shall be borne by Owners.
249 Should the vessel be driven into any port or anchorage by stress of weather hire shall continue to be due and
250 payable during any time lost thereby.
251   (d) If the vessel's flag state becomes engaged in hostilities, and Charterers in consequence of such
252 hostilities find it commercially impracticable to employ the vessel and have given Owners written notice thereof
253 then from the date of receipt by Owners of such notice until the termination of such commercial impracticability
254 the vessel shall be off-hire and Owners shall have the right to employ the vessel on their own account.
255   (e) Time during which the vessel is off-hire under this charter shall count as part of the charter
256 period.

第21条 — オフハイヤー

21. (a) 時間の喪失（本船業務の中断によるものであろうと，業務の能率の低下によるものであろうと，またその他いかなる原因によるものであろうと）が，

   (i) 乗組員の欠員または船用品の不足，修繕，修繕のためのガス・フリー，修繕のため入渠した期間およびその待ち時間，機関，汽罐または本船の他の箇所もしくは本船の属具（無条件にタンク・コーティング部を含む）の故障（部分的であると全体的であるとを問わない），分解検査，保守または検査，衝突，座礁，本船の事故もしくは損傷その他これに類する本船の効率的稼働を妨げる原因により生じ，かつ，そのような喪失時間が3連続時間を超えるとき（本船業務の中断による場合）または合計3時間を超えるとき（業務の部分的喪失による場合），または

   (ii) 船長，職員または部員の側の罷業，就航拒否，指図違反または業務怠慢のため生ずるとき，または

   (iii) 病人または負傷者（本契約第17条に基づき乗船している傭船者の代表者を除く）の診察，治療を得るため，もしくは下船させるために，または（傭船者の代表者を除く）遺体を下船させるために生じ，かつ，そのような時間の喪失が3連続時間を超えるとき，または

   (iv) 船長，職員または部員が，傭船者またはその代理人の書面による同意または指図なしに，伝染病流行地域に上陸したことにより検疫停船期間が延長することによって生ずるとき，または船長，職員もしくは部員の側の密輸その他現地法違反により，税関その他当局に抑留されるために生ずるとき，または

   (v) 本船もしくは本船船主に対する訴訟，または本船もしくは本船船主の規則違反（ただし，傭船者の行為または怠慢により生じたものでないこと）に起因して，国内または外国当局に本船

が抑留されたことで，生ずるときは，
いかなる場合にも，第3条に基づく傭船者の権利または本契約に基づき，もしくは本契約外での傭船者のその他の権利を損なうことなく，本船はそのような時間の喪失の開始時から，本船が再び準備を整え，稼働状態で，そのような時間の損失が始まった地点より傭船者に不利益とならない地点から本船業務を再開するまで，オフハイヤーとなるものとする。ただし，オフハイヤー期間に本船が提供した業務または短縮した距離は，傭船料の控除額の算定にあたり考慮するものとする。
　(b)　本船が第24条に基づく保証速力で航行できず，しかもそれが全面的であろうと部分的であろうと，上記第21条(a)に規定する原因のいずれかによるときは，本第21条に基づき本船がオフハイヤーとなる期間は，
　　(i)　本船がその担保速力で当該業務を遂行するのに要したであろう時間と
　　(ii)　その業務を遂行するのに実際に要した時間（同業務の遂行中断による時間の喪失を含む）との差とする。
　疑義を避けるため，上記(ii)に該当するすべての時間は，第24条に基づく一切の計算から除外するものとする。
　(c)　さらに，また前記権利を損なうことなく，本船が第21条(a)に記載されたいずれかの原因または目的のために，本船が離路（離路という語には本船が傭船者の指図によらずに港に引き返し，または指図以外の港に入港することを無条件に含む）する場合には，そのような離路の開始時から，本船が再び準備を整え，稼働状態で，その離路が始まった地点より傭船者によって不利益とならない地点から本船業務を再開するまで，本船はオフハイヤーとする。ただし，同オフハイヤー期間に本船が提供した業務または短縮された距離は，傭船料の控除額の算定にあたり考慮するものとする。本船が，第21条(a)に記載されたいずれかの原因または目的のために，傭船者の指図によらない港に入るときには，そのような港での港費，水先料その他の費用は船主負担とする。悪天候により，本船がどの港またはどの錨地であれ避難を余儀なくされるときは，傭船料は，それによって生ずる時間の損失についても中断することなく支払われるものとする。
　(d)　本船の旗国が参戦し，その戦争行為のため傭船者が本船を商業的に使用不可能と判断し，船主にその旨を書面で通知したときは，本船は，船主がその通知を受け取った日からその商業的に使用不可能の事態が終了するまで，オフハイヤーとし，船主は自己の費用で本船を使用する権利を有するものとする。
　(e)　本船が本契約に基づきオフハイヤーとなる期間は，傭船期間の一部に含めるものとする。

　第21条の205／206行は業務の中断だけでなく業務能率の低下も含むとして「時間の喪失」を定義する。これと一致して229／230行は，オフハイヤー時間の計算に際して「オフハイヤー中に本船のなした業務または短縮された距離は傭船料を減じる額を査定する際に考慮する」ことを求めている。したがってShelltime 4 の第21条は「正味喪失時間」オフハイヤー条項として案出された。

　対照的にShelltime 3 のオフハイヤー条項（第21条もまた）は「正味喪失時間」というより「期間」条項であると判示された（*The Bridgestone Maru No.3*［1985］2 Lloyd's Rep. 62 事件参照）。したがってShelltime 3 ではオフハイヤー発生の時から本船が準備完了し，時間の喪失が発生した位置ではなく傭船者に不利益とならない位置から業務を再開できる有効な状態になるまで傭船料は支払われない。オフハイヤー条項の一般的解説については前出427／446頁参照，特に「期間」と「正味喪失時間」については，前出429頁参照。

　Bridgestone Maru 号は，Shelltime 3 で 1 年間定期傭船された。傭船契約に基づき，船主は引渡時に本船は NKK の船級であることを保証し，ブタンかつ・またはプロパンの輸送に本船が適するよう相当の注意を尽くすことを船主は保証した。オフハイヤー条項（第21条）は，次のように規定していた。「人員の欠員または船用品の不足，修理，機械または汽罐の（部分的であるとないとにかかわら

ず）故障，衝突または座礁または事故または本船の損傷または本船が効率的に作動するのを妨げる何らかの他の原因による……時間の喪失の場合，そのような時間の喪失の開始時点より，本船が時間の喪失を開始した位置より傭船者に不利益とならない位置で，再び準備完了し効率的な状態で業務を再開するときまで，傭船料の支払期限は到来せずまた，支払義務は生じないものとする」。

傭船契約期間中，移動式ブースターポンプが貨物の揚荷の補助のため船上に装備された。プロパンを揚荷するため Livorno に到着したときに，安全規則の施行の公的管轄機関である RINA は，その規則上使用ポンプは据え付け式でなければならず，そのブースターポンプは規則に適合していないとの理由で，貨物の揚荷を許可しなかった。ブースターポンプの配備は事実上適度に安全であったが，RINA の規則に不適合なゆえの揚荷不可能という事態は，「本船の効率的な稼働を妨げるその他一切の原因」の文言の範囲内に含まれると判示された。Hirst 判事は，83頁で次のように述べた。「……本船の揚荷ができないことは本船自身の規則適合性を疑われる状態に起因する。結果として乗組員が機械すなわちそのポンプの関連する部分を使用できなかった」。

オフハイヤー期間の計算につき，傭船者は，当該条項は「正味喪失時間」条項であると主張した。したがって Livorno で揚荷できなかったときに発生した全喪失時間は勘定に入れられ，その計算は「揚荷不能となった時点まで遡ることができる」と主張した。しかしながら，同判事は同条項は「期間条項」であり，時間喪失は本船が Livorno でドックに入ったときに始まり，他の仕向地に進航すべく Livorno を出港する時点まで継続すると判示した。本船がその全能力を修復し，時間喪失が開始した位置より傭船者に不利益とならない位置で業務を再開したのは，Livorno を出港した時点であった。

The Bridgestone Maru No.3 [1985] 2 Lloyd's Rep. 62.

Shelltime 3 の第21条(i)項の文脈で「本船の効率的稼働を妨げるその他一切の原因」との表現は *The Manhattan Prince* [1985] 1 Lloyd's Rep. 140 事件で本船の物理的状態に関する事項に制限され，国際運輸労連（ITF）によるボイコットの結果としての喪失時間を除くものとして解釈された。

Manhattan Prince 号は，Shelltime 3 書式で傭船された。ITF のボイコットの脅威に対して船主は ITF 条件にあわせて乗組員を雇用することを保証した。その後，船主は ITF 賃金率で支払われない交代乗組員を雇用した。ITF 行動の結果として本船は Oxelsund でボイコットに遭い，遅延を被った。本船はオフハイヤーではないと判示された。Leggatt 判事は，Shelltime 3 書式の第21条(1)項の文脈で「効率的稼働」という文言は「効率的物理的な稼働」を意味し，ITF 行動により傭船者が望む方法で本船が稼働するのを妨げられたけれども，本船は全面的に稼働していたと判示した。

The Manhattan Prince [1985] 1 Lloyd's Rep. 140.

この事案において Shelltime 3 の第21条(i)項を解釈するにあたって Leggatt 判事は報告書の146頁に次のように述べた。「人は同種解釈（*ejusdem generis*）の原則を，特定される時間喪失の原因は実際に『本船の効率的稼働』という文言に基づく適正な意味を明らかにする観点で考慮するかも知れない」（同種解釈（*ejusdem generis*）原則の適用に関する詳細解説は前出439頁にある）。Shelltime 4 の第21条(a)(i)項は，また本船をオフハイヤーにする事由の範疇を拡大し，本船の効率的稼働を妨げる他の原因を決定する範疇は下位条項で参照の前条項に言及して「本船の効率的稼働を妨げるその他の**類似の**原因」という文言の使用により解釈されるべきであることを明示的に規定している。

594 Shelltime 4 の第21条(a)(i)項は，（本船の業務の中断から生じる）時間の喪失が連続3時間を超えて継続する場合，または（業務の部分的喪失から生じる）3時間を超えて累積する場合，本船は第21条(a)(i)項に基づきオフハイヤーとなるものとすると規定している点で Shelltime 3 の第21条(i)項と異なる。この規定は，ある表記の事由に起因する時間喪失が二つの定期入渠の

間に1年につき合計72時間までは，またはその按分時間まではオフハイヤーとして計算しないものとするという趣旨で，Shelltime 3 の第23条の規定に取って代わるものである。

Shelltime 4 の第21条(a)(i)項の効果が The Fina Samco ［1994］1 Lloyd's Rep. 153 事件で検討された。Fina Samco 号は日本の苫小牧と名古屋の2港で原油の揚荷の指図を受けた。本船は苫小牧で10月22日の午前1時12分に揚荷を開始した。その時点と同日の午前8時48分までの間に汽罐の不調のため揚荷を11回中断した。この中断は合計で3時間を超えた。午前8時48分から継続的中断となった。悪化した天候と海象のため離桟命令が出た午前11時15分まで，不調の原因の解析が行われた。原因は突き止められて，11月2日までに修繕されたが，不運な天候と海象のため本船は11月8日まで再度着桟できなかった。

3時間を超えた第21条(a)(i)項に基づく汽罐の故障による時間の喪失であるとの理由で，本船は10月22日の午前1時12分からオフハイヤーであると Fina Samco 号の傭船者は，主張した（補償についての傭船者の代替請求については前出第3条(ii)項を参照）。10月22日の午前1時12分から午前8時48分までの期間に関するオフハイヤークレームについて傭船者は，本船の汽罐はこの期間ずっと効率的ではなかったし，傭船者が求めたのは継続的揚荷であったので，3時間を超えて累積するという第21条(a)(i)項の意味の範囲内での「業務の部分的喪失」であり，したがって揚荷開始時点からオフハイヤーが開始すると主張した。しかしながら Colman 判事は，発生したことは「業務の部分的喪失」を構成せず，本船はこの期間オフハイヤーではないと判示した。同判事は160頁で次のように述べた。「同じ欠陥による業務の別の中断を業務の部分的喪失として同一視することは許すことができない。求められた業務は継続であり，したがって度重なる中断は継続すべきであったものを分断したとの主張は私の判断では第21条(a)項の文脈にはない意味を『業務の部分的喪失』に与える」。

10月22日の午前8時48分からの期間について傭船者は，汽罐の不調がなければ，苫小牧貨物の残りを名古屋で揚荷するようにとの指図を受けたであろうから，気象条件のため本船が3時間未満後の午前11時15分に離桟命令を受けたことは関係ないと主張した。同判事は，オフハイヤー請求において何が考慮されなければならないかは，何が即時に求められる業務であるかということであると強調してこの点についても傭船者の主張を退けた。午前11時15分まで即時に求められる業務は，本船が汽罐の不調のために履行できなかった揚荷である。しかし午前11時15分以降即時に求められる業務は錨地で天候の回復を待つことである。汽罐が11月2日まで修理完了しなかった事実にもかかわらず本船はこのことを履行できたのである。

「船長，職員，または部員の側の命令違反または義務懈怠」のための時間の喪失の場合，本船はオフハイヤーであるという Shelltime 3 の第21条(ii)項の規定は Shelltime 4 の第21条(a)(ii)項に再録されているが，同規定は The Aditya Vaibhav ［1993］1 Lloyd's Rep. 63 事件のオフハイヤー請求の基礎であった。同事件はパームオレイン油とパーム油の輸送後，本船のタンクを洗浄する際に船長と乗組員の側に「義務の懈怠」があったと申し立てられたものである。

The Sargasso ［1994］1 Lloyd's Rep. 412 事件で，乗組員の「義務の懈怠」のために Shelltime 3 の第21条(a)(ii)項に基づき本船はオフハイヤーであると申し立てられた。貨物の一部は汚損のために仕向港で揚荷できず2番目の港で揚げざるをえなかった。Clarke 判事は，汚損が乗組員の側の義務の懈怠による場合，本船は第2番目の港への航海と同港での揚荷の期間オフハイヤーであると考えた。選択的に同判事は，この期間の傭船料に相当する損害賠償請求は，衡平法上の相殺の法理に基づき傭船料と相殺できると考えた（前出306頁参照）。

Shelltime 4 の第21条(a)(ii)項に基づく命令違反のオフハイヤークレームに関する事案について The Houda ［1993］1 Lloyd's Rep. 333 および ［1994］2 Lloyd's Rep. 541 (C. A.) 事件参照。その事実関係は前出第13条に述べられている。

いくつかのタンカー定期傭船契約はオフハイヤー条項に「傭船者の過失により生じた」時間喪失の場合には本船はオフハイヤーにはならないものとすると規定している。*The Berge Sund* [1993] 2 Lloyd's Rep. 453 事件で控訴院は, Mobiltime 傭船契約のオフハイヤー条項の文脈でこの表現の意味を検討した。そして,その条項の「過失」は喪失時間と傭船者の作為または不作為のいずれかとの間の原因関係に言及しているに過ぎず,道義上責められることは言うまでもないが,たぶん契約違反の証明を必要とするようなものではない。*The Berge Sund* 事件はタンク洗浄に関連した別の事案であった。本船は長期傭船で使用された。その傭船契約は, Mobiltime 2 からオフハイヤー条項を含む多くの条項を摂取していた。傭船期間中本船は,傭船者と船長が汚損しているか,規格外であると承知していたブタンを積載するよう指図を受けた。その貨物の揚荷後,空船航海時にタンク洗浄が行われたが,他貨物の積込前の検査時にあるタンクが汚損していることが確認された。タンクが次の貨物の運送のため十分洗浄済として受け入れられるまでには,さらに大変な洗浄作業を要した。結果として本船は遅延した。傭船者は,「本船の効率的作動を妨げる他の一切の原因」による時間の喪失があったので本船の遅延の期間はオフハイヤーであると固執した。紛争を付託された仲裁人は,空船航海中のタンク洗浄につき乗組員側の過失はなかったと裁定したが,証拠に基づいて仲裁人は追加洗浄を必要とした相変わらず続いた汚損の原因に関して結論に到達できなかった。

仲裁人と第1審の Steyn 判事は ([1992] 1 Lloyd's Rep. 460), 本船は次の予期した業務を提供できる,つまり次の貨物の積込を開始できるほどに効率的な状態ではない,したがって本船は遅延の期間オフハイヤーであると決定した。控訴院は,本船の効率的稼働はタンクの追加洗浄を実行しても低下することにはならないとの理由で,その決定を覆した。タンクの追加洗浄の遂行は事実傭船者が必要とした業務そのものであった。Staughton 卿判事は,控訴院報告書の461頁で次のように述べた。「私の意見では,決定的な問題点は1982年の12月20日に本船にとり何が必要な業務であったのかということである。傭船者の指示は何であったのか？ 指図は貨物を積まないことであった。私が言ったように,それは銅片テストに落ちたので,傭船者が指図した最後の事項そのものであった。指図は部分的には明示的に必要に応じ常時黙示的に追加洗浄を遂行することであった。それは求められていた業務であり,本船はそれを遂行するのに十分適合していた。洗浄は通常の方法で定期傭船者が求める行為である。どの貨物を積み込み,その結果いつどんな洗浄が求められるかは傭船者の任意である。特定の事例では傭船者は追加,または特別の洗浄が行われるまで,積込を拒否する場合,求められる業務はその洗浄である。もちろん,そのような追加洗浄の必要性が船主の側の契約違反または『船長,職員または部員の側の義務の過失』に起因する場合もあろう。その場合,傭船者には救済手段があ|596|る。しかしここでは仲裁人は空船航海時の洗浄に過失があったかまたは注意義務が欠如していたとの傭船者の申立を退けた。仲裁人は一度その結論に達するや,本船はオフハイヤーであると,または傭船者は支払済みの傭船料を回収できると主張するが,それは私の考えでは間違いなく失敗すると思う」。

Clause 22 — Periodical drydocking

257   22. (a) Owners have the right and obligation to drydock the vessel at regular intervals of

258   On each occasion Owners shall propose to Charterers a date on which they wish to

259   drydock the vessel, not less than .... before such date, and Charterers shall offer a

port for
260 such periodical drydocking and shall take all reasonable steps to make the vessel available as near to such date as
261 practicable.
262 　　　　Owners shall put the vessel in drydock at their expense as soon as practicable after Charterers
263 place the vessel at Owners' disposal clear of cargo other than tank washings and residues. Owners shall be
264 responsible for and pay for the disposal into reception facilities of such tank washings and residues and shall have
265 the right to retain any monies received therefor, without prejudice to any claim for loss of cargo under any bill of
266 lading or this charter.
267 　　　　(b) If a periodical drydocking is carried out in the port offered by Charterers (which must have
268 suitable accommodation for the purpose and reception facilities for tank washings and residues), the vessel shall
269 be off-hire from the time she arrives at such port until drydocking is completed and she is in every way ready to
270 resume Charterers' service and is at the position at which she went off-hire or a position no less favourable to
271 Charterers, whichever she first attains. However,
272 　　　　(i) provided that Owners exercise due diligence in gas-freeing, any time lost in gas-freeing to
273 the standard required for entry into drydock for cleaning and painting the hull shall not count as off-hire, whether
274 lost on passage to the drydocking port or after arrival there (notwithstanding Clause 21), and
275 　　　　(ii) any additional time lost in further gas-freeing to meet the standard required for hot work or
276 entry to cargo tanks shall count as off-hire, whether lost on passage to the drydocking port or after arrival there.
277 　　　　Any time which, but for sub Clause (i) above, would be off-hire, shall not be included in any
278 calculation under Clause 24.
279 　　　　The expenses of gas-freeing, including without limitation the cost of bunkers, shall be for
280 Owners account.
281 　　　　(c) If Owners require the vessel, instead of proceeding to the offered port, to carry out periodical
282 drydocking at a special port selected by them, the vessel shall be off-hire from the time when she is released to
283 proceed to the special port until she next presents for loading in accordance with Charterers' instructions,
284 provided, however, that Charterers shall credit Owners with the time which would have been taken on passage at
285 the service speed had the vessel not proceeded to drydock. All fuel consumed shall be paid for by Owners but

286　Charterers shall credit Owners with the value of the fuel which would have been used on such notional passage
287　calculated at the guaranteed daily consumption for the service speed, and shall further credit Owners with any
288　benefit they may gain in purchasing bunkers at the special port.
289　　　　(d) Charteres shall, insofar as cleaning for periodical drydocking may have reduced the amount of
290　tank-cleaning necessary to meet Charterers' requirements, credit Owners with the value of any bunkers which
291　Charterers calculate to have been saved thereby, whether the vessel drydocks at an offered or a special port.

第22条 ─ 定期入渠

22. (a) 船主は、…………毎に本船を入渠させる権利および義務を有する。その都度船主は本船の入渠を希望する日を少なくとも…………前までに傭船者に申し出るものとし、一方、傭船者は定期入渠を行うための港を申し出、その期日に実務上可能な限り近い日に本船を利用できるよう合理的なあらゆる手続を取るものとする。

傭船者がタンクの洗浄液と残滓以外の貨物を揚げ切って、本船を船主の使用に委ねた後、船主は、実務的に可及的速やかに自己の費用で本船を入渠させるものとする。船主は、タンクの洗浄液および残滓を受入施設で処理する義務を負い、その費用を支払うものとし、またそれによって得られる金銭を収得する権利を有するものとする。ただし、これにより船荷証券または本契約に基づく積荷損害賠償請求権は損なわれない。

(b) 定期入渠が、傭船者の申し出た港（入渠を行うための適切な設備およびタンクの洗浄液と残滓の受入施設を有さなければならない）において行われるときは、本船がその港に到着したときより、入渠が終了して、あらゆる点で傭船者の業務を再開する準備が整い本船がオフハイヤーとなった地点または傭船者にとってそれより不利益とならない地点のいずれかに最初に到達するまで、本船はオフハイヤーとする。ただし、

(i) 船主がガス・フリーを行うのに相当の注意を尽くすことを条件として、船体の清掃と塗装の目的で入渠するために要求される基準までガス・フリーを行う際に生じた喪失時間は、（第21条にかかわらず）入渠する港に向かう途中で生じたものであろうと、その港に到着後に生じたものであろうと、オフハイヤーとして計算されないものとする。また

(ii) 火気工事をするため、または貨物タンクへ入るために要求される基準に合致するために、さらにガス・フリーの実施により喪失した追加時間は、それが入渠港への途上で生じたものであろうと、その港に到着後に生じたものであろうと、オフハイヤーとして計算する。

上記(i)による場合を除き、オフハイヤーとなる期間は、第24条に基づくいかなる計算にも含まれないものとする。

ガス・フリーの費用は、無条件に燃料費を含め、船主負担とする。

(c) 船主が、申出のあった港へ行く代わりに、自ら選んだ専用港で定期入渠を行うことを要求する場合には、本船がその専用港へ向かうために解放されたときから、次に傭船者の指図に従って船積のために提供されるまでの間は、本船はオフハイヤーになるものとする。ただし、本船がその船渠へ向かわなかったと仮定して、常用速力で航海するのに要したであろう時間については傭船者が船主に対し負担するものとする。消費した燃料は一切船主が支払うものとする。ただし、前記の仮定の航海で消費されたとみられる燃料を常用速力に要する1日当たりの保証消費量で算出し、その代価を傭船者は船主に対し負担するものとする。さらに傭船者は船主に対し、その専用港での燃料購入に際し得られる便益を供与するものとする。

(d) 本船の入渠が申出のあった港で行われるか、専用港で行われるかに関係なく、定期入渠を行うための清掃が傭船者の要求を満たすのに必要なタンク清掃の総量を減少する場合に限り、傭船者はそ

れによって節約されたと算定される燃料代を船主に支払うものとする。

　第22条(a)項に基づき傭船者が提示した入渠港が本船の入渠に必要なすべての設備を整えているが，傭船者が船主の自由に本船を委ねる時点またはその頃にその施設が使用中で利用できない場合には，本条項に基づく問題が生じ得る。第22条(b)項に基づき，そういう港には定期入渠に「適切な設備」とタンク洗浄水と残滓の受入「施設」がなければならない。港は適切な能力のある船渠を有するだけでなく，船渠は傭船者が船主の自由に本船を委ねる時点またはその頃に実際に利用できる要があるとの見解により，「適切な設備」の文言の使用は重要であろう。しかし，船主がどんな作業の遂行を計画しているか，または完了するまでにどれくらい時間を要するかを傭船者は通常承知していない。傭船者が適当な船渠が空いていない港を誠実に提示する場合，船主は空くまで入渠を待って遅延する危険を負担するか，または第21条(c)項に基づき自ら選んだ「特別」な港を選択しなければならない。

Clause 23 — Ship inspection

292　23. Charterers shall have the right at any time during the charter period to make such inspection of the
293　vessel as they may consider necessary. This right may be exercised as often and at such intervals as Charterers in
294　their absolute discretion may determine and whether the vessel is in port or on passage. Owners affording all
295　necessary co-operation and accommodation on board provided, however,
296　　　(i) that neither the exercise nor the non-exercise, nor anything done or not done in the exercise or
297　or non-exercise, by Charterers of such right shall in any way reduce the master's or Owners' authority over, or
298　responsibility to Charterers or third parties for, the vessel and every aspect of her operation, nor increase
299　Charterers' responsibilities to Owners or third parties for the same ; and
300　　　(ii) that Charterers shall not be liable for any act, neglect or default by themselves, their
301　servants or agents in the exercise or non-exercise of the aforesaid right.

第23条 ― 検　　船

　23. 傭船者は，本傭船期間中いかなる時でも，本船に対し自ら必要と考える検査を行う権利を有するものとする。この権利は，傭船者がまったく自らの任意で決定する都度または間隔毎に，かつ，本船が碇泊中であると航海中であるとを問わず，行使できるものとする。他方，船主は一切の必要な協力と船内便宜を提供するものとする。ただし，
　　(i) 傭船者がその権利を行使すると否とにかかわらず，またはその権利の行使，不行使によって何らかのことが行われると否とにかかわらず，本船および本船運航のあらゆる状況に対する船長または船主の権限ないしはそれらに関する傭船者または第三者に対する船長または船主の責任は，決して軽減しないものとし，かつ，同じくそれらに関する船主または第三者に対する傭船者の責任も増加しないものとする。また
　　(ii) 傭船者は，上記権利の行使・不行使による自己，その被用者または代理人によるいかなる行為，過失もしくは懈怠に対しても責任を負わないものとする。

第23条で傭船者は在港中であれ航行中であれ,必要と考える場合には本船を検船する権利を有する。しかし,第23条(ii)項の規定により,傭船者は権利の行使または不行使の際に傭船者自身,その被用者,または代理人の行為,過失または懈怠につき責任を負わない。この免責は狭く解釈されるべきであり,検船のための本船上における傭船者代表側の過失は,検船権限の実際の行使で生じたものでない限り免責されないと思われる。

Clause 24 — Detailed description and performance

302 24. (a) Owners guarantee that the speed and consumption of the vessel shall be as follows: —

303 Average speed   Maximum average bunker consumption
304 in knots   main propulsion—   auxiliaries
305   fuel oil/diesel oil fuel oil/diesel oil
306 Laden   tonnes   tonnes

307 Ballast

308   The foregoing bunker consumptions are for all purposes except cargo heating and tank cleaning
309 and shall be pro-rated between the speeds shown.
310   The service speed of the vessel is knots laden and knots in ballast and in the absence
311 of Charterers' orders to the contrary the vessel shall proceed at the service speed. However if more than one
312 laden and one ballast speed are shown in the table above Charterers shall have the right to order the vessel to
313 steam at any speed within the range set out in the table (the "ordered speed").
314   If the vessel is ordered to proceed at any speed other than the highest speed shown in the table,
315 and the average speed actually attained by the vessel during the currency of such order exceeds such ordered
316 speed plus 0.5 knots (the "maximum recognised speed"), then for the purpose of calculating any increase or
317 decrease of hire under this Clause 24 the maximum recognised speed shall be used in place of the average speed
318 actually attained.
319   For the purposes of this charter the "guaranteed speed" at any time shall be the then-current
320 ordered speed or the service speed, as the case may be
321   The average speeds and bunker consumptions shall for the purposes of this Clause 24 be
322 calculated by reference to the observed distance from pilot station to pilot station on all sea passages during each
323 period stipulated in Clause 24 (c), but excluding any time during which the vessel is (or but for Clause 22 (b) (i)
324 would be) off-hire and also excluding "Adverse Weather Periods" being (i) any periods during which reduction
325 of speed is necessary for safety in congested waters or in poor visibility (ii) any days,

noon to noon, when winds
326 exceed force 8 on the Beaufort Scale for more than 12 hours.
327   (b) If during any year from the date on which the vessel enters service (anniversary to anniversary)
328 the vessel falls below or exceeds the performance guaranteed in Clause 24(a) then if such shortfall or excess
329 results
330   (i) from a reduction or an increase in the average speed of the vessel, compared to the speed
331 guaranteed in Clause 24(a), then an amount equal to the value at the hire rate of the time so lost or gained, as the
332 case may be, shall be deducted from or added to the hire paid;
333   (ii) from an increase or a decrease in the total bunkers consumed, compared to the total bunkers
334 which would have been consumed had the vessel performed as guaranteed in Clause 24 (a), an amount equivalent
335 to the value of the additional bunkers consumed or the bunkers saved, as the case may be, based on the average
336 price paid by Charterers for the vessel's bunkers in such period, shall be deducted from or added to the hire paid.
337   The addition to or deduction from hire so calculated for laden and ballast mileage respectively
338 shall be adjusted to take into account the mileage steamed in each such condition during Adverse Weather
339 Periods, by dividing such addition or deduction by the number of miles over which the performance has been
340 calculated and multiplying by the same number of miles plus the miles steamed during the Adverse Weather
341 Periods, in order to establish the total addition to or deduction from hire to be made for such period.
342   Reduction of hire under the foregoing sub-clause (b) shall be without prejudice to any other
343 remedy available to Charterers.
344   (c) Calculations under this Clause 24 shall be made for the yearly periods terminating on each
345 successive anniversary of the date on which the vessel enters service, and for the period between the last such
346 anniversary and the date of termination of this charter if less than a year. Claims in respect of reduction of hire
347 arising under this Clause during the final year or part year of the charter period shall in the first instance be settled
348 in accordance with Charterers' estimate made two months before the end of the charter period. Any necessary
349 adjustment after this charter terminates shall be made by payment by Owners to Charterers or by Charterers to
350 Owners as the case may require.
351   Payments in respect of increase of hire arising under this Clause shall be made promptly after

352　receipt by Charterers of all the information necessary to calculate such increase.

第24条 ── 本船の細目および性能

24. (a) 船主は本船の速力および燃料消費量が次のとおりであることを保証する。

平均速力（ノット）	最大平均燃料消費量	
	主機	補機
	燃料油・ディーゼル油	燃料油・ディーゼル油
貨物積載時	トン	トン
	燃料油・ディーゼル油	燃料油・ディーゼル油
空船時	トン	トン

上記燃料消費量は，貨物の加熱とタンク清掃を除くすべての用途を含み，記載の両速力の間で比例按分するものとする。

本船の常用速力は，貨物積載時……ノット，空船時……ノットで，傭船者の別段の指図がない限り，本船は常用速力で航行するものとする。ただし，上掲の表に貨物積載時速力と空船時速力がそれぞれ二つ以上記載されているときは，傭船者は，その表に示された範囲内のいかなる速力（「指図速力」）でも本船に航行指図を出す権利を有するものとする。

本船が，同表に記載された最高速力以外の速力で航行するよう指図され，その指図の期間中に本船の実際に達成した平均速力が，指図速力プラス0.5ノット（「最大認知速力」）を上回るときは，本第24条に基づき傭船料の増減を計算する際，実際に達成した平均速力に置きかえて最大認知速力を用いるものとする。

本契約に基づく「担保速力」とは，いずれの時点にせよ，その時点での指図速力または常用速力を指すものとする。

本第24条に基づく平均速力および平均燃料消費量は，第24条(c)に規定された各期間における全航行水域上のパイロット・ステーションからパイロット・ステーションまでの測定距離を参照して計算するものとする。ただし，上記期間からは，本船がオフハイヤーとなった（または第22条(b)(i)がなければオフハイヤーとなっていたであろう）期間を除外し，また(i)輻輳水域や視界不良水域で安全のため減速が必要だった期間，(ii)ビューフォート風力階級で風力8を上回る強風が12時間以上にわたり吹いた日（正午から正午を基準）など，「荒天期間」も除くものとする。

(b) 本船が，業務を開始した日を基準とする年間（開始日から開始日までの年単位）を通じ，第24条(a)で担保された性能を上回った場合，または下回った場合には，そのような性能の過不足が，

　(i) 第24条(a)の保証速力に比較して，本船の平均速力が増加または減少したときは，節約または喪失された時間につき傭船料率によって算出した額に見合う金額を，それぞれ支払傭船料に上乗せするか，または傭船料から控除するものとする，

　(ii) 本船が第24条担保どおりの性能を出していた場合に消費したであろう総燃料油量に比較して，実際に消費した総燃料油量が増加，または減少するときは，余分に消費され，または節約された燃料油につき，当該期間に傭船者が本船の燃料油代に支払った平均価格に基づき算出した価額に見合う額を，それぞれ支払傭船料に上乗せするか，または傭船料から控除するものとする。

積載航行距離および空船航行距離につき各々以上のように計算された傭船料の増額または減額は，荒天期間の各状況の中で航海した距離を考慮して調整するものとする。すなわち，当該期間に対して支払うべき傭船料の増額ないし減額の総計を確定するために，当該の増額ないし減額を，当該の性能で航行した距離で除し，それに「同距離に荒天期間中に航海した距離を加算した数」を乗ずるものとする。

前記本条(b)に基づく傭船料の減額は，傭船者の取りうるその他のいかなる救済方法に拠る権利をも損なわないものとする。

(c) 本第24条に基づく計算は，毎年本船が業務を開始した日に応当する日を終了日とする1年間毎に，そして1年に満たないときは前回の応当日から本契約の終了日までの期間につき行うものとす

る。本傭船期間の最終年または最終の1年に満たない期間において本条に基づき生ずる傭船料の減額に関する請求は，まず最初に本傭船期間の終了2ヶ月前になされる傭船者の見積に従って精算するものとする。本契約終了後精算の必要があれば，場合に応じ船主が傭船者に，または傭船者が船主にそれぞれ支払うものとする。

　本条に基づき生ずる傭船料の増額についての支払は，傭船者がその増額を計算するのに必要なすべての資料を入手しだい速やかに行うものとする。

　Shelltime 3の第24条は，本船がオンハイヤー中の全期間の全航海につき計算した最大燃料消費量で担保平均速力を規定しているが，Shelltime 4の第24条(a)項は，本船の速力を輻輳した海域または視界不良で安全のため落とす場合，または風が12時間を超えてビューフォート風力階級8超となるような「悪天候期間」を性能計算から除外している。それから337／341行の第24条(b)項で，悪天候期間の航走を評価する罰金または報奨金の按分比例調整が規定されている。

　この論題に関する判決例にはShelltime 4第24条の検討を必要とするものは1件も存しない。これらの事案は主に悪天候期間についての傭船契約上の罰金・報奨金規定の適用が判然としないタンカー定期傭船契約に関係している。裁判所は，原則として荒天中の本船の性能は考慮されるべきであるとの立場に立ってこれらの事案を扱った。

　Didymi Corporation v. *Atlantic Lines & Navigation* [1987] 2 Lloyd's Rep. 166 および [1988] 2 Lloyd's Rep. 108 (C. A.) 事件で，乾貨物の定期傭船契約はタンカー定期傭船契約から典型的な追加条項を取り入れた。その条項は次のとおりである。

　「(1)　本傭船契約書に規定の速力と燃料は船主が表示する。傭船契約期間中の平均の本船の実際の性能がその表示の1つまたは複数を充足しないことが示された場合，傭船料は船主と傭船者で相互に合意した金額だけ公平に減額されるものとする。ただし，その金額は，その充足されない範囲で傭船者に補償するに足る金額をいかなる場合でも超えないものとする。

　(2)　本船は良好な気象条件の下で，本傭船期間中シーブイからシーブイまで（速力は航海日誌記載の全航走距離を全航走時間で除して計算される）全航海を最高粘性1500秒の最良質の燃料油を1日あたり40／41ロングトンの担保消費量で良好な気象条件の下（平穏な海上とビューフォート風力階級3より弱い風力）で担保平均速力15.5ノットを維持できるし，維持する義務がある，ただし本船は港および・または錨地にて長期間碇泊しないものとする，と船主は明記する。

　(3)　上記(2)で船主が担保した速力と燃料消費は本傭船契約の期間の満了時に傭船者により点検される。本船が上記記載の速力と燃料消費を本傭船契約期間中平均で維持できなかったことが判明した場合，傭船者は上記(1)に従って傭船料の減額により補償されるものとする。

　(4)　同様に，本船が上記(2)記載以上の速力かつ・また燃料消費を本傭船期間中平均で維持できたことが判明した場合，船主は前文で規定された減額計算と同じ方法で計算による追加傭船料の補償を受けるものとする」。

　この事案の判決に生じる問題の一つは，天候がビューフォート風力階級が3に達しない平穏な海上ではないときに同条項をいかに適用すべきかということである。Hobhouse判事と控訴院は，次のように判示した。「本船の性能の良成績・悪成績の程度を考慮する際に，風がビューフォート風力階級3以上である期間を含めるのは正しくない。しかし，性能の優劣が確定した場合，契約上の基準に従って計算された本船の性能の成績から生じた当事者の全傭船期間を通じての得失如何を評価することは必要である」。第1審の報告書の171頁でHobhouse判事は，次のように述べた。「良好な気象状況以外の海上の期間について，類似の論理を貫くことができよう。仮定によれば本船は，良好な気象条件の下で担保速力かつ・また燃料消費を維

持できないと証明された。そのため気象条件が良好なときだけでなく不良の場合にも損失を引き起こす。したがって一旦担保違反が良好な気象条件での性能に言及して立証された以上，損失はあらゆる気象条件で証明されたことになりうる。これが，担保速力を気象良好の状態で達成する本船の能力に関係する傭船契約速力担保の単純な形式の下での通常の運用である。その能力と結果としての一切の損失は気象不良状態の下での性能につき専門家の証拠を含む証拠により決定されねばならない。……したがって良好な気象条件の下での性能不足から生じる傭船者の損失が計算されるべき期間は同様に気象不良期間を含むことができるし，一応そうすべきである。専門家の証拠はこれがいかになされるべきかを証明するために必要とされるかも知れない」。

The Gas Enterprise [1993] 2 Lloyd's Rep. 352 事件で Beepeetime 2 の改訂第 5 条を解釈するにあたって，類似の原則が適用された。第 5 条の下位条項 1 は，引渡時に本船は添付の Gas Form C に記載の明細に合致するものとする，そして船主は「本契約に基づき業務期間中本船を……そう……維持する」との船主の担保を含んでいる。第 5 条の下位条項 2 および 3 は担保速力と燃料消費量の数字を記載している。さらに下位条項 4 と 5 は次のように規定する。

「4） 本船の性能の評価のために本船の平均速力と燃料消費はパイロットステーションからパイロットステーションの間でビューフォート風力階級 4 以下の風波で……傭船者の発した指図による各航海において本船の航走距離・時間および燃料消費量に基づいて計算されるものとする。本船が第23条に基づきオフハイヤーとなる期間または視界不良または輻輳した水域で……本船の安全航行のための必要な機関速力の低下による遅延の期間（およびその期間の本船の航走距離または燃料消費量）はこの評価から除外されるものとする。

　　5） 下位条項(4)に基づき精査された航海の期間
　　　(a) 本船の平均速力が 1 航海の間，時に傭船者の船長への指図に基づく平均速力を下回ったり，または超過する場合，時間単位かつ・またはその端数で表される生じた損失または得た時間の節約は，傭船料の時間料率で掛け算される。そして時間の喪失が生じる場合，計算結果の金額は船主から傭船者に支払われるものとする……
　　　(b) 本船の燃料の全消費量が上記の如き傭船者の指図により平均速力で本船が契約を履行する場合の燃料消費量を下回ったり，または超過し，この下位条項(2)に記載の表に従った速力に適用される場合，超過燃料消費の金額に等しい金額が船主から傭船者に支払われるものとする。……」

下位条項 5 は，時間の喪失の評価を「下位条項 4 に基づき精査された航海」に限定することを要求し，下位条項 4 に定義された「航海」は気象不良期間を排除しているので，評価はすべての悪天候期間を必然的に排除しなければならない，と船主の代理として法廷弁護士は主張した。下位条項 5 に基づき評価に気象不良期間を含めると損失の計算に不安定さを取り込むことになるであろうと，さらに船主側は主張した。控訴院は船主の解釈を退けた。Lloyd 卿判事は 366 頁で次のように述べた。「船主の法廷弁護士が拠った文言は，『下位条項 4 に基づき精査された航海の間に……場合』という文言であった。しかし私はこの文言を下位条項 5(a)の『生じた損失』すなわち担保違反から生じる損失を切り詰めるまたは計算を限定するものとして判断できない。計算演習の最初の段階は，気象が風力 4 以下の期間，下位条項 4 に従って各航海の平均速力を算定することである。この算定により，本船の問題の航海期間の速力（と燃料消費）を確定し，船主が違反しているか否かを決定する。……良好な気象の下での本船の速力が各航海について確定されれば，その担保の効果が顕著となる。確定速力が担保速力を下回る場合，または燃料の消費がその速力の担保消費量より大きい場合，傭船者は良好な気象の下で履

行された航海のその一部分ではなく問題の航海のすべての期間につき補償を回収する権利がある。……その担保は，本船が実際に履行する速力ではなく，本船の速力の履行**能力**に関する船主の約束である」。

The Al Bida [1986] 1 Lloyd's Rep. 142 および [1987] 1 Lloyd's Rep. 124（C. A.）事件で生じた問題は平均燃料消費量が計算される期間に関していた。Al Bida 号は，旧版の Standtime 書式に基づく１年間定期傭船により２回連続傭船された。傭船契約書には平均燃料消費量の計算方法に関する特別規定はなかった。傭船契約書の前文には，本船は「通常の稼働状態で穏やかな天候の下貨物満載で速力約15.5ノットを平均燃料消費量24hrs 当たり……満載で53トン IFO1,500，空船で50トンを維持する能力が」あると規定していた。傭船契約書が摂取した C. Gas 書式は「１年間の担保海上速力約15.5ノット」と言及していたが，C. Gas 書式の燃料消費の明細には期間についての言及がなかった。船主は平均燃料消費は傭船契約の２年間の全期間で計算されるので，担保消費量より悪い実績の期間を担保消費量より良い実績を本船が達成した期間で相殺する利益を享受すると船主は主張した。船主は，平均速力は１年間に亘り計算されるべきであるという事実は傭船契約の解釈を裏付けると主張した。仲裁人は船主の主張を退け，航海毎に消費量を平均して燃料消費の担保の違反につき損害賠償額を計算した。この点について Evans 判事と控訴院は仲裁人の裁定を支持した。裁判所は，燃料消費に期間についての言及がないが，速力に関しての１年間の言及は船主が主張した解釈を導くものではないと判断した。さらに，担保が特に記載の平均消費量を維持する本船の**能力**に向けられているので，関連する期間は本船が担保消費量まで達することができない期間したがって担保違反が存する時期であると，裁判所は判断した。担保違反が存しない期間を考慮するのは適切ではな

601 い。速力担保の「約」の意味を扱う判決のその部分に関する解説については前出156頁参照。

Shelltime 3 の第24条に関する２個の報告された事案は主としてそれ自身の特別な事実経緯に拠った。*The Larissa* [1983] 2 Lloyd's Rep. 325 事件で，その事案の Shelltime 3 傭船契約の修正第24条の関連ある部分は次のような規定であった。

>「……船主は本船の平均速力は１日当たり DO２トン FO42トンの最大燃料消費で……少なくとも14.6ノットであることを保証する。……
>　傭船期間の開始から１年間，本船は本条項の保証性能を下回るまたは上回る場合，……(b)ここに保証した１日当たりの平均消費量に関してここに定義した本船の平均消費量の増加または減少からそれぞれ，この不足または超過が生じる場合，傭船料は関連する燃料の超過または節約の価格に等しい金額だけ適当に減額または増額されるものとする。……」

傭船契約の開始前も傭船期間中も本船の実際の燃料消費量は１日当たり42トンではなく，32トンであった。第24条の適正な解釈によれば，本船が傭船業務を開始した時点から，燃料消費の減少はなかったのだから，第24条(b)項の「減少」という文言は，不実記載となるものではないというのが，傭船者の基本的な主張であった。しかしながら，第24条(b)項の「減少」は，第24条前半の保証最大消費量の不足を記述するために使用されているのであって，現実の消費量には言及していない，と判示された。

２番目の事案，*The Evanthia M* [1985] 2 Lloyd's Rep. 154 事件は修正 Shelltime 3 の第24条の燃料消費量保証についての追加条項の効果に関する事案であった。その追加条項により傭船者は浮体貯蔵庫としての本船の使用を許容された。

Clause 25 — Salvage

353   25. Subject to the provisions of Clause 21 hereof, all loss of time and all expenses (excluding any damage to
354   or loss of the vessel or tortious liabilities to third parties) incurred in saving or attempting to save life or in
355   successful or unsuccessful attempts at salvage shall be borne equally by Owners and Charterers provided that
356   Charterers shall not be liable to contribute towards any salvage payable by Owners arising in any way out of
357   services rendered under this Clause 25.
358   All salvage and all proceeds from derelicts shall be divided equally between Owners and Charterers
359   after deducting the master's, officers' and crew's share.

第25条 — 海難救助

25. 本契約第21条の規定を条件として，人命の救助またはその試みもしくは成功または不成功に終わった海難救助の試みから生じた一切の喪失時間および費用（本船の滅失もしくは損傷または第三者に対する不法行為責任を除く）は，船主と傭船者が等分して負担するものとする。ただし，傭船者は，本第25条に基づき提供される救助作業により何らかの点で生じた，船主が負担すべき救助料を分担する責任を負わないものとする。

すべての救助料ならびに遺棄物の売上金は，船長，職員および部員の受取分を控除した後，船主と傭船者の間で等分するものとする。

第27条(b)項に基づき本船は遭難船を曳航し，またはその支援に赴き，かつ人命または財物を救助するために離路する自由を有する。

第25条の仕組では，傭船者は財物または人命を救助する行為の費用を分担するが，本船の滅失損傷の費用，第三者への不法行為責任および船舶自身が救助報酬を支払う責任は分担しない。その結果は，他船の救助を企てる際に救助を根拠に曳航支援を得るとすれば，傭船者に分担する責任はないが，他船を救助する行為の結果として曳船契約で曳船を取る場合には，その費用は傭船者が分担するものと思われる。

Clause 26 — Lien

360   26. Owners shall have a lien upon all cargoes and all freights, sub-freights and demurrage for any amounts
361   due under this charter; and Charterers shall have a lien on the vessel for all monies paid in advance and not
362   earned, and for all claims for damages arising from any breach by Owners of this charter.

第26条 — リーエン

26. 船主は，本契約に基づき支払われる一切の金額に対して，すべての貨物，すべての運賃，再運送賃および滞船料の上にリーエンを有するものとし，傭船者は，反対給付が得られなかった一切の前払

金および船主の本契約違反により生じるすべての損害賠償請求につき，本船上にリーエンを有するものとする。

602 「船主は，本傭船契約上当然受け取るべき一切の金額につき，すべての積荷，再運送賃の上にリーエンを有するものとする」と，規定するニューヨーク・プロデュース書式のリーエン条項の文脈で「再運送賃（sub-freight）」の意味に関して第1審で矛盾する判決が出されている。The Cebu No.1 [1983] 1 Lloyd's Rep. 302事件と The Cebu No.2 [1990] 2 Lloyd's Rep. 316事件につき前出558頁参照。後者の事件で，判事は「運賃（freight）」の語の意味に関して現代的理解に拠って，「再運送賃（sub-freight）」には再傭船料は含まれないと判示した。Shelltime 4 第26条，360行の「滞船料（demurrage）」と「再運送賃（sub-freight）」とが連結しているので，この文脈での「再運送賃（sub-freight）」は船荷証券の運賃と再航海傭船の運賃に限定されるとの判断は支持されるものと思われる。

一般には前出555／556頁と『航海傭船』（Voyage Charters）の339／353頁参照。

Clause 27 — Exceptions

363　27. (a) The vessel, her master and Owners shall not, unless otherwise in this char-
364　ter expressly provided,
　　be liable for any loss or damage or delay or failure arising or resulting from any act, ne-
　　glect or default of the
365　master, pilots, mariners or other servants of Owners in the navigation or management of
　　the vessel; fire, unless
366　caused by the actual fault or privity of Owners; collision or stranding; dangers and ac-
　　cidents of the sea; explosion,
367　bursting of boilers, breakage of shafts or any latent defect in hull, equipment or machin-
　　ery; provided, however,
368　that Clauses 1, 2, 3 and 24 hereof shall be unaffected by the foregoing. Further, neither
　　the vessel, her master or
369　Owners, nor Charterers shall, unless otherwise in this charter expressly provided, be li-
　　able for any loss or damage
370　or delay or failure in performance hereunder arising or resulting from act of God, act of
　　war, seizure under legal
371　process, quarantine restrictions, strikes, lock-outs, riots, restraints of labour, civil commo-
　　tions or arrest or
372　restraint of princes, rulers or people.
373　　(b) The vessel shall have liberty to sail with or without pilots, to tow or go to
　　the assistance of vessels
374　in distress and to deviate for the purpose of saving life or property.
375　　(c) Clause 27 (a) shall not apply to or affect any liability of Owners or the ves-
　　sel or any other relevant
376　person in respect of
377　　　(i) loss or damage caused to any berth, jetty, dock, dolphin, buoy, mooring
　　line, pipe or crane
378　or other works or equipment whatsoever at or near any place to which the vessel may
　　proceed under this charter,
379　whether or not such works or equipment belong to Charterers, or

380   (ii) any claim (whether brought by Charterers or any other person) arising out of any loss of or
381 damage to or in connection with cargo. All such claims shall be subject to the Hague-Visby Rules or the Hague
382 Rules, as the case may be, which ought pursuant to Clause 38 hereof to have been incorporated in the relevant bill
383 of lading (whether or not such Rules were so incorporated) or, if no such bill of lading is issued, to the
384 Hague-Visby Rules.
385   (d) In particular and without limitation, the foregoing subsections (a) and (b) of this Clause shall not
386 apply to or in any way affect any provision in this charter relating to off-hire or to reduction of hire.

第27条 ― 免　　責

27.（a）本契約書に別段の明示の規定がない限り，本船，本船船長ならびに船主は，船長，水先人，船員その他船主の被用者の航行または本船の取扱に関する行為，過失または不履行，船主の故意または重過失に基づかない火災，衝突または座礁，海上の危険および事故，汽罐の爆発，破裂，シャフトの破損，船体または装備もしくは機関の隠れた欠陥により生じる，またはその結果によるいかなる滅失，損傷，遅延または不履行に対しても，責任を負わない。ただし，本契約第1条，第2条，第3条および第24条は上記によって影響を受けないものとする。さらに，本船，本船船長，船主または傭船者は本契約書に別段の明示の規定のない限り，不可抗力，戦争行為，裁判上の差押え，検疫上の制限，ストライキ，ロックアウト，暴動，労働制限，内乱，君主または統治者または人民による拘留または拘束から生じるまたはその結果によるいかなる滅失，損傷，遅延または本契約の不履行に対しても，責任を負わない。
　（b）本船は，水先人をつけてまたは水先人なしで航行し，遭難中の船舶を曳航し，またはその救助に向かい，また人命もしくは財産を救助するために離路する自由を有するものとする。
　（c）第27条(a)は，次のものについては船主，本船その他一切の関係者のいかなる責任に対しても適用されず，または影響を与えないものとする。
　　（i）傭船者の所有物であると否とを問わず，本契約に基づく本船の仕向地またはその近くにあるすべてのバース，桟橋，ドック，繋留柱，ブイ，繋船索，パイプ，クレーンその他一切の構造物または設備に与えた損害または損傷，または
　　（ii）貨物に対する，または貨物に関する一切の滅失もしくは損傷から生じるあらゆる賠償請求（傭船者またはその他の者によって提起されたかどうかを問わない）。かかるすべての損害賠償請求は，本契約第38条に従って当該船荷証券に摂取されることになるヘーグ・ヴィスビー・ルールまたはヘーグ・ルールにそれぞれ従うものとし（各ルールがその趣旨で摂取されているか否かを問わない），かかる船荷証券が発行されていないときは，ヘーグ・ヴィスビー・ルールによるものとする。
　（d）特に，かつ無条件に，上記本条(a)および(b)は，オフハイヤーまたは傭船料の減額に関する本契約のいかなる規定にも適用されず，またはいかなる点でも影響を与えないものとする。

　免責は過失責任を対象とするとの明確な意図が示されない限り，本条項は，免責は過失責任を対象としないという解釈の一般原則を条件とする。免責条項とその解釈について，前出489／496頁参照。
　Shelltime 3 第28条は，ヘーグ・ルール，またはヘーグ・ヴィスビー・ルールに言及していないとの意味で，Shelltime 4 第27条は Shelltime 3 免責条項（第28条）と異なっている。一方

Shelltime 4 第27条(c)(ii)項は,「貨物の滅失損傷からまたは貨物に関連して発生する」賠償請求は,ヘーグ・ルール,またはヘーグ・ヴィスビー・ルールを条件とすると規定している。Shelltime 4 第27条(a)および(b)項は,Shelltime 3 の第28条原文をほとんど同一の表現で再現しているが,一方Shelltime 4 第27条(c)(i)項は,本船が航行する場所またはその近くのバース,構築物,設備の滅失損傷を別個に扱っている。

　Shelltime 4 第27条(a)項の免責の多くの用語は,ヘーグ・ルールの第Ⅳ条2項の免責の用語を反映している。その用語は同じ意味を持つと思われる (その点については,『航海傭船』 (*Voyage Charters*) の752／770頁を参照)。

　しかしながら,第27条(a)項363／368行の免責の**趣旨**はおそらく異なるであろう。航海の開始時点またはその以前に本船を堪航性あるものとする際の運送人の注意義務の欠如が滅失損傷の603原因ではない場合のみヘーグ・ルールの第Ⅳ条2項の免責に拠ることができる。しかしながら,第1,2または第3条の違反が滅失損傷の原因ではない場合のみ,363／368行の免責に拠ることができる。第1条および第2条(a)項は,本傭船契約に基づく引渡時点の堪航性および適合性の**絶対的**要件である (前出668頁参照)。第2条(b)項は,傭船期間を通して業務につき**絶対的義務**を課している。そして,第3条(i)項は,傭船期間を通して第1条と第2条(a)項に記載の条件 (the conditions) を維持しまたは修復するため相当の注意を尽くすという継続的義務を課している。

　第27条(b)項に関して,1航海のための定期傭船に離路の概念は適用されるかも知れないが,離路の概念は通常の期間定期傭船に関連があるとは考えられない (航海傭船の文脈での離路に関する解説については,『航海傭船』 (*Voyage Charters*) の185頁を参照)。したがって第27条(b)項に含まれる自由は,極力迅速に全航海を遂行する第2条(b)項に基づく義務,および傭船者の指図と指示に適合する第13条(a)項に基づく義務とに,主として関連があるように見える。第27条(c)(ii)項によりヘーグ・ルール,またはヘーグ・ヴィスビー・ルールが適用される場合,人命または財物の救助のために離路する自由は同ルールの第Ⅳ条4項により拡張されるであろう (前出505頁参照。救助に関連する第25条参照)。

　第27条(c)(i)項の趣旨は,この下位条項に参照されたバース,構築物,または設備の滅失損傷の場合に,船主が第27条(a)項の免責の恩恵もヘーグ・ルール,またはヘーグ・ヴィスビー・ルールの免責の恩恵にも浴しないということである。船主は「船舶の航海または取扱における船長,水先人,船員,または船主の他の被用者の行為,過失または懈怠による……滅失損傷につき責任を負」わないという第27条(a)項の免責によりそういう一切の損傷から船主が責任を免除されるというこの下位条項は,一切の損害賠償請求に対処するためにShelltime 4 に導入された (*Australian Oil Refining* v. *Miller* [1968] 1 Lloyd's Rep. 448 事件と *The Satya Kailash* [1984] 1 Lloyd's Rep. 588 (C.A.) 事件および前出599頁参照)。したがって,傭船契約の条件 (terms) に対する船主の違反から,または船主に責任がある過失から傭船者に生じた滅失損傷に対して,この下位条項が対象とする状況の中で船主には責任がある。

　「貨物の滅失損傷からまたは貨物に関連して生じる」賠償請求に関して,第27条(c)(ii)項の効果により第1条および第2条の傭船契約の開始時点での堪航性の絶対的義務は,その時点で本船を堪航性あらしめるために相当の注意を尽くすという義務に減じるだけでなく,傭船契約に基づく各航海の開始時点までまたはその以前に堪航性につき相当の注意を尽くすという義務を課する (前出594頁および *Adamastos Shipping* v. *Anglo-Saxon Petroleum* (*The Saxon Star*) [1958] 1 Lloyd's Rep. 73 事件参照)。しかしながら,*The Saxon Star* 事件で,第27条(c)(ii)項におけるような特別な損害賠償請求にヘーグ・ルールの制限はなかったことは留意されるべきである。

ヘーグ・ルール,またはヘーグ・ヴィスビー・ルールの詳細解説については,『航海傭船』(*Voyage Charters*)の701／804頁と前出593／602頁参照。

第Ⅲ条の6項および6項の2に基づく出訴期限

The Stena Pacifica［1990］2 Lloyd's Rep. 234 事件で,Shelltime 4 の第27条(c)(ii)項が,ヘーグ・ヴィスビー・ルールまたはヘーグ・ルールの第Ⅲ条6項の1年の出訴期限を摂取するように適用されるかという問題が生じた。その事件で,傭船者は貨物の揚荷遅延につき船主に損害賠償請求をし,その損害賠償は,遅延に関して貨物関係者が傭船者に対して行った請求を参照して計算された。傭船者が船主に対して申し立てた傭船契約違反が,同ルール上の船主の義務に基づき生じたか,または同一面上の違反である場合,かつ損害賠償請求が貨物の滅失損傷または貨物に関連して発生する場合,その損害賠償請求は第27条(c)(ii)項の意味の範囲内で「同ルールを条件と」するということができると判示された。したがって1年の出訴期限が適用された。

Stena Pacifica 号は Shelltime 4 で傭船された。その傭船期間中,本船は定期傭船者によりポルトガルからナイジェリアへの航海に再傭船された。ナイジェリアで揚荷は非常に遅延した。定期傭船者は,これはポンプの欠陥によると申し立てた。再傭船者は,本来であれば貨物が揚げられたであろう時間と実際の揚荷完了の時間の間の貨物の市場価格の変動による損失につき定期傭船者に損害賠償の請求をした。揚荷後1年経過して,定期傭船者は再傭船者が提起し請求したのと同額を船主に対し遅延揚荷に関する損害賠償として請求し,船主に対する仲裁を開始した。船主は第27条(c)(ii)項によりその請求は期限を喪失していると主張した。

Evans 判事は,貨物の物理的滅失損傷でなくとも,貨物に関する金銭的損失は第27条(c)(ii)項の「貨物の滅失損傷,または貨物に関する滅失損傷」の定義の範疇に入るとの先例(*Goulandris* v. *Goldman*［1957］2 Lloyd's Rep. 207（同判例集222頁）事件および *Renton* v. *Palmyra*［1950］2 Lloyd's Rep. 379 事件）に疑問を抱かなかった。しかしそのこと自身ではその請求がヘーグ・ルールを「条件とする」には不十分であった。請求の基となる違反がヘーグ・ルールの船主の義務に基づき発生した,またはその同一面上に存することをさらに示す必要があった。請求がヘーグ・ルールに関連しない傭船契約の条件の違反に基づく場合には,その請求が「貨物の,または関連した滅失損傷」に関すると言えてもヘーグ・ルールは適用されない。

The Stena Pacifica［1990］2 Lloyd's Rep. 234.（［1993］1 Lloyd's Rep. 257 と［1994］2 Lloyd's Rep. 506（C. A.）と後出718頁の *The Fiona* 事件参照）

しかし,ヘーグ・ヴィスビー・ルールが第27条(c)(ii)項により,傭船契約に基づき提起される損害賠償請求に適用され,その請求は傭船者に生じた貨物責任に関しての船主に対する傭船者の賠償請求である場合,そういう賠償請求の期限はヘーグ・ヴィスビー・ルール第Ⅲ条6項の2が規定する期限であると思われる。第Ⅲ条6項の2は次のように規定する。「第三者に対する補償の訴訟は事案が係属している法廷地の法が許容する期限内に提起される場合,前節で規定の年数の終了後でも提起しうる。しかしながら許容期間は補償の訴訟を提起した者がその補償請求を解決したとき,またはその者自身に令状が送達されたときから3ヶ月未満であってはならない」。

この規則は,*The Xingcheng*［1987］2 Lloyd's Rep. 210 事件に関し枢密院で審理された。これは,ヘーグ・ヴィスビー・ルールを条件としない通し船荷証券に基づく第一次運送人が,貨物が接続運送人の手元にあるときに生じた貨物損傷に関する責任を招来した事件で,第一次運送人はヘーグ・ヴィスビー・ルールを条件とする接続船荷証券に基づき賠償を求めて出訴した。接続運送人はヘーグ・ヴィスビー・ルールの第Ⅲ条6項の1年の期限に拠った。第一次運

送人は第Ⅲ条6項2に拠った。Brandon卿は後者の適用を支持して、次のように述べた（同判例集213頁）。第Ⅲ条6項の2は第Ⅲ条6項の一般性に特別の例外規定を創り出すものである。したがって6項の2が適用される事案では、それは6項とは離れて、それ自身の別個の効果を持たねばならない。6項の2が適用される事案は、船主Aが貨物所有者Bに対し実際の、または潜在的な責任があり、船舶または船主Cに対し損害賠償の方法で賠償を請求する事案である。船主Aの船舶または船主Cへの請求が、ヘーグ・ヴィスビー・ルールが適用される運送契約に基づき行われる場合、請求を提起するのに許容される時間は、6項の2で記載の時間であり、6項記載の時間ではない。船主Aが船舶または船主Cに対して賠償を請求する貨物所有者Bへの責任は、ヘーグ・ヴィスビー・ルールが適用される運送契約に基づき生じる要があることは、6項の2の明示の要件ではない」。

　英国法の下でのそのような事案での6項の2に基づき適用される出訴期限は1980年出訴期限法により6年である。傍論ではあるが、ヘーグ・ヴィスビー・ルールが適用される第27条(c)(ii)605項に基づく傭船者による船主に対する同様の損害賠償請求も6年の出訴期限を条件とすると述べられた。

　第Ⅲ条6項と6項の2に関する解説については、『航海用船』（*Voyage Charters*）の732／743頁と前出509頁参照。

「戦争行為」

　Shelltime 3の免責条項（第28条）は *The Chemical Venture* [1993] 1 Lloyd's Rep. 508事件で、本船は良港で安全港間のみに使用されることを確実にするために相当の注意を尽くすというShelltime 3第3条に基づく傭船者の義務という文脈で考察された。その事案（事実関係は前出678頁で記述されている）で、傭船者が提出した主張の一つは、たとえ傭船者が第3条の義務に違反していると推定しうる場合であっても、それにもかかわらず第28条の免責に拠ることができる、そして特に「……本傭船契約に別途特段の規定がない限り、本船、船長、傭船者のいずれも戦争行為……から生じる……結果として生じる、本傭船契約に基づき滅失損傷、遅延、不履行につき一切責任を負わない……」という規定に拠ることができるということであった。

　この主張を拒否して、Gatehouse判事は船主の法廷弁護士の主張を採用して、次のように述べた（同判例集516頁）。「戦争行為の危険により港が非安全で、傭船者が第3条に違反していると推定しうる場合、第28条により傭船者は擁護されるのか。(a)戦争行為により非安全港で／間で本船が使用されないように相当の注意を尽くす義務が第3条に基づき傭船者にある。(b)第28条は一般免責条項であり、一義的に戦争危険を目指しているものではない。解釈の問題として、不履行（およびそれから結果として生じる一切の滅失損傷）が免責危険の一つにより、引き起こされたときのみ、第28条は傭船者を保護する。特に(i)傭船者自身の過失から生じる責任について傭船者は第28条により保護されない。*The Emmanuel C* [1983] 1 Lloyd's Rep. 310事件のBingham判事による312, 313および314頁。これは、*The Satya Kailash* [1984] 1 Lloyd's Rep. 588, 597（C. A.）事件で認められている。(ii)第28条は交戦のために非安全である港に関して第3条に基づく相当の注意を尽くす義務から傭船者を救済することを意図していない。(c)第3条に違反して本船を安全港間に使用することを確実にするために傭船者が相当の注意を尽くすことができずに本船が戦争行為の危険に曝されることになった場合に、戦争行為によるというよりも傭船者自身の過失により不履行となったのであり、第28条により傭船者は保護されない」。

Clause 28 — Injurious cargoes

387　28. No acids, explosives or cargoes injurious to the vessel shall be shipped and without prejudice to the
388　foregoing any damage to the vessel caused by the shipment of any such cargo, and the time taken to repair such
389　damage, shall be for Charterers' account. No voyage shall be undertaken, nor any goods or cargoes loaded, that
390　would expose the vessel to capture or seizure by rulers or governments.

第28条 ─ 有害貨物

28. いかなる酸類，爆発物または本船に有害な貨物も船積してはならず，前述の規定に拠る権利を損なうことなく，かかる貨物の船積に起因する本船への一切の損害，また同損害の修繕に要した時間は，傭船者の負担とする。統治者または政府によって本船が拿捕または差押えられる危険のある航海は引き受けないものとし，またそのような危険のあるいかなる物品または貨物も船積しないものとする。

　この条項と第27条の関係はいくぶん不安定をもたらすかも知れない。第27条(c)(ii)項の規定によると第27条(a)項（一般免責条項）は，「貨物の滅失・損傷または貨物に関連して発生する……一切の損害賠償請求」に関して船主または本船または他の一切の関係者の責任に適用されないし，影響しない。さらに第27条の下位条項によると「あらゆるそのような損害賠償請求は」ヘーグ・ヴィスビー・ルールまたはヘーグ・ルールに従う。したがって有害貨物に関するヘーグ・ルールまたはヘーグ・ヴィスビー・ルールの第Ⅳ条6項は，傭船者であろうと他の何者かが提起するにせよ（380行参照）「貨物の滅失・損傷からまたは貨物に関連して生じる」損害賠償請求がある場合のみに，適用されると思われる。後出 The Fiona 事件でヘーグ・ヴィスビー・ルールが法の定めるところにより船荷証券に適用される場合，第Ⅳ条6項は，有害貨物の船積に関してコモン・ローの黙示の義務に優先する排他的法典を構成する，と判示された。しかしながら Shelltime 4 の第27条と第28条の趣旨は，ある状況の下では第Ⅳ条6項ではなく，コモン・ローの原則に任せることを必要とするということかも知れない。さらに，第28条の387行は，「本船に危害を及ぼす貨物」に言及しているだけで他貨物に有害であるかも知れない貨物については，何も述べていないことを留意すべきである。第Ⅳ条6項に関する解説と有害貨物に関するコモン・ロー上の義務について前出221／225頁参照。

　　　Fiona 号は，1番タンクが爆発した。そのタンクには法の定めによりヘーグ・ヴィスビー・ルールが適用される船荷証券に基づき貨物の所有者が船積した燃料油があった。船積されたその燃料油は貨物火点以下の温度で本船のタンクの上方空間に爆発性のガス体を出す性質があり，これが発生した爆発の原因となったと船主は申し立てた。貨物所有者は，爆発は燃料油の前荷コンデンセートの残滓の混入によると主張した。Diamond 判事は，次のように判示した。(1)船積された燃料は，第Ⅳ条6項の意味での範疇において船主はその性質と特性を知って承諾したものではない爆発の原因となる危険な性質がある。(2)第Ⅳ条6項は，特に同ルールが法律により適用される場合には，コモン・ローに基づく黙示の義務にとって代わる排他的法典である。しかし(3)爆発の主原因は，燃料油にコンデンセートが混入したことである。この点につき船主は第Ⅲ条1項に違反し，本船を堪航性あらしめるのに，相当の注意を尽くすことはできなかった。(4)船主は第Ⅲ条1項に基づく堪航性につき義務違反しているので第Ⅳ条6項に拠ることはできない。
　　　第4番目の点について控訴院は Diamond 判事の判決を肯定した。
　　　The Fiona ［1993］1 Lloyd's Rep. 257 と ［1994］2 Lloyd's Rep. 506（C. A.）.

第28条の389/390行は，「統治者または政府により本船が拿捕または差押えに曝されるような」航海の引受，または貨物の積込を禁止している。「拿捕」または「差押え」の語は，保険法で十分に定義された意味を有する。*Cory* v. *Burr* (1883) 8 App. Cas. 393事件で次のように指摘された。「『拿捕』は，敵または交戦国による差押えまたは奪取のあらゆる行為を当然に含むものと思われる。『差押え』は，『拿捕』より広い語で，『拿捕』を超えると思われ，合法的権力，または圧倒的勢力により強制的に占領するあらゆる行為を含むものと合理的に解釈されるJ。しかし，定期傭船契約の文脈では，この用語はより広い商業的解釈を与えられるであろう。*Tonnevold* v. *Finn Friis* [1916] 2 K. B. 551事件で1914-1918年戦争（第1次世界大戦）の勃発の時点でまだ通用していた定期傭船契約は「支配者または政府による拿捕，差押え，本国送還，または罰金の危険を含む航海は引き受けられず，そのような書類，貨物，人員も船積されないものとする」と規定していた。1915年船主は敵国潜水艦の攻撃の危険のためにある航海を拒否した。船主は傭船契約の条項により拒否する正当な事由があるという仲裁人の裁定を支持して，Scrutton判事は，その報告書の552頁に次のように述べた。仲裁人は正当な商業的見解を持った。その見解は，「……当事者の意図は，『支配者または政府』により本船の占有権を奪われる危険に船主が曝される航海を船主に引き受けさせるべきではないということは明白である。そして，『拿捕』および『差押え』の語を使用する際に，それが船主から本船を奪う支配者または政府の行為を示していることは明白である。」ということであった。

Clause 29 — Grade of bunkers

391　29. Charterers shall supply marine diesel oil/fuel oil with a maximum viscosity of ... . Centistokes at 50
392　degrees Centigrade/ACGFO for main propulsion and diesel oil/ACGFO for the auxiliaries. If the Owners require
393　the vessel to be supplied with more expensive bunkers they shall be liable for the extra cost thereof.
394　Charterers warrant that all bunkers provided by them in accordance herewith shall be of a quality
395　complying with the International Marine Bunker Supply Terms and Conditions of Shell International Trading
396　Company and with its specification for marine fuels as amended from time to time.

第29条 — 燃料油の品質

29. 傭船者は，主機用として，摂氏50度において最大粘度………cs/ACGFOの舶用ディーゼル油・燃料油を，また補機用として，ディーゼル油・ACGFOを供給するものとする。船主が本船に，より高価な燃料油を供給するよう要求するときは，船主はその割増費用を負担するものとする。

　傭船者は，本条に基づいて供給する一切の燃料油がInternational Marine Bunker Supply Terms and Conditions of Shell International Trading Companyおよび随時改正される舶用燃料油に関するその細則に合致する品質であることを保証する。

Clause 30 — Disbursements

397　30. Should the master require advances for ordinary disbursements at any port, Charterers or their agents

398　shall make such advances to him, in consideration of which Owners shall pay a commission of two and a half per
399　cent. and all such advances and commission shall be deducted from hire.

第30条 ― 諸　　掛

30.　船長が，港において通常の諸掛のために立替金を要求するときは，船主がそれに対して2.5パーセントの手数料を支払うことを条件に傭船者またはその代理人は船長に立替払をなすものとし，かかる一切の立替金および手数料は傭船料から控除するものとする。

Clause 31 ― Laying-up

400　31. Charterers shall have the option, after consultation with Owners, of requiring Owners to lay up the
401　vessel at a safe place nominated by Charterers, in which case the hire provided for under this charter shall be
402　adjusted to reflect any net increases in expenditure reasonably incurred or any net saving which should
403　reasonably be made by Owners as a result of such lay-up. Charterers may exercise the said option any number of
404　times during the charter period.

第31条 ― 繋　　船

31.　傭船者は，船主と協議の後，傭船者によって指定された安全港において本船を係船するよう船主に要求する選択権を有するものとする。その場合は，本契約で定めた傭船料は，相当な理由によって生じた費用の純増分，またかかる繋船の結果船主によって合理的になされた純節約分を反映するように調整するものとする。傭船者は，傭船期間中，同上権利を何回でも行使することができる。

　傭船者が，本条項に基づく選択権を行使する場合，本船を繋船する安全な場所を指定する傭船者の義務の性質は論議となる事柄であるかも知れない。本傭船契約の第4条76／78行は，第4条または本傭船契約の他の条項の規定にかかわらず「傭船者は，自己が本船を仕向けるいかなる場所の安全性も保証するものではなく，上述の相当の注意を尽くさなかったことにより生じた滅失または損害を除いては，それに関し何ら責任を負わないものとする。」と規定する。しかしながら繋船場所に安全な場所を指定する第31条の義務は相当の注意を尽くすことに限定されないと思われる。第31条はそのような相当注意義務の限定に言及していないだけではなく，第4条の限定的相当注意義務は，特に本船の使用に関係している。然るに第31条は本船が使用されない状況を取り扱っている。それにもかかわらず，*The Evia (No.2)* [1982] 2 Lloyd's Rep. 307事件で，安全港担保義務の要件を，港の指定時に安全であると予測できることだけであると解釈することで納得した貴族院の考察は，第31条の義務にも適用できよう（*The Evia (No.2)* 事件の論議について前出242頁参照）。

Clause 32 — Requisition

405　32. Should the vessel be requisitioned by any government, de facto or de jure, during the period of this
407　charter, the vessel shall be off-hire during the period of such requisition, and any hire paid by such government in
408　respect of such requisition period shall be for Owners' account. Any such requisition period shall count as part of
409　the charter period.

第32条 ── 徴　　用

32. 本傭船期間中, 本船がいずれかの政府により, その政府が事実上または法律的に確立された政府であるか否かを問わず, 徴用された場合は, 本船はその徴用期間中オフハイヤーとする。その徴用期間に対してかかる政府により支払われた傭船料は, 船主の収得とする。かかる徴用期間はすべて傭船期間の一部として算入するものとする。

　徴用の意味は法律, または規則により定義されよう。例えば1939年賠償 (国防) 法の第17節(1)は, 徴用を「財産に関してその財産を占有し, またはその財産を徴用機関の自由にする要求を」意味すると定義した。関連する制定法上の定義はなかったが, 本船を政府の自由に委ねることが絡まない本船への単なる指図と徴用の区別が行われたものの, 裁判所はその用語自身の範囲を記述するのをためらった。*Bombay & Persia Steam Navigation* v. *Shipping Controller* (1921) 7 Ll.L. Rep. 226 事件で記録長官 Sterndale 卿は, 海運統制機関が戦時に船舶に出した命令を考察して, 次のように述べた (同判例集227頁)。「……[海運統制機関] が, 実際に行ったのは, 想定していた港へ直航する代わりに海運統制機関, またはある他の機関が必要とするときに, 船舶またはその貨物を占有する権限を行使できるように Port Said 行を本船に指示することであった。そしてその必要は生じなかった。生起したことは, 指図に従い本船は離路したということだけである。私は, *The Sarpen* [1916] P. 306 事件で広い意味での徴用を定義することを拒否した。そして私は拒否を続けるつもりである。しかしともかくそれは政府による政府の目的のためのある種の使用を想定している。そうでなければ行かなかった所へ本船が行くように指示しただけである。……私の考えではそれは徴用ではない……」

　Sutherland v. *Compagnie Napolitaine D'Eclairage* (1920) 36 T. L. R. 724 事件 (本船に対する英国政府のための貨物積込の指示は徴用を構成すると判示された) と *France Fenwick* v. *The Crown* (1926) 26 Ll.L. Rep. 52 事件と *Nicolaou* v. *Minister of War Transport* (1944) 77 Ll. L. Rep. 495 事件参照。

　命令または指図を代行して出す機関は政府とみなされるべきかという問題が, Gencon 傭船契約書の戦争条項の文脈で *Luigi Monta* v. *Cechofracht* [1956] 2 Lloyd's Rep. 97 事件 (その事実関係は前出660頁に記載されている) で考察された。この事案で設定された原則は第32条の「いずれの政府にせよ, その政府が事実上または法律的に確立された政府であるか否かを問わず」の語にも適用されると思われる。

　本船が徴用される場合, 何が起こるかについて明示の規定がこの条項になされているが, この条項にかかわらず本船の徴用はある状況では傭船契約の履行不能となる。履行不能の一般について461／479頁, そして徴用に関する先例について468頁参照。王国の国防のため, 必要な期間の占有に国の権限は限定されているので, 王の特権に基づく本船の徴用は単に一時的占有取得に過ぎないという, *Port Line* v. *Ben Line Steamers* [1958] 1 Lloyd's Rep. 290 事件の

Diplock 判事の所見を考慮することは履行不能の関係事案では適切であるのかも知れない。

Clause 33 — Outbreak of war

409　33. If war or hostilities break out between any two or more of the following countries; U.S.A., U.S.S.R.,
404　P.R.C., U.K., Netherlands-both Owners and Charterers shall have the right to cancel this charter.

第33条 ― 戦争の勃発

33. 戦争または敵対行為が次の国家のうちの二国またはそれ以上の国々の間で勃発した場合は，船主および傭船者は共に本契約を解約する権利を有する：米国，ソビエト，中華人民共和国，連合王国，オランダ。

事実関係が後出の *Kawasaki K. K. K.* v. *Bantham Steamship* 事件で，類似条項の「戦争」の用語は商業人により解釈されるような戦争を意味するとして解釈された。しかし，第34条と一緒に第33条を読めば，第34条は「(事実であれ，法律であれ) 戦争」を言っているのに対して第33条は「戦争」を定義していないゆえ，第33条の「戦争」は通俗的または商業的意味ではなく，厳密な意味合いがより強いものとして意図されていると主張できるのかも知れない。

日本の傭船者と英国の船主の間の *Nailsea Meadow* 号の定期傭船契約は次のように規定していた。「日本を含んで戦争が勃発する場合に，傭船者と船主は本傭船契約を解約する自由を持つものとする」。船主が傭船契約を解約しようとした1937年9月18日までに中国と日本の間で戦争が勃発したかという問題が生じた。審判人は，あらゆる証拠を考慮の上，関連の日付の時点で日本と中国の間で戦争が勃発したと裁定した。しかし，傭船者の法廷弁護士は，裁判所は戦争は２つの外国の間で勃発したかにつき，指針として英国政府に問い合わせねばならぬと主張し，「戦争」は国際法の原則に従って厳密に法解釈されなければならないと主張した。この主張を退けて，Goddard 判事と控訴院は，問題が連合王国が戦争状態にあるかとのことであれば，裁判所は行政府から指針を求めなければならないかも知れないことを認めるが，審理の対象である本傭船契約条項の「戦争」は，この状況で「商業的に理解される」用語として解釈されるべきであると判示した。

Kawasaki K. K. K. v. *Bantham Steamship* (1938) 61 Ll.L. Rep. 331および (1939) 63 Ll.L. Rep. 155 (C.A.).

609　保険証券と定期傭船契約の戦争危険保険条項の文脈で「敵対行為 (hostilities)」の用語は，交戦国により行われた敵対行動を意味し，戦争状態の存在を必要条件とすると判示された (*Spinney's* v. *Royal Insurance* [1980] 1 Lloyd's Rep. 406 (同判例集437頁) 事件参照)。そこで諸事案が引用されている。*Britain Stemaship* v. *The King* [1921] 1 A.C. 99 事件で T. 99 定期傭船契約書に基づき英国政府は本船に「宣戦布告の前であれ後であれ」敵対行為または軍事行動のあらゆる結果に対して船舶を付保する契約を結んだが，Wrenbury 卿は貴族院で次のように述べた (同判例集133頁)。「……『敵対行為 (hostilities)』なる語は『戦争状態の存在』を意味しないが，『敵対行動の行為 (acts of hostility)』または (次のように実詞を用いると)『敵対行動の作戦 (operations of hostility)』を意味する。この文は，『宣戦布告の前であれ後であれ (戦争の) 敵対行動作戦，または (戦争の作戦に類似した) 軍事行動のあらゆる結

果』と読まれるかも知れない。長い意味をその語に帰することは，つまり『戦争状態の存在のあらゆる結果』は，人が意図していたものとして心に抱いている何かをはるかに超える範囲をその表現に与えるであろう」。

したがって，戦争が法律上，特定の国々の間で宣言される場合，または特定の国の間に事実上の戦争状態が存在し，特定国の一つが他方の特定国に対して敵対行動を冒す場合，第33条は解約権を生じることを意図している。

第33条にソビエト連邦が言及されているが，しばしば「旧USSRの一部であった国または共和国（旧USSRの構成国であった複数の国，または共和国同士のみの宣戦布告は除かれる）」と言い換えられる。

Clause 34 — Additional war expenses

411　　34. If the vessel is ordered to trade in areas where there is war (de facto or de jure) or threat of war,
412　Charterers shall reimburse Owners for any additional insurance premia, crew bonuses and other expenses which
413　are reasonably incurred by Owners as a consequence of such orders, provided that Charterers are given notice of
414　such expenses as soon as practicable and in any event before such expenses are incurred. and provided further
415　that Owners obtain from their insurers a waiver of any subrogated rights against Charterers in respect of any
416　claims by Owners under their war risk insurance arising out of compliance with such orders.

第34条 — 戦争による追加費用

34. 本船が，（事実上であれ，宣戦布告がなされている場合であれ）戦争状態にあるまたはそのおそれのある区域へ就航するように指図された場合は，傭船者は，かかる指図に従う結果として，船主に当然に生じる保険料の割増料金，船員の特別手当ならびにその他の費用を船主に補償するものとする。ただし，傭船者はかかる費用につき，実務上できる限り速やかに，かついずれの場合にも，その費用が発生する前に，通知を受けるものとする。さらに船主は，かかる指図に従った結果生じる戦争危険保険に基づく船主の請求に関して，保険者が傭船者に対して有する代位請求権を，保険者より放棄せしめるものとする。

この条項は Shelltime 3 の傭船契約書の戦争による追加費用条項と戦争保険条項に取って代わるものである。この条項は二つの昔の条項をある程度融合したものであるが，重要な点で異なっている。Shelltime 4 の条項は戦争がある地域だけでなく，戦争の脅威のある地域へ航行する指図を扱っている。さらにその指図の結果として発生する追加戦争保険，乗組員の特別手当，他の費用を傭船者が支払うことを求めている。本条項の「戦争」の広い定義は，厳密なまたは法的意味の戦争だけでなく「事実上」の戦争を含み，「戦争の脅威」も広く解釈されるべきで，一国により他の一国に対して正式な戦争の脅威がもたらされるような状況に限定されるべきではないことを示唆している。船主と傭船者が広く本船が指図される地域を戦争の脅威が存する所とみなしたであろうことを示すことは十分であるのかも知れない。

本条項の扱う危険についての安全に関する一切の義務から傭船者を解放する「完璧な法典」

として本条項をみなすべきかという問題が生じるかも知れない（[1982] 2 Lloyd's Rep. 307 および前出242／243頁の The Evia (No.2) 事件および後出727頁参照）。しかし、いずれにせよ本条項は415／416行で、追加保険料、乗組員特別手当、その他費用につき船主に弁償する義務は、船主が保険者から代位求償権放棄を取り付けることを条件とすると規定する。しかしながら、傭船者が本船に航行を指図した位置が戦争または戦争の脅威以外の理由で非安全の場[610]合、傭船者はいずれにせよ第4条に基づく安全性に関する義務から逃れられない。

　Shelltime 3の対応する規定よりもある点で広いが、第34条に基づく追加保険料、乗組員特別手当、その他の費用を支払う傭船者の義務は、ある場合にはShelltime 3の戦争保険条項に基づく追加戦争危険保険を支払う義務より狭いかも知れない。標準戦争危険保険は「戦争……または戦争の脅威」から生じるもの以外の他の危険を含む。特に「戦争」の語は「内乱」を含むと判示されたが (Pesquerias y Secaderos de Bacalao de Espana v. Beer (1949) 82 Ll.L. Rep. 500 (H. L.) 事件、内乱を除いては暴力的内部抗争、または騒動は「戦争」の語の中に入らない (Spinney's v. Royal Insurance [1980] 1 Lloyd's Rep. 406 （同判例集427頁）事件参照。諸事案がそこに引用されている）。しかし、そういう抗争や騒動は標準海上戦争危険保険の填補範囲の中に入るであろう。標準海上戦争危険保険に基づく塡補危険に関する解説についてはMiller著、『海上戦争危険』(Marine War Risks (2nd edn.)) 参照。事実関係が前出617頁に要約されている The Taygetos [1982] 2 Lloyd's Rep. 272 事件でShelltime 3の戦争による追加戦争費用と戦争保険条項とほぼ同一のBeepeetime 2の第38条と第39条が考察された。しかし、その事案は第38条にタイプで追加された追加文言に拠って判決が出された。戦争保険および追加戦争保険料に関する他の事案について前出615／618頁参照。

Clause 35 — War risks

417　35. (a) The master shall not be required or bound to sign bills of lading for any place which in his or

418　Owners' reasonable opinion is dangerous or impossible for the vessel to enter or reach owing to any blockade,

419　war, hostilities, warlike operations, civil war, civil commotions or revolutions.

420　　　　　(b) If in the reasonable opinion of the master or Owners it becomes, for any of the reasons set out in

421　Clause 35 (a) or by the operation of international law, dangerous, impossible or prohibited for the vessel to reach

422　or enter, or to load or discharge cargo at, any place to which the vessel has been ordered pursuant to this charter

423　(a "place of peril"), then Charterers or their agents shall be immediately notified by telex or radio messages, and

424　Charterers shall thereupon have the right to order the cargo, or such part of it as may be affected, to be loaded or

425　discharged, as the case may be, at any other place within the trading limits of this charter (provided such other

426　place is not itself a place of peril).If any place of discharge is or becomes a place of peril, and no orders have been

427　received from Charterers or their agents within 48 hours after dispatch of such messages, then Owners shall be at

428　liberty to discharge the cargo or such part of it as may be affected at any place which

they or the master may in
429 their or his discretion select within the trading limits of this charter and such discharge shall be deemed to be due
430 fulfilment of Owners' obligations under this charter so far as cargo so discharged is concerned.
431　　　　(c) The vessel shall have liberty to comply with any directions or recommendations as to departure,
432 arrival, routes, ports of call, stoppages, destinations, zones, waters, delivery or in any other wise whatsoever
433 given by the government of the state under whose flag the vessel sails or any other government or local authority
434 or by any person or body acting or purporting to act as or with the authority of any such government or local
435 authority including any de facto government or local authority or by any person or body acting or purporting to
436 act as or with the authority of any such government or local authority or by any committee or person having under
437 the terms of the war risks insurance on the vessel the right to give any such directions or recommendations. If by
438 reason of or in compliance with any such directions or recommendations anything is done or is not done, such
439 shall not be deemed a deviation.
440　　　　If by reason of or in compliance with any such direction or recommendation the vessel does not
441 proceed to any place of discharge to which she has been ordered pursuant to this charter, the vessel may proceed
442 to any place which the master or Owners in his or their discretion select and there discharge the cargo or such part
443 of it as may be affected. Such discharge shall be deemed to be due fulfilment of Owners' obligations under this
444 charter so far as cargo so discharged is concerned.
445　　　　Charterers shall procure that all bills of lading issued under this charter shall contain the Chamber of
446 Shipping War Risks Clause 1952.

第35条 ― 戦争危険

35. (a) 船長は，封鎖，戦争，敵対行為，軍事的行為，内乱，暴動または革命が原因で，本船の入港または到着が危険または不可能であると，自らまたは船主が合理的に判断した場合は，いかなる場所であれ，そのような場所向けの船荷証券に署名を要求されることはなく，または署名を義務付けられることもない。

(b) 船長または船主の合理的な判断において，第35条(a)に規定されたいずれかの事由によりまたは国際法の適用により，本傭船契約上指図された場所への本船の到着，入港もしくは積揚が危険または不可能となり，または禁止された場合は（かかる場所を「危険地」という），傭船者またはその代理人はテレックスまたは無線機により連絡を受けしだい，その貨物をまたは影響をうけるその一部を本傭船契約上の就航区域内にある他の場所での，船積または揚荷を指図する権利を有するものとする（ただし，その場所自体が危険地でないものとする）。揚荷場所が危険地であるか，または危険地となり，かつ，その旨の連絡が発せられてから48時間以内に，傭船者またはその代理人が何らの指図も行

わなかった場合は，船主はその貨物をまたは影響をうけるその一部を，船主または船長の裁量により，本傭船契約中の就航区域内で選択するいかなる場所においても，揚荷することができる。かかる揚荷は，そのように揚荷された貨物に関する限り，本傭船契約上の船主の義務の正当な履行とみなすものとする。

(c) 本船は出航，到着，航路，寄港地，停船，仕向地，海域，水域，引渡その他一切の事項に関し，本船の旗国政府，事実上の政府もしくは地方官憲を含むその他の政府もしくは地方官憲またはそのような政府もしくは地方官憲の権限をもって行為しまたは行為すると称する者もしくは団体によって，または本船に関する戦争危険保険の条項に基づき指図または勧告をする権限を有する委員会もしくは者によってなされた一切の指図または勧告に従う権利を有する。そのような指図または勧告によりまたはそれに従った何らかの作為または不作為があっても，それは離路とはみなされない。

本船がそのような指図もしくは勧告によりまたはそれに従うことによって，本契約に基づいて指定された揚荷地へ航行しない場合は，本船は船長または船主がその裁量により選択する場所へ航行し，そこでその貨物をまたは影響を被るその一部を揚荷することができる。かかる揚荷は，そのように揚荷された貨物に関する限り，本傭船契約上の船主の義務の正当な履行とみなすものとする。

傭船者は，本契約に基づき発行されるすべての船荷証券に，1952年海運会議所「戦争危険」約款を含むことを保証する。

本条項は1952年海運会議所戦争条項に基づいている。傭船者は本条項の445／446行であらゆる船荷証券に海運会議所条項を摂取することを求められている。「事実上と法律上」としての前条第34条の戦争の定義にかかわらず，本第35条の「戦争」は定義されていないが，本条項の起源のゆえに厳密な法的意味の戦争だけでなく商業的に解される言葉としての戦争も含むと同[611]じように解釈されるべきものと思われる（*Kawasaki K. K. K.* v. *Bantham Steamship* (1939) 63 Ll.L. Rep. 155 事件と前出722頁参照）。封鎖，敵対行為，軍事的行為，内乱，騒乱，革命のような第35条(a)項に出てきた他の表現の分析について『航海傭船』（*Voyage Charters*）の514／520頁参照。

船長または船主の見解による「危険」

後出 *The Kanchenjunga* 事件で Shelltime 4 の第35条(b)項にいくぶん似た Essovoy 戦争危険条項の規定に基づき，船長は自らが危険であると誠実に判断した港で貨物の積込を拒否する権利がある一方，傭船者のその港への航行の指図が出た時点で，船主は当該港は非安全であると知っていながら，船主は傭船者の指図を拒否する権利を放棄したと判示された。

Kanchenjunga 号は，Kharg 島を含む複数積港の選択権付で連続航海傭船に Essovoy 書式で傭船された。傭船契約は安全港担保義務を含んでいた。本船は Kharg 島での積込を傭船者に指図された。船主の指図に従って本船はそこへ向かい，準備完了通知を出しバース待ちで港の沖に錨泊した。本船が錨泊地で待っている間に Kharg 島に空襲があり爆弾が投下された。そこで船長は Kharg 島から安全な所まで逃げ出し，Kharg 島へ引き返すことを拒否した。仲裁人は Kharg 島は傭船者の指図が出される前からずっと非安全港であると認定し，そして空襲があったときに起こったことは予測された危険の現れそのものであると認定した。仲裁人はさらに船主はずっと危険についてあらゆる重要な事実を知っていたと認定した。

Hobhouse 判事と控訴院と貴族院は，次のように判示した。本件の特定の状況の下で船主は諸事実のすべてを承知の上で傭船者の指図を明白に承諾しており，船主は Kharg 島へ航行せよとの指図を拒否する権利を放棄した。したがって安全港担保につき傭船者の契約違反はなかった。空襲の後 Kharg 島から逃げる際に船主に違反があったかという問題が生じた。

傭船契約の第20条(iv)項は次のように規定していた。

「(a) 本傭船契約に指定の積・揚荷港もしくは船荷証券の条項に従って本船が適切に指図される積・

揚荷港が封鎖される場合，または

　(b)　いかなる戦争，敵対行為，軍事的行為のために……そのような積・揚荷港への入港，またはそのような港での貨物の積・揚荷役が船長または船主が自らの判断で危険である，または禁止されると判断する場合，傭船者は本傭船契約の条項に基づき各々確定した複数の積・揚荷港のうちの他の安全な積・揚荷港で貨物の全部または影響を受ける貨物の一部を積み・揚げることを指図する権利を持つものとする（ただし，その他の港が封鎖されておらず，またはそこへの入港またはそこでの貨物の積・揚げは船長または船主の判断で危険ではない，または禁止されていないことを条件とする）」。

　控訴院と Hobhouse 判事の判断を維持して，貴族院は第20条iv(b)項は船主を損害賠償請求から保護すると判示した。Hobhouse 判事は第1審の報告書の518頁で次のように述べた。「船主は同条項に基づき船長（および船主）は危険であると自らが誠実に判断する港での積込を拒否できると申し立てた。……さらに船長はずっと必要で誠実な確信を抱いていたことは論議の余地がないと申し立てた。……しかし傭船者は，この条項が船長に Kharg 島での貨物積込を拒否する権利を与えるとの主張に反対した。私の判断では，船長は明確に当条項の文言により当然にその権利を暗黙裡に与えられている。同条項は船長が危険な状況下で行う判断に明確に言及している。船長は自らの評価に従って行動する権利を明確に持っているに違いない。仮に同条項を違った風に解釈するとすれば，ありそうもないこととはまったく異なる危険な状況に関連した場合の趣旨を同条項から奪うことになろう。同様に船長は禁止を突破しない権利を持つ。したがって仲裁人が認容した諸事実に基づいて私は，船長は Kharg 島で貨物の積込を拒否する権利があった，と判示する。船長の積込拒否により他の積荷港を指定する選択権が傭船者に生じたが，傭船者は選択権を行使しなかった。船長が Kharg 島での積込を誠実に拒否する権利がある状況下で傭船者は代わりに傭船契約を終了したが，船主の側のいかなる違反も訴えることはできない」。

　The Kanchenjunga〔1987〕2 Lloyd's Rep. 509，〔1989〕1 Lloyd's Rep. 354（C. A.）および〔1990〕1 Lloyd's Rep. 391（H. L.）。

612　放棄の問題に関するさらなる解説については前出142／144頁参照。

　Shelltime 4 第35条(b)項類似の他の戦争危険条項，Beepeetime 2 第40条(2)項は後出 *The Product Star* 事件で検討された。その事件で本船が積込を指図された港へ航行する際の危険は傭船契約締結時に広まっていた周知の危険を超えるものではないと判断された。同時に船主は戦争危険条項に拠ることができず，その指図に応じるのを拒否する正当な事由はないと判示された。

　Product Star 号は，6ヶ月延長の傭船者選択権付きの6ヶ月の期間で1987年4月に Beepeetime 2 で傭船された。船主は傭船契約締結時点で傭船者の配船航路のパターンは時には他のアラビア湾地区を含む航海だが，Ruwais を含むアラブ首長国連邦の諸港で積み込むということを知っていた。追加戦争危険保険条項に基づき傭船者はこの配船航路様式に対するそのときの追加基本戦争保険料と傭船契約時に支払うべき基本戦争保険料を超えるあらゆる戦争保険料を支払うこととなっていた。傭船契約の第40条(2)項は次のように規定していた。

　「(A)　本傭船契約に定める，もしくは本船が船荷証券条項に従って適切に指図された積・揚荷港が封鎖される場合，または

　(B)　戦争，敵対行為，軍事的行為，内乱，騒乱，革命，または国際法の行使のため(a)その積・揚荷港への入港またはその港での積・揚荷役が船長または船主の自らの判断で危険である，または禁止されると判断される場合，または(b)その本船がその積・揚荷港へ到着するのは，船長または船主の判断で危険である，または不可能であると判断される場合，

　その場合に傭船者は貨物のすべてまたは影響を受ける貨物の一部を他の積・揚港で積む・揚げることを指図する権利があるものとする。……」

　傭船契約開始前にアラビア湾の他の地域ではイラン軍・イラク軍の両方が多数の船舶を攻撃したが，アラブ首長国連邦のみに航行する船舶には全然攻撃がなかった。1987年の4月から8月末までの

間に *Product Star* 号は Ruwais から Bangladesh に4航海を遂行した。その間イラン軍とイラク軍の船舶への攻撃は続いた。しかしアラブ首長国連邦に航行する船舶が関係する危険の性質と範囲は増大しなかった。それにもかかわらず9月の始めに船主は傭船契約の第40条に拠って船主と船長の両方がRuwais に入港するのは危険であると判断したとの理由で，積込のため Ruwais に再び航行せよとの指図を拒否した。

　Diamond 判事の判決を維持して，控訴院は次のように判示した。(1)第40条に基づく判断は独断的気まぐれで無分別であってはならず正直に誠実に行使されなければならない。(2)第40条の「危険」を解釈するためには，本船はアラブ首長国連邦に航行すべきであるとの共通の意図が関係する。船主は傭船契約の条項で傭船契約締結時のその港の状況は第40条の目的にとって「危険」ではなかったことを認めた。船主がその危険は増大したとみなす妥当性を船主が証明できるときのみその条項に船主は拠ることができる。そして(3)事実，その危険は増大しなかったし，船主が航行を拒否する際に誠実に判断したかどうかは疑わしい。いずれにせよ船主の拒否は独断的で不当であった。

　The Product Star (*No.2*) [1991] 2 Lloyd's Rep. 468; [1993] 1 Lloyd's Rep. 397 (C. A.). (本事案につき Davenport [1993] LMCLQ 150参照)。

戦争危険と港の安全性

　Shelltime 4 第35条と類似しているが同一ではない Shelltime 3 の戦争危険条項（第36条）は *The Chemical Venture* [1993] 1 Lloyd's Rep. 508 事件で分析された。その事実関係は Shelltime 3 の他の戦争条項（第32条／第35条），安全港担保義務条項（第3条）と免責条項（第28条）の文脈において前出678頁に述べられている。Gatehouse 判事はこれらの条項は第3条の義務を無効にするように契約履行のなんらかの局面が戦争の影響を受ける際に当事者の諸権利を扱う包括的な法典を構成するような方法で成文化されていないと判示した。船主の法廷弁護人の主張を採用して同判例集516頁に同判事は次の文言でこの結論の理由を述べた。「(a)(i)第28条（「免責」）は，戦争の危険に根本的に繋がらない一般的免責条項であり，第35条（「戦争保険」）または第36条（「戦争危険」）と直接的にいかなる方法でも繋がらない。(ii)第32条（「徴用」）は，戦争の遂行に関連する（しかし関連は必要でない）目的のために政府により本船が船主の管理（そしてしたがって傭船契約の役務）から奪われる特別な状況を取り扱うが本船への敵対行為の直接の影響を扱ってはいない。(iii)第33条（「戦争の勃発」）は，ある国々の間の戦争に適用を限られ，そして傭船契約を解約する権利を与えるだけである。(iv)第34条（「戦争による追加費用」）第35条（「戦争保険」）と第36条（「戦争危険」）は本船の航行に関して敵対行為の影響のある側面を一般的に取り扱うが船主の権利を枯渇させるとか，または第3条に優先することを意図しているとは思われない。(b)さらに当該傭船契約に基づき，(i)船主は戦争区域に入るのを拒否する**無条件**の権利を有するものではない。本船が封鎖される（第36条(2)(A)項）か，戦争ゆえに危険な港に配船を指図される場合，第36条は船主が指示に応じるのを拒否するのを許容するだけである。(ii)第5条（「船主は……本船に関するあらゆる保険を支払うもの……」）と第35条に基づき戦争危険保険の基本的費用は船主の負担となる。傭船者は船体機関の協定価格に関連して傭船契約日の料率を超えるものを負担するだけである。(iii)第36条は船主の責任の範囲である傭船料の喪失または他の危険（例えば乗組員の負傷）に対する戦争危険保険を規定していない。(iv)第36条は敵対行為の結果として本船の損傷または乗組員の負傷による喪失時間を規定していない。(v)当該傭船契約の条件は，*The Concordia Fjord* [1984] 1 Lloyd's Rep. 385 事件で Bingham 判事が同判例集387頁で検討した傭船契約の条件とこの重要な面においてほぼ同等で……，そして *The Evia* [1983] 1. A. C. 736 事件で Roskill 卿が同判例集766頁で検討したボルタイム書式の条件とは，同じ点で実質的に異なる。……」（前出242頁参照)。

上記の論拠の多くはShelltime 4 にも適用されるが，Shelltime 4 （第34条）の戦争による追加保険費用条項は，Shelltime 3 の追加戦争費用と戦争保険条項（第34条と第35条）よりある面で範囲が広いことに注目することが重要である。つまり，Shelltime 4 は，船主は保険者から傭船者に対する代位求償権の放棄を取得するとのただし書き条件で戦争または戦争の脅威がある地域での航行の指図の結果として船主に発生した「割増保険料，乗組員の特別手当と他の費用」を傭船者が支払うことを求めている。その代位求償権の放棄の範囲は困難な問題を引き起こすかもしれないが，その範囲はおそらく傭船者が割増保険料を支払うその危険から生じる損失の範囲を超えないであろう。

Clause 36 — Both to blame collision clause

447　36. If the liability for any collision in which the vessel is involved while performing this charter falls to be
448　determined in accordance with the laws of the United States of America, the following provision shall apply:
449　　"If the ship comes into collision with another ship as a result of the negligence of the other ship and any
450　act, neglect or default of the master, mariner, pilot or the servants of the carrier in the navigation or in
451　the management of the ship, the owners of the cargo carried hereunder will indemnify the carrier against all loss, or
452　liability to the other or non-carrying ship or her owners in so far as such loss or liability represents loss of, or
453　damage to, or any claim whatsoever of the owners of the said cargo, paid or payable by the other or non-carrying
454　ship or her owners to the owners of the said cargo and set off, recouped or recovered by the other or non-carrying
455　ship or her owners as part of their claim against the carrying ship or carrier."
456　　"The foregoing provisions shall also apply where the owners, operators or those in charge of any ship
457　or ships or objects other than, or in addition to, the colliding ships or objects are at fault in respect of a collision or
458　contact."
459　　Charterers shall procure that all bills of lading issued under this charter shall contain a provision in the
460　foregoing terms to be applicable where the liability for any collision in which the vessel is involved falls to be
461　determined in accordance with the laws of the United States of America.

第36条 — 双方過失衝突条項

36. 本船の本契約履行中に生じた衝突に関する責任が，米国の法律に基づき裁定されることになる場合には，次の条項を適用する。
「本船が相手船の過失と，本船の航行または本船の取扱に関する船長，乗組員，水先人または船主の被用者の行為，過失または不履行の結果，相手船と衝突した場合には，本契約に基づき運送される貨物の所有者は，相手船，すなわち非搭載船またはその所有者に対して運送人が負う損失または債務に

つき次の限度において運送人に補償するものとする。すなわち，このような損失または債務が当該貨物の滅失，損傷または貨物所有者の有する一切の請求額に相当するものとして，相手船，すなわち非搭載船またはその所有者により相殺，控除もしくは回収されたものに限る。」

「前記の規定は，衝突船舶または衝突物体以外のいずれの船舶または物体の所有者，運航者もしくは管理者が，衝突または接触につき過失ある場合にも適用する。」

傭船者は，本契約に基づき発行されるすべての船荷証券に，本船が関係する衝突に関する責任が米国の法律によって裁定される場合には，上記条項が適用される旨の規定を含むことを保証する。

614 運送人はヘーグ・ルールにより運送船に対する貨物関係者による直接訴訟から保護されているが，その運送人が間接的に貨物関係者に責任を負うこととなる米国法の状況を取り扱うように企図されている本条項に関する解説につき前出607頁および後出778／779頁参照。

本条項は傭船者が本傭船契約に基づき発行されるあらゆる船荷証券は双方過失衝突条項の摂取を履行することを求める。傭船者が履行できず，同条項が含まれていれば保護された責任が含まれていないため，船主に責任が生じる場合には船主は補償を受ける権利がある。

Clause 37 — New Jason clause

462　37. General average contributions shall be payable according to the York/Antwerp Rules, 1974, and shall

463　be adjusted in London in accordance with English law and practice but should adjustment be made in accordance

464　with the law and practice of the United States of America, the following provision shall apply :

465　"In the event of accident, danger, damage or disaster before or after the commencement of the

466　voyage, resulting from any cause whatsoever, whether due to negligence or not, for which, or for the

467　consequence of which, the carrier is not responsible by statute, contract or otherwise, the cargo, shippers,

468　consignees or owners of the cargo shall contribute with the carrier in general average to the payment of any

469　sacrifices, losses or expenses of a general average nature that may be made or incurred and shall pay salvage and

470　special charges incurred in respect of the cargo."

471　"If a salving ship is owned or operated by the carrier, salvage shall be paid for as fully as if the said

472　salving ship or ships belonged to strangers. Such deposit as the carrier or his agents may deem sufficient to cover

473　the estimated contribution of the cargo and any salvage and special charges thereon shall, if required, be made by

474　the cargo, shippers, consignees or owners of the cargo to the carrier before delivery."

475　Charterers shall procure that all bills of lading issued under this charter shall contain a provision in the

476　foregoing terms, to be applicable where adjustment of general average is made in accordance with the laws and

477　practice of the United States of America.

第37条 — ニュー・ジェイソン条項

37. 共同海損分担金は1974年のヨーク・アントワープ・ルールに従って支払うものとし，かつLondonで英国の法律と慣習に従って精算するものとする。ただし，その精算が米国の法律と慣習に従ってなされる場合には，次の条項を適用するものとする。

「航海の開始前または開始後，事由の如何を問わず，過失によると否とを問わず，法律，契約その他により運送人が責任を負わない，またはその結果について責任を負わない事故，危険，損害または災害が発生したときは，貨物，荷送人，荷受人または貨物の所有者は，支払われるまたは支払うことになる共同海損の性質を有する犠牲，損害または費用を共同海損において運送人と分担し，貨物について生じた救助料および特別の費用を支払わなければならない。」

「救助船が運送人の所有または運航するものである場合も，救助船が第三者の所有下にある場合と同一の救助料全額を支払わなければならない。もし要求があれば，貨物，荷送人，荷受人または貨物所有者は，運送人またはその代理人が貨物の概算分担金ならびに貨物に関する救助料および特別の費用を塡補するのに足りるとみなす金員を貨物の引渡前に運送人に預託しなければならない。」

備船者は，本契約に基づき発行されるすべての船荷証券に，前記条項の規定を取り入れて，共同海損の精算が米国の法律と慣習によって行われる場合に，上記条項の規定が適用されるようにすることを保証する。

本条項は共同海損が，ヨーク・アントワープ・ルールに従って支払われ，その精算がLondonでなされることを規定する。本条項は1974年ルールの1990年改訂を含むものと修正されるかもしれないし，または1994年ヨーク・アントワープ・ルールの挿入で取り替えられるかも知れない。また，本条項は精算が米国法および慣習に従って行われる可能性の余地を残している。

米国ハーター法の第3条に含まれる船舶の航海および管理上の過失についての免責は，そのような過失が事故を引き起こした場合に，共同海損分担金を船主はもはや回収できないとした *The Irrawaddy*, 171 U.S. 187 (1897) 事件の米国最高裁の判決の網をくぐることをニュー・ジェイソン条項は意図している。ニュー・ジェイソン条項に関する解説について後出779頁を参照。

この条項はさらに，備船者が備船契約に基づき発行されたあらゆる船荷証券にニュー・ジェイソン条項を含むことを取り計らうように求める。備船者がそれをできずに，同条項が含まれていれば保護されるはずの責任を船主が負う場合には，船主は補償を受ける権利がある。

Clause 38 — Clause Paramount

478　　38. Charterers shall procure that all bills of lading issued pursuant to this charter shall contain the

479　　following clause:

480　　"(1) Subject to sub-clause (2) hereof, this bill of lading shall be governed by, and have effect subject

481　　to, the rules contained in the International Convention for the Unification of Certain Rules relating to Bills of

482　　Lading signed at Brussels on 25th August 1924 (hereafter the "Hague Rules") as amended by the Protocol signed

483　　at Brussels on 23rd February 1968 (hereafter the "Hague-Visby Rules"). Nothing contained herein shall be

484　　deemed to be either a surrender by the carrier of any of his rights or immunities or

any increase of any of his
485　responsibilities or liabilities under the Hague-Visby Rules."
486　　"(2) If there is governing legislation which applies the Hague Rules compulsorily to this bill of lading,
487　to the exclusion of the Hague-Visby Rules, then this bill of lading shall have effect subject to the Hague Rules.
488　Nothing herein contained shall be deemed to be either a surrender by the carrier of any of his rights or immunities
489　or an increase of any of his responsibilities or liabilities under the Hague Rules."
490　　"(3) If any term of this bill of lading is repugnant to the Hague-Visby Rules, or Hague Rules if
491　applicable, such term shall be void to that extent but no further."
492　　"(4) Nothing in this bill of lading shall be construed as in any way restricting, excluding or waiving the
493　right of any relevant party or person to limit his liability under any available legislation and/or law."

第38条 ── 至上条項

38. 傭船者は，本契約に基づき発行されるすべての船荷証券が，次の条項を含むことを保証する。

「(1)本条第(2)項を条件として，本船荷証券は1968年2月23日Brusselsで署名された議定書（以下「ヘーグ・ヴィスビー・ルール」という）により修正された，1924年8月25日Brusselsで署名された船荷証券に関するある規則の統一のための国際条約（以下「ヘーグ・ルール」という）の規則に準拠し，かつ同規則による効力を有するものとする。本証券中に，ヘーグ・ヴィスビー・ルールに基づく運送人の権利もしくは免責を放棄し，または運送人の責任もしくは義務を加重させるものは一切含まれていないものとみなす。」

「(2)ヘーグ・ヴィスビー・ルールを排除して，ヘーグ・ルールを強制的に本船荷証券に適用する準拠法がある場合は，本船荷証券はヘーグ・ルールにより効力を有する。本証券に，ヘーグ・ルールに基づく運送人の権利もしくは免責を放棄し，または運送人の責任もしくは義務を加重させるものは一切含まれていないものとみなす。」

「(3)本船荷証券の条項が，ヘーグ・ヴィスビー・ルールまたは準拠法がヘーグ・ルールの場合これに反するときは，その条件に反する範囲のみを無効とする。」

「(4)本船荷証券の条項は，いかなる場合においても，適用可能な制定法および・または法律に基づき当事者の責任を制限する当事者の権利を制限，排除または放棄するように解釈してはならない。」

本条項はヘーグ・ルールまたはヘーグ・ヴィスビー・ルールを本傭船契約書に摂取する効果を有しないが，傭船者が本傭船契約に従って発行されるあらゆる船荷証券に本条項を含めることを履行するよう求める。傭船者が履行できない場合，第36／37条に基づき既に言及した結果と共に契約違反となる。ヘーグ・ルールまたはヘーグ・ヴィスビー・ルールの摂取の限定範囲は前出第27条(c)項で検討されている。両ルールに関する解説につき『航海傭船』（*Voyage Charters*）の701／805頁を参照（前出593／602頁も参照）。

第38条は，ハンブルグ・ルールが強制的に適用となる限りにおいて，同ルールの摂取についても規定するように通常修正されている。

Clause 39 — TOVALOP

494   39. Owners warrant that the vessel is:
495   (i) a tanker in TOVALOP and
496   (ii) properly entered in   P & I Club
497   and will so remain during the currency of this charter.
498   When an escape or discharge of Oil occurs from the vessel and causes or threatens to cause Pollution
499   Damage, or when there is the threat of an escape or discharge of Oil (i.e. a grave and imminent danger of the
500   escape or discharge of Oil which, it if occurred, would create a serious danger of Pollution Damage, whether or
501   not an escape or discharge in fact subsequently occurs), then Charterers may, at their option, upon notice to
502   Owners or master, undertake such measures as are reasonably necessary to prevent or minimise such Pollution
503   Damage or to remove the Threat, unless Owners promptly undertake the same. Charterers shall keep Owners
504   advised of the nature and result of any such measures taken by them and, if time permits, the nature of the
505   measures intended to be taken by them. Any of the aforementioned measures taken by Charterers shall be
506   deemed taken on Owners' authority as Owners' agent, and shall be at Owners' expense except to the extent that:
507   (1) any such escape or discharge or Threat was caused or contributed to by Charterers, or
508   (2) by reason of the exceptions set out in Article Ⅲ, paragraph 2, of the 1969 International
509   Convention on Civil Liability for Oil Pollution Damage, Owners are or, had the said Convention applied to such
510   escape or discharge or to the Threat, would have been exempt from liability for the same, or
511   (3) the cost of such measures together with all other liabilities, costs and expenses of Owners arising
512   out of or in connection with such escape or discharge or Threat exceeds one hundred and sixty United States
513   Dollars (US $ 160) per ton of the vessel's Tonnage or sixteen million eight hundred thousand United States
514   Dollars (US $ 16,800,000), whichever is the lesser, save and insofar as Owners shall be entitled to recover such
515   excess under either the 1971 International Convention on the Establishment of an International Fund for
516   Compensation for Oil Pollution Damage or under CRISTAL ;
517   PROVIDED ALWAYS that if Owners in their absolute discretion consider said measures
518   should be discontinued, Owners shall so notify Charterers and thereafter Charterers shall have no right to
519   continue said measures under the provisions of this Clause 39 and all further liability to Charterers under this

520 Clause 39 shall thereupon cease.
521   The above provisions are not in derogation of such other rights as Charterers or Owners may have
522 under this charter or may otherwise have or acquire by law or any International Convention or TOVALOP.
523   The term "TOVALOP" means the Tanker Owners' Voluntary Agreement Concerning Liability
524 for Oil Pollution dated 7th January 1969, as amended from time to time, and the term "CRISTAL" means the
525 Contract Regarding an Interim Supplement to Tanker Liability for Oil Pollution dated 14th January 1971, as
526 amended from time to time. The terms "Oil", "Pollution Damage", and "Tonnage" shall for the purposes of this
527 Clause 39 have the meanings ascribed to them in TOVALOP.

第39条 ── TOVALOP（油濁責任に関するタンカー船主間自主協定）

39. 船主は本船が,
    (i) TOVALOP加入船であり，かつ，
    (ii) 正式に..............................P＆Iクラブに加入していること，
そして本契約期間中本船がこれを維持することを担保する。

　本船からの油の流出もしくは排出が油濁損害を発生させ，または発生させるおそれがあるときは，または油の流出もしくは排出のおそれがあるとき（すなわち，もし発生すれば，油濁損害の重大な危険を招来するであろう，油の流出もしくは排出の重大かつ切迫した危険であって，その後実際に流出もしくは排出が生じたと否とを問わない）は，傭船者は自らの選択により船主または船長に通知して，その油濁損害を防止または軽減するために，またはその危険を除去するために合理的に必要とされる措置を講ずることができる。ただし，船主が直ちに同様の措置を講ずるときはこの限りでない。傭船者は，自己のとった措置の種類と結果につき，また時間の許すときは自ら予定している措置の種類につき，船主に絶えず連絡するものとする。傭船者がとった上記のいかなる措置も，船主の代理人として船主の権限に基づきなされたものとみなし，かつその費用は，以下の場合を除き，船主の負担とする。

　(1) そのような流出もしくは排出またはそのおそれが，傭船者に原因があるか，または傭船者が寄与している場合，

　(2) 1969年の油による汚染損害についての民事責任に関する国際条約第3条第2項に規定された免責事項によって，船主がその流出もしくは排出またはそのおそれに関する責任を免除される場合，または同条約の適用により免除されたであろう場合，

　(3) そのような措置の費用とその流出もしくは排出またはそのおそれから生じ，またはそれらに関連して生じる船主のその他一切の責任および諸費用が，本船の1総トン当たり米貨160ドルまたは米貨1,680万ドルのいずれか低い金額を超える場合，ただし，船主が1971年油による汚染損害の補償のための国際基金の設立に関する国際条約またはCRISTALのいずれかにより，その超えた金額を回収する権利を有する場合を除く。

　ただし，船主は，まったく自らの任意で，上記の措置を続行すべきではない，と判断したときは，常に傭船者にその旨を通知する。その後は，傭船者は本条第39条の規定に基づく上記の措置を続行する権利を有せず，本条第39条に基づく傭船者に対するそれ以上の一切の責任は，そのときをもって終了する。

　上記の規定は，傭船者または船主が本契約に基づき有する，または法律もしくは国際条約もしくはTOVALOPによって有するまたは取得する，その他の権利を損なうものではない。

「TOVALOP」とは，1969年1月7日付け油濁責任に関するタンカー船主間自主協定であって，随時改正されたものをいう。また「CRISTAL」とは，1971年1月14日付けタンカーの油濁責任に対する臨時追加補償に関する契約であって，随時改正されたものをいう。「油」，「油濁損害」および「総トン」とは，本条第39条においては TOVALOP においてそれぞれの語に付した意味を有するものとする。

TOVALOP と CRISTAL に関する解説は『航海傭船』(*Voyage Charters*)の553／554頁参照。

616 Clause 40 — Export restrictions

528 　40. The master shall not be required or bound to sign bills of lading for the carriage of cargo to any place to
529 　which export of such cargo is prohibited under the laws, rules or regulations of the country in which the cargo was
530 　produced and/or shipped.
531 　　　Charterers shall procure that all bills of lading issued under this charter shall contain the following
532 　clause:
533 　　　"If any laws rules or regulations applied by the government of the country in which the cargo was
534 　　　produced and/or shipped, or any relevant agency thereof, impose a prohibition on export of the cargo
535 　　　to the place of discharge designated in or ordered under this bill of lading, carriers shall be entitled to
536 　　　require cargo owners forthwith to nominate an alternative discharge place for the discharge of the
537 　　　cargo, or such part of it as may be affected, which alternative place shall not be subject to the
538 　　　prohibition, and carriers shall be entitled to accept orders from cargo owners to proceed to and
539 　　　discharge at such alternative place. If cargo owners fail to nominate an alternative place within 72
540 　　　hours after they or their agents have received from carriers notice of such prohibition, carriers shall be
541 　　　at liberty to discharge the cargo or such part of it as may be affected by the prohibition at any safe place
542 　　　on which they or the master may in their or his absolute discretion decide and which is not subject to
543 　　　the prohibition, and such discharge shall constitute due performance of the contract contained in this bill
544 　　　of lading so far as the cargo so discharged is concerned".
545 　　　The foregoing provision shall apply mutatis mutandis to this charter, the references to a bill of lading
546 being deemed to be references to this charter.

第40条 — 輸出制限

40. 船長は，仕向地向けの貨物の輸出がその貨物の産出国および・または船積国の法律，規則または条例によって禁止されている場合は，その地向けの貨物運送に対する船荷証券への署名を要求されず，またその義務もない。

傭船者は本契約に基づき発行されるすべての船荷証券に次の条項が含まれることを担保する。

「貨物産出国および・または船積国の，またはその関係機関によって適用される法律，規則または条例が，本船荷証券に指定された，またはそれに基づき指図される揚地向けの貨物の輸出を禁止している場合は，運送人は直ちに荷主に対して，その貨物または影響を被るその一部を揚荷するために，代替揚地を指定するよう要求する権利を有する。その代替揚地は上記の禁止を受けない場所とし，かつ運送人は荷主よりかかる代替揚地へ航行し揚荷を行う指図を受ける権利を有するものとする。荷主またはその代理人が運送人からそのような禁止についての通知を受けてより72時間以内に代替地を指定しなかった場合は，運送人はその貨物または影響を被るその一部を，運送人または船長の絶対的裁量において決定した，上記の禁止を受けない安全な場所で揚荷することができる。かかる揚荷は，そのように揚荷された貨物に関する限り，本船荷証券が表象する契約の正当な履行を構成するものとする。」

上記の規定は本契約にも準用し，船荷証券の箇所は本契約と読み替えるものとみなす。

この条項は輸出規制条項があらゆる船荷証券に摂取されることを求めるだけでなく，傭船契約自身に適用されることを545／546行に定めている。

外国法下の禁制または違法の効果については Dicey & Morris 著の『法の抵触』（*The Conflict of Laws*（12th edn.））（1259／1264頁，1280／1284頁，1410／1413頁）参照。

Clause 41 — Law and litigation

547 　41. (a)　This charter shall be construed and the relations between the parties determined in accordance
548 with the laws of England.
549 　　　　(b)　Any dispute arising under this charter shall be decided by the English Courts to whose
550 jurisdiction the parties hereby agree.
551 　　　　(c)　Notwithstanding the foregoing, but without prejudice to any party's right to arrest or maintain
552 the arrest of any maritime property, either party may, by giving written notice of election to the other party, elect
553 to have any such dispute referred to the arbitration of a single arbitrator in London in accordance with the
554 provisions of the Arbitration Act 1950, or any statutory modification or re-enactment thereof for the time being
555 in force.
556 　　　　(i)　A party shall lose its right to make such an election only if:
557 　　　　　　(a)　it receives from the other party a written notice of dispute which—
558 　　　　　　　　(1)　states expressly that a dispute has arisen out of this charter;
559 　　　　　　　　(2)　specifies the nature of the dispute; and
560 　　　　　　　　(3)　refers expressly to this clause 41(c)
561 　　　　　　and
562 　　　　　　(b)　it fails to give notice of election to have the dispute referred to ar-

bitration not later than
563　　　　　　　　　　30 days from the date of receipt of such notice of dispute.
564　　　　　　(ii) The parties hereby agree that either party may—
565　　　　　　　　(a) appeal to the High Court on any question of law arising out of an award;
567　　　　　　　　(b) apply to the High Court for an order that the arbitrator state the reasons for his award;
568　　　　　　　　(c) give notice to the arbitrator that a reasoned award is required; and
569　　　　　　　　(d) apply to the High Court to determine any question of law arising in the course of the
570　　　　　　　　　　reference.
571　　　　(d) It shall be a condition precedent to the right of any party to a stay of any legal proceedings in
572　which maritime property has been, or may be, arrested in connection with a dispute under this charter, that that
573　party furnishes to the other party security to which that other party would have been entitled in such legal
574　proceedings in the absence of a stay.

第41条 ── 法および訴訟

41. (a) 本傭船契約は英国法により解釈され，当事者間の関係は英国法により決定される。
　(b) 本傭船契約に基づき生じるいかなる紛争も，英国裁判所により解決されるものとし，当事者はここにその管轄権に合意する。
　(c) 上記の規定にかかわらず，海上財産をアレストし，またはアレストを維持するいかなる者の権利も損なうことなく，いずれの当事者も，他の当事者に対し書面による選択の通知を交付することにより，1950年仲裁法またはその時に施行されているその修正法または改正法の規定に従ってLondonの単独仲裁人にその紛争の仲裁を付託することを選択することができる。
　　(i) 当事者は次の場合にのみその選択の権利を失う。
　　　(a) 当事者が，
　　　(1) 紛争が本傭船契約から生じたことを明記し，
　　　(2) 紛争の性質を記載し，かつ
　　　(3) 本条第41条(c)に明確に言及する
　　　　紛争についての通知書を相手方から受け取り
　　　そして
　　　(b) 当事者が紛争についての通知書の受領の日から30日以内に，その紛争を仲裁に付託する旨の選択通知を交付しなかった場合
　　(ii) 両当事者は，ここにいずれの当事者も次のことを行いうることに合意する。
　　　(a) 仲裁判断から生じる法律問題に関し，高等法院に上訴すること
　　　(b) 高等法院に対して，仲裁人がその仲裁判断に理由を付記する命令を申請すること，
　　　(c) 仲裁人に，理由を付した仲裁判断が要求されることを通知すること，かつ
　　　(d) 高等法院に対し，仲裁手続の過程で生じる法律問題の判断を申請すること。
　(d) いずれかの当事者が本傭船契約に基づく紛争に関連して，海上財産がアレストされたか，またはアレストされる法的手続を停止する権利を行使するためには，その当事者が，停止がない場合にそのような法的手続において相手方が提供を受ける権利を有することになるとみられる担保を相手方に提供することが停止条件となる。

本条項は本傭船契約が英国法を準拠法とすることを明確に規定している。第41条(b)項で紛争は英国裁判所で解決されるべきことを，第41条(c)項で一方の当事者の選択によりLondonの単独仲裁人に紛争の解決を委ねうることを規定する。

適用される出訴期限に関する解説については前出716頁参照。仲裁の開始と仲裁一般について507/517頁参照。

<u>617</u>　**Clause 42 — Construction**

574　42. The side headings have been included in this charter for convenience of reference and shall in no way
575　affect the construction hereof.

第42条 — 解　釈

42. 条項の見出しは，参照の便宜のため本傭船契約に挿入したものであって，本傭船契約の解釈にいかなる影響も及ぼすものではない。

タンカー定期傭船STB書式

STB書式によるタンカー定期傭船契約に関する米国法上の解説

3 IT IS THIS DAY MUTUALLY AGREED between ....
4 ....
5 as Owner/Chartered Owner (herein called "Owner") of the ....
6 .... (herein called "Vessel") and
7 ....
8 (herein called "Charterer") that the Owner lets and the Charterer hires the use and services of the
9 Vessel for the carriage of ...., in bulk, and
10 such other lawful merchandise as may be suitable for a vessel of her description, for the period and
11 on the terms and conditions hereinafter set forth.

　本日，…………号（以下，単に「本船」と称する）の船主／傭船船主………（以下，単に「船主」と称する）と……………（以下，単に「傭船者」と称する）との間で，……の撒積運送，およびその他本契約に表示する船舶に積載しうる適法な貨物の運送のために，以下の傭船期間，約定条件で本船を使用運航する権利を，船主は賃貸し傭船者は賃借りすることを合意する。

　輸送される石油あるいは他の液状製品の種類は，粘性とその他の特性が時により加わるが，慣習的に一般的な分類により表示される。だから表示は「原油と・または黒物製品」とか「白物製品」となる。もちろん，輸送される貨物の性質は，それが本船のタンクの状態，ポンプの容量および安全設備に関連する限りにおいて船主にとっては非常に重要なことである。記載されている種類に属さない貨物の船積は契約違反であり，傭船者は損害賠償を請求されることになる。*The Witfuel*, SMA 1381 (Arb. at N.Y. 1979) 事件参照。この場合，蒸留された白物製品の船積が傭船契約違反と判示された。契約では傭船者は原油および・または黒物製品積取しかできないことになっていた。他方もし傭船船舶が指定貨物を安全に輸送できなければ，船主は契約に違反することとなる（前頁226頁参照）。

TERM
12 1. (a) The term of this Charter shall be for a period of about
13 (hereinafter "Original Period") plus any extensions thereof as provided in (b) below. The Original
14 Period shall commence at the time when the Vessel is placed at the Charterer's disposal as provided
15 in Clause 5. The word "about" as used above shall mean "14 days more or less" and shall apply to
16 the term of this Charter consisting of the Original Period plus any extensions as hereinafter provided.

期　間
　1. (a). 本契約の期間は，約……………（以下，単に「原期間」と称する）であり，これに下記(b)

に規定する幾ばくかの延長期間が付加される。原期間は，第5条の規定に基づいて，本船が傭船者の使用に委ねられた時点より開始する。上記に使用した「約」という語は，「プラスマイナス14日」を意味し，原期間と，後に規定する幾ばくかの延長期間より成る本契約の期間に適用される。

STB書式は容認される「期間短縮」，「延長」の日数を14日と定めている。すなわち返船は原期間より14日未満なら「期間不足」でも「期間超過」でも可能ということになる。New York においてはこのことは次の判決の数々を基にたぶん厳正に守られるべき要件であると考えられているようである。すなわち *The Romandie*, SMA 1092 (Arb. at N.Y. 1977), *The Scaldia*, SMA 905 (Arb. at N.Y. 1975) および *The Elizabeth Entz*, SMA 588 (Arb. at N.Y. 1971) 各事件。しかしながら英国においては，*The Dione* [1975] 1 Lloyd's Rep. 115事件の原則により傭船者の手に余る事情の下では傭船者が返船を14日以上遅らせる権利を認められることがありうる。

EXTENSIONS

17　(b)　Charterers shall have the option of extending the term of this Charter for a period of
18　.......................... (hereinafter "Extended Period") by written
19　notice to Owner at least 30 days previous to the expiration of the Original Period. The term of this
20　Charter may be extended by Charterer also for periods (hereinafter "Off-Hire Extensions") of all or
21　any part of the time the Vessel is off hire during the Original Period and/or Extended Period, if any,
22　by giving written notice to Owner at least 30 days before the expiration of the Original Period or
23　Extended Period, as the case may be, and, if Charterer so elects and gives a further written notice to
24　Owner at least 30 days before the expiration of any such Off-Hire Extension, all or any part of the
25　time the Vessel is off hire following the previous notice shall be added to the term of this Charter.

延長

(b). 傭船者は，原期間満了の少なくとも30日前に，船主に書面により通知することによって，…………間（以下単に「延長期間」と称する），本契約の期間を延長する権利を有する。本契約の期間は，本船が原期間および／もしくは延長期間中にオフハイヤーとなった場合，原期間もしくは延長期間の満了の少くとも30日前に船主に対して書面により通知することにより傭船者はそのオフハイヤー期間の全部または一部につき，本契約の期間を延長する（以下，単に「オフハイヤー延長期間」と称する）ことができる。さらに，傭船者はオフハイヤー延長期間満了の少なくとも30日前に，船主に対しさらに書面により通知することにより，先の通知の後に本船がオフハイヤーになった場合，その期間の全部または一部を本契約の期間に付加することができる。

この条項の最初の文言により傭船者に賦与された固定期間に対する傭船期間延長の選択権は実際問題として（慣習上）ごくまれにしか認められないようである。つまり非常に多くの場合，この条文は削除される。

さらに重要なことは，2番目の条文は傭船者に対して合算した「オフハイヤー」期間の全部または一部を傭船期間に「加える」選択権を認めていることである。かかる条文がなければオフハイヤー期間を「加える」権利は生じない。

VESSEL PARTICULARS

26 　2. The following are particulars and capacities of the Vessel and her equipment:
27 　A. Cargo Carrying Capacity
28 　　I. Total cargo tank capacity when 100% full .... US Barrels
29 　　II. Weight of stores, etc., permanently
30 　　　deducted from cargo carrying capacity .... L. T.
31 　　III. a. Fresh water consumption per day .... L. T.
32 　　　b. Capacity of evaporators per day .... L. T.
33 　　　c. Quantity of fresh water deductible
34 　　　　from cargo carrying capacity on a
35 　　　　daily basis .... L. T.
36 　　IV. Estimated loss of cargo carrying capacity due
37 　　　to "sag" when fully loaded with light, medium,
38 　　　heavy cargo
39 　　　　　　　　　　　　　　　Light .... L. T.
40 　　　　　　　　　　　　　　　Medium .... L. T.
41 　　　　　　　　　　　　　　　Heavy .... L. T.
42 　　V. The Vessel can carry .... tons (of 2,240 lbs.) total deadweight (as
43 　　　certified by Classification Society) of cargo, bunkers, water, and stores on an assigned
44 　　　summer mean draft of .... ft .... in. and an assigned freeboard of
45 　　　......... ft .... in.
46 　B. Other Tank Capacities
47 　　I. Total capacity of fuel tanks for propulsion .... US Barrels
48 　　II. Total capacity of fresh water tanks .... L. T.
49 　　III. Total capacity of segregated ballast tanks .... L. T.
50 　C. Capacity of Pumps
51 　　I. Cargo Pumps
52 　　　a. Number ....
53 　　　b. Make ....
54 　　　c. Type ....
55 　　　d. Design rated capacity of each pump in
56 　　　　U.S. Barrels per hour and corresponding .... US Bbls/Hr.
57 　　　　head in feet .... Feet/Head
58 　　II. Stripping Pumps
59 　　　a. Number ....
60 　　　b. Design capacity of each pump in U.S.
61 　　　　Barrels per hour for the guaranteed .... US Bbls/Hr.
62 　　　　discharge head of .... Feet/Head
63 　　III. Segregated Ballast Pumps
64 　　　a. Number ....
65 　　　b. Design capacity each pump .... US Bbls/Hr.
66 　D. Cargo Loading/Discharge Manifold

67　The whole manifold is made of steel or comparable material and is strengthened and supported
68　to avoid damage from loading and discharge equipment and to withstand a maximum load from
69　any direction equivalent to the safe working load of the cargo hose lifting equipment.
70　I. a. Number of manifold connections ....
71　　　b. Diameter of manifold connections ....
72　　　c. Distance from centers of manifold connections ....
73　　　d. Distance from manifold connections to ship's side ......
74　　　e. Distance center of manifold connection to deck ....
75　　　f. Distance bow/center of manifold ....
76　　　g. Safe working load of cargo hose lifting equipment .... tons.
77　II. Cargo Manifold Reducing Pieces
78　Vessels from 16 to 60 MDWT are equipped with a sufficient number of cargo manifold
79　reducing pieces of steel or a comparable material to permit presenting of flanges of 8", 10"
80　and 12"(ASA) cargo hoses/arms at all manifold connections on one side of the vessel.
81　Vessels over 60 MDWT are equipped with a sufficient number of cargo manifold reducing
82　pieces of steel or a comparable material to permit presenting of flanges of 10", 12" and 16"
83　(ASA) cargo hose/arms at all manifold connections on one side of the vessel.
84　E. Heating Coils
85　　I. Type of coils and material of which manufactured ....
86　　II. Ratio heating surface/volume
87　　　a. Center Tanks .... Ft^2/40 Ft^3
88　　　b. Wing Tanks .... Ft^2/40 Ft^3
89　F. Cargo Loading Performance
90　　Vessel can load homogeneous cargo at maximum rate of .... B/H.
91　G. Vessel Particulars
92　　I. Length overall .... ft. .... In.
93　　II. Fully loaded summer draft in salt water of a density of 1.025
94　　......... ft. .... inches on an assigned freeboard of ....
95　　III. Fresh Water allowance .... In.
96　　IV. Light ship draft　　Forward .... Ft. .... In.
97　　　　　　　　　　　　　Aft .... Ft. .... In.
98　　　　　　　　　　　　　Mean .... Ft. .... In.
99　　V. Moulded Depth ....
100　VI. Light ship freeboard .... Ft. .... In.
101　VII. TPI on light ship draft ....
102　VIII. TPI on summer draft ....
103　IX. Extreme beam ....
104　X. Gross Reg. Tons ....
105　XI. Net Reg. Tons ....
106　XII. Suez Canal Tonnage ....
107　XIII. Panama Canal Tonnage ....
108　XIV. Flag of Registry ....
109　XV. Call letters ....
110　XVI. Classification Society ....

111   XVII. Maximum bunkers aboard when vessel is placed at Charterer's disposal to be
112   ....
113   XVIII. Owner shall provide Charterer with copies of the Vessel's plans upon Charterer's request
114   therefor, provided, in the case of a newbuilding, that Owner need not provide same until
115   such plans are available to him from the building yard.
116   XIX. Vessel is equipped with a fresh water evaporator which will be maintained in good
117   operating condition. Owners warrant that this evaporator is capable of making suffi- cient
118   fresh water to supply the vessel's needs.
119   XX. Owner warrants vessel is capable of heating cargo to 135° F. and of maintaining same
120   throughout entire discharge. Should vessel fail to heat cargo in accordance with Char-
121   terer's instructions, Charterer shall have the option to:
122   a) Delay discharge of the cargo
123   b) Delay berthing of the Vessel
124   c) Discontinue discharge and remove vessel from berth until cargo is heated in accord-
125   ance with Charterer's instructions.
126   All time lost to be considered as off-hire and for Owner's account. In addition, any
127   expenses incurred in moving vessel from berth will be for Owner's account.

本船要目

2．本船の要目，容量，装備は次のとおりである。

A. 貨物積載容量

I．100パーセント積載時の全積荷タンク容量.........USバレル
II．積荷積載容量から常時控除される船用品等重量.........ロング・トン
III．a．1日当たり清水消費量.........ロング・トン
　　b．1日当たり造水量.........ロング・トン
　　c．積荷積載容量より控除される清水1日当たりの量.........ロング・トン
IV．軽質油，中質油，重質油各満載時の「サグ」のための積荷積載容量の見積損失
　　　　　　　軽質油.........ロング・トン
　　　　　　　中質油.........ロング・トン
　　　　　　　重質油.........ロング・トン
V．本船は，夏期満載喫水.........フィート......インチ，乾舷......フィート.........インチで，積荷，燃料，水，船用品を，総載貨重量屯......トン（2,240ポンド）（船級協会証明），運送できる。

B. その他のタンク容量

I．推進用燃料タンク全容量.........USバレル
II．清水タンク全容量.........ロング・トン
III．バラスト専用タンク全容量.........ロング・トン

C. ポンプ性能

I．貨物ポンプ
　a．数量..............
　b．製造..............
　c．型式..............

d. 時間当たり US バレルでの各ポンプの定格容量..............US バレル／時間
　　　　　および対応する揚程..............フィート／揚程
　II. ストリッピング・ポンプ
　　　a. 数量..............
　　　b. 各ポンプの定格容量..............US バレル／時間
　　　　　およびこれに対応する保証吐出揚程..............フィート／揚程
　III. 専用バラストポンプ
　　　a. 数量..............
　　　b. 各ポンプの定格容量..............US バレル／時間
D. 積荷揚荷マニホールド
　　マニホールドは、すべて鋼製またはそれに準ずる材質製で、荷役設備による損害防止の補強がなされており、かつ荷役ホース昇降装置安全荷重と同等の、どの方向からの最大荷重にも耐えるだけの、強度を保持するものとする。
　I. a. マニホールド連結口の数量..............
　　　b. マニホールド連結口の径..............
　　　c. マニホールド連結口の中心間距離..............
　　　d. マニホールド連結口と舷側間の距離..............
　　　e. マニホールド連結口中心の甲板からの高さ......
　　　f. マニホールド中心・船首間距離..............
　　　g. 荷役ホース昇降装置安全荷重..............トン
　II. 貨物マニホールド・レデューサー
　　　16ないし60MDWT の船舶は、鋼製またはそれに準ずる材質製の十分な数の荷油マニホールド・レデューサーを装備しており、これによって船舶の片舷のマニホールド連結口全部に、8"、10"、12"（ASA）のフランジの荷役ホース／アームを連結できる。
　　　60MDWT を超える船舶は、鋼製またはそれに準ずる材質製の十分な数の荷油マニホールド・レデューサーを装備しており、これによって船舶の片舷のマニホールド連結口全部に、10"、12"、16"（ASA）のフランジの荷役ホース／アームを連結できる。
E. 加熱管
　I. 加熱管の型式および材質
　II. 加熱面積／容積比
　　　a. 中央タンク..............平方フィート／40立方フィート
　　　b. 両翼タンク..............平方フィート／40立方フィート
F. 荷油積込性能
　　本船は、同質荷油を最高レート..............バレル／時間で積み込むことができる。
G. 本船要目
　I. 全長..............フィート..............インチ
　II. 比重1.025塩水での夏期満載喫水..............フィート..............インチ
　　　その時の指定乾舷..............
　III. 淡水における喫水沈下量..............インチ
　IV. 空船喫水　舳..............フィート..............インチ
　　　　　　　　艫..............フィート..............インチ
　　　　　　　　平均..............フィート..............インチ
　V. 型深..............
　VI. 空船時乾舷..............フィート..............インチ
　VII. 空船時のトン・パー・インチ..............
　VIII. 夏期満載喫水でのトン・パー・インチ..............
　IX. 全幅..............
　X. 総トン数..............

XI. 純トン数................
XII. スエズ運河トン数...............
XIII. パナマ運河トン数...............
XIV. 船籍国................
XV. 信号符字................
XVI. 船級協会................
XVII. 本船の傭船者引渡時の最大積載燃料...............
XVIII. 船主は，傭船者の要求に応じて本船の図面の写を提供する。新造船の場合には船主は，造船所より図面を受け取った後，写を提供すれば足りる。
XIX. 本船は造水器を装備しており，それは良好に作動するように調整されるものとし，船主は，この造水器が本船に必要な量の造水能力を有することを保証する。
XX. 船主は，本船が荷油を華氏135度に加熱し，揚荷中継続してその状態を維持する性能を有することを保証する。もし本船が傭船者の指図どおりに，荷油を加熱できない場合には，傭船者は次のいずれかを選択する権利を有する。
 a) 揚荷を遅らせる。
 b) 本船の着桟を遅らせる。
 c) 揚荷を中止し，荷油が傭船者の指図どおりに加熱されるまで本船を離桟させる。
 これらの喪失時間すべては，オフハイヤーとみなされ，船主負担となる。さらに，離桟費用一切も船主負担となる。

　タンカーの傭船契約における船舶の詳細な記載は異常に包括的であるにせよ珍しいことではない。多くの書式は単に別個の明細書を参照し，摂取するだけである。
　記載された容量能力は疑いもなく英国法上「中間的義務」として，また米国法上「担保」として解釈される。したがって本船がこの記載要目のある部分に適合できない場合，契約違反となるが，結果的に容易ならざる事態を生じない限り，これは傭船契約の終了を正当化する事由とはならない（前出138／142頁参照）。
　記載された明細に関し，いくつかの点に注意すべきである。各種ポンプ（貨物，ストリッピング，専用バラスト）の容量は「定格上」の容量であるということである。比較的古い船舶の場合，実際上の容量は明確に少ないにもかかわらず，STB書式の第4条（後出752頁）に基づき船主は，本船が「第2条に示す性能を満たす」ことを保証し，傭船期間を通してその性能を維持するために「相当の注意」を尽くすことを保証する。ポンプの容量は，さらに第8条（後出757頁）により，さらに修正されて，船主は本船が指定の温度で毎時一定量の貨物を揚荷する能力を有することを保証することになる。
622　第2条（G. XX）は，また本船が貨物を135°F. まで加熱できるという保証を明示している。そこで，この規定により傭船者はこの温度維持ができない場合3つの選択権を有する。要するに，傭船者は単に揚荷作業を中断し本船が所要の温度に加熱できるまで，オフハイヤーにすることができる。
　しかしながら，傭船契約が輸送を目的とする種々の石油製品のすべてが加熱を必要としていない場合，本船の加熱保証はすべての貨物を無差別に，連続的かつ一律に保証温度まで加熱する約束として解釈できないことが注意されるべきである。*The London Confidence*, SMA 1257 (Arb. at N. Y. 1978).

HIRE
128　3. (a) The Charterer shall pay hire for the use of the Vessel at the rate of ......

129　in .... currency per ton (of 2,240 lbs.) on Vessel's deadweight as shown in
130　Clause 2. A. per calendar month, payment to be made in advance monthly at. ....
131　............... by check without discount commencing with the date and hour the Vessel
132　is placed at Charterer's disposal hereunder and continuing to the date and hour when the Vessel is
133　released to Owner at the expiration of this Charter except as otherwise expressed in this Charter.
134　Any hire paid in advance and not earned shall be returned to the Charterer at once. In no event will
135　initial payment of hire be made until Charter Party is signed and Vessel placed at Charterer's disposal
136　as herein provided.

傭 船 料

　　3．(a)．傭船者は，本船の使用に対して，第2条Aに表示する載貨重量トン1トン（2,240ポンド），1ヶ月当たり，......の通貨.........の率で，傭船料を支払う。本契約に別段の定めなき限り，支払は暦月毎に前払で，割引なし小切手にて，.........において，本船が傭船者の使用に委ねられた日時に始まり，傭船契約が満了し本船が船主に返船される日時まで，継続して支払われる。反対給付が得られなかった前払傭船料一切は，直ちに傭船者に返還される。本契約書に署名がなされ，本船がここに規定するように傭船者の使用に委ねられるまでは，いかなる場合にも，傭船料の第1期の支払はなされない。

　　古い傭船契約書式と異なり，現代の商業実務を反映してこの条項に基づく傭船料は「現金」ではなく「小切手」で支払われる。この規定はしばしば修正されて，船主の銀行口座に電信送金による傭船料の支払を要すると変更される。

　　最後の条文は，最初の傭船料の払込は契約書が「署名」され，本船が傭船者に引き渡されるまではなされなくてもよいと規定している。もちろん，傭船契約が，効力を生じ，拘束力を有するために書面にする必要はない。しかし，通常見られるように，書面による傭船契約が考えられている場合でも，実際の署名は引渡の数週間後，あるいは数ヶ月後に至るまで行われないことがありうる。仮に傭船契約書に署名がなされていなくても，本船が傭船者の自由に委ねられた時をもって傭船料が支払われる（傭船が開始する）との意図が存するのであれば，この条項は修正されるべきである。

DEDUCTIONS

137　(b) The Charterer shall be entitled to deduct from hire payments : (1) any disbursements for
138　Owner's account and any advances to the Master or Owner's agents, including commissions thereon,
139　(2) layup savings calculated in accordance with Clause 17, (3) any previous overpayments of hire
140　including offhire and including any overpayments of hire concerning which a bona fide dispute may
141　exist but in the latter event the Charterer shall furnish an adequate bank guarantee or other good and
142　sufficient security on request of the Owner, (4) any Clause 8 and 9 claims, and (5) any

other sums to
143 which Charterer is entitled under this charter. The Charterer shall be entitled to 2.5% commission on
144 any sums advanced or disbursements made for the Owner's account. However, the Owner shall have
145 the option of making advances to the Charterer or its designated agent for disbursements (provided
146 such advances are deemed adequate and reasonable by the Charterer), and, in such event, no
147 commissions shall be paid.

控　除

(b). 傭船者は，傭船料支払額から次に挙げるものを控除することができる。(1)船主負担となる立替金，船長または船主代理人への前払金一切。これには対応する手数料を含む。(2)第17条に基づき算出される係船割戻金。(3)傭船料の事前超過支払額一切。これにはオフハイヤー分，および善意の争いある傭船料超過支払額が含まれる。ただし，後者において傭船者は，船主の要求があれば，十分な銀行保証，または他の信用ある十分な担保を提供しなければならない。(4)第8条，第9条の求償。および(5)本契約上傭船者に控除権を与えたその他一切の金額。傭船者は，船主負担となる前払金，または立替金の2.5パーセントを手数料として取得する権利を有する。ただし，船主は立替金について，傭船者もしくはその指定する代理人に前払をなす権利を有する（ただし，かかる前払金を，傭船者が十分かつ妥当とみなすことを条件に）。この場合には手数料の支払を要しない。

　STB書式は，傭船料の控除に関するやっかいな問題を取り扱うに際して，傭船者に対してかなりの広範な控除の自由を与えている。だから，傭船者はオフハイヤーそのものが争われている場合でも，本船がオフハイヤーになるとして傭船料の過払分を控除することができる。これに対する唯一の抑制といえば，「善意の紛争」事実における船主請求に基づく（傭船者の）担保の提供義務である。

　第8条および第9条によって判断された履行の欠陥につき傭船者がオフハイヤーおよび他の控除を行うことは，たぶん同様に正しいということになる。上記の文言は「どんな第8条および第9条の求償」についても控除を許容している。このことは善意による「求償」が存在しさえすれば，「求償額」が最終的には縮小または無視されることになる場合でも控除を行うことはできるということを示唆する。したがって，傭船者は控除につき善意に基づく紛争の結果，傭船料の不払を理由とする本船の引揚について何の心配もいらない。

　最後に雑規定があり，「本契約上傭船者に控除権を与えるその他一切の金額」の控除を許容している。これは単なる「求償額」に対立するものとして傭船者が「権利を与えられた」金額に限られているので，傭船者はたぶん危険覚悟で（オフハイヤーおよび第8条および第9条に基づく求償とは異なる）係争中の額を控除することになろう。傭船者が結局係争金額に対する権利要求の正当性を実証できない場合，控除額は少なくとも不払傭船料の一部となり，したがって本船引揚の正当な事由となろう（前出330／340頁参照）。

FINAL VOYAGE

148　(c) Should the Vessel be on her final voyage at the time a payment of hire becomes due, said
149 payment shall be made for the time estimated by Charterer to be necessary to complete

the voyage
150 and effect release of the Vessel to Owner, less all deductions provided for in sub-paragraph (b) of this
151 Clause which shall be estimated by Charterer if the actual amounts have not been received and also
152 less the amount estimated by Charterer to become payable by the Owner for fuel and water on
153 release as provided in Clause 19. (b). Upon redelivery any difference between the estimated and
154 actual amounts shall be refunded to or paid by the Charterer as the case may require.

最終航海

(c). 本船が，傭船料支払期日に最終航海中である場合，当該支払は，当該航海を完遂し，本船を船主に返船するに必要であると傭船者が予定した期間についてなされ，そこから，本条(b)に規定する全控除額，もし実際の額が不明であれば傭船者見積額，および第19条(b)に規定する船主に支払義務のある返船時の燃料，清水代の傭船者見積額を控除する。返船時において，見積額と実際額の差額を，傭船者に返還するか，あるいは傭船者が追加支払しなければならない。

この節は単純に最終月の傭船料から概算の船主負担支払金，返船時の燃料油，その他の控除に関する規定で，明白に認定されているか否かにかかわらず，慣習上定期傭船契約のあらゆる書式に基づき広く追随されるところとなっている。

LOSS OF VESSEL

155 (d) Should the Vessel be lost or be missing and presumed lost, hire shall cease at the time of
156 her loss or, if such time is unknown, at the time when the Vessel was last heard of. If the Vessel
157 should become a constructive total loss, hire shall cease at the time of the casualty resulting in such
158 loss. In either case, any hire paid in advance and not earned shall be returned to the Charterer. If the
159 Vessel should be off hire or missing when a payment of hire would otherwise be due, such payment
160 shall be postponed until the off-hire period ceases or the safety of the Vessel is ascertained, as the
161 case may be.

本船の滅失

(d). 本船が滅失するか，もしくは行方不明で滅失と推定される場合，傭船料は滅失時，それが不明なら本船の最後の消息の時点で中止される。本船が推定全損となった場合には，傭船料は当該全損の原因たる事故の時点で中止となる。いずれの場合にも，反対給付が得られなかった前払傭船料は傭船者に返還される。もし本船が，傭船料支払時期にオフハイヤー中であるか，または行方不明である場合，傭船料支払は，場合によりオフハイヤー期間が終了するか，または本船の安全が確認されるまで延期される。

一般的な規則として船舶は修復および修理の費用が船価を超える場合,「推定全損」になる。前出488頁の履行不能に関する章の解説参照。

この条項の最後の文は,本来の傭船料支払期限の到来時に本船がオフハイヤーであれば,傭船料の支払は延期されると規定している。この規定により,時として例えば傭船料の支払時期に本船が修理中である場合,傭船者としてはオフハイヤー部分の傭船料をいくら控除するのが適当であるかといった困難な予測をしないでよいこととなる。オフハイヤー期間が終了するまで支払を延期することにより傭船者に必要なのは彼が知ることのできる本船の使用期間のみの傭船料の前払ということになる。

REDUCTION IN HIRE

162　(e) If the Vessel shall not fulfill the Owner's Warranty or any other part of her description as
163　warranted in Clause 4, Charterer shall be entitled without prejudice to a reduction in the hire to
164　correct for the deficiency and to any other rights the Charterer may have.

傭船料の減額

(e). 本船が,第4条の船主担保,その他の担保された船舶表示を満たさない場合,傭船者は,欠陥の是正その他傭船者が有すべき一切の権利を取得する。ただし,傭船者の傭船料減額の権利は,損なわれない。

この条項は第8,9条および第11条の明示のオフハイヤー規定には規定のない容積というような担保の違反を扱う「すべてを網羅した」条項のように思われる。

DEFAULT

165　(f) In default of punctual and regular payment as herein specified, the Owner will notify
166　..................................... at ....
167　........................... whereupon the Charterer shall make payment of the
168　amount due within ten (10) days of receipt of notification from the Owner, failing which the Owner
169　will have the right to withdraw the Vessel from the service of the Charterer without prejudice to any
170　claim the Owner may otherwise have against the Charterer under this Charter.

遅　滞

(f). ここに規定する期限どおりの定期の支払が遅滞した場合,船主は,.........所在の.........に通知をなす。この場合傭船者は船主からの通知受領後10日以内に支払をなさなければならず,これを怠った場合,船主は同人が傭船者に対して有する本契約上の他の請求権を害さずに,本船を傭船者の業務から引き揚げる権利を有する。

これは支払遅延がどのようなものであれ,傭船契約の終了を許容する伝統的な「本船引揚」

条項を部分的に修正するものである。支払遅滞の通知を要求し猶予期間を設けることにより、この条項は高い市場の中での本船の引揚によって生じる周知の難事を防いでいる。船主による正当な本船の引揚は、傭船者の支払遅延によって生じる損害賠償を求める権利と同様、傭船契約に基づき有するすべての損害賠償請求権を損なうことはない。

624 INCREMENT

171 　(g) The rate of hire set forth in sub-paragraph (a) of this Clause includes an increment of
172 　$ .... to cover in full any expenses for Charterer's account for extra victualling
173 　by the Master, telephone calls, radio messages, telegrams and cables and all overtime worked by the
174 　Vessel's officers and crew at Charterer's request.
175 　(h) The rate of charter hire set forth in this Clause 3 is equivalent to $ ....
176 　per hour.

増　　額

　(g). 本条(a)に規定する傭船料は、傭船者負担の、船長による臨時食事提供、電話、無線、電報、電信、および傭船者の要求でなした本船の職員、部員の時間外労働の費用を全額まかなう ....ドルの増額分を含むものである。

　(h). 本条第3条に規定する傭船料率は、時間当たり ......ドルに相当する。

　この条項は、通常船員の時間外手当を対象とする一括払の増額規定を拡大し、しばしば傭船者に個別に課される種々の少額費用を含めるものである。

WARRANTIES

177 4. Owner warrants that at the time the Vessel is placed at Charterer's disposal, the Vessel shall
178 fulfill the descriptions, particulars and capabilities set forth in Clause 2 above, and shall be tight,
179 staunch, and strong, in thoroughly efficient order and condition and in every way fit, manned,
180 equipped, and supplied for the service contemplated, with holds, cargo tanks, pipelines, and valves
181 clear, clean, and tight and with pumps, heating coils, and all other equipment in good working order.
182 Such description, particulars, and capabilities of the Vessel shall be maintained by Owner throughout
183 the period of the Vessel's service hereunder so far as possible by the exercise of due diligence.

担　　保

　4. 船主は、本船が傭船者の使用に委ねられたときに、上記第2条に表示した表示、要目、性能を満たすこと、堅牢、強固であること、完全に性能を発揮しうる状態でかつすべての点で適応性を持つこと、乗組員が配乗されていること、艤装されていること、さらには予定される運航のために積荷タ

ンク，荷油管，弁を清浄かつ堅牢な状態に，またポンプ・加熱管，その他すべての装備を良好な状態で提供することを担保する。船主は，本契約上本船が使用される全期間，相当の注意を尽くすことにより本船は上記表示，要目，性能をできる限り維持しなければならない。

第4条は，引渡当日における本船の記載要目と堪航性の両方につき担保を明示するものである。その後，この担保は「相当の注意」の一つまで減殺される。もちろん，性能不足が存すれば，船主が尽くした「相当の注意」の程度如何にかかわらず，第8，9および11条のオフハイヤー規定が適用されることになる。

The OMI Charger, SMA 2769 (Arb. at N.Y. 1991) 事件で仲裁審は，本船がジェット燃料積載に不向きであったのは，本船のタンクが担保されたとおり十分に上塗りされていなかった事実に原因の一部があると判示した。船主はさらに，積荷と次の航海の積荷の合間に不適当な洗浄を行うという過失を犯した。

HIRE

184　5. (a)　The use and services of the Vessel shall be placed at the disposal of the Charterer at
185　............................. (hereinafter "Port of Delivery") at such readily
186　accessible dock, wharf, or other place as the Charterer may direct. Charter hire shall commence when
187　the Vessel is at such dock, wharf, or place and in all respects ready to perform this Charter and ready
188　for sea and written notice thereof has been given by the Master to the Charterer or its Agents at the
189　Port of Delivery.

傭　　船

5. (a). 本船は傭船者の指示する............ (以下，「引渡港」という) の，直に接岸しうるドック，埠頭その他の場所で，傭船者の使用に委ねられなければならない。傭船料は，本船がかかるドック，埠頭または場所において，すべての点で本契約の遂行および航海の準備が完了し，船長が引渡港で傭船者またはその代理人に，その旨の書面による通知をなしたときより開始する。

本船が引渡時において，船積可能な状態にあるということに加え，「航海の準備完了」していることが要求されるのは，本船を航海可能ならしめるためにある種の修理が必要であるにもかかわらず，本船が積荷可能である場合，傭船が有効であると判示される事態の招来を避けるためである（前出215頁参照）。本条項はしばしば行われる船舶の洋上引渡の事実も考慮している。引渡後，航海のためだけに必要な装備の一時的欠陥は，時間の喪失ではないのだからたぶん積荷役中にはオフハイヤーとならないであろう。

LAYDAYS

190　(b)　Hire shall not commence before ....
191　................................., except
192　with Charterer's consent, and the Vessel shall be placed at Charterer's disposal in accor-

dance with
193　the provisions hereof no later than .... in default of which Charterer shall
194　have the option to cancel this Charter declarable not later than the day of the Vessel's readiness.
195　Cancellation by Charterer or acceptance of the use of the Vessel's services shall be without prejudice
196　to any claims for damages Charterer may have for late tender of the Vessel's services.

碇泊期間

(b).　傭船は，傭船者が同意する場合を除いては............以前には開始しない。本船は，ここに規定するところに従い.........より以前に傭船者の使用に提供されなければならず，これを怠った場合，傭船者は本船が準備完了となる日以前に宣言することにより，本契約を解約する権利を有する。傭船者による解約，または本船の運航業務の受領は，本船の運航業務の提供の遅延に対し傭船者が有する損害賠償請求権を害するものではない。

625　この規定の最初の文章は，ニューヨーク・プロデュース書式の第14条のごとく，他の標準的な「傭船開始・解約」条項とまったく同じである。最後の文章はそれらの条項の中ではほとんど見かけない。しかし，それはたぶん単純に引渡を受けたり，解約することによって何らかの損害賠償請求権の放棄に繋がることを避けること以外の何ものでもなかろう。極力迅速に引渡港へ向けた航海での（例えば引渡港への途中の不当な航海を行うことによって）義務の不履行によるとかあるいは，契約成立時の本船の所在地，または準備完了予定を不実表示したことがない限り，通常船主は引渡の遅延につき責任はないであろう（前出425頁参照）。

USE OF VESSEL

197　(c)　The whole reach and burthen of the Vessel (but not more than she can reasonably stow
198　and safely carry) shall be at the Charterer's disposal, reserving proper and sufficient space for Vessel's
199　Officers, Crew, Master's cabin, tackle, apparel, furniture, fuel, provisions, and stores.

本船の使用

(c)　本船の全載貨容積（ただし，本船が適切に積載し，安全に運送できる量を最大限として）は，本船の船長，職員，部員の船室，器具，装備，艤装具，燃料，食料，船用品のための十分かつ適当なスペースを保留して，傭船者の使用に供されなければならない。

これは定期傭船契約書式に見られる標準的な規定で解説不要である。

TRADING LIMITS

200　6.(a)　The Vessel may be employed in any part of the World trading between and at ports,
201　places, berths, docks, anchorages, and submarine pipe-lines in such lawful trades as the Charterer or
202　its agents may direct, subject to Institute Warranties and Clauses attached hereto but may be sent to

203　ports and places on the North American Lakes, the St. Lawrence River and tributaries between May
204　15 and November 15 and through the Straits of Magellan and around Cape Horn and The Cape of
205　Good Hope at any time of the year without payment of any extra premium. Notwithstanding the
206　foregoing restrictions, the Vessel may be sent to Baltic Sea ports not North of Stockholm, and to
207　Helsingfors and Abo, Finland, and other ports and places as set forth in the Institute Warranties and
208　Clauses, provided, however, that Charterer shall reimburse Owner for any additional premia proper-
209　ly assessed by Vessel's underwriters and payable by Owner for breach of such trade warranties.

航路定限

6. (a). 本船は，ここに添付する協会担保航路定限条款に従い，世界中のいかなる港，場所，埠頭，ドック，錨地，海中パイプラインおよびそれらの間の傭船者，またはその代理人が指図する適法な航海に使用される。ただし，5月15日から11月15日までの間の北アメリカの湖水，St. Lawrence 河およびその支流，年間を通じての Magellan 海峡通過，Horn 岬，喜望峰周辺への配船は，保険料割増金の支払なしにできる。上記の制限にかかわらず，本船を Stockholm 以南のバルト海諸港，フィンランドの Helsingfors, Abo, その他協会担保航路定限条款に規定する港，場所に配船することができる。ただし，傭船者は，当該航路定限違反に対して船主が支払うべき本船の保険者により適切に査定された追加保険料を船主に支払うものとする。

定期傭船においては船舶の航路を London の保険者協会が定めた航路定限である「協会担保航路定限」に限定することがほとんど全世界的な慣習となった。これを越えて航行する場合，船体保険の割増料が課せられる。上記規定は特別の協会担保航路定限条項が傭船契約に添付されており，傭船者が船舶船体保険で要求される特別割増料を支払わずに本船に担保定限を超えることになるかも知れない特定水域への航行指図を出すことを認めることを考えている。傭船者は保険業者から課せられる追加割増保険料を支払うことによってのみ，本船に対し他の特定の協会担保航路定限外への航行指図を行うことができる。

BERTHS

210　(b) The Vessel shall be loaded, discharged, or lightened, at any port, place, berth, dock,
211　anchorage, or submarine line or alongside lighters or lightening vessels as Charterer may direct.
212　Notwithstanding anything contained in this Clause or any other provisions of this Charter, Charterer
213　shall not be deemed to warrant the safety of any port, berth, dock, anchorage, and/or submarine line
214　and shall not be liable for any loss, damage, injury, or delay resulting from conditions at such ports,
215　berths, docks, anchorages, and submarine lines not caused by Charterer's fault or neglect

or which
216 could have been avoided by the exercise of reasonable care on the part of the Master or Owner.

碇泊場所

(b). 本船は，傭船者が指図する港，場所，バース，ドック，錨地，海底ラインにおいて，艀あるいは瀬取船に横付けして積荷，揚荷，瀬取をしなければならない。本条，その他本契約書の他の規定にかかわらず，傭船者が港，バース，ドック，錨地および／または海中パイプラインの安全を担保したものとはみなされない。また傭船者は，港，バース，ドック，錨地，海中パイプラインの状態を原因とするいかなる滅失，損傷，事故または遅延について，それが傭船者の過失，怠慢に起因しない場合，あるいは船長または船主が相当の注意を尽くせば回避しえた場合，一切の責任を負わない。

これは通常の「安全港」および「安全バース」の担保を変更するものである。STB書式ははっきりと安全の担保を否認する。そして代わりに傭船者の「過失または怠慢」による損失に対する傭船者の責任を限定する。加えて，この規定は，もし船主側または船長が相当の注意を尽くせば回避できたであろう損失を船主が負担することを明示している。例として，*The Athenoula*, SMA 1410 (Arb. at N. Y. 1980) 事件参照。この中で仲裁審は MOBILTIME 書式の第16条がバースの安全性を担保するものではなく，むしろ傭船者は本船が安全なバース間に就航することを保証する上での相当の注意を尽くす義務があるとの指摘をした。この規定は災害が傭船者と船主双方の過失に帰せられる場合の「損害平分負担」という結着の可能性に道を開くものである。かようにして傭船者の責任原則は，無過失責任からその者自身の過失へと変わってきたものの，海事に関する損害を均衡ある過失の原理に基づき配分するという傾向は消えていない。しかし，*The Halekulani*, SMA 1633 (Arb. at N. Y. 1981) 事件参照。

船主の船舶が指図を受ける多くの「港（ports：商港）」および「バース」が，これまで「港（harbor：天然または人工の地形によって波風を避けるのに適した港）」という概念と関連づけて考えられた気象や海象からの保護が皆無に等しい係留ブイに過ぎないため，今日，積荷時における安全性の問題はタンカーの船主にとってとりわけ深刻なものである。その上，原油の多くは港（port）の「政治的」安全性に配慮を要する地域から生産される。STB書式に基づき，これらの追加的な危険は船主に転嫁されてきたように思える。

FUEL

217 (c) The Charterer shall accept and pay for all fuel in the Vessel's bunkers at the time the
218 vessel is placed at Charterer's disposal not exceeding the maximum quantity stated in Clause 2 above.
219 Any excess quantity shall be removed by the Owner at its expense before such time unless the
220 Charterer elects to accept such excess at the price determined as hereinafter provided or at such
221 other price as may be mutually agreed. Payment for such fuel shall be in accordance with The Esso
222 International Contract Price List current for the date when and the port or place where the vessel is
223 placed at Charterer's disposal under the Charter or the nearest port to which such list

applies.

燃　料

(c) 傭船者は，本船が傭船者の使用に委ねられたときに積載している燃料を，上記第2条に表示した最大量を限度として，受け取り，その代金を支払わなければならない。超過量については，傭船者がその選択で，後に規定するところに従い決定される価格，または相互の合意に基づく価格で，これを受け取ることができるが，傭船者が超過分を受け取らない場合には，本船が傭船者の使用に委ねられる前に，船主は自らの費用で当該超過量を本船から移出しなければならない。燃料代金の支払は，本船が本契約により傭船者の使用に委ねられた日，およびその港，場所におけるエッソ国際契約価格表の値，または同表に掲載される最寄りの港における表値に従い行われる。

STBのこの言い回しは，大部分は引渡時の燃料代の支払に関連して生じる争いを超過燃料に対する明確な罰則（例えば，船主負担による移出）および燃料価格決定に関する明確な基準を明示することによって避けている。

CARGO

224　7. The Charterer shall have the option of shipping any lawful dry cargo in bulk for which the
225　Vessel and her tanks are suitable and any lawful merchandise in cases and/or cans and/or other
226　packages in the Vessel's forehold, 'tween decks, and/or other suitable space available, subject,
227　however, to the Master's approval as to kind and character, amount and stowage. All charges for
228　dunnage, loading, stowing, and discharging so incurred shall be paid by the Charterer.

貨　物

7. 傭船者は，本船およびそのタンクが適切にできる適法な撒，乾貨物の船積，および箱，罐，その他梱包された適法な商品を船首船艙，中甲板，その他適切な利用可能スペースへ船積する権利を有する。ただし，種類，特性，数量，載貨方法に関する船長の同意を条件とする。荷敷，積込，保管，揚荷についての費用一切は，傭船者が負担する。

この条項は傭船者に対して別途タンカーに適した乾貨物を船積する権利を単に留保せしめるものである。だから，例えば傭船期間中に原油または石油製品輸送のためのタンカーの需要が落ち込む場合，穀物の輸送を許可することになる。

SPEED, FUEL AND PUMPING WARRANTIES

229　8. The Owner warrants that the Vessel is capable of maintaining and shall maintain throughout
230　the period of this Charter Party on all sea passages from Seabuoy to Seabuoy a guaranteed average
231　speed under all weather conditions of .... knots in a laden condition and
232　.........knots in ballast (speed will be determined by taking the total miles at sea divided

233 by the total hours at sea as shown in the log books excluding stops at sea and any sea passage
234 covered by an off-hire calculation) on a guaranteed daily consumption of .... tons
235 (of 2,240 lbs.) of Diesel/Bunker C/High Viscosity Fuel Oil maximum .... seconds
236 Redwood No. 1 at 100 degrees F. for main engine, and .... tons (of
237 2,240 lbs.) of Diesel for auxiliaries for propulsion.
238　　For each day that heat is applied to cargo the guaranteed daily consumption is
239 .... bbls. of Diesel/Bunker C/High Viscosity Fuel Oil maximum ....
240 seconds Redwood No. 1 at 100 degrees F. per tank day. For each hour that tank cleaning is required,
241 the guaranteed consumption is .... bbls. of Diesel/Bunker C/High Viscosity Fuel Oil
242 maximum .... seconds Redwood No. 1 at 100 degrees F. per machine hour.
243　　The Charterer is entitled to the full capabilities of the Vessel and the Owner warrants that
244 the Vessel is capable of discharging a cargo of petroleum at the following minimum rates :
245 Light Petroleum (viscosity less than 320 SSU at 100° F.) .... bbls/hr
246 Medium petroleum (viscosity of 320 to 3200 at 100° F.) .... bbls/hr
247 Heavy petroleum (viscosity above 3200 SSU at 100° F.) .... bbls/hr
248 or of maintaining a pressure of 100 PSI at ship's rail should the foregoing minimum rates not be met.
249　　Charterer is to be compensated at $............... per hour or pro rata for each
250 part of an hour that Vessel takes in excess of the pumping rates as stipulated above. The owner
251 understands and agrees that he will receive no credit or compensation if the Vessel is able to dis-
252 charge at a rate greater than those specified above. Any delay to Vessel's discharge caused by shore
253 conditions shall be taken into account in the assessment of pumping performance. Pumping per-
254 formance shall be reviewed in accordance with Clause 9.

速力，燃料，ポンプ能力の担保

　8．本船は本契約期間中，シーブイとシーブイとの間の海上航行において，主機については最大粘度が華氏100度において.........秒レッドウッド No.1 のディーゼル油／C重油／高粘度燃料，.........トン（2,240ポンド），補機についてはディーゼル油.........トン（2,240ポンド）の1日当たり保証燃料消費量で，満載状態では.........ノット，空荷状態では.........ノット（速力は，オフハイヤーとして計算される航海時間および海上での停船を除き，航海日誌記載の全航走距離を全航海時間で除することにより算出される）を，あらゆる気象条件の下で維持することを船主は担保する。

　積荷が加熱されている間の1日当たり保証燃料消費量は，1タンク，1日当たり，最大粘度が華氏100度において.........秒レッドウッド No.1 のディーゼル油／C重油／高粘度燃料，.........バレルである。タンク清掃中の保証消費量は，1機1時間当たり，最大粘度が華氏100度において......秒レッドウッド No.1 のディーゼル油／C重油／高粘度燃料，.........バレルである。

　傭船者は，本船の全性能を使用する権利を有し，船主は本船が最低でも以下のレートで荷油を揚荷する性能を有することを担保する。

　　軽質油（華氏100度で粘度320セーボルト・ユニバーサル未満）......バレル／時間
　　中質油（華氏100度で粘度320セーボルト・ユニバーサル以上，3,200セーボルト・ユニバーサル以

下)......バレル/時間
　　重質油(華氏100度で粘度3,200セーボルト・ユニバーサルを超える)......バレル/時間
上記の値を満足しない場合には，舷側で100ポンド/平方インチの圧力を維持することができるもの。

　　傭船者は，上記揚荷レートを下回った所要時間につき1時間当たり.........ドル，1時間未満については，これを按分比例して補償を受ける。船主は，本船が上記レートを超えて揚荷できる場合にも，支払ないし補償を受けないことを了承し，これに同意する。陸側の状態に起因する本船の揚荷の遅延は，すべて揚荷実績の査定において考慮されるべきものとする。揚荷実績は，第9条に従い精査される。

　　ここでわれわれは，典型的なタンカーの定期傭船契約書式とニューヨーク・プロデュースおよびボルタイム書式との間の顕著な違いの一つを見ることになる。通常の乾貨物の傭船契約書式の場合，速力の性能は「良好な」，あるいは「普通の」気象条件の下で測定される。STB書式のようなタンカーの定期傭船は「保証した」あるいは「あらゆる気象での」速力概念が特に実際的な目的で使用され，そこでは風，波浪，潮流，霧のような外的な要因は無視される。この手法は平易という長所を持つ。そして船が長期間の普通の航路に就航する場合，これらの要因は結局，相当に良好で平均的な線に落ち着くことになる。しかしながら，この規定はいくつかの New York の仲裁審において文字どおりには適用されてこなかった。だから The Golar Kansai, SMA 1263 (Arb. at N.Y. 1978) 事件で MOBILTIME 書式の速力担保と傭船料調整規定が，「穏やかな(ビューフォート　1-5)」気象に適合すると判示された。また The Athenoula, SMA 1410 (Arb. at 1980) 事件および The Efplia, SMA 1359 (Arb. at N.Y. 1979) 事件参照。そこでは MOBILTIME および TEXACOTIME 書式に基づき，速力の遵守状況は「穏やかな」気象の下で測定されると判断された。

　The Ionic, SMA 2519 (Arb. at N.Y. 1988) 事件で争いは TEXACOTIME による傭船に基づく，さまざまな状況下での速力の低下についての責任に関して生じた。仲裁審の多数は速力の低下が海上衝突予防法に従ったものでないかぎり，性能の測定にあたり，気象条件に起因した視界不良の結果を喪失時間の対象から外すのは不適当であると裁定した。この仲裁審が満場一致で裁定したのは，本船が限定された規定の航路を航行しなければならず，そして機関速力を国際法規または地域特有の法に従い，減速した場合，性能を測定する上で，機関速力低下の期間は考慮の対象外とすべきであるということだった。しかしながら，仲裁審は特に言及し，本船があらゆる気象条件の下で，保証速力と燃料消費量を満たし，維持する能力を有することを証明することは機関性能条項に基づく船主の権利のための必要条件であると指摘した。仲裁審は，「本船は明確にシーブイ/シーブイ間就航を基準として傭船期間を通して要求された性能を満たすことができたはずであった。」と述べた。

　未解決の問題は，速力と燃料消費量についての性能保証を，意図的な減速(slow steaming)の期間にどの程度適用するかということである。超過消費に対するクレーム問題の可能な解決策の一つは，「グラフ (curve)」すなわち種々の速力に応じた燃料消費量の尺度を予め明記しておくことである。

　なお，別の問題は，VLCC を積地，または揚地の諸港において，数週間あるいは数ヶ月間にわたり留めおくことにより，実質上貯蔵施設として使用することによって生じる。このことにより船底に貝藻が付着するような事態が生じた場合，いかなる速力の低下も船主の単独責任であるか否かの紛争が生じる可能性がある。

　The Stolt Capricorn, SMA 2359 (Arb. at N.Y. 1987) 事件において，本船の貨物ポンプが良好な稼働状態にあって，第8条の規定に適合していたことを船主が証明できなかったことに

より，傭船者の損害に対し船主は責任ありとの結論に至った。仲裁人は，もし船主が，本船が第8条の規定に適合するとの証明さえできていたのであれば，本船の性能に関する一切のクレームから放免されていただろうと述べた。本事案で提起された問題の一つは陸上ターミナルの背圧であった。仲裁審は「船長が法廷に対し本船の性能に対する陸側からの影響による本船の遅延について異議を申し立てる義務があった」と裁定した。かかる異議の申立や記録不在の中で仲裁審は陸側の状態が強く揚荷に悪影響を及ぼしたとの立証を船主がなしえなかったとの結論を出した。

ADJUSTMENT OF HIRE

255 9. (a) The speed and consumption guaranteed by the Owner in Clause 8 will be reviewed by the
256 Charterer after three calendar months counting from the time of delivery of the Vessel to the
257 Charterer in accordance with this Charter Party and thereafter at the end of each three (3) calendar
258 month period. If at the end of each twelve (12) calendar month period (or at any time during the
259 term of this charter) it is found that the Vessel has failed to maintain as an average during the
260 preceding twelve (12) calendar month period (or for any other twelve month period during the term
261 of this charter) the speed and/or consumption warranted, the Charterer shall be retroactively
262 compensated in respect of such failings as follows:
263   (b) Speed-Payment to Charterer of $ .... per hour or pro rata for each
264 part of an hour that Vessel steams in excess of the equivalent time Vessel would have taken at the
265 guaranteed speed warranted in Clause 8 as calculated in accordance with Attachment 1-"Perform-
266 ance Calculations."
267   (c) Consumption-the Owner to reimburse the Charterer for each ton of 2,240 lbs. or pro
268 rata for part of a ton in excess of the guaranteed daily consumption for main engine and/or
269 auxiliaries and/or heating and/or tank cleaning including any excess not borne by the Owner in
270 accordance with the off hire clause of this Charter Party at the average price for the particular grade
271 of oil as set forth in the then current Esso International Contract Price List at ...... for
272 the total period under review provided that Vessel's actual speed is in accordance with Clause 8. To
273 the extent the Vessel's speed is less than that warranted, fuel consumption allowed will be
274 determined in accordance with Attachment-1 "Performance Calculations".
275   (d) The basis for determining the Vessel's performance in (a) and (b) above shall be the

276　statistical data supplied by the Master in accordance with Clause14. (b).
277　(e) Owner to have similar privileges under this Clause for receiving compensation as Char-
278　terers do should Vessel performance as concerns speed be in excess or consumption for propulsion
279　be below the descriptions outlined herein.
280　(f) The Charterer shall provide Owner with an opportunity to review any claim submitted by
281　Charterer under this Clause, and the Owner shall complete such review, and provide Charterer with
282　the results thereof within 30 days from the date such claim was mailed by Charterer to Owner.
283　Charterer may deduct from hire any amount to which it is entitled under this Clause after the
284　expiration of 40 days from the date of Charterer's mailing of a claim relating thereto to Owner.
285　In the event of Charterer having a claim in respect of Vessel's performance during the final
286　year or part of the Charter period and any extension thereof, the amount of such claim shall be
287　withheld from hire in accordance with Charterer's estimate made about two months before the end
288　of the Charter period and any necessary adjustment after the end of the Charter shall be made by the
289　Owner to the Charterer or the Charterer to the Owner as the case may require.

傭船料の調整

　9．(a). 第8条で船主が保証した速力および燃料消費量は，本傭船契約に従い傭船者に本船が引き渡されたときより3暦月後，以後3暦月毎に傭船者により精査される。各12暦月の期間の最終日に（または傭船期間中いつでも），本船がそれに先行する12暦月間（または傭船期間中の他のいずれかの12暦月間）の保証速力および／または保証燃料消費量を平均して維持できなかったことが判明した場合，傭船者は当該違反に関して，以下に従って遡及して補償を受ける。

　(b). 速力―傭船者に対し，第8条で担保した本船の保証速力での推定所要時間の超過分につき，1時間当たり………ドル，1時間未満は按分比例により支払う。超過時間は添付書1――「性能計算書」――により算定される。

　(c). 消費量―船主は傭船者に，本船の実際の速力が第8条に適合していることを前提として精査した上で，主機，補機，加熱および／またはタンク洗浄についての1日当たり保証消費量を超えるトン数（2,240ポンド）について，1トン未満は按分比例で当該全検査対象期間について………でのエッソ国際契約価格表の既述特定油種の平均価格に従い，償還する。超過分は，本傭船契約のオフハイヤー条項に従って，船主負担にならないものをも含む。本船の速力が保証速力を下回る場合，その程度に応じて燃料消費量は添付書1――「性能計算書」――により算定される。

　(d). 上記(a)および(b)における本船実績の判断基準は，第14条(b)に従って船長の提出する統計資料を基礎とする。

　(e). 船主は，本船の実績上，速力が保証を超えるか，または，燃料消費量がそれ以下である場合には，本条において傭船者が有すると同様の補償を受領する権利を有する。

　(f) 傭船者は，本条により提起する請求について，船主に検討の機会を与え，船主は検討後，傭船者が船主に当該請求書を郵送した日より30日以内に，その結果を傭船者に提出しなければならない。傭船者は，船主に対する請求書の郵送の日より40日経過後，本条により権利を認められる金額を，傭

船料より控除できる。

　傭船者が，傭船期間および延長期間の最終年または最終部分の間の本船実績に関し，請求権を有する場合，当該請求額は傭船期間終了約2ヶ月前になされた傭船者の見積に従い，傭船料より控除される。そして，傭船期間終了後，必要な調整は船主が傭船者に対し，場合により傭船者が船主に対しなすこととする。

　この条項は，性能維持不能の事態における傭船料調整の方法を規定するむしろ複雑高度な企ての一つといえる。速力と燃料消費の問題において，船主は本船の性能が保証した数値を上回っている場合，割増金の権利を与えられるということに注目すべきである（The Golar Kansai, SMA 1263 (Arb. at N.Y. 1978) と The Northern Star, SMA 1494 (Arb. at N.Y. 1980) 各事件参照）。しかしながら，The Golar Kansai 事件では，MOBILTIME 書式絡みの事案であったが，船主は本船が最低速力維持不能であった結果，燃料消費量が少なかったことについて割増金の権利はないと判示された。

　The Norhern Star 事件の判決は，ある状況の下で傭船料調整条項を適用することの困難性を例証している。本船は傭船の最初の2年間低燃料消費の下，優れた速力性能を実現した。紛争は残る数年の傭船者からの指示による「減速航海」期間について生じた。暫定裁定の中で仲裁審は次のごとく裁定した。

　減速または係船の傭船料算定のためのいかなる期間もその間本船が傭船者の指示に妨げられることなく維持できた速力で航走した直前3ヶ月間の実際の1日あたりの確定傭船料率を基準にして査定されるべきである。全速力時の燃料とディーゼル油の証明済最小消費についての船主の報酬は，傭船者の指示に妨げられることなく本船が速力性能を維持できた直前の3ヶ月間の報酬と同じ基準で減速期間および／または係船期間についても船主に与えられるべきである。

　かかる裁定を行うに際して，仲裁審は傭船料調整の条項は本船の証明された速力能力と燃料消費の特質につき船主または傭船者の損失を埋め合わせるが，そうでなければこの条項は一方のみの利益に偏する解釈を認めてしまうことになると指摘した。したがって，一度本船が担保能力を超えた速力を立証すれば傭船者は船主が割増傭船料を稼ぐのを効果的に防ぐために，本船に対して担保速力以上には航走しないよう単純な指示をすればよいということになる（The Columbia Liberty, SMA 2220 (Arb. at N.Y. 1986) 事件も参照）。

　第8条最後の規定に従って，最小保証量を超えるポンプの揚荷レートに対する割増料金は払われない。

　第9条(f)に基づき，傭船者は船主に対して統計に基づく補償請求書（そのクレームが係争中の如何を明らかに無視して）の郵送40日後に性能不足による損害賠償請求額を差し引くことができる。

　最後にかかる条項に基づく傭船料の調整は損害賠償と軽減についての通常の契約法概念を伴うものではないことに言及すべきである。それゆえに傭船者が速力不足による損害賠償額を軽減するための代船引渡を拒否することは代船規定がない中では傭船者の権利の正当な行使であって傭船料の調整に影響を及ぼすものではない（前出 The Golar Kansai 事件参照）。

LIENS

290　10. The Owner shall have a lien on all cargoes for all amounts due under this Charter, and the

291　Charterer shall have a lien on the Vessel for all moneys paid in advance and not earned, all disburse-
292　ments and advances for the Owner's account, for the value of any of Charterer's fuel used or
293　accepted for Owner's account, for all amounts due to Charterer under Clause 9, and other provisions
294　of this Charter and for any damages sustained by the Charterer as a result of breach of this Charter
295　by the Owner.

リーエン

　10. 船主は，本契約により支払われるべき全金額について，すべての積荷にリーエンを有する。傭船者は，反対給付が得られなかった前払全金額，船主負担となる立替金，前渡金，船主負担で使用された，または受け取られた傭船者の燃料一切の代金，第9条およびその他本契約の規定により傭船者に対して支払うべき全金額，および船主の本契約不履行の結果，傭船者が被った全損害金額について本船の上にリーエンを有する。

　この語はニューヨーク・プロデュース書式の第18条と類似のものである。通常リーエンは第三者所有の貨物にまで及ばない（前出568頁参照）。しかしながら，ニューヨーク・プロデュース書式の第18条と異なり「再運送賃」上のリーエンについて明らかに認めてはいない。そこで貨物が第三者に売却された場合，船主の保証についての立場は不安定なものになる。もちろん，もし船荷証券が定期傭船契約に言及し，この条件を摂取していれば，受荷主はリーエンの条件を知った上で貨物を購入したものということができよう。しかしタンカー取引においてそれは一般的慣習ではない。

　傭船者が本船に有するリーエンは明々白々である。米国法に基づき傭船者のリーエンが執行可能であることは明らかであり，合衆国地方裁判所で傭船者のリーエンにより本船は「対物」訴訟手続の対象とされる。

OFF-HIRE

296　11. (a) In the event of loss of time from breakdown of machinery, interference by authorities,
297　collision, stranding, fire, or other accident or damage to the Vessel, not caused by the fault of the
298　Charterer, preventing the working of the Vessel for more than twelve consecutive hours, or in the
299　event of loss of time from deficiency of men or stores, breach of orders or neglect of duty by the
300　Master, Officers, or Crew, or from deviation for the purpose of landing any injured or ill person on
301　board other than any person who may be carried at Charterer's request, payment of hire shall cease
302　for all time lost until the Vessel is again in an efficient state to resume her service and has regained a
303　point of progress equivalent to that when the hire ceased hereunder; cost of fuel consumed while the

304 Vessel is off hire hereunder, as well as all port charges, pilotages, and other expenses incurred during
305 such period and consequent upon the putting in to any port or place other than to which the Vessel
306 is bound, shall be borne by the Owner; but should the Vessel be driven into port or to anchorage by
307 stress of weather or on account of accident to her cargo, such loss of time, shall be for Charterer's
308 account. If upon the voyage the speed of the Vessel be reduced or her fuel consumption increased
309 by breakdown, casualty, or inefficiency of Master, Officers, or Crew, so as to cause a delay of more
310 than twenty-four hours in arriving at the Vessel's next port or an excess consumption of more than
311 one day's fuel, hire for the time lost and cost of extra fuel consumed, if any, shall be borne by the
312 Owner. Any delay by ice or time spent in quarantine shall be for Charterer's account, except delay in
313 quarantine resulting from the Master, Officers, or Crew having communications with the shore at an
314 infected port, where the Charterer has given the Master adequate written notice of infection, which
315 shall be for Owner's account, as shall also be any loss of time through detention by authorities as a
316 result of charges of smuggling or of other infraction of law by the Master, Officers, or Crew.
317 (b) If the periods of time lost for which hire does not cease to be payable under the
318 foregoing provisions of this Clause because each such period or delay is not of more than twelve (12)
319 hours duration exceed in the aggregate one hundred and forty-four (144) hours in any charter party
320 year (and pro rata for part of a year), hire shall not be payable for the excess and any hire overpaid
321 by the Charterer shall be repaid by the Owner.
322 (c) In the event of loss of time by detention of the Vessel by authorities at any place in
323 consequence of legal proceedings against the Vessel or the Owner, payment of charter hire shall cease
324 for all time so lost. Cost of fuel and water consumed as well as all additional port charges, pilotages,
325 and other expenses incurred during the time so lost shall be borne by the Owner. If any such loss of
326 time shall exceed thirty consecutive days, the Charterer shall have the option to cancel this Charter
327 by written notice given to the Owner while the vessel remains so detained without prejudice to any
328 other right Charterer may have in the premises.

オフハイヤー

11. (a). 傭船者の過失を原因としない機関の故障，官憲の介入，衝突，座礁，火災その他本船の事故もしくは損害により時間の喪失が生じ，それが本船の稼働を連続12時間を超えて妨げる場合，もしくは人員，船用品の不足，船長，職員，部員による指揮命令違反または義務不履行，または傭船者の要請で運送される者以外の船内傷病者を上陸させる目的での離路により時間の喪失が生じる場合，傭船料の支払は，本船がその運航業務を再開するに十分な状態となり，オフハイヤー開始時の原点に復帰するまでの全喪失時間中停止される。本契約に基づく本船のオフハイヤー期間中および仕向地以外の港，場所に向かったため生じた消費燃料代，港費一切，水先料，その他の費用は船主負担とする。ただし本船が気象状態により，もしくは積荷の事故のために港または錨地に入る場合，その喪失時間は傭船者負担とする。機関故障，災害，あるいは船長，職員，部員の非能率により，航海中本船の速力が低下し，または燃料消費量が増加した場合，それによって本船の次港到達が24時間以上遅延し，または消費量が1日分の消費量を超えた場合，その喪失時間または超過燃料消費量は船主負担とする。結氷による遅延，または検疫のための時間は，傭船者負担とする。ただし，傭船者が船長に伝染病流行についての十分な書面による通知をなしたにもかかわらず，その伝染病流行港で船長，職員，部員が，陸上と交通することにより生じた検疫による遅延は，船主負担とする。船長，職員，部員がなした密輸その他の法律違反の追及の結果としての，官憲の抑留による喪失時間についても同様とする。

(b). 本条前段により喪失時間または遅延が12時間以下であることを理由に傭船料支払が停止されなかった喪失時間が，各傭船契約年において（1年に満たない部分はその割合で）合計144時間を超えた場合，その超過分につき傭船料は支払われず，船主は過払傭船料を傭船者に返還する。

(c). 本船または船主に対する法的手段の結果たる官憲による抑留によって喪失時間が生じた場合，それがいかなる地においてであっても，その全喪失時間について傭船料支払は停止される。当該喪失時間中生じた消費燃料および水の代金，さらには追加港費，水先料，その他の費用一切は船主負担となる。この喪失時間が30日を超えて継続する場合，傭船者は，本船の抑留中に船主に，書面で通知することによって，本契約を解約することができる。この場合，傭船者の有する前述の他のいかなる権利も害されない。

STBのオフハイヤー規定とニューヨーク・プロデュース書式のような乾貨物を対象とした書式のオフハイヤー規定の間には幾つかの重要な違いがある。したがってSTB書式に基づき本船は「官憲の介入」によって生じた遅延についてオフハイヤーとなるが，これはニューヨーク・プロデュース書式のオフハイヤー条項の下では，オフハイヤーとはならない。もっとも「君主の拘束」により喪失した時間については同条項が適用される。

条文の最初の部分（すなわち機関の故障，衝突，その他）に基づきオフハイヤーが生じるのには遅延が少なくとも12時間を超えなければならない。一度12時間を超えた場合，本船は遅延の全期間につきオフハイヤーとなり，最初の12時間も含まれる。さらに「b」項は，12時間に満たない遅延の全期間につきその加算を求めている。そしてその合計が年間（1年に満たない場合は，その割合で）144時間を超えた場合，本船はその超過分につきオフハイヤーとなる。

この条項はまた，傭船者の要請で運送される者以外の傷病「者」を上陸させる目的での離路はいかなるものであれ，本船のオフハイヤーを構成すると規定している。これは一般的に身体傷害を受けた乗組員を上陸させるための離路を意味するものである。さらにこれはニューヨーク・プロデュース書式第15条の範囲外でのオフハイヤーの範疇に入る。その上，オフハイヤー（すなわち人員の不足，離路，その他）を前提としての遅延の2番目の語群には最低の「控除期間」がない。

オフハイヤーは本船の性能欠如の期間ではなく，むしろ本船の使用が傭船者に実際に与えた，すなわち故障または離路の始まりから故障が生じた時点または離路開始時の状態に戻るまでの時間の浪費によって測られる。これは本船の性能欠如期間のみをオフハイヤーとして扱っ

ているニューヨーク・プロデュース書式第15条を解明する事案の傾向とは対照的である。（前出447頁参照）

　船主に有利なSTB書式の一つの相違点は積荷の「事故」により避難港に入る場合の喪失時間は傭船者負担であるという条項である。ニューヨーク・プロデュース書式のもとでは，本船は「……積荷の海損となるべき事故」による時間の喪失につきオフハイヤーとなる。

　速力の低下または燃料消費量増加の場合には，1日（24時間）の「控除」期間がある。

　オフハイヤーの規定はすべて第8条と関連して解釈されるべきである。したがって適用されるべき最低2時間とか最低24時間に満たないためオフハイヤーが成立しないとしても本船の平均速力の算定に関する限りにおいて，喪失時間はもちろん「勘定に入る」。同様の理由により，実際のオフハイヤー期間は第8条に基づく速力と燃料消費量の計算から除外される。

　「a」項の最終文は検疫による遅延にもオフハイヤーの対象となる可能性があることを認めている。対応するニューヨーク・プロデュース書式では検疫についての特別な記載はない。そして検疫という事態が本船のオフハイヤーにつながる「人員の不足」あるいは「君主による拘束」のもととなったか否かについて多くの紛争が生じている。

　「c」項は本船のアレストまたは差押えがオフハイヤーとなるかどうかの問題につき（本船がアレストされるかまたは差押えられることが最終的に傭船者の責めに帰すべきクレームと関連している場合の状況には触れないまま）傭船者に有利な取決めとなる。この項はまた，アレストが連続して30日に及んだ場合に傭船者に対し解約の選択権を認めている。したがって必要な担保を提供する方策を持たない船主としては，本船が長期の法的拘束に身を曝す場合，貴重な傭船契約を失う危険を冒すことになる（前出455頁の論議参照）。

DRYDOCKING

329　12. (a)　Owner, at its expense, shall drydock, clean, and paint Vessel's bottom and make all
330　overhaul and other necessary repairs at reasonable intervals not to exceed twenty-four (24) months
331　for which purpose Charterer shall allow Vessel to proceed to an appropriate port. Owner shall be
332　solely responsible therefor, and also for gasfreeing the Vessel, upon each occasion. All towing,
333　pilotage, fuel, water and other expenses incurred while proceeding to and from and while in
334　drydock, shall also be for Owner's account. Fuel used during such drydocking or repair as provided
335　in this Clause or Clause 15 or in proceeding to or from the port of drydocking or repair, will be
336　charged to Owner by Charterer at the price charged to Charterer by its bunker supplier at such port
337　if bunkers are obtained there or at the next replenishment port.
338　(b)　In case of drydocking pursuant to this Clause at a port where Vessel is to load, discharge
339　or bunker, under Charterer's orders, hire shall be suspended from the time the Vessel received free
340　pratique on arrival, if in ballast, or upon completion of discharge or cargo, if loaded, until Vessel is

341 again ready for service. In case of drydocking at a port other than where Vessel loads, discharges, or
342 bunkers, under Charterer's orders, the following time and bunkers shall be deducted from hire : total
343 time and bunkers including repair port call for the actual voyage from last port of call under
344 Charterer's orders to next port of call under Charterer's orders, less theoretical voyage time and
345 bunkers for the direct voyage from said last port of call to said next port of call. Theoretical voyage
346 will be calculated on the basis of the seabuoy to seabuoy distance at the warranted speed and
347 consumption per Clause 8.

入　渠

12. (a). 船主は，自らの負担において24ヶ月を超えない適当な間隔をおき，入渠，清掃，船底塗装，すべての分解検査その他必要な修繕を行い，傭船者は，この目的のため本船が適当な港に向かうことを許容する。船主は，上記および本船のガス・フリーについてすべての責任をもつ。ドックへのおよびドックからの回航中および入渠中に生じる曳航費用，水先料，燃料費，清水代その他の費用もまた船主負担とする。本条または第15条に規定するドック中または修繕中，もしくはドックまたは修繕港への，またはそこからの航行中に消費された燃料は，それが当該地または次の補給港で得られたものである場合には，この燃料供給者が傭船者に請求した価格を，傭船者は船主負担として請求する。

(b). 本船が傭船者の指図に従い積荷，揚荷，燃料補給をする港で本条に基づき入渠する場合，傭船料は，本船が空船のときは，到着時点で検疫済証を得たときから，積荷あるときは揚荷終了のときから，再び運航業務の準備ができるまで，支払われない。傭船者の指図に従い，本船が積荷，揚荷，燃料補給をなす港以外の港で入渠する場合，以下の時間および燃料費用は，傭船料より控除される。すなわち，傭船者が指図した最終寄港地より次の寄港地までの修繕のための寄港を含む実際の航海所要時間および燃料費用より，当該最終寄港地より次の寄港地まで直航したと仮定した場合の航海所要時間および燃料費用を減じた時間および費用である。この仮定の航海は，シーブイからシーブイまでの距離を基準に，第8条の保証速力および保証燃料消費量で算定される。

第12条は，少なくとも2年に1回船主の時間と費用で本船を入渠させることを要求する公正で率直な規定である。しかしながら第8条に基づく注釈で示されているように，傭船者の本船使用方法による速力低下を防ぐため，特別な船底掃除が必要となる場合，紛争が生じることがある。

「b」項は，傭船者の使用時間の損失を入渠との関連でオフハイヤーにする努力の成果を表すものである。船渠の場所により指図の変更が生じるかも知れないので，まさにどのような「仮定の航海」が，船渠への離路に要する時間から差し引かれるべきかということは常に明白であるとは限らない。しかしながら，実際問題として，船主と傭船者は通常，入渠手配にあたり，傭船者の本船使用時間の喪失とオフハイヤーの期間を最小限にするため協力する。

OWNER PROVIDES

348 13. The Owner shall provide and pay for all provisions, deck and engine room stores, galley and
349 cabin stores, galley and crew fuel, insurance on the Vessel, wages of the Master, Offi-

cers, and Crew,
350 all certificates and other requirements necessary to enable the Vessel to be employed throughout the
351 trading limits herein provided, consular fees pertaining to the Master, Officers, and Crew, all fresh
352 water used by the Vessel and all other expenses connected with the operation, maintenance, and
353 navigation of the Vessel.

船主負担費目

13. 船主は，食料費，甲板部，機関部の船用品，厨房・船室の船用品の費用，厨房・船室の燃料費，本船保険料，船長・職員・部員の賃金，本船を本契約に規定する航行区域に運航させるために必要な証明書その他の書類一切の費用，船長・職員・部員に関する費用一切を負担しかつ支払う。

この条項はニューヨーク・プロデュース書式の第1条と似ている。しかしながら上記記述に基づき船主が許容される航行区域に本船を配船するために必要なすべての「証明書」の提供を引き受けるということに注目すべきである。これは疑いもなく，合衆国の油濁条例により求められる「賠償資力責任確認書」および現在あるいは今後他の法域で要求される類似の書類を含むものである。

MASTER'S DUTIES

354 14. (a) The Master, although appointed by and in the employ of the Owner and subject to
355 Owner's direction and control, shall observe the orders of Charterer in connection with Charterer's
356 agencies, arrangements, and employment of the Vessel's services hereunder. Nothing in this Clause or
357 elsewhere in this Charter shall be construed as creating a demise of the Vessel to Charterer nor as
358 vesting Charterer with any control over the physical operation or navigation of the Vessel.
359 (b) The Master and the Engineers shall keep full and correct logs of the voyages, which are to
360 be patent to the Charterer and its agents, and abstracts of which are to be mailed directly to the
361 Charterer from each port of call.
362 (c) If the Charterer shall have reason to be dissatisfied with the conduct of the Master or
363 Officers, the Owner shall, on receiving particulars of the complaint, investigate it and if necessary,
354 make a change in the appointments.

船長の義務

14. (a). 船長は，船主によって任命され，その被用者たる立場にあり，その指揮命令に従うが，傭船者の代理，運航手配，本契約による本船の運航業務利用に関しては傭船者の指図を遵守する。本条

および本契約のいずれの条項も，傭船者に対する本船の賃貸借を構成するもの，あるいは傭船者が本船の物理的管理または航海を支配する権限を傭船者に与えるものと解釈されてはならない。

(b). 船長および機関士は，航海日誌を脱落なくかつ正確に記載する。それは，傭船者およびその代理人の閲覧に供され，かつその抄録は各寄港地で傭船者に直接送付される。

(c). 傭船者が，船長または職員の行為を不満足とする理由がある場合，船主はその苦情内容聴を取後，直ちにそれを調査し，かつ必要あれば交代させるものとする。

これらの規定は，対応するニューヨーク・プロデュース書式の規定とまったく同じで，注釈の必要はない（前出361頁の論議参照）。

The Zacharia T, SMA 2224（Arb. at N.Y. 1986）事件で，本船はエクアドルの Esmeraldas からテキサスの Corpus Christi への原油輸送のため，傭船された。傭船契約は本船が「熱帯清水（TFW）における39'6"というパナマ運河安全通過喫水基準の下」原油を満載すると規定していた。この安全喫水の指令は後刻傭船者により訂正され，最深通過喫水38'11"TFW とされた。本船は一ヶ所だけの係船ブイで積荷を行った。そして強いうねりのあるところで，事実上正確な喫水表示を読みとることは不可能であった。船長は，積荷監督に51,000L/T がポンプで積荷された時点で通知するよう依頼した。積荷が終了したとき，検査人により積込量は53,435L/T と確認された。超過の積荷は本船のパナマ運河通航を妨げる喫水に及ぶことになるため，船長は抗議の手続きをした。Esmeraldas で積荷を揚げることはできそうにもなかった。代わりに本船は積荷を Balboa で艀に移し，本船と艀がパナマ運河を通過した後で，再び貨物が本船に積み戻された。船主と傭船者の間で艀の費用とオフハイヤーにつき紛争が生じた。仲裁審は本船が貨物を積み過ぎないようにするのは船長の責任であるがゆえに船主に責任ありと裁定した。仲裁審によれば，

本船が所期の航海を安全に遂行するために積荷を行い，貨物のバランスをとることに気をつけるのは常に船長の責任である。もし意図した航行が本事案のように海峡または運河の喫水制限により影響を受けるのであれば，これを考慮に入れ，航海を遅滞なく，余分な費用をかけずに達成するような方法で積荷を行うのが船長の義務である。

FUEL, PORT CHARGES, ETC.

365 15. (a) The Charterer (except during any period when the Vessel is off hire) shall provide and
366 pay for all fuel except for galley and Crew as provided in Clause 13. The Charterer shall also pay for
367 all port charges, light dues, dock dues, Panama and other Canal dues, pilotage, consular fees, (except
368 those pertaining to Master, Officers, and Crew), tugs necessary for assisting the Vessel in, about, and
369 out of port for the purpose of carrying out this Charter, Charterer's agencies and commissions
370 incurred for Charterer's account and crew expense incurred for connecting and disconnecting cargo
371 hoses and arms. The Owner shall, however, reimburse the Charterer for any fuel used or any
372 expenses incurred in making a general average sacrifice or expenditure, and for

any fuel consumed
373　during drydocking or repair of the Vessel.

燃料費，港費等

15. (a). 傭船者は，(本船のオフハイヤー期間を除き)，第13条で規定する厨房および乗組員のための燃料費以外のすべての燃料を手配し，その費用を支払う。傭船者はまた，すべての港費，艀賃，埠頭料，パナマその他の運河通行料，水先料，領事証明手数料(船長・職員・部員に関するものを除く)，本契約を実行するための出入港および港内碇泊のための必要な曳船使用料，傭船者負担分として生じる代理店費および手数料，荷役ホースおよびアームの連結，取りはずしより生じる乗組員の費用を支払う。しかし船主は，共同海損犠牲損害または費用として使用した燃料費ないし生じた費用，および入渠中または修繕中消費した燃料費を，傭船者に償還する。

この規定は通常燃料費を傭船者に割り当てることと調和している。共同海損犠牲損害の一部として消費された燃料が船主負担となるが，それは本船と貨物が共同海損費用の割り当てを律する確立した規則に基づきこの費用を分担するから筋が通ることであるということは注目すべきであろう。第23条に基づき，海難救助作業の間に消費された燃料油代は一切の救助費用から控除されることとなっている。海難救助努力があったにもかかわらず救助料が支払われない場合，その費用を傭船者が負担するという基本原則を変える規定は存在しない。

TUGS AND PILOTS

374　(b) In engaging pilotage and tug assistance, Charterer is authorized by Owner to engage them
375　on behalf of Owner on the usual terms and conditions for such services then prevailing at the ports
376　or places where such services are engaged, including provisions there prevailing, if any, making pilots,
377　tug captains, or other personnel of any tug the borrowed servants of the Owner.
378　(c) Neither the Charterer nor its agents nor any of its associated or affiliated companies, nor
379　any of their agents of employees, shall be under any responsibility for any loss, damage, or liability
380　arising from any negligence, incompetence, or incapacity of any pilot, tug captain, or other
381　personnel of any tug, or arising from the terms of the contract of employment thereof or for any
382　unseaworthiness or insufficiency of any tug or tugs, the services of which are arranged by Charterer
383　on behalf of Owner, and Owner agrees to indemnify and hold Charterer, its agents, associated and
384　affiliated companies and their employees harmless from and against any and all such consequences.
385　(d) Charter shall have the option of using its own tugs or pilots, or tugs or pilots made
386　available or employed by any associated or affiliated companies, to render towage or pilotage

387　services to the Vessel. In this event, the terms and conditions relating to such services prevailing in
388　the port where such services are rendered and applied by independent tugboat owners or pilots, shall
389　be applicable, and Charterer, its associated or affiliated companies and their pilots shall be entitled to
390　all exemptions from and limitations of liability, applicable to said independent tugboat owners or
391　pilots and their published tariff terms and conditions.

曳船および水先人

　　(b). 水先案内および曳船を使用する場合，船主は，当該業務を必要とする港または場所において，慣行となっている当該業務についての通常の条件で，水先人，曳船の船長その他乗組員を船主派遣被用者とする条件で，船主に代わってこれらを雇い入れる権限を傭船者に与える。

　　(c). 傭船者，その代理人，関連会社，子会社，それらの代理人または被用者は，水先人，曳船の船長その他乗組員の過失，無能力，不適任に起因する，あるいはこれらの者の雇用契約条件から発生する，さらには傭船者が船主に代わって手配した曳船の不堪航ないし性能不足に起因する責任，滅失，損傷につき何らの責任を負うものではない。そして船主は，かかる結果の一切について傭船者，その代理人，関連会社，子会社，その被用者に責任を負わせないこと，また損害を負担させないことに同意する。

　　(d). 本船に曳船ないし水先案内の業務を提供するについては，傭船者は，自己の曳船，水先人，あるいは関連会社ないし子会社が利用しているか，ないし雇用している曳船，水先人を使用する権利を有する。この場合，当該労務が提供される港に普及している，独立の曳船所有者ないし水先人が用いる当該労務に関する諸条件が適用され，そして傭船者，関連会社，子会社，その水先人には，上記独立曳船所有者ないし水先人に適用されるすべての免責，責任制限，およびその公表されたタリフ条件が認められる。

　第15条の「b」項は明らかにいわゆる「英国曳船条件」のような曳船および水先人の条件を目的とするものである。これらは標準的な契約条件で，船主に本船側の過失による損傷にとどまらず，曳船側の過失についても責任を負わすものである。かかる契約は合衆国では公序良俗に反するものとして無効とされる。しかし英国その他ではこれらは有効である。この条項により，この業務を必要とする特定の港またはターミナルで慣習となっているか，または要求される場合，傭船者は船主をこれらの条件に拘束する権限を与えられる。

　「c」項は，いずれにしても，何がもっともらしい一般的原則であるかを示す。すなわち傭船者は船主の代理として曳船や水先人を雇うのであって，本船の安全航行には当然責任がない。しかしながら，この規定は第6条の「安全港」および「安全碇泊場所」に限定される義務との関連で解釈されるべきである。これらは，傭船者が本船に対して，彼が十分な曳船設備がないと知っているか，または知っているべき港または碇泊場所向けの指示を出すことを不可能にすると思われる（*The Agia Erini II*, SMA 1602 (Arb. at N. Y. 1981) 事件参照）。

　Scholl v. *Chuang Hui Marine Co., Ltd.*, 646 F. Supp. 137, 1987 AMC 1162 (D. Conn. 1986) 事件において傭船契約にはSTB第15条c項と類似の条項が入っていた。傭船者と船主は石油検査官に訴えられた。彼はタンカーの甲板上で油性の物質で滑ってけがをしたとして賠償の請求を提起した。裁判所は簡易判決で傭船者を支持して，石油検査官の賠償請求を却下し，傭船者は検査官に対して甲板を安全な状態に保つべき義務はないと判示した。

　第15条の最後の規定「d項」は，不慮の災難時，責任の所在を決めるために，傭船者の曳船子会社を分離して独立した存在として扱うという努力の成果である。かかる曳船を巻き添えに

する損害賠償は傭船契約に基づき，New Yorkにおける仲裁を条件とすると判定されると思われる。その場合，船主は当該曳船条件は強制できないと主張することができよう。そのような条件が公表されているところではそれはたぶん有効であるように思えるから，かなり困難な抵触法の問題が生じることになろう。

ADDITIONAL EQUIPMENT

392 16. The Charterer, subject to the Owner's approval not to be unreasonably withheld, shall be at
393 liberty to fit any additional pumps and/or gear for loading or discharging cargo it may require
394 beyond that which is on board at the commencement of the Charter; and to make the necessary
395 connections with steam or water pipes, such work to be done at its expense and time, and such
396 pumps and/or gear so fitted to be considered its property, and the Charterer shall be at liberty to
397 remove it at its expense and time during or at the expiry of this Charter; the Vessel to be left in her
398 original condition to the Owner's satisfaction.

追加装備

16. 傭船者は，傭船開始時に本船にある積荷ないし揚荷のためのポンプおよび／または，設備の他に，必要なポンプおよび／または設備を追加設置する自由を有し，さらに必要な蒸気管または水道管と連結することができる。ただし，船主の同意を必要とするが，船主は理由なくこれを拒否できない。この設置は，傭船者の費用と時間でなされ，かつ設置されたポンプおよび／または設備は傭船者の財産とみなされ，さらに傭船者は，その費用と時間で本契約期間中，または満了時にこれを撤去する自由を有する。本船は船主の満足するよう，その原状に回復されなければならない。

ポンプのような装備の追加は第8条に基づく本船の性能の評価を複雑なものにする。さらに|634|装備は傭船者所有に帰するものとの主張にもかかわらず，それは本船に対する海事リーエンの対象となる (*Payne* v. *The Tropic Breeze*, 412 F. 2d 707 (1st Cir. 1969) 事件参照)。

LAY-UP

399 17. The Charterer shall have the option of laying up the Vessel for all or any portion of the term
400 of this Charter, in which case hire hereunder shall continue to be paid, but there shall be credited
401 against such hire the whole amount which the Owner shall save (or reasonably should save) during
402 such period of lay-up through reduction in expenses, less any extra expenses to which the Owner is
403 put as a result of such layup.
404 Should the Charterer, having exercised the option granted hereunder, desire the Vessel

again
405 to be put into service, the Owner will, upon receipt of written notice from the Charterer to such
406 effect, immediately take steps to restore the Vessel to service as promptly as possible. The option
407 granted to the Charterer hereunder may be exercised one or more times during the currency of this
408 Charter or any extension thereof.

繋　船

17.　傭船者は，本傭船期間の全部または一部にわたり本船を**繋船**する権利を有し，この場合，傭船料は継続して支払われる。しかし，この傭船料に対しては，船主は，**繋船**中の費用削減により節約する（ないし合理的にみて節約すべき）額から，**繋船**により船主が負担すべき増加費用を控除した額を，減額する。

傭船者が本条により付与された権利を行使した後に，本船を再び運航させることを希望するならば，船主は，傭船者からその旨の書面による通知を受領した後直ちに，本船をできるだけ，速やかに運航業務に復帰させる措置を講ずる。本条により付与された傭船者の権利は，本傭船期間またはその延長期間中，一度ないし数度行使することができる。

繋船はタンカー市場が不振のとき，頻繁に利用される特権である。節減額と経費の基本的な配分方式は実際問題としてはかなり複雑ではあるが単純で公正である。例えば保険料と維持費の「節減額」の計算は，もし本船が大船隊の部分をなすものであれば難しいことになろう。同様に長期**繋船**の後の本船の性能を正確に測定するのも困難である。そして「本船を元の状態に戻す（原状復帰）」ため，どの程度傭船者に責任を負わせるかということで紛争が生じるのは疑いのないところであろう。

REQUISITION

409 18. (a) In the event that title to the Vessel shall be requisitioned or seized by any government
410 authority (or the Vessel shall be seized by any person or government under circumstances which are
411 equivalent to requisition of title), this Charter shall terminate automatically as of the effective date
412 of such requisition or seizure.
413 (b) In the event that the Vessel should be requisitioned for use or seized by any government
414 authority on any basis not involving, or not equivalent to, requisition of title, she shall be off hire
415 hereunder during the period of such requisition, and any hire or any other compensation paid in
416 respect of such requisition shall be for Owner's account, provided, however, that if such requisition
417 continues for a period in excess of 90 days, the Charterer shall have the option to terminate this
418 Charter upon written notice to the Owner. Any periods of off-hire under this Clause shall be subject

419 　to the Charterer's option for off-hire extension set forth in Clause 1 (b) hereof.

徴　用

18. (a). 本船の権原が，いかなる政府当局により徴用，または奪取された場合にも（もしくは，本船が，いかなる人または政府当局によって権原の徴用と同じ状況の下で奪取を受けた場合にも），本契約は，当該徴用ないし奪取の実際の開始日を以て自動的に終了する。

　(b). 本船がいかなる政府当局により使用のため徴用，または奪取された場合にも，それが権原徴用または，それと同等のものでない限り，本船はその徴用期間中オフハイヤーとなる。そして，当該徴用に関して支払われる傭船料その他補償金一切は，船主勘定となる。しかしながら，当該徴用が90日を超えて継続するならば，傭船者は，船主に対し書面による通知をなし，本契約を終了させる権利を有する。本条によるオフハイヤー期間中については，本契約第1条(b)に規定するオフハイヤー延長期間についての傭船者の権利が適用される。

　この条項のような規定がなくても，船舶の権原徴用は伝統的に傭船契約を「履行不能にする」と判示されてきた（前出486頁参照）。

　船舶の使用の徴用に関する限り，履行不能の法理を適用することはそれほど確実なものではない。「b」項は選択権という言葉で，徴用が90日以上続いた場合，契約を終了させる権利を傭船者に認めている。選択権の行使を要する時期については規定がない。それゆえ，この条項では選択権が徴用の期間続くと解釈されることになろう。船主に対しては類似の選択権が認められていない。もっとも徴用が十分長期に亘る場合（もちろん，傭船者が自己の選択権の不行使を決定したと推測した上で）には一般的な法原則により傭船契約を「履行不能」と宣言できるであろう。

　船舶使用の徴用期間中の全オフハイヤー期間は，傭船者の任意で傭船期間に加算できることは，留意されるべきである。

REDELIVERY

420 　19. (a) Unless the employment of the Vessel under this Charter shall previously have been
421 　terminated by loss of the Vessel or otherwise, the Charterer shall release the Vessel to the Owner's
422 　use, free of cargo, at the expiration of the term of this Charter stated in Clause I (including any
423 　extension thereof provided in said Clause or elsewhere in this Charter), at ……………
424 　………………… (herein called "Port of Redelivery") and shall give
425 　written notice of the date and hour of such release. At the Charterer's option, the vessel may be
426 　released to the Owner with tanks in a clean or dirty condition.
427 　(b) The Owner shall accept and pay for all fuel in the Vessel's bunkers when this Charter
428 　terminates. Payment for such fuel shall be made in accordance with the Exxon International Company
429 　Contract Price List current for the date when and the port or place where the Vessel is redelivered
430 　by Charterer to Owners under this Charter, or the nearest port to which such list applies.

返　船

19. (a). 本契約による本船の業務が，本船の滅失その他により事前に終了したものでない場合，傭船者は，第１条に定める契約期間（同条または本契約の他の規定による延長期間を含む）の満了時に………（以下，「返船港」という）において，本船を空船状態で船主の使用に供すべく返船し，その返船日時を書面により通知する。本船のタンクを洗浄して，船主に返船するかどうかは傭船者任意とする。

(b). 船主は，本契約終了時に本船に積載されている燃料タンク内の燃料一切を受け取り，かつその代金を支払う。当該燃料代金支払は，エクソン国際会社契約価格表により，本船が傭船者から船主に返船された日付，および港または場所，もしくはその表が適用になる最寄り港の値に従ってなされる。

返船については特定の港よりもむしろ諸港の範囲と規定するのが慣習である。それにより傭船者に対し傭船契約に基づく，最終航海期間の柔軟性を与えることができる。

BILLS OF LADING

431　20. (a)　Bills of Lading shall be signed by the Master as presented, the Master attending daily, if
432　required, at the offices of the Charterer or its Agents. However, at Charterer's option, the Charterer
433　or its Agents may sign Bills of Lading on behalf of the Master. All Bills of Lading shall be without
434　prejudice to this Charter and the Charterer shall indemnify the Owner against all consequences or
435　liabilities which may arise from any inconsistency between this Charter and any bills of lading or
436　other documents signed by the Charterer or its Agents or by the Master at their request or which
437　may arise from an irregularity in papers supplied by the Charterer or its Agents.
438　(b)　The carriage of cargo under this Charter Party and under all Bills of Lading issued for the
439　cargo shall be subject to the statutory provisions and other terms set forth or specified in sub-
440　paragraphs (i) through (vi) of this Clause and such terms shall be incorporated verbatim or be
441　deemed incorporated by the reference in any such Bill of Lading. In such subparagraphs and in any
442　Act referred to therein, the word "carrier" shall include the Owner and the Chartered Owner of the
443　Vessel.
444　　(i) *Clause Paramount*. This bill of lading shall have effect subject to the provisions of the
445　Carriage of Goods by Sea Act of the United States, approved April 16, 1936, except that if this Bill
446　of Lading is issued at a place where any other Act, ordinance, or legislation gives statutory effect to
447　the International Convention for the Unification of Certain Rules relating to Bills of Lad-

ing at
448 Brussels, August 1924, then this Bill of Lading shall have effect subject to the provisions of such Act,
449 ordinance, or legislation. The applicable Act, ordinance, or legislation (hereinafter called "Act") shall
450 be deemed to be incorporated herein and nothing herein contained shall be deemed a surrender by
451 the Owner or Carrier of any of its rights or immunities or an increase of any of its responsibilities or
452 liabilities under the Act. If any term of this Bill of Lading be repugnant to the Act to any extent,
453 such term shall be void to that extent but no further.
454   (ii) *New Jason Clause*. In the event of accident, danger, damage, or disaster before or after
455 the commencement of the voyage, resulting from any cause whatsoever, whether due to negligence
456 or not, for which, or for the consequences of which, the Carrier is not responsible, by statute,
457 contract or otherwise, the cargo shippers, consignees, or owners of the cargo shall contribute with
458 the Carrier in General Average to the payment of any sacrifices, losses, or expenses of a General
459 Average nature that may be made or incurred and shall pay salvage and special charges incurred in
460 respect of the cargo. If a salving ship is owned or operated by the Carrier, salvage shall be paid for as
461 fully as if the said salving ship or ships belonged to strangers. Such deposit as the Carrier or its
462 Agents may deem sufficient to cover the estimated contribution of the cargo and any salvage and
463 special charges thereon shall, if required, be made by the cargo, shippers, consignees or owners of the
464 cargo to the Carrier before delivery.
465   (iii) *General Average*. General Average shall be adjusted, stated, and settled according to
466 York/Antwerp Rules 1950, as amended, and, as to matters not provided for by those rules,
467 according to the laws and usages at the Port of New York. If a General Average statement is
468 required, it shall be prepared at such port by an Adjuster from the Port of New York appointed by
469 the Carrier and approved by the Charterer of the Vessel. Such Adjuster shall attend to the settlement
470 and the collection of the General Average, subject to customary charges. General Average Agree-
471 ments and/or security shall be furnished by Carrier and/or Charterer of the Vessel, and /or Carrier
472 and/or Consignee of cargo, if requested. Any cash deposit being made as security to pay

General

473　Average and/or salvage shall be remitted to the Average Adjuster and shall be held by him at his risk
474　in a special account in a duly authorized and licensed bank at the place where the General Average
475　statement is prepared.
476　　　(iv) *Both to Blame.* If the Vessel comes into collision with another ship as a result of the
477　negligence of the other ship and any act, neglect or default of the Master, mariner, pilot, or the
478　servants of the Carrier in the navigation or in the management of the Vessel, the owners of the cargo
479　carried hereunder shall indemnify the Carrier against all loss or liability to the other or noncarrying
480　ship or her owners in so far as such loss or liability represents loss of, or damage to, or any claim
481　whatsoever of the owners of said cargo, paid or payable by the other or recovered by the other or
482　noncarrying ship or her owners as part of their claim against the carrying ship or Carrier. The
483　foregoing provisions shall also apply where the owners, operators, or those in charge of any ships or
484　objects other than, or in addition to, the colliding ships or object are at fault in respect of a collision
485　or contract.
486　　　(v) *Limitation of Liability.* Any provision of this Charter to the contrary notwithstanding,
487　the Carrier shall have the benefit of all limitations of, and exemptions from, liability according to the
488　Owner or Chartered Owner of vessels by any statute or rule of law for the time being.
489　　　(vi) *Deviation clause.* The Vessel shall have liberty to sail with or without pilots, to tow or
490　be towed, to go to the assistance of vessels in distress, to deviate for the purpose of saving life or
491　property or of landing any ill or injured person on board, and to call for fuel at any port or ports in
492　or out of the regular course of the voyage.

船荷証券

　20. (a). 船荷証券は，呈示どおりに船長により署名されるものとし，要求あれば，船長が，傭船者またはその代理人の事務所に毎日出頭する。しかし，傭船者の選択により，傭船者またはその代理人が，船長に代わって船荷証券に署名することもできる。いかなる船荷証券も本契約上の権利を害するものではない。また本契約と，船荷証券，その他傭船者その代理人，またはその要求によって船長が署名した書類との間の不一致，または傭船者またはその代理人の提供した書類の不備により生じるすべての結果ないし責任について，傭船者は船主に補償する。
　(b). 本傭船契約および積荷につき発行された船荷証券に基づく積荷運送は，制定法規およびその他本条(i)ないし(vi)に規定する条項に従う。また，これら条項は，すべての船荷証券に逐語的に摂取され，あるいは船荷証券上に引用されることにより摂取されたものとみなされる。上記当該条項および

法律にいう「運送人」とは、本船船主および傭船船主を含む。

(i) 至上条項。本船荷証券は、1936年4月16日承認された米国海上物品運送法に準拠し効力を有する。ただし、他の一定の法律、命令、規則が1924年8月Brusselsにおける船荷証券に関する若干の規則の統一のための国際条約を国内法化している地で発行される場合には、本船荷証券は、当該法律、命令、規則に準拠し効力を有する。適用される法律、命令、規則（以下、「法律」という）は、ここに摂取しているものとみなされる。そして、ここに規定するいかなる条項も、船主または運送人による当該法律上の権利ないし免責の放棄、もしくは責任の加重とみなされるものではない。本船荷証券中の条項が法律と矛盾する場合、その条項はその抵触する範囲およびその限度で無効となる。

(ii) ニュー・ジェイソン条項。航海開始の前後を問わず、また原因の如何、過失の有無を問わず、事故、危険、損害、災害が生じ、かかる事態およびその結果に対して運送人が法律、契約その他により責任を負わない場合、貨物、荷送人、荷受人、貨物所有者は、支払われるまたは支払われることになる共同海損の性質を有する犠牲、損害または費用を共同海損において運送人と分担し、かつ積荷に関して生じた救助料および特別費用を支払う。救助船が運送人により所有ないし管理されている場合、救助料は、当該救助船が第三者に属する場合と同等に控除なく支払われる。荷送人、荷受人、貨物所有者は要求があれば、貨物引渡前に運送人に対して、運送人またはその代理人が積荷分担金、救助料、特別費用を回収するために十分とみなす額を供託しなければならない。

(iii) 共同海損。共同海損は、1950年改正ヨーク・アントワープ・ルールおよびこれに規定なき事項については、New York港の法律および慣習に準拠し、精算され、書類が作成され、決済される。共同海損精算書が要求される場合には、それは、運送人が選任し、本船傭船者が同意したNew York港の精算人によって同港で作成される。当該精算人は慣行的報酬を得て共同海損の決済、徴収をなすものとする。本船の運送人、傭船者、積荷の運送人および／または荷受人は、要求があれば共同海損同意書または保証状を提出する。共同海損および／または救助料の支払保証としてなされる現金供託は、海損精算人に送金され、当該精算人により、またその責任において、共同海損精算書作成地の正当に認可され、免許を有する銀行の特別口座に保管される。

(iv) 双方過失。本船が、他船の過失および本船船長、船員、水先人その他運送人の被用者の航海もしくは船舶取扱上の行為、過失または怠慢の結果、他船と衝突した場合、本契約に基づき運送された積荷の所有者は、運送人に対して、相手船たる非積載船ないしの船主に対するすべての損失ないし債務を、次の限度において補償する。すなわちそれが積載船または運送人に対する求償の一部として相手船により支払われたかまたは支払われるべき、あるいは相手船、非積載船ないしその船主により回収された上記積荷所有者の全滅失、損傷ないし求償分に限る。以上の規定は、衝突船または衝突物体以外の、船舶または物体の所有者、運航者または管理者に、衝突、接触につき過失ある場合にもまた適用する。

(v) 責任制限。本契約中の反対の規定にもかかわらず、運送人は、現行の制定法ないし法の原則による船主または傭船者の責任制限ないし免責の利益を有する。

(vi) 離路条項。本船は、水先人の有無にかかわらず航行し、曳航し、または曳航され、遭難船の救助に向かい、人命、財産の救助または船上の傷病者を上陸させる目的で離路し、あるいは航海の通常航路上および航路外の港に燃料補給のため寄港する自由を有する。

STB書式は、船長が「呈示どおりに」船荷証券に署名するものと規定することで通常の慣習に従っている。しかしそれらの証券は傭船契約上の「権利を損なわない」ことになっている。本質的には、このことは証券の書式と規定は傭船契約そのものの条件から生じる義務よりも重い義務を「運送人」としての船主には課さないことを意味する。もちろん「b」項は傭船契約に基づく、すべての運送にCOGSA（海上物品運送法）の適用を、続けて規定している。したがって船主はもしCOGSAがそれ自体の力で準拠法となる場合に、貨物に対してたぶん負わされるであろう程度の責任を事実上負うことになる。ゆえに、傭船者が船荷証券を発行し、貨物に対する運送人の義務を増大させるような場合に限り、「a」項が活用されることになる。

「b」項は、ニューヨーク・プロデュース書式よりも、はるかに明確にCOGSAを参照し、

摂取することを規定している（前出603頁の論議参照）。したがって傭船者が荷送人であるにも拘らず，合意に従いCOGSAが当事者の権利と義務の免除を左右する。この規定はまた「至上条項」を「ii」から「iv」に亘って列挙した小段落の条項と併せて，傭船契約に基づき発行されるすべての船荷証券に摂取することを要求している。

かかる条項がすべての船荷証券に引用して摂取されていると「みなされる」べきだとの記述の意味ははっきりしていない。というのは，証券を所持する第三者は，これらの文言が証券に引用され摂取されていない場合，傭船契約の条件に縛られることはないからである。貨物がすべての段階で傭船者の所有である場合に関する限り，証券は単なる受取証であるが，また，権原証券でもある。そして傭船契約そのものが運送契約の条件を証する証拠となる。

「ニュー・ジェイソン条項」は，もちろん，共同海損の回収の障害になるとして，伝統的に運送人の過失を無視する手法である。The Jason, 225 U.S. 32 (1912) 事件での合衆国最高裁の判決により，契約による運送人の貨物の滅失あるいは損傷に対する責任の免除に限って，運送人は共同海損の回収の障害となるとして，過失を無視することを認められている。したがって，実際問題として，貨物はその割合に応じて「航海過失」から生じた共同海損の費用分担を免れない。しかし本船の堪航性を保持するための運送人の「相当の注意義務」の欠如によって生じた共同海損を貨物が分担することはない。

例えばThe Argo Merchant, SMA 2101 (Arb. at N.Y. 1985) 事件参照。この場合傭船者は共同海損の支払につき，責任ありと判示された。

現在のSTB書式に基づき，共同海損は改訂された1994年ヨーク・アントワープ・ルールよりむしろ1950年ヨーク・アントワープ・ルールによって書類が作成されることになっている。しかしながら，この規則には条約または法令としての効力がないので，当事者達は，同規則の特定版を適用することで自由に契約を交わすことができる。しかしヨーク・アントワープ・ルールのどの版が傭船契約の中で規定されていようともSTB傭船契約に基づき発行された船荷証券がこれを引用し摂取していることを確かめるために注意が払われるべきである。

「双方過失衝突条項」は，互いの過失による衝突事件で貨物側が非積載船から回収できる全金額の権利につき積載船の船主に補償するよう，貨物側に要請することを意図するものである。例えば，A船がB船と衝突し両船に過失がある場合，A船積の貨物はその損失を公正な不法行為理論に基づきBから回収できる。（A船の過失が怠慢な航海による場合，「航海過失」はCOGSAに基づき抗弁できるのでA船積の貨物は通常の双方過失事件においては，当然のことながらA船からは回収できない）しかしながら，B船からの貨物損害の回収はB船の損害の一部になる。その部分の一部はA船の過失の程度に比例してA船から回収可能となる。正味の結果は，A船がそれらの損害に直接的な責任はないとしても，間接的にA船積の貨物の損害の一部に責任があるということである。この条項がいっているのはこの間接的責任の回避である。

[637] 双方過失条項は長い間COGSAに基づき無効とされてきた（前出607頁の論議参照）。しかしながらAmerican Union Transport Inc. v. United States, 1976 AMC 1480 (N.D.Cal. 1976) 事件では，法廷は自家運送の場合，有効であると支持した。双方過失条項が「至上条項」との関連で用いられるとき，その有効性については疑問が残っている。なぜなら後者（至上条項）はそれ自らの用語でCOGSAと矛盾する双方過失条項を含むすべての条項を無効とするからである。しかしながらSTBがCOGSAを摂取するのはCOGSAと矛盾する条項をすべて無効にするとはっきり主張するものではなくて，**運送人**の権利を減ずる条項のみを対象としているに過ぎない。これゆえにSTB書式の中の双方過失条項が傭船者所有の貨物輸送の場合，その有効性については議論の余地がある。

米国法に基づき，責任の制限権は船主および裸傭船者だけが利用でき，定期傭船者と航海傭船者はこれを利用できない（46 U.S.C. §§183, 186)。船主または裸傭船者としての船主でさえ，傭船契約のような「個人の」契約に基づき生じる責任に関する限り，制限は認められない（*Pendleton* v. *Benner Line*, 246 U.S. 353 (1918)）。したがって，米国法の法令や規定が，傭船契約に基づき船主に責任制限の権利を認めないため，「(b)(v)」項は船主が「運送人」で，傭船者が貨物の所有者である場合においては，効力がないものと思われよう。かかる事態においては，船主は，傭船契約の条件に基づき免責されなかったことに起因する貨物の滅失または損傷につき責任制限権の適用はなく，傭船者に対して責任を負うことになりそうである。

しかしながら，その所持人に正当に譲渡された船荷証券が当該運送契約の証拠となる場合，船主は自分の「個人的関知あるいは知識 privity or knowledge」に起因せずに生じた貨物の滅失または損傷につき所持人に対する責任を制限できることが認められる。しかし，もし船荷証券が傭船者によって発行される場合，その所持人は貨物の滅失または損傷が，「運送人」としての傭船者と船荷証券の所持人との間の運送契約を証する船荷証券の準拠法である COGSA により免責されない事由に起因する場合，満額を回収する権利を認められる。もし損失の原因が本船の堪航性維持に関する相当の注意義務の不履行とか，最終的に傭船契約の条件によりその責任が船主に帰せられる他の諸要因によるものであるのであれば，傭船者はもちろん損害の補償を受ける権利を有する。そして補償請求権が「個人の」契約（傭船契約）から生じる場合，船主が傭船者に対しその責任を制限することは認められない。最終的な結論は，船主が滅失または損傷に対し，間接的に全責任を負うということであろう。だから，第20条の「(b)(v)」項は，船主が第三者に対する船主の責任を制限するために有する法的権利を，その船主から奪うものと解釈される余地が傭船契約の中に全く存しないということを明確にすること以外何らの効果もないように見える。

双方過失条項についていえば，船荷証券に基づき第三者の貨物が輸送される場合，COGSA の離路についての制限と STB 書式の第20条(b)(vi)のような「自由」の条項との間にはある種の矛盾があるようである。しかしながら運送が傭船契約の規定に従って傭船者のために行われるとき，自由の条項の規定に十分な効力が認められないわけがないように思われる。

```
493  21. War Risks. (a) No contraband of war shall be shipped, but petroleum and/or its
      products
494  shall not be deemed contraband of war for the purposes of this Clause. Vessel shall not,
      however, be
495  required, without the consent of Owner, which shall not be unreasonably withheld, to en-
      ter any port
496  or zone which is involved in a state of war, warlike operations, or hostilities, civil strife,
      insurrection
497  or piracy whether there be a declaration of war or not, where it might reasonably be
      expected to be
498  subject to capture, seizure or arrest, or to a hostile act by a belligerent power (the
      term "power"
499  meaning any de jure or de facto authority or any other purported governmental organi-
      zation main-
500  taining naval, military, or air forces).
501    (b) For the purposes of this Clause it shall be unreasonable for Owner to withhold
      consent
```

502   to any voyage, route, or port of loading or discharge if insurance against all risks de-
      fined in Article
503   21 (a) is then available commercially or under a Government program in respect of such
      voyage,
504   route or port of loading or discharge. If such consent is given by Owner, Charterer will
      pay the
505   provable additional cost of insuring Vessel against Hull war risks in an amount equal to
      the value
506   under her ordinary hull policy but not exceeding .... In addition, Owner may
507   purchase war risk insurance on ancillary risks such as loss of hire, freight disbursements,
      total loss,
508   etc., if he carries such insurance for ordinary marine hazards. If such insurance is not
      obtainable
509   commercially or through a Government program, Vessel shall not be required to enter or
      remain at
510   any such port or zone.
511   (c) In the event of the existence of the conditions described in Article 21 (a) subse-
      quent to
512   the date of this Charter, or while vessel is on hire under this Charter, Charterer shall, in
      respect of
513   voyages to any such port or zone assume the provable additional cost of wages and in-
      surance
514   properly incurred in connection with Master, Officers and Crew as a consequence of
      such war,
515   warlike operations or hostilities.

　21.　戦争危険条項。(a)．いかなる戦時禁制品も船積してはならない。ただし、石油および／または石油製品は、本条における戦時禁制品とはみなされない。しかしながら、本船は、船主の同意――それは理由なく拒否されるべきではないが――なくして、宣戦布告の有無にかかわらず戦争、軍事的行為、または敵対行為、内乱、暴動、海賊行為下にあり、拿捕、没収、アレスト、または交戦国（「国(power)」とは、陸海空軍を保有する法律上または事実上の政府その他政府機関一切を意味する）による敵対行為を受けることが合理的に予期される港、地帯に入港・入域することを要求されない。
　(b)．本条の趣旨に照らして、第21条(a)に規定する一切の危険についての保険を、その航海、航路、積揚港に関して商業上または政府の施策上、付保しうる場合には、船主の当該航海、航路、積揚港に関する同意拒否は不当なものとなる。船主が同意した場合、傭船者は、本船の普通船体保険証券上の保険価額につき本船を船体戦争保険に付保するについて相当の割増保険料を、.....................を超えない限度で支払う。さらに船主が、不稼働損失、運賃船費、全損等の付随危険について普通の海上危険に付保している場合、船主は、かかる危険につき戦争危険保険を付すことができる。もし当該保険が、商業上ないし政府の施策上得られない場合には、本船はそのような港または地域に入りまたは滞まるを要しない。
　(c)．本契約締結日以降または本船の本契約に基づく傭船中、第21条(a)に規定する状況が存在している場合、傭船者は、そのような港または地域への航海に関して当該戦争、軍事的行為、敵対行為の結果、船長、職員および部員に支払うべき正当な割増賃金および割増保険料を負担する。

　ニューヨーク・プロデュース書式および他の定期傭船書式に基づき、船主は通常本船またはその積荷に脅威を与えると懸念される敵対行為が進行している港向けの航行を拒否する権利を有する。そのような場合の船主の権利は明示の「戦争危険」規定というよりむしろ、傭船者の「安全港」を指定する義務に由来する。「安全」とは、港が航行上の安全と同様「政治的に」安

全であって，事実上捕獲される危険や，軍事的行為による損傷の危険が存在する港は，傭船者の義務を満たすものではない。しかしながら既に見たように STB 書式の第6条(b)項は「安全港」のいかなる保証も放棄し，傭船者の義務を相当の注意義務の行使に限定している。第21条は程度がさらに進んで，戦争危険保険が利用できるという条件付ではあるものの，事実上船主に戦争海域まで船を航行させる義務を負わせる。

「(a)」項は幅広い用語表現であり，法律上または事実上の政府の敵対行為だけでなく「陸・海・空軍を保有する政府機関と称する」ものによることさえも含めて，あまねく表示している。これはゲリラまたはテロリストの集団をも含んでいるように見える。他方これにはそのような機関と関わりのない妨害行為者および暴徒の行為は含まれていないようである。

「(b)」項に基づき，傭船者は付保することができるのであれば戦争危険船体保険割増料を支払う義務を負う。その場合，船主は現に敵対行為が進行している積揚港に本船を入港させる航海を許容することを要求されることになる。船主は，また不稼働損失，運賃，船費，全損を含む「付随危険」につき，戦争危険保険を付すことができる。船主がこのような危険につき海上保険を既に付保している場合，b 項は明白にそれを記述していないが，傭船者が敵対行為の生じている海域への航行を本船に命ずる結果支払われる戦争危険船体保険の割増料のような戦争危険保険の割増料が傭船者負担となることは明白な推論である（前出621頁参照）。

EXCEPTIONS

22. (a) The Vessel, her Master and Owner shall not, unless otherwise in this Charter expressly provided, be responsible for any loss of damage to cargo arising or resulting from : any act, neglect, default or barratry of the Master, Pilots, mariners or other servants of the Owner in the navigation or management of the Vessel; fire, unless caused by the personal design or neglect of the Owner; collision, stranding, or peril, danger or accident of the sea or other navigable waters; or from explosion, bursting of boilers, breakage of shafts, or any latent defect in hull, equipment or machinery. And neither the Vessel, her Master or Owner, nor the Charterer, shall, unless otherwise in this Charter expressly provided, be responsible for any loss or damage or delay or failure in performing hereunder arising or resulting from : act of God ; act of war ; perils of the seas ; act of public enemies, pirates or assailing thieves ; arrest or restraint of princes, rulers or people, or seizure under legal process provided bond is promptly furnished to release the Vessel or cargo ; strike or lockout or stoppage or restraint of labor from whatever cause, either partial or general ; or riot or civil commotion.

免　責

22. (a). 本船，その船長および船主は，本契約書に別段の規定ない限り，以下に起因する積荷の滅失，損傷に対しては責任を負わない。すなわち，船長，水先人，船員その他船主の被用者の本船航海あるいは船舶取扱上の行為，過失，怠慢または不履行，火災（ただし，船主自身の故意，過失を原因とするものを除く），衝突，座礁，海上その他可航水域における危険または事故，爆発，汽罐の破裂，シャフトの折損，その他船体，艤装，機器の隠れたる瑕疵。さらに，本船，その船長および船主あるいは傭船者は，本契約書に別段の規定がない限り，以下に起因する契約上の滅失，損傷，遅延または契約不履行について責任を負わない。すなわち，天災；戦争行為；海の危険；公敵，海賊，強盗の行為；君主，統治者，人民によるアレスト，抑留もしくは法的手続による差押え（ただし，本船または積荷を解放するために直ちに保証金が提供されることを条件とする）；原因の如何を問わず部分的または全般的たるとを問わず，ストライキ，ロックアウト，労働の停止，制限；暴動または内乱。

第22条(a)条の最初の条文に基づき，船主と本船船長は対人的，そして本船は対物的に，航海あるいは船舶取扱上の過失，船主自身の故意または怠慢に起因しない火災，海上の危険および隠れた瑕疵を含む列挙された原因により生じた貨物の滅失または損傷につき責任を免れる。

第2の条文は，ニューヨーク・プロデュース書式（第16条第2の条文）の対応する規定が掲げるリストよりもかなり多い一連の原因に起因する傭船契約に基づく「業務遂行上のいかなる滅失，損傷，遅延または不履行」に対する責任からも船主と傭船者の双方を保護する「相互」免責条項である。米国の法廷によって解釈されたように，「相互」免責条項は，その業務が免責の原因の一つが生じたことで影響を受けた当事者のみを免除するものである。したがって，船主が曳船のストライキにより，傭船者の航海指図に従うことができない場合，船主には損害賠償の責任はない。しかしこのストライキは傭船者の傭船料支払能力に影響するものではなく，オフハイヤー条項（第11条）には，曳船のストライキによる時間の喪失をオフハイヤーと規定するものがないので，傭船者はこの遅滞中の傭船料の支払義務を免れない（*Clyde Commercial S. S. Co.* v. *West India S. S. Co.*, 169 Fed. 275 (2d Cir. 1909) 事件参照）。

逆に，銀行のストライキで傭船者が支払日に傭船料を支払えない場合，傭船者はストライキが続く限り，傭船料の支払を免除される。しかし船主には航海，積揚荷役，その他に関し傭船者の指図に従う義務が残る。

NUMBER OF GRADES

529　(b) The Owner warrants the Vessel is constructed and equipped to carry ....
530　grades of oil. If for any reason the Vessel, upon arrival at a loading port, is unable to load the
531　required number of grades, the Charterer will do its utmost to provide a suitable cargo consistent
532　with Vessel's capabilities. However, if this is not possible the Vessel is to proceed to the nearest
533　repair port in ballast and will there repair all bulkhead leaks necessary, any time and expense being
534　for Owner's account.
535　(c) The exceptions stated in subparagraph (a) of this Clause shall not affect the Owner's
536　undertakings with respect to the condition, particulars and capabilities of the Vessel, or the

537 provisions for payment and cessation of hire or the obligations of the Owner under Clause 20 in
538 respect of the loading, handling, stowage, carriage, custody, care and discharge of cargo.

複数等級

(b). 船主は，本船が................等級の油を運送するために建造かつ艤装されたものであることを担保する。何らかの理由で，本船が積荷港へ到着したときに，要求された数の等級の異なる油を積載できない場合，傭船者は本船の能力に合致する適当な貨物を提供するため，最善を尽くすものとする。ただし，これが不可能であれば，本船は，空船状態で最寄りの修繕港へ向かい，そこで必要なすべての隔壁の漏れを修理する。当該時間および費用は船主負担とする。

(c). 本条(a)に述べた免責事由は，本船の状態，要目，性能，傭船料の支払および停止の規定，もしくは貨物の積込，取扱，保管，運送，管理，注意，揚荷についての，第20条に基づく船主の義務に何ら影響するものではない。

「(b)」項の最初の条文は，本船が運送可能な油の複数等級の明確な数を保証するものである。しかしながら，2番目の条文は要するに第11条のオフハイヤー条項の修正であって「いかなる理由」にしろ，本船がその保証に応じることができない場合でも，そのとき傭船者は本船の積取可能な貨物を提供するために「全力を尽くす」義務があって，必ずしも本船がオフハイヤーに至ることにはならない。それが，不可能なときだけ，船主は本船を空船で最寄りの修理港に行かせ，そこで必要な修理を施す義務を負う。その場合，喪失時間および費用は船主負担となる。

539 23. All salvage moneys earned by the Vessel shall be divided equally between the Owner and the
540 Charterer after deducting Master's, Officers' and Crew's share, legal expenses, hire of Vessel during
541 time lost, value of fuel consumed, repairs of damage, if any, and any other extraordinary loss or
542 expense sustained as result of the service, which shall always be a first charge on such money.

23. 本船が収得した救助料一切は，救助料に対して最優先権を有する船長，職員，部員の取得分，法的手続費用，喪失時間中の本船傭船料，消費燃料費用，もしあれば損害修理費，その他救助の結果として生じた特別損失および費用一切を控除した上で，船主，傭船者間で均等に分配される。

この規定については特に解説の必要はない。

OIL POLLUTION

543 24. Owner warrants that the Vessel is entered in TOVALOP and will remain so entered during
544 the currency of this Charter, provided, however, that if Owner acquires the right to withdraw from
545 TOVALOP under Clause VIII thereof, nothing herein shall prevent it from exercising

that right.
546　When an escape or discharge of oil occurs from the Vessel and threatens to cause pollution
547　damage to coastlines, Charterer may, at its option, and upon notice to Owner or Master, undertake
548　such measures as are reasonably necessary to prevent or mitigate such damage, unless Owner
549　promptly undertakes same. Charterer shall keep Owner advised of the nature of the measures
550　intended to be taken by it. Any of the aforementioned measures actually taken by Charterer shall be
551　at Owner's expense (except to the extent that such escape or discharge was caused or contributed to
552　by Charterer), provided that if Owner considers said measures should be discontinued, Owner may so
553　notify Charterer and thereafter Charterer shall have no right to continue said measures under the
554　provisions of this Clause and all further liability to Charterer thereunder shall thereupon cease
555　If any dispute shall arise between Owner and Charterer as to the reasonableness of the
556　measures undertaken and/or the expenditure incurred by Charterer hereunder, such dispute shall be
557　referred to arbitration as herein provided.
558　The provisions of this Clause are not in derogation of such other rights as Charterer or Owner
559　may have under this Charter, or may otherwise have or acquire by law or any International
560　Convention.

油　濁

　24. 船主は，本船がTOVALOPに加盟し，かつ本契約有効期間中，継続して加盟することを担保する。しかしながら，その規約第Ⅷ条により，船主がTOVALOPを脱退する権利を得る場合，本契約のいかなる条項も当該権利の行使を妨げるものではない。

　本船から油の流出，排出を生じ，海岸への油濁損害を生じるおそれがある場合，船主が速やかに措置を講じないときは，傭船者はその裁量で船主ないし船長に通知して，損害を防止し，または最小限に止めるために必要な合理的措置をとることができる。傭船者は，その講じようとする措置の内容を，常に船主に通知するものとする。傭船者が現実にとった上記措置の費用は，船主負担とする（油の流出，排出原因が傭船者にある場合，あるいは傭船者が流出，排出に寄与している場合は，その限りにおいて例外とする）。ただし，船主が当該措置を中止すべきだと考えるならば，船主は傭船者にその旨通知でき，その後傭船者は，本条項により当該措置を続行する権利を有せず，以後の行為に対する傭船者の責任は消滅することを条件とする。

　ここに規定した，傭船者によりとられた措置および／または生じた費用の妥当性に関して，船主・傭船者間に意見の不一致が生じた場合，当該紛争は本契約書に規定する仲裁に付託される。

　本条の規定は，傭船者または船主が本契約に基づき，あるいは別途法律または国際条約により有するか，もしくは取得する他の権利を害するものではない。

　TOVALOP協定に加盟しているタンカーの船主は，その無過失を証明できなければ，特定

の金額の範囲内で，政府に対して油濁浄化費用を弁償することを約束する。そしてさらに船主はこうして負担する契約上の責任について付保することも請け負う。

第24条の第2，第3の条文に基づき，傭船者は船主が即座に行動を起こさないときは，船主負担で漏油の後で浄化処置に着手する権限を与えられる。しかしながら船主は，傭船者にその処置を中止するよう，要求することができ，その場合，傭船者がそれ以上の処置をとれば，それは傭船者の負担となる。

第24条の最終条文は，傭船契約あるいは法律，または国際条約に基づき，両者が有する権利を単純に保護するものである。そして「油濁損害に対する民事責任に関する国際条約」が発効しているところでは，条項Ⅲに基づき油濁の責任は本船船主を経由することになるが，船主は油漏れに責任ある傭船者または第三者から賠償を受ける権利を有する。

CLEAN SEAS

561　25. The Owner agrees to participate in the Charterer's program covering oil pollution avoidance.
562　Such program aims to prevent the discharge into the sea anywhere in the world of all oil, oil water or
563　ballast, chemicals or oily waste material in any form if the said material is of a persistent nature,
564　except under extreme circumstances whereby the safety of the Vessel, cargo or life would be
565　imperiled.
566　　The Owner agrees to adhere to the oil pollution avoidance instructions provided by the
567　Charterer in the Charterer's Vessel Instruction Manual together with any amendments which may be
568　issued in writing or by radio to cover special cases or changes in International and National Regula-
569　tions or Laws. The Master will contain on board the Vessel all oily residues from consolidated tank
570　washings, dirty ballast, etc. Such residues shall be contained in one compartment after the separation
571　of all possible water has taken place by safe methods employing the use of settlement and decanting
572　or mechanic separation to approved and recognized standards.
573　The oily residue will be pumped ashore at the loading or discharge terminal either as
574　segregated oil, dirty ballast, commingling with cargo or as is possible for Charterer to arrange with
575　each cargo.
576　　If the Charterer requires that demulsifiers be used for the separation of oil and water, the
577　cost of such demulsifiers will be at the Charterer's expense.
578　　Owner will also arrange for the Vessel to adhere to Charterer's oil pollution program during
579　off-hire periods within the term of this Charter including the preparing of cargo tanks for drydocking
580　and repairs. In the latter case, the Charterer agrees to bear costs for the disposal of oil

residues.
581　Vessel will take all necessary precautions while loading and discharging cargo or bunkers as
582　well as ballast to ensure that no oil will escape overboard.
583　Nothing in the Charterer's instructions shall be construed as permission to pollute the sea by
584　the discharge of oil or oily water etc. The Owner agrees to instruct the Master to furnish Charterer
585　with a report covering oil pollution avoidance together with details of the quantity of oil residue on
586　board on arrival at the loading port.

汚染防止

25. 船主は，油濁防止に関する傭船者の計画に参画する。その計画は，本船，積荷または人命が危険に曝される極端な状況を除き，世界中どこであろうと，油，油濁水，バラスト，化学製品，その他いかなる形態であろうと，持続性残滓油の海洋投棄を防止する目的を持つ。

　船主は，傭船者の提供した，傭船者本船指図便覧中の油濁防止要領を，遵守することに同意する。当該指図便覧は，国際あるいは国内法規制上の特別の事態または変更を網羅するための書面または電信により発行される改定をも含む。船長は，本船上に集合タンク洗浄の油濁残水，汚濁バラスト等を保持する。かかる残水は，沈殿分離または機械的分離法を用いた安全な方法で，公認された水準にまで，可能な限り水分を分離した後に，1区画に保持する。

　油濁残水は，分離油，汚濁バラスト，積荷との混合物として，傭船者が各積荷を調整するのに可能な限り，積荷または揚荷ターミナルで陸揚される。

　傭船者が，抗乳化剤を油水分離のため使用することを要求するならば，当該抗乳化剤の費用は傭船者負担である。

　船主は，入渠または修理のための積荷タンク準備を含む，本契約期間内のオフハイヤー期間中に，傭船者の油濁防止計画を遵守すべく，本船を整備する。この場合には，傭船者は，油濁残水投棄の費用を負担する。

　本船は，積揚荷役，燃料補給，バラスティングの際に，油を船外に排出しないことを確実にするために，必要なあらゆる予防策を講ずる。

　いかなる傭船者の指図も，油または油濁水の排出等による海洋汚染の容認と解されるべきではない。船主は，船長に対し，傭船者へ積荷港到達時の船上油濁残水量の詳細も併記した油濁防止に関する報告書の提出を，指図することに同意する。

　この条項は傭船者からの指図があれば，海上油濁を最小限にするための努力として，石油会社の採用した「ロード・オン・トップ (load on top)」および他の方式に従うことを船主に要請するものである。

PRODUCTS

587　26. Owner hereby agrees to receive sales representatives of affiliates of Charterer which market
588　marine products. However, Owner is under no obligation to purchase from said affiliates, and said
589　affiliates are under no obligation to sell to Owner any of such products. Owner designates the
590　following as the appropriate persons or organizations with whom said affiliates should

deal :
641 591 Name ....
592 Address ....

製　品

26.　船主は，ここに船用製品を商う傭船者の子会社の販売部と接することに同意する。しかしながら，船主はこの子会社から当該生産物を購買する義務はなく，この子会社が船主に販売する義務もない。船主は，当該子会社と交渉する適当な人物ないし組織として次の者を指定する。

名称............................
住所....................................

この条項は傭船者に対して彼が生産した潤滑油および他の石油製品を努力して「売込む」ことを単に認めることを明らかに意図したものである。

CHANGE OF OWNERSHIP

593　27. Owner's rights and obligations under this Charter are not transferable by Sale or Assignment
594　without Charterer's consent. In the event of the Vessel being sold without its consent in addition to
595　its other rights. Charterer may, at its absolute discretion, terminate the Charter, whereupon the
596　Owner shall reimburse Charterer for any hire paid in advance and not earned, the cost of bunkers,
597　for any sums to which Charterer is entitled under this Charter, and for any damages which Charterer
598　may sustain.

所有者の変更

27.　本契約上の船主の権利および義務は，傭船者の同意なくして売却または譲渡により移転するものではない。本船がその同意なく他の権利と共に売却された場合，傭船者は，そのまったくの自由裁量で傭船契約を終了させることができる。その場合，船主は傭船者に対し，反対給付が得られなかった前払傭船料，燃料費用，本契約上傭船者に支払われるべき金額一切，および傭船者が被る損害一切を償還する。

この条項によりSTB書式は，本船を「傭船契約付」で売ることにより，高い料率の傭船から利益を売る船主の手法をはっきりと制限する。傭船者に対し評判のよい買手への売船に同意することを不当に抑える権利を与えるべきではないとの論議があるかも知れないが，にもかかわらず，同意なき譲渡が結局契約を終了させるという厳しい罰則が存するゆえに，慎重な船主であれば，先ず傭船者の明確な承諾を得ることなく売船を企てる以前に二の足を踏むことになろう。

この条項の中には，ある会社名義で登録された本船の船主が彼の所有するその会社の株式の持分を売ることで間接的に本船に対する権利を処分することを禁ずるものは何もないと思われる。

ARBITRATION

599 28. Any and all differences and disputes of whatsoever nature arising out of this Charter shall be
600 put to arbitration in the City of New York pursuant to the laws relating to arbitration there in force,
601 before a board of three persons, consisting of one arbitrator to be appointed by the Owner, one by
602 the Charterer, and one by the two so chosen. The decision of any two of the three on any point or
603 points shall be final. Until such time as the arbitrators finally close the hearings either party shall
604 have the right by written notice served on the arbitrators and on an officer of the other party to
605 specify further disputes or differences under this Charter for hearing and determination. The
606 arbitrators may grant any relief which they, or a majority of them, deem just and equitable and
607 within the scope of the agreement of the parties, including, but not limited to, specific performance.
608 Awards pursuant to this Clause may include costs, including a reasonable allowance for attorney's
609 fees, and judgement may be entered upon any award made hereunder in any Court having jurisdiction
610 in the premises.

仲　裁

　28．いかなる性質のものであれ，本契約から生ずる一切の紛議，紛争は，New York 市で効力を有する仲裁に関する法律に従って，New York 市において3名で構成する仲裁委員会に付託される。同委員会は，船主により任命された仲裁人，傭船者により任命された仲裁人，およびこの2人が選任した仲裁人により構成される。3名のうち，いずれか2名の，いかなる争点についての判断も最終のものとする。各当事者は，仲裁人が聴聞を終結するときまで，仲裁人または相手方に書面で通知することによって，本契約上の他の紛争または紛議を審問，裁決の目的として指定する権利を有する。仲裁人は，全員一致または多数決をもって，当事者の合意の範囲内で正当かつ衡平とみなされる救済を与えることができる。かかる救済は，特定の履行行為を含むがそれに限られない。本条による裁定額は諸費用を含み，そこには，妥当な弁護士費用も含まれる。本条による裁定に基づき当該事項につき管轄を有する裁判所において，判決を取得することができる。

　STB書式とニューヨーク・プロデュース書式の間には，仲裁条項で幾つかの重要な相違がある。後者によれば，仲裁人は「実務家」でなければならず，この用語の意味は New York では現役の法律家を除くものと解釈される。しかし STB 書式では，当事者は法律家，実務家のどちらからでも選べる。そしてしばしば仲裁審は法律家と法律家でない人で混成される。

　STB の仲裁条項は仲裁人に対し，特定履行命令の権利を含む広範囲の権限を与える。明示の権限がなければ，そのような裁定が有効で執行可能なものかどうかについては疑問が残る。しかしながら米国の法廷は，仲裁条項に彼らにそうする明示の権限を与えるに十分な外延が存する場合には，仲裁人が衡平法上有効な救済を与えることができると判示してきた。

　最後に STB 書式の仲裁条項は明白に裁定額に弁護士費用を含むことを認めている。この点に関して，ニューヨーク・プロデュース書式は触れていない。かかる明示の権限がない場合，

弁護士費用についての裁定は仲裁人の権限の範囲外のものであると裁定されてきた。一方，STB 書式によれば，そのような裁定は明確に有効であるということになる（*Transvenezuelian Shipping Co. S. A.* v. *Czarnikow-Rionda Co. Inc.*, 1982 AMC 1458 (S. D. N. Y. 1982) 事件前出529頁の論議参照）。

ASSIGNMENT SUBLET

611　29. (a)　Charterer, upon notice to Owner, may assign this Charter Party to any of its affiliates.
612　　(b)　Charterer shall also have the right to sublet the Vessel, but in the event of a sublet,
613　Charterer shall always remain responsible for the fulfillment of this Charter in all its terms and
614　conditions.

譲渡転貸

29. (a)　傭船者は，船主に対して通知の上，本傭船契約をその関連会社に譲渡できる。
　(b)　傭船者は，また本船を再傭船に出す権利を有する。しかし，この場合にも，傭船者は常に本契約全条項，全条件に基づく本契約の履行につき責任を負う。

642　これらの規定は，はっきりと傭船者に対して，傭船契約の譲渡と本船を「再傭船に出す」権利を認める。米国法に基づき，この権利はかかる明示の規定がない場合でも，傭船契約が明確に別途異なる規定をしていなければ，認められるものである。

LAWS

615　30. The interpretation of the Charter and of the rights and obligations of the parties shall be
616　governed by the laws applicable to Charter Parties made in the City of New York. The headings of
617　Clauses are for convenience of reference only and shall not affect the interpretation of this Charter.
618　No modification, waiver or discharge of any term of this Charter shall be valid unless in writing and
619　signed by the party to be charged therewith.

法　律

　30.　本傭船契約およびその当事者の権利，義務の解釈は，New York 市で締結された傭船契約に適用される法律に準拠する。各条項の見出しは引用，参考の便宜のためのものにすぎず，本契約の解釈に影響を与えるものではない。本契約書のいかなる条項の変更，権利放棄または取消も，書面によりなされ，かつ，その責任を負う当事者により署名されない限り無効とする。

　傭船契約は，海事契約であり，州法または地方の法律等とは係わりなく，合衆国の「一般海事法」に準拠する。この海事法は英国海事法の先例を加え裁判上形成された一組の法則であり，米国内で一律に施行されている（前出105頁参照）。かなりの程度まで，船荷証券に基づく

物品運送の実体法（例えばハーター法とCOGSA）は，連邦制定法により修正されてきた。しかし傭船契約に基づく運送は比較的，制定法上の規則にとらわれない。したがって主に，第30条により当事者は他のどの国の法律よりも米国の一般海事法の適用を単に受け入れているに過ぎない。

620　IN WITNESS, WHEREOF, THE PARTIES HAVE CAUSED THIS CHARTER TO BE
621　EXECUTED IN DUPLICATE THE DAY AND YEAR HEREIN FIRST ABOVE WRITTEN.

....　............................
　　WITNESS TO SIGNATURE OF
....　............................
　　WITNESS TO SIGNATURE OF

以上の証拠として本契約書は当事者により本契約書冒頭記載の年月日に2通作成された。
....　............................
　　………の証拠としての署名
....　............................
　　………の証拠としての署名

事項索引（Index）

該当頁は原書の頁を指す（原書頁数は訳文の左肩☐内に表記）。
イタリック体の頁数は米国法の頁を示す。

A

"About",	「約」	
charter period,	傭船期間	128, *135*
deadweight capacity,	載貨重量	102, *114*
speed,	速力	128, *135*
Act of God,	天災	
events amounting to,	〜に至るできごと	420, *428*
Agency,	代理	
Baltime form,	ボルタイム書式	552
charterers' duty to provide and pay for,	支給し支払う傭船者の義務	221
conflict of laws,	法の抵触	70
effect of,	〜の効果	61
Agent,	代理人	
actual authority,	実際の権限	*71, 72*
apparent authority,	表見権限	68, 69, *73*
approval of transactions,	取引の承認	*72*
authority, acting without,	権限のない行為	
apparent or ostensible authority,	外観上または表見的権限	68, 69
breach of warranty, agent liable for,	担保違反に責任ある代理人	67, 69
ratification,	追認	68
telegraphic authority,	電報による権限	69, 70
broker as,	〜としての仲立人	*72*
disclosed principal, contract for,	顕名された本人のために契約	
authority,	権限	61
basic rule,	基本規則	61
body of contract, agency indicated in,	契約書体文に示された代理関係	63, 64
foreign principal,	外国人が本人	64
guarantors,	保証人	64
liable and entitled, being,	責任を負うべき、かつ権利のある	62
party, agent not,	代理人は当事者ではない	*71*
rights of agent,	代理人の権利	64
signature as agents,	代理人として署名	62
unnamed principal,	氏名が表示されていない本人	64
words following signature,	署名に続く語句	63
employment clause, under,	使用条項に基づく	299
piercing corporate veil, *See* **Company**	法人格の否認、会社を参照	
principal, as,	本人として	
named,	氏名が表示された〜	65
unnamed,	氏名が表示されていない〜	65, 66
principal, liability to,	本人に対する責任	74
ratification of actions,	行為の追認	68, *74*
undisclosed principal, contract for,	隠された本人のための契約	
"as charterer", description of agent,	「傭船者として」代理人の表示	67
"as disponent", description of agent,	「管理船主として」代理人の表示	67

"as owner", description of agent,	「船主として」代理人の表示	66
enforcement of rights,	権利の行使	*74*
principal or agent suing under contract,	契約に基づき訴える本人または代理人	66
Arbitration,	仲裁	
abandonment of,	〜の放棄	*457*
agreement,	合意	
enforcement,	強制	*448*
law governing,	準拠法	*439*
matters in,	合意の事項	*447*
parties to,	合意の当事者	79
written,	書面による合意	*447*
appeals,	上訴	
application for leave, exercise of discretion on,	上訴申請に関する裁量行使	444, 445
consent of parties, with,	当事者同意の上の上訴	445
Court of Appeal, to,	控訴審への上訴	446
exclusion of right to,	上訴の権利の排除	445
High Court, to,	高等法院への上訴	444, 445
statutory provisions,	法令規定	*451*
arbitrator,	仲裁人	
appointment of,	仲裁人の指名	440,
"commercial men",	「実務家」	441, *454*, 455
costs, award of,	費用に関する裁定	*457*, *458*
court, appointment by,	裁判所による選任	443, *453*, *454*
failure of party to appoint,	当事者が仲裁人の起用を行わない場合	442
fees, award of,	弁護士費用の裁定	*457*, *458*
interest, award of,	利子の裁定	446, *457*
misconduct,	仲裁人の不当な管理	*468*, *469*
number not specified,	仲裁人の数が特定されていない	441
powers of,	仲裁人の権限	442, 443
powers, exceeding,	仲裁人が自らの権限を踰越した場合	*469*-*471*
punitive damages, award of,	懲罰的賠償の裁定	*458*, *459*
security, award of,	保証状の提出を命ずる裁定	*461*
single, reference to,	単独仲裁人の適用	441, *453*
"three persons",	「3名仲裁人」	441,
attachment or arrest of security,	担保の差押えまたはアレスト	*459*-*461*
award,	判断	
binding effect of,	判断の拘束効果	*477*
confirmation,	仲裁判断の確認	*462*, *463*
foreign, recognition and enforcement of,	外国仲裁判断の承認および執行	*474*-*477*
vacating. *See* vacating of award, *below*	〜判断の破棄，〜判断の破棄を参照	
Baltime form,	ボルタイム書式	571
bills of lading, clause in,	船荷証券の〜条項に	*448*
charter disputes, of,	傭船契約紛争の〜	56, 57
choice of law,	法律の選択	
arbitrators, applied by,	仲裁人によって適用される法律の選択	437
charters entered into after 1 April 1991,	1991年4月1日以降に締結した傭船契約	438
charters entered into before 1 April 1991,	1991年4月1日より前に締結した傭船契約	437, 438

New York,	ニューヨーク州法	*447*
Rome Convention,	ローマ条約	*437*
commencement,	〜の開始	*440*
extension of time for,	〜の開始のための期間の延長	*440,*
time for,	〜の開始の時期	*439, 523 - 525*
compelling,	〜の強制	*450 - 452*
conduct of proceedings,	〜手続の実施	*442-444*
consolidated,	〜の併合	*452, 453*
costs, award of,	費用に関する裁定	*457, 458*
court, powers of,	裁判所の権限	
arbitrators, appointment of	仲裁人の選任	*443, 453, 454*
conduct of arbitration, as to,	仲裁の実施に関する裁判所の権限	*444*
discovery before,	〜開始前の証拠開示手続き	*455*
dismissal for delay in,	遅延を理由に棄却	*443*
disputes subject to,	〜に付託を条件とした係争	*455 - 457*
English law, governed by,	英国法にて規制される〜	*441*
fees, award of,	弁護士費用の裁定	*457, 458*
interest, award of,	利子の裁定	*446, 457*
interim awards,	暫定仲裁判断	*446*
jurisdiction, law governing,	管轄を規制する法律	*439*
New York Produce Exchange Form,	ニューヨーク・プロデュース書式	*437, 447*
NYPE 93,	NYPE 93	*18, 446*
place of,	〜の場所	*437*
procedure, law governing,	〜手続を規制する法律	*439*
punitive damages, award of,	懲罰的賠償の裁定	*458, 459*
security in aid of award,	裁定実現を目的とする担保	*459 - 461*
statutory recognition of,	〜に関する制定法上の承認	*447*
stay of suit pending,	〜に付託されている場合の訴訟手続の停止	*442, 449*
STB Form,	STB 書式	*48, 641*
suit brought in, time of,	〜における「訴の提起」の時期	*440*
timeliness of demand,	〜付託の時機を得た要求	*450, 451*
United States Carriage of Goods by Sea Act,	米国海上物品運送法	
time limit, incorporation of,	出訴期限の摂取	*439, 440*
vacating of award,	〜判断の破棄	
bias, appearance of,	偏向の様子	*466, 467*
contract, misinterpretation of,	契約の解釈の誤り	*473*
corruption, award obtained by,	贈賄で得られた〜判断	*465*
final,	最終〜判断の破棄	*463, 464*
final and definite, not,	最終的, 明確ではない〜判断の破棄	*472*
grounds of attack,	攻撃の理由	*464 - 472*
manifest disregard of law, for,	明らかなる法の無視を理由とした〜判断の破棄	*472-474, 476*
misconduct of arbitrators,	仲裁人の不当な管理	*468, 469*
powers, arbitrators, exceeding,	仲裁人が自らの権限を踰越	*469 - 471*
relationship of party with arbitrator, effect of,	仲裁人と当事者の関係の効果	*467*
time limits,	時間の制限	*464*

undue means, award obtained by,	不公正な方法により得られた判断	465
violation of public policy, on,	公序良俗への違反に基づく〜	474
want of prosecution,	訴訟追行が為されない	443

Arrest, アレスト
arbitration, security in,	仲裁の担保	459-461
cause, preventing full working of vessel, as,	本船の完全な稼働を阻害する要因として〜	372
off-hire, whether resulting in,	オフハイヤーとなるか否か〜	372, 387, 388

Assignment, 譲渡
liens, of,	リーエンの〜	501
STB Form, under,	STB書式に基づく〜	48, 641
subfreights, of,	再運送賃の〜	485, 486

B

Bale capacity, 容積能力
statements of,	〜の表示	101, 112
trade evidence,	取引関係の証拠	103

Baltime exceptions clause, ボルタイム免責条項
delay,	遅延	551, 556, 557
misdescription,	誤表示	559, 560
personal want of due diligence,	船主または船舶管理人自身の相当な注意の欠如	557-559
physical loss or damage,	物理的滅失または損傷	556

Baltime Form, ボルタイム書式
commentary on,	〜に関する注釈	545-571
text of,	〜の本文	22-25

Berth, バース
nomination of,	〜の指定	546
NYPE 93, under,	NYPE 93に基づく〜	11
safe,	安全〜	195, 196
STB Form,	STB書式	41, 625, 626

Berth Standard of Average Clause, バース海損基準条項
effect of,	〜の効果	315

Bills of lading, 船荷証券
arbitration clause in,	〜の仲裁条項	448
authority of sub-charterers' to sign,	〜に署名する再傭船者の権限	147, 148
bareboat charter, under,	裸傭船契約に基づく〜	529
cargo loaded under deck, wrongly stating,	艙内積貨物と誤記載の〜	331
carrier, identification of,	運送人の同一性	346
charterers' right to issue,	〜を発行する傭船者の権利	553
clause required by charter, not incorporating,	傭船契約により要求される条項を摂取していない〜	329
condition of cargo, misrepresenting,	貨物の状態を不実表示している〜	329-331
demise clause in,	〜のデマイズ条項	331, 332, 346
destination,	仕向地	
alteration of,	仕向地の変更	585
outside charter limits, for,	傭船契約航路定限外の仕向地	329
extraordinary terms in,	〜の異常な性質の条件	328, 329
foreign jurisdiction clause in,	〜の外国裁判管轄条項	332
forum selection clauses,	裁判管轄条項	527

事項索引　　　　797

freight prepaid,	運賃前払	332
effect on lien,	リーエンの効果	486, *496*
functions of,	～の機能	*339*
greater liabilities, imposing,	大きな責任を課する～	
breach of contract,	契約違反	326
claim for indemnity, when arising,	補償の請求が生じるとき	328
express indemnity,	明示の補償	328
implied indemnity,	黙示の補償	326, 327, *344*
incorrect date on,	～の不正確な日付	331
issuance, express restrictions on,	発行時の明示の制限	*345*
NYPE 93,	NYPE 93	14
owners, binding on,	船主を拘束する～	336-338
production before delivery of cargo, master's right to demand,	荷渡前に～の呈示を要求する船長の権利	*346*
quantity or nature of cargo, misstating,	貨物の量または性状の誤表示の～	331
ratification,	追認	*343*
Shelltime Form,	シェルタイム書式	30, 585-587
shipper's right to demand,	～を要求する荷送人の権利	*346*
signing,	～に署名	
"as presented",	「呈示された」	325, *344*, *636*
bailees, by owners as,	受寄者としての船主による署名	334
Baltime form,	ボルタイム書式	336, 553
charterers, on behalf of,	傭船者のために署名	337
charterers or agents, by,	傭船者または代理人による署名	335, 336, 338, *340-342*
effect of,	署名の効果	333-338
indemnity arising from,	署名から生じる補償	295, 326, 327
indemnity, loss of,	補償の喪失	330
intermediate charterers, liability of,	中間傭船者の責任	*342*
master, by,	船長による署名	333, 334, *339*, 340
New York Produce Exchange Form,	ニューヨーク・プロデュース書式	325, *339*
NYPE 93,	NYPE 93	336
ostensible or apparent authority to bind owners,	船主を拘束する表見的権限	338
refusal by master,	船長の署名拒否	325, *344*, *345*
Shelltime Form,	シェルタイム書式	585
tanker charters,	タンカー傭船契約	336
STB Form,	STB 書式	45, *635-637*
terms "manifestly inconsistent" with charter,	傭船契約と「明らかに矛盾している」条件	328, 329
"without prejudice to the charter-party",	「傭船契約上の権利を損なうことなく」	333, *345*
Both-to-blame collision clause.	双方過失衝突条項	
See **Carriage of Goods by Sea Act.**	海上物品運送法を参照	
Bunkers,	燃料	
Baltime Form,	ボルタイム書式	548
bunkering place, safety of,	燃料補給場所の安全性	219
delivery and redelivery, quantity on,	引渡時と返船時の数量	223, 227, 588, *626*
domestic consumption,	船内消費	509, *510*
New York Produce Exchange Form,	ニューヨーク・プロデュース書式	227, *229*

NYPE 93, under,	NYPE 93に基づく〜	10, 219, 228
off-hire period, during,	オフハイヤー期間中の〜	222, *223*, 377
price for,	〜の価格	228, *229*
property in,	〜の性質	219, 228
quality,	質	218, *224*, *225*
quantity,	量	218, *223*, *224*
Shelltime Form,	シェルタイム書式	30, 33, 588, 589, 609
STB Form,	STB 書式	44, *626*
"while on hire",	「オフハイヤーの時に」	222, *223*, 377, 509

C

Cancellation, 解除
   wrongful, damages for,   不法な〜についての損害賠償   *277-279*

Cancelling clause, 解約条項
   Baltime Form,   ボルタイム書式   570
   cancelling date, 解約期日
     no absolute obligation to deliver by,   解約期日までに引き渡すことは絶対的義務ではない   358
     no right or obligation to cancel before,   解約期日前に解約する権利（義務）はない   359
     use before,   解約期日以前の使用   *355*
   damages, right to recover,   損害賠償請求権   360, *361*, *362*
   effect of,   解約条項の効果   355
   holds, condition of,   船艙の状態   357
   "in every way fitted for the service",   「あらゆる点で運送業務に適した」   356
   late tender, action for damages for,   本船提供の遅延により生じた損害の賠償請求の訴訟   *361*
   minor infringements, effect of,   軽微な違反の効果   356, 357
   misdescription of ship,   船舶の不実表示   357
   New York Produce Exchange Form,   ニューヨーク・プロデュース書式   355, *361*
   NYPE 93,   NYPE 93   12, 359
   option to cancel, exercise of,   解約選択権の行使   360, *361*
   other rights, and,   その他の権利   360
   readiness, notice of, 準備完了通知
     failure to give,   準備完了通知が出されない   355, 356
     premature,   要件を満たさない準備完了通知   358
     state of ship required for valid,   有効な準備完了通知に必要な本船の状態   154-158, **162**, 356
     writing, in,   書面による準備完了通知   356
   Shelltime Form,   シェルタイム書式   581, 582
   STB Form,   STB 書式   **624, 625**
   use before date stated,   約定日以前の使用   355

Captain. *See* **Master.**   船長。Master を参照

Cargo, 貨物
   charterers' orders, delivery in obedience to,   傭船者の指図に従った〜の引渡   292
   claims,   〜クレーム
     Inter-Club Agreement,   クラブ間協定   311
     NYPE 93,   NYPE 93   14
     settling,   〜クレームの解決   310-314
     Shelltime Form,   シェルタイム書式   602

clean-swept holds for,	清掃した〜船艙	155, *163*
condition, bill misrepresenting,	〜の状態を不実表示した証券	329-331
controlled substances,	麻薬	*173*
dangerous,	危険〜	
advising of dangers,	危険性の連絡	*173*
Baltime Form,	ボルタイム書式	170, 546
becoming,	危険となる〜	168
biological degradation,	生物学的品質低下	*173*
Carriage of Goods by Sea Act	海上物品運送法と	168-170, *174*
and Hague Rules, under	ヘーグ・ルールに基づく危険〜	*175*, 605
classification as,	危険〜として分類	*175*
extra remuneration for,	危険〜について特別報酬	170
implied obligations of charterers,	傭船者の黙示の義務	167
implied warranty, breach of,	黙示担保の違反	*173*
lack of information, due to,	知識の欠如による	170
NYPE 93,	NYPE 93	9, 166
owners' indemnity,	船主に対する補償	170
owners, rights of,	船主の権利	168
question of fact, as,	事実問題として	*175*
risks, anticipating,	予想される危険	167
shipper, liability of,	荷送人の責任	168, 169
spontaneous combustion, susceptibility to,	自然発火しやすい性質	*175*
warn, duty to,	警告の義務	*174*
deck,	甲板〜	
NYPE 93, indemnity,	NYPE 93，補償	283
responsibility for,	甲板〜に対する責任	308
discharge	揚荷	
bill of lading, place shown on,	船荷証券に表示された揚荷場所	586, 587
course of voyage, during,	航海途上で揚荷	304
responsibility for,	揚荷の責任	303
excess, preventing full working of vessel,	貨物を積みすぎて，本船の完全な稼働を阻害する	371
excluded under charter,	傭船契約に基づく除外〜	
acceptance, effect of,	傭船契約に基づく除外〜の引受の効果	166
NYPE 93,	NYPE 93	9
shipment of,	傭船契約に基づく除外〜の船積	165, 166
sub-charter,	再傭船	*172*
gear, NYPE 93,	荷役機器，NYPE 93	14
gear and equipment, readiness of,	荷役機器および装置の準備	155, 156
injurious,	有害〜	
Shelltime Form,	シェルタイム書式	33, 605
intermediate charterers, liability of,	中間傭船者の責任	*342*
lawful merchandise,	適法な貨物	
Baltime Form,	ボルタイム書式	546
excluded cargo,	除外貨物	165, 166
New York Produce Exchange Form,	ニューヨーク・プロデュース書式	165, *172*
lawful trades,	適法な航路	171
loaded under deck, misstating,	艙内積と誤表示の〜	331
loading, stowing, trimming and discharging,	〜の積込，積付，荷均と揚荷	

"and responsibility of the Captain",	「および船長の責任」	305, 306, *318*, *319*
Baltime Form,	ボルタイム書式	305, 547
Berth Standard of Average Clause,	バース海損基準条項	315
Carriage of Goods by Sea Act, effect of,	海上物品運送法の効果	304, 305, 313
charterer, reservation of stowage to,	傭船者の積付の確保	*319*
claims, estoppel,	主張の禁反言	308
contributory negligence,	寄与過失	309, 310
improper stowage, charterers' liability for,	積付不良についての傭船者の責任	*319*, *320*
Inter-Club New York Produce Exchange Agreement,	ニューヨーク・プロデュース書式に基づく貨物クレームに関するPIクラブ間協定	310-314, *322*
leading American case,	指導的米国判例	*316*
loss overboard, liability for,	船外落下についての責任	*318*
New York Produce Exchange Form,	ニューヨーク・プロデュース書式	303, *316*
NYPE 93, under,	NYPE 93に基づき	303
owner, liability of,	船主の責任	*316*, *317*
owners' P. & I. Cover, charterers to have benefit of,	傭船者が，船主のPI塡補の利益を得る	315
responsibility for,	〜の積込，積付，荷均と揚荷の責任	303, *316*
ship, damage to,	船舶の損傷	*321*
stevedoring operations, supervision of,	荷役作業の監督	*318*
"under the supervision of the Captain",	「船長の監督の下で」	305, 306, *317-322*
vouching-in,	訴訟告知	*323*
mate's receipts,	メーツ・レシート	330, *339*
order to load, nature of,	〜の積込指図の性質	297
owners' lien on. *See* **Liens**.	〜に船主のリーエン。リーエン参照	
quantity or nature, bill misstating,	量または性状を不実表示した証券	331
readiness to load,	〜を積み込む準備	154-158, *162*
safe carriage, responsibility for,	安全輸送についての責任	*175*, *176*
space,	スペース	
Baltime form,	ボルタイム書式	550
New York Produce Exchange Form,	ニューヨーク・プロデュース書式	282
NYPE 93,	NYPE 93	11
Shelltime Form,	シェルタイム書式	584
special equipment for,	〜の特別装置	158
STB Form,	STB書式	41, *626*
unlawful,	違法な〜	165
US legislation,	米国の法規制	*176*
Carriage of Goods by Sea Act 1936,	**1936年海上物品運送法**	
both-to-blame collision clauses, insertion of,	双方過失衝突条項の挿入	521, *526*, 613, *636*, *637*
commencement of proceedings, time for,	手続開始の時期	439, 520, *523-525*
exceptions in,	〜の免責事由	423, 518, 519
forum selection clauses, validity of,	裁判管轄条項の有効性	*527*
Harter Act, partially superseding,	〜はハーター法を一部改廃	513
incorporation,	〜の摂取	*522*
disregarded provisions,	無視される条項	517
effect of,	〜の摂取の効果	111, *112*, 514-516

limited right to deviate, giving,	～の摂取は離路を行う限定された権利を与える	520
manner of,	～の摂取の方法	516
other clauses, conflict with,	他の条項との衝突	517, 518
time limit provision,	出訴期限条項	439, 520, *523*
NYPE 93, incorporation of clauses in,	NYPE 93に諸条項の摂取	521
owner and charterer as carrier,	運送人としての船主と傭船者	*522*, *523*
owners and charterers, division of operations between,	船主と傭船者間の業務の分担	521
seaworthiness, obligation of,	堪航性担保義務	97, *112*, 514, 516, 517
voyages under New York Produce form, applicable to,	ニューヨーク・プロデュース書式に基づく航海に～は，適用となる	516
Charter,	**傭船契約**	
bareboat,	裸～	529
choice of law clause,	法の選択条項	*56*, 437-439, *447*
conditions, subject to,	条件として	58
demise,	デマイズ～	
effect of,	デマイズ～の効果	529
hire, contract for,	賃貸契約	530
time charter not,	定期傭船契約であり，デマイズ～ではない	529
frustration. See **Frustration of charter.**	履行不能。傭船契約の履行不能を参照	
governing or proper law,	準拠法またはプロパー・ロー	
generally,	原則的に	*56*, 437-439, 441
Shelltime Form,	シェルタイム書式	616
STB Form,	STB書式	*641*
insurance cover, See also **Insurance.**	保険填補。保険も参照。	531-535, *538*
maritime contracts, as,	海事契約としての～	*56*
option to continue,	～を継続する選択権	353, *354*
rules of construction,	解釈の規則	*57*
time,	定期～	
charterers' interest in vessel,	定期傭船者の本船に対する利害	*536*, *537*
demise charter, not,	定期～であり，デマイズ傭船契約ではない	529
effect of,	定期～の効果	530
officers and crew as servants of owners,	船主の被用者として職員と部員	530
owner, responsibility of,	船主の責任	*537*
provision of services, contract for,	役務提供の契約	530
trip, time charter,	1航海のための定期～	131, 531
voyage,	航海～	
consecutive,	連続航海～	531
effect of,	航海～の効果	530, 531
Charter period,	**傭船期間**	
Baltime Form,	ボルタイム書式	123, 129, 549, 550
delay in currency of,	～中の遅延	557-559
delivery, starting with,	引渡で開始	121
duration of trip, definition of period of hire by,	航海の継続期間をもって定める傭船期間	131, 531
early redelivery,	期限前返船	129, 130, *138*
final voyage,	最終航海	
Baltime Form,	ボルタイム書式	549

exceeding,	〜を超過する最終航海	121-123
invalid orders for,	違法な最終航海の指図	125
legitimate, whether,	適法な最終航海か	122-126, *138*
orders for,	最終航海の指図	123-125
Shelltime Form,	シェルタイム書式	590, 591
STB Form,	STB書式	*623*
last or final voyage clause, effect of,	最終航海条項の効果	128, 129, 591
late redelivery,	返船遅れ	123, *136-138*, 549, 550
"let" and "hire", meaning,	「賃貸」と「賃借」の意味	121
margin,	許容	
"about",	「約」	128, *135*, *136*
express,	明示の許容	127, *134*
extent of,	許容期間	128, *136*
implied,	黙示の許容	126, *132*
not implied,	黙示されていない許容	127
reasonable, extent of,	妥当な許容期間の範囲	*136*
maximum and minimum periods,	最長と最短期間	*133*
New York Produce Exchange Form,	ニューヨーク・プロデュース書式	121, *132*
NYPE 93,	NYPE 93	8
option to extend,	〜を延長する選択	129
overlap/underlap,	期間超過／期間不足	121, *132*
round voyage, definition,	往復航海の定義	*135*
trip, duration of,	航海の継続期間	131
true extent of,	〜の真の範囲	126-128
Charterers,	**傭船者**	
colors, NYPE 93,	社色、NYPE 93	17
duty to provide and pay for,	手配し支払う義務	
agencies,	代理	221
all other usual expenses,	ほかのあらゆる通常の費用	221
Baltime Form,	ボルタイム書式	547
bunkers,	燃料	*223-225*
continuation of responsibility,	責任の継続	*223*
fuel,	燃料	217-219
general nature of,	〜の手配し支払う義務の一般的性質	217
hold cleaning expenses,	艙内清掃費用	*226*
New York Produce Exchange Form,	ニューヨーク・プロデュース書式	217, *223*
off-hire periods, in,	オフハイヤー期間に	222
pilotages,	水先料	220, 221, *225*, *226*
port charges,	港費	219, 220, 547
Shelltime Form,	シェルタイム書式	582, 583
STB Form,	STB書式	*632*
inspection of ship,	検船	97
instructions, giving,	指図を出す	585
orders. *See* **Charter period ; Employment clause.**	命令。傭船期間、使用条項を参照	
responsibility of,	〜の責任	
Baltime Form,	ボルタイム書式	563
NYPE 93, under,	NYPE 93書式に基づく	9
Shelltime Form, under,	シェルタイム書式に基づく	29

事項索引　803

spaces available to,	～に利用可能なスペース	282, 550, 584
vessel, interest in,	船舶の利害	530, *536*, *537*
Class,	**船級**	
statement as to,	～に関する表示	101, *112*
Clause paramount. *See also* **Carriage of Goods by Sea Act.**	至上条項。海上物品運送法も参照	
Baltime Form, incorporated in,	ボルタイム書式に摂取された～	560, 561
New York Produce Exchange Form, in,	ニューヨーク・プロデュース書式の～	513, 515, *522*
NYPE 93, in,	NYPE 93の～	14
Shelltime Form,	シェルタイム書式	35, 614, 615
Collision,	**衝突**	
both-to-blame clause, incorporation of,	双方過失衝突条項の摂取	521, *526*
NYPE 93,	NYPE 93	15
Shelltime Form,	シェルタイム書式	34, 613, 614
STB Form.	STB書式	46, *636*, *637*
Commissions,	**歩金**	
address,	アドレスコミッション	542
NYPE 93,	NYPE 93	18
Baltime Form,	ボルタイム書式	571
broker, right of,	仲立人の権利	541, *543*, *544*
New York Produce Exchange Form,	ニューヨーク・プロデュース書式	541, *543*
NYPE 93, under,	NYPE 93に基づく～	18
premature termination of charter to avoid,	～を免れるため仮装の解約	541
Company,	**会社**	
corporate veil, piercing,	法人格の否認	
admiralty jurisdiction,	海事管轄	*75*
application of principles,	原則の適用	*76, 77*
appropriate form of relief, where,	適当な形式の救済	*76*
arbitration, in,	仲裁における法人格の否認	*78*
contract cases, in,	契約事案の法人格の否認	*78*
historic origins of,	法人格否認の歴史的起源	*75, 76*
prima facie case for, proving,	法人格否認の一応証拠のある事案を証明	*77*
tests for,	法人格否認の基準	*76*
tort cases, in,	不法行為の事案の法人格の否認	*78*
persons treated as *alter ego*,	分身として扱われる者	558
Contract,	**契約**	
applicable law,	適用法	*56*, *57*
breach of,	～違反	
affirmation after,	～違反の後の確約	93
damages for,	～違反について損害賠償	87
de minimis,	些細なことは問わない	86
discharge by,	～違反による解約	87, 88
fundamental,	根本的な契約違反	425, 426
injunction, order for,	差止命令	87
material,	重大な～違反	*108*
remedies,	救済策	86, 87
specific performance, order for,	特定履行命令	87
waiver,	権利放棄	92, 93
Carriage of Goods by Sea Act,	海上物品運送法の摂取	

804 事項索引

incorporation of,	～の解釈	*111, 112*, 513
construction of,	～の解釈	
deletions from standard form,	標準書式の削除	128, *133*
ejusdem generis rule,	同種解釈の原則	373, *385*
exceptions clauses,	免責条項	424, *427*
general principles,	一般原則	*57*, 420
de minimis breaches of,	些細なことは問わない違反	86
formation,	成立	
essential terms,	基本条項	
agreement to,	基本条項に合意	*57*, 58
clear agreement on,	基本事項に明確な合意	49-51
meaning,	意味	*58*
formal charter, terms of,	傭船契約書の条項	51, 52, *60*
interpretation of terms,	条項の解釈	49, 50
law determining,	契約の成立を決定する法	55
meaningless words and phrases, ignoring,	意味のない語句を無視する	50
New York Produce Exchange Form,	ニューヨーク・プロデュース書式	49, *56*
special form, no need for,	特別な形式は不要	49
"subject details" and "sub-details",	「細目を条件として」	53, 54, *59*, *60*
"subject to",	「を条件として」	
meaning,	「を条件として」の意味	52
use of,	「を条件として」の用法	54, 55
subsequent negotiation, providing for,	後日の交渉に委ねる	50, 51
survey, permission or approval, subject to,	検査結果，許可または承諾を条件に	52, 53
frustration of. *See* **Frustration of charter.**	～の履行不能。**傭船契約の履行不能を参照**	
Harter Act, incorporation of,	ハーター法の摂取	*111, 112*, 513
misrepresentation. *See* **Misrepresentation.**	不実表示。**不実表示を参照**	
parties,	当事者	
agency. *See* **Agency.**	代理人。**代理人を参照**	
contract principles, application of,	契約の原則の適用	71
corporate veil, piercing,	法人格の否認	75-78
guarantors,	保証人	**78**, *79*
New York Produce Exchange Form,	ニューヨーク・プロデュース書式	61, *71*
owner, charterer described as,	船主として記載された傭船者	71
owners and charterers,	船主と傭船者	61, *71*
promises, terms as,	約束としての条件	86
rules of construction,	解釈の規則	*57*, 424
terms,	条件	
cancelling clause, effect of,	解約条項の効果	91, 92
classification of,	条件の分類	88
commercial certainty and fairness, conflict between,	商業的確実性と公正の衝突	90
conditions,	条件	88, 89
treated as,	条件として扱われる条件	90-92
intentions of parties,	当事者の意思	91
intermediate,	中間条件	89
promises as,	条件としての約束	86

warranties, 担保		88, 89
Crew, 乗組員		
"deficiency of men",	「人員の不足」	368, *381*
"in every way fitted for the service",	「あらゆる点において業務に適した」	160
incompetence and insufficiency of,	〜の無能力と員数不足	97, 160
overtime, liability for,	時間外についての責任	
Baltime Form,	ボルタイム書式	565
NYPE 93, under,	NYPE 93書式に基づいて	14
Shelltime Form,	シェルタイム書式	30, 584
refusal to sail,	出港拒否	562
Shelltime Form,	シェルタイム書式	575, 576
stoppage by,	〜による停止	562, 563
strike by,	〜によるストライキ	*382, 383,* 562

D

Damages, 損害賠償（額）		
misdescription of capacity, for,	能力の不実表示の〜	103, *113*
misrepresentation, for,	不実表示の〜	83-85, *108, 109*
punitive, in arbitration proceedings,	仲裁手続における懲罰的賠償	*458, 459*
redelivery of damaged ship, for,	損傷を受けた船舶の返船の〜	237, *239*
substitute ship, windfall profit from,	代船による予想もしなかった利益	161
trading outside limits, for,	定限外航海に対する〜	142
waiver of right to,	〜の権利の放棄	92
wrongful withdrawal or cancellation, on,	不当な引揚または解約に関する〜 268, *277-279,* 360, *361, 362*	
Dangerous or injurious cargo. See **Cargo.**	危険または有害貨物。貨物を参照	
Deadweight capacity, 載貨重量		
"about", margin allowed by,	「約」で許容される範囲	102, *114*
lifting capacity, abstract measure of,	積載能力の抽象的計量	101, 102
misdescription, damages for,	不実表示の損害賠償	103
New York Produce Form, definition in,	ニューヨーク・プロデュース書式の定義	102
reduction in, reduction of hire for,	〜の減少に対する傭船料の減額	*113*
statements of,	〜の表示	101, *112-114*
tonnage, misdescription of,	〜トン数の不実表示	*114*
warranty as to,	〜に関する担保	*112, 113*
weight of dunnage, including,	積付資材を含む〜	102
Deductions from hire. See **Hire, payment of.**	傭船料の控除。傭船料の支払を参照	
Delivery, 引渡		
acceptance of,	〜の受諾	161
bunkers on,	〜時の燃料	*223, 227,* 588, *626*
delay in, Baltime Form,	ボルタイム書式，〜の遅延	556, 557
documents, requirements for,	〜書類の要件	158-160
meaning,	意味	121
NYPE 93, under,	NYPE 93に基づく〜	8
place of, New York Produce Exchange Form,	ニューヨーク・プロデュース書式，〜場所	151
redelivery. See **Redelivery.**	返船。返船を参照	
state of ship on,	〜時の船舶の状態	
cancellation, right of,	解約の権利	153

cancelling clause, readiness for purposes of,	解約条項のための準備	154
"clean-swept holds",	「清掃された船艙」	155, *163*
commercial judgment of readiness,	準備の商業的判断	156, 157
crew, competence and sufficiency of,	乗組員の能力と人員充足	160, *164*
damages, measure of,	損害賠償の測定	161
defects, effect of,	欠陥の効果	153, *162*
documentation,	書類	158-160
gear and equipment, of,	機器と装置の〜	155, 156
"in every way fitted for the service",	「あらゆる点において業務に適した」	154, *163*
minor deficiencies,	些細な欠陥	156, 157
New York Produce Exchange form,	ニューヨーク・プロデュース書式	153, *162*
physical state, obligation extending beyond,	物理的状態を超えて広がる義務	158
question of fact, as,	事実問題として	160
readiness to load,	積込準備	155, *162*
requirement, absolute nature of,	要件の絶対的性質	154
special equipment, of,	特別な装置の〜	158
tight, staunch and strong,	船体堅牢強固	154, *163*, *164*
time for,	〜の時	231, *233*
Description of ship. *See* **Ship**	船舶の明細。船舶を参照	
Deviation,	離路	
concept of,	〜の概念	435
lives of third parties, to save,	第三者を救助する〜	*386*
Discharge. *See* **Cargo.**	揚荷。貨物を参照	
Documentation,	書類	
"in every way fitted for the service",	「あらゆる点において業務に適した」	158
NYPE 93, under,	NYPE 93に基づく	17
Drydocking,	入渠	
New York Produce Exchange Form,	ニューヨーク・プロデュース書式	511
NYPE 93,	NYPE 93	13, 511
off-hire,	オフハイヤー	368, *384*
Shelltime Form,	シェルタイム書式	31, 596
STB Form,	STB 書式	43, *631*
Dunnage,	荷役資材	
redelivery with,	〜を船上に残して返船	*241*
Duration. *See* **Charter period.**	継続期間。傭船期間を参照	

―― E ――

Embargo,	輸出禁止令	
frustration of charter by,	〜による傭船契約の履行不能	*416*
Employment clause,	使用条項	
agents, appointment of, *See also* **Agency.**	代理人の指名。代理も参照	299
Baltime form,	ボルタイム書式	552, 553
cargo, orders to load,	貨物を積み込む命令	297
charterers' orders, obedience to,	傭船者の指図に従う	291-293, 300
deviation from orders,	命令からの逸脱	*300*, *301*
employment, meaning,	使用を意味する	296, 297
indemnity,	補償	
"all consequences or liabilities",	「あらゆる結果または責任」	170, *300*

事項索引　807

causation,	因果関係	297, 298
charterers' fault, not dependent on,	傭船者の過失に拠らない補償	295
dangerous cargo,	危険貨物	552
express,	明示の補償	295
implied,	黙示の補償	293-295, *301*
navigational risks, and,	航行危険と補償	298, 299
ordinary expenses, no recovery of,	通常費用の無補填	298, 299
owner and charterer, right between,	船主と傭船者の間の補償の権利	*301*
signing of bills of lading, arising from,	船荷証券に署名することから生じる補償	
		295, *342, 344*
New York Produce Exchange Form,	ニューヨーク・プロデュース書式	291, *300*
other clauses, relationship with,	他の条項との関係	295
Shelltime Form,	シェルタイム書式	585-587
ship, employment of,	船舶の使用	296
Enemies,	公敵	
actions of,	〜の行為	420
"Errors of navigation",	「航海上の過誤」	422, *432*, 516
Exceptions clause,	免責条項	
"Act of God",	「天災」	420, *428*
additional, in typescript,	タイプ書きで追加〜	560
Baltime Form,	ボルタイム書式	555-563
burden of proof,	立証責任	559
Carriage of Goods by Sea Act 1936, in,	1936年海上物品運送法の〜	419, 423, *432*, 518-520
construction, principles applied,	〜の解釈に関する原則	424-426
"dangers and accidents of the seas, rivers",	「海洋, 河川の危険および事故」	422, *431, 432*
enemies, actions of,	公敵の行為	420
"errors of navigation",	「航海上の過誤」	422, *432*, 516
fire,	火災	420, *428, 429*
"fundamental breach", effect of,	「根本的な契約違反」の効果	425, 426
Hague Rules, claims subject to,	ヘーグ・ルールに従うクレーム	602, 603
Hague-Visby Rules, claims subject to,	ヘーグ・ヴィスビー・ルールに従うクレーム	
		602, 603
loss of ship, not restricted to,	本船滅失に限らない	419
"machinery, boilers and steam navigation",	「機関, 汽罐, 蒸気航海」	422, *432*
misdescription, protection against,	不実表示に対する保護	559, 560
mutual exceptions,	相互に免責	423, *427*
New York Produce Exchange Form,	ニューヨーク・プロデュース書式	419, *427*
repayment of hire,	傭船料返還	424
"restraint of princes, rulers and people",	「君主, 統治者および人民による抑留」	
		421, *429-431, 570*
Shelltime Form,	シェルタイム書式	602-605
STB Form,	STB書式	*638, 639*
stoppage,	停止	562, 563
strikes,	ストライキ	561
time limits,	出訴期限	603-605
war, acts of, *See also* **War risks.**	戦争行為. **戦争危険**も参照	566-569, *569, 570*, 605
Export restrictions,	輸出制限	
Shelltime Form,	シェルタイム書式	35, 616
Extension of charter,	傭船期間の延長	

option to continue,	継続する選択権	353, *354*

F

Final voyage,	**最終航海**	
Baltime Form,	ボルタイム書式	549
charter period, exceeding,	傭船期間を超過する〜	121-123
invalid orders for,	〜の違法な指図	125
last voyage clause, effect of,	最終航海条項の効果	128, 129, 592
legitimacy of,	〜の適法性	122-126, *138*
orders for,	〜の指図	123-125
release from obligation to complete,	〜を完了する義務からの解放	124
Shelltime Form,	シェルタイム書式	590, 591
STB Form,	STB書式	*623*
Fire,	**火災**	
exception for,	〜に関する免責	420, *428*, *429*
"Fitted for the service",	**「業務に適した」**	
cancelling clause,	解約条項	356
crew,	乗組員	160
delivery on,	〜状態で引渡	154, *163*
documentation,	書類	158
seaworthiness,	堪航性	96, 100, 158, *164*
Flag,	**国籍**	
statement as to,	（〜に関する表示）	96, *109*
Freight,	**運賃**	
"freight prepaid" bills of lading,	「運賃前払」の船荷証券	332, 486, *491*
sub-freights,	再運送賃	
lien on. *See* **Lien.**	〜に対するリーエン。リーエンを参照	
payable to owners,	船主に支払われるべき再運送賃	483, 484
Frustration of charter,	**傭船契約の履行不能**	
breach of charter, caused by,	傭船契約違反に起因する〜	405
burden of proof,	立証責任	407
charterer contributing to event,	傭船者に帰属する事情	405, *414*
collision, effect of,	衝突の効果	*413*
constructive total loss, effect of,	推定全損の効果	417
contractual obligation incapable of being performed,	契約上の義務履行が不可能	393, 394
damage to ship, by,	本船の損傷による〜	396
dangerous zone, vessel in,	危険水域の船舶	568
delay, by,	遅延による〜	
commencement of charter, in,	傭船始期の遅延	396, 397
contractual route becoming impossible,	約定された航路が不可能	398, *413*
foundation of contract, loss of,	契約の基礎の喪失	396
prolongation of charter,	傭船期間の延長	397, 398, *413*
service, interruption to,	役務を中断させるもの	399, 400
deliberate act or election, by,	意図的な行為または選択による〜	405, 406
doctrine of,	〜の法理	393, 394, *410*
effect of,	〜の効果	394
embargo, by,	輸出禁止令による〜	*416*
events contemplated by parties,	当事者が考慮した事態	400
events provided for,	規定された事態	400, 401, *412*

extent of interruption, assessment of,	中断の程度の評価	
strikes,	ストライキ	402
time for,	評価を行うときの基準時点	401, 402
war,	戦争	403, 404, *411-413*
fact and law, as question of,	事実問題と法律問題として	394, 395
fault, effect of,	過失の効果	405-407, *414*
financial loss,	経済的損失	404, *412, 413*
foreign law, impossibility due to,	外国法であるがゆえに不可能	*415, 416*
Frustrated Contracts Act,	履行不能により消滅する契約に関する法	393, 408
impossibility, claim of,	不可能の主張	*410*
law, changes in,	法律の変更	*415, 416*
money paid in advance, return of,	前払金の報酬	407, *410*
negligence, by,	過失による〜	406, 407
New York Produce Exchange Form,	ニューヨーク・プロデュース書式	393, *410*
obligations following,	〜に伴う義務	
charterers' property, entitlement to,	傭船者の財産の権利	409
common law, at,	コモン・ロー上の〜に伴う義務	407
exclusion of provisions,	規定の排除	409
statutory provisions,	法的規定	408, 409
performance commercially impracticable, where,	商業的に実行不可能な履行の場合	393, *412, 413*
requisition,	徴用	399-401, 607, *634*
risk, allocation of,	危険の分担	*412*
self-induced,	自ら招いた〜	405-407, *414*
service, interruption to,	役務の中断	399, 400
ship, loss of,	船舶の喪失	393, 396, 417, 591
strict criteria for application of,	〜の適用の厳密な基準	*410*
substitution clause, effect of,	代船条項の効果	396, *417*
Suez Canal,	スエズ運河	397, 398, *410-413*
third party, default of,	第三者の債務不履行	*414*
total loss, effect of,	全損の効果	*417*
unforeseen, event to be,	予見不可能な事態	*411*
war,	戦争	403, 404, *411-413*, 568
Fuel,	燃料	
Baltime Form,	ボルタイム書式	548
bunkering place, safety of,	燃料補給場所の安全性	219
charterers' duty to provide and pay for,	〜を支給し, 支払う傭船者の義務	
Baltime Form,	ボルタイム書式	217
bunkers, property in,	燃料の所有権	219, 228
New York Produce Exchange Form,	ニューヨーク・プロデュース書式	217, *223*
NYPE 93, under,	NYPE 93に基づく	219, 228
quality,	質	218, 219, *224, 225*
quantity,	量	218, *223, 224*
Shelltime Form,	シェルタイム書式	30, 33, 588
consumption,	〜消費	
average,	平均〜消費	105, 106
average, assessing,	平均〜消費を計算	599-601
Shelltime Form,	シェルタイム書式	597-601
statements as to,	〜消費に関する表示	

		103-106, *118*, *119*, 597-601, *626-629*
delivery and redelivery, on,	引渡時および返船時の〜	223, 227, 588, *626*
domestic purposes, for,	船内用の〜	509, *510*
reduction in speed saving,	速力の低下と〜節約	379
STB Form,	STB 書式	41, *626*, *627*
"while on hire",	「オンハイヤーの時に」	222, *223*, 377, 509

G

General average,	共同海損	
NYPE 93, under,	NYPE 93に基づく〜	13
Guarantee,	保証	
"guaranteed" capability of ship,	船舶の「保証」性能	91, 576
obligation under charter, of,	傭船契約に基づく義務の〜	64
"without guarantee",	「保証なしに」	131
Guarantor,	保証人	
arbitration clause, whether bound by,	仲裁条項により拘束されるか	*78, 79*
party to contract, not,	契約当事者ではない	*78*
Hague Rules. *See also* **Carriage of Goods by Sea Act.**	ヘーグ・ルール。海上物品運送法も参照	
claims subject to,	〜に従うクレーム	602, 603
dangerous cargoes, as to,	危険貨物に関する	168-170, 605
incorporation of,	〜の摂取	515
effect of,	〜の摂取の効果	520
NYPE 93,	NYPE 93	14, 521
paramount clause. *See* **Clause paramount.**	至上条項。至上条項を参照	
protection under,	〜に基づく保護	518-520
time limits under,	〜に基づく出訴期限	439, 603
Hague-Visby Rules,	ヘーグ・ヴィスビー・ルール	
claims subject to,	〜に従うクレーム	602, 603
dangerous cargoes, as to,	危険貨物に関して	169-170, 605, 606
time limit, indemnity claim for,	補償クレームの出訴期限	603
Harbours,	港	
bars, with,	洲を伴う〜	555
Harter Act,	ハーター法	
applicability,	〜の適用	*111*, *112*, 513
Carriage of Goods By Sea Act, and,	〜と海上物品運送法	513, *522*
immunities, restrictions on,	免責の制限	519
incorporation,	〜の摂取	*111*, *522*
Hire,	賃借、傭船料、傭船期間	
adjustment of,	〜の調整	33, 42, 598, *628*
commencement of,	〜の開始	281, 282, *284*
owners' right to,	船主の〜の権利	243
rate of,	〜料率	
NYPE 93, under,	NYPE 93に基づく	10
Shelltime form, under,	シェルタイム書式に基づく	29, 583
STB Form, under,	STB書式に基づく	40, 41, 622
suspension of,	〜の支払停止	554
Hire, payment of,	傭船料の支払	
absolute obligation, as,	〜に関する絶対的義務	254
Baltime Form,	ボルタイム書式	548

bank errors,	銀行の過誤	275, 276
banker's drafts and payment orders, by,	銀行為替と支払指示による〜	244, 245
"cash", in,	「現金」で〜	243-246, 270
dangerous zone, vessel in,	危険水域の船舶	568
deductions,	控除	
amount of,	控除額	252
anticipated off-hire, of,	予想されるオフハイヤーの控除	*271*
Baltime Form,	ボルタイム書式	549
bona fide belief in right of,	控除する権利を誠実に信じる	252
charter, permitted by,	傭船契約で許容される控除	247, 248, *270-272*
claims for damages, of,	損害賠償請求金額の控除	248-251, *270, 271*
deficiencies in vessel, for,	船舶の欠陥に対する控除	577, 578
deprivation of use of ship, for,	船舶の使用の阻害に対する控除	249-251
equitable set-off,	衡平法上の相殺	248-251
other claims of charterers, for,	傭船者の他の請求に対する控除	251, *270*
"reasonable assessment made in good faith",	「誠実に行われた妥当な査定」	252
Shelltime Form,	シェルタイム書式	584
default of,	〜の支払懈怠	257, 549
failure to pay,	〜の支払不履行	*272*
"in advance",	「前払で」	253, *272*
"in default of payment",	「支払懈怠で」	257, 548
last half-month, for,	〜の最後の半月分	
Baltime Form,	ボルタイム書式	254
New York Produce Exchange Form,	ニューヨーク・プロデュース書式	254
NYPE 93,	NYPE 93	255
late,	〜遅延	
acceptance of,	〜遅延の受領	260, 261, *274*
bank errors,	銀行の過誤	275, *276*
effect on right to withdraw,	引揚権への影響	257
previous acceptance of,	〜遅延の事前の承認	256
repeated,	度重なる〜遅延	255
use of vessel, right to deny,	船舶の使用を拒否する権利	*279*
less than amount of full hire due, of,	満額以下の〜	246, *270-272*
modification of provisions by course of conduct,	態度による規定の変更	255, 256, *272, 273*
New York Produce Exchange Form,	ニューヨーク・プロデュース書式	243, *270*
NYPE 93, under,	NYPE 93に基づく	11
non-banking day, due on,	〜期日が銀行休日	254, *272*
off-hire. See **Off-hire**.	オフハイヤー。オフハイヤーを参照	
previously approved method, lateness arising from,	従前承認された支払方法に起因する支払遅滞	255, 256, *272, 273*
semi-monthly,	半月毎に	252, 253
Shelltime Form,	シェルタイム書式	29, 583, 584
ship off-hire at due date, where,	〜期日に船舶がオフハイヤーである場合	247
STB Form,	STB 書式	622, *623, 627-629*
telex transfers,	テレックスによる口座間の振替	245, 246
timely but insufficient, acceptance of,	期日どおりであるが、不足払の容認	261
use of ship withheld, where,	船舶の使用が妨げられた場合	247

variation of method, agreement on,	支払方法の変更の合意	246
withdrawal clause, invoking,	引揚条項の行使	255
withdrawal of vessel,	船舶の引揚	
anti-technicality clause,	反厳密解釈条項	259
cargo on board, with,	船上に貨物をもったまま船舶の引揚	264, 265, *275*
charter, ending,	傭船契約を終了させる船舶の引揚	263-265
damages, right to,	損害賠償の請求権	268, 269, *276*, *277*
delay in exercising right of,	船舶の引揚権の行使の遅滞	262, 263
effect of,	船舶の引揚の効果	263-265, *276*, *277*
final, to be,	船舶の引揚は最終的なもの	256, 257
forfeiture, equitable relief from,	権利消滅に対する衡平法上の救済	258
injunction,	差止命令	269
late payment,	遅れた支払	
acceptance of,	遅れた支払の受領	260, 261, *274*
effect of,	遅れた支払の効果	257, *274*
late tender of payment, after,	期限遅れの支払提示の後で引揚	*274*
notice of,	船舶の引揚通知	258, *274*
"on any breach of this charter",	「本傭船契約の違反により」	265-267, *276*
repudiation, failure to pay amounting to,	履行拒絶に至る～不履行	268, *277*
repudiation, failure to pay not amounting to,	履行拒絶に至らない～不履行	268, 269
waiver of right,	船舶を引き揚げる権利の放棄	260-263
warning, whether required,	警告が必要か	*273*, *274*
wrongful, damages for,	不法な船舶の引揚に対する損害賠償	268, *277-279*
Holds,	**船艙**	
"clean-swept",	「清掃された」	155, *163*
cleaning expenses,	清掃費用	*226*
responsibility for,	清掃費用の責任	*214*
NYPE 93, under,	NYPE 93に基づく	17
"customary assistance",	「慣習上の助力」	286, 288
grab damage,	グラブによる損傷	240
ladders, installation of,	梯子の装備	*215*
readiness of,	～の準備	155-157, *162*, *163*, 357
readiness to load,	積込準備	152, *162*
redelivery, condition on,	返船時の状況	236, 240

I ─────────────────────────

Ice clause,	**氷条項**	
Baltime Form,	ボルタイム書式	564, 565
effect of,	～の効果	*536*
NYPE 93,	NYPE 93	16
Indemnity,	**補償**	
bills of lading, liability under,	船荷証券に基づく責任	
claim, when arising,	～請求が生じる場合	328
express,	明示の～	327, 328
implied,	黙示の～	326, 327, *344*
measure of damages,	損害賠償の基準	520
signing, arising from,	署名から生じる～	295, 330
time limit for claim,	クレームの出訴期限	603

事項索引　　　　　　　　　　813

cargo,	貨物	
dangerous, in respect of,	危険貨物に関する〜	170
deck,	甲板貨物	283
employment clause, arising under,	使用条項に基づき生じる〜	
See **Employment clause.**	**使用条項**を参照	
irregularities in papers, as to,	書類の不備に関する〜	586
loss of right to,	〜を受ける権利の喪失	330
Shelltime form, under,	シェルタイム書式に基づく	585, 586
signing bills of lading "as presented",	「呈示された」船荷証券に署名	325
imposing greater liability than charter,	傭船契約以上の責任を課す	325, 326
"without prejudice to the charter-party",	「傭船契約上の権利を損なうことなく」	333
Injunction,	**差止命令**	
remedy of,	〜の救済	87
Instructions,	**指図**	
Shelltime Form, under,	シェルタイム書式に基づく	30
Insurance,	**保険**	
Baltime Form,	ボルタイム書式	532
cover, effecting,	〜の付保	531
damages to ship, owners' claims against charterer for,	本船の損傷に関する船主の傭船者に対するクレーム	532
New York Produce Exchange form,	ニューヨーク・プロデュース書式	531, *538*
NYPE 93, laid-up returns,	NYPE 93, 係船戻し〜	17
owner, responsibility of,	船主の責任	*538*
reimbursement of premiums by charterer,	傭船者による保険料の払戻	
discounts,	割引	533
provision for,	傭船者による保険料の払戻の条項	532, *538*
war risks, See also **War risks.**	戦争保険。戦争危険も参照	533-535, *538*
vessel, of,	船舶の〜	211
war risks,	戦争危険	567
Inter-Club New York Produce Excahnge Agreement,	**ニューヨーク・プロデュース書式に基づく貨物クレームの船主・傭船者に関するPIクラブ間協定**	
cargo claims, division of liability for,	貨物クレームの責任の割合	310
contractual agreement, as,	契約上の合意	*322*
incorporation of,	〜の摂取	313, 314
text of,	〜の本文	311-313
International Transport Workers Federation (ITF),	**国際運輸労働者連盟**	
boycott by,	〜によるボイコット	372, *382*

L ────────

"Last voyage". See **Final voyage.**	「最終航海」。**最終航海**を参照	
"Lawful merchandise". See **Cargo**	「適法な貨物」。**貨物**を参照	
"Lawful trades". See **Voyage.**	「適法な航海」。**航海**を参照	
Layday/Cancelling.	**「傭船開始・傭船解除」**	
See also **Cancelling clause.**	**解約条項**も参照	
Shelltime Form,	シェルタイム書式	581, 582
STB Form,	STB書式	*624, 625*
Laying-up,	**係船**	
Shelltime Form,	シェルタイム書式	34, 607
STB Form,	STB書式	44, *634*

Liberties, 自由
    NYPE 93, under, NYPE 93に基づく 13

Liens, リーエン
    amounts due under charter, for, 傭船契約において支払われるべき金額に 486, 487
    arrest, アレスト
        obligation to free vessel from, アレストから船舶を解放する義務 504, 505
        perfected by, アレストにより完璧 497
    assignment, 譲渡 501
    Baltime Form, ボルタイム書式 565, 566
    cargo damage, for, 貨物損害についての〜 503
    charterers' property subject to, 〜がついている傭船者の財物 505
    charterers', on ship, 船舶に対する傭船者の〜
        breach of charter, for, 傭船契約違反につき船舶に傭船者の〜 497, 498
        meaning, 定義 487
        priority, 船舶に対する傭船者の〜の優先権 498, 499
        prospective lost profits, for, 得べかりし利益についての〜 498
        right of, 船舶に対する傭船者の〜の権利 487, 488
    common law, コモン・ロー 479
    contractual, 契約上の〜 479
    English and American law distinguished, 英国法と米国法の違い 479
    equity, under, 衡平法に基づく〜 479
    executory contract, under, 未履行の契約に基づく〜 490, 491
    in rem action against goods, 貨物に対する対物訴訟において 497
    maritime, 海事〜 479, 490
    New York Produce Exchange Form, ニューヨーク・プロデユース書式 479, 490
    NYPE 93, NYPE 93 13, 489
    owners', on cargo, 積荷に対する船主の〜
        American courts, recognition in, 米国裁判所の認定 491
        Baltime form, ボルタイム書式 480
        cargoes over which exercised, 船主が〜を行使しうる貨物 480
        exercise of, 積荷に対する船主の〜の行使 493-496
        nature of, 積荷に対する船主の〜の性質 479, 491, 492
        New York Produce Exchange Form, ニューヨーク・プロデユース書式 480, 481
        possessory, 積荷に対する船主の留置権 480
        scope of, 積荷に対する船主の〜範囲 492
        third party, cargo owned by, 第三者の所有する積荷に対する船主の〜 492
        when exercised, 積荷に対し船主が〜を行使する時期 493
        where exercised, 積荷に対し船主が〜を行使する場所 481
    owners', on sub-freights, 再運送賃に対する船主の〜
        bill of lading, owners party to, 船主が船荷証券の契約の当事者 483, 484
        charge, registrable as, 担保権として登記される船主の〜 486
        charterers, sub-freights payable to, 傭船者に支払われるべき再運送賃 484
        constructive notice of, 再運送賃に対する船主の〜通知の擬制 495
        discharge of, 再運送賃に対する船主の〜の消滅 494
        exercise of, 再運送賃に対する船主の〜の行使 493-496
        freight pre-paid bills of lading, 運賃前払の船荷証券の効果
            effect of, 486, 496
        nature of, 再運送賃に対する船主の〜の性質 482
        non-possessory, 留置権ではない 493

事項索引　　　　　　　　　　　　　　　　　　　　　　815

NYPE 93,	NYPE 93	483
payable to owners,	船主に支払われるべき	483, 484
payment twice,	二重払	494
priority of claims,	請求の優先	485, 495
scope of,	再運送賃に対する船主の～の範囲	492
sub-charterers, freights payable to,	再傭船者に支払われるべき運賃	485
sub-freight, meaning,	再運送賃の意味	482
perfecting,	～が完璧になる	497
Shelltime Form,	シェルタイム書式	33, 601, 602
statutory,	制定法上の～	479
STB Form,	STB書式	43, 629
stevedore, of,	荷役業者の～	500
sub-charterers',	再傭船者の～	504
subrogation, acquired by,	代位により取得される～	501
supplies ordered by charterer, for,	傭船者の発注による物品供給についての～	
assignment,	譲渡	501
necessaries, for,	必需品についての～	500, 501
no-lien clause, knowledge of,	リーエン禁止条項の知識	502, 503
precluding,	排除	499
priority,	優先権	504
statutory provisions,	制定法上の規定	499, 500
waiver of,	～の放棄	502
third party, ship arrested in respect of,	第三者に関連してアレストされた船舶	488
Loading. See **Cargo**.	積込。貨物を参照	
Logs,	公用日誌	
Baltime form,	ボルタイム書式	554
New York Produce Exchange Form,	ニューヨーク・プロデュース書式	349
NYPE 93, under,	NYPE 93に基づく	12
Shelltime Form,	シェルタイム書式	30, 585
voyage, of,	航海の～	350, 351

M

Machinery,	機関	
physical risks of,	～の物理的危険	422, 432
Maintenance clause,	保守条項	
capital improvements, responsibility for,	資本的改善の責任	215, 216
changed legal requirements, effect of,	変化した法的要件の影響	214-216
continuing obligation,	継続する義務	211, 212
damage, making good,	損傷を修理する	235
due diligence, duty of,	相当の注意を尽くす義務	213, 576, 577
hold cleaning expenses, responsibility for,	船艙清掃費用の責任	214
insurance of vessel,	船舶保険	211
New York Produce Exchange Form,	ニューヨーク・プロデュース書式	211, 213
NYPE 93,	NYPE 93	212
Shelltime Form,	シェルタイム書式	576-578
types of,	～の類型	212
wages, meaning,	賃金，意味	211
warranty of seaworthiness, reinforcing,	堪航性の担保の強化	213
Maritime cases,	海事事案	
federal jurisdiction,	連邦裁判管轄	56

事項索引

Master, 船長
  "and responsibility of the Captain", 「および船長の責任」 306-308, *318*, *319*
  Baltime form, ボルタイム書式 550-552
  bills of lading, signing, 船荷証券に署名
    See also **Bills of lading.** 船荷証券も参照
    Shelltime Form, シェルタイム書式 585
    STB Form, STB書式 *635*, *636*
  charterers' orders, obedience to, 傭船者の指図に服従 291-293
  conduct of, Shelltime Form, ～の態度，シェルタイム書式 587
  "customary assistance", 「慣習上の助力」 286, 288
  navigation and ship management, 航行および船舶取扱の責任
    responsibility for, 296
  negligence, liability for, 過失に対する責任 293
  orders and directions of charterer, under, 傭船者の命令と指図の下で 585, 586
  Shelltime Form, シェルタイム書式 575, 576, 585, 589
  STB Form, duties under, STB書式に基づく義務 *631*, *632*
  "under the supervision of the Captain", 「船長の監督の下で」 305, 306, *317*, *318*
  "utmost despatch", 「極力迅速に」 285, 286
Misrepresentation, 不実表示
  Baltime clause, ボルタイム条項 13, 559, 560
  breach of collateral contract, as, 付随契約の違反として～ 84, 85
  damages for, ～に基づく損害賠償 83-85, *108*
  description of ship, in, 船舶の明細の～ 82, *108*
  exclusion of liability for, ～の責任の排除 85
  false statement, as, 虚偽の表示として 82
  fraudulent, 詐欺的～ 84
  inducing entry into contract, 契約を締結させる～ 82
  negligent, 過失による～ 84
  parol evidence rule, 口頭証拠の法則 86
  part of contract, as, 契約の一部となる～ 85, 96
  rescission for, ～による契約の解除 82, 83
  right to terminate for, ～を理由として契約を終了する権利 *108*

N

Navigation, 航行，航海
  both-to-blame collision clause, 双方過失衝突条項 521, *526*, 637, 638
  errors of, 航海上の過誤 422, *432*
  master's and owners' responsibility for, 船長と船主の～に対する責任 221, 298, 299
  negligence of pilot, 水先人の過失 193, 208, 220, 225, 226, 531
  NYPE 93, under, NYPE 93に基づく 14
New Jason clause, ニュー・ジェイソン条項
  NYPE 93, in, NYPE 93で 15
  Shelltime Form, シェルタイム書式 34, 614
  STB Form, STB書式 636

O

Off-hire, オフハイヤー
  "any other cause", 「その他一切の事由」 370-375, *385*
  arrest, vessel under, アレストされた船舶 *387*, *388*
  average accidents, detention by, 海損事故による滞船
    average accident, meaning, 海損事故の意味 369, *383*, *384*

事項索引　　　　　　　　　　　　　　817

cargo, to,	貨物の海損事故による滞船	*384*
detention, meaning,	滞船の意味	369
NYPE 93,	NYPE 93	369
period of detention, hire ceasing for,	滞船期間中傭船料は停止	366
Baltime Form,	ボルタイム書式	548, *554*, 555
beginning of charter period, event occurring before,	傭船開始前に発生した事由	368
bottom fouling,	船底の汚れ	379
breach of orders, claim for,	指図違反に対する請求	595
breakdown, resulting From,	故障から生じる〜	369
bunkers, while off-hire,	オフハイヤー中の燃料	222, *223*, 377, 509
cause preventing full working of vessel, by,	本船の完全な稼働を阻害する原因による〜	
any other cause whatsoever,	その他一切のいかなる事由	374, 375, *385*, *386*
arrest of cargo,	貨物のアレスト	372
ejusdem generis rule,	同種解釈の原則	373, 374
excess quantity of cargo,	貨物の積み過ぎ	371
fortuitous,	偶発性の	375
hull, machinery or equipment, breakdown or damages to,	船体，機関または装備の故障または損傷	*384*, *385*
meaning,	意味	370
NYPE 93,	NYPE 93	374
outside agencies, action by,	外部の機関がとった行動	372
physical efficiency, as,	物理的に有効な稼働	373
service required by charterers, efficient to perform,	傭船者の要求する業務を有効に遂行する	370-373
Shelltime Form,	シェルタイム書式	593
typhus, ship carrying,	発疹チフスの船舶	372
winches, refusal to operate,	ウィンチ操作の拒絶	*385*
charterers' breach, incident caused by,	傭船者の義務違反による事由	376, 386
clause,	〜条項	
Baltime Form,	ボルタイム書式	554
breach of contract, independent of,	債務不履行から独立した〜条項	363
excluding charterer's fault,	傭船者の過失を除外する〜条項	595
"net loss of time",	「正味喪失時間」	364, 365, 592, 593
New York Produce Exchange Form,	ニューヨーク・プロデュース書式	363, 380
NYPE 93,	NYPE 93	367
option to cancel, giving,	解約の選択権を付与する条項	*391*
"period",	「期間」	364, 365, 592, 593
Shelltime Form,	シェルタイム書式	592-596
deductions on withdrawal,	引揚の際の〜の控除	378
"deficiency of men",	「人員の不足」	
gunners, not including,	砲兵を含まない	369
illness, incapability through,	病気により遂行できない	368
incapacity,	不適格	*381*, *382*
NYPE 93,	NYPE 93	369
refusal to work,	業務遂行の拒否	368
unwillingness to work,	就労忌避	*382*, *383*
drydocking,	入渠	*384*

events constituting,	〜を構成するできごと	554, 555
fire, loss of time due to,	火災により時間喪失	*384*
fuel used during,	〜中に使用された燃料	509, *510*
general principle,	一般原則	363, *380*
hire becoming payable again,	傭船料支払義務が再開する	365-367, *380*, *381*
ITF boycott, by,	ITFボイコットによる〜	372, *382*
lives of third parties, deviation to save,	第三者の生命の救助のための離路	*386*
loss of time,	時間の喪失	364, *380*
NYPE 93, under,	NYPE 93に基づく	12
obligations during period of,	〜期間中の義務	377
obligations of charterer, not suspending,	傭船者の義務を停止しない	*389*
other remedies, effect on,	その他の救済についての効果	
charterers, claims by,	傭船者の損害賠償請求	377, 378, *389*-*391*
owners, claims by,	船主の損害賠償請求	378
partial inefficiency, on,	部分的業務不能	367, 368
payment of hire ceasing on,	〜中の傭船料支払の停止	377
reduction in speed, deduction for,	速力の低下に対する控除	378, *379*, *389*
refusal to berth vessel,	接岸拒否	*386*
resumption of hire,	傭船料の再開	*380*, *381*
Shelltime Form, under,	シェルタイム書式に基づく	31, *592*-*596*
STB Form,	STB書式	43, *629*-*631*
tacking,	〜期間を加える	*620*
Turkish waters, refusal to cross,	トルコ領海域を通過拒否	*386*
unseaworthiness, effect of,	不堪航の効果	364
"while on hire", effect of,	「オンハイヤーの時に」の効果	222, *223*, 377, 509
Oil Pollution,	油濁	
Shelltime Form,	シェルタイム書式	615
STB Form,	STB書式	47, *639*, *640*
On-off hire survey,	オン・オフハイヤー検査	
NYPE 93, under,	NYPE 93に基づく	9
"Ordinary wear and tear". *See* **Redelivery.**	「通常の損耗」。返船を参照	
Owners,	船主	
due diligence, personal want of,	〜自身の相当の注意の欠如	555-559
duty to provide and pay for,	支給し, 支払う〜の義務	
Baltime Form,	ボルタイム書式	547
New York Produce Exchange Form.	ニューヨーク・プロデュース書式	
See **Maintenance clause.**	保守条項を参照	
NYPE 93, under,	NYPE 93に基づく	9
Shelltime Form,	シェルタイム書式	29, *582*
STB Form,	STB書式	631

P

Paramount clause. *See* **Clause paramount.**	至上条項。至上条項を参照	
Payment of hire. *See* **Hire, payment of.**	傭船料の支払。傭船料の支払を参照	
Period of charter. *See* **Charter period.**	傭船期間。傭船期間を参照	
Pilotage,	水先, 水先料	
charterers' duty to provide,	〜を手配する傭船者の義務	220, 221, *225*, *226*
NYPE 93, under,	NYPE 93に基づく	221
Pilots,	水先人	

employment of, Shelltime Form,	〜の使用，シェルタイム書式	589
responsibility for,	〜に関する責任	220, *225*, *226*, 531
safe port and,	安全港と〜	193, *208*
Shelltime Form, under,	シェルタイム書式に基づく	30
STB Form,	STB 書式	44, *632*, *633*
Port charges,	港費	
Baltime Form,	ボルタイム書式	220
charterers to provide and pay for,	〜を傭船者が手配し支払う	219, 220, 547, *632*
meaning,	意味	219
Ports,	港	
bars, with,	洲のある〜	555
excluded,	除外された〜	564
icebound,	氷で閉ざされた〜	564
named, liability for unsafety,	指定の〜の非安全に対する責任	194, 195, *206*
safe. See **Safe ports.**	安全な〜。安全港を参照	
Proper or governing law of charter.	傭船契約のプロパー・ローまたは準拠法	
See **Charter.**	傭船契約を参照	
Protective clauses,	保護条項	
NYPE 93, under,	NYPE 93 に基づく	14-16

R

Readiness. See **Cancelling clause ; Delivery.**	準備。解約条項；引渡を参照	
Redelivery,	返船	
areas and notices, NYPE 93, under,	NYPE 93 に基づく区域と通知	10
Baltime Form,	ボルタイム書式	549
bunkers at,	〜時の燃料	588, 589
damaged ship, of,	損傷を受けた船舶の〜	236, 237
dunnage, with,	積付資材とともに〜	*241*
early,	期限前〜	129, 130, *138*, 237
end of charter period, after,	傭船期間満了後の〜	*136-138*, 549, 550
"hire to continue",	「傭船料支払は継続する」	122, 124, 235
hire, payment of,	傭船料の支払	*136-138*
late,	期限後〜	123
"like good order", in,	「同様に良好な状態」で	235, 236, *239*
New York Produce Exchange Form,	ニューヨーク・プロデュース書式	235, 239
notice of,	〜の通知	*139*
ordinary wear and tear, damage as,	通常の損耗としての損傷	237, *240*
place of,	〜の場所	*138*, *139*
place other than that agreed, at,	合意以外の場所で〜	237, *238*, *241*
STB Form,	STB 書式	45, *634*
Requisition. See also **Frustration.**	徴用。履行不能も参照	
NYPE 93, under,	NYPE 93 に基づく	16
Shelltime Form,	シェルタイム書式	34, 607, 608
STB Form,	STB 書式	45, *634*
Restraint of princes,	君主による拘束	
exception for,	〜の免責事由	421, *429-431*
war risks,	戦争危険	*570*
Rivers,	河，川	
bars, with,	洲のある〜	555
perils peculiar to, exceptions,	〜に固有の危険，免責	422, **431**, **432**

S

Safe ports,	**安全港**	
abnormal occurrences, responsibility for,	異常事態に対する責任	184, 185
action to depart, ability to take,	出港の行動をとる可能性	181
adverse weather, local warnings of,	悪天候の気象警報	182
afloat, vessel lying,	常に浮揚状態で碇泊する船舶	197, *199*
approach, safety of,	接近時の安全性	180, 181, *201-203*
berth, safety of,	バースの安全性	195, 196
berthing and mooring facilities,	着岸，繋船設備	182
charterers,	傭船者	
primary obligation of,	傭船者の第一義的義務	187, 188
restriction of obligations,	義務の制限	198
secondary obligation of,	傭船者の第二義的義務	188
unsafety not known to,	傭船者の知らない非安全性	189
danger zone, withdrawal of vessel From,	危険区域から船舶を引き揚げる	*204*
definition of,	〜の定義	177
delays rendering unsafe,	非安全にする遅延	179
departure, safety in,	出港時の安全性	183, 184, *201-203*
due diligence clauses,	「相当の注意」条項	189, *200*, 579-581
efficient navigational aids in,	〜で有効な水路標識	183
employment clause, claim under,	使用条項に基づく請求	197, 198
express warranty of,	〜の明示の担保	*199-201*
good navigation and seamanship, dangers avoidable by,	適切な航海技術により回避可能な危険	186, 187, *205, 206*
hostile seizure or attack, risk of,	敵国の拿捕または攻撃の危険	180, 181
ice, effect of,	氷の影響	*203*
implied term of safety,	安全性の黙示の条件	194
law, matters of,	法の問題	187
named,	指定の〜	194, 195, *206*
negligence by crew or master, effect of	乗組員または船長の過失の効果	
apportionment of damage,	損害の分割	193
causation,	因果関係	192, 193
contributory,	乗組員または船長の寄与過失	193, *208, 209*
effect of,	乗組員または船長の過失の効果	192
intervening,	乗組員または船長の過失の介在	*207, 208*
New York Produce Exchange Form,	ニューヨーク・プロデュース書式	177, *199*
nomination, becoming unsafe after,	指定の後で非安全となる	188
nomination by owners,	船主による指定	581
NYPE 93,	NYPE 93	177
particular ship, for,	特定の船舶の〜	179, 180, *201*
political risks,	政治的危険	183, *204, 205*
political unsafety,	政治的な非安全	185, 186
prospectively unsafe port, consequences of order to,	非安全と予見される港への配船の結果	190-192
question of fact, as,	事実問題として	187
relevant period of time for judging,	判断するための当該期間	178
"safely lie always afloat",	「常に浮揚した状態で安全に」	151, 195, 196, *199*
safety, elements of,	安全性の要素	177
Shelltime Form,	シェルタイム書式	579-581

state of war, danger due to,	戦争状況による危険	185, 186
temporary dangers in,	〜の一時的危険	178
unsafe berth or port, nomination of,	非安全バースまたは港の指定	*199*
unsafe, refusal of order to,	非安全港への配船の拒否	190
use, safety in,	使用上の安全性	181-183, *203*, *204*
voyage charters, criteria applicable to,	航海傭船に適用される基準	197
war clauses, interaction with,	戦争条項との相互作用	198
war risks,	戦争危険	612, 613

Sailing orders, 航海指図
  NYPE 93, under,   NYPE 93に基づく   12

Sale of ship. *See* **Ship.** 売船。船舶を参照

Salvage, 海難救助
Baltime Form,	ボルタイム書式	566
division of,	〜料の分配	507
New York Produce Exchange Form,	ニューヨーク・プロデュース書式	507
NYPE 93, under,	NYPE 93に基づく〜	13
Shelltime Form,	シェルタイム書式	33, 601

Seas, 海
  perils peculiar to, exceptions,   〜に固有の危険, 免責   422, *431*, *432*

Seaworthiness, 堪航性
breach of warranty,	担保違反	110, 111, 164
bunkers, sufficiency of,	十分な燃料	218, *223*
cancelling clause and,	解約条項と〜	100, 153, 356
Carriage of Goods by Sea Act 1936 incorporation of,	1936年海上物品運送法の摂取	111-112, 514
classification society certificate as evidence of,	〜の証拠として船級協会証書	*214*
crew, competence and sufficiency of,	乗組員の能力と人員の充足	97, 160
documentation,	書類	159
maintenance clause reinforcing,	〜を強化する保守条項	*213*
meaning,	意味	97, *164*
undertaking or warranty of,	〜の保証または担保	
absolute nature of,	〜の絶対的保証または担保	96, *115*
express or implied,	明示または黙示の〜の保証または担保	96, 97, *110*, *163*
effect of incorporation of COGSA and Hague Rules,	国際海上物品運送法またはヘーグ・ルールの摂取の効果	97, 100, *111-112*, 513-521, *522*
nature of contractual term,	契約条件の性質	97
"tight, staunch, strong and in every way fitted for the service",	「船体堅牢強固であらゆる点において運送業務に適した」	96, 100, *110*, 158, *163-164*
when taking effect,	〜の保証または担保の効力を生じる時	
at time charter entered into,	定期傭船契約を締結する時	96
at time of delivery,	引渡時	96-97, 163
each voyage,	各航海	514-517
"with hull machinery and equipment in a thoroughly efficient state",	「船体, 機関および装備を完全な稼働状態に保持すること」	96, *110*

unseaworthiness, 不堪航
cargo owner, direct liability of owner to,	貨物所有者に船主が直接責任	343
off-hire, and,	不堪航とオフハイヤー	364

refusal or failure to remedy,	堪航性回復の拒絶または回復不能	99
unseaworthy ship, delivery of,	不堪航な船舶の引渡	98
Shelltime Form,	シェルタイム書式	
commentary on,	注解	573-617
text of,	本文	28-36
Ship,	船舶	
condition, Shelltime Form,	状態，シェルタイム書式	573-575
description of,	～の明細	
bale and deadweight capacity,	ベール容積と載貨重量	101, *112-114*
characteristics, of,	～の特徴	*108*
class, statement as to,	船級に関する表示	101, *112*
Coast Guard letter of compliance,	コーストガイド適合証書	*108, 109*
conditions, not being,	条件ではない	94
flag,	国籍	96, *109*
gross/net tonnage, as to,	総トン・純トンに関して	*114*
legal label,	法的位置づけ	*108*
misdescription, cancellation on,	不実表示に基づく解約	357
misrepresentation,	不実表示	82-86
See also **Misrepresentation**	不実表示も参照	
name, by,	船名	94, *109*
New York Produce Exchange Form,	ニューヨークプロデュース書式	81, *108*
requirement to comply with,	明細に適合する要件	93
Shelltime Form,	シェルタイム書式	573-575
ship not meeting, delivery of,	明細に合致しない船舶の引渡	93, 94
speed and fuel capacity,	速力と燃料消費性能	103-106, *114-118*
statements in course of negotiation,	交渉の過程でなされる表示	81-86
STB Form,	STB書式	*620-622*
expected ready to load,	船積準備完了見込	107
fitness, questions of,	適合性の問題	575
hull, machinery and equipment in thoroughly efficient state, undertaking of,	船体，機関および装備を完全な稼働状態に保持することの保証	96-101, *110*
See also **Seaworthiness.**	堪航性も参照	
inspection, Shelltime Form,	検船，シェルタイム書式	597
loss of,	～の喪失	
Baltime Form,	ボルタイム書式	565
Shelltime Form,	シェルタイム書式	591
STB Form,	STB書式	*623*
misdescription, exemption clause,	不実表示，免責条項	559, 560
name, description by,	船名による明細	94, *109*
present position, statement as to,	～の動静に関する表示	106, 107, *119*, 120
sale during charter,	傭船期間中の売船	95, 96
substitution,	代船	95
use of, STB Form,	～の使用。STB書式	*625*
Smuggling,	密輸	
NYPE 93. under,	NYPE 93に基づく～	18
Specific performance,	特定履行	
Contract, of,	契約の～	87
Speed,	速力	
"about",	「約」	

modification by use of term,	「約」の語句を付して修飾	*116*
qualification of warranty with,	〜の担保の規定	105
average,	平均〜	105, 106
assessing,	平均〜の評価	599-601
bottom fouling, effect of,	船底汚損の効果	117, *118*, 379
claim, methods of determining,	〜クレームを決定する方法	*115*
compliance with description,	明細に適合	104
continuing warranty of,	〜担保の継続	104
good weather, in,	好天時の〜	*117*
guaranteed average,	保証した平均〜	598
maintenance of vessel in efficient state, and,	〜とおよび十分な稼働状態に船舶を保守	*116*
reduction in,	〜の低下	
bottom fouling, for,	船底汚損による〜の低下	379
deduction for,	〜に対する控除	378, *389*
fuel, saving,	燃料の節約	379
reduction of hire for,	〜の低下による傭船料の減額	*115*
Shelltime Form,	シエルタイム書式	597-601
statements as to,	〜に関する表示	103-106, *114-118*
warranty as to,	〜に関する担保	*114, 115*
weather conditions, effect of,	気象の影響	599
STB Form,	**STB 書式**	
text of,	〜の本文	38-48
commentary on,	〜の注解	*619-642*
Stevedores,	荷役作業、荷役作業員	
damage, NYPE 93,	損害,NYPE 93	16
employment of, Shelltime Form,	〜の使用,シェルタイム書式	589
lien,	リーエン	*500*
Shelltime Form, under,	シェルタイム書式に基づく	30
Stowage. See **Cargo.**	積付。貨物を参照	
Stowaways,	密航者	
NYPE 93, under,	NYPE 93に基づく	17
Strikes,	ストライキ	
crew, of,	乗組員の〜	382, *383*, 562
definition,	定義	562
frustration of charter by,	〜による傭船契約の履行不能	402
loss or damage arising From,	〜から生じる損害	561
Sub-charter,	再傭船	
bills of lading, authority of sub-charterers' to sign,	船荷証券に署名する再傭船者の権限	147, 148
effect of,	〜の効果	147
sub-freights. See **Freight.**	再傭船料,再運送賃。運賃を参照	
Subletting,	再傭船	
Baltime Form,	ボルタイム書式	566
bills of lading, authority of sub-charterers' to sign,	船荷証券に署名する再傭船者の権限	147, 148
freight, payment of,	運賃の支払	148
liberty to,	〜の自由	
charterer, responsibilities of,	傭船者の責任	**149**

824　事項索引

New York Produce Exchange Form,	ニューヨーク・プロデュース書式	147
sub-charter, effect of,	再傭船の効果	147
NYPE 93, under,	NYPE 93に基づき	13
Shelltime Form,	シェルタイム書式	30, 589
STB Form,	STB 書式	48, **641**
Substitution of ship. *See* **Ship.**	代船。船舶を参照	

T―――――――――――――――――――――――――――――――

Tanker time charters,	タンカー定期傭船契約	
additional equipment, provision of,	追加装備の規定	633, 634
arbitration,	仲裁	641
assignment,	譲渡	48, 641
berths,	バース	625, 626
bills of lading,	船荷証券	585-587, 635-637
signing,	署名	336
both-to-blame collision clauses,	双方過失衝突条項	613, 614, 636, 637
bunkers,	燃料	
at delivery and redelivery,	引渡時および返船時の燃料	588, 589
grades of,	複数等級の燃料	607
cancelling clause,	解約条項	581, 582
cargo,	貨物	626
injurious,	有害貨物	605, 606
warranty as to heating,	貨物加熱に関する担保	622
change of ownership, effect of,	所有権の変更の効果	641
charterer provides,	傭船者が手配する	582, 583
clause paramount,	至上条項	614, 615
clean seas program,	汚染防止計画	640
default,	滞納	623
description and condition of vessel,	船舶の明細と状態	573-575, 597
disbursements,	諸掛	607
drydocking,	入渠	596, 631
exceptions clauses,	免責条項	602-605, 638, 639
export restrictions,	輸出制限	616
extensions,	延長	619, 620
final voyage,	最終航海	590, 623
fuel,	燃料	626
consumption,	消費	597-601
provision by charterer,	傭船者の支給	632
warranties,	担保	626, 627
governing law,	準拠法	642
grades of oil carried,	運送される複数等級の油	639
hire,	傭船, 傭船料	
adjustment of,	傭船料の調整	628, 629
commencement of,	傭船の開始	624
deductions,	傭船料の控除	622
increment,	傭船料の増額	624
payment of,	傭船料の支払	583, 584, 622
rate of,	傭船料率	583
reduction in,	傭船料の減額	623
inspection of ship,	検船	597

instructions,	指図	585
law and litigation,	法および訴訟	616
lay-up,	係船	607, *634*
laydays,	備船開始	581, 582, *624*, *625*
liens,	リーエン	601, 602, *629*
logs,	公用日誌	585
loss of vessel,	船舶の滅失	591, *623*
maintenance clause,	保守条項	576-578
master, duties of,	船長の義務	*631*, *632*
New Jason clause,	ニュー・ジェイソン条項	614
off-hire,	オフハイヤー	592-596, *629*-*631*
oil pollution warranties,	油濁保証	*639*, *640*
overtime,	時間外手当	584
owner provides,	船主が手配する	582, *631*
period and trading limits,	期間と就航区域	578-581
port charges, payment of,	港費の支払	*632*
products, sales of,	製品の販売	*640*
pumping systems, description of,	ポンプ・システムの明細	*621*
pumping warranties,	ポンプ能力の担保	*626*, *627*
redelivery,	返船	*634*
requisition,	徴用	607, 608, *634*
salvage,	海難救助	601
Shelltime Form, commentary on,	シェルタイム書式の注解	573-617
shipboard personnel,	乗組員	575, 576
conduct of,	乗組員の行為	587
space available to charterers,	貨物積載場所	584
speed,	速力	597-601, *626*, *627*
STB Form, commentary on,	STB書式の注解	*619*-*642*
stevedores,	荷役業者	589
sub-letting,	再備船	589, *641*
supernumeraries,	定員外の乗船	589
term,	期間	*619*
TOVALOP,	油濁責任に関するタンカー船主間自主協定	615, *639*
trading limits,	航路定限	*625*
tugs and pilots,	曳船および水先人	589, ***632***, ***633***
use of vessel,	本船の使用	*625*
vessel, particulars of,	船舶の明細	573-575, *620*-*622*
war,	戦争	
additional expenses,	追加費用	609
outbreak of,	戦争の勃発	608, 609
war risks clauses,	戦争危険条項	610-613, *637*, *638*
warranties,	担保	*624*
Taxes,	税金	
NYPE 93, under,	ニューヨーク・プロデュース書式に基づく	17
Time,	期間、時、時間	
computation of,	期間の計算	231, 232, **233**
local or elapsed,	地方標準時または経過時間	231, 232
New York Produce Exchange Form,	ニューヨーク・プロデュース書式	231
NYPE 93, under,	NYPE 93に基づき	232

Tonnage,	トン数	
misdescription of,	〜の不実表示	114
TOVALOP,	油濁責任に関するタンカー船主間自主協定	
Shelltime Form,	シェルタイム書式	35, 615
STB Form,	STB書式	639, 640
Trade,	航路	
Baltime Form,	ボルタイム書式	546
Trading limits,	航路定限	
agreement to break,	〜外航行に関する協定	142, 143
breach of obligations,	義務の違反	144
broad,	広範囲の〜	144
charter more narrowly defined,	より狭められた航海を対象とする定期傭船契約	141, 142
consent to trade outside,	〜外の航海に同意	579
New York Produce Exchange Form,	ニューヨーク・プロデュース書式	141, 144
NYPE 93, under,	NYPE 93に基づく	9
obedience to charterers' orders,	傭船者の指図に服従	142
orders to trade outside,	〜外の航海の指図	141
purpose of,	〜の目的	141
Shelltime Form,	シェルタイム書式	578-581
STB Form,	STB書式	625
trading outside, damages for,	〜航海に対する損害賠償	142
Trimming. See **Cargo.**	荷均。貨物を参照	
Tugs,	曳船	
employment of, Shelltime Form,	〜の使用。シェルタイム書式	30, 589
STB Form,	STB書式	44, 632, 633

U─────────────────

U.S. trade drug clause,	米国航海麻薬条項	
NYPE 93, in,	NYPE 93の〜	15
"Utmost despatch". See **Master ; Voyage.**	「極力迅速に」。船長；航海を参照	

V─────────────────

Vessel. See **Ship.**	船舶。船舶を参照	
Vouching-in,	訴訟告知	
procedure,	手続	323
Voyage,	航海	
charterers' instructions,	傭船者の指図	349, 350
last or final.	最終〜	
See **Charter period ; Final voyage.**	傭船期間；最終航海を参照	
"lawful trades",	「適法な航海」	165, 171
log,	公用日誌	350, 351
performance of, NYPE 93,	〜の遂行, NYPE 93	10
utmost despatch, prosecution with,	極力迅速に遂行	
Baltime Form,	ボルタイム書式	551
breach of obligation, protection From,	義務違反から保護	559
customary assistance,	慣習上の助力	286, 288
delay in currency of charter,	傭船期間中の遅延	557-559
engineers, duty of,	機関士の義務	285
exceptions,	免責	285, 286
New York Produce Exchange Form,	ニューヨーク・プロデュース書式	285

事項索引

NYPE 93,	NYPE 93	285
purpose of,	〜の目的	*287, 288*

W

Wages, — 給与
  meaning, — 意味 — 211

Waiver, — 権利放棄
  breach of contract, — 契約違反 — 92, 93
  damages, right to, — 損害賠償請求権 — 92
  lien, — リーエン — *502*
  withdrawal of vessel, right to, — 船舶を引き揚げる権利 — 260-263

War, — 戦争
  frustration of charter by, — 〜による傭船契約の履行不能 — 403, 404
  Shelltime Form, — シェルタイム書式 — 34
    additional expenses, — 追加費用 — 609, 610
    exceptions clause, — 免責条項 — 605
    outbreak, cancellation on, — 〜勃発による解約 — 608, 609
    cancellation, NYPE 93, — 解約、NYPE 93 — 16

War risks clause, — 戦争危険条項
  any other government, meaning, — 他のいかなる政府, 意味 — 568, 569
  Baltime Form, — ボルタイム書式 — *566-569, 569, 570*
  dangerous, port considered to be, — 危険と考えられる港 — 611, 612
  insurance of, — 戦争危険の保険 — 567
    premiums for, — 戦争保険の保険料 — 533-535
  NYPE 93, — NYPE 93 — 15
  safe ports clause, interaction with, — 安全港条項との相互作用 — 198
  safety of ports, — 港の安全性 — 612, 613
  Shelltime Form, — シェルタイム書式 — 610-613
  STB Form, — STB 書式 — *637, 638*

Warranty, — 担保
  STB Form, — STB 書式 — *624*
  term of contract, as, — 契約条件として — 88

Withdrawal of vessel. — 船舶の引揚
  See also **Hire, payment of** — 傭船料の支払も参照
  wrongful, damages for, — 不法な〜に対する損害賠償 — 277-279

Words and phrases, — 語句
  "about", — 「約」 — 102, 105, *114, 116, 119,* 128, *135*
  "act of God", — 「天災」 — 420, *428*
  "act of war", — 「戦争の行為」 — 605
  "affirmation", — 「確約」 — 93
  "all consequences or liabilities", — 「あらゆる結果または責任」 — 170, *300*
  "all other usual expenses", — 「その他すべての通常費用」 — 221
  "always mutually excepted", — 「常に相互に免責される」 — 423
  "and responsibility of the Captain", — 「および船長の責任」 — 305, 306, *318, 319*
  "any other Government", — 「他のいかなる政府」 — 568
  "any other cause preventing efficient working of vessel", — 「船舶の有効なる稼働を妨げる一切の事由」 — 373-375, *385*, 593
  "any reasonable deviation", — 「合理的ないかなる離路」 — 435
  "as agents", — 「代理人として」 — 62
  "as charterer", — 「傭船者として」 — 67

"as disponent",	「管理船主として」	67
"as owner",	「船主として」	66
"as presented",	「呈示された」	325, *344*, *636*
"average accident",	「海損事故」	369, *383*
"bareboat charter",	「裸傭船契約」	529
"by telegraphic authority",	「電報の授権により」	69
"cancellation",	「解約」	88
"cash",	「現金」	243, *270*
"charterers shall accept and pay for",	「傭船者が承認し支払うべき」	588
"clean-swept holds",	「清掃した船艙」	155, *163*
"commercial men",	「実務家」	441, *454*, 455
"commercially impracticable",	「商業的に実行不可能な」	*410*, *412*
"conditions",	「条件」	88, 89
"customary assistance",	「慣習的助力」	286, *288*
"customary quick despatch",	「可及的迅速荷役」	*288*
"dangers and accidents of seas and rivers",	「海洋，河川の危険および事故」	422, *431*, *432*
"deficiency of men",	「人員の不足」	368, *381*
"delivery",	「引渡」	121
"disclosed principal",	「隠された本人」	61
"due despatch",	「相当な迅速」	285, *287*
"due diligence",	「相当の注意」	189, 579
"efficient working",	「有効なる稼働」	373
"employment",	「（船舶の）使用」	296
"enemies",	「公敵」	420
"equal benefit",	「均等の利益」	507
"errors of navigation",	「航海上の過誤」	422, *432*, 516
"essential terms",	「基本的条項」	*58*
"expected ready to load",	「船積準備完了見込」	107
"expenses",	「費用」	507
"final award",	「最終判断」	*463*
"fire",	「火災」	420, *428*, *429*
"fundamental breach",	「根本的な違反」	425
"good weather",	「良好な天気」	*117*
"grates and stoves",	「暖炉やストーブ」	509
"hire to continue",	「傭船料の支払は継続する」	122, *124*, 235
"hostilities",	「敵対行為」	609
"in advance",	「前もって」	253, *272*
"in default of payment",	「支払懈怠」	257, 548
"in every way fitted for ordinary cargo service",	「あらゆる点で通常の貨物運送業務に適している」	98, 160
"in every way fitted for the service",	「あらゆる点で運送業務に適している」	
		154, 158-160, 356, 574
"inordinate delay",	「極端な遅延」	179
"lawful merchandise",	「適法な貨物」	165, *172*
"lawful trades",	「適法な航路」	165, 171
"like good order",	「同様に良好な」	235, 236, *239*
"loss of time",	「時間喪失」	592
"loss or damage",	「滅失または損傷」	519

"machinery",	「機関」	*432*
"machinery, boilers and steam navigation",	「機関，汽罐および蒸気航海」	422, 432
"manifest disregard of law",	「明らかな法の無視」	*472*, *476*
"manifestly inconsistent",	「明らかに矛盾している」	328, 329
"misrepresentation",	「不実表示」	82
"necessaries",	「必需品」	*500*
"net loss of time",	「正味喪失時間」	364, 365, 592, 593
"on any breach of this charter",	「本傭船契約の違反により」	265-267, *276*
"ordinarily incurred",	「通常に発生」	237
"ordinary wear and tear",	「通常の損耗」	237, *240*
"per calendar month",	「歴月当たり」	231
"preventing full working of vessel",	「船舶の完全な稼働を妨げる」	370
"reasonable assessment made in good faith",	「誠実に行われた妥当な査定」	252
"redelivery in like good order",	「同様に良好な状態で返船」	*239*
"rescission of contract",	「契約の解除」	88
"restraint of princes, rulers and people",	「君主，統治者，人民による抑留」	421, *429-431*, 570
"risks of steam navigation",	「蒸気航海の危険」	422
"safe port",	「安全港」	177, *205*
"safely lie always afloat",	「安全に碇泊し常時浮揚状態で」	151, 195, 196, *199*
"second safe port",	「2番目の安全港」	*200*
"stoppage",	「停止」	562
"strike",	「ストライキ」	562
"sub-freights",	「再傭船料」「再運送賃」	482, 602
"subject details",	「細目を条件として」	53, 54, *59*
"subject superficial inspection",	「外見上の検査の上で」	53
"subject to contract",	「契約締結を条件として」	52
"subject to government permission",	「政府の許可を条件として」	52
"subject to satisfactory completion of two trial voyages",	「2試験航海の満足行く結果を条件として」	53
"subject to shipper's approval",	「荷送人の承諾を条件として」	52
"subject to survey",	「検査結果を条件として」	52, 53
"subject to war risks clause",	「戦争危険条項の定めるところによる」	54
"termination of contract",	「契約の終了」	88
"three persons",	「3名」	441, 659
"tight, staunch and strong",	「船体の堅牢強固」	154, 158, 159, *163*, 574
"under the supervision of the Captain",	「船長の監督の下に」	305, 306, *317-322*
"undisclosed principal",	「隠された本人」	66
"undue hardship",	「不当な困難」	440
"unsafe",	「非安全」	179
"utmost despatch",	「極力迅速」	285, 286
"vouching-in",	「訴訟告知」	*323*
"wages",	「給料」	211
"waiver",	「権利放棄」	92
"war",	「戦争」	608
"warranty",	「担保」	88, 89
"while on hire",	「オンハイヤーの時に」	222, *223*, 377, 509
"withdraw",	「引揚」	256

"without guarantee",　　　　　　　「保証なく」　　　　　　　　　　　　　　131
"without prejudice to charter-party",　「傭船契約上の権利を損なうことなく」　333, *345*

【監訳者】
郷原資亮（ごうはら　もとすけ）
　　1934年　福岡県生まれ。神戸大学法学部卒業，三井船舶株式会社（現（株）商船三井）入社。
　　1966年　大阪商船三井船舶株式会社ロンドン支店勤務，1976年〜83年　大阪商船三井船舶株式会社法務保険部勤務，1983年〜87年　国連アジア太平洋経済社会委員会（ESCAP）事務局，海運，港湾，内水路部勤務，1988年〜89年　大阪商船三井船舶株式会社審議役。
　　1989年　摂南大学法学部教授に就任，現在に至る。
　　主　著　『定期傭船契約（初版）』（成山堂，1981年，共訳），『国際運送と新しい企業責任』（成山堂，1994年共訳），『海運の法理と実務』（近藤記念海事財団，1999年単著）

【共訳者】
石井達夫（いしい　たつお）
　　1948年　広島県生まれ。京都大学経済学部卒業，大阪商船三井船舶株式会社入社。（株）エム・オー・エル　アジャストメント　クレイムグループ調査役。

小川　優（おがわ　まさる）
　　1957年　熊本県生まれ。京都大学法学部卒業，大阪商船三井船舶株式会社入社。（株）商船三井総務部法務・保険チーム課長

白水　隆（しろうず　たかし）
　　1960年　東京都生まれ。富山高等商船高校卒業，国際エネルギー輸送株式会社入社。国際エネルギー輸送株式会社海技安全グループ課長

定期傭船契約［第四版］

2001年11月20日　第1版第1刷発行

Ⓒ 監訳者　郷原資亮
発行者　今井　貴・稲葉文子
発行所　（株）信山社
〒113-0033　東京都文京区本郷 6-2-9-102
TEL 03-3818-1019　FAX 03-3818-0344
制作：編集工房 INABA

2001, Printed in Japan　　印刷・製本／松澤印刷・大三製本

ISBN4-7972-9029-3 C3030

現代企業法の新展開	小島康裕教授退官記念 泉田栄一・関英昭・藤田勝利編	15,000円
中国国有化企業の株式会社化	虞建新著 名古屋大学法学研究科専任講師	5,000円 新刊
現代企業法学の研究	筑波大学大学院企業法学専攻十周年記念論集	18,000円 新刊
手形法・小切手法入門	大野正道著 筑波大学企業法学専攻教授	2,860円
現代企業・金融法の課題(上)(下)	平出慶道・高窪利一先生古稀記念	各15,000円
閉鎖会社紛争の新展開	青竹正一著 小樽商科大学商学部企業法学科教授	10,000円
商法改正[昭和25・26年]GHQ/SCAP文書	中東正文編著	予38,000円 近刊
企業結合・企業統合・企業金融	中東正文著 名古屋大学法学部教授	13,800円
株主代表訴訟の法理論	山田泰弘著 高崎経済大学講師	8,000円
株主代表訴訟制度論	周劍龍著 青森県立大学助教授	6,000円
企業活動の刑事規制	松原英世著 関西学院大学	3,500円
グローバル経済と法	石黒一憲著 東京大学教授	4,600円
会社持分支配権濫用の法理	潘阿憲著 横浜市立大学商学部助教授	12,000円
金融取引Q&A	髙木多喜男編 神戸大学名誉教授 大阪学院大学教授	3,200円
国際私法2000	年報2 国際私法学会編	3,000円
IBL入門	小曽根敏夫 弁護士	2,718円
金融の証券化と投資家保護	山田剛志著 新潟大学法学部助教授	2,100円
企業形成の法的研究	大山俊彦著 明治学院大学教授	12,000円
現代企業法の理論	菅原菊志先生古稀記念論文集 庄子良男・平出慶道編	20,000円
取締役・監査役論[商法研究Ⅰ]	菅原菊志著 東北大学名誉教授	8,000円
企業法発展論[商法研究Ⅱ]	菅原菊志著 東北大学名誉教授	19,417円
社債・手形・運送・空法[商法研究Ⅲ]	菅原菊志著 東北大学名誉教授	16,000円
判例商法(上)-総則・会社-[商法研究Ⅳ]	菅原菊志著	19,417円
判例商法(下)-商行為・手・小-[商法研究Ⅴ]	菅原菊志著	16,505円 全5巻セット79,340円
商法及び信義則の研究	後藤静思著 元判事・東北大学名誉教授	6,602円
アジアにおける日本企業の直面する法的諸問題	明治学院大学立法研究会編	3,600円
企業承継法の研究	大野正道著 筑波大学企業法学専攻教授	15,534円
中小会社法の研究	大野正道著 筑波大学企業法学専攻教授	5,000円
企業の社会的責任と会社法	中村一彦著 新潟大学名誉教授	7,000円
会社法判例の研究	中村一彦著 新潟大学名誉教授・大東文化大学教授	9,000円
会社営業譲渡・譲受の理論と実際	山下眞弘著 立命館大学法学部教授	2,600円
会社営業譲渡の法理	山下眞弘著 立命館大学法学部教授	10,000円
国際手形条約の法理論	山下眞弘著 立命館大学法学部教授	6,800円
手形・小切手法の民法的基礎	安達三季生著 法政大学名誉教授	8,800円
手形抗弁論	庄子良男著 筑波大学企業法学専攻教授	18,000円
手形法小切手法読本	小島康裕著 新潟大学法学部教授	2,000円
要論手形小切手法(第3版)	後藤紀一著 広島大学法学部教授	5,000円
有価証券法研究(上)(下)	高窪利一著 中央大学法学部教授	14,563円 9,709円
振込・振替の法理と支払取引	後藤紀一著 広島大学法学部教授	8,000円
ドイツ金融法辞典	後藤紀一他著 広島大学法学部教授	9,515円 品切
金融法の理論と実際	御室龍著 元札幌学院大学教授・清和大学講師	9,515円
米国統一商事法典リース規定	伊藤進・新美育文編	5,000円
国際商事仲裁法の研究	高桑昭著 元京都大学教授 帝京大学教授	12,000円
改正預金保険法・金融安定化法	新法シリーズ 信山社編	2,000円